Ehud Ben Zvi
Social Memory Among the Literati of Yehud

Beihefte zur Zeitschrift für die alttestamentliche Wissenschaft

Edited by
John Barton, Reinhard G. Kratz, Nathan MacDonald,
Sara Milstein, Carol Newsom and Markus Witte

Volume 509

Ehud Ben Zvi

Social Memory Among the Literati of Yehud

DE GRUYTER

ISBN 978-3-11-076292-1
e-ISBN (PDF) 978-3-11-054714-6
e-ISBN (EPUB) 978-3-11-054651-4
ISSN 0934-2575

Library of Congress Control Number 2018967606

Bibliographic information published by the Deutsche Nationalbibliothek
The Deutsche Nationalbibliothek lists this publication in the Deutsche Nationalbibliografie;
detailed bibliographic data are available on the Internet at http://dnb.dnb.de.

© 2021 Walter de Gruyter GmbH, Berlin/Boston
This volume is text- and page-identical with the hardback published in 2019.
Printing and binding: CPI books GmbH, Leck

www.degruyter.com

This volume is dedicated to the memory of Profs. Gene M. Tucker, Philip R. Davies and Gary N. Knoppers who passed away as this volume was being prepared and with whom I had many thought-provoking, enjoyable conversations on many of the issues discussed here for a long time. May their memory be a blessing.

Foreword

The essays included in this volume are an integral part and representative of a larger project on Social Memory in/and of Ancient Israel, mainly in the late Persian/early Hellenistic period. This project has been supported by grants from the Social Sciences and Humanities Research Council of Canada. I am most thankful to the Council.

Some of the ideas and the correlated essays emerged out of papers given at and in conversations held in workshops, including those co-organized by Faculties of Catholic Theology and Protestant Theology at Ludwig-Maximilians-Universität (LMU) Munich on the one hand and the Dept. of History and Classics at the University of Alberta on the other. Again, the Social Sciences and Humanities Research Council of Canada supported some of these workshops and the Fritz Thyssen Stiftung others.

Most of the other essays emerged out of a papers and conversations at EABS, SBL, IOSOT and CSBS meetings in the last ten years. I wish to express my gratitude to all the organizers of these sessions and to the scholars who work tirelessly to make these meetings possible, and whose contribution is rarely acknowledged. I would like to stress my debt of gratitude to all the colleagues who participated in these sessions. I learned much from the all. Needless to say, especial thanks also to those who co-edited volumes with me, on this or related subjects, and to those who invited me to the volumes and conferences they organized. Working with all of them and thinking with them has benefited my work, and needless to say, enriched myself personally, time and again.

I have also learned much from my students at our Social Memory seminars at my institution. I feel much gratitude to them all and to my department at the University of Alberta, for it continuously supported my work on this subject in any possible way.

I wish to thank the editors of BZAW for accepting this volume in the series, De Gruyter for publishing it, and to all the publishers who allowed republication of previously published work. I am most indebted to Dr. Sophie Wagenhofer, Senior Acquisitions Editor (Religious Studies, Jewish and Islamic Studies, De Gruyter), who went well beyond her call of duty to help me, to Dr. Albrecht Döhnert (Editorial Director, Theology and Religion, De Gruyter), to Aaron Sanborn-Overby (Content Editor, Ancient Near East, De Gruyter) Anett Rehner (Production Editor, De Gruyter) and all the editorial staff for all the work they have done for this project. This volume would not have come to life without them and their support.

To all those who have shared this journey with me over the last years, thank you!

Table of Contents

Introduction —— 1

On Social Memory and Identity Formation in Late Persian Yehud: A Historian's Viewpoint with a Focus on Prophetic Literature, Chronicles and the Deuteronomistic Historical Collection —— 28

Remembering the Prophets through the Reading and Rereading of a Collection of Prophetic Books in Yehud: Methodological Considerations and Explorations —— 80

Prophetic Memories in the Deuteronomistic Historical and the Prophetic Collections of Books —— 109

The Yehudite Collection of Prophetic Books and Imperial Contexts: Some Observations —— 134

The Memory of Abraham in Late Persian/Early Hellenistic Yehud/Judah —— 162

Exploring the Memory of Moses 'The Prophet' in Late Persian/Early Hellenistic Yehud/Judah —— 199

Squaring Circles and The Social Benefits of Squaring Them: Joshua as a Case Study for Constraints, Preferences, Balances and Flexibility within the Complex Memory System of the Literati of the late Persian/early Hellenistic Period —— 232

Isaiah, a Memorable Prophet: Why was Isaiah so Memorable in the Late Persian/Early Hellenistic Periods? Some Observations —— 253

Remembering Hosea: The Prophet Hosea as a Site of Memory in Persian Period Yehud —— 274

Reading the Book of Hosea, Remembering Hosea and Thinking of Exile in Yehud —— 294

Readers, Social Memory, Deuteronomistic Language and Jeremiah: The Roles of Deuteronomistic Language in Shaping Memories of Jeremiah among Late Persian / early Hellenistic Readers of the Book of Jeremiah —— 304

Chronicles and Samuel–Kings: Two Interacting Aspects of one Memory System in the Late Persian / Early Hellenistic Period —— 317

Shaping and Remembering an Arch-Villain in the Late Persian / Early Hellenistic Period: The Case of Ahaz in Chronicles and its Implications —— 332

Reshaping the Memory of Zedekiah and His Period in Chronicles —— 342

Reading Chronicles and Reshaping the Memory of Manasseh —— 367

Toward a Sense of Balance: Remembering the Catastrophe of Monarchic Judah/(Ideological) Israel and Exile through Reading Chronicles in Late Yehud —— 387

Chronicles and Its Reshaping of Memories of Monarchic Period Prophets: Some Observations —— 407

Contributions of the Genealogies in Chronicles to the Shaping of the Memory of the Monarchic Period: The Case of Some Simeonites's Vignettes —— 428

A Balancing Act: Settling and Unsettling Issues Concerning Past Divine Promises in Historiographical Texts Shaping Social Memory in the Late Persian Period —— 440

A Contribution to the Intellectual History of Yehud: The Story of Micaiah and Its Function within the Discourse of Persian-Period Literati —— 459

When Yhwh Tests People: General Considerations and Particular Observations Regarding the Books of Chronicles and Job —— 472

Exploring Jerusalem as a Site of Memory in the Late Persian and Early Hellenistic Periods —— 482

Remembering Pre-Israelite Jerusalem in Late Persian Yehud: Mnemonic Preferences, Memories and Social Imagination —— 504

Re-Negotiating a Putative Utopia and the Stories of the Rejection of Foreign
Wives in Ezra–Nehemiah —— 527

The "Successful, Wise, Worthy Wife" of Proverbs 31:10–31 as a Source for
Reconstructing Aspects of Thought and Economy in the Late Persian/
Early Hellenistic Period —— 546

Monogynistic and Monogamous Tendencies, Memories and Imagination in
Late Persian/Early Hellenistic Yehud —— 566

Othering, Selfing, 'Boundarying' and 'Cross-Boundarying' as Interwoven with
Socially Shared Memories: Some Observations —— 580

Total Exile, Empty Land and the General Intellectual Discourse in
Yehud —— 599

The Voice and Role of a Counterfactual Memory in the Construction of Exile
and Return: Considering Jeremiah 40:7–12 —— 612

Potential Intersections Between Research Frames Informed by Social-Memory
and 'Bourdieusian' Approaches/Concepts: The Study of Socio-Historical
Features of the Literati of the early Second Temple Period —— 631

Social Sciences Models and Mnemonic/Imagined Worlds: Exploring Their
Interrelations in Ancient Israel —— 655

Bibliography —— 674

Index of Authors —— 722

Index of References to Ancient Sources —— 730

Introduction

This volume is a collection of thirty-one essays addressing matters of Social Memory among the Literati of Yehud selected to familiarize or further familiarize readers with a particular socio-anthropological approach that sheds significant light on the world of ideas (and memories) shared by these literati. The essays here were chosen so readers may engage with a variety of research outcomes emerging from this approach, and thus raise observations, reservations, or think of complementary or alternative potential outcomes that this approach might lead to. All in all, the essays in this volume showcase a research path that historians may take to reconstruct the thought of the literati of the period. It also exemplifies potential uses of this approach for the study of the thought of other groups.

In addition, the volume includes some essays (see esp. the last two in this volume) that address potential intersections and complementarities between approaches informed by Social Memory studies like the one advanced here and those informed by other social-anthropological approaches. This volume thus invites the readers to explore some larger methodological questions involving historical method and social-anthropological approaches.[1]

The essays included in this volume are representative of a larger, ongoing project on Social Memory in/and of Ancient Israel (mainly in the late Persian/ early Hellenistic period) in which I explore what happens when a historian of ancient Israel wears the critical lenses of Social Memory to construct reasonable reconstructions of the cultural world of an ancient group.[2] I hope that at least some of the readers of this collection, be they specialists in the history of ancient Israel or of other ancient societies, whether they agree or disagree on the particular points I am advancing, would reach the conclusion at the end of their readings that these lenses are indispensable for historians of the social and cultural world of societies.

---

[1] For my basic approach on these matters, see also my "Clio Today and Ancient Israelite History: Some Thoughts and Observations at the Closing Session of the European Seminar for Historical Methodology," Lester L. Grabbe (ed.) *'Even God Cannot Change the Past' Reflections on Seventeenth Years of the European Seminar in Historical Methodology* (LHBOTS, 663; London: T&T Clark, 2018), 20–49. (The volume was just published, but the relevant essays go back to 2012).

[2] I would like to stress that this project has been supported over several years by various grants from the Social Sciences and Humanities Research Council of Canada. This support of my research has made a substantial difference in my ability to carry it out.

https://doi.org/10.1515/9783110547146-002

As part of this project I have given numerous talks in academic conference settings, and to the general educated public, on four continents. I talked to colleagues in the field of ancient Israel and 'Biblical Studies' and to colleagues in departments of History. I have taught seminars and low undergraduate courses at my university, involving students of a substantial variety of periods and cultures. In addition, along with dear fellow travelers, I co-organized workshops and sessions on these matters and co-edited a significant number of (mainly thematic) volumes dealing with various aspects of this project. I have learned much through this process from all of my colleagues and students, from all those who interacted with my papers and from all the participants in the talks I have given to specialists and to the general public, especially from those who asked questions and took me aside after talks. I am thankful to them most of all.

The collection comprises, for the most part, essays already published in a variety of academic venues, mainly various collected essay volumes, but also six that are published here for the first time. None of the essays is from earlier than 2010. Since I tend to believe in the importance of case studies, provided that they incorporate some explicit reference to and acknowledgment of the methodological approach underlying them, the majority of essays focus on either a diverse set of significant characters of memory remembered by these literati (e.g., Abraham, Moses, Joshua, Isaiah, Jeremiah, Hosea, Ahaz, Zedekiah, the successful, wise, worthy wife of Prov 31:10–31) or central topics, that were often explored through the memories of them that were shared by the literati. These topics include matters such as exile, boundaries around Israel and crossing them or establishing in-between areas, divine promises, ideological responses to life under the Persian Empire and related issues involving hybridity and mimicry, and the limits of human knowledge.

Of course, not all sites of memory (on the term, see below) within a community involved figures of the past. Thus, in this volume, I have included two essays that deal explicitly, though from different angles, with the Jerusalem of the literati's mind and memory. A volume such as this one without reference to Jerusalems of memory would have been truly unthinkable.

Moreover, although considerations about the methodological approach guiding these essays are explicitly included in all these essays, two of them (see chapters 30 and 31) focus especially on potential intersections and complementarities between approaches informed by Social Memory studies and those informed by other social-anthropological approaches and which raise interesting methodological issues of relevance to all historians of ancient societies.

To be sure, neither all the central characters of the memoryscape of the literati nor all core issues explored through memories of them held by the literati can be addressed in one single volume. Some crucial sites of memory are not mentioned at all in this volume and some areas remain by necessity grossly underrepresented in this collection. This holds true, even if I discussed some of these issues/sites elsewhere.³ Given my own expertise, the focus of the collection

---

3 The volume does not include, *inter alia*, the following essays: "Memories of Female (and Male) Sages in late Persian/Early Hellenistic Yehud Considerations Informed by Social Memory and Current Cross-and Trans-Disciplinary Trends in the Study of Wisdom," Stephanie Antonioz and Sebastian Fink (eds.) *Representing the Wise – A Gendered Approach. Melammu Workshop 1*; Lille, 4–5 April 2016 (scheduled for publication later this year); "Were YHWH's Clothes Worth Remembering and Thinking About among the Literati of Late Persian/Early Hellenistic Judah/Yehud? Observations and Considerations," Antonios Finitsis (ed.), *For All Her Household are clothed in Crimson: Dress in the Hebrew Bible* (LHBOTS; London: T&T Clark: forthcoming, 2019); "Memories of Kings of Israel and Judah within the Mnemonic Landscape of the Literati of the Late Persian/early Hellenistic Period: Exploratory Considerations," *SJOT* 33 (2019) (forthcoming); "Remembering Three Nehemiahs in Late Second Temple Times: Patterns and Trajectories in Memory Shaping" (co-authored with Sylvie Honigman), *JHebS* 18, (2018) article 10 available at http://www.jhsonline.org; "Chronicles and Social Memory," *ST* 71 (2017), 69–90; "Remembering Twelve Prophetic Characters from the Past," Elena Di Pede and Donatella Scaiola (eds.), *The Book of the Twelve – One Book or Many?* (FAT II; Tübingen: Mohr-Siebeck, 2016), 6–36; "Memory and Political Thought in the Late Persian/Early Hellenistic Yehud/Judah: Some Observations," Diana V. Edelman and Ehud Ben Zvi (eds.) *Leadership, Social Memory and Judean Discourse in the 5th-2nd Centuries BCE* (WANEM; London: Equinox, 2016), 9–26; "Late Historical Books and Rewritten History," Stephen B. Chapman, Marvin A. Sweeney (eds.) *The Cambridge Companion to the Hebrew Bible/Old Testament* (New York, NY: Cambridge University Press, 2016), 292–313; "Introductory Centre/Core-Periphery Considerations and the Case of Interplaying of Rigid and Flexible Constructions of Centre and Periphery among the Literati of the Late Persian/Early Hellenistic Period," Ehud Ben Zvi and Christoph Levin (eds.), *Centres and Peripheries in the Early Second Temple Period* (FAT, 108; Tübingen: Mohr-Siebeck, 2016), 21–41; "Purity Matters in the Book of Chronicles: A Kind of Prolegomenon," Carl S. Ehrlich, Anders Runesson and Eileen Schuller (eds.), *Purity, Holiness, and Identity in Judaism and Christianity* (WUNT, 305, Tübingen: Mohr-Siebeck, 2013) 37–52; "The Study of Forgetting and the Forgotten in Ancient Israelite Discourse/s: Observations and Test Cases," P. Carstens, T. Hasselbach and N. P. Lemche (eds.) *Cultural Memory in Biblical Exegesis* (Perspectives on Hebrew Scriptures and its Contexts 17; Piscataway, N.J.: Gorgias Press, 2012), 139–57; "How 'Historical' is Ancient Israel?," Alan T. Levenson (ed.) *The Wiley-Blackwell Companion to the History of Jews and Judaism* (Malden, MA: Wiley-Blackwell, 2012), 25–34; "Constructing the Past: The Recent History of Jewish Biblical Theology," I. Kalimi (ed.), *Jewish Bible Theology. Perspectives and Case Studies* (Winona Lake, Ind.: Eisenbrauns, 2012) 31–50. One may add to these a number of forthcoming articles, including "Reading Chronicles and Remembering Saul in the Late Persian/early Hellenistic Period," and "Chronicles' Reshaping of Memories of the Ancestors Populating Genesis Among (late) Persian-Period Literati" (to be published in 2019 in two collected essays volumes in honour of distinguished colleagues), "Alexander as a Site of Memory in Hellenistic Judah in the Context of Mnemonic Appropriations of 'High-Value' Outsiders," "Leadership in the World of Memories Evoked by Chronicles in the Context of the Late Persian/Early Hellenistic Period," "Matters of Authorship, Authority and Power from the Perspective of a Historian of the World

is mainly on memories shaped, evoked and explored through readings of prophetic books, Chronicles and the Deuteronomistic Historical Collection, but significantly, not exclusively (see, e.g., the chapter of the Abraham of memory, or chapters 24–26).

As in all single-author collections of this type, two questions emerged early in the preparation of this volume, namely (a) should the essays undergo substantial revision in terms of content? and (b) should the essays remain understandable as stand-alone contributions as they originally were, or should the volume avoid any possible repetition at the cost of rendering each individual chapter readable *only* as an integral part of the volume and with the knowledge of what is stated in the other chapters?

Concerning (a), I have preferred to keep the contributions as they were. This does not mean that today I would still write every single word or develop every single argument as I did when I wrote them originally, nor that, despite the fact that all essays are relatively recent—none pre-2010, there are no new works that have appeared since the original publication, and which demand engagement. Obviously, there are. My preference for keeping the contributions as they are is grounded in a number of factors. Most significantly, many of these contributions were shaped in various ways by the original context in which they emerged, such as talks at conferences or workshops convened around a particular topic, at a specific location, involving certain groups of scholars.[4] Removing all of this context in order to achieve some kind of 'homogenization' seems to me the wrong way to go. The essays included here made a contribution to research in the way and in the setting in which they emerged.

As for the second question, I have decided that each chapter should remain fully readable as a stand-alone work within this volume. The reasons are simple. First, although all authors may (fervently?) wish for readers who would read their books from cover to cover, leaving no page unturned, the reality today is that few would do so. Second, turning the essays into chapters that are understandable *only* as integral parts of a book requires removing them from their original settings in which they emerged, and regarding this, see above. Thirdly, single chapters may (and will hopefully) be included as such in reading lists for top undergraduates and graduate students, and thus *must* remain understandable as stand-alone essays.

---

of Yehudite/Judahite Literati," and "The Pentateuch as/and Social Memory of 'Israel' in the Late Persian Period" (to appear in the Oxford Handbook of the Pentateuch). Several of these are likely to be published next year.

[4] Bibliographic details and at times additional information within the relevant chapters provide the readers with the relevant information.

Introductions to collections of essays tend to consist mainly of a sequential list of brief summaries of each one of them. In this introduction, however, I would like to follow a different path. I would like to explicitly address a basic set of questions about the historical project of which this book is representative. My decision to do so is grounded in my experience with academic presentations on the topics discussed. I noticed that despite the different settings, there were sets of basic questions, concerns, and doubts that tended to play a central role in the question period following my talks, and in the subsequent conversations. These questions or issues were not focused on particular arguments I advanced about the way this or that personage or place was remembered, or even about particular readings of texts. Instead the queries, concerns and at times, outright uneasiness were grounded on more basic matters, such as the most basic question of all, why to bother with Social Memory and Social Memory approaches at all?

Moreover, when it was agreed that these approaches might indeed be helpful, then other questions would follow:

(a) why the strong focus on the literati of Yehud, as opposed to the memory shared by any other group in ancient Judah or Samaria/Israel, such as Judahite literati during the time of Josiah, (northern) Israelite literati during the time of Omri, or even rabbis from the Talmudic period, for that matter?

(b) Even more generally, why should one focus only on 'literati' of one kind or another, that is, just a few 'intellectuals' who constituted only a very small percentage of the population, and which were from a sociological perspective certainly not representative of most of the population? Is this not an elitist approach?

(c) Is this 'memory' just a new 'fancy' term for 'tradition'? In which way is it different from the old 'tradition-history" method?

(d) Does a focus on social memory work against a focus on historical analysis?

(e) Is 'memory' an alternative to 'history' and thus, are not memory-based approaches necessarily or mainly anti-historical, and if so, something that 'good historians' should either avoid or even categorically oppose?

Let me address first the last three points (c-d-e). Using the term memory, at least within this project, conjures a set of socio-anthropological approaches advanced to work on what has been referred to as collective, social or cultural memory. These approaches work across multiple cultures and time periods and bring with them a set of central heuristic questions. They serve as indispensable critical lenses for historians of the social and cultural world of societies, as the following chapters in this volume demonstrate.

This is not the place to discuss all the intricate differences between the concepts of (critical, professional) history as it is understood today and the memories of the past shared by a particular group.[5] It suffices to say that social memories that suit well the main metanarratives and social mindscape of a particular group[6] tend to be preferred by the relevant group over potential others. These memories were 'true' to the group, but not 'historically true' in the sense contemporary critically-trained historians use this term. In fact, often they were not 'historically true' in that sense at all. At times, even the remembering community or many within it were aware at some level that these socially shared, central memories stood in clear tension with what they 'knew' to have happened to them or their ancestors (see, e.g., chapters 28 and 29).

It is clear that most ancient historians were what we may call memory agents: that is, people who wanted to shape and impart memories of the past to particular groups to which they belonged or with whom they interacted and hoped to socialize them accordingly. They were certainly not what we may today consider 'professional historians'.[7] The world of memories that these mem-

---

[5] The last decades have witnessed a renewed interest in matters of historical methodology and philosophy of history. The field of 'history and theory' has blossomed and substantial, new perspectives have been advanced and debated. Of course, it is impossible to engage this conversation in any meaningful form in the context of this introduction, or the volume in general. Readers interested in my own position may consult E. Ben Zvi, "Clio Today."

[6] For the concept of "social mindscapes" see E. Zerubavel, *Social Mindscapes. An Invitation to Cognitive Sociology* (Cambridge: Harvard University Press, 1997); E. Zerubavel, *Time Maps: Collective Memory and the Social Shape of the Past* (Chicago: University of Chicago Press, 2003). The concept of "mindscape" precedes, of course, Zerubavel and goes back to M. Maruyama who used "the term 'mindscape' to mean a structure of reasoning, cognition, perception, conceptualization, design, planning, and decision making that may vary from one individual, profession, culture, or social group to another," M. Maruyama, "Mindscapes and Science Theories," *Current Anthropology* 21 (1980): 589–99 (591). The study of social mindscapes involves, inter alia, that of accepted and shared ways of thinking in a group, generating ideas, questions and ways of addressing them, providing meaning to 'data' and actually construing 'data' by focusing on particular matters and not others, assigning significance to memories, stories, and actually shaping the production of memories according to particular patterns. Moreover, it involves the study of how all these are deeply interconnected.

[7] As I have developed elsewhere, one may also conceptualize professional history in terms of a preferred set of social memories held by trained historians when they act as such, that is, as a socially validated (construction of the) past that is held by those who follow the rules governing the discipline of history and as a consequence are construed and evaluated, from a pragmatic perspective, as a 'reasonable' reconstruction of a likely (though necessarily partial) past. This approach raises, of course, interesting methodological issues about the relation between History and Social Memory that have at least a potential bearing on matters of ancient Israelite historiography; see my "Clio Today." But in any case, the rules governing the discipline of history

ory agents shaped was in accordance with their own large metanarratives and the ideological significance and social roles that they associated with these (see, e.g., Josephus).

It is also true that scholars like myself who follow the type of approach exemplified time and again in this volume are not focused on finding 'historical' kernels in, for instance, stories in which Abraham, Joshua, David or for that matter Josiah serve as the main human characters, but on discussing with the help of these texts how a later community construed and remembered these periods, and why. But such an approach is certainly not a rejection of history; rather, it is a necessary step for studying the history of thought of the remembering community.

In what follows, and within the constraints of an introduction, I would like first to elaborate a bit more on what happens when a historian of ancient Israel wears Social Memory lenses and what kind of contributions it makes. Then, I will follow with a response to the type of questions marked as (a) and (b) above, both of which relate to the focus on the Yehudite literati and their socially-construed and socially-shared memories that strongly characterizes this volume.

A good starting point for beginning to address these matters is the 'simple' observation that all social groups are, among others, mnemonic communities, that is, groups shaped around a set of shared memories. No social group has ever existed without sharing memories about their past or future.[8] Moreover, the self-understanding of a group and their understanding of the world around them is grounded on the world of memory they share. A socially shared memory (and accepted patterns of shaping memories) is necessary for social reproduction and essential for 'proper' socialization of the group.

It is undeniable that historical, social groups often tend to root themselves and their future in their past.[9] To be sure, they tend to root themselves not in any past, but in *their* past as they remember it. This is the past that they collectively imagine to have happened and which they are socialized to remember, whether such a past is historically (in our professional, contemporary terms) 'true' or not. This is a socially validated 'past' not a professionally, historically

---

today were not in existence in ancient times, but those governing the writing of ancient historians are similar to those shaping social memories.

8 One may claim that even a group of one (that is, an individual) cannot construct a sense of self without memory. Of course, the collective is housed within individual memory structures as we share, e.g., space, time, language, society.

9 Of course, these considerations apply across cultures and societies, see, e.g., Ron Eyerman, "Social Movements and Memory," in Trever Hagen and Anna Lisa Tota (eds.) *Routledge International Handbook of Memory Studies* (London: Routledge; 2015), pp. 100–105.

validated past. In fact, it is for these groups a socially validated, present past. It is a past that is reshaped by the remembering group to support it in the present. This is true, even if the ongoing process of reshaping and re-signifying works much better when it is 'invisible' for the community, that is, when people are unaware of the ongoing, constructed character of their past or successfully bracket their knowledge of the process.

Particularly important for historians is the fact that historical agents continuously process not only their own identity and knowledge of the world in terms of their (ever-adapting) present past, but also their actual historical behavior in their present in terms of examples and lessons learned from *their* past and the social messages conveyed by *their* memories.

At the same time, it is worth stressing that social agents are also informed by their socially shared images of the future (i.e., their present future/s), or in other words, by vicarious 'memories' of future events and circumstances that they share along with memories of the past. Collective mental time travel works both ways within historical communities.[10] The study of memories of the future

---

[10] Both remembering the past and imagining the future involve 'mental time travel' (MTT) and according to some scholars, memory actually evolved to facilitate imagination of the future. All in all, the area of studies connecting memory of the past and imagination of the future, both at the individual and collective levels, has exploded in recent years and become more interdisciplinary. See e.g., P. M. Szpunar and K. K. Szpunar, "Collective Future Thought: Concept, Function, and Implications for Collective Memory Studies," *Memory Studies*, 9 (2016), 376–389; Kourken Michaelian and John Sutton, "Collective Mental Time Travel: Remembering the Past and Imagining the Future Together," *Synthese. An International Journal for Epistemology, Methodology and Philosophy of Science*. Special issue: Thinking (about) groups; 2017; doi.org/10.1007/s11229-017-1449-1; Denis Perrin and Kourken Michaelian, "Memory as Mental Time Travel," in Sven Bernecker & Kourken Michaelian (eds.), *Routledge Handbook of Philosophy of Memory* (London: Routledge; 2017), 228–239; Johannes B. Mahr and Gergely Csibra, "Why Do We Remember? The Communicative Function of Episodic Memory," *Behavioral and Brain Sciences* 41 (2018) E1. doi:10.1017/S0140525X17000012; Sinéad L. Mullally and Eleanor A. Maguire, "Memory, Imagination, and Predicting the Future: A Common Brain Mechanism?", *The Neuroscientist* 20 (2014), 220–234. For a different perspective, see the earlier summary: Paolo Jedlowski, "Memories of the Future," in Trever Hagen and Anna Lisa Tota (eds.) *Routledge International Handbook of Memory Studies* (London: Routledge; 2015), pp. 145–54. This introduction will not dwell in detail on these developments. For the present purposes, it suffices to say that the essays in this volume—many of which were written earlier than these developments—premise that the social processes and generative grammars involved in the production of images/memories of the past and images/memories of the future are similar. Moreover, the term 'memories of the future' stresses the affective impact of conjuring and 'seeing'/'vicariously experiencing' the future. The memories that are created through these acts of shared imagination and experience are of a kind with the memories that emerge from conjuring and 'seeing'/'vicariously experiencing' the past. Both acts involve 'mental time travel' to particular, socially accepted events, times and locations.

of a particular group is as important as those of memories of the past (and complementary to it) for historians who are interested in the ways in which a group thought, the questions and issues that drew their attention, the governing rules/ generative grammar that led to the preference of some types of memories over others and the like. This is even truer for historians of societies in which memories of (utopian) futures serve crucial roles for hope, for managing a worldly marginality that was inconsistent with their own ideological understanding of themselves, and for social reproduction, such as the literati whose world of memory and mindscape this volume explores.[11]

It follows then that attention to the world of socially produced, reproduced, evoked, shaped and reshaped memories is a basic requirement for historians of ideas and cultures whose focus is not on individuals and their actions,[12] but on how social groups construed the world, themselves and others and their respective 'spaces' and acted accordingly. Or how said social groups explored matters ranging from the character of the divine to human leadership in a polity or how they understood the limits of human knowledge—all subjects that cannot avoid dealing with the socially shared memory of the group they are studying.

A few additional observations are in order at this point. First, the worlds of memory socially shaped and socially shared within a group represent the outcome of acts and processes of remembering certain matters and *forgetting* (or "bracketing) others. In fact, much more is 'forgotten' (or bracketed) than 'remembered'. Studying the social memory of a group necessarily involves noticing, researching and advancing generative grammars for forgetting/bracketing. Moreover, just as there is 'induced remembering', there is also 'induced forgetting'.[13]

Second, memories of individuals, places and the like never stand alone. Thus, for instance, it is impossible to remember one figure without remembering

---

[11] Memories of the future are explored in almost all the essays in this volume.

[12] Social memory lenses, along with other socially focused approaches that emphasize 'social systems' tend to be less helpful for contemporary historical studies whose focus is on individuals. These lenses, however, are often of much help for understanding how individuals (see, e.g., the case of figures ranging in time from Alexander of Macedon to Lincoln to J. F. K.) were remembered by some trained historians, who by necessity were products of their own times.

[13] Recent socio-cognitive approaches to and observations on the matter of induced forgetting in contemporary societies may be fine-tuned in order to serve, at least, as helpful heuristic tools for studying induced forgetting. (Induced forgetting is to be differentiated from *damnatio memoriae* that most often involves remembering that a particular person is not worthy of being remembered). On recent approaches to 'induced forgetting' in contemporary contexts, see, e.g., Charles B. Stone and William Hirst, "(Induced) Forgetting to Form a Collective Memory," *Memory Studies* 7 (2014), 314–27.

other figures with whom the first interacted in the world of memory of the remembering group. Similarly, a reference to one particular 'place' carries no significance unless other places exist in the memory world. To illustrate, and in terms of the world of memory of the literati on whom this volume focuses, their memories of kings had to be intertwined with, and were fully interdependent with memories of other figures that existed in the same mnemonic landscape. Moreover, all of these memories were shaped in the context of main metanarratives that were strongly internalized within the world of the literati and which fit well and exemplified core aspects of their social (and ideological) mindscape.

Moreover, remembering even particular kings (or prophets, etc.) and assigning significance to these memories was only possible within the parameters and messages conveyed by these large metanarratives.

Put another way, within any remembering group, memories can exist and bear significance only within the general mnemonic system of which they are an integral 'component' and in which they partake. This system is a cultural/mnemonic system that evolves as such. Consequently, what we may call collective or comprehensive social memory refers to a large, integrative system or array of multiple social memories and sites of memories that are constantly interacting and informing each other. By 'site of memory' I refer here and throughout this volume to any socially constructed space, place, event, figure, text or the like—whether it is manifested "materially" or only in the mind of members of a social group—whose presence in the relevant cultural milieu evokes or was meant to evoke core images or aspects of images of the past held by the particular social group who lives in that cultural milieu. Most of these sites act as ciphers to be activated within a particular social discourse, and as places to be visited and revisited, even if only mentally, as part of a self-supportive mechanism of socialization and social reproduction.

Like all social systems, the large, integrative system mentioned above is partially chaotic to be sure, but also follows some implied sets of rules, or systems of preferences and dis-preferences for the inclusion or exclusion of particular memories or types of memories. Even when the main rules are abandoned, it is because a competing or complementary set of rules becomes more dominant. In the essays in this volume, I tend to refer therefore to underlying generative grammars of preference and dis-preference regulating the production and reproduction of memories within the system. These underlying grammars are so internalized within the group that they become invisible to the agents and, like all matters that are so internalized, they provide important clues about the social mindscape of the remembering community.

Third, as the last paragraph suggests, it is impossible for a historian to study memories that are socially produced, reproduced, shaped, reshaped and re-signified among members of any group without paying attention to historical social agents. Memory entrepreneurs – people with mnemonic capital and the like – were involved in the social processes mentioned above. Without them, these social processes could not function. Single memories – much less an eco-system of memories – can neither be produced nor reproduced or even exist in a reified social vacuum.

Fourth, memories may be referred to as – and might have been assumed by historical communities to be – 'encoded' in texts. But the very term 'encoded' calls attention to the need of a 'code' to decode them, and of course, an act of 'decoding'. When read, texts that shape images of the past or future serve to construe, recall and reconfigure memories. Moreover, they may allow their readers to vicariously experience the worlds they conjure when reading them, and when they do, they shape (socially-valuable) emotional attachments to these memories of the past and future.[14] The key, however, is the very act of reading and the latter requires a community with a particular world of knowledge, including an existing repertoire of texts, images and memories. Again, it is easy to notice, from a historian's perspective, the importance of an interrelated eco-system that includes the world of knowledge, ideology, socially acceptable modes of reading, socially shared memoryscape and the social mindscape of the agents.

Fifth, paying attention to social agents and their actions within the social system in which they exist also means that the study of the pragmatic, social meaning of acts of remembering and of virtually experiencing these worlds of the mind, across time – in contradistinction to the semantic meaning of some the recalled narratives – must be strongly taken into account and is likely to be more helpful for the historical purposes envisaged here than simple semantic meanings.[15]

---

[14] Empathy plays an important, transcultural role in reading (literary) texts. If one understands empathy as "the ability to put oneself into the position of some other person ... and imagine the sensation of being in that situation" or "visualizing what the world looks like from another's vantage point," we have to assume that readers can vicariously experience what the character in the story, as construed by the reader, experiences. Not only that, readers can share vicariously the experience of a character, but also share with each other the experience of having vicariously experienced it through their readings. The literature on empathy and reading/literature is quite large. See, e.g., Meghan Marie Hammond and Sue J. Kim (eds.), *Rethinking Empathy through Literature* (Routledge Interdisciplinary Perspectives on Literature, 31; London/New York: Routledge, 2014) and literature cited there.

[15] I explored these matters also in my "Leadership in the World of Memories Evoked by Chronicles in the Context of the Late Persian/Early Hellenistic Period."

In what precedes, I have discussed some of the main features of a Social Memory approach, such as the one taken up in the essays included in this volume and in the general project of which these essays are representative. I made the point that such approaches informed by Social Memory studies are necessary, at least, for historians who are primarily focused on how certain historical groups thought and imagined themselves and others. But if historians should involve themselves in reconstructing a reasonable construction of the past and future as it was construed, remembered and shared by a particular historical group, how may they go about doing precisely that?

As in all cases involving matters of history and method, any critical approach that only 'works' within the parameters of a particular social-historical group is not a real critical approach, but an exercise in circular thinking. Although all historical settings are unique, only an approach that contributes to historical research across multiple cultures and societies may be considered good historical methodology. Since Social Memory studies have been shown to contribute to historical knowledge of multiple social-historical groups, across time and space, an approach informed by Social Memory studies to the study of the world of the ancient literati provides an excellent platform for countering the dangers of circular thinking that threaten historical studies that focus narrowly or solely on a number of texts. An approach that is informed by Social Memory studies would be most helpful by drawing attention to patterns of social memory construction, reproduction and function across a number of societies, by allowing us to see 'similarities' and 'dissimilarities' with other socio-historical groups, and by raising heuristic questions for research (for a good example, see e.g., chapter 14).

There exist multiple approaches in the field of Memory Studies, as even the most cursory reading of any 'handbook' or 'companion' to Social or Cultural or Collective Memory clearly shows to be the case. My own approach is strongly informed by (though not identical, partially due to my focus on ancient societies) those developed by scholars such as Eviatar Zerubavel, Barry Schwartz, Gary Alan Fine, and James W. Wertsch,[16] and in our field, by my colleague Diana V.

---

[16] See, e.g., Eviatar Zerubavel, *Social Mindscapes: An invitation to Cognitive Sociology* (Cambridge, Mass.: Harvard University Press, 1997); idem, *Time Maps: Collective Memory and the Social Shape of the Past.* (Chicago: University of Chicago Press, 2003); *Ancestors and Relatives: Genealogy, Identity and Community* (Oxford: Oxford University Press, 2011); Barry Schwartz, *Abraham Lincoln and the Forge of National Memory* (Chicago: Chicago University Press, 2003; idem, "Collective Forgetting and the Symbolic Power of Oneness: The Strange Apotheosis of Rosa Parks," *Social Psychology Quarterly* 72 (2009), 123–42; Gary Alan Fine, *Difficult Reputations. Collective Memories of the Evil, Inept and Controversial* (Chicago: Chicago University Press, 2001);

Edelman.[17] I have chosen this (mainly) socio-anthropological approach and remained consistently within its main parameters because, as I hope to demonstrate in this volume as well as in the larger project, it is most helpful from a heuristic viewpoint for the present studies.[18] In what follows I will summarily introduce a few key terms and cross-cultural observations strongly informing this approach.

Let me begin with the 'narrativity' of social memory. Socially shared memories tend to be structured as (implicit or explicit) narratives. As such they have a plot, beginnings and ends. They have main characters, including main heroes and villains, secondary characters that shed light on the main ones, and the like.

Beginnings and ends (i.e., periodization) play a substantial role in shaping social memories. They attribute prominence to certain events and characters and draw much attention to them as key signifiers, while drawing attention away from others.[19] Multiple mnemonic narratives, each with its own beginnings and ends, structures and meanings, may co-exist and complement each other within the general memoryscape of a group and at times, even within the world of the past evoked by reading particular books. For instance, in Chronicles one may notice a narrative/memory trajectory that moves from Adam to Cyrus, from the first (and clearly gendered) *man* and the beginning of creation and order and the rebuilding of the temple in Jerusalem. But there are complemen-

---

idem, *Sticky Reputations: The Politics of Collective Memory in Midcentury America* (New York: Routledge, 2012); James W. Wertsch, "Collective Memory and Narrative Templates," *Social Research* 75 (2008), 133–56; idem, *Voices of Collective Remembering* (Cambridge: Cambridge University Press, 2002).

17 See especially her "Introduction" in Diana V. Edelman and Ehud Ben Zvi (eds.) *Remembering Biblical Figures in the Late Persian & Early Hellenistic Periods: Social Memory and Imagination* (Oxford: Oxford University Press, 2013), xi–xxiv. See also Ian D. Wilson, *Kingship and Memory in Ancient Judah* (New York: Oxford University Press, 2017).

18 On various potential approaches to memory studies within the context of ancient Israel, see also Daniel Pioske, "Retracing a Remembered Past Methodological Remarks on Memory, History, and the Hebrew Bible," *BibInt* 23 (2015), 291–315. I am aware that in some fields, the memory approach advanced by Aleida and Jan Assmann is very popular. I tend to prefer slightly different socio-anthropological approaches to historical research, even if all these approaches go back to Halbwachs and eventually to Durkheim.

19 It is not the same to read a collection of books that begins with Genesis and ends with Deuteronomy as it is to read one that begins with Genesis and ends with Joshua. Of course, the same community may shape their comprehensive social memory in a way informed by both. See below.

tary trajectories as well, such as from Adam to David, from Saul to Cyrus, from David to Cyrus, among many others.[20]

Similarly, the selection of main heroes (rarely heroines) and villains[21] and particularly the attributes that are narratively and imaginatively associated with them, play a central role in social memory and what the group is socialized to learn from its past. Conversely, these choices tell us a lot about the remembering group. For instance, it is significant that despite the role of the priests at the temple in Jerusalem and the role of the Temple itself, including its support for the literati, that the main human hero of their past was Moses, the lawgiver and prophet, not Aaron, the priest, or David, the king of a polity, conqueror of Jerusalem and in Chronicles, the one whose ordinances establish the temple. Similarly, it is not by chance that their authoritative repertoire included books associated with individual prophets, but none associated with a king or priest, as such.

Likewise, selecting and constructing a memorable first/founding leader/ ruler and its counterpart 'the last leader/ruler' and their characterizations shed much light on the remembering community and its social mindscape. Of course, the 'first' is not necessarily the most important character within a memory space. The 'second Adam' is far more important in Christian memory than the 'first Adam', but this tell us much about the remembering group. Chapter 14 addresses directly the matter of remembering 'last rulers.'

Comparative memory studies are most helpful, not only for identifying these matters, but also for noticing general tendencies within them that hold across different cultures. They provide a necessary heuristic tool and lessen the danger of falling into circular thinking.

Comparative memory studies have also drawn attention to the so-called tendency toward 'oneness,' that is, a strong tendency for and a 'reproductive' bias in favor of constructing (implicit or explicit) narratives about particular events, processes, and periods in which there is *one* main character (hero or villain), which, of course, necessitates drawing attention away from others.[22] Given that this tendency is grounded in reasons of cognitive economy, it is not surprising that it is widely attested. But precisely because this is the case, when it is not

---

[20] These and the considerations just mentioned above are explored in most of the chapters in this volume. See also my "Reading Chronicles and Remembering Saul."
[21] On the matter of the arch-villain of memory see esp. chapter 13.
[22] A classical work on this is Barry Schwartz, "Collective Forgetting and the Symbolic Power of Oneness".

followed, there is a need for historians to explore why. What was gained by the group and by its memory system that justified the additional cognitive costs?[23]

To be sure, one might have expected also the existence of one main memory narrative about any main period or about any main character. Within the repertoire of the literati discussed here, however, the most common situation is an array of narratives informing and balancing each other. In the cases of the main characters, one of the results is a sense of fuzziness (see also below). Whether all this multiplicity and multivocality is the result of long diachronic processes or not,[24] the outcome is still the same; the literati who read and reread their repertoire construed a past in which main characters were multi-vocal, multiple narratives existed about supposedly the same event, and as mentioned above, there were multiple memory trajectories. Moreover, often reading one single book brought all of the above to light. Since all of these involve higher cognitive costs, a historian should raise the question about gains that more than balanced the costs. Numerous essays in this volume discuss from a variety of perspectives the ideological and social gains brought by this system of preferences.

The characters of the past mentioned above are usually described in this volume as sites of memory, but this term refers to more than only them. Comparative memory studies show some level of diversity in terms of the referent of 'site of memory'. This concept plays an important role in this approach, both in the current volume and in the entire project as well.

'Site of memory' is used here to refer to any socially constructed space, place, event, figure, text or the like—whether it is manifested 'materially' or only in the mind of members of a social group—whose presence in the relevant cultural milieu evokes or was meant to evoke core images or aspects of images of the past held by the particular social group who lives in that cultural milieu. The moment one accepts this understanding and pragmatic use of the term, then one

---

[23] For instance, what did the community gain by having to remember three major characters of memory, namely Isaiah, Jeremiah and Ezekiel, instead of only the first two who could have covered and shaped an image of the same period? Why have fifteen prophetic characters with whom to associate books? These issues are discussed, inter alia, in chapter 2.

[24] It is extremely unlikely that the literati went about reading texts within their repertoire by first separating each of them into its multiple redactional layers, assigned each of them to a particular period in their construed past, and then looked for and reconstructed the other texts that populated each one of these periods and which may have informed that particular layer. In other words, their mode of reading texts was not like the mode of our redactional critical colleagues and for a reason. The latter do not ask the same questions from the text than the former did. One may say that the historical literati of the period read their texts in a mode of reading akin to what we tend to call 'synchronic'.

must accept that all memory groups have sites of memory, and since all groups are, inter alia, memory groups, that all groups have their sites of memory.

Sites of memory are necessary for encapsulating – embodying as it were – and for communicating and evoking memories. Of course, memories, and all memory narratives, necessarily shape sites of memory. Moreover, the more important the memories were for the group, the more important the relevant sites for it become, and *vice versa*. Memories become central for a group in direct relation to the degree in which they relate to matters that are at the very core of the group and its worldview and understanding of itself. For instance, *torah*, prophecy, the deliverance from Egypt, proper prophetic leadership, and godly commands about how the cult of YHWH should proceed were all central concepts within the ideological world of the literati. Conversely, Moses who as a site of memory serves as a mnemonic node connecting them all, becomes the most central site of memory associated with a figure of the past for them. As mentioned above, neither Aaron the priest nor Joshua the conqueror, nor, for that matter, David, the king most associated with Jerusalem, could compete with Moses as a site of memory. All of these figures were considered secondary to him. They were construed as helpers of, or necessary complements to, Moses.

The reference to complementarity above raises another important issue. Central sites of memory serve as nodes connecting core ideological concepts/memories but also must be deeply connected to numerous other sites populating the memoryscape of the group. Just as in a narrative, the main character cannot exist alone, so memory studies show that remembering a main character requires remembering others, and the others also shed much light on the main.

In addition, and not surprisingly, main sites of memory (e.g., Moses, Lincoln, Peter the Great) are likely to embody as it were periodizations of the remembered past. In the case of Moses, the emerging periodization, clearly attested by the boundaries around the Pentateuch, drew attention to the period of birth of Israel (torah and deliverance from Egypt). At the same time, it required a prelude (the patriarchal period) and the ensuing fulfillment of Moses' prophecies (i.e., the history of Israel from Joshua to 2 Kings), thus shaping not only the period of the 'birth of Israel', but the entire memory narrative about Israel.[25]

---

[25] Although these matters are discussed in various essays in this volume (see esp. chapter 6), it is worth stressing that periodizations, because of their significance for ideological socialization, may become in some communities sites of mnemonic struggles, while in other communities, multiple periodizations may balance and inform each other, shaping the comprehensive social memory of the group. In the case of the literati discussed here, the latter option was taken, and this is fully consistent with their strong tendency to shape a kind of consistency grounded on seemingly consistent inconsistency (or as I refer at times, the coherence grounded on seeming,

Comparative cases of "exemplar" or "founding" figures, or both, within the memoryscape of other groups across cultures and societies not only help us to notice what is transculturally common in Moses, the site of memory that was held by the literati, but also what is uncommon. For instance, Moses is not imagined, in the main, as a leading warrior, or as a general.[26] Significantly, the same thing happens with Abraham—with one 'minority report'—and the warrior aspect of Joshua is substantially downplayed in the book of Joshua and in the memory of the literati reading this book, contrary to what one may have expected from the main human leader involved in the conquest of the land.[27] In other words, here one begins to notice the influence of (an implied) strong set of preferences and dispreferences for the production and reproduction of memories and the shaping of sites of memory.

Central sites of memory are transculturally a most useful communal tool for social cohesion, and for the integration of various memories (and the implied ideologies that they evoked) that are seemingly in tension with each other. Thus, to bring an example from the memoryscape of the relevant literati, it is not surprising that their Moses spoke 'D' and 'P' and advanced seemingly contradictory, but actually socially complementary positions. Of course, Moses is not alone in this. Jeremiah had more than one diction, and above all, YHWH, the most central site of memory of the literati, was 'overhead' by the literati, as they read the books in their repertoire and vicariously experience the narrated events, as speaking in multiple dictions and advancing multiple, and at times seemingly contradictory, positions. One may ask then why the central figures of memory of the group are so multivocal and one may say 'fuzzy'?

In the essays in this volume, I demonstrate time and again that there was a strong, systemic preference for this type of integrative fuzziness, both in terms of shaping central sites of memory and at the very level of the texts within the repertoire, including, for example, narratives, and images. Scholars working with more commonly used redactional methods would work with the relevant texts, notice their 'contradictions' and try to 'solve' them by stringing together a diachronic chain of 'logically self-consistent' texts associated with particular sources, authors, redactors and the like. Each of these textual chains, then, would voice a particular – and for the most part coherent – viewpoint, often in a coherent diction. In the case of narratives, this tendency shapes narratives that 'work logically' and do not self-contradict at various points or details.

---

consistent incoherence). On these issues see below in this Introduction. They are discussed and exemplified also in most essays in this volume.
26 Of course, later Hellenistic period literature will 'normalize' his image in this aspect.
27 See, e.g., chapters 5, 6 and 7.

For historians whose work is strongly informed by a Social Memory studies perspective, the world looks much more difficult to grasp, at least at first. The reason is simple: the literati who read and reread a particular repertoire of authoritative texts[28] and were socialized through this process, could not but imagine and vicariously experience their past through their readings. But their repertoire included and integrated all the voices that our redaction criticism-oriented colleagues have rightly noticed. From the perspective of the reading (and remembering) community, all these voices and tensions become representative of a set or sets of multiple voices that the community cannot but end up associating with the implied author of the text they are reading[29] (or when appropriate some central character as portrayed by the implied author in the book), whose intent they are supposed to grasp. Thus, from the perspective of the reading community, all of these voices had to be construed as complementary, at least at some level, since they all go back to the same implied author or central character.[30]

The preceding discussion pointed to just one mnemonic (and literary) preference, but as the studies in this volume show, there are many sets of preferences and dis-preferences shaping memories and thus, from a systemic viewpoint, what emerges is a complex generative grammar preferring the production and reproduction of some types of memories, sites of memory, and central narratives and dis-preferring others. To be sure, an examination of such (underlying) gen-

---

28 The term 'authoritative,' as used here and in the volume in general, has at times raised misinterpretations. The point I want to make is that a community cannot conceive itself to be 'text-centered' if it has no 'text' to be centered on. The Israel construed by the literati was a 'text-centered' world and the adjective 'authoritative' signifies that the texts so marked were, even if in slightly different ways, an integral part of the 'text' around which the literati's Israel was centered. As such these texts carried 'authority' within their worldview. Moreover, since these texts appear in the form of books or collections (and at times both; see for example, the prophetic book collection, the deuteronomistic historical collection) that implicitly or explicitly claim to communicate a sense of social and ideological authoritativeness, then the voices of the implied authors, narrators of these works, as the readers construed them to be, were characterized as authoritative as well, and within this ideological/theological context, as godly too.
29 Of course, here, in the rest of the volume and in the general project, by implied author I refer to the author that readers construe to be the author of the text. All readers, knowingly or unknowingly, construe implied authors as they read texts and the way in which they construe them strongly influence the way in which they read them and *vice versa*. I explore further this concept of (socially) implied (and socially construed) author in my "Matters of Authorship, Authority and Power."
30 These issues are widely discussed and exemplified in the essays included in this volume.

erative grammars cannot but shed much light into the social mindscape of the literati.[31]

Memories also represent a wide field – or one may call it a 'playground' – for safely exploring central ideas (e.g., divine promises, the significance of the catastrophe at the end of the Judahite, monarchic polity, or the future kingdom of YHWH[32]), as well as other types of matters important to the community, such as a preference for monogyny in a patriarchal society, or issues that today we would label as economic thought, political thought, or even what constitutes being wise.[33] Memory studies alert us to these roles of memory.

Remembering, of course, cannot exist without a remembering group; it takes place within social locations associated with agents of memory and remembrance and serves social roles for them. Acts of remembering constitute implicit claims for mnemonic capital, for cultural capital and often also social capital. Remembering complex arrays of images of the past, all informing each other and constituting the mnemonic landscape of the group, requires expertise and knowledge, and conveys claims concerning them.[34]

As mentioned above, the work of scholars such as E. Zerubavel, B. Schwartz, G. A. Fine, J.V. Wertsch and most socio-anthropological researchers in the field of Social Memory focuses on relatively recent societies. Although their methods may be applied to multiple historical societies and groups within them, one must keep in mind the historical specificity of the remembering community: in this case, that of the literati in late Persian/early Hellenistic Yehud. Equally important, there is an obvious and significant gap in the type of sources available to us to reconstruct for more ancient communities their socially construed and shared memories, the grammars governing their production and reproduction and the pragmatic roles of remembering particular stories in certain social settings.

The question of sources is certainly crucial. The main source for historians of the world of the literati informed by Memory Studies, and certainly for the approach taken here, is the authoritative repertoire of texts that they had. But how can any historian know what constituted their core or authoritative repertoire?

---

[31] Needless to say, it also allows us to recognize its limits and particular cases in which counter-grammars were at work. By drawing attention to these issues, this approach also shed a necessary, complementary light on the social mindscape of the literati.
[32] See, e.g., chapters 19, 16 and 4 respectively.
[33] Several of these matters are explicitly discussed in the essays included here, see esp. chapters 25 and 26. See also my forthcoming "Memories of Female (and Male) Sages."
[34] See, e.g., chapter 30.

The underlying assumption here is that the Pentateuchal collection, the Deuteronomistic Historical collection, the prophetic books collection, Chronicles, most of Psalms and Proverbs and a few other books included today in the Hebrew Bible (e.g. Lamentations, Ruth) are approximately *representative* in more-or-less their known present forms[35] of the general authoritative repertoire of the literati in the late Persian/early Hellenistic period. It bears stating that this collection does not extend to all of the books currently included in the Hebrew Bible (see for example, Daniel and Esther, which are later than the late Persian/early Hellenistic period).

This assumption is reasonable given the small number of literati, the relatively large and sophisticated corpus of texts referred to here, and the substantial agreement among scholars that these books and collections existed in some form that resembles their present compositional forms at least by the Early Hellenistic period.[36]

One may add that the assumption of an authoritative, textual repertoire is not out of place given that within the ideological discourse of the literati, texts occupy a central position. In fact, Israel was conceived as a text-centered group.[37] In addition, the social location of the literati is worth keeping in mind, including the lengthy training they had to undergo to achieve the necessary level of high literacy they had. Moreover, their training had to include reading these high-literacy texts. After all, to be able to compose prophetic books, for example, one has to have an idea of what a prophetic book is; and to achieve the latter one, has to read prophetic books.[38]

---

35 Readers should notice the plural form, 'present forms'.

36 It is true that additional books, now lost, might have been part of the core, but the alternative option, namely that the extant entire corpus is completely unrepresentative of the authoritative repertoire of the literati and thus cannot serve even as an approximation is difficult to maintain.

37 The literati's ability to construe, evoke and identify with a text-centered Israel was strongly facilitated by the fact their authoritative repertoire (i.e., the 'text' around which Israel was centered) conjured into being a past and a future that provided them with a sense of who they were, a memoryscape by which they could explore matters close to them, such as those that were directly and indirectly related to social, ever ongoing processes of shaping identity, and the correlated issues of constructing 'others' and in-between areas and the whole spectrum between more and less porous boundaries. They contributed also to explore matters of how to lead a godly life as a group and the associated issues of proper (and improper) leadership, instilling hope by providing meaning to memories of the past and enjoy memories about idyllic, but for them 'certain to come' worlds in the far future of Israel that provided them with the necessary hope required for proper social reproduction.

38 Cf. also the issues discussed in ch 30.

Of course, written texts or collections of texts are not themselves memories. They may, inter alia, encode, communicate, shape, reshape, recall memories, but they are not memories. Only people can have memories. But people do not live alone. They are socialized in particular ways, including ideological worldviews, worlds of knowledge, and even patterns for constructing memories. Reading texts always requires previous knowledge, including that of other texts, but also an internalization of 'proper' modes of reading. All readings are historically and socially contingent, as are all memories that are shaped, reshaped, and vicariously experienced (via empathy) through readings of texts within a group. They belong to a specific group in a particular social and historical location, with its own distinct social mindscape and ideological discourse, and thus its own mode of reading.[39] For instance, the Genesis of Calvin was substantially different from the Genesis of Rashi, Ibn Ezra or, for that matter, the targumists (see, esp. Neofiti, Pseudo-Jonathan, Fragment Targums), even if all had access to essentially the same Hebrew text.[40] In other words, it is not the text as a collection of graphemes, but as the 'read' text that counts for the present purposes.

If constructing reasonable, historical reconstructions requires some imagination, my task here is to imagine the world of memory that these literati must have shared when they read and reread their texts and thus construed an array of images about their past and vicariously experienced it (and the future memories also encoded in them). And it is clear that they did indeed read and reread these texts.[41] If this were not the case, then it is difficult to explain, inter alia, (a) the long compositional and redactional processes that the books in the repertoire underwent, (b) the existence of multiple textual versions of at least some of these books, (c) the crucial role assigned to memories of material texts and acts of writing within the literati's authoritative repertoire for the community and their socially constructed and shared memory (see, esp. Exod 24:12; Deut 27:3,8; 31:9,24; Josh 8:31–34; 24:6; 2 Kgs 17:37), all of which are associated within the memoryscape and social mindscape of the group with an implied notion that what a godly text contains must be followed, which in turn, implies that they must be read, (d) the repetitions and inner and inter-book allusions that serve as signposts which guide reading and provide contexts, and (e) the height-

---

39 Cf., e.g., Lowell K. Handy, "One Problem Involved in Translating to Meaning: An Example of Acknowledging Time and Tradition," *SJOT* 10 (1996), 16–27.
40 Of course, there are also limits to what the readers may construe the text to be. I proposed a heuristic theoretical frame for analyzing different readings of a book in my *Signs of Jonah* (JSTOTSup, 367: London: Sheffield Academic Press, 2003), 129–54.
41 Of course, they most likely read these books, or portions of them, to others who were not able to do so without the literati's intermediation. On these issues see below.

ened sophistication and complexity of these books, both of which attest to higher textual training, which by necessity involves reading texts at this level.

To be sure, it is not enough to say that the literati read their authoritative, textual repertoire. One must also provide an image of how they read them. What would be a reasonable, approximate reconstruction of their way of readings texts given the existing evidence of the texts themselves and taking into account comparative studies?

The most reasonable answer to this question is that they read their authoritative texts, to a large extent, in such a manner that each text (and each section even within a book or a literary subunit in it) was informed by and in turn informed the other texts. The widespread, and widely acknowledged, system of evocative cross-references among many books, characters and the like supports the idea that texts were read this way.[42] Since reading went together and was closely intertwined with imagining a past and future, many of the issues raised in memory studies, and particularly by the type of approach to memory studies adopted here, are relevant (see discussion above).

The literati could not but read also in ways strongly informed by and at the same time informing and balancing central ideological grand narratives or metanarratives about the past and future of Israel that were held by the group, and the same about the way in which they imagined and vicariously encountered, via reading and empathy, their main heroes of the past (and future in some cases).

In other words, they read their authoritative texts as an integral part of a cultural, textual center around which they construed Israel. They were informed by their world of knowledge – as all readers are – and tended to accept readings in

---

[42] The Book of Chronicles provides much evidence of this reading. For instance, it assumes knowledge of other texts and books in the repertoire, and, in addition, reading Chronicles reflected the viewpoint and taught the literati that the meaning of a text in Exodus can be obtained only by reading it in a way informed by one in Deuteronomy and vice versa. See Ehud Ben Zvi, "Revisiting 'Boiling in Fire' in 2 Chr 35:13 and Related Passover Questions Text, Exegetical Needs, Concerns, and General Implications," in Isaac Kalimi and Peter J. Haas (eds.), *Biblical Interpretation in Judaism and Christianity* (LHBOTS, 439; London and New York: T&T Clark, 2006) 238–50. See also Ehud Ben Zvi and Diana V. Edelman (eds.), *What is Authoritative for Chronicles* (Winona Lake, Ind.: Eisenbrauns, 2011) and in this volume also "Chronicles and Samuel-Kings: Two Interacting Aspects of one Memory System in the Late Persian/Early Hellenistic Period." To be sure, it is not only Chronicles that provides such evidence. For instance, reading the superscriptions of many of the prophetic books (e.g., Isa 1:1) was clearly tantamount to activating the reading literati's knowledge of the periods of particular kings in the past. I discussed some of these matters in "Towards an Integrative Study of the Production of Authoritative Books in Ancient Israel," in Diana V. Edelman and Ehud Ben Zvi (eds.), *The Production of Prophecy. Constructing Prophecy and Prophets in Yehud* (London: Equinox, 2009), 15–28.

ways that helped them with central issues. They favoured readings that were socially acceptable, just as memories are more likely to produce and reproduce in a group if they are socially acceptable by a group, in light of its own ideology and social mindscape.

Modes of reading support or undermine social tendencies. For instance, social cohesion among the relatively few, highly educated literati in Jerusalem, despite whatever personal differences they might have had, was served by sharing a sea of (a) texts, (b) allusions, (c) acts and memories of reading these texts, (d) memories of a communal past and future, (e) social self-ascribed roles, (f) socialization and social mindscape, and (g) performance of shared pragmatic roles when reading these texts. Above all, they shared a preference for the type of coherence grounded in seeming incoherence that characterized their discourse and was embodied in their main sites of memory, as discussed above and throughout this volume. Significantly, this strong preference is well-suited to, not only small social groups for which a substantial level of social coherence facilitates social reproduction, but also and mainly to those that do not see themselves threatened by strong existential anxieties (see already chapter 1 in this volume).

In addition to all of the above, one has to take into account the 'pragmatic' roles of reading certain texts and of remembering the worlds they conjure (and remembering that they remembered and virtually experienced them as well) within the context of a social location within a particular socio-historical setting. For instance, what is the pragmatic meaning of producing and reading past-shaping texts by temple-centered literati living in a subordinate, local polity, within an empire whose hegemonic center is elsewhere?

As in the somewhat comparable case of cuneiform literature in temples in Babylonia during the Persian and Seleucid periods, reading these texts served not only as acts performing a social position, but also as acts that evoked and connoted – and to an extent, brought into being – a sense of Israel-ness (or 'Babylonian-ness' in the case of literati in Babylon or Ur). More or less at the same time, these ethno-cultural groups were construed in terms of their 'essential' association with a literary corpus that shaped memories of the past and hopes for the future.[43] It is not surprising either that they were construed in such a way by functionally comparable elites.

---

[43] See, e.g., Caroline Waerzeggers, "Facts, Propaganda or History? Shaping Political Memory in the Nabonidus Chronicle," in Jason M. Silverman and Caroline Waerzeggers (eds), *Political Memory in and after the Persian Empire* (ANEM/MACO, 13; Atlanta: SBL Press, 2015), 95–124; Geert De Breucker, "Heroes and Sinners: Babylonian Kings in Cuneiform Historiography of the Persian and Hellenistic Periods," in Silverman and Waerzeggers (eds), *Political Memory*, 75–94; Michael Jursa, with contributions by Céline Debourse, "A Babylonian Priestly Martyr, a King-like Priest,

Before concluding this introduction, two of the common questions mentioned at the outset may be addressed. The present approach may be used for historical reconstructions of the world of thought and memory of literati other than those in Yehud in the late Persian and early Hellenistic period. If this were not the case, that is, if it were to 'work' only for those literati, then, as mentioned above, this approach would not be methodologically sound to begin with.

To be sure, as in any other case, one has to be aware of the social and historical circumstances of the group, and its 'uniqueness.' Particularly important is the matter of sources. The approach advanced here, although grounded in social-anthropological approaches to memory studies, has been, by necessity, designed to work with literati whose shared memory was shaped mainly by reading a repertoire of texts or, one may say, the contents of a conceptual, mental library.

Unless historians have access to something that may serve as representative or a reasonable approximation to this library, the type of project (and approach) advanced here would not work. For this reason, for instance, I have not tried to reconstruct the memoryscape, social mindscape and the like of literati in monarchic Judah or Israel. I have no doubt that they existed, had memories, and wrote and read texts that encoded, shaped, and recalled their socially shared memory. But I do not think that historians have access to the necessary approximation to the library of literati in, for example, Ahab's Israel or Josiah's Judah. I would like to stress that even if I were to grant the possibility that at least some of the texts that our redactional-critical colleagues have proposed to have existed in, for instance, Hezekianic or Josianic Judah, or for that matter, the exiled court of Jehoiachin in Babylonia,[44] we still would not have anything close to an approxima-

---

and the Nature of Late Babylonian Priestly Literature," *Wiener Zeitschrift für die Kunde des Morgenlandes* 107 (2017), 77–98. Significantly, in both cases, there was a tendency to accept logical tension, ambiguity and multivocality within the corpus. I address a few similarities and differences in terms of generative grammars between the Mesopotamian and the Yehudite literati in my "Leadership in the World of Memories Evoked by Chronicles in the Context of the Late Persian/Early Hellenistic Period" (forthcoming).

44 To be sure, I have argued for a long time that we do not have access to texts from the monarchic period *in the ways they existed then*. To be sure, texts did exist, but the redactional-critical methods we use to construct and date an original textual forerunner of later texts and all the subsequent editorial layers are unable to provide them. For a recent publication in which I address these matters, see Ehud Ben Zvi, "Remembering Twelve Prophetic Characters from the Past," esp. pp. 7–12. This said, even if I were to grant that we had access to a few texts as they existed in that period, it would not be enough to use the approach advanced here. To be sure, I am aware that the approach taken here ends up, by necessity, construing hypothetical readings, even if the process of generating them is supported at one level or another by comparative, social anthropological approaches to production and reproduction of social memory. This

tion of the comprehensive mental library of core texts shared by these literati. A few texts held by a group do not necessarily represent their synchronic, mental library of core texts.⁴⁵ Further, within this approach, texts do not evolve (nor are they read) separately from others. Instead, it is the entire eco-system of texts that evolves over time (and its co-related system of socially shared images of the past and future, social mindscapes, worlds of knowledge), and in response to the vicissitudes of history in general and in the social roles of literati as a result of them in particular.⁴⁶

Of course, none of this means that nothing about memory may be said about the monarchic period (Judah or Northern Israel) or monarchic period texts. For instance, one may develop the old tradition of trying to find historical kernels helpful to reconstruct earlier periods in later texts into one that focuses on echoes of ancient memories that, even if they are resignified in later texts, may still inform about earlier periods.⁴⁷ This approach to memory is, however, substantially different from the one advanced here.

Limitations concerning sources also explain the exclusive focus on the literati rather than the whole community in Yehud, or at least a much larger group during that period. As in the case of monarchic Judah, the desire to know presses us all, but the sources limit what we can do.

---

approach, however, deals with one layer of readers (i.e., the literati) who were aware of all the other books in the repertoire. Redactional-critical approaches must deal with multiple layers of readers/redactors-authors and with an unclear repertoire of (other) texts for each one of the layers of readers/redactors-authors for each one of the texts that they dealt with. In other words, redactional critical approaches *exponentially* increase the perils for critical historians that are associated with generating hypothetical readings in comparison with the model advanced here.

45 It is very doubtful too that the literati of this earlier monarchic period conceptualized Israel as a community centered on authoritative texts and allowed no room for royal institutions to play a role in shaping a sense of identity for the people living in the relevant monarchic polities. If they did not conceptualize Israel as (solely or even mainly) a text-centered community, then significant concerns arise for the use of the approach delineated here.

46 Cf. Umberto Eco's concepts of the 'encyclopedia' and 'encyclopedic knowledge.' Although no historian can reconstruct the full encyclopedia (in Eco's sense) of the literati of the late Persian/early Hellenistic period, the approach taken here seems the best way to reconstruct an approximation of their 'encyclopedia'. Moreover, like Eco, I would argue that each new book that is added to the library reshapes, to an extent, the meaning of the other books in the library and vice versa. The implications of these concepts for historical research about the world of thought of the literati are vast. Many of the essays in this volume may be seen as indirect explorations of these issues, see e.g., chapter 12.

47 See, e.g., several of the essays on the special issue on Jeroboam (II) in *HebAI* 6 (2017), such as Nadav Na'aman, "Memories of Monarchical Israel in the Narratives of David's Wars with Israel's Neighbours," *HebAI* 6 (2017), 308–28.

It is extremely likely that the literati communicated some of the texts in their authoritative repertoire to those in the larger community who were unable to read them by themselves, that is, the immense majority of the community. This is so because, as elaborated in, for example, chapter 30 in this volume, the text-centered vision of the literati and, at least, some of the meanings and related memories associated with it *had* to be successfully communicated to and shared by groups other than the literati, if it was to be maintained.

Moreover, the story of Jehoshaphat's mobile teaching committee in 2 Chr 17:7–9, and references to public readings of divine teachings (e. g., Deut 31:9–13; cf. Neh 8) show that communication to the larger group was indeed associated with important memories of the past and part of the memoryscape of the community. Further, these texts indicate also some of the ways in which such a communication might have actually been carried out, and how it is controlled by an authoritative centre as well.

The problem, however, is that there is no way for current historians to reconstruct the acts of social performance and socialization through which the texts were communicated, nor the way the texts were read to the gatherings and the meanings attributed to these texts that were communicated to the larger group. Setting aside all the obvious differences, a contemporary example helps to understand the depths of the problem. Today's USA is one the countries with one of the highest levels of literacy, but the Bible that most people 'know' is not that which is based on a careful analysis of what this or that English translation states, but on what they heard in churches and synagogues, and on social media. It changes from religious denomination to denomination, within various denominations, on the personal and socially structured filters that individuals use when listening to biblical texts or explanations of them in religious settings or elsewhere. It even changes depending on the ritual season of the year, current events, and the identity of the preacher. It is certainly not uncommon today in America that the same text may be used to communicate one meaning and exactly its opposite. Future historians more than two millennia from now would be extremely lucky if they have access to full copies of the NRSV, the KJV, the NKJV, the NIV and the NJPSV. But if this all they have, they will certainly be unable to reconstruct the 'heard' Bibles of Americans today.

To be sure, the small population of Yehud was far more homogeneous than that of the USA today. But we still do not have knowledge of which texts were read to the public or when. We have no way to reconstruct the oral, aural and visual features (including pauses, stresses, facial expressions) that strongly impacted the meaning of the text read to some of the public. We do not have access to the contextual setting in which readings took place, or with which co-texts they were read. As the case of the *haftarot* clearly shows, the meaning of a text is substantially impacted by the other texts with which it is read.⁴⁸

Further, if the situation was, at least from time to time, that the text was ritually read (in Hebrew) to all and shown in a scroll as an iconic, revered object, and then explained (in Aramaic?),⁴⁹ we still have no idea if it was translated from Hebrew to Aramaic, in which case the unknown translation would have been key for the interpretation. In any event, we cannot reconstruct the mental 'library' of explanations heard by the public, nor what they made of it.⁵⁰

In sum, like any historian I know, I wish also to know far more than I can know about ancient Israel. At times, it makes methodological sense to remain wishing and acknowledge our limitations in pursuing historical knowledge. At times, however, as I demonstrate in the following chapters, critical lenses such as those of approaches informed by Social Memory may allow us to see the potential richness of our sources, even if within the limits of one social group (i.e., the literati) and one era (i.e., the late Persian/early Hellenistic period in Yehud). Much more work remains to be done, though, and hopefully this volume will encourage further research on these matters.

---

48 On the *haftarot*, see Michael Fishbane, *Haftarot* (JPS Bible Commentary; Philadelphia: The Jewish Publication Society), 2002.
49 Cf. Neh 8; 2 Chr 17:7–9.
50 To be sure, one might argue that the basic 'global semantic contents' (or 'macro-structure,' following scholars in discourse comprehension; see, e.g., Teun A. van Dijk and Walter Kintsch, *Strategies of Discourse Comprehension* [New York: Academic Press, 1983]; Teun A. van Dijk, *Macrostructures* [Hillsdale, NJ: Erlbaum, 1980]) that characterize some 'simple' narratives (such as the very basic plot of the story of Hosea and his wife/ves) might have been used time and again for 'public education' purposes in the larger community, as they could encapsulate in memorable ways the basic plot of Israel's past and future. See references to potentially relevant examples in chapters 2, 9 and 10. Of course, all this assumes that the relevant historical community was strongly patriarchal, but such was indeed the case. Although this might have been the case in some occasions, (a) we will still remain without a comprehensive approximation to the mental 'library' of the general population, (b) even these narratives are not so simple at all and were likely read in multiple, complementary ways by the literati (see mentioned chapters in this volume), and (c) the 'global semantic contents' contribute, but certainly do not alone define which interpretation a text would be given. See, Ben Zvi, *Signs of Jonah*, 129–54.

On Social Memory and Identity Formation in Late Persian Yehud: A Historian's Viewpoint with a Focus on Prophetic Literature, Chronicles and the Deuteronomistic Historical Collection*

A Preliminary Considerations

I To begin with

Prophetic Literature, Chronicles and the Deuteronomistic historical collection all had an impact on the formation of communal identity in late Persian Yehud.[1] They did so not as historiographical or prophetic literature directly,[2] but through their contribution to the shaping of the community's social memory, or at least that of the literati who read and reread these books.[3] Given (a) the size of the community, (b) the fact that the maintenance of a literati group required social resources, (c) the likely role of the Jerusalem temple in supporting the production of highly sophisticated Jerusalem-centred texts and their authorships and

---

* First published in *Texts, Contexts and Readings in Postexilic Literature: Explorations into Historiography and Identity Negotiation in Hebrew Bible and Related Texts* (ed. L. Jonker; Tübingen: Mohr Siebeck, 2011), 95–148.

1 It is worth noting that communal identity involves an array of features, from a sense of shared ancestry, to cultural patterns and shared world of knowledge and ideological worldviews, to the construction of the group in terms of fulfilling a role in the world and vis-à-vis its deity/ies. Cf. (and contrast) J. Berquist, "Constructions of Identity", 53–66. Significantly, the statement above holds true not only for ancient social groups/ethnies, but often also for contemporary groups.

2 This is the reason I prefer to write about "social memory" and "identity" rather than "historiography" and "identity", despite the fact that "ethnic" or "national" historiography always contribute to the shaping and constant reshaping, and reflect "ethnic" or "national" identities. They do so along with other texts that construe the past but that can hardly be defined as historiography (e.g. the prophetic books) because of their impact in the shaping and reshaping of social memory and the creation of a social mindscape that has important cognitive roles. On these matters, see below.

3 Thus, had I been the editor of the recent and excellent collection of essays entitled *Historiography and Identity (Re)formulation in Second Temple Historiographical Literature*, I would have probably called it *Social Memory and Identity*. The point of this comment is not to criticise the editor, who prepared a very thoughtful and helpful volume, and is none other than the editor of the volume in which the present essay was first published and the convenor of the original workshop (i.e. Louis Jonker), but to raise already the underlying issues of terminology and perhaps methodology.

(re)readerships, and (d) that the literati's Jerusalem-centred ideology promoted and was fully consistent with the historical process that led to an incipient Jerusalemite temple in a Benjaminite-centred early Persian Yehud gaining the status of the central institution that it became already by the mid-/late Persian period,[4] it is reasonable to assume that the collective memory of the community was not far removed from that of the literati.

Some of the ways in which readings of the mentioned books contributed to the shaping of memory and through memory to the formation of identity are easy to discern. For instance, a main metanarrative in prophetic literature is: (a) YHWH chose Israel long ago and became its patron; (b) Israel – the client – broke its obligations towards its patron, or in theological terms, Israel sinned against YHWH; (c) YHWH punished Israel (a stage associated with the fall of the monarchic polities and socio-cultic systems), but since YHWH still "loves" Israel, the deity will not exterminate Israel or abrogate its patronship/"fathership," which from an ideological perspective would be tantamount to its ceasing to exist as such and losing its "identity;"[5] and (d) since YHWH did not abrogate its patronship, at an undefined but certain future time, YHWH will bring this relationship to its proper (ideal) form.[6] This general metanarrative shapes and informs a construction of the past and future of Israel, identifies the community of Yehud with this transtemporal Israel and characterises the latter in terms of a relationship with YHWH, which in turn serves to characterise YHWH as well.[7]

Similarly, it is relatively easy to note that a construction of the past influenced mainly by the primary historical collection (Genesis – 2 Kings) would tend to place much mindshare in the Mosaic period, as pertinent in a community

---

[4] Note, for instance, the asymmetry between the Samarian and Yehudite addressees of the letters sent by Jedaniah and his colleagues, the priests in Elephantine, which unequivocally points to the high status of the Jerusalemite temple in Yehud by 407 BCE. The letters were sent to "Delaiah and Shelemiah, sons of Sanballat, governor of Samaria" and in first instance, to "Jehohanan the High Priest and his colleagues the priests who are in Jerusalem, and to Ostanes the brother of Anani and the nobles of Judah," and later to Bagavahya, the governor of Yehud. See B. Porten et al., *The Elephantine Papyri*, 139–149; B. Porten and A. Yardeni, *Textbook*, 68–75.

[5] For example, and to use common metaphors in the literature of Yehud and in the social mindscape of the community, the "child," and mainly, though not exclusively, "son" (Israel), can be the child, because he (or she) has a father (YHWH); similarly, the "wife" (Israel) can be the wife, because she has a husband (YHWH). All these are relational identity constructions.

[6] See E. Ben Zvi, *Hosea*, 8.

[7] Israel and YHWH characterise each other at both the notional and the narrative/social mnemonic level. See note 5 and ubiquitous reference to YHWH as the God of Israel, and the latter as YHWH's people.

that is text-centred and whose main "text" is construed as YHWH's *torah* communicated through Moses.

Chronicles, in turn, influenced the balance of social memory towards an increased mindshare for the closely related themes of David and Davidic temple, and associated both with proper worship at the temple. By doing so, Chronicles not only appropriated the memory of Moses, but associated it with that of David.[8] Elsewhere, Chronicles associated the place with the temple with Mt. Moriah (2 Chr 3:1), and thus associated the figure of Abraham with both the place and with David.[9] It is worth mentioning that in Chronicles Jerusalem is portrayed as the capital of YHWH's kingdom (1 Chr 28:5; 29:23), that is, a kingdom whose subjects constitute "Israel." Thus, Jerusalem is presented as neither a Judahite nor a Benjaminite city, but a city that "belongs" to all Israel (see, for instance, the explicit reference to peoples from "all the tribes of Israel" in 2 Chr 11:13–17). Of course, this means also that the concept of Israel is shaped as Jerusalem-centred and deeply associated with the memory of David, David's house and the kingdom of Judah. It is in this context of appropriation and assimilation that kings of Judah could rightly and explicitly be referred to as kings of Israel (e.g. 2 Chr 21:2; 28:19, 27).[10]

Through all this, Chronicles contributed much to Yehudite self-identity as being not only or merely "Israel", but the very heart of Israel just as the kingdom of Judah was, and compared to which any manifestations of Israel contemporaneous to either one could only be imagined as "marginal" Israel.[11] Of course, these claims stood both by themselves and against opposing Samarian claims.

In different ways, the Deuteronomistic historical collection informed the entire Pentateuchal tradition and contributed in late Persian Yehud to the shaping of a reading of it that was Jerusalem-centered that, in turn, supported the mentioned Yehudite self-understanding as being not only or merely "Israel" but the

---

[8] E.g. 2 Chr 23:18; see also De Vries, "Moses and David", 619–639. Significantly, this is not substantially different from what the Dtr. historical collection does. The gap between this collection and Chronicles has sometimes been exaggerated. See E. Ben Zvi, "Are There Any Bridges Out There?", 59–86.
[9] An association between these two characters is communicated also by the way in which the story of Abraham's purchase evoked that of David's purchase of the site of threshing floor of Araunah/Ornan, that is, the place of the future temple (1 Chr 21:21–22:1; cf. 2 Sam 24:20–25) and vice versa. On the relation between the two stories see, among others, Y. Zakovitch, "Assimilation in Biblical Narratives", 181; Japhet, *1 & 2 Chronicles*; S. McDonough, "And David was old", 128–131; cf. J. E. Harvey, *Retelling the Torah*, 60.
[10] Cf. I. Kalimi, *An Ancient Israelite Historian*, 125–141; I. Kalimi, *The Reshaping of Ancient Israelite History*, 19–22.
[11] Cf. E. Ben Zvi, *History, Literature and Theology*, 195–209.

very heart of Israel. One may note also that the Deuteronomistic historical collection placed much emphasis on explaining the catastrophe of 586 BCE and saw it already envisioned by Moses and Joshua, thus again appropriating these figures for their own local discourse.

But more than historiographical texts were involved in this process. Prophetic literature was also very Judah- and Jerusalem-centred and so were many of the Psalms in the evolving, authoritative collection. Even wisdom literature became associated with kings of Judah. This consistent and multiple reinforcement of the issue, across collections and literary genres, suggests that a self-understanding of the Yehudite community as being not only or merely "Israel" but the very heart of Israel, and the related stress on the unique, exclusive and exclusionary status of Jerusalem were are the centre of the discourse at the time. This emphasis may be explained, at least in part, in terms of a need to address potential or real counter-claims, both in Yehud (e.g. from Benjaminite areas) and from Samarians.

All these issues require further studies and clearly much more can be written on any of these basic observations, even in this contribution and on the roles and functions of particular memories within the general collective memory of Israel at the time and its impact on the formation of social/group identity.[12]

This said, it seems that there is another layer of analysis that demands much attention as well, namely the one dealing with the array of underlying generative structures and systemic preferences that led to the construction of, and to partiality for, particular memories in Yehud. This type of analysis would attempt to identify these structures and systemic preferences, discuss their historical significance and the ways in which they reflected what the community assumed itself to be, and particularly so when it did not engage in an intentional or self-aware process of identity formation; or to phrase it differently, it would have to emphasise the study of what was so "natural" or "obvious" that became totally transparent or unseen to the community. This is so because the underlying principles governing social imagination (including identity formation) as well as practical and intellectual behaviour often bear more information (and more reliable infor-

---

[12] Diana Edelman and I are currently organising a substantial volume of studies on particular social memories associated with different characters that populated the past of Israel, as construed in the Persian/early Hellenistic period in Yehud, and their social roles. [Editor's note: Published as D. V. Edelman and E. Ben Zvi, eds. 2013. *Remembering Biblical Figures in the Late Persian & Early Hellenistic Periods: Social Memory and Imagination.* Oxford: Oxford University Press.]

mation) about the actual way in which society understood itself and shaped its identity at any particular time, than any explicit, self-aware statement.[13]

Thus, one has to deal not only with how and why social memory was organised in a particular way, or how and why it played its central role in questions of self-understanding, but also with matters of social memory and group identity in terms of a general discourse that seemed at least to the literati "natural" and thus was "transparent" to them. To approach this discourse, and particularly the generative elements in it, requires an examination of some elements of their social mindscape,[14] which in itself provides much information about their group identity and the social "mental fences" that they develop to maintain it. To discuss these issues some general preliminary considerations are in order.

II Social group and social memory

It is quite common to refer to Israel/Yehud as a good example of an ancient ethnic group. A bit less common is to dwell on what exactly do we mean in this case by "ethnic group" and, as particularly relevant to the present endeavour, how particular definitions of Israel as an "ethnic group" may contribute (or not) to a better understanding of the social processes involved in identity formation in Yehud.

A. D. Smith, for instance, has defined ethnic group or ethnie as "a named human population with myths of common ancestry, shared historical memories, one or more elements of shared culture, a link with a homeland, and a measure

---

13 For instance, to mention an obvious example, the well-known "we hold these truths to be self-evident, that all men are created equal, that they are endowed by their Creator with certain unalienable Rights, that among these are Life, Liberty and the pursuit of Happiness" in its original historical setting implied the existence of social mental fences that made the existence of many people invisible. This invisibility tells us a lot about identity formation in the group within which these words were originally expressed. Of course, the words themselves have a long history (and became a site of memory) that was re-configured and re-signified by those remembering them, according to their own current circumstances.
14 On "social mindscapes" see E. Zerubavel, *Social Mindscapes* and *Time Map*. The concept of "mindscape", of course, precedes Zerubavel and goes back to M. Maruyama, who used "the term 'mindscape' to mean a structure of reasoning, cognition, perception, conceptualisation, design, planning, and decision making that may vary from one individual, profession, culture, or social group to another" ("Mindscapes and Science Theories", 589–599 [citation 591]).

of solidarity, at least among the elites."[15] According to him, "memories of territory, heroes, and golden ages form important elements of what we may term the *ethnohistory* of each ethnie, its own self-understanding as these events have been remembered and handed down by successive generations of the community ... [t]hey are all the more powerful in scope and intensity when they are linked to particular institutions like the law, the church, the state, or the schools ..."[16]

Whether we accept this basic definition of ethnie and apply it to a historical group in Yehud and to those outside Yehud who saw themselves as Israel as well, or whether we prefer simply to refer to the historical community in Yehud as they imagined and construed themselves, that is, their ethnie of the mind, there can be no doubt that memories of the past dealing with origins, golden ages or catastrophic events, paradigmatic heroes and villains, as well as mental maps turning space into a wide array of interwoven spatial sites of memory, are all part and parcel of the particular social memory of the group.[17]

This is not surprising since an ethnie is a particular type of a mnemonic community,[18] that is, a community that socialises its members both to (a) remember particular events, characters, places and the like, and (b) learn how to remember, i.e. how to construe memories, which includes, among other things, learning about what is worth remembering, how to create basic plotlines and metanarratives, and the like.[19] Surely, without some form of shared memory, there could be no sense of social continuity through time (whether short or long) and therefore no communal reproduction or even simply maintenance. All historical communities – even at the basic level of family and kin – are imagined communities based on a shared memory. They are brought together not only by sharing memories about a shared past, but also by an underlying shared approach to and about constructing memories (see previous section).[20]

---

15 A. D. Smith, *The Nation in History*, 65. This definition is not substantially different from, for instance, the one discussed in J. C. Miller, "Ethnicity and the Hebrew Bible", 170–213 (particularly 171–175).
16 A. D. Smith, *The Nation in History*, 68.
17 And, needless to say, provide what – according to Smith's definition – an ethnie requires to be an ethnie.
18 A family is, for instance, another type of mnemonic community. See E. Zerubavel, *Social Mindscapes*, 17–18, 90; *Time Maps*, 3–5. See also B. A. Misztal, *Theories of Social Remembering*, 15–19.
19 See E. Zerubavel, *Social Mindscapes* and *Time Maps*.
20 Incidentally, one may mention that language is to a large extent an embodiment of shared, social memory. As such, it often exists in multiple versions, a "national" one associated with central structures and (sub-)group versions that may arise in particular regions, or among people of shared social status or background, all of which embody and secrete as it were (sub)group

Since memories shape an image of what the group is about, they play a crucial role in terms of identity formation and self-legitimisation, and particularly so given the common ideological role of "the past" as a legitimising factor in traditional societies. Moreover, even the communal, social act of remembering a similar past plays an important role in social cohesion. A society that "remembers together" is far more likely to "remain together," that is, to socially reproduce itself in a successful way.

Of course, neither ethnies (or other social groups) nor their self-identities are static and, accordingly, their memories are not static either. Thus, selfidentity, related conceptualisations of boundaries and social memories are all shaped and reshaped again, always in a process of (re)configuring themselves, sometimes in minor but at times major ways; and thus, the emphasis is on identity formation, rather than just "identity."

III Reconstructing ancient social memory and the processes involved in its production and reproduction: social memory and socialisation

The present essay does not intend to "prove" that social memory in ancient Israel was essential to identity formation in ancient Israel. This can be safely assumed.[21] Instead it is meant to begin to explore what studies of social memory in the late Persian Yehud may contribute to a better understanding of what and how the relevant community imagined itself to be and the social roles that such acts of social imagination had in the community, or at least its literati (see below). It is not only the "what" and the "how" that are important, but also the "how," which often carries much indirect information about the "what."

But before any such exploration is undertaken, the question of how to reconstruct even some semblance of the social memory of the community must be addressed. Obviously, there is no direct access to social memory of the community

---

segmented memories that relate in a variety of ways to the central, "national" memory. In addition, one has to keep in mind the (representation of) languages that an inner group may associate in its own mind and memory with the Other (or historical or imaginary "others"). Although all these issues relate quite obviously to matters of identity formation, the scope of the essay does not allow them to be discussed here. For a minor example of what a partial application of this approach may mean for studies of ancient Israel, see E. Ben Zvi, "The Communicative Message", 269–290.

21 The evidence from studies in social memory is just overwhelming. In addition, there is no possible sense of group identity without a sense of group memory, just as there is no sense of personal identity without a memory of oneself. Further the evidence from texts that provided much of the ground for social memory in Yehud supports this assumption.

in ancient Yehud, but it seems reasonable to assume that there was some significant relation between the contents of the (authoritative) texts that constructed the past of the community and its social memory, or at least the social memory of the literati who read these very texts. After all, through the process of reading these texts, the literati came to imagine a set of characters, spaces and events from the past. These acts of reading and "reading-originated" imagination created social memories and sites of memory that were shared among the community of readers and re-readers of these texts. Significantly, and particularly when they read prophetic literature, these (re-) readers were able to (imaginatively) visit and revisit not only their past, but also their future. Thus, social memory in the Yehudite community, or its literati at least, included memories of a shared future.

In light of the aforementioned citation from A.D. Smith about memories being "more powerful in scope and intensity when they are linked to particular institutions,"[22] it is worth noting that the social memory shaped by reading and creating mental images of the past and future was likely reinforced by central institutions in Yehud. Since I have discussed these matters elsewhere,[23] it suffices for present purposes to note that the production and consumption of highly sophisticated literature such as the books that were part of the authoritative repertoire of the community would not have been possible without some social and institutional support. For one, this required the existence of a group of people with a very high level of literacy. Their continuous existence in Yehud would not have been possible without an appropriate educational infrastructure. The latter ranged from the necessary instructional personnel to a curriculum of texts to be read and learned – after all, how could people learn about how to write or edit prophetic books, except by reading and rereading them? – and, needless to say, an ability to archive and retrieve texts. The very existence of a substantial repertoire of authoritative texts in such a small community proves beyond doubt that resources were allocated to allow for the continuous production and "consumption" of highly sophisticated literature.

It is impossible to think of this long-term, systemic allocation of resources without institutional mediation and intervention. Given the historical circumstances in Yehud and the content of the extant literature, it is most reasonable to assume that the institution involved in, and mediating, this allocation of resources was the Jerusalemite temple.[24] Since the temple, and its likely associated

---

22 See above, fn. 16.
23 E.g. E. Ben Zvi, "The Concept of Prophetic Books", 73–95 and bibliography.
24 It is hard to imagine the office of the (Persian) governor of Yehud fulfilling these functions. A temple or cultic centre is the most likely candidate (cf. contemporary Egypt). It is also difficult to

or supported "school" for future literati, provided the social resources for the production of the texts and above all of their readings, and given the quite small size of the Jerusalem of the time, it is certainly reasonable to assume that these institutions strongly supported and, to a large extent, controlled the production of these texts/readings, and thus social memory. This is in fact to be expected, since this social memory served to socialise the group into the proper identity, behaviour and ideology. Since collective memory is always involved in this process of socialisation, the centre of the community, whose role includes ensuring social reproduction, tends to shape or control, at least to some extent, its production.

Although, at times, this may involve direct action, the most efficient way of shaping and controlling the production of social memory was through a process of socialisation that inculcated, among many other things, an accepted and shared way of thinking, of generating ideas, questions and ways of addressing them, of assigning significance to stories and imagining them, competence at knowing what to see and being socialised to build mental fences to render other matters "invisible," patterns of organisation of knowledge and a shared world of knowledge, which included "facts" agreed upon within the community about the world, the community's past and future and, in ancient societies, the world of the divine. We may refer to this "system" governing and shaping the production of social memory as its general, central discourse or from a different but complementary methodological perspective, to approach it in terms of the shared social mindscape of the member of the literati and those in society who shared their view. In either case, there is a close relation between social memory and this social "system." This being so, an historical exploration of social memory in ancient Israel carries the potential to contribute much not only to an analysis of particular remembered facts (e.g. Israel consists of the children of Abraham, Isaac and Jacob) or particular concepts involving in Yehudite (or its literati) self-understanding (e.g. Israel is Y𝐇𝐖𝐇's people), but also to shed light on the entire discourse or social mindscape, its "generative grammar" and its underlying patterns, which are in turn related to historically contingent circumstances – none of them exists in any kind of "vacuum."[25]

Although a study of particular textual pericopes or books, historiographical or not, is certainly helpful, a focus on the discursive system or, if one prefers, the social mindscape of the literati in Yehud, is required for a general study of social

---

imagine a Yehudite cultic centre other than Jerusalem (Mizpah? Bethel?) carrying out these functions (see the contents of the literature). Cf. K. Van der Toorn, *Scribal Culture*.

25 For numerous examples of the historical contingent character of social mindscapes see E. Zerubavel, *Social Mindscapes* and *Time Maps*.

memory. Clearly, the latter cannot be identified with any book, since it is not a book. More to the point, social memory cannot be identified either with what evolved in the minds of "appropriately socialised" individuals in a community as they read any single book, even if they did so within the boundaries of a socially accepted ideology and mode of reading. Instead, social, comprehensive memory refers to a large, integrative system or array of multiple social memories and sites of memories constantly informing each other. This array included memories evoked and relived through multiple readings of multiple books. But in each of these readings the literati could not but bring to bear the social and socially agreed knowledge that they possessed, and in a text-centred community this implied many other authoritative texts, and along with this a large set of concepts, images and ways of organising knowledge, in addition to anything that was explicitly mentioned in the book they were reading. This situation led to a social memory that was shaped by, and reflected in, the global discourse of the remembering community. It also led to a social memory consisting of a polyphony of memories, whose shifting mindshares depended on the text being read, remembered, evoked and, most importantly, the particular circumstances in which this happened.

The preceding observation leads us to our final preliminary remark: books that may have influenced mindshare about the past in Yehud at one time may not have existed in another. Thus, some element of diachronic thinking is necessary. For the present contribution, and given that the focus is on Prophetic Literature, Chronicles and the Deuteronomistic historical collection, it is particularly worth stressing that only the repertoire of the late Persian (or early Hellenistic) period included all three groups, and that of the early to mid-Persian the first two.[26]

---

26 Given the long tradition of reconstructing the historical Persian Yehud and its intellectual discourse on the basis of Ezra-Nehemiah, one may raise the question of why this study focuses on prophetic literature, Chronicles and the Dtr. historical collection. The answer is in part that I was asked by Louis Jonker to focus on these corpora and that is already a quite wide field. But this would be only a partial answer. It is my contention that the reconstruction of the historical discourse of Yehud can be better advanced by focusing on the wide repertoire of authoritative books that emerged from the period and were read and re-read at the time (e.g. the books in the Dtr. historical collection, the Pentateuch, the prophetic books and, towards the end of the era, Chronicles) than by turning to a fairly unique, post-Persian-period book (at least in its present form) that purports to describe some events of the period.

B Particular Observations

I Introduction

The goal of these observations is not to attempt to reconstruct an approximation of the comprehensive social memory of the community in Yehud or its literati, or its underlying discourse or social mindscape. This endeavour requires a multifaceted research programme that will take decades to develop and a large number of researchers. Instead, the goal of this section is to present some observations about key issues in the study of social memory in Yehud, the general discourse of the community and the cognitive social mindscape of, at least, its literati that clearly and directly have a bearing on identity formation in Yehud. Moreover, the goal is not to provide a thorough discussion of any of them, as each one of them demands a separate study but, as appropriate in a workshop, to provoke further thoughts and suggest some paths for future research. This holds particularly true for some commonly held positions about why the community in Yehud, and particularly the literati, remembered what they remembered, and to which social and historical concerns was the social memory they developed supposed to respond. This contribution also wishes to draw attention and further thought to issues concerning the organisation of memory, how the images of the past that the literati revisited time and again as they read and re-read prophetic and historical books (i.e. past and future-constructing texts) were generated, and to the ways in which all these issues had relevance to identity formation and self-understanding in late Persian Yehud.[27]

It should be stressed from the outset, however, that these observations do not deal with absolutes. Instead they deal with *trends* to stress particular aspects of social memory in ancient Israel, to shift mindshare to or away from certain issues and constructed memories, or to *preferences* for organising and linking memories in a particular way. As will become clear, in none of these cases was there a totalising situation that precluded the existence of any potential alternative or complementary memory or memory pattern. It cannot be overstressed that the collective memory of ancient Israel/Yehud consisted of a complex array of sites of memory balancing and informing each other; this feature is not consistent with a strong totalising tendency.[28]

---

[27] I would like to add that the cumulative weight of these observations demands some attention in itself as well.
[28] See E. Ben Zvi, "The Study of Forgetting". On some implications of this tendency see section VIII below.

II Social memory and self-identity in late Yehud from a perspective of communal anxiety/security about its own existence and their interrelation with perceptions of risk

There is no doubt about the extent of the catastrophe that befell Judah around 586 BCE. There is also no doubt that the community in early to mid-Yehud was obsessed with ideological constructions and memories dealing with the fall of the monarchic polity, exile and its counterpart images of a future return, redemption and related visions of utopian futures.[29] The prophetic corpus, the Deuteronomistic historical collection, and even the more comprehensive primary historical collection clearly demonstrate the point. But is the social memory of Yehud characterised by a sense of "communal (ontological) anxiety" as opposed to "communal (ontological) security"? And if so, did this anxiety have a strong impact on the process of identity formation in late Persian Yehud?

This is not the place to engage at length with the concept of "ontological security." Suffice it to note that, according to A. Giddens, it "has to do with being." He characterises ontological security as an important form of "feelings of security" and maintains that the concept refers to "the confidence that most human beings have in the continuity of their self-identity and in the constancy of the surrounding social and material environments of action".[30] For present purposes it is heuristically helpful to use a somewhat similar concept as it pertains to communities, not individuals. A community with a strong sense of ontological security would consider that the very continuity of the group is not at risk and trust the basic reliability of its institutions. One may reasonably assume that the level of ontological anxiety was quite elevated in 701 BCE Judah and during the periods just before and following the fall of the monarchic polity. The quite extreme depopulation of the land may have contributed to that in the early years of the neo-Babylonian period, and certainly immediately after the assassination of the Babylonian-appointed governor, Gedaliah. But what about late Persian period Yehud?

On the surface, it may be claimed that the memory of the catastrophe raised anxiety about the ability of the community in Yehud to survive. The corollary of this position would be that the ubiquity of promises of a utopian future for Israel and the equally ubiquitous "didactic" explanations of the catastrophe in the discourse of Persian-period Yehud served to counter this anxiety. In other words,

---

29 I discussed these matters to some extent in "Toward a Sense of Balance" in this volume, pp. 387–406.
30 A. Giddens, *The Consequences of Modernity*, 92.

according to this proposal, the social memory of the community at that time was, at least in part, shaped to address a severe need to create a sense of communal security in Persian Yehud. To be sure, there might be some degree of historical truth to this position. Certainly, social memory in Yehud ended up buttressing a sense of communal security, but to what extent did the community in Persian Yehud develop its social memory and the related sense of self-identity that characterised it as a response to its deeply ingrained sense that its very existence was largely at risk?[31]

Although feelings of (ontological) communal security or anxiety do not have to correlate directly with "objective" reality, it is reasonable to assume that they tend to reflect at least in some way the level of risk that the historical society confronted. For instance, the (late) kingdom of Judah faced the risk of devastating military campaigns, the destruction of the polity, exile, destruction of its basic institutions and the like. Their inhabitants and certainly its elite were well aware of these risks, and the fate of contemporary polities and their populations. The province of Yehud did not face these "existential" risks. It was a very poor and marginal province, whose elite could not in any way contest militarily any imperial power or its neighbours for that matter. None of the highly elevated risks that characterised late monarchic Judah politics applied to it. For the same reasons and given its geographical location, Yehud was during the Persian period an unlikely place to draw the sustained attention of large enemy armies and the related "existential" risks that such campaigns brought about.[32]

---

31 Cf. the reading of Chronicles advanced in D. J. Chalcraft, "Sociology and the Book of Chronicles". My own understanding of Chronicles differs at substantial points from Chalcraft's. For instance, he maintains that "the Chronicler can create an ongoing sense of ontological security and a method for dealing with risk through a world view that very clearly links cause and effect in the realm of behavior and its consequences ... [t]he Chronicler would not be alone in this quest for a theodicy of relative simplicity," (215) while I maintain that Chronicles did not advance such a simple theodicy or a predictable cause and effect relation. In fact, I would maintain, Chronicles often destabilises, when it counts the most, expectations of a cause and effect in the realm of behaviour and its consequences. I, however, agree with Chalcraft that "[t]he experience of chaos and the disruption to ongoing narrative has been overcome through the creation of a communal sacred space that cannot be placed before or after the disaster but on another plane," (223) but again I would not refer in the case of Chronicles to any direct experience, but to a social memory of disruption long ago and to which the book as a whole tends to draw less attention than the prophetic books, the Dtr. historical collection, the primary historical collection and Lamentations, which is also a past-constructing text.

32 To be sure, Yehud like any other province, could have faced temporary risks of over-taxation, but temporary over-taxation does not constitute an *existential* risk; the neo-Assyrian and neo-Babylonian campaigns against Judah and Jerusalem did posit such a risk.

Of course, but perhaps even more importantly, the community in Yehud could not but be highly aware that "Israel" survived *even* the catastrophe of 586 BCE. This was a fundamental constituent of their social memory and essential for the formation of their self-identity. They were Israel and thus Israel must have survived the catastrophe. This central memory of resilience was manifested (and at work) in various additional ways within the discourse of the community. For instance, in Chronicles it is expressed in a balancing (and in itself, balanced) shift towards reducing the mindshare about the catastrophe and its status as a watershed in Israel's past.[33] In prophetic literature it is expressed directly in claims about YHWH's unwillingness (or even self-enforced) inability to destroy Israel (e.g. Hos 11:8–9; Mic 7:8) and indirectly by evoking memories of YHWH's announcements of salvation in the monarchic period, and in particular at times during which Israel was construed as grievously sinning against YHWH and "meriting" destruction (e.g. Hos 1–3). These images of a certain glorious future and the fact YHWH decided to proclaim them at the very nadir of Israel's behaviour communicated a sense that Israel will never disappear, no matter how sinfully it may behave or how much it will be punished by YHWH.

It is in this context that it is worth stressing that reading and rereading prophetic books in Yehud evoked images of a remnant that may indeed be "lowly" (e.g. Zeph 3:11–13) but not dead or dying;[34] on the contrary, such a lowly Israel embodied as it were, and its memory constituted, a shared site of memory among the literati that communicated a sense of "rebirth." To be sure, the future rebirth was imagined and vicariously felt in multiple ways by readers who identified themselves as Israel/the remnant (and at times, by the very same readers and even within the same literary sub-unit, Mic 5:6–8), but there was no debate that Israel continued after the catastrophe, would face a certain great future, and that being reduced to a remnant was associated with a potential for greatness in the manifold ways in which the latter may have been imagined within the discourse of Yehud.

Similarly, an ideological mindscape characterised, at least in part, by the idea that there is nothing *really* new in the world as is (exemplified in different ways in Chronicles, Qohelet) is one in which *real* watersheds cannot exist and

---

33 On this issue see "Toward a Sense of Balance" in this volume, pp. 387–406.
34 There are, of course, texts such as 2 Kgs 21:14 ... ונטשתי את שארית נחלתי, but given both the historical setting in which the texts were read in Yehud and their literary context, it is clear that even these texts did not evoke an image or memory of a permanent divine abandonment of the remnant.

therefore it is one in which the risk of undergoing one vanishes.[35] Within this mindscape there is a place for social anxiety about potential future disasters/divine judgement – they did happen before, so they may still happen again, and call for "proper" socialisation and behaviour (see below) – but not anxiety about the very existence of Israel or even its identity, namely as a text-*torah*-centred community that is supposed to follow YHWH's commandments.[36]

Recent studies on social memory in contemporary societies have pointed out that groups which understand themselves as being "endangered" tend to emphasise images of (righteous) victimhood. These images reinforce both a sense of "national/ethnic" cohesion and a sense of existential risk for the community. Thus they serve (and are used by political elites) to mobilise the group towards actions that from their perspective would allow it to overcome the risk to its existence.[37] Against this background, it is worth underscoring that, despite the stress on the catastrophe, the social memory of the community of Yehud did not emphasise the motifs of righteous victimhood and martyrdom at the hands of enemy. To be sure, there were plenty of sites of memory referring to the catastrophe that were evoked in the community through the reading of prophetic literature and the book of Kings (e. g. 2 Kgs 21:12 – 14; 25:1 – 21; Jer 25:9 – 11; Ezek 12; Hos 2:5 – 15; Zeph 1:2 – 6; see also Lamentations). These texts, however, did not emphasise or shape memories of righteous sufferers and victimhood but, on the contrary, of sinful behaviour that justified the catastrophe.[38] Clearly, there was nothing comparable to stories that emerged in, for instance, the Maccabean period (see As. Mos 5:1 – 6; 8:1 – 5; 9:1 – 10:10; 1 Macc 1; 2 Macc 6).

---

[35] Of course, Qohelet gave expression to some anxiety (and even angst) about a world in which nothing actually changes, but this is not the kind of communal "existential" anxiety that we are discussing at this point. I briefly referred elsewhere to some discursive connections between Chronicles and Qohelet. This matter demands a separate study that cannot be undertaken here.
[36] See below on "political" memory as in a sense akin to "political" history, rather than stating the quite obvious point that all memory is political.
[37] There are multiple attestations of these tendencies. Just one example is A. Oberschall, *Conflict and Peace*, 102; cf. M. Levene, "Introduction", 27. Needless to say, memories of victimhood played a role not only in Serbia but in Croatia as well. Memories of victimhood play important roles in the respective social memories of contemporary Israelis and Palestinians.
[38] This holds true even in texts meant to evoke strong memories of social distress and cause their readers to fall for fallen Jerusalem, such as Lamentations. See, for instance, Lam 1:5, 8 – 9, 14, 18; 3:42; 4:13, 22; 5:7. Lamentations when read against the (late) Persian context did not communicate a need to close ranks and mobilise against a contemporary enemy; instead it conveyed a clear message that YHWH has not abandoned or rejected Israel, has heard Jerusalem's plea and a full restoration is still to come (e. g. Lam 5:21 and cf. the prophetic books).

Even the enemy that caused the destruction was not always emphatically construed as the sinful Enemy/Other.[39] In fact, the community even held some memories and texts that commanded much mindshare that characterised the Babylonians who carried out the catastrophe in a positive light (see the reference to Nebuchadnezzar as Yhwh's servant in Jer 25:9; 27:6;[40] and its Jeremianic characterisation in Jer 40:1–6[41]).

Pious victimhood and even martyrdom played a role in the social memory created through the reading and rereading of the prophetic and the historical books in Yehud, but it was imagined in the main as inflicted on the righteous from *inside* not outside the community, and its recipients were for the most part prophetic figures.[42]

A society striving to mobilise a strong sense of "national/ethnic" cohesion to face some existential risk from an external empire is less likely to develop this systemic memory preference – which existed well before the time of Chronicles in the late Persian period – than a society that is internally focused and which elevates the importance of *mobilising internal resources for internal didactic purposes*. This emphasis may be seen as a (systemic) response to a perceived risk concerning the potential to lose control over "proper" socialisation and behaviour (see above). In fact, the production and, above all, the reading and rereading of texts such as the prophetic and historical books, which are above all di-

---

39 On the "Other," see below. Of course, there are texts in which those who contributed to the fall of Judah and Jerusalem are portrayed in very negative terms (see, for instance, Obadiah and Lamentations).
40 On elevated (but not Jeremianic) characterisations of Nebuchadnezzar in the book of Jeremiah, see J. Hill, "Your Exile Will Be Long", 152–156; and esp. Hill, *Friend or Foe?*, 103–110, 130–139, 198–199, 203–205. Significantly, unlike Nebuchadnezzar, no such texts or memories existed about Sennacherib. On this matter, see below.
41 "The author wants to persuade us that Nebuzaradan was a pupil of Jeremiah (40:2–3)" (K. A. D. Smelik, "The Function of Jeremiah", 97). Cf. also Jer 40:2 with Jer 32:23. The characterisation of Nebuzaradan, the officer in charge of the destruction of the temple, the city and the exile, as a pupil of Jeremiah served to characterise, indirectly, the person whom he actually represented in Judah, King Nebuchadnezzar.
42 E.g. 1 Kgs 18:4, 13; 2 Kgs 9:7; Jer 11:18–21; 20:1–2; 26:7–9, 11; 37:12–21; 2 Chr 16:10; 24:20–22; 36:15–16; for an example of pious victimhood of a non-prophetic character, see Naboth. To be sure, the most memorable "righteous sufferer" in ancient Israelite memory was David at the hands of Saul. In this case, the story follows a well-known ANE narrative pattern. See M. Liverani, "Memorandum", 184–186. But if Persian-period Israel could see itself in the story of David, it would have been the sinful David of the post-Bathsheba period, who was worthy of death but not executed, severely punished, humiliated and weakened, and yet maintained so as to lead to a glorious continuation, namely Solomon and the building of the temple. Cf. F. H, Polak, "David's Kingship", 119–147.

dactic literature, may be seen as a response to the same perceived, internal need.⁴³

Before developing this matter further, it is worth noting that since the authoritative books themselves were related to central institutions (authoritative texts, literati to read them, the educational processes of the latter and their curriculum, and most likely the Jerusalemite temple, both directly and indirectly), we have to conclude that we are dealing with a mindscape that on the whole conveys a sense of trust (not distrust) in the roles of the central institutions of Yehud. This is a significant observation, since groups that have internalised a sense of much insecurity about their own future tend to distrust their central institutions.⁴⁴

A community that tends to perceive risks (to its welfare, not to its survival, which is not deemed to be at stake) as internal and communal rather than as external would tend to develop a social mindscape according to which the actions of agents external to the community do not substantially matter; only internal actions and behaviours matter at the end. This tendency is clearly attested in Chronicles – in which even the actions of Israel outside Judah are of, at best, marginal importance, but is also well attested in the earlier, pre-Chronicles Persian-period repertoire, and is clearly and saliently at work in the prophetic literature.

If the behaviour of the inner groups is what actually counts and, therefore, the main source of risk for the community, one would expect a tendency to shift attention and mindshare within social memory not only to the existence of authoritative texts communicating divine instructions (after all, it is a text-centred community), but also to teachers (or "sages") able to teach these instructions to the community. One would expect that this attention to those who count at the end – that is, teachers – would at least partially balance the traditional emphasis on the heroic characterisation of "heroes" (i.e. warriors) of the past.⁴⁵

---

43 E. Ben Zvi, "Analogical Thinking", 321–332.
44 The same holds true for those who experienced directly or indirectly the reality of group catastrophe. Chronicles was composed many generations after 587 BCE; in the late Persian (or perhaps early Hellenistic Judah).
45 Needless to say, such act of balancing will have an impact on constructions of masculinity in the community and would tend to enhance the masculine/heroic character of the literati *vis a vis* images of masculinity that emphasise warrior capabilities and achievements. Cf. the partial transformation of David from a mighty warrior to "the singer and master of ceremonies at the head of a swarm of priests and levites" (J. Wellhausen, *Prolegomena*, 182). Cf. the construction of the important and successful man in Sirach.

This anticipated tendency is actually attested in social memories about Abraham, whose "heroic/warrior" character is on the whole clearly de-emphasised,[46] certainly in memories of Moses, who is not only the main teacher but also whose "heroic/warrior" features are substantially downplayed,[47] and influenced even memories about Joshua, the conqueror par excellence, and see his transformation into a "literatus" persona in Josh 1:8. The characterisation of David in Chronicles and the roles attached to prophetic figures in the book provide additional examples. It is worth stressing, however, that this tendency is not an innovation of Chronicles or the late Persian period. In fact, the characterisation of prophetic figures as teachers/preachers who attempted to shift Israel from its sinful behaviour in monarchic times (and as per the main metanarrative about monarchic Israel, failed) is not only well attested in Kings, but central to the prophetic books. Moreover, in the latter, the most central image of YHWH is that of teacher.[48]

III Intentional creation or systemic expression of social memory? Was a particular social memory intentionally created to create self-identity in Yehud?

These questions, although they cannot be answered in a definitive way, bear much importance for understanding social memory and its role in Yehud, as well as for the history of Yehud and the history of identity formation in Yehud. The prophetic books, the Deuteronomistic historical collection, and Chronicles were intentionally didactic texts, but were they intentionally written to create a sense of self-identity in Yehud? Clearly, from the fact that the prophetic books, the Deuteronomistic historical collection and Chronicles each contributed much to the formation of social memory, and the latter to the shaping (and re-shaping) of group identity, this does not mean that they were the result of some purposeful, well-guided, authorial/agent intentionality. This may be the result of systemic processes in the society, which were invisible to an extent at least

---

[46] The only tradition about Abraham the general in the HB is in Gen 14. He shows no military power anywhere. I discussed these matters at length in "The Memory of Abraham" in this volume, pp. 162–98.
[47] For Moses as a conqueror see only Num 21:21–35; Deut 2:26–3:13. The image of Moses as a successful mighty general is on the whole downplayed in the Hebrew Bible. For the non-warrior-like figure of Moses in the Pentateuch and the warrior traditions about him, see T. Römer, "Moses outside the *Torah*." See also the discussion in "The Memory of Abraham."
[48] On this matter, see E. Ben Zvi, "Reading Hosea", 43–57 and esp. 53–57.

for most, if not all, members of the said society.⁴⁹ In other words, historiographical (and other past-constructing) texts may have been (a) written consciously to create a particular social memory to shape society and its policies, or (b) systematically preferred texts that emerged within a society: given that any (image of the) past that a community construed was directly influenced by the community's present – i.e. every past was a present past – then images of the past that responded well to the needs of the community and cohered well with what they thought and wanted to think about their past were naturally preferred.

At times it seems that some scholars approach the past-construing texts from a perspective informed by the well-known role of modern "national" (and nationalising) historiography, which was clearly written with the intention of developing a social memory that could mobilise support for nation (or nation-state) building enterprises. Of course, in all the modern cases the very existence of the enterprise was proof positive of a present perceived lack and a need to respond to that lack. On the analogy of modern times, one might argue that if there was an intentional ethnie/polity-*building* enterprise in Yehud, then perhaps, as part of this process, historiographical and other works constructing the past were intentionally written and communicated to the community mainly for that purpose. But was there an intentional ethnie/polity-building enterprise?

On the surface one might argue that if Yehud was a kind of Persian colony founded by "returnees" over and against the "remainees,"⁵⁰ then one may imagine some kind of effort on the side of the returnees to develop a collective memory that sets ideological foundations for their new polity (and their priority over the "remainees"). Yet, as I discussed elsewhere, there is little to support this historical reconstruction.⁵¹

In a nutshell, despite the fact that it is reasonable to assume that some people came to Yehud relatively early in the Persian period with the support of the Persian centre, and that for a while there could have been tensions between the newcomers and those who remained in the land – particularly if the former came

---

49 To perceive them they would have to develop critical skills to allow them to study their own society from the "outside" or at least from a comparative, methodological perspective. To illustrate, we may easily observe instances of "hybridity" in traditions and behaviour in local societies in antiquity, the locals (including those in societies supposedly influenced by "nativist" movements, e.g. Hasmoneans), however, were far less likely to consider these products of "hybridity."

50 This position, though expressed in many different ways, has a long history in research.

51 See "Total Exile" in this volume, pp. 599–611; cf. E. Ben Zvi, "Inclusion in and Exclusion", 95–149. Cf. and contrast, J. Weinberg, *The Citizen-Temple Community*; J. Kessler, "Persia's Loyal Yahwists", 91–121.

with support from forces "outside" the local community (i.e. the imperial centre) – one has to keep in mind, among other things, that (a) no massive migration took place; (b) most of the population in Yehud were not returnees of any kind, but descendants of those who remained in the land; (c) Haggai and Zech 1–8 (and even Ezra-Nehemiah, for that matter) do not give the impression that severe, permanent conflicts arose between the small group of returnees and the majority of the population; in fact, the general image is one of unity;[52] (d) the seemingly exclusionary concept and social memory of the "empty land" did *not* arise as an expression/justification of worldly ambitions for power of a colonising or elite group who wanted to discursively erase (and thus forget) the presence of the Other in Yehud, but was a concept adopted by the "remainees" in response to an array of discursive and ideological needs;[53] (e) the most central Yehudite institution that evolved and grew in importance during the Persian period was the Jerusalemite temple; this historical process would have been impossible had the temple intentionally, systematically and consistently excluded most of the population of Yehud – in fact, it is difficult to imagine why a temple without land would have systematically chosen this policy and how such a temple would have been able to maintain it in the long run; (f) the main tendency in the authoritative literature of Yehud and the social memory it evokes is one of *not* excluding or othering Benjaminites – who formed most of the population of Yehud and who (at least for the most part) were descendants of "remainees" – but of integrating them into a Jerusalem-centred Israel; and (g) the main formative texts for the constitution of collective memory in Yehud were the Pentateuchal texts; these are clearly not the kind of texts that a Yehudite returnee elite would create intentionally to advance their exclusionary ethnie-building enterprise.

Moreover, one may ask whether is it reasonable to assume that Yehudites were likely consciously engaged in an enterprise of self-identity creation, be it for political or ethnie purposes. To begin with, this would assume a sense of

---

52 Of course, earlier texts may be brought in to the discussion as well, cf. D. Rom-Shiloni, "Exiles and Those Who Remained", 119–138 [Hebrew]; "Group Identities in Jeremiah", 11–46. It is worth noting that literati in late Persian Yehud did not read the (scholarly reconstructions of) different redactional layers in Jeremiah (or other prophetic books), but a book they associated with a communicative voice (i.e. that of the implied author) that included all the putative voices of each of the proposed layers. See also J. Kessler, "Images of Exile".
53 See in particular, "Total Exile" in this volume, pp. 599–611. Cf. the (partial) erasure of the Canaanites in the book of Joshua, which certainly could not have evolved out of a colonising discursive strategy adopted by any invading Israelites, since historically (as opposed to mnemonically) Israel neither came from Egypt nor conquered Canaan.

lack regarding proper self-identity that had to be remedied. In traditional and ancient societies people are not likely to ask (theoretical or abstract) questions about ethnic self-identity. This is because of their sense of belonging to a social group, most often construed in kinship or locality-based terms, was, most often again, seen as a given. Moreover, in these societies and certainly in ancient Israel society was not seen as a system to be understood only in "social" or "historical" (or "immanent") terms in isolation from the divine realm.[54] Thus it is difficult to imagine some group of literati in Yehud deciding that *they* have to write past-construing texts (and/or future-construing texts for that matter) so as to create a sense of "national" or group identity. It is more likely that they felt that their identity was "self-evident" – even if we know that it was constructed and basically an act of shared social imagination). From their perspective it was certain that their group (i.e. Israel/Yehud/Judah) was created by YHWH, not by literati like themselves writing texts.

The foregoing considerations provide support for an approach grounded on the generative role of systemic preferences in the production of past-constructing texts meant to evoke or partially shift the weight in social memory. If, at the end of the day, the past was construed to a significant extent in the ways in which it was – because the community (or its literati) as a social group preferred to think that it was so – then one has to assume that at some underlying level there was a preference in the community or its literati, as a whole, for the images of the past that occur in these works.

But significant preferences in the shaping and reshaping of social memory were not restricted to the main characters (e.g. Moses, David, etc., all of whom became central sites of memory that embodied and communicated messages at the core of the community's beliefs), or to the main metanarratives (see above), or to agreed upon "facts" about the past (e.g. the triad Abraham, Isaac, Jacob as the forefathers and thus as a main marker of group identity), but also to a shared social mindscape that shaped, among other things, how time and temporal continuities and discontinuities were conceived, and how they led to the creation of a particular distribution of relative density of memories across time.[55]

This social mindscape contributed in other ways to the construction and significance of social memory. For instance, the basic concept (widely shared in the ANE, but characteristic of many other societies through history) that the distant

---

54 This stands in clear contrast to the situation in contemporary times. On these matters, cf. C. A. Taylor, *A Secular Age*, 149; M. G. Brett, "National Identity", 29–40.
55 I.e. what Zerubavel calls "sociomnemonic density of history".

past carries a legitimising value well integrated into the social mindscape of the literati. Needless to say, this concept was particularly significant in the formation of social memory and the allocation of meaning to shared memories.[56]

Some other aspects of the social shared mindscape of the literati that are relevant to the construction and organisation of social memory are also clear. For instance, the literati's social mindscape would be supportive of the ubiquitous tendency in past- and future-constructing texts to develop "fuzzy" (and at times seemingly contradictory) but integrative rather than clear-cut, logically consistent concepts and memories. One may note in this regard the tendency to remember multiple images of events and periods (cf. the Deuteronomistic historical collection, Chronicles, and some prophetic books set in the monarchic period), multiple evaluations of kings (cf. Kings and Chronicles), multiple stories of origin, seeming contradictions within the same book and at times the very same literary unit within it, as well attested in prophetic literature, the Deuteronomistic historical collection and Chronicles, and even at times the blurring of clear boundaries between Israel and the Other (see, for instance, Chronicles, both in the genealogies and the main narrative).

All these features are relevant to matters of social memory and self-understanding/identity. They and their possible significance will be addressed below, but before doing so some counter-arguments to the general approach mentioned above must be addressed. For instance, one might argue that given that, obviously, the literati were not able to simply imagine any past they wished,[57] there is no point in emphasising systemic preference in these matters. After all, the argument is, there was no "real" freedom in the system and without that it is meaningless to speak of underlying, generative choices within the system. Without the latter, in turn, there is no ground from which to attempt to reconstruct the (underlying) preferences of the literati of the time.

Although there were obvious restrictions to the shaping of the past in ancient Israel and in any other society for that matter, both grounded in the world of knowledge and cognitive social mindscapes, this does not mean that

---

[56] See, for instance, Judg 11:12–24(/26). The construction of the past as legitimising normative situations in the present was related to the idea that "history" reflects the final agency and will of the divine. It is worth stressing that the aforementioned text clearly portrays a mnemonic battle as part and parcel of a politico-military conflict. Also in antiquity, mnemonic battles were an integral part of discourses justifying positions in such conflicts – be they internal or external to the polity. Of course, mnemonic wars are well attested and all too obvious in many contemporary conflicts. For some illustrations, see E. Zerubavel, *Time Maps*, 103–110.

[57] There were always facts agreed upon in the community about the past that were not malleable.

there were no degrees of freedom within the system. The intricate web of at times logically inconsistent images about the past that the different books and at times the very same book evoked in the Jerusalem-centred, late Persian (and early Hellenistic) community in Judah (or its literati, at least) already demonstrates the existence of very substantial degrees of freedom within the system.

Moreover, even when, for instance, some facts agreed about the past were not malleable (e.g. Moses – not David – was the one who led Israel from Egypt and received divine instruction/*torah*), this does not mean that remembering them did not represent the will of the literati. It is true that they could not have imagined a (hi)story of Israel in which David led the people out of Egypt, but it is also true that the literati wanted to tell and retell a (hi)story in which Moses (and Yhwh!) did so. It is also true that the literati who authored and read the prophetic and historiographical texts shifted attention at times towards, and at times away from, particular periods and events, even if the "facts" about them were not malleable (e.g. Chronicles did not lead to an increase in the relative mindshare of stories about Joshua's conquest of the land among its primary and intended readers, and most likely not by chance).

The second, general concern that might be raised is that systemic analyses and their results in terms of tendencies among the literati (at least) to prefer or dis-prefer features and contents of past constructing texts – as advanced above – tend to downplay the importance of diachronic studies. Of course, not all the books that existed in the repertoire of the late Persian period were composed at that very time.[58] Moreover, most, if not all, of them underwent some compositional and redaction process.

Readers of the Book of Kings who lived before the late Persian period could not have read it in a way informed by Chronicles, because they could not have been aware of a book that did not exist at the time. But the primary readers of Chronicles were aware of Kings and readers of Kings in the late Persian (or early Hellenistic period, that is, once Chronicles became accepted, read and re-read in the community) were aware of Chronicles. Social memory was then shap-

---

[58] It must be acknowledged that we do not have access to the full repertoire of authoritative texts of Persian Yehud at any time. This said, there is no reason to assume that the repertoire of books from the period to which we have access (i.e. those books that eventually became part of the Hebrew Bible), as a whole, was particularly unrepresentative of the actual repertoire of the community, to the point that we cannot even approximate or tentatively approach the main systemic features of the Persian-period repertoire in Yehud through an analysis of the texts to which we have access. It must be kept in mind that the society in late Persian Yehud and Jerusalem was very different from that of late Second Temple, so we may not necessarily infer anything from the situation in Qumran. See section VIII below.

ed by images evoked by both works (though with shifting weightings/saliency, depending on the issue and circumstances of the reading). This consideration only emphasises the point that for the purpose of reconstructing social memory and the general discourse in Yehud about the past, one must approach sources such as Chronicles, Kings, Isaiah, or Jonah for that matter, as *read* texts, that is, in the way in which they were likely read and understood within the discourse of particular historical communities. In other words, we have to pay attention to their respective (and at times diachronically different) *Sitze im Diskurs*.[59]

IV Social memory, past-constructing texts, historical "degrees of freedom", temple and self-identity.

As mentioned above, the community, including its literati, most likely did not engage in an (intentional) search for self-identity, nor thought that their self-identity needed texts to shore itself up. There was no need for texts to explain to them that they were not Persian, Phoenicians, Egyptians, Assyrians, Amalekites, or Reubenites for that matter. Yet there were areas in which some choices could be made and the past-constructing texts within the repertoire of late Persian Yehud show clear preferences on the matter.

For instance, although Benjaminites were Benjaminites, there could have been a salient tendency to refer to the entire community in Yehud (including Benjaminites) as יהודים, that is to use Judah/Yehud as a high-level, inclusive and inclusivist category. Such a tendency would have re-asserted and reshaped traditions about the former kingdom of Judah and the Exile of their inhabitants/elite/those who "actually counted" and, above all, the sense of continuity between that kingdom and the Persian province of Yehud. This tendency, of course, existed at the time (consider already the name of the province) and eventually led to the use of the term יהודי for "Jew" rather than Judahite,[60] so prominently at work in Esth 2:5–6, which foregrounds the social memory of this feature and

---

[59] As for redactional concerns, one may note that even when a particular book underwent compositional or redaction development, the readers of the "(temporarily) finished product" did not read the "last addition/layer" alone, but the entire book. The communicative voice speaking to them through the book, as it were, carried the voices of all the layers and their interactions. Additions may inform and balance pre-existing voices, but never stand on their own. Moreover, the "(temporarily) finished product" was read in a way informed by the discourse of the community, including all the other texts that the readers had in their authoritative repertoire and that were relevant as background to their reading of this "(temporarily) finished product".
[60] Judahite here is meant to refer to a category that excludes Benjaminites.

the way in which it helped to construct both identity and a classifying social mindscape.[61]

Yet within the *inner intellectual discourse* of the literati in late Yehud, and thus in their authoritative repertoire, the most preferred tendency was to use the term Israel as their main self-identifying label.[62] This is not the place to discuss the origin of the use of the term Israel for and by a Judah/Jerusalem-centred community,[63] but to emphasise that it was at least the literati's preferred label for identifying their community and ethnie within the world created by their authoritative repertoire, and within the social memory that reading and rereading this repertoire shaped, reflected and activated. Of course, as they chose the term Israel as their main identifier label, they shaped this term in a very clear Jerusalem-centred form. Thus, for instance, the Jerusalem temple was construed as the successor of the Tabernacle; the temple priests as those of Aaron; "judgment" against northern Israel as secondary to and informative of the main "judgment" against Judah in 586 BCE (prophetic literature, Kings); the utopian polity of the future as centred in Judah/Jerusalem, even though it was conceived as inclusive of the north; the history of Israel in Judah/Jerusalem – but not outside it – as the one to be most remembered because it is the only one that is crucial for "Israel" since David (Chronicles); and "the land" that must rest its sabbaths as the land of the former kingdom of Judah, not that of Israel (Chronicles).

The identification of the Yehudite literati and their (ideological, imaginary) text-centred society with Israel and the reshaping, reformulation (and appropriation) of the concept of Israel were all involved in the process of constructing social memory through their effect on the weighting and re-signification of existing memories. The identification of the Yehudites as Israel was not open for discussion in the discourse of the late Persian period, but the relative weight given to expressing self-identity in this manner was; and so also were the associations that the term "Israel" may carry and their respective mindshare. Choices made in this regard had an impact on, and co-related with, the promotion of certain

---

61 This tendency may have been at work already by the time of the Elephantine papyri. See the use of the term יהודי there as a gentilic. This matter, of course, requires a separate discussion.
62 The term "Judah and Benjamin" and related terms are also used, but like "Judah" and its associated terms, they were less dominant than "Israel" as self-identifying label.
63 For two positions on the matter see, for instance, P. R. Davies "The Origin of Biblical Israel", 141–148 and N. Na'aman, "The Israelite-Judahite Struggle", 1–23; "Saul", 211–224 and 335–349. Whatever the origin of the use of the term might have been, Israel was used as a group name and identifier in the *inner intellectual discourse* of the Jerusalem-centred community in late Persian Yehud.

aspects of the self-understanding of the group. The latter issue brings up the matter of the temple in Jerusalem.

Whereas being Israel was accepted as self-evident and in no need of any explanation, and linked directly to Israel's association and definition in terms of a relationship with Yhwh (and memory of its manifestations, which is conceived as "Israel's history"; see Genesis–Kings), there was competition among different cultic centres for Yhwistic groups (i.e. Israel). It is not by random chance that the Persian period saw both (a) the development of the Jerusalemite temple from a minor incipient temple in a marginal area within Yehud itself – in terms of population, economic and political power, though rich in memory – into the main institution of Yehud; and (b) the production and consumption of a corpus of authoritative literature, comparatively large and very sophisticated given the quite minimal size and resources of the population that in one way or another construes Jerusalem and its temple as central for Israel. Moreover, it is not by chance that this literature and the literati necessary to develop it were, most likely, directly or indirectly supported by the temple as an institution.

If there was a social project in Persian Yehud, it was developing a central position for the Jerusalemite temple (and therefore, for Jerusalem as the city of the unique temple). The development of social memory supporting this project was then only to be expected. If there was anxiety among temple-centred literati during the early to mid-Persian period that reflected actual historical circumstances, it was about the success of the temple project within Yehud. But this anxiety most likely disappeared by the late Persian period, when Jerusalem was the capital and the temple became central focal point (already by the time of the Elephantine Papyri). Yet the production of past-constructing texts and their roles in a social memory that emphasised the centrality of Jerusalem and above all the temple continued in that period (see Chronicles), and even in later periods in which there could not have any doubt about the centrality of the Jerusalemite temple in Judah (see Sirach). This situation may be explained in terms of the social mindscape of the literati, or in other words, the ideologically temple/Jerusalem-centred literati constructed a past that is, not surprisingly, temple/Jerusalem-centred.

In addition, the fact that groups within Israel (i.e. other Yhwistic groups) in the vicinity of Yehud (esp. in Samaria) did not accept the supremacy of Jerusalem and its temple and its exclusive claims most likely created an inner *discursive* need to reaffirm this time and again within the literature of the Jerusalem-centred community; in other words, something akin to the well-attested and cross-cultural phenomenon of "preaching to the choir." Of course, "preaching to the choir" presupposes and reaffirms the existence of "the choir," that is, the inner group, and the boundaries around shaped by an implicit or explicit construction of the Other (i.e. those outside "the choir"). The very act of shared and repeated listening to, and confirming of, the "truth" of the preached message by the choir and the memory of doing so time and again re-enact the allegiance of the members of the choir to the group. Thus, "preaching to the choir" plays a substantial role in identity formation and increases social cohesion within the group. In the present case reading and writing these texts by the literati for primarily their own use served in late Yehud to reinforce the literati's construction of Israel – which they imagined as an extension of their own circle – as a text-centred community. It also allowed them to expand the scope of the texts included in "the text" around which their community was imagined to be centred (e.g. including Chronicles in the repertoire) and, by doing so, rebalancing a social memory based on them.

The temple was, of course, understood by the literati as the exclusive temple of Yhwh, the god of Israel (not of Judah or Benjamin alone). This understanding explains why the Yehudite literati tended to speak of the community in Yehud as (a manifestation of) Israel and construed Jerusalem and by extension Yehud (and the related area and population of the former kingdom of Judah of social memory) as standing at the core of Israel and decisive for its historical record and future. Since the temple was Israel's temple, then they were Israel and thus they were embodied in the triad Abraham, Isaac and Jacob, and left in the Exodus and stood at Sinai, suffered Exile and will enjoy living in the (prophetic books') utopias to materialise in the future. They remembered this past and future, of course, through acts of imagination involving vicarious experiences through the reading of the shared past/future constructing texts.

But to be Israel meant also to share essential texts and social memories with non-Yehudite groups, even if they were re-signified through interaction with uniquely Yehudite texts and social memories. Similar considerations, however, most likely applied outside Yehud too. For instance, to be Israel meant for the Yhwistic population of the province of Samaria to share essential texts and social memories with non-Samarian (e.g. Yehudite, Benjaminite groups). It is this discursive background that enables us to understand why the Pentateuchal books[64] not only were shared by these two groups, but also retained this status through their compositional and redactional processes in the Persian period, despite the fact that Samaria and Yehud constituted two different polities/com-

---

64 That is, those past-constructing books from the Persian period that were crucial for a formation of a social memory that allowed for the identification of Samarians and Yehudites as Israel.

munities, each with its own leadership, self-identity, social memory and ideological discourse.[65]

Needless to say, shared memory is conducive to the imagination of a (partially) shared identity. Since this identity cannot be associated only with Yehud, it generates a sense of porousness of Yehudite self-identity. It also generates a counter-balancing sense of identity that is not bound, in the main, to shared remembering of (agreed upon) "facts" about the past per se, including genealogical data, but rather to a Yehudite interpretation of these "facts." Identity formation is not necessarily about shared facts, but about proper interpretation and, therefore, it necessitates (a) a proper set of authoritative texts to inform the reading of the shared texts and the significance of the events, laws, places and the like that they evoke, and (b) proper interpreters.

Finally, a temple cannot but lead to the creation of a cultic community around itself and thus establish boundaries. This obvious fact had, however, some generative potential of interest to the present purpose. The Yehudite literati of the late Persian period were socialised to associate Jerusalem closely in their minds with the temple.[66] They certainly saw Jerusalem as the symbolic centre of both Israel (the people) and Yehud (the province). This shared social mindscape carried a substantial potential for the development of images in which the temple's cultic community becomes symbolic and eventually an embodiment of Israel. To illustrate, this tendency allowed the development of the concept that "exilic/returnee Israel" equals "Israel" that played an important role in the discourse of Yehud, once the entire cultic community (most of which consisted of

---

65 Of course the texts could be shared, because each community could read them in an "unshared" manner, as each of them read them in a way informed by other texts, social memory and general ideological discourse. Historical processes that lead to a shared text and an unshared reading of it by two diverse communities are often the result of an existing text that is then "appropriated" by either the two communities (in their own respective ways) or of an existing text associated with a community that is "appropriated" by a second community that sees itself as supplanting the former. Both models have been proposed for the development of a corpus of scriptures that were shared by early Judaism and early Christianity. It is worth noting, however, that this basically diachronic model assumes the existence of the shared text prior to the two-communities situation. It is difficult, however, to use to explain the sharing of the Pentateuchal books by Samarians and Yehudites according to these models, since the texts emerged (at least in their present form) in the Persian period. [Editor's Note: I further explored these issues in E. Ben Zvi, "The Pentateuch as/and Social Memory of 'Israel' in the Late Persian Period," in J. Baden and C. Nihan (eds.), *The Oxford Handbook of the Pentateuch* (forthcoming)
66 After all, from their perspective, the city was important because of the temple, that is to say, because Yhwh's choice of Jerusalem as the city in which Yhwh's appropriate temple should be located. The generative role of the association of Jerusalem and temple played a role in the extension of some attributes of the temple to the city (e.g. Isa 52:1).

the descendants of people who never left the land) there adopted as part of its social memory the concept that they were all returnees from Babylonian exile who came to an empty land.[67]

V Identity and social memory: how, what or who should be remembered in late Persian Yehud – temporal, spatial and main narrative considerations

The last section referred explicitly or implicitly to the issue of what was to be socially and collectively remembered in late Persian Yehud and its bearings on questions of group identity. Of course, the "what" was directly related to the "how," i.e. the kind of mental maps that the community had to develop to remember, organise and provide with significance the "what."

A community must construe a sense of time to construe and remember its past. There can be no concept of past without a concept of time. Moreover, since ancient Israelite memory included a (text-evoked) memory about future events about which the community read and reread, just as it did for past events, a concept of time was necessary for the construction of 'memories' of the future. Time is usually construed in a linear and cyclical or quasi-cyclical terms. Both organisations are at work in the social mindscape of Yehud.

Certainly the Deuteronomistic historical collection, the primary historical collection and Chronicles, as most historiographical works, socialised their readers and the community into a strong sense of linear time. When social memories and the historiographical works that reflect and shape them are organised around linear time, a number of basic plotline types become available (e.g. progress, decline, rise-fall-rise, etc.)[68] Since (a) the population in Yehud understood itself as the descendants and the remnant of those who suffered the calamity of 586 BCE, (b) ruins were probably seen in the area throughout the Persian period[69] and served to bring home the presence of a past nowhere to be physically seen in the present and (c) the discourse of the community was "obsessed" with the

---

[67] When the narrative of empty land, exile and return became the founding myth of the community Yehud, all Yehudites "remembered" themselves as if they participated in it. (Cf. the case of the Mayflower in social memory in America and the number of Americans who are able to construe, at least partially, their identity as descendants of those in the Mayflower.) On the Yehudite case, see "Total Exile" in this volume, pp. 599–611.

[68] For a general discussion and application of several of the concepts underlying this section to contemporary societies see E. Zerubavel, *Time Maps*; for references to plotlines, see, in particular, 11–25.

[69] Cf. D. Ussishkin, "The Borders", 147–166.

cluster of the 586 BCE catastrophe, Exile and related themes, decline had to dominate the narrative plotline of the past. This is clearly the case in the Deuteronomistic historical collection, the primary historical collection and Chronicles.

Moreover, the very idea that there is a corpus of pre-existing texts that are to be *interpreted* (already at work in Chronicles), the very concept of a text-centred community, the distinction between "classical" and "non-classical" texts communicated by the SBH and LBH contrast,[70] and the unique authority and status of Moses – and along with Moses, David's concerning the regulations of the temple, in Chronicles – all together conveyed a sense of decline, in which the early generations had more authority than present ones.

This general approach was consistent with a social mindscape in which antiquity was associated with legitimacy, which was common in the ANE.[71] This association is responsible for the common ANE narrative, propagandistic, but also cognitive pattern of the "restorer." The "restorer" is needed because positive change is associated with bringing back that which was in antiquity. The prophetic literature is, of course, suffused with references to "restoration." Unlike "historiographical" texts and related memories that turn to the motif of the "restorer" to characterise former kings (e.g. Hezekiah and Josiah are the major examples, but see also Asa, Joash and Jehu) and narrate their actions, prophetic literature's restorer is Yhwh and the restoration is in the future – note incidentally, that the same holds true for Lamentations.[72]

Whereas human restorers cannot stand aside completely from the decline plotline (e.g. Josiah cannot be a new Moses; he must find an already existing book, not write one; Hezekiah cannot be Solomon, he can only reopen the temple that the former built (see Chronicles); Jehu may not be Jeroboam, but cannot be the David of Kings, and the like), the divine restorer can create a plotline of rise-fall-rise in which the future rise is not only different but in some ways (though not necessarily all) superior to the previous rise, and which may involve, among other things, a new and better creation, a transformation in Israel so it may not sin again, or images of Jerusalem that are as exalted as commensurate

---

70 I expanded on this particular issue in E. Ben Zvi, "The Communicative Message", 269–290.
71 This pattern is still at work in many contemporary groups.
72 This is not the place to discuss ancient Yehudite "messianism." Clearly, some prophetic texts included images of an elevated, supra-human Davidic king, while other prophetic texts fail to mention any Davidic king, human or supra-human for that matter, in the image of the future. In either case, the fundamental slot of the restored is kept for Yhwh – the supra-human, future David is part of the restoration himself, rather than its initiator.

with its being "the city in the centre of the world."[73] The association of the "Rise-Decline-Rise" pattern with memories about the future and YHWH are directly related to the actual historical conditions of the community in Yehud. Clearly, it could not have imagined itself as being in the "Rise" period. The best it could do was to think that some faint markers pointing towards a future rise (e.g. YHWH's anointing of Cyrus for the sake of Israel (see Isa 45:1–4), the rebuilding of the temple, and the like).

The "Rise-Decline-Rise" plotline moves by necessity into cyclical (historical) time. It is worth noting, however, that in the relevant past- and future-constructing texts and in the memory of Yehud, this cyclical time is not a "circular" but a "helical" time, since the previous circumstances never exactly return. This holds true both in the case of the helical narratives about past restorers, which keep themselves within a general decline plotline and in the case of the helical turn towards a "Return" that does not simply undo Exile, but leads to a full utopian world, and thus while still within a basic "Rise-Decline-Rise" plotline, the final "Rise" shapes it as an incommensurably positive helical plotline.

It goes without saying that each of these constructions of time (i.e. linear and helical) conveys a message about who the remembering community is. Significantly, they do that together, balancing and informing each other and, to be sure, also along with the clearly circular, cultic configuration of time that characterises (and is communicated by) the festival and seasons calendar and the daily life of any agrarian society.

As mentioned above, linear time creates a sense of "beginnings" and "ends." Historiographical texts grounded on an underlying understanding of time as linear tend to shape and create a mental map in which there is "history" and there is "pre-history." Many historical narratives about the Americas begin (in earnest at least) with Columbus; about California with its annexation to the USA; and about Western Canada with the first trading posts. Similarly, narratives about many mountain peaks, lakes and rivers in North America (and in many other continents) begin at the moment they were "discovered" or "found" by a European explorer. Even if some note is made of preceding periods, this organisation of time is crucial for the development of social memory and reflects the (basic) self-understanding of the remembering community.

Chronicles led its intended and primary readers to imagine David as such a crucial beginning, and thus reflected and shaped a self-understanding of a community for which Jerusalem and temple are at the very centre of their identity.

---

73 On the common ancient Near Eastern, ideological, propagandistic, but also cognitive pattern of "the city at the centre of the world" see M. Liverani, "Memorandum", 189–191.

The Pentateuchal books reflected and communicated (to both Samarians and Yehudites) a sense that the crucial beginning was the creation of "Israel" through the Exodus and Sinai experience (e. g. Lev 11:45; 22:33; Num 15:41; Deut 4:6; 7:6). This reflected and shaped a self-understanding of the remembering community as "Israel."

From this perspective Genesis is in some way akin to the genealogies in Chronicles; it provided a background to understand the main central narrative to be remembered, and above all dealt with a central requirement of the shared mental map of the community, namely the matter of ancestry. They provided, among other things, the necessary answer to the implicit question about who those were who became Israel through the Exodus and Sinai, and who those were over whom David reigned, that is, and from the perspective of Yehudites: "Who are we?" Genesis allowed the information provided by Exodus-Deuteronomy to fit better into the mental maps held by the community.

Genesis was an integral part of the Pentateuch collection, but also stood saliently aside from the Moses-centred Exodus-Deuteronomy one.[74] The readers of Genesis were asked to imagine and construe time in such a way that associated the crucial beginning with Abraham, the divine call to return to the land and the covenant between YHWH and Abraham that involved the promise of land and progeny. It reflected and shaped a self-understanding of a community for which lack of possession of the promised land and promised progeny and a sense of seeming powerlessness along with faith in the promise to overcome these things in the future were core attributes of their identity. It is also a self-understanding of the community that emphasised it as a community of trust and obedience to YHWH. This is the community of those who "fear YHWH" (and were chosen by YHWH).[75]

The readers of the Deuteronomistic historical collection were asked to construe Moses as the central beginning point. This reflected and shaped a self-understanding of a community for which *torah* (associated with Moses), and to

---

[74] It is reasonable that some books were placed in several "shelves" in the "mental library" of late Persian Yehud. For instance, Deuteronomy was in the Pentateuch shelf, but also in that of the Dtr. historical collection. The Pentateuchal books occupied an important shelf, but were also part of the "Primary History" shelf and the Hexateuch shelf. Genesis was part of the last three mental shelves, but also stood by itself. The result, of course, is a web of readings, each of which is informed by a different set of books within the repertoire of the community, and all of which informed each other, even if at particular times, according to circumstances and purposes, one may have weighed more than another.

[75] There is more, of course, associated with remembering Abraham in the late Persian period. I addressed these matters in "The Memory of Abraham" in this volume, pp. 162–98.

some extent prophecy as well, were at the core of the self-understanding of the community.

The corpus of prophetic literature acknowledged all these beginning points directly or indirectly (e.g. Hos 2:17; 12:3), but on the whole the central period that opened the world to which the attention of the readers of the prophetic corpus was drawn started with the beginning of the process that led to the catastrophe of 586. The Assyrian period thus became a pre-figuration (and counterpoint in the case of Hezekiah) to the destruction of Jerusalem and Exile. This was a fitting beginning for books that reflected from different perspectives on the main story of Israel's deserved judgment, its suffering and its Return, which was partially fulfilled by the re-establishment of the temple but in the main still in the future, as the divinely promised utopia(s) has not yet been manifested in the world. The saliency given to this "beginning" (of downfall) time in the prophetic books reflected and shaped a community whose self-understanding evolved in the light of an awareness of a colossal past catastrophe and its counterpart, a (often colossally imagined) utopian future.

It is worth stressing that all of these beginnings contributed to the social memory of the community. The crucial beginnings that each of them drew attention to, and complemented each other within the discourse of a remembering community that (vicariously) experienced them as they read and reread all these books, which were simultaneously part of their authoritative repertoire in the late Persian period. By doing so, all of them together provided a fuller image of the ways in which the community viewed itself.

Moreover, their very co-existence and the way in which they informed each other carried generative potential for a cross-diffusion of images. Thus, for instance, if Abraham was the site of memory par excellence that embodied fearing and loving YHWH, then Abraham must have kept משמרתי מצותי חקותי ותורתי (Gen 26:5; cf. Deut 11:1), because "fearing YHWH" was associated in the mindscape of the community with observing YHWH's teachings and commandments.

As is well known, the association of the beginning of Israel, that is, within this discourse, of YHWH's people with the narrative of the Exodus tended to influence several narratives of "re-creations" of Israel after Exile (Cf. Isa 52:12a with Deut 16:3 and Exod 12:11, 31–34; Isa 52:12b and Exod 14:19 [and Exod 13:21–22]).[76]

Another example: the Deuteronomistic historical collection and the prophetic books shared an "obsession" with the catastrophe, its prefiguration during the

---

76 It is worth noting that in Isa 52:11–12 YHWH, not Pharaoh, commands the people to leave. Cf. J. Goldingay, *The Message of Isaiah 40–55*, 458–460, and from a different perspective, see J. Van Seters, *The Pentateuch*, 153.

Assyrian period, and its aftermath. They expressed a similar mental map of density of memories that focused on the period. Chronicles and some Pentateuchal texts attempted to temper this concentrated, obsessive focus on the catastrophe and related themes, despite the different beginnings to which they draw particular attention.[77]

The difference between "history" and "pre-history" reflects a distribution within the mental map of the community of temporal continuities and discontinuities.[78] Turning points at the end of "historical works" are another good marker for them. The conclusion of the books of Kings and Chronicles is suggestive of a way of thinking that distinguishes between (a) a *political* past of Judah worth of continuous remembering, but that ends with the events of 586 BCE and its aftermath and which "requires" historiographical works (see Kings and Chronicles), and (b) a later past worth remembering as well, but which is not a *political* past and can thus be evoked through the reading of prophetic books but not of (narrowly defined) historiographical works.[79]

This distinction seems to suggest that there was agreement within the community, or better, its literati: there was a particular literary genre that was an appropriate vehicle to communicate "political" history (i.e. historiography) and that "political" history is about kings and their deeds.[80] If so, books like Kings

---

[77] See "Towards a Sense of Balance" in this volume, pp. 387–406.
[78] On the general bearing of these matters on the study of social (or collective) memory in contemporary times, see E. Zerubavel, *Time Maps*, 89–110.
[79] Eventually Ezra-Nehemiah were (and later "was") written, but they are only in a partial way a kind of continuation of the main historiographical narrative – note their "episodic" rather than continuous narrative that characterises the monarchic period in both Kings and Chronicles. This and other differences between Ezra-Nehemiah, on the one hand, and Chronicles, on the other, demand a separate study that cannot be advanced here. As mentioned above, it is my contention that whether the imperial centre forced upon the local elite of Yehud the historical Nehemiah as a governor for a comparative brief period (from the perspective of the Persian period as a whole) or not, the present Ezra-Nehemiah is later than Chronicles and later than the Persian period.
[80] Significantly, there are still students today who think within a similar social mindscape and for whom "history" is a story about kings. To be sure, this position is partially balanced in Yehud by the memories of sovereign, "kingly" rulers of the "nation" who were not kings, but rather prophets or prophets/priests (e.g. Moses, Samuel). It is worth noting that these figures were placed in a far away, pre-monarchic past. It is in this context that the somewhat later, but still relatively early, Hellenistic construction of Israel's past in Hecateus is worth mentioning, since it illustrates the generative power of this kind of social mindscape concerning past leadership and its potential manifestations in the present of the community. On Hecateus's testimony in Diodorus Siculus 40.3 see D. Mendels, "Hecataeus of Abdera", 96–110. Note also the recent challenge to the widely accepted claim that the text in Diodorus Siculus 40.3 goes back, at least in the main, to Hecateus of Abdera in D. R. Schwartz, "Diodorus Siculus", 181–198.

and Chronicles cannot go beyond the end of the monarchy. Except that this boundary had to be breached somehow, since the community of readers felt that a kind of narratively minor (but ideologically very significant) appendix could not be avoided, for after all, the past existed so it may be brought to bear upon the present of the readership.[81]

It may be noted that the Deuteronomistic historical collection evoked a long narrative about the failure of all types of political, human leadership to provide a *stable*, socio-political foundation for the establishment of the Israel that should be.[82] All kinds of forms of political leadership had been tested and none provid-

---

[81] The end of Kings serves as a site of memory that "embodied and secreted" the potential well-being and "high-status" (see 2 Kgs 25:28) of Israel within the foreign-run Empire. Of course, this was not the end-point of Israel's history from a perspective informed by the dtr. historical collection. The fulfilment of the prophecy of Deut 30:1–5 was still in the future, and its certainty only emphasised by the fact that the catastrophe and Exile were also foreseen and explained by Moses. (It is most significant that by the conclusion of Deuteronomy and the Pentateuch the most hopeful references do not point to the new beginning that will follow the crossing of the Jordan which is about to happen in the narrative world, but rather to the new beginning that will follow the fall of the society that the Israelites are about to create (see, for instance, Deut 30:1–10, and cf. Deut 29:28). A similar situation occurs in Deut 4, where the target readership is first asked to read Deut 4:25–31 and, then in the light of these verses, to understand the subsequent reports about the establishment of Israelite rule in Transjordan, i.e. Deut 4:41–49). The end of Chronicles not only explains the catastrophe and Exile, but also diminishes the "watershed" value of Exile, while at the same time (a) reminding its target readership of the role of Empire as an instrument to fulfil Yhwh's wishes for Israel and to restore Yhwh's temple, and (b) evoking among the readers who live in the late Persian (or early Hellenistic) period the image of the yet to be fulfilled return of Israel, which will take place only when Yhwh wishes it to happen (i.e. the same attitude is present in the prophetic corpus). I wrote about the ending of Chronicles elsewhere, see E. Ben Zvi, *History, Literature and Theology*, 201–203, 208–209; for a different approach to the conclusion of Chronicles, see I. Kalimi, *Ancient Israelite Historian*, 143–157. On Chronicles' beginning of the story to be remembered with Adam and concluding it with Cyrus, see below.

[82] Moses (the highest prophet and lawgiver, explicitly selected by Yhwh) is explicitly presented as someone who knew that after his death, Israel will act corruptly (see Deut 4:25–28; 31:16), i.e. even a leader such as Moses cannot establish the "required" leadership. Joshua (the leader appointed by the highest prophet and lawgiver) does not even appoint a successor and certainly does not create a stable community in which the people follow Yhwh's teachings (see Judg 2:6, 13; see also Josh 23:12–26; 24:15–20 in which the future actions of Israel are prefigured). The book of Judges expresses in unequivocal language that the Judges (i.e. charismatic leaders) who follow Joshua did not provide the mentioned foundation (see, for instance, Judg 2:18–19; 3:12; 4:1; 6:1). The leadership of the House of Eli, the hereditary priest/ruler, is presented as a dead end, but so is the House of Samuel, the priest/prophet/ruler (see, for instance, 1 Sam 2:22–34; 4:10–18; 8:1–3). Significantly, the report about the sinful behaviour of Samuel's sons immediately precedes and explains the people's request for a king. But clearly neither the

ed a lasting solution. The corollary was that the solution for Israel's woes was not to be found in political leadership. What actually counted was whether the people follow Yhwh's commandments/teachings. Although Chronicles did not relate the story of successive (and failed) political systems, it reflected and inculcated a similar ideological attitude. The political "history" of kings may end, but Israel will continue, provided that it has proper teachers of Yhwh's teachings and proper authoritative texts. This is consistent with a self-understanding that emphasised Israel as Yhwh's people and therefore bound to Yhwh, which within their discourse also meant a text-centred community, over and against any polity-based self-identity.[83]

The prophetic books conveyed a similar attitude, but in some places they looked towards the end of "history as is" and "Israel as is," as their utopian solutions involved a substantial change in the nature of the world and/or Israel.[84]

In sum, the topography of the mental temporal map/s of the literati in late Persian Yehud (and possibly, other societies influenced by it) was indicative of underlying core concepts held by the group that had a significant bearing on its sense of self-identity.

Of course, this was not the only kind of topography that the mental maps of the literati in Yehud carried. The preceding observations have made the point that several personages of old (e.g. Abraham, Moses, David) served as main sites of memory. Personages such as these embodied and communicated core messages to the community and enjoyed much mindshare. The Pentateuchal texts, the Deuteronomistic historical collection, Chronicles, and the prophetic books shaped images of several of these major characters of the past and numerous relatively minor figures. Given that there was (most likely) a significant relation between (authoritative) texts constructing the past of the community and its social memory, or at least the social memory of the literati who read these texts,

---

judge/charismatic/king Saul can provide the political leadership that leads Israel to a stable situation of wellbeing, which within this ideology can only be based on obeying the divine will/teachings. The disastrous end of the Saulide dynasty led to the establishment of the Davidic dynasty, which led in turn to the divinely caused catastrophe of 586, Exile and the Israelite behaviour that justified both.

83 Of course, the very same literati also emphasised the continuity between Persian Yehud and monarchic Judah. There were always several partial self-understandings informing each other. For instance, continuity between Persian Yehud and monarchic Judah could be discursively positioned as continuity between two temporal manifestations of trans-temporal Israel.

84 See, for instance, Isa 11; 65:17, and note the changed Israel that is reshaped by the deity as unable to sin because it is "programmed" to follow Yhwh (e.g. Deut 30:6; Jer 31:31–34; 32:38–41; Ezek 11:19–20; 36:25–28; cf. Hos 2:21; Jer 24:7), and the peaceful world in which all the nations will flow to Jerusalem (e.g. Isa 2:2–4; Mic 4:1–5).

one may assume that the characters about whom much was written and therefore much was read and reread were evoked more frequently, secured more mindshare, and tended to serve to attract to themselves numerous important messages (e.g. Moses is, among others and for late Persian period Yehudite, the prophet, lawgiver, leader of the "nation" and to some extent "priest;" both the central motifs of Exodus and *torah* are closely associated with him, and even the catastrophe of 586, Exile and a future Return were foreseen by him).[85]

It would be relatively easy to construe the list of personages that social memory included among the "must be remembered and remembered often" list of the community in late Persian Yehud, but it is worth stressing that despite all this, the main characters in the primary historical collection the Deuteronomistic historical collection, Chronicles and the prophetic books include none of the individualised characters (whether Moses, Joshua, David, Solomon, Isaiah or Jeremiah, to mention only a few of the salient figures), but (transtemporal) Israel and Yhwh. Basically, all these texts shape a social memory in which the most important past was imagined and conceptualised in terms of the interactions between Israel and Yhwh. This is the reason why the primary historical collection, the Deuteronomistic historical collection and Chronicles, can be considered "national" histories.

This phenomenon of "national" histories is important in two ways. First, since no matter how important individual personages may be, they are always secondary to a "collective" (transtemporal) Israel. This phenomenon is consistent with and contributes to a social mental map of society in which a horizontal (rather than vertical or hierarchical) approach is dominant. This mental map is manifested in many other places in the authoritative texts of late Persian Yehud, including the Pentateuchal laws, the idea of a divine covenant with the people (rather than with the king alone), the understanding that the entire people should be should be holy (e.g. Lev 19:2) and the multiple references to the agency of the people and consultation with the people in Chronicles.

This observation brings to mind the often-quoted words of B. Anderson, namely "the nation is always conceived as a deep horizontal comradeship."[86] Leaving aside for a moment the differences between ancient "nations" or ethnies and modern nations, and that this emphasis on the horizontal, both in modern and ancient times, is a *discursive* phenomenon or, if one wishes, a necessary act

---

[85] Deuteronomy is above all a book of restoration (and so is Gen–Deut). See, among many others, K. A. Deurloo, "The One God", 31–46, and esp. 32–33. Of course, David is not only or simply a "king" (and see in particular Chronicles) and Abraham is associated with plenty of central motifs. See "The Memory of Abraham" in this volume, pp. 162–98.

[86] B. Anderson, *Imagined Communities*, 7.

of imagination that may take place against a background of exclusions (e.g. women, lower strata in society) and historically hierarchical organisation and even tends to mask these exclusions by filtering them out of what it is to be noticed and remembered, the point remains that national/ethnie identity tends to require some level of horizontal construction of the nation/ethnie. Here the "national" histories of ancient Israel, the social memory that they created and the ways in which they socialised the community to focus on and remember certain matters, and not to "see" others,[87] all were deeply related to processes of self-identity construction.[88]

Second, national histories in ancient Israel (and other places in the Hellenistic period; cf. Berossus, Manetho) represented a response of cultural 'peripheries' in interaction with imperial centers (e.g. the Achaemenid or later Hellenistic empires),[89] and served as an ideological tool of resistance, aimed at maintaining and enhancing local traditions, power centres and their viewpoints, including those involved in maintaining self-identity and a sense of heightened self-worth. Transcultural historical studies lead to an expectation that in such cases ideas, symbols and images pertaining to the imperial discourse would be re-configured to support the claims of groups on the periphery; in other words, hybridity is expected.[90] Not all aspects of hybridity and their relation to social memory and self-identity/understanding can be explored, but an important example will be discussed in section 7 below.

Even a mini-survey of prominent topographies in mental maps of the literati, such as this one is, cannot but include a reference to the topography of the spatial map of the literati in late Persian Yehud. It goes without saying that it was heavily tilted towards Jerusalem and Judah in the prophetic literature, the Deuteronomistic historical collection and Chronicles.[91] This point may seem so obvious that it requires no discussion, but it is still worth stressing that no prophetic text/book was associated with a character who was born or grew up in Babylon and that the density of references to Mizpah or Benjamin in general in the Deu-

---

87 The Decalogue provides an excellent, and quite obvious, example.
88 Cf. the positions advanced in M. G. Brett, "National Identity", 29–40 and J. L. Wright, "Continuing These Conversations", 149–167.
89 Cf. A. Momigliano, "Eastern Elements", 25–35. Compare and contrast A. Kuhrt, "Israelite and Near Eastern Historiography", 268–276. For examples of historiographical works by and about 'peripheries' in Hellenistic times, see the works of Berossus and Manetho.
90 See E. Ben Zvi, "Late Historical Books".
91 And not surprisingly in other corpora within the authoritative repertoire of the community. See Psalms, Lamentations, Ruth and the references to kings of Judah in wisdom literature. See even Songs of Songs. There are exceptions to the rule, e.g. Job, but a discussion of these is beyond the scope of this contribution.

teronomistic historical collection is extremely low in comparison with those to Jerusalem/Judah, even if Mizpah/Benjamin was the political (and economic) centre of Yehud in the early Persian period.

Given the association of Israel with "the land" in the discourse of the period, when it comes to space, a conceptual map in which the Other was construed as "Outside the Land" emerged. In addition to the expected constructions of outside space in comparative or absolute negative terms, either implicitly or explicitly, that are so common in mental maps that serve to enhance inner social identity and that were clearly attested in ancient Israel (e.g. Exod 3:8; 15:13; Lev 25:23;[92] Deut 8:7–9; Josh 22:19 [note the boundaries of "the land" implied there]; Amos 7:17) and the related characterisation of living outside the land with shame (e.g. Ezek 36:20; Amos 7:17; Zech 9:11), there was second type of constructions that demands attention.

The logic of the conceptual, related associations of "the land" with YHWH, Israel with YHWH, and "the land" with Israel carried a generative potential for the development and flourishing of memories of Israel in which it needs to reside in the "Other space" so as to prepare itself for the "Inner Space," that is, to achieve a status commensurate with being in the land. For instance, Israel must be first aware of the divine teachings governing its behaviour and then not only socialise itself to follow them but actually do so to "fit" in the land.[93] Significantly numerous texts and main metanarratives about "*torah*" are proof positive of the existence and salience of memories evoking directly or indirectly these matters in the primary historical collection and the prophetic books.

It may be noted, however, that Chronicles emphasised not only the need of the people to purify themselves so that they may return to the land, but also the need for the land to purify itself (2 Chr 36:21; cf. Lev 26:34–35). By doing so, Chronicles did not attempt to negate the other memories held in the community, but shifted their relative mindshare to emphasise it more.

---

92 Note that in H, "the land" is "holy." See below.
93 See, for instance, explicit texts such as Exod 13:5; implicit attestations of this principle are ubiquitous. The concept of the holiness of the land (and the people) has bearings on these matters as well. These issues, however, are discussed in section 6 below.

VI Social memory, some Israelitising tendencies in construction of the Other, boundaries and self-understanding

Christine Mitchell recently stressed the importance of the Other in ancient historiographical writing.[94] Of course, constructions of the Other are deeply involved in the process of constructing the self-image of the group by depicting what the group is not. Moreover, in an approach based on binary logic, attributes assigned to the Other are often selected so as to highlight their opposites, which are then associated with the inner group. For instance, when the enemy of the Assyrian king is depicted as the enemy of the gods, or as someone who damaged temples or who relies on his own army or the terrain he holds, or who illegally encroached on someone else's territory, or as one who brings chaos to the world, the Assyrian king is imagined not only as a negation of all these attributes, but as an embodiment of their opposite – and so he is loyal to the gods, relies on them, rebuilds their temples, never encroaches illegally on the territory of another polity, and brings order to the world.[95] Similarly, when Persian men are depicted as "soft" and effeminate, then the Greek men who defeated them are construed as "tough" and truly manly.

This logic of binary opposition and construction of the Other so as to create a positive image of the inner group through inversion is at work in, among others, Deuteronomy, the Deuteronomistic historical collection and the primary historical collection, as well as in works that, although they may be past-constructing, can hardly be considered historiography (e.g. Ps 115; note the characterisation of the Other in multiple prophetic texts, none of which can be considered historiography; Isa 44:9–20; Ezek 38:10–12; Obad 3; Nah 3:4; *passim*).

This observation demonstrates that, although the national/ethno-cultural Other is commonly present in historiography, this is not the result of any unique feature of historiography, but to the inclusion of such texts within a wider group of texts. The national/ethno-cultural Other may be construed and remembered for its roles in the imagined past or future; its presence is characteristic of past- and future-constructing texts, that is, social memory-constructing texts. This is hardly surprising given that constructions (and memories of) the Other play a necessary role in distinguishing the inner group from the others, and given that "without memory, groups could not distinguish themselves one from another, whether family, friends, governments, institutions, ethnic groups,

---

[94] See C. Mitchell, "Otherness and Historiography", 93–109.
[95] On the characterisation of the enemy/Other in Assyrian texts, see B. Oded, *War, Peace and Empire*, 43–66.

or any other collectivity, nor would they know whether or how to negotiate, fight or cooperate with each other."[96]

Moreover, it is worth stressing that the Other is often used to construct binary pairs of social subgroups within the same ethno-cultural group (e.g. the righteous vs. the transgressors (see Ps 1, numerous other psalms and proverbs), or the men vs. women, which is implicitly conveyed in much of the literature of the Hebrew Bible). In all these cases there is no inherent reason why historiographical texts would play a central role in identity-creation through Othering.

In sum, it is the basic character and behaviour of the Other as shaped and reshaped in social memory that contributes to identity formation. This said, it is worth keeping in mind that the opposite of the Other is not necessarily (or even often) an actual social group, but an ideal social group, as perceived and communicated by the remembering community involved in Othering. This being the case, Othering may be (rhetorically) used to shame the inner group or a subgroup within it for failing to meet its expected standards, which in the case of the Jerusalem-centred literati would be for being "unfaithful" to the ideologically proper image of what Israel should be.[97] In other words, Othering serves to a large extent to reflect inner worries about the character and thus indirectly, at some level, the "actual" identity of the inner group.[98]

Given its role in shaping and reshaping identity, social memory as a whole tends to create mental maps of "Otherness." For instance, one of these maps involved Othering time: the radical utopian time can be seen as the Other of regular historical time. Given space constrains here and given the central discursive topos of the (promised) land and Israel that prevailed in the late Persian period in Yehud, I will briefly explore only those topoi concerning "lands" and "peoples."[99]

It is to be stressed from the outset that the discursive topos of the (promised) land, although significant for identity formation, had nothing to do with the actual extent of the province of Yehud or any historically possible expansion of it. It did not express any operational policy that the province might have considered

---

96 M. G. Cattell and J. J. Climo, "Meaning in Social Memory", 1–36 (here 1).
97 E.g. much of the construction of the Other (nations) who was (were) removed from the land because of their sins served the rhetorical purpose of portraying Israel as worthy of being exiled.
98 E.g. is Israel like the Canaanites? One may mention that similar processes are at work even in present-day society. The (regrettably) common case of the coach of a boys' team that shouts at them "not to play like girls" makes the point.
99 It goes without saying that the existence of mental maps of the Other that emphasise lands and peoples is certainly not something peculiar to Yehud. They do exist and very prominently so up to contemporary times.

on these matters. As much as it does not deal with the world of realpolitik, it deals in important ways with an ideological world that existed in the minds of the literati (and those who followed them in this regard) through an act of shared imagination.

This attitude and set of preferences is consistent with a group for which identity is not a challenge in everyday interaction or closely related to practical political or administrative action.[100] Instead the main "challenges" to identity are those that occur when people explore their *own* mental landscape and social memory.

The most fertile ground to explore the underlying complex mental landscape that governs the construction (and undermining/encroachment) of boundaries consists of cases that may be described as "on the edge," because they test the very conceptualisation of borders within the mindscape of the community.[101] In the late Persian period, "the land" (i.e. "inner space") was considered to be holy. But as Milgrom wrote, "the promised land" is holy (in H), and "all other land is impure (Josh 22:19; Amos 7:17), *except* where a theophany has occurred (Exod 3:5; Josh 5:15)" (emphasis added).[102] The "except" clause is of particular significance for the present purposes, since it means that "outside space" can be seen and remembered by the community as if it were "inside space," because it became a particular site of memory for Israel because of its direct association with Yhwh's theophany. In other words, considerations of social memory could outweigh seemingly solid geographical considerations and lead to the creation of a hybrid conceptual category, namely places that are clearly and permanently outside "the land" (e.g. Horeb) and therefore never promised to the patriarchs, but which share the most salient character of "the land," its holiness.

Turning to another very important mental map of Otherness in Yehud, Yhwh's teachings and the requirement to follow them were among the most characterising features associated with being Israel within the discourse of late Persian Yehud (cf. Deut 4:5–6).[103] Other features included the related concept of knowing Yhwh (i.e. acknowledging the authority, deeds and power of Yhwh) and receiving Yhwh's prophecy/communication.

As is well-known, Chronicles partially Israelitises a significant number of foreigners, by describing them as performing Israelite roles (e.g. serving as pro-

---

100 See above.
101 Thus, for instance, there is no point in providing examples to demonstrate that people in Yehud did not consider Egypt to be part of "the land," or to illustrate that they did not ponder whether they were Assyrians or Egyptians or Persians.
102 See J. Milgrom, *Leviticus 23–27*, 2412.
103 Cf. Jer 51:19.

phetic voices; see Neco [2 Chr 35:21]; Cyrus [2 Chr 36:23]) or voicing what pious Israelites where supposed to voice, and even using typical Israelite expressions (e.g. Huram [2 Chr 2:10–15]; the Queen of Sheba [2 Chr 9:5–8]).[104]

To be sure, some of the cases (e.g. Cyrus) can be explained in terms of a well-known process of local resistance in cultural imperial systems by which famous external figures are used to provide (additional) legitimacy to the local traditions of the group,[105] but this does not hold for all of these cases. Moreover, the account of Amaziah in 2 Chr 25 both assigns Israelitising features to those supposed to be the Other and in a rhetorical reversal, partially foreignise the king while conveying that being a Jerusalemite by itself does not convey any particular status.[106] The genealogies in Chronicles both link Israel to, and separate it from, the "Other," but most importantly for present purposes they at times blur boundaries, and particularly so in the case of Judah, which is the dominant tribe.[107] Mitchell has claimed that "most of Chronicles is just not that concerned with foreigners."[108] I would suggest that the intended and primary readers of Chronicles were asked to remember a significant number of cases that could not but problematise the simplistic boundaries that often occupy the default position in society.

Moreover, Chronicles is not alone within the general discourse of the late Persian period in emphasising that boundaries separating categories may be more fuzzy and problematic than simplistic default positions may suggest, as the voice in Isa 56:3–7 clearly shows.[109] To be sure, all these voices not only inform but are also informed by other voices and by an implied default tendency to draw boundaries.[110] Significantly, this system of balancing voices reflects a multifaceted system of mental constructions of what Israel is that prevailed in late Persian Yehud. Israel was at the same time conceived in terms of, among other things, shared ancestry (as almost normative within the expected mind-

---

104 See E. Ben Zvi, *History, Literature and Theology*, 270–288.
105 Cf. the tradition of the meeting between Alexander and Jerusalemite High Priest. See Josephus, *Ant.* 11.325–339. On this tradition, see, for instance, T. H. Kim, "The Dream", 425–442 and S. J. D. Cohen, "Alexander the Great", 41–68.
106 See E. Ben Zvi, "A House of Treasures", 77–84.
107 G. N. Knoppers, "Intermarriage", 15–30; "Great Among His Brothers"; *I Chronicles 1–9*, 302.
108 See C. Mitchell, "Otherness and Historiography in Chronicles", 93–109.
109 Among the many examples of past memories that partially Israelitise foreigners one may mention the characterisation of Abimelech in Gen 20; Jethro in Exod 18; Rahab in Josh 2, and even see Deut 4:5–6. It is worth mentioning that later Judaic tradition takes up the characterisation of Rahab in Josh 2 and fully Israelitises her.
110 It goes without saying that texts that seem to undermine or render porous boundaries imply and necessitate the very existence of these boundaries in the discourse of the community.

scape of ancient ethnies),[111] but also as (a) a group characterised by a particular worldview that was associated with the deity, (b) certain cultural and behavioural patterns and a shared memory, (c) an identification with a particular sacred space (as almost normative within the expected mindscape of ancient ethnies/ "national" groups), and (d) a group with a role to play, which within their own discourse was assigned to them by YHWH. Of course, all these associations related to and informed each other; but again, it is significant that political realities, i.e. being part of the Persian empire, are not part of these ideological acts of imagining and re-imagining Israel and its boundaries, at least not explicitly.

VII Remembering earlier and future polities and the question of the Central Empire

The last comment raises the issue of the Empire. Berquist recently wrote about a reading of the Deuteronomistic history among Yehudite scribes of the late Persian period:

In this reading, the scribes discover a past, a time before the empire. Although they live at empire's geographic edge and in the approach of the Persian Empire's chronological end, they first experience the end of the Empire through reading about the time before the Empire. The text of the Deuteronomistic History, in this sense, resists Empire; the text imagines a world without the empire. In particular, the text celebrates heroes of the past, for whom the reader can yearn. These characters such as David, Solomon, Josiah, and others are then seen as persons who resisted empire or ran their own politics.[112]

It is true that the literati remembered a world before the Assyrian, neo-Babylonian and Persian empires. They also remembered a world well before David and Solomon, for that matter. All these memories were not only important in terms of the past, but also in terms of their generative potential to frame expectations of utopian futures of different kinds and thus for the memories of these futures that the readers activated as they read and reread the relevant books in their authoritative repertoire.

Yet, it is worth noting that despite the clear influence of memories of the past on the shaping of memories of the future, the latter were not in the main shaped in terms of a return to the political circumstances evoked by the for-

---

111 Of course, the myth of a shared ancestry is still at work in many contemporary nations.
112 J. Berquist, "Identities and Empire", 3–13.

mer.¹¹³ Thus, for instance, the very prominent patriarchal stories evoked images of a future Israel in possession of "the promised land," which was not in the hands of Israel at all during the period of the patriarchs.

Memories of the original failure to conquer the entire land and remove its previous residents (see, for instance, Num 33:55; Josh 13:1–7; 15:63; 16:10; 17:12–13; 23:13; Judg 1; 2:1–3; 2:20–23¹¹⁴) helped develop memories of an (imaginary) future in which the entire land is inhabited by Israel (see, for instance, Obad 19–21, the ideological topos of the empty land that assumes that non-Israelites would not settle in the land, even if it stands empty for decades, and the memories of future fulfilment of the promises to the patriarchs), but not of a return to a failed attempt to conquer the land.

Memories of the Davidic-Solomonic polity had much mindshare but, for instance, Obad 19–21 brings Israel back to a "territory similar to that of the traditional Davidic Israel" in a future era reminiscent of that of the Judges (cf. Neh 9:27; the period of the Judges is portrayed in positive terms in Ruth), not the Davidic polity.¹¹⁵

Just as memories about David and Solomon had a significant mindshare in late Persian Yehud,¹¹⁶ so did memories of a future Davidide at the time (e.g. Isa 9:5–6; 11:1–9; Jer 23:5–6; 30:8–11; 33:14–26; Ezek 34:23–30; 37:15–28; Hos 3:5; Amos 9:11–15; Mic 5:1; cf. Zech 9:9–10). But very often the future Davidide or the circumstances of his reign are portrayed as highly elevated.¹¹⁷ Most significantly, the memories of this future are far different from the memories

---

113 This is so despite a quite pervasive rhetoric of return (e.g. Zeph 3:20; passim) and despite the general ANE (and cross-cultural) tendency to emphasise return to a previous, ideal period. See above.

114 But contrast with Josh 11:23; 21:43. There are, of course, many other instances of "logically" contradictory statements within the very same book in ancient Israelite historiography (e.g. Judg 1:8 but see 1:21; 1 Kgs 5:27–32; 11:28 but see 1 Kgs 9:20–22; 2 Chr 14:2, 4 but see 2 Chr 15:17; 2 Chr 17:6 and see 2 Chr 20:33). Texts in tension with one another also appear in prophetic literature (cf. Mic 4:1–5; 7:17), and at times one in the textual vicinity of the other (e.g. Mic 5:6, 7–8). On the bearing of these observations on the general issues discussed here see section 8.

115 See E. Ben Zvi, *A Historical-Critical Study of the Book of Obadiah*, 228. See also P. R. Raabe, *Obadiah*, 255–273 (esp. 269); cf. J. Renkema, *Obadiah*, 215–219; J. Barton, *Joel and Obadiah*, 157.

116 One way to approach relative mindshare in late Persian Yehud is to assume that the more written space was devoted to a given a story, character, place within the authoritative literary repertoire of the literati, the more the latter read about them. This being so and since memories were shaped by the literati's vicarious encounters with these characters, events and places of their mind, it is reasonable to assume that the more they read about them, the more they imagined and remembered them.

117 For a highly elevated David see Isa 9:5–7; 11:1–9; Hos 3:5.

of the reign of David (or Solomon) reflected in the books of Samuel, Kings or even Chronicles, which in its own way lionises the past David (and Solomon).

Moreover, given the relative mindshare of all these memories about past and future involving Davidides, it is remarkable that the same community held many other memories of the future that were saliently devoid of any reference to the future Davidide, elevated or not (e.g. Isa 40–66;[118] Jer 50:4–5, 19–20; Hos 2:18–22; 14:6–9;[119] Obad; Zeph 3) The literati in late Persian Yehud could imagine, vicariously experience, and certainly 'remember' many different utopian futures. This wide range of images and memories, informing and complementing each other[120] and all of them contributing and shaping social memory, is of importance for matters discussed in section 8, but at this point it is worth stressing that none of them involved an actual restoration of a past period or characters.

Given that trends towards univocality were rare in the discourse of late Persian Yehud and dealt only with central matters (e.g. the importance of Jerusalem), this is not a minor observation.[121] As mentioned above, historical time (i.e. the time that links memories of the past and the future) was not construed in ancient Israel as circular but helical, and in fact in the form of a highly twisted helix. This being so, and despite the importance of images of the past, it is probably as appropriate (or more so) to focus on 'memories' of the future, if one wishes to discuss how social memory could have contributed to Israel's construction of its identity and particularly the ways in which it used its imagination and memory to resist or adapt for its purposes the imperial discourse of its time.

If so, probably the most significant and salient set of memories about the future that emerge as relevant to this question is the very widespread memory of the future Israelite empire (e.g. Isa 2:2–4; 42:1, 6; 45:14; 49:7, 23; 51:4–5; 56:6–7; 60:9; Mic 4:1–3; Zeph 2:11; Hag 2:7–8; Zech 8:20–22; 9:10; Ps 22:30; 68:30; 72:8–10; 96:7–10; 97:6–7). This is a memory about Israel's king, Yhwh, or an elevated future Davidide or Israel as embodying "the king" who will rule the nations from Jerusalem; peoples will flow to the new imperial centre (Zion) and will

---

118 See H. G. M. Williamson, "The Messianic Texts", 239.
119 See E. Ben Zvi, *Hosea*, 307–308 and note that the Targum felt it necessary to add an explicit note about a messianic king in v. 8 ("they shall dwell in the shade of the Anointed One").
120 See E. Ben Zvi, "Utopias", 55–85.
121 This trend is probably associated with, and perhaps explained by, the idea that unless the future is substantially different from the past, the latter might or will re-occur, and therefore Israel will again suffer justified and severe divine punishment. Cf. the cyclical conception of time in Qohelet. Chronicles may have shared some of the mindscape conveyed in Qohelet, but the issue requires a separate discussion.

bring their gifts to Zion and to the king, which is an adaptation and reversal of the common imperial image of the nations paying homage to the king of kings (i.e. the emperor). It is Israel not the Assyrian king who is remembered as "a light to the nations" (Isa 42:6) and, like Darius, Israel's king is one king for many, one lord for all, the king who is over kings, a king of numerous countries containing all kinds of peoples, the king of all the earth and the like (cf., for instance, DE, DNa, DSb). Like imperial capitals (e.g. Babylon), Jerusalem is imagined as the city "at the centre of world."[122] This is a future world in which the many "others" (and the Other) are partially Israelitised, that is, they are, through an act of imagination, culturally "colonised" by Israel; this future world is one in which the main features shaping the character of nations other than Israel are replaced by those typical of Israel, and thus in which the very identity of these nations is reformulated. It is an imperial world and dream of cultural conquest and assimilation of the Other to the centre of the discourse of the future empire and of the community that dreams about it.[123]

Moreover, this empire of the mind and dreams, like "real" ancient empires, has to deal with the issue of the ideological and functional role of the imperial central socio-cultural or ethnic group (e.g. Persians, and to some extent, but substantially less so, Medes in the Persian empire) and that of all the other peoples who accept the king of kings as their king. This involves negotiating boundaries around the potential role of their "children" at core institutions of the empire or ideological-administrative matters (e.g. and from substantially different perspectives, Isa 56:6–7; Deut 32:8, according to 4QDeut^j and the LXX, a version supported also by Sir 17:17)[124] and at times emphatic expressions of the *partial* character of the integration (which may also represent a mitigated imperial dream that still allows for some still significant level of local differentiation even if tinged with some sense of inferiority to the standards of the imperial centre, e.g. Mic 4:5).

Within this context, the memory that all humanity has a common pair of ancestors who were created by Yhwh – thus implying it all belongs to Yhwh (cf. Ps 100:3), along with the entire world created by Yhwh (e.g. Ps 24:1; 89:12) – provided an additional layer of ideological support for the future empire.

---

[122] On this motif, see M. Liverani, "Memorandum", 189–191.
[123] See, among many examples, Isa 56:1–8. Needless to say, these (underdog) dreams of empire are both proof positive of an internalisation (and adaptation) of the imperial discourse and of the ways in which a local community may use the adapted version of this discourse to express and shape a sense of local identity and resistance to imperial claims that may contradict the self-understanding of the community.
[124] See, for instance, J. H. Tigay, *Deuteronomy*, 303, 513–518 and bibliography cited there.

Of course, this future imperial system on earth is related to an imperial structure among the deities, who like vassal kings are subordinate to the hegemonic king, if they are allowed to remain "kings" (e.g. [4QDeut^j and 4QDeut^q and LXX] Deut 32:8, 43; Zeph 2:11; Ps 29:1; 82; 97:7b; and cf. Exod 15:11; Ps 96:5).

Many of the basic imperial topoi that were used to imagine and remember this future empire resembled, as expected, the image that the actual empire of the time (and through it, previous empires)[125] projected through its ideology. Of course, differences are expected too. Significantly, there are differences that go beyond a simple transfer of the centre from the Persian king and his divine imperial counterpart, Ahura Mazdā, to its Israelite counterpart. As in other cases of hybridity and ideological resistance to empire, the importance of these differences for historical studies rests on the fact that they tend to call attention to the particularities of the local discourse and thus to shed light on the ways in which they imagined core aspects of who, they thought, they were.

For one, the future empire of Yhwh (/Israel) was not ephemeral as the one in which the Yehudites lived or any other foreign empire that may replace the Achaemenid.[126] Memories of the establishment of the future empire were not memories of a simple replacing or succession of empires, as had happened before, but of memories of a substantial change in Yhwh's way of governing the world.

In the period before the establishment of this empire, as construed within the social memory of Yehud, Yhwh controlled the world, but through kings like Cyrus (e.g. Isa 44:28; 45:1–4; 2 Chr 36:22–23) and by extension the Persian king, even if for the sake of Israel (Isa 45:5).[127] The image of Yhwh controlling the world through non-Yhwistic monarchs was bound to generate some potentially ideological concerns, but the latter could have been easily allayed (see already Isa 45:1–7). The image, of course, allowed for an accommodation of Israel, its elite and its (imperial) hegemonic discourse to the actual world of the Persian

---

125 The Achaemenid empire used and reshaped ideological motifs that go back to the neo-Assyrian empire.
126 Or for that matter, ephemeral, territorially limited, versions of empire that the literati associated with particular periods in the past of Israel (e.g. 1 Kgs 5:1). Again, the future empire is not like any Israelite "empire" of the past. Time is not cyclical and what has happened is not what will happen. There will be something new under the sun – a new type of empire.
127 Within this discourse the catastrophe of 586 was *also* construed as another of Yhwh's actions for the sake of Israel (cf. Jer 25:9; 27:6; note the implied notion that the fall of the northern kingdom should have carried a didactic benefit for the core of Israel, namely Judah that appears in the Dtr. historical collection and prophetic literature), but a study of the web of constructions and images associated with that calamity is beyond the scope of this contribution.

empire, and to the remembered world in which previous empires (e. g. Babylon) were dominant.

This said, a world permanently run by Yнwн through others than Israel or its king (see below) and with a marginal Jerusalem was, within the logic of the discourse of the community, inherently unstable. It did not fit well with the cosmic order. For one, Jerusalem eventually had to be "the city at the centre of the world" and known as such. Moreover, lack of knowledge was associated with the chaotic or "uncivilised" realm and seen as a permanent source of instability in the "orderly," "civilised" world. But the divine order governing the world was a secret, unknown to anyone (including the Persian king who does not "know" Yнwн; e. g. Isa 45:5) except Israel and its Yehudite literati.[128]

Another central difference: at the centre of the Persian empire were the figures of the king and Ahura Mazdā.[129] There is, however, a very strong current that remembers a future empire at whose centre the traditional kingly and divine figure collapse into one: Yнwн is king in that empire. Moreover, often also Israel as a whole is imagined with royal attributes (see above). In addition, at times when non-Yнwн royal figures are imagined, they are in terms quite opposite to those associated with worldly kings (e. g. the servant of Yнwн in Isa 40–55; the king of Zech 9:9–10).

All these considerations point to the existence of a very strong trend towards drawing memories of the future empire away from the known "political-worldly" realm and towards a world in which the latter does not necessarily constrains social imagination and the generative power of theology/ideology. It is precisely in that world that the literati of Yehud could "compete and beat" the actual Empire,[130] while at the same time, and partially because of their success in that endeavour, be able to adapt well to it in their regular, but ideological and discursively "less significant" life.

Finally, it is worth noting that this trend to shift the focus of competition and resistance to the imperial discourse, through adaptation and reformulation, away from the realm of the polity was at work in the organisation of other social memories. For instance, it is not the remembered monarchic David of Samuel-Kings (or Chronicles) who was implicitly compared and shown within the dis-

---

[128] It is worth noting that even when the literati imagined the existing imperial world as peaceful, they could not construe it as stable. They had to imagine a deity that will not let it stand, because in this world neither Israel nor Jerusalem can be imperial, and therefore, such a world is doomed to fall (see Zech 1:8–17).
[129] And those of the king and Marduk and Assur, in the neo-Babylonian and neo Assyrian empires.
[130] Of course, in their own sight; this was a "game" that they played and could only play alone.

course of the community as superior to Cyrus, but Moses – see the stories of their birth,[131] and his role as servant of Yhwh. Moreover, not only did Moses' salient role as the Prophet provide a counterpart to Persian/Zoroastrian memory,[132] but so do explicit references to Yhwh as the creator of both light and darkness, good and evil (see Isa 45:7)

VIII Multiple views, portrayals, fuzziness and social memory

The above observations time and again indicate a very common preferred trait of the *general* discourse of late Persian Yehud which was well reflected in its past-constructing and other authoritative texts. From a system's perspective, it is clear that there was a strong preference for the presence of multiple voices and for a collective memory that included vast arrays of seemingly contradictory memories (and thus and by implication, a de-emphasising of the mimetic aspect of both memory and historiography).[133] An Israel that imagined itself through the reading of the authoritative literature of the late Persian period was an Israel that imagined itself as constantly balancing and thus integrating different viewpoints, memories, statements and even law texts. This is an Israel in which texts kept informing other texts and in which, within limits to be sure, multiple perspectives were allowed.

This understanding of Israel is consistent with a group of literati who pondered and "played" with texts, and had time to do so. The presence of such a group was necessary for the self-image of Israel as a text-centred community to emerge and become as dominant as other identity formations (e.g. those based on ancestry).

In a seemingly counterintuitive way, this relative openness was consistent with and perhaps required the existence of a small group of literati in a poor, resource-deprived Yehud. For one, in such group social cohesion would most likely trump "logical" coherence. The practical impossibility of developing (permanent) *sects* within the very few literati in Yehud meant that the social process of raising boundaries and the development and solidifying of divisive issues that characterised the emergence of sects, could not have taken place (contrast with the situation in the late Second Temple period).

---

131 Cf. H. Zlotnick-Sivan, "Moses the Persian?", 189–205.
132 Cf. E. S. Gerstenberger, "Persian Empire", 110–130.
133 Note not only tensions within the same book (and at times chapter), but also among different books that were all part of the authoritative corpus and which reflected and generated memories. Cf. Samuel–Kings and Chronicles.

Moreover, given the small size of the literati group, and their role in central institutions (most likely, the Jerusalemite temple) in educating, socialising and sustaining the group, it is reasonable to assume that the centre could exert social control among the literati, most likely through an ingrained and socially reinforced sense of self-control. A big and much wealthier city such as late second temple Jerusalem, with its greater number of literati and multiple resources to train and socialise them, cannot exert such a degree of control and, as a result, permanent sects may emerge and develop their own boundaries, identities and memories.[134]

The comparison with the late Second Temple period raises another difference between the two concerning a central enabling factor for the development of social sects, namely the "eschatological temperature" of the period.[135] The considerations advanced above suggest that the eschatological temperature of the late Persian period that is the focus of this chapter was very cold indeed.[136]

In addition, it is worth noting that the tendency to balance tension and develop an approach of "both-and" rather than "either-or" may also have been consistent with elements of the "Persian" imperial worldview and early Zoroastrianism; see, for instance, the concrete example of burials as implied by sepulchral tombs such as those of the Achaemenid kings and the seeming requirement for exposure of the dead body, and the general background of (within limits) "tolerance" of "deviation."[137]

These last considerations draw attention to a substantial feature of the general social mindscape of the literati of late Persian Yehud and, most likely, to some extent other groups in the same community (e.g. those who supported the literati and identified even partially with their worldview). This feature may been shared in other regions of the empire as well,[138] namely a tendency towards some level of flexible or fuzzy thinking as opposed to rigid single-mind-

---

134 Cf. A. Baumgarten, *The Flourishing of Jewish Sects*.
135 Cf. A. Baumgarten, "But Touch the Law", 301–315.
136 It is worth stressing that stating that the "eschatological temperature" in a society or period was low does not mean that there were no eschatological expectations or hopes for a distant (even if certain) future. It means that there was no sense of an imminent or close enough eschaton to influence the way in which people organised their thinking, or related to each other or to shape their discourse. Cf. A. Baumgarten, "But Touch the Law." These considerations have practical implications for the work of historians of ancient Israel. A discussion of, for instance, the eschatological temperature of a work such as Chronicles seems more heuristically helpful than one about whether the concept was present or not.
137 See O. Basirov, "The Achemenian Practice", 75–83.
138 A most obvious case would be the Jewish community in Elephantine, but see the example from the centre rather than the periphery of the Empire mentioned above.

edness, that is, a preference for a way of organising knowledge, memory and "the world" into somewhat flexible or fuzzy categories that may allow for overlapping structures, tensions and the like.[139] This preference is conducive to a more fluid construction of identity and to placing seemingly rigid categories in proportion when needed (cf. 2 Chr 30:18–20), though even such "placing in proportion" is at times set "in proportion" itself.[140]

It is worth noting that a preference for some degree of flexibility or fuzzy mindedness is more likely to develop within a group that does not see a strong need to adopt tough defensive positions, or insular attitudes. This is far less likely to be the general preference of a group that sees itself under attack. These considerations apply to the literati as a subgroup in Yehud, but very likely, to some extent to Yehud as a whole.[141] It is reasonable to assume that the community as such implicitly saw itself shielded from any potentially dangerous attack by and through the shared universe of thought and memories that it developed; and, to be sure, because in the Persian imperial context (and in the context of Yehud's marginality) they did not perceive any substantial threat to the long-term physical survival of the community.

These considerations, and those advanced in previous sections, shed much light on the processes of shared imagination that played a substantial role in the formation of identity and the related development of social memory in the late Persian Yehud. They open paths for future research on the ways in which the literati of the period constructed and organised the past in general as well as for studies on particular memories.[142] All of this will contribute not only to a better understanding of the general discourse of the period, but of the multiple threads that were interwoven – in ever-shifting ways, as they informed each other time and again, and at times in very contingent patterns – in the production of a fuzzy/flexible and multi-layered self-understanding of Israel in the late Persian period.

---

139 Cf. E. Zerubavel, *Social Mindscapes*, 58–63. It is worth stressing that the outcomes of these tendencies to organise the world are strongly contingent on historical circumstances. After all, these are *social* tendencies. This being so, the examples that Zerubavel provides are a far cry from what the literati in Yehud would have thought. Yet the issue is not an outcome, but a general cognitive *tendency* to organise (and shape) knowledge whose strength or lack thereof is related to the historical circumstances in which a group finds itself. (Note also that I am referring to a tendency, not to an exclusive or exclusivist mental attitude.)
140 See E. Ben Zvi, "Purity Matters".
141 Again, cf. the Jewish community in Elephantine.
142 Cf. "The Memory of Abraham" in this volume, pp. 162–98.

Remembering the Prophets through the Reading and Rereading of a Collection of Prophetic Books in Yehud: Methodological Considerations and Explorations*

This essay consists of two sections. The first discusses how and why to explore the matter of remembering the prophets through the prophetic books. It deals with general issues concerning the use of approaches informed by Memory Studies for a better understanding of the memoryscape and social mindscape of the literati in Yehud (and those who followed them), and the implications associated with the use of these approaches. The second section explores some results that emerge from using these approaches to better understand how and why fifteen prophetic characters (Isaiah, Jeremiah, Ezekiel and twelve others) were remembered, and remembered in particular ways. This second section is not and cannot be comprehensive, but rather illustrative.[1] Moreover, its focus is not on the par-

---

* First published in *Remembering and Forgetting in Early Second Temple Judah* (eds. E. Ben Zvi and C. Levin; Tübingen: Mohr Siebeck, 2012), 17–44.
1 This essay is part of a larger project I am undertaking on matters of Social Memory and Ancient Israel. I have written about remembering particular characters (Abraham, Moses, Isaiah) in *Remembering Biblical Figures in the Late Persian and Early Hellenistic Periods: Social Memory and Imagination* (eds. D. V. Edelman and E. Ben Zvi; Oxford: Oxford University Press, 2013) and in separate chapters/articles that have appeared elsewhere (Hosea, the Manasseh of Chronicles – see "Remembering Hosea: The Prophet as a Site of Memory in Persian Period Yehud," and "Reading Chronicles and Reshaping the Memory of Manasseh," in this volume, pp. 274–93, 367–86, as well as, *inter alia*, on issues of social memory and identity formation, memories of exile in Chronicles, memories of prophetic figures in Chronicles, issues of social mindshare of purity in Chronicles, and questions of social memory and historiography in ancient Israel; see, for instance, "On Social Memory and Identity Formation in Late Persian Yehud: A Historian's Viewpoint with a Focus on Prophetic Literature, Chronicles and the Dtr. Historical Collection," in this volume, pp. 28–79; "The Memory of Abraham in Late Persian/Early Hellenistic Yehud/Judah" in this volume, pp. 162–98; "Purity Matters in the Book of Chronicles: A Kind of Prolegomenon," in *Purity, Holiness, and Identity in Judaism and Christianity* (ed. C. S. Ehrlich, A. Runesson, and E. Schuller; WUNT I 305; Tübingen: Mohr Siebeck, 2013), 37–52; "Chronicles and its Reshaping of Memories of Monarchic Period Prophets: Some Observations," "Toward a Sense of Balance: Remembering the Catastrophe of Monarchic Judah/(Ideological) Israel and Exile through Reading Chronicles in Late Yehud" and "Reading Chronicles and Reshaping the Memory of Manasseh," 407–27, 387–406, 367–86 respectively in this volume; "Late Historical Books and Rewritten History" in *The Cambridge Companion to the Hebrew Bible/Old Testament* (eds. S. B. Chapman and M. A. Sweeney; Cambridge: Cambridge University Press, 2016), 292–313; "The Study of Forgetting and the Forgotten in Ancient Israelite Discourse/s: Observations

ticular memories associated with this or that prophet – which would each demand a separate study – but on the general, systemic features of this particular group of remembered characters of the past and what explorations of their memories at that time might contribute to a better understanding of the mindscape of the literati of the period.

Section I: How to Explore These Matters, and Why?

1 Introduction

The prophetic books[2] were didactic, meant to socialize their intended readers into a general, shared mindscape. One of the main ways in which they did so was to shape and evoke social memory. This shared social memory contributed much to the process of constant formation of communal identity. At the same time the particular shared social memory instilled in the remembering group ways of thinking, organizing knowledge, construing questions and ways to address them – in other words, an ideological, comprehensive viewpoint that we may call social mindscape.[3]

It is worth noting that the majority of books within the authoritative repertoire of the literati in Yehud were, among many other things, past-construing works. These include the prophetic books, the dtr. historical collection, the primary historical collection, Chronicles, and some Psalms (e.g., Ps 78, 105, 106). The strong social preference towards past construing texts also manifests itself in notes that turned, at least in part, non-past construing into past-construing texts, either in the Persian or Hellenistic period (e.g., Prov 1:1; 25:1; Ps 51:1; Qoh 1:1; Song 1:1).

---

and Test Cases," in *Cultural Memory in Biblical Exegesis* (ed. P. Carstens, T. Hasselbach and N.-P. Lemche; Gorgias Press, 2012), 139–157; "Prophetic Memories in the Deuteronomistic Historical and the Prophetic Collections of Books," in this volume, pp. 109–33; "How 'Historical' is Ancient Israel?" in *The Wiley-Blackwell Companion to the History of Jews and Judaism* (ed. A. T. Levenson; Malden, Mass.: Wiley-Blackwell, 2012), 25–34. This project is supported by a grant from the Social Sciences and Humanities Research Council of Canada.
2 By "prophetic books" I refer here to works that belong to a particular literary genre that existed in the repertoire of the Yehudite literati. These books are those that eventually and much later were referred to as "the Latter Prophets."
3 On the concept of social mindscapes, see, for instance, E. Zerubavel, *Social Mindscapes: An Invitation to Cognitive Sociology* (Cambridge: Harvard University Press, 1997). See also, idem, *Time Maps: Collective Memory and the Social Shape of the Past* (Chicago: University of Chicago Press, 2003).

The observation that most of the books that eventually ended up in the Hebrew Bible are, among other things, about memories of a past, and about memories of images of a future that, though it is still to come, can be engaged and visited through the power of imagination and which, most significantly, are learned within the community as memories of words uttered in the past is particularly significant in and by itself. This observation may seem, to a large extent, a reformulation of characterizations of the HB as a kind of "history book," that which by themselves have a very long history.[4] The reformulation here, however, carries important heuristic and hermeneutical implications. For the present purposes, it suffices to state that it directly and explicitly raises the issue of social memory, and thus, the question of whether contemporary studies on social memory and some of the concepts used in this kind of research may be heuristically helpful for historical studies that focus on the construed/imagined past that was brought to the present of the literati (and those who were influenced by them) in Yehud through their reading and rereading of their authoritative literature. Certainly, it is this socially shared past that constantly shaped the way in which they understood the world, their deity and they themselves, i.e., "Israel" as they conceived it.

2 The Heuristic Potential and Implications of Approaches Informed by Memory Studies

To ask whether approaches informed by Memory Studies may be heuristically helpful to understand the past that communities of readers (and mainly rereaders) constantly construed for themselves in Yehud as they read and reread the books in their authoritative repertoire in general and the prophetic books in particular, is to ask whether approaches informed by Memory Studies can help us to reconstruct approximations not only to their social memory but also to their social mindscape. Social memories are constantly shaped within a certain social mindscape, exemplify aspects of it time and again, and illuminate its fabric; for instance, the memories point at assumptions so ingrained that they are never questioned or tested (i.e., "transparent" and unnoticed assumptions), including those at work in the organization of knowledge within the community and matters such as the differentiation between what is worthy of being remem-

---

4 Cf. G. von Rad, *Old Testament Theology*, vol. 2 (tr. D. M. G. Stalker; Edinburgh: Oliver and Boyd, 1962), 356; and there is, of course, the pre-critical characterization of "the *Torah*" as a ספר דוכרניא "book of records/memories." See Tg Neofiti, Tg Pseudo Jonathan, and Frag. Tg to Exod 12:42.

bered and what is not, what is reasonable and what is unreasonable. This being so, to ask whether approaches informed by Memory Studies can be helpful to reconstruct memories of prophets, kings, events or places is basically to ask a very fundamental methodological question for studies of how at least some ancient Israelites, namely the literati of Yehud, thought.

In practical terms, asking whether these approaches can be heuristically helpful involves two related questions: (a) are these memory-studies informed approaches able to help us to formulate questions, heuristic frameworks, and explanatory hypotheses that may not have been raised otherwise, and thus substantially contribute to our historical knowledge of the period and of the books as they were read and understood at that time – in other words, do these approaches provide far more than a new "lingo" that just rephrases what has been already known?[5] and (b) do approaches common to Memory Studies today require some "fine-tuning" to become heuristically helpful for the study of ancient Israel in general and prophetic literature in particular?

At present, studies on ancient Israelite books have not been influenced much by work in the field of Memory Studies. This is hardly surprising, since most studies in social or cultural memory have focused on modern societies or communities. But social memories are obviously not a uniquely contemporary phenomenon. Even the most cursory look at ancient Near Eastern texts demonstrates that ancient societies and their ruling elites and associated groups constructed images of the community's past, remembered heroes, fools and villains, crucial events, symbolic objects, and sacred spaces. Moreover, the social act of collectively remembering memories about a shared past served important roles in polities and communities in terms of identity shaping, which is always a dynamic and continuous process of self-legitimization and social cohesion.

In fact, there could not have been any sense of social continuity through time (whether short or long) without some form of shared memory, and there could not be any way of social, communal reproduction or even polity maintenance without some form of shared memory. All historical communities – even at the basic level of family and kin – are to a large extent imagined communities based on a shared memory.

---

5 As in other guilds in the humanities and social sciences, the development of subgroups within the guild of ancient Israelite historians or academic biblical researchers is a normal process. It is anticipated that in many of these cases, each group will display its own lingo and tend to refer to a set of foundational (methodological) heroes and a set of texts in order to provide "authority" to methodological approaches. Moreover, each subgroup will often create connections to subgroups in other guilds. The study of these processes is within the realm of sociology of knowledge/academic research and as such stands outside the scope of this essay.

All this said, a simple transfer of concepts that work well for the study of contemporary societies or generalizing claims about "social memory" that pay no serious attention to particular historical circumstances is extremely problematic. Certainly, there is a very substantial difference between the number and the kinds of sources available for the study of present-day memories and those of ancient Yehud. To illustrate, let's think about the sources available for the study of the social memory of Reagan's or JFK's days among the myriad of diverse groups that exist within the USA, never mind outside it. While the same holds true for sources about Canadian social memories of Pierre Trudeau's days, there is certainly nothing comparable for ancient Yehud.

Another issue: studies on contemporary memories focus on the construed past, for obvious reasons. Yet, in ancient Israel, and particularly, but not exclusively, in relation to the prophetic books, the communally shared memories of places and events developed through reading these books involved events, spaces and characters set in both the past and future of the reading community. In fact, one of the important functions of these books was to provide mental memories and vicarious experiences (or taste of experiences) of utopian futures – even if set in the past – often alongside dystopian pasts. While social memory in contemporary societies is all about the past, in ancient Yehud it encompassed vicarious experiences of the future as well as the past. One may say that ancient Israel remembered its future in Yehud.

There are also significant differences among ancient societies that impacted their shaping of social memories, even if the relevant communities existed more or less at the same time. I have already pointed to one of them. Not all ancient societies placed so much emphasis on memories of the future, and particularly the distant future, as Yehud did. There are many other differences. For instance, constructions of the past were not legitimized in the same way in the Greek and ancient Israelite historiography – a point that Erhard Blum recently stressed.[6] Moreover, the creation and re-enactment of the central collective memory (and of counter memories or partial reconfigurations of that collective memory by some subgroups) involved matters of power within a society and actual or perceived power relations of that society with other societies. It involved social structures – issues of self-definition most often in the form of claimed continuity and the setting of boundaries separating in and out-group, those who share and don't share a particular collective memory. This being so, issues of structure, re-

---

6 E. Blum, "Historiography or Poetry? The Peculiarities of the Hebrew Prose Tradition," in *Memory in the Bible and Antiquity: The Fifth Durham-Tübingen Research Symposium (Durham, September 2004)* (eds. L. T. Stuckenbruck, S. C. Barton, and B. G. Wold; WUNT 212; Tübingen: Mohr Siebeck, 2007), 25–45.

sources, and the size of a society, as well as matters of center and periphery, hybridity, resistance, and hegemony are all involved in the production and reproduction of social memories.

All these considerations require us to take seriously the particular historical circumstances of each community of shared remembrance and be very cautions of over-generalizations. Thus, while it is true that studying the ancient social memory of the literati and those influenced by them in Persian Yehud draws attention away from questions about the "historicity" – in our terms – of what is reported or evoked in their books (e.g., questions such as: "Did Isaiah say such and such?" "Did Hezekiah defeat King Sennacherib?" "Who precisely was Shalman [Hos 10:14]?"), it is also true that social memory approaches demand that we pay much more attention to the historical circumstances of the remembering community. In fact, it is the focus on the remembering community and what it imagined that calls us to pay less attention to whether the narrated events historically happened or not. What counts within this approach is what the historical community "remembered."

On the surface, the most cautious approach of the study of memory in ancient Israel seems to be to focus on *explicit* notes about remembering at the level of the world portrayed in biblical texts. To be sure, there is a very substantial number of texts in which explicit calls to remember are advanced. In many of them, it is Israel or some subgroup within it which is called to remember (e.g., Exod 13:3; 20:8; Deut 7:18; 9:7; 24:9; 25:17; Josh 1:13; Isa 44:21; 46:8, 9; Mic 6:5; Mal 3:22; Qoh 12:1; Neh 4:14; 1 Chr 16:12, 15); in many others, it is the deity who is asked to remember (e.g., Exod 32:13; Deut 9:27; 2 Kgs 20:3; Neh 5:19; Ps 74:2; 137:7, Lam 5:1; 2 Chr 6:42; 13:22). There are texts that include references to a particular day to be remembered yearly from generation to generation (e.g., Exod 12:14), to "monuments" that were supposed to serve as material sites of memory within the world of the text (e.g., Gen 31:52; 35:20; Josh 4:20–24; 5:3; 22:26–28; 2 Sam 18:18; Zech 6:14), and explicit references to ways of maintaining memory (e.g., Exod 13:8–10). There are many texts in the prophetic books that explicitly evoke and shape memories of a past (e.g., Hos 2:17; 9:10; 11:1; Zech 1:4–5).

To be sure, the fact that books containing all these references to memory emerged and were read and reread within Persian Yehud is proof positive that memory was central to the discourse and life of that society (cf. Ps 78). But numerous as these texts are, and *as important as they are*, they shed only a very narrow ray of light on the social memory of the community and, as it will be argued below, they do not provide the most promising path for historical reconstructions of social memory or the social mindscape that it reflects.

As mentioned above, the intended readership of most of the books that eventually ended up in the HB deeply involved themselves in a project of imagining and remembering a past, in fact, multiple related pasts, all of which together constituted the general, comprehensive social memory of the community. The main contribution of approaches informed by Memory Studies to research in ancient Israel and its prophetic books is *not* circumscribed or even, in the main, directly related to their heuristic role for understanding some particular references to remembering that are explicitly reported in the world portrayed in the books that were read by the community. It is the books themselves, not a few scenes here or there, that serve as the main source for reconstructing social memory in Yehud.

Moreover, it is not necessarily a question of exploring explicit constructions of the past, i.e., what the text says about this or that event in the past, but of why the text construes the past in the way it does, or what makes some characters or periods more memorable than others. One may begin by asking seemingly simple questions: which social roles were fulfilled by collective/social acts of imagination of the past that resulted from reading a shared set of texts, within a particular historical context? Why did the community develop some images of the past (or future) and not others? Why did certain memories appear again and again, while others did not? What made some memories preferred and some dis-preferred and did that ever change, and if so, why? These questions already point at the emphasis on the social and systemic engendered by that approaches informed by Memory Studies.

In addition, books, prophetic or not, may embody memory, but they do not remember. Social memory does not equal a book, a section thereof, or a collection of books. As members of the Jerusalemite community in Yehud read and re-read, or had others read to them, the books that the community agreed that carried authority, that is, their authoritative books, they imagined, configured and reconfigured sites in their minds. They brought to life characters, events, material objects, and buildings and the like, whether set in the past or the future. As these readers went through their repertoire of authoritative books and other relevant sources they may have had, they shaped a shared, central social memory through multiple particular memories.

Even individual characters of the past came to embody and integrate multiple memories, which at times were seemingly at tension with one another. For instance, the remembering community imagined Isaiah and his political counterparts (e.g., Ahaz, Hezekiah), Manasseh, David, and Moses in ways informed by multiple books. To be sure, even when a prophetic character, e.g., Hosea, is imagined on the basis of one single book, there are still multiple viewpoints.[7]

These observations indicate that approaches to prophetic literature substantially informed by Memory Studies will shift the emphasis away from the work of proposed individual authors and redactors that is so predominant in historical studies of the prophetic books, and towards the *read text*, and thus, towards readers, society, general discourse and what we may call systemic, social, and ideological preferences and dis-preferences, for, as it is well known, readings are strongly influenced by the world of knowledge, ideology and general discourse of the readers – that is, all the things that made readers competent to read particular books in a given society and thus able to partake in the project of imagining it into being – which is another way of saying, of participating in the project of ideologically construing their present community by construing/imagining its pasts and futures through the reading of socially approved books.[8]

These considerations have substantial implications. In fact, they call for a serious study of the *Sitz im Diskurs* of each of the authoritative books of ancient Israel. In other words, these considerations indicate that to understand how books were *read*, and therefore, how they contributed to the configuration and communication of social memory, we have to understand them in terms of their place and function within the general discourse of the period.[9]

To illustrate this matter in practical terms, this means that if we work within this social memory framework for historical research, when we find a reference to, for instance, Exile or the Exodus in a particular prophetic book, we must con-

---

[7] See "Remembering Hosea: The Prophet Hosea as a Site of Memory in Persian Period Yehud."
[8] I address directly matters of literary competence in Yehud elsewhere; see my "Would Ancient Readers of the Books of Hosea or Micah be 'Competent' to Read the Book of Jeremiah?" in *Jeremiah (Dis)Placed. New Directions in Writing/Reading Jeremiah* (eds. A. R. P. Diamond and L. Stulman; LHBOTS 529; London: T&T Clark, 2010), 80–98. It goes without saying that reading and remembering the past and the future was an activity carried out by socially located people, within a particular historical group (Yehud's literati) and as members of that group. The construction and maintenance of central social memory required social support, resources, and ability to channel these resources. Above all, social memory was a social construction and the outcome of social processes, not the work of solitary, segregated authors/geniuses. It involved social institutions and served to legitimize them. Of course, as in any society there might be counter memories, or social memories of segments in a general society, but these also emerge out social processes and institutions, even if the latter are "peripheral."
[9] By "discourse" here I mean the vast realm that includes the ways of thinking, webs of images, texts, "common" knowledge and linguistic registers that shaped (a) which issues or set of issues were likely to come up in a community, and (b) the ways in which the community went about thinking about these issues when they arose and the range of possible responses and interactions within these responses.

tinue analyzing the reference within the inner context of the book (*Sitz im Buch*) and search for allusions and references to other texts that existed in the same repertoire. But we should also analyze the reference to Exile and Exodus within the context of the meanings that these two sites of memory or ciphers came to embody in the discourse of the community, along with the multiple functions that these two concepts played, and reasons for the kind of obsession with these two memories in the repertoire of Yehud. Moreover, these memories were not isolated. They were interwoven with a number of connective ciphers/sites of memory (e. g., the wilderness; Israel's sin; land; Egypt, Babylon, *torah*) and only along with them shaped comprehensive memory.

Central, comprehensive social memory was not what happened when someone in ancient Yehud read a particular book (see above), but rather an integrative system that included memories evoked and relived through multiple readings of multiple books. Within this multivocal system (though not without boundaries) every reading informed every other reading in some way or another. Literati had to be competent to read these highly sophisticated books, but this competence means that they were supposed to bring their previous social and socially agreed knowledge to bear on their readings, and in a text centered community, this implies many other authoritative texts. Thus this research framework leads us to the conclusion that we cannot study the meaning of a prophetic book in a particular society, including Persian Yehud, by focusing on the book only as a stand-alone historical entity. Instead we must look at it in terms of the general discourse (which includes more than a simple repertoire of books) of the period. In other words, we must pay attention to the book's *Sitz im Diskurs*.

Let me illustrate with a further example: the prophetic books shaped images of the late monarchic past. However, Persian period literati reading them imagined this period not only by reading the prophetic books, but also by reading Kings and, in the late Persian period (perhaps early-Hellenistic), by reading Chronicles as well. Looking at the *Sitz im Diskurs* of the prophetic books and at the memories that they evoked draws attention to questions such as: how did the same community of readers deal with the multiple and, at times, substantially different, partial memories? How did these readers "integrate" all these memories into a more or less central, comprehensive social memory, and at what price to what we today may call "historicity" or "external referentiality"? Above all, which systemic advantages offered the complex system of seemingly partially contradictory images of the past over its potentially more simple counterparts in such a small group as that of the literati in Yehud? Moreover, why is there such a density of references to memories of the monarchic period compared to other periods? Memory obsession is an important piece of information for historical reconstructions of historical discourses.

It goes without saying that an approach that focuses on social memory and takes matters of *Sitz im Diskurs* into account necessarily draws attention to the multiple images of what a prophet in the monarchic period was or was supposed to be or do that are evoked by the prophetic and historiographical books. It will raise not only the question of how these images informed each other, but also the related, but independent question of what a prophetic book was meant to be and how that may relate to the multiple images of prophets of the past.

One of the most heuristically helpful concepts for historians dealing with prophetic literature (and the historiographical books) that seems to emerge from Memory Studies frameworks and for studies of their *Sitz im Diskurs* is a version of the concept of "site of memory."[10] As a working definition most appropriate for the present goals, "site of memory" refers here to any constructed space, place, event, figure, text or the like – whether it exists "materially" or only in the minds of members of a social group – whose presence in the relevant socio-cultural milieu evokes or was meant to evoke core images or aspects of images of the past held by the social group living in that socio-cultural milieu. Most of these sites act as ciphers to be activated within a particular social discourse, and as places to be (mentally) visited and revisited as part of a self-supportive mechanism of socialization and social reproduction.

The process of reading prophetic literature necessarily involved the creation of multiple mental spaces/sites of memory that were associated with particular times, characters, and events. In a way akin to modern and contemporary common physical memorials, these mental spaces served to celebrate, mourn and, above all, construct events and spaces and imbue them with meaning. For instance, the temple that the intended readers imagined when they read Ezek 40–43 (or the larger unit, Ezek 40–48) served as such a site of memory,[11]

---

10 The term "site of memory" goes back to the work of Pierre Nora, who wrote: "If the expression lieu de mémoire must have an official definition, it should be this: a lieu de mémoire is any significant entity, whether material or non-material in nature, which by dint of human will or the work of time has become a symbolic element of the memorial heritage of any community." See his "General Introduction: Between Memory and History," in *Realms of Memory Volume 1: Conflicts and Divisions* (ed. P. Nora; New York: Columbia University Press, 1996), 1–20 (xvii). Nora, however, advanced a relatively restrictive understanding of the term; op. cit., 14–19. Nora's essay appears also, with a slightly different English translation as P. Nora, "Between Memory and History: Les Lieux de Mémoire," *Representations* 26 (1989): 7–24.

11 On this issue see H. Liss, "'Describe the Temple to the House of Israel': Preliminary Remarks on the Temple Vision in the Book of Ezekiel and the Question of Fictionality in Priestly Literatures," in *Utopia and Dystopia in Prophetic Literature* (ed. E. Ben Zvi; PFES 92; Helsinki: Finnish Exegetical Society, 2006), 122–143. Her concluding paragraph is worth citing in full: The literary account in Ezek 40–43 (or the larger unit, Ezek 40–48) is thus far more than a written testimo-

but so did many other references to the temple in other prophetic books and, needless to say, Kings and Chronicles, and some Psalms. The imagined monarchic temple was one and many at the same time. It was associated with both celebration and abomination. It was both destroyed and eternal, as it could exist forever in the minds of the readers.[12] Of course, the imagined, monarchic temple of social memory always stood in close association to other imagined Jerusalemite temples, including temples of the future (Ezek 40–48, Hag 2:6–9) and those associated with the beginning of the Second Temple (e.g., Hag 2:2–3), and, of course, was imagined in close association with the tabernacle. All these temples interacted with the actual temple of the community. The site of memory (or array of sites of memory) embodied and signified by "temple" contributed much toward organizing, structuring and shaping meaningful memory. It is one of the sites that bound multiple texts and images together and, by attracting attention to itself in the process, it conveyed a strong sense of identification with the past and future of the community; "temple" helped to tell the community its own narrative about itself and thus contributed much to its self-identity. In addition, this particular site of memory facilitated the integration of multiple viewpoints, hopes, worries, didactic messages and the like by anchoring them into a particular space, even as it leaves the imagination to flow unanchored through all remembered/imagined times. In other words, temporally-related temples, all of which serve as sites of memory, become illustrations of a comprehensive cross-temporal site of memory, namely the "cross-temporal" and to some extent "trans-temporal" temple.

Before I move to another type of site of memory, I would like to underscore that there are plenty of references to the Temple in prophetic literature. This is again a reflection of an important aspect of the social memory of the period and of its discourse. Not all sites of memory show the same level of mindshare, that is, not all sites are allocated the same "mental space" in the community. Much more "mental space" was allocated to the Temple than to any other

---

ny of prophetic visionary experience. It replaces reality, taking place in the realm of history, by a reality in the "realm of the text." Moreover, the three-dimensional "U-Topia" of a temple that does not have a spatial existence becomes a "literary utopia", having the *kābôd* dwell in Israel's literature forever, the literary fiction being a realization of the temple and the presence of the *kābôd* among Israel. It is the only way to keep the divine promise ושכנתי בתוכם לעולם ["I will dwell among them forever," Ezek 43:9] upright, and, at the same time, create a new "place" for Israel to turn to (143).

12 The latter could visit it as they recreated in their mind the descriptions in 1 Kgs 6–7 and 2 Chr 3–4, which in a sense served a role similar to m. *Middot* after the destruction of the second temple—or as they vicariously relived the many events that occurred in that temple according to the prophetic and historiographic books.

space related concepts, with the possible exception of "the land." This reflects the centrality of the Jerusalemite Temple in the social memory of Israel during the Persian period, and indirectly in the self-identity of Israel as construed by Jerusalemite-centered literati. Mindshare is expressed in terms of the relative amount of references to particular sites of memory, but mindshare is a central reason for the development of more and more stories about particular sites, including prophetic characters, each with their own mindshare.

Section II: Remembering Prophets in Persian Yehud

1 Some Observations on Sites of Memory and Social Mindshare

The literati in Yehud, as members of a reading community, read the prophetic books, and as they read, they construed and imaginatively encountered and interacted not with the books themselves, but with characters such as Isaiah, Jeremiah, Hosea, Micah and the like. Each prophetic book was associated with a single prophet and each carried a particular voice, because the books were supposed to make the prophets of old present in the community.

The prophetic books thus became memorials for the prophets, who in turn, as sites of social memory, accrued and broadcasted meaning. Sirach, illustrates the case as he remembers and glorifies prophets, not the prophetic books (see Sir 48:23–25 [Isaiah]; 40:6–7 [Jeremiah]; 49:8 [Ezekiel]; 49:10 [the twelve prophets]). In other words, the prophetic books served to bring the prophets to the community, not the other way around.

As I discussed elsewhere, this role of the prophetic books explains not only why each of them is associated with a *single* prophetic character and carries an *individual* voice marked by a particular idiolect[13] that served to characterize him as an individual personage, but why the twelve prophetic books remained independent, each with their own opening and closing notes, even if they were written on one single scroll. No single prophet could have been imagined or construed to embody "the Twelve." Had the scroll been read as one book, it would have failed to make present any particular prophet from the past within

---

[13] Of course, all these idiolects are part of the general sociolect of the community, or in Yehud and far more precisely to the main sociolect that the community of readers of authoritative books, that is, the remembering community attributed to the past societies within which these prophets were imagined to speak.

the reading community. But when the scroll was read as constituting twelve prophetic books, it raised twelve prophets and their voices within the community.¹⁴

Of course, all fifteen prophets were remembered, but the relative weight that the different prophets held in the imagination and, accordingly, in discourse of Yehud, was not uniform. It stands to reason that there was a connection between mindshare and the size of the book associated with the prophet; if people made Isaiah present in their midst far more than Obadiah, for instance, it is more likely that the book associated with the former will develop much more than the book associated with the latter and conversely, the more they read about a prophet, the larger his mindshare. In general terms, we are dealing with well-known processes of positive feedback: the more a person is recognized within a group as memorable, the more s/he will tend to attract new memories and conceptual associations, which in turn make the person even more memorable.¹⁵ In sum, it is reasonable to think in terms of a relation between the social mindshare of a prophet and the textual space allocated in the repertoire of the community to that prophet. (Of course, the same applies to kings and other types of figures.)

The collection of prophetic books shaped a set of three main prophetic characters and twelve others to remember. To be sure, these numbers indicate a process of remembering some and forgetting others. Even if one were to take into account only the selected periods and spaces to which these characters are associated (I will deal later on with matters of space and time), there were surely many more historical prophets, but social processes of remembering and forgetting led to the construction of a set of three and twelve.

Memory studies show the existence of tendencies towards oneness, that is, trends favoring the construction of a single *main* great hero/site of memory that

---

14 E. Ben Zvi and J. D. Nogalski (with an introduction by T. C. Römer), *Two Sides of a Coin: Juxtaposing Views on Interpreting the Book of the Twelve/the Twelve Prophetic Books* (Analecta Gorgiana 201; Piscataway, N.J.: Gorgias Press, 2009).

15 There are multiple examples of the application of the principle of positive feedback in Memory Studies. For instance, scientists who were awarded a Nobel Prize tend to be much more remembered and their achievements much more emphasized, celebrated and funded than the runners up and their work, even if in 'objective' terms their differences may be minimal and could have been easily evaluated by the Nobel committee (and were at the time evaluated by other members of the scientific community) the other way around. This effect is often called the "Matthew Effect" ("for to all those who have, more will be given, and they will have an abundance; but from those who have nothing, even what they have will be taken away," Matt 25:29) and has been proven to be at work in numerous fields. See D. Rigney, *The Matthew Effect: How Advantage Begets Further Advantage* (New York: Columbia University Press, 2010). This principle has often been used to study why some people and events became memorable and others of (clearly "historically") similar or even higher importance were not.

embodies central images, ideas, events, processes and the like. This is a common way to shape knowledge and symbolize knowledge (e.g., Bolivar, as "El Libertador" of the Americas – but not in Argentina, where San Martín takes that role; Lincoln as the "Great Emancipator;" and close to our field, Moses as the "Lawgiver" and "Foundational Prophet," and David as the "Foundational Yhwistic King").[16]

To be sure, one may claim that there was at least some tendency towards "oneness" at work in the present case, as there was only one major prophet associated with the deliverance of Jerusalem from Sennacherib (Isaiah) and one with its destruction at the hands of Nebuchadnezzar (Jeremiah) – that is, one for each of the two crucial events that shaped much of the memory of the late monarchic period (on this see below).[17] But one still has to account for Ezekiel. This may not be difficult since Ezekiel was a site of memory that embodied and communicated messages and images with which neither Isaiah nor Jeremiah could be associated (e.g., ideal temple and land, life within the diasporic community in Babylon, etc.), but this observation is already helpful since it draws attention to important aspects within the social mindscape of late Persian Yehud that constrained tendencies towards "oneness."

In addition, there were twelve other prophetic characters. To be sure, their mindshare was less than Isaiah, Jeremiah and Ezekiel, but they were still part and parcel of the social mindscape of the period. The plurality of prophetic characters (even if constrained and perhaps not by chance eventually including the notion of a group of *twelve* prophets) reflects and reinforces a tendency to set them apart from the great and exemplar prophet: Moses. There was *only one*

---

[16] For a study providing a discussion of the underlying reasons for this tendency towards "oneness" and a good case study, within the frame of contemporary Memory Studies, see B. Schwartz, "Collective Forgetting and the Symbolic Power of Oneness: The Strange Apotheosis of Rosa Parks," *Social Psychology Quarterly* 72 (2009), 123–142 and bibliography. At times, the tendency towards the construction of one main site of memory cannot lead to a single site, but still leads to a condensation of sites that to a large extent complement each other (e.g., Pearl Harbor and D-Day as main sites of memory for WWII in America; Sir John A. Macdonald [Conservative] and Sir Wilfrid Laurier [Liberal] as main founding figures of today's Canada). Turning the gaze to our area, Abraham and Jacob, David and Solomon, Hezekiah and Josiah, and most relevant to this essay, Isaiah and Jeremiah.

[17] I wrote elsewhere on remembering Isaiah in the late Persian period and the importance of the pairs deliverance/destruction, Sennacherib/Nebuchadnezzar (and their respective subordinate representatives, Rabshakeh and Nebuzaradan) and, of course, Isaiah/Jeremiah; Hezekiah/Zedekiah elsewhere. See "Isaiah, a Memorable Prophet: Why Was Isaiah So Memorable in the Late Persian/Early Hellenistic Periods?" in this volume, pp. 253–73.

Moses, but fifteen late prophets, even if some of them were Isaiah, Jeremiah and Ezekiel.[18]

It is particularly worth noting that the community could and did construe a memory-scape in which no prophetic figure with mindshare similar to that of Isaiah, Jeremiah or Ezekiel, and certainly none of the stature of Moses, occupies the time of the actual building of the "Second Temple," as the example of Haggai and Zechariah – who not coincidentally is construed only partially in terms of the actual establishment of the Yehudite temple in Jerusalem – clearly show. This mnemonic situation reflects and communicates a worldview and social memory in which the temple was in fact established through the divine instruction given to Moses[19] and thus is anchored in the foundational period of Israel.[20] Building the Jerusalem temple in Persian Yehud is important, but not on par with what transpired in Moses' period. Moreover, Isaiah and especially Ezekiel take much more mindshare than Haggai on Temple matters. The future, utopian temple that existed in their minds and their memories of the future/s takes a far more central role within the social mindscape of this literati than the one they could actually visit, despite the fact that this temple was the social institution that made their work *and works* possible.[21] This very same aspect of the social mindscape of the literati is responsible for the tendency to focus on either the past or the future but not their present, and for their consistent self-effacement within their literary output/repertoire.

Another important observation: even the twelve prophetic personages who did not draw as much mindshare as Isaiah, Jeremiah and Ezekiel were construed in this community as complex sites of memory. As the case of Obadiah (the prophet associated with the briefest book in the collection) clearly shows, each prophet embodied multiple perspectives and evoked numerous core concepts, images and the revisiting/reimagination of memories of crucial past and future events among the remembering community. After all, remembering Obadiah was, *inter alia*, remembering the fall of Jerusalem and its future glory, advancing an image of a future Return that differs considerably from and balances

---

[18] On Moses the Prophet see "Exploring the Memory of Moses 'The Prophet' in Late Persian/Early Hellenistic Yehud/Judah," in this volume, pp. 199–231.

[19] Cf. with the portrayal in Chronicles of the temple as based on the instructions of Moses and David and the image of David as founding the temple in every important aspect, even if Solomon is the builder, a godly activity, but still secondary in importance.

[20] And vice versa that their temple is the true manifestation of Yhwh's only legitimate cultic centre. See below.

[21] See, among others, K. van der Toorn, *Scribal Culture and the Making of the Hebrew Bible* (Cambridge, Mass.: Harvard University Press, 2007).

the most common in the discourse of the period, re-imagining and positively re-signifying the period of the judges (cf. Ruth), and balancing out images of an utopian future in which Davides play an important role that appear in other texts within the repertoire of the community. Remembering Obadiah involved exploring the "brotherhood" between Israel and the nations represented by Edom/Esau and organizing memories about them. Encountering the imagined Obadiah meant dealing with constraints on human wisdom and power, and therefore on the ability to act. In addition, as the text was read and reread, it evoked echoes of Jeremiah while at the same time distanced Obadiah from him (and the book of Jeremiah) and let the remembering community wonder whether this Obadiah could have been the Obadiah they remembered as a prophet during the reign of Ahab. Encountering Obadiah through reading also reminded the reading/remembering community that construing images of the prophets of the past involved careful reading and awareness of multiple meanings, ambiguities, and networks of meanings; above all it required the presence of highly sophisticated readers – the literati responsible for these works and those who could conjure the figures from the past and bring them to the present along with the instance of YHWH's word that was associated with them and which provides hope for the future and meaning for the past.[22]

As much as the prophets were the main sites of memory that emerged out of the reading and rereading of the prophetic books among the literati, at some point, some of the utterances associated with them became sites of memory in and of themselves. The process probably started as phrases appearing in texts within the sea of texts to which the authors and redactors of books in Yehud had access were reused and completely resignified in another text, with or without much attention to their original association with particular speakers from the past. These texts carried a meaning directly related to their new literary context, but at the same time, at least from the perspective of the readers, evoked or echoed other texts that were within their repertoire. By the time of Chronicles, at least, some phrases clearly had become sites that evoked memory by themselves not only outside their original context but in sets that reportedly *preceded* the

---

[22] Cf. Jerome's often quoted words, *quanto brevius est, tanto difficilius* (Commentary on Obadiah, on v. 1). I addressed these issues in Obadiah in my *A Historical-Critical Study of The Book of Obadiah* (BZAW 242; Berlin: De Gruyter, 1996). For other works on Obadiah see, among others, B. Dicou, *Edom, Israel's Brother and Antagonist: The Role of Edom in Biblical Prophecy and Story* (JSOTSup 169; Sheffield: JSOT Press, 1994); J. Renkema, *Obadiah* (Historical Commentary on the Old Testament; Leuven: Peeters, 2003) and P. R. Raabe, *Obadiah* (AB 24D; New York: Doubleday, 1996); J. Barton, *Joel and Obadiah: A Commentary* (OTL; Louisville, Ky.: Westminster John Knox Press, 2001).

putative time of the prophetic character with whom they were associated in their original context.²³ Prophetic words came to have a life of their own, as it were, and might then apply to future and past events,²⁴ in ways that might be and at times were construed as unbeknownst to those speaking them. Thus, these prophetic expressions became multi-temporal and could then be imagined as being fulfilled and yet to be fulfilled numerous times. Later Qumran *pesher* exegesis, the exegetical approach underlying, for instance, the praise of Simon in 1 Macc 14:4–15, and concepts about a pre-existing *torah* are later and far more developed expressions of this tendency, but it existed already by the late Persian period, at least.²⁵

Of course, imagining a prophet is also imagining space, or better, spaces. Encountering the prophetic figures through the reading and rereading of the prophetic texts meant to encounter, that is, to imagine places. The concept of mindshare seems heuristically helpful in this context as well. It goes beyond the obvious, e. g., remembering the prophets is remembering that none of them was born or grew up outside the land, that the space of Exile is very important symbolically, but less mindshare is given to it as a space populated by Israelites who live their own lives there, as expected within a general mindscape in which life in Exile is far less worth remembering than life on the land, which, if at all, is remembered mainly in terms of a process leading to the end of the Exile (cf. the textual allocation to Israel in Egypt from the time of Joseph to the raising of the "new Pharaoh").²⁶

---

23 See, for instance, in Azariah's speech, during the time of King Asa: 2 Chr 15:3 (cf. Hos 3:4), 5 (cf. Zech 8:10 and Amos 3:9), 6 (cf. Zech 11:6), 7 (cf. Jer 31:16; Zeph 3:16); in king Jehoshaphat's prayer: 2 Chr 16:9 (cf. Zech 4:10); 20:20 (cf. Isa 7:9). See E. Ben Zvi, "Who Knew What? The Construction of the Monarchic Past in Chronicles and Implications for the Intellectual Setting of Chronicles," in *Judah and the Judeans in the Fourth Century BCE* (eds. O. Lipschits, G. N. Knoppers and R. Albertz; Winona Lake: Eisenbrauns, 2007), 349–360.

24 E. g., A. Warhurst notices, for instance, that some of "Isaiah's descriptions of a future restoration after exile are read back into the account of Hezekiah's reign" in Chronicles, but still these descriptions remain as prophecies for the future. See A. Warhurst, "The Chronicler's Use of the Prophets," in *What is Authoritative in Chronicles* (eds. E. Ben Zvi and D. V. Edelman; Winona Lake, Ind.: Eisenbrauns, 2011), 165–181.

25 It goes without saying that even within the repertoire of the prophetic books there were clear cases of reversals of meanings as well, informing each other, see, for instance, Joel 4:10 and cf. Isa 2:4 and Mic 4:3.

26 K. Stott, "A Comparative study of the Exilic Gap in Ancient Israelite, Messenian, and Zionist Collective Memory" in *Community Identity in Judean Historiography: Biblical and Comparative Perspectives* (eds. G. N. Knoppers and K. A. Ristau; Winona Lake, Ind.: Eisenbrauns, 2009), 41–58.

Finally, using the concept of mindshare we may ask what the primary readers of primary readers imagined themselves as watching when they virtually visited places that came to life as they read the prophetic books. To use again the example of the Temple: what did the same readers see in the House of YHWH that they imagined as they read the prophetic books and imagined the prophets speaking? Did they see mainly vessels, priests, animals, matters of purity and impurity, prophets making speeches, song, and praise? What about present, past and future temples?

An exploration of these matters within the framework of the entire set of memories associated with the fifteen prophets is clearly beyond the scope of this essay, but obviously there is a very substantial diversity (cf. Isaiah, Ezekiel and Haggai).[27] One may conceive of the comprehensive, central, collective memory of Yehud concerning these matters as a multivalent, shifting array of multiple sites of memory, each bringing attention to certain images and away from others, and each influencing social mindshare in different ways and up to its capabilities within the discourse of the community.[28] In any event, this research path carries much potential for a better understanding of the ways in which the literati in Yehud, who read and reread all this literature and imagined all these prophets, conceived and imagined "their" past, present and future, including central institutions/spaces such as the Temple.

2 Some Observations on Memorable Prophetic Narratives

Social memories tend to be organized as narratives, but prophetic books are not (with the exception of Jonah, which is, in fact, a meta-prophetic book). Remembering the prophets contributed much to the shaping of a mnemonic narrative

---

27 I began to explore these questions in the case of the memories of the past that Chronicles evoked in late Persian Yehud or early Hellenistic period in my "Purity Matters."

28 The capability of a text and the characters whose memory it evoked to influence mindshare was directly proportional to how much the text was read. Some texts were more influential than others. Of course, it is impossible to develop any kind of scale of "reception." How can a historian today know whether Amos was more or less read than Micah in Persian Yehud? This said, it is clear that some books and their respective characters were most likely very influential. For instance, given the number of allusions to the work, the lengthy editorial history, and suggestive data from the late(r) Hellenistic period, one may assume that Isaiah was a substantial character with much mindshare. A similar argument may be made for Jeremiah, and needless to say, for Moses. I discuss these matters elsewhere insofar as they relate to memories of Isaiah and Moses (see "Exploring the Memory of Moses 'The Prophet'" and "Isaiah, A Memorable Prophet," in this volume, pp. 199–231 and pp. 253–73 respectively.

(or a set of related narratives) about the past and future of the community. Since no site of memory was or could serve as a singular, stand-alone site, imagining a prophet was often imagining a period too. To think of Isaiah is to think of Hezekiah and his days and of Cyrus; to think of Jeremiah is to revisit the last days of monarchic Judah, and to bring to them to the present of the remembering community, which also imagines, remembers and vicariously experiences the same period differently when they remember and interact with Ezekiel. To think of Zephaniah is to evoke some images of Josiah's reign that cast a shadow on glorious memories of the period evoked by Kings and Chronicles; and to think of Haggai is to think of Zerubabbel and Joshua son of Jehozadak and of the Persian period Jerusalem temple.

I discussed elsewhere at some length the main contours of this narrative in terms of plot and starting and end points, and the existence of a kind of preface or pre-history to that main narrative. It suffices here to say that the main narrative moves from the Assyrian crisis and Jerusalem's deliverance, to the catastrophe of the fall of the monarchic polity in Judah, then to the beginning of the return and the building of the temple, and finally to the utopian future. The main characters are always Yhwh and Israel, with the nations other than Israel as secondary characters. Monarchic Israel is sinful and tends to reject prophets and certainly deserves divine punishment, but Yhwh will bring Israel to a utopian future and in fact, Yhwh announced it in the midst of sinful Israel during the monarchic period.

Obviously, the mindshare of particular prophets is directly associated with that of certain periods within the social mindscape of the community. This is not surprising, but also points at a more general feature of the remembered prophets. Prophets as successful sites of memory must be unique and carry their own voice, but they must also reflect and to, at least some extent, embody, integrate in one personage and communicate concepts, ways of thinking, core discursive issues, and images at the core of the general mindscape of the community, which as such tend to be encoded in additional sites of memory. In fact, had this not been the case, the prophetic figures would not have been of much significance for the community and would not have been remembered to begin with.

Thus it is not mere chance that the memory-scape created by the prophetic figures shows so much density around the fall of Jerusalem to the Babylonians and its counterpart, the "salvation" of Jerusalem during Hezekiah's time, and their preludes and aftermath, or that it deals constantly with the catastrophe of 586 BCE, directly and indirectly, and hammers down the motif of Exile, all from multiple perspectives. All these issues and tendencies are well attested elsewhere within the repertoire of the community and reflected what the

Jerusalem-centered literati of the period thought worth thinking and imagining, and their ways of structuring knowledge. It is not by chance either that imagining the fifteen prophetic books meant bringing strong messages of hope, and certitude of the deity's plans for Israel to the present, both in spite of and against the background of ubiquitous memories of Israel's sinful past and its well-deserved punishment. Similar messages are conveyed in pentateuchal texts and not surprisingly the Return from Exile was imagined in terms evocative of the Exodus from Egypt, as is very often noted. Perhaps it is as important to note some less obvious generative tendencies at work in the ways in which prophetic and other books shaped memory and implied mnemonic narratives which reflect sets of preferences within the mindscape of the community.

To illustrate, the Hexateuch ends with the conquest of the land and does not describe the ongoing life of the community in the land; the same general attitude to stop the mnemonic narrative at the beginning of the "new world" is also at work in the Pentateuch.[29] The world of memories of the past evoked by prophetic figures tends to stop with the "new temple" (cf. Chronicles, which shows the same tendency). Of course, when remembering prophetic figures brings memories of future events, a similar tendency is apparent. Reaching the "new utopian world" tends to be the preferred boundary, though in this case, at times, there might be boundaries to the imagination as well.

Constructions of time are often intertwined with constructions of space. Thus, for instance, one may notice similar (implied) generative grammars shaping similar systems of preferences at work in the processes that led to (a) an image of Joshua reaching the "new world" and establishing it as he proceeds to re-organize/Israelitize the land and allocating it to the tribes, and (b) a book such as Ezekiel that brings to memory the image of a (future) divine "conquest" of the land, and its re-organization/re-Israelitization. Of course, memory studies may contribute to an explanation of these tendencies. They may point out that constructed glorious beginnings tend to be more memorable than more mundane and at times heavily disappointing following periods, but it is worth noting that while this reasoning may explain well the case of Joshua, there is more at work in the case of analogical constructions involving both the Second Temple and the utopian future. The building of the Jerusalemite temple in Persian Yehud was hardly imagined by the community as "the most glorious beginning" and even in Isaiah, the focus is on a/the utopian future, which

---

29 Similar tendencies to prefer future potential and key turning points that would lead to new beginnings rather than the actual beginning is at work in, for instance, the emphatic association of (the promise of) the land to Abraham, Isaac and Jacob rather than to Joshua. (The land is never referred to as Joshua's.)

at least, according to most prophetic books would not and could not lead to disappointing results. (Future utopia is not utopia at all if it is understood as unstable and leading by necessity to dystopia or to an eternal cycle of recurrent "utopias" and "dystopias"; this matter raises concerns that are explicitly addressed in, for instance, Jer 31:31–34; Ezek 36:26; Hos 2:21–22.)

Although, similar sets of (implied) preferences were at work in all types of past construing books/collections, because they were grounded on preferences set at the level of a common social mindscape, the prophetic books were not like any other past-construing books/collections in the repertoire of the community. For one, prophetic books lead their readers much more easily to vicariously experience utopian futures and to increase the social mindshare of these futures. Remembering the prophets provided an opportunity for the community to imagine both a past and future in ways that are not so easily realized while imagining other characters (cf. remembering Isaiah with remembering Hezekiah; Zephaniah and Josiah; Jeremiah and Zedakiah).

But as important, since prophetic books provide the community with (a) particular manifestations of Yhwh's word whose meaning was construed as relevant to the past community that the remembering community imagined as interacting with the prophetic character they were also imagining as they read these books, and (b) particular manifestations of Yhwh's word with direct significance to them, that is, the imagining/remembering community, and not only to them, but also to a future Israel which stands in continuity with them and which was supposed to continue reading the prophetic books, these factors lead to (c) a strong tendency to understand the words of the prophets and of Yhwh to them as carrying a multi-temporal dimension. Associating prophetic characters with multi-temporality allows for the possibility of imagining them as less temporally bound than other characters populating the memory-scape of the community. Thus, one notices *partial* de-historicizing tendencies especially among the twelve prophetic characters, with the exception of Haggai. For example, there exists the possibility of imagining a prophet such as Joel, who is not clearly associated with a period and lacks any clear temporal reference. The same holds true, though, within the boundaries of the Persian period and after the rebuilding of the temple, for Malachi.[30] In other words, remembering the prophets in-

---

[30] For the full argument supporting the preceding statements, see my "De-historicizing and Historicizing Tendencies in the Twelve Prophetic Books: A Case Study of the Heuristic Value of a Historically Anchored Systemic Approach to the Corpus of Prophetic Literature" in *Israel's Prophets and Israel's Past: Essays on the Relationship of Prophetic Texts and Israelite History in Honor of John H. Hayes* (eds. B. E. Kelle and M. Moore; LHBOTS 446; London: T&T Clark, 2006), 37–56. (I have revisited this essay in a forthcoming contribution entitled "Balancing

volved construing a past and imagining the world of the prophet, but also, at times, structuring meaningful knowledge about the past in ways far less focused on particular events and far more interested in social attitudes, behaviors, and beliefs. Remembering the prophets does not require the remembering community to forget about kings and political events, but brings some mindshare to images of the past at whose center stood societies; as such it balances the more (and necessarily so) political/king-oriented constructions of the other past-construing texts in the community.

Remembering the prophets and construing "historical narratives" also facilitated the formulation of symbolic, metaphorical and highly memorable condensations of a long "history" of the past (and future) in ways that were not as feasible within the worlds evoked through the readings of books such as Kings and Chronicles. To illustrate, the entire gamut of experiences in the "history" of YHWH and Israel, past and future, is reformulated and made memorable in Hosea (Hos 1–2) as the story of the transformation of a woman who by nature tends to sin/to engage in illegitimate sex (אשת זנונים) into one whose attributes are divinely given righteousness, justice, steadfast love, mercy and faithfulness. The entire story is a variant of the *Chaoskampf* motif in which the struggle is over a woman in which Chaos (i.e., sin/promiscuity) took hold, but is defeated by YHWH, resulting in a permanent orderly world. Most significantly, Israel/the woman takes the structural slot of the Cosmos, thus promoting a sense of cosmic centrality for Israel and guaranteeing a sense of "ontological security" in the world imagined and populated (vicariously) by the literati, and also in the world of all those who accepted these memorable stories, be they literati or not.

Although the language and the details are different – as they should be, since now the readership brings Jeremiah and not Hosea from the past to their present – a similar pattern is at work in Jer 31:31–34. The entire story of Israel past and future is condensed as the story of Israel/a woman (the gendered image is saliently marked by וְאָנֹכִי בָּעַלְתִּי בָם in 31:32)[31] who is transformed as her deficient "heart/mind" is replaced with a new "heart/mind" that is "wired," as it were, with YHWH's teachings/*torah*. (Note that these teachings

---

shades of 'historical', 'historically-blurred' and 'trans-historical' contexts and temporal contingency in Late Persian/Early Hellenistic Yehudite memories of YHWH's Words and prophets of old in the Prophetic Book Collection and its Subcollections," to be published in a collected essays volume in the near future.

31 The image of husband and wife is, of course, one of the common and most memorable ways to symbolize hierarchical patron-client relations. Husband-wife imagery tends to appear along with that of father-son and other related semantic pairs that served so well to pragmatically condense the gamut of relations associated with (male) deity and his people in ancient Israel.

do not have to be taught anymore, that is, brought from outside to bear into the "heart/mind".) The agent that leads to Chaos, in this case, a deficient heart, is utterly removed and Chaos made impossible.[32]

These basic schemas organize the whole past, present and future experience. They remove all the gamut of "unnecessary" details that may "hamper" understanding or remembering of the meaning of all past, present and future history. They also reflect cognitive tendencies that favor similar, condensed and (over)simplified, symbolic and mythological narratives with very few central characters (most often only one or two) that tend to influence much how different groups construct and remember the past, and even how some media today shapes memories of current events.[33]

It is within this context that a sense of proportion in Yehud comes to the forefront. On the one hand, remembering prophetic characters went hand in hand with and facilitated these schematic, very memorable, metanarratives; on the other hand, prophetic literature and the other past-constructing literature that existed in Yehud was abundant with detail, multiple meanings, complex networks of meaning balancing each other, and the like. Just as the former lessened cognitive demands, the latter much heightened them. The collective, social memory of the literati, that is, the mentioned array of multiple and ever-shifting sites of memory is not an easily transmittable socio-cultural complex.[34] It can only be the social memory of a very sophisticated and highly educated cadre, which certainly did not consist of many members at any given time in Persian period Jerusalem. It is not surprising, however, that this cadre would also in-

---

[32] YHWH is the hero who defeats Chaos and leads to the creation of a stable, proper world/Israel, but YHWH achieves victory through YHWH's *torah*. From the perspective of the literati in late Persian Yehud and at a general conceptual level, YHWH's *torah* was associated with Hosea's divinely given righteousness, justice, steadfast love, mercy and faithfulness.

[33] Cf., among others, B. Schwartz, "Collective Forgetting"; S. E. Bird and R. W. Dardenne, "Myth, Chronicle and Story: Exploring the Narrative Quality of News" in *Myths, and Narratives: Television and the Press* (ed. J. W. Carey; London: Sage, 1988), 67–85; M. Coman, "New Stories and Myth – The Impossible Reunion?" in *Media Anthropology* (eds. E. W. Rothenbuhler and M. Coman; Thousand Oaks, Calif.: Sage, 2005), 111–120.

[34] This raises the question of the benefits that may have accrued to the literati and those who supported them from developing and maintaining such a system. A discussion on these issues stands well beyond the scope of this essay. It suffices here to state that there were benefits beyond the quite obvious issues of perceived social/cultural capital and also involved matters such as a social mindscape that placed much value on a sense of continuity and strongly favored fuzziness and discursive integration, within limits. I discussed these issues elsewhere and in particular in my "Social Memory and Identity Formation in Late Persian Yehud," in this volume, pp. 28–79.

clude types of (mythological) narratives and constructions of the past whose reception did not involve such high cognitive demands.

3 Yehud and Samaria

The Persian period literati of Yehud imagined time and again various worlds, but they also lived in one: Yehud, a small and poor province, with a small and poor temple in Jerusalem, with Samarian neighbors who worshiped Yhwh but did not share the Jerusalem-centered ideology of these literati and their temple, which, in any event, had to first establish itself in Yehud.

The comprehensive, central, collective memory of Yehudite literati may be conceived as a multivalent, shifting array of multiple "sites of memory" that, as a whole, provided a mechanism for socialization and social reproduction consistent with and supportive of the general goals and worldview of the institutions and sectors at the center of a particular community. After all, matters of power and institutions are always involved in the production of central, comprehensive memories. Of course, this means that similar types of arrays for external/internal counter-groups with the ability to create social memories (e.g., Samarians).

Both Yehud and Samaria shared a Pentateuch[35] and the memory of Moses, the Lawgiver and Prophet. We have no access to texts that may suggest to us how Samarians in the Persian period imagined their past,[36] which prophets they remembered (Elijah? Elisha?) or, even more important, how they remembered them.[37] Remembering the prophetic characters evoked by the Yehudite

---

[35] Cf. C. Nihan, "The *Torah* between Samaria and Judah: Shechem and Gerizim in Deuteronomy and Joshua," in *The Pentateuch as Torah: New Models for Understanding Its Promulgation and Acceptance* (ed. G. N. Knoppers and B. M. Levinson; Winona Lake, Ind.: Eisenbrauns, 2007), 187–223. Samarian-Yehudite issues have been the focus of much recent research. See, for instance, G. N. Knoppers, "Aspects of Samaria's Religious Culture During the Early Hellenistic Period" in *The Historian and the Bible. Essays in Honour of Lester L. Grabbe* (eds. P. R. Davies and D. V. Edelman; LHBOTS 530; London: T&T Clark, 2010), 159–174, and earlier, idem, "Revisiting the Samarian question in the Persian period" in *Judah and the Judeans in the Persian Period* (eds. O. Lipschits and M. Oeming; Winona Lake, Ind.: Eisenbrauns, 2006), 265–289.

[36] It is impossible to know whether Samaria had a strong cadre of (relatively few) literati as those centered (at least ideologically) and probably supported by the Jerusalemite temple. In addition, one can always wonder what would have happened if the Samarian leadership would have dealt with Alexander's armies as Yehudites did and *vice versa*.

[37] Significantly, even if they remembered an Elijah, it is very unlikely that their Elijah would have been similar to the one evoked in Chronicles, or that they would have imagined a Hosea

prophetic books was tantamount to appropriating Moses and the Pentateuch for the Jerusalem-centered ideology of the literati. The tabernacle as a site of memory blurs with the Jerusalemite temple as it establishes an exclusive line of continuity. Moses leads to Mosaic prophets who are those remembered in Judah/Yehud and conversely some of the latter (most notably, Jeremiah) evoke Moses and shape him as superior. Even northern prophets are construed so as to share the discourse of Jerusalem (see the Davidic and therefore Jerusalem-centered Hosea), and Malachi, likely imagined as the last of the great prophets of the past, brings to memory both Moses and Elijah in Yehud and as they were imagined in Yehud.

One may maintain, of course, that there was no *need* to imagine the prophetic characters to appropriate Moses and the Pentateuch and to turn them into unshareable characters and texts respectively through this appropriation. Clearly, the deuteronomistic historical collection did this job admirably.[38] But, as mentioned above, sites of memory evolved and became more and more memorable as they embodied, integrated and communicated that which stood at the core of the general mindscape of the community. Conversely, there was a strong tendency to attach that which was considered central within the community to central characters of the past. As a result, these matters tend to be embodied and broadcasted in different ways in multiple sites of memory. That the two, non-pentateuchal, main collections within the authoritative repertoire of the community in late Persian Yehud (and one should add to them also Psalms, Lamentations, and Chronicles) address the issues mentioned above only show their centrality for the community.

Of course, different sites of memory and types of sites of memory may carry similar and converging messages, but sites of memory are never simply copies of each other. (If they were, they would lose their appeal to imagination and their hold in the memory-scape of the community.) Making pentateuchal books and the memories and places they evoke Jerusalemite-centered through reading prophetic books and imagining their prophets is transforming them by means of YHWH's word. The prophetic books and their characters bear YHWH's word in a way that the book of Kings, for instance, could not claim, at least not directly. This is not a minor claim, which is amplified by conceptually, partially porous boundaries between (Jerusalem-centered construed) YHWH's word and

---

who strongly advances an ideological Yehudatization of northern Israel and prophecies about a new Davidic kingdom including both North and South.

38 To some extent the same is also achieved by the book of Psalms as well.

(Jerusalem-centered construed) Yhwh's teaching (see Isa 2:3; Mic 4:2) and their associations with memories of the Mosaic prophets and Moses respectively.

4 Yehud, Jerusalem, Strong Sets of Preference and Social Reality

The literati were ideologically centered on Jerusalem and its temple, but were still focused, as reality would have forced them, on Yehud (and in terms of memory, Judah) as a whole. The Jerusalem temple worldview *had* to be construed as inclusive of Yehud (and including Benjamin).[39]

The system of preferences (and dis-preferences) that generated prophets who were worthy (or unworthy) of being remembered as part the group associated with prophetic books ended up including only male prophets, despite the fact that memories of them were evoked in the deuteronomistic historical collection. No prophet who was born or grew up outside the land was included; there was only one prophet clearly assigned to the monarchic North and none to the North after the fall of its monarchic polity. It is also clear that certain periods were preferred over others at significant costs (e.g., there was no prophet during the time of Manasseh, despite its characterization in Kings and Jeremiah; see 2 Kgs 21:1–20; 23:12, 26; 24:3; Jer 15:14 and the common motif of Yhwh's prophets as warning voices calling for repentance; none from the putative time of David and Solomon despite its foundational role in images of the past). But it included prophets from Judah (and Benjamin) and relatively few prophets who were from Jerusalem.[40]

---

[39] Benjamin was the demographic, economic and even political center of early Yehud. It remained the most populated area within the province throughout the period. The incipient temple in Yehud could have never succeeded if it had excluded Benjamin. For bibliography on demographic data and above all on the inclusion of Benjamin in Jerusalem-centered Yehud and from a different perspective, see "Total Exile, Empty Land and the General Intellectual Discourse in Yehud" in this volume, pp. 599–611.

[40] Does this distribution have something to do, directly or indirectly with the demographic and political situation in Yehud? Did it play a role on or reflected local politics of memory in Yehud or in processes of socialization, appropriation and incorporation of Yehudite local elites and their traditions into a Jerusalem-centered discourse and the social institutions that embodied and propagated it? These matters are beyond the scope of this essay, but deserve analysis.

5 Forgetting, Remembering, and Counterfactual Memories

Approaches informed by memory studies can be particularly helpful in terms of understanding processes of forgetting. Sites or sets of sites of collective memory evoke and shape particular memories; as they do so, they cannot but urge their visitors to forget or render dormant, or reduce the mindscape of some images, memories, associations and the like. But that which is remembered and forgotten stands at times interwoven in particular and significant ways. To illustrate, Exile is a central ideological concept in Yehud and remembering the prophets was remembering their warnings and announcements of Exile.[41] At the same time actual life under Exile is something whose mindshare is minimized, though as whole imagined in negative terms of alienations for YHWH and YHWH's land (cf. Hos 9:3) but this happened in a community that often imagined itself as constituted only by those who returned from Exile (see the motif of empty land) and at times imagined in particular exiles to Babylon in a positive light (e.g., Jer 24; Ezek 11:14–21; 33:21–29). On the whole, the group in Yehud construed itself in terms of a close cultural relation with a construed/remembered group that existed outside its borders, in a place outside the land and in alienation from YHWH, but with whom they imagined to be directly related and as ideologically close,[42] while at the same time they bracketed out the memory of this group. In other words, they both evoked and bracketed them out, at the same time.[43]

Of course, there are other cases of memories that are both recalled and forgotten through the process of remembering and vicariously encountering the prophets of old. Literati who encountered their Hosea were both reminded and asked to bracket out the future Davide (compare the messages of Hos 2:2 and

---

[41] Cf. M. A. Halvorson-Taylor, *Enduring Exile: The Metaphorization of Exile in the Hebrew Bible* (VTSup 141; Leiden/Boston: Brill, 2011). Whether some of the text were originally as earlier as she proposes or not, all the crucial texts she discusses were simultaneously part and parcel of the repertoire of late Persian (or early Hellenistic) Yehud/Judah and I would claim informed each other at the time.

[42] Incidentally, process of identity formation in which a group adopts as markers of its identity features that they associate with an external group they construe as particularly close to them (in a quite counterfactual way, one may add) are not so rare or unique to antiquity. See the case of the Garifuna of Honduras and US African American rap music; that of the Sepharadic converso community of Holland and external and quite removed, sociologically, geographically and ideologically, rabbinic leadership.

[43] For similar processes, note that Ezra and Nehemiah do not dwell much on the community within which they were socialized; later on, in rabbinic literature, much is made of Hillel who came from Babylon and brought back *torah* to Israel, but almost nothing is said/remembered of Hillel in Babylon.

3:4–5 with those of 2:16–25, esp. vv. 20–22, and 14:2–9). At times, however, matters are more definite (e.g., the necessary forgetting of Aram in Hosea in accordance with a social mindscape that preferred a consolidated schema of dyads [Assyria-Egypt; Babylon-Egypt], which served to construe and evoke lands of exile and exilic events and communities associated with them) but even there, one finds the minor reference to Hos 12:13 that creates a kind of pre-history to the main implied narrative.[44]

Reading and rereading a particular text meant that the community recalled some sites or sets of sites and that as it did so, it bracketed, made dormant or temporarily forgot other sites or sets of sites. When reading either another portion of the very same text or other texts that existed within the very same cultural milieu, the process reversed. I would argue – especially in the case of very small communities – that this situation does not necessary involve the creation of "sectarian memories" or "counter cultural memories" opposed to the collective memory developed by and at the center of the society. Instead, the situation may reflect a state in which a collective memory that shapes social identity and enhances social integration includes shifting arrays of memories, of matters forgotten or dormant, all interacting with one another and, at times, seemingly oblivious of each other. This system does not have to be logically consistent, since it has to bring about socially shared acts of imagining the past that contribute much to a shared imagining of the community, or in the case of Yehud, "the nation" (i.e., transtemporal Israel). Thus, polyphony often characterizes the system, even if it is, by necessity, restricted to that which is consistent with group's core beliefs.[45] Moreover this polyphony is a dynamic one, in which mindshare can be balanced, according to, for instance, particular rhetorical needs and specific settings, only to rebalanced again and again.[46]

6 A Final Observation

The Persian period literati of Yehud lived in small, poor province with a small, poor temple in Jerusalem – a city in which remains of past "grandeur" and of past "defeat" were most likely abundant. Thus it is not surprising that the proph-

---

[44] See "Remembering Hosea" and to some extent, my previous, "Study of Forgetting and the Forgotten in Ancient Israelite Discourse."
[45] Cf. P. R. Davies, *Memories of Ancient Israel: An Introduction to Biblical History – Ancient and Modern* (Louisville, Ky.: Westminster John Knox; 2008), 113.
[46] Cf. "Study of Forgetting and the Forgotten in Ancient Israelite Discourse."

ets they chose to remember were for the most part ones who explained the past catastrophe and used it as a powerful didactic tool for the community.

This said, remembering the prophets was not only remembering a painful, almost dystopian past, it was also remembering that Y{HWH} proclaimed a great, utopian future precisely in the midst of that sinful period; thus, these memories reaffirmed a social mindscape within which Y{HWH}'s decision to bring the promised future was not the result of, or dependent on human actions, and as such unreliable. Remembering the prophets was an exercise in comforting and instilling hope for a future (cf. Sir 48:24–25; 49:10), and it was a didactic enterprise whose goal was to learn about Y{HWH} and what is godly, so as to develop the best possible (human) Israel and perhaps avoid another catastrophe, until Y{HWH} changes their hearts, endows them with divine attributes, or in other words elevates them above common human existence, so they may become an appropriate wife/son to the deity. Of course, at that time, the entire world will change, but matters of utopian worlds in Yehud and Y{HWH}'s empire must be the subject of a separate essay.

Prophetic Memories in the Deuteronomistic Historical and the Prophetic Collections of Books*

Introductory Issues

This essay is not about what monarchic or, for that matter, premonarchic prophets might have been or what they did or did not do. It is about how they were imagined by Persian period Jerusalem-centered literati whose memories of prophets of old were based on their readings of the Deuteronomistic historical and the prophetic collections of books. This essay is about why these prophets of old were imagined and remembered in certain ways and about the basic, general conceptual prototypes of prophecy and prophets that these literati shared among themselves, and about their social mindscape, which was underlying, generating, and reflecting itself in these memories

This type of exploration is consonant with the actual historical roles of Deuteronomistic and prophetic collections of books in Persian Yehud. They served above all as tools for didactic instruction and socialization among the literati who produced, read, and reread them, and likely– through the intermediation of these literati–for other groups in Yehud as well. These collections could serve such a role because reading these collections brought to the present of their rereading communities memories of the past and of the characters that populated it. These remembered, and thus constantly construed characters became sites of memory within the community. The collection of fifteen prophetic books (hereafter PBC) and the Deuteronomistic historical collection (hereafter DHC) served to a large extent as platforms for a crucial social activity: evoking, exploring, and instilling a shared social memory. Through the process, readers construed and remembered characters. Connective features shared by characters in some group (e.g., prophets, priests, etc.) created a web of attributes that reflected the implied understanding of the basic nature of the group, or one may say of a conceptual prototype of what a "generic" (non-individualized) member of the group was (e.g., a prophet). Conversely, this prototype contributed to the shaping of social memories of members of the group (e.g., prophets).

---

* First published in *Israelite Prophecy and the Deuteronomistic History. Portrait, Reality and the Formation of a History* (eds. M. R. Jacobs and R. F. Person Jr.; SBLAIL 314, Atlanta: SBL, 2013), 75–102.

It is worth stressing that for the most part the main sites of memory were not the very books in either the DHC or the PBC that evoked these central figures of old (e.g., the book of Judges, or the book of Isaiah), but the places, events and, above all, prophetic characters whose memory the books were seen to encode, and which the literati decoded as they imagined and vicariously experienced the past in their present. Thus, it is not by chance that, for instance, although all (or almost all) the information the literati in the Persian and later periods could gather about their main prophets of old was based on the prophetic books in their repertoire, they constantly referred to prophets and to their words, *not* to the prophetic books associated with them (see, for instance, Jer 26:18; Zech 1:4; 7:7; 2 Chr 24:19).¹ This is not to say that the prophetic books were not important as such, but that the "person" of the particular prophet that the readers shaped in their minds through shared readings and social interaction symbolized–and embodied, as it were–the contents and messages of the book. The book was the means to recreate and encounter the "person." Reading the book made such a "person" of old present in the remembering community.²

This holds true, of course, for the DHC as well. The collection did not call attention to itself directly, but to what happened to Israel, the main protagonist of the history, through time. Through reading and rereading the DHC, the literati in Yehud imagined and vicariously experienced main events of Israel's past, and encountered time and again the multiple characters that populated the past as remembered and construed. All of these characters evoked memories of particular places, events, concepts, and even texts. Remembered characters became signs embodying and secreting meanings. Of course, much social mindshare

---

1 The case of the ספר התורה or ספר תורת יהוה/משה (e.g., Josh 1:8; 2 Kgs 14:6; 22:10–11; cf. 2 Chr 17:9; 34:14) is different. This "book" served both as a core site of memory by itself–unlike books of, e.g., Isaiah, Ezekiel or fudges–and as a book whose reading brought to the present of the remembering community central figures, events, and texts from the past. To the extent that this book was imagined only as Deuteronomy, in itself a problematic assumption in some cases (e.g., 2 Kgs 22:10–11; see E. Ben Zvi, "Imagining Josiah's Book and the Implications of Imagining It in Early Persian Yehud" in *Berührungspunkte: Studien zur Sozial- und Religionsgeschichte Israels und seiner Umwelt* [eds. R. Schmitt, I. Kottsieper, and J. Wöhrle; AOAT 250; Minister: Ugarit, 2008], 193–212, here 201–8), this characterization would have been a unique case of a prophetic book calling much mindshare to itself (see below), and as such it would have accentuated existing patterns of similarities and dissimilarities between Moses and the other prophets. See "Exploring the Memory of Moses 'The Prophet' in Late Persian/Early Hellenistic Period Yehud/Judah," in this volume, pp. 199–231.

2 This process may have facilitated redactional activities in the books. After all, the books were meant to provide the messages of the prophets of old. An exploration of this point is, however, beyond the scope of this essay.

was devoted to those that evoked and embodied concepts and events that were at the core of the collective social memory of the literati and that played important roles for identity formation. Thus, for instance, Abraham, Jacob, Moses, Joshua, David, and the like were sites that commanded much memory mindshare, while others, for instance, עדיה, Adaiah, (the father of ידידה, Jedidah, the mother of Josiah; see 2 Kgs 22:1) had very little. To be sure, a positive feedback loop was at work as well: the more important the character, the larger the mindshare that was associated with him or her, and conversely, the larger the mindshare he or she commanded, the more likely that some core concepts and images would end up being embodied in the character. Of course, these characters, or sites of memory, were imagined and (virtually) encountered within particular contexts associated with particular periods of the agreed-upon, shared, and remembered past. Thus they drew meaning, at least in part, within the context of the remembered circumstances of their relevant period. This memory-anchoring principle plays a central role in the shaping of both characterizations of core personages in "historical" (i.e., social memory) narratives about the past that existed in ancient Yehud (see below) and of crucial periods as remembered by the community. As it did both, it contributed much to the construction of their discursive significance.[3]

Prophetic characters were as a group among the most salient sites of memory in the memoryscape of the Yehudite literati, and they appear in dramatically different periods within the basic narrative of Israel about itself. It is impossible to engage thoroughly with memory of each of monarchic or premonarchic prophetic figures in Yehud, even if one restricted the scope of the analysis only to those who were strongly evoked by the reading and rereading of the DHC, the

---

[3] To be sure, (human) personages who were anchored to particular periods that existed in the memory of the community did not constitute all the (main) sites of memory that shaped the mentioned memoryscape. Particular (construed and remembered) spaces (e.g., Jerusalem, temple, "the land"), and transtemporal or perhaps panchronic characters such as YHWH and Israel were also among the main sites of memory. Yet *particular* periods, as socially construed and remembered by the community, became reenacted, as it were, as the literati who read, for instance, the prophetic books actually had to speak the voices of the prophets of old and YHWH's words to them. To do so implied vicariously experiencing the context in which the words were set (within the remembered past agreed upon by the literati). Even when the process of speaking voices of the past was not at work (e.g., in third person narratives), the readers still imagined a past and closely identified with many of the main characters, their experiences, and the spaces they walked through within the mentioned circumstances (e.g., the monarchic temple they construed as they read many texts set in that place).

PBC, or both in a way that informed each other in Yehud.[4] It is feasible, within the boundaries of a chapter, to explore *some* of the ways in which prophets and prophetic figures were remembered, the basic narratives that shaped their characterizations, and some aspects of the system of preferences that shaped the representation of prophets and prophecy in the DHC and the PBC.

Of course, this line of research will not tell us much about any "historical" Elijah or Zephaniah. But it will help us understand why prophets were remembered the way they were, and why they tended to be associated with certain periods and not others. Above all, it will shed some light on what it does to the literati to continuously remember a past in which monarchic or premonarchic prophets were imagined and vicariously encountered the way they were.[5] The point is to go beyond the obviously correct, and widely acknowledged understandings such as (1) that the shared social activity of creating a *present* past contributed much to identity formation and social cohesion among the literati; (2) that it influenced non-literati members of the community whose discourse was influenced by the former, and (3) that it set some boundaries between in-groups and out-groups. After all, like other communities, this one was one comprised of shared memory and imagination. Instead, I plan to begin to explore, for instance, some aspects of the grammar implied in the structure of the social memory that was shared and reenacted through shared readings and rereadings of these collections and its generative powers.

The emphasis above on remembering and shaping so-called "historical"– but actually social memory–*narratives* is not accidental. As is well known, social memories take the form of narratives or interrelated sets of narratives informing and balancing each other.[6] Readers assign significance to the characters populating a narrative as they internalize the basic plot and the communicative messages they find in it. Social memory among the literati in Yehud was construed as an interrelated set of narratives structured and, above all, remembered in terms of many individuals, heroes and villains, each of whom became a site of

---

[4] That is. even if one leaves aside prophetic characters that are evoked primarily in Genesis–Numbers, Chronicles, or Ezra–Nehemiah. Even if one restricts the endeavor to those in the PBC alone, the matter would be well beyond the scope of even a lengthy monograph.

[5] Or, in other words, what kind of impact such continuous remembering had upon the literati engaged, time and again, in this process of remembering the past and, large extent, of mentally reenacting it within a socially shared imagination.

[6] On the cross-cultural construction of social memories as narratives see, for instance, E. Zerubavel, *Social Mindscapes: An Invitation to Cognitive Sociology* (Cambridge: University Press, 1997); idem, *Time Maps: Collective Memory and the Social Shape of the Past* (Chicago: University of Chicago Press, 2003).

memory in a large, socially shared memoryscape of the literati (although from a later period, cf. Sir 44–49). In this context, prophetic memories in Yehud should be explored for the present purposes.

To explore the matters mentioned above, I will refer to prophetic memories, basic narratives, connective features, and underlying system of preferences shaping the representations of prophets and prophecy in the DHC and will look into the social mindscape about prophecy that they suggest. I will focus mainly on (1) a few highly salient personages, because the more centrally they figured as sites of memory for the community the more they attracted to themselves and thus embodied and communicated what was crucial for the community and because, conversely, the more they embodied and communicated these crucial concepts, the more central they became; and (2) "generic" prophetic characters or groups that reflect more clearly central conceptual images of what a prophet of old should be–that is, more than highly individualized portrayals of a certain individual or group.[7] Then I will continue with a similar study of the PBC. I will conclude with some observations about the interplay between the discussed features, since both PBC and DHC were read as part of one ideological discourse, namely that of the (at least ideologically) Jerusalem-centered literati of Yehud, and since the memories evoked by each of these collections informed each other and together shaped the comprehensive memory of the very same remembering community of literati.[8] Needless to say, this exploration will have to focus on paradigmatic (or at least potentially paradigmatic) cases, and to refrain from any attempt at comprehensiveness.

Two related caveats must be addressed before embarking on this exploration. First, the reconstructed "remembering community" of literati stands for an "ideal" community that conflates a number of historical communities of literati in Yehud that existed for a few generations. The crucial features that charac-

---

[7] For a fuller explanation of this approach, which is particularly relevant to the case of Kings, see E. Ben Zvi, "The Prophets," republished with minor changes under the same title in *The Books of Kings: Sources, Composition, Historiography, and Reception* (eds. B. Levine and A. Lemaire; VTSup 129; Leiden: Brill, 2010), 387–99.

[8] Whatever the origin of the sources or literary forerunners of each of books in their respective collections might be, the PBC and the DHC were read by the same literati and *together* shaped the comprehensive social memory of the late Persian, Jerusalem-centered, Yehudite literati. It is worth stressing that the approach proposed here is a "bird's-eye view" approach. A colleague–who is both an historian and a field archaeologist–compared it to focusing on patterns that emerge when a helicopter overviews a site and its region, in contradistinction to advancing a detailed (ground-perspective) study of each building or room in a particular site. Of course, both approaches are necessary to advance knowledge on the site or issue, because they raise different questions.

terized these related communities are (1) a shared intellectual discourse; (2) a repertoire of central or authoritative books that included the DHC and the PBC or something very close to them; and (3) social memories about prophets that were shaped mainly by the two collections mentioned above, but not Chronicles.

These considerations lead to the second caveat: The "ideal" community discussed here must be a pre-Chronicles community. The comprehensive social memory of the pre-Chronicles period cannot be equated with that of the Chronicles and of post-Chronicles Yehud, because the composition and, above all, the reading and rereading of Chronicles by itself shaped and drew attention to complementary sets of memories of prophets that balanced, informed, and were in turn also balanced and informed by, the memories evoked by the two other collections. As a result, a new system of social memory interactions emerged. Texts construed as encoding memory are decoded within their *Sitz im Diskurs*. Or from a slightly different perspective, sites of memory become meaningful to the community not as standalone sites, but as part of a large memoryscape populated by other sites of memory. As the memoryscape shifts, by the reading and rereading of Chronicles, to some extent so does the meaning of each site of memory. This said, a significant result of the present study is that Chronicles follows, in a number of substantial cases, (ideological) generative grammars, and responds explicitly to implied questions and issues that existed within the pre-Chronicles communities and, conversely, that many features associated with prophecy and prophetic characters in the DHC particularly–but also in the PBC–come strongly and explicitly to the forefront in Chronicles. To put it in other words, Chronicles did not represent a radical departure from the pre-Chronicles discourse in Yehud, but quite the opposite: it shows significant continuity, at least in terms of prophecy and prophetic and prophetic characters.[9]

---

[9] See E. Ben Zvi, "Observations on Lines of Thought Concerning the Concepts of Prophecy and Prophets in Yehud, with an Emphasis on Deuteronomy–2 Kings and Chronicles," in *Words, Ideas, Worlds: Biblical Essays in Honour of Yairah Amit* (eds. A. Brenner and F. H. Polak; Sheffield: Sheffield Phoenix, 2012), 1–19; idem, "Are There Any Bridges Out There? How Wide Was the Conceptual Gap between the Deuteronomistic History and Chronicles?" in *Community Identity in Judean Historiography: Biblical and Comparative Perspectives* (eds. G. N. Knoppers and K. A. Ristau; Winona Lake, Ind.: Eisenbrauns, 2009), 59–86.

The DHC, Memories of Prophetic Characters, and Their Implications

The DHC communicated and shaped social memory in the form of a narrative. As is well known, the starting point of a "national" narrative is often particularly meaningful. To illustrate with a present-day example, whether the historical narrative of "modern Germany" begins with Bismarck or with a plethora of great philosophers, writers, and musicians is clearly not a minor issue devoid of any discursive importance. The DHC begins with Moses the prophet. Significantly, he is *also* a prophet. Moreover, the opening of Deuteronomy (1:1) is reminiscent of those of prophetic books. Deuteronomy is *also* a prophetic book. These basic observations already suggest blurred or fuzzy boundaries. Moses is a prophet *and* a lawgiver, *and* a few other things (e.g., a [super]kingly and priestly figure);[10] Deuteronomy is a prophetic book *and* a historical book *and* a pentateuchal book and so on. In addition, memories of Moses the prophet were encoded not only in Deuteronomy, but also in other pre-Chronicles texts (Exodus–Numbers). Obviously, this essay is not the appropriate place for any kind of significant study of the memories of Moses.[11] For present purposes, a few observations suffice. First, Moses was a central site of memory that came to embody in one person virtually every feature associated with prophecy. He was, among other things, a foreteller, a wonder maker, a historian, a teacher, a writer, a singer, an intercessor; a person who prayed for people, who admonished them, who suffered rejection, a conveyor of divine messages for the people, a doom announcer, and a hope maker.[12]

In other words, Moses was construed as the prophetic exemplar; he embodied all possible attributes assigned to prophets. Thus, it comes as no surprise that neither the DHC nor any other book available within the community evokes the image of another prophet to whom the full range of attributes is attached. In fact, only a few of them fulfilled even a significant number of them, and some features (e.g., singer) were not embodied in entire books (e.g., "singer" in Kings).

To remember Moses, presented at the beginning of historical narrative as extremely worthy of being remembered, was to remember and to internalize a par-

---

[10] See, for instance, J. Lierman, *The New Testament Moses: Christian Perceptions of Moses and Israel in the Setting of Jewish Religion* (Tübingen: Mohr Siebeck, 2004), which discusses perceptions of Moses in Yehud as well.
[11] For my contribution to the topic, see "Exploring the Memory of Moses" in this volume, pp. 199–231.
[12] See note above.

ticular organization of the past. There was (1) a pre-Mosaic and thus primarily nonprophetic period; (2) the time of Moses the paradigmatic prophet period; and (3) the post-Moses period or, better, the period of the Mosaic prophets (Deut 18:15, 18).[13] Prophets are intermediaries, and since the main divine communication that Moses transmitted to the people was "the *torah*," this structural periodization of the memory of the past was tantamount to the following: (1) the (mainly) pre-*torah* era (2) the period of Moses' prophetic communication, or *torah*, and (3) a torahic period (cf. 2 Kgs 17:13). The overlap of these structures was consistent with the way in which Israel figured as a "*torah*-centered community" within the social mindscape of the literati. It created a clear overlap between the torahic period and the period of the Mosaic prophets.

This being said, it is particularly worth noting that, on the *surface,* the historiographical narratives addressing the beginning of the torahic period of Mosaic prophets in the DHC did not draw the attention of its primary readers and rereaders toward memories of prophets. To illustrate, Joshua is never called a prophet or even "man of god,"[14] and the term נביא does not appear in the book at all. The crossing of the Jordan, although clearly reminiscent of the crossing of the Sea of Reeds,[15] was shaped in social memory far more as a liturgical enterprise than as "divine miracle" associated with a prophetic intermediary

Yet Joshua was remembered as a leader who followed Moses as the main divine intermediary (see Josh 1:1–2). Moreover, the memory of Joshua is that of a person who consistently referred to Moses and to the contents of the divine message that he communicated, namely "*torah*" He was imagined as learning "*torah*," reminding people of "*torah*," encouraging them to follow it, admonishing them about the consequences of abandoning it, writing its words, and so on (e.g., Josh 1:8; 8:31–32; 22:5; 23:6). Thus, Joshua becomes an exemplar of a Mosaic prophet as construed by texts such as 2 Kgs 17:13, which reads:

שבו מדרכיכם הרעים ושמרו מצותי חקותי ככל התורה אשר צויתי את אבתיכם ואשר שלחתי אליכם ביד עבדי הנביאים

("Turn back from your wicked ways, and observe my commandments and my laws, according to all the *torah* that have I commanded *your ancestors* and which I have sent *you* through my servants, the prophets;" emphasis mine)

---

[13] For the point that these prophets can only be Mosaic, not equal to Moses, see Deut 34:10.
[14] The only one referred to as a "man of God" in Joshua is Moses (see Josh 14:6; cf. Deut 33:1).
[15] On these matters, see, among others, J. Wagenaar, "Crossing the Sea of Reeds (Exod 13–14) and the Jordan (Josh 3–4): A Priestly Framework for the Wilderness Wandering Studies in the Book of Exodus," in *Studies in the Book of Exodus: Redaction, Reception, Interpretation* (ed. M. Vervenne; BETL 126; Leuven: Peelers, 1996), 461–70 and bibliography.

This text communicates Yhwh's memory of "the prophets" as a chain of transmission for the Mosaic *torah*. The community of readers was supposed to orient their memory to Yhwh's and to make Yhwh's their own collective memory (cf. Zech 1:6).

The texts of 2 Kgs 17:13 and Zech 1:6, along with others, reflected and shaped a sense of *partial* conceptual blending between prophetic characters and Yhwh's servants within the discourse of the community.[16] One may note the use of the *exact epithet* עבד יהוה in the book of Joshua. It was associated time and again with Moses.[17] But significantly, it was also used for Joshua. This choice, especially given the context in which the exact epithet was used (see Josh 24:29–30; see also Judg 2:8–9), served pragmatically to underline the role of Joshua as the successor of Moses, as Yhwh's intermediary–similar to Moses, but not his equal (compare and contrast with Deut 34:5–10).[18] The expression evoked also a

---

16 Other texts include 1 Kgs 14:18; 15:29; 2 Kgs 9:7, 36; 10:10; 14:25; 17:13,23; 21:10; 24:2; Isa 20:3; Jer 7:25; 25:4; 26:5; 29:19; 35:15; 44:4; Ezek 38:17; Amos 3:7. I emphasize "partial" because the realm of Yhwh's servants included nonprophetic characters (see, for instance, Isa 41:8–9; 56:6; Jer 27:6; 30:10; Job 1:8). A partial blending of concepts of Yhwh's servants and prophets is well attested in later literature as well. See for instance Ezra 9:11; Dan 9:6,10.
17 See, e.g., Josh 1:1,13,15; 8:31, 33; 11:12; 12:6; 13:8; 14:7; 18:7; 22:2,4, 5.
18 For the use of עבד יהוה as an epithet of Moses, see also 2 Kgs 18:12; 2 Chr 1:3; 24:6 (cf. 1 Chr 6:34; and see also Neh 10:30; Dan 9:11). Among the intended primary readers of the DHC (and Chronicles), the epithet brought up associations with the figure of Moses. In Psalms, the epithet of עבד יהוה evoked the image of David; see Ps 18:1; 36:1 (cf. 1 Kgs 8:66; Isa 37:35; Ezek 34:23; Ps 132:10; 2 Chr 6:15–17; 6:42). In the PBC, there is, of course, Isa 42:39 (cf. Isa 42:1; 52:13; 53:11). The question of whether, within the discourse of Persian-period Yehud, readers of Isaiah would have read some play, at least at some level, between the image of servant Israel and their own image of Moses, the servant of Yhwh (inasmuch as in Greek literature Achilles was "the swift of foot") is beyond the scope of this essay. But it relates directly to the investigation of the concept "Israel" in the shared social mindscape of the literati, which involved both transtemporal Israel and the literati themselves, as they identified with it. The matter should be addressed in a separate essay. Many other personages populating the past were characterized as Yhwh's servants (e.g., Abraham, Caleb, Ahijah, Elijah, Isaiah, Nebuchadnezzar and Zerubbabel) but the epithet עבד יהוה was not associated with them. There are additional texts that underline the role of Joshua as the successor of Moses, though clearly not his equal. One may note, for instance, the command to Joshua in Josh 5:15 to remove his sandals, which evokes the memory of Moses' removal of his sandals (Exod 3:5). One may note, however, that, among other differences, it was Yhwh who gave the command to Moses, but an angelic figure, namely, שר צבא יהוה to Joshua. For another example, compare and contrast Deut 34:7 with Josh 24:29.

sense of participation in a long chain of prophets who were remembered as YHWH's עבדים, even if the exact epithet was not used in relation to them.[19]

Joshua was remembered as one who was contacted directly by the deity, not through an intermediary, just as Moses was (cf. Deut 31:23; Josh 1:6 with Deut 31:7).[20] Moreover, the literati imagined that YHWH explicitly chose to inform Moses, in Joshua's presence, of the future exile and the promise of restoration afterwards (see Deut 31:14–21 and cf. Amos 3:7; and note the obligation to teach this prophecy in Deut 31).[21] One may note also the choice of the plural verbal form כתבו in reference to this prophecy in verse 19. This choice explicitly asks the readers to imagine Joshua as included, despite the expected use of singular form in verse 22 that signals the centrality and in comparability of Moses.

The memory of Joshua is evoked and clearly "prophetized" in 1 Kgs 16:34. One may note that the clause X כדבר יהוה אשר דבר ביד is used elsewhere, with prophets standing for X (see 1 Kgs 14:18; 15:29; 17:16; 2 Kgs 24:2).

Moreover, Persian-period readers of Joshua likely understood Josh 24:19–20 as prophetic, in the sense of foreseeing the future. Within the discourse of the period, Joshua's construction of the present of his time in terms of the fulfillment of all YHWH's good promises (Josh 21:45; 23:14) was pregnant with significance, since from their perspective, all the "bad" promises were fulfilled as well.

In fact, the literati were supposed to construe Joshua's great present in a way reminiscent of that of Solomon, and *vice versa* (cf. Josh 21:45; 23:14 with 1 Kgs 8:56). The purposeful use of the same language drew attention to some narrative/mnemonic similarities. In both cases, once the remembered narrative reaches its highest point, memories of the following periods had to be structured in terms of a genera! decline plot. In the case of 1 Kgs 8, the underlying concept of (future) exile, bubbles quite saliently to the surface of the "highest point" narrative (see 1 Kgs 8:46–53 [cf. 2 Chr 6:36–39]; cf. 1 Chr 16:35). Likewise, the dramatic future downturn is implied and clearly evoked in Persian-period readings of Josh 21:45; 23:14. Moreover, both speakers (Joshua and Solomon) were con-

---

[19] See, for instance, 2 Kgs 9:7; 17:13; 21:10; Jer 7:25; 26:5; 35:15; 44:4; Ezek 38:17; Zech 1:6; see also 1 Kgs 14:18; 15:29; 2 Kgs 10:10; 14:25; Isa 20:3. As mentioned above, not only prophets were characterized as "servants of YHWH," but, leaving aside patriarchal figures that belong to an earlier period in Israel's mnemonic map and David, the vast majority of *persons* who were remembered as YHWH's servants and who populated the period from Moses to the catastrophe were prophets.
[20] One may still note a difference in the choice of verbal forms, namely, ויאמר versus ויצו. The first tends to be used in this literary unit for YHWH's talk with Moses; the second for YHWH's talk with Joshua, and for Moses' talk with the people (see Deut 31:10, 14, 16, 23, 25), but see Josh 1:1.
[21] Note the motif of the prophet as teacher. This motif is clearly assumed and considered central in 2 Kgs 17:13, and later on in Chronicles.

strued as sharing an understanding of history (future and past) as a sequence of fulfillments of YHWH's promises. This message was clearly "prophetic."[22] In addition, both Joshua and Moses were characterized as prophetic because they foresaw the future,[23] and because they explained to the people the causality governing history (namely, YHWH's will and responses).

Joshua was also imagined as a memory maker or "national" historian, a person telling the people of his generation their (hi)story, and indirectly the Persian-period literati who overhear him–as they virtually "experience" the event through their readings, so they may learn from it (see Josh 23:3–4; 24:2–13). Although "summaries of history" may appear in different contexts,[24] within the DHC, they tend to be associated with prophetic voices (see 1 Sam 12:8–15; Judg 6:8–10; see also Judg 10:11–14, in which a prophetic personage is implied).[25] Along with the construction of prophets as those who admonished Israel by recalling their past (e.g., Jer 16:10–13; Ezek 20), this tendency contributed to the prophetization of the memory of Joshua.

Like Moses, Joshua is not remembered only as a prophet, but *also* as a prophet. It is worth noting that in this case the prophetization of Joshua does not lead to memories of a miracle-worker, healer, or king-maker prophet (though he is a covenant-maker),[26] but implies some of the characteristic features of

---

22 See Deut 18:14–22; 1 Kgs 12:15; 14:18; 15:29; 16:12; 17:16; 2 Kgs 9:36; 10:10; 14:25; 17:23; 24:2; cf. 1 Kgs 11:31–35 with 1 Kgs 12:15; 1 Kgs 14:7–11 with 1 Kgs 15:29; 2 Kgs 15:12 with 2 Kgs 10:30. These texts carry a potentially "misleading" interpretation that had no place in the discourse of the community (e.g., things simply happened because prophets prophesied them). As one would expect, this potential generated the development of notes and comments meant to counter such potential "misinterpretation." For a discussion of these and other aspects see E. Ben Zvi, "Prophets and Prophecy in the Compositional and Redactional Notes in I–II Kings," *ZAW* 105 (1993): 331–51.
23 On 1 Chr 16:35 and David's knowledge of the future see E. Ben Zvi, "Who Knew What? The Construction of the Monarchic Past in Chronicles and Implications for the Intellectual Setting of Chronicles," in *Judah and the Judeans in the Fourth Century BCE* (eds. O. Lipschits, G. N. Knoppers, and R. Albertz; Winona Lake, Ind.: Eisenbrauns, 2007), 349–60.
24 See, for instance, Jer 16:10–13; Ezek 20; Ps 78, 105, 106, 107, 136; Neh 9:6–37; Jdt 5:3–23; 1 Macc 2:50–68.
25 The alternative, that is, to imagine a kind of direct divine revelation to the entire people as in Sinai, seems very unlikely.
26 Joshua, like Moses, is a covenant maker. He also writes a covenantal text (Josh 24:25–26). Memories of Samuel evoked by 1 Sam 12 were clearly reminiscent of those of Moses and to a minor extent those of Joshua. (See also Jer 11.) The question of whether prophetic roles and covenant making were closely associated within the mindscape of the literati cannot be discussed here. To be sure, the usual presence of historical reviews in the introduction to covenants, of statements exhorting the subordinate to fulfill its obligations, and common warnings about

prophecy that are similar to those that emerge as dominant in Chronicles.²⁷ Significantly, Chronicles depicts characters who fulfill clear prophetic roles, and thus are imagined as "prophetic," but who are not explicitly designated as "prophets," and who fulfill other roles as well.²⁸

The fact that there are no explicit references to "prophets" in Joshua is significant,²⁹ but so is the fact that Joshua was imagined as a prophetic character, that is, as one who embodies and fulfills attributes associated with prophecy. It is also significant that several of the prophetic attributes associated with Joshua point at a trend that emerges saliently and explicitly in Chronicles.

The situation is not essentially different in Judges.³⁰ To be sure, Deborah is designated אשה נביאה in Judg 4:4. Significantly, she is *also* a prophet (like others, she "judges" Israel; see Judg 4:4–5) and her most memorable prophetic contribution is singing a song that construes memory (cf. Deut 31:22,30; 32; and Exod 15:20; note the characterization of singers as prophets in 1 Chr 25:1).³¹ More-

---

the punishments that would fall on those who break it, created a certain amount of overlap between prophetic roles and figures and covenant making. However, it is unclear whether connections between the two went beyond these shared generic roles within the Persian-period literati's mindscape.

27 I have dealt elsewhere with prophets in Chronicles. See "Chronicles and Its Reshaping of Memories of Monarchic Period Prophets" in this volume, pp. 407–27.

28 Yairah Amit, among others, maintains that in Chronicles, "a king, a Levite or any other person, functions as prophet when he utters prophetic statements in the Chronistic sermonizing style," Y. Amit, "The Role of Prophecy and Prophets in the Chroniclers World," in *Prophets, Prophecy, and Prophetic Texts in Second Temple Judaism* (eds. M. H. Floyd and R. D. Haak; LHBOTS 427; London: T&T Clark, 2006), 80–101, here 89. The "Chronistic sermonizing style" to which she refers is the style of the "Levitical sermon" as discussed in G. von Rad, "The Levitical Sermon in I and II Chronicles," in *The Problem of the Hexateuch and Other Essays* (Edinburgh: Oliver & Boyd, 1966), 267–80. Contrast Amit's position with Schniedewind's, for whom prophets are *only* those that Chronicles explicitly designate as such (e.g., W. M. Schniedewind, "Prophets and Prophecy in the Books of Chronicles," in *The Chronicler as Historian* [eds. M. P. Graham, K. G. Hoglund, and S. McKenzie; JSOTSup 238; Sheffield: Sheffield Academic Press, 1997], 204–24, here 214). Suffice it to say that Chronicles reflects and shapes a conceptual field populated by both "prophets" and prophetic characters who deliver prophecies, even if they are not *explicitly* called prophets. This shared conceptual field strongly associates one image with the other. On these matters, see "Chronicles and Its Reshaping of Memories" in this volume, pp. 407–27.

29 See my previous "Prophets and Prophecy in the Compositional and Redactional Notes."

30 On prophecy in Judges, see C. Levin, "Prophecy in the Book of Judges," paper presented at the 2002 Annual Meeting of the Society of Biblical Literature, November 23–26, 2002.

31 The memory "category" of singing prophetess includes Miriam and Deborah. But due to Hannah's song (1 Sam 2:1–10), her memory was at least partially "prophetized." Clearly within the book of Samuel, her song was presented as proleptic, and thus likely read as "prophetic"

over, it is worth noting that in Judg 5:1 the song is associated with both Deborah (the main character and the "prophet") and Barak the military leader, who partakes in a prophetic role (cf. Chronicles' characterization of some kings and military leaders as people who uttered prophetic speeches).[32]

The only other explicit reference to a נביא is in Judg 6:8–10, in which, significantly a "summary of history" along with the its lessons is communicated (and see Chronicles and see above).[33]

It may be noted also that in Judg 6:8–10 the role of the prophet is reminiscent of that of the מלאך יהוה of Judg 2:1–3, and reflects a social mindscape in which these two conceptual realms already partially overlap and partially "blend" with one another (see Isa 44:26; Hag 1:13; Mal 1:1; 2 Chr 36:15–16).

In addition, within the discourse of the Persian period, people upon whom רוח יהוה descended included not only judges but prophets (see Isa 61:1). The community was asked to remember Gideon as one who consulted the deity through a kind of trial to ascertain whether to wage war or not, an activity usually associated with prophecy (see 1 Kgs 22; cf. 2 Chr 18).

More importantly, the community was supposed to remember that, in the period of Judges of their shared memory, Jotham played a crucial role as speaker who made sense of the events described in the historical narrative (cf. 1 Sam 12; prophetic speeches in Chronicles). In addition, within the context of

---

from the perspective of a remembering community in late Persian Yehud and early Hellenistic Judah (see, e.g., v. 10). At a later time, Targum Jonathan made the implicit association of Hannah and her song with prophecy explicit. See Tg. 1 Sam 2:1: צליאת חנה ברוח נבואה ("And Hannah prayed in a prophetic spirit"; E. Van Staalduine-Sulman, *The Targum of Samuel* (Leiden: Brill, 2002], 204–5). On evidence for a characterization of Hannah as a prophetess in Septuagint traditions (e.g., L), see S. D. Walters, "Hannah and Anna: The Greek and Hebrew Texts of 1 Samuel 1," in *JBL* 107 (1988): 400 n. 24. On Hannah's partially prophetic characterization in 1 Sam 2, see J. W. Watts, *Psalm and Story: Inset Hymns in Hebrew Narrative* (JSOTSup 139; Sheffield: JSOT, 1992), 30–32.

32 See Amit, "Role of Prophecy," and "Chronicles and its Reshaping of Memories" in this volume, pp. 407–27.

33 The text of Judges preserved in 4QJudg[a] demonstrates the existence of a text of Judges in which Judg 6:11–13 immediately followed 6:2–6. It is possible that the note mentioned above was a late addition to the text. If this is the case, it would only demonstrate the discursive generative power of the considerations advanced in this essay. Certain approaches to memories of prophets existed that would tend to create explicit, particular memories like those expressed in these verses. On the possible text-critical issues, see J. C. Trebolle Barrera, "Textual Variants in 4QJudg[a] and the Textual and Editorial History of the Book of Judges," in *RevQ* 14 (1990): 229–45; and R. S. Hess, "The Dead Sea Scrolls and Higher Criticism of the Hebrew Bible: The Case of 4QJudg[a]," in *The Scrolls and the Scriptures: Qumran Fifty Years After* (eds. S. E. Porter and C. A. Evans; Sheffield: Sheffield Academic Press, 1997), 122–28.

a Persian-period remembering community, the core of Jotham's speech, namely the parable in Judg 9:8–15 was most likely construed as significant not only to its immediate context in the world portrayed in Judg 9, but also as a prophetic comment about future kings. This speech, oriented to the long-term future, is clearly at work in the prophetic characters in the PBC, and in Moses and Joshua. This case also attests to a tendency to construe a multi-temporality of prophetic words: Jotham clearly refers to Abimelech, but his words could apply to numerous other events.[34]

The most memorable prophet in the book of Samuel is Samuel himself, even though he is preceded by the איש אלהים of 1 Sam 2:27–36. A substantial study of the memory of Samuel in Yehud demands a separate research venue. A few observations about memories of him, however, suffice for the present purpose. He was among the individual prophets in Samuel–Kings with largest narrative space, and one with highest evaluation and mindshare (see not only the narratives about him in 1 Samuel, but also Jer 15:1; Ps 99:6). The tendency to remember such a great prophet of the past in ways reminiscent of Moses is at work here too, just like the tendency to shape him as a great figure, though still of less stature than Moses (cf. the case of Elijah, another individual prophet with much mindshare; see below).

Given the focus in this essay on general systemic trends and tendencies rather than on particular individual traits, it is worth stressing that Samuel is reminiscent of Moses–as is usually noticed[35]–but that, unlike Moses, he begins a long line of named individual prophets associated with the establishment of kings and royal dynasties.[36] This chain of prophets plays an important role for the Saul-David-Solomon transition, and for the basic narrative about the northern kingdom reflected in and remembered in Yehud on the basis of the book of

---

34 The concept of multitemporality of prophetic words is clearly at work in Chronicles. See Ben Zvi, "Who Knew What?"

35 See, for instance, A. Breytenbach, "Who Is Behind the Samuel Narrative?" in *Past, Present, Future: The Deuteronomistic History and the Prophets* (eds. J. C. de Moor and H. F. van Rooy; OTS 44; Leiden, Brill, 2000), 50–61.

36 Moses does not appoint kings, but he is a kingly figure himself, far more than Samuel. In fact, in the Hebrew Bible Moses is also characterized as a royal figure, one far more powerful than the deuteronomic king envisaged in Deut 17:14–20, as I discussed in "Exploring the Memory of Moses." On the royal image of Moses in the Hebrew Bible see Lierman, *New Testament Moses*, 79–89. Moses is clearly a royal figure in some later Second Temple texts, e.g., Philo, *De vita Mosis* 1:334 (see W. A. Meeks, *The Prophet-King: Moses Traditions and the Johannine Christology* [NovTSup 14; Leiden: Brill, 1967], 107–16), and later on in some rabbinic texts (see Exod Rab 40:2; 48:4; Num Rab 15:13; Midr. Tehillim Ps 1; b. Zebah. 102a).

Kings.³⁷ Conversely, a systemic preference for emphasizing this aspect within memories about monarchic prophets developed.³⁸ Given that the book of Kings and the memories it evoked were structured around kings, it is only to be expected that this chain of prophets should be given salience, and that eventually the rereading community should develop a mindshare commensurate with the narrative space given to the relevant prophetic characters in Samuel–Kings. It is also to be expected that it would cause a substantial decrease in the number of individualized prophets associated with Judah after Nathan, and certainly after Rehoboam, for neither the agreed-upon collective and comprehensive memory of the period nor its basic ideological discourse could have allowed for a story about a prophet of YHWH anointing a new dynasty in Judah instead of the Davidic/Solomonic one. This lack of individualized prophetic memories for monarchic Judah, with the salient exception of Isaiah,³⁹ characterizes the book of Kings. Of course, it was balanced by the PBC for the crucial late monarchic period (see below), and later in a less memorable, but from a temporal perspective far more comprehensive way by Chronicles.

Nathan, the most salient prophet in the second part of the book of Samuel and 1 Kgs 1, is, of course, a central member of the mentioned chain of prophets. But the Nathan of memory, like all larger characters, fulfills more than one memory role. To remember Nathan was to remember the temple and David. Yet it is also to remember the role of the prophet in leading David to recognize his past sin and in announcing his punishment. This is particularly relevant within the context of a Persian-period community. The latter likely saw a reflection of themselves in the suffering, weakened בן מות David, fully aware of having grievously sinned⁴⁰ and thoroughly humiliated, as he is characterized in the latter part of Samuel. This David stood typologically for "their" Israel. Nathan as a

---

37 The chain of violent replacements of leaders begins actually with the איש אלהים of 1 Sam 2:27–36. Yet this prophet, whose role was narratively and mnemonically necessary to allow for the rise of Samuel, did not depose a reigning king. This said that the presence of the crucial temporal term עַד־עוֹלָם in both 1 Sam 2:30 and 2 Sam 7:16 suggests that at some level 1 Sam 2:30 served as an interpretive note looking forward to the rest of the DHC and balancing other positions there. The issue is, regrettably, beyond the scope of this essay.
38 Note, for instance, how the image of Elijah suddenly departs from its comparative Mosaic framework in 1 Kgs 19:15b–16. On Moses and Elijah see below.
39 Significantly, even Jeremiah is not mentioned in Kings.
40 For a reading of the David of Samuel that develops, among others, a portrayal in which David's "consciousness of having sinned" plays an important role, see F. H. Polak, "David's Kingship–A Precarious Equilibrium," in *Politics and Theopolitics in the Bible and Postbiblical Literature* (eds. H. G. Reventlow, Y. Hoffman and B. Uffenheimer; JSOTSup 171; Sheffield: Sheffield Academic Press, 1994), 119–47.

site of memory embodied and reminded the community of the suffering, humiliated David of the present, and of the great temple of the future, and of the late monarchic period prophets of the PBC.

Since I have written elsewhere about prophets and prophecy in the book of Kings,[41] only a few observations are in order for present purposes. The first is that Kings reflects and contributes to the shaping of a general concept of the prophets of old as a group–to be distinguished from particular highly individual prophets–who are: (1) a faithful minority of servants of Yhwh who were likely to become an object of persecution if the ruling leader was sinful; (2) a group that was aware of Israel's history of misconduct that justified the extreme divine punishment against monarchic Israel, and that unsuccessfully tried to bring Israel to Yhwh; (3) a group that embodied a reminder of Israel's history of rejecting Yhwh and of disregarding the advise of Yhwh's servants; and (4) a group associated with transmission of Yhwh's teachings, standing at the earliest spot in the chain of transmission of these teachings and leading directly to the remembering community (see, explicitly 2 Kgs 17:13).[42] In other words, these "generic" prophets were clearly and explicitly Mosaic prophets.[43]

As for the strongly individualized prophets, the two most memorable prophets that populated the book were Elijah and Isaiah.[44] Not surprisingly both characters, or sites of memory, were encoded in other books in addition to Kings (see the book of Isaiah; Mal 3:23 [most ET. 4:5]; 2 Chr 21:12–15). Many stories contribute to the construction of Elijah and Elisha, but it is particularly noteworthy that Elijah's narrative, and thus his memory, was shaped so as to be reminiscent in many ways of that of Moses the prophet, while at the same time making sure that Elijah remains secondary to him.[45] The focus on remembering Isaiah and on his worthiness to be remembered, so strongly encoded in Kings, directly relates to the fact that he (along with Hezekiah) embodied the memory of the glorious deliverance of Jerusalem in 701 BCE that stood as a direct counterpoint to

---

[41] See Ben Zvi, "Generic Prophets"; idem, "Prophets and Prophecy in the Compositional and Redactional Notes."
[42] See Ben Zvi, "Generic Prophets."
[43] See ibid.
[44] As important as Elisha is, he remains the person who "poured water on the hands of Elihu" (2 Kgs 3:11) and secondary to his master. Note Mal 3:23 [most ET 4:5], which mentions Elijah not Elisha, and 2 Chr 21:12–15 of which, "theoretically," the sender should have been Elisha, but which was attributed to Elijah, most likely because he was more saliently in the mindshare of the community.
[45] For some comparisons between memories associated with Elijah and Moses see, for instance, J. T. Walsh, *1 Kings* (Berit Olam; Collegeville, Minn.: Liturgical Press, 1996), 284–89. The presence of a significant number of "parallels" has been widely acknowledged.

the catastrophe of 586 BCE This issue, as will be noted below, is central to the way in which the PBC organizes knowledge about the past and its prophetic voices.

But before turning to the PBC, another important aspect of the ways in which the DHC contributed to the shaping of social memory about prophets and prophecy demands attention. The memory world of the community could not have started with the catastrophe of 586 BCE, but had to go back to the remembered establishment of a *torah*-centered community in the days of Moses, the prophet who mirrored their ideological image of themselves as a *torah*-centered community It could not have concluded with the events of 586 or those narrated in 2 Kgs 25:27–30. To be sure, there were genre and discursive reasons to conclude the collection with the fall of the polity and its aftermath,[46] but the collection served as a tool to organize knowledge and shape a general social mindscape, including those involving prophecy and prophets. Although the DHC, like any historiographical collection, evoked memories of past prophets, it also generated tendencies towards the shaping of memories about prophetic characters in the pre-utopian future.[47] Reading the DHC suggested to the remembering community that these future personages, unlike many of the former prophets, would most likely not be involved in deposing and anointing Israelite kings, but would be Mosaic and absolutely necessary in the future as well. This is so because they are required to warn Israel and urge it to keep Yhwh's commandments and statutes, in accordance with all the *torah* that Yhwh commanded Israel and that was sent to Israel by the prophets, to paraphrase 2 Kgs 17:13. Within the underlying ideological discourse of the community, the prophets were associated with the divine teaching, and they were and necessary for its transmission.

---

[46] E.g., Kings being a book about, and structured around (Israelite) kings; the centrality of the catastrophe of 586 BCE within the discourse of the community, and its construction as a watershed, etc.

[47] Like most historiographical narratives, the DHC does not address the real utopian future. These matters are addressed by the PBC, and it is the latter that evokes many memories of utopian futures.

The PBC, Memories of Prophets, and Their Implications

Even if there is little explicit narrative in the prophetic books, the PBC contributed much to the creation of social memories, which were organized and remembered in narrative form.[48]

Narratively shaped social memories behave as all narratives do. They have beginnings and endings, and their plots are rarely uniform in terms of temporal density. They emphasize certain periods and deemphasize others. Since each prophetic book within the collection was meant to bring to the present a particular prophetic character of the past, it could not but structure time in terms of prophetic figures. Although this is an obvious genre requirement, it does something to the community to remember a past that is structured around prophetic characters, and it does tell something about the mindscape of the community that it developed a strong social preference for books about prophets of old rather than about other possible characters (e.g., priests, sages, or the like).

Unlike the DHC, the main narrative implied and communicated by the PBC, as a whole, begins with the crisis in the Assyrian period, mainly in terms of both a prefiguration of and a counterpoint to the catastrophe of 586 BCE (e.g., Micah, Hosea, Isaiah). The second period it draws attention to is set around that catastrophe, preceding and directly leading to it, and including its immediate aftermath (e.g., Zephaniah, Jeremiah, Ezekiel). The third main period with which prophetic characters were associated was that of the early restoration.

To be sure this does not mean that readers of these books had to imagine that there were no prophets before Amos or Hosea–in fact, they could not have done so–but it means that these books focused the readers' and rereaders' mindshare mainly on prophetic characters associated with these three periods. As such, they reflect a mnemonic narrative shaped around the catastrophe, explaining time and again its causes and the didactic lessons to be learned from it, and providing hope for the future.

The PBC shaped a social mnemonic narrative about the late monarchic past characterized by a guiding concept of decline and constant slide toward the catastrophe from the period of Hezekiah on. Significantly, there was no room in that narrative for Josiah as a salient, positive site of memory. In fact, it is particularly worth noting that the second main period did not begin with the time of Manasseh (which is fully ignored) but with that Josiah.[49] Even the glorious period of

---

48 As memories usually are. See above, n. 5.
49 See E. Ben Zvi, "Josiah and the Prophetic Books: Some Observations," in *Good Kings and Bad Kings* (ed. L. L. Grabbe; LHBOTS 393; EABS 5; London: T&T Clark, 2005), 47–64.

Isaiah and Hezekiah was seen as inexorably leading toward the destruction (Isa 39:1–8; this section directly leads the reader to Isa 40). Within this implied narrative about the past, the late monarchic prophets had to be imagined as: (a) aware of the incoming and justified catastrophe–after all, Yhwh had informed the prophets of the deity's plans for Israel (cf. Amos 3:7); (b) warning voices (both of this attribute and the previous one are consistent with a mindscape in which Yhwh is construed as a deity who warns before punishment); (c) on the whole unsuccessful in terms of their generation, since the catastrophe did happen; and (d) successful in the sense that their words as encoded in the relevant books, and they themselves, became important sites of social memory for the later community, which stood in both continuity and discontinuity with late monarchic Israel/Judah.

The latter point is worth elaborating. Of course, within this scheme late monarchic Israel/Judah had to be imagined as on the whole rejecting their prophets, so as to fulfill their role as sinners meriting the catastrophe that came to them (cf. Jer 35:15; Zech 1:4–6; cf. 7:12–14). This explicitly reflects and communicates a central feature of the collective memory of monarchic-period prophets: they voiced unsuccessful warnings to their own time and society (cf. also Jer 7:25; 25:4; 26:9; 35:15; 44:4).[50] Yet, because they were unsuccessful, they and their contemporaries became successful sites of memory for the remembering community in Yehud. In fact, memories of both the prophets of old and of those who rejected them were structured and didactically used to communicate what, within the story, the late monarchic prophets could not accomplish in their own generation. Thus, matters of continuity and discontinuity between the literati in Yehud and monarchic Israel/Judah were negotiated.

This narrative clearly reflected and reinforced the crucial role of the memory of the catastrophe and the related concept of exile and overcoming exile had in the discourse of Yehud. This is not surprising, given the general ideological discourse of the period and the numerous material reminders of the catastrophe that confronted Yehudites and especially Jerusalemites at the time, since the ruins of monarchic Judah that were all around them. It is also fully consistent with the very basic metanarrative directly evoked by the collection, namely, that late monarchic Israel sinned, was severely punished. But, loved by Yhwh, they will be led to an utopian future. In the meantime, there exists a measure of partial relief to Israel in the form of a Jerusalemite temple and community in Yehud.

---

50 See also, for later periods, Neh 9:30.

Yet it is worth stressing that the implied narrative and the underlying systemic preferences that led to the above-mentioned temporal mindshare within the collection of prophetic books, and the organization of memories of the past in terms of individual prophetic characters, as powerful and significant as they were to the community, had to be, and were, placed on proportion within the PBC itself because of other features within their *Sitz im Diskurs*. In other words, demands that were implied in the discursive logic of the community and the "rules" of social memory called for and required that the above-mentioned features be balanced.

As central as a catastrophe may have been in the collective memory of a particular group, Israelite memory could not have its starting point in the catastrophe itself or in its surrounding era, just as Armenian and Jewish arrays of social memories cannot begin with their respective catastrophes in the last century, but must include a very substantial and substantive pre-catastrophe period. Similarly, remembering and explaining Israel's catastrophe in 586 BCE required a story about Israel that well preceded the events of 586 BCE, and those directly related to them in terms of the social memory of the period (e. g., Sennacherib's invasion and the non-destruction of Jerusalem in 701, and the rebuilding of the temple in the Persian period). Not only did the PBC require other memory-evoking texts within the community to balance itself, but even within the PBC there are crucial references to sites of memory situated well before the late monarchic period (e. g., Isa 63:11–12; Hos 2:15; 9:9–10; 10:9; 12:14; Mic 6:4; Mal 3:22 [most ET 4:4]).

In addition, and most importantly, the community was to remember the figure of Moses, the prophetic exemplar par excellence within its ideological discourse and social memory. The prophetic book of Moses (i. e., Deuteronomy) already called into question any implicit claims that the Prophets worthy of being remembered are only those in the PBC. In fact, it called into question the temporal boundaries of the PBC, since Deuteronomy was to some extent *also* a prophetic book.

Moreover, the figure of Moses clearly influenced the ways in which the prophetic characters in the PBC were construed and vice versa, creating a sense of connection among all these prophetic figures. This is true not only a more or less obvious cases such as Jeremiah and Ezekiel,[51] but also at a more basic level, given that within the social memory of the community, all worthy prophets, ex-

---

51 See H. McKeating, "Ezekiel the 'Prophet Like Moses'?" in *JSOT* 101 (1994): 7–109; C. R. Seitz, "The Prophet Moses and the Canonical Shape of Jeremiah," in *ZAW* 101 (1989): 3–27. For a brief survey of research (with bibliography) on the potential link between the figures of Jeremiah and Moses, see M. Roncace, *Jeremiah, Zedekiah, and the Fall of Jerusalem: A Study of Prophetic Narrative* (LHBOTS 423; London: T&T Clark, 2005), 20.

plicitly or implicitly, called Israel to follow Yhwh's Mosaic teachings, and they therefore had to be construed as Mosaic as well.[52] Within the discourse of the community, reading prophetic books was remembering to follow these teachings, as is stated explicitly in Mal 3:22 [most ET. 4:4] and implicitly elsewhere. This interrelation within the collective memory of the community between Moses, the prophetic exemplar, and the later Mosaic prophets is explicitly reflected and encoded in Deuteronomy, which was presented to the community as *also* the prophetic book of Moses, and thus as expanding and breaking the temporal constraints of the PBC.[53]

The discursive necessity both to keep a relatively narrow temporal focus in the PBC while at the same time expanding the temporal focus toward the past probably generated a tendency toward potential time fuzziness, in which sites of memory embody at least potential temporal slippage. For instance, the book of Obadiah might have evoked a reading of the book in which the prophetic character was imagined in a way informed by 1 Kgs 18.[54] The book of Jonah almost certainly asked its primary and intended readerships to imagine the prophetic character in a way informed by 2 Kgs 14:25–27, but not always or necessarily so,[55] and thus contributed to the development of multiple images of the prophet informing each other and a general sense of fuzziness that was, not incidentally, consistent with one of the basic communicative messages of the book, namely that there are serious and systemic limits to the literati's ability to construe "secure" knowledge from authoritative texts, even though this is their role in society. A book like Joel may be read against multiple temporal backgrounds.

But even more important than balancing the message of the collection by selecting memories of the past was the balancing of the past with images of the future. Remembering a past in which Yhwh announced Israel's future utopias in the midst of, and against the background of, a particularly sinful Israel was especially significant because it shaped the fundamental relationship between Yhwh and Israel as unconditional, and thus provided unconditional

---

[52] See "Exploring The Memory of Moses" in this volume, pp. 199–231.
[53] It goes without saying that temporal relations shaped in a memoryscape belong to this memoryscape. To illustrate, whereas a particular representation/social memory of President Lincoln may be historically later than one of President Obama, from the perspective of the remembering community, their remembered President Lincoln always precedes their remembered President Obama.
[54] See E. Ben Zvi, *A Historical-Critical Study of The Book of Obadiah* (BZAW 242; Berlin: De Gruyter, 1996).
[55] See E. Ben Zvi, *Signs of Jonah: Reading and Rereading in Ancient Yehud* (JSOTSup 367;: Sheffield: Sheffield Academic Press, 2003), 40–64.

hope. Therefore, to remember such a terrible past was also to remember the future, that is the utopian future. The PBC is at the very same time focused on a relatively narrow past and exuberantly, far more than any other ancient Israelite collection, enmeshed in the future.[56]

Most significantly for the present purposes of understanding the conceptualization of prophets and prophecy, whereas the prophets evoked by the PBC served as central sites of memory in the pastscape of the remembering community, the very same books asked them to imagine and remember a future devoid such characters. Memories of prophets structured and organized the past, but memories of future prophets played no role in utopia.

This was not a minor matter. It went well beyond matters of balancing continuity and discontinuity between past and future Israel. It directly relates to core features of the community's conceptualization of prophets and prophecy, as temporary features, historically contingent institutions necessary at particular times, but not others.

Some of the reasons for the absence of prophets in utopia are obvious, such as the following: (1) voices warning Israel were not imagined as part of utopia; (2) since the prophecies of the monarchic prophets about a utopian future were imagined as fulfilled, then there would be no need for new prophecies; moreover, (3) prophecies about utopia were remembered as closely associated with periods constructed as sinful.

But there is more. Other factors have more to do with the generative logic of utopian future. For instance, prophets were intermediaries, but when utopia was imagined and remembered in terms of a successful marriage between YHWH and Israel (e.g., Hos 2), there was no possible role for intermediaries between husband and wife. In these instances, the intellectual discourse of the community required that divine gifts be endowed to Israel so as to allow her to become a faithful wife. These gifts would perform the job that the prophets of old could not. They would turn Israel into a necessarily faithful wife (Hos 2:21–22). A similar generative logic, though without the marital imagery, was at work when Israel was imagined as being divinely endowed with a new heart, unable to sin (e.g., Jer 31:31–34; 32:38–41; Ezek 11:19–20; 36:25–28), or living in a radically reshaped, idyllic world (e.g., Isa 11; 65:17). In none of these cases could there be any significant role for prophets like those populating the PBC. The authorities that commanded the mindshare of the future remembering community were

---

[56] It is precisely this close association of memories of the tragic past and the utopian future that provided significance to both from the perspective of the remembering community.

king Yhwh (e. g., Isa 40–66;⁵⁷ Jer 50:4–5, 19–20; Hos 2:18–22; 14:6–9;⁵⁸ Obadiah; Zeph 3), at times a highly elevated Davidic king, who did not look like any previous king in either the PBC or the DHC⁵⁹ and, very rarely, judge figures (see Obad 19–21; cf. Neh 9:27).⁶⁰ Prophets were conspicuous for their absence.

What about the prophetic books? Were they also imagined as temporary, or as historically contingent institutions or sites of memory meant to play no significant role in the future? Certainly, a utopian future without conspicuous prophets was one in which new prophetic books would not be written. But what about those that were so central to the present community? Texts such as Jer 31:31–34 may suggest that there might be no need for them.

Yet even the very activity of remembering and imaginatively experiencing these periods was grounded upon reading prophetic books. Prophetic books were implicitly present in the pre-utopian, worldly future that looked not much different from the present of the remembering community, and in which, certainly, prophetic memories played a major role. Significantly, even within the PBC, these memories might refer to characters whose memories were encoded primarily outside the PBC (e. g., Moses and Elijah, as in Mal 3:22 [most ET 4:4]). A process of setting memories of past and future, multiple collections, and roles of prophecy is at work here as well.⁶¹

---

57 See H. G. M. Williamson, "The Messianic Texts in Isa 1–39", in *King and Messiah in Israel and the Ancient Near East: Proceedings of the Oxford Old Testament Seminar* (ed. J. Day; JSOTSup 270; Sheffield: Sheffield Academic Press, 1998), 238–70, here 239.
58 See E. Ben Zvi, *Hosea* (FOTL 21a.1; Grand Rapids: Eerdmans, 2005), 307–8; and note that the Targum felt the necessity to add an explicit note about a messianic king in v. 8 ("they shall dwell in the shade of the Anointed One").
59 For memories of a future David see, e.g., Isa 9:5–6; 11:1–9; Jer 23:5–6; 30:8–11; 33:14–26; Ezek 34:23–30; 37:1–28; Hos 3:5; Amos 9:11–15; Mic 5:1; cf. Zech 9:9–10). Very often the future David and the circumstances of his reign are portrayed as highly elevated (e.g., Isa 9:5–7; 11:1–9; Hos 3:5). Most significantly, the memories of this future are far different from the memories of the reign of David (or Solomon) reflected in the books of Samuel, Kings, or even Chronicles, which in its own way lionizes the past David (and Solomon).
60 See Ben Zvi, *Obadiah*, 197–229 (228). See also P. R. Raabe. *Obadiah* (AB 24D; New York: Doubleday, 1996), 255–73, here 269; cf. J. Renkema, *Obadiah* (HCOT; Leuven: Peeters, 2003), 215–19; and J. Barton, *Joel and Obadiah: A Commentary* (OTL; Louisville: Westminster John Knox, 2001), 157. It is worth noting that even in a text such as Isa 19:20, in which the portrayed world clearly evokes images of the exodus, the prophetic Moses is replaced by a מושיע.
61 Much more can be written about "memories of prophets" in the PBC. After all, the entire collection is about creating such memories. This said, the selected observations advanced here suffice for the argument advanced in this particular essay. See below.

A Few Final Considerations

Explorations may raise significant issues and point at lines for future research. The present study is just an exploration, as befits the scope of a chapter in a collected essays volume, but it brings up substantial issues. For instance, it not only indicates that the DHC and the PBC shaped prophetic memories in Yehud, but also points at the multiple, closely intertwined ways in which their roles as prophetic memories and memory shapers were fulfilled. The PBC shaped prophetic memories, but it could not have done so or emerged in the present form within a community in which the DHC, or some similar large historiographical, memory-evoking narrative, were absent. This is true not only at the basic level of shaping an image or a monarchic past to provide a mnemonic background for the prophetic characters and statements set in the books included in the PBC—which is obvious—but also at a deeper discursive level, because the balancing role of the historical narrative allowed for the development of a more temporally concentrated corpus of prophetic books. A community without the DHC or any similar narrative would have been a community in which the PBC would have never emerged.

Yet both collections balanced and informed each other. The PBC provided the most memorable examples of the late monarchic warning: unheeded prophets that the DHC called for. Both collections shared basic ideological tenets and central memory structures and sites of memory. Among these, one may mention the importance of the catastrophe, the hope for a new beginning after the catastrophe, a similar sense of causality in history similar constructions of the character of YHWH, the centrality of *torah* and Moses, the necessity (in the pre-utopian period) of Mosaic, or torahic, prophets, the potential multitemporality of prophetic utterances (i.e., their words' relation to the circumstances in which they were reportedly uttered, but also potentially to other circumstances in both the future and the past, fulfilled multiple times), and a certain preference for fuzziness about boundaries concerning collections, prophecy, prophetic characters, and even between *torah* and דבר יהוה (cf. Isa 2:3; Mic 4:2; and note the multiple roles of Deuteronomy as a book of legislation, a prophetic book, and a historiographical book as well). Coming from differing perspectives and literary genres, these two collections mutually reinforced their central messages and shaped a memory of prophetic figures and prophecies that was supportive of them. Moreover, it shaped together a conceptual realm for prophetic figures and prophecies within the shared social mindscape of the remembering community.

At the same time, each collection made some particular contributions to the shaping of the comprehensive memory of the remembering community concerning the prophets of old, going beyond patterns of temporal density or tendencies emerging from the highly individualized characters of the various prophets appearing in these collections. In fact, some of these particular contributions touched on central aspects of what was evoked by terms and concepts such as prophetic character or prophecy.

To illustrate, it is easier to notice in the DHC trends toward prophetizing characters and toward providing prophetic figures with many of the attributes that become explicitly and saliently associated with prophetic characters in Chronicles (see above). But one is to take into account that both the DHC and Chronicles are historical narratives, unlike the PBC.

More importantly although the prophets of the prophetic books may address worldly matters directly relevant to the people populating the world in which the books and the prophetic characters were set, much of their message was focused in the far future and the hope that remembering this future provided to the present community. To be sure, these features set the prophets who were remembered through the reading of the prophetic books, and the latter to some extent, in contradistinction with many of the memories evoked by the DHC concerning monarchic period prophets and their messages. Of course, it does not follow from this observation that there did not exist a socially shared mindscape within the Persian period community in which both collections were read and reread. First, the DHC is a historiographical work, and as such has clear genre constraints in terms of its ability to ask its readers to experience and remember a future. Moreover, the main prophetic character in the DHC, Moses, was remembered as actually foreseeing and teaching (along with Joshua) a far future, well beyond the horizon of his time. The entire DHC may in fact be seen as a detailed elaboration of the fulfillment of Deut 30:1; 31:26–29. This would suggest that, from the perspective of the readers of Joshua–Kings, the subsequent chapter in their history is pregnant with the fulfillment of Deut 30:2–10.

One may mention also that, unlike the PBC, the DHC does not bring up memories of a future without prophets and without need for them. As such, it does not raise a concept of prophetic characters and books as temporary, contingent features that while absolutely necessary in the pre-utopian period have no role in the utopian. Yet historiographical narratives, unlike prophetic books, were not supposed to focus on the far future. Neither, for the most part, could their prophets do so. From the perspective of the remembering community, each collection made its contribution to the shaping of social memory. Each contribution was understood simultaneously in terms of the literary genre in which it was written and in terms of the larger *Sitz im Diskurs* in which it was read. An awareness of both interpretive lenses contributed to the significance given to the memories of the prophetic figures and books that the collections evoked among the Persian period literati, and allowed for the construction of a basic, shared conceptual range for what was prophetic within their intellectual discourse.

The Yehudite Collection of Prophetic Books and Imperial Contexts: Some Observations*

I Introduction

The proper starting point for advancing any observations on a topic such as "the Yehudite Collection of Prophetic Books and Imperial Contexts" is an explicit statement of what is meant by the relevant key terms. By "the Yehudite Collection of Prophetic Books" I do *not* refer to a collection consisting only of Haggai, Zechariah (or some proposed Haggai-Zechariah corpus, or Zech 1–8) and Malachi; *nor* do I refer to a collection including these books and sections from Isaiah (esp. Isa 14–27 and Isa 56–66), some "additions" to other prophetic books (esp. Jeremiah and Ezekiel) and perhaps Jonah and Joel.[1] Instead I refer to the collection of prophetic books that likely existed and was read and reread in the Late Persian (or the early Hellenistic) period. This collection, as well as *most* of the ancient Israelite books that eventually ended up in the Hebrew Bible, emerged, at least in something close to their present form, among the *literati* of a small community in a small and marginal province within a large empire.[2] It is reasonable to assume that the compositional versions of the present fifteen prophetic books (Isaiah-Malachi) constitute a corpus that is representative of the contents of that collection and may be used as such.[3]

---

* First published in *Divination, Politics and Ancient Near Eastern Empires* (eds. Jonathan Stökl and Alan Lenzi; ANEM/MACO 7; Atlanta: Society of Biblical Literature, 2014), 145–69.
1 As commonly done; cf., among many others, L. L. Grabbe, *A History of the Jews and Judaism in the Second Temple Period, Volume 1. Yehud: A History of the Persian Province of Judah* (LSTS 47; London/New York: T&T Clark, 2004), 85–97.
2 On the marginal importance of Yehud for the Achaemenid empire, see, for instance, P. Briant, "Histoire impériale et histoire régionale: À propos de l'histoire de Juda dans l'Empire achéménide," in *Congress Volume: Oslo 1998* (eds. A. Lemaire and M. Sæbø; VTSup 80; Leiden: Brill, 2000), 235–45 (238 and passim). The lack of substantial growth in terms of settlements and population within the province throughout the Persian period also supports the marginality of Yehud in the Persian imperial eco-system.
3 I would like to stress that I am dealing with the collection of prophetic books as they were likely read and reread in this social context. This implies looking at them within their *Sitz im Diskurs* at the time. Moreover, I am looking at this collection of books as texts that reflected and shaped memory of past and future events. (Readers could remember events from the future as well as from the past; they vicariously experienced them through their readings and rereadings.) Since the collection is, among other things, one of past and future construing texts, it is reasonable to use approaches informed by memory studies as heuristic tools. The latter can help us to understand generative grammars that make certain memories more likely to be remem-

The choice to focus on the entire collection of prophetic books read and reread by the community, rather than on a relatively small set or potential subsection thereof, which are construed all on the basis of possible dates of authorship, is of crucial importance for the reconstruction of the social mindscape and intellectual history of the community in the relevant period.⁴ Communities shape and express their discursive world through their repertoire of texts as they are *read* by the community and as they shape and evoke social memories in the group.⁵ Texts are not read in a way un-informed by other texts within the repertoire of the community (thus, the importance of the *Sitz im Diskurs* for understanding how a text was actually read within it) nor according to exclusive and exclusivist

---

bered than others. In other words, they help us understand systemic tendencies that influenced what was remembered and the reasons that certain memories were shaped in the ways in which they were. It will be shown that imperial contexts played numerous roles in these processes. All these matters are critical for any historical reconstruction of the intellectual discourse of Yehud in the late Persian (or early Hellenistic) period. (It goes without saying that historians of the intellectual discourse of Yehud, as historians of any discourse for that matter or historians in general can only construct their own scholarly reconstruction of the relevant readers and their readings and rereadings. Of course, some reconstructions are better than others, according to historical standards. On my own take on historical methodology in general and in particular in relation to historical studies of ancient Israel see my "Clio Today and Ancient Israelite History: Some Thoughts and Observations at the Closing Session of the European Seminar for Historical Methodology," in *Even God Cannot Change the Past: Reflections on Seventeen Years of the European Seminar in Historical Methodology* (ed. Lester L. Grabbe; LHBOTS 663; London: T&T Clark, 2018), 20–49. See also the bibliography on historical methodology cited there.)

4 On "social mindscapes" see E. Zerubavel, *Social Mindscapes. An Invitation to Cognitive Sociology* (Cambridge: Harvard University Press, 1997); E. Zerubavel, *Time Maps: Collective Memory and the Social Shape of the Past* (Chicago: University of Chicago Press, 2003). The concept of "mindscape" precedes, of course, Zerubavel and goes back to M. Maruyama who used "the term 'mindscape' to mean a structure of reasoning, cognition, perception, conceptualization, design, planning, and decision making that may vary from one individual, profession, culture, or social group to another," M. Maruyama, "Mindscapes and Science Theories," in *Current Anthropology* 21 (1980): 589–99 (591). The study of social mindscapes involves, *inter alia*, that of accepted and shared ways of thinking in a group of generating ideas, questions and ways of addressing them, of providing meaning to 'data' and actually construing 'data' by focusing on particular matters and not others, of assigning significance to memories, stories, and actually shaping the production of memories according to particular patterns. Moreover, involves the study of how all these are deeply interconnected.

5 The stress on "historical authors" and "historical redactors" rather than on "community" and "communally read texts" is probably a remnant of a "great men," traditionally modernist historiographic tendency. Significantly, the "real" authors and characters with which the community interacted as they read and reread these books were those they construed to be as such, that is, a communal, implied author of the text. It is worth noting that it is very unlikely that they ever construed a lengthy series of implied redactors.

subsets constructed on the basis of their chronological claims or (supposed) dates of authorship.⁶ To use a metaphor, the various texts that exist within the repertoire of a community are comparable to "words" or "sentences" within a general language. To understand the language and its underlying "grammar," one cannot limit oneself to "new words." Significantly, even most of these "new words" were presented to and read by Yehudite *literati* as "old words" (e.g., Isa 14–27 and Isa 56–66). In any case, as they reread their texts, they kept construing the (implied) authors of these texts and its main characters.

The meaning of the other crucial term/concept, namely "empire," also demands some clarification. Certainly not all empires are the same but first, and most important, there is no agreement on what an empire is or was.⁷ Second,

---

6 If comparison with historical work on contemporary social groups, despite all its obvious problems and limitations, may still have an element of relevance, one may note that historians today would not attempt to reconstruct the general social mindscape of Canadians (or a particular subset of Canadians) in any region of the country in 2013, or in the last decade for that matter, by looking only at texts (in its most comprehensive meaning) "published" only in the relevant group and only in that region. The reason is simple: Canadians in any region are informed by, construe the meaning of, and "consume" (and thus construct) far more texts than those published in a single year or decade or only those in their region. Yehud is different and certainly did not participate in a world similar to ours, but still, it is very unlikely and contradicted by their very texts that they would construe their ideological world on the basis of texts that they read (and were asked to read) as written in the Persian period (e.g., Haggai, Zechariah, and Malachi) or on a set of sections that they would have to extract out of books that presented themselves from earlier periods (i.e., texts that *we today* tend to identify as "additions" and "supplements").
7 There is, indeed, a significant debate on how to define "empire." One of the most cited or referenced observation concerning the plethora of definitions is: They [numerous definitions of empire] share in common a view of empire as a territorially expansive and incorporative kind of state, involving relationships in which one state exercises control over other sociopolitical entities (e.g. states, chiefdoms, non-stratified societies), and of imperialism as the process of creating and maintaining empires. The diverse polities and communities that constitute an empire typically retain some degree of autonomy–in self- and centrally-defined cultural identity ..., and in some dimensions of political and economic decision making. Most authors also share a conception of various kinds of empires distinguished by differing degrees of political and/ or economic control, viewed either as discrete types or as variations along a continuum from weakly integrated to more highly centralized polities (C. M. Sinopoli, "The Archaeology of Empires," in *Annual Review of Anthropology* 23 [1994]: 159–80 [160]). For citations of or explicit references to this observation, see, for instance, E. R. M. Dusinberre, *Aspects of Empire in Achaemenid Sardis* (Cambridge: Cambridge University Press, 2003), 196; A. C. Hagedorn, "Local Law in an Imperial Context: The Role of *Torah* in the (Imagined) Persian Period," in *The Pentateuch as Torah: New Models for Understanding its Promulgation and Acceptance* (eds. G. N. Knoppers and B. M. Levinson; Winona Lake: Eisenbrauns, 2007), 57–76 (59–60). Sinopoli, "Archaeology of Empires," summarizes and discusses also the large variation among empires. Cf. M. Chavalas,

in the last decades there has been a considerable debate about models of ancient empires and perhaps even an interpretive shift in terms of which models are more appropriate for historical reconstructions of actual, historical empires (as opposed to its representation in some of the literature emanating from the center). To illustrate, there is considerable debate about how these empires actually worked and in particular on how they, once these became well-established, (tended to) administer their territories in particular. Did they (tend to) rule *over* a plethora of various local societies or also and perhaps even in the main *through* these societies, or more precisely, their elites. To what extent were ancient imperial polities run, in practical terms, by and according to "universal," "rational," royal policies and general "laws" enacted to fulfill particular imperial aims and alternatively, to what extent did ancient empires represent a polity based on processes of ongoing "negotiations" with a plethora of different local leaderships leading to outcomes that may or may not be similar to one another, even if always involving unequal partners?[8] Unsurprisingly, there is considerable debate about how to understand the referent of "the Achaemenid Empire" among contemporary historians.[9]

Moreover, just as "nations" are imagined communities, so were empires. Being part of the "Persian Empire"[10] was above all an act of social imagination

---

"The Age of Empires: 3100–900 BCE," in *A Companion to the Ancient Near East* (ed. D. C. Snell; Malden/Oxford: Blackwell, 2005), 34–47.

8 This chapter is clearly not the place to discuss at any length these general matters, even if the results of these discussions have an impact on reconstructions of how ancient empires, once established, were likely experienced by local populations and particularly local elites outside the main center of power. On these issues and with examples, see, for instance, M. M. Austin, "Hellenistic Kings, War and the Economy," *Classical Quarterly* 36 (1986): 450–66; J. G. Manning, *The Last Pharaohs: Egypt under the Ptolemies, 305–30 BC* (Princeton: Princeton University Press, 2010), 1–19; and J. Ma, *Antiochos III and the Cities of Western Asia Minor* (Oxford: Oxford University Press, 2000). A common critique to the "legalistic" model of ancient empire is that it is anachronistic. I thank Sylvie Honigman for her comments on these matters (personal note). Matters, of course, do not change in any significant way if instead of using the abstract term "empire" one uses terms such as the kingdom/household of "the great king, king of kings, king of countries containing all kinds of men [and women], king in this great earth far and wide," "one king for many, one lord for all" (see DE; i.e., Darius Inscription on Mount Elvend, and the "parallel" inscription of Xerxes [XE] on the same place, one next to the other; for an English translation of the text see A. Kuhrt, *The Persian Empire: A Corpus of Sources from the Achaemenid Period* [2 vols.; London: Routledge, 2007], 1:301, 304).

9 See, for instance, P. Briant, *From Cyrus to Alexander: A History of the Persian Empire* (Winona Lake: Eisenbrauns, 2002), 1.

10 As opposed to simply paying (forced) taxes and the like.

on the part of the community of Yehud.¹¹ As all acts of social imagination, this is an act of imagination of a particular historical community, and thus contingent on, for instance, the social mindscape of the community, its memories, its self-understanding, etc. Different groups in the Persian Empire likely imagined their being part of the Persian Empire in substantially different ways. Different groups developed different imperial experiences, even if they include some undisputable overlaps.

This said, references to "imperial context" and its importance for reconstructions of the historical matrix within which prophetic books–and other books within the authoritative repertoire of Yehud–emerged can be extremely helpful, provided that it is clear what, even if only heuristically, is meant by "imperial context." Here, and for pragmatic reasons only, I refer to (willing or unwilling) participation in *an unequal network of multiple ethnocultural groups that includes numerous contact areas* (e.g., cultural, economic, political, social), and *various dynamic processes affecting different aspects of the life of these groups* (e.g., acculturation and perceived resistance to acculturation, economic flows of goods and material–including taxes and trade, complex processes involving the build-up, maintenance and projection of permanent, seemingly overwhelming military power, etc.), which is *sustained by the presence of a central authority and its main socio-political and symbolic structures*.

To be sure, "imperial context" in that sense, and even "universal" imperial context, was nothing new to communities in the ancient southern Levant, but a long-standing reality in the area.¹² No one alive in Persian-period Yehud would have had anyone in his or her family, for generations, who lived outside some sort of "universal" imperial context. To imagine a world in this social context was, by default, to imagine one characterized by "imperial contexts," even if these contexts could be imagined in different ways.

As suggested above, living in an imperial context impacted multiple aspects of the life of the community. This contribution, however, is an attempt to explore *some* of the ways in which the imperial context of the community was intertwined with processes of social memory formation and re-formation, concerning past and future events that were evoked through the reading and rereading of the prophetic books. In other words, and from a slightly different but closely related

---

11 The same applies, of course, to any other community that existed "within" such an empire.
12 I am using the adjective "universal" here to distinguish "world hegemony" empires such as Assyria, Babylon (even if its center *formally* refused to imagine/present itself as a "universal" empire until the reign of Nabonidus), Persia, Alexander, Rome and the like from non-world hegemony empires (e.g., the Ptolemaic or Seleucid empires, or the socially remembered, imagined regional empire of David and Solomon).

perspective, it is about (discursive) "generative grammars" that created systems of preferences and dis-preferences that contributed much to the shaping of images and texts within the collection of prophetic books.

Certainly, the imperial experience of the Yehudite *literati* could not but strongly affect, directly and indirectly, in ways known or unbeknownst to them, their literary activities. The importance of this seemingly trivial observation for the social and intellectual history of Yehud becomes apparent once one takes into consideration that these activities were central to processes of identity formation and negotiation within the community, and that, at least from the *literati*'s perspective, this community was construed as centered around divine teachings contained in the very authoritative literature of the community that represents the outcome of their literary activities (both as writers/composers/editors and as readers and re-readers).

It is also hardly surprising that cultural trends, images and conceptual frames, some of which had a *longue durée* and which may be identified with "empire," were internalized and, through this process, re-signified by Yehudites; just as later Judahites certainly did so in the late Second-Temple period and most certainly earlier Judahites did as well, each according to their own imperial context. As historical cross-cultural studies indicate, ethnocultural groups that participate, willingly or unwillingly, in a "world" cultural and socio-political system tend, over time, to appropriate and internalize discourses, images, and concepts present in their "world" socio-cultural system, but that originated outside the inner group. As they do so, they re-signify the images and concepts so as to enhance their ability for social reproduction. In other words, what we may call hybridity regularly emerges in such cases.[13] It is worth noting, however, that these

---

[13] One may note that hybridity, in this sense, is not only a matter of Yehudite Israel. It is the hallmark of social discourses within later Jewish communities through time. A few examples suffice: the Hasmonean state and its discourse, Alexandrian Hellenistic Jewish intellectual discourses, medieval thinkers such as Ibn Ezra and Rambam, the emergence of Reform Judaism and neo-orthodox Judaism in the 19th century, discourses such as the neo-Kantian philosopher Hermann Cohen in late 19th- and early 20th-century Germany, the emergence of Jewish (political) nationalism in Eastern and Central Europe and Zionism in particular, Lubavitcher Messianism of the 20th century, and present-day American Jewish discourses (e. g., signs such as "Occupy Oakland not Palestine" that embody and communicate the [religious] discourse of groups such as those around the bi-monthly Tikkun and rabbi Michael Lerner, or the phenomenon of Orthodox Jewish rock [or folk] music). From this perspective, one might say that a history of Jewish thought or Judaic systems/discourses is or even can only be a history of multiple forms of hybridity through time and geographical and social space. But Jews were/are certainly not alone in this respect. In fact, cultural interactions, appropriations and re-significations are the norm, not the exception.

groups would rarely see and most rarely internalize their discourses as some form of "hybrid"; for them, it is their very own culture, and as such it serves to shape their sense of identity. Moreover, they would tend to see trajectories of continuity linking their present with their past. To be sure, issues of legitimization are involved in the matter, but also of self-identity.[14]

Of course, imperial centers are also influenced by, appropriate, and resignify substantial cultural aspects of ethnocultural groups outside the original imperial center and thus create their own forms of hybridity, which dynamically shape the center through intercultural interactions at the interface between different ethnocultural groups.[15]

As per its title, the point of this contribution is not to discuss hybridity in general, but particular manifestations in a very particular community. To do so, it has to deal with particular "generative grammars" that caused certain social memories of past and future empires to be preferred or dis-preferred within Persian Yehud, or at least among its *literati*.[16] This said, a final, general, cross-cultural consideration is in order. Social memories tend to be preferred or dis-preferred in a community according to the degree to which they are consistent, evoke or even serve to embody central meta-narratives or sections thereof that stand at the core of the collective memory, and that serve important roles in processes of formation of social identity within and for the community.

---

[14] One example, among the myriad of possible examples, is the Hasmonean presentation of their rule as in continuity with a "biblical" past; see 1 Macc 9:22; 16:23 and very extensively in 1 Macc 14:4–14.

[15] Cultural influences of the type mentioned above are all too present in the Achaemenid, Roman, Parthian and Mughal empires, to mention a few. Leaving aside "global" empires, Syrian/Levantine influence on New Kingdom Egypt is well known and so is Egyptian influence in the Ptolemaic empire, and, of course, there is Kassite Babylon. Although, since the first Aramean migration to Northern Mesopotamia, there was a process of Arameanization of Neo-Assyrian culture and language, which obviously preceded the expansion of the empire to control the Aramean heartland, there was strong Aramean influence in Assyria; the Assyrian empire became so influenced by the Arameans that it could be characterized as an Assyrian-Aramean empire. Similar tendencies are at work in recent empires. It is probably not perchance that current Indian historians are emphasizing not only how much the UK influenced India, but how much India has influenced the UK. To be sure, this is not necessarily the case in other (formerly) colonized groups, but still shows that cultural influences may go in multiple directions even today.

[16] To use a metaphor suggested to me by a colleague, who is an archaeologist and historian, my approach here is to focus on patterns that emerge from a view from above the surface, that is, from a helicopter overview of a site and its region, rather than focusing on a detailed (ground-perspective) study of each building or room at a particular site. Both approaches are necessary to advance knowledge on the site/issue, but they require different methodological approaches and raise different questions.

Turning now to the collection of prophetic books, even the most cursory analysis of the memory-scape shaped and evoked by the prophetic books shows that: (a) one city, Jerusalem, stands at the very center of this "memory-scape"; and (b) two imperial powers, Assyria and Babylon, dominate the mindshare of the community that read and reread these books and in the process shaped its memories of the community's *past*.[17] Observation (a) is the starting point for the next section of this essay and observation (b), for section three.

II On Jerusalem, Empires, and Kings in the Constructed and Remembered (Mainly) Present and Future of the Yehudite Literati

A comprehensive analysis of the multiple aspects associated with remembering Jerusalem in the Achaemenid period is well beyond the scope of this or any essay.[18] Given that this contribution is about "imperial contexts" and prophetic books, a more helpful starting point is to note that Jerusalem and its temple were, among many other things, local manifestations of Achaemenid imperial

---

[17] A word about mindshare in the context of studies of the intellectual world of the early second temple period is in order. The concept of mindshare is important in memory studies, because obviously not all memories show the same level of mindshare in a community. Some carry much weight and are activated much more than others. For instance, and close to our area, much more mindshare was allocated to the monarchic Temple than to any other building in Jerusalem within the social memory about the monarchic period that existed at least among the Jerusalem-centered *literati* of the late Persian period in Yehud; similarly, the mindshare of a site of memory like Moses, the lawgiver and the greatest prophet was far larger than Joshua, even if the latter conquered the land, within the world of knowledge of the community. Both observations teach us a lot about the discourse and the social mindscape of the *literati* in Yehud. In general, one may say that usually there is a degree of correlation between social mindscape and social mindshare. Social memories with relative large mindshare in a particular group, are most often those that fit well with the general social mindscape of the mnemonic community. I discussed the importance of the concept of social mindshare for studies of social memory in ancient Israel in my "Remembering the Prophets through the Reading and Rereading of a Collection of Written Prophetic Books in Yehud: Methodological Considerations and Explorations," in this volume, pp. 80–108.

[18] I explored *some* of these aspects in three separate essays: "Exploring Jerusalem as a Site of Memory in the Late Persian and Early Hellenistic Periods," in this volume, pp. 482–503, "Remembering pre-Israelite Jerusalem in late Persian Yehud: Mnemonic Preferences, Memories and Social Imagination," here pp. 504–26, and in "Jerusalem as a Mnemonic System and the Social Mindscape of Late Persian/Early Hellenistic Yehud/Judah," to be published in a future volume. A full exploration of these aspects would require several monographs.

will and control. The re-building of the temple and of Jerusalem and their rise to prominence in Yehud (over the previous Benjaminite center, which had been prominent during Neo-Babylonian times) were deeply involved in and associated with imperial power, allocations, and even with taxation, since temples served directly or indirectly also as tax centers and "sanctuaries" for goods.[19] Certainly, the shift of the capital of the province of Yehud to Jerusalem, and the likely construction of some type of wall around it,[20] required imperial decisions.[21] The situation that results stands then, among others, as a marker of Achaemenid power.

Leaving aside the highly debated proposal of a "Persian imperial authorization" of the Pentateuch,[22] the entire authoritative literature–including the collection of prophetic books–adopted by the Jerusalem-centered *literati*, was to some

---

19 Of course, this is not to deny that Ramat Raḥel did serve as an imperial taxation center, which is evident from the recent excavations led by O. Lipschits. On the Jerusalemite temple and taxation, see also J. Schaper, "The Jerusalem Temple as an Instrument of the Achaemenid Fiscal Administration," in *VT* 45 (1995): 528–39; idem, "The Temple Treasury Committee in the Times of Nehemiah and Ezra," in *VT* 47 (1997): 200–206. For an argument against the position that the Jerusalem Temple played a role in imperial taxation; see P. R. Bedford, "The Economic Role of the Jerusalem Temple in Achaemenid Judah: Comparative Perspectives," in *Shai le-Sara Japhet: Studies in the Bible, its Exegesis and its Language* (eds. M. Bar-Asher et al.; Jerusalem: Bialik Institute, 2007), 3*-20* (14*-20*). A serious discussion of Bedford's argument is beyond the scope of this contribution. It may be noticed that during Hellenistic times, the temple played, in one way or another, an important role in taxation see, for instance, "the tribute and taxation demanded by the Seleukid kings from Judaea are often expressed in the sources as a lump sum of silver, to be provided by the high priest acting as tax collector" (G. G. Aperghis, "Jewish Subjects and Seleukid Kings: A Case Study of Economic Interaction," in *The Economies of Hellenistic Societies, Third to First Centuries BC* [eds. Z. H. Archibald, J. K. Davies, and V. Garielsen; Oxford/New York: Oxford University Press, 2011], 19–41, here 35). In any event, even if for the sake of the argument one were to accept Bedford's position concerning Achaemenid Yehud, there can be no doubt that ("rebuilt") Jerusalem would still be remembered as also an Achaemenid project.
20 On the (highly debated) matter of the walls of Jerusalem, see I. Finkelstein, I. Koch, and O. Lipschits, "The Mound on the Mount: A Possible Solution to the 'Problem with Jerusalem'," in *JHebS* 11 (2011): article 12 (which is freely available online at http://www.jhsonline.org/Articles/article_159.pdf) and the bibliography mentioned there. The essay appears under the same title in *Perspectives on Hebrew Scriptures VIII* (ed. E. Ben Zvi; Piscataway: Gorgias Press, 2012), 317–39.
21 Even if taken at the level of satrapy. Not everything in an empire has to go to the highest level of central administration.
22 On the matter, see, in particular, K. Schmid, "Persian Imperial Authorization as a Historical Problem and as a Biblical Construct: A Plea for Distinctions in the Current Debate," in *The Pentateuch as Torah: New Models for Understanding its Promulgation and Acceptance* (eds. G. N. Knoppers and B. M. Levinson; Winona Lake: Eisenbrauns, 2007), 23–38 and bibliography there. Cf. *Persia and Torah: The Theory of Imperial Authorization of the Pentateuch* (ed. J. W. Watts; SBLSymS 17; Atlanta: Society of Biblical Literature, 2001).

extent the outcome (and representation) of locations and institutions directly associated and representing, among other things, imperial power.

The association of *torah*, proper cult, the welfare and centrality of Jerusalem with imperial power (and control) is, as is well known, most explicit in Ezra-Nehemiah. The book is later than the Persian period, but it is difficult to assume that the underlying discursive "grammar" of the book evolved only and *ex nihilo* after the fall of the Persian empire. In addition, the book of Isaiah puts such a position to rest with the glorification of Cyrus for the sake of Israel and Jerusalem (see below). Also, one has to take into consideration that the Achaemenid empire was remembered as the worldly power that commanded the rebuilding of temple, enabled the restoration of the settlement in the land (see memories of "the return")[23] and of the city, and thus, indirectly, what emerged from them.[24]

Out of this background, a "generative grammar" of images and memories emerges, with a strong preference for constructing and remembering the Persian empire (in contradistinction to other universal empires of the past) in a very positive light. This "grammar" generates both active acts of imagination and substantial discursive omissions. This was, however, not the only "generative grammar" at work. Processes of formation of self-identity conducive to social

---

23 For the present purposes it is irrelevant that the land was historically not completely "empty" or that the "return" could not have involved massive migration to the "empty land." What is relevant is that the Persian empire was construed and remembered as the power that allowed the "return," and thus, "the return" was construed and remembered as (*inter alia*) a manifestation of the worldly power of Persia; even if the latter was construed, as expected, as ultimately stemming from YHWH's power). I discussed the matter of the *memory* of the return to the "empty land" elsewhere. See "Total Exile, Empty Land and the General Intellectual Discourse in Yehud," in this volume, pp. 559–611.
24 I want to stress that I am *not* maintaining that the community in Yehud was a colonial institution that forcefully colonized Judahites who remained in the land after the destruction of Jerusalem. In fact, elsewhere I argued against historical reconstructions of the Persian period based on claimed long-term conflict between returnees and remainees. See, for instance, "Total Exile"; and my earlier "Inclusion in and Exclusion from Israel as Conveyed by the Use of the Term 'Israel' in Postmonarchic Biblical Texts," in *The Pitcher is Broken: Memorial Essays for Gösta W. Ahlström* (eds. S. W. Holloway and L. K. Handy; JSOTSup 190; Sheffield: JSOT Press, 1995), 95–149. Similarly, I am *not* maintaining that ancient Israel (as understood in Yehud) was a (colonial) Persian invention. Persian activities may have facilitated the development of certain (theological, text-centered) ideas of Israel, but this is a far cry from invention. This (theological, text-centered) Israel was the "invention" of Jerusalem-centered Yehud, a province that existed, as any other, within an imperial system. Its discourse and the social/political conditions in which it evolved could not but reflect "imperial circumstances." To say that Israel was an invention of the Persian center is as absurd as stating that because the persecutions of Antiochus IV facilitated the development of late Second Temple discourses, Antiochus IV invented the latter.

reproduction required that Israel be imagined as the (adopted) "son" of its own deity, that Jerusalem and its temple be construed as the cosmic center and the place from which the divine instruction will come, and that Israel itself be (self-)imagined as a primary worldly agent, not a secondary (or lower) one. These considerations led to preferences to remember a future that goes well beyond the Persian empire and to the allocation of far more mindshare to these memories of the future than to those of re-foundation under the Persian empire.

All these general observations require further elaboration. To begin with, the lack of explicit criticism and above all lack of memories about any announcements of punishment/judgment against Persia by Yhwh in prophetic literature is, no doubt, a salient feature of the collection of prophetic books. It stands in sharp contrast with the treatment allocated to Assyria and Babylon (see section III) and to any country or people of any significance known to the remembering community, temporally located within the time-frame portrayed in the collection of prophetic books, *including* Israel and Judah.

At times, it has been suggested that little can be learned from this observation, beyond the perils for the community that arise from criticizing the ruling power, and the actual impossibility of such criticism. But several considerations argue against this position. First, although one should not disregard concrete perils that historical agents might have faced if they criticized the empire, from a systemic perspective, any strong emphasis on the *impossibility* of criticism is problematic. There are numerous cross-cultural examples of explicit and implicit acts of cultural resistance.[25] Moreover, the existence of a "public transcript" does not negate the possibility of a "hidden transcript/s." In addition, even if, during Achaemenid days, one were to grant that it was impossible for Yehudites to criticize in any way or form or to construe divine pronouncements that would involve the fall of the Persian Empire, even if in the far future, why would that be impossible during the early (or for that matter later) Hellenistic times?[26] These

---

[25] Historians of Judaism/s cannot but bring to mind the extreme case of *Toldot Yeshu*. This very polemical text was kept for centuries. For recent discussion, see *Toledot Yeshu ("The Life Story of Jesus") Revisited: A Princeton Conference* (eds. P. Schäfer, M. Meerson, and Y. Deutsch; TSAJ 143; Tübingen: Mohr Siebeck, 2011). Of course, *Toldot Yeshu* itself was an excellent case of (polemical) hybridity, as it appropriated Christian narratives and in polemical ways turned them upside-down. The same holds true for *Sefer Zerubavel*. See D. Biale, "Counter-History and Jewish Polemics Against Christianity: The *Sefer Toldot Yeshu* and the *Sefer Zerubavel*," in *Jewish Social Studies* 6 (1999): 130–45.

[26] One may add further: Should we imagine that the Persian center would consistently care about Yehudite prophecies about a distant future, or even care enough to read and reread prophetic books that existed only in Hebrew and could be read only by Yehudite *literati*? One has to

considerations indicate that the lack of memories of announcements of doom against Persia or negative characterizations of it was not only the result of imperial coercion. There existed in Yehud a strong preference to set the Persian empire aside from those of other nations (e.g., Babylon, Assyria) and glorify it, because by doing so the community was, within their own discourse, indirectly legitimizing and enhancing positive self-constructions of Jerusalem, its temple, Israel, and its Jerusalem centered divine instruction along with the authoritative literature that encoded it.

To be sure, a salient positive character is not created only through the lack of negative characterization, as remarkable as this may be in this particular context. To begin with, as I discussed elsewhere,[27] studies on social memory show that there exists a cross-cultural tendency to organize memory so as to coalesce around a few main symbolic figures/sites of memory; these are the "great heroes" of the past who draw the attention of the remembering community to their own (construed) personal figures and to what they had done, including institutions that they had established.[28] Since Cyrus served as the greatest and the most positive site of memory of a Persian in Yehud (and in Greece as well,[29] and perhaps in other ethnocultural groups at around this time), it is only expected that his figure would symbolically embody all Persians[30] and that he would be associated in Yehud's social memory with the beginning of the rebuilding process.[31] The re-builder of the Temple could not but be construed as a very positive

---

keep in mind that Yehud was a marginal, poor province which in reality could not revolt against Persian rule and that the Achaemenid empire was not a 20th-century totalitarian state.

27 "Exploring the Memory of Moses 'The Prophet' In Late Persian/Early Hellenistic Period Yehud/Judah," in this volume, pp. 199–231.

28 Although social memory is historically contingent, the mentioned processes tend to be comparable (though not identical) across different cultures and societies (though certainly not all). This is so because they relate to the ways in which social memory and social mindscapes are likely to be shaped. For comparative purposes, with processes in a very different society and time, but still focused on the importance of main figures for social memory, one may look at C. Kaplonski, *Truth, History and Politics in Mongolia: The Memory of Heroes* (London: Routledge, 2004), esp. 182–86.

29 See L. Mitchell, "Remembering Cyrus the Persian: Exploring Monarchy and Freedom in Classical Greece," in *Remembering Biblical Figures in the Late Persian and Early Hellenistic Periods: Social Memory and Imagination* (eds. D. V. Edelman and E. Ben Zvi; Oxford: Oxford University Press, 2013), 283–92.

30 See the contribution by Joseph Blenkinsopp to this volume and particularly his analysis of Isa 55:3–5 (cf. J. Goldingay, *The Message of Isaiah 40–55: A Literary-Theological Commentary* [London: T&T Clark, 2005], 549–50).

31 See Isa 44:28; 45:1–7, 12–13; 2 Chr 36:22; cf. Ezra 1; 4:3. Note also "[t]he expectation that the city devastated by the Babylonians will be restored by Cyrus is frequently expressed (45:13;

character.³² He was not of Israel, since he had to be Persian, but a mnemonic tendency to *partially* Davidize him is to be expected.³³ It is thus not the result of random chance that Cyrus is presented and remembered as Yhwh's shepherd and anointed,³⁴ or that both David and Cyrus (the "founder" and the "re-founder" of the temple, respectively) serve as sites of memory that embody their respective peoples.³⁵ One may add also explicit references to the elevated character of

---

49:14–18; 51:3)," as stated by J. Blenkinsopp, *Isaiah 40–55: A New Translation with Introduction and Commentary* (AB 19 A; New York: Doubleday, 2002), 247. If, for the sake of the argument, one were to grant Albertz's position that originally the Persian king in Isa 40:1–52:12 was Darius not Cyrus, that Cyrus eventually became "the king" would be most meaningful and, needless to say, consistent with the systemic preference for a memory that has Cyrus in that role. See R. Albertz, "Darius in Place of Cyrus: The First Edition of Deutero-Isaiah (Isaiah 40.1–52.12)," in *JSOT* 27 (2003): 371–83.

32 Central institutions in antiquity tended to develop social memories within which they were founded by great personages of the past, not by "nobodies" or "evil characters." It is not by chance that the temple in Jerusalem was associated with the figures of David and Solomon and that on the whole these characters tended to be lionized.

33 Note that Zerubabbel, the Israelite/Yehudite associated with building the temple, ends up being evoked as a Davidide in 1 Chr 3:19 and is elevated in Hag 2:21–22. Centuries later, other central figures were partially Davidized: Jesus, Hillel, and Rabbi Yehuda HaNasi (sometimes referred to as "Rabbi Judah the Prince"). In all these cases, the construction and the remembering of these figures as Davidides served important discursive and ideological functions in the relevant social groups. On general matters of social memory, mindscape, and socially construed genealogies, see E. Zerubavel, *Ancestors and Relatives: Genealogy, Identity, and Community* (Oxford: Oxford University Press, 2012).

34 See, for instance, Isa 44:28; 45:1; cf. 2 Sam 5:2 (// 1 Chr 11:2); 7:7 (// 1 Chr 17:6); Ps 78:71–72; 2 Sam 19:22; 23:1; 2 Chr 6:42.

35 David is the real "founder" of the temple in Chronicles. In Kings, the story is different as Solomon has a more important role. Given general, transcultural mnemonic tendencies, one would have expected a preference for a memory of David as both founder of the dynasty and founder of the temple, and particularly so since he is the "founder" of Israel's Jerusalem (i.e., his conqueror). The existence of a truncated expectation in Samuel-Kings went hand in hand with the need of a memorable story explaining why the expectation was truncated and, of course, removing any possible stain on David, at least concerning this matter. Chronicles goes further as it characterizes David as the "founder" (though not the actual "builder") of the temple and by communicating a close association of the temple with both David and Solomon, but there is already a strong echo of this in 2 Kgs 21:7. Moreover, one has to keep in mind that Chronicles and Samuel-Kings shaped together a single general mnemonic system in the late Persian/early Hellenistic period. The social memory of the community at the time was influenced by both, and its readings of one corpora could not but inform and be informed by readings of the other. I am currently completing an essay for a collected essays volume on this topic. In the meantime, and on converging lines between Chronicles and some voices in Samuel-Kings see my previous, "Are There Any Bridges Out There? How Wide Was the Conceptual Gap between the Deuteronomistic His-

Cyrus[36] and the implied central mnemonic narrative conveyed by the trajectory from Isaiah chapters 36–39 to chapters 40–48, i.e., from Hezekiah to Cyrus. All these contribute much to the construction of an important site of memory, namely, the foreign king who was worthy of being selected by Yhwh to initiate the rebuilding of city and temple.[37]

Against this background of the lionization of Cyrus, the most heuristically helpful question seems to be (at least to me) not whether one may find somewhere some underlying or implied criticism of Cyrus or the Persians in the prophetic or other books, or in general in the discourse of the period.[38] It is also not whether one may argue that Cyrus's image could have been somewhat downgraded because he was remembered among Yehudite *literati* as one whose mission was just for the sake of Israel, or whose success reflects the power of Yhwh, a deity whom he does not know (Isa 45:4). In fact, that is difficult to argue. His characterization as one who does not know Yhwh is basically a way to keep him Persian and, in fact, as a kind of embodiment of Persia.[39] None of the other observations about his characterization portray Cyrus in a negative light. The statement that he was chosen by Yhwh for the sake of Israel is not only to be expect-

---

tory and Chronicles?," in *Community Identity in Judean Historiography: Biblical and Comparative Perspectives* (eds. G. N. Knoppers and K. A. Ristau; Winona Lake: Eisenbrauns, 2009), 59–86.
36 See, for instance, Isa 44:(24–)28; 45:1–8, 12–13. Goldingay, *Message of Isaiah,* 253–300, describes all of Isa 44:24–45:25 as "the triumph of Cyrus." See also Cyrus's background presence in Isa 40–48, which is correctly stressed by Blenkinsopp (see his essay in this volume); cf. esp. Isa 48:12–15.
37 It is worth noting that I am focusing neither on the putative words of a prophet called Deutero-Isaiah nor on the world portrayed in these sections of the book of Isaiah, but on memories evoked by reading this book in late Persian (or early Hellenistic) Judah. The readership most likely imagined Cyrus as the beginning of the "reconstruction." That Cyrus was imagined in Judah as having a "warm spot" in his heart for Jerusalem and as Yhwh's victor, was not categorically different, from a social memory perspective, from the case of a later community imagining and remembering something very similar in relation to Alexander (see *Ant.* 11.325–39).
38 See the thoughtful contribution of E. S. Gruen, "Persia Through the Jewish Looking-Glass," in *Cultural Borrowings and Ethnic Appropriations in Antiquity* (ed. E. S. Gruen; Oriens et Occidens 8; Stuttgart: Franz Steiner, 2005), 90–104; and in an extended version, under the same title, in Jewish *Perspectives on Hellenistic Rulers* (eds. T. Rajak et al.; Hellenistic Culture and Society 50; Berkeley: University of California Press, 2007), 53–75.
39 Both in Greece's and Yehud's memory, Cyrus is always a *Persian* king. This said, Cyrus may be "elevated" within this discourse by texts that evoke a memory of him as similar to Israel/Jacob; see the image envelope in Isa 48:12–15 created by the use of forms from the root קרא, but notice also the presence of a difference as well. Note also the similarities and differences evoked by קְרָאתִיו in the book: Isa 48:15 (the caller is Yhwh, and the called is Cyrus) and Isa 51:2 (the caller is Yhwh, and the called is Abraham); and see also Isa 41:9; 42:6; 49:1 (the caller is Yhwh, and the called is the Servant/Israel).

ed, given that the text is written for and by Israel, but also would have been appreciated by the empire itself and its propaganda.[40] It is also an excellent example of appropriation and reshaping of imperial memories. Cyrus's success was turned, discursively, into Yhwh's and Israel's success. Such appropriations, needless to say, facilitated both adaptation to and participation in the imperial world and the kind of resistance to "foreign" ideology and even mindscape that allowed for inner group self-valorization and social reproduction.

From a heuristic perspective, it seems to me that the most helpful question for the purpose of understanding the discourse of the period is of a different kind: namely, given that he was so great, why is there relatively little about Cyrus in the prophetic literature (and in the general repertoire of authoritative texts in Yehud)?

To be sure, part of the answer is that the collection of prophetic books drew much of the attention and mindshare of the reading community to: (a) the catastrophe of 586 BCE (and thus also to its forerunners [the fall of Samaria] and counterparts [the deliverance of Jerusalem in 701 BCE]); and (b) the utopian future. Cyrus and the entire process of rebuilding the city and temple were thus sandwiched between the two and, according to the system of preferences governing social memory in Yehud, they were left with less social mindshare and textual space.

This answer, as correct as it is, raises an even more important underlying issue. Just as the existing second temple of the Persian period was construed as far less important in the broad scheme of things, and thus far less worthy of being "remembered" than the one of the past and the future utopian one that would replace it, so Cyrus was far less important than the future utopian king who would replace him (Yhwh, or in some versions, a highly elevated, more-than-human Davidide).[41] And so the future empire that would replace the Persian empire was much more important and worthy of being remembered than the Persian empire itself.

The last observation is particularly important for any study of the impact of "world" imperial circumstances in the production of the prophetic books collec-

---

40 Cf. the Cyrus Cylinder or the Verse Account of Nabonidus.
41 For memories of a future in which Davidides are absent see, for instance, those evoked by Isa 40–66; Jer 50:4–5, 19–20; Hos 2:18–22; 14:6–9; Obad; Zeph 3. For memories of a future with a Davidide, see, for instance, those evoked by Isa 9:5–6; 11:1–9; Jer 23:5–6; 30:8–11; 33:14–26; Ezek 34:23–30; 37:15–28; Hos 3:5; Amos 9:11–15; Mic 5:1. It is worth noting that this Davidide was already imagined as highly elevated and very different from any image of a monarchic David or Solomon that existed in the social memory of the community (see Isa 9:5–7; 11:1–9; Hos 3:5).

tion. A future world without a world-empire was probably beyond the imagination of the community and its ability to experience (virtually, of course) the future through their readings of (authoritative) future-constructing texts. This being so, the logic of the situation and of the discourse in Yehud led to a clear outcome: the "good" empire must be superseded by a utopian empire, YHWH's empire, with its capital in Jerusalem.

Within the logic of the discourse of Yehud, a world permanently run by YHWH through kings and empires other than Israel or its king, with a marginal Jerusalem, was inherently unstable, even if these kings (and, indirectly, YHWH) ran it for the sake of Israel (Isa 45:5). An orderly and stable world was conceived as one that could only be grounded on "true" not illusory knowledge. But in the Achaemenid imperial world, even the great Cyrus, YHWH's anointed, does not know YHWH, does not know the reason for his successes or the "real" purpose of his endeavors. Cyrus's own knowledge is illusory and, in fact, mis-knowledge. He is certainly not alone, however. YHWH is the creator and ruler of the world, but this deity is mostly unknown throughout the earthly world. Jerusalem is the city truly at the center of the world, but it is a very small village unknown to most inhabitants of the "world," and thus it cannot fully fulfill its cosmic roles. This Jerusalem of the Persian empire is not, in the earthly world, a universal source of wisdom/*torah* (e.g., Isa 2:3; Mic 4:2). It is not light or the place of light to the world (Isa 60:1–3, 19–20). Thus, the Persian imperial world is one in which the "truth" was a "secret" known only to those in Yehud who are able to read the authoritative books or have others who read these books to them. This secret is not manifested in the world; in fact, it is hidden by a world that actually looks like a book of mis-knowledge. Such a world cannot stand forever, even if Cyrus is its earthly king.

Such a world is explicitly contrary to YHWH's wishes (see, for instance, Isa 45:5–7). Even when this world was imagined as peaceful and seemingly stable, it was remembered as one doomed to fall (see Zech 1:8–17) and to be replaced.

The alternative, future, yet continuously remembered empire of Israel/YHWH (see below) was, of course, not a minor site of memory with marginal social mindshare. Not only was it evoked by numerous texts in prophetic literature (e.g., Isa 2:2–4; 42:1, 6; 45:14; 49:7, 23; 51:4–5; 56:6–7; 60:9; Mic 4:1–3; Zeph 2:11; Hag 2:7–8; Zech 8:20–22; 9:10), but also it was indispensable for developing the concept of what a prophetic book was supposed to be. It was the ultimate end-point of the plot in the main ("historical") meta-narrative of ancient Israel, and a source of hope for the community.

These memories of the future facilitated accommodation to present imperial circumstances, in practical terms, by resisting hegemonic claims on what the community considered of most importance from their own perspective. It rejected any aspect of imperial hegemonic narratives and world constructions that contradicted the self-understanding of the Yehudite community. These memories of the future, so commonly evoked by prophetic books, produced alternative narratives that allowed the community to hold fast to its sense of self and thus its social reproduction over time.

Since these memories of the future empire were such core features of Yehud's social mindscape (or at least that of its *literati* and likely its elite), their explicit presence could not have been restricted to prophetic texts. One would anticipate that they would appear in other types of texts, within which memories of the future could be encoded, and this is actually the case (e.g., Ps 22:30; 68:30; 72:8–10; 96:7–10; 97:6–7).

The *literati* in Yehud, and those who were influenced by them, imagined a future empire, but how did they imagine it?[42] Certainly, and despite reference to "David," it was not in terms of their (social) memories of the Davidic/Solomonic empire, despite the general tendency in the ancient Near East towards restorationist images. For Yehud, the imagined future would not be like the imagined (glorious) past. Several reasons account for this choice: for one, within their main historical narrative, this "glorious" past led to catastrophe. Moreover, the Davidic/Solomonic empire was not construed as a "world" or universal empire.[43] Yet, Yʜᴡʜ was a universal "king" and thus his kingdom had to be construed as "universal."

Many of the basic imperial topoi that were used to imagine and remember this future empire resembled the image of the actual empire of the time, and through it, those of previous empires.[44] A few examples will suffice to make the point.

Images such as those of peoples flowing to the new imperial center (Zion) and bringing their gifts to Zion and to the king, gifts of treasures from various peoples or human resources gathered to and for the sake of the new imperial

---

[42] I have previously discussed some features of this ideal future or sets of related futures. In the following paragraphs I will revisit and further develop some highlights of my previous discussion that are particularly relevant to the discussion here. See "On Social Memory and Identity Formation in Late Persian Yehud: A Historian's Viewpoint with a Focus on Prophetic Literature, Chronicles, and the Dtr. Historical Collection" in this volume, pp. 28–79.

[43] Texts such as 1 Kgs 5:9–14 and 1 Kgs 10 shape a larger horizon to Solomon's fame and cultural influence, but his empire was not imagined/construed as a world/universal empire.

[44] As is well-known, the Achaemenid empire used and reshaped ideological motifs that go back to the Neo-Assyrian empire.

city,⁴⁵ do involve adaptations and reversals of the common imperial image of the nations paying homage to the king of kings, despite the substantial variety among them.⁴⁶ The construction of Jerusalem/Zion as the imperial city at the center of the world, is another case of appropriation and reversal of common imperial images, with a very *longue durée*. The royal garden in which the king is supposed to spend time is now in future Jerusalem (and the Temple) and evokes Eden.⁴⁷ Certainly, Yhwh was imagined as "the great king, king of kings, king of countries containing all kinds of men, king of this earth far and wide."⁴⁸ It is Israel, not the Assyrian king, who is remembered as "a light to the nations" (Isa 42:6). The empire, once it is established, is orderly and without conflict; in fact, it is one in which "history" reaches its end, as the world becomes intrinsically stable (and peaceful). This is again a (modified) version of the image that the Achaemenid empire tried to project.

From a heuristic perspective, it is perhaps more interesting to note the ways in which this new empire might have been imagined as structurally different from existing empires or empires of the past. One obvious difference is that, at the center of the Persian empire, there were the separate figures of the king and of Ahura Mazda.⁴⁹ There was, however, a very strong current in Yehudite discourse (and in its prophetic books) that remembered a future empire at whose center the traditional kingly and divine figures would collapse into one; Yhwh alone is king, in that future empire.

Significantly, often Israel as a whole is also imagined with royal attributes.⁵⁰ In which way might this "royal" role for Israel as a whole be implemented in the

---

45 See, for instance, Isa 2:2–4; 45:14; 55:3–5; 60:10–16; Jer 3:17; Mic 4:1–4; Hag 2:7–8; Zech 10:20–22.
46 See, e. g., DNa, DE, DZc. For an English translation of DNa, the inscription in the upper registrar in his tomb in Naqš-i Rustam, see A. Kuhrt, *The Persian Empire*, 2:502–3; for one of DZc, the inscription of Darius I on a stela set up at Kabret in Egypt, see A. Kuhrt, *The Persian Empire*, 2:486; for DE, the inscription of Darius on Mt. Elvend; see A. Kuhrt, *The Persian Empire*, 1:301, 304. The latter is almost identical to the inscription of Xerxes (XE) that stands next to it.
47 See Xenophon, *Oec.* 4.13 (cited in A. Kuhrt, *The Persian Empire*, 2:510); and on Jerusalem, see T. Stordalen, "Heaven on Earth – Or Not? Jerusalem as Eden in Biblical Literature," in *Beyond Eden: The Biblical Story of Paradise (Genesis 2–3) and Its Reception History* (eds. K. Schmid and C. Riedweg; FAT II/34; Tübingen: Mohr Siebeck, 2008), 28–57, (36–40); and "Exploring Jerusalem as a Site of Memory" in this volume, pp. 482–503.
48 On this motif, see M. Liverani, "Memorandum on the Approach to Historiographic Texts," in *Or* 42 (1973): 178–94 (189–91).
49 And those of the king and of Assur and of Marduk, in the Neo-Assyrian and Neo-Babylonian empires, respectively.
50 See, for instance Isa 55:3–5; note the characterization of Israel as the "son" of the deity, e. g. Hos 11:1. Israel may take the traditional slot of a king (e. g., Isa 45:14; and outside prophetic lit-

new Empire, since it could not be, in the traditional sense, "king"? And what does it say about how "kingly-ness" is construed in the discourse of the *literati* in Yehud? I will return to this question, but at this point it is worth noting that, at times when non-YHWH royal figures are imagined, they are imagined in terms quite opposite to those associated with worldly kings (e.g., the servant of YHWH in Isa 40–55; the king of Zech 9:9–10). There is here a clear tendency to imagine an imperial world different from any present or even elevated form of the present imperial world.

For instance, at times, the community imagined and remembered dramatic military confrontations in the period leading to the establishment of the empire,[51] but unlike the cases of present and past empires, no human hero/king took a central role as the successful warrior (and most masculine male) who established the empire through his military might (with the help of the gods, of course). Instead the successful warrior is YHWH.

Significantly, most great kings set their path to establishing their empire by waging offensive wars, not by defending their capital,[52] yet YHWH is often imagined in these terms. This is not an empire based on any heroic actions by humans, but by YHWH and his actions. The social memories associated with the foundation of YHWH's empire were very different from those associated with the foundation of the Persian empire (or any other empire).

At the center of YHWH's (future) empire stands Jerusalem, not as the city of a human king, but as YHWH's city, and as the city of the temple. People will flow to Jerusalem to receive *torah* (in the sense of true divine teachings) and wisdom from Zion, not from a new Solomon (contrast Isa 2:2–4 and Mic 4:1–4 with 1 Kgs 5:9–14 and 1 Kgs 10). It is a wisdom that is institutionalized (temple and *literati*, representing Israel) not personalized (a human king). The temple/Zion is the source of blessing in this imperial world. To be sure, this future empire was YHWH's but within the discourse of the community, this meant that it had to be construed as a Zion/Temple/*torah*-centered (world) empire.

Of course, it was also Israel's empire, but Israel was also construed as Zion/Temple- and *torah*-centered, and to a large extent as encapsulating the very nature of the empire. This means, of course, that in practical terms, this is an empire in which at its center are priests and *literati*. To imagine that Israel was kingly in this context meant that, from a discursive and ideological perspective, a

---

erature, see, for instance, social memories of Israel's covenant with YHWH) and see the attributes of Israel in Hos 2:21.
51 See, among many others, Ezek 39; Joel 4:9–21; Zeph 3:8–20; Hag 2:6–7; Zech 14.
52 Or, even failing initially to successfully defend it. See Zech 14:1. For YHWH's defeating the enemy in Israel's/YHWH's land, see also Ezek 39:1–20 and Isa 14:24–27.

torah centered community⁵³ was kingly. Of course, it also meant, from a different perspective, that the *literati* themselves, indirectly, were kingly, too.

Since this is an empire at whose center stood Temple and *torah*, the community in Yehud had to deal with the issue of the partial acculturation of the nations other than Israel. It is worth noting that in this regard, the empire of Yhwh was imagined as somewhat different from the Achaemenid empire. In the latter, ethnocultural groups were not *required* to partially (but significantly) Persianize themselves, nor were they required to acculturate themselves by following a single path that leads to a common end-stage for all non-Persian groups.

In the future world empire imagined in Yehud, however, the many "others" (and the Other) had to be partially Israelitized. In this future world, the main features that were associated with nations other than Israel were replaced by those typical of Israel, and thus in this universal empire the very identity of these nations is re-formulated.

This is an imperial world that reflects a dream of cultural conquest and assimilation of the Other to the center of the discourse of the future empire, and of the community that dreams such dreams.⁵⁴

It is worth noting that in the universal empire of Yhwh, the king (Yhwh) was imagined as actively desiring and acting towards the acculturation/partial Israelitization of the Other. Kings in historical world empires, be they Assyrian, Babylonian, or Persian, did not champion cultural and identity shifts that would turn entire "peripheral" populations into partially "inner groups." Kings did not have world-wide cultural missions.⁵⁵ To be sure, processes of acculturation

---

53 One may say that sociologically, the Jerusalemite temple had an important hand in legitimizing the community's *torah*, but discursively and ideologically, *torah* legitimized the temple. For the present purposes, the latter is the crucial observation. On these matters, see E. Ben Zvi, "Imagining Josiah's Book and the Implications of Imagining it in Early Persian Yehud," in *Berührungspunkte: Studien zur Sozial- und Religionsgeschichte Israels und seiner Umwelt: Festschrift für Rainer Albertz zu seinem 65. Geburtstag* (eds. R. Schmitt, I. Kottsieper, and J. Wöhrle; AOAT 250; Münster: Ugarit Verlag, 2008), 193–212. Cf. T. C. Römer, "Transformations in Deuteronomistic and Biblical Historiography: On 'Book-Finding' and other Literary Strategies," *ZAW* 109 (1997): 1–11; idem, "Du Temple au Livre: L'idéologie de la centralization dans l'historiographie deutéronomiste," in *Rethinking the Foundations: Historiography in the Ancient World and in the Bible: Essays in Honour of John Van Seters* (eds. T. C. Römer and S. L. McKenzie; BZAW 294; Berlin: De Gruyter, 2000), 207–25; idem, *The So-Called Deuteronomistic History: A Sociological, Historical and Literary Introduction* (London: T&T Clark, 2005), 55, 175–83.
54 See, among many examples, Isa 56:1–8.
55 As shown, concerning Assyria, in A. Berlejung, "The Assyrians in the West: Assyrianization, Colonialism, Indifference, or Development Policy?" in *Congress Volume Helsinki 2010* (ed. M. Nis-

did happen, but they were for the most part the outcome of processes of "intergroupal" exchanges. Although they were likely influenced by matters of prestige, "social capital" and the like, they were not the result of central, monarchic planning.[56]

YHWH's/Israel's future empire was remembered in this respect as having at its center priorities that were not those of past or future kings of universal empires. This again says much about the way in which Israel conceived its future "kinglyness" (see above).

The construction of YHWH's/Israel's empire discussed here represents underdog dreams of empire. They are proof positive of an internalization (and adaptation) of the imperial discourses. They represent a clear case of resistance through the creation of meta-narratives and the act of remembering and experiencing (virtually) what they tell. It may also be some form of social (over?)response (even if not necessarily self-conscious) to the partial "Arameanization" of

---

sinen; VTSup 148, Leiden: Brill, 2012), 21–60. Of course, the same is true of the Hellenistic kingdoms. Neither Alexander nor any of the later Hellenistic kings engaged themselves in a world mission of "Hellenization." In fact, Hellenistic kings often showed an ability to adapt and appropriate local ideologies and cultures; see, for instance, the famous Borsippa Cylinder of Antiochos I (268 BCE). On these issues and the problematic historical character and background of once common claims about Hellenistic kingdoms as promoters of forced, institutional Hellenization and related positions about the nature of these kingdoms/empires, see, among others, A. Kuhrt and S. M. Sherwin-White, *From Samarkhand to Sardis: A New Approach to the Seleucid Empire* (London: Duckworth, 1993), 141–87; J. G. Manning, *The Last Pharaohs,* esp. ch. 2 (29–54). See also J. Ma, "Kings," in *A Companion to the Hellenistic World* (ed. A. Erskine; Oxford: Blackwell, 2003), 177–195. It must be kept in mind that empires were based on negotiation, not negotiation among equals to be sure, but still negotiation with local groups and particularly their elites. This is certainly true of the Hellenistic empires, see, for instance, Manning, *The Last Pharaohs,* J. K. Davies, "The Interpenetration of Hellenistic Sovereignties," in *The Hellenistic World: New Perspectives* (ed. D. Ogden; London: Duckworth and The Classical Press of Wales, 2002), 1–21; R. Strootman, "Kings and Cities in the Hellenistic Age," in *Political Culture in the Greek City After the Classical Age* (ed. R. Alston, O. van Nijf, C. Williamson; Groningen-Royal Holloway Studies on the Greek City After the Classical Age 2; Leuven: Peeters, 2011), 141–53. Through these processes of negotiations, kings tended to appropriate and partially resignify local cultural traditions and locals tended to appropriate and resignify some Hellenistic traditions; both groups thus tended to create a kind of ever shifting "third-space" in which both could interact each for their one benefit. Similar considerations apply not only to ancient empires, but modern as well.

56 This explains, for instance, why the initiative to become a polis most often originated within local groups, not Hellenistic kings. Concerning the general cultural processes see note above.

Yehud during the Persian period,[57] now turned into a memory of a future partial (but far more substantial) Israelitization of the entire world.

The question of the partial Israelitization of the Other was bound to raise the question of whether the Other may change enough to be able to join the center of the future empire. Although foreigners loyal to the Persian king served in peripheral roles in the court of the Persian king, could be awarded honors and rewards and even invited to the King's table, they could not become members of the imperial inner circle. Not incidentally, intermarriage at the level of the Persian king was not allowed, whether involving foreign women or even Persian women who were not from the nobility.[58] What about future Israel? Would they be able to live in the imperial court (i.e., Jerusalem) and receive royal rewards? What about joining the King's table? Would they be able to become full members of the inner circle (i.e., priests) and intermarry with members of this circle? These questions require a separate analysis, but suffice it to say that multiple answers co-existed and balanced each other in the discourse of late Persian/early Hellenistic Yehud/Judah.[59]

---

57 Note both the use of Aramaic in Yehud and the introduction of the Aramaic lapidary script. On the latter, see O. Lipschits and D. S. Vanderhoft, *The Yehud Stamp Impressions: A Corpus of Inscribed Impressions from the Persian and Hellenistic Periods in Judah* (Winona Lake: Eisenbrauns, 2011), 63–73; but note also that discontinuity in script is balanced with continuity in design. Note also that despite the introduction and prevalence of Aramaic, the authoritative texts of the community continued to be written in Hebrew. Cf. E. Ben Zvi, "The Communicative Message of Some Linguistic Choices," in *A Palimpsest: Rhetoric, Ideology, Stylistics and Language Relating to Persian Israel* (eds. E. Ben Zvi, D. V. Edelman, and F. Polak; Piscataway: Gorgias Press, 2009), 269–90. The question of the partial "Arameanization" of Yehud requires a separate in-depth study. It is worth stressing that the Aramaic language was only one of the important languages of the empire. A simple example suffices: the vast majority of the Persepolis Fortification Texts were not in Aramaic. Processes of partial "Arameanization" varied among the different groups constituting the Persian empire in both contents and extent. On Aramaic in the eastern part of the Achaemenid empire, see J. Wiesehöfer, *Ancient Persia: From 550 BC to 650 AD* (London: Tauris, 1996), 118, in which the matter is approached from the perspective of our knowledge of the situation in the later Parthian empire.

58 See, for instance, M. Brosius, "Greeks at the Persian Court," in *Ktesias' Welt = Ctesias' World* (eds. J. Wiesehöfer, R. Rollinger, and G. B. Lanfranchi; Classica et orientalia 1; Wiesbaden: Harrassowitz, 2011), 69–80.

59 To be sure, there are texts such as Isa 66:21 and Isa 14:1 or Isa 56:1–8, but on the other hand also like Ezek 44:7; and there are, of course, Pentateuchal texts (e. g., Lev 17:8–9; Num 15:14), but there are many different types of non-Israelites and all these texts require careful exegesis. Moreover, there is also the traditional concept of a hereditary priesthood, but at the same time, the line may be expanded to include "adopted sons" into the lineage, as in the case of Samuel, implied by the fact that he is an Ephramite in Samuel but a Levite in Chronicles. I discuss further this particular case and its implications in "A Balancing Act: Settling and Unsettling Issues Con-

Another aspect of the memories of the future world empire of Yhwh/Israel as construed in late Persian Yehud: It is clear that dreams of the Yehudites did not focus on the basic structures of worldly world empires (e. g., central administration, regional administrations, army, communications, regular collection of taxes), and as mentioned above, they did not focus on human military heroes. When people in Yehud imagined and remembered the future empire of Yhwh and Israel, their mindshare was not occupied by the usual functions and personages of any historical polity (or state). Instead their attention focused on *torah*, temple, priests, teachers of *torah* and the like. They were at the center of the new empire. Their imagination and memories drew them away from the known "political, worldly" realm and towards a world in which the latter does not necessarily constrain social imagination and the generative power of their ideological discourse. As I mentioned elsewhere, it is precisely in that world that the *literati* of Yehud could "compete and beat" the actual empire, while at the same time, and partially because of their success in that endeavor, be able to adapt well to it in their regular, but ideological and discursively, "less significant" life.[60] Yet, at the same time, their very ability to do so, to think in this way, was dependent on the very imperial circumstances in which they lived. The existence of the community neither required nor depended on the kind of "state" structures and institutions (including a standing and thus, costly army) that were vital for even a vassal kingdom such as monarchic Judah. They were a province in a larger Persian empire.[61]

III On the Remembered Main Empires of the Past

Turning from the "universal" remembered empire of the future to those of the past, as mentioned above (end of section I), two imperial powers grabbed most of the mindshare of the community in the set of social memories encoded and evoked by the collection of prophetic books: Assyria and Babylon. Assyria

---

cerning Past Divine Promises in Historiographical Texts Shaping Social Memory in the Late Persian Period," in this volume, pp. 440–58.
60 "Social Memory and Identity Formation" in this volume, pp. 28–79.
61 The basic critique and even rejection of "state" structures appears too in historiographical books (e. g., 1 Sam 8:11–18 may reflect a similar imperial context). But this is also an issue that demands a separate discussion. It suffices for the present purposes to note that an ideal future reminiscent of the non-state period of Judges is projected into the ideal future not only in relation to Judah (see Obad 20), but also and paradigmatically in relation to Egypt (see Isa 19:20). These two images, however, demand a separate discussion as well.

was a universal empire which was associated in the main narrative of Israel's past with the fall of the northern kingdom and its failure to conquer (and destroy) Jerusalem during the time of Hezekiah. Both Assyria's success against the northern kingdom and its (remembered) failure before Jerusalem contributed much to its negative characterization. In the case of the former, this held true for obvious reasons. The latter held true because military failure was associated with moral failure. The salience of the deliverance of Jerusalem before the Assyrian army in social memory shaped a strong mnemonic (and narrative) preference for the presence of great heroes (YHWH, Hezekiah, Isaiah) and their counterpart, great villains (Sennacherib), confronting each other at the central world place at a crucial time. Thus, the story of the deliverance of Jerusalem evolved so as to evoke in the community in Persian Yehud not only the pious behavior of Hezekiah and the successful role of the prophet Isaiah (contrast with the pair Zedekiah/Jeremiah)–and a sense that Israel has agency and its actions influence history–but also the figure of a hubristic enemy bent on fighting and mocking YHWH, who was thus surely to fall.[62]

To be sure, there was a strong "generative grammar" within the discourse of Yehud that generated an association between universal empire and hubristic behavior. Clearly the king of such an empire occupied the structural/mnemonic slot of YHWH, the real universal king; moreover, there was the discursive and ideological expectation that the king of a universal empire be constructed/imagined in Yehudite social memory as one who boasted of his power and trusted those elements (divine, natural, social) upon which he relied (his gods, terrain, fortifications, army and the like)–the worst of them went to the extreme of thinking themselves as para-gods.[63] Needless to say, this would constitute hubristic behavior, from the perspective of the *literati* in Yehud. In fact, the same holds true even for less than "traditional" universal empires within their social memory, as the case of Tyre in Ezek 27 and 28 shows.[64] But as the case of the Persian empire (see above) demonstrates beyond any doubt, a strong "generative grammar" may exist, but it produces no substantial outcome if other "generative

---

[62] See, for instance, Isa 10:10–11; Isa 37:23–29 // 1 Kgs 19:22–28.
[63] See, for instance, Isa 14:3–23; Ezek 31; 32. This motif is also part and parcel of imperial discourses. See M. Liverani, "Kitru, kataru," in *Mesopotamia* 17 (1982): 43–66.
[64] On Ezekiel 27, see J. B. Geyer, "Ezekiel 27 and the Cosmic Ship," in *Among the Prophets: Language, Image and Structure in the Prophetic Writings* (eds. P. R. Davies and D. J. A. Clines; JSOTSup 144; Sheffield: JSOT Press, 1993), 105–26. Tyre trusts its wealth and the sea; Jerusalem has the Temple. See I. D. Wilson, "Tyre, a Ship: The Metaphorical World of Ezekiel 27 in Ancient Judah," in *ZAW* 125 (2013): 249–62.

grammars" hinder or pre-empt such an outcome.⁶⁵ Conversely, in the case of the negative characterization of Assyria, tendencies to cast it as hubristic are reinforced by strong preferences to cast it in the most negative terms, due to the social memory dynamics of remembering the events in the 14ᵗʰ year of Hezekiah and by social memories of catastrophes suffered by Israel at Assyrian hands, which in turn create a preference for more mindshare for and high descriptions of its fall.⁶⁶

The Babylonian empire was mnemonically associated for the most part with the catastrophe of 586 BCE. This association, along with the very fact that Babylon was a world "empire" and that it was defeated by Cyrus, generated a strong preference for negative memories and constructions of Babylon.⁶⁷

To be sure, memories of Egypt are also evoked in the collection of prophetic books, but not so much as a successful universal empire, but rather as the unsuccessful foil to the winning world empires, Assyria and Babylonia. Of course, if we include Deuteronomy as the "prophetic book of Moses" among the prophetic books–in addition to being part of the pentateuchal, hexateucal, deuteronomistic historical, and primary history collections⁶⁸–Egypt becomes the prototypical house of bondage, the place out of which YHWH had to extricate Israel, so Israel could come into being. Leaving Egypt was thus imagined as leaving the (Egyptian) empire, as leaving Babylon was imagined as leaving the Babylonian empire. This set of memories and sites of memories shaped a strong preference for the development of negative characterizations of Egypt, as the archetypal "evil empire," and liberation from it, as the archetypal case of deliverance from this type of "imperial" subjugation.

An aspect of the imperial construction of Egypt, Assyria, and Babylon is, of course, their transformation into geographical/spatial sites of memory associated with Israel's exile. Significantly, one can observe a significant shift in the basic narrative about leaving exile. In two cases, leaving physically the territorial heart of the empire was remembered as a crucial step towards the establishment of a *torah*/temple-centered community. In the first and foundational instance, it

---

65 It is worthwhile to stress that the contrast between images of Assyria and Babylonia as cruel, pitiless powers, on the one hand, and Persia as a kind and generous one, on the other, is the product of particular social memory processes in Yehud. They are not a reflection of essentially divergent attitudes towards rebellions; see the way in which Darius I put down the rebellions against him at the beginning of his reign (DB 32–33).
66 See above all Nah 2; for other examples, see Isa 14:21–24; 30:27–33; Zeph 2:13–15 (and note the placement and relative extent of the reference to Assyria in Zeph 2:4–15).
67 E.g., Isa 13; 14:3–24; Jer 50; 51:24–28.
68 See "Exploring the Memory of Moses 'The Prophet'" in this volume, pp. 199–231.

was Egypt, but its slot is taken in the re-foundation part of the main meta-narrative by Babylon. The plot that the community remembers is thus helical, not cyclical.

To be sure, there are references to other empires. But they were assigned less textual space in the collection of prophetic books and in the social mindshare of the community (e. g., Tyre).[69] Far more important for historical reconstructions of the full scope of the intellectual discourse of late Persian Yehud are the substantial memories encoded in and evoked by the prophetic book collection that balance the thrust of the memories of empires mentioned before. To illustrate, and focusing again on the two main universal empires of the past, there are texts that asked the community to construe and remember the Babylonian empire (and characters that represented and symbolized it) in extremely positive light, not when Babylon is fallen or when it is about to be replaced as the center of the world by Jerusalem, but at the height of its power, just when it destroyed Jerusalem, the Temple, and sent Israel into "exile."

Babylonia at its zenith, the very universal empire that destroyed Jerusalem, was also generally imagined containing at its heart the very territory most suitable for Israel's exile.[70] Although a somewhat elevated figure of Nebuchadnezzar,[71] particularly as Yhwh's servant, is to be expected (see Jer 25:9; 27:6–cf. Isa 10:5–and in Jer 25:1–14, note also vv. 11–12), and particularly since he successfully destroyed Jerusalem, which in the discourse of Yehud could have only been understood as having been selected by Yhwh to do so, the same cannot be said of Nebuzaradan, who is explicitly characterized as a pious foreign leader, who not only acknowledges Yhwh's power and justice, but also thinks

---

[69] Tyre was imagined and remembered in prophetic literature as the center of what we may call today a commercial empire and Tyre, the city, and its king as at the center of a world, like imperial kings and cities. Of course, from the perspective of the remembering community this is a kind of "anti-world" and Tyre is a kind of "anti-Jerusalem." See, for instance, Ezek 27–28 and also cf. Ezek 26:16–18 and note 64 above. Given Aram's importance in the historical process that led to the fall of Samaria, the tendency to "bracket" it, particularly in Hosea, is worth noting. On this matter, see E. Ben Zvi, "The Study of Forgetting and the Forgotten in Ancient Israelite Discourse/s: Observations and Test Cases," in *Cultural Memory in Biblical Exegesis* (eds. P. Carstens, T. Hasselbach, and N. P. Lemche; Perspectives on Hebrew Scriptures and its Contexts 17; Piscataway: Gorgias Press, 2012), 155–74.
[70] See, for instance, Jer 29; Ezek 33:21–29; and contrast with how Egypt, which did not destroy Jerusalem, was imagined in this regard: see Jer 40:7–41:18; 42:1–22; 43:1–13; 44:1–30.
[71] See J. Hill, "'Your Exile Will Be Long': The Book of Jeremiah and the Unended Exile," in *Reading the Book of Jeremiah: A Search for Coherence* (ed. M. Kessler; Winona Lake: Eisenbrauns, 2004), 149–61 (152–56); idem, *Friend or Foe? The Figure of Babylon in the Book of Jeremiah MT* (BibIntSup 40; Leiden: Brill, 1999), 103–10, 130–39, 198–99, 203–5.

and talks like a pious Israelite/Judahite/Yehudite. In fact, Jer 40:2–3 asks the community to remember a Nebuzaradan, the very same person who burned the temple and Jerusalem and deported Israel and the temple vessels (2 Kgs 25:8–11; Jer 39:9; 52:12–27), as a person who thought and talked as a godly disciple of the prophet, as Jeremiah would have thought and talked.[72]

Turning to Assyria, although there is Nahum, there is also Jonah. Significantly, the "king of Nineveh" is not to be imagined as the king of a falling polity, but of one at the height of its power (see Jonah 3:2–3). Clearly, the book of Jonah, among many other things, serves to balance, to the best of its potential within the community, the memories associated with Nineveh.

These are not some odd cases one can "safely ignore" in reconstructions of the intellectual discourse of the period, nor are the perspectives that they raise restricted to texts in the prophetic book collection.[73] These memories served to balance the mindshare of extremely negative constructions of past, universal empires. While positive constructions of their present "universal" empire may have contributed to the images of past empires,[74] these texts shaped an image of the past empires and their populations[75] as containing the seed of their transformation into loyal members of the future empire of YHWH/Israel, as (discursively necessary) pre-figurations of that future. At the same time, Babylon and Assyria

---

[72] "The author wants to persuade us that Nebuzaradan was a pupil of Jeremiah (40:2–3)," writes K. A. D. Smelik in "The Function of Jeremiah 50 and 51 in the Book of Jeremiah," in *Reading the Book of Jeremiah: A Search for Coherence* (ed. M. Kessler; Winona Lake: Eisenbrauns, 2004), 87–98 (97). Compare also Jer 40:2 with Jer 32:23.

[73] Chronicles (and books in the deuteronomistic historical collection, and the book of Genesis) shaped memories of several virtuous, powerful foreign kings. See E. Ben Zvi, *History, Literature and Theology in the Book of Chronicles*, 270–88; previously published as "When a Foreign Monarch Speaks," in *The Chronicler as Author: Studies in Text and Texture* (eds. M. P. Graham and S. L. McKenzie; JSOTSup 263; Sheffield: Sheffield Academic Press, 1999), 209–28.

[74] Note, for instance, the case of the positive characterization of the Other in the land, before Israel could take possession of it, that is, during the patriarchal period. One may also compare these positive others with those populating constructions of the Persian empire in Yehud. On these matters, see "The Memory of Abraham in the Late Persian/Early Hellenistic Yehud/Judah," in this volume, pp. 162–98. A Persian-period connoted flavor might be at work also in the portrayal of the sailors in Jonah's ship. Note the multiplicity of gods/cultural backgrounds associated with them, which is balanced by their shared behavior, which provides a pre-figuration of the behavior of "the Others" at the time of the future empire of YHWH/Israel.

[75] In Jonah, see the partial Israelitization of not only the king of Nineveh, but also the entire population of the city and earlier within the book's story that of the sailors in the ship.

are past empires and as such they have to pass. Even Jonah, as read and reread in Yehud, has two endings.[76]

IV Final Observation

These observations do not and cannot address within the boundaries of a single essay the gamut of issues associated with "empire" and "imperial conditions," the prophetic collection of books, and matters of social memory and mindscape in late Persian/early Hellenistic Yehud. It is hoped, however, that they provide a fruitful and somewhat distinctive springboard for multiple, future conversations on these matters.

---

[76] As I maintained in E. Ben Zvi, *Signs of Jonah: Reading and Rereading in Ancient Yehud* (JSOTSup 367; London: Sheffield Academic Press, 2003). I discussed there also the motif of *partial* Israelitization of "the Other" in Jonah at some length.

The Memory of Abraham in Late Persian/Early Hellenistic Yehud/Judah*

Introduction

There is no doubt that by the late Persian/early Hellenistic period the figure of Abraham played a prominent role in the memory of ancient Israel.[1] By that time, the authoritative repertoire of the Jerusalem-centred *literati* included the Pentateuchal books, the Deuteronomistic historical collection, the book of Chronicles, and most or all of the fifteen prophetic books in a form or forms similar to those we know. As the *literati* and those who heard their readings imagined the past evoked by reading and re-reading these books, they encountered Abraham as one of Israel's most important founding figures.[2]

This essay is not meant to reconstruct a kind of narrative 'biography' of Abraham that the *literati* of the time could have construed on the basis of their readings and re-readings of these authoritative books—by necessity, such

---

* This chapter initiated the conversation out of which this volume emerged. It was first published, under the same title, in *The Reception and Remembrance of Abraham* (eds. P. Carstens and N. P. Lemche; Piscataway, NJ: Gorgias, 2011), 13–60 and was then republished with minor changes and with the explicit permission of Gorgias Press, and under the same title in *Remembering Biblical Figures in the Late Persian & Early Hellenistic Periods. Social Memory and Imagination.* (eds. Diana V. Edelman and Ehud Ben Zvi; Oxford: Oxford University Press, 2013), 3–37. The chapter here follows the latter, slightly revised version.

1 The level of continuity between the late Persian and the early Hellenistic periods in Yehud/Judah, particularly in terms of intellectual discourse, allows and perhaps demands that the study of the main aspects of the cultural memory of the relevant Jerusalem-centred community, as reflected in its stories about Israel's past, be carried out without separating the two. One may also bear in mind the notorious problem of dating some of the books within the authoritative repertoire precisely; e.g. Chronicles, and the fact that, to some extent, Alexander was 'the last' Achaemenid (e.g. P. Briant, *From Cyrus to Alexander* [Winona Lake, IN: Eisenbrauns, 2002], 2); P. Briant, "Des Achéménides aux rois hellénistiques: continuités et ruptures," in *Annali della Scuola Normale Superiori di Pisa* 9 [1979]: 1375–414 [see explicitly, 1414] = *Rois, Tributs et Paysans* [Paris: Les Belles lettres, 1982], 291–330. For a different position, though, see R. L. Fox, "Alexander the Great: 'Last of the Achaemenids'?," in *Persian Responses* (ed. C. Tuplin; Swansea: Classical Press of Wales, 2007), 267–311 and bibliography there. Too strict a differentiation between the two periods and their respective, Jerusalem-centred intellectual discourses is bound to encounter insurmountable problems.

2 Within the Jerusalem-centred discourse of the period, other founding figures include Moses, Jacob/Israel and also David, and to a lesser extent Solomon, since Israel became ideologically associated with Jerusalem and its temple. Within this discourse, YHWH, though not an Israelite, established/founded Israel and as such was its 'father/ruler/highest-level patriarch'.

a 'biography' would end up being largely a re-narration and interpretation of Gen 11:27–25:10. Nor is it a comprehensive analysis of a particular set of references to Abraham in various biblical books.[3] More importantly, and for reasons that soon will become clear, this essay does not focus on the figure of Abraham in terms of the possible intentions of their respective authors.

There is room for all that, but this study is about social/cultural memory. Social memory is certainly not a book, nor what happened when an individual in Yehud read or wrote a particular book or short sections of text here and there. Rather, it is the public, integrated, and socially integrative representation of the past that is held, shaped, and negotiated within a social group, and which holds it together. Social memory is about the past that is constantly present within the community and about the present of the community that is legitimized by that past. Different social groups have different cultural memories and thus different 'Abrahams'.[4] The focus here is on the small, poor community in Yehud by the late Persian period and its descendants in the early Hellenistic period. Since the accessible traces of their social memory are all in written texts, the focus is primarily on the community's *literati*, who were the only group in society competent to re-read time and again the repertoire of authoritative books held by the community at large. However, since social isolation was not an option for these *literati*, one may assume their social memory trickled into the community at large.

It is reasonable to assume that by the late Persian or early Hellenistic period, a repertoire of (authoritative) books existed that included, more or less in their present forms, the Pentateuchal, prophetic, and historical books (including Chronicles) as well as many Psalms.[5] Reading and re-reading these books

---

[3] See, for instance, J. Van Seters, *Abraham in History and Tradition* (New Haven, CT: Yale University Press, 1975) and more recently, L.-S. Tiemeyer, who discusses references to Abraham in Isa 41:8; 51:2; 63:16; Ezek 11:15; 33:23; and Neh 9 ("Abraham–A Judahite Prerogative", in *ZAW* 120 [2008]: 49–66).

[4] Christian, Jewish, and Muslim groups each have their own 'Abraham/Ibrahim'. Likewise, reconstructions of ancient remembered Abrahams vary substantially according to the remembering community the historian associates with the figure of Abraham. Compare and contrast this essay with, for example, R. S. Hendel, *Remembering Abraham* (Oxford: Oxford University Press, 2005). For constructions of Abraham in the late Second Temple period, see, for instance, S. Sandmel, *Philo's Place in Judaism* (New York: KTAV, 1971); L. H. Feldman, *Josephus's Interpretation of the Bible* (Berkeley: University of California Press, 1998), 223–89.

[5] Most of these books likely had a history prior to the late Persian period history; the patriarchal and Exodus traditions originally may well have been two separate corpora, but this observation is not relevant to the study of the social memory of an Israel who understood itself in terms of the Primary History (Genesis–2 Kings). It was the mental world evoked by reading this collection

made present within the 'remembering community' multiple images of a shared, construed past and a shared, imagined future (especially in prophetic books). The central, collective memory of this group, which included a vast array of interwoven, mutually informing, partial memories, represents a comprehensive cultural system upheld by the group. These memories were evoked and relived by the *literati* as they read and re-read authoritative texts within the context of the world of knowledge of the community. The shared discourse included basic assumptions, identity, and boundaries, cultural norms, and fears and hopes. It asked questions and shared ways to address them and a repertoire of potential answers. It also included generative tendencies for preferred and rejected ways of thinking about the world, the self, and about textual features and characterization of personages from the past. Cultural memories are part and parcel of this *general* discourse and had to be approached from that perspective.

A study of the collective memory of the *literati* in Yehud cannot focus on a single book or subsection as if it were a stand-alone, historical entity. To reconstruct the social memory of Yehud or its *literati* in the late Persian or early Hellenistic periods, one must deal with the comprehensive cultural horizon of the group. This means mapping the basic convergences among very diverse books within the repertoire that cut across the particular exigencies and idiosyncrasies of a given text and point to the general discursive matrix to which each belongs and attests. One must deal not only with the repertoire of authoritative texts of the period–rather than a particular, isolated text–but above all, must also analyse each of these texts in light of their *Sitz im Diskurs* (their setting in the discourse)–for examples, see below.

A full reconstruction of the memories of Abraham that existed within the community cannot be achieved.[6] But more importantly, the less pretentious goal of reconstructing the memories associated with Abraham whose traces can be found in the extant sources is well beyond the scope of a single essay. Therefore, the more modest goal of this contribution is to draw attention to several central *topoi* and core concepts in the *general ideological discourse* of the relevant community/ies (hereafter, 'the community') that became associated with the figure of Abraham so that he became a core site of memory[7] that embodied

---

within a particular discourse and world of knowledge–which included a specific repertoire of books–that shaped and reflected the shared, imagined and imaginative social memory of the rereading community.

6 Such a goal belongs to the same category of unachievable goals as 'total historical reconstruction'.

7 I use the term 'site of memory' to refer to any constructed space, place, event, figure, text, or the like–whether it exists 'materially' or only in the mind of members of a social group–whose

and 'broadcasted' them. This chapter demonstrates that Abraham became a site of memory or cipher intended to evoke and reinforce matters and images at the core of the community's self-characterization and self-understanding.

In addition, this chapter suggests ways to approach the characterization of other core figures of the Israel's past in the same community. The process leading to the construction of Abraham as a central node in the collective memory network involved a positive feedback loop: the more central a figure was, the more it became a 'magnet' for issues and images at the community's core (including self-characterization, identity, and ideology). Conversely, the more such matters and images were associated with Abraham, the more central he became. The same feedback was at work in relation to a few other core figures in ancient Israelite discourse, such as Jacob, Moses, and in a different way, David and Solomon.[8] All became central and connective memory nodes in the community's collective memory, functioning as sites of memory that embodied and communicated most of the basic tenets of the community, if sometimes in an abbreviated but memorable form. Implicitly or explicitly, all were deeply connected to and evocative of other such sites of memory. Functioning in this way, these sites/central nodes created a fully interwoven mental landscape that encapsulated the community's construed past and future and its ideological discourse and made them memorable. Making these central figures of the past present served as much to shape images of the past and future as to construct a community and socialize people to its core values and ideology while providing hope and contributing to the community's accommodation to the world in which it lived.[9]

---

presence in the relevant cultural milieu was meant to evoke core images or aspects of images of the past held by the particular social group living in that cultural milieu. Most of these sites act as ciphers to be activated within a particular social discourse and as places to be visited and revisited, even if only mentally, as part of a self-supportive mechanism of socialization and social reproduction. See E. Ben Zvi, 'The Study of Forgetting and the Forgotten in Ancient Israelite Discourse/s: Observations and Test Cases', in *Cultural Memory in Biblical Exegesis* (eds. P. Carstens, T. Hasselbach, and N. P. Lemche; Perspectives on Hebrew Scriptures and its Contexts 17; Piscataway, NJ: Gorgias Press, 2012), 155–74.

8 In this essay I focus solely on Abraham and some of the most salient characteristics of social memories associated with him within the context of the relevant historical community.

9 The convergence and coexistence of all these core concepts, images, and *topoi* within the remembered persona of Abraham and other central characters communicated a sense that, not only could they coexist, but that they were at some level deeply connected to each other.

The Triad 'Abraham, Isaac, and Jacob' and Related Matters

The memory of Abraham often evoked the triad Abraham, Isaac, and Jacob, which was well known to the *literati* of the time. In fact, participation in the triad and the entire set of stories and associations with the triad constantly informed the ways the memory of Abraham was construed in late Persian/early Hellenistic Yehud.

The triad was remembered as the (mythical) biological ancestors of Israel; these *literati* construed Israel, and thus themselves, as 'the seed' of these ancestors (e.g. Deut 1:8; Jer 33:26; and the basic narrative of Genesis). Genealogies played (and still play) an important role in the construction of cultural memory in traditional, kingship-oriented societies. Among other functions, genealogies shaped and created a necessary sense of kinship and shared primordial memory within ancient Israel, while advancing the claim that the community constituted the legitimate descendants of the patriarchal heroes of the past. Genealogies also construed and communicated the place of the community in a larger frame of global and regional genealogical communities. Finally, they provided the community with (mythical) ancestors who might assist it in the present.

Since Abraham was remembered as the father of many nations (Gen 17:5), his name was bound together with those of Isaac and Jacob to create a genealogy that construes the remembering community (i.e. 'ancient Israel') as the primary legitimate heir of the patriarch and the promise associated with him. Since Abraham occupied the foundational, first slot in the genealogy, it is also understandable why sometimes his figure–and that of the last member of the triad–embody the entire line (see 2 Chr 20:7; Ps 47:10 – cf. Ps 47:5).[10]

Given the theological discourse of the *literati* of late Persian early Hellenistic Yehud, the motif of ancestral assistance tended to be shaped in terms of ancestral merit, which in turn, was often associated with divine promises to the ancestors (Gen 22:16–19; Exod 32:13; Lev 26:42; Deut 4:31; 9:27; 2 Kgs 13:23; Isa 41:8; Jer 11:5; Ps 105:42). The theme of ancestral assistance led, however, to its discursive counterpart when the community imagined itself, through reading, as lamenting its own situation. If Israel is in such lamentable shape, the patriarchs must have (temporarily) rejected it and, therefore, have refused to assist Israel (see Isa 63:16).[11]

---

[10] Just as all Israel became embodied in 'Jacob', Abraham, Isaac, and Jacob could become embodied in 'Abraham'.

[11] See R. J. Bautch, *Developments in Genre between Post-exilic Penitential Prayers and the Psalms of Communal Lament* (AcBib 7; Atlanta, GA: SBL, 2003), 37–8; 61–2 and literature cited there.

In addition, as a group and individually, the triad embodied and reminded the community of its image of itself and of the patriarchs as involved in a particular and exclusive mutual relation with the deity–see, for instance, the phrase 'the god of Abraham, the god of Isaac, and the god of Jacob' in Exod 3:6,15; 4:5; 1 Kgs 18:36; 1 Chr 29:18; 2 Chr 30:6 and references to 'the god of our ancestors' (Deut 26:7; 1 Chr 12:18). Within the hierarchical metaphors of the time, this exclusive characterization evoked an image of Yhwh as the ultimate head/patriarch of Israel[12] and of Israel as Yhwh's son (see, among others, Exod 4:22–3; Deut 14:1; Isa 1:2; Jer 31:9,20; Hos 2:2; 11:1). As is usual in these cases, memory not only creates a link to the deity but also an inner discourse about boundaries separating those who share this memory and those who do not, shaping a sense of a privileged inner group and a less privileged 'other' (i.e. Yhwh is the god of Abraham, Isaac, and Jacob, not of Abraham, Isaac, and Esau, or of Ham, Canaan, and Sidon, or of Nahor, for that matter). Within the discourse of these *literati*, however, this claim had to be informed by the stance that their deity was actually the great (and only) god ruling the universe and all in it, including all the nations. As a result, it is balanced, for instance, by imagining that the leaders of the peoples form the retinue of the god of Abraham (i.e. Yhwh) in Ps 47:10.

The memory of the triad, and particularly of Abraham, was emphatically associated with the land and the promise of the land (Gen 12:7; 13:15, 17; 15:18; 24:7; 26:3; 28:13; 50:24; Exod 3:8; 6:8; 13:5,11; 32:13; 33:1; Lev 26:42; Num 14:23; 32:11; Deut 1:8; 6:10; 9:5; 30:20; 34:4; Jer 11:5; cf. Ps 105:9–11; 1 Chr 16:15–18). The cipher, or better, site of memory 'Abraham–Isaac–Jacob' was saliently associated with the land in the memory of Israel and contributed to a construction in which the land stood at the centre of the relationship between Israel and Yhwh.

On the surface, this explicit and underscored association seems odd, given that none of the triad held the land at any time nor is portrayed to have been able to conquer it. Abraham was not born in the land, and Jacob died outside it. Both had to leave it for substantial periods of time.

Moreover, the prioritization of the association of the land with Abraham (and Isaac and Jacob) runs contrary to a general tendency in collective memory (or even literary representations of collective memory) but, at the same time, highlights the ideological construction of the space by those who inhabit it. When socio-political spaces such as lands and cities become strongly associated

---

[12] Imagining Yhwh as father was among the preferred metaphors used to construe the relationship between Israel and Yhwh in the discourse of the period (e.g. Deut 32:6; Jer 31:9; Isa 63:16; 64:7); comparable images appear elsewhere in the ancient Near East. See, for instance, the Sumerian Prayer of King Sin-Iddinam to Utu, in which Utu is referred to as 'the father of the black-headed ones' (W. W. Hallo, *The Context of Scripture (COS)* [3 vols.; Leiden: Brill, 2003], 1.165, 534).

with an individual, most often they activate, directly or indirectly, the memory of the person who 'created' them either through conquest or 'founding'[13] (e.g. Gen 4:17; Deut 3:14; 2 Sam 5:9; cf. Alexandria, Rome–the biblical references show this tendency existed within the discourse of ancient Israel). Against this background, it is particularly noticeable that the land was not primarily associated with Joshua–as one might have expected–or even with Moses for that matter,[14] but was construed as primarily linked to Abraham–Isaac–Jacob in ancient Israelite discourse, who certainly neither conquered nor possessed it at any time.

A secondary trend in social memory was to associate socio-political spaces with those who lost control over them. Through this process the 'losers' (e.g. Gen 17:8; Exod 3:8; Lev 8:3; Num 21:25, 31; Ps 105:11; 2 Sam 24:16; 1 Kgs 16:24; 2 Kgs 9:21; *passim*) become sites of memory that symbolize and constantly re-enact subordination and celebrate both the displacement of the previous owners

---

[13] The motif of founding a city is a variant of the conquest motif; the founder takes over control of the site from nature and turns a 'non-cultural' or 'chaotic' space into a cultural, 'ordered' space within a new polity that stands over and against a previous situation of 'chaos'. The founder 'defeats' nature/chaos, just as the conqueror defeats a human enemy, whose rule over the city is contrary to (divinely set) 'order'.

[14] For Moses as a conqueror, see Num 21:21–35; Deut 2:26–3:13. The image of Moses as a successful general is, on the whole, downplayed in the Hebrew Bible. For possible reasons, see "Exploring the Memory of Moses "The Prophet" In Late Persian/Early Hellenistic Yehud/Judah" in this volume, pp. 199–231. Moses could have been seen as the founder of the community in the land because the blueprint for the society to be established was associated with him. Yet, neither the land, or any polity or any important space in the land was directly or particularly associated with Moses; instead, *torah* ('teaching') was. On the difference between Abraham and Moses in this respect, see T. Römer, "Moses, the Royal Lawgiver" in the same volume, 81–94. The 'anticipated' role of Moses as 'founder' in the metanarrative is explicitly assigned to him in the recounting of Israelite history by Hecateus of Abdera (as cited in Diodorus Siculus, *Bibliotheca Historica* 40.3). On this text, see M. Stern, *Greek and Latin Authors on Jews and Judaism, Volume One* (Jerusalem: Israel Academy of Sciences and Humanities, 1974), 26–35; D. Mendels, "Hecataeus of Abdera and a Jewish "Patrios Politeia" of the Persian Period (Diodorus Siculus XL, 3)", *ZAW* 95 (1983): 96–110; R. Albertz, "An End to the Confusion? Why the Old Testament Cannot Be a Hellenistic Book", in *Did Moses Speak Attic?* (ed. L. L. Grabbe; JSOTSup 317; Sheffield: Sheffield Academic Press, 2001), 30–46 and, for a very different assessment of this text, see D. R. Schwartz, "Diodorus Siculus 40.3–Hecataeus or Pseudo-Hecataeus?", in *Jews and Gentiles in the Holy Land in the Days of the Second Temple, the Mishnah and the Talmud* (eds. M. Mor et al.; Jerusalem: Yad Ben-Zvi, 2003), 181–97. See also B. Bar-Kochva, *Pseudo-Hecataeus, On the Jews* (Berkeley: University of California Press, 1996), 18–43. On the non-warrior figure of Moses in the Pentateuch and the warrior traditions about him, see T. Römer, "Moses outside the *Torah* and the Construction of a Diaspora Identity", *JHebS* 8 (2008), article 15; available at http://www.jhsonline.org and in print in *Perspectives in Hebrew Scriptures V: Comprising the Contents of Journal of Hebrew Scriptures, vol. 8* (ed. E. Ben Zvi; Piscataway, NJ: Gorgias Press, 2009), 269–81. See also Römer, "Moses, the Royal Lawgiver".

and the founding of the 'new world'.¹⁵ At times, the remembrance of the previous world and its destruction reflects a level of anxiety about the long-term stability of the 'new world', which in turn creates a positive feedback loop as it fuels a need for remembering the early displacement/founding *topos* and for stressing the 'unbridgeable gap' between the former and present 'owners'. This rhetorical strategy both eases identity worries and feeds them, leading again and again to a revisitation of the memory/ies of displacement.

There are multiple references to the dispossession of the previous dwellers of the land in the social memory of ancient Israel (e. g. Exod 3:8,17; 13:5; 33:2; 34:11; Deut 4:47; 7:1; Josh 3:10; 1 Kgs 14:24; 2 Kgs 16:3; 17:8,11; 21:2; Amos 2:10; Ps 105:44; Neh 9:8; 2 Chr 8:7–8), but significantly, none of them can be related to a celebration of their actual dispossession by Abraham or any other figure in the triad. In fact, within the memory of Israel, the dwellers of the land were not dispossessed, peacefully or otherwise, by any of the members of the triad.¹⁶

The main reason for the ubiquitous preference for an association of the land with the figure of Abraham (and Isaac and Jacob) rather than Joshua is that the former makes salient the element of *promise* over and against that of present or past fulfilment. Had the land been associated primarily with Joshua, the emphasis would have been in a past fulfilment that is no longer present in the life of the community. For the same reason, the land was not primarily referred to as the land held by the figures David and Solomon. The memory of Abraham (Isaac, and Jacob) served to bring to the present of the remembering community a promise and, above all, memories of a future that its *literati* and those who followed them could imagine and experience vicariously as they read the relevant authoritative books.

It is only in this virtual world that they could imagine themselves (i. e. 'Israel') enjoying 'the Promised Land'. It is particularly worth stressing that 'the Promised Land' is not Yehud.¹⁷ It is not even Yehud and Samaria, but the

---

15 The case in 1 Kgs 16:24 combines the two trends, evoking both a previous owner and a foundational deed by Omri. Compare the reference to the 'threshing floor of Araunah/Ornan' in 2 Sam 24:18; 1 Chr 21:22; 2 Chr 3:1. In both cases, the memory of the displaced character causes the community to remember and re-enact in their minds an act of transfer.

16 On signposts associated with them that may evoke a future dispossession, see the section 'Memories of a Token of Possession/Landmarks' and texts such as Gen 49:29–33; 50:5,13.

17 Scholars who interpret Abraham's interaction with the land in terms of (supposedly) long-term tensions between 'returnees' and 'non-returnees' in Yehud in the early Persian period and their struggle over land not only face the problem that there was no historical massive return and that by the late Persian period Yehudites–the majority of whom had remained in the land–developed a collective memory of leaving and returning to the land as a whole, but also that the memory of Abraham was directly related to the promise of a land far larger than

whole land of Canaan (see, for instance, Gen 17:8). Whatever its exact borders, this is a land whose possession by the small and poor community in Yehud stood well beyond any possible or even imaginable political development within the community.[18] The 'impossibility' of the claim was what made it so appealing.

Yehud. See my "Total Exile, Empty Land and the General Intellectual Discourse in Yehud", in this volume, pp. 599–611. Abraham is not primarily an immigrant to Yehud but an immigrant to a vast land that his descendants, construed to be 'all Israel', are going to possess–by dispossessing others. The ancient readers of these stories in late Persian/early Hellenistic Yehud associated these stories with territoriality and territorial claims. Compare F. Stavrakopoulou, "Ancestor Ideologies and the Territoriality of the Dead in Genesis", in *A Palimpsest* (eds. E. Ben Zvi et al.; NJ: Gorgias, 2009), 61–80. I agree with her that images of an 'ecumenical', 'foreigner-friendly', or 'non-territorial' Abraham–no matter how helpful for contemporary theological thought– are not likely to have dominated the intellectual discourse of late Persian–early Hellenistic Yehud, at least, if the latter was based on or reflected in readings of the entire corpus of authoritative books that existed at the time–including Genesis–Deuteronomy in more or less their present compositional form. Needless to say, stories about territoriality, of possession and their counterpart, the loss of land by previous inhabitants, were part and parcel of constructions of the past of peoples not construed/imagined as indigenous, see Hdt. 4.11, 173. Stavrakopoulou's Abraham, however, is too narrowly related to the territory of Judah/Yehud in my opinion, though this may be an accidental side effect of her focus on Abraham's purchase of the Cave of Machpelah rather than on the memory of Abraham as shaped and reflected in the *entire* repertoire of authoritative books. Similarly, the Abraham that emerges from a reading of the reconstructed 'P' document alone or in a way that is not strongly informed by other texts lead will look different. See, for instance, A. de Pury, "Abraham: The Priestly Writer's 'Ecumenical' Ancestor," in *Rethinking the Foundations: Historiography in the Ancient World and in the Bible* (eds. S. L. McKenzie and T. Römer; BZAW 294; Berlin/New York: De Gruyter, 2000), 163–81; J. Blenkinsopp, "Abraham as Paradigm in the Priestly History in Genesis", in *JBL* 128 (2009): 225–41. While the 'P' Abraham as it emerges from recent research is likely to be the most helpful of all Abrahams for theological thought within many Christian and Jewish groups today, it carries no weight in any historical analysis of the discourse of late Persian/early Hellenist Yehud. For the image of Abraham as emblematic of the '*gola* community' in Yehud in contradistinction to the 'remainees' during the Persian period, see, among others, J. L. Ska, "Essai sur la nature et la signification du cycle d'Abraham (Gn. 11,27–25,11)," in *Studies in the Book of Genesis* (ed. A. Wénin; Leuven: Peeters, 2001), 153–77; and M. Liverani, *Israel's History and the History of Israel* (London: Equinox, 2005), 258–61.

18 See Gen 10:15–19; 15:18; Num 34:1–12; Josh 13:1–13; Ezek 47:13–20; 48:1,28. All these texts created a net of mental maps of the land of Canaan/'the Promised Land' within the discourse of ancient Israel. For present purposes, the point is neither the precise borders–which are a matter of debate–nor the degree to which the latter correspond with those of an Egyptian 'Canaan' that existed about 1,000 years before the Persian Empire and the early Hellenistic era, but that all the mental maps that the *literati* in Yehud drew of this land included much more than the territory of Yehud or even the two provinces of Yehud and Samaria together. Members of the community in Yehud, and certainly its *literati*, were certainly aware that there was no imaginable, worldly political development that might lead them to rule over 'the Promised Land'. They

The remembering community needed, produced, and experienced mental maps of the entire land and images of Israel possessing it that could displace the actual maps with which the community was all too familiar, which were thought to be far from what the 'real world' should be.

It is worth stressing that neither Joshua nor David or Solomon was imagined as controlling the entire land.[19] There seems to have been a strong tendency to imagine no past, no matter how great it was conceived, as fulfilling the community's utopian map of the ideal future. Remembering Abraham was remembering that future.

Of course, the appeal that a mental map of the land to be possessed, a land that cannot be destroyed, invaded, or polluted by enemies since it exists only in the minds of those who read the authoritative texts of the community, went hand in hand with other but related mental 'realities' that involved claims that were impossible to advance or fulfil within the 'real world', such as the imperial dream that all the nations of the world will flow (one day) to the small temple of one of the poorest provinces in the Persian Empire and along with the nations, their treasures too, or that the deity governing the world and the destiny of 'global' empires is that of a minuscule group of people and 'enjoys' one of the poorest 'houses' (i.e. temples) in a vast, multi-ethnic empire.

The very impossibility of any of these images in the 'real' world raises the importance of the imagined, mental world shaped through the reading of the authoritative texts in the community. This mental world was populated with sites of shared memory created by reading shared books. These sites embodied and communicated ideological fulfilment and, all together, created a new world in which the greatness and power of YHWH and the deity's particular gifts to Israel were openly manifested.

This mental, imaginary world represents the ideologically 'real' world, and since it differs from the 'actual' world the community is experiencing, the latter

---

were like Abraham in this regard. On historical reconstructions of the boundaries of Canaan and discussions of the 'biblical borders', see N. Na'aman, *Canaan in the Second Millennium BCE. Collected Essays, Volume Two* (Winona Lake, IN: Eisenbrauns, 2005), 110–33; N. Na'aman, *Ancient Israel and Its Neighbors: Interaction and Counteraction* (Winona Lake, IN: Eisenbrauns, 2005), 265–78; N. Na'aman, *Borders and Districts in Biblical Historiography* (Jerusalem Biblical Studies 4; Tel Aviv: Simor, 1986); Z. Kallai, "The Patriarchal Boundaries, Canaan and the Land of Israel: Patterns and Application in Biblical Historiography," in *IEJ* 47 (1997): 69–82; idem, "The Boundaries of Canaan and the Land of Israel in the Bible," in *ErIsr* 12 (1975): 27–34 and bibliography cited in these works. Compare N. P. Lemche, *The Canaanites and Their Land* (JSOTSup 110; Sheffield: JSOT, 1991); Y. Aharoni, *The Land of the Bible* (rev. ed.; Philadelphia: Westminster, 1979), 54–80.

19 On David and Solomon, see, for instance, Van Seters, *Abraham in Tradition*, 265–6.

can only be, at some deep level, (ideologically) deceitful. It is certain to fall and be replaced by the 'truthful' world, which in this case, is the world the *literati* imagine as they read the relevant repertoire of books. They 'know' this is the case because they are endowed with godly knowledge (i.e. the authoritative books of Yehud) and, therefore, can figure out which world is ultimately 'real'. To be sure, through the process, all cognitive dissonances vanish. This mental world emerges as an embodiment, symbol, and expression of hope associated with local 'secret' but 'ultimately truthful' knowledge. Through its ideological characterization of the 'actual' world as 'ultimately deceitful' and thus less important, this mental world not only contributes to a local ideological resistance to main imperial narratives but also to the ability of the local community to find an accommodation with the empire in the actual, less important world.

The point advanced here becomes evident when one uses a cognitive model represented in the following variant of a 'veridiction' diagram (see Figure 1.1). The diagram shows that when the realms of '(truthful) reality' and those of the external appearance of the world are understood as consistent, the community believes that the latter sends a true message about reality. Conversely, when external appearances are imagined to be consistent with non-reality (e. g. cases of ideological resistance such as those mentioned above), then the message the world conveys to the community is considered 'deceitful'. In such cases, the community 'knows' that '(truthful) reality' is actually consistent with what does not appear in the world as it is. They 'know' this is the case only through a secret knowledge they possess.[20] The world 'as is' from the perspective of the community in Yehud included a minuscule Jerusalem but many large non-Israelite cities; a very poor Jerusalemite temple but splendid non-Yahwistic temples; a powerful imperial centre to which the wealth of the nations flows but a globally insignificant, meagre provincial centre in Jerusalem/Yehud. The implied message, the hierarchy and the sense of an essential lack of potential for any substantial change in the status of Israel/Jerusalem/Yehud vis-à-vis 'the nations' that this world conveyed was, however, understood by the community in Yehud as dangerously misleading–even if grounded in Yhwh.[21] It stood contrary

---

[20] This diagram is a variant of Greimas's semiotic square. The form I have used is similar to what I used in *A Historical-Critical Study of The Book of Zephaniah* (BZAW 198; Berlin: De Gruyter, 1991), 337–46. Compare D. Maddox, *Semiotics of Deceit* (Lewisburg, PA: Bucknell University, 1984), 24–5.

[21] Within this discourse, Yhwh governs the world and anything that happens in it, including the presence of powerful non-Yahwistic empires/temples and minuscule Yahwistic centres. From their perspective, the status quo members of the community experienced was also ground-

to what they considered to be the '(truthful) reality'. While unseen in the external world, the latter was, from their perspective, approachable through reading the godly texts they had and by visiting the sites of memory that these texts evoked (i.e. the community's particular and unique 'knowledge') in their imaginations.

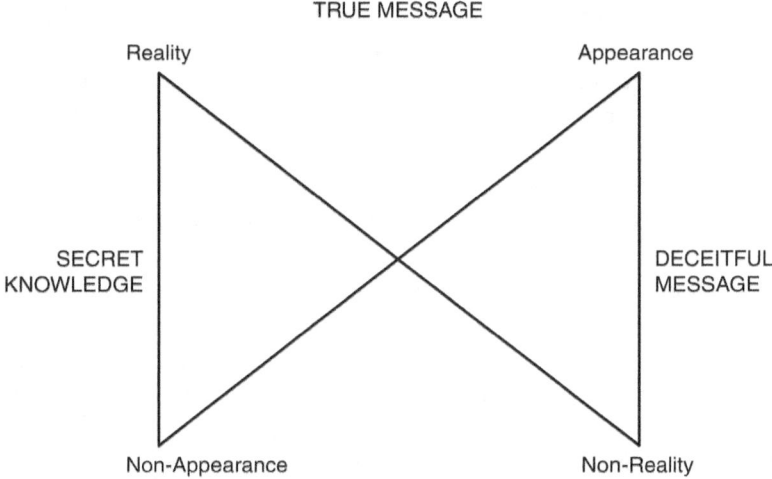

Figure 1.1

The impossibility under any worldly turn of events of the community's desire to 'inherit' the land in the 'actual' world finds a direct parallel in the impossibility of Abraham (and Isaac and Jacob as well) to 'inherit' it within the world portrayed in the patriarchal narratives and their associated memories.[22] Abraham's family was no match for the many and numerous peoples who lived in the land (see the explicit construction of the circumstances at the time of the promise in Ps 105:12 // 1 Chr 16:19), and to make matters worse, its very biological continuity hung on a thread. According to the story that the community in Yehud shaped and remembered about itself, their ancestors/Israel were few and powerless until they became a mighty nation in Egypt, just before the Exodus and the subsequent conquest of much of the land[23] (see Deut 26:5; cf. Deut 1:10, whose

---

ed in Yhwh, but they maintained that this deity provided them with texts that allowed them to see through the 'falsity' of worldly appearances.
22 See Gen 34:30; this refers to only one city in the entire 'Promised Land'/Beyond the River.
23 The social memories of ancient Israel stressed that the conquered land fell well short of the promised land/land of Canaan (see Josh 13:2–6; Judg 1; 3:1–5). Moreover, the common construction of the territory of 'Israel's' settlement during the monarchic period as 'from Dan to Beer-

very language shaped in the community a memory of the [first, but partial] fulfilment of the promise of progeny to the patriarchs [see Gen 22:17; 26:4; Exod 32:13; Deut 10:22; 28:62]). Within this construction of the past, they remained a numerous people through the monarchic period (Deut 28:62; 1 Chr 27:23; and see population numbers implied in the books of Kings and Chronicles), but following the fall of the monarchy, because of its sins, Israel again became few in number (Deut 28:62–the cross reference to the memory of Abraham's promise is clear in this verse–see Gen 22:17 and related verses–and see also Deut 4:27) and remained so, from the perspective of the remembering community. The text of Ps 105:8–15 // 1 Chr 16:15–22 refers to the patriarchs but has a multi-temporal capacity, since, from the perspective of the remembering community, it applies to its members as well. They are like Abraham (and Isaac and Jacob). They may be few, powerless, and seemingly dependent on powerful rulers, but their descendants will inherit the land in the future. Just like in the case of Abraham, as Yhwh promised, their progeny will grow exponentially and then when it does, with Yhwh's help and leadership, it will be able to take hold of the land. They remembered that seventy people went down to Egypt (Exod 1:5; Deut 10:22) and in a few generations, due to Yhwh's promise and action, they became a people with about 600,000 mature males, which likely meant a group of two to three million people in total (Exod 12:37–38; cf. Num 1:46–47; 2:32; 11:21; 26:51). Such a memory was particularly relevant for them (see Isa 51:1–3).[24]

Sheba' (see 1 Sam 3:20; 2 Sam 3:10; 17:11; 24:2; 1 Kgs 5:5) was a far cry from all of Canaan. Thus, even when the community in Yehud imagined 'Israel's' power to have seen much better days than their own, the images they construed bear a sense of lack, which emphasizes how their utopian territory stands fully in the future, as do those construed for Abraham, Isaac, and Jacob. In addition, memories of these 'lacks' communicate the point that 'worldly power' alone is not enough; an issue clearly advanced in the conquest book par excellence, Joshua.

24 Ezek 33:24 shows awareness of Abraham as a relevant site of memory as well. In this text, however, those characterized as making 'use' of it are the 'bad guys' who consequently, are portrayed as misapprehending the memory of Abraham's promise and assigning it a wrong and 'ungodly' meaning (see following verses). They are portrayed as missing the point of Abraham's being one (i.e. future power to the divinely chosen, but presently powerless) and multiplying their mistake by stating that they are 'many' (i.e. powerful) in the present (see the discursive concepts and social memory underlying Deut 7:7, also known in the community). The description of the speakers in Ezek 33:24 uses the common pattern of having a group condemn itself with its own words by characterizing the enemy as hubristic and stupid. Significantly, the speakers are not imagined as holding their own counter-memory of Abraham but of completely missing the meaning of a shared memory. Thus, Ezek 33:24 indirectly raises the issue of interpretative competency in social memory. (A re-readership community in which both Ezek 33:24 and Isa 51:2 are part of the authoritative repertoire–like the late Persian/early Hellenistic Jerusalem-centred

In addition, and in the meantime, they also remembered that when Israel was small and powerless (in the patriarchal period), 'Yhwh allowed no human person to oppress them (i.e. the patriarchs [and matriarchs] and by extension those who identify with them) and rebuked kings on their account, saying, "Do not touch my anointed ones; do my prophets no harm"' (Ps 105:14–15; 1 Chr 16:21–22). The remembering community likely learned that even if they seem to be powerless, there is a limit to how much they may be oppressed, and that if oppressed too much, Yhwh may and will intervene to save them and bring disaster to the oppressors (see the Exodus narrative).[25]

Memories of a Token of Possession/Landmarks and Their Meanings within the General Discourse of the Community

Given the emphasis on the lack of possession of the land at the time of Abraham and the tendency of communities in the ancient Near East to construe forerunners for their present conditions, it is not surprising that some token possession be associated with Abraham in the memory of the remembering community. Such stories balance his memory and allow his reported actions to create 'ancient' references/signposts that explain 'future' possession of landmarks for the community he metaphorically and typologically represents. Moreover, since these reported actions are associated with particular places that are integral to the community's social memory, they are construed as pointing to future events and landmarks. The more important the 'ancient' figure is, the more important are the memory-bonds this figure is likely to shape and reflect within the discourse of the community.[26]

---

literati–would see these texts as informing one other. From their perspective, Isa 51:2 reflects a proper understanding of Abraham and Sarah as 'sites of memory'.)

25 To some extent this motif may be seen as an extension or variant of the powerless, oppressed individual, which tends to be more 'universal' than 'oppressed peoples'. The preferred option for the identity of the oppressed collective in social memory is the 'self'. Within the social memory of the communities in this essay, the 'oppressed' is 'Israel' while among those Babylonians who supported Cyrus and opposed Nabonidus–perhaps after his defeat, the oppressed is 'Babylon'. Within the discourse of the period in Yehud, the concept that there was a limit to Israel's oppression had to interact with the idea that Israel's oppression was often associated with its just punishment and that the ultimate punishing authority/king is Yhwh. Yet, even here, for obvious reasons, the preferred choice was to set divine limits to punishment/oppression (see, for instance, Hos 11:8–9).

26 The same holds true for Jacob, the other main patriarch to whom the land is promised, who could not even remain dwelling in it. It is probably not by chance that Jacob is associated with

The two main landmarks associated with Abraham are Mt Moriah (Gen 22) and Abraham's purchase of burial place in Gen 23 from Ephron, which is the only plot he came to possess in the land.[27] Although the story refers to territorial possession and to a shift in ownership from a Hittite to Abraham, it suits well, on the one hand, the emphasis on his inability (and that of the remembering community) to possess the land: the limits of the transaction are clear. What changes possession is a small piece of land, not 'the land', and, importantly, the piece of land bought by Abraham becomes an אֲחֻזַּת־קָבֶר, a perpetual place to bury members of Abraham's family–from the perspective of the readers, Israel. He did not come to possess a dwelling place but a burial place.[28] On the other hand, burial places are sites of memory and serve to advance a social continuity that is directly related to territoriality.[29]

Moreover, and most importantly, by the time of Chronicles at the latest and likely earlier, the story of Abraham's purchase was associated with David's purchase of the site of the threshing floor of Araunah/Ornan, the place of the future temple (1 Chr 21:21–22:1; compare 2 Sam 24:20–25).[30] The bond created between the two stories and more importantly, between the two sites of memory, Abra-

---

Beth-El and his sons with Shechem (they kill Shechem and plunder the city). An analysis of these stories and the memory webs they evoke cannot be developed within the limits of this chapter.

27 For bibliography on the study of the ancient legal background of the deal and a discussion of a crucial term, see V. A. Hurowitz, "kæsæp 'ober lassoher (Genesis 23,16)," in *ZAW* 108 (1996): 12–19; for a literary study of the pericope, see M. Sternberg, "Double Cave, Double Talk: The Indirections of Biblical Dialogue", in *'Not in Heaven'* (eds. J. Rosenblatt and J. C. Sitterson, Jr; Bloomington, IN: Indiana University Press, 1991), 28–57; see also R. L. Cohn, "Negotiating (with) the Natives: Ancestors and Identity in Genesis," in *Harvard Theological Review* 96 (2003): 147–66; Blenkinsopp, "Abraham", 239–40.

Another significant spatial landmark associated with Abraham is Shechem, though he never buys land there. Gen 12:5–6; 33:18–19 seem to construe it as the main city in the land for those who come from Aram. Since Shechem is far more associated with memories about Jacob and his sons, it lies outside the purview of this essay.

28 One may note Abraham's advanced age at the time and the extremely high price he pays (see esp. vv. 14–20). Both contribute to the aura of impossibility surrounding his possession of the land.

29 Cf. Stavrakopoulou, "Ancestor Ideologies".

30 See, among others, Y. Zakovitch, "Assimilation in Biblical Narratives", in *Empirical Models for Biblical Criticism* (ed. J. H. Tigay; Philadelphia: University of Pennsylvania Press, 1985), 175–96 (181); R. Alter, *The David Story* (New York: W. W. Norton, 1999), 358–9; S. Japhet, *1 & 2 Chronicles* (OTL; Louisville, KY: Westminster John Knox, 1993); S. McDonough, "'And David was old, advanced in years': 2 Samuel xxiv 18–25, 1 Kings 1, and Genesis xxiii-xxiv", in *VT* 49 (1999): 128–31; cf. J. E. Harvey, *Retelling the Torah* (JSOTSup 403; London: T&T Clark, 2004), 60.

ham and David, is strongly reinforced by the identification of the threshing floor with Mt Moriah (2 Chr 3:1 and cf. Gen 22:2),[31] the other main landmark in the land associated with Abraham. Thus, the patterns of social memory preferred in Yehud construed relations between Abraham and David (and Solomon), between the (Abrahamic) sacrifice of Isaac and the proper (Davidic) sacrificial order of the temple, and between Abraham's obedience to the authority of YHWH–the main motif in the story in Gen 22 (for a fuller discussion, see the section, 'Divine Choice, Obedience and Test')–and (Davidic) ritual as obedience to the authority of YHWH.[32]

Two other landmarks associated with Abraham are worthy of note in this context. Within this array of memories, the only space that Abraham purchased in the land and held control over was imagined to be Hebron (Gen 23:19). The memory of Abraham's incipient possession of the land becomes intertwined with David's incipient kingdom. The other landmark directly relevant to the present discussion is embedded in the memory of the encounter between Abraham and the king-priest of Salem (Gen 14:18–20). Clearly, the remembering community in the late Persian/early Hellenistic period identified Salem with Jerusalem (see Ps 76:3; compare 110:2–4), which reinforced the bond linking memories of David, Jerusalem, and temple to Abraham.[33]

The association of Mt Moriah with the Jerusalemite temple and of Abraham with David create a 'read Pentateuch' that is unequivocally aligned with the ideology of the remembering community. The Pentateuchal books were shared by both Samaria and Yehud, but not their interpretation. These associations con-

---

[31] Abraham is an important character not only in the social memory reflected in and evoked by Chronicles as this case demonstrates but also, and quite explicitly, in the genealogies that open the book, which set him (and Noah) as the main figures in 1 Chr 1:1–2:2. See G. N. Knoppers, *1 Chronicles 1–9* (AB 12; New York: Doubleday, 2003), 277–8.

[32] The cultic ritual at the temple served as sign of obedience to YHWH in both Chronicles and the so-called Deuteronomistic History. See D. Janzen, *The Social Meanings of Sacrifice in the Hebrew Bible* (BZAW 344; Berlin: De Gruyter, 2004).

[33] On David and Abraham, see R. E. Clements, *Abraham and David* (Naperville, IL: Allenson, 1967). On the identity of Salem, see J. A. Emerton, "The Site of Salem, the City of Melchizedek (Genesis XIV 18)," in *Studies in the Pentateuch* (ed. J. A. Emerton; VTSup 41; Leiden: Brill, 1990), 45–71. It is possible that there was an alternative tradition associating Salem and Shechem (for a possible trace, see Gen 33:18), but even if such a tradition existed, the community whose memory is studied here clearly identified Salem with Zion. If the place of ancient Salem was a matter of debate between Yehudites and Samarians–as it was later among late Second Temple Jews [see, for instance, 1Q GenAp col. 22 l. 13 'Salem, which is Jerusalem'] and Samaritans and later groups evolving from them–then the memory of Abraham held in the Yehudite community helped to further the case for the Jerusalem interpretation and weaken contrary claims, at least within the own discourse of the Jerusalem-centred community.

tribute to the shaping of a social memory about Abraham in Yehud that was not and could not have been shared with Samaria. This memory played a central role in the appropriation of a potentially shared founding figure and its transformation into a founding hero of 'Israel' as understood within Yehudite ideology. This, in turn, served to legitimize the very notion of 'Israel' held by the remembering community–and delegitimize alternative notions, e.g. those in Samaria.[34]

Abraham and the Nations in the Land: Practical Accommodations and Future Replacement

For the remembering community, Abraham/the patriarchs stood for Israel and so they identified with him/them in their tribulations, powerlessness, and promise. The patriarchal Israel of their memory was small vis-à-vis the well-established, infinitely more powerful peoples of the land, who held all the power in the area. Neither Egypt nor any Mesopotamian empire is portrayed as ruling or controlling the area.[35] Who in the world in which the remembering community lives is the overwhelmingly powerful 'other' who actually rules 'the land' and compared to whom Israel is like a single family? The answer is, of course, the Persian Empire. Abraham/Israel/Yehud accommodates to the powerful other (the previous residents of the land/the Persians). They can negotiate only a minor tract of land, and certainly cannot even think of expelling 'the other' in any practical way.

Within the discourse of the remembering community, such collaboration is presented/imagined not only as a practical necessity but also as a kind of response to the positive 'other'.[36] Just as the Persians are construed in the discourse of the period as an 'other' that is not an evildoer nor one whose religious practices are considered an abomination, the Canaanites, with whom Abraham interacts, are not evildoers, nor are their religious practices condemned. In

---

34 The element of controversy continued in later tradition. On this matter, see I. Kalimi, *Early Jewish Exegesis and Theological Controversy* (Assen: Van Gorcum, 2002), 33–58.

35 Even the 'minority report' in Gen 14 makes this point. The servants of one person, Abraham, defeat a mythical coalition of four kings headed by the king of Elam. On the character of this note as a 'minority report', see the section, 'Tensions, Minority Reports and Preferences and Disfavours'.

36 See the memory of a covenant associated with the interaction of three positive sites of memory (Abraham, Abimelech, and Beer Sheba; and, as expected, Yhwh) in Gen 21:22–34, which concludes with Abraham living peacefully as a *ger* = 'non-citizen') for 'many days in the land of the Philistines' in the story-world's present, but creating a landmark for an 'Israelite' town far in the future.

fact, an opposite tendency is clearly at work. For instance, the remembering community cannot but understand that the 'fear of God' exists in Gerar (Gen 20:11) and that it is wrong and risky for Abraham (/themselves) to think this is not the case. The community had every reason to imagine that the deity who talked to Abimelech in Gen 20:3–7 was YHWH and to associate YHWH with Melchizedek's 'El 'Elyon (Gen 14:18–22; and see the explicit statement in v. 22).[37] The very same community remembered that YHWH stirred up the spirit of Cyrus (the paradigmatic Persian king) and talked to him (Isa 44:28; 45:1,13; 2 Chr 26:22–3) and that Cyrus responded in a very positive way. It is in this context of the positive 'other' and the intellectual atmosphere of the period among the *literati* in Jerusalem that they remembered that Abraham and, therefore, they themselves are (supposed) to be or to carry a blessing for the 'other' and should assume that 'the other' will behave wrongly just because it is other.

At the same time, there are clear ideological limits to this collaboration. First, there is the stance that Abraham/Israel must remain distinct and that the 'other' must remain other. The Abraham narratives clearly carry this sense of boundaries (see esp. Gen 23). Since social memory served to create a sense of self-identity and boundaries, this is to be expected.

Secondly, there is the element of higher 'self-characterization'. YHWH communicates to Abimelech that Abraham is a prophet and his prayer is necessary and successful (Gen 20:7). Abraham is portrayed as *nasi' 'elohim* (Gen 23:6) and since the term *nasi'* can be associated with the figure of a king in the discourse of the community (see Ezek 37:25; 44:3), it is not surprising that Abraham and the other patriarchs could be imagined as prophets and anointed in Ps 105:14–15; 1 Chr 16:21–22.[38] The presence of this tendency and the association of explicit statements of inner-group grandeur to 'the other' (cf. Melchizedek's response to Abraham) are typical of peripheral groups in imperial systems.[39]

Thirdly, there is the obvious case of projecting the local deity into the 'other' and the latter's quasi-Israelitization. This is at work in the construction of positive foreign kings in Chronicles (including Cyrus) and is also anticipated in this

---

37 Cf. L. K. Handy, "Biblical Bronze Age Memories: The Abraham Cycle as Usable Past," in *Biblical Research* 42 (1997), 43–56 (51–3).
38 Conceptual associations between king and head of the (enlarged) house of the father are at work too, allowing and setting generative rules for the creation of potentially acceptable images in the community.
39 See the emphasis on external (mainly 'Greek' and Roman), positive evaluation of the Jews in Josephus. I discussed this phenomenon in terms of Chronicles in E. Ben Zvi, *History, Literature and Theology in the Book of Chronicles* (London: Equinox, 2006), 270–88.

type of circumstance.⁴⁰ In some way, this is a kind of discursive reverse imperialism in which 'the Other' is imagined as culturally 'colonized' by the 'ingroup'.⁴¹

Fourthly and most importantly, however, is the vision of the future. Abraham/Israel is promised the land. The 'other' will be dispossessed of the land. The direct relation between promise and future dispossession is emphatically communicated in the stories (see, for instance, the transition between Gen 15:18 and Gen 15:19). To be sure, images of (future) dispossession may lead to multiple scenarios,⁴² and they conjure images of sins justifying the latter (cf. the images of the inhabitants of Canaan in Abraham's time with those there during the time of Moses or Joshua, see Gen 15:16), but the point remains the same: the land will be Abraham's/Israel's.

These memories embody and communicate a clear, ideologically shaped construction of territorial space. Abraham/Israel will not inherit the 'four corners of the earth' but a certain land–even if the latter is much larger than whatever territory past 'Israel' was imagined to have held. The limitation to a particular land is part of a discourse in which YHWH was construed as ruling over all nations and lands but has chosen a particular land (Hos 8:1; 9:15; Jer 12:7; Zech 9:8, in which at least one of the meanings of *bêt yhwh* ['the house of YHWH'] is 'YHWH's land') and within it, a particular place (Jerusalem, Mt Moriah) just as it was conceived that YHWH, the deity who created and governed heaven and earth and all in them, had a particular people that was 'his'.

The memory of Abraham evoked territoriality, election, YHWH's election of a land, and a future utopia. It communicated within the remembering community in Yehud a sense of accommodation and collaboration for the present and near future, but of displacement, replacement, and supersession for the distant and, from their perspective, utopian future. Abraham served as a site of memory that interwove and secreted both messages.

---

40 See Ben Zvi, *History in Chronicles*, 270–88.
41 This discursive reverse imperialism is at work in the creation of memories of a future in which far away nations and peoples will acknowledge and worship YHWH.
42 These scenarios include removal from the land due to natural causes, to forced expulsion, to physical elimination. On these scenarios, see M. Weinfeld, *Deuteronomy 1–11* (AB 5 A; New York: Doubleday, 1991) 382–4; B.J. Schwartz, "Reexamining the Fate of the 'Canaanites' in the *Torah* Traditions," in *Sefer Moshe* (eds. C. Cohen et al.; Winona Lake, IN: Eisenbrauns, 2004), 151–70 and bibliography. Since social memory does not have to be logically consistent, all these scenarios could and, in fact, did coexist within the memory of the community in Yehud during the late Persian/early Hellenistic period. They all relate to 'the Other' in the land of Canaan, not to 'the Other' in any other land.

The stories about Abraham do not explain what the future status of 'the Other' will be in their 'other' lands once Israel takes over the land. But the same community was aware of images of a utopian future in prophetic literature and experienced them as they mentally visited these future worlds in which Israel and Jerusalem/Zion were exalted (see Isa 2:2–4; 51:4; 56:1–8; Mic 4:1–5; Hag 2:6–9; Zech 8:20–23). In these worlds, 'the Other' is (partially) Israelitized,[43] and as such, it resembled 'the Other' with which Abraham interacted. In these worlds, the centre that provides peace, order, and happiness to humankind, to whom goods and people from all nations flow, does not stand at the heart of the Persian Empire but in Jerusalem at Mt Moriah, a landmark associated with Abraham. It is in this context that the characterization of Abraham as 'father' of many peoples assumes a very pregnant meaning–and so do texts such as Gen 12:3; 18:18 (cf. 28:14).[44]

Divine Choice, Obedience, and Test

Unlike the situation in later texts and their related remembering communities, YHWH's selection of and promise to Abraham is presented within the repertoire of the community, at least at one level, as unrelated to any deed Abraham may have done before his selection (see Gen 11:31–12:3).[45] Thus, remembering Abraham was also remembering and construing a deity that for no humanly intelligible, logical reason chose Abraham (and thus 'Israel').[46] The concept that YHWH selected 'Israel' because of the deity's love (*'ahavah*) for Abraham (and

---

[43] The (future) 'colonization' of 'the Other' is saliently present in Isa 56:1–8 as well. All these may be seen as imperial dreams of a feeble underdog. On the one hand, they are tools of resistance, but on the other, they assume an internalization (and adaptation) of the imperial discourse. All of them involve an ideological subordination of 'the Other' and a replacement of main features of its character by those of the 'dreamer' group. In other words, they involve cultural conquest and assimilation of 'the Other to the 'centre' of the (dreamt) empire discourse.
[44] Compare with the message of Isa 49:6–7.
[45] See Jon D. Levenson, 'The Universal Horizon of Biblical Particularism', in *Ethnicity and the Bible* (ed. M. G. Brett; Leiden: Brill, 2002), 143–69.
[46] A tendency to associate divine 'unmerited' gifts with the most important choices is present also in Chronicles, despite the popular belief that the book is about merited 'individual retribution', whether in terms of reward or punishment. See Ben Zvi, *History in Chronicles*, 22–3, 124, 160–73, *passim*. Cases of convergence among clearly different books constitute the best pointers we may have to the general, intellectual discourse of the community. See E. Ben Zvi, "Reconstructing the Intellectual Discourse of Ancient Yehud," in *Studies in Religion/Sciences Religieuses* (2010): 7–23.

Isaac and Jacob)/Israel/the remembering community was widely accepted in the latter (see, for instance, Deut 4:37; 7:7–8,[47] 13; 10:15; 23:6; Isa 41:8; 2 Chr 20:7; cf. Hos 11:1; 14:5; Ps 47:5; Mal 1:2, and see also, among others, Jer 31:2; Hos 2:16–17).

The love of Y$_{HWH}$ for Abraham was understood as pointing to and embodying the concept of 'Israel'. As a result, the love of Y$_{HWH}$ for Israel was directly associated in the community with their 'loving' Y$_{HWH}$ in return,[48] though this was never imagined as a symmetrical relationship. Although both involved a commitment (/covenant), Y$_{HWH}$'s commitment to Israel was understood, in the main, in terms of promises of land, offspring, wise guidance (i.e. divine instruction), and an elevated role in a utopian future.[49] Israel's commitment was understood primarily in terms of obedience (see Gen 26:3–5).

Although the motif of Abraham's obedience to Y$_{HWH}$ in response to divine promise already appears in Gen 12:4a (i.e. immediately after 12:1–3) and plays a significant role in other places within the memory of Abraham held by the community, the most salient memorial for his obedience is the sacrifice of Isaac (Gen 22).[50] Not surprisingly, and given the foundational role of Abraham in the memory and myth of origin of the remembering community, his sacrifice of Isaac evolved into a central nodal site for social memory that encapsulated and secreted several ideological core *topoi* that, on the surface, seemed unrelated. Moreover, the convergence of these *topoi* into a single site of memory created a sense of 'embodiment' though not necessarily logical coherence for their dis-

---

[47] The reference to Israel as 'very few' in the text is part of the construction of the past (and the underlying ideological world) mentioned in the section, 'Abraham and the Nations in the Land'. From the perspective of the remembering community, it points at both 'patriarchal' Israel and the community itself in late Persian Yehud. It points at Abraham who is one person who still embodies Israel and also at those who live in one of the smallest and poorest provinces of the Persian Empire around a lightly populated, very small Jerusalem.

[48] The point is made repeatedly in Deuteronomy (e.g. 6:5; 11:1,13,22) but is also expressed in a stylistically sophisticated way in Isa 41:8; 2 Chr 20:7. These texts state that Y$_{HWH}$ loves Abraham but also connote a secondary meaning: Abraham loves Y$_{HWH}$. Thus, they encapsulate and communicate a sense that the two are deeply interwoven.

[49] Needless to say, they do not involve protection from disaster. To the contrary (compare Amos 3:2), Y$_{HWH}$ may serve as the agent that brings disaster against Israel, but the commitment involves protection from extermination, since the latter would preclude the fulfilment Y$_{HWH}$ promises.

[50] The narrative has served as a focal point for constructions (and deconstructions) of obedience and morality in numerous communities up to this day. See, for example, the continuous debate about Kant's and Kantian interpretation sketched by S. R. Palmquist and P. McPherson Rudisill, "Three Perspectives on Abraham's Defense against Kant's Charge of Immoral Conduct," in *JR* 89 (2009): 467–97 and bibliography there.

course and communicated that all these core *topoi* are interwoven facets in a single theological/ideological discourse.[51]

To illustrate the preceding, remembering Abraham's sacrifice was remembering a paradigmatic story about full and complete obedience to Yhwh that explicitly concludes with a divine confirmation that 'now I know that you (Abraham– and by extension any Yehudite who mentally visits this site of memory and fully identifies with Abraham) fear God' (Gen 22:12). Within the discourse of the community, 'fearing God' was directly associated with obedience to the deity[52] and with serving the deity (e.g. 1 Sam 12:14). Significantly, Abraham was the first personage characterized as Yhwh's servant (Gen 26:24; Ps 105:6,42; cf. Exod 32:13; Deut 9:27) within the world of this remembering community.[53]

Remembering Abraham's sacrifice was remembering a founding event directly related to the establishment of the temple, the selection of Mt Moriah as the site of the temple–and thus, by implication, that Yehud's concept of 'Israel' and Yhwh is the correct one–and the establishment of the temple offerings– which in turn is, by itself, an expression of obedience to Yhwh.

Remembering Abraham's sacrifice also brings forward the tenuous character in the 'worldly' world of the promise, both at the time of (their imagined) Abraham[54] and at that of the remembering community. This indirectly is seen to reaffirm the belief that the community is 'Abraham', has been chosen by Yhwh, knows about it through texts and memories that provide (only) them with true knowledge, and reinforces the certitude that a utopian future will come to be at some unknown time.

Remembering Abraham's sacrifice involved developing an awareness that the fulfilment of the divine promise was advanced by Abraham's willingness to act in a way that from any logical perspective would have precluded its fulfilment and, thus, was tantamount to showcasing and developing (vicarious) experiential knowledge about human/logical modes of understanding cause and effect and their value to anticipate or control the future.[55]

---

[51] Cf. the 'embodiment' of core aspects of early Christian discourse in the figure of Jesus in general, and in the memory of his crucifixion/sacrifice more specifically.
[52] And to following the ways and commandments of the deity. On this, see the next section.
[53] The other two patriarchs follow, and then Moses. The 'Israel' paradigmatically represented by Abraham (and the triad) was also understood as 'Yhwh's servant'.
[54] Note the setting of the story of the sacrifice of Abraham and particularly, the preceding narratives about promises. See K. Schmid, "Abraham's Sacrifice: Gerhard von Rad's Interpretation of Genesis 22," in *Interpretation* 62 (2008): 268–76 and bibliography.
[55] The *literati* placed claims to knowledge derived from their access to authoritative literature in perspective but emphasized the limitations of human understanding and ability to predict. Cf.

Remembering Abraham's sacrifice also meant placing the memory that the divine promise to Abraham (and thus 'Israel', including the remembering community) has nothing to do with the actions of the latter in perspective (see Gen 22:16–18; 26:5; note also the textual system of textual signposts linking 22:18b to 26:5a and vice versa; cf. Neh 9:8). The issue at stake is the balance between the hope conveyed to the community by its belief that Yhwh loves them and will fulfil the promise no matter what Israel will do or fail to do and the ideological and didactic value of maintaining some relation between human actions and divine responses. This issue and the balance that it requires stand at the core of the prophetic books and underlie the historiographical narratives.

Remembering Abraham's sacrifice meant also to remember Abraham as the 'tested' par excellence[56] and Yhwh as a testing deity who particularly tests the righteous and 'Israel'. This facet of the deity played an important role in the discourse of the period (see Job and Chronicles). It served to explain numerous events in the (construed) past of the community.[57] Moreover, the remembering community may have wondered if they (i.e. the tiny community in Yehud) were not being tested.

Obedience and 'Torah'

Within the discourse of the community, the related *topoi* of obedience to, fearing, and loving Yhwh were all directly associated with following Yhwh's teachings, which were in turn associated with the foundational figure of Moses (i.e. *'torah'*, see, among others, Exod 20:6; Deut 5:10; 11:1). This being the case, it is only anticipated that Abraham, the paradigmatic case of obedience and 'fear of God' be imagined as one who 'kept Yhwh's charge, commandments, statutes, and laws' (Gen 26:5; cf. Deut 11:1; and among many others, Exod 15:26; 16:28; 24:12; Lev 26:15; 1 Kgs 11:38; Deut 5:31; 6:1–2; 2 Kgs 17:13; 2 Chr 7:19).[58]

Job 38, 40 and books as diverse as Chronicles and Jonah; on these two books, see respectively, Ben Zvi, *History in Chronicles* and idem *Signs of Jonah* (JSOTSup 367; London: Continuum, 2003).
56 For the expression 'Abraham the tested' and a study of the development of the motif in Second Temple Judaism, see J. L. Kugel, *Traditions of the Bible* (Cambridge, MA: Harvard University, 1998), 296–9.
57 I discussed this issue in "When Yhwh Tests People: General Considerations and Particular Observations Regarding the Books of Chronicles and Job," in this volume, pp. 472–81.
58 On the relation between 'fearing Yhwh' and observing the commandments, following the deity's ways and the like see, for instance, Deut 5:29; 6:2; 8:6; 13:5; 17:19; 31:12.

The result is that a set of related memories informing each other–at times, for rhetorical purposes, making another dormant but often recalling each other–evolved together within the general cultural memory of the community. Abraham, the first servant and 'lover/friend' of YHWH and the paradigm of 'fearing YHWH', had to follow *torah*, but *torah* had to be given to Moses, who lived several generations after Abraham. The interrelation between the two memories constituted a site of memory that raises among its visitors important issues about the nature and contents of *torah*. Given the centrality of the concept, it is not surprising that these issues continued to be discussed for generations as later communities remembered Abraham and Moses.[59] In addition, this nodal convergence of memories contributed to the necessary discursive closeness between the two foundational figures of the community, Abraham and Moses, and is addressed in numerous references within the repertoire of the community (e.g. Exod 2:24; 3:6,15,16; 6:8; 12:40–41[cf. Gen 15:14]; 32:13; Deut 30:20, *passim*).[60]

Circumcision

Remembering Abraham was remembering YHWH's statement: 'This is my covenant that you shall keep between me and you and your offspring after you: every male among you shall be circumcised. You shall circumcise the flesh of your foreskins, and it shall be a sign of the covenant between me and you' (Gen 17:10–11). It was remembering circumcision, its function as a sign of the covenant, and establishing it at the foundational period. To the concentration of 'firsts' that characterize the image of Abraham in the memory of the commun-

---

[59] Clearly, among the matters at stake in this memory-interaction is the issue of a pre-Mosaic *torah*. The motif of Abraham as an ideal person who observes *torah* is present in Ben Sira and becomes important and a source of debate in later Judaism. See B. C. Gregory, "Abraham as the Jewish Ideal: Exegetical Traditions in Sirach 44:19–21," in *CBQ* 70 (2008): 66–81. For a study of other texts, see J. D. Levenson, "The Conversion of Abraham to Judaism, Christianity and Islam," in *The Idea of Biblical Interpretation* (eds. H. Najman and J. H. Newman; JSJSup 83; Leiden: Brill, 2004), 3–40. On Abraham's Sirach, see P. C. Beentjes, "Ben Sira 44:19–23 –the Patriarchs: Text, Tradition, Theology," in *Studies in the Book of Ben Sira* (eds. G. G. Xeravits and J. Zsengellér; JSJSup 127; Leiden: Brill, 2008), 209–28.

[60] Thus, it is to be expected that some of elements of the portrayal of the one would be associated with the other (e.g. their designation as 'servant of YHWH'; for Moses, see, for instance, Exod 14:31; Num 12:7; Josh 1:2,7,13,15). This tendency continued to influence the development of images of these personages after the period under discussion. For instance, the reference to Abraham as 'lover/friend' of YHWH, which is very popular in later literature, shifts to Moses in Pseudo-Philo, *Biblical Antiquities*. See Kugel, *Traditions of the Bible*, 258.

ity (e. g. first servant of Yhwh, first embodiment of Israel in the land, first to be a 'friend' of Yhwh, first to receive the promise of the land, etc.), one had to add that he was the first to be circumcised, to circumcise the males in his household (including his son Ishmael) and most importantly, the first 'Israelite' father to fulfil the commandment to circumcise his son when he is eight days old (Gen 21:4; cf. Gen 17:12; Lev 12:3).[61]

Remembering Abraham the circumciser/circumcised involved remembering the covenant (Gen 17). It was also remembering a particular construction of boundaries around Israel (see, among others, Gen 34:14; Judg 14:3; 15:18; 1 Sam 14:6; 17:26, 36; 31:4; Isa 52:1; Jer 9:25; Ezek 44:7,9)[62] in which to be uncircumcised was not only a marker of 'being the other' but also of shamefulness. Thus, the demarcation is not only 'ethnic' but also value-laden. As expected in the discourse of the period, circumcision was also used to mark the (required) partial Israelitization (and the avoidance of the 'shame' of being uncircumcised) of the 'others' who dwell or are associated with 'Israel' (see, for instance, the case of Ishmael and later the legislation in Exod 12:48 that was also remembered in the community).

In addition, the positive associations of being circumcised that existed in the discourse of the community allowed for an additional semiotic association of the concept, symbolized in the expression, 'to circumcise one's heart'. From a cultural memory perspective, it is not surprising that Yhwh's circumcision of the heart of the Israelites is meant to cause them to love the deity (Deut 30:6) and that the first person circumcised was Abraham, who was the paradigmatic 'lover/friend' of Yhwh.[63] The community certainly imagined Abraham as having both a circumcised penis and a circumcised heart. Yhwh's promise to him can be fulfilled only by his descendants, who are to be circumcised like him (cf. Lev 26:41; Deut 30:6–9; Jer 4:4).

---

[61] From the perspective of a readership well aware of the entire repertoire of authoritative books, there is a system of links partially connecting, despite all their difference, the circumcision of Abraham, of Moses (Exod 4:24–6), and of the children of Israel under Joshua's leadership (Josh 5:2–8). The underlying discursive concept connecting them seems to be that circumcision is a precondition to perform certain godly/god mandated tasks (cf. Exod 12:48). Note also the metaphorical language of Lev 19:23.

[62] Negative associations with the concept 'uncircumcised' are present in the mentioned texts and in, for instance, Ezek 32.

[63] Note also the memory associations activated by Deut 10:15–16.

Individual and Collective Punishment?

Abraham was also remembered for his debate with Yhwh in Gen 18:23–32. Stories, particularly popular, easy-to-remember ones, tend to provide a discursive way to relate to 'truths' that are explicitly or, more often, implicitly agreed upon within the group but whose members find it difficult to express or to express sharply by other means.[64]

The story in Gen 18:23–32 reminded the readers that the Abraham they remembered tried to persuade Yhwh (and the readers themselves) through a rational argument that (a) to 'sweep away the righteous with the wicked' is wrong, unjust, and a behaviour unworthy of 'the judge of all the earth'; (b) there are standards concerning what Yhwh ought and ought not to do; (c) these standards may be known to a human being; and (d) divine justice (as well as human justice) implies individual retribution. This memory of Abraham is activated within a text that implicitly asks its readers to imagine Yhwh as unable to save the righteous from divinely initiated destruction of wicked cities (Gen 18:23–32).[65] This is an important matter, given that the destruction of Jerusalem was a central site of memory within the community. Were *all* those who died at the time to be imagined as sinners like those of Sodom, or was Yhwh unable to save the few pious? Significantly, the text in Gen 18:23–32 is set in a context that places the validity of some of the (implicit and explicit) assumptions governing the logic of the dialogue in perspective. Note, for instance, that the narrative that follows this dialogue (Gen 19) explicitly demonstrates Yhwh's power to save a righteous person from disaster and that the preceding one is about what Abraham does not know.[66] Within its *Sitz im Buch* (setting in the book), is Gen 18:23–32 at least in part about what Abraham cannot fully understand? And vice versa, is the story in Gen 18:23–32 a way of placing in perspective the implicit ideological underpinnings of the surrounding stories? In any event, remembering this dialogue between Yhwh and Abraham serves as a cultural memory node/site of memory that allows the remembering community

---

[64] Excellent examples of other memorable stories serving these purposes admirably include the story of Micaiah, the son of Imlah and Jonah. See "A Contribution to Intellectual History of Yehud: The Story of Micaiah and Its Function within the Discourse of Persian Period Literati in this volume, pp. 459–71 and my *Signs of Jonah*, 1–3, respectively.

[65] All the 'bargaining' concerning the fate of the city would be irrelevant if Yhwh could have snatched fifty, or forty, or any number of righteous out of Sodom.

[66] For a fuller discussion of these matters, see my "The Dialogue between Abraham and Yhwh in Gen 18:23–32," in *JSOT* 53 (1992): 27–46.

to address very important ideological issues within its discourse through a seemingly simple, memorable narrative.

Certainly, remembering the Abraham of Gen 18:23–32 is remembering him as one who fears, loves, serves, and obeys YHWH but who also is able to enter into a rational debate with the deity on ideological matters. Is this Abraham a projection of the *literati* of the period and their desire to enter into debate with their deity? Are they part of a long tradition in the ancient Near East of (limited) intellectual freedom within which kings can be held accountable?[67]

Abraham, Exile, and Return (Mesopotamia, Egypt)

The remembering community discussed in this chapter had an array of related myths of origins, including the Exodus, which they understood as leading to *torah*/Sinai and then the possession of (much of) the land, the myth of the Return from Babylonia to an empty land that led to the 'return' of YHWH's presence to, and rebuilding of, the Jerusalemite temple (and in Ezra's version, imagined also in terms of the return of the book of *torah*), the myth of Abraham, the myth of Jacob,[68] the myth evoked by Ezek 16:3, and others. From a systemic perspective, one can easily discern some rules governing preferred and dis-preferred scenarios within the array as a whole. There was strong preference for the image that the origin of Israel was outside the land and a clear preference for a myth that involved overcoming exile. In addition, there was a strong preference for myths that evoked and typologically resembled the other myths, thereby creating a generative tension between what is basically the same but different in each case. This drew attention to each myth and to the meanings generated by (virtually) reliving each of them in a way informed by the others.

The Return (from Babylonia), which became the collective memory of the community–whether or not their ancestors were returnees or had never left the land,[69]–was typologically associated with the Exodus of Egypt. This is to be expected since this myth served, to a large extent, as the founding myth of Israel in the land, and the other, again to a large extent, as its refounding myth. Both reflected and shaped a sense that Israel came from outside the land.

---

[67] Cf. D. C. Snell, "Intellectual Freedom in the Ancient Near East?" in *Intellectual Life of the Ancient Near East* (ed. J. Prosecky; Prague: Academy of Sciences of the Czech Republic-Oriental Institute, 1998), 359–63.

[68] This myth is clearly similar to that of Abraham and at times related to it but is not identical. It cannot be discussed here in any detail.

[69] A point I discussed in "Total Exile, Empty Land".

There were, of course, some differences that could not be prevented. The Exodus led to Sinai and *torah* before the people reached the land. Thus, within this discourse not only the origin of Israel but also what makes Israel unique, i.e. *torah*, originated outside the land. The Return could not conjure up the image of a new Moses but managed a second and secondary Moses (i.e. Ezra). In addition, the Exodus led to the settlement of much of the land, whereas the Return led to the settlement of Yehud only. Yet, on one point, the Return seemed to shine more. Isa 52:11–12 constructed the return of the temple vessels, which symbolized the return of the deity and those who carried them, not only as a reversal of the exile of the vessels and people[70] but also in terms that clearly evoked and surpassed the image of the 'return' associated with the Exodus (cf. Isa 52:12aa with Deut 16:3 and Exod 12:11; 31–34; Isa 52:12b and Exod 14:19 [and Exod 13:21–22]; note also that in Isa 52:11–12 Yhwh, not Pharaoh, commands the people to leave).[71] Significantly, unlike the first 'return' (i.e. the Exodus), in the book of Isaiah Yhwh brings the symbols marking his and the people's presence not to the land in general, but to Jerusalem. The Exodus leads directly to the land, but the Return leads directly to the temple in Jerusalem.

In which ways did the Abraham myth of origins of Israel interact with the other two main myths (Exodus and Return)? Like the others, it was consistent with the rule that Israel must come from outside the land. Whereas Exodus evoked Egypt[72] and the Return Babylonia, Abraham's memory evoked and combined both. Like the Exodus, Abraham's story was directly associated with the large (promised) land; like the Return, Abraham's memory was directly associated with the founding of the Jerusalemite temple.

Unlike Exodus and Return, the narrative about Abraham did not require him to leave the land to be in exile. Yet he does, and since he does, his story allows a convergence of the motif of exile in the north with that in the south. The memory of Abraham's march into exile to Egypt is, moreover, emblematic of the lack involved in exile outside the land. Abraham, the patriarch, must leave the land– the alternative is to perish–but to do so involved his wife's transfer to Pharaoh. (Within the logic of the story, and from Abraham's perspective, if he says, 'She is my sister', Pharaoh takes possession of her; if he says, 'She is my wife', he is killed and Pharaoh takes possession of her. Either way, Pharaoh takes possession of her.) In a patriarchal society in which men's honour depends to a large extent

---

70 See Jer 27:22; Lam 4:15.
71 See J. Goldingay, *The Message of Isaiah 40–55* (London: T&T Clark, 2005), 458–60. From a different perspective, see J. Van Seters, *The Pentateuch* (Sheffield: Sheffield Academic Press, 1999), 153.
72 And vice versa, see Amos 9:7.

on their control of 'their woman/women', the portrayed situation conveyed a sense of extreme powerlessness and shamefulness. The matter required YHWH to intervene and 'save' Abraham's honour (Gen 12:17).[73] From the perspective of a community in which the memory of Abraham is associated with constructions of Israel and vice versa, this story served as a cultural memory node (or site of memory) that encapsulated and reminded the community of the shamefulness of 'exile from the land', of the clear priority to remain alive even in the face of extreme shame, of hope for divine help and, within the general context of their knowledge of Abraham/Israel, of trust in the fulfilment of the promises–even when they seem impossible (see Sarah's position as Pharaoh's concubine). In addition, this memory created a semiotic system that associated the loss of 'wife' with that of the 'land' and the related, seeming loss of potential for the future. It also created a scenario in which prominent differences raised significant issues in the discourse of the group. For instance, Abraham left the land for Egypt because of famine, not sword, but both were imagined as essentially dependent on YHWH's will. Both sinners (late monarchic Judah) and the pious (Abraham) may be removed from the land, directly and indirectly, by YHWH (see the underlying conceptual world of 2 Sam 24:12–13). Didactically, the well-established cause-and-effect relationship between sin and exile was put into perspective. Exile may coexist with piety.

In addition, Abraham lived in 'exilic conditions' inside the land–a point emphatically made by the partial parallel between the memory of Abraham (and Sarah) in Egypt and Abraham (and Sarah) in Gerar. The idea that Israel can be in exile in the land was, as is well known, another central and generative concept within the discourse of late Persian/early Hellenistic Yehud–and much later periods.

Significantly, Abraham was remembered as leaving Egypt with wealth (Gen 12:16, 20; 13:1–2) in a way reminiscent of Israel's Exodus (Exod 12:25–36) and of some related memories of Israel's Return (see Ezra 1:4). When Abraham leaves Gerar, the same motif appears, though somewhat less prominently (Gen 20:14). In addition, 'the Other' acknowledges him as a prophet, and he in

---

[73] I am discussing the story within the cultural parameters within which it was likely understood by the relevant (male) *literati* in late Persian/early Hellenistic Yehud, as pertinent to a historical study like the one advanced here. To be sure, the story (Gen 12:10–13:2) may carry a very different meaning when it is understood against present-day contexts and within the cultural and social systems in which we live today. Every time I deal with this text, my students raise the image of 'Abraham, the pimp'. (This portrayal is shared by scholars as well; e.g. B. L. Visotzky, *The Genesis of Ethics* [New York: Crown, 1996], 25–8.) Yet, it is very unlikely the mentioned *literati* imagined Abraham, the obedient servant/friend of YHWH, as a pimp.

turn becomes a conduit of blessing for them (Gen 20:7,17–18). The community also remembered that Abraham's (and symbolically, Israel's) blessing of progeny in the form of Isaac (symbolically continuity for Israel) followed his intervention on behalf of 'the other' and its own blessing of progeny. Given the emphasis in the discourse of Yehud about Abraham/Israel as conduits of blessing for 'the Other', including the far more powerful in worldly terms than Abraham/Israel (e.g. the king of Gerar), and the related emphasis on the relationship between YHWH (and thus Israel) and the Persian imperial centre in the pre-utopian world, these considerations are particularly important.

Remembering the Aram Connection

The Abraham of memory provided also a necessary, connective nexus between narratives of origin that focused on Mesopotamia (see Gen 11:31 and the previous section) and those that emphasized the Aramean start of Israel (Gen 11:32–12:1; 24:4,10; 25:20; cf. Deut 26:5) and allowed them to be bound together with those of Egypt (e.g. Deut 26:5; Josh 24:2–4, and the general Genesis–Exodus narrative). Remembering Abraham was remembering that to go to *his country, his kindred and his father's house* (cf. Gen 12:1) is to go Aram-naharaim, to the city of Nahor: Haran.[74] It was to remember that the kinsmen of 'Abraham' (and the other patriarchs, and thus, of Israel) are Arameans (see, esp. Deut 26:5).

Whatever the origin of traditions that construed in-group memory that saw Israel as a 'particular' offshoot of an Aramean population and Arameans as close kin, the meaning of this cultural memory within milieu of the late Persian period could not be disassociated from the use of Aramaic by the remembering community and other Yahwistic groups (e.g. Samaria, Elephantine). Linguistic markers tend to be construed as group/ethnic markers. It is worth noting, for instance, that in Elephantine the same person may be characterized in one document as Aramean and as a Jew in another.[75]

---

[74] See Gen 24:4,10; compare Gen 12:1. On Aram-naharaim, the Aramean territories by the Euphrates river, see J. J. Finkelstein, "Mesopotamia," in *JNES* 21 (1962): 73–92; Cf. J. Van Seters, *Abraham in Tradition*, 33–4.

[75] 'Meshullam son of Zaccur, an Aramean' (TAD B 3.3/B 36) and cf. 'Meshullam son of Zaccur, a Jew' (TAD B 3.6/ B 39); 'Mahseiah son Jedaniah, an Aramean' (TAD B 2.1/B 23; TAD B.2.7.3/B 29 and cf. 'Mahseiah son of Jedaniah, a Jew' (TAD B 2.2/B 24). "B" numbers refer to B. Porten, *The Elephantine Papyri in English* (Leiden: Brill, 1996), while TAD refers to B. Porten, and A. Yardeni, *Textbook of Aramaic Documents from Ancient Egypt*, 4 vls. (Jerusalem: Hebrew University, 1986–1999).

Remembering Abraham the Aramean was imagining him (and his household, e.g. his servant) speaking Aramean, just as the remembering community did. It is also linking him (and the community) to the administrative tongue of the empire. This aspect of cultural memory linked the remembering community also with the largest cultural group in the area and with empire. At the same time, like any 'bridge', this memory also called attention to differences; Abraham the 'Aramean' was envisioned as substantially different. The Arameans were not promised the land, were not servants of Yhwh nor 'friends/lovers' of the deity and did not obey it. In addition, the Arameans populating the era of the patriarchs in the cultural memory of the community were not perishing, homeless, or landless, but the patriarchs were portrayed as such (see Deut 26:5).[76]

Abraham the Aramean served as a site of memory that embodied and communicated both a sense of (partial) belonging to, and separateness from, the dominant cultural group and the ways they informed each other within the community in Yehud.

Tensions, Minority Reports, and Preferences and Disfavours

Cultural memories of heroes do not have to offer a fully consistent image. Tensions may exist among different images of a hero, since they may fit diverse rhetorical and discursive needs. This is certainly expected within the context of late Persian Yehud. Salient tensions, statements that are logically contradictory, or reports about events that are inconsistent with the explicit world portrayed in the text occur time and again among the books included in the repertoire of the community. In fact, all of these contributed to the shaping of the message of these books and suggested modes of reading them.[77]

For purposes of reconstructing the intellectual discourse of the period and the associated cultural memory held by the community, it is helpful to focus on the generative processes or discursive/ideological needs that led to, or were reflected in, these tensions. At times, some discursive/ideological needs are reflected in very few vignettes within the general cultural memory of the hero. They appear, as it were, as a minority report. Why? What rules of preference and disfavour would lead to their minority status within the memory of the com-

---

76 See J. G. Janzen, "The 'Wandering Aramean' Reconsidered," in *VT* 44 (1994): 359–75; J. H. Tigay, *Deuteronomy* (Jewish Publication Society Commentary; Philadelphia: Jewish Publication Society, 1996), 240; compare A. R. Millard, "A Wandering Aramean," in *JNES* 39 (1980): 153–5.
77 I have discussed these features and their meanings extensively through the years. See, for instance, my *History in Chronicles, passim*.

munity reflected in the traces it left in the authoritative literary repertoire of the community? Of course, disfavour may lead to full or partial omission. In what follows, I will deal with two concrete, illustrative examples.

The first example deals with the salient tension between attaching Abraham to both worldly powerlessness and military might. The preceding discussion has emphasized the many important roles the memory of Abraham (/Israel) lacking worldly power served within the discourse of the community. But the same remembering community knows the Abraham of Gen 14 (see esp. vv. 14–15), who is a mighty and clever (experienced?) military leader able to defeat a coalition of King Chedorlaomer of Elam, King Tidal of Goiim, King Amraphel of Shinar, and King Arioch of Ellasar with his private, well-trained servants. The report about Abraham the military hero is clearly a 'minority report' within the book of Genesis and elsewhere.

Given the common and anticipated associations between founder and hero and, in the particular case of Abraham, given also some of the links between memories about Abraham and matters later associated with David, the crucial question is clearly why Abraham (and Moses, see below) tended *not* to be remembered as the usual 'manly hero' as opposed to why he occasionally was.

The answer to this question seems quite obvious. The tendency to prefer Abraham the powerless to Abraham the powerful general is easy to understand: powerlessness was a requirement for the remembering community's identification of Abraham with (exilic) 'Israel'. It was necessary for binding the memory of Abraham to those of Exodus and Return and to emphasize promise over fulfilment. These considerations alone suggest that the Abraham the *literati* responsible for the community's books and for shaping its intellectual discourse remembered had to be, for most purposes and in most occasions, powerless. He had to be surrounded by mighty 'Others', but unlike them, he alone held Yhwh's promise. This Abraham was perishing and landless but obedient to Yhwh and a lover/friend of the deity.

There was also a complementary tendency at work to disfavour military power within the discourse of the community. Contrary to the general trend to attribute a heroic–and thus a strong 'manly' character–to figures of the past that embody a nation/city/dynasty/polity (e.g. Gilgamesh; David; Cyrus, Aeneas), the two main 'founders' of Israel, Abraham and Moses, were not portrayed as mighty military leaders in the Pentateuchal books.[78] This is hardly a coinci-

---

78 On Moses, see n. 14 above. The lack of emphasis on Moses the general in the Hebrew Bible necessitated the development of Joshua the general, yet the construction of Joshua is balanced and informed by Josh 1:8. The same holds true for Jacob.

dence. The reason for this disfavour was likely related to the actual socio-political situation of the community, including–but not limited to–its relation with the imperial centre and its internal hierarchical organization. In addition, the related values (and concepts of what a 'man' is) held by its *literati*, and likely some other groups in the community, played an important role. This tendency was not restricted to Moses and Abraham. Even the image of Joshua the Conqueror, necessary to the narrative, was balanced and informed by Josh 1:8, among others. The ideal king in Deut 17:14–20 and esp. vv. 18–20 is certainly not a king like those of the nations (cf. v. 14). The images of David in Chronicles and Psalms and the ways in which they inform those of Samuel are also consistent with this trend.[79] All these examples point to an image of what a (Yahwistic, that is, a 'true/godly') hero/leader/ruler (and one may say also a 'man') is that was counter to traditional conceptions but appropriate for the discourse and worldview of the *literati* responsible for these texts and for the shaping of the community's collective memory, and their historical circumstances.

Against this background, it is still worth noting that 'minority reports' occurred in the Hebrew Bible, for both Moses and Abraham, and had a role to play in the collective memory of Israel. They suggest a not fully repressed need to balance the image of the foundational figures of Israel with 'traditional' attributes for maleness, greatness, and power.[80]

These considerations lead to the unavoidable question of whether 'minority reports' such as those in Gen 14 and Num 21:21–35; Deut 2:26–3:13[81] are remnants of a larger corpus of memories in which founding figures were characterized as more 'traditional' heroes.[82] If this is the case, then the cultural memory reflected and shaped by the present texts would represent the *literati*'s successful endeavour to construct a particular memory of Israel that was consistent with

---

[79] One may add also that Israel identified itself with Jacob, the smooth tent-dweller, not Esau the hairy hunter. Significantly, some later literature (e.g. Jub 38) made Jacob more 'heroic' than Esau–Jacob kills Esau in battle and defeats his forces. Of course, Jubilees constructs a different memory of Israel than the one reflected and communicated by the Pentateuchal books.

[80] The same holds true on the matter of wealth. The patriarchs had to be imagined as poor, perishing, landless, and homeless but at the same time, as very wealthy individuals enjoying the status of a mighty prince (Gen 23:6; נשיא אלהים carries a double meaning in this verse). Despite all the differences, from a typological perspective, one may compare the situation to the 'need' to associate the obviously poor, newborn Jesus with gold, frankincense, and myrrh because he was a 'king' (Matt 2:11).

[81] Note also the hero-centred horizon of thought implied and communicated in Gen 24:60. The defeat the sons of Jacob inflicted on Shechem is condemned in the text and used to emphasize Jacob's ultimate powerlessness.

[82] Römer, "Moses outside the *Torah* and Diaspora Identity".

their worldview and values by limiting exposure to some sites of memory,[83] enhancing the importance of others and imbuing remaining problematic sites with 'appropriate' meanings,[84] either directly or indirectly, by setting them in the context of a large corpus of texts that turned them into 'minority reports'. All these questions are as interesting as they are impossible to answer with any degree of certainty. Yet they are important, because the *literati*-shaped, collective memory represented in the authoritative repertoire of books was most likely selective–as all collective memories are. Some texts and images were included and others excluded. Although historians of ancient Israel cannot reconstruct what was excluded, they should attempt to reconstruct at least some of the 'rules' governing the game of 'exclusion and inclusion' in the collective memory of the period.

In later times, to be sure, there appeared (reappeared?) images of Moses the conqueror and of Abraham the 'masterful general' as well.[85] There is nothing surprising about that; communities adapt and develop memories according to their present needs. The past is always present among those remembering it as their 'present' past, even if they maintain and very often need to maintain that it existed in the 'past' as well.

---

[83] Enoch can be included in the list of possible traditions that could have been selected for limited participation in the collective memory of Israel construed by that authoritative repertoire of the community. It seems reasonable to assume that the text in Gen 5:24 (cf. 5:22) is the tip of the iceberg of a large tradition not included in the book of Genesis. The principle of relative exclusion that could have operated here may also have been at work in Chronicles, in which this character neither walks about with the deity nor disappears.

[84] Note, for instance, the characterization of Moses in Exod 17:8–14. Readers of these texts were not asked to imagine General Moses but Moses as Yhwh's intermediary and as a leader/writer. He is the 'religious' leader, Joshua is the general, and as important as it is for readers revisiting the battle scene and its immediate aftermath to imagine Joshua, he is far less important than Moses and victory does not depend on his skill but on Yhwh's help through Moses.

[85] Concerning Abraham, see, *Ant.* 1.177–179 and see L. H. Feldman, *Flavius Josephus Translation and Commentary, Vol. 3* (Leiden: Brill, 2000), 67, esp. n. 562 (cf. *Ant.* 2.213–214). Feldman's long list of references shows the clear contrast between later rabbinic reconstruction of the Abraham of Gen 14 and Josephus'. There is also the text that Josephus attributes to Nicolaus of Damascus in *Ant.* 1.159–160. For Moses, see Römer, "Moses outside the *Torah* and Diaspora Identity".

Preferences and Disfavours: The Case of a Substantial Omission

Joshua 24:2–3 explicitly reflects a reconstruction of the past in which Israel's ancestors worshipped 'other gods'.[86] The presence of such a memory was to be expected, since the community remembered that Israel's ancestors were Arameans (for a fuller discussion, see the section, 'Remembering the Aram Connection'). Yet, the story of the origin of Israel embodied in the Abraham of the Hebrew Bible contains no reference to the beginning of one of the most defining features of Israel as imagined by the remembering community: the worship of Yhwh alone. It seems extremely unlikely that the community imagined the Abraham of Gen 12:1–3 as a worshipper of 'other gods'. Moreover, this would have precluded Abraham from signifying and embodying 'Israel', Yhwh's servant. What about the Abraham of Gen 11:27–32? As a child did not Abraham worship the gods of his father/ancestors (see Josh 24:2–3; cf. v. 15)?[87] At some point the fateful shift to serving and obeying Yhwh, that is, to becoming 'Israel', must have happened.

A story of origins that includes no reference to the origin of this 'Israel' raises the question why this could have been the case in the official, collective memory of the community discussed here and represented in their repertoire of authoritative books. Certainly, this situation seems odd, and significantly, it did not hold in communities later than the one discussed here.[88]

The remarkable exclusion of stories about Abraham's rejection of the worship of 'other gods' in the Hebrew Bible and the collective memory of the community being discussed here is consistent with two important ideological positions. The first has been touched on above. It is the matter of *not* grounding Yhwh's choice of Abraham (and Israel) on merit. At work is a core concept in the discourse of the period involved in different ways with most of the central divine choices (e.g. the selection of the land, of Jerusalem, site of the temple, of the Davidic dynasty, of Solomon as the man of peace able to build it in Chronicles; note also that the crucial event of the Exodus is not predicated on the merit of the Israelites there–Yhwh is portrayed in Exod 3:7 as seeing the misery of the

---

[86] The reference in vv. 2–3 serves a clear rhetorical purpose, as is clear from Josh 24:15. Within a Jerusalem-centred reading of the text, the importance of the speech's delivery at Shechem lies in its status in the constructed geography of the community as the first city in the land for those who come from Aram (Gen 12:5–6; 33:18). As such, it is associated with 'our ancestors'.

[87] If one were to claim Abraham's father did not worship 'other gods', then one would only move the crucial shift by one generation.

[88] For example, Jdt 5:6; Jub 11:16–17; 12:2–8; 12:12–14; *Ant.* 1.154–157, *Gen. Rab.* 38.13, among many others.

people, not their merit).⁸⁹ Within this discourse, the selection transforms the one being selected, and in the case of individuals or the people, carries obligations to the one who made the selection, but the selection itself is left unexplained in human reason, and thus rhetorically unassailable.

The second reason is that shaping memories about Abraham before Gen 12 would, by necessity, involve imagining an Abraham before the land and the promise, weakening a crucial component in the Abraham of the site of memory reflected and shaped by the book of Genesis. As a matter of mindshare, Genesis asked its primary readership to focus on the Abraham transformed by the divine selection, the promise, and strongly connected in his own 'landless'/exilic way, with the land. Only the transformed Abraham could embody Israel in this discourse, no matter how meritorious the untransformed Abraham could have been.

Genesis provides a segmented story of Abraham that may be seen as a kind of segmented history of Israel. The book does not claim that Abraham kept worshipping other gods until the events reported in Gen 12:1–3, nor could it have done so. It suggests, however, that what happened before is not worth remembering as much as what happened later to Abraham. In many ways, the same principles governing this segmented history/story are similar to those in place in Chronicles. This book does *not* claim the world was not created by YHWH as described in Genesis, or that there was no garden of Eden, no Exodus, no wandering in the desert, no conquest of the land, no period of Judges and the like. Instead, it suggests the readers should focus on other matters, to create additional paths for their virtual or mental tour of central sites of memory that do not include the garden of Eden and the like and to walk these paths in order to reconfigure some aspects of the social memory held by the group. In the case of Chronicles, they are to read in a way that informs and is being informed by other texts existing in the community.⁹⁰

The two observations advanced above provide grounds for choosing not to include stories about Abraham's rejection of the worship of 'other gods'. They do not, however, provide sufficient grounds for exclusion. As shown in the pre-

---

89 As mentioned in the section entitled 'Divine Choice, Obedience, and Test', there are texts that inform and somewhat balance this position, and some aspects of 'remembering Abraham' are also involved in the process. To contextualize an idea by introducing complementary positions, some of which might create logical tensions, does not discredit that idea.

90 We simply cannot know if this was the case for Genesis in the late Persian/early Hellenistic period, since we do not have 'the other story'. 'The other story' of Chronicles was textually inscribed in the books included in the Primary History. We do not have books from the period that describe the pre-selection Abraham, nor can we be sure that they even existed.

vious section, different and contradicting tendencies may exist, so it would not have been difficult to imagine a tendency to stress Abraham's rejection of any worship of 'other gods'. The long list of elaborations of this motif appearing in works later than those of this period only reinforces the point.

Yet, unlike the previous cases in which some balance between inclusive and exclusive trends developed, leading to main memories and what I have called 'minority reports', there is no such balance about the 'pre-selection' Abraham, but rather, omission. This situation seems to speak loudly about the importance of the issues at stake within the world of the *literati* responsible for the Pentateuchal books and for the cultural memory they wanted to shape.[91]

In Sum

This essay has shown how the memory of Abraham served as a central site of memory that encapsulated and evoked a large number of central issues and images in the discourse of the community, and how the latter related to the actual historical circumstances in which it lived. It has shown that this site of memory served as a memory node binding several other core sites together into a well-crafted web of sites of memory, informed and shaping each other. It has pointed at tendencies towards preference for and disfavour of certain motifs and explored what these can tell us about the world of the community. It has also raised questions about memories that were de-emphasized and mindshare. All in all, it is illustrative of the contribution that studies on cultural memory can bring to the historical study of the world of ancient societies in general and late Persian/early Hellenistic Yehud. Of course, Abraham was not the only figure remembered. Reconstructions of the intellectual discourse of this society (or at least its *literati*) must take into account the memories of all the other central personages of Israel's past.

---

[91] The same holds true even if no stories existed about 'pre-selection' Abraham within the community. If this were the case and no one ever thought of how, when, or why Abraham rejected the worship of 'other gods', this lack would speak volumes about the intellectual discourse of the period and about the actual power the centre of the community held over its members, be they literate or not.

Exploring the Memory of Moses 'The Prophet' in Late Persian/Early Hellenistic Yehud/Judah*

Introduction

Moses was one of the most salient sites of memory in ancient Yehud. As was the case with similar sites (e.g. Abraham), a positive feedback loop developed: the more central a figure was, the more it became a 'magnet' for issues and images that stood at the community's core (including and involving matters of self-characterization, identity, and ideology). Conversely, the more such matters and images were associated with Moses, the more central he became.

The positive feedback loop is consistent with the tendency to organize memory to coalesce around main symbolic figures/sites of memory. Remembering the 'great heroes' of the past draws the attention of the remembering community to their (construed) personality, their main (assigned) attributes, and the outcome of their actions, such as the establishment of institutions, the creation of cities, particular events like battles or political reforms, central texts associated with them, and the like.[1] From time to time emphasis may shift from one pole to the other, and in Yehud there was a strong tendency to focus on the outcome and lasting significance of the Mosaic events (e.g. Exodus, *torah*, etc.). Nevertheless, this does not mean the figure of Moses and the attributes associated with him were not important.

As a most central hero in Yehud, Moses was construed as the central exemplar. He was both (a) a personification of a set of ideal standards that, while highly desirable, were not achievable and (b) a central example of what the ideological system and discourse of Yehud was likely to develop by bringing together its main concerns in a figure that could embody and communicate them. Of course, meaning (b) only emphasizes the importance and potential of meaning (a).

---

* First published in *Remembering Biblical Figures in the Late Persian Period & Early Hellenistic Periods. Social Memory and Imagination* (eds. D. V. Edelman and E. Ben Zvi; Oxford: Oxford University Press, 2013), 335–64.

1 Although social memory is historically contingent, the mentioned processes tend be comparable, though not identical, across different cultures and societies (though certainly not all). This is because they relate to the ways in which social memory and social mindscapes are likely to be shaped. For comparative purposes, with processes in a very different society and time that still are focused on the importance of main figures for social memory, one may look at C. Kaplonski, *Truth, History and Politics in Mongolia* (London/ New York: Routledge, 2004), 182–6.

Remembering (and thus constructing) Moses in Yehud brought up within the community the most central exemplar they had, for remembering Moses became identified with remembering (and thus constructing) who Yhwh and Israel were. Remembering Moses involved remembering, among other things, (a) that Yhwh brought Israel out of Egypt with mighty, unequalled deeds to establish the deity's unique relationship with Israel (e. g. Lev 11:45, *passim*), which was a central concept for the formation of Israel's identity as Yhwh's people and of Yhwh as Israel's god. It also meant (b) that Yhwh provided Israel with distinctive teachings (e. g. Deut 4:5–6, *passim*) and particularly, the central text of this text-centred community,[2] which again was a central concept for the formation of Israel's identity as a text-centred community; (c) that Yhwh provided Israel with a blueprint for achieving a degree of purity/holiness consistent with their association with Yhwh and Yhwh's land, which was necessary for the formation of Israel's identity as a 'holy' people; and (d) the main historical metanarrative of Israel, in which Yhwh brought Israel out of exile in Egypt, led Israel to the land, eventually sent it into exile because of sins but will once again bring it back to the land (e. g. Deut 31:16–21 [cf. Deut 28]; Deut 30:1–10; cf. Deut 32:19–43), which was essential for the construction of Israel's identity as a continuous, social group based on shared ancestry, a shared history and a shared future hope and certainty about it. Of course, remembering Moses was also remembering and mentally re-enacting the power of Yhwh (e. g. Deut 7:18–21, *passim*) and the deity's incomparability (e. g. Deut 4:32–34) that, given the unique relationship between Yhwh and Israel, indirectly and at the discursive and imaginative level, empowered Israel and made it incomparable among the nations.

The memory of Moses brought together, like no other figure, the concepts of Exodus, *torah*, land, exile, sin, and hope. It is in this context that I would like to stress that Moses was saliently remembered also as a prophet and explore some of the implications of his characterization as such. To remember Moses as a prophet was to associate his memory with prophecy; in which ways did such

---

[2] On Israel as a text-centred community, see, for instance, T. Römer, "Du temple au livre: L'idéologie de la centralization dans l'historiographie deutéronomiste," in *Rethinking the Foundations* (eds. T. Römer, and S. L. McKenzie; BZAW 294; Berlin/New York: De Gruyter, 2000), 207–25. I have written on this matter elsewhere; see E. Ben Zvi, "Observations on Josiah's Account in Chronicles and Implications for Reconstructing the Worldview of the Chronicler," in *Essays on Ancient Israel in Its Near Eastern Context* (eds. Y. Amit et al.; Winona Lake, IN: Eisenbrauns, 2006), 89–106 and "Imagining Josiah's Book and the Implications of Imagining it in Early Persian Yehud," in *Studien zur Sozial- und Religionsgeschichte Israels und seiner Umwelt* (ed. R. Schmitt; AOAT 250; Münster: Ugarit, 2008), 193–212.

a memory serve to embody, inform, and perhaps contribute to the organization of knowledge about (past) prophecy/prophets in Yehud?

Moses was consistently remembered as a prophet in late Second Temple communities—and in Jewish, Samarian, and Christian groups as well after the destruction of the Jerusalemite temple in 70 CE.[3] At times, simple references to him as a prophet indicate that the 'fact' that Moses was prophet was common 'knowledge' in the social memory (e.g. Sir 46:1; Wis 11:1; *Tg. Ps* 90:1). At times, the matter might have been somewhat emphasized to serve the particular purposes of a writer, as in the writings of Philo and Josephus.[4] But remembering Moses as a prophet was not an innovation of Sirach or the late Second Temple period. Moses the prophet played a prominent role in the social memory of late Persian Yehud as well.[5]

Moses the Prophet and the Exodus Node of Memories

Some of the texts within the repertoire of late Persian Yehud or early Hellenistic Judah that explicitly referred to Moses as a prophet emphatically brought to the minds of the *literati* of Yehud the concept of prophet in conjunction with the

---

[3] See, for instance, J. Lierman, *The New Testament Moses* (Tübingen: Mohr Siebeck, 2004), 32–64. As for Judaism, see Rambam's *Thirteen Principles* (esp. principle 7). The same point is made in Qaraite theology. Moses is construed as an important prophet in Islam as well.

[4] For examples of the multiple, explicit references to Moses as a prophet in their respective works, see Philo, e.g., Decal. 175; Gig 56, Mut. 103, 125; and Josephus, *Ant.* 2.327; 4.165, 320, 329. On the Moses of Philo, see L. H. Feldman, Philo's Portrayal of Moses in the Context of Ancient Judaism (Notre Dame, Ind.: Univ. of Notre Dame Press, 2007. Concerning Josephus, L. H. Feldman notes also, 'Josephus highlights the role of Moses as a prophet, twice identifying him as a prophet when the biblical text does not (*Ant.* 2.327 vs Exod 14:13; *Ant.* 4.320 vs Deut 33:1) ... so also Philo (*Legum Allegoriae* 2.1.1)'; citation from L. H. Feldman, *Judean Antiquities 1–4* (ed. S. Mason; Flavius Josephus Translation and Commentary 3; Leiden: Brill, 2000), 471. This said, Josephus tends to add the explicit word 'prophet' (or 'prophesied') to many other biblical characters. See L. H. Feldman, "Prophets and Prophecy in Josephus," in *Prophets, Prophecy, and Prophetic Texts in Second Temple Judaism* (eds. M. H. Floyd and R. D. Haak; London/New York: T&T Clark, 2006), 210–39 (213). In any event, Josephus explicitly refers to Moses as the greatest of all prophets (*Ant.* 4.329). In the later Samaritan tradition, Moses is the prophet par excellence and this might have held true for Persian-period Samaria as well, but there is no way to prove or disprove the matter.

[5] There is a long history of interpretation that emphasized the role of Moses as the archetypal prophet in the Hebrew Bible. For a recent brief survey and bibliography, see M. Widmer, *Moses, God, and the Dynamics of Intercessory Prayer* (FAT 2.8; Tübingen: Mohr Siebeck, 2004), 72–5.

memory of the Exodus.⁶ The point, of course, is not that Moses was associated with the Exodus–this was a given–or that memories of 'the greatest event' conjured memories of 'the greatest leader' in the community and, vice versa,–a commonplace–but that Moses was explicitly remembered as 'the prophet' of the Exodus and, vice versa, that the Exodus was seen as a paradigmatic case of prophetic activity. The key texts in this regard are Deut 34:10–12 and Hos 12:14. The latter reads: 'By a prophet Yнwн brought Israel up from Egypt, and by a prophet it was guarded/guarded itself.'⁷

The text is in a particular literary setting where it evokes memories of Moses and Jacob, presents a paradigmatic contrast between Yнwн and Jacob, and raises a number of interesting issues.⁸ In addition, it clearly and explicitly evoked and shaped a memory of the Exodus in which the main human agent was Moses the prophet. To be sure, Moses was imagined as a tool and intermediary of the 'real' historical agent, the deity, as explicitly expressed by the preposition *be*. Moreover, Moses was imagined as related to, but on the whole secondary in importance to, the event. But memories about intermediaries are, by necessity, deeply intertwined with memories about those they stood for and whose

---

6 The repertoire included, at least in a form very close to the present one, most of the books that eventually became part of the Hebrew Bible (e. g. the prophetic books, those included in the collection Genesis–2 Kings, Chronicles, Ruth, Lamentations, Proverbs). These books were most likely read in a way informed by their late Persian/Early Hellenistic discursive setting such that they shaped and reflected the social memory of the reading community. Their compositional/redactional history was not likely to have been influential in their reading and interpretation. There may have been other authoritative books in the discourse of the community, but there is no reason to assume that, as a whole, the repertoire of books from the period to which we have access (i. e. those that eventually became part of the Hebrew Bible) was non-representative of the actual repertoire of the community to the extent that we could not even approximate or tentatively approach the main systemic features of the Persian-period repertoire in Yehud by analysing the texts to which we have access. The conditions in the poor society of late Persian Yehud and the existence of a particularly very small circle of *literati* (likely around the Jerusalemite temple) was a far cry from anything in the late Second Temple, so inferences from the library situation at Qumran are not particularly germane for reconstructing the situation in Yehud.
7 On the reflexive meaning of the *niph'al* see, for instance, Joüon-Muraoka (P. Joüon, *A Grammar of Biblical Hebrew* [trans. and rev. by T. Muraoka; SubBib, 27; 2nd ed.; Rome: Pontifical Biblical Institute, 2006]), 51a, c; B. K. Waltke and M. O'Connor, *An Introduction to Biblical Hebrew Syntax* (*[IBHS]*; Winona Lake, IN: Eisenbrauns, 1990), 23.4b. The *niph'al* form of the root שמר carries a reflexive meaning in most of its occurrences in the Hebrew Bible.
8 See E. Ben Zvi, *Hosea* (FOTL 21 A. 1; Grand Rapids, MI: Eerdmans, 2005), 255–56, 260–62. For different positions, see the bibliography there and E. K. Holt, *Prophesying the Past* (JSOTSup 194; Sheffield: Sheffield Academic Press, 1995), 49; K. van der Toorn, "The Exodus as Charter Myth," in *Religious Identity and the Invention of Tradition* (eds. J. W. van Henten and A. Houtepen; STAR 3; Assen: Royal Van Gorcum, 2001), 113–27 (120–22).

deeds they performed; as a result, such memories tend to show some blurring of boundaries between representatives and those they represent. Significantly, within the authoritative texts that encode and evoke the social memory of Moses, it is not only sinful Israel who might refer to him as the one who brought Israel up from Egypt (see Exod 32:1, 23), but Yhwh was imagined and remembered as shaping a memory of the events in similar language (Exod 33:1 cf. Exod 33:12). Likewise, in Deut 34:12 (and cf. 34:11), Moses is associated with Exodus motifs that were usually associated with Yhwh (see Deut 4:34; 26:8 and cf. Exod 7:3; Deut 6:22; 7:19; 29:2; Jer 32:20 – 21).

This said, since the memory of the hero was encoded in memories of the event, attributes assigned to the latter inform the characterization of the hero. For instance, the event was explicitly construed in the discourse of the community as unlike any other, greater in splendour, more memorable, and of greater significance.[9] When social memory construes a past event to be without equal and with long-term significance, then the very same social memory would tend to consider the human agent involved, in this case, Moses the prophet and his Exodus-related deeds, also as without equal and greater than other prophets, who certainly did not lead Israel out of Egypt. Within this system of organizing

---

9 See, for instance, Deut 4:32–34 and note the way in which Yhwh was remembered to have characterized himself in Exod 20:2 and Deut 5:6; see, among others, Exod 6:7; Lev 11:45; 22:33; Deut 13:6; Josh 24:17; Judg 2:12; 2 Kgs 17:7; and compare Deut 4:37. This chapter is not the place to dwell on the social memory of the Exodus and its importance. To discuss this issue requires a separate volume. For present purposes, it suffices to state that the Exodus likely served as the most central node of social memory for the community in Yehud. Remembering the Exodus continuously brought to the present of the community the paradigmatic narrative that exemplified and communicated the full and sole dominion of Yhwh over the entire earth, the deity's supremacy over other gods, the related the supremacy of Yhwh's intermediaries over all others, and Yhwh's unique relationship with Israel. See A. Rofé, "The Monotheistic Argumentation in Deuteronomy 4,32–40: Contents, Composition and Text," in *VT* 35 (1985): 434–45; reprinted in A. Rofé, *Deuteronomy: Issues and Interpretation* (London/New York: T&T Clark, 2002), 15–24. Exodus is a foundational narrative for both Israel and for Israel's construction of Yhwh. The very high mindshare of the Exodus within the community and its central role in the social memory of the period is indicated by the sheer number of references to it in the authoritative literature of the period. As R. S. Hendel wrote, 'Israelite law, ritual and ethics are often grounded in the precedent and memory of the Exodus' (*Remembering Abraham* [Oxford/New York: Oxford University Press, 2005], 57). Prayer should be added to the list (e.g. Jer 32:20 – 21). Texts like Exod 13:8 – 9 and Deut 6:20 – 25 (compare Exod 10:1 – 2) explicitly refer to the importance of remembering and reliving the Exodus from generation to generation, even within the world that the text evoked among the readers in late Persian or early Hellenistic Judah. The numerous references to how memorable the Exodus was and the unparalleled narrative space attached to it and its related motifs in the Pentateuch indicate its centrality.

memory and of interlinking particular sites of memory (e. g. Moses, the prophet, and Exodus), not only were the deeds of the deity at the time remembered as incomparable but also those of the intermediary, as clearly stated in Deut 34:10–12 (see Deut 4:34; 26:8 and cf. Deut 34:10a, 11–12).

Even when the memory of the Exodus was used to organize and shape memories of other events such as the 'return',[10] very basic elements that characterize the narrative are not retold, even though enough ciphers are activated to evoke the memory of the Exodus. The story of 'the return' has no Pharaoh, no plagues, no new set of teachings to be received at Sinai, and no Moses the prophet leading the people back. The new story is never as memorable as the original one within the repertoire of the community.[11] I will return to this point, but here I want to stress that not only were the incomparability elements of the Exodus and of Moses the prophet deeply intertwined, but they continuously fed each other within the discourse of the community, each carrying its own subset of particular significances.

But why did the discourse of the period show such a preference for bringing together the prophetic character of Moses and the memory of the Exodus to begin with? After all, many other types of human agents theoretically could have fulfilled the role of the intermediary. Why not, for instance, a warrior-like leader, a מושיע ('saviour') as in the period of the Judges (cf. Isa 19:20), or a priest?

A number of considerations shaped the memory of the mythical human hero of Exodus as a prophet. For one, memories of Moses were encoded in the narratives about the Exodus that existed in the community. These narratives contained salient references to great signs and portents (אותות ומפתים)[12] that directly evoked the image of a prophet (see Deut 13:2; compare 1 Sam 2:34; 2 Kgs 20:9; Isa 7:14;

---

10 Compare Isa 52:12aa with Deut 16:3 and Exod 12:11, 31–34; Isa 52:12b and Exod 14:19 (and Exod 13:21–22).
11 Note also that Isa 19:20, in which motifs related to the Exodus reverberate, refers to a מושיע 'deliverer', not a second Moses. When readers of Ezek 20:33–38 were asked to evoke the motif of the Exodus and de-familiarize it–the divine action is now not against the external 'Other' (i.e. Egypt/Pharaoh) but an Israel that turned itself into the 'Other'–they are not asked to imagine a prophet like Moses as the intermediary through which Yhwh executes punishment (cf. Deut 34:12). Ezra, which in some ways is portrayed as a second Moses, is neither a prophet nor a second Moses. He may bring back the divine teachings associated with Moses to the community, but he does not receive them directly from Yhwh.
12 E.g. Exod 7:3, 10; 10:1–2; Deut 4:34; 6:22; 7:19; 11:3; 26:8.

8:18).¹³ The importance of this *topos* for the characterization of Moses as the greatest prophet is explicitly advanced in Deut 34:10–12.

Signs and miracles were considered features of a process of prophetic authentication (e.g. 1 Kgs 13:16; Isa 7:11), even if not sufficient by themselves (see Deut 13:1–12), within the discourse of the late Persian period and in the later Second Temple period as well. As expected, the greatest prophet Moses was associated with the greatest signs and wonders in the repertoire (Deut 34:10–12), but the role of the prophet was not exhausted by his (and far less likely, her) authentication as such; quite the opposite! The authentication and the elevation it brings ensure the success of the communication of the divine message the prophet is tasked to convey.¹⁴ Within the discourse of the community in the late Persian and early Hellenistic periods, the very purpose of the liberation from Egypt was conceived to be the establishment of YHWH as Israel's god (e.g. Lev 11:45; 22:33). This was tantamount to the foundation of Israel and required the disclosure of the teachings, without which Israel becomes 'the Other'. The display of YHWH's power in Egypt, the liberation of the Israelites and the self-glorification of YHWH through these actions, along with that of Moses, all lead to the purpose of remembering the mighty deeds that disclose the divine teachings (e.g. Deut 6:20–25, *passim*).

This is not surprising, given that the *literati* of the period shaped an identity for Israel in terms of a text-centred community. As a result, its foundational memory would most likely be the (mythical) origin of the text around which the community is centred. Within the discourse of the period, the core of that text consisted of the divine teachings the community construed as having been communicated by YHWH through Moses. Thus, Moses had to be imagined as the intermediary par excellence of YHWH; not only did he have to be a prophet, but *the* prophet par excellence, with no equal (see Exod 34:29–35; Num 12:6–8; Deut 34:10).

This also is consistent with the claim that the transmission of the divine teachings (i.e. the contents of Moses' prophecy) from YHWH to Moses was more direct ('face to face', 'mouth to mouth') than communications made via other prophets/prophecies (see Exod 33:7–11; and esp. Num 12:6–8¹⁵ and Deut 34:10). Moreover, the community remembered that this direct communication was part of a larger pattern: YHWH and Moses shared a particular space for

---

13 Not all prophetic sign-acts serve only to authenticate the prophet. On a type of prophetic sign-act different from the one discussed here, see, for instance, K. Friebel, *Jeremiah's and Ezekiel's Sign-Acts* (JSOTSup 283; Sheffield: Sheffield Academic Press, 1999).
14 Although a bit late for the period, this idea is conveyed explicitly in Sir 45:3–5.
15 See B. Levine, *Numbers 1–20* (AB 4 A; New York: Doubleday, 1993), 329–32; 341–2.

meeting and talking. Unlike any other prophet, they virtually saw Moses going whenever he desired to the tent of meeting to converse with a deity who was always willing to talk to him (Exod 33:7–11).[16] The two talked as friends to each other (Exod 33:11). This uniquely close connection between Moses the prophet and Yhwh was further reinforced by the construction of a shared, ad hoc conceptual domain of memories. For instance, the signs and wonders were explicitly construed as serving not only to authenticate Moses but as ways to authenticate Yhwh, as it were, before Israel and the nations (e.g. Exod 7:2–5; Lev 11:44–45; 22:31–33; Deut 4:32–40; 6:22–25; *passim*). This authentication of Yhwh before Israel and the memory of that authentication was construed as instrumental for socializing Israel according to the divine teachings conveyed directly and through Moses, due to the inability or reluctance of Israel to communicate directly with Yhwh (e.g. Exod 20:18–21; Deut 5:22–33; 18:16). Despite their differences, Moses and Yhwh were authenticated by similar narratives; both communicated divine teachings, both needed a prophet to be able to communicate (see Exod 7:1), though for different reasons,[17] and both were teachers. Significantly, the image of Yhwh as a teacher is the most basic metaphor in the prophetic books, which were mainly didactic works. I will return to the image of Moses the prophet par excellence as the teacher par excellence (Deut 4:14).

The memory of Moses as the incomparable prophet cannot but construe his image as a '*sui generis*' prophet while at the same time, associating numerous other attributes with him that the discourse of the period linked to prophets more generally. Moses foresees the future of Israel (e.g. Deut 30:1; 31:16–22; 32:19–25), admonishes (*passim*), prays and pleads for the people, including important individuals (e.g. Exod 32:21–33; Num 12:13), teaches them how to behave (*passim*, and cf. above all with Chronicles' concept of prophecy), sings (Exod 15; cf. the singers as prophets in 1 Chr 25:1),[18] is rejected by the people (e.g.

---

[16] In addition, the community vicariously experienced and remembered the events portrayed in Exod 34:34–35. 'The verbal forms used [here] to describe these activities imply repetition of the actions, indicating that from the time that Moses returned to the camp from Mt Sinai until his death his face remained radiant' (N. M. Sarna, *Exodus* [The JPS Torah Commentary; Philadelphia: Jewish Publication Society, 1991], 221). There seem to be no restrictions on Moses' entry to the Tent of the Meeting. Contrast the situation with Aaron in Lev 16:2.

[17] Moses needs a prophet because of his inability to express himself properly while Yhwh needs one because of his inability to reach the target audience directly. From the perspective of the *literati* in Yehud, Yhwh's limitation (or better, Israel's) can be solved by the presence of written texts encoding Yhwh's message; Moses' limitation can be solved by having *literati* who can interpret and communicate the existing texts.

[18] On Chronicles and its prophets, see my "Chronicles and its Reshaping of Memories of Monarchic Period Prophets: Some Observations," in this volume, pp. 407–27 and bibliography.

Exod 14:11–12) and physically threatened (Exod 17:4; cf. 2 Chr 24:20), writes a historical narrative (cf. prophets in Chronicles),[19] and must have a proper call narrative, including portrayals of his attempts to reject the role assigned to him by YHWH (e.g. Exod 4:10; 6:12, 30).

I will return to these points, but before dealing with them, it is worth stressing that Moses cannot be *the* prophet par excellence of the collective memory of the community if he is their only prophet. Construing him as such was tantamount to organizing memories about other prophets within a pattern based on both continuity and discontinuity (and cf. already Deut 34:10 with Deut 18:15, 18) and to shaping memories of later prophets in the historical narrative of Israel in a way that was informed by the memory of Moses. It also meant a move toward reconfiguring the concept of prophet and prophecy–after all, Moses must also be *sui generis*–and introducing some level of fuzziness in the construction of the concepts of prophets and prophecy.

Continuity and Discontinuity: Moses and Mosaic Prophets in Late Persian/Early Hellenistic Judah

'By a prophet YHWH brought Israel up from Egypt, and by a prophet it was guarded/guarded itself.' Hos 12:14 shows some of the ways in which the image of Moses as a prophet informed the memory of other prophets and the concept of prophecy. The text conveys more than one meaning, even if they are complementary. On one level, it asked the readership to remember that through a prophet (i.e. Moses), YHWH brought Israel from Egypt, and by a prophet (i.e. Moses) it was guarded (cf. Deut 4:14–19).[20] At this level, the entire memory of the period from leaving Egypt to the moment the people were prepared to enter the land is evoked, including the divine teaching, social organization, and leadership. Moreover, when the text was read in this way, the basic roles of the מלאך '(divine) messenger' in Exod 23:20 (and cf. Exod 23:21–22) and those of Moses become interrelated.[21]

---

19 In Chronicles, prophets recorded (and interpreted) monarchic history (e.g. 1 Chr 29:30; 2 Chr 9:29; 12:15; 13:22; 23:32; 33:19) and conversely, books consisting of historical records included prophetic texts (2 Chr 20:34; 32:32; 33:18).
20 See especially the language of v. 15 and the role of the prophet as teacher envisaged there and note the choice of language in v. 14: ללמד אתכם 'to teach you'.
21 There is a difference as well; the מלאך leads the conquest of Canaan (cf. Exod 23:23; 32:34; 33:2), whereas Moses does not or, at least, does not directly. But both are messengers/intermediaries of the divine whose job is to protect Israel. These texts create an *ad hoc*, shared concep-

On a different level, Hos 12:14 suggested to the readership that through a prophet (i.e. Moses) Yhwh brought Israel from Egypt, and by a prophet (i.e. someone other than Moses and in period later than the Exodus) it was guarded. Although some scholars reading the text in this way have attempted to identify the other prophet,[22] the text avoids such a move by referring to 'the prophet' generically (i.e. the prophetic office), raising the image and memory of a guardianship role for 'the prophet' at a point or points in the past.[23] As a third complementary option, the text can also be understood to say, 'By a prophet Yhwh brought Israel up from Egypt, and by a prophet it has guarded itself.' Read in this way, the text conveyed an association between the foundational prophet and the prophetic office on the one hand, and the actual prophets who were necessary to Israel to guard itself after the foundational event, on the other. Continuity between Moses and the later Mosaic prophets was emphasized by the repetition of בנביא 'by a prophet'; a counterbalancing element of discontinuity was provided by the reference to the Exodus, which was historically unique, as was its prophet.

One may compare the organization of the remembered past here with that in, for instance, 2 Kgs 17:13. The readers of the text learned that Yhwh remembered the prophets of old as a group who, from a long-term, historical standpoint, attempted to teach and 'guard' Israel (though with no success). Particularly significant for the present purposes is the explicit mention of 'all the *torah* that I commanded your ancestors [during Moses' times] and which I communicated/sent to you through my servants, the prophets'. Here Yhwh remembers 'the prophets'[24] as constituting a chain of transmission for the Mosaic *torah*, and the community of readers was supposed to orientate their memory with Yhwh's and to make Yhwh's memory their own collective memory.

---

tual domain populated by memories of Moses and the divine messenger labelled מלאך. Compare Amos 2:10, in which Yhwh is evoked as the agent for the period. Note also that by the late Persian and early Hellenistic periods, prophets were imagined as מלאכים ('messengers') of Yhwh. See already the name Malachi ('my messenger'), and see Isa 44:26; Hag 1:33; 2 Chr 36:15.

22 See F. I. Andersen and D. N. Freedman, *Hosea* (AB 24; New York, NY: Doubleday, 1980), 621.

23 By not mentioning any name, the text shifts the attention of the readers to 'the office' of the prophet, away from the memory of any prophet in particular. It is likely that this emphasis on the office is at work in the lack of mention of the name of Moses in Hos 12:14 (Van der Toorn, "Exodus as Charter Myth," 120).

24 'The prophets', that is, the 'generic prophets', are the best indicator of the general concept of prophet or its mental prototype in the social mindscape of the community in late Yehud. See my "'The Prophets'–Generic Prophets and their Role in the Construction of the Image of the 'Prophets of Old' within the Postmonarchic Readership of the Book of King," in *ZAW* 116 (2004): 555–67.

The notion that prophets (or prophetic voices) were needed to lead Israel to behave in YHWH's ways was clearly expressed in many of the works included in the authoritative repertoire of the community. Indirect references also occurred in passages that reminded the readers time and again in the authoritative literature of the period of the many prophets YHWH sent to turn Israel back to the deity before the destruction of the monarchic polities (e.g. 2 Kgs 17:13; Jer 35:15; Zech 1:4; 2 Chr 36:15–16). In Chronicles, for instance, it is also conveyed by multiple examples in the historical narrative and by the presence of prophetic voices in most of the regnal periods of Judah. In addition, it is expressed in the negative portrayal of periods without prophets or prophecy (e.g. 1 Sam 3:1; Ezek 7:26; Amos 8:11–12; Ps 74:9; Lam 2:9).[25] The necessity of prophets to lead the people in YHWH's ways is also implied in the memory about the 'creation' of the prophetic Mosaic office encoded in Deut 18:15–19, where prophets are necessary because the people as a whole need an intermediary to receive divine messages. The presence of numerous sites of memory associated with multiple periods and contexts, all of which communicate a similar conceptual message about the prophets of the past, points to the very high proportion of mindshare of the relevant concept and its nodal and generative role in the discourse of the community.

The concept that at some level, all proper prophets have to be Mosaic[26] is not restricted to Hos 12:14 or Deut 17:1 but is integral to the entire discourse of the late Persian and early Hellenistic periods. It is embedded in both the conceptualization of Moses as *the* prophet par excellence and of Israel as a text/*torah*-centred community. Within a community for whom to behave in YHWH's ways was to behave in accordance to YHWH's *torah*[27] and in which this *torah* was associated

---

[25] Note also the implied, panchronic link in Prov 29:18 between the lack of prophecy and of *torah* (in the wider sense of the term, as opposed to priestly instructions, as in Ezek 7:26) as read within the *torah*-centred discourse of the late Persian and early Hellenistic periods.

[26] For a narrow meaning of the term 'Mosaic', see below and see my "On the Term 'Deuteronomistic' in Relation to Joshua–Kings in the Persian Period," in *Raising Up a Faithful Exegete* (eds. K. L. Noll and B. Schramm; Winona Lake, IN: Eisenbrauns, 2010), 61–71.

[27] This position that following YHWH (and YHWH's ways) was tantamount to following YHWH *torah* is well attested in the book of Chronicles and was integral to the general social mindscape of this book's authorship and primary readership, both of which are to be found in the late Persian or early Hellenistic period. See, for instance, 2 Chr 6:16 and cf. 1 Kgs 8:25. In Ps 119, which likely was part of the authoritative repertoire of the community by either the late Persian or early Hellenistic period, 'YHWH's *torah*' is placed in the expected structural and ideologically laden slot of YHWH. It might even be indicative of a kind of *torah*-religiosity that existed in the late Persian or early Hellenistic periods.

with Moses,[28] proper prophets cannot but be construed as Mosaic in one way or another.

Deut 13:2–6 not only asks its readers to compare future prophets with Moses (see Exod 4:28–31; Deut 34:10–12), but its very logic implies that their teachings will deal with similar kind of matters. It issues its warning about prophetic teachings that may differ from those of Moses. The line of thought expressed there leads to two conclusions. First, there cannot be a prophet like Moses, because either (a) prophets reaffirm the already known Mosaic message and therefore are at best secondary to him, or (b) they are sent by Yhwh to test Israel and should/may be killed.[29] The second conclusion is that prophets are potentially dangerous. Their prophecies must be dealt with caution and pass the test of consistency with the Mosaic divine teachings. The text creates among the readers a panchronic reality in which what the prophet says must be approved by others as consistent with the commandments as understood by the late Persian or early Hellenistic readers on the basis of their readings of the authoritative texts they have. All prophets must be Mosaic in that sense (cf. 2 Kgs 17:13; Mal 3:22–24).

In addition, the notion that there were prophets like Moses after his death, i.e. Mosaic, but not really 'like' Moses, was evoked as well by Deuteronomy within this particular *Sitz im Diskurs* (setting in the discourse of the community). Whereas Deut 18:15 explicitly states, 'Yhwh your God will raise up for you a prophet from among your own people; you shall obey such a prophet' (see also Deut 18:18–19), which pragmatically could only mean for readers in this period that there were Mosaic prophets in Israel, Deut 34:10 clearly stated that 'never again has a prophet arisen in Israel like Moses'. The latter passage reinforced what they already knew: that these prophets were not and could not have been like Moses.[30]

---

[28] E.g. Josh 1:7–8; 22:5; 23:6; 1 Kgs 2:3; 2 Kgs 14:6; 21:8; 23:23. Within the world of Chronicles, e.g. 2 Chr 23:18; 25:4; 30:6; 33:8, 14; 35:12, along with the references to laws in Exodus–Deuteronomy that were associated within the discourse of the community with Moses.

[29] In Deut 8:2 Yhwh also is construed as testing the Israelites. The concept of the testing deity is common in the discourse of Persian-period Israel and plays important roles in Chronicles and Job. The fact that Deuteronomy deems prophets to be excellent testing 'agents' is noteworthy. Significantly, these prophets are among the only divinely sent, testing agents that may/should be killed. On the concept of Yhwh's testing, see my "When Yhwh Tests People: General Considerations and Particular Observations Regarding the Books of Chronicles and Job," in this volume, pp. 472–81.

[30] It is perhaps possible to explain away the seeming tension between Deut 18:15, 18–19 and Deut 34:10 by narrowing the term 'prophet' in the first and the incomparability idea in the second. By associating the term 'prophet' in the former with those who fulfil the roles of the diviners mentioned in Deut 18:14 and postulating Moses was conceived as an incomparable proph-

The statement in Deut 34:10, however, does more than inform those in Deut 18:15,18–19 or interweave itself with other explicit and implicit expressions of the incomparability of Moses the prophet.[31] It explicitly shapes and reflects on the social memory of the remembering community. It brings together the implied author of the book of Deuteronomy and the late Persian readers to organize the past in terms of a foundational period associated with the Exodus, *torah*, and the prophet Moses and a post-foundational period in which there cannot exist a prophet like Moses. It is particularly significant that the conclusion of Deuteronomy framed the watershed in terms of prophetic hierarchy: the period of Moses the prophet and the post-Moses period in which there are other prophets who must be Mosaic but not like Moses.[32]

Continuity and Discontinuity: Periodization of 'National' History and Issues of Prophecy

Periodization is a social mnemonic activity. It is about organizing memory so a temporal continuum may be segmented so as to create sets of binary polarities that reflect and draw attention to particular issues that the remembering community considers to be of very high significance. The mentioned organization of the past into Moses' period and one of Mosaic prophets expresses a central tendency in the organization of memories of the past within late Persian and

---

et only in terms of the mighty deeds mentioned in Deut 34:11–12, one can perhaps reconcile the two statements, though there remains the issue of Deut 34:10b. Even if this were the case, references to 'prophet' here, particularly given the setting of Deut 34:10–12 within the larger book, most likely were evocative of the large conceptual field signified by the term 'prophet'. In addition, see also Deut 34:10b, Exod 33:11, the construction of Moses as entering the tent of meeting to receive divine teachings and the lack of references to Moses as one upon whom the 'word of Yhwh' came. The latter contrasts with Gen 15:1; 1 Sam 15:20; 2 Sam 7:4; Jer 1:2, 4; Ezek 1:3 and *passim*, where 'Yhwh speaks to Moses' instead. All these considerations suggest there is much at stake in differentiating between Moses and the Mosaic prophets. This issue will continue to be discussed in the following sections.

31 Much has been written about Deut 34:10–12. On this pericope and its potential implications see, for instance, S. B. Chapman, *The Law and the Prophets* (FAT 27; Tübingen: Mohr Siebeck, 2000), 113–31, and bibliography there, esp. J. Blenkinsopp, *Prophecy and Canon* (Notre Dame, IN/London: University of Notre Dame Press, 1977). See also A. H. J. Gunneweg, "Das Gesetz und die Propheten: eine Auslegung von Ex 33,7–11; Num 11,4–12,8; Dtn 31,14f.; 34,10," in *ZAW* 102 (1990): 169–80.

32 Cf. Deut 13:1–12; Mal 3:22–24 and the general discourse of the period about a text/*torah*-centred Israel. Moses was not the only prophet during the Mosaic period (see Num 11:25–9; 12:6), but he was *the* prophet of the period.

early Hellenistic Yehud/Judah. It was consistent with the most basic thrust and message of the Pentateuchal and Exodus–Deuteronomy collections and the boundaries they created. Although, on the surface, Moses seems to be imagined as the crucial mnemonic organizing principle, he actually stood for the related concepts of Exodus and *torah*–with the former authenticating the latter–and given that both the Pentateuch and Exodus–Deuteronomy[33] are 'national histories' whose main characters are Israel and Yhwh,[34] they were really about the 'birth' of Israel, i.e. about the process of the transformation of an ethnie into a *torah*/text-centred community/people through the agency of Yhwh and the mediation of Moses the prophet.[35]

Like all periodizations, this one reflects and brings attention to a number of somewhat related oppositions.[36] Three in particular are related to the present endeavour: (a) the absence of possession of the land by Israel–possession of the land; (b) Moses–other prophets; (c) prophecy (i.e. divine utterances communicated to a prophet so s/he may communicate them to Israel or a sub-group among it, which also are encoded in books) that includes basic laws–prophecy that is encoded in prophetic books but contains didactic teachings that rarely expand on law. Other matters that do not shape or reflect binary oppositions are de-emphasized by this periodization. For instance, and in particular in terms of the present endeavour: (a) the image of prophets as pleading for Israel or some important sub-group, (b) the image of prophets as singers, and (c) the motif of the people's rejection of the prophet.[37]

Before addressing these matters, it is worth stressing that multiple periodizations informing each other existed at least among the *literati* who read and re-read the authoritative literature of the period. The mentioned periodization-mak-

---

[33] The point is emphasized time and again in Exodus–Deuteronomy. See, for instance and among many others, the messages on the matter conveyed at the beginning of the collection, the motif of the liberation of the people (not of Moses), and the motif of the covenant with the people (not with Moses).

[34] This point is emphasized by the way in which the Pentateuch organized the social memory of Israel in itself and by the way in which the Pentateuch informed understandings of the Exodus–Deuteronomy in the community.

[35] Within the discourse of Yehud, the rhetorical complaint of Moses in Num 11:12, namely 'did I get pregnant and conceive all this people, did I give birth to them?' reflects, in an ironic way, a symbolic metaphor to which many of the intended and primary readers may have answered 'yes'. Through the intermediary role of Moses, Yhwh gave birth to Israel, then provided it with divine teachings.

[36] Cf. E. Zerubavel, *Time Maps* (Chicago: University of Chicago Press, 2003), 82–100.

[37] Other motifs are de-emphasized as well by this periodization, like the Davidic dynasty, but these matters lie beyond the scope of this chapter.

ing collections are better understood as 'shelves' in the 'mental library' of late Persian Yehud. Deuteronomy was on the Pentateuch shelf but also was part of the Deuteronomistic historical collection and in the Exodus–Deuteronomy collection. The Pentateuchal books occupied an important shelf but were also part of the 'Primary History' shelf and the Hexateuch shelf. The result is a web of readings, each of which is informed by a different set of books within the repertoire of the community, all of which informed each other even if, at particular times and according to circumstances and purposes, one may have carried more weight than another. The binary opposition between, for instance, the absence of possession of the land by Israel; possession of the land shaped by the Pentateuch was balanced by, among others, the periodization communicated by the Hexateuch and in turn, both–though in different ways–by Genesis–2 Kings.

Continuity and Discontinuity: The Prophet, Prophetic Books, and Moses the Prophet as a Site of Memory

The prophetic books were meant to bring to the present of the community the memory of the prophets of old. The reading community in Yehud construed and imaginatively encountered and interacted with prophets such as Isaiah, Jeremiah, Ezekiel, and Zephaniah by reading the prophetic books that were associated with them. If prophetic books belong to a genre subset of authoritative ancient Israelite books that is characterized by a claim of association with a prophetic personage of the past and which present themselves as communicating YHWH's word to its readers, then Deuteronomy was *also*, among other things, the prophetic book of Moses. In fact, Deuteronomy was textually inscribed as such by its title/introduction. The reading community of the period could have hardly missed that the book opens in a way similar to that of the other prophetic books, thus raising in the readership similar expectations about its contents.[38] The characterization of the book as 'the words that Moses spoke' is not substantially different from that advanced in Jer 1:1: 'the words of Jeremiah' or in Amos 1:1: 'the words of Amos'.[39] In all these cases, the opening words of the

---

[38] This is one of the main functions of an introduction. It elicits among the intended, primary readership of the book a provisional 'schema' of what the following text is about and suggests to the readers or learners of this text a set of questions and issues to be dealt with through their interpersonal, communal reading of the book. The introduction serves to evoke the memory of the read material for re-readers of the book.
[39] For the preference of this formula in Deuteronomy over 'the word of YHWH that came to' (cf. Hos 1:1; Mic 1:1; etc.) see later in this section.

book elicit a provisional schema about what the following text is about, associate it with a prophetic figure whose memory it evokes among the readers, and let the readers know the book will include divine messages.[40] This is clearly the case in Deuteronomy.

Prophetic books tended to carry a particular linguistic flavour, or a choice of particular expressions, or the construction of a deeply interrelated and unique network of expressions and the like that served to provide each book with a sense of uniqueness that the readership associated with the prophetic voice they encountered as they read the book. Deuteronomy not only fulfils this expectation but carries matters to a level substantially higher than the other prophetic books. Moreover, as in the prophetic books, the voice of the prophet, of YHWH and the implied author all share this flavour and tend to blur.

Like all prophetic books, Deuteronomy contained numerous references to divine messages and like all the large prophetic books that evoked figures that carried a high proportion of mindscape in the community (i.e. Isaiah, Jeremiah, and Ezekiel), it contained 'biographical' elements. Finally, Deuteronomy, like all prophetic books, shows a clear and basic structure: (a) an introduction, (b) a body consisting of didactic prophetic readings (i.e. readings that carry an association with a prophet) and (c) a clearly marked, textually inscribed conclusion.

When Deuteronomy is approached from the perspective of the requirements for inclusion in the genre of 'prophetic book',[41] it fits easily in that category. Most significantly, it does so because of clear and multiple, textually inscribed markers in the text that a readership aware of this genre hardly could have missed. To be sure, Deuteronomy fit in other collections of books (e.g. the Deuteronomistic historical collections, the Pentateuch, the Hexateuch, the Enneateuch), but it was most likely construed *also* as a prophetic book.

Yet the community remembered that Moses was different from any of the other, later Mosaic prophets. His prophetic book, Deuteronomy, was, not surprisingly, a prominent site of memory that embodied and communicated this difference. Deuteronomy did so through texts explicitly stating the dissimilarity between Moses and the later prophets (see Deut 34:10 and discussion above),

---

40 The prophet will be presented as one who received YHWH's communication so as to transmit it to 'Israel' within the world portrayed in the book, so the readers of the book may read and thus remember that.

41 For a discussion of the genre of 'prophetic book', see E. Ben Zvi, "The Prophetic Book: A Key Form of Prophetic Literature," in *The Changing Face of Form Criticism for the Twenty-First Century* (eds. M. A. Sweeney and E. Ben Zvi; Grand Rapids, MI: Eerdmans, 2003), 276–97; compare Ben Zvi, *Hosea*, 319.

through somewhat trivial differences, as at the very outset of the book,[42] but also, if not more importantly, by shaping a world of pervasive difference. Five significantly different examples illustrate this point.

First, the prophetic book of Moses contained a very substantial amount of legal material. This is clearly not the case in the other prophetic books. Moses was the prophet/site of memory that embodied legal material, unlike the others.

This is consistent with the memory of Moses that other books (Exodus–Numbers) evoked in the community. But this is a second area of pervasive difference: the memory of none of the fifteen other prophetic figures that were associated with books was not substantially encoded outside 'their' books. The matter directly relates to the construction of the memory of Moses as such a central figure that all the foundational legal material became associated with the divine teachings he received from Yhwh in the foundational period of Israel, whether they are encoded in one book or another. As a result, memories of both Yhwh's communication of these foundational teachings to Moses and Moses' communication of them to the people became part of a biography of Moses and were informed by other aspects of his biography, none of which were all encoded, even in the main, in one book. Finally, since different books may carry different voices, Moses was imagined as a person embodying multiple (and at times significantly different) voices and dictions, which, through their association with him, became deeply intertwined. None of this held true for the memory of any of the fifteen prophets associated with the other prophetic books.

Third, the opening expression, 'Yhwh spoke to Moses' or a variant of it such as 'Yhwh spoke to me', meaning Moses, is very common in texts shaping memories about Moses. It is present in Deuteronomy, but the other prophetic books fail to contain parallel expressions (e.g. 'Yhwh spoke to Ezekiel'). Conversely, 'the word of Yhwh came to X' and the like are very common in prophetic

---

[42] See Deut 1:1 and contrast it with Jer 1:1 and Amos 1:1. There was no need to identify Moses by reference to his ancestors, occupation, or place of birth; from the beginning of the book he was assumed to be unique and well known to the readership. Incidentally, no other person is called Moses in the Hebrew Bible. The same holds true of several other main figures in Israel's social memory (e.g. David), which is consistent with tendencies to reserve the names of these figures as sites of memory. One may note the memory evoked by Sargon II when he chose the name Sargon and the contribution of the very large temporal gap to the message that remembering Sargon of Akkad conveyed at the time. For cross-cultural comparisons of tendencies to dis-prefer the use of names of past heroes in the workings of social memory within the communities in which these heroes serve as central sites of memory, compare the removal of the 'numbers' that characterized elevated sport heroes from those available to teams in contemporary North America; Gretzky's jersey number, 99, has been retired from all NHL teams; Gretzky is the most famous/memorable ice hockey player of this generation in North America.

books but are not used in relation to Moses in Deuteronomy or elsewhere. This is consistent with the tendency to characterize Moses as the prophet with whom, unlike all others, Yʜᴡʜ spoke like a friend (Exod 33:11; cf. Num 12:8; Deut 34:10b). It is particularly worth noting that this tendency was so embedded in the memory of the community that it became embedded in the very language used to encode memories of Moses and the other prophets.[43]

Fourth, Moses' prophetic book contained numerous markers that invited its readership to read it *also* as an integral part of larger collections of books that construed 'national' historical narratives (e.g. Genesis–2 Kings; Genesis–Deuteronomy; Exodus–Deuteronomy; Genesis–Joshua; Exodus–Joshua). Although individual texts in the other prophetic books included historical narratives, none of the fifteen books contains markers that would suggest their readers should approach *the book as a whole* as an integral part of any of the 'national' historical narratives.

Fifth, the fifteen prophetic books are all set on a relatively narrow span of historical time, from the beginning of the process that led to the catastrophe of 586 BCE to the very beginning of the re-establishment of the temple. The central temporal focus around which this pattern was created was the fall of the temple and the exile. The prophetic book of Moses is set in a period far earlier.[44]

Turning to the last observation, a corpus of sixteen prophetic books organizes memories of the past in such a way that a bridge leading directly from Moses to Hosea is created (cf. Hos 12:14 and equally importantly, Hos 2:16–25). Moreover, it is one in which the fact that Moses was remembered as one who foresaw the catastrophe of 586[45] acquires enhanced significance and serves to link Moses to the other prophets. At the same time, it turns their messages of judgment and salvation into subsequent echoes of Moses' own message.[46]

---

[43] The expression occurs in Deut 4:12. There it is embedded in Moses' speech and in the context of a reminder to Israel that Yʜᴡʜ spoke to the people 'out of the fire', that they 'heard the sound of words but saw no form; there was only a voice.' The reference appears then within a context that stresses the difference between the way in which Yʜᴡʜ communicated with Moses and the people. It also stresses the separate status of Moses, the prophet as teacher of the people. See Deut 4:14.

[44] As is the case with every memory-created separating wall in the discourse of a community, it has some pores. Interstitial material and its patterns are, by themselves, indicators of how the memory of Moses the prophet informed other prophetic memories and vice versa, within the discourse of the community.

[45] See Deut 30:1–5, and, among others, the pragmatic message in late Persian Yehud of Deut 28:15–68; 29:13–27; 30:17–19; 31:19–22.

[46] On the importance of this issue for the construction of historical narratives, see the next section.

The existence of a strong tendency to remember that the foundational character already foresaw from the beginning the crucial catastrophe that will befall the people and even saw beyond it toward future restoration is worth noting. Chronicles, in which Moses and David were foundational characters, implied a past world in which David, and to a large extent 'all Israel' at his time, were aware of the catastrophe to come and of the Exile.[47] The issue is not just about lionizing the foundational figures of the past but about allowing the foundational character to identify, even if partially, with the Persian period community of readers; and conversely, allowing the community to identify better and partially with their foundational figure–through their shared knowledge of a crucial historical event. These tendencies contributed to the shaping of a generative grammar for the development of social memory.

Certainly no prophetic book was included in another collection, but not only do memories of some major prophetic characters appear in other collections (the most salient case is Isaiah), but some prophetic books include sections that reminded the community of events narrated in a different collection (see, for instance, Jer 39:1–10 and cf. 2 Kgs 25:1–18; Jer 52:1–27 and cf. 2 Kgs 24:1–25:21) or of events that continue narratives that appear elsewhere (see Jer 40–41/42). No prophetic book is part of another collection, but Jeremiah carries a strong Deuteronomistic flavour. Although the book is not part of the Deuteronomistic historical collection, Jeremiah was remembered as a prophet who *at times* used a Deuteronomistic voice–that is, a voice that sounded similar to Moses in Deuteronomy[48]–that was similar to the voices present (along with others) in the Deuteronomistic historical collection, which it occasionally supplements.

All these voices were evocative of, though not identical to, Moses in his prophetic book. These voices asked the readers of the Deuteronomistic historical collection to be mindful of the memory of Moses the prophet and the book associated with him. They asked those involved in remembering (and construing) Jeremiah to be informed by their memories of Moses and to negotiate similarities and differences between the two, imagining in the process what a good exemplar of a late monarchic, Mosaic prophet might look like. To be sure, to engage in such a process involves shedding light and shadow on the site of memory we can label 'Moses the prophet', partially and momentarily reconfiguring it. In the case of Jeremiah, this process would result in increased salience to aspects

---

[47] See 1 Chr 16:35. I discuss this matter in my "Who Knew What? The Construction of the Monarchic Past in Chronicles and Implications for the Intellectual Setting of Chronicles," in *Judah and the Judeans in the Fourth Century BCE* (eds. O. Lipschits et al.; Winona Lake, IN: Eisenbrauns, 2007), 349–60 (349–54).
[48] See Ben Zvi, "On the Term 'Deuteronomistic'," 59–69.

like the sin of the community addressed by Moses, his intercessions on behalf of Israel, his own fate to die outside the land, the transmission of leadership,[49] and the after-life influence of Moses' voice in Israelite historiography. Many other facets of this site of memory (e.g. the legal contents of much his prophecy, his ability to talk with YHWH as a friend, his prophetic/political leadership or his prophetic singing, for that matter) will become, by necessity, less prominent.

But Jeremiah was not the only case. As mentioned above, the prophetic book of Moses was the only one that included a very substantial amount of legal matters and Moses was the only prophet to whom YHWH revealed so much law for communication to Israel. Yet, the book of Ezekiel, especially chs 40–48 (see also Ezek 18), brings to the community a prophetic figure to whom legal matters also were communicated. The remembering community could hardly miss obvious markers of difference between the two, such as the emphatically conveyed distinction in the ways in which YHWH communicated with Moses and with Ezekiel and the prophetic hierarchy that such an emphatic dissimilarity conveyed. But they could also notice some similarities between the two. For instance, remembering both brought to the community vivid mental images of Israel, its land, its ritual, leadership, and the like. The community was also asked to remember that in both cases these images were conveyed by YHWH to the prophet outside the land. But Ezekiel and the *literati* remembering him through their readings of Ezek 40–48 were asked to imagine a utopian, stable future; whereas Moses and the *literati* vicariously visiting his world and identifying with him knew all too well that the people will sin and eventually lose the land, go into exile, repent and only then come back.

More examples may be brought, but the point is, as in the previous case, the remembering community was involved in negotiating similarities and dissimilarities between the two, and as they did so, they imagined again what a good exemplar of a late monarchic, Mosaic prophet might look like.[50] This also meant partially and momentarily reconfiguring the site of memory we can label 'Moses the prophet'. The result of the reconfiguration in this case would be unlike the previously discussed, however. It would include increased salience to aspects such as the hopeful image of establishing the community in the land and providing it with a blueprint, on the uniqueness of the mode of revelation to

---

[49] Cf. C. R. Seitz, "The Prophet Moses and the Canonical Shape of Jeremiah", in *ZAW* 101 (1989): 3–27. For a brief survey of research and bibliography on the potential link between the figures of Jeremiah and Moses, see M. Roncace, *Jeremiah, Zedekiah, and the Fall of Jerusalem* (LHBOTS 423; London: T&T Clark, 2005), 20.
[50] Cf. H. McKeating, "Ezekiel the 'Prophet Like Moses'?," in *JSOT* 101 (1994): 97–109.

Moses and the higher authority of his prophecy.[51] As they encounter the mental image of Moses the prophet that is evoked when they approach it from a perspective strongly informed by their reading of Ezekiel, other issues, including those made prominent by the Jeremianic light on Moses the prophet, became less prominent to the virtual visitor of this site of memory. And, the very same Jerusalem-centred *literati* of the period keep visiting the site and watching it at times with Jeremianic and at times with Ezekielian light, and the site keeps bringing them together, balancing and informing each other, as well as all the other sights that result from looking at Moses the prophet from a perspective influenced by another memory.

Some of the particular markers that distinguished Moses from the Mosaic prophets and Moses literature from the fifteen prophetic books that were mentioned above shed light on the ways in which features associated with Moses the prophet contributed to the shape of memories of characters outside the genre of prophetic books, and in the process, shed momentary light and shadow on the memory of Moses. One example suffices. The seemingly simple, opening expression 'YHWH spoke to X' is rarely used for figures other than Moses in the Hebrew Bible (see Josh 20:1) and does not appear in the other prophetic books, but Chronicles uses it in 1 Chr 21:9 and 2 Chr 33:10. In the first occurrence, Chronicles turns an original and usual 'the word of YHWH came to the prophet Gad, David's seer' (see 2 Sam 24:11) into a very uncommon 'YHWH spoke to Gad, David's seer'. Here YHWH speaks to 'Gad, David's seer', and indirectly to David within the context of the story that leads to the choice of the place of the temple and which emphasizes the importance of repentance–a central ideological *topos* in Chronicles.[52] By doing so, it places David within a structural slot similar to Is-

---

[51] On the surface, hierarchy carries particular significance here because of some tension between the 'Mosaic' and 'Ezekielian' 'law'; see, for instance, Ezek 45:24 and cf. Num 28:20–21; 29:3–4, 14–15; or Ezek 44:31 and Lev 22:8. This tension eventually led to the rabbinic legend about Hananiah, the son of Hezekiah, who could manage to harmonize them; see *b. Šabb.* 13b; *b. Ḥag.* 13a. Yet multiple images of laws, utopias, past and future events were a common feature in the discourse of Persian-period Israel, as its authoritative repertoire as a whole, and some of its books by themselves, clearly show. In addition, Ezekiel's temple and general vision belonged to the realm of what can be imagined, not about what is to be built. See H. Liss, "'Describe the Temple to the House of Israel': Preliminary Remarks on the Temple Vision in the Book of Ezekiel and the Question of Fictionality in Priestly Literatures," in *Utopia and Dystopia in Prophetic Literature* (ed. E. Ben Zvi; Publications of the Finnish Exegetical Society 92; Helsinki: Finnish Exegetical Society and Göttingen: Vandenhoeck & Ruprecht, 2006), 122–43. The realm of what can be imagined is very prone to multiple images.
[52] On David as a paradigmatic repentant sinner, see G. N. Knoppers, "Images of David in Early Judaism: David as Repentant Sinner in Chronicles," in *Bib* 76 (1995): 449–70.

rael, to which Yʜᴡʜ speaks through the prophet Moses, while at the same time emphasizing that Gad was David's seer. The very same text includes what might be a second reverberation of stories associated with Moses: in a diminished version of a fearsome theophany, David and the elders of Israel face a threatening messenger of Yʜᴡʜ, not Yʜᴡʜ; see 1 Chr 21:16. The importance of David and the temple in Chronicles, the existence of several other examples where the text of 1 Chr 21 evokes memories of other events in the world of knowledge of the intended and primary readership and links to the texts in which these events are encoded,[53] along with the very rare use of 'Yʜᴡʜ spoke to X' for characters other than Moses suggest that the choice of language here is not due to chance or read as such within the context of the literarily sophisticated Jerusalemite *literati* of the period. Here, the 'leakage' of terms and memories associated with Moses the prophet may be significant.

But Chronicles uses 'Yʜᴡʜ spoke to X' one more time, in relation to Manasseh, the other major figure embodying and communicating repentance, who is shaped in this book. Whereas Yʜᴡʜ is portrayed as sending messengers calling for repentance during Zedekiah's reign (2 Chr 36:15), Yʜᴡʜ himself addresses Manasseh and his people and calls them to repent (2 Chr 33:10). (Note also the minor changes between the language of 2 Chr 33:12b and that 2 Chr 36:12b, which reinforce the point.) According to Chronicles, Manasseh, the great sinner, and along with him the sinful Israel of his time, was treated by Yʜᴡʜ in a way partially reminiscent of Moses the prophet. This Manasseh was taken into exile to Babylon, repented, and was brought back so he could undo his wrongdoing. As a result, prophets decided to keep for posterity, i.e. for memory, his prayer among their records.

Manasseh is also a symbol for Israel. The text evokes a sense that not only did Yʜᴡʜ send Mosaic prophets to warn Israel before the catastrophe as usually remembered (e.g. Jer 35:15; Zech 1:4) and encoded in Chronicles itself (2 Chr 36:15–16), but that he talked to it directly, as if it were Moses the prophet. Again, partially because of the markers of discontinuity that it contains, the memory of Moses the prophet served as a central informing beacon shedding light on significant constructions of past events and contributing to identity formation and self-understanding for Yehud/Israel.

---

53 E.g. the evocative links to Mt Moriah and to the purchase of a burial place by Abraham.

Continuity and Discontinuity: The Prophet and Historical Books as Prophetic Books

The presence of Deuteronomistic voices in Joshua–2 Kings, that is, voices that sound similar to Moses in Deuteronomy, conveyed to the readers a sense of association between their 'national' history and *the* prophet par excellence. These voices brought more than a whiff of Mosaic authority to the historical narrative and reinforced the sense that Moses was a kind of historian too. This is not only because of texts like Num 33:2, but above all, because within a discourse in which the role of the (prophetic) historian is to interpret the 'national history' according to Yhwh's teaching, Moses not only foresaw but provided an explanation of the basic guideline of the history of Israel to unfold in Joshua–2 Kings.[54]

All these conveyed a sense that Joshua–2 Kings is a continuation of a prophetic book, blurring the divide between the genres of historiography and prophetic book. A tendency towards blurring the divide was already noticed in the case of Jeremiah, the prophet whose voice at times reminds the community of Moses the prophet, but here it is made prominently noticeable and memorable through its direct connection with the figure of Moses and his prophetic book. This tendency is consistent with the construction of historiography as a prophetic task encoded to some extent in 1 Samuel–2 Kings and very clearly in Chronicles. Conversely, this tendency would likely be conducive to an association of the large-scale 'national' history with the earliest and the greatest of all the prophets rather than with important but still secondary Mosaic prophets such as Isaiah, Ezekiel, Hosea, and Zechariah.

Reading Joshua–2 Kings in a way that is strongly informed by the presence of Moses the prophet in Deuteronomy renders the former collection of books prophetic in another sense. According to Deuteronomy, whatever a true prophet prophesies is fulfilled (Deut 18:22).[55] Given that prophets were supposed to prophesy about important issues for the 'nation', this approach generated a mnemonic organization of the past in terms of fulfilled prophecies (e.g. 1 Kgs 12:15;

---

[54] In other words, he was a historian of a certain future about which he had knowledge and which he could encounter already imaginatively. The community in Yehud that read and reread the prophetic books had many memories of (this time) utopian futures to come. Whether events are in the future or past of the group, they could be interpreted by 'historians' if they knew about them—and, of course, provided they were able to interpret their meaning in accordance with the expectations of the discourse of the time.

[55] It is worth noting that Deut 18:22 does not state that fulfilment of the prophecy proves the prophet was a true prophet sent by Yhwh but rather, that the lack of fulfilment of the prophecy proves that the prophet was not sent by Yhwh and is therefore false. Cf. Deut 13:2–4.

14:18; 15:29; 16:12; 17:16; 2 Kgs 9:36; 10:10; 14:25; 17:23; 24:2).[56] This organization of the past reinforced the ideological message that YHWH is in control of history and that the deity cares about Israel by sharing information about the future via prophets (e.g. Amos 3:7). Finally, this organizational mindscape generates a record that authenticates the figure of the true prophets of the past and of their messages.[57]

Reading Joshua–2 Kings in a way informed by the fact that the voice of Moses resonates (among others, to be sure) in Joshua–2 Kings and that this collection of books is preceded by a prophetic book (and esp. that of Moses) was to construe the 'national' history of Israel as a long and elaborate fulfilment of Moses' statements about its future (see Deut 30:1–5; 32:19–25 and, among others, the pragmatic message in late Persian Yehud of Deut 28:15–68; 29:13–27; 30:17–19; 31:19–22). Most significantly, this also meant construing and making memorable within the community a 'historical' plotline that leads directly to the fulfilment of Deut 30:2–10 (and cf. Deut 32:26–43). Thus construed, the Deuteronomistic historical collection ends on an implied but recognizable high note. Chronicles' more positive ending becomes not an innovation but an attempt to make explicit what its source conveyed implicitly: that Israel's history will move from catastrophe to a new beginning.[58] It means reading Deuteronomy–2 Kings as conveying a message akin to that of most of the prophetic books.

All these readings shed light and shadow on Moses the prophet as a site of memory. As *literati* construe their mental image of the Moses the prophet that they encounter when they approach texts from this perspective, they would tend to make particularly salient some aspects of his role as prophet, such as foreseeing events and providing hope for the future, and they would tend to project an image of a line of Mosaic successors who are involved in writing historiographical works. At the same time, by necessity, they would pay less attention to other aspects of the same site prominently advanced elsewhere, like Moses' authentication through incomparable and memorable signs and wonders, the em-

---

[56] Cf. G. von Rad, "The Deuteronomistic Theology of History in the Books of Kings," in *Studies in Deuteronomy* (trans. from 1948 German original; London: SCM Press, 1953), 74–91.

[57] I discuss these issues and other discursive generative tendencies concerning prophecy in general at this period in my "Observations on Lines of Thought Concerning the Concepts of Prophecy and Prophets in Yehud, with an Emphasis on Deuteronomy–2 Kings and Chronicles," in *Words, Ideas, Worlds in the Hebrew Bible: Essays* (eds. A. Brenner and F. H. Polak; Sheffield: Sheffield Phoenix, 2012), 1–19.

[58] In fact, one may claim that the *pragmatic* purpose of the ending in Chronicles within its late Persian Yehud setting was to temper the community's expectations for the near future while maintaining hope for a utopian end to the exile. See E. Ben Zvi, *History, Literature and Theology in the Book of Chronicles* (BibleWorld; London: Equinox, 2006), 195–209.

phasis on legal material in the prophecy of Moses, and the other markers of substantial difference between Moses and the other prophets. The latter include the fact that the memory of Moses is not encoded in only one book and that his voice, and the divine voice that merges with his in Deuteronomy, does not necessarily have to sound similar to a Deuteronomistic one (see Leviticus). It also means drawing attention away from the presence of speakers in Joshua–2 Kings that do not carry a Deuteronomistic voice. Of course, the power of the site of memory is that it can be seen from multiple perspectives and shifting arrays of light and shadow and thus can embody, balance and communicate all of them.

Of course, tendencies towards balancing images had limits too. The latter are often indicative of central issues in the world of remembering community. For instance, visiting and revisiting a site of memory that closely links images of Moses the prophet to the Deuteronomistic historical collection and to images of the fifteen main prophets to whom the Yehudite prophetic books were associated (see also Mal 3:22) clearly shaped an image of Moses as integral to, and as the founding hero of, the discourse and claims of the Jerusalem-centred *literati* of the late Persian and early Hellenistic periods. Remembering Moses in this way was tantamount to appropriating the memory of a hero shared, in principle, with Samaria and turning his memory into the central component of an unshared and unsharable Jerusalem-centred viewpoint.[59]

---

[59] I expanded on this matter elsewhere, see my 'On the Term "Deuteronomistic"'. The memory of Abraham was appropriated in a similar manner; see "The Memory of Abraham in Late Persian/Early Hellenistic Yehud/Judah" in this volume, pp. 162–98. Although other figures were appropriated as well, Abraham and Moses served foundational roles in the discourse of these Jerusalem-centred *literati*. Processes of appropriation of the memories of central heroes of the past to turn them into sites of memory that embody and communicate the discourse of a remembering community are only expected when the discourse of such a community stands in contradistinction to another group that claims the same heroes (or in more general terms, the 'same' sites of memory) for itself. Similar processes took place, for instance, when both rabbinic Judaism and early Christianity appropriated biblical characters from the Tanak/Old Testament. Moreover, multiple examples in contemporary social memory studies attest to this very common tendency. See, for instance, the case of Alexander as a main site of memory in Greece and in the Republic of Macedonia or that of Kiev in common foundational historical narratives in Russia and in the Ukraine.

Continuity and Discontinuity: The Prophet and Leadership

Moses was a prophet who was prominently remembered as a political leader. Deut 33:4–5 states, 'Moses charged us with the law, as a possession for the assembly of Jacob. There arose a king in Jeshurun, when the leaders of the people assembled–the united tribes of Israel.' Verse 5 could be easily read as referring to YHWH or Moses as king, and likely to both, though at different levels, thus construing another conceptual domain populated by both Moses and YHWH. In any event, the text nominally connoted a royal image for Moses. References to Moses as the holder of the staff of the deity (Exod 4:20; 17:9; which are suggestive of a position as YHWH's viceroy) granted the image of Moses a kind of kingly aura as well. This quasi-royal image of Moses is consistent with many of the roles he fulfils in the past remembered by a community of readers of the Pentateuchal books (e.g. Exod 18) and with common images of the roles of the divine viceroy = human king in the ancient Near East. In fact, the remembering community could not but notice that Moses was far more powerful than the king described in Deut 17:14–20, who, by design, was subordinate to the divine *torah* that Moses communicated and taught.

Moreover, since Deut 17:14–20 associates the office of king with being in the land, *torah*, which must be given outside the land, cannot be transmitted from YHWH to the people by a king. A king/ruler can only learn and teach *torah*, and incidentally, in the process, becomes a prophetic voice (see constructions of Joshua in Josh 1:8[60] and some royal characters in Chronicles). Yet the image of the prophet-king plays no important role in construction of Israelite past in late Persian Yehud. To be sure, this may be due in part to memories of the monarchic period, but even if this were the case, these memories could have been reshaped or the image of a prophet-king could have been shifted to earlier time. In fact, the latter has been done to a large extent in the construction of the memory of Samuel.[61] Yet, as the book of Samuel explicitly and strongly communicated, this type of leadership was superseded by others and not too successful. Although Moses the prophet-king was remembered as very successful in office, social memory again construed him as a special case that could not be repeated

---

[60] For Joshua's role as a prophet, see E. A. Knauf, "Remembering Joshua" in *Remembering Biblical Figures in the Late Persian and Early Hellenistic Periods: Social Memory and Imagination* (eds. D. V. Edelman and E. Ben Zvi; Oxford: Oxford University Press, 2013), 106–27.
[61] It is worth mentioning that Samuel was portrayed in the book of Samuel as less powerful than a king, whereas Moses is portrayed in Deuteronomy as far more powerful than a king, and the same holds true when Deuteronomy was read in a way informed by the Pentateuchal collection as whole.

at any time in Israelite history. Not only could no other prophetic figure be associated with incomparable wonders or with communicating YHWH's *torah* to Israel, but also, none could match his ability to be the prophet-king/ruler.⁶²

This observation may be understandable in light of the tendency toward constructions of the Israelite past in which causality is understood as divine causality and deeply related to the question of whether Israel followed or did not follow the divine *torah* communicated by the prophet Moses. Since no superseding *torah* can be given, there is no place for a new Moses, and the welfare of Israel depends far more on Mosaic prophets/teachers who should lead the king and Israel to follow *torah* during the monarchic period and Israel to follow it alone during the postmonarchic era than on the office of a political king. Significantly, the *literati* of the period who read and re-read the authoritative books and shaped the community's memory of the past saw themselves, along with the implied authors of the prophetic and historical books that they construed through their readings of these works, as those fulfilling this Mosaic, prophetic role.

Finally, it is noteworthy that while the office of Moses the prophet-king did not set the precedent for the monarchic king, the virtues of Moses the prophet set the example for the virtues of David. As B. Levine has observed, 'in Num 12:7 Moses [the prophet] is characterized in virtually the same way as is David in 1 Sam 22:14!'.⁶³ Memories of the greatest prophet end up evoking those of an ideal king and vice versa.

(Main) Continuity Markers and Their Significance

A few facets of the memory of Moses the prophet tended to emphasize continuity over discontinuity. These facets are particularly significant since they suggest features of the general concept (or an array of related, complementary, and mutually informing concepts) of prophet/prophecy held by the community that

---

62 On the royal image of Moses in the Hebrew Bible, see J. Lierman, *The New Testament Moses* (Tübingen: Mohr Siebeck, 2004), 79–89. As is well-known, Moses is clearly a royal figure in some later Second Temple texts, e.g. Philo, *Mos.* 1:334, in the New Testament (W. A. Meeks, *The Prophet-King* [NovTSup 14; Leiden: Brill, 1967], 107–16), and later on in some rabbinic texts; see, for instance, *Exod. Rab.* 40.2; 48:4; *Num Rab.* 15:13; *Midrash Tehillim* on Ps 1; *b. Zebaḥ.* 102a.
63 According to B. Levine, *Numbers 1–20*, 342 (parenthetical comment mine). He concludes that "*Torah* literature embodies both in the characterization of Moses' virtues and in God's stated evaluation of Moses, a model of the upright Davidic monarch" (342–3).

were imagined as either non-contingent on particular settings or contingent on circumstances that tend to appear all along Israel's past. In these cases, Moses as a site of memory points at what is permanent about prophecy or, at the very least, very common to it.

There was a strong preference in Yehud to remember prophets as being rejected by the people and physically threatened. Even the prophet par excellence cannot avoid that preference (Exod 14:11–12; 17:4). This motif is present in Zech 1:4, which construes this approach to past prophecy as the collective memory of Israel about that matter. Most of the memories activated/evoked by the prophetic books whose background is set in the monarchic period contributed to this construction of the past, either explicitly (e.g. Jer 7:25; 25:4; 26:9; 35:15; 44:4) or implicitly, since the destruction proclaimed in these books did happen from the perspective of the Persian-period readership and the book of Kings clearly supports it (e.g. 1 Kgs 18:4; 2 Kgs 9:7, 17:13–15).[64] Within the late Persian-period setting, the emphasis on this particular construction of the prophets is directly associated with its construction of Israel as sinful and antagonistic to both YHWH and the deity's prophets, which played an important part in the explanation of the catastrophe of 586 BCE. The memory of the prophet Moses contributed to this trend and made him the first in a very long chain of prophets who were challenged or derided by the people. The very act of continuously remembering this tradition was seen as a learning exercise meant to avoid the perpetuation of the chain of rejection and a better socialization of Israel.

In Chronicles, prophets sing (1 Chr 25:1), and so does Moses (see Exod 15; cf. Exod 32:1–44). Of course, one does not have to be a prophet to sing (see Num 21:17), but the role of Moses in Exod 15 and in the 'Song of Moses' (Exod 32:1–44) brings to the forefront their prophetic character.[65] It is possible that these memories endow the role of prophets/singers in cultic services with additional significance.[66]

As intermediaries, prophets plead and pray for Israel (e.g. Exod 5:22–23 [cf. 1 Kgs 17:20]; 32:11–14; Num 11:2; 21:7; Deut 9:18–19, 25–29; 10:10–11). Numerous examples encoding this memory of the prophets of old appear in the prophetic books and historical books (e.g. Gen 20:7, 17; Amos 7:2–3, 5–6; Jer 37:3;

---

[64] Chronicles, however, attempted to balance this approach; see my "Chronicles and its Reshaping of Memories". It could do that because Chronicles tended to reduce the role of the catastrophe and the exile in Israel's social memory. See "Toward a Sense of Balance: Remembering the Catastrophe of Monarchic Judah/(Ideological) Israel and Exile through Reading Chronicles in Late Yehud," in this volume, pp. 387–406.

[65] The prophet Miriam also sings in the event portrayed in Exod 15 (see Exod 15:20–21).

[66] One may note that Moses and the prophetic singers are Levites.

2 Kgs 4:33; 2 Chr 32:20) and in fact, in Jer 27:18, intercession is construed as the main prophetic feature.[67] Of course, it is not only a prophetic role, and since kings are prominent characters in both the book of Kings and of Chronicles, these books evoked multiple memories of kings praying (e.g. 1 Kgs 3:6–9; 2 Kgs 19:15; 20:2; 2 Chr 14:10; 20:6–12; 32:20, 24; 33:13, 19), but prophets are prominent in this role and particularly so in prophetic literature. It is significant that Moses the prophet is also presented as *the* prophet par excellence in this regard.[68]

At times, prayer goes together with teaching and admonishing (see Deut 9), which brings us to a main facet of the memory of Moses the prophet: being *the* human teacher par excellence (e.g. Deut 1:5; 4:1, 4, 10, 14; 5:1, 31; 6:1; 31:12, 19, 22). A text-centred community is, in practical terms, a teacher-centred community. As Israel's identity was construed and re-enacted through the collective memory of its past as a *torah*-centred 'nation', it became in practical terms a 'teacher-centred' nation. Since the central text/*torah* consists of divine teachings, it brought to the forefront the image of Yhwh as the teacher and of Moses, the deity's representative, as regent-teacher.

Teaching was conceived as involving both (a) a foundational era in which the *torah* is communicated to Israel through Moses the prophet and through his teaching and (b) a long process of expounding the text and continuously instructing Israel about Yhwh's *torah* and socializing it to follow it. This long process was construed as involving the deity as teacher as well, because the deity continued to provide teachings through prophets. The prophetic books contain didactic readings associated with Yhwh and a particular prophet. They also communicate an image of Yhwh as, above all, a teacher.[69]

Joshua–2 Kings shaped and reflected memories of sermons in a Deuteronomistic, i.e. Mosaic-like, voice. Chronicles contributed memories of many prophetic voices that exhorted the people to follow Yhwh and the deity's teachings. Moreover, the implied author of Chronicles was construed by the remembering community as one who expounded the meaning of *torah*, thereby following in the footsteps of Moses the prophet (see Deut 1:5).

Moses was remembered as the (human) teacher par excellence because, unlike anyone after him, he communicated to Israel the foundational teachings of Yhwh. In addition, he was the first exemplar of a very long line of Mosaic, pro-

---

67 According to R. P. Carroll, Jeremiah is the prayer prophet par excellence.
68 See Widmer, *Moses, God, and Intercessory Prayer* and its bibliography.
69 See E. Ben Zvi, "Reading Hosea and Imagining Yhwh," in *Horizons in Biblical Theology* 30 (2008): 43–57.

phetic teachers, be they prophets by 'office' or because they conveyed godly teachings that originated, within the discourse of the community, in YHWH.

Teaching within the discourse of the community required written texts (cf., among others, Deut 28:58; 29:19–20; 29:26; 30:10; Josh 1:8; 8:34; 2 Kgs 14:6; 22:6–20; 2 Chr 17:7–8). It is not surprising, therefore, that YHWH the teacher was remembered as a scribe[70] or that Moses the prophet was also remembered as the (human) scribe par excellence[71] and the first in a long chain of scribes that led to the *literati* who wrote, read, re-read, and expounded the authoritative repertoire of the community and the divine teaching/*torah* embodied in it. Their presence was conceived, in fact, as the only safeguard from undoing Israel as a text-centred community and making it unfit to be in the land (cf. Deut 4:1–15; 5:31–33; *passim*).

Remembering Moses the Prophet and Constructing Integrative Fuzziness

Moses was one of the most central characters in the social memory of Israel during the late Persian and early Hellenistic periods (and later periods as well). More was read and re-read about him at the time than about any other Israelite figure of the past. Therefore, one can easily imagine that his mindshare had no equal among them. Such a central figure tends to embody and communicate all the central *topoi* in the discourse of the community. A full study of the memory of Moses and all the links it had in the discourse of late Yehud is beyond the scope of a single essay and would require several volumes. This chapter has explored some connective aspects of a set of features associated with the memory of Moses the prophet. Most of the literary units and texts mentioned here deserve a full study that could not be undertaken in the restricted space available. Nevertheless, I have presented a very general picture of the multiple and intertwined ways in which the memory of Moses the prophet informed and was informed by memories of other figures, how it served to draw attention to particular central ideological and identity-forming *topoi* in the community, how it construed and balanced 'historical' plot-lines, how it provided a generative and organizing logic to memories of the past and the roles of different groups in the past and

---

[70] See Exod 24:12; 31:18; 32:15–16, 32; 34:1; Deut 4:13; 5:22; 9:10; 10:2, 4, and notice the explicit connection between writing and teaching in Exod 24:12.
[71] Exod 34:27–28; Num 33:2; Deut 27:3, 8; 31:9, 19, 22, 24, and notice the characterization of Moses' writing in Deut 27:8 and the transmission of the role to Joshua in Josh 8:32.

of the *literati* in the present, and even how it led to hope and to constructions of the character of YHWH.

The remembered Moses came to embody in one person virtually every feature associated with prophecy. He was, among others, a foreteller, a wondermaker, a historian, a teacher, a writer, a singer, an intercessor; a person who prayed for people, who admonished them, who suffered rejection, a conveyor of divine messages for the people, an announcer of doom, and a provider of hope. Memories of him also reminded the readers that non-prophets could fulfil some of these prophetic roles–or, one may say, prophetic non-prophets–thus blurring the category of prophet.

In addition, Moses was a prophet who was commissioned to transmit a substantial amount of legal material. His prophecy is *torah* and, like that of all the other prophets, it is YHWH's word. The social memory of Moses brought together prophet and lawgiver, *torah* stipulations and prophetic utterances and roles, or better, the memory of both.[72] The memory of Moses brought together prophetic books, historical books, and Pentateuchal books. All foundational voices, both in terms of contents, ideology, and even diction,[73] are embodied in Moses and he voices them all.

The figure of Moses served to (partially) integrate all these voices, images, and ideas in one person. By doing so, Moses served as a site of memory that made boundaries among the voices fuzzy. As they remember him, they cannot but imagine a world in which, among other things, *torah* is prophecy and prophecy is *torah*, a book is prophetic but also is part of a historiographic collection, a man speaks with multiple voices and conveys multiple messages (and to some extent, worldviews), concepts that serve to characterize YHWH partially apply to Moses and vice versa, Moses is unlike all other prophets but the latter are (and should be) similar to him (that is, Mosaic) and vice versa, he is to resemble them and embody most of the features that may characterize these prophets. A very significant aspect of the contribution of the social memory of Moses the prophet as a whole to the discourse of the community and to the social mindscape of its members (or at least, its *literati*) was precisely the contribution of this site of memory (i.e. Moses the prophet) to fuzziness (or a level of fuzziness) in their world.

To be sure, one may debate the mode/s of reading through which the *literati* engaged particular texts. It is possible that they tended to bracket their knowl-

---

[72] Cf. the position advanced about Chronicles in E. S. Gerstenberger, "Prophetie in den Chronikbüchern: Jahwes Wort in zweierlei Gestalt?" in *Schriftprophetie* (eds. F. Hartenstein et al.; Neukirchen-Vluyn: Neukirchener Verlag, 2004), 351–67.
[73] Cf. the so-called Deuteronomic ('D'), Priestly ('P'), and Holiness ('H') dictions.

edge of some texts and images encoded in them when reading others–though bracketing is never total. Yet, it is difficult to argue that when they came to think about and remember their greatest prophet they would not be aware that he spoke in both 'D' and 'H', thought and communicated multiple messages, even if on the surface some of them might seem contradictory, and certainly served multiple prophetic roles for the community. Moreover, Moses' memory had the largest mindshare in the community, besides YHWH's. But most significantly, the memory of YHWH encoded in the repertoire of books that were authoritative in the community also contributed to a sense of fuzziness. After all, YHWH was construed and remembered as saying many things, expressing multiple ideologies, and speaking in numerous dictions. A discussion of the memory of YHWH in Late Persian and early Hellenistic Judah is beyond the scope of this chapter, but it is worth noting in this regard that the memory of Moses the prophet resembles that of YHWH, except the latter has even further diversity and thus encoded even more distinctly a systemic tendency towards fuzziness. As before, the remembered YHWH shows, in larger scale, *some* of the features that the remembered Moses shows in a minor scale.

Reading about and remembering Moses (and YHWH), time and again could not but affect the habits of mind of the *literati* and their social mindscape. It 'did' something to visit and revisit that central site of memory and encounter a central character that embodied and encoded so much fuzziness in many significant areas.[74] As I have discussed elsewhere, the presence of a preference for organizing knowledge, memory and 'the world' in somewhat flexible or fuzzy categories carries substantial implications for reconstructing the entire discourse of the period and, to some extent, the self-perception of the *literati*. Certainly, such a tendency to accept fuzziness contributed to the formation of an integrative discourse and thus, to social cohesion within the community (or at least among its *literati*).[75] In addition, such an approach was more likely to develop within a group that did not see a strong need to adopt tough defensive positions, sharpen existing boundaries and create new ones, or develop insular attitudes. It is more likely to be developed in a group that did not see itself as under attack. These considerations seem to apply to the *literati* in Yehud, who saw themselves

---

[74] It is to be stressed that somewhat fuzzy boundaries and partial overlaps among categories not only were a way of organizing difference but also were limited to particular ranges of differences. To illustrate, Moses was never imagined as a Philistine, as someone who lived before Abraham, or as unconnected to the Exodus and *torah*.

[75] Cf. my earlier "Towards an Integrative Study of the Production of Authoritative Books in Ancient Israel," in *The Production of Prophecy* (eds. D. V. Edelman and E. Ben Zvi; London: Equinox, 2009), 15–28.

to some extent (necessarily, in a substantially reduced form) as 'successors' of the Moses of their memory, but this goes beyond the scope of this general exploration of the memory of Moses the prophet in Yehud in the late Persian and early Hellenistic periods.[76]

---

[76] See my "On Social Memory and Identity Formation in Late Persian Yehud in this volume, pp. 28–79; and compare my "Towards an Integrative Study," 15–28.

Squaring Circles and The Social Benefits of Squaring Them: Joshua as a Case Study for Constraints, Preferences, Balances and Flexibility within the Complex Memory System of the Literati of the late Persian/early Hellenistic Period[1]

Introduction

When I submitted the title for this presentation, I was politely asked to find a 'catchy' title. At the time I could not think of one, but I finally came to understand that "Squaring Circles and The Social Benefits of Squaring Them" reflects exactly the core of the matter to be explored in this address. Of course, I am not these issues in the abstract, but from perspective of a substantial site of memory among the literati of the late Persian/early Hellenistic period in Yehud/Judah, namely Joshua, which although necessarily unique is not so unique as not to serve as a good representative for a general mnemonic trend at the heart of the production and reproduction of memories among these literati, and their social mindscape.[2] In fact, the main reason I selected Joshua as a case study is that it is likely to be a familiar figure to all of us, wherever our personal expertise may lay.

Few Hebrew Bible stories are more 'familiar' than the story of the Exodus and the strongly related story of conquest. These foundational stories are, of course, not only 'familiar' now, but were very much familiar among a plethora of historical groups that encoded them as part of their "Bible," all across time

---

[1] Presidential Address at the 2016 Meeting of the European Association of Biblical Studies held in Leuven, Belgium.
[2] I am well aware also that the figure of Joshua is fundamentally problematic in and for many contemporary discourses. In fact, there is an abundance of literature (academic and popular) on these issues. As much as I refuse to assign the historical period and society I discuss here any primacy over any other society or period, it is simply not feasible to address these matters and the relevant literature on this occasion, while at the same time dealing with ancient Israel. The basic fact is that addressing these contemporary discourses and constructions of Joshua requires, at the very least, a separate paper that focuses on matters other than this one. It is important, in this context, to keep in mind that this paper deals only with the memories of Joshua that existed in an ancient society that is substantially different than our own or any other contemporary society in all aspects, including ethical and moral discourses.

https://doi.org/10.1515/9783110547146-009

and space. In fact, we could have decades of sessions in our program devoted to readings and interpretations of these stories over time, by particular historically-contingent groups and the impact that their re-tellings and re-constructions of these stories had on them, from ancient times to the present.

Given my own area of expertise, I will focus today on one historically contingent group, namely the Jerusalem-centered literati in the late Persian or early Hellenistic period and I will approach the matter at stake here from a social memory perspective.[3]

The choice of approach is particularly relevant to the title of this paper. Scholars working with more commonly used redactional methods would propose and discuss a diverse string of relatively 'logically self-consistent' texts associated with particular sources, authors, redactors and the like. Each of them would voice a particular, for the most part, coherent viewpoint.

For historians who work like me from a social memory perspective, the world looks much more difficult to grasp, at least at first. The reason is simple: the literati who read and reread a particular repertoire of authoritative texts and were socialized through this process, could not but imagine and vicariously experience their past through readings. But their repertoire included and integrated all the voices that the mentioned colleagues have noticed. Unless, one assumes that they read the texts in a way strongly informed by the textual processes that eventually led to the books they were reading, as we reconstruct them, they could 'resolve' tension and contradictions by allocating them to different authors, periods and the like. But there is nothing to support this assumption.

Thus, historians like me have to construct a reconstruction of the literati as facing a multiplicity of voices, all relevant and all embodied (and thus integrated) in the same characters populating their memory-scape including their Yнwн, and in the authoritative implied authors that they construed when reading these books in a way informed by their world of knowledge, agreed ideology and social mindscape.

---

[3] Soon after the meeting, Zev Farber published a comprehensive volume dealing with "images of Joshua', focusing on a much larger range of time and places—he addresses also early Christian, Rabbinic and Samaritan constructions of Joshua—and from a different methodological perspective. Despite the differences, including that the present, by necessity non-comprehensive, study turns to memories of Joshua *as a relevant case study* for a larger discussion, this chapter and the lines of thoughts advanced/implied here on the one hand and Farber's work, on the other, may be considered partially complementary and readers of the present chapter are invited to read Zev Farber, *Images of Joshua in the Bible and Their* Reception (BZAW, 457; Berlin: de Gruyter, 2016) and compare the approaches.

Further, these literati, like all readers, did not approach their texts in a vacuum. When they construed, imagined and vicariously experienced what they believed to be "their" past, through their readings, they did so in a way strongly informed by their authoritative textual repertoire. The emphasis here is on the word 'repertoire.' To construct reasonable reconstructions of the social memory of a group in the ancient past, one needs more than one or a few memory shaping texts available to the community, because one has to have an idea of their general world of knowledge, social mindscape, and the ways in which the texts could have interacted with each other in ways known and unbeknownst to the literati when they construed and remembered their past.

In other words, from a social memory perspective, although separate texts might be idiosyncratic and seemingly contradictory, all together shape and attest to a system, a mnemonic system. This system, like all systems, is governed by some underlying grammar, even if complex and in itself a set of interrelated simpler grammars. This grammar carries preferences, dispreferences and is above all generative. Any knowledge of the grammar or lower level grammars that were involved in the production and reproduction of social memories for a group are particularly helpful for historians of the world of knowledge and social mindscape of that group.

To be sure, one cannot fully reconstruct the entire repertoire of the mentioned literati, but a corpus consisting of collections of books such as the Pentateuch, the Hexateuch, the Deuteronomistic (hereafter, dtr.) historical collection, the Primary History, the Prophetic book collection, many of the Psalms, and probably Proverbs and Chronicles is reasonably representative, in its broad strokes at least, of the mentioned authoritative textual repertoire. This being so, we do have a reasonable 'library' or more precisely a 'literary system' that allows us to construct plausible reconstructions of the social memory of a historical group who construed its own image of its past, to a large extent at least, through the reading and rereading of these very texts, in a way informed by their knowledge of the other texts in this library/system.

Before I continue, some caveats are in order. First, I am dealing today, as an historian with an aspect of the intellectual history of an ancient society, whose culture and social values were by necessity different than ours. I am not doing more than that, but also no less than that. The second caveat is that I am not attempting to construct a reconstruction of the whole Joshua imagined and remembered by these literati.[4] My goal is here is much more narrow, namely to dis-

---

4 Readers interested on one such a reconstruction of the Joshua of memory, see E. Axel Knauf, "Remembering Joshua," in Diana V. Edelman and Ehud Ben Zvi (eds.). (Oxford: Oxford Univer-

cuss the importance of 'squaring circles' in the particular community of readers I am discussing. I will dwell on seeming incoherences, all embodied in the literati's Joshua of memory, and show that their particular Joshua, to a significant degree, diverged from the character of memory that one might have anticipated to emerge given the basic constraints created by his place in the general narrative about Israel and by general trends in the construction of heroes of memory who fulfil similar functions.

If their Joshua of memory seemed, at first look, a bit 'ungrammatical', it is not because the generation of such Joshua is devoid of rules. Just like sentences in a language, social memories are not really ungrammatical, but products and reflections of additional sometimes alternative and sometimes complementary generative grammars. Needless to say these grammars are subsumed into a larger systemic grammar that incorporates and regulates them from a systemic perspective.

Constraints and Their Concomitant Expectations

My first observation is that although we are all familiar with the figure of Joshua, from a perspective informed by memory-studies, the very existence of a Joshua-like figure seems a bit of an anomaly. The foundational narrative of the Israel construed and remembered by the literati had to include their being in Egypt, then the desert and *torah* outside the land, but it could not include only that. At some point, Israel was supposed to take possession of a land that within this very narrative was settled by others. Given the discourses of the time and a strong generative grammar that preferred mnemonic narratives of total population replacement, the necessity of taking over an inhabited land was very much conducive to the development of stories and memories of successful military exploits at the original time of the establishing of the commonwealth in the land.[5]

---

sity Press, 2013), 106–27; cf. idem, "Why 'Joshua'"?, 73–84 in Diana V. Edelman (eds.), *Deuteronomy -Kings as Emerging Authoritative Books. A Conversation* (ANEM, 6; Atlanta, Ga.: SBL; 2014), 73–84. Knauf is also the author of an important commentary on Joshua, namely, *Josua* (ZB, 6; Zürich: Theologischer Verlag Zürich, 2008).
5 To be sure, military conquest is not the only option. The land could have been imagined as suddenly emptied of its inhabitants just before the conquest, but in these relatively rare, from a comparative viewpoint, cases in which this is imagined, the question arises why would the land be 'emptied.' If the reason is that a mighty enemy that they cannot stand against is about to conquer the place, then it is a conquest story too. See Hdt. 4.11. Within the memory-world of the Yehudite literati, there were multiple versions of the manner in which the population of Canaan at the time of the invasion was replaced. This aspect of their memory world re-

The main foundational leaders of new polities whose control over a particular area was achieved by military means (e.g., Sargon, Cyrus, Alexander) tended to be remembered as those whose war exploits secured the relevant area, even if, needless to say, they did so with divine support. Against this background the usual paths of memory-shaping would have led to constructing a Moses who not only provided the people with divine laws to be effective upon the possession of the land, but actually led the people in war to achieve the said possession. The closest one may get to that Moses is in Hecateus of Abdera, as quoted by Diodorus Siculus. There Moses "led out military expeditions against the neighboring tribes" and annexed their lands, but, for reasons we cannot discuss here, he was still imagined as a leader who took possession of Judea and the area around Jerusalem peacefully, because this particular area was utterly uninhabited when he arrived.[6]

---

quires a separate discussion that cannot be carried out within the frame of this essay. For a study of the various 'fates' of the 'Canaanites' in Pentateuchal traditions, informed by source critical approaches, see Baruch J. Schwartz, "Reexamining the Fate of the 'Canaanites' in the *Torah* Traditions,' in Chaim Cohen, Avi Hurvitz and Shalom M. Paul (eds.), *Sefer Moshe: The Moshe Weinfeld Jubilee Volume: Studies in the Bible and the Ancient Near East, Qumran, and Post-Biblical Judaism* (Winona Lake, Ind.: Eisenbrauns, 2004), 151–70.

6 The differentiation between Judea (and Jerusalem) and the rest of the land of Canaan in this text requires a separate discussion that cannot be carried out here. The relevant section of the text of Hecateus (as per Didodorus) reads: "... the greater number [of the foreigners driven out of Egypt] were driven into what is now called Judaea, which is not far distant from Egypt and was at that time utterly uninhabited The colony was headed by a man called Moses, outstanding both for his wisdom and for his courage. On taking possession of the land he founded, besides other cities, one that is now the most renowned of all, called Jerusalem. In addition, he established the temple that they hold in chief veneration, instituted their forms of worship and ritual, drew up their laws and ordered their political institutions. He also divided them into twelve tribes ... He led out military expeditions against the neighboring tribes, and after annexing much land apportioned it out, assigning equal allotments to private citizens and greater ones to the priests..." (GLAJJ I, 11 = M. Stern, *Greek and Latin Authors on Jews and Judaism* [Jerusalem, 1974], 26–35. For studies on Hecateus' account of the foundational history of Judea (as cited in Diodorus Siculus *Bibliotheca Historical* 40.3), see, e.g., D. Mendels, "Hecataeus of Abdera and a Jewish "patrios politeia" of the Persian period (Diodorus Siculus XL,3)," *ZAW* 95 (1983), 96–110; D. R. Schwartz, "Diodorus Siculus 40.3 – Hecataeus or Pseudo-Hecataeus?," in M. Mor et. al., *Jews and Gentiles in the Holy Land* (Jerusalem, 2003), 181–197; R. Albertz, "An End to the Confusion? Why the Old Testament Cannot Be a Hellenistic Book," in L. L. Grabbe (ed.), *Did Moses speak Attic?* (Sheffield, 2001), 30–46; idem, "Hecataeus of Abdera and the Jewish law: the Question of Authenticity," in Ingo Kottsieper, Rüdiger Schmitt and Jacob Wöhrle (eds.) *Berührungspunkte. Studien zur Sozial- und Religionsgeschichte Israels und seiner Umwelt. Festschrift für Rainer Albertz zu seinem 65. Geburtstag* (AOAT, 350; Münster, Ugarit-Verlag, 2008), 613–626; Claudio Zamagni, "La tradition sur Moïse d'Hécatée d'Abdère d'après Diodore et Photius," in

In any event, Moses the general was not the Moses of memory among the literati discussed here. Their Moses never entered the land, never mind, conquered it and thus raised the need for a Joshua-figure. In sum, a kind of mnemonic anomaly concerning their Moses required a kind of anomaly in the form of a Joshua-like figure.

A study of the underlying ideological grammars of preference that resulted in a strong de-emphasizing of Moses the warrior/mighty hero and the meanings communicated by such a reluctance also demand a separate discussion.[7] But for the present purposes, it suffices to note that, by the late Persian period, the relation between Moses and Joshua was remembered as bearing some resemblance to that between David and Solomon.[8] The presence of Joshua served, *inter alia*, to subdue the need for an image of a warrior-like Moses (a matter already attested in Exod 17:8–14) and in that sense the role of Joshua might be seen as comparable to the role of David the warrior whose success allowed Solomon to be the required man of peace to build the temple.

David, whatever else he was remembered for—and there was much more he was remembered for—was undoubtedly remembered as a legendary military hero whose achievements expanded the putative territory controlled by Israel

---

Thomas Römer et al. (eds.), *Interprétations de Möise: Égypte, Judée, Grèce et Rome* (Leiden/Boston: Brill, 2010), pp. 133–69.

[7] On the non-warrior figure of Moses in the Pentateuch and the warrior traditions about him, see T. Römer, 'Moses outside the *Torah* and the Construction of a Diaspora Identity', *JHebS* 8 (2008) article 15; available at http://www.jhsonline.org and in print in *Perspectives in Hebrew Scriptures V: Comprising the Contents of Journal of Hebrew Scriptures, vol. 8* (ed. E. Ben Zvi; Piscataway, NJ: Gorgias Press, 2009) 269–81. This tendency is at work in other foundational figures of ancient Israel, such as Abraham and Jacob. In all these cases there are 'minority reports' within the repertoire of the community that attests directly to the existence of a significant potential for alternative constructions of these characters and indirectly to the existence of a strong grammar of dis-preference for shaping these core sites of memory as evocative of mighty warriors/generals. In other words, it is not by chance, that images of them as 'mighty warriors/generals' are marginalized. I will return to this point. For 'minority reports' about Moses the general/warrior see Num 21:21–35 (and note how the text emphasizes the role of Israel and subdues to some extent that of Moses; e.g., "Israel took..."); Deut 2:26–3:13; Josh 12:6. On these issues, see "The Memory of Abraham in Late Persian/Early Hellenistic Yehud/Judah," in this volume, pp. 162–98 and "Exploring the Memory of Moses 'The Prophet' in Late Persian/Early Hellenistic Yehud/Judah," in this volume, pp. 199–231.

[8] Cf., inter alia, H. G. M. Williamson, "The Accession of Solomon in the Books of Chronicles," *VT* 26 (1976), 351–71; R. L. Braun, "Solomon, The Chosen Temple Builder. The Significance of 1 Chronicles 22, 28 and 29 for the Theology of Chronicles," *JBL* 95 (1976) 581–90 and Christa Schäfer-Lichtenberger, *Josua und Salomo. Eine Studie zu Autorität und Legitimität des Nachfolgers im Alten Testament* (VTSup, 58; Leiden: Brill, 1995).

to its largest extent within the social memory of the community. He was the one who confronted Goliath, killed lions and bears (1 Sam 17:36), and who was pleased to be asked to pay a bride price of a hundred foreskins for Michal and happy to pay it (1 Sam 8:25–27). As the literati were reminded, time and again, David was the man who killed tens of thousands of enemies (1 Sam 18:7; 21:11; 29:5) and he certainly made a name for himself as a military leader/warrior (2 Sam 8:13; cf. 2 Sam 7:9). Although, within the world of knowledge of the literati, the territory conquered by David began to be lost already during the days of Solomon. There are no "ifs or buts" about the conquests of David.

Thus, whatever else Joshua was also remembered for, and to be sure one would expect him to be remembered for much else, the 'familiar' expectation is that he would be strongly characterized as a military hero, a mighty warrior similar to David.

This expectation is fulfilled in Ben Sira, who begins his portrayal of Joshua with "Joshua son of Nun was mighty in war (Heb, גבור חיל)... as his name implies, a great savior of God's elect, to take vengeance on the enemies that rose against them, so that he might give Israel its inheritance" (Sir 46:1 NRSV). It is also, no doubt, part and parcel of Josephus' portrayal of Joshua, the general in Josephus.[9] Within the world of the literati of the late Persian period, it is clear that Josh 1–11 not only recalls military victories of the Israelites under the leadership of the character Joshua, but also assigns to this Joshua well-known ideological/literary topoi usually assigned to neo-Assyrian (and much earlier) kings in texts communicating their mighty power. Topoi, such as, the image of the hero who overcomes natural barriers, the characterization of the one pious leader standing against the many impious rulers who oppose divine will and the divine support with which this great hero was provided.[10]

---

9 One may note, *inter alia*, that Josephus refers explicitly to Joshua as 'general' (στρατηγὸς) ten times (*War* 4.459; *Ant.* 3.59; 4.165, 324; 6.84; 7.68; 7.294; 9.207, 280; 11.112). On Josephus's Joshua see esp. Louis H. Feldman, "Josephus's Portrait of Joshua," *HTR* 82 (1989), 351–76.

10 Cf. John Van Seters, "Joshua's Campaign of Canaan and Near Eastern Historiography," *SJOT* 2 (1990), 1–12. Van Seters claims argues that DtrH, who is for him the author of Josh 1–11*, shaped a narrative of "a great military campaign using the model offered by the Assyrian royal inscriptions" (11). On Josh 9–12 within this context, see the detailed analysis of K. Lawson Younger, Jr., *Ancient Conquest Accounts: A Study in Ancient Near Eastern and Biblical History Writing* (JSOTSup, 98; Sheffield: Sheffield Academic Press, 1990), esp. 195–237 and his conclusion where he argues that "it appears that the text of Josh 9–12 is structured on a transmission code similar to that of other ancient Near Eastern royal inscriptions ... [s]ince the account utilizes similar literary and ideological aspects to the ancient Near Eastern conquest account, as well as similar syntagmic structuring, this conclusion seems justified" (p. 237). See also Thomas Römer, "Joshua's Encounter with the Commander of Yhwh's Army (Josh 5:13–15): Literary Construction or Re-

Joshua, as a site of memory among these literati, embodied and communicated the image of that military hero, and to be sure, its associated concept of masculinity.[11] Moreover, and as to be expected in the case of founding military leaders, Joshua as a site of memory integrated, embodied and communicated a number of related images, such as being a ruler/king-like figure. Further, the central sites of memory within any group tend to integrate, embody and communicate particular concepts that stand at the very core of communal self-identity. Thus, it is not surprising that Joshua was remembered as a student and writer of a copy of the *torah* (Josh 1:8; 8:32), a follower of Yhwh's commandments, prophet and teacher of them. To be sure, these basic attributes draw attention to matters other than 'Joshua the general', but not only that these attributes are not in tension with the image of Joshua the general, and mighty hero, but on the contrary, they actually support it. As in Assyria, the hero king is also (and must be) a pious king. David was remembered as a mighty hero and the designer of the temple and its service (see Chronicles), as a great general and singer (and dancer) of praises to Yhwh, as mighty hero and as a prophet (Qumran). Within particular social mindscapes and ideological discourses, all these partial images were mutually supportive.

Finally, the fact that the Joshua recalled and remembered by the literati when reading the book of Joshua could evoked and carry voices and themes associated with dtr., P or the Holiness 'School', hereafter HS,[12] is also to be expect-

---

flection of a Royal Ritual?," in Brad E. Kelle, Frank Ritchel Ames, and Jacob L. Wright (eds.), *Warfare, Ritual, and Symbol in Biblical and Modern Contexts* (AIL, 18; Atlanta: SBL, 2014), 49–64.
11 It is worth noting that this construction of masculinity is not necessarily coupled with images of procreation or even sexual activity. It is all about male hierarchy and the leading general is at the top. Cf. Ovidiu Creangă, "Variations on the Theme of Masculinity: Joshua's Gender In/stability in the Conquest Narrative," in idem (ed.), *Men and Masculinities in the Hebrew Bible and Beyond* (The Bible in the Modern World, 33; Sheffield: Sheffield Phoenix, 2010), 83–109.
12 Ada Taggar-Cohen maintains that the Achan story in Josh 7 and Josh 24 are at home with HS. See, Ada Taggar-Cohen, "Between Ḥerem, Ownership, and Ritual: Biblical and Hitttite Perspectives," in Roy Gane and Ada Taggar-Cohen (eds.), *Current Issues in Priestly and Related Literature: The Legacy of Jacob Milgrom and Beyond* (Society of Biblical Literature. Resources for Biblical Studies, 82; Atlanta: SBL Press, 2015), 419–34 (433); idem, "The Holiness School—Creativity and Editorial Activity in the Book of Joshua: The Case of Joshua 24," in Shamir Yona et al. (eds.), *Marbeh Hokma: Studies in the Bible and the Ancient Near East in Memory of Victor Avigdor* Hurowitz (Winona Lake, IN: Eisenbrauns, 2015), vol. I, 541–557. Although there are multiple differences in the details there is general agreement that dtr. and P texts, or as I would prefer voices, exist in Joshua. Of course, there is much debate about the significance of the presence of these texts for the reconstruction of the history of the book of Joshua, but since this essay deals with the Joshua of memory shaped by reading the book that eventually came into existence by the

ed. After all, the same occurs in the case of Moses and in both cases this feature is consistent with the Pentateuch that already existed at that time, and with the tendency towards integrative fuzziness that characterized the social mindscape of these literati.[13]

There is no doubt that all of these anticipated features serve to construct a more balanced image of Joshua: he is the successful general of the foundational period—as he had to be given his role in the narrative from Exodus to conquest and settlement of the land, but also much more. The fact that, as they began reading the book and thus evoking and shaping their memory of Joshua, the literati found and recalled that Josh 1:1–6 is immediately followed by Josh 1:7–8 only emphasizes the point.

Balancing, Rebalancing, and Interweaving Memories

None of the observations made above point to anything that may seem, at least on the surface, 'strange' in the way Joshua was remembered by these literati given their world of knowledge, social mindscape and the basic constraints of the narrative from Exodus to Settlement in the land. But there is something very substantial in the Joshua of memory of this group that is a least on the surface a 'odd', that is, something that defies the expected generative grammars at work in the group. As it is often the case with seemingly 'ungrammatical' but important social memories, the existence of such seemingly 'ungrammatical' constructions concerning the character Joshua demonstrates the existence of additional generative grammars at work in the group and draws attention not only to their weight, but also to their significance as reflections of core underlying ideological constructions.

Let me begin with a simple comparative remark about the other mighty hero/ great general par excellence, namely David. The literati were never asked to contemplate and remember that David conquered Jerusalem but failed to do so; that he expanded his kingdom in all directions and also that he failed to do so. To do

---

late Persian/early Hellenistic period, these matters do not have direct bearing on the issues discussed here.

13 See, e. g., "Exploring the Memory of Moses 'The Prophet'," "On Social Memory and Identity Formation in Late Persian Yehud: A Historian's Viewpoint with a Focus on Prophetic Literature, Chronicles and the Dtr. Historical Collection," in this volume, pp. 28–79, and "Readers, Social Memory, Deuteronomistic Language and Jeremiah: The Roles of Deuteronomistic Language in Shaping Memories of Jeremiah among Late Persian/early Hellenistic Readers of the Book of Jeremiah," in this volume, pp. 304–16.

so, even within a social mindscape that tends to favor a substantial degree of fuzziness would be to undermine the basic heroic aspect of the hero. A strong systemic dis-preference made these options unviable within the memory-scape shared by the literati. The same can be said for memories of a Samson defeated by a single Philistine warrior, or since these systemic dis-preferences occur not only for this type of heroes, for any construction of Solomon as wise, but less knowledgeable and wise than, e.g., the Queen of Sheba.

But when it comes to their Joshua, the literati were well aware that although several texts reminded them that Joshua was successful in conquering the entire land (e.g., Josh 11:23; 18:1; 22:43; cf. 10:41–42), several others in the books of Joshua (e.g., Josh 13:1–6; 15:63; 16:10) and the very beginning of Judges (Judg 1) emphatically and unequivocally reminded them that Joshua was not able to do so; that in fact, not all the land was conquered by Joshua or Israel under his leadership by a wide margin. Further, additional texts in the book of Joshua recalled the story of Judg 1 (e.g., Josh 15:13–19, 63; 16:10; 17:11–13; 19:47).

The literati were competent readers who seem to have been aware of genre conventions of royal inscriptions, and thus they were likely aware that explicit references to matters such as complete conquests, destructions of whole areas and populations or deportations often are not to be understood in the narrowest literal way. Instead, these references fulfil literary and rhetorical functions and tend to be hyperbolic.[14] In fact, similar cases, actually occur in their own historiographic works (see, e.g., 2 Kgs 24:13–14, which the following narrative conclusively demonstrate that competent readers should not take them literally).

Their conclusion that, in what they imagined to be their 'actual' past, Joshua failed to conquer the whole land was not without consequences for their construction of Joshua. After all, they knew that when Joshua was appointed, a crucial attribute for the candidate was his ability to serve as a military leader (see Num 27:16–17 and esp. v 17; cf. 2 Sam 5:2; 1 Chr 11:2 which refer to David as a military leader). They knew that Joshua was mandated to lead Israel in the conquest of the whole land (see, e.g., Josh 1:1–5 and the explicit portrayal of the land to be conquered, including its boundaries in vv 3–4; cf. Deut 11:24; 1:7). He was supposed to completely replace the existing local population with Israelites[15] and, along with the priest Eleazar, he was supposed to allocate the entire

---

14 See also e.g., Younger, *Ancient Conquest Accounts*, 246.
15 According to Deut 7:2; 20:16–17; cf. Deut 7:16, 23; 9:3, this population replacement was mandated to include utter physical annihilation. Within the discourse of the literati, the failure of the Israelites at the time of Joshua to utterly destroy the local population was construed as a substantial failure of Israel with important implications (see, e.g., Ps 106:34; Other voices asked the

land (see, e.g., Num 34:17; Deut 1:38; 31:7–8; Josh 1:1–6).¹⁶ In this light, and keeping in mind not only Yhwh's opening words in the book of Joshua and Joshua's own words at the beginning of account of the invasion of the land (Josh 3:10), Joshua the general could not have been construed or remembered as being too successful in achieving this task.¹⁷

Moreover, when the gates to reconsider the success of Joshua the general open, particular memories associated with putative events in his campaign, although still positive seem to draw less attention to Joshua's prowess as military leader or his heroism and far more to other aspects of this site of memory. For example, Joshua's crossing of the Jordan is certainly consistent with the common topos of the mighty king overcoming mighty barriers (e.g., rivers, mountains), but the two spies Joshua sent to Jericho seem to have crossed it without much problem (Josh 2:1, 23) shortly before Joshua's crossing, as the readers of the text know well.¹⁸ Even accounting for the sudden reference to "the Jordan overflows all its banks throughout the time of harvest" (Josh 3:15), the fact is that the story of the crossing of the Jordan does not focus on Joshua the military hero or mighty warrior able to defeat 'nature', but on other aspects of his leadership, along with the role of the priests and the ark. Moreover, the main point of the narrative at this point is to legitimize Joshua as the true successor of Moses in the eyes of the Israelites, as Yhwh himself was remembered explicitly telling Joshua, and indirectly the readers of the book (Josh 3:7). Moreover, since the military prowess of Moses is downplayed in the memory-scape of literati, empha-

---

literati to imagine other, still violent alternatives, but not necessarily involving utter physical annihilation (e.g., being forced to flee the land, forced exile [e.g., Lev 18:25–28; cf. Lev 20:22] and so on). See Baruch Schwartz, "Reexamining." It is worth noting that Num 33:54 construes and communicates an image of a Yhwh who judges the 'potential' inability of the Israelites to "drive out the inhabitants of the land from before you" as a deep failure for them and as one that would cause them substantial problems in the future. Even if the literati were to construe Joshua as not personally responsible for this failure, they would have to construct his leadership, to a significant extent at least, as a failure.

16 In a world of knowledge that included as an agreed fact that Joshua did not conquer the entire land, there will be a strong preference for raising the question of whether he may virtually allocate that which he and the Israelites have not conquered. Josh 23:4 is proof positive for the existence of such a tendency. Vicariously overhearing Joshua talk to the people by reading Josh 23:4 provided the literati with a positive answer to their question. This response whereas allows for Joshua's failure to conquer the land, minimizes the damage to his character, as does ch. 23 in general and see below.

17 Cf. Knauf, "Remembering Joshua;" idem, "Why 'Joshua'?."Cf. the case of the battle against Amalek in Exodus (see below).

18 See Knauf, "Why 'Joshua'"?

sizing the Mosaic character of Joshua at this conjuncture downplayed the warrior heroism of Joshua.

The conquest of Jericho, the first and most memorable conquest evoked by the book of Joshua also does not call particular attention to the military leadership or individual prowess of Joshua. In the case of Ai, the idea for the crucial ambush was not Joshua's but Yhwh's (Josh 8:1–2), and Joshua requires Yhwh to tell him when to launch the attack (Josh 8:18). Significantly, the MT of 8:26 (cf. MT Josh 8:18) unlike the LXX,[19] points at the existence of a memory-shaping tendency towards constructing the act of Joshua here as reminiscent of that of Moses during the battle against Amalek in Exod 17:11, which by placing Joshua and Moses on the same 'slot,' undermines the construction of either one as the mighty warrior engaged in battle and implicitly draws attention to the fact that when it comes to the conquest of Ai someone else fulfilled a role similar to that of the younger, Joshua (see Exod 17:9–10, and esp. v. 13) and takes the city (Josh 8:19).

Even narratives such as Josh 10 that clearly construed Joshua as a war-hero,[20] although necessarily secondary to Yhwh (e.g., Josh 10:10–11) become open to re-balancing when the text was read in a way informed by the failure to conquer the whole land. After all, the literati cannot but remember that although Joshua defeated and killed the king of Jerusalem and all his allies and achieved great military success with Yhwh's help, he still did not conquer Jerusalem (see below).

In addition, the memorable story in Josh 10:12–14 about the sun standing still at Gibeon and the moon in the valley of Aijalon, in the book read by these literati, does not emphasize Joshua battle skills, but that the deity was willing to go to 'unparalleled' lengths to help him and Israel.[21]

I would like to conclude this set of observations with one that is particularly important for any historical understanding of the social mindscape of the literati: the land is *never referred* to as the land conquered by Joshua and there are no narratives about his (or his companions') personal acts of heroism.[22]

---

19 The LXX lacks v 26. (There are minor differences between LXX and MT 8:18). Whether MT 26 is a later addition or not, it still points at the mentioned memory-shaping tendency.
20 Of course, within the terms of the discourse of the time. Current international law would consider any leader doing what the Joshua and the Yhwh of the text did to be a war-criminal.
21 On Josh 10:12–14 and its proposed forerunners, see, e.g., Thomas B. Dozeman, *Joshua 1–12* (AB, 6B; New Haven, Conn.: Yale Univ. Press, 2015), 441–45.
22 I expanded on similar issues in "Memory of Abraham" and "Remembering Pre-Israelite Jerusalem in Late Persian Yehud: Mnemonic Preferences, Memories and Social Imagination", in this volume, pp. 162–98 and 504–26 respectively.

Significantly, these observations are not restricted to the main narrative about Joshua in the Book of Joshua. The most memorable story about Joshua the warrior found outside the book of Joshua appears in Exod 17:8–14. The account there seems to exalt Joshua the military leader, but ends up opening the gates for communal reconsideration, for re-evaluation of this aspect of his leadership and rebalancing the image of Joshua. Although the text states that Joshua overwhelmed (חלש, qal) Amalek (v. 13), it is not only that the fate of the battle depended on the position of Moses' hand/s, and of course, YHWH, rather than the warrior heroism of Joshua, but also that the report ends in v. 14 with YHWH (via Moses) reminding the community that the deity "will utterly blot out the memory of Amalek from under heaven!" The remembering community was asked thus to recall, even in the context of this text, that Joshua's victory was only partial, because as they know well, Amalek continued to exist. Moreover, Joshua is told that such were the words of YHWH, and even he had to be imagined as acknowledging the partial character of the victory.[23] His greatness in the text is not to be found in his military capabilities, but in his willingness to serve Moses and, by doing so, YHWH. Joshua the servant is far more important and successful than Joshua the general within a community remembering the past narrated in Exod 17:8–14 and Exodus in general.

In sum, whereas the figure of Joshua had to be construed as a that of a military conqueror, not only that he is construed as much more than simply a military leader—a move which is expected—but also that his aura as a successful battle hero and warrior is strongly balanced and diminished, even in the context of memories of his main conquests. The latter is, on the surface, less expected and demands an explanation. Which factors were responsible for the development of such a tendency to undermine his characterization as a top Israelite warrior of memory? Why was there a generative grammar that preferred this type of characterization, of all cases, in that of Joshua?

Converging Factors

A number of converging and to large extent systemically interrelated reasons contributed to the emergence of a system of preferences and dis-preferences for the shaping and reproduction of the memory of Joshua among the literati that resulted in the seemingly 'odd' aspects of Joshua as a site of memory men-

---

23 Cf. Farber, *Images of Joshua and Their Reception*, 16 n. 40.

tioned above. Of course, in turn, these seemingly 'odd' aspects could not but draw the attention of the literati to the underlying issues that led to them.

First, the concept that it was Yhwh led the conquest, that Yhwh not Joshua was the real general of Israel[24] and its war hero and that the military skills of Joshua or the Israelites play no role (e.g., Josh 24:11–12; Ps 44:1–3) contributed to the emergence of this system. The point is not so much that divine presence and intervention were crucial to the success of the military endeavors—this was taken as a given in Israel and other ancient near Eastern cultures – but within the logic of this view, there is no point in expanding on or remembering Joshua's skills (or lack thereof, for that matters) as general or warrior, since they really did not matter at all.

This approach allowed the literati to consider that the failure to conquer the whole land is not due to Joshua's fault or of his leadership (a point made clear by Josh 23) and is not even the people's fault. From that perspective, the ultimate deciding factor on the matter is Yhwh's will, and thus, at the end of the day, Yhwh decides to do whatever Yhwh decides to do and the only thing Joshua and Israel can practically do is follow Yhwh and hope for a future settlement on the whole land, if they follow him.

Moreover, Yhwh may have reasons for not allowing the full conquest. In fact, one may argue, that some form of partial conquest served to instill the point that *torah* is a pre-condition for the complete fulfillment of Yhwh's promises (see Josh 23; cf. Josh 1:7–8).[25] Of course, Yhwh could and was imagined at times as having additional reasons (e.g. Judg 3:1–2).

Within this approach, remembering Joshua followed Yhwh and his commandments and led Israel as much as he could to follow them was worthwhile because this provided a good didactic example for community leaders. Moreover, remembering the events of retold in Josh 1–12 was also worthwhile, because this memory served didactic purposes. For one, and beyond simply exalting Yhwh and conveying Yhwh's power, the memory inculcated a sense of indebtedness

---

[24] The literati remembered that the idea of a divine intermediary, rather than Yhwh, who may lead the conquest of the land was actually raised by Yhwh to the consternation of the people and as a form of partial divine rejection (see Exod 33:1–6). Of course, they also remembered that Yhwh announced that he will lead the invasion (see Exod 34:11) and cf. Deut 9:3. But see also the voices and memories encoded and communicated by Exod 23:20–23. Not surprisingly multiple memories informing, balancing and interacting with each other existed on these matters, as in probably all important matters within the general discourse of these literati. On Josh 5:13–15 see Thomas Römer, "Joshua's Encounter with the Commander of Yhwh's Army," and cited bibliography.

[25] See Dozeman, *Joshua 1–12*, 396.

and gratitude to Yʜwʜ, and alongside it, a directly related demand for the community's loyalty to him (cf. the world portrayed in Josh 24:2–13).[26] Although the Exodus remained the most commonly used node of memory for these purposes within the authoritative repertoire,[27] the conquest of Canaan undoubtedly served as an important secondary node (cf. the case in the world portrayed in Josh 24:2–13).

This general approach to remembering Joshua and the conquest tends to strongly de-emphasize the battle/war hero dimension of Joshua as a site of memory. It is not only that focusing on Joshua military prowess would have been tantamount to focusing on what, in the end, does not matter all, but at times, too much emphasis on Joshua's success as a military leader would have been potentially damaging for the overall characterization of Joshua – as when the literati construed and remembered the failure of Joshua's generation to fully destroy the local population as sign of disloyalty to Yʜwʜ (cf. Ps 106:34). The generative grammar emerging from this underlying approach is quite clear and consistent with what was discussed above in terms of the lack of full conquest.

A second factor that contributed to the emergence of a system of preferences and dis-preferences for the shaping and reproduction of the memory of Joshua among the literati was the multiplicity of memories associated with the replacement of the existing population. The construction of the Israelites coming from somewhere else required the creation of memories of settlement in the land. Although historical processes of migration and resettlement are well attested, historical cases of immediate complete population replacement over a large area are not. To be sure, there were cases of, and narratives about, relatively circumscribed areas that were contested between groups and in which one of these groups carried some form of 'ethnic cleansing' (see, e.g., Mesha), but not over very large areas. Migration and resettlement often led to various forms of unequal integration between local and migrant populations. Moreover, it was more common to construe the beginning of the process of colonization in a somewhat distant land as taking place in some empty space than a place fully inhabited with mighty people and cities. To be sure, the new place may be construed as empty, because the local population fled in advance, and there are multiple instances in which a settlement that began in 'empty land' led down

---

[26] Cf. Jon D. Levenson, *The Love of God: Divine Gift, Human Gratitude, and Mutual Faithfulness in Judaism* (Princeton: Princeton University Press, 2016), 44–57 and passim.

[27] Some general accounts of the mighty deeds of Yʜwʜ for Israel (and despite them, its lack of loyalty to Yʜwʜ) even completely omitted or barely mentioned the conquest of the land under the human leadership of Joshua (see, e.g., Pss 78; 136; and cf. Neh 9:24–25 with the attention given to other sections of the basic foundational story of Israel

the road to the displacement of the local population, but stories like the most familiar narrative of the Conquest by Joshua are rare.²⁸

It is worth noting in this regard that, although all memories about the settlement of Israel in the land involve the displacement of mighty populations, some of them seem to work within the parameters of a story of empty land or partially empty land, in which Yhwh 'drove out' (Heb. גרש) the local peoples gradually (e.g., Exod 23:27–31; 34:11) and thus the need to forbid Israel from entering into a covenant or intermingling with them; or in which 'the land' (Lev 18:25–28; cf. Lev 20:22) itself exiled/removed the local peoples, in the wake of Israel's entrance.²⁹ The story of the 'return' from Babylonia, which was mnemonically shaped to echo the stories of the Exodus and the entrance to the land, also constructs the land as empty, and Hecateus references to the empty land of Judah are all suggestive that there was certain generative grammar working in that direction and over time.

As an aside, it is usually forgotten but important to stress that just as the literati remembered multiple partial images of the past, ranging from those evoking total to partial population replacement, they also remembered that Joshua's Israel included non-Israelites from the beginning, even if bound to *torah*, as demonstrated by the explicit reference to the presence of the *gēr* at the *torah* event described in Josh 8:30–35.³⁰

Moreover, whether the land was imagined as empty,³¹ in the process of emptying itself or being forcefully emptied by Israel, with Yhwh's support or any combination of the above, the main didactic message for late Persian literati remained the same: (a) no matter how strong these local peoples were, their fate

---

28 For Greek evidence, see Robert Garland, *Wandering Greeks: The Ancient Greek Diaspora from the Age of Homer to the Death of Alexander the Great* (Princeton, NJ: Princeton University Press, 2014), esp. pp. 46–51.

29 On these issues see Baruch Schwartz, "Reexamining." Note that he argues that "J imagined the promise to have been one of miraculous expulsion of the Canaanites; Israel's only task was not to get in the way" (157). From the perspective of the literati discussed here, J is not a source, but a voice (one among others) that they hear and whose tenor is part and parcel of their integrated, though diverse system of memories about these events.

30 This text informs and is informed by Deut 27:1–8, In fact, the 'stones' on which Joshua writes the copy of the *torah* were likely understood in reference to the stones mentioned in Deut 27:2–4 rather than on those of the altar referred to in Josh 8:31. If Deut 27:4 read rather than Mt. Ebal, the reference to Ebal in Joshua may be consistent with a pro-Jerusalem bias. See below and on this issue cf. Reinhard Müller, "The Altar on Mount Gerizim (Deuteronomy 27:1–8). Center or Periphery?," in Ehud Ben Zvi and Christoph Levin (eds.), *Centres and Peripheries in the Early Second Temple Period* (FAT, 108; Tübingen: Mohr-Siebeck, 2016), 197–214.

31 Cf. Hdt. 4.11

was sealed, because of their sinful ways in the sight of Yhwh—pious non-Israelites can remain in the country with the Israelites, see above—and they serve as a memorial warning Israel not to follow their path; (b) Israel did follow their path and was exiled; and (c) unlike these dis-inherited peoples, Yhwh brought back Israel from exile, because he gifted the land to their ancestors; a gift that demands gratitude in the form of loyalty.[32]

Within this logic, the role of the Israelites during the conquest is to a significant degree comparable to the role of the Babylonian armies (and Assyrians before). In other words, their military power was only a secondary, contingent and transient component of a far more important, and from the perspective of the literati, constant narrative. Reports about their military prowess may make for more vivid and memorable stories and, from a systemic perspective, enhance their efficiency as socializing tools, but no more. This may explain why Joshua was remembered as a general. At the same time, given that (a) these were one-time-events in the very distant past and (b) military prowess and the ability to lead vast armies were not among the traits that the literati considered most necessary for themselves or for the *torah*-centred, Jerusalem-centred Israel that they imagined in the Persian period, it follows that a strong tendency to balance them with more relevant traits from their perspective, such as leading people to *torah*, serving as proper, Mosaic, human 'guardian' of Israel in his generation and so on.[33]

Of course, the foundational, human 'guardian' of Israel was Moses (see, e.g., Hos 12:14), and here one encounters another factor that contributed to the mentioned system of mnemonic preferences. Joshua was and had to be remembered as much as reminiscent of Moses as possible, without being his equal, of course. Given that the motif of General Moses or General Abraham (the other main foundational figure of Israel) or General Jacob for that matter was downplayed in the core textual repertoire of the literati of the period, one may anticipate also a strong tendency to downplay as much as possible, and within the constraints of the role given by the main narrative, the weight of General Joshua in the Joshua of memory held by these literati. To be sure, this has to do with the contingent historical circumstances of these literati (see above) and as changes on these matters in the Hellenistic period concerning all three of these characters demon-

---

[32] Cf. J. D. Levenson, *Love of God*, 44–57 and passim.
[33] On the concept of 'guardian' see my "Memory and Political Thought in the Late Persian/Early Hellenistic Yehud/Judah: Some Observations," in Diana V. Edelman and Ehud Ben Zvi (eds.) (WANEM; London: Equinox, 2016), 9–26.

strate.³⁴ But there is more than that in the case of Joshua and Moses. The more Joshua has to look reminiscent of Moses, the more that being a teacher of *torah*, a covenant maker, a warning prophet and the like has to be highlighted in the construction of their Joshua of memory.

Moreover, the literati knew well that the land was taken by both Moses and Joshua was lost, just as Moses and Joshua had anticipated.³⁵ But *torah* and the relevant promise to the land remained unassailable and, within their worldview, a crucial source of hope and utopian thinking for the community. For this reason, the land is never the land that Joshua conquered (a temporary attribute), but the land Yʜᴡʜ promised to the ancestors (a permanent trait).

Moreover, if Persian-period memories of Joshua and king Josiah informed and shaped each other,³⁶ then, in both there is the element of what a leader should do, even when what his 'material' main achievement will be lost, namely still teach and follow *torah*. Thus Josh 1:8; 8:30–35 and 23–24 acquire increased mindshare while remembering Josiah and his military achievements may be downplayed.

Earlier I mentioned that scholars have noticed that the relationship between Moses and Joshua was imagined in a way informing and informed by that of David and Solomon. Significantly, whereas the military aspects of these pairs would tend to associate David and Joshua, for the most part the strongest link is between the memories of Joshua and Solomon. The link between Solomon and Joshua goes, however, well beyond the basic narrative constraint that both were successors. In both cases, they transformed a chaotic space into an ordered well-organized place by conceptually appropriating and reshaping the whole territory into well-organized systems of districts or tribe allotments depending on the case, and far more importantly, by explicitly marking it for Yʜᴡʜ (and indirectly, for Yʜᴡʜ's people), through the building of the temple

---

34 See note 7 above, to which one may add the portrayal of Jacob in Jub 34:1–9; 37:1–38:14), and see Atar Livneh, "With my Sword and Bow: Jacob as Warrior in Jubilees," in Deborah Dimant and Reinhard Kratz (eds.), *Rewriting and Interpretation: The Biblical Patriarchs in Light of the Dead Sea Scrolls* (BZAW 439; Berlin: de Gruyter, 2013), 189–213.
35 Concerning Moses, see Deut 30:1–5; 32:19–25; and, among others the pragmatic message in late Persian Yehud of Deut 28:15–68; 29:13–27; 30:17–19; 31:19–22. For Joshua, see, the pragmatic message of Josh 24: 19–21; cf. 23:14–16.
36 See and cf. Josh 8:34 and 2 Kgs 23:2; significantly, whereas Joshua fulfills the task of the king of Deut 17:18 to write a copy of the *torah*—in fact he is the only royal character who fulfills it within the memory scape of community, whereas Josiah 'finds' one. This matter cannot be explored in this context. On Joshua and Josiah, see Richard Nelson, "Josiah in the Book of Joshua," *JBL* 100 (1981), 531–540; Marvin A. Sweeney, *King Josiah of Judah. The Lost Messiah of Israel* (Oxford: Oxford Univ. Press, 2001), 25–26; 134–136.

in Jerusalem in the case of Solomon and memorials marking the land for YHWH in places such as Gilgal (Josh 4:1–24), Mt Ebal (Josh 8:30–35), Shiloh (Josh 18:1); East of the Jordan (Josh 22:10–34), Shechem (Josh 24:1–28). Moreover, in both cases, they could transform the chaotic, still un-ordered space, because the period of disorder came to an end, as marked in references to the reaching of the required state of 'rest' and safety (e.g., Deut 12:10–12; Josh 23:1 (cf. Josh 13:1); 1 Kgs 5:4; 8:56).

When approached from this perspective, what is most worth remembering of Joshua (and of Solomon) is not Josh 1–12, but chapters 13–24 and texts such as Josh 8:30–35. The outcome is, of course, a trend towards downplaying the relative saliency of the image of Joshua the general/warrior. Significantly, a mnemonic preference for 'building' the space over conquering it was at work in the case of David where it matters the most, i.e., in the case of Jerusalem. As I discussed elsewhere, the construction of David as the mighty warrior and hero is not emphasized in this instance, unlike many other cases, and despite the existence of clear differences in the way in which the conquest of the land was remembered compared to memories of the conquest of Jerusalem, when each is viewed as a whole.[37]

One may argue that this still does not explain why Joshua was so explicitly and so saliently remembered also as unable to conquer the whole land, but once we keep in mind the social location of the Jerusalemite literati, the issue becomes clear. Within a Jerusalem-centered ideology, all the places that were marked for YHWH by Joshua could only be construed as temporarily correct. Remembering Joshua, the northerner, included that the narrative of Israel required a Judahite David, who would conquer Jerusalem and a Judahite (/Jerusalemite) Solomon to properly mark the land with a material temple and above all with the memorial that such a temple created in the minds of the literati.

It is not surprising then that whereas David was remembered as the great general who conquered and controlled the whole land, Joshua was not; that whereas the usual topos of the nations coming to Israel due to the fame of their ruler and of YHWH is applied in a positive way to memories of Solomon (see esp. 1 Kgs 10:1–13, 24–25), but functions as a parody in Josh 9 (see esp. vv 9–10). In sum, within a Jerusalem-centered ideology, the role of Joshua as servant of Moses had to be kept; Joshua had to remain one of the most respected Israelites of memory, but his memory had to be balanced, particularly to reflect the ideological status of Jerusalem and the related mnemonic roles of David and Solomon. This tendency is clearly evident, and strongly communicated through

---

37 See "Remembering Pre-Israelite Jerusalem."

the contribution of a book such as Chronicles to the partial rebalancing of Israel's comprehensive social memory.[38]

Squaring Circles

The present discussion has shown that, to some extent, the literati were involved in social processes of squaring circles. They often shaped, engaged and maintained multiple partial memories that contradicted each other from a logical viewpoint. Moreover, some of these memories were meant to bring to the fore exactly what others downplayed, and *vice versa*. Further, some of these memories were 'grammatical' within a particular generative grammar, but ungrammatical in relation to others.

Some of us may recoil at all of this. But when it comes to mnemonic systems, coherence may well be overrated. Most historical systems, ideological representations and the like are not fully coherent nor can they be if the system is supposed to be somewhat stable. In fact, we may be advised as historians to talk about a systemic coherence of incoherence, of systemic congruity of incongruity or of the grammatically of the overall outcome of multiple different generative grammars.

The ability to allow the interplay and intertwining of multiple memories and generative grammars provided the ability to construe and remember a past that served the present of the literati and social coherence. It allowed them to also turn memory into a language to explore multiple ideas and fuzzy hierarchies of conceptual meanings. It allowed them to develop creative, ideological in-between areas which linked various aspects of memories embodied in one site of memory and aspects of memories embodied in separate sites of memory, thus facilitating a process in which they mutually inform each other and add new potential meanings to be embodied and conveyed by them. All this demanded, of course, a group whose social mindscape was comfortable with flexible thinking, ambiguity and fuzziness. Of course, these were precisely the hallmarks of the literati of the period. In addition, one cannot but notice that all of these activities

---

[38] The only reference to Joshua is in 1 Chr 7:27, in the genealogical line of Ephraim. Of course, Chronicles partakes into a larger mnemonic system. For my position on these issues, see "Chronicles and Samuel-Kings: Two Interacting Aspects of one Memory System in the Late Persian/Early Hellenistic Period," in this volume, pp. 317–31.

construed, by necessity, a conceptual world in which they (i.e., the literati) enjoyed much cultural and mnemonic capital.[39]

In sum, squaring circles may seem a strange activity to engage in, but as an historian I would conclude that it provided the literati with many benefits. It involved high cognitive costs, to be sure, but its benefits, at multiple levels, far outweighed any such costs for this group.

---

[39] I expanded on these matters in "Potential Intersections Between Research Frames Informed by Social-Memory and 'Bourdieusian' Approaches/Concepts: The Study of Socio-Historical Features of the Literati of the early Second Temple Period," in this volume, pp. 631–54.

Isaiah, a Memorable Prophet: Why was Isaiah so Memorable in the Late Persian/Early Hellenistic Periods? Some Observations*

Introduction

Isaiah was a very memorable character.[1] There can be no doubt that Isaiah served as a central site within the memory landscape of late Persian/early Hellenistic Judah and of the late and early post-Second Temple period. The number of Isaiah scrolls in Qumran and of allusions and references to the book of Isaiah in the literature of the period argue the point beyond any possible doubt concerning the last two periods.[2]

---

* First published in *Remembering Biblical Figures in the Late Persian & Early Hellenistic Periods: Social Memory and Imagination* (eds. D. V. Edelman and E. Ben Zvi; Oxford: Oxford University Press, 2013), 365–83.

1 I use 'Isaiah' to designate a character in the memory of the community. This character was imagined, shaped, and reshaped on the basis of the *entire* book of Isaiah and some other texts (e.g. relevant sections in Kings, Chronicles). This character is to be distinguished from any (reconstructed) historical Isaiah of Jerusalem and any contemporary reconstruction of Deutero-Isaiah and Trito-Isaiah, who may well be characters in our social memory but not in that of readers in the late Persian or Hellenistic periods. The book of Isaiah, as a whole, evoked in antiquity the image of one prophet, as did all the other prophetic books; see E. Ben Zvi, "Is the Twelve Hypothesis Likely from an Ancient Readers' Perspective?," in *Two Sides of a Coin* (eds. E. Ben Zvi and J. D. Nogalski; Analecta Gorgiana 201; Piscataway, NJ: Gorgias, 2009), 47–96 (80–4). Cf. Sir 48:18–25 and note that if there was a marked division in the manuscript of the book of Isaiah, it was after ch. 33, not ch. 39.

2 See Sir 48:18–25 and see P. W. Skehan and A. A. Di Lella, *The Wisdom of Ben Sira* (AB 39; Garden City, NY: Doubleday, 1987), 538–9. See, among others, M. A. Knibb, "Isaianic Traditions in the Aprocrypha and Pseudepigrapha," in *Writing and Reading the Scroll of Isaiah* (eds. C. C. Broyles and C. A. Evans; VTSup 70.2; Leiden/ New York: Brill, 1997), 633–50; republished in M. A. Knibb, *Essays on the Book of Enoch and Other Early Jewish Texts and Traditions* (SVTP 22; Leiden/New York: Brill, 2009), 289–306; M. A. Knibb, "Isaianic Traditions in the Book of Enoch," in *After the Exile* (eds. J. Barton and D. J. Reimer; Macon, GA: Mercer University Press, 1996), 217–29. There are more Isaiah mss (twenty-one, *not* including the one found in W. Muraba'at) among the 'biblical' Qumran mss than mss for all the other books in the PBC combined and more mss than for all the historical books (Joshua–2 Kings + Chronicles) combined. Isaiah is the third most represented book among the 'biblical' Dead Sea Scrolls, after Psalms and Deuteronomy. There are more than 400 references, allusions, and echoes to Isaiah in the New Testament. See C. A. Evans, "From Gospel to Gospel: The Function of Isaiah in the New Testament" in *Writing and Reading the Scroll of Isaiah* (eds. C. C. Broyles and C. A. Evans; VTSup 70.2; Leiden/ New York: Brill, 1997), 651–91 (esp. 651 and the bibliography there).

https://doi.org/10.1515/9783110547146-010

As for the late Persian/early Hellenistic period in Yehud/Judea, which is the topic addressed here, the repertoire of books held as authoritative by the community, or at least by its *literati*, attests clearly to the importance of Isaiah in the reading/remembering community. By either the late Persian or early Hellenistic period, the mentioned repertoire included the fifteen prophetic books (i.e. the prophetic books collection, hereafter PBC, the Deuteronomistic historical collection, hereafter DHC, and the book of Chronicles).[3] All things being equal, it is reasonable to assume a direct correlation between the textual space allocated to characters within that repertoire and their relative mindshare in the group. Not only is it more likely that greater space was devoted to more prominent figures in the group, but reading about Isaiah could not help but draw attention to the character, to bring him to the present of the community, as it were. Thus, the larger the corpus of reading material about him that is read in the community, the more prominent Isaiah becomes in its mnemonic landscape. Conversely, the more important the character becomes, the more likely it is that additional texts about him will emerge in that community.

The proviso above about 'all things being equal' addresses the likelihood that not all texts (or books) within the repertoire would have been read equally or would have carried the same weight. Since one may safely assume that the relative mindshare of the memories evoked by a text correlated directly with its relative influence in the community, texts that were widely read were more influential than those that were not. While it is difficult to assess the relative weight of readings of and images shaped in Samuel–Kings vs their counterpart in Chronicles in the late Persian/early Hellenistic Judah,[4] there is no reason to

---

[3] Although there is some debate about the date of the book of Chronicles, most scholars tend to associate it with the late Persian or early Hellenistic periods (i.e. in the fourth century BCE). See, among many others, H. G. M. Williamson, *1 and 2 Chronicles* (New Century Bible Commentary; Grand Rapids, MI: Eerdmans, 1982), 15–17; S. J. De Vries, *1 and 2 Chronicles* (Forms of Old Testament Literature 11; Grand Rapids, MI: Eerdmans, 1989), 16–17; S. Japhet, *I & II Chronicles* (OTL; Louisville, KY: Westminster John Knox, 1993), 23–8; J. E. Dyck, *Theocratic Ideology* (Biblical Interpretation Series 33; Leiden: Brill; 1998), 31–3; K. Peltonen, "A Jigsaw without a Model? The Date of Chronicles," in *Did Moses Speak Attic?* (ed. L. L. Grabbe; JSOTSup, 317; Sheffield: Sheffield Academic Press, 2001), 225–71; I. Kalimi, *Ancient Israelite Historian* (SSN 46; Assen: Van Gorcum, 2005), 41–65; G. N. Knoppers, *I Chronicles 1–9* (AB 12; New York, NY: Doubleday, 2004), 101–17; R. W. Klein, *1 Chronicles* (Hermeneia; Minneapolis, MN: Augsburg Fortress, 2006), 13–17.

[4] It is not a foregone conclusion that *in toto*, Samuel–Kings was more influential than Chronicles. Matters may vary from episode to episode and from figure to figure. Moreover, at times–though certainly not always–Chronicles may partially represent the way in which Samuel–Kings was actually read/received among the *literati*. Each of these books evoked a multiplicity of contrasting but complementary memories of many characters and events and sometimes, a

doubt that the book of Isaiah was very, and not peripherally, influential among the *literati*. The number of texts outside Isaiah that evoked Isaianic texts and vice versa is proof positive of its mindshare and the associated mindshare of the main character, Isaiah.[5] Moreover, the extensive redactional history of the book of Isaiah suggests a continuous process of engaging, remembering, and reshaping the figure of the prophet for generations, down to the final shaping of the present form of the book of Isaiah, probably by the late Persian period.[6] There is no reason to assume the *literati* ceased to read the book or to think of Isaiah, just because the compositional process more or less reached a final state (probably) by the end of the Persian or the early Hellenistic period.

Moreover, there was plenty to read about Isaiah and plenty to evoke and thus shape and reshape memories of Isaiah and his messages in the community. In addition to the book of Isaiah, which most significantly and deliberately evolved into one of the larger books in the Hebrew Bible, there were references to Isaiah in 2 Chronicles that assumed an already existing memory of a great prophet Isaiah within the intended readership of the book and which was placed

---

particular, seemingly 'minor' memory in one book was reinforced by a similar one in the other book. See my "Are There Any Bridges Out There? How Wide Was the Conceptual Gap between the Deuteronomistic History and Chronicles?," in *Community Identity in Judean Historiography* (eds. G. N. Knoppers and K. A. Ristau; Winona Lake, IN: Eisenbrauns, 2009), 59–86.

5 The list is vast and goes well beyond the parallel texts in Kings and Isaiah or Isa 2:1–4 // Mic 4:1–3 (cf. Joel 4:10); see, among others, Exod 15:2; Isa 12:2; Ps 118:14; and note the influence of the text of the book of Isaiah in some sections of Chronicles, see A. Warhurst, "What was Prophetic for the Chronicler?," in *What is Authoritative in Chronicles?* (eds. E. Ben Zvi and D. V. Edelman; Winona Lake, IN: Eisenbrauns, 2011), 165–81. On the matter of allusions, or what I would prefer to describe, in focusing on the perspective of a late Persian period/early Hellenistic period *literati*, networks of texts recalling and informing each other, see B. D. Sommer, *A Prophet Reads Scripture* (Stanford, CA: Stanford University Press, 1998). For a similar network occurring in Sirach and thus, from a later period, see R. L. Schultz, *The Search for Quotation* (JSOTSup 180; Sheffield: Sheffield Academic Press, 1999), 153–9.

6 The book of Isaiah reached its compositional form well before Sirach; see Sir 48:18–25, which assumes a memory of the prophet shaped by (and reflecting) a reading of the book of Isaiah as a whole and as a book encoding memories about the monarchic-period prophet Isaiah. An earlier *terminus ad quem* for the book of Isaiah is, however, more likely, given that the book of Isaiah most likely pre-dated the book of Chronicles, which, in turn, is dated to the Persian or early Hellenistic period. As for the *terminus a quo*, it is obvious that the present compositional cannot be dated earlier than Isa 56–66, which is often assigned to the (mid-to-late) Persian period. Although some prophecies in Isaiah likely ended up being read as being fulfilled in the Seleucid period (e.g. LXX Isa 14, 23, 25, 26), they were not composed in the Seleucid period (cf. R. L. Troxel, *LXX-Isaiah as Translation and Interpretation* [JSJSup 124; Leiden/Boston: Brill, 2008], 209–34 and the bibliography there).

there to lionize Hezekiah.[7] Above all, there were the very substantial references to Isaiah in 2 Kings.

Isaiah is the prophet to whom the most extensive amount of textual space was allocated in Kings, with the exception of Elijah, who was not featured in a prophetic book. Moreover, the only two prophets whose memories were encoded in and evoked by substantial texts, who appear in crucial places in both prophetic and historiographic texts, were Isaiah and Jeremiah, but again, the number of overlapping texts concerning Isaiah is much larger than those about Jeremiah.

This observation is not only relevant for matters of social mindshare but also for the potential to construe a highly complex, multifaceted image of the prophet that in turn facilitates its ability to 'absorb' and 'communicate' multiple sets of meanings that stand at the core of the community. A prophetic character whose memory was shaped primarily by the interweaving of partial images and aspects of images that emerged from the *literati's* reading of *both* a prophetic book (i.e. Isaiah) and the book of Kings has more potential than a character imagined on the basis of only one book.[8] Two different, highly developed books, each evoking and communicating multiple messages informing each other, were read in turn within the remembering community as significantly informing each other–or in the very least, as providing a meaningful background for understanding the other.

Moreover, although all prophets were construed as unique, Isaiah was construed as exceptional in ways that drew particular attention to him, his place, and his role in the memory landscape of the *literati* in Yehud. Three prophetic characters within the PBC drew the highest level of mnemonic mindshare: Isaiah, Jeremiah, and Ezekiel. Yet, whereas Jeremiah was partially characterized by speaking with a voice whose diction evoked Moses and carried some

---

[7] On the reshaping and uses of the memory of Isaiah in Chronicles, see S. Kostamo, "The Prophet Isaiah of Chronicles," a (still unpublished) paper delivered at the 2011 EABS meeting in Thessaloniki, Greece.

[8] It is to be kept in mind that social memory is not identical with the contents of a book, even if the book contributes to the shaping of social memory; the remembered Isaiah of the community was not solely the Isaiah of Kings, or of the book of Isaiah, or of Chronicles or Proverbs for that matter. The remembered Isaiah, that is, Isaiah as a site of social memory not only included all of these but integrated them into a single unit through dynamic processes that allowed for different emphases in the particular situations in which the memory of Isaiah was brought to the present of the remembering community. Compare contemporary cases in which memories of presidents such as Jefferson, Jackson, and Lincoln are brought to bear in the present-day American discourse.

Deuteronomic-Mosaic flavour[9] and Ezekiel's voice carried a Priestly/Holiness Code Mosaic flavour, the late Persian (or early Hellenistic) community remembered an Isaiah who explicitly reminded them of the Exodus and who was remembered as *the* prophet of the 'Second Exodus'.[10] He overwhelmingly carried a very distinctive voice, with its own particular diction and non-Mosaic flavour (whether Mosaic D or Mosaic P/H), even if at times it interacted with and evoked some Mosaic-sounding voices.[11] Such a distinctive voice draws particular attention to itself and to what the memory of Isaiah evoked, including, for instance, a memory of a prophet leading an Exodus whose language (and the language of YHWH when he speaks to him)[12] did not cast him as a second Moses.

In addition, although the prophetic characters populating the PBC tend to be anchored in particular historical periods and prophecies that not only are about the near but also the far future of Israel, their words are equivocally associated with explicit regnal periods of kings widely separated in time. But the Isaiah of the late Persian/early Hellenistic period was remembered in terms of both Hezekiah and Cyrus, of monarchic and postmonarchic kings, of the monarchic, about-to-be rebuilt, and rebuilt Jerusalem/temple. Again, although all prophets were unique, Isaiah was to a large extent an exceptional prophetic character and this exceptionality is a type of attention-grabber, even within a field of several, important, late monarchic characters.

Salient sites of memory tend to develop positive feedback: the more it becomes a 'magnet' for issues and images at the community's core (including matters of self-characterization, identity, ideology, attitudes towards 'the Other', and main narratives about the past) and conversely, the more such matters and images were associated with Isaiah, the more central the latter became. This holds

---

9 On Mosaic and other voices, see E. Ben Zvi, "On the Term Deuteronomistic in Relation to Joshua–Kings in the Persian Period," in *Raising Up a Faithful Exegete* (eds. K. L. Noll and B. Schramm; Winona Lake, IN; Eisenbrauns, 2010), 59–69; and "The Communicative Message of Some Linguistic Choices," in *A Palimpsest* (eds. E. Ben Zvi et al.; Piscataway, NJ: Gorgias, 2009), 269–90.

10 See the section, "Matters of Gaps and Emphasis in Social Memory of the Triad Catastrophe, Exile and Return as well as of a Second Exodus."

11 See, for instance, R. Levitt Kohn, *A New Heart and a New Soul* (JSOTSup 358; London/New York/ Sheffield: Sheffield Academic Press, 2002) and the bibliography there.

12 When addressing a prophetic figure in the prophetic books, the language of YHWH tends to show a diction that resembles that of the prophet associated with the book. This feature creates a sense of convergence between the reported speech of the prophet and that of YHWH within a book; both speeches were to be considered godly and complementary since together, both bring forward to the community YHWH's word, that is, a prophetic book.

true for figures such as Abraham, Moses, and David,[13] but also for Isaiah. However, unlike Moses, Abraham, or David for that matter, Isaiah could not be construed by the community as either the main ancestor of the nation or the first or central exemplar of a prophet, lawgiver, or king. Despite his strong association with the memory of a 'Second Exodus', he was not imagined as a kind of second Moses, even if theoretically, the community could have done so, as it did in the cases of Jeremiah and Ezekiel.[14] His voice[15] could have theoretically carried a Mosaic flavour (e. g. Jeremiah) or he could have been associated with a complementary set of godly legal/cultic instructions (cf. Ezekiel or David in Chronicles),[16] but nothing like this evolved for Isaiah, even though and despite the fact that in the sense discussed in the chapter about Moses 'the Prophet', Isaiah like any other prophet, remained to a large extent a Mosaic prophet.[17] A mnemonic, systemic preference for developing a memory of Isaiah that did not evoke that of a second Moses and by doing so underscored a sense of emphatic individuality around Isaiah, 'the prophet of the Second Exodus', seems to have been at work.

Both the large mindshare assigned to Isaiah, particularly in relation other prophets associated with the late monarchic period, and the exceptional features associated with remembering and the remembered Isaiah[18] lead to two related, basic questions: (a) why was Isaiah remembered so extensively and (b) why was he remembered the way he was? From a more precise and methodologically aware perspective of social memory, one may rephrase these questions to ask which features of the social mindscape of the community or what kind of 'generative grammar' within the discourse of the community was conducive to the

---

[13] See "The Memory of Abraham in Late Persian/Early Hellenistic Yehud/Judah", in this volume, pp. 162–98; "Exploring the Memory of Moses 'The Prophet' in Late Persian/Early Hellenistic Yehud/Judah" in this volume, pp. 199–231, and D. V. Edelman, "David in Israelite Social Memory" in *Remembering Biblical Figures* (eds. E. Ben Zvi and D. V. Edelman), 141–157.

[14] See C. R. Seitz, "The Prophet Moses and the Canonical Shape of Jeremiah," in *ZAW* 101 (1989): 3–27; M. Roncace, *Jeremiah, Zedekiah, and the Fall of Jerusalem* (LHBOTS 423; London: T&T Clark, 2005), 20 and the bibliography cited there; H. McKeating, "Ezekiel the 'Prophet Like Moses?'," in *JSOT* 101 (1994): 97–109.

[15] In the sense of diction. Diction plays an important role in the characterization of prophets in the PBC as individuals, giving each his own voice and individuality. Moreover, as mentioned above, even YHWH's voice tends to merge with that of the prophet in each of these books.

[16] See, for instance, Ezek 18, 40–48; 1 Chr 28:19; 2 Chr 23:18.

[17] See "Exploring the Memory of Moses".

[18] Note also that among the characters encoded in prophetic books, he was imagined as the most successful. On this matter, see the section, "Remembering Isaiah and Narrative Plots in Memory: Central Contrastive Pairs as Main Structural Mnemonic/Narrative Devices".

development and wide acceptance of such an unusual but prominent site of memory?

Although we can never know why it was the memory of Isaiah (and, not, for instance, that of Micah) that developed in the form it did, given the importance of positive feedback in the development of central sites of memory, it is reasonable to assume that once the process started, it fed itself.[19] But we can pinpoint some characteristic and exceptional features of Isaiah that may help us begin to understand why Isaiah was remembered so extensively in that period and why a prophet who was greatly remembered could evolve into something similar to the remembered Isaiah of the late Persian or early Hellenistic period.

Remembering Isaiah and Narrative Plot in Memory: Matters of Continuity, of a Widely Shared, Condensed Narrative, and its Temporal Structure

The shared communal memories of places and events that developed through the reading of the prophetic books involved events, spaces, and characters set both in the past and future of the reading community. Isaiah served as a site of memory that brought together King Hezekiah, King Cyrus, and the future Davidide. It brought together monarchic Jerusalem, destroyed Jerusalem, about-to-be-rebuilt Jerusalem, and a future Jerusalem; the monarchic temple, the Persian period temple, and the future temple. It brought together into one figure memories from late monarchic Judah at its zenith (the defeat of Sennacherib), little Yehud, and Yhwh's empire, with Jerusalem as its capital, in the future.

By doing so, Isaiah embodied, and to a large extent symbolized, a main trajectory of Israel's past and future history as construed in Yehud. Remembering Isaiah provided a sense of continuity with the past and future as well as a temporal map to organize knowledge within the social mindscape of the community.

---

[19] Research on processes of construction of memories in present-day societies has drawn attention to a general preference toward the development of a single main site of memory to evoke, construe, commemorate, and symbolize entire socio-historical processes and the role of positive feedback shaping this preference. For a good case study, see B. Schwartz, "Collective Forgetting and the Symbolic Power of Oneness: The Strange Apotheosis of Rosa Parks," in *Social Psychology Quarterly* 72 (2009): 123–42 and the relevant bibliography.

Social memories take the form of narratives or interrelated sets of narratives informing and balancing each other.[20] Narratives have beginnings and ends and their plots are rarely uniform in terms of temporal density. They emphasize certain periods and de-emphasize others, according to a certain grammar that reflects the general social mindscape of the remembering group. Although here and there the community's encounter with Isaiah through readings of texts encoding him (e.g. the book of Isaiah) could evoke images of Moses[21] or Abraham, and although an awareness that Israel existed well before the Assyrian period and that its history as construed by the community are all assumed in the book of Isaiah, it is clear that remembering Isaiah was tantamount to drawing a tight temporal focus: to structuring social memory around a main narrative whose beginning is in Assyrian times and whose end is in the utopian future.[22] Most significantly, these are the very end and beginning of the main narrative implied in and communicated by the PBC *as a whole*. Isaiah not only fits this narrative as a whole but also serves as a paradigmatic example.

Although many other prophets remembered by the community brought together memories of past and future events, Isaiah, the site of memory, was unique in its strong and explicit reference to figures that encompass the entire trajectory from the Assyrian period to the Babylonian period, the Persian period, and to the future empire. Once Isaiah began to develop in this way, once it embarked on that path and began to become a central node of core memories (and concepts), it became likely that a positive feedback loop increased mindshare for Isaiah and led to the growth and further development of memories about Isaiah.

---

[20] On the (cross-cultural) construction of social memories as narratives see, for instance, E. Zerubavel, *Social Mindscapes* (Cambridge, MA: Harvard University Press, 1997); E. Zerubavel, *Time Maps* (Chicago: University of Chicago Press, 2003).

[21] For example, general allusions to the Exodus story and explicitly in Isa 63:11–12; as for Abraham, see, Isa 51:2; cf. 41:8; 63:16.

[22] Which are exactly the temporal limits of the implied narrative about Israel communicated by the PBC. See "Prophetic Memories in the Deuteronomistic Historical and the Prophetic Collections of Books," in in this volume, pp. 109–33. The reference to the year in which Uzziah died in Isa 6:1 and references to the reign of Ahaz in Isa 7 and Isa 14:28 create a sense of 'pre-history,' i.e. a period that precedes and leads to the main 'history'. Clearly, Isaiah was remembered primarily as the main prophet of the Assyrian period, but he was imagined as coming into this period with a 'past', just as Israel came into that period with a past. Micah, another prominent prophet associated with the Assyrian crisis (see not only the book of Micah, but also Jer 26:18), was also imagined as having a past prior to the Assyrian crisis (see Mic 1:1). Comparatively minor references to a 'pre-history' do not disrupt the main narrow temporal mnemonic focus around 'history'; they just create a background out of which 'history' emerges.

Remembering Isaiah and Narrative Plots in Memory: Central Contrastive Pairs as Main Structural Mnemonic/Narrative Devices

Hero and villain, success and defeat, sin and righteousness; although real life tends not to be reducible to simple binaries, these binaries are very common devices to structure social memories.²³ A set of central binary contrasts played a major role not only in the construction of the memory of the late monarchic past but also in the shaping of its significance. One can easily discern a pattern of closely related sets of contrastive pairs set around two major events in ancient Israel's social memory of the period: (a) the Assyrian crisis of 701 BCE and (b) the Babylonian crisis that led to the catastrophe of 586 BCE. The narrative moves then from deliverance to catastrophe. It moves from, among others, (i) Sennacherib, a blaspheming foreign king who cannot be successful against a pious Jerusalem to (ii) YHWH's servant Nebuchadnezzar,²⁴ who cannot but be successful against sinful Jerusalem; from (i) Rabshakeh, Sennacherib's subordinate substitute, who fails to understand and thus ridicules what constitutes godly behaviour to (ii) Nebuzaradan, Nebuchadnezzar's subordinate substitute, who not only ac-

---

23 For examples of ancient constructions of social memory around binaries, albeit without using memory studies terms, see the now classical work, M. Liverani, "Kitru, kataru," in *Mesopotamia* 17 (1982): 43–66. Of course, this way of structuring memories is not restricted to ancient societies. For an example of a recent case study of 'Manichean' memories, see A. S. Seniavskii and E. S. Seniavskaia, "The Historical Memory of Twentieth-Century Wars as an Arena of Ideological, Political, and Psychological Confrontation," in *Russian Studies in History* 49 (2010): 53–91. Given the often-made remark that ancient historians resemble today's journalists far more than contemporary, professional historians (e.g. P. Veyne, *Did the Greeks Believe in Their Myths?* [Chicago: University of Chicago Press, 1988], 5), it is worth noting that a significant sector of today's media tends to shape memory along these lines. On issues concerning the narrative and mythical framework of some contemporary media, see, for instance, S. M. Barkin, "The Journalist as Story-teller. An Interdisciplinary Perspective," in *American Journalism* 1 (1984): 27–33; S. E. Bird and R. W. Dardenne, "Myth, Chronicle and Story: Exploring the Narrative Quality of News," in *Myths, and Narratives* (ed. J. W. Carey; London: Sage, 1988), 67–85; M. Coman, "New Stories and Myth–The Impossible Reunion?" in *Media Anthropology* (eds. E. W. Rothenbuhler and M. Coman; Thousand Oaks, CA/London/New Delhi: Sage, 2005), 111–20.

24 See Jer 25:9; 27:6. See also J. Hill, *Friend or Foe?* (BibInt 40; Leiden: Brill, 1999) esp. 106–10. On elevated characterizations of Nebuchadnezzar in the book of Jeremiah, see J. Hill, "'Your Exile Will Be Long': The Book of Jeremiah and the Unended Exile," in *Reading the Book of Jeremiah* (ed. M. Kessler; Winona Lake, IN: Eisenbrauns, 2004), 149–61 (152–6) and Hill, *Friend or Foe?*, 103–10, 130–9, 198–9, 203–5. See also the characterization of Nebuchadnezzar in Josephus, and even from a general perspective in Daniel. None of these characterizations could have ever applied to Sennacherib, ironically, since he did not destroy Jerusalem.

knowledges Yhwh's power and justice but also thinks and talks as a godly disciple of the prophet Jeremiah would have thought and talked.²⁵

Related to all these pairs and even more central to the narrative are the contrastive pairs Isaiah/Hezekiah and Jeremiah/Zedekiah. These closely intertwined sites of memory serve to shape and make memorable a plot that moves from the central prefiguration of and a counterpoint to the catastrophe itself, while at the same time conveying its 'meaning' to the community.

Historiographical texts, with their focus on kings, tend to emphasize the latter in their shaping of the story through the pairs Hezekiah/Isaiah and Zedekiah/Jeremiah. Within these stories Zedekiah is to be portrayed as an anti-Hezekiah (see Jeremiah's interactions with him and compare with those of Isaiah), or, because of the influence of ideological/discursive considerations, see its role (partially) taken by Manasseh, creating a paradigmatic narrative in which the antipode of Hezekiah is Hezekiah's own son, Manasseh (and see the counterpart development of the figure of Ahaz, Hezekiah's father, as an anti-Hezekiah).²⁶ But the underlying, structuring role of the contrastive pairs Hezekiah/Isaiah and Zedekiah/Jeremiah is at work not only in the memories evoked by the reading of the books of Isaiah and Jeremiah within the same community of *literati* but also in the historiographical books as well.

The centrality of the opposition between the Assyrian and Babylonian crises was certainly highly conducive to the development of Isaiah and Jeremiah as two main prophetic sites of memory and two main books, each embodying, evoking, and communicating the meaning of these crucial events. But the contrast between Isaiah and Jeremiah served another related function.

In postmonarchic Israel there was a widespread and very strong discursive and ideological preference for imagining monarchic period prophets as unsuccessful warning voices in their own times and society. Members of the latter had to be imagined as rejecting them and their words in order to fulfil their role as sinners who merited the catastrophe that befell them. Jeremiah is the

---

25 See esp. Jer 40:2–3. 'The author wants to persuade us that Nebuzaradan was a pupil of Jeremiah (40:2–3)' (K. A. D. Smelik, "The Function of Jeremiah 50 and 51 in the Book of Jeremiah," in *Reading the Book of Jeremiah* [ed. M. Kessler; Winona Lake, IN: Eisenbrauns, 2004], 87–98 [citation from 97]). Also see Jer 40:2 with Jer 32:23.

26 The main generative 'grammar' mentioned here was never the only 'generative grammar' at work in Kings, Chronicles, and the PBC. Different sets of ideological concerns (e.g. doctrines about divine distribution, the role of kings, the construction of the figure and memory of king Josiah and its larger significance, particularly in the DHC) also influenced the shaping of Persian period narratives about the late monarchic era and were in this case responsible for the shaping of Manasseh as the antipode of Hezekiah.

main exemplar of this type of the rejected, unsuccessful monarchic period prophet.[27]

To be sure, Jeremiah and his counterparts become successful sites of memory for the remembering community in Yehud because both the prophets of old and those who rejected them now participate in a didactic memory that communicates what the remembered late monarchic prophets could not accomplish in their own generation. Needless to say, matters of continuity and discontinuity between the *literati* in Yehud and monarchic Israel/Judah were thus negotiated.

At the same time, there were reasons to balance that negative image of the unsuccessful and persecuted prophet. Monarchic Israel could not be imagined as always and constantly sinful, rejecting and mocking godly prophets.[28] Just as Jeremiah is the paradigmatic, unsuccessful, rejected prophet,[29] Isaiah is, within the discourse of the community, the successful one.[30] Just as the rejection of Jeremiah was deeply associated with the catastrophe, Isaiah's success was associated with the great deliverance before Sennacherib. Remembering Jeremiah was (also) remembering the dangers involved in rejecting godly prophets and their messages; remembering Isaiah was (also) remembering that an Israel guided by godly prophets and following their messages can and actually did withstand even the greatest imaginable challenges.

---

27 See 2 Kgs 17:13; Jer 35:15; Zech 1:4–6; 7:12–14; Neh 9:30; 2 Chr 36:12, 15–16; see also Jer 7:25; 25:4; 26:9; 35:15; 44:4. Cf. J. O'Brien, "Nahum-Habakkuk-Zephaniah: Reading the 'Former Prophets' in the Persian Period," in *Interpretation* 61 (2007): 168–83. She maintains that 'Hosea-Zephaniah so closely conform to Zechariah's description of the "former prophets" that these books may have been written or edited as a prelude to Zechariah' (168).

28 For similar reasons, numerous instances of successful prophets were added to the historical narrative of Israel in Chronicles. See "Chronicles and its Reshaping of Memories of Monarchic Period Prophets: Some Observations," in this volume, pp. 404–27.

29 For more on Jeremiah in biblical social memory, see M. Leuchter, "Remembering Jeremiah in the Persian Period" in *Remembering Biblical Figures* (eds. E. Ben Zvi and D. V. Edelman), 384–414.

30 Note his most memorable role during the (highly remembered) Assyrian crisis. Isaiah and Micah (see Jer 26:18) are the only two prophetic characters set in the monarchic period in the PBC that are construed as successful. Of the two, Isaiah enjoyed much more mindshare in Yehud during the Persian period. Among others, see their respective shares in 2 Kings, in which one is heavily mentioned and the other not at all. To be sure, and raising a number of very interesting questions, the book of Isaiah also asked its readers to inform their construction of the successful Isaiah by Isa 6:9–10. A discussion of these issues is beyond the scope of this chapter.

Additional Considerations about the Narrative Structure of Memories of Israel Informed by Remembering Isaiah and The Assyrian Crisis

On the surface, one may wonder about the role played by remembering the period of the Assyrian crisis within a society in which the memory of the (Babylonian) catastrophe was omnipresent.[31] But remembering the Assyrian crisis provided a sense that things might have ended up differently; that people have an agency.

Most importantly, for readers informed by both the book of Isaiah and Kings, the Assyrian crisis shaped the narrative envelope of Yhwh's actions that brought salvation to Israel/Jerusalem in the time of Sennacherib and in the time of Cyrus. The presence of a discursive association linking Assyria and Persia (with Persia being a kind of successor of Assyria)[32] contributed as well to the emergence and mnemonic strength of this envelope created by the figures of Assyria and Persia. Remembering Isaiah was remembering the narrative shaped by the contrastive pairs: (a) most sinful Sennacherib and (b) pious Cyrus, but also between (a1) past salvation *against* foreign kings and (b1) present salvation *through* foreign kings (and eventually through Yhwh as the king of kings). At the same time, it facilitated the shaping of another narrative and ideological contrast that encapsulated a complementary core narrative beginning with Nebuchadnezzar, Yhwh's servant, as a destroyer and ending with Cyrus, Yhwh's servant, as rebuilder. This narrative could not cover the entire discourse within the community about who might be Yhwh's servant, and remembering Isaiah was remembering another servant of Yhwh, Jacob (see also the section, 'A Final Consideration: A Site of Memory as a Place in which Various Approaches Inform (and Balance) Each Other and Related Fuzziness'). Again, it is not surprising how a central

---

[31] See "Total Exile, Empty Land and the General Intellectual Discourse in Yehud," in this volume, pp. 599–611.

[32] See Ezra 6:22. See also A. Kuhrt, "The Cyrus Cylinder and Achaemenid Policy," in *JSOT* 25 (1983): 83–97; A. Panaino, "The Mesopotamian Heritage of Achaemenian Kingship," in *The Heirs of Assyria* (eds. S. Aro and R. M. Whiting; Melammu 1; Helsinki: The Neo-Assyrian Text Corpus Project 2000), 35–49; and note that according to Ctesias and Herodotus, the Assyrians were followed by the Medes and the latter by the Persians. See R. Bichler, "Some Observations on the Image of the Assyrian and Babylonian Kingdoms within the Greek Tradition," in *Commerce and Monetary Systems in the Ancient World* (eds. R. Rollinger and C. Ulf; Melammu 5; Stuttgart: Steiner, 2004), 499–518. The relative lack of memories about the Neo-Babylonian Empire in Greek sources is an interesting issue for ancient social memory studies but cannot be addressed here.

site of memory becomes a magnet for explorations of central narratives about Israel's past and future and core ideological motifs.

In addition, and given that exile within the discourse of the community was both partially overcome and still to be overcome after Cyrus,[33] as exile was conceived not only as being outside the land but also as a state of alienation from YHWH or as state of distress that can be fully resolved only by YHWH's deliverance,[34] one faces within the narrative embodied in Isaiah as a site of memory not only an envelope between deliverance at the time of the Assyrian crisis and of Cyrus, but between the former and the complete, stable, utopian deliverance. The implied historical memory plot associated with and evoked by Isaiah began with Assyria's threat and YHWH's deliverance at that time, which leads from the reign of Sennacherib to that of Cyrus but continues into that of YHWH and utopia.[35]

These envelopes were not only comforting and consistent with the general discourse of the Persian (and early Hellenistic) period; since they were embodied in and communicated by the site of memory Isaiah, they served to address and above all, to *balance* ideological needs concerning (a) the role and importance of Israel's agency (see Isaiah/Hezekiah in 701 BCE) and (b) YHWH's enduring relationship/love of Israel that led to a second Exodus. Like the first, this new exodus is not presented as substantially conditioned by or as a reward for Israel's godly behaviour. It is the latter that eventually was conceived as leading to a situation in which Israel would not (be able to) alienate itself from YHWH.

---

[33] Exile was conceived not only as beginning outside the land but also as a state of alienation from YHWH, as a state of distress that only could be resolved by YHWH's deliverance; see M. A. Halvorson-Taylor, *Enduring Exile* (VTSup 141; Leiden/Boston: Brill, 2011). Alienation from YHWH can only be fully and permanently resolved when YHWH brings Israel to any of the different utopias evoked by the prophetic books; see for instance, Isa 2:2–4; 11; 51:4–5; 56:1–7; 60 (and note vv. 19–22).

[34] So, for instance, Isa 43:1–2. See Halvorson-Taylor, *Enduring Exile*, 110–19 and *passim*. The general concept of exile as alienation from YHWH *includes* the notion that outside the land Israel is pre-empted from fully relating to YHWH through cultic ritual, to which multiple texts within the repertoire of the community draw much attention (e.g. Hos 9:3–4; Ps 137:4 and Deuteronomy as read in the community). Yet, overcoming exile is not restricted to a return to the land and the potential to renew worship; see, for instance, Isa 42:5–7, Hos 2, and similar texts.

[35] See, for instance, Isa 2:2–4; 11; 51:4–5; 56:1–7; 60 (and note vv. 19–22).

Matters of Gaps and Emphasis in Social Memory of the Triad Catastrophe, Exile, and Return as well as of a Second Exodus

The prophetic characters in the PBC are associated with three main periods: (a) the Assyrian crisis; (b) the period of the fall of monarchic Judah, including the time preceding and leading to it and the one that immediately follows it; and (c) the beginning of the 'restoration' period. Bringing the memory of Isaiah to the present of the community was tantamount to drawing attention to period (a) and, unlike other prophetic books, drawing attention also to period (c). However, aside from prophetic references to the (forthcoming) catastrophe for Judah that appear in all the prophetic books and some references to the future destruction of Babylon–which in the context of the book of Isaiah serve to open the path towards (c), Isaiah does not draw *particular* attention to period (b). A simple contrast with Jeremiah and Ezekiel demonstrates the point.

Remembering Isaiah in this way shaped, in the main, a mnemonic narrative whose focus moves directly from the world encountered in Isa 39 to that of Isa 40.[36] This is a narrative in which life under exile is bracketed to a large extent and as such, it is a narrative that tends to be preferred in the discourse of Yehud, in which actual references to life outside the land or the pre-'restoration', post-586 Babylonian period in Judah tend to be marginal.[37] Isaiah reflects well and reinforces the social mindscape of Yehud in terms of what is worthy of being remembered.[38]

The way in which the 'Return' in Cyrus's time is construed in Isaiah also contributed to the centrality of this character in the social mindscape of Yehud, as it brought attention to central issues in the discourse of the community.[39] For in-

---

[36] On the trajectory that moves straight from the world of Isa 39 to that of Isa 40, see the section, "A Final Consideration", below. The narrative path that it creates skips over Josiah–who in the PBC, unlike the DHC, represents a marginal character–but more importantly, gives other explanations for the catastrophe, besides, for instance, Manasseh (2 Kgs 23:26; Jer 15:4) and Zedekiah (see Jeremiah, *passim*, Chronicles). On Josiah in the PBC, see my "Josiah and the Prophetic Books: Some Observations," in *Good Kings and Bad Kings* (ed. L. L. Grabbe; LHBOTS 393; European Seminar in Historical Methodology 5; London: T&T Clark International, 2005), 47–64 and "Prophetic Memories".

[37] Cf. K. M. Stott, "A Comparative Study of the Exilic Gap in Ancient Israelite, Messenian and Zionist Collective Memory," in *Community Identity in Judean Historiography* (eds. G. N. Knoppers and K. A. Ristau; Winona Lake, IN: Eisenbrauns, 2009), 41–58.

[38] For the methodological background underlying these considerations, see E. Zerubavel, *Social Mindscapes* and *Time Maps*. His approach pervades much of the discussion in this chapter.

[39] R. Albertz maintains that the anonymous oracles associated with the Persian salvific king in Isa 40:1–52:12 refer not to Cyrus but to Darius ("Darius in Place of Cyrus: The First Edition of

stance, the temple vessels and their return are referred to in Isa 52:11–12.⁴⁰ Within the world of the text and the memory of those who experience the event–as it were–time and again through their reading of the text, YHWH walks with and guards (the representatives/priests of) 'YHWH's people' as they return with the symbol of YHWH. In other words, the text strongly legitimizes the vessels, which one may assume were claimed to be those in the Persian-period, Jerusalemite temple, as YHWH's and emblematic of YHWH's returning presence. Moreover, since YHWH guards the people who carry the vessels, the text associates their return with that of the deity.⁴¹ It constructs the return of the vessels and those who carry them not only in terms of a reversal of their joint exile but also in terms that evoke yet surpass the image of the 'return' associated with the Exodus (cf. Isa 52:12aα with Deut 16:3 and Exod 12:11; 31–34; Isa 52:12b and Exod 14:19 [and Exod 13:21–22]). One may note also that in Isa 52:11–12 YHWH, not Pharaoh, commands the people to leave. Significantly, unlike the first 'return' (i.e. the Exodus), in the book of Isaiah YHWH brings the symbols marking the divine presence not to the land in general but to Jerusalem, the place where the vessels (and by association, the people) belong. Remembering Isaiah of Jerusalem, the one who saved Jerusalem during the reign of Hezekiah (and Sennacherib), is also remembering a new kind of Exodus that although not foundational as the first is imagined in some regards as superior to that one, because it explicitly leads to and legitimizes the temple in Jerusalem.

Significantly, the text mentioned above–the remembered Isaiah–conveyed Jerusalem-centredness that fitted well with the ideological discourse of Yehud at a different but not unrelated level. In Isa 52:11 the intended readership was

---

Deutero-Isaiah (Isaiah 40.1–52.12)," in *JSOT* 27 [2003]: 371–83). Although I agree with Albertz and others that these texts were not written in Cyrus's day but much later (see esp. 372–3 and nn. 5 and 6), I still maintain that the readership of the book of Isaiah in the late Persian/early Hellenistic period would more likely have assumed the king to be Cyrus rather than Darius, especially given Isa 44:24–45:7 and the lack of any explicit reference to Darius in the book. Moreover, Cyrus may well have been imagined as the archetype of the godly Persian king at that time.

40 On Isa 52:11–12 see, among others, J. Goldingay, *Isaiah 40–55*, Volume II (ICC; London/New York: T&T Clark, 2006), 269–72; J. Goldingay, *The Message of Isaiah 40–55* (London/New York: T&T Clark, 2005), 458–60; J. Blenkinsopp, *Isaiah 40–55* (AB 19 A; New York: Doubleday, 2002), 343–4; and compare J. L. McKenzie, *Second Isaiah* (AB 20; Garden City, NY: Doubleday, 1968), 124; K. Baltzer, *Deutero-Isaiah* (trans. from 1999 German original; Hermeneia; Minneapolis: Fortress, 2001), 386–91 and the bibliography cited there.

41 The vessels fulfil a role comparable to that of the deity statue in other narratives about the return of the deity to the temple. Any reference to the statue of YHWH would have been impossible within the discourse of the period and particularly, in the book of Isaiah.

asked to imagine itself and the authorship of the book they were reading as living already in 'the land': 'depart, depart, go out from *there*' (compare Ps 137:1). The readers were Israel in the land (i.e. in Yehud),[42] and the great Isaiah of Jerusalem reminded them not only that their ancestors were not expelled from the land to Babylonia but that they returned in a kind of (ritual) 'procession' headed and protected by YHWH himself, which led to the building of the Jerusalemite temple of their own times.

Finally, one is to keep in mind Mesopotamia as the locale from which the second Exodus leaves. On the whole, that region is construed as a mental place that tends to rank higher than Egypt in Yehudite social memory. This spatial hierarchy contributes much to and is interwoven with constructions of Israel. Postmonarchic Mesopotamian Israel (i.e. the Babylonian *gola*) is consistently construed as ranking higher than postmonarchic Egyptian Israel (i.e. the Egyptian *gola*) within the central texts of the community.[43]

Additional Considerations

The issues and networks of concepts considered in the previous sections were certainly not the only ones that influenced the relative popularity of the memory

---

[42] For a recent study with a different goal and approach that, nevertheless, makes a strong point for Isa 40–55 as the product of the people in Yehud, see L.-S. Tiemeyer, *For the Comfort of Zion* (VTSup 139; Leiden/Boston, 2011).

[43] See, for example, the cumulative weight of the symbolic and mnemonic power of the *topos* of the servitude in Egypt, which has a significant counterpart; the lack of a counterpart for the explicit, divine prohibition in Deut 17:16; and the memory of a Mesopotamian origin and a prefiguration of the Exodus in Abraham (and contrast with the story of Abraham in Egypt). On the postmonarchic Egyptian Israel, see, for instance, Jer 40:7–41:18; 42:1–22; 43:1–13; 44:1–30; compare Jer 24. On the latter, see J. Kessler, "Images of Exile: Representations of 'Exile' and 'Empty Land' in Sixth to Fourth Century BCE Yehudite Literature," in *Concept of Exile* (eds. E. Ben Zvi and C. Levin; BZAW 404; Berlin/New York: De Gruyter, 2010), 308–51 (316–18; 323–6) and the bibliography there. On the general negative image of Egypt, which, to a significant extent, is the paradigmatic 'Other' in the Pentateuch, see F. V. Greifenhagen, *Egypt on the Pentateuch's Ideological Map* (JSOTSup 361; Sheffield: Sheffield Academic Press, 2002). To be sure, the socio-political situation of Yehud in the Persian period may have contributed to this tendency to prefer, on the whole, Mesopotamian over Egyptian space, but it would be too reductionist to think that this is the main or only factor at work. Likewise, it is obviously the case that historical and mnemonic reasons dictated that the 'first Exodus' be associated with leaving Egypt and the 'second Exodus' with leaving Babylonia, but this in no way removes the ideological significance of the contrast within the discourse of the community or the evocative networks that it activated within the social mindscape of the period.

of Isaiah. This study is illustrative and represents a call to continue to further this type of research. This said, a reference to three additional networks of meanings associated with the figure of Isaiah cannot be avoided.

First, Isaiah is certainly not the only prophet remembered as drawing attention to 'former things' known within the community (that is, to social memory), advancing the argument that since prophecies of punishment have been fulfilled in the view of the readership, salvific prophecies will come to pass as well. In so doing, he not only evoked many other texts within the sea of authoritative texts that the community held but also, and even more importantly, significantly resignified them. Yet, Isaiah explicitly and systematically stresses these issues that play central roles within the discourse of Yehud and is probably the paradigmatic prophet in this regard.[44]

Second, there can be no doubt that remembering Isaiah involved remembering and drawing attention to a self-understanding of Israel as a *wretched* servant.[45] It is a self-understanding that involves accommodation to sociopolitical realities through ideological resistance and a certainty about a future worldly implementation of utopia by YHWH's decision. It accepts that Israel looks stricken and lowly in the present but squares it with a self-perception of unique divine selection, kingly attributes,[46] and a central role to acculturate 'the Other' (in the

---

44 Cf. P. T. Willey, *Remember the Former Things* (SBL Dissertation Series 161; Atlanta, GA: Scholars Press, 1997). The *entire* book of Isaiah, regardless of its long redactional history, brought to the present of the community an image of Isaiah, the prophet from the past.
45 E.g. Isa 41:8–10; 42:1–7; 44:1–5, 21–22; 45:4; 48:20; 49:1–6. A study of the image of YHWH's suffering and yet glorious servant in Isaiah is well beyond the scope of this essay. A few issues mentioned here suffice, however, for present purposes. The list of works discussing the wretched servant is immense. Among many others, see Tiemeyer, *For the Comfort of Zion, passim* and bibliography mentioned there.
46 It has been proposed that some 'servant texts' may carry some Davidic motifs (e.g. Isa 52:13–15; Goldingay, *Message of Isaiah 40–55*, 488–91; some of these motifs were 'traditionally' interpreted as messianic in both Jewish and Christian communities for centuries). Many of the images used to portray the servant were royal, using general ancient near Eastern motifs like divine adoption–*passim*–to particular expressions such as 'light to the nations,' in itself a kind of secondary and subordinate association with the divine as 'source of light'. Royal images could be associated within the discourse of the time not only with Israel but also with 'David' in the discourse of the period. It is very significant, however, that whereas the identification of the servant with Israel is explicitly and repeatedly hammered down (Isa 41:8–9; 44:21; 45:4; 48:20; 49:3–4) not a single, explicit reference to a Davidide is advanced in these texts. They may well reflect a general tendency in the discourse of the period to associate proper royal and implied 'Davidic' motifs with 'Israel'; see, among many others, these texts in Isaiah; Hos 2:21–22; the idea of a covenant with Israel as a whole, not with the king, and texts 'democ-

future) into viewpoints held by the Yehudite *literati* (i.e. a dream of a cultural/ ideological empire in which Yhwh serves as the high king and the servant as his chosen officer; cf. Isa 2:1–4). Significantly, it is for the sake of this servant that Yhwh governs history and for the sake of this servant the Persian Empire came into being (Isa 45:1–5). This type of approach to resolving cognitive dissonance, developing the ideological resistance to imperial cultures necessary for social reproduction, is ubiquitous in the PBC and the social mindscape of Yehud yet finds in Isaiah a site of memory that evokes it in very memorable terms. At the same time, the fact that the memory of Isaiah is substantially associated with such a memorable image[47] contributes to making Isaiah such a memorable prophet.

Third, Isaiah was also remembered as a central and memorable voice for a monotheizing tendency that shaped much of the discourse of Yehud, and for a co-related tendency toward a complete rejection of 'idols'.[48] Since these tendencies resonated greatly with the central ideological discourse of the *literati* of the period, it is reasonable to assume that they also contributed to the popularity of memories of Isaiah and to his relative mindshare among the very same *literati*.

A Final Consideration: A Site of Memory as a Place in which Various Approaches Inform (and Balance) Each Other and Related Fuzziness

Up to this point the focus has been on Isaiah as a central mnemonic node, cipher, or site of memory embodying, evoking, and communicating, as it were, core narratives, central images, and crucial ideological positions that played an important role in shaping the social mindscape of the community, or at least its *literati* and those influenced by them. This section draws attention to

---

ratizing' the 'Davidic promise' in Chronicles. Any substantive discussion on this issue is clearly beyond the scope of this chapter, but see Edelman, "David in Israelite Social Memory".

47 Note the density of such references once the text moves into references to postmonarchic circumstances.

48 See Isa 43:10–11; 44:6, 9; 45:5–7, 14, 18, 21; 46:9; as for 'idols' see, for instance, Isa 40:18–20; 44:9–15. For a good discussion of monotheism in Isaiah (chs. 40–55), see M. S. Smith, *The Origins of Biblical Monotheism* (Oxford/New York: Oxford University Press, 2001), 179–94. For Smith's more recent treatment of 'biblical' monotheism, see his *God in Translation. Deities in Cross-Cultural Discourse in the Biblical World* (Grand Rapids, MI: Eerdmans, 2010; first published by Mohr Siebeck in 2008); see also the issues raised in S. M. Olyan, "Is Isaiah 40–55 Really Monotheistic?" in *JANER* 12 (2012): 190–201.

the vital and well-attested tendency in the community to balance different positions and set them in proportion by associating them all with a single site of memory that was also at work in the case of Isaiah.

To illustrate, remembering Isaiah was remembering a lionized Hezekiah. The substantial generative network of evocative *topoi* and mnemonic narratives associated with their positive interrelationship has been mentioned above. Yet, remembering Isaiah was also remembering that Hezekiah had played a very significant role in the process that led to the catastrophe; see Isa 39 and note that in the book of Isaiah it leads directly to Isa 40.[49]

Remembering Isaiah was recalling him as the paradigmatic successful prophet, but Isaiah also evoked the image of the wretched servant of YHWH and a voice reminding people of the redemptive nature of the servant's suffering and prophetic martyrdom.[50] The prophet who was remembered as the most successful in the monarchic period is, not coincidentally, also remembered as the one who was commanded, 'Go and say to this people: "Keep listening, but do not comprehend; keep looking, but do not understand. Make the mind of this people dull, and stop their ears, and shut their eyes, so that they may not look with their eyes, and listen with their ears, and comprehend with their minds, and turn and be healed"' (Isa 6:9–10; NRSV).

Remembering Isaiah was remembering a nearly utopian, second Exodus superior in some ways to the first, yet it was also remembering that the community in Yehud was far from fulfilling utopia (see, for instance, Isa 56–66),[51] and that

---

[49] The parallel text in 2 Kgs 20:12–19 is followed by the account of Manasseh in 2 Kgs 21. Although 2 Kgs 20:12–19 raises the issue of the culpability of Hezekiah, this becomes one of several voices on the matter in Kings and not the most important one. Chronicles, a work that lionizes Hezekiah much more than Kings and attempts to reshape the social memory of the narrated event (2 Chr 32:25–26), diminishes its significance. Yet, as mentioned above, in the book of Isaiah, Isa 39 directly precedes Isa 40. Hezekiah is a marker pointing at both exile and the eventual return as well.

[50] See and compare J. L. Crenshaw, *Prophetic Conflict* (BZAW 124; Berlin: De Gruyter, 1971), 66.

[51] 'The reader of 56–66 soon becomes aware that the dominant frame of mind of the people being addressed is one of disorientation and disillusionment (see especially 59:9–15a; and 63:7–64:11). Even if we make due allowance for homiletic hyperbole, the message is that engagement in traditional religious practices–fasting, sacrifice, Sabbath–remains at the level of mere formality (see esp. 58:1–14). There are few if any signs of moral regeneration. Religious leaders are self-indulgent and neglect their responsibilities (56:9–12). There is rampant injustice in the workplace and in the exercise of the judicial system. Murder is being committed, and there is no thought for the poor (58:3–4, 6–10; 59:1–15a). Worst of all, from the point of view of the prophetic author or preacher, the syncretized state religion of the last decades of the Judahite kingdom, including mortuary rites and cults with a strong sexual orientation, is still being practiced,

he, Isaiah, was *no* Moses. Remembering Isaiah was remembering the salvation associated with the Assyrian crisis but remembering that he also prophesied the catastrophe of 586 BCE. Remembering Isaiah was remembering that Israel (and within this discourse, the world/creation as a whole) needs a more-than-human Davidide (e.g. Isa 11), can work well with a pious but human Davidide (e.g. Hezekiah), but does not need a king at all, since YHWH is its king (see Isa 33:17–24).[52]

Examples like these can be multiplied. It is possible that these multiple, contrastive positions emerged as a result of a long redactional process, but whatever their history, from the perspective of a community in the late Persian or early Hellenistic period that construes its Isaiah in their own present mainly on the basis of their readings of the book of Isaiah (and 2 Kings and to a lesser extent Chronicles), multiple voices become embodied in one person; they become integrated. Of course, Isaiah was not an exceptional case in this regard (see the chapter on Moses in this volume and note that the figure of Moses embodied and integrated D, H and P voices). Within the discourse of the community there was a very significant preference in this regard and this preference teaches us much about the social mindscape of the community in late Yehud (e.g. the tendency towards some degree of fuzziness).[53]

A Kind of Epilogue

Random or accidental developments that can only be approached from the perspective of chaos theory might explain why some prophetic figures began to become more central than others (e.g. Isaiah vs Micah),[54] but the present basic observations show that approaches focusing on social memory may help us

---

and the practitioners still include the temple priesthood (57:3–13; 65:1–12; 66:17).' (J. Blenkinsopp, *Isaiah 56–66* [AB 19B; New York: Doubleday, 2003], 77).

52 Note that this unit is the conclusion of the first section of the book of Isaiah in 1QIsaᵃ. On YHWH as king in Isa 44–55 see T. N. D. Mettinger, "In Search of the Hidden Structure: YHWH as King in Isaiah 40–55," in *Writing and Reading the Scroll of Isaiah* (eds. C. C. Broyles and C. A. Evans; VTSup 70; Leiden/New York: Brill, 1997), 143–54. For a different, redactionally oriented reading of Isa 33, see C. Balogh, "'He Filled Zion with Justice and Righteousness.' The Composition of Isaiah 33," in *Bib* 89 (2008): 477–504 and bibliography.

53 See "Exploring the Memory of Moses," especially the section "Remembering Moses the Prophet and Constructing Integrative Fuzziness".

54 It is even *possible*, though just a matter of speculation, that the 'outsized' development of Isaiah as a site of memory partially pre-empted or removed social and discursive incentives for a similar development of the figure of Micah.

recognize features that explain some of the ways in which the memory of a central prophet such as Isaiah was shaped and why such a shape brought to Isaiah a strong mindshare in the community. It was this type of feature that facilitated the development of a positive feedback process, which repeatedly enhanced and further developed the memory of Isaiah. Through this process, the remembered Isaiah became a magnet that attracted voices, mnemonic narratives, and images that were salient in the social mindscape of the community and as he did so, he became an even stronger magnet. Moreover, as a site of memory Isaiah evoked, integrated, and balanced all these voices, images, narratives while at the same time maintaining a sense of individuality; that is, a sense of an Isaianic voice[55] that marked him as a singular, prominent, and exceptional site of memory within a larger landscape of memory.[56]

---

[55] Not incidentally, and as mentioned above, there is a clear 'Isaianic' flavour in the language of the book as a whole that sets it apart from books such as Jeremiah, Ezekiel, Hosea, and Deuteronomy. In each of these cases, the 'individuality' of the book's language serves to communicate the 'individuality' of the prophet whose memory is encoded in the book and decoded and evoked through its reading.

[56] My thanks to Sonya Kostamo for reading and commenting on a draft of this chapter.

Remembering Hosea: The Prophet Hosea as a Site of Memory in Persian Period Yehud*

1 Introducing the Topic

Francis and I have worked together for a bit more than twenty-five years at the University of Alberta. We developed our own research and teaching paths in conversation and collaboration with each other and we learned much from one other. Of course, we asked different questions and thus proposed or toyed with different answers Although our approaches and emphases changed a bit over time, they always remained substantially different. The outcome was, of course, a more exciting intellectual adventure for us and our students. I used to ask may students to compare our respective commentaries on Hosea[1] so as in experience how the questions we ask and the approaches we take shape what we see and what we argue for, and how much one can learn from a scholar with a different approach.

Since Francis and I devoted so much attention, thought, and time to "Hosea," I decided that it is most appropriate to write about this topic in a Festschrift honoring him. As Francis would anticipate and certainly expect from me, I am writing within the realm of my own approaches and, not surprisingly, about Hosea as a site of memory in Persian Yehud and about a grammar of preferences and dis-preferences that contributed to the shaping of the Hosea of memory (and imagination) of the literati of Persian Yehud.[2] This topic is even more appropriate

---

* First published in *Poets, Prophets, and Texts in Play. Studies in Biblical Poetry and Prophecy in Honour of Francis Landy* (eds. E. Ben Zvi, C. V. Camp, D. M. Gunn and A. W. Hughes; LHBOTS, 597; London: Bloomsbury T&T Clark, 2015), 37–57.
1 See especially F. Landy, *Hosea* (2nd ed. Sheffield: Sheffield Phoenix, 2011; 1st ed.; Sheffield: Sheffield Academic, 1995); E. Ben Zvi, *Hosea* (FOTL 21 A/1; Grand Rapids, Mich.; Eerdmans, 2005). (See also "Reading the Book of Hosea," pp. 294–303 in this volume.)
2 I have been working on matters of social memory in ancient Israel for a number of years. Among the most recent publications are: "Reshaping the Memory of Zedekiah and his Period in Chronicles," in this volume, pp. 342–66; "Chronicles and Samuel–Kings: Two Interacting Aspects of One Memory System in the Late Persian/Early Hellenistic Period," in this volume, pp. 317–31; "The Memory of Abraham in Late Persian/Early Hellenistic Yehud/Judah," in this volume, pp. 162–98; "Exploring the Memory of Moses 'The Prophet' in Late Persian/Early Hellenistic Yehud/Judah," in this volume, pp. 199–231; "Isaiah, a Memorable Prophet: Why Was Isaiah so Memorable in the Late Persian/Early Hellenistic Periods?," in this volume, pp. 253–73; "Chronicles and Its Reshaping of Memories of Monarchic Period Prophets: Some Observations," in this volume, pp. 404–27; "Remembering the Prophets Through the Reading and

https://doi.org/10.1515/9783110547146-011

for this volume because Francis contributed hit own methodological take on matters of memory and enriched our conversation on these issues.[3]

The focus of this essay is thus on the Hosea of memory that existed in Persian Yehud, among the literati. It is meant to explore *some* of the significant images and meanings[4] embodied and "broadcasted" as it were by this site of memory, general social and mnemonic tendencies that influenced the way in which Hosea was actually construed and remembered within the community, and why a character such as Hosea was worth remembering for the literati in Yehud.

The starting point of this exploration is that the prophetic books were read in Yehud, in part, to evoke the memory of prophetic characters of old.[5] As the literati read and reread the book of Hosea they could not but imagine and vicariously encounter their "own" Hosea, a Hosea construed and remembered within the context of their own worldview, world of knowledge, and social mindscape. This is the Hosea whose memory was, from their perspective, encoded in the book, as they understood it. This Hosea–evoked time and again, remembered time and again–served as a significant site of memory, and populated their mnemonic "landscape" along with other prophetic and non-prophetic characters/sites of memory (e.g., Jacob, Moses), and along with sites of memory that are not embodied in personages of the past (e.g., cities, buildings, crucial events such as the Exodus or Sinai).

In any event, the remembered prophet of old did not exist in solitude, For one, this construed figure was recalled in association with a particular period, as construed and remembered by the community, and thus with other figures/sites of memory. In addition, the ways in which the prophet was remembered were strongly influenced by the social mindscape of the remembering community, including its grammar of preferences and dis-preferences for particular types of memories. This grammar was at work in the shaping of multiple prophets of

---

Rereading of a Collection of Prophetic Books in Yehud: Methodological Considerations and Explorations," in this volume, pp. 80–108

3 See especially F. Landy, "Notes Towards a Poetics of Memory in Ancient Israel," in Ben Zvi and Levin, eds., *Remembering and Forgetting*, 331–45.

4 A discussion of the plethora of meanings that (likely) emerged from reading and rereading the book of Hosea within the mentioned historical context is well beyond the scope of this essay. For extended discussions, see, for instance, J. M. Trotter, *Reading Hosea in Achaemenid Yehud* (JSOTSup 328; Sheffield: Sheffield Academic, 2001) and J. M. Bos, *Reconsidering the Date and Provenance of the Book of Hosea: The Case for Persian Period Yehud* (LHBOTS 580; London: Bloomsbury T&T Clark, 2013). See also my own commentary, Ben Zvi, *Hosea*.

5 I assume that Francis would agree with me in that regard, just as I assume also that the books were also read, at least by some, for the joy of reading. Francis would probably tend to emphasize the latter aspect.

memory and other central characters, construals that worked together to embody and communicate matters and metanarratives that are at the core of the discourse of the remembering community.

When, as it was often the case in the late Persian and early Hellenistic period in Yehud/Judah, some core concepts and even metanarratives are actively and substantially negotiated, such socially constructed sites of memory (or a combination of related sites of memory) often provide a socially appropriate, "safe" playground for exploring and integrating multiple voices. The fact that all these voices become embodied in one single personage of the past/site of memory reinforces their integrated and, even more importantly, integrative message, making them better able to reflect the general discourse of the community and its social mindscape.[6]

Although much more can be said about these matters, this brief and necessarily limited introduction suffices for the present purposes, as I wish to allocate the rest of the space assigned to this essay to an explicit exploration of how and why Hosea was remembered as he was in Yehud, at least among the literati.

2 Remembering Hosea and Some Basic Mnemonic Patterns in the Prophetic Book Collection

Hosea was remembered as one of a group of selected prophetic figures associated with prophetic books within the authoritative repertoire of the community. Like all these figures, he was a male. This observation is particularly relevant given that female prophets existed in ancient Israel's memory (e.g., Judg 4:4; 2 Kgs 22:14; 2 Chr 34:22; Neh 6:14), but still no book in the prophetic book collection (hereafter, PBC) was devoted to evoking the memory of a female prophet. Although this matter requires a separate study that cannot be carried out here, it is not unreasonable to think that the tendency of the most likely male literati of Persian Yehud to identify with the prophets of old and to voice their voices as they read these books contributed to this strong mnemonic preference.[7]

---

[6] One may say that each site of memory serves as a node in an integrated social memory-scape whose meaning and significance emerged in relation and interaction with other sites of memory. The shifting array of multiple, connective, and connected sites of memory shapes the comprehensive social memory of the group.

[7] To be sure, there were many contributing factors. One may mention, *inter alia*, the tendency to remember YHWH as male, the male-oriented metaphors and perspectives that abound in these books and the world of memory they evoke, the facts that these were books written (at the very least in the main) by males and to be read and reread by males (even if at times portions of them

Like all the prophets evoked by the PBC, Hosea lived during one of the few, selected periods of the communally construed past to which the PBC drew particular attention and helped give shape. As I discuss elsewhere, the PBC as a whole creates a narrative about the past in which three periods are strongly emphasized.[8] The first is the period of the Assyrian crisis, including as its main mnemonic highlights the destruction of the northern Israelite polity and the divine deliverance of Jerusalem before Sennacherib; the second is the period directly leading to, during, and following the destruction of Jerusalem; and the third is that of the beginning of the restoration of Jerusalem. The deliverance of Judah from the hands of the Assyrians at the time of Hezekiah serves clearly as a contrastive topos to the final destruction at the hands of the Babylonians. Since the social memory grammar that generated this preference belonged to the community, not to a literary genre, it is not surprising that its influence was by no means restricted to the PBC, as even a cursory reading of Kings clearly shows.[9]

Not only a time range, but also a spatial range was at work in the construction of these prophets of old. Like all the other main prophetic figures evoked in the PBC, Hosea was not remembered as a person who was born in Exile or grew up there. Rather, the Northern character of Hosea reflected and reinforced a construction of the territory of Northern Israel as included in "the land." Samaria is not "Exile" (see further below).

Like all the other main fifteen prophetic figures "memorialized" in the PBC, Hosea's memory was evoked mainly through the reading of the relevant book in the PBC, and like the majority of them, *solely* by reading that book.[10] Like them, too, with the exception of Isaiah and Jonah, he was remembered as a prophet whose utterances did not turn his (imagined/remembered) contemporaries to Yhwh, leading them to repent from sin and avoid punishment. Finally, like the others, he is remembered not only as a prophet who voiced Yhwh's announcements of doom–which are construed within the basic mnemonic narrative as fully justified–but also as one voicing Yhwh's announcements of a yet to come, but certain, utopian future or futures, precisely at that time of imminent and well-deserved punishment for severe sin.

---

were read to males and females), in a process that socializes into an androcentric perspective, as is the case for the vast majority of world literature until very recent decades and only in particular regions of the world.
8 E.g., "Remembering the Prophets" in this volume, pp. 80–108.
9 See "Prophetic Memories in the Deuteronomistic Historical and the Prophetic Collections of Books," in this volume, pp. 109–33.
10 The exceptions are Isaiah and Jeremiah.

Prophetic characters (and the Yhwh that was remembered as interacting with them) were imagined as carrying a characteristic voice (cf. for instance, Isaiah, Jeremiah, and Ezekiel). Hosea's voice and Yhwh's voice in the book associated with Hosea carried a particular linguistic flavor, with "a high density of 'odd' Hebrew features within a book whose language on the whole is similar to that of other prophetic books."[11] This combination is not itself "odd" because any prophet's characteristic voice could be construed as including a particular range of dictions. For instance, Jeremiah was remembered as using deuteronomistic and non-deuteronomistic dictions.[12] The characteristic voice of Hosea uses both common and "odd" Hebrew features.

The utterances of these prophets, or Yhwh's utterance voiced by them as reported in some place in the book, were reminiscent of other utterances of them reported elsewhere in the book, even if within putatively different circumstances. Moreover, these utterances recalled other texts, outside the relevant prophetic book, that existed within the authoritative repertoire of the reading community by, at least, the late Persian period. The outcome was that memories of their sayings became intertwined with, and served as mutual signposts to, other community-shaping memories. Memories of Hosea's sayings fulfill well this pattern.[13]

As with the other prophetic characters evoked by the PBC, and one may say any major site of memory in ancient Israel or elsewhere, Hosea served as a magnet for issues and images at the community's core, including matters of self-characterization and identity, as well as constructions of a shared past, future utopias, space, Exile, and otherness. Conversely, the more such matters and images were associated with Hosea, the more the Hosea of memory became worth remembering. Most significantly, positions on and images related to these issues were not selected according to a criterion of logical consistency with each other. To the contrary, the tendency was to evoke images and approaches that often stood in tension, within the basic limits set by the shared discourse of the community (see further below).

The examples mentioned above are by no means exhaustive, but representative enough to show beyond a doubt the existence of a strong grammar of socially shared preferences and dis-preferences that shaped the ways in which the prophets of old evoked by the books included in the PBC were remembered. This

---

11 Ben Zvi, *Hosea*, 17.
12 See "Readers, Social Memory, Deuteronomistic Language and Jeremiah: The Roles of Deuteronomistic Language in Shaping Memories of Jeremiah among Late Persian/early Hellenistic Readers of the Book of Jeremiah," in this volume, pp. 304–16.
13 Ben Zvi, *Hosea*, passim.

tendency towards "sameness" was strongly balanced, as one may anticipate from memory studies, by the need to make the character "unique," and thus memorable as an individual. In fact, one of the most consistent traits of the prophets evoked by reading and rereading these books was their individuality.

The very presence of fifteen memorable prophetic characters by itself speaks volumes about the literati who constituted the (direct) remembering community in late Persian Yehud. This is the case because of a general, transcultural tendency towards limiting the number of main sites of memory associated with a particular event, period, or group, either to one or, alternatively, a few sites that to a large extent complement each other in terms of their message.[14] When this is not the case, just as among the literati in Yehud, one would expect some mnemonic reward for the community to compensate for the increased cognitive and social effort of multiplying main sites of memory. Why did the community have to remember fifteen main prophetic figures, unless each of them contributed something somehow unique to their memory-scape?

These considerations raise the question of what made Hotel particularly worthy of being remembered within this historical and social setting. What effect did it have on the community to remember Hosea as one among the other prophetic characters, and what would have been lost, if he were to be forgotten? In which particular way did the necessary tendencies towards "uniqueness" and "sameness" become interwoven so as to shape a memory of a prophet of the past that was worthy of being remembered? Each of the following sections will provide paths and potential case studies to explore these questions.

3 Remembering Hosea and Shaping a Pro-History to the Main Yehudite Narrative About Judah's Destruction

Communities tend to create time maps to organize their past sometimes as here by means of books and collections of books that directly or indirectly reflect and shape narratives about the past and draw attention to some periods and away from others. They often create a "central history/story" with a start and end point.[15] At the same time they may include some pre-history and at times an epilogue to then main historical narrative. Both the prologue and the epilogue serve

---

14 See "Remembering the Prophets," in this volume, pp. 80–108 and the bibliography there.
15 Cf. E. Zerubavel, *Time Maps: Collective Memory and the Social Shape of the Past* (Chicago: University of Chicago Press, 2003); *Social Mindscapes: An Invitation to Cognitive Sociology* (Cambridge, Mass.: Harvard University Press, 1997).

to shed light into their main memorable "history," becoming "usable" memory for under-standing that which is most worth remembering.

Remembering Hosea was remembering that the North fell to the Assyrians (see Hos 11:5; cf. 9:3; 10:5–6), that there was no Hezekiah for them (cf. Hos 1:7), and that Northern Israel's fall was both an unheeded warning to Judah and a direct pre-figuration of fallen Judah (see below). Remembering Hosea meant attaching a prologue to the main narrative of late monarchic Judah constructed and communicated by the PBC. Remembering Hosea and, above all, the instance of YHWH's word that he embodied, both shed light on the main narrative (e. g., the characterization of Judah is influenced by their presumed knowledge of the sin of Samaria and its consequences) and created a sense of continuity. Images of sinful Northern Israel are interwoven with those of sinful Judah; the destruction of one is now intertwined with the other. Most significantly, the Judah of the main mnemonic metanarrative of the literati is construed as deeply inter-related with Northern Israel; both are imagined as particular manifestations of the (ideological and mnemonic) Israel that the literati in Yehud imagined, conceptualized, and with which they identified themselves.

Remembering Hosea, the northern prophet, was an exercise in remembering the fluidity of the term Israel, as well as that of Judah itself.[16] One may easily notice, for instance, the link between עם ישבי הארץ כי ריב ליהוה (Hos 4:1), "for YHWH has a quarrel/indictment against the inhabitants of the land," and וריב ליהוה יהודה, "for YHWH has a quarrel/indictment against Judah," in Hos 12:3. In the latter, however, monarchic Judah comes to embody "the inhabitants of the land." Likewise, the Yehudite readers of Hos 12:3–5 could not but associate Judah with Jacob and its traditions–that is, with Israel–or notice that Jacob and Judah are two who are one in Hos 10:11.

At the same time, remembering Hosea served as a reminder to the literati of their belief that Northern Israel and Judah were not exactly equal in YHWH's sight. Remembering Hosea served to construct the fall of the North as a prefiguration to that of Judah/Jerusalem and as a warning that should have been heeded by Judah/Jerusalem, but was not. The Hosea of old reminds the literati not only of their common mnemonic construction of monarchic Judah as a community of blind, obstinate sinners, but also of a deity who makes an example of Samaria/Israel, in part, so Judah may learn and avoid a similar fate.

One may claim, correctly, that this is all at work in the books of Kings, and in some way, in other prophetic books (cf. Ezek 23, among others). This observation only proves the point that many underlying core concepts, images, and ideas

---

[16] Cf. Chronicles, in which this fluidity is explicitly attested multiple times (e. g., 2 Chr 28:18).

that some memorable characters came to embody, integrate, and communicate were not and *could not* be unique to them, because they were grounded in the general mindscape of the community and its memory-scape. Nonetheless, reading Hosea and remembering Hosea drew far more focused attention to Samaria and Northern Israel than reading any other book or recalling any other prophetic character whose memory is encoded in the PBC. This focused, singular attention to Samaria and Northern Israel makes the Hosea of memory excellent ground for shaping, reflecting, and communicating central ideological constructions about the North among the Jerusalem-centered literati of Yehud.

4 Remembering Hosea and Constructing and Othering the Literati's Past and Present Northern Israel

Although other prophets within the PBC refer to Northern Israel, Hosea is the prophetic figure *par excellence* among the fifteen that brings to the present of the community the memory of late monarchic, Northern Israel, In fact, he is the only prophetic figure among them who was most likely imagined as a northern prophet, with the possible exception of Jonah, whose book is metaprophetic and which in any case does not address the North.

The community reading about and thus imagining and encountering Hosea and his world easily noticed that the two main speaking characters–both divine and human–expressed themselves in a manner somewhat different from that in other prophetic books. The fact that YHWH and the prophet shared a diction is nothing strange; it is quite common in prophetic literature and contributes to a sense of convergence within the realm of godliness. But the high density of "odd" Hebrew features within a book whose language on the whole is similar to that of other prophetic books–and the ways in which the speakers of Hosea differ in this regard even from those in the book of Amos, in which the speakers are constructed as addressing a northern Israelite readership– certainly impacted the readers' characterization of Hosea. It is reasonable to assume that these literati were supposed to decode these odd linguistic forms as pointing to some form of non-Judahite, and given the context, presumably Israelian diction, as they construed it to be.[17]

---

[17] See Ben Zvi, *Hosea*, 16–17. On the more general issue of the communicative roles of linguistic choices see my "The Communicative Message of Some Linguistic Choices," in *A Palimpsest: Rhetoric, Ideology, Stylistics and Language Relating to Persian Israel* (eds. E. Ben Zvi, D. V. Edelman, and F. Polak; Piscataway, N.J.: Gorgias, 2009), 269–90. It is worth stressing that the textually inscribed characterization of Hosea as a northern prophet in the book of Hosea is so

The stressed inclusion of a prophet from Northern Israel in the collection is *not* a minor issue. No non-Israelite prophet was constructed as worth including among the main prophetic figures populating the PBC, nor was any prophetic figure born and/or brought up in Exile. To remember that Hosea was part of the group was to remember not only that the "Northerners" are Israel, but also that "the land" (i.e., YHWH's land) includes the North. Moreover, remembering Hosea was to draw attention to the fact that the past of the North and of the Northerners was worth remembering and of significance to Yehud.

To be sure, this point may seem quite obvious given the memories evoked by the Deuteronomistic Historical Collections (hereafter, DHC) and the Pentateuch; however, within the PBC, northern Israel's past would only have been marginally evoked without Hosea. Remembering Hosea within this collection of characters balanced the social memory it evoked and brought it more in line with the memory-scape reflected in the DHC; it thus contributed indirectly to making Hosea particularly worth remembering within the PBC.

Of course, social remembering does not exist for its own sake. The literati's Israel was construed as a Jerusalem-centered and temple-centered Israel and it is in this context that the memory of the *exemplar* of the northern prophet carries additional significance in terms of its potential to reflect and communicate the discursive world of the remembering community and to reassure itself of its consistency with YHWH's viewpoint.

To fulfill these needs, the Hosea of old *had* to be construed and recalled as a prophet who shared the basic tenets of the ideological Jerusalem temple-centered literati. These tenets are accordingly projected into Hosea's putative historical past through the Hosea of memory of the Yehudite literati. In other words, remembering Hosea meant for them, *inter alia,* creating a past for Northern Israel that matches well with the Yehudite ideological world.

Thus, the mnemonic community remembered that there was a great prophet in the North who identified with and who brought to the present of his community (and, indirectly, to that of the literati overhearing and vicariously experiencing that world from their own location in Yehud) a utopian image of a future in which Northern Israel joins Judah and both are ruled by a *Davidide* (Hos 3:4–5), that is, by the dynasty explicitly and uniquely associated with Jerusalem and its temple. This mnemonic vignette is consistent with, reflects, and reinforces the Yehudite construction of a past Northern kingdom in which good Northerners

---

strong that most scholars have considered Hosea a northern prophet, even if a significant number of them posited a later Judahite edition of the book. See, for instance, G. I. Emmerson, *Hosea: An Israelite Prophet in Judean Perspective* (JSOTSup 28; Sheffield: JSOT, 1984); A. A. Macintosh, *Hosea* (ICC; Edinburgh: T&T Clark, 1997).

were well aware already then that the Davidides were the only legitimate, Yhwhistic dynasty (cf. Hos 8:4; 10:7; 13:11; cf. 2 Chr 11:13–17; 13:4–12, passim).[18]

Within the memory-scape of the literati community, David was associated with the Jerusalemite temple. The cypher the "house of Yhwh" conjured the image of that temple, and then Hosea made references to it. Hos 8:1 envisions a scene of danger to the house of Yhwh, using multiple images to intertwine past and future, North and South, and temporal and a-temporal (see Hos 8). In Hos 9:4 a cessation of offerings at the temple in Jerusalem is evoked.[19]

All in all, remembering Hosea brought much attention to the construction of Northern Israel and Judah as the two who are one and the one who is two. Ephraim/Northern Israel was not equaled not could have been fully equated with Judah or vice versa (see, for instance, Hos 1:7; 10:9; 12:1) and even the diction of the remembered Hosea suggests constructions of difference with the South. But those who remembered Hosea in ideologically Jerusalem-centered Yehud construed and vicariously experienced both a past and a future in which North and South were intertwined: both were Israel, the object of Yhwh's original love, the perpetrator of sin, and the future recipient of elevated status. In the utopian Israel of the Yehudite literati's dreams, the people, Israel, would receive Yhwh's blessing in the whole land, including both the territories of Samaria and Yehud (see Hos 2:16–25).

Reading the book and remembering Hosea in Yehud. moreover, brought to the present of that Jerusalem-centered literati a godly prophet from monarchic Northern Israel who proclaimed these "truths" long ago to the ancestors of the Samarians of their own day. This was a prophet whose words and position represented Yhwh's and whose prophecies of punishment were already fulfilled. This Hosea was the literati's prophet of old Samaria, but simultaneously also a prophet whose message was impossible to imagine as acceptable for their contemporary Samarians. Thus their remembering of Hosea reinforced and mnemonically enlivened the Yehudite motif of Israel's rejection of Yhwh's worthy prophets in the past and brought it up to date in relation to the Samarians.

---

18 Within the discourse of the community, though, just accepting a Davidide as king does not make Israel (North or South) pious. Northern Israel's rejection of David was construed as a rejection of proper cult and of Yhwh, and contributed to shaping a memory of northern kings and their elites and subjects as bound to idolatry, apostasy, improper cultic places and the like (e.g., Hos 8:4–6; cf., among others, 2 Kgs 17:7–18). Significantly, the literati could not but recall that such sins also occurred in monarchic Judah, despite the fact that a Davidic king ruled over them. Reading and rereading the PBC reminded that there is more than one way to that outcome, and rejecting the prophets appears in all them.
19 On these matters, see Ben Zvi, *Hosea*.

Remembering this Hosea allowed the community not only to construct the Samarians as Other, but to *appropriate* the North and shape its memory so as to legitimize their own ideological world and, conversely, delegitimize crucial aspects of the worldview and traditions of the Samarians. Significantly, Hosea and the Yhwh experienced by Hosea were imagined by the literati in Yehud as aware of a past of Israel by means of rhetoric that evoked and claimed control over Hexateuchal traditions (e. g., Hos 2:16–17; 11:1; 12:4–5,10,13–14). Thus the latter were also, albeit implicitly, Yehudized, and retrojected as such, to the putative time of Hosea in monarchic Israel.[20]

Hosea, like all the prophets in the PBC, was remembered as a prophet of hope, and particularly of a hope that Northern Israel would become an integral part of a future Israel that represented the ideals held by Yehudite literati. It is this Israel who is Yhwh's future bride, and she embodied both Northerners and Southerners. But this hope is a dream of appropriation, of a divinely caused socialization of the "Other" to the ideal terms of the insider's community. Within the logic of that world, anyone of Israel who did not share this worldview (e. g., Persian period Samarians) were rejecting Yhwh and could not be imagined as embodied in Yhwh's future, elevated bride (see below). Such matters are well attested in numerous texts within the repertoire of the Yehudite community. The entire DHC may be seen as an example of appropriation and otherization of Northern Israel and contemporary Samarians. But again, Hosea draws attention to these matters far more than the other prophetic characters in the PBC.

It is to be stressed that none of the observations advanced above require or even strongly suggest the existence of any actual intense animosity between Yehudites and Samarians at the time. A strong investment in ideological boundaries and on claims about Jerusalem/Judah's centrality in Yhwh's economy may well suggest the opposite, namely, the existence of strong social interactions between Samarians and Yehudites, even as they point at ideological competition. It is particularly significant in this regard that the Pentateuch emerged as a shared core literary collection for both Samarians and Yehudites, and that unshared and unsharable readings of it actually facilitated the shared adoption of the Pentateuch.[21]

---

[20] A similar process of appropriation of Northern prophets is at work in the case of the Elijah of Chronicles (2 Chr 21:12–15).

[21] Obviously any significant discussion of these issues requires a separate study that goes well beyond the boundaries of this essay. For recent publications on these matters, see in particular G. N. Knoppers, *Jews and Samaritans: The Origins and History of Their Early Relations* (New York: Oxford University Press, 2013) and bibliography.

Moreover, remembering Hosea was not only remembering his polemic against Samaria, but also his polemic against Benjaminite cultic centers (Mizpah, Bethel, Gilgal).²² Certainly this does not mean that the Yehudite literati did not have strong social interactions with Benjaminites. In fact, the eventual rise to prominence of the temple of Jerusalem required the support and inclusion of Benjaminites, for they constituted the demographic and economic center of Yehud for much of the Persian period, if not in its entirety. The very literati who read about the condemnation of Benjaminite cultic centers of the past in Hosea were also aware of multiple texts that brought together Judah and Benjamin and emphasized social and regional cohesion between the two (see the memory evoked by Josh 18:28). The negative construction of these cultic sites in Hosea plays out in an evocative world that does not promote a mnemonic association of all the sinful cultic places with "Judah and Benjamin," but instead with Samaria. Negative images of the Benjamin of the past were associated with Samaria, while a far more positive Benjamin was associated with "Judah and Benjamin" within this discourse. Remembering Hosea meant engaging, even unconsciously, such a world of conceptual and mnemonic associations.

5 Remembering Hosea for the Sake of Forgetting: Shaping a Foundational Plot Concerning the Late Monarchic Period

There is no remembering without forgetting; there is no drawing attention to something without drawing attention away from something else. Remembering and shaping narratives about the past involved by necessity useful forgetting (or "bracketing"). An analysis or memories of Hosea should attend to what becomes "forgotten" or "bracketed" when remembering the Hosea of the Yehudite literati, and why.

Here I shall note briefly an example I discussed elsewhere at some length,²³ namely, that Hosea contributed to collective forgetting about Aram's hegemonic role in the eighth century. In fact, up to 732 BCE. Aram, not Egypt, was the main regional superpower confronting Assyria, but the remembered Hosea never spoke against reliance on Aram. His world was shaped by the dyad Egypt–Assy-

---

22 See Bos, *Reconsidering the Date and Provenance of the Book of Hosea*, esp. 70 – 101.
23 See E. Ben Zvi. "The Study of Forgetting and the Forgotten in Ancient Israelite Discourse/s: Observations and Test Cases," in *Cultural Memory in Biblical Exegesis* (eds. P. Carstens, T. Hasselbach, and N. P. Lemche; Perspectives on Hebrew Scriptures and Its Contexts 17; Piscataway, N.J.: Gorgias, 2012), 155 – 74.

ria (Hos 7:11; 12:2).²⁴ For the purpose of exploring the grammar of mnemonic preferences and dis-preferences at work is the forgetting of the powerful Aram that existed at the putative time of Hosea (see Hos 1:1), it is important to note that the Hosea of the community, and the only Northern prophet in the PBC, communicated a basic organization of the late monarchic past in which the two main earthly powers were first Assyria and Egypt and then Babylon and Egypt. This periodization of the period reflected a central narrative about that past structured around two main Judahite, contrastive events: (a) the delivery of Jerusalem by YHWH in the fourteenth year of Hezekiah and (b) its fall at the hands of the Babylonians. In addition, it reflected a social mindscape in which all the remembered, central external powers (namely Egypt, Babylon and Assyria) are construed as places of Exile and starting points for a future Return.²⁵ Hosea's silence on Aram–along with his multiple references to the dyad Assyria–Egypt and the construction of their lands as spaces for Exile and its counterpart, a future, utopian Return (e.g. Hos 9:3; 11:5, 11)–was consonant with and strengthened a core Yehudite narrative about the place of Exile and the overcoming of Exile, in a way that both included Northern Israel (see Assyria as a place of Exile) and undermined its separate existence.

6 Remembering Hosea and Gendered Acts of Imagination

Stories about sex, whoring, and violence tend to be memorable and to make characters memorable. No one would dispute that one of the features that made Hosea, as a character, unique among the fifteen prophets is the story (or stories) of YHWH/the prophet and his wife (or wives). Evoking the presence of Hosea among the Yehudite literati involved at one level an exercise of imagining Israel as the sinful wife, who is punished by the deity, rejected, and eventually reshaped as a godly wife and "restored." This is a version of the basic Yehudite narrative of destruction due to sin, Exile, and future utopian return, in which the alienation between the couple, i.e., YHWH–Israel, is removed forever.

---

24 In Hosea, Aram is mentioned only in Hos 12:13 as the place to which Jacob escaped in the far past. The importance of Aram at the time was not completely forgotten in the world of the literati who read the books of Kings, Isaiah, and perhaps Amos 1:3–5.
25 It is worth noting that the only reference to Aram in the book of Hosea (Hos 12:13) features it as the temporary place of "exile" of the patriarch Jacob. Aram as a site of memory could only be related to Jacob's stay in Laban's house, not as a place or agent of deportation for monarchic Israel.

In fact, the entire gamut of experiences in the "history" of Yhwh and Israel, past and future, is reformulated and made memorable in Hos 1–2 as the story of the transformation of a woman selected in the days of old by Yhwh who by nature tends to sin–that is, to engage in illegitimate sex (i.e., זנונים אשת)–into one whose attributes are divinely given righteousness, justice, steadfast love, mercy, and faithfulness (2:21–23).²⁶ The entire story is a variant of the *Ckaoskampf* motif; in this case, the struggle is over a woman in whom Chaos (i.e., sin/"promiscuity") first lakes hold,²⁷ but is then defeated by Yhwh, resulting in a permanent orderly world. Here Israel/the woman takes the Structural slot of the Cosmos, thus conveying (and reflecting) a sense of cosmic centrality for Israel and guaranteeing a sense of ontological security in the world imagined and populated (vicariously) by the literati, and also in the world of all those who accepted these memorable stories.

At the same time, the literati imagining this world identified not only with the woman, but also with Hosea, the godly northern (but ideologically Yehudized) prophet. Remembering Hosea was remembering and vicariously experiencing the role of the husband. This being the case, it was also, to some extent, an exercise in being in Yhwh's image, or imagining being as it were in "his shoes," thereby construing and remembering the past of Israel in a way akin to that experienced by Hosea/Yhwh, and suffering accordingly (see Hos 11:1–4, 8). Such remembering thus allows the community to imagine their past as two radically different experiences,²⁸ both grounded in the story of sin and punishment (and future de-alienation) but seen and experienced from opposite sides. A similar process was at work when the main metaphor recalled by those imagining and remembering this aspect of their own Hosea was not husband/wife, but father (Hosea/Yhwh) and children, which complements the

---

26 Understanding the crucial text as "I [i.e., Yhwh] will betroth you [i.e., Israel] to me for ever; I will betroth you to me with righteousness and with justice, with kindness and mercy. I will betroth you with faithfulness."
27 Her nature as אשת זנונים makes her by necessity inimical to Yhwh and Yhwh's desired, stable order (i.e., his marriage to her). A complete erasure of that nature becomes a necessary condition for the establishment of that ordered world within this discourse.
28 In fact, there are three perspectives and vicarious experiences to remember, one based on the literati's identification with Israel/wife, another with Hosea/husband and a third with Yhwh/husband, since Hosea was not and could not have fully identified with Yhwh–even not to the extent that Israel could have (partially) imagined itself as embodied in both Gomer and the future Israel who is the elevated bride of Yhwh. Yet, there is no doubt that the story conveys a sense of structural and symbolic convergence between the roles played by Yhwh and Hosea in these chapters.

husband/wife metaphor in terms of hierarchical constructions and familiar expectations.

Remembering Hosea was thus cresting an image of the past that integrated and balanced two different perspectives. The strong affective rhetoric involved in imagining oneself as at once both the woman and her husband creates a past that evokes strong emotions in both sides and thus is even more memorable. Further, the memorable past was deeply intertwined with memories of an equally emotion-laden future, vicariously experienced by the literati recalling their Hosea.

This is certainly a story about Yhwh's love for Israel–represented by various reported memories of Yhwh (e.g., Hos 2:16–17; cf. 11:1–4; 13:5–6), despite its rejection of Yhwh, its sin, and about Israel's justified punishment (passim). But it is also a story and vicarious memory of a future, elevated Israel, who at the time of her betrothal becomes permanently endowed by Yhwh with five godly attributes, namely, צֶדֶק, חֶסֶד, מִשְׁפָּט, and רַחֲמִים and אֱמוּנָה (Hos 2:21–22), all of which belong to and characterize her husband as well. There is nothing too strange in this construction. After all, one is to expect that a woman who is imagined and remembered as the true, constant, and worthy female companion of the deity would not be imagined as a "regular," completely human woman. Remembering Hosea was not only an invitation to identify with Hosea the prophet or his wives, but also with a future, somewhat goddess-like, or (so to speak) goddess-light Israel, a female figure "remembered" in such a way as to make her fit to be the deity's proper and eternal consort.

The logic of the future elevation of Israel and her new status distinguishes her from all other "women" also populating that future. But what about them? Certainly, the literati neither imagined nor "remembered" a future (or past, for that matter), equally valid marriage of Yhwh to other women/nations (e.g., Assyria, Egypt, Edom). Such "memories" would have been strongly dis-preferred within the discourse in Yehud, for obvious reasons. At the same time, although these other future "women" remain unseen in the textual scenes remembered by the literati, it is very unlikely that the latter imagined a world in which there existed no other nations/women except Israel. In fact, from a general perspective of the dreamed (and vicariously experienced) future hierarchies, the issue at stake is similar to that emerging when future Israel is construed as a (deputy) "king" or "priest" meant to provide the other humans with Yhwh's instruction, order, and contentment with the world.[29] But in Hosea these issues remained es-

---

29 See, e.g., Isa 2:2–4; 55:3–5; 56:1–8; cf. Exod 19:5–6.

sentially unseen and unexplored. To be sure, Hosea was an important site of memory, but this did not mean that it had to serve as a playground for the exploration of every possible issue within the discourse of the community or that might emerge from remembering Hosea and his putative world.[30]

7 Remembering Hosea and Exploring "the Land"

This said, there are additional substantial issues within the discourse of the community that were explored by thinking through images of Yhwh as husband and Israel as his wife in the context of remembering Hosea and the godly words associated with him. Remembering the latter involved imagining the land also as Yhwh's female consort (see Hos 2:23–25) and, therefore, deeply intertwining images of the land and (future) Israel, i.e., Yhwh's wife (see Hos 2:21–25). Yet at the same time, remembering Hosea was constructing and remembering a past within which Israel's relation with Yhwh was at its best when Israel was in the wilderness, outside the land, and within which coming close to or entering into the land were associated with sin and rejection of Yhwh (Hos 9:10, 15). It is remembering, on the one hand, that the potential for proper offerings and purity was bound to existence within the land (Hos 9:3–5), but that Yhwh must bring Israel back to the desert, outside the land, for only there may Yhwh seduce her and return her to himself. And it is only there, outside the land, that Yhwh will elevate her to a new status through his betrothal gifts (Hos 2:16,21–22), thereby inoculating her, as it were, from the dangers of the land that necessarily brought down her predecessor, the less elevated Israel.

The memorable and unique first chapters of the book shaped a remembered Hosea who served as an excellent site of memory for safely exploring a multifaceted construction of the relation of the land and Israel, within a Persian period, Yehudite context. Equally importantly, it served as a site of memory that brought together voices that were in seeming tension with one another and embodied them all within a single character, the Hosea of their memory.

---

[30] To be sure, Hosea as a site of memory was not as developed or comprehensive as more central sites, such as Isaiah, but still, no site has or can save as a playground for every single important matter in the discourse of the community.

8 Remembering Hosea and Remembering Yʜᴡʜ as a Teacher

The central image of Yʜᴡʜ as "the teacher" that permeates the PBC– and other core collections in Yehud as well–allowed the literati reading the books in the PBC to construe Yʜᴡʜ as addressing simultaneously two different social groups: (a) the one populating the book and (b) the one overhearing, as it were, everything that transpired in that world. The deity and the prophet evoked in Hosea were remembered as using didactic language, including socially memorable stories involving sex, whoring, and violence; as employing familiar familial images and metaphors such as father, husband, son; and as turning to references to trees, animals (e. g., lion), and commonly experienced phenomena like dew to make their point clear. They were also remembered as using pathos to persuade their "students," and both assumed the potential teaching efficacy of constructing and reminding them of a shared memory of the past and future so as to socialize them properly.[31]

Of course, the literati in Yehud were very well aware of the calamities that ended the monarchic past, and thus could not but imagine that both Yʜᴡʜ and the prophets, despite all their memorable, didactic stories, failed miserably in their teaching mission insofar as it concerned the monarchic communities construed and remembered by the Yehudite literati. They hoped, however, that they would succeed in enabling the community to remember and experience vicariously their previous failure, through their readings of the PBC in Yehud, while at the same time reminding them that no full and permanent success is achievable until Israel is elevated and provided with some divine attributes (see Hos 2:21–22; cf. the logic governing Jer 31:33–34). Hosea not only fits well within this ideological, mnemonic pattern, but also draws particular attention to it.

Every book in the PBC concludes with an emphatic and unique ending. But the book of Hosea is unique in its uniqueness, insofar as it concerns matters of instruction. It does not conclude with some utopian image as it could have easily done (see Hos 14:5–9), but with דרכי יהוה וצדקים מי חכם ויבן אלה נבון וידעם כי ישרים ילכו בם ופשעים יכשלו בם "whoever is wise, let him understand these things [i. e., the teachings voiced by Yʜᴡʜ and Hosea as the literati of the time construed them to be]; whoever is discerning, let him know them; for the ways of the Yʜᴡʜ are right, and the upright walk in them, but transgressors stumble in

---

[31] The idea that communities must be bound by a sense of shared past and future to be "successful" and the related social processes of ongoing, active construction and inculcation of memories of the past and of a future by an elite for socialization purposes have both been attested in many different cultures and historical periods.

them" (based on the RSV). Thus Hosea served as a unique and focused reminder of the role of the literati and of the prophetic literature in their hands. It explicitly stressed both the importance of teaching דבר־יהוה (one of whose instantiations is identified with the prophetic book of Hosea in Hos 1:1) and also of wise students (i.e., the literati themselves) who stand in strong opposition to the fools of the past (monarchic Israel) but also to the fools of the present, inside and outside the community (see previous discussion of Samarians).

Notice as well the opposition between the "righteous people" and the sinners and transgressors.[32] Since only the former may succeed, remembering Hosea and the book associated with him was reminding the community that the presence of the righteous literati becomes an absolutely necessary requirement for Israel if it is to avoid the calamities of the past. But there is more: the literati have to remember the Hosea of old and discern the messages of the deity by reading the book that evoked both their shared teaching and the calamities that follow from failing in that endeavor. Significantly, and from our perspective perhaps counter-intuitively, this teaching is to a substantial extent a lesson on socializing the literati as a group into fuzziness, within socially and ideologically set boundaries.

9 Fuzziness

Remembering Hosea was remembering that Israel is/was both a "luxuriant vine" and also a "damaged vine"; likewise, that its "fruit is similar to it" and thus also luxuriant or damaged (Hos 10:1); that prosperity brings about both the rejection of YHWH and YHWH's ways (e.g., Hos 2:4–15; 10:1–2; 12:9), but is also a worldly manifestation of YHWH's future blessing when utopia will be realized (e.g., Hos 2:16–25). It is remembering that Israel's space is in YHWH's land (e.g., Hos 2:1–3; 3:3–5; 7:16; 9:3–5; 9:6; 11:5–6, 11; 14:6–8),[33] but evoking memories of reaching the land that are associated with disaster, while YHWH's past "happy days" with Israel are imagined outside the land (e.g., Hos 2:10–15; 9:10; 11:1–4; 12:9–10, 14; 13:4–6; cf. Hos 10:11–13).

Remembering Hosea and the godly words that he embodied was remembering that repentance is necessary for divine deliverance and also that it is not (cf.

---

32 This is a commonplace in wisdom literature; see, for instance, Ps 1:6; Prov 2:20–22; 3:33; 4:18–19; 10:28; 11:21, 23; 24:16.
33 See ארץ יהוה in Hos 9:3; vv. 4–5 state that no (proper) worship can take place outside YHWH's land.

Hos 1:2–2:25 and esp. Hos 2:1–2, 16–25; 11:7–11 with Hos 3:5; and see Hos 14:2–9);³⁴ that Israel needs and will have a future Davidide king who will be a highly elevated figure (Hos 2:2; 3:4–5) and also that Israel does not need a Davidide, because Israel would be the elevated figure (2:16–25, esp. vv. 20–22); further, the image of YHWH as Israel's king obviates the need for a Davidic king in the utopian future (see Hos 14:2–9) and is coherent with the widely attested image that Israel is YHWH's (adopted) son (e. g., Hos 11:1).³⁵

Many more examples can be added, but these suffice to make the point: Hosea as a site of memory was a site of some significant fuzziness. Remembering Hosea was constructing and communicating a sense of fuzziness and socializing the literati into it. It meant constantly balancing and thus integrating different viewpoints, statements, and memories of past and future events, all embodied and integrated in one figure from the past that was brought to the present of the community.

Again, Hosea is not unique in this regard. The same can be said of any one of the fifteen prophetic characters encoded in the PBC, of Moses and of the implied authors of most (if not all) books in the authoritative repertoire of the community. There was a very strong systemic preference for remembering characters imagined as embodying, integrating, and communicating multiple perspectives. It is not by chance that Hosea was remembered this way, nor that remembering him this way contributed to his memorability.³⁶

10 Final Comments

Although many more examples and topics may be brought up in relation to remembering Hosea in Yehud, I hope those mentioned above suffice as an exploration into Hosea as a site of memory in Yehud; into why Hosea was very much

---

34 See Ben Zvi, *Hosea*, 303–4.
35 All these examples are discussed at length in Ben Zvi, *Hosea*.
36 This tendency towards fuzziness on a very larger number of issues (though, of course not all) is a major issue for historical reconstructions of the intellectual history of the Yehudite literati and their social context. As shown elsewhere, this tendency is consistent with the social location of this discourse among a small group of literati in Yehud who did not conceive themselves as being under a substantial existential threat to their survival as a community, as tendencies toward organizing knowledge and memories in fluid rather than rigid concepts are more common in communities without high levels of existential anxiety. On these issues see "On Social Memory and Identity Formation in Late Persian Yehud: A Historian's Viewpoint with a Focus on Prophetic Literature, Chronicles and the Deuteronomistic Historical Collection," in this volume, pp. 28–79.

worth remembering among the (ideologically) Jerusalem-centered literati of the time; and into generative grammars of preferences and dis-preferences that played a substantial role in the shaping of memories about Hosea as one of the fifteen prophets evoked by the PBC. Such shaping included the ever-present balancing act between a uniqueness that made the character of Hosea memorable and a lack of uniqueness that allowed him to fulfill a set mnemonic patterns without which he could not have been construed as a memorable, godly prophet. I hope it also suffices as an exploration into some core matters embodied and communicated by Hosea as a site of memory, including the tendency to socialize the literati into fuzziness. Above all, may the Hosea of social (/communal) memory proposed in this essay have interesting conversations with the prophet Hosea about whom Francis writes, or at least, as interesting as those Francis and I have had through the years.

Reading the Book of Hosea, Remembering Hosea and Thinking of Exile in Yehud

Introduction

The Yehudite literati who read and reread the Book of Hosea construed and remembered a Northern prophet of the old monarchic era and the instance of YHWH's word associated with him. As they did so, they could not but think and explore Exile, both (a) from the temporal perspective of the putative characters populating the world of the book, which was informed by the way the literati remembered monarchic Israel, and from (b) their own temporal location, in the late Persian period.

Moreover, Exile was not a self-standing concept, neither within the world of the implied author of the book, as the readers construed (most likely) him to be, nor within the discourse of the literati, or their Hosea of memory. Instead, it was a concept and node of memory which was meant to evoke and interact with other concepts, images, and central nodes of memory within their own discourse and within the discourse in which they imagined the characters in the book they were reading and its implied author partook.

In what follows, I will explore a number of texts within the book of Hosea that explicitly raise matters of Exile and Exile's construction, and for obvious reasons, the examination of these texts carried out here must focus narrowly on what they can inform us about constructions of Exile conveyed to the literati through these readings and the memories that they shape. These examples will lead us to several general observations, which will then be placed into the context of major themes within the ideological world and memory world of these literati.[1]

---

[1] I have discussed all these texts in E. Ben Zvi, *Hosea* (FOTL 21 A, part 1; Grand Rapids, MI: Eerdmans, 2005). For an extended study of these texts see Ben Zvi, *Hosea*. Here I build on and further develop some issues from my previous analysis of these texts so as to be able to build an argument on the matter of "reading the Book of Hosea, remembering Hosea and thinking of Exile in Yehud."

Crucial texts encoding and communicating a concept of Exile in the Book of Hosea as likely read by Yehudite literati

Hos 1:2–2:2 is an extremely rich and multivocal text. This said, the basic mnemonic, narrative plot shaped and communicated by the text is still clear. It moves from Israel's sin, to its divine punishment, exile and overcoming exile.

One of the key terms in this text is יזרעאל (Jezreel), the name of the first son. For one, it marks an inclusio between 1:4–5 and 2:2 and draws attention to a 'day' that consists of two days. The first, in Hos 1:4–5, is day of judgement and calamity for Israel and the second in 2:2 is one of redemption; both days are intrinsically associated with Jezreel. In addition, the name Jezreel itself connotes a meaning of "El/God sows" and evokes both a divine promise to the patriarchs concerning the multiplication of their "seed" that comes to the forefront in 2:1, and the images of seeding the land that comes to the forefront in 2:15. At the same time, "sowing" means "scattering seed," and as such the term hints at images of exile, as it is explicitly manifested in, for instance, Zech 10:9 ואזרעם בעמים ובמרחקים יזכרוני וחיו את בניהם ושבו ("though I scattered/seeded them among the peoples, yet in the far countries they will remember me, and they and their sons will live, and they will return"[2]), a text that not accidentally, also closely links Exile to Return.

As a site of memory, Jezreel serves as a nexus to explore Exile and Overcoming Exile, and embodied and exemplified the reasons for the calamity (see 1:4) within the construed 'historical' circumstances of the character Hosea, i.e., a Northern prophet from the time of Jeroboam II.[3]

In addition, since Jezreel is both the name of the eldest child of Hosea and Gomer and of a city and a valley, the choice of the term 'Jezreel' reminded the literati that the child stands both for the people and the land. This close association amongst the children, the people and the land, is, of course, strongly communicated in Hos 2:23–25, in which not only the term 'Jezreel' occurs (v 24), but also the related form וּזְרַעְתִּיהָ לִּי ("I will seed her for myself") in v 25.

To be sure, Jezreel is one of three children. The other two have names, Loruhamah (Unpitied) and Lo-ammi (not-my-people), that while pointing in their own ways to 'Exile,' also clearly associate the latter with a future in which Exile has been overcome, for Unpitied conjures the image of and recalls memo-

---

[2] This translation is based on the one advanced in Paul Reddit, *Zechariah 9–14* (IECOT; Stuttgart: Kohlhammer, 2012), 58. See there for discussion.
[3] For more on this matter, see "Remembering Hosea: The Prophet as a Site of Memory in Persian Period Yehud," in this volume, pp. 274–93.

ries of the future 'Pitied' and 'Not-My-People' of the future 'My People' (see 2:1–3, 22–25).

In sum, Exile and Overcoming Exile are here construed as deeply associated with one another. For the most part one is conceived as the inverted image of the other, and conjuring images of this dyad involved communicating a sense of connection between people and land at multiple levels.

But there is much more in this prophetic reading of relevance to our present purposes. The expression וְעָלוּ מִן־הָאָרֶץ in Hos 2:2, at the very least, activated images of a return from exile evocative of the Exodus[4] that were common in the general social mindscape of the community. If the phrase *also* conveyed some remote, secondary echo of 'underworld'[5] then it carried an additional act of signaling towards a mythical horizon. In either case, it is important that the text did not actually ask the literati to constrain their imagination and shared memory when reading this text to any particular concrete land of exile (וְעָלוּ מִן־הָאָרֶץ). The identity and particular characteristics of that land are not worth remembering, and if anything, the expression might have actually hinted at some conceptual sense in which the land of exile and the land of, and represented by the children converge.

It is also worth noting that Jezreel in 1:4–5 is directly associated with and points to the fall of the House of Jehu. This was a historical fact from the perspective of the readership of the book, but still clearly stood in the future for the prophet and his audience within the world of the book. The future circumstances in which Exile is overcome in this prophetic reading included the image of Judah and Israel unified under one ruler/king, which in the context of the world of the literati could only be a Davide (Hos 2:2; for ראש as king see, e. g., Isa 7:8–9). This world was very much in the future of the literati. The main point I want to make is not that recalling that the first of two prophecies was fulfilled is a way to construe hope that the second will be fulfilled too. Although this is obviously correct, the relative importance of this observation for the present purposes is limited, particularly given that the entire literary unit as a whole was a strong expression of hope. Instead, the point I want to emphasize in this context is that the text asked the literati of the Persian period to construe themselves as

---

[4] Cf. Targum, Peshitta, and most modern translations. This position has a long history in research, see e. g., J. Wellhausen, *Skizzen und Vorarbeiten Fünftes Heft. Die Kleinen Propheten* (Berlin: Georg Reimer), p. 97.

[5] On cases of ארץ as 'underworld,' see Scott B. Noegel, "God of Heaven and Sheol: The 'Unearthing of Creation," *HS* 58 (2017), pp. 119–44 and bibliography. On ארץ as 'underworld' in Hos 2:2, see F. I. Andersen and D. N. Freedman, *Hosea* (AB 24; New York: Doubleday, 1980), pp. 208–9.

living before the Return, still in Exile, even if they lived in Jerusalem and even if they have in their midst a proper temple.

Moreover, since the text stresses in multiple ways that Exile is the inverse image of Overcoming Exile, it signaled to the literati that Exile *also* began with the split of the unified kingdom, as remembered by the community. It is worth noting that reading the Book of Hosea in this historically contingent context often meant encouraging the literati to engage in acts of shaping and recalling memories of sinful Israel from various times, all of which were much earlier than the putative time of the character Hosea (cf. Hos 9:9–11, 15; 11:1–2). This prophetic reading is just one in a series of readings in the book, each drawing attention to particular sites of memory comprising a set of infamous memories ('the days of Gibeah; Gilgal, Baal Peor, early in the Wandering period, the division of the monarchy), all of which were considered complementary turning points in the grand narrative of Israel moving forwards towards Exile and Overcoming Exile.

The second prophetic text to be addressed here within the boundaries of the present topic is Hos 2:4–25. Textual markers linked this text to the preceding unit (see vv 24–25) and vice versa. Further, this text required the readers to engage in a reconceptualization of the basic meta-narrative of the latter, and vice versa. The end result is that by mutually informing each other, some messages and didactic points were reinforced, but others were reconfigured.

For the present purposes, it is worth stressing first that Exile and Overcoming Exile were again conceptualized as intrinsically and essentially related. Thinking of one necessitated thinking of the other. Again, no attention is drawn to any concrete place of Exile. The message was again that these matters were not really worth remembering and perhaps even unhelpful for conceptualizing Exile and Overcoming Exile.

Hos 2:4–25 forcefully communicated an association between the conceptual dyad of Exile and Overcoming Exile on the one hand and memories of the Exodus, Wilderness, and Possession of the fruitful land on the other. This text and particularly the mentioned associated memories, strongly communicated a construction of Overcoming Exile in which all Israel *necessarily* takes part as one group—not just Judah or Northern Israel, and therefore, it shaped and communicated the same messages and implications of the image of the future unification of Israel as the previous prophetic reading in the book of Hosea.

In addition, not surprisingly given our preceding observations, no attention is drawn in this prophetic reading to Egypt, the concrete place of Exile in the recalled narrative of the Exodus. But, significantly, attention is certainly drawn in the narrative to the Wilderness. It is *there*, in the Wilderness, that the crucial act of Overcoming Exile takes place. To be sure, the land will be fruitful, and Israel's.

Moreover, the concluding act of Overcoming Exile will take place in the land (see 2:25; "I will say to Not-My-People, you are my people").

It is worth noting that whereas the literati were asked to conceptualize Exile and Overcoming Exile through acts of recalling memories of Exodus and Wilderness, they were also asked to engage in significant reformulations. In the world of imagination and memory of Hos 2:4–25, the possession of the fruitful land comes about through YHWH's actions as a fertility deity who bans war and strife (see esp. 2:20), not as the Warrior, nor through the empowerment of a human hero or heroes as in the Conquest narrative.

It is also worth noting that within the world of imagination and memory shaped and embodied in this text, when YHWH was imagined as "seeding her (Israel) in the land for the deity" (see וּזְרַעְתִּיהָ לִּי בָּאָרֶץ in 2:25), there were no other 'seeds' around. Within this world, the land was 'virgin'/empty, just waiting for YHWH's creative action, unlike the case in the Conquest narratives, but similar, at least in this regard, to other mnemonic narratives of Overcoming Exile that existed among the literati.

Another important difference: within this world of memory shaped by the Primary Historical Collection (Gen-2 Kings) and its sub-collections, the turning point that shaped Israel 'forever' was YHWH's granting of *torah* to Israel.[6] In Hos 2:4–25, however, the structurally similar turning point consists of YHWH's gifting Israel some divine attributes (righteousness, justice, kindness and mercy) that make her into a new, higher-than-human 'person', now unable to betray her husband, YHWH (cf. Jer 31:31–34; 32:38–41; Ezek 11:19–20; 36:25–28).[7]

The point the text conveyed is that for the process of Overcoming Exile to achieve permanent success, nature had to be changed, and the previous אֵשֶׁת זְנוּנִים ("a promiscuous woman") had to be reconfigured by YHWH. Although Overcoming Exile was construed and built on the concept Exile and its associated narratives, and although both concepts shaped each other, Exile was still conceived as integral to the world of common 'human history,' i.e., a history in which normal humans interact. For the literati reading Hosea, to imagine and remember Exile Overcome permanently meant to envision the end of usual, human history and of Israel's regular, un-enhanced humanity, and the beginning of the now a-historical, stable era of an elevated Israel. (Significantly, not an elevated Davide, but an elevated Israel).

Reading the text also meant that the literati constructed an implied hierarchy of what is most worthy of being remembered when they thought of the proc-

---

6 See Hos 4:6; 8:1 as understood by the literati and cf. esp. Hos 8:1 with Ps 78:10.
7 The בְּ carries both the meaning of 'in' and 'with' in Hos 2:21–22.

ess from Exile to Overcoming Exile. The transformation of Israel, the new possession of the now fertile land, and the peaceful world were all explicitly evoked and stood at the top of the list. But the reversal of the stoppage of Israel's festivals, new moons and sabbaths and appointed festivals (Hos 2:13) was not explicitly mentioned. No space was allocated to this in the text. To be sure, it does not mean that the literati imagined a future utopian world without them, but that that these were given less mindshare when they virtually experienced the beginning of the new permanent era through their readings and socially shared imagination.

If Hos 2:4–25, and for that matter, Hos 14:5–8 towards the conclusion of the book, shaped among the literati an image of a future world in which there was no need for a Davide, Hos 3:1–5 balanced this trend by construing not only a future Davide, but a uniquely elevated one. This is the case because, whereas seeking YHWH is not uncommon, seeking a human king is very much so (see 3:5); and one may compare with Mal 2:7 in which people are supposed to seek instruction from the priest, rather than seek the priest.

All in all, the image of Exile and Overcoming Exile were again closely linked, in this case with the lack of Davide on the throne of Israel leading the image and memory of a future, highly elevated Davide, and, not surprisingly, with no explicit reference to the return of the sacrifices[8] or the royal officials, as both are matters that were *not* considered at the centre of what is to be remembered.

Brief references to two additional texts in the Book of Hosea suffice for the present purposes. The first, Hos 9:1–13, devotes most of its space, as typical in the Book of Hosea as a whole, to the explanation of the reasons for Exile (i.e., Israel's behaviour and to a large extent nature), but allocates more textual space and encourages the literati to increase the relative mindshare of some features of the conceptualization and imagination associated with remembering Exile (see vv 3–6) among the readers and their implied author.

The Exile referred to here was explicitly and more prominently associated with Egypt (cf. 8:13b[9]), even as an important reference to Assyria is advanced.[10] The image of life in Exile vicariously experienced by the literati reading this text is one in which at the center stands, as before, the lack of proper cult, sacrifices

---

[8] The issue of sacrifices is more complex, because the reference to them is within a context that carries ambiguous connotations. See E. Ben Zvi, *Hosea*, 90–91.
[9] Hos 8:13b brings forward again the image of Exile as a Return to Egypt and creates a system of mutual signposts with Hos 9:3 (מִצְרַיִם יָשׁוּבוּ referring to 'Ephraim' in the former and וְשָׁב אֶפְרַיִם מִצְרָיִם).
[10] The Exile is that of Ephraim but from the perspective of the literati, also of all Israel, as it will be clear in a moment

and festivals, but also matters of purity of food that emerge from the construction of the impurity of the lands outside Yhwh's land (v 3; cf. Josh 22:19 [MT])[11] that, to be sure, from the perspective of the literati included Judah and at whose center stood the proper Temple of Yhwh.[12] Within the world construed in prophetic reading, Overcoming Exile was conceptualized as requiring, at the very least, a proper Temple and cult in Jerusalem and settlement in Yhwh's land. This is not surprising, given that these two ideological tenets were ubiquitous within the discourse of the Yehudite literati of the time.

The final text to be discussed in this context is Hos 11:1–11.[13] The most interesting reference for the present purposes is in vv 10–11. The text refers to Israelites about to come back from exile. As one may anticipate in the book of Hosea, when the book concretely mentions places, they are based on the South/North axis shaped by dyad of Egypt and Assyria that is so well attested in the book and this indeed happens v 11. But in v 10, the literati were asked to also evoke the motif of Israelites returning from the west, which appears elsewhere in the discourse of the community (cf. Isa 11:11; Obad 20; and cf. Isa 60:8–9), but usually is a minor element and is not directly associated with any of the memories that the book evoked involving Israel and its dealings with Assyria or Egypt. The seemingly unexpected reference to the west indicates that an underlying, ideological tendency towards generalization and universalization of the spaces associated with both Exile and Overcoming Exile was at work here.

In addition, it is worth noting that this text asked the community to imagine and vicariously experience the memory of a future event in which those who were exiled will return to their 'houses' in the land, seemingly undoing well-remembered divine acts such as those described in Jer 6:12, namely "their houses

---

[11] Cf. also Ezek 4:13; Amos 7:17.

[12] Within the world of the literati בֵּית יהוה in v 4 could not but be understood as a reference to the temple in Jerusalem.

[13] I am leaving aside the polyvalent text of Hos 11:5 (לֹא יָשׁוּב אֶל־אֶרֶץ מִצְרַיִם וְאַשּׁוּר הוּא מַלְכּוֹ כִּי מֵאֲנוּ לָשׁוּב and the potential relation of its first word with Hos 11:4; cf. LXX), because it does not add much to the matters discussed here. The text may be understood as (a) "he will not return to the land of Egypt, but rather it is Assyria who will be his king;" (b) "No, he shall return to the land of Egypt, but Assyria shall be their k/King;," (c) "he will not have to go back to Egypt, Assyria will be his k/King instead!"; (d) and including the end of v. 4 "... I fed them him, but he will return to Egypt, and [as a result] Assyria will be his k/King; and perhaps (e) ... I prevailed over him. He will return to Egypt, but/and Assyria will be his k/King. Whether in the world shaped by Hos 11 as understood by the literati, there was or there was not a partial return to Egypt, the latter would not have meant forfeiting the creation of Israel as Yhwh's adopted child in 11:1. The main focus of this verse is to shape a memory of Israel foolishly making Assyria rather than Yhwh its k/King

shall be turned over to others," except that in the world evoked in Hos 11, there are no others to imagine or remember. In any event, in both cases references to the Exile are brought in the context of Return, of Overcoming Exile.

The conceptualization of Exile communicated by the (implied) author of the Book of Hosea to the Yehudite literati

The discussion above clearly leads to the conclusion that the conceptualization of Exile was deeply intertwined with that of Overcoming Exile and *vice versa*. The literati reading Hosea were not asked to imagine, remember or conceptualize one without doing the same for the other.

Conceptualizing and remembering Exile and Overcoming Exile as deeply intertwined meant, from a memory perspective, to place them within some helical plots governing the construction of memories of Israel. Precisely this helical structure as opposed to a cyclical one allowed the literati to develop a range of complementary memories informing each other, which allowed the literati reading Hosea to explore and play with memories of the Exodus, the Wilderness, the Conquest of the land and the like so as to explore ideological matters close to the heart of the community in a way which that not only advances a conceptualization of the dyad Exile and Overcoming Exile, but also turns the latter into mnemonic nodes embodying and communicating all these central ideological issues.

In addition, the literati could not but notice that much of the textual space in Hosea was devoted to explaining the reasons for exile, the didactic lessons to learn from it, and exploring, in various ways, the inseparable dyad of Exile and Overcoming Exile as well as substantial matters in their own ideological landscape.

There was, however, no real interest in the experience of what we would define as actual exiles in the Persian period. The lives of, for instance, Judahites in Elephantine or Al-Yahudu and their worlds and memories, if known to the literati, were considered not worth remembering or even discussing.[14] If the ancestors of these Judahites were traumatized by their forced relocations, their traumatic experiences were also not at the center of the literati's consciousness. I will return to the issue of trauma.

---

14 Even when a seemingly, small vignette of life in Exile was mentioned in passing, the Jerusalem-centrism of the supposed experience is all too obvious.

Exile and Overcoming Exile were also conceptualized in such a way that concrete, historical places of Exile were not at the mnemonic or ideological centre. In fact, the main land in which those in Exile dwelt in the Persian period within the world shaped by the literati's reading Hosea and similar books, consisted of Judah and Jerusalem. The literati reading Hosea in Yehud were those who were in Exile and longed for the manifestation of Overcoming Exile.

The close connection between Exile and Overcoming Exile that they conceptualized may have marginalized the singularity of the historical exiles, but provided much hope for the Yehudite literati, and sense of identity around a shared narrative that was grounded, in part, on remembering a past calamity associated with the fall of the monarchic polity, for which there were numerous concrete memorials around them in the form of ruins and general material markers of a much larger Jerusalem than the one of their days and a much larger settlement.

It is true that remembering such a calamity involved recalling (socially transmitted) traumatic memories.[15] It is also true that the social sharing of the traumatic event in the past referred to as Exile by the group helped it to bond together and further a sense of self-identity as Israel. Therefore, it seems appropriate to consider, at least in part, Exile (at large) as the chosen trauma of the literati and those who identified with them, and use the conceptual framework associated with this term.[16]

This said, and leaving aside that this chosen trauma was certainly just one of the factors that bonded them together and helped to shape their identity as a group—Overcoming Exile and their construed relation to YHWH also served central roles—it is crucial to stress that in a manner very much unlike most (if not

---

[15] In recent years a significant number of scholars of prophetic literature in general and of the three larger prophetic books in particular (e.g., Kathleen M. O'Connor, Ruth Poser, Julia M. O'Brien, Louis Stulman, L. Juliana Claassens, Daniel L. Smith-Christopher, Gale Yee) have used the lenses of Trauma Studies to analyze traumatic memories encoded and reflected in the relevant literature. See, e.g., Kathleen M. O'Connor, *Jeremiah: Pain and Promise* (Minneapolis: Fortress, 2011); idem, "Reclaiming Jeremiah's Violence," in Julia M. O'Brien and Chris Franke (eds.), *The Aesthetics of Violence in the Prophets* (LHBOTS, 517; New York: T&T Clark, 2010), 37–49; Ruth Poser, *Das Ezechielbuch als Trauma-Literatur* (VTSup, 154; Leiden: Brill, 2012); L. Juliana Claassens, "God and Violence in the Prophets," Carolyn Sharp (ed.), *The Oxford Handbook of the Prophets* (New York: Oxford University Press, 2016), 334–49) and cited bibliography. See also the various essays about prophetic characters in Elizabeth Boase and Christopher G. Frechette (eds.), *Bible Through the Lenses of Trauma* (Atlanta: SBL Press, 2016) and cited bibliography. All this said, it is worth keeping in mind that when studying the literati reading Hosea in the Persian period, the focus can only be on socially transmitted group trauma.

[16] I am using here the concept of 'chosen trauma' developed by Vamik D. Volkan; see, e.g., idem, "Transgenerational Transmissions and Chosen Traumas: An Aspect of Large-Group Identity," *Group Analysis* 34 (2001), pp. 79–97, esp. 87–95 and the bibliography cited there.

all) cases of contemporary groups displaying some form of 'chosen trauma', when they recalled their own concept of Exile and their socially shared mnemonic landscape associated with the concept, the literati reading Hosea in Yehud certainly did not understand themselves as (innocent) victims, nor dwelled on a sense of powerlessness to change 'history'.[17]

To the contrary, since reflecting on and shaping images of Exile meant also reflecting on and shaping images of Overcoming Exile, their reading of Hosea strengthened a self-understanding at whose focus stood hope and the certitude of some form of utopia awaiting Israel. Not only did these literati neither see themselves as powerless nor construe themselves around a self-image of victimhood and injustice perpetrated against them in the past—as usual in instances of groupal 'Chosen Trauma'—but within their world they developed an image of themselves as a select elite group that had unmatched knowledge about YHWH and YHWH's (final) decision to bring Israel to an exalted, utopian future. Within their own world, they were at the top, not at the bottom. They were, as it were, the beloved bride of YHWH, the most powerful character they could imagine, the one with no rival; just as Israel had no possible rival at that time, within their ideological perspective.[18]

These constructions were, of course, an integral part of the social-cultural environment in which the mentioned literati lived and they reflected their social mindscape. This being so, one would anticipate that similar positions would have emerged when they read other books within the sub-collection consisting of the twelve prophetic books. The issue, however, is beyond the scope of this contribution.

---

17 See Daniel Bar-Tal, Lily Chernyak-Hai, Noa Schori and Ayelet Gundar, "A Sense of Self-Perceived Collective Victimhood in intractable Conflicts," *International Review of the Red Cross* 91/874 (2009), pp. 229–258. See also Daniel Bar-Tal, *Intractable Conflicts: Socio-Psychological Foundations and Dynamics* (Cambridge: Cambridge University Press, 2013).

18 It is worth noting also that this "Chosen Trauma" was not activated among members of this group in any of the ways that had been noticed in contemporary times, perhaps because the group certainly did not saw themselves under threat or in crisis. See "On Social Memory and Identity Formation in Late Persian Yehud: A Historian's Viewpoint with a Focus on Prophetic Literature, Chronicles and the Dtr. Historical Collection," in this volume, pp. 28–79.

Readers, Social Memory, Deuteronomistic Language and Jeremiah: The Roles of Deuteronomistic Language in Shaping Memories of Jeremiah among Late Persian / early Hellenistic Readers of the Book of Jeremiah

A few years ago, in a Festschrift for Richard D. Nelson, I expressed my views about whether an implied concept somewhat akin to what we may label 'deuteronomistic' may have existed and what it may have meant for literati in late Persian or early Hellenistic Judah who read and reread Joshua-Kings as part of their repertoire of core communal texts.[1] I explored in that occasion whether they would have recognized a *separate* conceptual realm that overlaps even if partially with our usual 'dtr' or better, 'dtrs' and if so, what would have been the pragmatic or communicative meaning of *their* encountering 'dtr' features in these texts.

The present contribution is a response to an invitation to address the question of what would happen if instead of focusing on Joshua-Kings,[2] we turn our attention to the book of Jeremiah, in some version or versions for which the present versions of the book may be considered representative.[3] In other words, what did encountering 'dtr' features 'do' to these readers of Jeremiah; how did it affect their readings, the social memories evoked by these readings and the ability of both, readings and memories to reflect, shape and explore their general worldview? In sum, what would have been the significance and social and communicative role of dtr features *in this particular context*.[4]

---

[1] E. Ben Zvi, "On the Term Deuteronomistic in Relation to Joshua–Kings in the Persian Period," in K. L. Noll and B. Schramm (eds.), *Raising Up a Faithful Exegete: Essays in Honor of Richard D. Nelson* (Winona Lake, Ind.: Eisenbrauns, 2010), 61–71. Cf. also my "The Communicative Message of Some Linguistic Choices," in E. Ben Zvi, D. V. Edelman and F. Polak (eds.), *A Palimpsest: Rhetoric, Ideology, Stylistics and Language Relating to Persian Israel* (Piscataway, NJ: Gorgias Press, 2009), 269–290.

[2] This contribution originated in an oral, invited presentation for an SBL session devoted to Jeremiah.

[3] The present analysis requires only that these texts are *representative* of the texts that existed in the repertoire of the community. Whether the relevant community existed in the late Persian or early (or at least, pre-Hasmonean) Hellenistic period has no significant bearing on the discussion here, since the argument does not depend on a precise dating of the texts.

[4] It is worth stressing at this point that the lengthy and complex textual history of Jeremiah, as interesting as it may be, has no real bearing, even if one were to grant that it can be fully and

Before addressing these questions, a few remarks are necessary to clarify the approach taken here and the type of research questions and issues that it raises, which are not necessarily those raised by other approaches. First of all, my approach stresses, and needs to stress, reading because the text that impacts the community, the one that reflects and contributes to its worldview is *the community's read text*, that is, the text that members of the group *read/understood/remembered*.[5] In addition, at least in our case, the communities not only or even mainly remembered 'texts,' but also, through the process of reading them, they evoked and shaped their memories of the past and their main sites of memory (which included central prophetic figures of the past, e. g., Moses, Jeremiah, Isaiah).[6] These socially shared memories contributed much not only to socialization and social cohesion but also shaped and provided a general playground on which to explore matters that interested the community.[7]

No community (or individual for that matter) ever read texts in a vacuum. Communities read texts in ways informed by their world of knowledge, their ideological viewpoints and social attitudes.[8] Moreover, texts are read in a way informed by the other texts that exist within the community. While this is true in general, this is even truer within a small community of literati who construed themselves as a text-centered Israel. In other words, when these literati read Jeremiah, they did so in way informed by other texts included in the repertoire of the community and, *vice versa*, reading Jeremiah contributed to their readings of the other texts.

There is no evidence whatsoever that when the literati of the early Second Temple period read their texts, they did so as contemporary redactional critical scholars. It is extremely unlikely that their reading process involved first dividing each text into multiple redactional layers, then assigning each to a particular period in their construed past, and then approaching each text in a way informed by other texts they reconstructed in the said manner, and which they thought belonged to the same repertoire as the particular layer of the text they were read-

---

faithfully reconstructed, because it is extremely unlikely that the literati read the text and imagined the character Jeremiah in way that was substantially informed by knowledge of such a history. See below.

5 A strong awareness of the historical contingency and the social character, roles and impact of readings underlies the recent flourishing of the field of 'reception history.'
6 The prophetic books served to draw attention to and shape memories of prophetic characters of the past; in other words, the prophetic books served to bring the prophets to the remembering community, certainly not the other way around.
7 See below.
8 Even if, or likely even more so since the process was dynamic, and the reading of texts contributed to the shaping of the latter.

ing.⁹ Instead, it is reasonable to assume that from the perspective of the relevant ancient readers, as well as from that of the vast majority of readers transculturally, the *implied author* of a book/text was the communicator whose intention they needed to grasp.¹⁰

Before we continue another fundamental aspect of the community of readers discussed here must not only be taken into account, but also placed at the center of any study of the present matter. I am referring to the historical fact that neither Jeremiah nor Joshua-Kings was read in late Persian or early Hellenistic Judah by some *socially separate* 'dtr' group that read, wrote and thought only in dtr language and expressions. For one, it is very problematic to re-construct sociallyseparate, exclusive groups within the few Jerusalem-centered, at least ideologically, literati of the time on the basis of the use of particular linguistic expressions,¹¹ or for that matter, to reconstruct historical, socially exclusive groups on the grounds of language alone.¹²

But even more importantly for our purposes, as the literati read Jeremiah, they construed and remembered a prophet Jeremiah who could easily speak with a dtr flavour or without it. Moreover, Jeremiah is certainly not unique in this matter. The implied authors of Joshua, Judges, Samuel and Kings could

---

9 To be sure, to read texts this way is a good and appropriate academic endeavor today, but not what ancient Israelites did. Although diachronic analyses may help us to construct reconstructions of how the relevant books reached their present form/s, they are not the best tool to study the ways in which the texts were likely read by the relevant reading communities. Just as etymology is not the best tool for studying the pragmatic meaning of a conversation, the mentioned approaches are not the best for the particular endeavour advanced here.

10 Cf. G. Rusch, "Comprehension vs. Understanding of Literature," in S. Tötösy de Zepetnek and I. Sywenky (eds.), *The Systemic and Empirical Approach to Literature and Culture as Theory and Application* (Siegen: Siegen University, 1997), 107–119 (p. 115).

11 When sociolects (or even languages in multi-lingual societies) are used that way, they serve to construe and enforce social boundaries. They construe, exclude and marginalize the 'other' and produce a sense of social cohesion binding together the inner-group.

12 As it is well-known, people may and do actually use various 'sociolects' and choose which one to use (often even in a non-self-conscious way) according to the need of particular social performances and communicative acts. I discussed some of these issues in E. Ben Zvi, "On the Term Deuteronomistic," idem, "Communicative Message" and idem, "Towards and Integrative Study of the Production of Authoritative Books in Ancient Israel," D. V. Edelman and E. Ben Zvi (eds.), *The Production of Prophecy. Constructing Prophecy and Prophets in Yehud* (London: Equinox, 2009), 15–28; cf., e.g., Konrad Schmid, *The Old Testament. A Literary History* (Minneapolis: Fortress, 2012), 31; R. Rezetko, "The (Dis)Connection between Textual and Linguistic Developments in the Book of Jeremiah: Hebrew Bible Textual Criticism Challenges Biblical Hebrew Historical Linguistics," R. F. Person Jr. and R. Rezetko (eds.), *Empirical Models Challenging Biblical Criticism* (SBLAIL, 25; Atlanta: SBL Press, 2016), 239–69 and bibliography.

use dtr dictions or not use them and, needless to say, Moses was remembered as speaking and embodying D and P. [13]

Although neither textual characters or the related personages of memory that the texts evoke nor the implied authors of the books that the community reads are just masked projections of the readers, it stands to reason that the literati did not construe ancient authors, with whom they were supposed to identify, as completely different from themselves. If their heroes and their implied authors did not use dictions to represent and reinforce boundaries between an in-group and an out-group, why would they? If their heroes and their implied authors actually embodied a mixture of dictions,[14] why would these literati not be able to activate multiple dictions, as they deem appropriate for their particular communicative or performance needs, and even as a performance by itself?[15]

But matters do not stop at multiple 'dictions'. Jeremiah (and Moses and Abraham and many others central sites of memory) were construed and remembered as characters expressing and even embodying multiple and at least seemingly contradictory views. The point is well-known and therefore, only a few examples are necessary for the present purposes. For instance, and selecting only those that deal with Jeremiah, and with core, not marginal, issues in the discourse of the community, readers of Jer 15:1–4 remembered that the destruction of Jerusalem was made unavoidable by the sins of Manasseh and no amount of pleading (or repentance) would have helped (cf. Jer 11:14), but is this fully consistent with a central memory of Jeremiah as the last monarchic prophet in a long series of prophets calling for repentance (see Jer 26:2–3; 36:2–7; cf. Jer 7:25; 25:4–5, passim) or is it fully consistent with other sections of Jeremiah

---

[13] It may be mentioned that the words of the remembered Jeremiah—including those associated with the voice of Yhwh as reported by him—were at times reminiscent of words associated with a number of other prophets of memory that populated the community and, as importantly, vice versa, e.g., Jer 31:29 and cf. Ezek 18:2 (and Ezek 3:18; 33:8); Jer 34:5 and cf. Ezek 23:34; 26:5; 28:10; 39:5; Jer 49:7–22 and cf. Obad 1–7; Jer 2:15; 4:7; 9:11; 26:9 and cf. Zeph 3:6; and cf. the oracle against Moab in Isa 15 and Jer 48. This is, again, not unusual within the core repertoire and memory of the community. Cf. also Jer 10:13 and Ps 135:7; Jer 10:25 and Ps 79:6–7. As for Moses being remembered as speaking 'P' and 'D' and its implications, see "Exploring the Memory of Moses 'The Prophet' in Late Persian/Early Hellenistic Yehud/Judah," in this volume, pp. 199–231.

[14] Within the same or similar 'register'.

[15] It is worth mentioning that the literati were not only involved in the 'consumption' of prophetic and other types of core literature within the repertoire of the community, but also in their productions. How would they know how to produce texts, unless by reading similar texts and by imitating their implied authors, knowingly or unknowingly? But, if so, what does it say, about the texts they produced?

(e. g., Jer 4:1–2; 5:1; 18:1–11/12)? But this is not all, they also remembered that Zedekiah and the people of his time could have avoided the catastrophe (e. g., Jer 27:12–15; 34:8–22; 38:17–23) and that also Jehoiakim could have behaved differently and ensured that kings from David will remain on the throne (e. g., Jer 22:1–5). Another example, the readers remembered that there will be a great future for the Davidic dynasty and that this future is at least at the connoted level associated with Zedekiah (Jer 33:15–17),[16] but also that his sons were killed; that Jehoiachin holds the/a potential for the restoration of the House of David, but also that "none of his [Jehoiachin's] offspring shall succeed in sitting on the throne of David, and ruling again in Judah" (Jer 22:28–30).[17] In addition, they remembered and associated with their Jeremiah a future utopian world in which a future 'David' or even the monarchy are absent (Jer 31:31–40; cf. Jer 50:4–5). A final example, the readers imagined and remembered Jeremiah as the post-Moses prophet par excellence who urged the people, and though implicitly, but most importantly, the readers, that is, the community remembering Jeremiah and his deeds to follow the ברית (Jer 11:1–8[18]), and thus as fulfilling one of the roles of Moses and actually becoming a second—though necessarily secondary—Moses. Yet they also remembered him as the figure who embodied the hope of a different ברית that would obviate the need for teachers of the covenant and likely of prophets like Jeremiah himself (Jer 31:31–34).[19] We may call

---

16 The name of the future king in the LXX version is Iosedek. Cf. J. Lust, "Messianism and the Greek Version of Jeremiah: Jer 23,5–6 and 33,14–26," in J. Lust and K. Hauspie (eds.), *Messianism and the Septuagint: Collected Essays* (BETL, 178; Leuven: Leuven University Press, 2004), 41–67 (42–54, 66) and Hermann-Josef Stipp, "Zedekiah in the Book of Jeremiah: On the Formation of a Biblical Character," *CBQ* 58 (1996), 627–648 (644, n. 36). The point is that for the present purposes what counts is how the literati of the Late Persian or early Hellenistic Judah likely read this text, both at the denotative and connotative levels, and in this context, it is reasonable to assume that the reference was understood as both pointing at a future king and at the same evoking the last king of Judah. On memories of Zedekiah as last ruler among the literati we are discussing here, see "Reshaping the Memory of Zedekiah and his Period in Chronicles," in this volume, pp. 342–66.
17 On these issues from a redactional approach, see J. Pakkala, "Zedekiah's Fate and the Dynastic Succession," *JBL* 125 (2006), 443–452.
18 Verse 7 and most of 8 are not in the LXX. Their absence may influence the setting of the world portrayed in the book, but they have no bearing on the fact that the reading community imagined Jeremiah as (also) talking to them and urging them to follow the ברית.
19 Readers probably wondered if this is not the בְּרִית עוֹלָם promised in Jer 50:4–5 and which they certainly hoped. Also cf. Jer 31:31–34 and Ezek 36:26–27. I discussed likely underlying discursive reasons for emergence of this type of utopian thinking, in my "Analogical Thinking and Ancient Israel Intellectual History: The Case for an 'Entropy Model' in the Study of Israelite

this latter image, post-deuteronomistic, or even anti-deuteronomistic, but doing so would only stress the point that Jeremiah is remembered as both voicing and embodying 'deuteronomistic' and a 'non-' or 'anti- or 'post-deuteronomistic' approaches at the same time.

Examples can easily be multiplied. In fact, any scholar who differentiates between dtr and non-dtr texts within the book of Jeremiah makes this point time and again.[20] But a crucial detail, or at least, its significance, is frequently missed, namely the very fact that the community imagined and remembered Jeremiah as a character who was (in our terms) 'dtr' and 'non-dtr' at the very same time. If their Jeremiah was both 'dtr' and 'non-dtr,' why not they themselves, the readers, who after all, were supposed to identify with and learn from their Jeremiah (of memory)?

Further, there is nothing strange about the shaping of such a multivocal, multi-diction and one may say 'fuzzy' site of memory we may label Jeremiah among the literati of the time. Many of the great figures of the past that populated their memory, including the 'forerunner' of Jeremiah, Moses, were precisely constructed like that. In fact, there was a systemic preference for this type of memories insofar it concerns main sites of memory.[21]

Multi-diction contributed much not only to the shaping the prophetic characters of memory as fuzzy and integrative but also as distinct, and thus more memorable individuals, because each shows a different multi-diction spectrum. For instance, the overall multi-diction spectrum of Moses was different from that of Jeremiah, and the latter from that of Isaiah and so on. The very prominent exception to this system of individualizing by means of a particular multi-diction is YHWH who was imagined and remembered as talking to each prophet within the multi-diction spectrum that characterized such a prophet. But, in fact, this 'universal' multi-diction spectrum is by itself an 'individualized' spectrum. In fact, it is not surprising at all that YHWH was imagined and remembered as distinct from human beings, including prophets, by having a kind of 'omni'-multi-diction spectrum.

Where does all this leave us? If the concept of particular dtr dictions and ideologies is to be heuristically helpful for the study of this Jeremiah of memory, its social roles within the community and they ways in which it reflected and

---

Thought," in T. J. Sandoval and C. Mandolfo (eds.), (JSOTSup, 384; London: T&T Clark International, 2003) 321–332.
20 Almost all contemporary scholars are involved, in one way or another, in this project of differentiation or simply imply it.
21 I wrote on these matters elsewhere. See, e. g., "Exploring the Memory of Moses 'The Prophet' in Late Persian/Early Hellenistic Yehud/Judah" and bibliography.

contributed to the shaping of the intellectual discourse of the literati discussed here, I would say that its helpfulness resides precisely in its ability to draw prominent attention to the multivocal, fuzzy character of such a Jeremiah of memory. It is this Jeremiah who, by bringing together all these various 'voices' into one mnemonic figure, shaped a (play)ground in which the relevant community could explore, negotiate and integrate these, at times seemingly contradicting, Jeremianic voices.²²

But, of course, there is more. The relatively high density of occurrences of dtr diction in Jeremiah has been noticeable to readers of any period,²³ including, of

---

22 Of course, not everything was fuzzy and open for serious negotiation within the discourse of the community. For instance, in a Jerusalem/temple centered community one is to expect a strong dis-preference for authoritative texts that reject in principle the legitimacy of the Jerusalem Temple. Neither Jer 7:25 nor for that matter 1 Sam 15:22; Hos 6:6; or Ps 50 or Ps 51:16 raise any problem in this regard, and in general Jer 7:1–15 reminded the community of a rather self-evident point from the perspective of the literati in the late Persian or early Hellenistic period, namely that the temple itself cannot (and did not) protect wrongdoers from YHWH's justified judgment. To be sure, it made sense for them to imagine a proper prophet living at the time proclaiming these matters to the people and that served a didactic purpose, and so did the list of wrongdoings associated with the sinning community (which not surprisingly, included a combination of what we would call 'ethical' and 'ritual' wrongs). Perhaps, more interesting, for the purpose of exploring the social mindscape of the community, is the implied construction of a conceptual realm expressed by the term מקום in which the temple, Jerusalem and the land overlap (vv. 3, 7, 12, 14), allowing for the symbolic encompassment of the last two by the temple, rather than the usual of the land by its capital city. In a backhanded way, from the perspective of the literati the text may well shape and reflect a very temple-centred perspective. These matters, however, require a separate discussion. For Jer 7 as not an anti-temple text *per se* in recent decades see, e.g., R. P. Carroll, *Jeremiah* (OTL; Philadelphia: Westminster, 1986), 214–217; T. Römer, "How Did Jeremiah Become a Convert to Deuteronomistic Ideology?," in L. S. Schearing and S. L. McKenzie (eds.), (JSOTSup, 268; Sheffield Academic Press: Sheffield, 1999) 189–199; M. Avioz, "A Rhetorical Analysis of Jeremiah 7:1–15," *Tyndale Bulletin* 57 (2006), 173–189 and bibliography mentioned there. See also M. Leuchter, "The Temple Sermon and the Term מקום in the Jeremianic Corpus," *JSOT* 30 (2005), 93–109. For a different approach, see, E. K. Holt, "Jeremiah's Temple Sermon and the Deuteronomists: An Investigation of the Redactional Relationship between Jeremiah 7 and 26," *JSOT* 36 (1986), 78–81.

23 B. Bab. Bat. 15a. Isaac Abravanel proposed that Jeremiah compiled the book of Samuel and that Samuel in turn wrote Joshua and Judges, perhaps showing an incipient sense of what we may refer as the 'deuteronomistical' historical collection). It is interesting also that Isho'dad of Merv (mid-ninth century C.E., Syrian father of the Church) maintained that the Hilkiah who found the סֵפֶר הַתּוֹרָה in Josiah's days (see 2 Kgs 22:8–10) was the father of the prophet Jeremiah. Isho'dad claimed that the book was not only Deuteronomy, but the copy that Moses had placed in the Ark as a precaution. It seems that some connection between Jeremiah and Deuteronomy and even Kings was perceived. (Incidentally, Isho'dad explains that the reason for Moses' precaution was the danger in which the book would have been had it been found at another

course, the literati of the early Second Temple period. From the perspective of the reading community the main communicative effect of this diction was to shape reminiscences and evoke memories. Dtr style and phraseology was most likely understood by the literati as reminiscent of the language of Deuteronomy and of the particular Moses to which reading and remembering texts and events reported in Deuteronomy drew particular attention; a sense of 'Mosaic-like'.[24]

Beyond the (obvious) observation that such a sense connoted a sense of 'authority,' the significance of the conveyed association varied depending on the text the community was reading. For instance, the presence, at times, of a Mosaic-like voice resonating through the dtr historical collection played a substantial role in appropriating the figure of Moses for the Jerusalem-centered discourse of Yehud and rhetorically and ideologically undermining the connection between Moses and Samarian claims, because this collection is certainly not advancing Samarian claims. It goes without saying that the same can be said of the book of Jeremiah.

But not everything has to do with Samaria. Texts that evoked or were reminiscent of Moses' voice served also to appropriate in some way his figure and thus to *partially shift* the contents of his message to increase its compatibility and ideological coherence with certain positions or particular personages of old populating the relevant Moses-evoking text and thus, *inter alia*, increase their relative weight (and mindshare) within the reading community. A good example of this tendency is the known trend to *partially* construe Ezekiel as a second (and necessarily secondary) Moses[25] and the presence of Mosaic-like expressions, though certainly not confined to the Moses evoked in Deuteronomy.[26]

There is no doubt that the same can be said of Jeremiah. The differences are only that in the case of Jeremiah the process is even more obvious, due to the

---

time; Isho'dad explicitly compares the potential fate of this copy of Deuteronomy with the fate of the burnt prophecy of Jeremiah.)

24 To be sure, this was a partial memory of Moses that informed and was informed by other partial memories of Moses as all together shaped, evoked and reflected the comprehensive and integrative Moses of the community, but these matters necessitate another layer of analysis that cannot be explored in this essay. For the present purposes it suffices to note that these linguistic choices communicated a sense of 'Mosaic-like.'

25 See H. McKeating, "Ezekiel the 'Prophet Like Moses'?," *JSOT* 101 (1994), 97–109.

26 For 'dtr' examples, see e.g., Ezek 20:5; 32:9; the use of the term גילולים. One may note a sense of appropriation and reshaping of memories evoked by reading Deuteronomy and some texts in Joshua-Kings in, for instance, Ezek 20. On these type of issues, cf. C. L. Patton, "Pan-Deuteronomism and the Book of Ezekiel," in L. S. Schearing and S. L. McKenzie (eds.), (JSOTSup, 268; Sheffield Academic Press: Sheffield, 1999) 200–215 (esp. 205–208).

higher frequency of Mosaic-like expressions, and that the text draws attention mainly to the Moses evoked within the community by reading Deuteronomy.²⁷

These observations work not only at the level of books or general characterization of personages such as Jeremiah or Ezekiel. They work also at the level of particular readings or literary units within a prophetic book. For example, (a) the language of Jer 31:31–34 and (b) its association with (i) the YHWH that was experienced by the character Jeremiah within the world of the book, and indirectly but more importantly, by the readers of the book of Jeremiah as well, and (ii) with the Mosaic-like figure of Jeremiah held by these readers, contributed much to the ability of this text to evoke, inform and shape the potential range of significance of the concept of בְּרִית that the literati construed when reading Deuteronomy.²⁸

To be sure, the process worked both ways: the other texts also informed and thus partially shaped the potential range of significance evoked by Jer 31:31–34. In other words, the 'Mosaic-like' features of Jer 31:31–34 facilitated the creation of an in-between mnemonic playground within the general sites of memory of Jeremiah and Moses in which important ideological concerns could be explored, including human and thus Israelite tendencies to transgress, the problematic character of education and its limitations, and the absolute centrality of YHWH's *torah* for well-being.

It is important to keep in mind that a 'Mosaic-like' voice resonating in a text did not evoke only associations with Moses and thus with Deuteronomy, but also with other texts within which such a voice resonated and with their implied authors. In the case of Jeremiah, the presence, at times, of such a voice evoked an association between Jeremiah, the prophet who the readers reconstructed and virtually encountered when reading the text, and the implied author of the Book of Kings. But where does this observation lead us in terms of memories of Jeremiah and of the book of Jeremiah as read by the community? ²⁹

---

27 To be sure, the mnemonic generative grammar creating these 'appropriations' and 're-significations' of both the 'new' and the old 'Moses' is at work not only in prophetic books and there is no reason why it should be restricted to them. See, among many others, Ezra as second Moses (and second Joshua?), Stephen in Acts 7. This mnemonic generative grammar continues in fact, in some attenuated ways, even in contemporary times (e. g., the multiple cases of 'new Moses' in US mnemonic and ideological discourses that shape the constructions of memories not only of the 'new' but also of the 'old' Moses).
28 Of course, this is true, to the extent of the mindshare that Jer 31:31–34 had in the community.
29 To be sure, in later periods in which matters of individual authorship were important, there might have emerged some preference to address these issues from such a perspective; but none of the books in the primary historical collection (Gen–2 Kgs), the deuteronomistic historical collection (usually called, the 'deuteronomistic history') and I would add the collection of prophetic

To begin with, the communicative effect of mutually echoing 'Mosaic-like' phraseology between these two books led to the creation of a blended mental space in which the remembered Jeremiah and the voice of the implied author of Kings could participate and interact in the creation of meanings. Moreover, such a connection was, undoubtedly and mutually reinforced, by the presence of shared texts, namely 2 Kgs 24:18–25:21 and Jer 52:1–27 and 2 Kgs 25:27–30 //Jer 52:31–34 and by what the literati likely understood to be a kind of expansion of 2 Kgs 25:22–25 into a larger story in Jer 40:1–43:7, and *vice versa*, namely as they read 2 Kgs 25:22–25 as a kind of summary of what the implied author of Kings suggested to the readers was particularly worthy of being remembered about the story of Jer 40:1–43:7.

In any event, the end result of these processes is a blurring of boundaries. 'Historical' texts become 'prophetic' and *vice versa*, 'prophetic texts' and even books become a proper venue for 'historical' texts. This observation has significant implications for the discourse of the community. Moreover, it is consistent with other trends within the discourse of the late Persian or early Hellenistic Yehud/Judah such as constructions of prophets as 'historians' (see Chronicles[30]) and of the 'national' history of Israel expressed in the dtr historical collection "as a long and elaborate fulfillment of Moses' statements about its future (see Deut 30:1–5; 32:19–25 and, among others, the pragmatic message in late Persian Yehud of Deut 28:15–68; 29:13–27; 30:17–19; 31:19–22)." To be sure, this "meant construing and making memorable within the community a 'historical' plotline that leads directly to the fulfillment of Deut 30:2–10 (and cf. Deut 32:26–43)"[31] and thus shaping and expressing an overarching metanarrative that moves from past catastrophe to a new beginning. Significantly, this is the very same overarching meta-narrative that the collection of prophetic books communicated time and again, including, of course, the book of Jeremiah as well.

---

books (Isa-Mal) have marked individual authors, even if they have central characters. Obviously, this is not a 'random' phenomenon but of a strong preference for emphasizing the communal character of these books and collections which went hand in hand with a strong ideological and social preference to shape self-effacing literati, including actual writers and readers. On these matters and their possible implications, see, e.g. E. Blum, "Historiography or Poetry? The Peculiarities of the Hebrew Prose Tradition," in L. T. Stuckenbruck, S. C. Barton and B. G. Wold (eds), *Memory in the Bible and Antiquity: The Fifth Durham-Tübingen Research Symposium (Durham, September 2004)* (WUNT, 212; Tübingen: 2007), pp. 25–45.

30 See 1 Chr 29:29; 2 Chr 12:15; 13:22; 32:32.

31 This and the previous citation are from "Exploring the Memory of Moses" in this volume and see discussion there.

The blurring of boundaries between 'historical' and 'prophetic' texts by the community and at some level the attenuation of the gap between the voice of the implied author of Kings and that of the book of Jeremiah shaped an in-between space that facilitated the exploration of additional issues concerning main mnemonic narratives of Israel and the calamity of the destruction and its aftermath.

Reading Jer 40:1–43:7 meant imagining a (counterfactual) past in which Gedaliah could have succeeded; a past in which Israel could have remained in the land and prospered under a non-Davidic governor and as a loyal province of a foreign king, appointed by Yhwh to control 'the world,' which at that time meant the Babylonian king.[32] Certainly such a point resonated within a Persian or later community and from that perspective Jer 51 may be seen as a memory that allowed the community to transition from a Babylonian to a Persian empire, and thus reshape the message of Jeremiah concerning the importance of accepting Yhwh's decision to appoint a foreign 'world king' into a general, cross-temporal/cross-empire message valid to the community, as much as it was to those in the world in which the prophet Jeremiah, as they construed him, lived. In others, it meant removing the element of historical contingency from these messages.[33] Reading Kings in a way strongly informed by Jer 40:6–12 meant also reading 2 Kgs 25:22–25 within this perspective.[34]

But there is more, in Jeremiah, unlike Kings, Gedaliah is not alone (40:6). A true prophet, Jeremiah, is with him and Gedaliah (clearly, though implicitly) follows his advice. A community could exist and prosper in the land without a Davidic king, without Jerusalem, even without a temple, even after Gedaliah's assassination, but only if they had listened to Yhwh's word through Yhwh's prophet, Jeremiah (Jer 42:7–12). Conversely, within this mnemonic narrative

---

[32] See "The Voice and Role of a Counterfactual Memory in the Construction of Exile and Return: Considering Jeremiah 40:7–12," in this volume, pp. 612–30.

[33] The point was balanced, as usual in the discourse of the community, by references to utopian futures. See the common notion of a future empire of Yhwh centered in Zion that existed at the time within the community. These notions allowed for ideological resistance while at the same time facilitating the political accommodation of the local elite with the empire.

[34] Of course, reading one text in a way informed by the other and noticing that the read text was 'their text' that the community thought it has contributed much to remove the uneasiness created among contemporary scholars, but not necessarily among ancient readers discussed here, by the lack of explicit reference to Jeremiah in Kings. 2 Chr 36:12 is most likely not a drastic innovation, but a reflection of at least one version of how literati very well aware of Jeremiah would have imagined the world evoked in 2 Kgs 25.

the land becomes empty when that true prophet, who is again rejected, is forced into exile.³⁵

To some extent, Jeremiah becomes a figure similar to that of the Chronicles' prophet Oded (2 Chr 28:9–15), who also prophesied to a kingless Israel. But significantly, the Northern Israelites of Oded's time become a reverse image of the Judahites of Jeremiah's, because the former listened to the prophet and the others rejected him. Both Oded and Jeremiah come to exemplify a particular aspect of the political thought of the community in the late Persian or early Hellenistic period, namely kings may come and go, political structures may come and go, even the temple may momentarily disappear—it was closed in the world evoked by 2 Chr 28, but one thing must remain: there must be 'prophetic' guardianship within the community. Only when there exists both (a) a prophet/guardian/teacher/preacher of Yhwh's will and (b) a leadership and a people in general willing to listen to Yhwh, the basic, necessary—though not necessarily sufficient—requirement for the well-being of the community is fulfilled.³⁶

The inclusion of 'history' into 'prophetic texts' mentioned above is consonant with this development in political thought and the eventual characterization of the dtr historical collection as 'prophetic.' The existence of a communal sense of resemblance between Jeremiah and the implied author of Kings discussed above smoothed' the process and by doing so facilitated the adoption of its message.

The emergence of an in-between space for historical narration between Kings and Jeremiah led to a situation in which communal, preferred generative grammars governing the production of these stories could work across book boundaries. Thus, for instance, one may easily notice the structuring of an oppositional mnemonic pattern linking Sennacherib (the foreign king who was de-

---

35 Note also the precise language in Jer 43:6 אֶת־גְּדַלְיָהוּ בֶּן־אֲחִיקָם בֶּן־שָׁפָן וְאֶת־יִרְמְיָהוּ הַנָּבִיא וְאֶת־בָּרוּךְ בֶּן־נֵרִיָּהוּ and the very meaningful double meaning shaped around אֶת. It is worth stressing that up to this point, Jeremiah was, as it were, a physical symbol of his own message, because he, through obeying Yhwh's commands, became an embodiment of both the latter and the importance of obeying Yhwh; cf. C. Levin, "The 'Word of Yahweh': A Theological Concept in the Book of Jeremiah" in idem, Re-Reading the Scriptures (FAT, 87; Tübingen: Mohr Siebeck, 2013), 221–243. But Jer 43:6 is a turning point in the story. Jeremiah's very presence in Egypt stands not only as an embodiment of the people's disobedience, but also of their act of forcefully making the prophet behave, even if involuntarily, against Yhwh's will. Given that he is partially construed as a second Moses, this would be equivalent to a story about the Exodus not only coming back to Egypt, but also taking Moses with them.
36 I discussed the concept of prophetic guardianship in Israel in my "Memory and Political Thought in the Late Persian/Early Hellenistic Yehud/Judah: Some Observations," in Diana V. Edelman and Ehud Ben Zvi (eds.) (WANEM; London: Equinox, 2016), 9–26.

feated before Jerusalem) and Nebuchadnezzar (the successful foreign king who conquered Jerusalem). Significantly, there is a closely related, secondary pattern of their main servants, who symbolically take their role, namely Rabshakeh, the one who mocked 'dtr' teachings and its worldview—at a time when Hezekiah accepted them—and Nebuzaradan 'the one who followed 'dtr.' teachings'—at a time when the Judahite elite rejected them. This pattern emerged across the boundaries separating books, thus reflecting a social memory that goes beyond them, a process facilitated by the binding together of these stories and the relevant memories by a shared 'dtr'/Mosaic-like bond.[37]

To be sure, other mnemonic narrative existed in the community about exile and its reasons. Moreover, as mentioned above, Jer 40:1–43:7 and the memories it evoked informed the readings and memories evoked by 2 Kgs 25:22–25, but the process also worked the other way around, and when it did, other meanings emerged. The overall result of the workings of these balancing processes is that social memory constituted a shared ground (and one may say a 'language') by means of which central concepts within the community could be explored and negotiated. There is nothing odd about this, since a common transcultural way to explore and negotiate concepts is by means of mnemonic narratives about particular events or personages of the past.[38]

I hope that these preliminary considerations suffice to show the heuristic value of perspectives that emerge when, instead of focusing on ancient authors and editors, we focus on the texts as they were likely read by the literati of the late Persian (or early Hellenistic) period, the message conveyed by the placement of 'deuteronomistic' language in the mouth of particular characters whose memory was evoked through the reading of a book like Jeremiah, and the community that read such a book as part of a larger repertoire of texts and which remembered (and thus construed) Jeremiah and multiple other characters of the past.

---

[37] The presence of generative grammars working and shaping memory across book boundaries is easily noticeable in other instances. See, for instance, "Reshaping the Memory of Zedekiah." This phenomenon also makes far less important for the literati discussed here the absence of any explicit reference to Jeremiah in the text of Kings. After all, for them memory works as a system encompassing multiple images. See also note above. A full discussion of the absence of an explicit reference to Jeremiah in Kings goes beyond the scope of this paper and as mentioned here was most likely not a problem for the community whose memory and intellectual world I am exploring here.

[38] As I discussed in some recent essays, e. g., "Reshaping the Memory of Zedekiah," Period" and "Chronicles and Samuel-Kings: Two Interacting Aspects of one Memory System in the Late Persian/Early Hellenistic Period," in this volume, pp. 317–31 and in "Memory and Political Thought."

Chronicles and Samuel–Kings: Two Interacting Aspects of one Memory System in the Late Persian / Early Hellenistic Period*

1 Introduction

A main social role of the Yehudite historiographic writings in Late Persian/early Hellenistic Yehud/Judah was to encode, evoke, and contribute to processes of shaping social memory.[1] The latter served important roles for identity formation, communal social reproduction and provided tools and concepts to explore and to "make sense" of the world. To be sure, it was the historiographic writings as "read" texts that evoked and shaped social memory.[2] This almost self-evident observation raises, however, less self-evident issues. Communities never read books in a vacuum.[3] When the remembering community read these historiographic texts, they did so informed by their world of knowledge, ideological viewpoints and social attitudes, even if, or likely even more so since the process was dynamic and the reading of texts contributed to the shaping of the latter.

Moreover, when the remembering community read these historical works, they proceed to construe what their "authorial voices" or "communicators" were saying to them. They recognized that each communicator (i.e., the communally-shaped, implied authors of Samuel–Kings and Chronicles) spoke

---

* First published in *Rereading the Relecture? The Question of (Post)chronistic Influence in the Latest Redactions of the Books of Samuel* (eds. U. Becker and H. Bezzel; FAT II, 66; Tübingen: Mohr Siebeck, 2014), 41–56.

1 It is worth mentioning from the outset that in terms of social memory, my approach is particularly informed by the work of scholars such as E. Zerubavel and B. Schwartz and less by those of, for instance, A. and J. Assmann. Of course, all are intellectual descendants in one way or another of M. Halbwachs. For basic literature about these approaches see Zerubavel, *Social Mindscapes*; idem, *Time Maps*; idem, *Ancestors*; B. Schwartz, *Abraham Lincoln*; idem, *Collective Forgetting*; A. Assmann, *Cultural Memory*; J. Assmann, *Religion*. See also Wertsch, *Voices*. For my own approach to social memory in ancient Israel, see, the introduction to this volume.

2 Of course, other texts also shaped and evoked social memory, but this essay focuses on historiographic books, and in fact, only on a selection of them, Samuel–Kings and Chronicles.

3 The (by necessity, reconstructed) reading community discussed in this essay consists, of course, of the literati of Late Persian/Early Hellenistic Yehud/Judah. To be sure, their readings may have been communicated, even if in a partial way, to other groups in society. The ability of contemporary historians to reconstruct the historical "passed on" meanings of various groups is minimal. A study of these matters goes, in any event, well beyond the scope of the present essay.

in his voice or his range of voices,[4] evoked particular memories, shaped narrative paths connecting them usually according to preferred types of mnemonic plots,[5] and drew attention to or away from some aspects of central communal sites of memory (e.g., David, Samuel, Saul, and Jerusalem). Of course, at the same time, the community construed these "communicators" in a way informed by their world of knowledge and general social mindscape.[6] All of these are normal procedures in processes of reading.[7]

It is particularly noteworthy in this context that the literati's main sites of memory tended to include and express multiple voices and that all of these voices were often embodied in and communicated by one mnemonic figure, and thus interrelated and integrated. For instance, the Moses remembered by a community of readers of the late Persian/early Hellenistic period spoke in both D and P and said a variety of things that may be seem in logical tension, but the community associated them all with Moses; in fact, Moses was the embodiment of them all. The same tendency held true for the literati's implied authors. These observations point to a crucial characteristic of the social mindscape of these literati, namely a tendency to favor, within limits, integrative and integrated diversity and the related sense of fuzziness without which the latter cannot exist.[8]

The literati in late Persian/Early Hellenistic who read both Samuel–Kings and Chronicles from within the very same social location, shared not only the mentioned preference for fuzziness and integrative mnemonic constructions, but also other socially preferred ways of constructing memories, including, inter alia, preferences for particular mnemonic plots and types of narratives and mnemonic expectations in terms of characterizations of main heroes and villains, or holy spaces. Perhaps even more importantly, they shared a similar set of underlying matters to voice and explore through memories. In fact, mnemonic narratives and sites of memory became one of the main tools available to the community to formulate and explore, whether in ways known or unbeknownst to the literati, concepts, conceptual tensions and a wide variety of issues in

---

4 Very unlikely to be "her", given their historical gendered constructions of the period.
5 By preferred plots, I refer to socially-preferred plots. It is worth noting however, that there are strong cross-cultural preferences for particular types of plots, and often it is among them that societies arrange their preferences, which, of course, shift according to the circumstances in which these societies exist, on whom they interact and their prevalent social mindscape. See, for instance, Zerubavel, *Social Mindscapes*; cf. idem, *Time Maps*.
6 Such a social mindscape included, inter alia, ways of thinking, generating ideas, raising questions and means of addressing them, of providing meaning to "data" and generative grammars for developing and constructing social memories in certain preferred ways.
7 Cf. Rusch, *Comprehension*, 107–119, esp. 115.
8 See, for instance, "Exploring the Memory" in this volume, pp. 199–231.

their ideological discourse. Given that (a) none of the above is contingent on the particular book the literati happen to read at a moment but a reflection of their shared, social world of knowledge and general mindscape, (b) the Yehudite literati of the time shared all the above, (c) there was more or less a set range of socially possible ways of addressing these matters that was also shared,[9] and (d) the better some memories provided a socially appropriate "language" to approach these matters, the more likely such memories were to be accepted and transmitted by the community, then should we not anticipate parallel and interacting mnemonic formations to develop in readings of texts across the boundaries of Samuel–Kings on the one hand and Chronicles on the other?

In what follows, I would like to provide concrete examples that show the value, at the very least the heuristic value, of the previous considerations for historical studies of the intellectual world and ideology in the largest possible sense of the ideologically, Jerusalem-centred literati of the period. Given the genre constraints and length limitations that characterize essays, I will bring forward only a few selected examples. The usual risk in these cases, namely of focussing on unrepresentative or sui generis cases has been minimized as much as feasible. None of the selected examples relate to marginal issues or characters. Additionally, a wide variety of matters, types of issues and characters will be discussed and the examples relate to different periods within the past construed and remembered by the community.

2 Illustrative Examples

Given the importance of the concept of *torah* among the mentioned literati, it is appropriate to involve *torah* in the first example. It is generally agreed that the literati of the late Persian or early Hellenistic period construed Israel as a text-centered community.[10] A core issue for text-centred communities is, obviously, what is included in what we may cross-culturally call "Scripture" and this has much to do with the basic fact that the community's "Scripture" is actually its "read" text. The community's *torah* consisted of its own readings of the texts

---

9 Responses to these issues had to be consistent with the social mindscape of the group and its main ideological tenets. This left room for a variety of responses, but within a restricted set of what would have been considered by the community as appropriate responses.
10 E.g. Römer, "Du Temple". I wrote on this matter elsewhere; e.g., E. Ben Zvi, "Observations", and idem, "Imagining".

to which they granted the status of *torah*.¹¹ Such readings were certainly informed by the community's worlds of knowledge and social mindscape. Proof positive of the central social role of read-in-context texts is the way in which the Jerusalem-centred literati shaped a Jerusalem-centered reading of the Pentateuch and Deuteronomy by approaching the relevant books in ways which were informed by works such as Samuel–Kings, Chronicles, prophetic books and many Psalms. When the Pentateuch and Deuteronomy were read in that light, there could be no doubt about which city (and temple) Yhwh has chosen. Significantly, this is not what Deuteronomy or the Pentateuch actually stated if read as stand-alone works, but it was what the community read. Keeping this example in mind, let us turn our attention to some aspects of what *torah* evoked when the community read Samuel–Kings and Chronicles.

Reading Samuel–Kings was about shaping and communicating memories.¹² Reading Samuel–Kings as a separate corpus involved encountering a *torah* that was evocative of Deuteronomy, because, among others, (a) the use of "deuteronomistic" language,¹³ which in turn led to a frequent shared aural experience that was evocative of Deuteronomy and which was conducive the construction of a web of mental allusions; (b) the importance of a Jerusalem-centred reading of laws concerning cult centralization in Deut 12:13–14, a text which, of course does not mention Jerusalem; (c) texts such as 2 Kgs 14:6 (cf. Deut 24:16) that suggest that סֵפֶר תּוֹרַת־מֹשֶׁה is Deuteronomy, a recognition reinforced by the occurrence of the very same phrase, סֵפֶר תּוֹרַת־מֹשֶׁה within a context that was again clearly evocative of Deuteronomy in Josh 8:31 (cf. Deut 27:5), and (d) reading Samuel–Kings involved recalling a series of condemned cultic practices (/"abominations") in which Israel was often involved and that Deuteronomy and social memory influenced by this book associated, for the most part, with the peoples who were dispossessed by Yhwh in Joshua's time (e.g. 2 Kgs 21:6 and cf. Deut 18:10–14), thus drawing up and exploring an important simile between Israel and the nations that were dispossessed from the land.

---

11 Although the corpus of texts around which the community was supposed to be centered included various types of works, one has to keep in mind that at the core of the community's discourse was the concept that Israel was required to follow Yhwh's instructions, commandments and the like. These instructions and commandments were considered to be at the core of what made Israel to be Israel (e.g., 2 Kgs 17:34). These were also understood to be "directly" written in texts referred to as Yhwh's *torah*, the *torah* of Moses, this *torah*, the book of the *torah* and the like (e.g., 1 Kgs 2:3). Both Samuel–Kings and Chronicles reflected and reinforced this *torah* discourse.
12 To be sure, it was about shaping and communicating memories for a variety of purposes, but still about the shaping and communicating memories.
13 This language evoked the flavor of the voice of Moses of Deuteronomy. I discussed the communicative message of this language in the late Persian period in Ben Zvi, "On the Term," 61–71.

But, of course, reading Samuel–Kings in this way by the late Persian-Early Hellenistic period was not without problems. First, the *torah* of the literati of the time included not only Deuteronomy, but the Pentateuchal books in more or less their present compositional form. Second, the portrayal of the pious kings and their actions were at odds with the law of the king in Deut 17:14–20 and much of Deuteronomy was not applied either.[14] This being the case, a systemic perspective informed by memory studies would lead one to anticipate the development of a social tendency within the community towards addressing these issues through the generation of texts, readings and memories so as to manage these tensions.[15] Against the background of the period, it is not surprising then, that Chronicles evoked memories of monarchic Israel in which the terms associated with *torah* were evocative of a pentateuchal *torah*. This is true in the way of reshaping memories of events according to some narrative patterns and motifs present in Pentateuchal texts other than Deuteronomy (e. g., the case of fire from heaven, see 2 Chr 7:1 and 1 Chr 21:26 (see below) and cf. Lev 9:24). Moreover, as the case of 2 Chr 25:4 shows, Chronicles suggested to its readership that although the texts in Exod 12:9 and Deut 16:7 were both authoritative, their true meaning could not be found by reading each one of these texts in a way informed only and separately by their respective books. Instead, their true meaning emerges once texts when the two texts are read as informing each other. It is worth noting that this means that some of the content and meaning of some authoritative texts could be and at times had to be dissociated from the text itself, if read in isolation from other related authoritative texts in the repertoire of the community.[16] If this consideration is relevant to legal texts in Exodus and Deuteronomy, it stands to reason that it is also relevant at least to some degree and in some cases to the reading of Samuel–Kings and Chronicles within the same community of readers and social mindscape.

At times, matters are quite clear. For instance, remembering the divine promise to David in 2 Sam 7 in a way that is informed by 2 Chr 13:5; 21:7 means reading it as a ברית. But most significantly, 2 Chr 13:5; 21:7 are not alone in that regard (see 2 Sam 23:5; 1 Kgs 8:23–24 [implicitly]; Jer 33:17–21; Ps 89). This reading tendency and the preferred memory associated with it came to be expressed not only in a variety of texts external to the book of Samuel, but also within the book itself. Social memories are not constrained by book or even genre boundaries.

---

14 Cf. Knoppers, "Relationship."
15 Attempts at eliminating these tensions are far less likely to emerge within a social mindscape that favored multiplicity of voices and fuzziness, even if within limits. See above.
16 Cf. Ben Zvi, "One Size."

A more complex case concerns the Levitical and Ephraimite features of the Samuel of memory. The book of Samuel suggests that he was a priest and an Ephraimite. Chronicles portrays him not as an Ephraimite but as a Levite (1 Chr 6:13,18) and reflects an understanding of the Samuel of Samuel as a priest. Remembering him as a Levite was a way to respond to a seemingly problematic memory; after all, priests should be from Levi. When such a reading informs the community's reading of 1 Sam 1:1, this text tends to become devoid of a strong connotation of Ephraimite origin for Samuel.[17] But conversely, keeping in mind the mentioned suggestion advanced by the Book of Samuel while reading Chronicles draws particular attention to the entire question of in which sense should a priest be of Levi, and can an adopted son of a Levite (/priest) be a Levite (/priest)[18]? What about adopted sons of YHWH, can they be Israel?[19] Memory becomes a language within which to approach and explore these matters.

Returning for a short while to the issue of *torah*, I claimed elsewhere that readers of Samuel–Kings in the Persian period likely imagined the book found in Josiah's days in their story to be similar to Deuteronomy but not necessarily identical to Deuteronomy, even without Chronicles' influence and even without assuming that *torah* includes more texts than their book of Deuteronomy. It goes without saying that the reading of Samuel–Kings while keeping Chronicles in the back of the mind and being well aware that within the discourse of the community *torah* was not restricted to their present book of Deuteronomy, the readers would likely be less "fixed" on exploring whether the book found was the(ir) scroll of Deuteronomy. Conversely readers of Chronicles who may be influenced by their readings of Kings may tend to explore the salience of D and D-like language and ideas in their *torah*. Again, memory becomes a kind of language that allows exploring underlying matters concerning the meaning of *torah*, its extent and some of its features, and conversely, these matters generate systemic preferences for memories addressing them, in the main, narratively.

Additional and subtle changes occur when Samuel–Kings is read from a perspective strongly informed by notions of *torah* similar to those encoded in Chronicles. For instance, a text such as שמרו מצותי חקותי ככל התורה אשר צויתי את אבתיכם "observe my commandments and my laws/statues in accordance with all the *torah* that I have commanded your ancestors" in 2 Kgs 17:13, which in its own context is reminiscent of Deuteronomy and of Moses' role, becomes

---

17 The preferred reading would construe him as an Ephrati and his family is just "residing" in the hill country of Ephraim. Cf. Leuchter, *Samuel*, 22–24.
18 Samuel becomes a kind of adopted son of Eli in the Samuel story. On genealogies and social memory in general, see Zerubavel, *Ancestors*.
19 Cf. Isa 56:3–8.

also reminiscent of Gen 26:5 וישמר משמרתי מצותי חקותי ותורתי "he [Abraham] observed my commandments, my laws/statues and my *torah*." When these two texts and the memories they evoke inform each other, they surely draw attention to Deuteronomy and its language (cf. Deut 11:1). But, at the same time, they convey a concept of *torah* and of commandments that does not construe them as necessarily originating at Sinai and most importantly as being both Mosaic but also as being (at least in part) pre-Moses and pre-Sinai.

One more example within this set of "*torah* examples" suffices: readers of Samuel–Kings who were informed by Chronicles and by a larger concept of *torah* mentioned above would have been more inclined to construe or underscore the construction of the memories evoked by 1 Kgs 8:10–11 as reminiscent of those evoked by texts such as Exod 40:34–35; Lev 9:4, 6, 23–24 and thus they would have activated the concepts and images associated with the term כבוד יהוה and develop mnemonic plots linking all the above around the presence of כבוד יהוה and eventually its absence and return (cf. Ezekiel).[20] In other words, reading Samuel–Kings from a perspective informed by Chronicles facilitated certain types of potential readings. But "facilitation" is not necessarily "creation". Could the readers of Samuel, without any influence from Chronicles and the concept of *torah* that it encodes, still develop such readings? And if so, what does it say about some voices in Samuel–Kings?

Earlier I mentioned the tension between the roles of kings in social memory and the putative role of kings in Deuteronomy. This is addressed in Chronicles at least in part by evoking a memory of David as completing the work of Moses in terms of setting the basic regulations by which the community should exist, and particularly in regards to the temple and its service, including music and joy during its service (e. g., 2 Chr 23:18; 29:25; 35:4,15).[21] To be sure, this is not surprising because Israel, as understood by the community in Yehud, was imagined to be not only *torah*-centered, but Jerusalem-centred and Jerusalem temple-centred as well. Setting up two complementary founding fathers, Moses and David and, through the process, relating one to the other went hand-in-hand with interweaving Jerusalem, temple and *torah* at the conceptual core of the community and in

---

[20] The bibliography on כבוד יהוה is extensive. For a survey of the use and meaning of the term in these contexts, see E. Jenni and C. Westermann, *Handwörterbuch*, Art. 600, כבד f.
[21] On the explicit pairing of Moses and David, see Chronicles. On the matter, see De Vries, "Moses;"; Riley, *King*, 61–63; cf. Kleinig, *Divine Institution*; Schniedewind, *Chronicler*, 177 f.; Ben Zvi, "One Size,", 29–32. This construction of the past may not have been a "radical" innovation of Chronicles, but rather Chronicles may have voiced and developed basic approaches to the past that might have existed before its writing and that emerged in response to the tensions mentioned above.

its past and future memories and vice versa. The partial Mosaicization of the memory David[22] provided David with prophetic (cf. 2 Chr 29:25 and see also 1 Chr 16:35[23]) and law-giving features. These features cannot but set him apart from the king of Deut 17:14–20 and closer, to some extent, to the royal-like type of leadership associated with Moses.[24] Other pious Davidic kings who restored the "proper" cult and thus David's regulations, became in the imagination of the community, a kind of second and secondary Davids. A readership of Samuel–Kings that constructs its past with background knowledge of Chronicles and the memories it evokes, would tend to find the tensions between the king portrayed in Deut 17:14–20 and the pious (indirectly partially Mosaicized) kings they vicariously encounter and imagine when reading Samuel–Kings far less problematic.

But there is more, to remember David as the "builder" of the temple involves by necessity closely associating the sites of memory embodied in David and Solomon and both of them with the establishment of the temple. As is well known, Chronicles does so, but it is significant that the generative grammar of memories underlying the emergence of this set of memories was at work also in Samuel and even in Kings (see 2 Kgs 21:7).

To be sure, such an association was also another way of "normalizing" as much as possible a somewhat "anomalous" aspect of Israel's social memory about the building of the temple.[25] From a memory perspective the default expectation would have been that the main founding figure be the founder of the central, mythic temple. That such was the case in ancient Israel is clear from the emphatic, repeated presence of memorable reports about how much David wanted to build the temple and why he could not. The community simply could not have imagined David as conquering Jerusalem and not caring about building the temple. Moreover, the very memory of David's frustrated desire to build the temple and his willingness to accept fully and without debate Yhwh's decision, not only lionized David, and made him even more worthy to

---

[22] The differences between Moses and David as sites of memory in ancient Israel are many and obvious; note also the restricted "lawgiver" character of David compared to Moses.

[23] See the context of 1 Chr 16:35. I discussed these matters elsewhere; see Ben Zvi, "Who Knew What," 349–360.

[24] See Römer, "Moses." It is paradoxical that having no king over Israel facilitated the construction of Moses (and not a human king) as the (human) lawgiver and that the latter facilitated the construction of David as a (restricted) lawgiver.

[25] Cross-culturally, "anomalous" memories tend to be, at least in part, "normalized" over time. That is, made to fit commonly preferred mnemonic plots and tendencies for shaping important sites of memory, and to be sure, to fit well into the discourse of the community.

be a kind of co-founder to Moses, but also contributed another layer of partial Mosaicization of David and partial Joshuaization of Solomon. Just as Moses could not enter the land, David could not build and enter the temple.

As mentioned above, to associate both David and Solomon with the founding of the temple, and thus closely associating a core feature of how they were remembered, was another way of "normalizing" within the limits of the feasible the memory of the founding of the temple.[26] The fact that the same (implied) mnemonic preferences were at work and were well reflected not only in Samuel and Chronicles, but also in Kings (see 2 Kgs 21:7) clearly indicates that a general generative grammar of memories and thus of texts meant to shape memory worked in both corpora.

But what about readings of Chronicles informed by Samuel–Kings on kingship? Samuel–Kings reminded the reading community in late Persian/early Hellenistic Judah that monarchy was not a "natural" situation for Israel. In fact, the first chapters of Samuel may be considered half-hearted apologia for the institution; one that does not even refrain from reminding the community of the close interrelation that once existed between priestly/prophetic rule over Israel and YHWH's rule of over it (see the explicit claim in 1 Sam 8:7). When Chronicles was read in a way informed particularly by 1 Sam 1–8 and 12, several memories reflected in and evoked by Chronicles became more relevant and more pregnant in meaning. Among these memories, one may mention the association of royal images with Jehoiada (2 Chr 24:15), the priest with a prophetic voice and role. In this case, it is worth stressing that the community was asked to remember that Jehoiada died even older than Moses and Joshua and that his presence, not the king's presence, was crucial for the well-being of the people during his

---

[26] Neither Samuel–Kings nor Chronicles could claim that David actually built the temple anymore that Moses (not Joshua) conquered the land across the Jordan. Memories are malleable but have to be consistent with central aspects of what the remembering group agreed that happened. In other words, in ancient Israel, as in most – and likely all – societies there are limits to malleability. These limits on malleability are grounded on a social mindscape within which "usable" social memories have to be construed as "accurate" from the perspective of the remembering community, or using methodologically more precise language, the remembering community would tend to minimize the social "cost" involved in rejecting some widely accepted "facts" about the past that the community already agreed upon. Thus a remembering community would tend to shape an acceptable mnemonic narrative in such a way that does not explicitly contradict or, from its own perspective, "appropriately" incorporates at least in the main some core "agreed upon facts" that already exist within the world of knowledge. Significantly, not all "agreed upon facts" are necessarily "core facts." See Ben Zvi, "Malleability." On general issues of "accuracy" and "usable memory" in contemporary memory studies, see, for instance, Wertsch, *Voices*, 10–40 and bibliography.

time. Other memories to mention in this context include that of the rebuilding of the temple without a local king over Israel, or even the one encoded in a text such as 1 Chr 9:22 which reminds the community that the gatekeepers were established in their offices by Samuel and David.

Such a text not only closely associates David and Samuel to each other and both to the founding of the cultic order in Jerusalem, but also reflected and shaped an underlying mnemonic narrative in which David is to be understood as (also) the successor of Samuel. In other words, to be understood as a symbolic son of Samuel,[27] the prophetic/priestly political leader. But is this mnemonic tendency to link Samuel and David not more saliently reflected in the Book of Samuel?[28]

It is in this context that it is particularly worth noting that a text that appears only in Chronicles, i.e., 1 Chr 9:22, which seems to be in tension with other memories encoded in and evoked by Samuel–Kings and which deals with a character about whom not much is written in Chronicles (as opposed to the Book of Samuel), actually reflected (and one may say emerged out of) a mnemonic tendency that was strongly present in Samuel–Kings. Moreover, from the perspective of the remembering community that associated David with the founding of the temple, the note in 1 Chr 9:22 serves to address a particular void. If the two characters (Samuel and David) were to be imagined as being close to one another and as one being the proper successor of the other, should the community not tend to imagine them, even if occasionally, as sharing some link in relation to one of the most defining aspects of David?[29]

Imagining David as successor of Samuel and a parallel process of imagining David as a successor of Melchizedek (see Ps 110), along with the partial Mosaicization of David could not but priestsize the David of memory, to some extent.[30] To be sure, within the world portrayed in the text of Samuel–Kings as construed

---

[27] Cf. the association of David and Solomon in terms of building the temple (and cf. 2 Kgs 21:7).
[28] Elsewhere I wrote, "the traditional mnemonic narrative of a new ruler (i.e., the 'usurper') who brings down an impious regime and brings back order had to be extensively modified in this case. The ideological, generative grammar underlying Samuel–Kings could not allocate to David the traditional role of the 'usurper' bringing down Samuel, the last priestly ruler; instead it had to construe him as a kind of restorer of order supported by Samuel. In other words, it needed a transitional Saul figure to gloss over the fact that David's 'restoration' of order is not a return to Samuel's days, but a new beginning, by constructing Samuel himself as an active agent supporting David's kingship." See "Balancing" in this volume, pp. 440–58.
[29] Cf. Leuchter, *Samuel*, 22–24.
[30] See for instance, the pattern of occurrences of אֵפוֹד בַּד and of those wearing it, namely 1 Sam 2:18 (Samuel), 22:18 (priests), 2 Sam 6:14 (David) and 1 Chr 15:27 (David) (cf. Lev 16:2).

by reading it in a way not particularly informed by Chronicles and separate from much of the discourse of the late Persian/early Hellenistic kingdom, the association of some priestly or priestly-like traits did not represent a problem (cf. 2 Sam 6:13–18; 24:17; 8:18 [MT];³¹ 1 Kgs 8:14,55–56; the verses concerning אֵפוֹד בַּד see n. 30 and cf. Ps 110:4 and 1 Chr 15:27 as well). But within the discourse of the late Persian/early Hellenistic period in Jerusalem, a king who serves as an Israelite priest was a problematic memory to have, and one that had to be balanced and contained. Thus a mnemonic need or "void" to be filled emerged. The story of Uzziah in 2 Chr 26:16–21, for instance, served, from a systemic perspective, to address that void. The speech of Abijah, though in a less direct way given its context, communicated a similar message (see 2 Chr 13:9–12). In addition, Chronicles, for the most part, and the Pentateuchal traditions, for the most part, tended to de-emphasize the priestly character of David and Moses respectively, and to emphasize that of the Aaronides (or as the texts were read, likely the Zadokites).³² Reading Samuel with this frame of mind certainly lessens the potential mindshare of images of David as priest, despite texts such as 2 Sam 8:18 וּבְנֵי דָוִד כֹּהֲנִים הָיוּ and even raises questions about it (see LXX, "and David's sons were chiefs of the court" [NETS]).

Reading Chronicles within a frame of mind that included a strong awareness that David was associated with priestly traits in the book of Samuel, contributed to the construction of the potential meaning of the texts too. For one, they reinforced the voice of similar verses in Chronicles that connoted a quasi-priestly aura to the remembered David (e.g., 1 Chr 15:27 and cf. 1 Sam 2:18; 6:14; 22:18). But above all, they served to draw attention to and explore a main cultic/ideological issue, the role and characterization of the human king in Yehud against the background of a relatively common, long durée, ancient Near Eastern construction of the king as being at least occasionally a priest, which in itself was occasionally contested too.³³ It is worth stressing that all these readings were in-

---

31 Neither the LXX nor the parallel text in 1 Chr 18:17 agree with MT 2 Sam 8:18; cf. also 2 Sam 20:23–26. There was a tendency to disprefer the type of reading exhibited MT 2 Sam 8:18, but this tendency is certainly not circumscribed to Chronicles.
32 Priestly features in the memory of Moses were de-emphasized during the late Persian/Early Hellenistic period; once the priesthood was clearly established as a function of *torah* and prophecy, it remained a distinct domain delegated by Moses to Aaron. The priesthood of Moses became a more salient memory later on, under different circumstances. See Lierman, *Moses*, 66–70. See also "Exploring the Memory" in this volume, pp. 199–231.
33 E.g., the Verse Account of Nabonaid and cf. with the description of the sinful kings of Israel.

terwoven, influenced each other[34] and bore their own significance as part and parcel of a well interconnected mnemonic system that included both.

Another example of similar processes concerns Jerusalem. The lack of reference to the selection of Jerusalem in the Pentateuch led to a myriad of texts and memories in Yehud that address that void directly or indirectly and serve all to shape a Jerusalem-appropriate reading of the Pentateuch on this very crucial matter for the Jerusalemite literati. In fact, one may say that the Pentateuch could be shared between Samaria and Yehud, because Yehud (and possibly Samaria as well,) developed an unshared and un-sharable reading of it. Samuel–Kings played an important role in these matters, but so did prophetic literature, many of the Psalms, and to be sure, Chronicles is no different. For the purposes of this chapter, it is particularly noteworthy that the construction of Moses and David as the two founding figures of Israel, which has been mentioned above, is a paradigmatic case of this tendency. The development of partially converging mnemonic attributes between these two sites of memory served well to appropriate and reshape the memory of Moses so as to fit well in the Jerusalem-centered discourse of Yehud. Appropriation by means of a past central hero is a common transcultural mnemonic feature (and thus often the source of mnemonic struggles among different and often competing, contemporaneous "appropriating" groups).[35]

There is also a (trans-cultural) common mnemonic tendency for spatial appropriation through social memory that involves the construction of a sense of temporal continuity to foster the legitimization of the claims of a particular group over a place or over its importance for all. Thus, within the memory world of Yehud and its ideological discourse, the land becomes Israel's during Joshua's time, but was explicitly marked as being chosen for Israel already during Abraham's time. One would anticipate the development of a similar set of memories linking Jerusalem to pre-David times.[36] This tendency was certainly and explicitly encoded in 2 Chr 3:1,[37] and for that matter in Ps 110:4.[38] It is

---

[34] Perhaps even at the textual level, see the case of 2 Sam 8:18.
[35] Cf. the contemporary case concerning the memory of Bolivar in Venezuela, or of the "founding fathers" in the United States. One may safely assume that Moses was not closely associated with David in Samaria.
[36] See "Remembering Pre-Israelite Jerusalem" in this volume, pp. 504–26.
[37] Of course, this claimed association is at the core of mnemonic struggles between Yehud and Samaria (and their ideological discourses), as Samarian texts consistently associated Mt. Moriah with Mt. Gerizim. On the struggle over the memory of Mt. Moriah (and of Abram) see Kalimi, *Exegesis*, 33–58.
[38] Social mnemonic tendencies are at work not only in the shaping of historiographical narratives, but also of any past-construing text.

worth noting that all these memories created a mnemonic spatial overlap involving (some of) David's sites of memory with those of Abraham's.[39] On the surface, such a mnemonic connection could have drawn attention towards Hebron. It is in this context that it is particularly noteworthy that a memory encoded in Chronicles is deeply involved in shifting attention from Hebron to Jerusalem (see e.g., 1 Chr 11) and explicitly to the place of the temple. Moreover, the story of David's purchase of the site of threshing floor of Araunah/Ornan, the place of the future temple (1 Chr 21:21–26; cf. 2 Sam 24:20–26) is strongly reminiscent of that of Abraham purchasing a burial place in Gen 23 from Ephron, but now the space has been shifted to Jerusalem and the temple, and the generic Hittite has become a Jebusite. Both features convey the spatial shift towards Jerusalem.[40] To be sure, the similarities between the accounts are far more pronounced in Chronicles than in Samuel, but one must consider not only that a reading of Samuel informed by Chronicles would find these similarities in Samuel as well, but also consider that Chronicles may have made the implicit connotations that may have already be associated with readings of Samuel in the late Persian period far more explicit. In any event, the shift from Hebron to Jerusalem is saliently expressed in well-known mnemonic narratives about the shift of David's seat from Hebron to Jerusalem (see, for instance, 2 Sam 2:11; 1 Kgs 2:11; 1 Chr 3:4; 29:27).

Catastrophic ends are magnets for social memory. Social memory approaches would point to a general (cross-cultural) tendency to associate the fall of a polity to its last memorable ruler and to characterize (usually) him as the person responsible for the catastrophe. Thus, for instance, the fall of Aggade was associated with Naram Sin, that of the neo-Assyrian empire with Sardanapalus (in Greek sources), and in much later times, the traditional image of king Muhammad XII (/Boabdil) of Granada. The book of Kings anomalously and thus saliently refrains from constructing a mnemonic narrative that places (at least a significant) responsibility for the fall of Jerusalem on Zedekiah and reinforces the message by even construing the last king of Northern Israel as being not necessarily the worst (see 2 Kgs 17:2). Of course, this is not unheard of and one may compare this mnemonic attitude with Greek explanations of

---

Of course, there were also mnemonic struggles over Salem and texts such as Ps 76:3 addressed them. On the identity of Salem, see also Emerton, "Site of Salem."
39 Links between David and Abraham were recognized long ago in academic research, see, for instance, Clements, "Abraham."
40 See, among others, Zakovitch, "Assimilation in Biblical Narratives," 181; Alter, "David Story," 358 f.; Japhet, *Chronicles*; McDonough, *David*, 128–131; cf. Harvey, *Retelling*, 60 and "Memory of Abraham" in this volume, pp. 162–98.

the fall of the Achaemenid empire that do not, in the main, focus on Darius III. In the latter case, the point was to draw attention to a trans-generational fault in the Persians (i.e., the ideal "other" for the culturally proper "Greek") and to the "crimes" of Xerxes.[41] But the point here is that there is a point (i.e., a rhetorical/ideological/mnemonic purpose) in this type of "anomalous" mnemonic narratives. Chronicles and Jeremiah and Ezekiel, on the whole partially normalize the situation by placing at least some of the responsibility on Zedekiah, but the plethora of mnemonic voices and readings, each informing and interacting with the other, and by involving multiple voices not only among various books but often within books, along with the attention to the issue drawn by Kings' avoidance of a common mnemonic path and the textual encoding of attitudes closer to one book in another (e.g., Jer 15:4), all show that a complex system of interwoven memories emerged as a language to think about a central issue in the discourse of the community. That being, the why of the calamity of 586 BCE, the implications of various possible answers, and general issues of causality, responsibility and divine economy and justice.

A good number of examples of additional examples may be brought to bear, from seemingly narrow cases to larger issues. It is interesting to note, for instance, that Chronicles and Samuel–Kings often mnemonically complement each other. For instance, a common mnemonic attitude towards memories and sites of memory that are considered very negative or as embodying sinful behavior is both to dwell on them and strongly condemn them or to avoid mentioning them, so their memory will be no more in the community. Prophetic and psalmic statements about that which will be no memory of in the future, actually combine the two. It is worth noting that strongly negative memories to which Samuel–Kings devotes much space and to which it draws much attention are often not so strongly mentioned or not mentioned at all in Chronicles and vice versa. Similarly, and turning to positive matters, Chronicles tends to bring more memories of royal domestic building activities to bear and thus it complements, from a mnemonic system perspective, the relative scarcity of such references in Kings and significantly contributes to shaping an image of good (old) kings more in conformity with the usual ancient near East motif of the king as a builder and as continuing a divine work (see, esp. 2 Chr 26:10).[42] This image is balanced, of course, by Kings. Significantly, Kings itself seems to acknowledge the positive character of royal domestic building activities when it avoids assigning the building of the Garden of Uzza to Manasseh (2 Kgs 21:18).

---

41 There is also the matter of the lionization of Alexander.
42 Cf. D. J. Green, *Ideology*.

In sum, there were multiple interactions between the read Samuel–Kings and the read Chronicles of the community/the literati in the Late Persian/Early Hellenistic period that shared (a) both texts and (b) the social memories that emerged from these interactions in a continuous process of back and forth. A study of these requires a study of Samuel–Kings and the Chronicles of the literati of the time as part of one mnemonic system. Mnemonic generative grammars, typical mnemonic plots, expectations and voids to be managed were all at work in this mnemonic system and all shaped and reflected the social mindscape of these literati. These memories served also as a kind of a necessary language for thinking and exploring core concepts, tensions and the like, that would be difficult to approach without these mnemonic stories. Significantly, both Chronicles and Samuel–Kings also had to shape and evoke their own particular mnemonic stories so as to allow the development of the mentioned and socially very significant continuous loop of memory interactions that facilitated the above. It is worth noting also that often similar underlying generative ideas and basic mnemonic narratives and preferences frame the production of particular memories in both books, even if they tell, at least on the surface, a different story.[43]

---

[43] A final comment: the present essay is informed by social memory approaches and deals with social memory among the literati of the late Persian/early Hellenistic period, who included among their authoritative repertoire of books both Samuel–Kings and Chronicles in something close to their present form, which is another way of stating that the present Samuel–Kings and Chronicles are sufficiently representative of their Samuel–Kings and Chronicles so we may use the former as a good approximation of the latter. Thus the focus is on reading and remembering communities rather than with individual authors or redactors and their particular intentions. Likewise, this essay does not deal with potential forerunners of Samuel, Kings or Chronicles or of particular literary units that eventually, in a modified way, ended up in these books. The approach here is and must be both strongly historical, (after all it is an exercise in reconstructing the community's intellectual history) and synchronic. To be sure, the books of Samuel and Kings had a redactional and "textual" (in the sense of text criticism) history, and Chronicles is likely later than at least some form of Samuel–Kings and may also have undergone some redaction. There is room for diachronic analysis and redactional and text critics may find some of the observations advanced here potentially relevant for their endeavors, but I would leave this for them to decide.

Shaping and Remembering an Arch-Villain in the Late Persian/Early Hellenistic Period: The Case of Ahaz in Chronicles and its Implications

I

The study of the most heroic characters populating the mnemonic landscape of a particular group provides a helpful window into its social mindscape. But as important at least is the window provided by a careful examination of the ways in which arch-villains are construed and remembered. Moreover, societies may long and hope for their heroes, but detest and are terrified by the possible (re-)appearance of arch-villains. This is significant since transculturally more emotional weight and thus memory weight is usually given to negative than positive events and personages.

Yet, scholars have usually given much more attention to the heroes than villains of memory and this holds true not only in relation to relatively contemporaneous societies but also in the case of ancient societies. Only in recent years, some scholars of memory have begun to focus on villains.[1]

This contribution is, to large extent, an illustrative case-study that focuses on one prominent arch-villain, namely the Ahaz whose memory was encoded in and evoked through the literati's reading and rereading of Chronicles in the late Persian/early Hellenistic period. But just as no hero exists alone in social memory, no villain does either. Sites of memory carry their significance only within a general mnemonic landscape and therefore, in what follows, I will situate the Ahaz evoked through the reading of Chronicles within the context of other arch-villains that existed within the memory-world of the very same remembering community. Moreover, one must keep in mind that the relevant literati community read Chronicles, but again, not only Chronicles; their memories are those evoked by Chronicles, but not only those.

Let me conclude this introduction by stressing two matters: first, that just like the heroes, the arch-villains shape sites of memory that embody and communicate values at the core of the worldview of the remembering community. Moreover, both, of course, involve 'othering', but again a stronger form of 'othering' takes place in the case of arch-villains. Additionally, 'in-between' areas and po-

---

[1] See esp. Gary Alan Fine, *Sticky Reputations: The Politics of Collective Memory in Midcentury America* (New York: Routledge, 2012); cf. idem, *Difficult Reputations. Collective Memories of the Evil, Inept and Controversial* (Chicago: Chicago University Press, 2001).

https://doi.org/10.1515/9783110547146-015

rous boundaries become substantially more threatening than the usual and obvious reminders that although regular people should attempt to imitate as much as possible the great heroes, they are not arch-heroes and that any attempt to blur that line is not only silly, but tantamount to hubris.

Second, the goal of this contribution is not to offer a comprehensive study of the Ahaz of Chronicles, nor of the literary account in 2 Chr 28.[2] Instead the focus here is on exploring and demonstrating the potential of focusing on arch-villains such as Ahaz within the frame of an approach informed by memory studies.

II

It is widely agreed that, whereas in Kings, Manasseh is the main Judahite villain, in Chronicles, the most prominent archvillain is Ahaz. Within the general memory scape of the community, these two figures balanced each other, and both contributed to the shaping of an image of what a late-monarchic archvillain was all about. From the perspective of the community, one may say that remembering these two exemplars of archvillains was a way to explore what an archvillain is about.

It is also widely agreed that the shift from Manasseh to Ahaz was consistent with the shift from Josiah to Hezekiah as the main hero of the 'post-division' king of Judah, in the historical narratives that each of these books evoked among the readership.[3] Manasseh of Kings was construed, in part, as an anti-Josiah, whereas the Ahaz of Chronicles was construed as anti-Hezekiah.[4] The 'higher' the

---

[2] On the latter see, e.g. Itzhak Amar, "Chaotic Writing as a Literary Element in the Story of Ahaz in 2 Chronicles 28," *VT* 66 (2016), 349–364 and bibliography. Amar's conclusions about the manner in which at the literary level the unit reinforces a negative image of Ahaz "as a wicked transgressor who never ceases to do evil" (364) are consistent with the arguments developed below. For a study comparing the Ahaz of King and the one in Chronicles, see, e.g., K. A. D. Smelik, "The Representation of King Ahaz in 2 Kings 16 and 2 Chronicles 28," in Johannes C. de Moor (ed.), *Intertextuality in Ugarit and Israel* (OtSt, 40; Leiden: Brill, 1998), 143–185.
[3] Reasons for this change include, *inter alia*, an increased lionization of Hezekiah, partially due to the fact that he was mnemonically associated with the deliverance of Jerusalem during the time of Sennacherib, which in turn served as a counter-type for the destruction of Jerusalem at the hands of Nebuchadnezzar. (A lionization of Hezekiah can be observed in groups living in other times, places, and historical circumstances; see, e.g. how his image is shaped in rabbinic literature, see, e.g. b. Sanh. 99a; cf. b. Sanh. 94a; b. B. Bat. 15a. Of course, the attributes assigned to the lionized Hezekiah reflect always the discourse of the relevant social group).
[4] This is not the place to dwell on the shift in their relative weight as heroes of memory from Kings to Chronicles, nor how the two hierarchies balanced and complemented each other within

heroic character of one, the higher the negative characterization of its counterpart had to be construed.

But, arch-villains are rarely just mirror figures of their corresponding heroes.[5] In fact, they will fail to serve their social and mnemonic roles if they were merely mirror negative images of heroes. What makes them important is that they embody that which the community finds most threatening. Moreover, a successful process of arch-villainizing is supposed to bring up a sense of emotional disgust and, through disgust, impact in-group social behavior.

Transculturally, general assessments of characters of old are far more memorable than the multiple particular details supporting the evaluation of the character, even if social negotiations about these details are undoubtedly important. The Manasseh of Kings (see 2 Kgs 21:1–20; 23:12, 26; 24:3) and of Jer 15:14 was an arch-villain, above all, because he was responsible for the worst calamity that befell Israel within the memory-scape of the community: namely destruction of the temple, of Jerusalem and the end of the monarchic, Davidic polity (see explicitly, 2 Kgs 23:26; 24:3; Jer 15:14). This makes for a memory of a despicable person, but also for that of a powerful agent—after all, his actions led to a calamity of great proportions, with even a cosmic aspect, due to the cosmic functions of the temple.

Significantly, within this memory-scape there was nothing anyone could have done to avoid the incoming catastrophe by the time Manasseh finally died. Moreover, this construction of Manasseh included socializing the remembering community to accept that neither the piety of his great predecessor (see implicitly Jer 15:14), nor that of his great successor Josiah could do anything to avoid such a catastrophe, even when the latter is explicitly remembered as undoing some of the exempla given for the kind of deeds of Manasseh (cf. 2 Kgs 21:3–7 with 2 Kgs 23:4–14 in general and notice the explicit language of 2 Kgs 23:12 in particular). In fact, by stressing that Josiah removed the cultic material objects and did away with the cultic performances and behaviours (e.g., worshiping the host of heaven) for which Manasseh was responsible, but Judah still remained as condemned as before, a message was communicated: it is not their presence or absence per se that doomed Judah and the Jerusalemite Temple. It was a divine memory (i.e., YHWH's memory) of Manasseh's actions.

---

the general mnemonic system of literati whose memories of the past were shaped by reading these two works (along with other relevant past-shaping books such as the prophetic books).
5 E.g., Hitler is not remembered as a mirror negative image of Roosevelt in the USA or of Churchill in the UK; even in fiction, heroes and their villains are rarely just mirror negative images.

Details about what Manasseh did were less important and memorable than this basic characterization, but still shaped a memory and created a category, namely that of actions and behaviours that are worthy of such a punishment. The general characterization in 2 Kgs 21:2 explicitly constructs a basic cognitive and mnemonic category and its main prototypical members, namely (a) the divinely banished Canaanite 'nations' whose behaviour Israel was commanded not to follow (Deut 18:9; cf. 20:18), (b) northern Israelites and their non-Davidic kings (2 Kgs 17:8) and in this context, particularly Ahab, who is mentioned explicitly by name in the next verse (2 Kgs 21:3) and who is one of the two Northern arch-villain kings and significantly, (c) Ahaz (2 Kgs 16:3).

The existence of this cognitive/mnemonic *ad hoc* category and its main axes is re-affirmed in multiple ways. For instance, Ahab is a site of memory explicitly evoked in 2 Kgs 21:13. The memory of the other Northern arch-villain king, namely Jeroboam, was indirectly, but clearly evoked by the cypher 'caused to sin Judah' in 21:16.[6] Memories of Manasseh, Ahaz and the northern Israelites (and their king) are all linked together through the recalling of their shared practice of consigning their sons to the fire (2 Kgs 16:3; 21:6; 2 Kgs 17:17).[7] This is not surprisingly also associated with the banished 'nations' in Deut 18:10 (see also 2 Kgs 21:11), in which the practice stands at the head of exempla of behaviors that will doom Israel—a list in itself, not surprisingly evoked among what was worth remembering about Manasseh's behavior (see 2 Kgs 21:6),[8] and to which memories of Ahaz and Manasseh are linked from a rhetorical and cognitive viewpoint in 2 Kgs 23:12.

This said, although a cognitive and mnemonic realm that included as prominent exempla sites of memory such as Ahab, northern Israelites, the pre-Israelites residents of the land as construed in Deuteronomy was clearly construed, none of them was remembered as responsible for the destruction of Jerusalem, its temple and Judah's calamity, except Manasseh. In other words, Manasseh was construed as a fully developed arch-villain, not only in the sense that he stands opposite to all that is good and pious within the discourse of the community, but also because his actions were remembered as powerful enough to cause such a historical calamity.

To be sure, this focus on personal causality was problematic within the discourse of the remembering community and required balancing in the form of

---

6 Cf. 1 Kgs 15:26, 34; 16:26; 22:53; 2 Kgs 3:3; 10:29, 31; 13:2, 11; 14:24; 15:9, 18, 24, 28; 21:16; 23:15. The exact cypher was not associated with anyone else.
7 Note that the practice is 'democratized' in 2 Kgs 17:17; for a comparative democratization see Ezek 20:31.
8 Cf. the text of 2 Kgs 21:6 with that of Deut 18:10 and 2 Kgs 17:17.

multiple causations. Indeed, already in Kings and in the DHC (i.e., the Deuteronomistic Historical Collection) in general, multiple explanations of the calamity informing each other are present. For instance, the sins of the people also caused the calamity (see, e.g., and within the same pericope, 2 Kgs 21:15; and the point is implied in the 'democratization' of the sin of the Northern Israelites expressed in 2 Kgs 17), or the latter is the result of a long trajectory of sin that characterized Israel from the beginning (again, 2 Kgs 21:15), or even great heroes such as Hezekiah may fail and be, at least, partially responsible for the catastrophe (2 Kgs 10:16–19; cf. the mnemonic trajectory in the book of Isaiah that directly links Isa 39:6–8 to Isa 40:1). But multiple causations in this case do not imply exoneration.

Moreover, whereas the remembering community was asked to remember that the people rejected the prophets/*torah* teachers of their time (a typical motif in the landscape of the community, abundantly present in the Prophetic Book Collection [i.e., Isa-Mal, hereafter PBC] and elsewhere, see, e.g., 2 Kgs 21:9), it was also asked to remember that they did not listen to *torah*, because Manasseh misled them (וַיַּתְעֵם מְנַשֶּׁה; 2 Kgs 21:9).[9] At a conceptual level, the case may be compared to that of the successful misleading teacher in Deut 13:14–17.

Against this background, Chronicles evokes a social, complementary memory. On the one hand, it plays well within the basic cognitive, mnemonic realm mentioned above. Moreover, since it construes Ahab and his family as exerting some irrational attraction for the Davidic kings—even among the best of them; see, the extreme case of Jehoshaphat—it turns the Ahabites into a quasi-mythical symbol of the potentially fatal allure of evildoers for true followers of Yhwh, and thus enhances the conceptual connection between Ahab and Ahab's house and the prototypical group that serves this purpose within the discourse of the community, namely, the 'nations' dispossessed by Yhwh (e.g., Exod 23:31–33; Deut 7:16; 12:30–31; 20:16–18).[10]

But on the other hand, Chronicles drastically reshuffles some of main exempla that characterize this shared realm of meaning and memory. Thus, the Manasseh of memory, the exemplar for the most sinful, despicable, and most dangerous leader of the remembered past, becomes the exemplar of the repentant. Although the motif of drastic reversal is quite common in the construction of so-

---

[9] The image of Manasseh as, *inter alia*, a misleading teaching of *torah* is developed in Rabbinic literature (see b. Sanh. 99b). Ahaz is imagined, *inter alia*, as a king who forbid the study of *torah* (e.g., b. Sanh. 103b).

[10] I discussed this issue in E. Ben Zvi, "The House of Omri/Ahab in Chronicles," L. L. Grabbe (ed.), (LHBOTS, 421/ESHM 6; London and New York: T&T Clark, 2007), 41–53.

cially shared mnemonic narratives,[11] a reversal in the case of the arch-villain responsible for the destruction of the temple cannot but carry much meaning and draw attention to itself. Moreover, such a change would involve a very significant risk of high social costs for those advocating it.[12] The fact that the change was accepted strongly suggests that there was more than enough compensating social rewards for the group that engages itself in such a change.

This is not the place to discuss the Manasseh of Chronicles in any detail,[13] but suffices for the present purposes to note that the image of Manasseh reflected in and communicated by Chronicles, converged and overlapped symbolically with 'Israel'. Like monarchic Israel, he was extremely sinful. Like Israel, he was punished and exiled to Babylon. There, he repented and returned to the land to become an important reforming king of memory and the prototype of repenting Israel/pious returnees. To some extent, he even stands for a future Israel, better than the present but not yet at the 'end of history,' because Manasseh directly rules the land—even if as a vassal—unlike the present Israel of Chronicles.[14]

The fact that the known arch-villain ends up associated with Israel is not so strange as it may seem within this discourse, since the main villain of the main mnemonic narratives about Israel within the discourse of Yehud, including the Pentateuch is actually Israel. Moreover, since Israel is also the hero of its own story in general, it is not so surprising that it repents. In addition, the importance of repentance and the possibility of repentance, even in the worst cases, becomes thus associated with the hope of Israel to overcome exile in its multiple connotations (cf. PBC). Rather than being the cause of the exile, Manasseh becomes the symbol of overcoming exile, in all its possible meanings. The person

---

11 Cf. the 'conversion' of Antiochus IV in 2 Macc 9:13–17; and the cases of Saul/Paul (see Acts 8:1–3; 9:1–18; 26:9–18) and rabbinic figures such as R. Akiva (e. g., b. Pes. 49b; cf. the case of the daughter of the 'evil Turnus Rufus' whom R. Akiva eventually marries, see. b 'Abod. Zar. 20a).
12 A point made time and again in Gary Alan Fine, *Sticky Reputations*.
13 See "Reading Chronicles and Reshaping the Memory of Manasseh," in this volume, pp. 367–86. For a different (and to a significant extent complementary) study and set of questions about the Manasseh in Chronicles see Gary N. Knoppers, "Saint or Sinner? Manasseh in Chronicles," Jeremy Corley and Harm van Grol (eds.), *Rewriting Biblical History: Essays on Chronicles and Ben Sira in Honor of Pancratius C. Beentjes* (Deuterocanonical and Cognate Literature Studies 7; Berlin: de Gruyter, 2011), 211–29. See also Lowell K. Handy, "Rehabilitating Manasseh: Remembering King Manasseh in the Persian and Hellenistic Periods," in Diana V. Edelman and Ehud Ben Zvi (eds.), (Oxford: Oxford University Press, 2013), 221–235 and bibliography.
14 See "Reshaping the Memory of Zedekiah and His Period in Chronicles," in this volume, pp. 342–66.

who led Israel astray, will lead it back; Israel led itself to exile and it will lead itself out of it, through repentance.

I would like to stress that from the perspective of the remembering community, the point is not that the Manasseh of Kings is replaced by that of Chronicles or *vice versa*. The two constructions worked, because the community was not supposed to remember one and forget the other. In fact, remembering the Manasseh of Chronicles required remembering that he was the worst villain, for only by being so he could become the hero of repentance after punishment, a cypher of return and restoration, following exile. In addition, by embodying pre-exilic, exilic and post-exilic Israel in one single person, the three become one, Israel.

Whereas there is much to be gained for the community through this re-shaping of memories of Manasseh advanced by Chronicles, something is lost: namely, the clear-cut arch-villain of the late monarchic period has been dissolved in the process. Thus, from a memory-system approach, the need for a new arch-villain emerges. The choice of Ahaz to fulfill that role was clearly grounded on and emerges out of the already existing conceptual and mnemonic realm of associations mentioned above. The generative power of, inter alia, the previous associations between Ahaz and Manasseh, which are only enhanced in Chronicles (e.g., he clearly led his people astray; see what happens when he dies), was clearly at work in the choice of Ahaz as the new archvillain of memory. But this does not mean that the choice of Ahaz carried no serious implication or did not substantially re-signify the mentioned realm of association. In Kings, the latter clearly has to do with exile, but within the world of Chronicles, characterizing Ahaz as the main villain, necessarily meant refocusing the *ad hoc* realm of archetypal negative behaviours, at least in part, away from images of exile and the catastrophe of 587. It meant that the deeds of the arch-villain were conceptually set apart, at least in part, from the memories of catastrophe involving the destruction of the temple, Jerusalem and the monarchy.[15] Extreme evil may still be associated with dispossession of the land (as it is in other texts within the repertoire of the community), but now not necessarily so.

---

[15] Chronicles' evoked a memory that rebalanced, in the general social memory of the community, the weight of the overwhelming memory of the 587 BCE catastrophe. See "Toward a Sense of Balance: Remembering the Catastrophe of Monarchic Judah/(Ideological) Israel and Exile through Reading Chronicles," in this volume, pp. 387–406. In addition, within the world of Chronicles, there would have been a strong dis-preference against the construction of the misdeeds of a long-gone king as the reason for the destruction of the temple several generations later (contrast with the Manasseh of Kings) and the role of the people, Zedekiah, and of generations of Israel in bringing this calamity about is now considered very much worthy of being remembered. (See "Reshaping the Memory of Zedekiah" in this volume, pp. 342–66.)

Ahaz, the archvillain, is never remembered as the cause for the exile in the world evoked by reading Chronicles. But if even a late monarchic arch-villain cannot be remembered on the whole as the one who caused the destruction of the temple, how may such an archvillain be remembered, and what does it do to remember such an archvillain in the context of the discourse conveyed by Chronicles?

Within the world shaped and communicated by this book, Ahaz voluntarily closed the temple doors (2 Chr 28:24). Although, at some level, destruction and closure are conceptually similar (e. g., both result in a lack of a functioning temple), the difference between the outcomes of the actions of these arch-villains (Ahaz in CHR and Manasseh in Kings) carries important implications. Ahaz's actions can be easily undone. Hezekiah opens the doors of the temple in the first month of the first year of his reign (2 Chr 29:3) and while Cyrus makes his proclamation on the first year of his reign (cf. 2 Chr 36:22), there are still substantial differences: re-opening does not require material be-building; Cyrus is not necessarily Hezekiah, and simply closing the temple does not involve emptying the land so it may be purified (see 2 Chr 36:21), which is a pre-condition for the rebuilding of the proper temple.

There is far more to Ahaz as the arch-villain in the world evoked by Chronicles and the social mindscape of the literati engaged in constructing and recalling such Ahaz. Cross-culturally arch-villains tend to end up badly. They are punished, and their punishment tends to be become exemplary. But the community in this case was asked to remember that unlike the many sinners of Ahaz's time who were punished by death, Ahaz was not. To be sure, he was punished with disasters for his kingdom, but he himself continued to live and sin, unlike his underlings. If villains such as his officers and warriors were killed because they abandoned Yhwh (2 Chr 28:6–7), why was it worth remembering that Ahaz was not killed? The case is very prominent and from a communicative perspective, an obvious case of a strong 'attention-getter'. But attention-getters do not stand for themselves, rather they draw attention to some important message.

As usual in the case of Chronicles, there is not one but multiple, complementary, and partial messages. For instance, remembering Ahaz in such a way draws attention to an important ideological point advanced elsewhere in Chronicles, namely that humans in general and the literati in particular cannot predict the course of events on the basis of even the most explicit and clear starting conditions, because they cannot assume to predict Yhwh's deeds.

Moreover, remembering that the arch-villain was not killed meant remembering that even arch-villains may have a chance to repent. If arch-villains will always die after they committed their serious crimes, the potential for repentance would be drastically curtailed. Some of the arch-villains, of course, will repent (e.g., Manasseh), some would not (Ahaz). It is worth stressing that in this case, what is at stake is not a relatively marginal issue of (ideological) world-construction, but a quite visceral matter for the literati within their own discourse, because monarchic Israel was often considered an arch-villain who deserved to 'die' in this discourse, but was still given a chance (and so was 'David'/'Israel' in Samuel). In a world in which Manasseh/sinful monarchic Israel, becomes after exile, repentant, pious Israel; Ahaz cannot but represent unrepentant, repeatedly sinful, pre-cataclysmic punishment, monarchic Israel. As such Ahaz/ his Israel cannot be remembered as going into exile, because if he had, he would have repented. Moreover, like monarchic Israel, and like Israel in general, he must be construed as liable to be punished with death, but he cannot be really executed. Like all those killed, because of David's sin, warriors and people may and should die, but he/Israel must remain alive.

But there is far more to this construction of Ahaz. Whereas in the world of Chronicles, the former arch-villain Manasseh embodies the 'historical' Israel of the literati and their hopes for it (sinful, then exiled/punished, then repentant and finally returned to the throne), the new arch-villain Ahaz embodies their 'counterfactual' monarchic Israel, which is sinful, continually punished, and *not* exiled and thus never repentant. For the literati to imagine such a 'counterfactual' Israel was an exercise in exploring a horrific image of Israel, one with no real hope for the future and a continuous dreadful life in its present. From their perspective, divine avoidance of Israel's exile would have been a nightmarish scenario.

There is an additional underlying systemic and mnemonic association of monarchic, pre-cataclysmic punishment Israel with Ahaz and *vice versa* that may shed light on the issue of remembering arch-villains seriously and repeatedly punished, but not killed. The community may have construed the case, even if in a way unbeknownst to them, according to the basic pattern governing the construction of Pharaoh in the plagues story. The point of the plagues is clearly not to warn Pharaoh or teach him a lesson. The opposite is true, since Pharaoh was made unable to understand what 'normal' people would (see Exod 8:15, 32; 9:7, 34; 10:1; cf. 1 Sam 6:6). The repeated plagues are in themselves a way of further punishing the evildoer, and this requires a very much alive Pharaoh. In the case of Ahaz as Israel, the discourse of the literati would have evoked the common images of a warning that does not lead to repentance.[16] Of course, the very re-

---

[16] A case for a mnemonic, underlying association between the two sites of memory may be strengthened by noting that Pharaoh was remembered, implicitly, as a very rational/real-politik character, if Yhwh is not acknowledged, and who needs a 'miracle' to be made dumb enough not to send Israel out of Egypt, so he may be repeatedly punished; whereas Ahaz was remem-

peated rejections necessary contribute to the shaping of this Ahaz/the mentioned Israel as an arch-villain, and the price is that, like Pharaoh, he must remain alive.

Remembering Ahaz as *the* arch-villain was important for the literati for an additional significant reason. It was a strong and memorable way—archvillains are always memorable characters—to substantially balancing the weight given to individuals as agents in terms of the long-term, 'historical' trajectory of Israel, at least after the foundational Davidic-Solomonic period. This is an important issue strongly intertwined with numerous other issues within the social mindscape of a group. When the literati reading Chronicles evoked and vicariously experienced a world in which Ahaz not Manasseh was *the* arch-villain, they moved into a world in which the worst an individual archvillain can do shifts from inexorably causing the exile, the destruction of the temple, of Jerusalem and the like, to something that another individual king (in this case, Hezekiah) can easily undo already in his first year. In fact, as soon as he died, and Hezekiah assumed the throne, the Judahites (i.e., Israel) immediately perceived that the ways of Ahaz were despicable and they, along with their new king, refused to provide royal honours to Ahaz. Within this world-view, past arch-villains are indeed worth remembering, but also that their actions do not matter much in the long run.

---

bered also as a rational character, whose actions seem thoughtful, in a world that does not acknowledge Y<small>HWH</small> and Y<small>HWH</small>'s power and who is repeatedly punished as well, always missing the lesson of what happened to him because of his failure to acknowledge Y<small>HWH</small>. I addressed these matters elsewhere, see my "A Gateway to the Chronicler's Teaching: The Account of the Reign of Ahaz in 2 Chr 28,1–27," 7 (1993) 216–49.

Reshaping the Memory of Zedekiah and His Period in Chronicles*

1 Introduction and Basic Considerations

As per its title, the goal of this contribution is not to shed light on the details of the historical events around 586 BCE or to shape a historically accurate mini-biography of King Zedekiah. Instead, the goal is to reconstruct another historical king Zedekiah, namely the Zedekiah of memory that existed within a particular community that consisted of early Second Temple literati who encountered, constructed, and remembered their own Zedekiah through social acts of imagination grounded on their readings and re-readings of (past shaping/evoking) texts that existed within their core, authoritative repertoire, and in our case, especially, Kings, Chronicles, Jeremianic, and Ezekielian texts.[1] In particular, this essay focuses on the contribution of reading and rereading Chronicles to the shaping of this socially shared Zedekiah of memory. Since the contribution made by Chronicles can be reconstructed only against the background of the contributions of other texts, this work touches, even if in general strokes, on the latter as well.

Given the crucial role of matters of and approaches about (a) social memory and (b) readings and re-readings in the present endeavor, it is 'good practice' to state explicitly from the very outset some general remarks that provide the grounds out of which the approach taken here emerges. Four key observations, none of which is controversial in any way but whose implications are not always thoroughly thought out, are particularly important in this context.

---

* First published in *Congress Volume 2013* (ed. C. M. Maier; VTSup; Leiden: Brill, 2014), 370–395.
1 I locate these literati at the earliest in the late Persian period and at the latest in pre-Hasmonean times. We may refer to this period as the Early Second Temple period or perhaps and more precisely, the late Persian/early Hellenistic period. An exact date for each of these texts and more relevantly for the mnemonic system that emerged out of and became reflected in readings of each one of these texts in a way informed by all the others within one community (see below) is impossible to prove. But such a precise date is neither required nor relevant to the present study. The general time range established by the temporal boundaries mentioned above suffices. It is to be stressed also that the analysis advanced here does not require that the relevant texts existed exactly in their present forms at the time. It assumes, however, that the present forms–note the plural–of the books are significantly *representative* of the texts read by the community at that time. Most scholars would grant that point.

First, social memories exist in all human groups. Significant transcultural trends can be discerned, as studies in social or cultural memory have shown.[2] This being so, it stands to reason that approaches raised by (transcultural) social memory studies are likely to be, at least, a good heuristic tool for the reconstruction of the memory of Zedekiah in our particular group. Minimally, these approaches would suggest issues to bring up, questions to ask, and 'particularities' that can be noticed only against the existence of general trends. In other words, it is not reasonable to dismiss 'memory studies' when one conducts research on ancient Israel's social memory.[3]

Second, no group, or individual for that matter, can construe and possess a memory of one individual without involving memories of others. Memories of any person or place are always set in a large mnemonic landscape that not only involves, but also intertwines multiple memories. Very often, the very significance associated with the relevant memory is grounded in and depends on the ways in which it is intertwined with others. In other words, we are always faced with some mnemonic system of interrelated memories, not with a stand-alone memory of a person, place, or event.

Third, communities interact with the text 'as they read it,' that is, they interact with the text that emerges in their own readings. For the community their

---

2 E.g., E. Zerubavel, *Social Mindscapes: An Invitation to Cognitive Sociology* (Cambridge: Cambridge University Press, 1997); idem, *Time Maps: Collective Memory and the Social Shape of the Past* (Chicago: University of Chicago Press, 2003). My approach to social memory is more informed by those of Zerubavel and Barry Schwartz than those of, for instance, Aleida and Jan Assmann. Of course, all are intellectual descendants, in one way or another, of Maurice Halbwachs. For basic literature about all these approaches, in addition to the works mentioned above, see, for instance, E. Zerubavel, *Ancestors and Relatives: Genealogy, Identity and Community* (Oxford/New York: Oxford University Press, 2012); Barry Schwartz, *Abraham Lincoln and the Forge of National Memory* (Chicago: University of Chicago Press, 2000), idem, "Collective Forgetting and the Symbolic Power of Oneness: The Strange Apotheosis of Rosa Parks," in *Social Psychology Quarterly* 72 (2009): 123–42; A. Assmann, *Cultural Memory and Western Civilization: Functions, Media, Archives* (Cambridge/New York: Cambridge University Press, 2011); J. Assmann, *Religion and Cultural Memory* (Stanford: Stanford University Press, 2006). I am also influenced by approaches such as those present in J. V. Wertsch, *Voices of Collective Remembering* (Cambridge/New York: Cambridge University Press, 2002).

3 This is not to deny that on certain areas one needs to 'fine-tune' some common approaches and concepts that emerged within a field of Memory Studies in which social studies of ancient communities are still in a clear minority. I have addressed these issues elsewhere, cf. "Remembering the Prophets through the Reading and Rereading of a Collection of Prophetic Books in Yehud: Methodological Considerations and Explorations," in this volume, pp. 80–108.

own *read* text is 'the text.'⁴ It is only their *read* text that evokes the memories of the figures of the past that the community itself construes and remembers. Of course, no text was ever read by a community in a vacuum. Reading communities read texts in a way that is informed by (a) other texts that exist in their repertoire–to be sure, as each of them is read and understood by the reading community–and (b) their general social mindscape, or to use a different terminology (and approach), their general discourse.⁵ Since social readings and memories are historically contingent, one must state clearly whose readings and memories one is attempting to reconstruct. In this case, as stated above, the focus in this essay is on a community of, at least, ideologically, Jerusalem-centered literati in either the late Persian or the early Hellenistic period who encountered, constructed, and remembered their Zedekiah through social acts of imagination grounded on their readings and re-readings of texts within their core repertoire, and especially, Kings, Chronicles, Jeremianic, and Ezekielian texts.⁶

Fourth, communities strongly tend to read their texts synchronically. It is extremely unlikely that the literati of the early Second Temple period went about reading these texts by first separating each of them into its multiple redactional layers, assigned each of them to a particular period in their construed past, and then looked for and reconstructed the other texts that populated each one of these periods and which may have informed that particular layer. In other words, their mode of reading texts was not like the one of our redactional critical colleagues and for a reason. The latter do not ask the same questions from the text than the former did. One may say that the historical literati of the period read their texts in a mode of reading akin to what we tend to call 'synchronic' and that, as they read the text before them, even in ways that they were not fully aware of, they were informed by their world of knowledge, including their repertoire of texts.

To be sure, this does not mean at all that the kind of textual tensions that redactional critical scholars tend to highlight simply vanish or become irrele-

---

4 In fact, the community of readers construes its own 'implied author,' as it reads the book in its own way. If authorial intention is considered significant within the discourse of the community, then they would strongly tend to identify the intention of their 'implied author' with the intention of the 'author' of the book. In other words, the construed character of their implied author becomes invisible to them and thus they trust and imagine that they are reading according to the intentions of 'the author.'

5 This is the reason that there is a need for a careful study of the *Sitz im Diskurs* alongside with and to large extent in a way interwoven with that of the (more traditional) *Sitz im Leben* of texts, and *vice versa*.

6 See n. 1.

vant. To the contrary, these tensions become, from the viewpoint of the community reading the whole book, representative of a set or sets of multiple voices that the community cannot but end up associating with the implied author of the text they are reading. A corollary from these considerations is that from the perspective of the reading community, all these voices had to be construed as complementary, at least at some level, since they all go back to the same implied author or central character.

2 Social Memory and Last Rulers

Rulers who are construed and remembered as (the real) 'last rulers,'[7] just as those remembered as (real) 'first rulers,' tend to be memorable characters, or in more precise language, they tend to carry substantial mnemonic mindshare in the relevant mnemonic communities. A number of processes converge to create such a systemic preference to turn last and first rulers into memorable characters. For one, they are associated with turning points within core narratives about the past upon which the group agrees. Turning points draw attention to themselves because of the crucial role they play in shifting the trajectory of the plot in core mnemonic meta-narratives and because of their associated role in the shaping of periodization. The latter (i.e., periodization) is a crucial structuring device in mnemonic narratives and plays important roles in conceptualizing the past. Last rulers whose memories are intrinsically associated with those of turning points become thus memorable signposts for these discontinuities and at times even an embodiment of the pre-change society.

The more memorable a character becomes, the more likely it will turn into a 'magnet' for different attributes, positive or negative, that are important to the remembering community and the more likely central issues and images in the community will become associated or 'embodied,' as it were, in the character. As a result, that which the remembering society strongly values or rejects tends to be associated with these characters. In turn, this very feature makes the character even more memorable and thus an ongoing positive feedback tends to emerge.

Moreover, mnemonic (meta)narratives tend to provide the community with explanations for what happened at the turning points, i.e., to construe a sense of reasonable causality that contributes to the socialization of the group. Thus memories of first and last characters tend to become an important

---

[7] E.g., last rulers within a dynasty, or of a polity; last leaders of particular groups or the like.

mnemonic playground for negotiations between various proposals concerning why the community reached the turning point and the significance or lack thereof of the turning point itself in the large scale of things, as construed by the community. This very process generates a strong tendency to turn memories of the last and first rulers into didactic lessons. It is not surprising then that at times memories of last rulers become involved in constructions and negotiations of 'self' and 'other.' Implied questions such as "why did 'we' (notice the element of identification of the remembered group) suffer that upheaval?" or "what can 'we' learn from it?" or, alternatively, "why did 'they' (notice the element of 'otherization') suffer such a calamity and what can 'we' learn from it?" often play important roles in the social construction and use of memory.

In sum, last rulers are often memorable characters, populate relatively memorable times, and provide good didactic reasons. Since memory is the main language in many societies, including ancient Israel, for thinking of and exploring core concepts and sets of concepts, the particular ways in which these characters were remembered at particular times and by particular groups provides significant information about the remembering groups themselves, their world-views, and one may say their shared social mindscape.

Finally, turning points, by their very virtue of being such, evoke a sense of discontinuity between what was before and what followed. This said, when the remembering community identifies with the one it imagines as experiencing the turning point, the turning point, as a site of memory and particularly because it serves as a marker of discontinuity, conveys also a strong, implied sense of a higher-level, trans-temporal continuity that transcends the vagaries of time, including temporal turning points. After all, the remembering community identifies with and to some extent 'is' also (another temporal manifestation of) the remembered community and *vice versa*.[8] These considerations cannot but affect the ways in which, at least sometimes, last rulers, strongly associated with these turning points, are remembered.

Given all the above, it is not surprising that last rulers tend to be remembered as characterized by certain sets of attributes. For instance, since they em-

---

8 A good example of the *vice versa* aspect of the mentioned relation: the David that the literati imagined, construed and remembered when reading הוֹשִׁיעֵנוּ אֱלֹהֵי יִשְׁעֵנוּ וְקַבְּצֵנוּ וְהַצִּילֵנוּ מִן־הַגּוֹיִם in 1 Chr 16:35 is one who identified himself with, reflected, and reinforced the self-perception of the remembering community. I expanded on this example and the general issues associated with it, in the context of Chronicles, in E. Ben Zvi, "Who Knew What? The Construction of the Monarchic Past in Chronicles and Implications for the Intellectual Setting of Chronicles," in *Judah and the Judeans in the Fourth Century BCE* (eds. O. Lipschits et al.; Winona Lake: Eisenbrauns, 2007), 349–60.

body endings of polities, they are often remembered as evil, weak, or both. Good examples, and across times and cultures, are Naram-Sin, "Sardanapolus," Nabonaid, King Jié (the last king of the Xia dynasty, the first dynasty in Chinese records), and King Zhou (=Di Xin; the last king of the Shang dynasty that followed the Xia dynasty), Nero, Domitian, "Boabdil"/Abu 'Abdallah Muhammad XII, George III, the last king of the "American colonies," and to use relatively contemporary example, Gorbachev as he is often remembered within significant sections of the population in present day Russia.[9]

King Jié and King Zhou became both archetypical tyrannical emperors in Chinese memory.[10] Interestingly enough, in this case, some memories associated with one became associated with the other, including references to sexual wantonness and the negative influence of women on them. Similar mnemonic roles lead to partial mnemonic overlaps. The Naram-Sin of memory becomes, for the most part, an archetype of the sinful king who defies the gods rather than submitting to their will, as painful as the latter might be in ancient Near Eastern lore, though he was also imagined as a repentant king to be emulated by future generations (see the Cuthaean Legend). Sardanapalus is a Greek version of Ashurbanipal that stands as a primary example of the oriental "Other" in Greek literature. Nabonaid is mad, thinks that he is wise but is a fool and acts against the proper cult. Nero is crazy and bloodthirsty, Boabdil cries like a woman instead of fighting like a man, whereas George III is a tyrant (and a mad man). In all these cases, the remembering community construes the last king as the Other who embodies features that the remembering group considers negative.

Significantly, the way in which these last rulers are remembered may have little and, at times, nothing to do with 'history' as we know it; some may not

---

9 Just a few days after I read the paper at the Congress in Munich, a false rumor about Gorbachev's death spread in Russian social media. Most of the reactions to his (alleged) death in Russia, as posted in Russian social media, were virulent and strongly confirmed the point made above. See http://www.spiegel.de/international/world/false-story-about-gorbachev-death-unleashes-wave-of-hate-a-915670.html [cited 8 January 2014]. (It is worth noting that Gorbachev is usually remembered very differently in 'Western' countries. Social memory is always contingent.)

10 Additional last kings were considered particularly bad rulers. See S. H. Chang, *History and Legend: Ideas and Images in the Ming Historical Novels* (Ann Arbor: University of Michigan Press, 1990), 148–49; X. Guo, *The Ideal Chinese Political Leader: A Historical and Cultural Perspective* (Westport, Conn.: Praeger, 2002), 9–10. The following examples involve, for the most part, well-known characters among the target readership of this volume. For the sake of brevity and space, I have included below notes only for figures who may not be as well-known among, at least, significant sectors of readers.

even be historically speaking last kings (e. g., Naram-Sin and Ashurbanipal), but all of them were remembered in ways that served didactic purposes for those remembering them and that suit well their own narratives about themselves. This is not surprising, since social memories that suit well the main metanarratives and social mindscape of a particular group tend to be preferred by the relevant group over potential others.

But, of course, evil and/or weak last rulers are not the only option. At times, other patterns may end up being preferred, exactly because these characterizing patterns fit better the main meta-narratives and social mindscape of the remembering group. Thus, last rulers may be imagined as doomed, but defiant heroes embodying resistance. Clear examples are Cuauhtémoc in contemporary Mexican society,[11] Boudica, the Celtic queen, some twentieth century constructions of Bar-Kochba (or of the leaders of the first war against Rome), and Prince Lazar who fell in the Battle of Kosovo in 1389 in a widespread version of Serbian social memory.[12] Often, in these cases, the last leader becomes not only a heroic martyr to be remembered and to some extent an embodying symbol of the entire remembering group, but also a type of a future leader or leader to come, thus creating a narrative that moves from calamity in the remembered past to a glorious period in the remembered (and socially imagined/construed) future.[13] The 'last of' is thus a pre-figuration of the next great first. Remembering the past be-

---

[11] On Cuauhtémoc, see, e. g., L. L. Johnson, "Digging Up Cuauhtémoc," in *Death, Dismemberment, and Memory: Body Politics in Latin America* (ed. idem; Albuquerque: University of New Mexico Press, 2004), 207–44. There are numerous places and individuals carrying the name Cuauhtémoc in contemporary Mexico. (Not surprisingly, there are almost no places carrying the name 'Cortés'). Cf. also O. Paz, *The Labyrinth of Solitude: Life and Thought in Mexico* (New York: Grove Press, 1961), esp. 83–86; significantly, Paz's detractors in Mexico have maintained that he is no Cuauhtémoc but 'La Malinche,' that is, the very opposite of Cuauhtémoc; cf. S. M. Cypess, *Uncivil Wars: Elena Garro, Octavio Paz, and the Battle for Cultural Memory* (Austin: University of Texas Press, 2012), 33. In other words, the Cuauhtémoc of memory serves to construe and adjudicate important issues in contemporary Mexico.

[12] See, e. g., S. P. Ramet, "Dead Kings and National Myths: Why Myths of Founding and Martyrdom are Important," in *Civic and Uncivic Values: Serbia in the Post-Milošević Era* (eds. O. Listhaug et al.; Budapest/New York: Central European University Press, 2011), 267–98, esp. 281–92; cf. L. Johnston, "Religion and the Balkans–Blessing or Curse?" in *Understanding the War in Kosovo* (eds. F. Bieber and Ž. Daskalovski; London/Portland, Oreg.: Frank Cass, 2003), 184–95; 187.

[13] While–one may add–at the same time advancing a self-understanding of the present-day remembering community as a current manifestation of a long-suffering/martyred group and often, when appropriate, as even a Christ-like community. To be sure, self-identification with the suffering Christ carries in all these cases, even if in an implicit way, also a self-understanding as a future victorious Christ. Within these narratives, suffering and death lead to resurrection and victory. In fact, the suffering is seen as a pre-condition for the eventual final victory.

comes a way of constructing and remembering the future, and thus necessarily the latter conditions much of the former.

At times, however, last kings or rulers are relegated to very secondary mnemonic roles or practically forgotten. Such a process also says much about the main mnemonic narrative of the community, the construction of turning points in its plot, and about its identity. An obvious example is the case of Charles X who was the last king of France–Louis Philippe was king of the French, but even he is nowhere as remembered as Louis XVI and Marie Antoinette. The obvious issue at stake here is, of course, the centrality of the French Revolution. The much higher social mindshare allocated in ancient Israel to Saul over Ish-Ba'al is another example. Not surprisingly, from a perspective of social memory, Chronicles moves the narrative from Saul directly to David (1 Chr 10:13–11:1).[14]

Let me summarize the discussion up to this point: Last rulers tend to be memorable and when they are not, it is worth exploring why this is the case. When they are memorable, they are construed and remembered according to several main 'types,' some around the realm of images of the evil, sinful, weak, tyrannical ruler and some around that of the tragic, heroic leader, and even in some cases, the type of the future leader or leaders. When the last ruler tends to be construed as sinful and the like, this tends to involve some process of otherization, which at least, helps us as historians to construe what the remembering community considers to be the most negative traits. When the leader is linked to the future, constructions of that future play a generative role for the development of memories of the last king.

To be sure, there will always be cases in which these patterns are not present, and there will always be cases in which multiple patterns seem to be at work. These are the most interesting cases. It is possible that such complex sites of memory evolved as such because they emerged, originally, out of mnemonic struggles within a community or between communities or through processes of social or at least discursive encompassment of the 'other' (see the

---

14 As the case of Saul demonstrates, multiple patterns may also be at work in the same community. There is no doubt that he was remembered as a sinner, worthy of death and 1 Chr 10:13 contributes to the shaping of his memory particularly by emphasizing this very aspect, but this is not the entire story. Readers of Chronicles were also readers of other texts in the community and vice versa. Saul was also remembered along the lines of a tragic and heroic last leader. Moreover, there existed also an underlying, minor mnemonic tendency reflecting and activating a connection between Saul and some form of future leadership (see Esth 2:5).

case of General Lee).¹⁵ Whether this is the case or not in a particular instance, when these complex sites of memory become an integral part of the social memory of a group that is removed from those in which the original mnemonic struggles or encompassment processes may have taken place, and likely has not much or any awareness of these past circumstances, a very different situation emerges. In such cases, various features, at times, in tension with each other co-exist within a particular figure of the past. The result is a sense of fuzziness and an inherent process of continuous balancing created by the embodiment of multiple, and at times seemingly contradicting, images in one single mnemonic figure.¹⁶

In what follows these considerations will guide the present construction of a reasonable reconstruction of the memory of Zedekiah within the frame of the general comprehensive and integrative social memory of the literati of the early Second Temple and the contribution of Chronicles to the shaping of such a Zedekiah of memory. Since shaping and negotiating the memory of Zedekiah among these literati had to involve, whether directly or indirectly, an engagement on matters such as the catastrophe of 586 BCE, constructions of exile, constructions of the Davidic dynasty, divine ('historical') causality, political thought, and crucially important, also images of Israel's future, this Zedekiah of memory is very much worth exploring. This holds true whether Zedekiah was minimized, maximized, characterized as wicked or as pious, as a type of a future leader or not; whether he was partially or fully 'demoted' from being the last king of Judah or not at all. Since all the above hold true to some extent within the remembering community discussed in this contribution, the figure of the Zedekiah of memory that existed among these literati serves in many ways as an excellent ground to explore memories, worldviews, and key issues within the social mindscape of the community.

3 The Mnemonic Environment of the Zedekiah of Chronicles

To understand the contribution of Chronicles to the shaping of the memory of Zedekiah within the general mnemonic system of the community, it is imperative that, even if necessarily just from a bird's-eye view, the contributions of other

---

15 On grammars of encompassment, see G. Baumann, "Grammars of Identity/Alterity: A Structural Approach," in *Grammars of Identity/Alterity: A Structural Approach* (eds. idem and A. Gingrich; EASA Series 3; New York/Oxford: Berghahn Books, 2006), 18–50.
16 E.g., the case of Saul, see n. 14. See also "Exploring the Memory of Moses 'The Prophet' in Late Persian/Early Hellenistic Yehud/Judah," in this volume, pp. 199–231.

texts to that image be explored, both for what they say by themselves and what they say about the mnemonic system at work within the community.[17]

Even the most cursory study of the partial memories of Zedekiah[18] evoked by reading Kings shows–in the light of the transcultural mnemonic trends to construe last rulers discussed above–a very strong tendency to minimize the impact of this last king. To be sure, he was remembered as sinful, but readers of Kings were asked to understand that neither the end came about because of him nor tentative new beginnings have any connection with him; in fact, as much as Kings hints at them, they are connected to a previous king, Jehoiachin (2 Kgs 25:27–30).[19] Obviously, the Zedekiah evoked by reading Kings was not patterned as a heroic resisting figure,[20] but also not even as a tragic but still positive character. In fact, the real, 'good' tragic hero in the story of Kings is Josiah, whose great deeds cannot stop the calamity from coming and who is well

---

17 This is so, because the community read and was aware of all these texts and considered the implied authors of all of them to be godly and authoritative voices. Thus all the partial memories about Zedekiah evoked by reading one of these texts were directly or indirectly informed by and informing one another, drawing attention to or away from features associated with Zedekiah in each of the works, while at the very same time, integrating them by embodying them all in their Zedekiah of memory. The same holds, of course, for any important figure of ancient past whose memory was reflected, shaped and evoked by more than text considered to be 'authoritative'/ 'godly' within the community (e.g., David, Isaiah, and Moses).

18 Obviously, this is not the place for a comprehensive analysis of the account of Zedekiah in Kings. See, e.g., E. Abate, *La fine del regno di Sedecia* (Textos y estudios "Cardenal Cisneros" 76; Madrid: CSIC, 2008). On the account in Kings, and the question of its historicity and its relation to other accounts, see also J. Pakkala, "Zedekiah's Fate and the Dynastic Succession," in *JBL* 125 (2006): 443–52. On redactional and text critical issues in the relevant text in Kings see also R. F. Person, "II Kings 24,18–25,30 and Jeremiah 52: A Text-Critical Case Study in the Redaction History of the Deuteronomistic History," in *ZAW* 105 (1993): 174–205.

19 On the surface, one may have anticipated that in a community or at least in a text that asked the community to associate new beginnings with Jehoiachin, a tendency to remember, at least, this king as not an evil-doer–and as a substantially memorable character would have emerged. But such a tendency would have been strongly dis-preferred by the ideological and narrative grammar at work in a book such as Kings. After all, in Kings, the kings following Josiah had to be evil-doers and not very much worth remembering. The basic evaluation of Jehoiachin in 2 Kgs 24:9 is not explicitly balanced elsewhere in Kings and certainly this book does not draw particular attention to any attenuation of such evaluation. It is worth noting that the tendency to positively characterize Jehoiachin as a king eventually emerged, though not in Kings. For instance, Josephus explicitly depicts monarchic period Jehoiachin in positive terms in *Ant.* 10.100; see also 2 Bar 1:3 ("for the former tribes were forced by their kings to sin, but these two [Judah and Benjamin] have themselves forced and compelled their kings to sin"), which likely refers to both Jehoiachin and Zedekiah.

20 See 2 Kgs 25:4–5; a point even heightened in the parallel text in Jer 52:7; see Abate, *La fine del regno di Sedecia*, 189.

aware of this fact.²¹ It is particularly noteworthy that whereas the previous great reforming king Hezekiah is remembered as followed by a memorable villain who undoes his reforms (Manasseh) in Kings, there is no room for such a character following Josiah. After the king dies, the gates of calamity open and neither memorable villains nor heroes have a place.

Of course, all this requires an emphatic rejection of the position that the last king is the worst and the very reason for the calamity. Interestingly, Kings communicated to its target readership that actually this is more of a rule than an exception. To be sure, this is the case insofar as it concerns Hoshea, the last king of the Northern Kingdom (see 2 Kgs 17 and esp. 2 Kgs 17:2). Ahab is a complex figure in Kings, but still the main villain for the house of Omri within Kings and in the accepted memory of the period among the literati (see 2 Kgs 21:3, 13; cf. Mic 6:16 and *passim* in Chronicles²²). Of course, Ahab was not the last king of the Omrite dynasty. The same pattern holds true for Jeroboam I, who is the king remembered for causing the fall of his dynasty, but not its last king. Neither Elah (see 1 Kgs 16:8–10) nor Zechariah (2 Kgs 14:29; 15:8–11), who are actually last kings of their respective dynasties, are remembered as main or memorable vil-

---

21 I discussed elsewhere the Josiah of the Persian period. See E. Ben Zvi, "Imagining Josiah's Book and the Implications of Imagining it in Early Persian Yehud," in *Berührungspunkte. Studien zur Sozial- und Religionsgeschichte Israels und seiner Umwelt. Festschrift für Rainer Albertz zu seinem 65. Geburtstag* (eds. R. Schmitt et al.; AOAT 250; Münster: Ugarit, 2008), 193–212; idem, "Observations on Josiah's Account in Chronicles and Implications for Reconstructing the Worldview of the Chronicler," in *Essays on Ancient Israel in Its Near Eastern Context: A Tribute to Nadav Na'aman* (eds. Yairah Amit et al.; Winona Lake: Eisenbrauns, 2006), 89–106 and idem, "Josiah and the Prophetic Books: Some Observations," in *Good Kings and Bad Kings* (ed. Lester L. Grabbe; LHBOTS 393; European Seminar in Historical Methodology 5; London: T&T Clark, 2005), 47–64. For another reconstruction of the Josiah of the Persian Period, see Joseph Blenkinsopp, "Remembering Josiah," in *Remembering Biblical Figures in the Late Persian and Early Hellenistic Periods* (eds. D. V. Edelman and E. Ben Zvi; Oxford: Oxford University Press, 2013), 236–56. For Josiah in Chronicles, see also L. C. Jonker, *Reflections of King Josiah in Chronicles: Late Stages of the Josiah Reception in 2 Chr 34f* (Textpragmatische Studien zur Hebräischen Bibel 2; Gütersloh: Gütersloher Verlagshaus, 2003); H.-S. Bae, *Vereinte Suche nach JHWH. Die Hiskianische und Josianische Reform in der Chronik* (BZAW 355; Berlin: De Gruyter, 2005) and K. A. Ristau, "Reading and Rereading Josiah: The Chronicler's Representation of Josiah for the Postexilic Community," in *Community Identity in Judean Historiography: Biblical and Comparative Perspectives* (eds. G. N. Knoppers and K. A. Ristau; Winona Lake: Eisenbrauns, 2009), 219–47.

22 I discussed elsewhere the house of Ahab in Chronicles, see my "The House of Omri/Ahab in Chronicles," in *Ahab Agonistes: The Rise and Fall of the Omri Dynasty* (ed. L. L. Grabbe; LHBOTS 421; European Seminar in Historical Methodology 6; London/New York: T&T Clark, 2007), 41–53.

lains. In fact, the Kings suggests that there is very little worth remembering about these two, except for their being assassinated.

This strong and repeated emphasis on the last king as neither the worst monarch nor the reason for the fall of a dynasty or polity informed the reading community. This sustained preference for constructions of the last king as neither a memorable great villain nor an heroic character, but actually someone whose actions are not something that is so worth remembering (note the lack of details in 2 Kgs 17:2), could not but create an expectation within that readership for a somewhat similar construction of Zedekiah, the last king of Judah, as neither the worst king of Judah nor the real cause of the fall of Judah. The book of Kings delivers on that expectation.

When one encounters consistent, strong deviations from usual, cross-cultural mnemonic grammars of construing last rulers, it makes sense to examine them carefully, for usually there is a reason for the divergence (see above, section 2). Often deviations from common cross-cultural mnemonic patterns are explainable by and point at some important and crucial feature of the discourse of the remembering society. Such deviations from 'normal' patterns of memories of last rulers are often associated with or a response to a lack of correspondence between (a) significant aspects of the community's main mnemonic (meta-)narrative or some important section of it and (b) any substantial stress on the figure of the 'actual' last ruler.

Clearly, this is the case in Kings. The slot of the sinful king whose evil brings about the end is not only allocated to Manasseh in Kings, but also, and to a large extent, *has* to be assigned to him. This is so, because Manasseh and Josiah are, in this book, the main two characters of the late monarchic period and they are shaped as heightened opposite figures. In other words, the main mnemonic narrative is partially structured around and remembered in terms of a 'hero' and a corresponding 'villain' (and *vice versa*)–a situation common to many memorable narratives. The hero and the villain complement and necessitate each other. In Kings, Manasseh plays the role of the evil king whose actions bring about the end and Josiah that of the tragic pious character. The former multiplies wrongness and ensures that Yhwh will act against Jerusalem and Judah, whereas the other although successfully removes all worldly signs of the previous wrongdoing, still cannot remove their lasting effects on Judah, in Yhwh's economy, as construed in this book.

Of course, there is a reason for structuring the memory of the past in such a way in this particular book. It serves well to maximize the social mindshare for the pious hero, and above all the remembered reform of Josiah–whether historical or not. It ensures that the reform becomes the high point of the remembered late monarchic period and strongly legitimizes it, against any potential counter-argument.[23] Preference for such structuring of the mnemonic narrative of the fall of the monarchic polity and Jerusalem goes together (and cannot but go together) with a strong preference for minimizing the chances for the development of extremely memorable, royal characters after the death of Josiah.

There are, of course, additional and complementary plots at work. For instance, the community is also asked to remember that the people from the very beginning behaved in sinful ways and caused the well-anticipated calamity, which was already foreseen by Moses (e.g., Deut 30:1–5; 32:19–25 and, among others, the pragmatic message in late Persian Yehud of Deut 28:15–68; 29:13–27; 30:17–19; 31:19–22). This plot serves to emphasize agency in postmonarchic Israel, the figure of Moses, the primacy of *torah*–a point strongly communicated also by the central role the reform of Josiah–and the importance of prophetic voices teaching *torah* (2 Kgs 21:8–9; cf. 2 Kgs 17:13), who in the past were rejected, but hopefully will not be in the future if further calamity is to be avoided.

Within this mnemonic narrative, there is again little room for Zedekiah to become a major character. Thus it is not surprising that the reference to the failure to listening to *torah* and commandments is explicitly mentioned within Manasseh's account not within Zedekiah's; although Zedekiah was presented as an evil-doer, nothing explicit about the evil he did was construed as worth remembering, and even the crucial decision to rebel was framed primarily as an outcome of Y<small>HWH</small>'s pre-existing decision to destroy the temple (lit. to "expel the people of Judah and Jerusalem from Y<small>HWH</small>'s presence," see 2 Kgs 24:20) rather than as the (real) cause of its destruction. Finally, since the book of Kings associates hope for the future with Jehoiachin, it is not surprising that the text would create memorable images of the end of Zedekiah's line. He is a dead end and may be counted as 'childless' (contrast with Jer 22:28–30; see below).

Jeremianic texts also evoked images of Zedekiah.[24] Readers of the prophetic books encountered and learned from and about the prophetic characters that

---

[23] On these matters, see esp. H.-J. Stipp, "Remembering Josiah's Reforms in Kings," in *Remembering and Forgetting in Early Second Temple Judah* (eds. E. Ben Zvi and C. Levin; FAT 85; Tübingen: Mohr Siebeck, 2012), 225–38. The (partial) 'Mosaic' portrayal of Josiah, obviously, reinforces this point.

[24] For studies of Zedekiah in (the book of) Jeremiah, mainly though not only from redactional critical perspectives, see, e.g., H.-J. Stipp, "Zedekiah in the Book of Jeremiah: On the Formation of a Biblical Character," in *CBQ* 58 (1996): 627–48; J. Applegate, "The Fate of Zedekiah: Redactional Debate in the Book of Jeremiah," in *VT* 58 (1998): 137–60; idem, "The Fate of Zedekiah: Redactional Debate in the Book of Jeremiah. Part II," in *VT* 58 (1998): 301–8; E. Di Pede, "Jérémie et les rois de Juda, Sédécias et Joaqim", in *VT* 56 (2006): 452–69; J. Pakkala, "Zedekiah's Fate"; Abate, *La fine del regno di Sedecia;* Rannfrid I. Thelle, "Babylon in the Book of Jeremiah

they evoked as they read the different books. A crucial role of the prophetic books was actually to bring to the present of the community, as it were, the prophets of old. Reading Jeremianic texts was bound to turn Zedekiah into a secondary, but still necessary character to remember, because of his many interactions with Jeremiah. In other words, to construe, remember, and encounter vicariously Jeremiah, the literati had, at times, to remember, construe, and encounter Zedekiah. This not only allowed Jeremianic texts to encode and communicate memories whose inclusion in Kings would have been strongly dis-preferred, but actually required them to do so.

This said, clearly there is a Jeremianic voice evoking memories of Zedekiah that recalls among the literati the voice of Kings on the matter, as extensive parallels occur (cf. 2 Kgs 24:18–25:21 and Jer 52:1–27; see also Jer 39:1–10). At times, there are, however, substantial differences between some Jeremianic voices and those in Kings. Reading Jer 38:17–18 and remembering Zedekiah is remembering that had Zedekiah acted differently, the city would not have fallen. Doing so is bringing memories of Zedekiah in line with a common tendency in memories about last rulers, that is, the last ruler and his or her deeds cause the 'end.' In other words, reading Jer 38:17–18 and remembering Zedekiah involves 'normalizing' social memory and 'correcting' the strong deviation communicated by Kings, on precisely these matters. A tendency to stress that Zedekiah was responsible for the calamity is likely to go ahead with tendencies to heighten a negative characterization of the king, and this actually happens within a voice within the Jeremianic tradition.

But there are other voices also embodied in the Jeremiah of the literati's memory. Reading Jeremiah meant also that Zedekiah was to be imagined and remembered *also* as a ruler who was not necessarily so much an evil king, but an ineffective one (see, for instance, MT Jer 37:17–21).[25] Remembering him as a king who is not in control of his subjects or at least the elite among them (e.g., Jer 34:8–11) and whose will in practice was subordinated to that of his officers who actually lorded over him (e.g., Jer 38:4–28) is remembering a king who may not necessarily be evil, but who let disorder overcome order and whose image is

---

(MT): Negotiating a Power Shift," in *Prophecy in the Book of Jeremiah* (eds. H. Barstad and R. G. Kratz; BZAW 388; Berlin/New York: De Gruyter; 2009), 187–232, esp. 224–32.

25 The LXX text presents a more negative image of Zedekiah. For a comparative study of MT Jer 37:18–21 and its LXX counterpart, LXX Jer 44:18–21 and for a similar case between MT Jer 38:9 and LXX Jer 45:9, see Stipp, "Zedekiah," esp. 638–41; cf. E. Tov, *The Text-Critical Use of the Septuagint in Biblical Research* (Jerusalem: Simor, 1981), 296–98. Both versions could have co-existed within the repertoire of the Jerusalem-centered literati of the early Second Temple period.

to some extent, within the discourse of the period, partially feminized and certainly far removed from the 'masculine' warrior king. He is the weak ineffective king who ends up paying for his weakness with his kingdom and his life (e. g., Jer 34:21–22).²⁶

This aspect of the Zedekiah of memory associated with Jeremiah's voice serves also to shape a partial contrast to Jehoiakim that in itself encapsulated a significant narrative: Whereas Jehoiakim overrules the wishes of, at least, some of his advisors, to do evil (Jer 36:10–26; esp. vv. 19, 25), Zedekiah is overruled by (some of) his officers and thus still evil doing prevails and catastrophe ensues.²⁷ Whether the king is an evil-doer or a weak and perhaps even pathetic character, calamity awaits. Although the images of the evil and the weak king are in this case divided between two figures, from a conceptual and communicative perspective, they converge and together conform to some typical patterns of constructing last kings.

Yet at the same time, the not necessarily evil Zedekiah may evolve to fulfill another one of the basic characterizations of last kings. By listening to Jeremiah's voice through their readings, the literati activated also memories that at the very least hinted at a construction of Zedekiah as a positive character and thus one who is worthy of providing a link to the future (see Jer 23:5–6).²⁸ This tendency ended up being clearly manifested in 4Q470.²⁹ But it is unlikely to have emerged out of nothing in the late Second Temple period. It builds on Jer 23:5–6, and on Jer 32:5 and Jer 34:2–5 that communicated to the literati that the end of Zedekiah portrayed in Kings was probably not the end of his story in YHWH's view. To be sure, this development was facilitated by memories of Zedekiah as a weak, over-

---

26 Although the context suggests that Zedekiah was not among those who "turned around and took back the male and female slaves they had set free and brought them again into subjection as slaves" (Jer 34:11; NRSV), he is still punished.
27 Cf. with memories of Zedekiah reflected, shaped in and evoked by *Ant.* 10.103–105, 10.120 or, 2 Bar 1:3 and in an even later society, *b. 'Arak. 17a; b. Sanh. 103a*.
28 The name of the future king in the LXX version is *Iosedek*. Cf. J. Lust, "Messianism and the Greek Version of Jeremiah: Jer 23,5–6 and 33,14–26," in idem, *Messianism and the Septuagint: Collected Essays* (ed. K. Hauspie; BETL 178; Leuven: Leuven University Press, 2004), 41–67; 42–54, 66; and also Stipp, "Zedekiah," 644. Note, however, that for the present purposes what counts is how the literati of the Late Persian or Early Hellenistic Judah may have read this text, both at the denotative and connotative levels.
29 On 4Q470 see E. Larson, "4Q470 and the Angelic Rehabilitation of King Zedekiah," in *DSD* 1 (1994): 210–18; E. Larson, L. H. Schiffman, and J. Strugnell, "4QText Mentioning Hezekiah," in *Qumran Cave 4, XIV: Parabiblical Texts, Part 2* (eds. M. Broshi et al.; DJD 19; Oxford: Clarendon Press, 1995), 235–44; F. García Martínez, *The Dead Sea Scrolls Study Edition* (Grand Rapids: Eerdmans, 1997–1998).

powered, but not necessarily a villain king that were mentioned above, but was not necessitated by them.

At the same time, the book of Jeremiah, just as Kings shaped a link between Jehoiachin and hope in the post-calamity future that clearly and explicitly skips Zedekiah. This tendency taken to its full potential would entail demoting the latter from the slot of the last king in social memory. Significantly, this generative mnemonic tendency to skip Zedekiah finds its most clear expression in yet another book, Ezekiel, in which the last king is actually Jehoiachin.[30]

Moreover, even within this mnemonic tendency there are some differences. Kings, as one would expect, along with the parallel text in Jeremiah (see 2 Kgs 25:27–30 and Jer 52:31–34), emphasizes Jehoiachin himself and the royal family as an opening for the future. Jer 24 shifts the focus from the king to the people who are symbolically associated with the king. Of course, from a system perspective, both interact with a text such as Jer 22:28–30, which concludes by stating "none of his [Jehoiachin's] offspring shall succeed in sitting on the throne of David, and ruling again in Judah." Here we have yet another Jeremianic voice to which the literati cannot but pay attention and which also influences their memories of the past and the future that they vicariously experience through their readings and social imagination.

Obviously, this analysis may be further developed, but the main picture suffices for the present purposes. The mnemonic environment in which the Zedekiah of Chronicles functions is characterized by multiple voices that mutually inform, highlight, and activate or balance others. All these Jeremianic voices reflect, in one way or another, common generative grammars for memories of last rulers. Whereas the various images were, on the surface, in 'logical' tension with one another, all of them were embodied in one single character of the past (Jeremiah). The result is that Jeremiah becomes a site of memory characterized by integrative fuzziness. This, however, is actually to be expected within the discourse of these literati and fits well the tendency within their social mindscape

---

[30] Following Christophe Nihan, we may note that "the oracles and visions in Ezekiel are dated according to the year of the deportation of this king (see 1:2), as though he were still the legitimate ruler in Judah"; idem, "The Memory of Ezekiel in Postmonarchic Yehud," in *Remembering Biblical Figures in the Late Persian & Early Hellenistic Periods: Social Memory and Imagination* (eds. D. V. Edelman and E. Ben Zvi; Oxford: Oxford University Press, 2013), 415–48; 441. Significantly, there is a voice in Ezekiel, according to which he (embodying, of course, his descendants) is to be imagined as the last who becomes the new 'first' (see Ezek 17:22–24). Significantly, there is no negative portrayal of Jehoiachin in Ezekiel. As for Zedekiah, in contrast, see Ezek 12:12–14; 17:11–21; 21:30 and Nihan, "The Memory of Ezekiel," 440–41.

towards a substantial degree of fuzziness, particularly in relation to their main sites of memory.[31]

Finally, similar images may be expressed in different books and embodied in more than one communicator in the past of the community. This is so, because, after all, the underlying grammars generating preferences (or dispreferences) for certain types of memories are, above all, society bound.

4 Chronicles' Contribution

What did Chronicles bring to the mix? How did remembering the Zedekiah of Chronicles contribute to the shaping of a multi-faceted, communal site of memory, a Zedekiah who integrates all these perspectives and embodies all these images in one person?[32] At one level, just as Kings, Chronicles communicates to the community that the last four kings of Judah should not occupy a lot of its mindshare and thus reinforces this message. Certainly, once Josiah dies, the story moves quickly into the calamity. In fact, in Chronicles only twenty verses separate between the crowning of Jehoahaz, Josiah's successor, and the burning the temple (2 Chr 36:1–19). This is less than the narrative space assigned to a story ending with a non-functioning, but still standing temple, namely the account of Ahaz (2 Chr 28:1–27), or for that matter, to the story of Manasseh (2 Chr 33:1–20). It is certainly far less than the space allocated to the account of Hezekiah, the king who re-opened the gates of the temple, after Ahaz, or that of Josiah. Chronicles suggested to its readership that all these periods contained more matters worthy of being mentioned in the book, that is, remembered by the community, than the account of all the last kings together.

The point of Chronicles, here, is that as soon as Josiah died, the gates that withheld the divine punishment promised by Huldah, and understood by Josiah, were finally broken. On these matters, Chronicles and Kings mutually reinforce

---

[31] Cf. with their Moses, who spoke in 'D', 'H' and 'P' and communicated multiple messages, some of them in logical tension with each other, and still all of them were associated with Moses, embodied and integrated all in their Moses of memory. Cf. with the community's image of YHWH. I discussed these matters in "Exploring the Memory of Moses," in this volume, pp. 199–231.

[32] For recent approaches and questions about Zedekiah and Chronicles other than those advanced here, see, e.g., B. Becking, "More than a Pawn in Their Game: Zedekiah and the Fall of Jerusalem in 2 Chronicles 36:11–21," in *Rewriting Biblical History: Essays on Chronicles and Ben Sira in Honor of Pancratius C. Beentjes* (eds. J. Corley and H. van Grol; Deuterocanonical and Cognate Literature Studies 7; Berlin: De Gruyter, 2011), 257–71; idem, "Zedekiah, Josephus and the Dating of the Books of Chronicles," *SJOT* 25 (2011): 217–33.

the points communicated by the other and a particular preferred trend in social memory in ancient Israel is noticeable.[33]

Moreover, it is even more remarkable that even within the little narrative space assigned to the last four kings, the account of Zedekiah proper which covers eleven regnal years is allocated in Chronicles only three verses (2 Chr 36:11–13). This is exactly the same number of verses assigned in the book to the account of Jehoahaz that covers only three months (vv. 1–3) and just one more than Jehoiachin's, which covers a bit less than 100 days (vv. 9–10). Even Jehoiakim, who reigned eleven years like Zedekiah, is allocated five verses (vv. 4–8). Most significantly, the longest section within 2 Chr 36 begins with the *disappearance* of Zedekiah from the story and the concurrent appearance of the priests and the people and ends, of course, with the exile. This section is, however, only eight verses long (vv. 14–21).[34]

As we all know, allocations of narrative space are only a part of the story. Chronicles contributed to the shaping of the memory of Zedekiah not only by what it did not directly evoke, but also by what it did ask the community to remember about his reign. Japhet has maintained that Chronicles attributes the destruction of Jerusalem exclusively to Zedekiah's generation.[35] It is clear that reading and rereading Chronicles conjured within the reading/remembering community a memory of Zedekiah as responsible for the fall of Jerusalem. Chronicles did so by stressing that he "did not humble himself before the prophet Jeremiah who spoke from the mouth of Yhwh" (2 Chr 36:12b) and that he "rebelled against King Nebuchadnezzar, who had made him swear by God" (2 Chr 36:13a).

The first reference not only conforms Zedekiah to the well-known pattern of those who rejected the godly prophets, but also draws attention to and activates the memories evoked within the community through the reading of numerous Jeremianic texts. Remembering Zedekiah through the act of reading Chronicles was remembering his relation to Jeremiah and activating memories such as those evoked by Jer 38:17–18. Thus reading texts such as Jer 38:17–18 in Jeremiah informed the community that Chronicles was particularly on target, but also *vice versa*, reading Chronicles reinforced memories evoked by some voices and texts

---

33 See n. 21.
34 The length of the section has something to do with Chronicles' construction of exile. Clearly this is not the place for addressing the matter and in any case, I discussed the matter elsewhere. See "Toward a Sense of Balance: Remembering the Catastrophe of Monarchic Judah/(Ideological) Israel and Exile through Reading Chronicles," in this volume, pp. 387–406.
35 See S. Japhet, *I and II Chronicles* (OTL; Louisville: Westminster/John Knox Press, 1993), 1069.

in Jeremiah. In other words, a mutually reinforcing mnemonic loop emerged and reinforced the involved voices.

The reference to Zedekiah's breaking an oath of loyalty sworn by God shaped another mutually reinforcing mnemonic loop, this time between the memory of Zedekiah evoked in Chronicles and that in Ezek 17:19. This loop, just as the one mentioned above, carried a strong didactic message. In addition, the fact that Chronicles parallels Kings, but did not directly ask the readers to recall the crucial statement in 2 Kgs 24:20, contributed to the shaping of an important message: Zedekiah was responsible for the destruction.[36]

From the perspective of the larger mnemonic system, one may say then that some Jeremianic and Chronistic voices mutually reinforced each other, and even integrated Ezekielian memories and all served to shift the memory of Zedekiah to a more 'normalized' situation, that is, one in which the last ruler is blamed for the ruin of his (or her) polity.

Since this construction of Zedekiah is one of the preferred outcomes of a transcultural mnemonic generative grammar, it is not surprising that this Zedekiah of memory will keep appearing in various remembering communities across time, and, for instance, it populates some memories encoded in some rabbinic material.[37] But this does not mean that this is the only potentially preferred characterization of Zedekiah as a last ruler, and it is clearly not the only voice that the literati of the late Persian or early Hellenistic period 'heard' when reading and rereading Chronicles.

For one, the reference to 70 years of Sabbath rest that is so crucial to the explanation of exile in Chronicles (see 2 Chr 36:21) implies both a span of 420, not 11 years–the length of Zedekiah's reign according to 2 Chr 36:11–preceding the catastrophe and a clear notion of a cumulative burden of impurity caused by sin.[38] Significantly, within this perspective neither the land's cumulative impurity can be cleansed by Josiah's or anyone's reign, for that matter, nor can be caused only by one generation (cf. 2 Chr 36:14; cf. also Ezek 36:17). Finally, the explan-

---

[36] But so was his generation (see 2 Chr 36:14–16) including those who were particularly responsible for maintaining the purity of the temple and the people in general, who also rejected the prophets. I will address to this point and its significance in what follows. Second Chronicles 36:14–16 raises similar memories to those in, for instance, Ezek 36:17, raising thus another mutually reinforcing mnemonic loop, though advancing a complementary but still different message than those discussed above.

[37] E.g., Deut. Rab. 5.11.

[38] Cf. for instance, H. G. M. Williamson, *1–2 Chronicles* (NCB; London: Marshall Morgan & Scott and Grand Rapids: Eerdmans, 1982), 418; J. Milgrom, *Leviticus 23–27: A New Translation with Introduction and Commentary* (AB 3B; New Haven/London: Yale University Press, 2008), 2324–25.

ation given in 1 Chr 9:1 for the exile of Judah (and Israel; cf. 9:3)–בְּמַעֲלָם–cannot refer only to the "unfaithfulness" of those living during the reign of Zedekiah.

In addition, Chronicles adds to the mnemonic marginalization of the blame of Zedekiah and his generation by allocating a small amount of text (and social mindscape) to Zedekiah or to the post-Josianic period for that matter (see above). Had Chronicles wanted to convince its intended and primary readership that the fall of Jerusalem, the exile and the worst catastrophe in Israelite history were all the results of Zedekiah's sins and those who followed him during his relatively short rule, the community would have expected a substantial recounting of them. Nothing of the sort appears in Chronicles. As mentioned above, the sins of Zedekiah receive, if anything, less narrative attention than those of other kings (e.g., Ahaz;[39] see above).

One may be tempted to maintain that from a mnemonic system perspective, memories of Zedekiah evoked by Chronicles and Kings mutually reinforce each other in terms of marginalizing Zedekiah's blame. While this is true, an important distinction has to be made. A strong voice activated when reading 2 Kgs 24:3, and mutually reinforcing with the Jeremianic voice activated by reading Jer 15:4, assigned the blame to Manasseh. In Chronicles, Manasseh partially stands for Israel. Like Israel, he is punished and goes to Babylon, but there he repents and returns to the land and becomes an important reforming king and the prototype of repenting Israel. To some extent, he is even a prototype of a future Israel that is still living in the current world–not the world at the 'end of history,' but one who directly rules the land, even if as a vassal unlike the present Israel of Chronicles.[40]

As it is well known, since social memory tends to be organized in terms of narratives, personages from the past are most often remembered as characters within particular memorable plots and in relation to other important figures. It is not surprising thus that features of the remembered Zedekiah were interwoven with those of Manasseh/Israel, but the particular ways in which this is manifest-

---

[39] It is worth mentioning that in Chronicles, the main 'hero' – 'anti-hero'/'villain' pair of the late monarchic period consists of Ahaz and Hezekiah, not Manasseh and Josiah. A study of reasons for and implications of this shift in terms of social memory requires a separate discussion that cannot be taken up here.

[40] The construction of Manasseh in Chronicles strongly suggests that from the perspective communicated by this book, Israel repented in exile. Although the return of Israel and Manasseh to the land parallel each other and conveyed a sense that the figure of the 'king' is overtaken by that of the 'people' (see below), there is still the issue that Manasseh was remembered as ruling Judah in a way that was *not* fully comparable with the political roles of the 'people' in Yehud, during the time of the Chronicler. Manasseh thus provides a sense of hope for a future increase in local autonomy, within the general imperial frame.

ed and communicated in Chronicles are worth exploring. In fact, the first and most significant deed that the community was asked to remember about Zedekiah when reading Chronicles is that "he did not humble himself before the prophet Jeremiah who spoke from the mouth of Yhwh" יהוה ולא נִכְנַע מִלִּפְנֵי יִרְמְיָהוּ הַנָּבִיא מִפִּי (2 Chr 36:12b). The crucial turning point in Manasseh's/Israel's story, however, was that when taken captive to Babylon, "he humbled himself greatly before the God of his ancestors" וַיִּכָּנַע מְאֹד מִלִּפְנֵי אֱלֹהֵי אֲבֹתָיו (2 Chr 33:12b).[41] The connections are obvious and the language of these texts draws the reading community's attention to them.

On the one hand, the plot moves temporally from Manasseh to Zedekiah, from the pious to the sinful king and as it does so, it goes along the grain of common temporality and communicates an explanation of the calamity, namely Zedekiah/Israel failed to listen to Yhwh's word just as Manasseh/Israel did before exile (2 Chr 33:10). To be sure, according to Chronicles, Manasseh/Israel humbled itself, but only after he/it was deported to Babylon. Zedekiah and his people in 2 Chr 36:11–13, however, are not yet deported in the world of the story and so they cannot humble themselves. When read in this way, a plot moving from Zedekiah/Israel before exile to Manasseh/Israel after the exile was shaped and given that the second section of Manasseh's reign is better than the one in the present of the community (note the proliferation of prophets implied in 2 Chr 33:18, Manasseh's rule over the land), it is also a plot whose trajectory led into a hoped and hopeful future. As such, it converged with and activated plots that the community was aware of (see Jer 32:5, cf. Jer 34:5) and with images of Zedekiah as a link to the future, which again reflected common, transcultural processes of memory formation meant to bridge the discontinuity created by the figure of the 'last ruler.'

But there is more, since Manasseh/Israel must leave the land for exile, Manasseh could not be mnemonically associated only with Zedekiah in Chronicles. The figure of Zedekiah had to be complemented for these purposes by that of Jehoiakim (cf. 2 Chr 36:6 with 2 Chr 33:11). Zedekiah is thus construed not only as a counterpoint to Jehoiakim (as in some Jeremianic memories about Zedekiah), but

---

41 A full discussion on the Manasseh evoked by Chronicles cannot be carried out within the scope of this contribution. The argument here is simply build upon some of the points developed in "Reading Chronicles and Reshaping the Image of Manasseh," in this volume, pp. 367–86. For a different (and to a significant extent complementary) study and set of questions about the Manasseh in Chronicles see G. N. Knoppers, "Saint or Sinner? Manasseh in Chronicles," in *Rewriting Biblical History: Essays on Chronicles and Ben Sira in Honor of Pancratius C. Beentjes* (eds. J. Corley and H. van Grol; Deuterocanonical and Cognate Literature Studies 7; Berlin: De Gruyter, 2011), 211–29.

also and mainly as a complement to him, and both of them together, provide a type of pre-exile Manasseh.[42]

This is consistent with and reflects strong preference for a mnemonic pattern that closely associates the last kings of Judah. This tendency will eventually be expanded to almost all kings in Sirach (see Sir 49:4–7).[43]

Returning to the issue of responsibility for the destruction, Chronicles conveys a sense that the temple and Jerusalem were destroyed because of the actions of Zedekiah and in multiple and quite emphatic ways also that what he did actually did not matter much. This is not surprising because Chronicles emerged out of a well attested worldview reflected in multiple mnemonic narratives in which dual causality plays a central role. A few examples suffice to make the point: on the one hand the 'reason' that Amnon raped Tamar and Absalom killed Amnon, rebelled against David and had intercourse with his wives is David's sin and Yhwh's punishment for that sin, but on the other, this never relinquished Amnon or Absalom from their deeds. In fact, the community remembered that they were punished for them. Likewise, Yhwh decided that the king of Babylon has to destroy Jerusalem, but Babylon will still be punished for destroying Jerusalem; Jacob has to cheat Esau, according to Yhwh's plan, but this does not exonerate Jacob.

Double causality plays an important role in socializing the community, by means of mnemonic narratives, because it inculcates (and balances) both Yhwh's determination of the future and human agency and responsibility. The community knows that the temple had to be destroyed and the land purified, knows of the divine announcement communicated to Josiah, but still has to remember the responsibility of Zedekiah. Moreover, and, as mentioned above and see 2 Chr 36:14–16, not only his responsibility, but also that of his generation.

To be sure, as Chronicles brought up saliently the generation of Zedekiah it shaped within the community a network of multiple and mutually reinforcing images involving memories encoded in Jeremianic and Ezekielian texts (e.g.,

---

[42] Since Chronicles does not report and thus does not ask the remembering community to remember anything particular about the eight-year-old Jehoiachin (2 Chr 36:9), besides the usual statement וַיַּעַשׂ הָרַע בְּעֵינֵי יהוה, Jehoiachin could not have taken the role of Jehoiakim as counterpart of Zedekiah for these purposes.

[43] In Sirach all the kings, except David, Hezekiah, and Josiah are considered one group of unworthy rulers who were great sinners, because they abandoned the law of the Most High and thus justifiably, the kings of Judah came to an end (Sir 49:4–7), to be replaced eventually by a High Priest like Simeon (see below). The explicit reference to Jeremiah (vv. 6–7) suggests that to some extent all these kings have been 'Zedekianized.'

Ezek 36:17). But reinforcement points at mnemonic significance, it is not 'significant' by itself.

Foregrounding the role of the people and the priests during Zedekiah's time was not only a reflection of a trend to a more consultative/collaborative monarchy in a strand of political thought,[44] but also a way to connote identification between the Israel of Zedekiah's time and Israel in general. After all, rejecting prophets was associated with Israel already during Moses times. Moreover, 2 Chr 36:13b reads וַיֶּקֶשׁ אֶת־עָרְפּוֹ וַיְאַמֵּץ אֶת־לְבָבוֹ מִשּׁוּב אֶל־יהוה אֱלֹהֵי יִשְׂרָאֵל. The explicit and salient reference to the "stiffening the neck" recalled and activated memories that go well beyond Zedekiah and his generation. They evoked and activated those of Moses and the Israel of his time, and actually turned Zedekiah into a type of sinful 'all' (trans- and cross-temporal) Israel" and *vice-versa* (see Exod 32:9; 33:3, 5; Deut 9:6, 13, 16; 31:27; 2 Kgs 17:14; Jer 7:26; 17:23; 2 Chr 30:8).

But there is more at stake from the perspective of social memory in the way in which Chronicles asked the community to consider shaping the past. The readers of Chronicles were asked to draw particular attention neither to memories of Zedekiah the deportee (unlike 2 Kgs 25:7; Jer 39:7; Ezek 12:13; 17:16) nor to memorable images of the punished Zedekiah evoked by 2 Kgs 25:3–7; Jer 39:2–7; 52:6–11. The literati reading and rereading Chronicles were 'told' that whatever happened to Zedekiah the person was not worth remembering. In fact, after 2 Chr 36:13, he is not mentioned again, and even v. 13b more than hints at its transition into Israel (see above).

Zedekiah's presence fades from the text and from activated memory once he rebelled against the King of Babylon, as he both had to and chose to do. After that event that set in motion the next narrative move, he is construed as irrelevant in terms of social memory. As the historical narrative of Chronicles moves towards the calamity, it is the people who come to the forefront and take the leadership role, beginning with the heads of the priests. The king, the kingdom, and the monarchic polity begin thus their transformation into priesthood and temple-oriented community.[45]

Moreover, just as Kings highlights the message that the last is not the worst by shaping and recalling various and diverse memories all converging on that point, Chronicles highlights its point by construing and communicating memories of another falling and fading king and kingdom, namely that of Northern Israel (see 2 Chr 28). Significantly, within that narrative/memory, as the king fades

---

44 Cf. S. Japhet, *The Ideology of the Book of Chronicles and its Place in Biblical Thought* (2d rev. ed.; BEATAJ 9; Frankfurt a. M.: Peter Lang, 1997), 416–28.

45 Cf. Sirach (see n. 43).

among Northern Israelites, those who are first imagined to be in positions of authority are tribal chiefs and army leaders (see 2 Chr 28:9–15). But when it comes to Judah and Jerusalem, as in the case discussed here, the heads of the priests, the priests and the people come to the forefront. This said, it is as important to notice that Chronicles reminded the readers that the priests and the people failed, unlike the heads of Ephraim, because the Judahites did not listen to their "Oded" (i.e, their prophetic voice) and because they, at this stage in the narrative, have *not yet* been in exile. In other words, those who take the place of Zedekiah have yet to become Manasseh, humble themselves and listen to the prophets (2 Chr 33:18).

Chronicles used a mnemonic narrative to make a major point: the community stands now for the previous, faded king. The temple stands now for the faded palace; the Davidic line becomes Israel and the latter is both partially kingized and priestized.[46] The collective tragedy takes over that of the last ruler, and a collective image of hope for the future takes over the image usually associated with the last ruler (contrast with 2 Kgs 25:27–30//Jer 52:31–34).

But as we all know, this is not the only voice in Chronicles or in the discourse of the community.[47] To be sure, this is certainly one important voice present and activated through memories, both inside and outside Chronicles, but just one voice, again both inside and outside Chronicles.[48]

---

46 To be sure, images of a kingized and priestized Israel are not unique to Chronicles (cf. with the image of the covenant between YHWH and Israel; or see a text such as Exod 19:6). Basic concepts are bound to be manifested in multiple works, because they are not essentially book-dependant, but a reflection of an ideological world and its corresponding generative grammar for preferred memories of the past or the future.

47 There is considerable debate as to whether Chronicles shows a royalist, messianic tendency or a non-royalist, non-messianic, communal and temple-centered tendency, and to what extent these agendas are future and possibly utopian or present focused–the latter in particular, but *not exclusively,* for the non-royalist, communal/temple-centered agenda. For a recent survey of many of the important positions taken in research on the matter and substantial bibliography, see M. Boda, "Gazing Through the Cloud of Incense: Davidic and Temple Community in the Chronicler's Perspective," in *Chronicling the Chronicler: The Book of Chronicles and Early Second Temple Historiography* (eds. P. Evans and T. Williams; Winona Lake: Eisenbrauns, 2013), 215–46. Although I tend to stress the communal, non-messianic voice, I would argue that all these "voices" are present in Chronicles and that they complement and balance each other, but certainly do not "cancel" each other out. I would further argue that it is the intertwining of these multiple voices that represents both the discourse of the period and the "voice" of the implied author of Chronicles as construed by the literati in the late Persian/early Hellenistic period.

48 Compare and contrast with the emphasis on the continuation–even if in a very substantially diminished state–of the genealogy of David. See G. N. Knoppers, *1 Chronicles 1–9* (AB 12; New York: Doubleday, 2003), 333–36. Both the continuity and the potential that it connotes and the

Chronicles here participated in a larger social and ideological endeavor of exploring, balancing and above all, negotiating various positions on the matter of the future of Israel (and the Davidides) and of shaping integrative fuzziness through the memories it evoked in the community. To be sure, Chronicles was not alone. These activities involved interacting in various ways with multiple 'godly' voices shaping memories of the past that were evoked within the community by texts and sets of texts–within and across literary genre boundaries– that existed within the core textual repertoire of the community. Needless to say, these voices informed each other and at times were 'embodied' as it were in single characters of the past that turned into important sites of memory (e.g., Zedekiah, Jehoiakim, David, Josiah, Jeremiah).

In other words, we have here a complex mnemonic system at work. Memories within that system become a language to explore (though not necessarily to decide) matters that are important for the remembering community–directly the literati, and possibly and indirectly any other social group at the time that was strongly informed by the literati's construed past. Exploring these memories, participating in the ongoing process of balancing them, and the act of doing so as a group bound them together and indirectly, from their perspective, to the 'Israel' of their times, and the latter to their 'transtemporal Israel' across time. Remembering Zedekiah in the early Second Temple period was part of that process, and Chronicles contributed its share to it.

---

low status that it also communicates are present in the text and read by the community. Likewise, associating kings with Israel is an enterprise that may work in both ways.

Reading Chronicles and Reshaping the Memory of Manasseh*

1 Introduction

Manasseh was certainly a memorable king of Judah for those who had read and reread the books of Kings and Chronicles. Both books draw much attention to him, but there can be no doubt that the figure of Manasseh as portrayed in Chronicles was significantly different from the king evoked by the book of Kings (see 2 Kgs 21:1–20; 23:12, 26; 24:3) and reflected in Jer 15:4 as well.[1] Reading

---

* First published in *Chronicling the Chronicler. The Book of Chronicles and Early Second Temple Historiography* (eds. P. S. Evans and T. F. Williams; Winona Lake, Ind.: Eisenbrauns, 2013), 121–40.

[1] On the contrasting portrayals, see, for instance, P. Abadie, "From the Impious Manasseh (2 Kings 21) to the Convert Manasseh (2 Chronicles 33)," in *The Chronicler as Theologian: Essays in Honor of Ralph W. Klein* (eds. M. P. Graham, S. L. McKenzie, and G. N. Knoppers; JSOTSup 371; London: T&T Clark, 2003), 89–104. For a detailed and helpful contrastive analysis of the two texts, see K. A. D. Smelik, "The Portrayal of King Manasseh," in *Converting the Past: Studies in Ancient Israelite and Moabite Historiography* (ed. K. A. D. Smelik; OtSt 28; Leiden: Brill, 1992), 129–89. For a study that explains the difference between Kings' and Chronicles' portrayals of Manasseh in terms of cultural wars that were waged at the time of the exilic edition of Kings but that were all but won by the time of Chronicles, see B. Halpern, "Why Manasseh Is Blamed for the Babylonian Exile: The Evolution of a Biblical Tradition," in *VT* 48 (1998): 473–514. Cf. H.-J. Stipp, "Remembering Josiah's Reforms in Kings," in *Remembering (and Forgetting) in Early Second Temple Judah* (eds. E. Ben Zvi and C. Levin; FAT 85; Tübingen: Mohr Siebeck, 2012), 225–38. The tension between the two different portrayals of Manasseh construed by these texts continued to impact the construction of the memory of Manasseh centuries after these texts were composed and first read. See, for instance, "Said R. Yohanan, 'Both authorities [who dispute the fate of Manasseh] interpret the same verse of Scripture, as it is said, "And I will cause to be removed to all the kingdoms of the earth, because of Manasseh, son of Hezekiah, king of Judah" (Jer 15:4). ... "*One authority takes the view that it is* 'on account of Manasseh,' who repented, while they did not repent." ... "The other authority takes the view [103 A] that it is 'because of Manasseh,' who did not repent"'" (b. Sanh. 102b–103a; J. Neusner's translation). Two important essays that emerged after this essay was written should be mentioned here as well: (1) Gary Knoppers, "Saint or Sinner? Manasseh in Chronicles," in *Rewriting Biblical History: Essays on Chronicles and Ben Sira in Honor of Pancratius C. Beentjes* (eds. J. Corley and H. van Grol; Berlin: De Gruyter, 2011), 211–29. Knoppers addresses matters from a different, though complementary perspective from my perspective here. (2) L. Jonker, "Manasseh in Paradise, or Not? The Influence of Persian Palace Garden Imagery in LXX 2 Chronicles 33:20," in *Thinking of Water* (eds. E. Ben Zvi and C. Levin; BZAW, 461; Berlin/New York: De Gruyter, 2014), 339–58, draws particular attention to the burial notices in MT 2 Chr 33:20 and in LXX 2 Chr 33:20 (compare and con-

https://doi.org/10.1515/9783110547146-017

Chronicles affected the way in which literati in the late Persian (or early Hellenistic) period remembered Manasseh. Reading Chronicles and (mentally) visiting and (imaginatively) experiencing, as it were, the Manassic period that it evoked, balanced the social memory of the period that these literati (and those whose views were strongly influenced by them) would have had, if they had read and known only about the books of Kings and Jeremiah.

Although Manasseh was portrayed first in Chronicles in a way *roughly* similar to the portrayal in Kings (see 2 Chr 33:1–10),[2] the book asked its readers to imagine and remember, time and again, that Manasseh repented and carried out a "godly" cultic reform (2 Chr 33:11–17). Moreover, Chronicles reminded the readers that Manasseh's prayer was worth remembering for generations and, since the book does not provide the text of the prayer, it opened the prayer's contents to the imagination of the readers.[3]

---

trast with MT and LXX 2 Kgs 21:18) and suggests that these notes may have been part of a process of "upgrading" the figure of Manasseh.

2 Note, for instance, that 2 Chr 33:5 refers to "sons," plural, whereas 2 Kgs 21:6 (MT, but not LXX[B] and LXX[L]) has "son," singular; and that it carries a slightly longer list of misdeeds although, significantly, like 2 Kgs 21:6 it does not fully or explicitly reproduce the entire list from Deut 18:10–11. Note also the removal of the explicit reference to the rejected prophets in 2 Chr 33:10, so as to make Manasseh reject YHWH directly (see 2 Chr 33:10 and cf. 2 Kgs 21:10). In general, despite the fact that Manasseh is construed in extremely negative terms in 2 Kgs 21:1–10, the changes in 2 Chr 33:1–10 seem further to enhance the negative portrayal of the king. One may note also that 2 Chr 33:7 replaces the explicit reference to the Asherah in 2 Kgs 21:7 with a reference *to the* סמל (and cf. Deut 4:16; Ezek 8:3, 5). This change requires separate study. There are also minor additional changes; for example, compare 2 Chr 33:4 וּבָנָה מִזְבְּחוֹת בְּבֵית יהוה אֲשֶׁר אָמַר יהוה בִּירוּשָׁלַם יִהְיֶה־שְׁמִי לְעוֹלָם with 2 Kgs 21:4 וּבָנָה מִזְבְּחֹת בְּבֵית יהוה אֲשֶׁר אָמַר יהוה בִּירוּשָׁלַם אָשִׂים אֶת־שְׁמִי. On the "reprobate" section of the account of Manasseh in Chronicles, see W. Johnstone, *1 and 2 Chronicles*, vol. 2: *2 Chronicles 10–36: Guilt and Atonement* (JSOTSup 254; Sheffield: Sheffield Academic Press, 1997), 222–26.

3 Not surprisingly, texts that purported to be the prayer of Manasseh eventually emerged, as clearly evidenced by 4Q381, frg. 33, 8–11. Compare and contrast the position advanced in W. M. Schniedewind, "The Source Citations of Manasseh: King Manasseh in History and Homily," in *VT* 41 (1991): 450–61. For the (most likely) later (and "canonical" in some groups) "Prayer of Manasseh," see J. H. Charlesworth, in *Old Testament Pseudepigrapha* (ed. J. H. Charlesworth; New York: Doubleday, 1985), 2:625–38. On these and related matters, see F. Stavrakopoulou, *King Manasseh and Child Sacrifice: Biblical Distortions of Historical Realities* (BZAW 338; Berlin: De Gruyter, 2004), 130–33 and bibliography cited there. For a recent study of the "Prayer of Manasseh" and its background, see J. Davila, "Is the Prayer of Manasseh a Jewish Work?" in *Heavenly Tablets: Interpretation, Identity and Tradition in Ancient Judaism* (ed. L. R. LiDonnici and A. Lieber; JSJSup 119; Leiden: Brill, 2007), 75–85.

This essay is not about the historical King Manasseh who lived in the 7th century BCE[4] or about potential sources other than Kings that might or *might not* have been available to the flesh-and-blood author/s of Chronicles.[5] It is about the Manasseh evoked by Chronicles and the ways this character influenced the construction of the community's narrative about what "their" late monarchic past was and what they learned from it. It is about why the memory of Manasseh as evoked by Chronicles was shaped as it was.

2 The Usual Approach and Its Limitations

The usual approach to addressing these questions has been to focus on the historical (flesh-and-blood) author/s of Chronicles that we, as contemporary historians of ancient Israel or as historical-critical commentators of Chronicles, construct.[6] Once attention is turned to this author, on the surface, a response to the questions set at the conclusion of the previous section seems easy and quite straightforward: the portrayal of Manasseh's repentance and transformation from villain to reformist hero was simply the author's response to the tension that emerged from the length of the reign of Manasseh–55 years, the longest reign in Judahite history, even longer than the reigns of David and Solomon–as

---

[4] See, among others, I. Finkelstein, "The Archaeology of the Days of Manasseh," in *Scriptures and Other Artifacts: Essays on Bible and Archaeology in Honor of Philip J. King* (eds. M. D. Coogan et al.; Louisville: Westminster John Knox, 1994), 169–87; Y. Thareani-Sussely, "The Archaeology of the Days of Manasseh Reconsidered in the Light of Evidence from the Beersheba Valley," in *PEQ* 139 (2007): 69–77; A. Faust, "Settlement and Demography in Seventh Century Judah and the Extent and Intensity of Sennacherib's Campaign," in *PEQ* 140 (2008): 168–94; contrast with O. Lipschits, O. Sergi, and I. Koch, "Judahite Stamped and Incised Jar Handles: A Tool for Studying the History of Late Monarchic Judah," in *TA* 38 (2011): 5–41. See also my "Prelude to a Reconstruction of the Historical Manassic Judah," in *BN* 81 (1996): 31–44; E. A. Knauf, "The Glorious Days of Manasseh," in *Good Kings and Bad Kings* (ed. L. L. Grabbe; LHBOTS 393; London: T&T Clark, 2005), 164–88; F. Stavrakopoulou, "The Blackballing of Manasseh," in ibid., 248–63; and idem, *King Manasseh*. Compare and contrast B. Kelly, "Manasseh in the Books of Kings and Chronicles (2 Kings 21:1–18; 2 Chr 33:1–20)," in *Windows into Old Testament History: Evidence, Argument, and the Crisis of "Biblical Israel"* (eds. V. Philips Long, D. W. Baker, and G. J. Wenham; Grand Rapids, MI: Eerdmans, 2002), 131–46 and bibliography cited there.
[5] Among those proposing the existence of sources other than Kings behind the Chronicles' account of Manasseh, see, for instance, Schniedewind, "Source Citations"; S. Japhet, *I and II Chronicles: A Commentary* (OTL; Louisville: Westminster John Knox, 1993), 1009.
[6] This author was responsible for Chronicles but not for Ezra–Nehemiah or any section in that book. Given the distribution of social roles according to gender in Yehud, this author was most likely male and thus will be referred to as male in this essay.

stated in Kings and his characterization as extremely impious. Since length of days was considered a blessing within the social mindscape of the community (and as expressed in numerous texts in the discourse of the community; e.g., Exod 20:12; Deut 5:16, 6:2; Ps 91:14–16; Prov 3:1–2; 10:2; 12:28; cf. 2 Kgs 20:1–7; 2 Chr 24:15) and was construed as a blessing by the author, he felt it was necessary to resolve the inconsistency between Manasseh's long reign and life and the principles governing a divine economy of divine rewards and punishment; thus, he reshaped the portrayal of Manasseh.[7]

But matters are not as simple and straightforward as they seem to be. The observations mentioned above indeed shed light on some aspects of the emergence and role of the Manasseh of Chronicles in late Persian Yehud but obscure or oversimplify other aspects. To begin with, the generative tension between the 55 years' regnal period and the overwhelming impiety did *not necessitate* the construction of a narrative about a pious Manasseh and most certainly not the particular narrative advanced in Chronicles.

To be sure, a simple observation of literary and ideological tendencies (and constraints) at work in Chronicles shows that: (1) Chronicles could not have construed the span of Manasseh's reign any differently from the span stated in the (MT) book of Kings;[8] (2) Manasseh's piety was implicitly presented as consistent with his lengthy life; and (3) Chronicles shaped other regnal accounts around a narrative plot in which the reign of the king was divided between a period of piety and divine rewards and another of impiety and punishment (see the accounts of Asa, Joash, Amaziah, and Uzziah). But questions emerge.

Despite the fact that, on the whole, Chronicles valued length of life as a blessing,[9] the very same Chronicles assigns to its most sinful king a life of about 36 years (see 2 Chr 28:1), not much shorter than the life of one of its most pious kings, Josiah, to whom it assigns about 39 years (2 Chr 34:1). Moreover, if one were to claim that there is a difference in that Josiah enjoyed

---

[7] This has been the most common approach since, at least, J. Wellhausen. See his *Prolegomena to the History of Israel* (trans. J. Sutherland Black and Allan Menzies; Edinburgh: Black, 1885; orig. German pub., 1878) 206–7. See S. L. McKenzie, *1–2 Chronicles* (AOTC; Nashville: Abingdon, 2004), 353–54.

[8] See my *History, Literature and Theology in the Book of Chronicles* (London: Equinox, 2006), 78–99 (esp. 82–83). This chapter was first published as "Shifting the Gaze: Historiographic Constraints in Chronicles and Their Implications," in *The Land That I Will Show You: Essays on the History and Archaeology of the Ancient Near East in Honor of J. Maxwell Miller* (eds. M. Patrick Graham and J. Andrew Dearman; JSOTSup 343; Sheffield: JSOT Press, 2001), 38–60.

[9] Note that the great hero Jehoiadah the priest, to some extent as kingly a figure as a priest can ever be, lives 130 years, longer even than Moses; see 2 Chr 24:15. The portrayal of Jehoiadah in Chronicles requires a separate study that cannot be carried out here.

many more regnal years than Ahaz, one still must keep in mind that Abijah, a most pious king in Chronicles, reigned only 3 years (2 Chr 13:2), far less than Ahaz's 16 years (2 Chr 28:1).

In fact, Chronicles had no problems with construing a world in which sinners may, at times, outlive the pious (see 2 Chr 24:20–22); and even more importantly, it asks its readers to imagine a world in which the worst sinner (Ahaz) *is not necessarily* punished with premature death. The fact that he remains alive when sinners around him die because of their sins (see 2 Chr 28:5–7) makes the point emphatically. These are not minor issues or accidental examples bearing little meaning. They are integral to shaping and communicating that, while longevity and long regnal periods are a blessing, not all pious were blessed this way, and conversely, not all sinners had to die (prematurely).

The latter considerations reflect an important aspect of the ideological approach in Chronicles: a world in which sinners must be punished with (premature) death is a world that allows no room for repentance. However, repentance plays a central role in the ideological discourse of postmonarchic Israel (for obvious reasons) and in Chronicles. Ahaz is thus portrayed as being surrounded by examples of divine justice and consistently rejecting the lesson. His lack of repentance strengthens the negative characterization of the personage, which in turn, is a necessary feature for the shaping and communicating of an extreme example of the potential availability of repentance.

Manasseh, who is portrayed as the worst king in Kings, could have been construed in Chronicles as consistently doing wrong, never repenting for 55 years, and thus "besting" (as it were) Ahaz. Chronicles could have but, significantly, did not construct him that way.

Another consideration is that, although the division of a regnal period into two diametrically different eras is a common ideological and narrative-structuring device in Chronicles, the sequence is always a "good period" followed by a "bad period" (see the accounts of Asa, Joash, Amaziah, Uzziah, and to some extent Josiah). The account of Manasseh is a glaring, unique exception.[10] However,

---

10 On the surface, one might be tempted to consider the account of Rehoboam as another example, particularly given the report of his ascension to the throne. But that section of the account of Rehoboam is about the secession of the North and is substantially different from the accounts of the kings of Judah in the post-Davidic/Solomonic period. For my work on the secession of the North in Chronicles, see my *History, Literature and Theology in the Book of Chronicles*, 117–43; first published as "The Secession of the Northern Kingdom in Chronicles: Accepted 'Facts' and New Meanings," in *The Chronicler as a Theologian*, 61–88. On the account of Rehoboam in Chronicles, see G. N. Knoppers, "Rehoboam in Chronicles," in *JBL* 109 (1990): 423–40. Of course, many scholars have noticed the contrast between the trajectories in the accounts of

the strong preference for the good-turns-bad plot over its counterpart (i.e., bad-turns-good) is not random. It reflects a central ideological viewpoint and, one may say, a particular social mindscape. I discussed this issue at some length elsewhere,[11] but for the present purposes, it suffices to note that Chronicles could have construed a good period in which Manasseh followed the counsel of his father Hezekiah's advisors and then a bad period in which he rejected them (see Chronicles' account of Joash). Moreover, had Chronicles shaped its account of Manasseh's reign in such a way, not only would it have "explained" his lengthy reign, by assigning many of its years to the good period, but it also would have created a Manasseh whose image would have been much more easy to reconcile with that advanced in Kings than the image Chronicles actually developed. Given that the readership of Chronicles was well aware of Kings, social memory would have tended to prefer an image of Manasseh that could more easily been reconciled with the image in Kings than an image that can hardly be reconciled. But Chronicles did not follow this path; instead, it created an *exceptional* sequence that as such cannot but draw attention to itself, to the figure of Manasseh *as evoked by Chronicles*, and to the messages that this figure/site of memory communicated to the remembering community.

A third consideration: it is easy to recognize that the Manasseh of Chronicles is the paradigmatic Judahite king who repents and that he prefigures Israel, considering that he is exiled to Babylon because of his sins and returns to Judah.[12] But one may wonder, why Manasseh? Why does Chronicles join Manasseh to David in such a way that the two become the two paragons of repentance?[13] To be sure, the communicative point may be that they represent two extremes of kingly behavior, the best and worst king–that is, a kind of polar construction.

Asa, Joash, Amaziah, and Uzziah, as well as in Manasseh. For instance, P. Abadie maintains that the difference "gives the narrative of Manasseh a particular tonality" (Abadie, "From the Impious Manasseh," 95). See also Japhet, *I and II Chronicles*, 1001.

11 E. Ben Zvi, "A House of Treasures: The Account of Amaziah in 2 Chronicles 25: Observations and Implications," in *SJOT* 22 (2008): 63–85, esp. 69–75.

12 On discussions of Manasseh as a "type" or prefiguration of Israel in Chronicles, see, among many others, R. Mosis, *Untersuchungen zur Theologie des chronistischen Geschichtswerkes* (Freiburger theologische Studien 92; Freiburg: Herder, 1973), 192–94; Schniedewind, "Source Citations," 451–55; H. G. M. Williamson, *1–2 Chronicles* (NCB; Grand Rapids, MI: Eerdmans, 1982), 389–90; S. J. De Vries, *1 and 2 Chronicles* (FOTL 11; Grand Rapids, MI: Eerdmans, 1989), 399–400; Stavrakopoulou, *King Manasseh*, 55–56; Abadie, "From the Impious Manasseh"; etc.

13 On David, see G. N. Knoppers, "Images of David in Early Judaism: David as Repentant Sinner in Chronicles," in *Bib* 76 (1995): 449–70. For a different position, see J. W. Wright, "The Innocence of David in I Chronicles 21," in *JSOT* 60 (1993): 87–105.

As one would anticipate, the most ideal human king is imagined as a great "repentant" as well.[14] But, probably more important from a communicative and ideological perspective is the image of the most sinful king as repentant, for it carries more persuasive appeal as a site of memory encouraging repentance within the community and as a potential site with which Israel can identify.[15]

This said, Ahaz, not Manasseh, is the worst king in Chronicles. If the point is (1) that the worst Davidic king is comparable with Israel and (2) to convey a sense that both can repent (and that monarchic Israel did not, and thus it fell), then, again, why not use Ahaz, the most sinful king in Chronicles, for that purpose?[16] Moreover, given that the Ahaz evoked by Kings and particularly Isaiah is not such a bad king, it would have been "easier" to construe him as re-

---

14 Assuming, of course, that all humans, even highly lionized individuals such as David, will occasionally fail and sin. This position is attested in and communicated by Chronicles (remember David) and is common in the entire discourse of Yehudite Israel, which construed even Moses as occasionally sinning (see also 1 Kgs 8:46; Qoh 7:20).

15 Although at some level, Israel was identified with David, the "Israelites" probably did not imagine themselves as pious as Chronicles' David but also not as sinful as the Manasseh of memory and, if he could have repented, then so could they. See the text from *b. Sanh.* 102b–103a cited in n. 1.

16 On the surface, one may claim that Ahaz ended up being the worst king only by default, because Chronicles made Manasseh repent. Even if this were the case, the message would have remained, but this is very unlikely to have been the case. The main argument against such a position is that Ahaz's image was very actively shaped as that of the worst king in Chronicles (compare with his image in Kings and see, for instance, 2 Chr 28:24; note the action of closing the temple that is attributed to him in Chronicles; even the Manasseh of Kings was not imagined as planning or carrying out such an extreme deed). Moreover, the maximization of the negative characterization of Ahaz in Chronicles goes together with the lionization of Hezekiah, which is certainly not an accidental result of the "cleansing" of Manasseh but a very important point in Chronicles. It is not by accident that the most important contrastive pair of kings (the worst and the best) in Chronicles is Ahaz and Hezekiah, whereas in Kings, it is Manasseh and Josiah. This has much to do with the general mnemonic and ideological differences between Chronicles and Kings (see below). Finally, one might also add that Chronicles could have used an available common narrative pattern meant both to portray and to remember within a community a particular king in a saliently negative way and still allow for his repentance at a late stage (see, for instance, Naram Sin's legend; Dan 4 [esp. v. 34]; and 2 Macc 9:12, 17). There was no need to lionize Manasseh or characterize Ahaz extremely just to construe the former as repentant. The story, however, had to portray Manasseh and Ahaz in the way it actually did if Chronicles were to evoke certain important mnemonic narratives about the past (see below). There were no accidents here, nor did the community construe the implied author of Chronicles as communicating any accidents.

penting and withstanding the enemies who were attacking him and Jerusalem than to "clean up" Manasseh.[17]

Just to be clear, the point of these observations is *not* to advance or reject any hypothesis regarding causality as it applies to the actual author of Chronicles. The discussion above is not meant to propose or reject any particular answer to the question why the actual author of Chronicles wrote the account of Manasseh the way he did instead of some other potential way that would have been as consistent or more consistent with the general message and historiographical tendencies of Chronicles. Instead, the point of the present discussion is that the shape and contents of the report about King Manasseh in Chronicles do not represent a *necessary, inevitable* outcome. The actual author had a significant amount of freedom to reshape the narrative from Kings in different ways. Although we may *explain* the "final outcome," we certainly could not have predicted it. In other words, the best we can do is to develop good descriptive, post-event explanations rather than pre-event, causality-centered frameworks.[18]

---

[17] To be sure, there is the issue of the deportation to Babylon, but if this is, as most likely, a story contrived to make a particular point, it could have been used for other kings as well.
[18] The preceding discussion has focused on historiographical/ideological tendencies and constraints that characterize Chronicles. It must be admitted, however, that on the surface another type of consideration must be addressed: one might claim that the simplest position is that the author of Chronicles portrayed Manasseh the way he did, simply because such was the historical Manasseh. But first, the resulting reconstruction of the historical Manasseh is highly problematic (see references in n. 4). Second, even if for the sake of the argument one were to accept the idea that some aspects of the portrayal of Manasseh in Chronicles reflected the circumstances of the historical Manassic period, accepting this approach requires us to ignore the complex processes involved in history writing in general and the very evidence of Chronicles itself about the way in which it dealt with its sources. Moreover, ancient (as well as contemporary writers, one may argue) history writers, including the author of Chronicles, do not include stories in their historiographical narratives *simply* because they (believe that they) happened. They recount or fail to recount matters, and they shape their accounts the way they do for a large variety of historiographical reasons. Close to the case at hand–can we imagine that the author of Chronicles failed to include a single reference to Josiah's building activities just because he believed that Josiah did not build anything in his 31-year reign? Or that Asa and Jehoshaphat, both of them, did and did not remove the *bamot*? Or that Asa indeed had two different mothers? Or that this author included prophetic speeches such as Abijah's because they simply happened? Or that this author shaped an image of Elijah in the particular way that he did in Chronicles (which stands in sharp contrast to Kings) just because Elijah was actually like that? (For a discussion of these and related matters, see my *History, Literature and Theology in the Book of Chronicles*, 44–77). Likewise, claims that Chronicles described Manasseh the way it did because this was the description of Manasseh that existed in the author's sources not only face what we know all too well about the way Chronicles dealt with its sources but also simply shift the question to another "author" rather than "answering" the claim. Finally, as I show in § 3, the very

(Of course, these observations apply to authors of historiographical works other than Chronicles as well. See the book of Kings, for example; the book itself presents multiple approaches balancing each other and thus allowing multiple potential stories to be consistent with the book. At best, we would be able to "explain" how *any* text that the author/s eventually actually wrote/composed fit other aspects of the book rather than addressing the question of why he/they decided to write this but not any other potential texts.)

Moreover, the issue is not only that entering into the mind of the long-dead author to discern predictive, deterministic *causality* (as implied in some of the usual historical explanations about the construction of the figure of Manasseh in Chronicles) is in itself an impossible task but also–and far more important, even if this task were possible–that it would *not* shed much light on the memories evoked by the book.

It is the implied author as construed by the intended readership of the book, not the flesh-and-blood, "actual" author that has an impact on the construction of social memories shaped by reading texts, for it is with this author that the readership communicates. It is to *this* implied and socially construed author that they listen and whose characters they bring into existence through imagination and memory.[19]

---

focus on the historical author and on matters of direct correspondence between the narrative reported in Chronicles and contemporary potential narratives about the history of the Manassic period is not the most helpful way to approach the question of how a late-Persian-period community construed memories of Manasseh by reading Chronicles. This is the reason that this essay does not focus on the historical Manasseh but on the remembered Manasseh, and even more narrowly, on the remembered Manasseh evoked by reading Chronicles within a late-Persian/early-Hellenistic, Jerusalem-centered community–that is, in late Yehud. For general surveys or discussions on the historicity of the account of Manasseh in Chronicles, see, in addition to the works mentioned in n. 4, from different perspectives and among many other scholars: R. H. Lowery, *The Reforming Kings: Cults and Society in First Temple Judah* (JSOTSup 120; Sheffield: JSOT Press, 1991), 185–89; M. A. Sweeney, "King Manasseh of Judah and the Problem of Theodicy in the Deuteronomistic History," in *Good Kings and Bad Kings* (ed. L. L. Grabbe; LHBOTS 393; London: T&T Clark, 2005), 264–78 (esp. 268–72). Concerning the putative building activities of Manasseh, see also P. Welten, *Geschichte und Geschichtsdarstellung in den Chronikbüchern* (WMANT 42; Neukirchen-Vluyn: Neukirchener Verlag, 1973), esp. 31–34, 72–78.

19 It should be stressed that ancient readerships did not read texts that they considered authoritative (or as carrying reliable, godly knowledge about Yhwh and Israel) against the grain. In other words, readers of authoritative books imagined themselves as following the communicative wishes of the authors as they thought them to be. See Y. Amit, "'The Glory of Israel Does Not Deceive or Change His Mind': On the Reliability of Narrator and Speakers in Biblical Narrative," in *Proof* 12 (1992): 201–12.

As we turn to this implied author, an indirect but clear offshoot of the preceding discussion and its examples is that the literati reading and rereading the book in late-Persian Yehud had *no substantive reason to imagine the author of the book–the voice talking to them, as it were–as constrained either to invent or to report the story of Manasseh's exile to Babylon and his repentance*, so as to make sense of his long life. In fact, had their "historian" (i.e., their implied author of Chronicles) been construed in such a manner, he would not have been too credible in the community, and the book attributed to him would have been unlikely to survive. The implied author/historian *was not imagined as forced to tell anything*; rather, he simply narrated what is worth remembering of the things that "happened."

Concerning these matters, the intended (re)readership of Chronicles construed itself in ways similar to those of their implied author. The intended readership was not required to imagine that Manasseh *had* to repent to avoid premature death, even if their mindscape would have been dominated *only* by the ideology and narratives of Chronicles. Taking into account that they were also influenced by the book of Kings, which was part of their repertoire of authoritative books as well, and which actually evoked a memory of Manasseh as evil and long-lived, the case is even more evident.[20]

In other words, the literati who read and reread Chronicles were to evoke and remember Manasseh the way in which he is construed in Chronicles, because a Manasseh of this sort was worth remembering. But why did it make sense to remember this Manasseh, alongside the other Manasseh–the Manasseh in Kings and Jeremiah–in this community?

3 The Memorable Manasseh Evoked by the Target Readership of Chronicles

Before addressing this question, I must stress that, from the perspective of the reading community, the implied author wanted them to imagine and remember well the Manasseh of Chronicles. Time and again and in multiple ways, the text draws particular attention to Manasseh. The target readership is repeatedly re-

---

[20] Note again that the link between length of days and proper behaviour on earth is *not* an invention of Chronicles, but a basic feature of an existing social mindscape that came to be explicitly expressed in texts that predated Chronicles and remained within the authoritative repertoire of the community. See, for instance, Exod 20:12; Deut 5:16, 33; 17:20; 22:7; 25:16 and cf. Prov 10:2; 11:4.

minded that their Manasseh is an exceptional character, to whom they should pay much attention. In other words, theirs is a very memorable Manasseh.

At first glance, one might be tempted to dismiss *some* of the salient and unique ways that Manasseh is evoked as simple accidents, but the cumulative weight of all these observations is undeniable. Moreover, each of them in its own way serves to portray or draw attention to some significant aspect of the memory of Manasseh evoked by Chronicles.

The exceptional, bad-turns-good plot that shapes the account of Manasseh has been mentioned above. Whereas most kings either remain as bad as they are or turn from good to bad due to hubris or other reasons, the exceptional nature of the shift toward good in Manasseh makes him a salient exemplar for repentance. Moreover, the fact that he is described as a terrible sinner before his repentance communicates the message that Yhwh does not necessarily "execute" those worthy of being executed and that even some of the worst sinners may repent and their repentance be accepted by Yhwh. I will return to these points, but at this stage it is important to note the presence of many other markers of uniqueness and salience in Chronicles' Manasseh.

2 Chr 33:10 reads וַיְדַבֵּר יהוה אֶל־מְנַשֶּׁה וְאֶל־עַמּוֹ. Given that the syntax here is very common and so are the key words, it is particularly worth noting that the exact phrase X- אֶל יהוה וַיְדַבֵּר is rare in the HB used with any "X" other than Moses.[21] Moreover, in most of the exceptions, the slot of X is assigned to someone directly associated with Moses.[22] The other two exceptions are (1) in 1 Chr 21:9, where X is Gad, David's seer but, interestingly, not David himself; and (2) in 2 Chr 33:10. Furthermore, the occurrence in 1 Chr 21:9 is in the context of the story about David's census, the plague, David's repentance, and the place of the temple. At the very least, therefore, the use of this precise phrase in 2 Chr 33:10 prepares the reader for the fact that the next account will narrate "something of importance."[23]

The readers of Chronicles were also asked to remember a past in which various kings received godly advice through a special prophet or two at particular (potential) turning points. Chronicles evokes an image of a Manassic period in which *multiple* prophets continuously advised him (see the reference to וְדִבְרֵי הַחֹזִים הַמְדַבְּרִים אֵלָיו בְּשֵׁם יהוה אֱלֹהֵי יִשְׂרָאֵל in 2 Chr 33:18). Moreover, Chronicles informs its readers that the words of these prophets were worthy of being recorded for posterity and referred and see הִנָּם ... וְדִבְרֵי הַחֹזִים הַמְדַבְּרִים אֵלָיו ... וְיֶתֶר דִּבְרֵי מְנַשֶּׁה

---

[21] With "X" being Moses, it is very common in the Pentateuch.
[22] See Aaron in Lev 10:8; Num 18:8 (and Moses and Aaron in Lev 13:1; 15:1; Num 16:20; 19:1) and Joshua in Josh 20:1, within a text where Joshua clearly stands in continuation with Moses.
[23] Moreover, the text here may have hinted at a potential connection to David, the other main exemplar of repentance.

עַל־דִּבְרֵי מַלְכֵי יִשְׂרָאֵל "now the rest of the acts of Manasseh, ... and the words(/acts) of the seers who spoke to him ... these are in the Annals of the Kings of Israel (2 Chr 33:18). The contrast with the absolute absence of Manassic-period prophets in the worlds construed by the collection of prophetic books and the Deuteronomistic Historical Collection, with which the readership of Chronicles was acquainted as well, only emphasizes and draws attention to references about these prophets in Chronicles and about Manasseh himself.

Personages from the past are most often remembered as characters within particularly memorable plots and in relation to other figures populating the memory-scape of the community.[24] The Manasseh whose image was evoked by reading Chronicles was constructed parallel with and in contrast to a combination of images evoked about two kings of the late period—namely, Jehoiakim and Zedekiah. Like the first king, Manasseh is taken captive to Babylon (compare the precise language in 2 Chr 33:11b with that of 2 Chr 36:6, which stresses the point and weaves a network of meanings for the intended readers of the book), but in contrast to Zedekiah, he humbled himself (compare 2 Chr 33:12b with 2 Chr 36:12b).

Significantly, the general tendency was to construe major characters as encompassing, in a contrasting or non-contrasting way, several minor characters rather than vice versa. Manasseh is presented through these allusions to kings such as Jehoiakim and Zedekiah as a major character, more memorable and more important than either one of the latter. Note also that, whereas Yhwh is portrayed as sending messengers calling for repentance during Zedekiah's reign (2 Chr 36:15), Yhwh addresses Manasseh (and his people) "himself" and calls them to repent (2 Chr 33:10). This matter is not trivial or just a product of random chance and is consistent with the (contrastive) minor differences in the language of 2 Chr 33:12b and 2 Chr 36:12b and the other "peculiarities" of Manasseh's account in Chronicles.

Even as the memory of Jehoiakim and (especially) Zedekiah is strongly connected to the catastrophe of 586 BCE in Chronicles (in contrast to Kings, where Manasseh's memory is connected as much or even more), it is Manasseh and his repentance that consume more textual space and mind-share in Chronicles.[25]

---

24 This is so because social memory tends to be organized in terms of narratives.
25 This is consistent with the tendency in Chronicles to balance the overwhelming centrality of exile and the catastrophe in other works in the repertoire of the community. I have discussed this matter elsewhere: see "Toward a Sense of Balance: Remembering the Catastrophe of Monarchic Judah/(Ideological) Israel and Exile through Reading Chronicles in Late Yehud," in this volume, pp. 387–406. I discussed the importance of the concept of *social mindshare* for studies of social memory in ancient Israel see "Remembering the Prophets through the Reading and Re-

The target readership is asked to remember that Manasseh's prayer was worthy of being recorded in both the chronicles of the kings of Israel and the prophetic records (2 Chr 33:18, 19).[26] I will return to the issue of Manasseh's prayer and repentance, but at this point it is worth stressing that his is the only prayer, and the only text for that matter, that was putatively composed by a post-David/Solomon king of Judah and that was meant to be recorded for posterity. Also in this regard, the Manasseh evoked by Chronicles is exceptional and uniquely draws attention to himself.[27]

Of course, given the basic facts about the past agreed upon in the community and the large mind-share of the figure of Josiah (as construed in Kings), Manasseh could not have been remembered as the last reformer king, but only as another reforming king. However, the Manasseh of Chronicles was to be remembered as the last Judahite building king in a book in which building activ-

---

reading of a Collection of Written Prophetic Books in Yehud: Methodological Considerations and Explorations," in this volume, pp. 80–108.

26 This understanding of the text holds true regardless of the precise reading one adopts concerning דִּבְרֵי חוֹזָי in 2 Chr 33:19; on this matter, see Japhet, *I and II Chronicles*, 1012.

27 Manasseh's repentance and prayer were considered memorable and continued to affect and influence Jewish and Christian readers from early periods to recent times. A few examples from different times suffice. As I mentioned in n. 2, texts in Qumran purported to contain the prayer of Manasseh. A Hebrew version of the traditional "Prayer of Manasseh" was found in the Cairo Geniza. Voices in Rabbinic Judaism that attributed the fall of Jerusalem to the fact that, even Manasseh could repent but Judah did not, were mentioned above. Jerome wrote: O happy penitence which has drawn down upon itself the eyes of God, and which has by confessing its error changed the sentence of God's anger! The same conduct is in the Chronicles attributed to Manasseh, and in the book of the prophet Jonah to Nineveh, and in the gospel to the publican. ... The first of these not only was allowed to obtain forgiveness but also recovered his kingdom, the second broke the force of God's impending wrath. (Jerome, *Epist.* 77) David, the Ninevites, Hezekiah, and Manasseh are considered the eminent exemplars of repentance in *Apostolic Constitutions*, II, section 3, § 22. For much later times, see, for instance, the inclusion of Manasseh among six great kings of Judah in the statues at the royal chapel in El Escorial (the other kings are David, Solomon, Jehoshaphat, Hezekiah, and Josiah; see J. C. Endres, "The Spiritual Vision of Chronicles: Wholehearted, Joy-Filled Worship of God," in *CBQ* 69 [2007], 1–21 [esp. 6–12]). Turning to the twenty-first century: S. Tuell wrote, Manasseh serves as a compelling illustration of the extraordinary grace of God, offered freely to penitents whatever their offenses–and a firm rebuttal to those who would see a firm divide between 'Old Testament' *law* and 'New Testament' *grace*. In fact, the grace of God is the living heart of the whole Scripture. The forgiveness of sins in Jesus' ministry ... builds on the foundation laid in the Hebrew Bible ... the life of Paul, persecutor of the church turned apostle, forms an intriguing parallel to the Chronicler's life of Manasseh." (S. Tuell, *First and Second Chronicles* [Interpretation; Louisville: John Knox, 2001], 233).

ities was considered important and very much worth remembering.[28] In a manner reminiscent of the actions of his father, he built the walls of the city and strengthened the fortified cities (compare 2 Chr 33:14 with 32:5; 32:1), yet clearly the actions of Manasseh are portrayed as being carried out in a period of peace and blessing and as a mark of blessing, rather than being hasty actions meant to stop an invading army by worldly means.

There are additional textual markers that suggest that remembering the Manasseh of Chronicles involved evoking the memory of Hezekiah. For instance, the language זִבְחֵי שְׁלָמִים וְתוֹדָה in 2 Chr 33:16 is unique but reminiscent of the also-unique מְזַבְּחִים זִבְחֵי שְׁלָמִים וּמִתְוַדִּים in 2 Chr 30:22. Conceptually, the sentence וַיֹּאמֶר לִיהוּדָה לַעֲבוֹד אֶת־יהוה אֱלֹהֵי יִשְׂרָאֵל (2 Chr 33:16) may be seen as an expansion on 2 Chr 30:22 and similar texts.[29] In addition, the idiom, לַעֲבוֹד אֶת־יהוה אֱלֹהֵי יִשְׂרָאֵל (2 Chr 33:16) links the figure of Manasseh to that of Josiah, the other great reforming king; and see לַעֲבוֹד אֶת־יְהוָה אֱלֹהֵיהֶם (2 Chr 34:33).[30] In addition, Manasseh was imagined in some ways as being similar to the reforming kings within the memory-scape of the community that preceded Hezekiah and Josiah (cf. 2 Chr 33:17 with 1 Kgs 22:44; 2 Kgs 12:4; 14:4; 15:4).

The above considerations make the point that much attention was drawn in Chronicles to its Manasseh. But since he was made so memorable, the question is: why? What basic meanings and associations were embodied in the Manasseh of Chronicles as a site of memory for late-Persian/early-Hellenistic literati (the people who read and reread the book and for whom it was [directly] intended) that made him so central?

The Manasseh of Chronicles was construed as partially embodying Israel. To be sure, he was a sinner who, for his sins, was removed to Babylon and then restored to Judah and Jerusalem, just as Israel was (as construed by the literati in Yehud).[31] Unlike postmonarchic Israel, however, he returned to Judah and Jerusalem to rule the land as well as to live in it (compare and contrast with 2 Chr 36:23). The story of Manasseh inspired not only repentance but also hope for a future.

---

28 In Chronicles, Manasseh, not Josiah is the last building king. I wrote elsewhere on building activities in Chronicles: *History, Literature and Theology,* 100–116; originally published as "The Chronicler as a Historian: Building Texts," in *The Chronicler as Historian* (eds. M. P. Graham, K. G. Hoglund and S. L. McKenzie; JSOTSup 238; Sheffield: JSOT Press, 1997), 132–49.
29 See also the opening language in 2 Chr 32:26; 33:12.
30 It is worth noting that the precise expression לַעֲבוֹד אֶת־יְהוָה appears only in 2 Chr 33:16; 34:33.
31 An association between sinful Israel/Judah and sinful Manasseh is conveyed, indirectly, in Kings as well. See Smelik, "The Portrayal of King Manasseh," 149–51.

As the construed metaphor of Israel in the Persian period, Manasseh was not punished as harshly as he could have been.[32] Remembering Chronicles' Manasseh was indirectly hammering the common but important point in the discourse of postmonarchic Israel that Yhwh had been just *and merciful* with Israel, even when Yhwh exiled it; after all, Yhwh allowed a remnant to survive, who in turn could be "restored." Remembering Manasseh and seeing him as Israel was also remembering that the turning point that caused Manasseh's/Israel's change of heart was divine punishment in the form of exile. Needless to say, this construction reflected, supported, and communicated the role given to the exile in the discourse of Persian Yehud and the idea that post-repentance Israel/Manasseh is post-Babylonian Israel.[33]

Significantly, following his deliverance by Yhwh's mighty hand, Manasseh as construed and evoked by reading Chronicles, acknowledges that Yhwh is God, just as Israel does following its deliverance from Egypt–even if the Sinai-nomad Israelites were not brought to Jerusalem. One may note even the use of the phrase כִּי יהוה הוּא הָאֱלֹהִים in 2 Chr 33:13, taken word for word from Deut 4:35 and binding these two memories together. Thus, on some symbolic level, Manasseh is Israel and thus, when Yhwh talks to Manasseh, Yhwh is talking to Israel as well–a point implied in the logic of the text but also made explicit (2 Chr 33:10). Moreover, as Moses in Deut 4, Manasseh commands the people to serve Yhwh (2 Chr 33:16).

To remember the Manasseh of Chronicles is to remember that he was an example of the repentant Israel of 2 Chr 7:14 and of Yhwh's promise to forgive and heal. Significantly, some key wording and concepts in this text reverberate in

---

[32] Japhet correctly notes that, "in view of the extraordinary and unprecedented transgressions, this arresting of Manasseh presents a relatively mild reaction of the Lord, disproportionate to the immensity of sin" (*1 and 2 Chronicles*, 1009). But the same can be said of Manasseh's companions as paragons of repentance in Judah. David in the discourse of the literati was also influenced by Samuel, was construed as בֶּן מוּת, and was severely punished, but he was kept alive and eventually bore Solomon and engendered the temple. Postmonarchic Israel identified with both. Chronicles maintains the characterization of David as a paragon of repentance who existed within the discourse of the community, but it shifts the main event from the sin associated with Bathsheba and Uriah to the sin of the census: the story of Bathsheba is not mentioned in Chronicles and thus is indirectly considered not worthy of retelling and remembering. More importantly, the book tries to diminish the weight of the story within the mindshare of the community, while at the same time keeping David as a central site for repentance. Japhet concludes that Chronicles reports a relatively mild response of Yhwh, because it follows extrabiblical sources that report Manasseh's removal to Babylon at the hands of the Assyrians.
[33] See "Total Exile, Empty Land and the General Intellectual Discourse in Yehud," in this volume, pp. 599–611.

2 Chr 33:12–13. Notice the crucial role of Niphal verbal forms of כנע in both texts to communicate the turning point[34]–the importance of prayer and of turning from (what are considered to be) wicked ways–which is detailed and exemplified in the case of Manasseh (2 Chr 33:15–16).

Of course, the memory of Manasseh, like almost anything else in Chronicles, had to be set in proportion. Given his "history," Manasseh at the very end could not be imagined as great as Hezekiah or as Josiah, even in Chronicles (compare 2 Chr 33:15–17 with 2 Chr 34:33; and above all the reports about the kings' respective reforming activities and their level of success).[35] After all, Manasseh cannot overcome socially agreed-upon, core memories that exist in the community.[36] Moreover, not only his good deeds are worth remembering but also his evil ones (note the balance explicitly communicated in 2 Chr 33:19). But again, even this contrast makes the Manasseh of Chronicles a unique site of memory.

Studies on social memory show that, the more a character comes to embody, integrate, and communicate multiple matters that were at the core or close to the core of the discourse of the community, the more memorable the character turns out to be; and vice versa, memorable characters serve as magnets for issues and images that are central to the community. Moreover, although each character is construed and remembered as unique and his/her singularity is necessary to be a memorable figure, able to communicate all the matters integrated in and evoked as sites of memory (e. g., ideas, images, conceptualizations, basic narratives), many of these matters cannot be unique to him/her but must reflect the general mindscape of the period. Consequently, these memorable characters

---

34 See 2 Chr 12:22 (Rehoboam's repentance that allowed for the continuation of the Kingdom of Judah and David) and 2 Chr 32:26 (Hezekiah's repentance that postponed the fall of Monarchic Judah).

35 The "problem" that Manasseh's reform would not have left much for Josiah to purge/reform was *not* a problem for the target readership of Chronicles. Similar "logical" inconsistencies appear elsewhere in Chronicles (e. g., Asa's reform) and, in any case, emerge out of modes of reading Chronicles other than those the intended readers were asked to follow as they read the book, or at least many sections of it. I have discussed these matters elsewhere; see my *History, Literature and Theology in the Book of Chronicles*, 44–77.

36 It is particularly noteworthy that the motif of the people's continuing to sacrifice and make offerings in the *bāmôt* that is so common in Kings appears only here in Chronicles, in a place that could not have had any direct parallel in Kings but had a rhetorical function quite similar to what is in Kings. In Chronicles, the note explicitly sets Manasseh's reform in proportion, especially in terms of the reforms of his father, Hezekiah, and his most memorable successor, Josiah.

tend to be encoded elsewhere, in other sites of memory. In fact, had this *not* been the case, the character would not have been worthy of being remembered.[37]

The Manasseh of Chronicles was a unique site of memory that embodied both grave sin and great repentance. Thus, he served not only as a site of memory, standing symbolically for Israel, but also as a site of memory for Yehudite Israel. From the latter's perspective, Manasseh, to a large extent, encapsulated a central aspect of its main narrative about itself as reflected in the historical and prophetic books, and more importantly, for its present purposes.

To imagine the Manasseh of old was also to recall that both the good and bad deeds must be remembered by the community and that the good do not cancel the memory of the bad, even if explicitly imagined as "undoing" the bad. In this way, the Manasseh of Chronicles encapsulated again the general discourse of the period and the basic notions expressed in the authoritative repertoire of the community.

Remembering Manasseh was not only a way to remember the place of Jerusalem in Israel, especially the fact that its temple and the return from the second exile were to Jerusalem, not to the land in general (see Isa 52:11–12; 2 Chr 36:23; and contrast these with the original return–that is, the exodus). But also, in his own way, Manasseh served as a site of memory, embodying and broadcasting a core aspect of the community's ideology that was expressed elsewhere.

To remember the Manasseh of Chronicles was, of course, to remember Yhwh and the deity's interaction with Israel. Significantly, the Manasseh of Chronicles brings attention to Yhwh's willingness to give enough time to Israel to repent but also calls attention to the fact that Israel should repent and acknowledge Yhwh. Considering that, for the most part, the narratives about deliverance from Egypt and Babylon do not emphasize Israel's need for repentance prior to deliverance, and elsewhere Chronicles suggests that exile is by divine decision (temporally restricted and, in any case, of limited–though not inconsequential–significance),[38] remembering Manasseh serves to balance matters. This more balanced, multivo-

---

[37] On these trends in relation to the figures of Abraham, Moses, Isaiah, and Hosea in the late-Persian/early-Hellenist period, see "The Memory of Abraham in Late Persian/Early Hellenistic Period Yehud," "Exploring the Memory of Moses 'The Prophet' in Late Persian/Early Hellenistic Period Yehud/Judah" and "Isaiah, a Memorable Prophet: Why Was Isaiah So Memorable in the Persian/Early Hellenistic Period?," and "Remembering Hosea: The Prophet as a Site of Memory in Persian Period Yehud" in this volume, pp. 162–98, 199–23, 253–73, 274–93 respectively.
[38] On exile in Chronicles, see "Toward a Sense of Balance: Remembering the Catastrophe of Monarchic Judah/(Ideological) Israel and Exile through Reading Chronicles in Late Yehud," in this volume, pp. 387–406.

cal approach to the issue is far more consistent with and representative of the larger spectrum of voices encoded in the prophetic corpus on this very matter.

The preceding observations show that Manasseh was reshaped in Chronicles to reflect a set of positions expressed in the general authoritative repertoire of the community and reflective of its general social mindscape. Manasseh's reshaping in Chronicles also played important roles in the reshaping of the structure of the remembered narrative about Israel's late monarchic period. Kings encoded and communicated a narrative in which the two main characters were Hezekiah and Josiah, in that order. Each was preceded by a villain who served as the expected foil and, since Josiah was the most positive king in this plot, the one preceding him needed to be the most negative king. Thus the narrative in Kings was structured to a large extent around the pairs Ahaz-Hezekiah and Manasseh-Josiah. The heightened image of Josiah required and the lack of a slot for a "great villain" following him contributed much to the characterization of Manasseh as a king whose actions decided the fate of Judah–to the point that even Josiah's deeds could not change it.

The narrative in Kings played an important role in the formation of memories about the period in the community, but Chronicles rebalanced this period in the social memory of the community by creating a different, and to a large extent, complementary main plot. Here the main hero was Hezekiah, and the main villain then had to be Ahaz. To characterize late Manasseh as Israel, not as villain but a hero, erases the possibility of strongly structuring the narrative around the pairs Ahaz-Hezekiah and Manasseh-Josiah.[39] To have Manasseh as a complex and, to a large extent, very positive figure is conducive to a reshaping of the narrative in order to have one heightened point: Hezekiah's time (note the space allocated to his reign in Chronicles, which is much more than that allocated to any king since the foundational Davidic/Solomonic period).

---

[39] On the Hezekiah of Chronicles, see, for instance, M. A. Throntveit, "The Relationship of Hezekiah to David and Solomon in the Books of Chronicles," in *The Chronicler as Theologian: Essays in Honor of Ralph W. Klein* (eds. M. P. Graham, S. L. McKenzie, and G. N. Knoppers; JSOTSup 371; London: T&T Clark, 2003), 105–21 (and previous literature cited there); L. Jonker, "The Chronicler's Reinterpretation of Hezekiah's Reformation Efforts," in *From Ebla to Stellenbosch* (eds. I. Cornelius and L. C. Jonker; Wiesbaden: Harrassowitz, 2008), 116–40; A. Warhurst, "The Chronicler's Use of the Prophets," in *What Was Authoritative for Chronicles?* (eds. E. Ben Zvi and D. V. Edelman; Winona Lake, IN.: Eisenbrauns, 2012), 165–82. I elaborated elsewhere on Josiah in Chronicles; see my "Observations on Josiah's Account in Chronicles and Implications for Reconstructing the Worldview of the Chronicler," in *Essays on Ancient Israel in Its Near Eastern Context: A Tribute to Nadav Na'aman* (eds. Y. Amit et al.; Winona Lake, IN: Eisenbrauns, 2006), 89–106 and the references cited there.

This narrative, in fact, is a case of resignifying another main narrative that existed in the discourse of the community—the one in which Hezekiah and the Assyrian crisis served as the prefiguration and counterpoint of the catastrophe of 586 BCE, which is reflected in, among others, the book of Isaiah and much of the prophetic literature. Chronicles resignifies the narrative so as to draw more attention to Hezekiah as a reformer and pious king rather than as the king who was delivered by YHWH from the hands of the Assyrians. Although this is not the place to analyze the Hezekiah of Chronicles (and its aftermath in the quasi-messianic Hezekiah of Rabbinic Judaism),[40] it is worth stressing that the reshaping of the memory of Manasseh in Chronicles is part of a larger project of replotting and restructuring the late monarchic past and constructing a particular memory of Hezekiah. This project aims at creating a memory landscape that is different from the one evoked by reading Kings or most of the prophetic books—which also construct a late monarchic past, but not Isaiah, which moves straight from Hezekiah (see Isa 39) to Cyrus and the return (Isa 40–55).[41] This project constructs a late monarchic past that rebalances and informs the other two, just as it is rebalanced and informed by them. The fact that, through this project, the main villain—who was at times construed and remembered as responsible for the destruction of Jerusalem[42]—is now identified with Israel, is seen as quite a hero, becomes a shared embodiment of the extremely sinful and very pious; and a call to remember both turns out to be a cipher for a return to Jerusalem and the temple and is, above all, a cipher for (the potential of) repentance. This is clearly not to be underestimated.[43]

---

40 Compare with the (partial) "Hezekianic" characterization of Jesus in Matthew (see T. L. Thompson, *The Messiah Myth: The Near Eastern Roots of Jesus and David* [New York: Basic Books, 2005], 84). As for rabbinic sources, see b. Sanh. 94a, 98b, 99a; also M. Hadas-Lebel, "Hezekiah as King Messiah: Traces of an Early Jewish-Christian Polemic in the Tannaitic Tradition," in *Jewish Studies at the Turn of the Twentieth Century*, vol. 1: *Biblical, Rabbinical, and Medieval Studies* (eds. J. Targarona Borrás and A. Sáenz-Badillos; Leiden: Brill, 1999), 275–81 and bibliography there. On the relationship between the accounts of Ahaz and Hezekiah in Chronicles and the lionization of the latter, see P. R. Ackroyd, "The Biblical Interpretation of the Reigns of Ahaz and Hezekiah," in *In the Shelter of Elyon: Essays on Ancient Palestinian Life and Literature in Honor of G. W. Ahlström* (eds. W. Boyd Barrick and J. R. Spencer; JSOTSup 31; Sheffield: JSOT Press, 1984), 247–59.
41 For a discussion of the ways that social memory structures plot and its significance, see "Isaiah, a Memorable Prophet."
42 See the voice in Kings that comes to the forefront in 2 Kgs 23:26, 24:3; and see Jer 15:14.
43 And certainly not explained away in terms of "necessities" that befell a relatively single-minded author, or a matter that is peripheral to "historical" issues, such as: "Did Manasseh rebel or think to rebel against Assyria or not?" "Was Manasseh taken to Babylon or not?" To be sure, these questions are important for historical reconstructions of the Manassic period,

Of course, through this very process, Manasseh becomes a paradigmatic case of a multivalent (and yet integrated and integrating)[44] site of memory within the social memory of an Israel who reads and rereads Kings, the prophetic literature, *and* Chronicles. In fact, one may say that Manasseh becomes a main site of memory embodying and communicating the potential multivalence of other sites of memory in the memory landscape of the community.[45] The presence of multiple markers' drawing the attention of the target readership of Chronicles to its Manasseh and making him such a memorable figure can be understood as a reflection of the centrality of the messages that are both embodied and communicated by this site of memory and the need to increase the relative weight or better social mind-share of this Manasseh *vis-à-vis* other Manassehs that existed in the memory-scape of the community. They both competed with and complemented the memory evoked by Chronicles (and vice versa). Needless to say, the more important the messages that Manasseh evoked, the greater would be the tendency in Chronicles to increase its mind-share within the community. The present discussion brings to the forefront the proof of this process. At the same time, the status of Chronicles–which presented itself as secondary to the books of the Deuteronomistic Historical Collection and was meant to complement and balance the memories that this collection (and the Primary History) evoked rather than erase them–set some limits on its capability to shape the comprehensive social memory of Manasseh.[46]

---

but for the reasons mentioned above, far less relevant to historical reconstructions of the world of thought and the social memory-scape of literati in late-Persian/early-Hellenistic Jerusalem and Yehud/Judah. The primary readership and historical community that imagined its past as it read Chronicles included the latter but not the former (i.e., the historical Manassic Judah).

44 After all, all the mentioned attributes and associations were interwoven into one single character from the past. On this issue, see "Exploring the Memory of Moses 'The Prophet.'"

45 The presence of such sites of memory contributes to and is consistent with a certain preference for "fuzziness" in the social mindscape of the community. A study of these matters, however, stands well beyond the scope of this essay. I briefly dealt with these issues in "On Social Memory and Identity Formation in Late Persian Yehud: A Historian's Viewpoint with a Focus on Prophetic Literature, Chronicles and the Dtr. Historical Collection," and "Exploring the Memory of Moses 'The Prophet'" respectively in pp. 28–79 and 199–231 in this volume.

46 See J. Van Seters, "Creative Imitation in the Hebrew Bible," *SR* 29 (2000): 395–409; E. Ben Zvi, "One Size Does Not Fit All: Observations on the Different Ways That Chronicles Dealt with the Authoritative Literature of Its Time," in *What Was Authoritative for Chronicles?* (eds. E. Ben Zvi and D. V. Edelman; Winona Lake, IN.: Eisenbrauns, 2012), 13–36.

Toward a Sense of Balance: Remembering the Catastrophe of Monarchic Judah/(Ideological) Israel and Exile through Reading Chronicles in Late Yehud*

This essay and its companion, "Chronicles and Its Reshaping of Memories of Monarchic Period Prophets: Some Observations,"[1] address the potential contribution of Chronicles to a process of balancing the relative mindshare of different memories and sets of memories about monarchic events and figures in the late-Persian (or early-Hellenistic) Yehudite community in which its primary readership was located. As revealed by its title, this paper deals with remembering through reading and rereading. This remembering becomes memorable through the acts of mental imagination involved in re-creating and vicariously living the imagined past that was evoked by the text being read. Since reading evokes and activates memory within the community, within a text-centered community such as (at least) the literati in Yehud, texts to be read and reread affected mindshare. The more the community read (and reread) about a certain event, character, situation, the stronger the tendency to remember them. Conversely, the less something in the (construed) past of the community was mentioned in its authoritative repertoire, the less (we assume) its memory was evoked and the less mindshare it held in the community.

This paper is devoted in particular to what reading Chronicles, in the discursive context of the community within which and for which it emerged, may have contributed to its social memory about the exile, its significance, and the significance of closely associated clusters of social memories around the catastrophe at the end of the monarchic period, of which the exile was the outcome. The approach taken here has, at least, the potential to shed additional light on these social memories and the roles they played within the intellectual discourse

---

* First published in *Chronicling the Chronicler. The Book of Chronicles and Early Second Temple Historiography* (eds. P. S. Evans and T. F. Williams; Winona Lake, Ind.: Eisenbrauns, 2013), 247–65.
1 Published in another collection of works emerging from this seminar—namely, *Prophets and Prophecy in Ancient Israelite Historiography* (eds. M. J. Boda and L. M. Wray Beal; Winona Lake, IN: Eisenbrauns, 2013), 167–88 and republished in this volume, see pp. 407–27.

that characterized the community, and more light on what the reading of Chronicles may have "done" to the community.[2]

Contemporary historical studies on how Chronicles dealt with the concept of the exile have tended to focus on relatively few common issues.[3] An excellent illustration is provided by Rainer Albertz, who summarized the matter as follows:

> Except for the statement that the exiles became the servants or slaves of Nebuchadnezzar and his sons, the Chronicler does not find any concrete historical information concerning the period of the exile worth reporting. Instead, he embeds his meager account of the exilic period in a complex of theological interpretations. First, the exile is the fulfillment of a prophecy spoken by Jeremiah; second, it served as a Sabbath of rest for the land; third it had to last seventy years.[4]

The three central issues mentioned in the quotation arise from a very brief note in 2 Chr 36:20–21. As expected in our field, each one of the three has been the subject of some significant debate. For instance, among the many explicit or implicit research questions that have been raised and addressed in various ways, one may mention: (1) Does the reference to Jeremiah's prophecy point to the beginning or to the end of the exile, or to both?[5] (2) How does one understand the reference to the 70 years? (3) What was the history of this seemingly chronologically odd concept?[6]

This said, there seems to be widespread agreement that Chronicles brings together Lev 26:33/34–35, 43; and Jer 29:10 (see also Jer 25:12) and by doing so cre-

---

[2] It is common in our field that new light on texts and ancient intellectual discourses is shed, not through the discovery of "new evidence," but by asking new questions and looking at the "old evidence" from new perspectives.

[3] With the possible exception of S. Japhet, who emphasizes also "the uninterrupted settlement in the land" (*The Ideology of Chronicles and Its Place in Biblical Thought* [BEATAJ 9; 2nd ed.; Frankfurt am Main: Peter Lang, 1997], esp. 364–86). Her positions are discussed below, when relevant to the issue at stake.

[4] R. Albertz, *Israel in Exile: The History and Literature of the Sixth Century BCE.* (Studies in Biblical Literature 3; Atlanta: Society of Biblical Literature), 13.

[5] E.g., ibid.; L. C. Jonker, "The Exile as Sabbath Rest: The Chronicler's Interpretation of the Exile," *OTE* 20 (2007): 703–19 (esp. 708); idem, "The Chronicler and the Prophets: Who Were His Authoritative Sources?" in *What Was Authoritative for Chronicles?* (eds. E. Ben Zvi and D. V. Edelman; Winona Lake, IN: Eisenbrauns, 2011), 145–64; S. Japhet, *I and II Chronicles: A Commentary* (OTL; London: SCM, 1993), 1075–76; and cf. S. Frolov, "The Prophecy of Jeremiah in Esr 1,1," *ZAW* 116 (2004): 595–601.

[6] E.g., M. Leuchter, "Jeremiah's 70-Year Prophecy and the לב קמי/ששך *Atbash* Codes," *Bib* 85 (2004): 503–22; J. Jarick, *2 Chronicles* (Readings; Sheffield: Sheffield Phoenix, 2007), 192–95; H. G. M. Williamson, *1 and 2 Chronicles* (NCB; Grand Rapids, MI: Eerdmans, 1982), 417–18 and bibliography.

ates a new text,⁷ and that this new text conveys a sense of (1) the importance of the fulfillment of prophecy in history and particularly of the prophetic words associated with Moses and Jeremiah;⁸ (2) the presence of the concept of the exile as the sabbath of the land, which in itself implies a temporal limitation, which in turn is explicitly and saliently communicated by the reference to the 70 years that sets clear temporal limits on the exile; and (3) that all this means, as Sara Japhet puts it: "Exile only creates a necessary hiatus, after which life will return to its regular course; with the conclusion of the 'land's sabbaths' the time will come for its 'redemption'."⁹ Of course, this means also that the terrible judgment "has fully passed and no longer stands as a threat to his readers," to state this in the words of H. G. M. Williamson.¹⁰ Needless to say, this Chronistic approach to the exile communicates, as Louis Jonker has maintained, a sense that the Persian-period community that emerges after this exile represents a new, positive beginning.¹¹

Finally, even the most cursory survey of contemporary research on the concept of the exile in Chronicles cannot avoid noticing that 2 Chr 36:20–21 portrays an image of an "Empty Land." This is not the place to discuss the motif of the "Empty Land" in the postmonarchic period, its history and significance in the discourse of the late-Persian period, or its importance for the self-understanding of a Jerusalem-centered polity.¹² It suffices for the present purposes to say that (1) Chronicles reflected and communicated this common, postmonarchic motif (i.e., the "Empty Land"); (2) as did any other reference to the motif in the discourse of the primary community of readers, it evoked among them an image of the entire land or at least Judah (not just Jerusalem) as empty; and (3) most clearly was not an invention of Chronicles.¹³

---

7 E.g., M. Fishbane, *Biblical Interpretation in Ancient Israel* (Oxford: Clarendon, 1985), 482–83 (cf. 488–89); I. Kalimi, *The Reshaping of Ancient Israelite History in Chronicles* (Winona Lake, IN: Eisenbrauns, 2004), 222, 314; E. Ben Zvi, *History, Literature and Theology in the Book of Chronicles* (London: Equinox, 2006), 150–51, 156–57.
8 E.g., I. Kalimi, *An Ancient Israelite Historian: Studies in The Chronicler, His Time, Place and Writing* (SSN 46; Assen: Van Gorcum, 2005), 148–51.
9 Japhet, *1 and 2 Chronicles*, 1075. See, among others, Jonker, "The Exile as Sabbath Rest;" S. L. McKenzie, *1–2 Chronicles* (AOTC; Nashville: Abingdon, 2004), 371.
10 Williamson, *1 and 2 Chronicles*, 417.
11 Jonker, "The Exile as Sabbath Rest."
12 The matter has been extensively discussed. For an illustrative bibliography and my own take on the matter, see "Total Exile, Empty Land and the General Intellectual Discourse in Yehud," in this volume, pp. 599–611.
13 *The "empty land" of all Judah:* Japhet, among others, has maintained that Chronicles constructs a world in which only Jerusalem suffers from destruction at the hands of the Babylonians

I do not intend to contest in any substantive way the positions just mentioned.[14] They are widely accepted for good reasons—namely, they are all well grounded in 2 Chr 36:20–21. This very observation, however, serves as the starting point for my own exploration of the exile in Chronicles and the way that Chronicles may have influenced social memory about the exile. All these comments are based on just 2 verses in a historiographical work that spans 1,765 verses.[15]

To be sure, there are explicit references to the exile in a *very small number* of other verses in Chronicles, particularly in the genealogies. 1 Chr 5:6, 25–26 refer to the exile of the Transjordanian tribes. Unlike the exile of Judah, their exile is presented as still not being revoked (see "to this day" in v. 26) and thus their lands as not being populated by "Israel" since the days of Tiglath-pileser III, King of Assyria. Chronicles' portrayal of the demographic situation here stands

---

(see Japhet, *Ideology*, 364–68; idem, *1 and 2 Chronicles*, 1074). Whether this is the case or not, it is very unlikely that the primary readers of Chronicles would have read the book as stating that only Jerusalem became an "empty land" for 70 years, because there was no reason to understand the sabbath of the land as meaning only the sabbath of the urban area of Jerusalem. The number 70 and the implied 490 years system contradict this position, as well as the *Sitz im Diskurs* of Chronicles. *Regarding Chronicles' not inventing the "empty land,"* note, for instance, 2 Kgs 25:21–26; numerous images in prophetic books of complete desolation that in Yehud served to imagine the situation in Judah after the calamity of the Babylonian wars (e.g., Jer 32:43; 33:6; 44:2; cf. Isa 6:11–12; Zeph 1:2–3; see also Lev 26:34–35; Deut 29:21–23, 27 as read in Yehud); references to the land's purging itself (Lev 18:24–28; 20:22; 26:33–35); and the implied logic of images such as YHWH's divorce or at least expulsion from the marital home of Israel. All of these precede Chronicles. On the significance of a particular aspect of this "empty land" motif, see below.

14 However, I would certainly claim that the mentioned ideological positions are placed in proportion within Chronicles itself, as is usually the case in this book in particular and in the repertoire of the authoritative books of Yehud in general. For instance, within the discourse of the period (and even later periods), exile could be seen as both ending with the rebuilding of the temple (or the "return" and, therefore, as a matter of the past) and ongoing. In Chronicles, exile lasts 70 years and ends with Cyrus, but continues as well. See, for instance, the pragmatic meaning of מִי־בָכֶם מִכָּל־עַמּוֹ יְהוָה אֱלֹהָיו עִמּוֹ וְיָעַל in 2 Chr 36:23 (on the matter, see Kalimi, *An Ancient Israelite Historian*, esp. 153; Ben Zvi, *History, Literature and Theology*, 202–9). Clearly, neither the authorship nor the intended and primary readerships of Chronicles thought that the return of Judah had been complete by the "70 years" and thus "exile" had been banished from Israel. See also 1 Chr 5:6, 26; notice that the return envisaged in 1 Chr 16:35 can be only in the future of the community of readers. (The present discussion deals with "exile" in Chronicles; for a recent study from a different methodological perspective on different concepts of "exile" and what "exile" entails in other texts, see M. A. Halvorson-Taylor, *Enduring Exile: The Metaphorization of Exile in the Hebrew Bible* [VTSup 141; Leiden: Brill, 2011].)

15 D. N. Freedman, A. D. Forbes, and F. I. Andersen, *Studies in Hebrew and Aramaic Orthography* (BibJS 2; Winona Lake, IN: Eisenbrauns, 1992), 304.

in sharp contrast to the situation of Cisjordanian northern Israel (see, for instance, 2 Chr 30:1–31:1; 34:6–9).[16] Given the tendency in Chronicles to construe "the land" as populated (only) by "Israel" (and those who associate themselves with "Israel"),[17] this portrayal evokes a sense of boundaries or peripherality. It is not by chance that Transjordanian tribes and space play a substantially less significant role in Chronicles than their counterparts in northern Cisjordanian Israel[18] and, needless to say, incommensurably less than those in Judah.[19] The marginal character of these tribes and their land, along with the rather generic explanation of their exile (1 Chr 5:25) explains why these three verses played only a peripheral role in scholarly reconstructions of the concept of the exile in Chronicles, other than recognizing the rhetorical use of terms from the root מעל (cf. 1 Chr 9:1b; 10:13; 2 Chr 12:2; 26:16; 28:19, 22; 29:6; 30:7; 36:14).

There are two more explicit references to exile in the genealogies. 1 Chr 9:1b contains a *very brief note* that explicitly mentions Judah's exile and explains it in terms of 'their unfaithfulness' (במעלם). Not only is the explanation "generic," but also and perhaps more importantly, the main function of this note is clearly not to dwell on the exile, the reasons and historical processes that led to it (see the space given to it in the book), but to introduce (in an extremely sparse way, to be sure) the main themes of restoration and continuity, which are clearly expressed in a way that fits the genre of these chapters in 1 Chr 9:2–34. The second reference occurs in 1 Chr 5:41. Here Jehozadak is described as the Aaronide who "went into exile when the LORD sent Judah and Jerusalem into exile by the hand of Nebuchadnezzar." The addition of Jehozadak to the list of "high priests"–he is not mentioned in Kings–and the reference to him as the Aaronide in exile served not so much to dwell on exile or its causes but mainly to construe

---

16 It is worth noting that Chronicles shifts images/memories associated with the exile of (mainly) Cisjordanian Israel to the exile of Transjordanian tribes (cf. 1 Chr 5:26 and 2 Kgs 17:6; 18:11) and thus activates them in an, at least by connotation, more restrictive environment. In other words, it reshapes the target group and land associated with these images/memories in the social memory of the community of readers and, therefore, their relative mindshare.
17 See Japhet, *I and II Chronicles*, 46; R. W. Klein, *1 Chronicles* (Hermeneia; Minneapolis: Fortress, 2006), 46.
18 It is worth noting that different views about the actual extent of "the land" and particularly the inclusion of Transjordan existed in the authoritative literature of the period. Compare the mentioned tendency in Chronicles with Num 34:1–15; Ezek 47:13–23; and cf. 2 Kgs 14:25. A discussion of these issues is beyond the scope of this contribution. For studies on this matter see, for instance, M. Weinfeld, "The Extent of the Promised Land: The Status of Transjordan," in *Das Land Israel in biblischer Zeit* (ed. G. Strecker; Göttingen: Vandenhoeck & Ruprecht, 1983), 59–75.
19 On the issue of land/people peripherality in Chronicles, see my previous work in *History, Literature and Theology*, 195–209.

an ideological narrative and memory of continuity, because within the world of knowledge and the discourse of the community of readers of Chronicles, he was the father of Joshua, the "high priest" at the time of the rebuilding of the temple (see Hag 1:1, 12, 14; 2:2, 4; Zech 6:11). As in the previous case, it is easy to understand why 1 Chr 5:41 has served, at best, a very peripheral role in scholarly reconstructions of the concept of the exile in Chronicles.[20]

In sum, the exile is (unavoidably) acknowledged in 1 Chr 1–9, but the book allocates minimal space to references that evoke memories of exiles. Moreover, in two of the cases it does so for the purpose of conveying a sense that the exile was overcome, and that continuity prevailed in Israel. In the other two, it refers to peripheral space. In none of these four brief references is there anything remotely similar to the treatment of the exile in 2 Chr 36:20–21 in terms of an explicit and substantive message about the exile. Moreover, the concept of "the sabbath of the land," which with good reason is considered to play a central role in the explanation of the exile and its significance, is not mentioned elsewhere in the historical narrative of Chronicles, except in these 2 verses.

Although there are still a very *few* references (e.g., 1 Chr 16:35; 2 Chr 34:23–28) or typological allusions (2 Chr 29:6–9)[21] to the exile in Chronicles besides the aforementioned instances in the genealogies and 2 Chr 36:20–21, none of them addresses the nature of the exile as these two verses or has the exile as its main focus.[22] Thus and returning to the brief summary of the present understanding of the concept of the exile in Chronicles advanced by Albertz, it is with very good reason that scholars focused their attention and developed their positions on the matter on the basis of two crucial verses–namely, 2 Chr 36:20–21.

---

20 1 Chr 8:6–7 does not seem to refer to exile (that is, exile outside "the land") at all. There is no reason, therefore, to discuss this text here.

21 2 Chr 29:6–9 directly comments on and construes the reign of Ahaz, both in terms of the king's deeds (note the explicit reference to גַּם סָגְרוּ דַּלְתוֹת ... וְעֹלָה לֹא־הֶעֱלוּ בַקֹּדֶשׁ לֵאלֹהֵי יִשְׂרָאֵל "they shut the doors ... did not make burnt offerings in the holy place to the Israel's god" in v. 7 and cf. 2 Chr 28:24; and see the putative setting of the speech as explicitly and saliently expressed in vv. 3–5; see also the explicit, contrast between פָּתַח אֶת־דַּלְתוֹת "he opened the doors" in v. 3 and סָגְרוּ דַלְתוֹת in v. 7). Thus, it deals with events more than 100 years earlier than the exile. This said, the particular choice of language used to portray the situation is evocative of images of exile that existed in the discourse of the community (cf. Jer 25:9, Neh 8:17, among others). On Ahaz in Chronicles see the relevant chapter in this volume.

22 To avoid any misunderstanding, the point I want to make is *not* that Chronicles contains no explicit references to exile but that these are few and brief (i.e., that they do not occupy much "space" in this book) and that none of them develops the matter as 2 Chr 36:20–21 does.

But, this being the case, two questions emerge: (1) What may all the other verses that do not refer directly to the exile contribute to the impact of Chronicles on the construction of social memory about the exile? And (2) may the fact that only two verses out of 1,765 speak directly about exile insinuate something significant in itself on these matters, especially given (a) the social setting of the emergence and first readings and rereadings of Chronicles and (b) the fact that reading involved remembering the past evoked in the reading (and bracketing or momentarily forgetting, or at least displacing one's active memory of, what was not being read)?

Needless to say, Chronicles was not the only book the literati of the period read, nor could it have carried its intended message to the community had this been the case. This, of course, raises the need to take into consideration the implications of the *Sitz im Diskurs* of Chronicles on the matters to which this essay is devoted.[23] Chronicles emerged within and was read by its primary readership, whose discourse was to a large extent obsessed with the exile and with its related ideological constructions and memories (including those dealing with the fall of the monarchic polity) and with a future return, redemption, and related visions of utopian futures. The prophetic corpus saliently attests this concentration of social attention—or more precisely, of mindshare—which reaches the point of what may be called (though not in any pejorative meaning) memory obsession.

Outside the prophetic corpus, but still inside the relevant authoritative repertoire, the shadow of the catastrophe and the exile loomed large throughout the Deuteronomistic historical collection, and allusions to it are not only common but at times key interpretive notes for the historical narrative and its didactic/ideological significance.[24] In fact, one can easily discern a teleological trajectory running throughout the Deuteronomistic (and even in the primary) historical collection. The narrative moves toward a widely announced, anticipated, and at times even prefigured catastrophe and exile, even as it also implicitly points to hope and certitude about their reversal following a dystopian period.[25]

---

[23] Considerations regarding the *Sitz im Diskurs* of Chronicles apply to any historical study of the significance that reading the book had for the literati of the time. In the present contribution, only considerations that have direct bearing on the issues at stake can be discussed.
[24] Some of the instances even involve the creation of memory nodes connecting multiple central threads (e.g., the site/s of memory evoked in 2 Kgs 17:7–23; incidentally, this text informed and was, by the time of Chronicles, informed by Chronicles).
[25] From the perspective of the readers of Joshua–Kings, who knew Deuteronomy (as was the case with the literati of the Persian period), the historical narrative from Joshua to Kings becomes a detailed and strongly didactic elaboration of the fulfillment of the prophecies of

There are good reasons for this memory obsession. In a short period, Judah suffered a reduction of 70–75% in its population, and close to 90% in some areas (e.g., Jerusalem environs, eastern strip). This was due to war, famine, associated diseases, deportation, and migration caused by the economic collapse that followed and was engendered by the sociopolitical collapse. Even in Benjamin, who was the least affected of all regions, the population dropped by more than 50%. A catastrophe of this magnitude could not but be remembered and become a site of memory or cipher bearing a weighty significance for generations after the event, particularly among those whose self-identity was grounded on a close identification with the individuals who were afflicted by the disaster and within any polity or community that imagined itself and was understood as standing in continuation with the community that suffered such a calamity.[26] In addition, one must assume that ruins were probably seen in the region

---

Moses in Deut 30:1; 31:26–29. This being the case, the subsequent chapter in their history had to deal with the fulfillment of the promises of Deut 30:2–10.

26 Cf. H.-J. Stipp, "The Concept of the Empty Land in Jeremiah 37–43," in *The Concept of Exile in Ancient Israel and Its Historical Contexts* (eds. E. Ben Zvi and C. Levin; BZAW 404; Berlin: De Gruyter, 2010), 103–54, esp. 136–50. Stipp compares this shrinkage of population to that caused by the Thirty Years' War (which was far less dramatic). To put it in today's numbers, this would be equivalent to the loss of about 25 million Canadians or more than 230 million Americans. It is worth stressing that the demographic (or economic) recovery was nowhere even close to the population or economy of late-monarchic Judah during the Persian and early-Hellenistic periods, that is, the time in which Chronicles was composed and first read and reread. On demographic data about these periods, see, among others, O. Lipschits, "Persian Period Finds from Jerusalem: Facts and Interpretations," in *JHebS* 9 (2009) article 20, http://www.jhsonline.org; idem, *The Fall and Rise of Jerusalem: Judah under Babylonian Rule* (Winona Lake, IN: Eisenbrauns, 2005), esp. 258–71; idem, "Demographic Changes in Judah between the Seventh and the Fifth Centuries BCE" in *Judah and the Judeans in the Neo-Babylonian Period* (eds. O. Lipschits and J. Blenkinsopp; Winona Lake, IN: Eisenbrauns, 2003), 323–76; I. Finkelstein, "Persian Period Jerusalem and Yehud: A Rejoinder," in *JHebS* 9 (2009) article 24, http://www.jhsonline.org; idem, "Jerusalem in the Persian (and Early Hellenistic) Period and the Wall of Nehemiah," in *JSOT* 32 (2008): 501–20; idem, "Archaeology and the List of Returnees in the Books of Ezra and Nehemiah," in *PEQ* 140 (2008): 7–16; H. Geva, "בתקופותיה הקדומות: ההצעה המינימליסטית אומדן אוכלוסיית ירושלים" ("Estimating Jerusalem's Population in Antiquity: A Minimalist View"), in *ErIsr* 28 (Teddy Kollek Volume; 2007): 50–65 (Hebrew); A. Kloner, "Jerusalem's Environs in the Persian Period," in *New Studies on Jerusalem* (eds. A. Faust and E. Baruch; Ramat Gan: Ingeborg Rennert Center for Jerusalem Studies, 2001), 91–95 (Hebrew); cf. C. E. Carter, *The Emergence of Yehud in the Persian Period: A Social and Demographic Study* (JSOTSup 294; Sheffield: Sheffield Academic Press, 1999); A. Faust, "Judah in the Sixth Century BCE: A Rural Perspective," in *PEQ* 126 (2003): 37–53. See also the summary of the situation in K. Valkama, "What Do Archaeological Remains Reveal of the Settlements in Judah during the Mid-Sixth Century BCE?" in *The Concept of Exile in Ancient Israel and Its Historical Contexts* (eds. E. Ben Zvi and C. Levin; BZAW 404; Berlin: De Gruyter, 2010), 39–59.

throughout the Persian period[27] and served to bring home the presence of a past and of its catastrophic fate.

Against this background, Chronicles' relegation of its *main*, explicit messages concerning its concept of the exile to about two verses warrants some consideration. Of course, one may maintain that Chronicles did not expound much on the exile because, by definition, the exile involved living outside the land of Judah, and anything that happened outside the land of Judah was not conceived within the logic of Chronicles as determinative for the fate of Israel and thus not worth narrating.[28] In this position, thus, Israel in the exile was construed as somewhat akin to Israel in what was the Northern Kingdom–that is, a kind of Israel whose actions are removed from and essentially irrelevant to the main historical narrative of Israel (and the causality governing it).[29] But even if this position is correct (and I think it is), a communicative (implied, but clear) statement that something is not worth writing about in a book meant to instill memory of the past is tantamount to stating that this very something is not worth remembering much, which in itself is a significant observation.[30]

Moreover, and following the logic of the position mentioned above, whereas life in the exile may not be worth remembering much, because it takes place outside "the land," the actions in "the land" that led to the greatest national calamity in "the land"–and whose outcome was the exile, that is, the abandonment of "the land," the place where "history" took place–are not only memorable but very much worth remembering. In fact, an analysis of these grave actions could only serve as one of the best possible didactic examples for the commun-

---

[27] Cf. D. Ussishkin, "The Borders and *De Facto* Size of Jerusalem in the Persian Period," in *Judah and the Judeans in the Persian Period* (eds. O. Lipschits and M. Oeming; Winona Lake, IN: Eisenbrauns, 2006), 147–66.

[28] Cf. Japhet, *Ideology*, 371.

[29] Of course, Israel in the North was in the periphery of the land, whereas Israel in exile was outside the land altogether, but this difference did not have much bearing on the matter discussed here. See my discussion in my *History, Literature and Theology*, 195–209.

[30] There was a general, systemic tendency within Yehud to write, read, and therefore to remember far more about life and events in "the land" than about life and events in the Babylonian or Egyptian Exile. This tendency is attested across literary genres in the repertoire of the community and is certainly not limited to Yehud. On the matter of "skipping" periods in historiographical works, see K. Stott, "A Comparative Study of the Exilic Gap in Ancient Israelite, Messenian, and Zionist Collective Memory," in *Community Identity in Judean Historiography: Biblical and Comparative Perspectives* (eds. G. N. Knoppers and K. A. Ristau; Winona Lake, IN: Eisenbrauns, 2009), 41–58.

ity.³¹ The systemic, generative power of this line of thought is indeed widely attested in both the Deuteronomistic historical collection and the prophetic corpus. But the situation is strikingly different in Chronicles. Moreover, the difference cannot be explained in terms of glossing over negative images. Chronicles allocates substantially far less space than Kings not only to the narrative of the destruction but also to its discursive and ideological counterpart within Israel's social memory—namely, the non-destruction of Jerusalem during the reign of Sennacherib. In addition, the difference on the matter between Chronicles, on the one hand, and the Deuteronomistic historical collection and the prophetic books set in the monarchic period, on the other, goes far beyond a few literary units in Chronicles. Unlike the other books, Chronicles does not ask its readers to imagine a community walking for generations, as it were, toward a well-deserved but catastrophic judgment.³² The fall of Jerusalem and the exile do not hang over the narratives or the metanarrative of Chronicles.

This being so, these questions arise: Why is Chronicles—which after all is a didactic book that emerged within a social discourse strongly informed by these two corpora and sharing much with them³³—unlike them in this respect? And why does the book fail to make the most of the memories about the central catastrophe of the community for didactic purposes?

A potential answer to these questions is that the historical narrative in Chronicles was not shaped around a progression toward the calamity, or—and above all—as an explanation for that central catastrophe, because, unlike the Deuteronomistic historical narrative, Chronicles rejected the concept of cumulative sin and, therefore, whatever happened to Judah in the times of Zedekiah could not have been presented in Chronicles as the culmination of a long process of cumulative sin. Moreover, since supposedly in Chronicles sinners are punish-

---

31 This is an important point since Chronicles, like much of the authoritative literature in Yehud, was a didactic book. Moreover, Chronicles shows an extensive array of "persuasive techniques" meant to make memorable not only events of the past as construed in the book but also the ideological messages that they embodied and communicated.

32 Cf. Japhet, *Ideology*, 364–73; but also contrast the position advanced here with Japhet's concluding statement, "[In Chronicles,] foreign armies come and go, but the people's presence in the land continues uninterrupted" (*Ideology*, 373). On this matter, see, for instance, 1 Chr 9:1; 2 Chr 36:20–23, and also 1 Chr 9:2–44 and the discussion advanced here.

33 I discussed matters of sharing elsewhere; see "Reconstructing the Intellectual Discourse of Ancient Yehud," *SR* 39 (2010): 7–23; and "Are There Any Bridges Out There? How Wide Was the Conceptual Gap between the Deuteronomistic History and Chronicles?" in *Community Identity in Judean Historiography: Biblical and Comparative Perspectives* (eds. G. N. Knoppers and K. A. Ristau; Winona Lake, IN: Eisenbrauns, 2009), 59–86. It is precisely against a background of shared discursive tendencies that differences are particularly significant.

ed for their own sins, not for those of others, even the claims about Manasseh's responsibility for the catastrophe, which are advanced by one voice in Kings (2 Kgs 24:3; cf. 2 Kgs 21:11–14; 23:26–27; Jer 15:4) cannot hold. Within this logic, then, Chronicles had no option but to place the blame for the fall of Judah and the exile on Zedekiah or on Zedekiah and his people. In other words, there was simply no room within the ideology of Chronicles for the ubiquitous presence of the exile looming large on the historical narrative of Israel, from any of its multiple (discursive) origins to the fall of Jerusalem.

To be sure, even if for the sake of argument one would accept this explanation, still the lack of references to the exile would have had an impact on the relative mindshare of the exile in a community that was reading and rereading Chronicles. But this explanation of the relative absence of the exile in Chronicles must be rejected because of the cumulative weight of the following reasons.[34]

First, it assumes an authorship that lacks the ability to create and rhetorically use exceptions and is unable to stand seeming contradictions. Nothing can be so far from the truth in the case of Chronicles–but, significantly, neither is it the case in any prophetic or historical book within the repertoire of late-Persian Yehud.[35]

Second, this explanation fails the test of Chronicles' own explicit explanations of the catastrophe. Most evidently, the reference to the 70 years of Sabbath rest that is so crucial to the explanation of the exile in Chronicles implies both a span of 420, not 11 years (the length of Zedekiah's reign according to 2 Chr 36:11), preceding the catastrophe and a clear notion of cumulative burden or sin.[36] The explanation given in 1 Chr 9:1 for the exile of Judah (and Israel; cf. 9:3)–that is, במעלם–does not need to refer only to the 'unfaithfulness' of those living during the reign of Zedekiah and, given its context in the text, it is unlikely to have been so narrowly understood.

Third, within the world of Chronicles, the prophecy of Huldah (2 Chr 34:23–28) at the time of Josiah announced the divine judgment that would fall on Judah after the death of Josiah. The account of Josiah in Chronicles requires a separate discussion that goes well beyond the scope of the present

---

34 Some of these reasons by themselves would have provided sufficient ground to reject this position. The combined weight of all together makes the case even stronger.
35 I discussed numerous examples of seeming contradictions and exceptions elsewhere. See my *History, Literature and Theology in the Book of Chronicles*.
36 Compare, for instance, Williamson, *1–2 Chronicles*, 418; J. Milgrom, *Leviticus 23–27: A New Translation with Introduction and Commentary* (AB 3B; New Haven, CT: Yale University Press, 2008), 2324–25.

contribution³⁷ but, for the present purposes, suffice it to say that (1) the prophecy of Huldah explicitly refers to a full destruction that is about to happen following the death of Josiah, as it actually does in the world of the book, which moves quickly from his death to the fall of Jerusalem; and (2) the text nowhere states that the announcement of judgment can be averted or cancelled, and it clearly implies a notion of cumulative sin. Significantly, the text is about what a pious leader is supposed to do in the face of an unavoidable catastrophe.

Fourth, the notion that one generation may suffer because of the sins of a previous one is explicitly communicated in 2 Chr 29:6–9 and implicitly (and most relevant to the present purposes) communicated by the exile: people who were not even born at the time that monarchic Jerusalem existed experience it and suffer from it.

Fifth, this explanation fails to account for the relatively little narrative space allocated to Zedakiah or to the post-Josianic period for that matter. Had Chronicles wanted to convince its intended and primary readership that the fall of Jerusalem, the exile, and the largest catastrophe in Israelite history were all the results of Zedekiah's sins and those who followed him during his relatively short rule, one would have expected a substantial recounting of these sins.³⁸ Nothing of the sort appears in Chronicles. The sins of Zedekiah receive, if anything, less narrative attention than those of other kings (e. g., Ahaz). In addition, Chronicles does not draw particular attention (and readers' mindshare) toward the figure of Zedekiah or turn him into one of the most salient kings of Judah.³⁹

---

37 I have discussed this account in "Observations on Josiah's Account in Chronicles and Implications for Reconstructing the Worldview of the Chronicler," in *Essays on Ancient Israel in Its Near Eastern Context: A Tribute to Nadav Na'aman* (eds. Y. Amit et al.; Winona Lake, IN: Eisenbrauns, 2006), 89–106.

38 Similarly, the point cannot merely be that the catastrophe was simply caused by Zedekiah's revolt against its Babylonian suzerain. To be sure, Chronicles reflects a point similar to that of, for instance, Ezek 17:15 (see 2 Chr 36:13a), but this was not construed in the book (or elsewhere in the discourse of Yehud) as the only, main, or even primary reason/cause for the exile and catastrophe.

39 Compare the narrative about him in Kings and Chronicles. Although, unlike Chronicles, the former contains a strong voice that blames Manasseh (not Zedekiah) for the fall of Jerusalem and the exile, it still devotes more narrative space and makes Zedekiah a more memorable personage than Chronicles. Other considerations further strengthen the case for the relatively low-key characterization of Zedekiah in Chronicles. For instance, the same Manasseh is relatively central but clearly not the most central character in Chronicles' narrative of the post-Davidic/Solomonic Kingdom of Judah–for reasons other than those in Kings; the Manasseh of Chronicles serves as a "site of memory" that embodied and communicated the ideological motif of repentance. An analysis of the image of Manasseh in Chronicles shows that it was construed at the crucial time in his life (as per the account in Chronicles) as standing parallel with and in contradistinc-

Sixth, had Chronicles consistently communicated to these readers a doctrine of proportional, individually assessed, full coherence between sin and punishment, why would Chronicles not only fail to mention in any direct way the individual punishment of King Zedekiah but also draw the community's social memory away from the memorable images shaped by 2 Kgs 25:5–7?

And seventh, not only does Chronicles devote little narrative space to the fall of Jerusalem and its circumstances, but it clearly reduces the focus on its social-memory counterpart, the non-fall of Jerusalem during Hezekiah's days. The tendency to diminish the treatment of both closely related events in the discourse of the period suggests that something more than a narrow focus on the sins of the king and the people during the reign of Zedekiah was at stake.

This being so, especially considering the failure of the aforementioned approach to explain it away, the questions raised above call for an explanation. Against the background of a society whose memory was obsessed with the exile and its related themes and sites of memory, Chronicles emerged and was

---

tion to the combined image of two kings of the late period: namely, Jehoiakim and Zedekiah. Like the first, he is taken captive to Babylon (and compare the precise language in 2 Chr 33:11b with that of 2 Chr 36:6), but in contrast to the second, he humbles himself (compare 2 Chr 33:12b with 2 Chr 36:12b). The general tendency was to construe major characters as encompassing (in a contrasting or non-contrasting way) several minor characters rather than vice versa (compare Manasseh and Josiah in Kings). In other words, the more central the character is, the more s/he tends to attract features/partial images associated with several other characters (thus acquiring a larger mindshare among the intended readers). This tendency suggests that Manasseh was portrayed as a more central character than Zedekiah–that is, someone to whom more attention is drawn than Zedekiah. This suggestion is supported by the relative length of the two regnal accounts in Chronicles and by subtle changes in contrastive references; for instance, whereas Yhwh is portrayed as sending messengers calling for repentance during Zedekiah's reign (2 Chr 36:15), Yhwh himself addresses Manasseh (and his people) and calls them to repent (2 Chr 33:10). The matter is not trivial or just a product of random chance, because it is consistent with the (contrastive) minor difference in the language of 2 Chr 33:12b; 36:12b. A comprehensive study of Manasseh in Chronicles is beyond the scope of this contribution, but the preceding considerations along with the comparison between the accounts of Zedekiah in Kings and Chronicles suffice to make the point that (and perhaps contrary to some narrative expectations–after all, he is the king at the time of the catastrophe) Chronicles does not focus attention on the figure of Zedekiah in a way that is commensurate with what would have been required had the "sins of Zedekiah" been construed as the main (or only) reason for the calamity. Of course, a study of each (the Zedekiah and the Manasseh of Chronicles) not only deserves but requires a separate discussion that goes well beyond the scope of the present essay. For the Manasseh of Chronicles, see "Reading Chronicles and Reshaping the Memory of Manasseh," in this volume, pp. 367–86 and bibliography there. For the Zedekiah of Chronicles, see "Reshaping the Memory of Zedekiah and His Period in Chronicles," in this volume, pp. 342–66 and bibliography there.

read and reread as a national historical narrative in which the fall of Jerusalem and subsequent exile were mentioned, of course, but not provided with the salience given elsewhere. Within Chronicles, neither these events nor their ideological or theological underpinning were given the prominence granted in other texts meant to create and shape social memory (e.g., the Deuteronomistic historical collection, the prophetic corpus) or allowed to inform time and again central narrative accounts or large-scale metanarratives. Neither catastrophe nor the exile nor the theological notions associated with them were hammered down to the readership in Chronicles (note, for instance, the lack of reference to the sabbath of the land anywhere in Chronicles, outside the two mentioned verses).

The result from the perspective of the impact of reading and rereading Chronicles on social memory seems clear. By creating a landscape of social memories to be evoked by a community in which the exile, the catastrophe of 586 BCE, and associated sites of memory figured far less prominently, Chronicles rebalanced to the best of its possibilities the mindshare allocated to these common topoi. Of course, Chronicles did not ask its intended and primary readership to forget about the fall of monarchic Judah or the exile. It could not have done that, given the social location in which it emerged and the discourse of the period. In fact, Chronicles reminded the readership of the catastrophe not only in its expected location in the narrative (that is, the reign of Zedekiah and its immediate aftermath) but also in places such as 1 Chr 16:35[40] and within the genealogies in 1 Chr 5:6, 26,[41] 41; 9:1 (and by implication, 1 Chr 9:2–34). It even contains an explicit reference to the common early-Second-Temple motif of the rejected, monarchic prophets (2 Chr 36:15–16; cf. Zech 1:4; 7:7, 12; and the general image of the monarchic prophets that emerged from the prophetic corpus). But Chronicles was about setting these topoi in proportion and subtly decreasing their mindshare. As I mentioned elsewhere, this attitude is typical of Chronicles and is probably necessary for any "national" history that must conform with a

---

[40] I discussed this text elsewhere; see my "Who Knew What? The Construction of the Monarchic Past in Chronicles and Implications for the Intellectual Setting of Chronicles," in *Judah and the Judeans in the Fourth Century BCE* (eds. O. Lipschits, G. N. Knoppers, and R. Albertz; Winona Lake, IN: Eisenbrauns, 2007), 349–60.

[41] 1 Chr 5:6, 26 refer to the exile of the Transjordanian tribes. Unlike the exile of Judah, their exile is seen as still not being revoked (see "to this day"). These tribes play a substantially less-significant role in Chronicles than the Cisjordanian northern tribes. The differentiation between the Cisjordanian and Transjordanian northern tribes may reflect debates about the actual extent of "the land" or degrees of regional peripherality within the discourse of the community. See n. 18 above. 1 Chr 8:6–7 does not refer to the exile, not even "exile" in the sense of removal from "the (promised) land." See G. N. Knoppers, *I Chronicles 1–9: A New Translation with Introduction and Commentary* (AB 12; New York: Doubleday, 2003), 482.

set of "facts" about the past that was already agreed upon in the community and fit its general discourse.

But why would Chronicles draw (in relative terms) attention *away* from the calamity of 586 BCE and its surrounding images and concepts? Or in other, more-precise words: which general, systematic, ideological positions within the range of what was potentially acceptable for the community could have generated (or at least been consistent with) the attested Chronistic trend toward a shift on social memory *away* from the catastrophe, including the themes of Sennacherib's campaign and an idyllic restoration?

An array of diverse but related notions seems to answer this question. To begin with, from the perspective of Chronicles there was nothing of essential value for the community that changed because of the catastrophe. YHWH's teachings certainly did not change, nor did YHWH's way of governing the world, nor did Israel's obligation to follow YHWH.[42] The portrayal of Josiah in Chronicles as a person who acted in accordance with YHWH's will while fully aware of the calamity that would follow his death becomes an archetype for proper behavior. For Chronicles, knowing about the impending or already fulfilled destruction does not and could not change what a person should do–that is, follow YHWH and follow YHWH's teachings, which are conceived as the same thing.[43] Neither the catastrophe nor the exile constitutes any kind of watershed in this respect.

The actual temple may come and go and come again. As important as it is in Chronicles, it may be run properly, be polluted, cleansed, closed, destroyed, and rebuilt through the vicissitudes of history, yet Israel remains.[44] Moreover, no matter how many times the proper temple may cease to exist in actual Jerusalem, it is always re-buildable, because the community's knowledge of the temple and worship is always available through YHWH's teachings, in the form of authoritative texts held by the literati of the community. These texts provide them with a

---

[42] In this sense, and despite its obvious differences, Chronicles reflects an ideological response to the calamity of 586 BCE. that is partially comparable with the Mishnah's response, much later, to the catastrophe that ended the Second Temple period. On the latter, see J. Neusner, *In the Aftermath of Catastrophe: Founding Judaism 70–640* (McGill-Queen's Studies in the History of Religion 2/51; Montreal: McGill-Queen's University Press, 2009).

[43] Compare 1 Kgs 8:25 and the rendering of its meaning in 2 Chr 6:16. The concept is already implied in 1 Kgs 9:6, but see Ps 119.

[44] And, of course, along with it, the divine teachings about how it should behave and what should it remember. Within the world view of Chronicles (and probably of all the discourse of the literati of its original time), these teachings were considered to be what made Israel self-aware, and as such, were not only a key attribute of Israel but also an essential possession for its future and present. (See also "Reading the Book of Hosea," pp. 294–303 in this volume.)

mental temple, accessible through reading and imagination, that cannot be polluted, destroyed, or the like. In addition, although the "worldly" temple (as opposed to the temple in the shared imagination of the literati) may certainly be destroyed, closed, or polluted, it will always be cleansed and rebuilt eventually, because of Yhwh's will, as demonstrated in the history and prophecy within the world of Chronicles. The calamity of 586 BCE and its eventual aftermath thus provide a good didactic example, but certainly do not constitute a crucial watershed. Nothing in any of these issues that really matters was changed because of the catastrophe.

Of course, life according to Yhwh's wishes is possible without (access to) the temple, as the authorship and readership of Chronicles know, and as the case of the northern Israelites at the time of Oded (2 Chr 28:8–15) exemplified well.[45] What is necessary for society is a successful teacher/prophet who knows Yhwh's teachings and is successful enough to be able to lead the people to follow them in practical ways.

The land itself may be momentarily lost and partially regained. As much as Chronicles teaches that only life in the land is determinative for the history of Israel and worth remembering, and as much as Chronicles consequently shifts, to the best of its ability, the mindshare of the community toward memories of Israel in the land, temporary losses are no watershed and cannot be construed as such. They are part of a long-term system of sabbaths and to a large extent even necessary for purification.

Moreover, the notion of the "Empty Land" works to shape, not only the image that all Israel came back from exile, but also that the land was not available to anyone other than Israel for settlement. The land imagined as "empty of Israel" is imagined as remaining "empty"–as though Yhwh had set what we would call a "force field" around it.[46]

The Davidic Dynasty was certainly important to Chronicles, but again not indispensable. Israel could live and follow Yhwh without a Davidic king, because the readership within which and for which Chronicles emerged certainly knew how and needed to imagine. This was possible because there was no need for

---

[45] I discuss this passage elsewhere; see my *History, Literature and Theology*, 223–28.

[46] It is worth mentioning that many areas in Judah were not resettled but remained in ruins during the Neo-Babylonian period. This said, the development of the concept of the "Empty Land" should not be understood primarily as dependent on historicity in the narrow sense. Note that it involved forgetting that the majority of the population in Yehud consisted of descendants of the people who never left the land. The issue, however, is beyond the scope of this work, and I address it elsewhere. See "Total Exile, Empty Land and the General Intellectual Discourse in Yehud," pp. 599–611 in this volume.

a second David to institute instructions for the establishment of the proper (i.e., Davidic) temple and its worship. They were already set, and thus Israel could follow them in the absence of a David. The fact that both temples were established by kings other than David makes the point even more memorable. Again, as devastating as the fall of the monarchy was, it was not a crucial watershed as far as what matters most within Chronicles' ideology.

There are additional considerations that contributed to Chronicles' tendency to rebalance the weight of the overwhelming memory of the catastrophe in the community. For instance, a community whose mindshare is partially locked onto the catastrophe and who sees monarchic (or even premonarchic) history as greatly informed by the calamity and, to a large extent, as a long trajectory heading toward it is a community whose image of the Israel of the remembered past must on the whole be negative. Their past Israel must be very sinful, because its actions merited extreme divine punishment; in fact, it "forced" a reluctant YHWH to finally punish Israel as it fully deserved. This image of past Israel is present in the discourse of the community and finds clear expression in both the Deuteronomistic historical collection and the prophetic corpus. But this is a problematic image. Recounting Israel's sins may be appropriate in confessions of sin, prayers, and the like (e.g., Ps 106), which serve rhetorical roles. But a social memory that focuses for the most part on the inherently and irremediably sinful character of Israel and the extreme catastrophe that is the unavoidable, just outcome of this sin is not the best image with which to develop hope for the postmonarchic community. Neither does it help develop Israel's sense that it can follow YHWH's teachings, even if imperfectly, or its ability to avoid disasters in the future. Although in times of crisis or calamity, this characterization is necessary to maintain a sense of agency for the community within its own discourse, it is not the best construction for maintaining hope for the future. And hope is necessary for the community and widely attested as a systemic need in the discourse of Yehud, as demonstrated by the production and reception of prophetic literature.

Some texts in the repertoire of the Yehudite community advanced a solution to the problem: Israel will be changed by YHWH in the future (see Deut 30:6; Jer 24:7; 31:31–34; 32:38–41; Ezek 11:19–20; 36:25–28; Hos 2:21), so it will not be able to sin. But Chronicles–partially because as historiography it creates sites of memory in the past rather than the future, and partially because it promotes a "down-to-earth" utopia–addresses the issue differently, by rebalancing the remembered past. Thus, for instance, Chronicles adds numerous monarchic-period prophetic voices that were heard in their own putative times and remembered.⁴⁷ Thus, past Israel sinned, of course, but from time to time. In addition, Chronicles implicitly constructs an Israel that, when it is free from sinful leadership, tends to accept Yhwh and his ways⁴⁸ –that is, an Israel that tends by default, as it were, to follow Yhwh.

Summing up, Chronicles influenced the social mindshare about the catastrophe and exile within the community of readers. Chronicles did not attempt to erase the memory of the exile or catastrophe of 586 BCE. In fact, it recalled this memory and contributed to reshaping its meaning (e.g., the concept of the sabbath of the land), but it tried to put it into proportion and diminish the exile's mindshare within the community. This trend can be explained as emerging out of (or at least as being consistent with) the ideological agenda of Chronicles.⁴⁹ Within this agenda, the issue is not only or merely that nothing that essentially or categorically (not contingently) matters changed after the catastrophe or the exile. The issue is also, relatedly, that attention is turned toward–not away from–a sense of essential (though not contingent) continuity with the past. Furthermore, social memory is nudged to serve this goal better. Within this ideology, this sense of continuity is conceived as being directly related to the continuity throughout the calamity of Yhwh's teachings and what is required to follow them. It is related to Yhwh's ways of governing the world that characterizes Chronicles' world–pre- and post-catastrophe; before, in the middle of, and after the exile.

Of course, the continuity of Yhwh's teachings was predicated on the teachings of foundational written texts and appropriate readings of them as implied and communicated by Chronicles and its authoritative characters, including its implied author. Likewise, the possibility of learning about Yhwh's ways in dealing with the world and about what is required to follow Yhwh in the present and future of the community are presented as available for learning through the

---

47 I expanded on this matter in "Chronicles and Its Reshaping."
48 See my "A House of Treasures: The Account of Amaziah in 2 Chronicles 25–Observations and Implications," in *SJOT* 22 (2008): 63–85.
49 It also reflects the fact that some time has passed since the catastrophe itself. As Chronicles was written within and for a community that lived far more than a century after the events, it easily passes this test. At the same time, it is worth stressing that Chronicles was probably not the first text within the community to reflect and engage in this type of discourse about the catastrophe of the fall of Jerusalem and the exile. Moreover, there is no need to go as far as the end of the Persian period (or early Hellenistic), the most likely date of Chronicles, to imagine a community in Yehud and even in Jerusalem with the same or a similar viewpoint on the matter. The question of how much temporal distance was necessary in this and similar cases cannot be answered in any categorical way.

study of Chronicles, within its appropriate *Sitz im Diskurs* in late-Persian Yehud (or early-Hellenistic Judah).

Taking into consideration the facts that (1) Chronicles was essential and significant to the community precisely because it was essential to a larger shared, communal discourse; and that (2) the foundational and connective[50] issues led Chronicles to draw less attention to the catastrophe and the exile–these facts indicate that it is unlikely that Chronicles emerged as the only voice in the discourse of the period to influence the social memory toward rebalancing the weight of the exile and catastrophe. Despite all the differences between the Pentateuch and Chronicles, the latter as a whole may have fulfilled a comparable function,[51] but this is an issue for another essay. Moreover, the general outlook reflected in Chronicles' tendency to draw less attention to supposed watersheds and more attention to a sense of continuity based on following Yhwh, no matter what happens, and in the underlying attitude that nothing really new can be learned from even the largest catastrophe that befell Israel is consistent with the general outlook of Qoheleth (cf. Qoh 12:13), despite the obvious differences in literary genres. The presence of similarities in the underlying outlook of these two works is less surprising once one takes into account that both emerged (likely) within decades of each other and in a comparable setting–that is, a very small group of Jerusalem-centered literati. Further research on the respective *Sitz im Diskurs* of these two works and on the intellectual discourse of late Persian or early Hellenistic Judah is warranted.[52]

A final consideration: multiple voices informing and balancing each other were characteristic of the general discourse of Yehud, the related repertoire of authoritative books, and the books themselves. Chronicles was a prominent example of this feature. This observation is particularly relevant to the present discussion as well. Reading and rereading Chronicles led to a shift in social memory in particular directions. But reading and rereading Chronicles, not only in a way informed by other texts, but even by itself set this shift in proportion.

---

50 That is, core issues or positions that are strongly connected to a significant number of other matters or positions in the discourse of the community.

51 And compare Sirach's outlook on this matter.

52 The issues to be discussed are not constrained to the presence of similar or dissimilar underlying concepts (for the latter see "When Yhwh Tests People," in this volume, pp. 472–81), but also reveal the ways in which a readership well aware of Qoheleth may have read Chronicles and vice versa. For instance, to some extent and granted a substantial element of reductionism and exaggeration, it might be claimed that this chapter presents a partial "Qoheleth-light/like" reading of Chronicles, but what would have been a partial "Chronicles-light/like" reading of Qoheleth?

Thus, for instance, the exile is over after the "seventy years" but not over.[53] The relative mindshare of the catastrophe decreased as the literati of the time read and reread Chronicles, but the same book still reminded them of the catastrophe, its reasons, meaning, and nature (see above). Israel was not always sinful, but at times it certainly was, as Chronicles itself reminded its readers. The fall of the monarchy may not be a "big deal" because Israel knows how to establish and run a proper temple and because YHWH can charge a foreign king to build a Davidic temple, but somehow it is still a "big deal," as demonstrated by the numerous memories about the roles of kings and their importance in Judah that the text evokes.[54] No reconstruction of the impact of Chronicles on social memory about the exile and the circumstances that led to it can ignore the fact that, as much as Chronicles conveyed to the best of possibilities in the discourse of the time, a sense of balance regarding the exile and the catastrophe of the fall of Jerusalem and the monarchic polity, its communication was not only a *balancing* message but also a *balanced* message.[55]

---

[53] For example, when the readers of Chronicles imagined the YHWH who caused the catastrophe, they were asked to imagine a deity who had compassion on the people and on the divine dwelling place, the temple in Jerusalem (see 2 Chr 36:15; חמל על־עמו ועל־מעונו). The readers knew that the temple was rebuilt, but they were also aware that Yehud was still depopulated. And, of course, Transjordanian exile remained to "this day." The image of an exile that was overcome but was not overcome, both at the same time, played important roles in many if not most of the discourses that evolved during the Second Temple period, from the Persian to the Roman era.

[54] Obviously, the entire matter of Chronicles' message about the Davidic line has some bearing on this matter as well. Personally, I maintain that Chronicles communicated to its readership a sense that a Davidide is not necessary for Israel (only *torah* is) and reminded them of the sharp decline in the status of the Davidides in the post-catastrophe period. None of this, however, means that Chronicles necessarily conveyed (1) a categorical opposition to hopes for a Davidide (in fact, it may have reflected or communicated some [muted] hope for a future Davidide in the genealogy); or (2) a sense that the promise to David had to be, was, and would be fulfilled–all three tenses are correct in Chronicles–*only and under any circumstances* in terms of the community (compare the exile that was overcome and not overcome at the same time). These matters, however, are well beyond the scope of this essay and deserve a separate discussion. See M. Boda, "Gazing through the Cloud of Incense: Davidic Dynasty and Temple Community in the Chronicler's Perspective", in *Chronicling the Chronicler* (eds. P. S. Evans and T. F. Williams), 215–45.

[55] See my *History, Literature and Theology*. I would like to thank the participants in the CSBS seminar in which this paper was read for their helpful comments, in particular John Wright.

Chronicles and Its Reshaping of Memories of Monarchic Period Prophets: Some Observations*

Several important studies on prophets in Chronicles have appeared in recent years.[1] Of course, these studies built on a significant corpus of research that deals directly or indirectly with these matters since the early 1970s.[2] Many issues

---

* Originally published in *Prophets, Prophecy, and Ancient Israelite Historiography* (ed. Mark J. Boda and Lissa M. Wray Beal; Winona Lake, Ind.: Eisenbrauns, 2013), 167–88. Reprinted with permission.

[1] E.g., Y. Amit, "The Role of Prophecy and Prophets in the Chronicler's World," in *Prophets, Prophecy, and Prophetic Texts in Second Temple Judaism* (ed. M. H. Floyd and R. D. Haak; OTS 427; London: T&T Clark, 2006) 80–101. In fact, this is an updated version of the work by the same title published in *Beth Miqra* 93 (1983) 113–33 [Hebrew], which was overlooked in research, for the most part; P. C. Beentjes, *Tradition and Transformation in the Book of Chronicles* (SSN 52; Leiden: Brill, 2008), esp. pp. 90–98 and 129–39 (pp. 129–39 consist of a revised version of P. C. Beentjes, "Prophets in the Book of Chronicles" in *The Elusive Prophet: The Prophet as a Historical Person, Literary Character, and Anonymous Artist* [ed. J. C. de Moor; OTS 45; Leiden: Brill, 2001] 45–53); E. S. Gerstenberger, "Prophetie in den Chronikbüchern: Jahwes Wort in zweierlei Gestalt?," in *Schriftprophetie: Festschrift für Jörg Jeremias zum 65. Geburtstag* (ed. F. Hartenstein, J. Krispenz, and A. Schart; Neukirchen-Vluyn: Neukirchener Verlag, 2004) 351–67; L. C. Jonker "The Chronicler and the Prophets: Who Were His Authoritative Sources?" in *What Was Authoritative for Chronicles?* (ed. E. Ben Zvi and D. V. Edelman; Winona Lake, IN: Eisenbrauns, 2011) 145–64; A. Warhurst, "What Was Prophetic for the Chronicler?," in *What Was Authoritative for Chronicles?* (ed. E. Ben Zvi and D. V. Edelman; Winona Lake, IN: Eisenbrauns, 2011) 165–82.

[2] E.g., T. Willi, *Die Chronik als Auslegung; Untersuchungen zur literarischen Gestaltung der historischen Überlieferung Israels* (FRLANT 106; Göttingen: Vandenhoeck & Ruprecht, 1972); J. D. Newsome, "Toward a New Understanding of the Chronicler and His Purposes," *JBL* 94 (1975) 201–17; S. Japhet, *The Ideology of the Book of Chronicles and Its Place in Biblical Thought* (BEATAJ 9; 2nd ed.; Frankfurt am Main: Peter Lang, 1997; first published in Hebrew: Jerusalem: Bialik, 1977); D. L. Petersen, *Late Israelite Prophecy: Studies in Deutero-prophetic Literature and in Chronicles* (SBLMS 23; Missoula, MT: Scholars Press, 1977) 55–96; I. L. Seeligmann, "Die Auffassung von der Prophetie in der Deuteronomistischen und Chronistischen Geschichtsschreibung," *VT* 29 (1978) 254–84; J. P. Weinberg, "Die 'ausser kanonischen Prophezeiungen' in den Chronikbüchern," *Acta Antiqua* 26 (1978) 387–404; R. Micheel, *Die Seher- und Prophetenüberlieferungen in der Chronik* (BBET 18; Frankfurt am Main: Peter Lang, 1983); S. J. de Vries, "The Forms of Prophetic Address in Chronicles," *HAR* 10 (1986) 15–36; C. T. Begg, "The Classical Prophets in the Chronistic History," *BZ* 32 (1988) 100–107; idem, "The Chronicler's Non-mention of Elisha," *BN* 45 (1988) 100–107; Rex Mason, *Preaching the Tradition: Homily and Hermeneutics after the Exile* (Cambridge: Cambridge University Press, 1990); J. Kegler, "Prophetengestalten im Deuteronomistischen Geschichtswerk und in den Chronikbüchern: Ein Beitrag zur Kompositions- und Redaktionsgeschichte der Chronikbücher," *ZAW* 105 (1993) 481–97; H. F. van Rooy, "Prophet and Society in the Persian Period according to Chronicles," in *Second Temple Studies*, vol. 2: *Temple Community in the Persian Period* (ed. T. C. Eskenazi and K. H. Richards; JSOTSup 175; Sheffield: Sheffield Academic Press, 1994)

have figured prominently in this now-substantial corpus. Among them, one may mention: (1) the role and status of historical prophets at the time of the author(s) of Chronicles, including the question of whether ("classical") prophecy had ceased at that time, or even what a statement such as this may mean; (2) Chronicles' representations of prophets as "preachers" and/or "historians"; (3) the sources that the author(s) of Chronicles may have used or purposefully ignored when writing about prophets and prophecy; (4) the question of who is a prophet in Chronicles, and the related issues of "ad hoc" or "temporary" prophets, Levitical singers as prophets, and whether divinely inspired messengers were conceptually understood as "prophets"; (5) prophecy and cult; and (6) the status of prophetic utterances vis à vis Mosaic *torah* and the general question of what was authoritative for Chronicles. Every (or almost every) contemporary work on Chronicles and prophets/prophecy has implicitly or explicitly dealt with or assumed a position on these issues.

This essay is no exception, but its main goal is not to revisit these debates but to explore the issue of Chronicles and prophecy/prophets from a perspective informed by a strong focus on social memory. What did Chronicles, or better, what did the reading and rereading of Chronicles within the Jerusalem-centered community of the late Persian (or perhaps, early Hellenistic) period, within which the book emerged, contribute to social memory in that community, or at least among its literati, in terms of *their* memories about the prophets of the monarchic period?[3]

163–79; J. B. Burns, "Is Neco Also among the Prophets?" *Proceedings, Eastern Great Lakes and Midwest Biblical Society* 14 (1994) 113–22; W. M. Schniedewind, *The Word of God in Transition: From Prophet to Exegete in the Second Temple Period* (JSOTSup 197; Sheffield: Sheffield Academic Press, 1995); idem, "Prophets and Prophecy in the Books of Chronicles," in *The Chronicler as Historian* (ed. M. P. Graham, K. G. Hoglund, and S. L. McKenzie; JSOTSup 238; Sheffield: Sheffield Academic Press, 1997) 204–24; P. Höffken, "Der Prophet Jesaja beim Chronisten," *BN* 81 (1996) 82–90; R. W. Klein, "Prophets and Prophecy in the Books of Chronicles," *TBT* 36 (1998) 227–32; G. N. Knoppers, "Review of W. M. Schniedewind, *The Word of God in Transition: From Prophet to Exegete in the Second Temple Period*," *JJS* 49 (1998) 133–35; A. Hanspach *Inspirierte Interpreten: Das Prophetenverständnis der Chronikbücher und sein Ort in der Religion und Literatur zur Zeit des Zweiten Tempels* (Arbeiten zu Text und Sprache im Alte Testament 64; St. Otillien: EOS, 2000). An earlier and foundational work was, of course, G. von Rad ("The Levitical Sermon in I and II Chronicles," in *The Problem of the Hexateuch and Other Essays* [G. von Rad; Edinburgh: Oliver & Boyd, 1966] 267–80); idem, "Die levitische Predigt in den Büchern der Chronik," in *Festschrift für Otto Procksch* (ed. A. Alt; Leipzig: Deichertsche Verlag und Hinrichssche Buchhandlung, 1934) 113–24.
3 The question whether the book emerged in the late Persian period or early Hellenistic does not have a significant bearing on the observations advanced here. For the sake of convenience, I will continue referring to the era in which the book emerged and in which one is to find its primary readership as "late Persian period," but with an understanding that the early Hellenistic era is

I would like to stress that the focus here is not on particular memories about individual prophets but on the image of what a "monarchic-period prophet" looked like[4] and its importance in terms of social memory for the community within which Chronicles emerged.

Chronicles, like any other historiographical or prophetic book within the repertoire of ancient Israel/Yehud, was meant to evoke memory, to bring *particular* figures of the past to the present of the community and to allow members of the latter to shape and vicariously visit specific sites of memory (that is, people, places, events), which were construed through communally (more or less) shared acts of imagination as they read and reread the book. But bringing prophetic personages to the present of the community had to go hand in hand with and, in fact, necessitated at the level of general discourse the existence of a concept (or prototype) of what a "monarchic period prophetic persona" looked like, or, in other words and from a slightly different perspective, of a social memory of what monarchic prophets as a group were about.[5]

Given the importance of prophecy and prophets in the intellectual discourse of the Yehudite literati, this social memory could not but play an important role and much was at stake in its shaping. The very existence of the corpus of prophetic books, the centrality of figures such as Isaiah, Jeremiah, and Moses,

---

also a possibility. In fact, it is worth considering whether strong distinctions between the two are not based on a misguided use of external historical events (as opposed to social developments internal to the relevant society) as a base for historical periodization. After all, how drastic was the change in Judah, its society, and, as appropriate in this essay, its ideological discourse, when Alexander became the "last Achaemenid emperor"? (The characterization of Alexander as the "last Achaemenid" was advanced by P. Briant in 1979 ("Des Achémenides aux rois hellénistiques: Continuités et ruptures," *Rois, tributs et paysans: études sur les formations tributaires du Moyen-Orient ancient* [Annales littéraires de l'Université de Besançon 269/Centre de recherches d'histoire ancienne 43; Paris: Les Belles lettres, 1982] 291–330) and was accepted by many since then, for example, M. A. Dandamaev, *A Political History of the Achaemenid Empire* (trans. W. J. Vogelsang; Leiden: Brill, 1989) 331.

4 That is, in more precise terms, the focus is on the socially shared prototype of what a "monarchic period prophet" looked like, or, if one wishes, on the (mental or cognitive) concept associated with "monarchic prophet" within the relevant community.

5 There is no doubt that memories of particular prophets (for example, Isaiah) contributed to the creation of that prototype, but one has to take into account that these memories are by necessity very individualized, and many features, events, and the like associated with a particular figure are unique to that personage. On some of these matters, from the perspective of the book of Kings, see my "'The Prophets': Generic Prophets and Their Role in the Construction of the Image of the 'Prophets of Old' within the Postmonarchic Readership of the Book of Kings," *ZAW* 116 (2004) 555–67.

who is also characterized as a prophet, attests to that matter and so does the prominent role of prophets in both Samuel–Kings and Chronicles.

At this point, it is important to stress that social memory cannot be identified with any book, since it is not a book. Moreover, it cannot be identified with what evolved in the minds of an 'appropriately-socialized' individual as s/he read any single book, even if s/he did so within a socially accepted ideology and mode of reading. Instead, social, comprehensive memory may be understood as a large, integrative system or array of multiple social memories and sites of memories constantly informing each other. This array included memories evoked and relived through multiple readings of multiple books. In each of these readings, the literati could not but bring to bear the social and socially agreed knowledge that they possessed, and in a text-centered community, this implied many authoritative texts, concepts, and images in addition to those explicitly mentioned in the book they were reading. This being so, to understand the ways in which Chronicles contributed to the reshaping of the conceptual range of what a monarchic-period prophet was about, one must deal with the general discourse of the period and with the *Sitz im Diskurs* of Chronicles' images and positions. This is hardly surprising because readings of texts are always advanced within a general social discourse, and it is within that discourse that they are imbued with significance. To be sure, it is the text *as read* by the community that counts toward any reconstruction of the contribution of the book to the community's social memory.

In sum, images of monarchic prophets and prophecies were evoked through reading and rereading the book. These images served as memorials, that is, as sites of memory that existed in the minds of the readers, but which were socially shared. The Chronicler[6] asked his implied and primary (re)readers—hereafter, for the sake of simplicity, target readers or target readership—to visit and revisit these sites of memory. The questions at the center of this essay are: What did these visits "do" to and for the community? What difference did these visits, and indirectly the book of Chronicles, make in society in terms of social memory?

The target readers of Chronicles developed and encountered the mentioned sites of memory, that is, textually evoked memorials that in turn embodied, reminded them, and above all drew their attention to particular sets of attributes that the community associated with their implicit concept of "monarchic proph-

---

[6] By "Chronicler," I mean the implied author of the book as construed by its primary or intended readership; in other words, the communicator or communicative voice they "heard" when they read the book. (Given the gender constructions of the period, this Chronicler was most likely imagined as male.)

et." As they did so, they had no choice but at times to reinforce and at times to draw attention away from the attributes that were embodied and communicated by other images evoked by different books.

Thus, the approach I am advancing here must take into account the *Sitz im Diskurs* of the readings of the text of Chronicles within its target readership in the late Persian period[7] but also must address the question of mindshare in the historical community, or to be more precise, in the approximation of the historical community that its texts suggests to us.[8] In practical ways, this means that an approach that raises the question of what effect Chronicles had on social memory in the late Persian period should bring up time and again the question of whether and how Chronicles reshaped or rebalanced the relative mindshare of features or common topoi associated with the images of the monarchic prophets.[9]

A full, comprehensive study of all these features and topoi is beyond the scope of any paper or even of a single monograph. To make the study manageable in the present setting, five issues have been selected. These are central enough, however, to carry, at the least, the potential to make a significant contribution to a better understanding of both social memory within Yehudite Israel

---

[7] The definition of "Chronicler" advanced above is consistent with this approach.
[8] There is no access to the actual community of flesh-and-blood Israelites, but historians can reconstruct "textual communities," which in turn are likely to reflect, even if in very imperfect ways, the actual communities of readers or at the very least their own image of themselves. See L. C. Jonker, "What Constitutes Society? Yehud's Self-Understanding in the Late Persian Era as Reflected in the Books of Chronicles," *JBL* 127 (2008) 703–24; and my own discussions about the partial resemblance between intended and actual readerships in Yehud and the possibility of approximating in some ways ancient readings, for example, "Is the Twelve Hypothesis Likely from an Ancient Readers' Perspective?" in *Two Sides of a Coin: Juxtaposing Views on Interpreting the Book of the Twelve/the Twelve Prophetic Books* (ed. E. Ben Zvi and J. D. Nogalski; Analecta Gorgiana 201; Piscataway, NJ: Gorgias, 2009) 47–96, esp. pp. 54–63.
[9] It is worth noting that, unlike some present-day marketing struggles over consumers' mindshare, in which one company may set as its goal to obliterate the mindshare of its competitor, the tendency in Yehud was toward balancing mindshare. Chronicles was not aimed at convincing people that they should not read Kings or Samuel but sought to offer complementary memories that informed and were informed by those evoked by Kings or Samuel. Tendencies toward mainly monochromous memories and ideologies are more likely to develop within sectarian groups defining themselves and their boundaries and struggling against each other than within socially cohesive societies. In the latter, social cohesion is supported by both a centralization of resources and a significant range of allowed variety, which in turn is not seen as "dangerous" due to strength of cohesive tendencies. Needless to say, there were not enough literati or social resources in late Persian Jerusalem to allow for the development of sects and their more rigid and antagonistic viewpoints.

and its intellectual discourse and thus to contribute to the intellectual history of the period.

Remembering That Monarchic Prophets Could Also Be Successful in Their Own Times and Its Significance

אל־תהיו כאבתיכם אשר קראו־אליהם הנביאים הראשנים לאמר כה אמר יהוה
צבאות שובו נא מדרכיכם הרעים ומעלילכם הרעים ולא שמעו ולא־הקשיבו אלי
נאם־יהוה

> Do not be like your ancestors, to whom the former prophets proclaimed, "Thus says the Lord of hosts, 'Return from your evil ways and from your evil deeds.'" But they did not hear or heed me, says the Lord (Zech 1:4, NRSV).

The prophets of the monarchic past were remembered in Yehud, for the most part, as unsuccessful in their own monarchic historical contexts. This motif, which is explicitly stated in the text cited above (cf. Zech 7:7, 12),[10] played a central role in the construction of "the (generic) prophets" in Kings.[11] Most of the memories activated/evoked by the prophetic books whose background is set in the monarchic period contributed to this construction of the past, either explicitly (e. g., Jer 7:25; 25:4; 26:9; 35:15; 44:4) or implicitly because the destruction proclaimed in these books did happen from the perspective of the Persian-period readership.[12]

---

10 J. O'Brien ("Nahum-Habakkuk-Zephaniah: Reading the 'Former Prophets' in the Persian Period," *Int* 61 [2007] 168–83) has maintained that "Hosea–Zephaniah so closely conform to Zechariah's description of the 'former prophets' that these books may have been written or edited as a prelude to Zechariah" (p. 168) and

> [t]he scenario that I have described supports a redactional scheme in which Hosea through Zephaniah were consciously edited as a preface to Zechariah, providing a portrayal of the "former prophets" useful to the writer of Zechariah … [w]hile the contrary argument could be made (that Zechariah simply quoted from earlier prophetic books rather than helped create them), this latter scenario would account for neither 1) why the books have been put in this particular order, nor 2) why Zechariah has so many connections with the "happy endings" of the earlier books, which are widely recognized to reflect postexilic sensibilities. (p. 180)

Immaterial of whether one agrees with her redactional proposals or not, the point that Zechariah's description of the "former prophets" is fully consistent with the image that the books associated with prophetic characters ascribed to the monarchic period is certainly well taken and illustrates the point about a shared social memory about these prophets that shaped these books and is reflected in them.
11 As I discuss in "'The Prophets.'"
12 There is only one salient exception to this construction of the prophets of old, namely, Isaiah. He was the only major late monarchic period prophetic character who was construed

This social memory of the failed prophets was an integral and ideologically necessary part of a central node of social memories that (1) brought together social memories of exile, justified divine punishment, the correlated sinful character of monarchic Israel and (2) due to its *Sitz im Diskurs*, was strongly informed by widely accepted notions of a deity that warns before punishment and uses prophets as its messengers.[13] This node of related and mutually reinforcing memories and related ideological concepts provided significance to the remembered, central catastrophe and also served clear didactic purposes in Yehud.

Chronicles is no stranger to any of this. In fact, it reminded its target readers of these notions about YHWH as it asked them to remember multiple past cases that embodied and communicated this set of notions, that is, by creating multiple, appropriate "sites of memory." Moreover, in addition to asking its readers to experience vicariously instances in which prophets were unsuccessful in the past (e.g. 2 Chr 24:19), the Chronicler also and most significantly chose to conclude his key interpretive preface to the narrative that leads up to and includes Jerusalem's destruction and exile, with a heightened note (2 Chr 36:15–16) that reflected and shaped a memory consistent with that in Zech 1:4, namely,

---

as successful. The positive heightening of the character of Isaiah (and Hezekiah) is related to the significance of the memory of the "salvation" of Jerusalem at the time of Hezekiah, which served as the contrasting site of memory for that of the destruction of Jerusalem at the time of Zedekiah. This contrast of sites of memory plays a very important role in the general metanarrative of the fall of Jerusalem and exile and their ideological/theological significance in Yehud. This issue, however, is beyond the scope of this essay; see my "Malleability and Its Limits: Sennacherib's Campaign against Judah as a Case Study," in *'Bird in a Cage': The Invasion of Sennacherib in 701 BCE* (ed. L. L. Grabbe; JSOTSup 363; European Seminar in Historical Methodology 4; Sheffield: Sheffield Academic Press and Continuum, 2003) 73–105. It goes without saying that this unique characterization of Isaiah raises very interesting questions about the array of memories associated with him in the Persian and Early Hellenistic periods and their relative mindshare (cf. Sir 48:24–25). A good dissertation waits to be written on the matter. A second, and far less salient, exception to the characterization of the monarchic prophets as ineffectual at their time within the corpus of prophetic book is the brief reference to the memory of Micah within the world portrayed in Jer 26:18–19. Significantly, this text is about comparing the Assyrian crisis with the Babylonian and their contrasting outcomes.

13 Clearly, this is not an innovation of the Chronicler but part and parcel of the discourse of the late Persian period. It is implicitly and explicitly attested in the prophetic books (e.g., Jer 7:25; 25:4; 26:9; 35:15; 44:4; Ezek 3:16–27) and in Kings (e.g., 2 Kgs 17:13). The "principle" is, as most principles in Chronicles, not absolute, as demonstrated, for instance, by the absence of any narrative about warning in the paradigmatic case of Ahaz or in the very first reference to YHWH in Chronicles (1 Chr 2:3). On the principle of warning before punishment in Chronicles, see Japhet, *Ideology*, 176–91. The argument that most "principles" in Chronicles are not absolute is developed in my *History, Literature and Theology in the Book of Chronicles* (Bible World; London: Equinox, 2006); for a discussion of the account of Ahaz, see pp. 160–73.

וישלח יהוה אלהי אבותיהם עליהם ביד מלאכיו השכם ושלוח כי־חמל על־עמו
ועל־מעונו: ויהיו מלעבים במלאכי האלהים ובוזים דבריו ומתעתעים בנבאיו עד
עלות חמת־יהוה בעמו עד־לאין מרפא

> The LORD, the God of their ancestors, sent persistently to them by his messengers, because he had compassion on his people and on his dwelling place;[14] but they kept mocking the messengers of God, despising his words, and scoffing at his prophets, until the wrath of the LORD against his people became so great that there was no remedy (2 Chr 36:15–16, NRSV).

It is only expected that widespread memories about prophets being rejected, mocked, and the like would lead to memories of their persecution and even murder at the hands of their enemies. Chronicles, Kings, and the prophetic books, all of which evoke memories about rejected prophets in the monarchic period, shape and communicate a topos of (monarchic period) prophetic martyrology.[15] This topos is reflected also in Neh 9:26, which reminds its readers that their ancestors killed the prophets who had warned them in order to turn them back. In turn, memories of martyrdom make even more memorable (that is, increase the mindshare of) the motif of rejection of the monarchic prophets. In sum, themes both of prophetic lack of success and of persecution are well ingrained in social memories about monarchic Judah and Israel in Yehud and play important roles.[16]

All this said, it is worth stressing that Chronicles *balances* this construction of the memory of the prophets with a very substantial number of stories about

---

14 One point I advanced in *History, Literature and Theology in the Book of Chronicles.*
15 For Chronicles, see 2 Chr 16:7–10, 24:19–25, and esp. 24:20–22. I discuss the matter in relation to Kings in "'The Prophets.'" See the portrayal of the prophet Jeremiah there. On prophetic martyrology, see also A. Rofé, *The Prophetical Stories: The Narratives about the Prophets in the Hebrew Bible, Their Literary Types and History* (Publications of the Perry Foundation for Biblical Research in the Hebrew University of Jerusalem; Jerusalem: Magnes, 1988) 197–213. The generative power of the topos becomes evident (and the topos even more dominant) in the late Second Temple period, in which even Isaiah (the most "successful" monarchic prophet within the social memory of Yehud) was imagined as suffering martyrdom. It is worth noting that traditions about Isaiah's martyrdom captured the imagination for centuries and had a very long history of reception (for example, note the midrashic characterization of his killer Manasseh as Isaiah's grandson; or the persistent images in medieval Vulgate manuscripts; see R. Bernheimer, "The Martyrdom of Isaiah," *The Art Bulletin* 34 (1952) 19–34.
16 A study of the ideological and didactical role of the martyrdom of the pious one/few stands well beyond the scope of this essay. It suffices here to say that, although this motif became central later on, and particularly since the persecutions of Antiochus IV, it did exist before and is well attested in the discourse and repertoire of the community in late Persian Yehud. To a large extent, in all these cases, the "one/few" pious stood for what Israel should have been and should be.

prophets (or prophetic characters) who were successful in the monarchic period, for example, Shemaiah (twice during the days of Rehoboam, see 2 Chr 11:1–4; 12:5–6), Azariah in the days of Asa (2 Chr 15:1–7), Jehoiada in the days of Joash (note that his role is explicitly assigned to prophets in 2 Chr 24:19), the "man of God" in the days of Amaziah (2 Chr 25:7–9), Zechariah in the days of Uzziah (2 Chr 26:5), and Oded in (narratively and ideologically "kingless") northern Israel during the reign of Ahaz (2 Chr 28:8–15). Each of these stories created a particular site or memory for the readers of Chronicles, that is, a kind of memorial that reminded them that monarchic prophets were often successful.

These memorials do not populate the world evoked by Kings or by the prophetic books in the repertoire of Yehud. Had social mindshare on these matters been shaped *only* on the basis of the Deuteronomistic historical collection (hereafter, DH) and the prophetic corpus, the memory of the prophets of the monarchic period would have been very strongly shaped around the topos of the rejected, unsuccessful prophet and its logical counterpart, the usually sinful Israel. Chronicles, however, rebalanced, to the best of its capabilities, the mindshare of such a common topos. It did so not by denying or asking its readers to forget about it—in fact, it actively participated in its promotion—but by setting the topos in proportion. This attitude is typical of Chronicles and is probably necessary for a "national" history that must conform with some set of "facts" about the past that were already agreed on in the community and that can inform and be informed by other constructions of the past in the community, but not replace them.[17]

The ideological and social implications of the mentioned shift in social memory toward which Chronicles led are significant. The shift helped to construe and remember an image of Israel as not necessarily, or not in some essential way, sinful. Remembering monarchic Israel as not necessarily sinful was a consistent, underlying theme in Chronicles.[18]

---

[17] One point I advanced in *History, Literature and Theology in the Book of Chronicles.*

[18] In fact, as I suggested in my previous work ("A House of Treasures: The Account of Amaziah in 2 Chronicles 25—Observations and Implications," *SJOT* 22 [2008] 63–85), the Chronicler raised among its target readership an understanding that Israel, including of course their kings, tend by default to behave properly, that is, to follow Yhwh, if the rule of a bad king is removed from upon them. Significantly, kings are more likely to begin their reign piously than impiously till the death of Josiah, at which time Yhwh decided that a drastic purge is needed and will be fulfilled. Of course, initially pious kings and the people they lead show such a strong tendency to go astray at some point or another, but the putative default behavior of Israel may explain, or contribute to an explanation for a resetting of the entropic clock after the death, that is, the removal from power of a sinful king whose presence interfered with the "natural" tendency of the Israelites. Thus, as soon as Ahaz dies, the people, who previously followed his paths, recognize

There was also a practical implicature to Chronicles' tendency to shift the relative balance of mindshare on these issues in the community. As the Chronicler reminded the community of numerous cases of prophets and instances of prophetic preaching and teaching that were successful in their own time, it contributed to expectations about the success of preachers in their own time. As it did so, it conveyed an implied sense of continuity between (the Chronicles' construed) monarchic Israel and the (also construed) late Persian-period community as it should be in the view of the Chronicler.

There is another aspect of this particular tendency to balance social memory in this regard that converged to some extent with the preceding observation. As Chronicles drew, to the best of its capabilities, attention to stories of prophetic success, it drew some attention away from the topoi of prophetic rejection and persecution. The latter, however, was deeply linked in the discourse of the period to the ideological construction of the catastrophe of 586 BCE. As a result, Chronicles ended up drawing, indirectly, *some* attention away from the overwhelming focus on the catastrophe itself that would have characterized the social memory of Israel,[19] had social mindshare in late Yehud been shaped *only* by the DH and the prophetic books. This was consistent with the tendency in Chronicles not to deny but to place in proportion the significance of the catastrophe of 586 and "exile." This tendency cannot be discussed here, but it suffices to state that Chronicles conveyed to its target readership that nothing essential changed because of this catastrophe and that, in fact, the latter did not matter much in the long run. After all, nothing changed in terms of YHWH's teachings/*torah*, Israel's obligation to follow them, the need for godly preachers, the essential character of Israel, the centrality of Jerusalem, or YHWH's ways of governing the world.[20]

None of these positions are really innovations of the Chronicler. They did exist in one way or another within the general discourse of the period. The Chronicler's effect on the relative mindshare of memories of the monarchic

---

that this sinful king does not deserve to be buried with the kings of Israel/Judah (cf. 2 Chr 28:27; cf. 2 Chr 29–31 and note the date in 2 Chr 29:3). See also the beginning of the reign of Amaziah in 2 Chr 25. When a sinful king rules over Judah, the Judahites (/Israel) tend, however, to sin (see, for instance, 2 Chr 33:1–9).

19 Instances of implicit or explicit ideological engagement with the significance of the catastrophe, the use of its memory for didactic purposes and as a framing historical event in historiography attest to the mentioned focus, in addition to any direct or indirect report or image relating to the events themselves, to those that led to them and to their immediate aftermath.

20 On the concept of exile in Chronicles, see "Towards a Sense of Balance: Remembering the Catastrophe of Monarchic Judah/(Ideological) Israel and Exile through Reading Chronicles in late Yehud," in this volume, pp. 387–406.

past, however, exemplified a tendency to advance memories consistent with and promoting these positions and with *balancing* other memories that lent themselves to other (seemingly contradictory, but discursively complementary) ideological narratives.

Remembering Also That the Prophets Were Not Necessarily Focused on the Far Future of Their Community and Its Significance

There is no doubt that had the mindshare of the community been shaped by the prophetic books alone, images of monarchic period prophets announcing utopian futures would have played a highly prominent role. To be sure, remembering these announcements played a very substantial role in the creation and social impact of a basic and hopeful meta-narrative that moved from a just punishment in the past to a utopian future. Moreover, because in this meta-narrative YHWH's announcements about Israel's utopian future are set in the period of its extreme sinfulness, it reminded the community that YHWH's great promises for Israel's future are not conditional on their behavior. This memory contributed to a sense of hope and certitude about the future. Utopia will come and cannot but come; the community can be sure of that, because of the dystopian character of the monarchic past.

But Chronicles kept bringing its target readership to other sites of memory. Those embodied in monarchic period prophets whose messages to their addressees were not about some idyllic situation in the far future of their community or Israel in general, but about what they, that is, the addressees should do in their present and the possible implications of their actions for their immediate future. It is not the far future that figures prominently in all these instances but the very near future.

By doing so, Chronicles led, to the best of its influence, to a shift in the relative mindshare of memories about the main contents of past prophetic utterances in monarchic Judah, which was shaped in the main by the prophetic books.[21] This shift is consistent with the tendency in Chronicles to raise the prominence

---

21 Of course, the books of Samuel and Kings contain examples of utterances that are not utopian and have immediate significance. Again, Chronicles is clearly not "inventing" the prophet who spoke about matters of immediate significance. Yet, when it comes to mindshare about postsecession prophets in Judah, the prophetic books clearly carried the day, until Chronicles contributed to a partial rebalancing. On Kings, see pp. 179–180 below.

of issues such as following Yhwh's teachings.²² Although there is a tendency in Chronicles to portray vignettes of the monarchic past as utopian to some extent, and as veiled models for the future of its community,²³ these are a far cry from images such as those of a world in which "the wolf will live with the lamb" (Isa 11), of new heavens and a new earth (Isa 65:17), or of a changed Israel that is reshaped by the deity as unable to sin because it is 'programmed' to follow Yhwh (e. g., Deut 30:16; Jer 31:31–34, 32:38–41; Ezek 11:19–20, 36:25–28; cf. Hos 2:21; Jer 24:7), or of a peaceful world in which all the nations will flow to Jerusalem (e. g., Isa 2:2–4, Mic 4:1–4/5) or in which Jerusalem will become the imperial capital (e. g., Isa 60:11–12).

All the utopian futures evoked by prophetic books mentioned in the preceding paragraph involved a drastic transformation of the world in which the primary readers of Chronicles lived.²⁴ But Chronicles did not ask them to imagine these changes. On the contrary, it tended to reduce the emphasis that the general discourse of the period placed on these memories of a future, utopian transformation. Instead, Chronicles drew attention toward imagining a world better than the present, but not categorically discontinuous with it. The good future world that Chronicles tended to bring to prominence was still a mundane world in which godly speakers are needed and so are authoritative texts. This approach of Chronicles is again consistent with its inclination to reduce attention and soften—though certainly not eliminate—the discursive heights usually associated with the dystopic catastrophe of 586 BCE and its counterpart, the heightened images of "earth shattering" changes in the world as known to the community.

Kings, like Chronicles, did not draw particular attention to the utopian images of the prophetic books, but unlike Kings, Chronicles did provide many salient memorials (or sites of memory) leading its readers to imagine many particular (post-David/Solomon) Judahite prophetic characters and their speeches.²⁵ This remark leads us to the next main observation.

---

22 Including, of course, those relevant to proper worship.
23 See S. J. Schweitzer, *Reading Utopia in Chronicles* (OTS 442; New York: T&T Clark, 2007); J. Blenkinsopp, "Ideology and Utopia in 1–2 Chronicles," in *What Was Authoritative for Chronicles?* (ed. E. Ben Zvi and D. V. Edelman; Winona Lake, IN: Eisenbrauns, 2011) 89–104. Remembering utopian elements as facts in the monarchic past is consistent with the tendencies mentioned in the previous sections concerning remembering monarchic Israel as not necessarily sinful and about the essential continuity of Israel that bridges and reduces the salience of the fall of Jerusalem and its temple and its exile.
24 One has to keep in mind that the target readership of Chronicles was aware of and most likely read the repertoire of authoritative books of late Persian or early Hellenistic Yehud/Judah.
25 The exception in Kings concerns Isaiah.

Constructing a Temporally and Geographically Additional Distribution of Prophetic Sites of Memory and Its Significance

The book of Kings did not develop a strong mindshare among its target readership for memories of individual prophets in the (separate) Kingdom of Judah from the period it became well established (as a result of the successful secession of the north) to its fall along with that of its capital, Jerusalem.[26] To be sure, generic references to prophets conveyed a general sense that there were always prophets, but the text did not lead to the formation of prominent sites of memory that drew very substantial mindshare. The corpus of prophetic books provided a significant number of central monarchic period characters to remember, but concentrated them around either the late northern Israelite period and its counterpart in Hezekianic Judah (e. g., Hosea, Amos, Micah, Isaiah) or the late Judahite monarchic period or its immediate aftermath (e. g., Zephaniah, Jeremiah, Ezekiel). As mentioned above, both periods were closely associated with each other, because they provided the framework to understand the catastrophe of exile and draw significance from it.[27]

Chronicles asked its target readership to remember a significant number of prophets, who are not mentioned elsewhere but who cover precisely the gaps in the geographical or temporal distribution of prophetic images evoked by the

---

26 As mentioned above, the most salient exception for Judah is Isaiah; see also the case of Hulda. It goes without saying that Kings asked its target readership to remember and imagine multiple prophets in the North and construes some of them as very memorable (for example, Elijah and Elisha) but there are no counterparts to them in Judah. This situation may be explained, but *only in part* by the roles assigned to prophets in reports concerning the ascension or rejection (and disposal) of northern dynasties, which for obvious reasons had no counterpart in Judah's historical narrative once the Davidic dynasty is established. There is a need for a kind of sibling essay to this one, but dealing with prophetic memories in the Deuteronomistic Historical and the prophetic collections and their *Sitz im Diskurs*. It is worth stressing that Chronicles emerged later than these two collections, and for a substantial period of time social memory about prophets was shaped, in the main, by these two collections. I plan to write an essay on this in the near future.

27 It is worth noting that, unlike the emphasis on Manasseh as responsible for the Exile in some voices in Kings (see 2 Kgs 24:3), there is no prophetic book allocated to that period. Kings drew attention to Manasseh in its metanarrative of exile; the prophetic corpus—just as Chronicles—drew attention away from his reign in their own general metanarratives of exile. A full discussion of this matter and its implications is beyond the scope of this essay.

other authoritative corpora.²⁸ In other words, its effect, to the best of its influence, was to rebalance the mindshare of different images of the past in the community and through this rebalancing act to shape a general social memory of the monarchic period in Judah. In this social memory prophets appear as consistent sites of memory throughout the entire temporal and spatial landscape of Judah, as at least the literati in the late Persian period imagined it.²⁹ This is consistent with two ideological messages that Chronicles frequently communicated to its target readership: (1) Israel could exist without Jerusalem or temple or king, but not without divine instruction or guidance, and (2) the principle of warning mentioned above. Both, within the world construed by Chronicles, required the presence of prophetic voices.

Moreover, by filling the temporal and (theo)polity-bound gaps, Chronicles contributed to balancing mindshare in such a way that resulted in softening of the "heights and valleys" distribution of memorable prophetic figures in the social memory of the community in late Yehud. This in turn was fully consistent

---

28 See, for instance, 2 Chr 13:22 (reign of Abijah), 15:8 (reign of Asa), 16:7 (reign of Asa), 19:2 (reign of Jehoshaphat), 20:14 (reign of Jehoshaphat), 20:37 (reign of Jehoshaphat), 24:20 (reign of Joash), 25:7–10 (reign of Amaziah), 28:9 (kingless northern Israel). Jehoiada, the priest, serves the roles often associated with prophets during the reign of Joash, as he directs him to follow in Yʜᴡʜ's ways. After Jehoiada's death, when the king abandons his counsel, prophets are called to bring him and his elite back, though they fail to do so (2 Chr 24:19). (As required by the narrative world, Jehoiada is also a kind of kingly figure who restores to Judah the laws and regulations of both Moses and David, reestablishing the temple and the Davidic dynasty). The role of the prophetic voice during the reign of Uzziah is taken up by Azariah, the priest, and the other priests. L. Jonker associates most of these prophets with reports about war or cult. See Jonker, "Refocusing the Battle Accounts of the Kings: Identity Formation in the Books of Chronicles," in *Behutsames Lesen: Alttestamentliche Exegese im Gespräch mit Literaturwissenschaft und Kulturwissenschaften: Festschrift für Christof Hardmeier zum 65. Geburtstag* (ed. S. Lubs et al.; Arbeiten zur Bibel und Ihrer Geschichte 28; Leipzig: Evangelische Verlagsanstalt, 2007) 245–74. While this might be true, much of the narrative space of the nonformulaic section of the regnal accounts in Chronicles is devoted to these matters.

29 Of course, Chronicles also places prophets in periods that in the memory of the community are already populated by prophets, such as the David-Rehoboam period (cf. DH), the Ahabite period (cf. DH), the Hezekian period (cf. DH and the prophetic books), the Josianic period, and the relatively brief account of the three kings leading to the fall of Jerusalem. It is worth noting, however, that at times Chronicles draws attention to prophets known from existing sources that fit the period but advances a reconfiguration of the social memory of the community about them. The most obvious example is the case of Elijah and his letter to Jehoram in 2 Chr 21:11–15. In fact, there is hardly any period within the monarchic past to which the readers of Chronicles were not explicitly asked to associate prophetic voices. (Unlike Kings, in which he is never explicitly mentioned, Chronicles draws attention to Jeremiah in the context of the reign of Zedekiah; see 2 Chr 36:12). The most salient exception is the period of Ahaz.

with the tendency in Chronicles to soften—though certainly not eliminate—the heights and valleys associated in other literature with the post-Davidic/Solomonic past. After all, for Chronicles, neither exile nor for that matter the reported deeds of Josiah or Hezekiah[30] mattered so much in the long run.[31]

Remembering Also the Wide Range of Potential Intermediaries of Divine Knowledge and of Divine Knowledge and Its Significance

Chronicles also rebalanced the existing memories of the community in terms of who can be intermediaries of the divine for Israel and what they may do. It reminded its target readers that YHWH's intermediaries did not have to be "professional" or "permanent prophets" to fulfill the roles of prophets.[32] It reminded them that these intermediaries may be kings, even a foreign king, priests, or Levites (e. g., 1 Chr 28:19; 2 Chr 20:14–17; 24:20–22; 29:25; 35:20–24; 36:22).[33] It re-

---

30 I wrote elsewhere on the account of Josiah in Chronicles. See my "Observations on Josiah's Account in Chronicles and Implications for Reconstructing the World View of the Chronicler," in *Essays on Ancient Israel in Its Near Eastern Context: A Tribute to Nadav Na'aman* (ed. Y. Amit et al.; Winona Lake, IN: Eisenbrauns, 2006) 89–106.
31 The same holds true, of course, for the deeds of kings viewed in an extremely negative way, for example, those of Ahaz, who shut the doors of the temple, among his many other acts of impiety.
32 Y. Amit, among others, maintains that, in Chronicles, "a king, a Levite or any other person, functions as prophet when he utters prophetic statements in the Chronistic sermonizing style" ("The Role of Prophecy and Prophets," 89). The "Chronistic sermonizing style" to which she refers is the style of the "Levitical sermon" as discussed in G. von Rad, "The Levitical Sermon in I and II Chronicles." Contrast Amit's position with Schniedewind's, for whom prophets are *only* those whom Chronicles explicitly designate as such (e. g., W. M. Schniedewind, "Prophets and Prophecy," 214). Suffice to say that at the very least, Chronicles reflected and shaped a conceptual field populated by both "prophets" and prophetic characters who deliver prophecies, even if they are not *explicitly* called prophets. This shared conceptual field strongly associated one image to the other.
33 *Foreign king:* The text in 2 Chr 35:22 states מפי אלהים, but within the discourse of the target readership of Chronicles, אלהים could only be understood as a reference to YHWH. Most likely, in response to this understanding, in the text in 1 Esd 1:28, Jeremiah replaces Neco as the intermediary for YHWH's words. Note that mediation in the case of 1 Chr 28:19 is through a written text. This is one of the cases in which David is construed as a kind of necessary complement to Moses, given the importance of the temple and temple cult and above all of the divine instructions necessary for establishing and maintaining it. See S. J. de Vries, "Moses and David as Cult Founders in Chronicles," *JBL* 107 (1988) 619–39; and my own discussion of these matters in

minded them that monarchic-period prophets may compose and perform cultic music (1 Chr 25:1–8) or laments (2 Chr 35:25). It asked them to keep in mind that these prophets recorded (and interpreted) monarchic history (e.g., 1 Chr 29:30; 2 Chr 9:29; 12:15; 13:22; 23:32; 33:19) and conversely that books consisting of historical (royal) record included prophetic texts (2 Chr 20:34; 32:32; 33:18).³⁴

Thus, Chronicles contributed to a reconfiguration of the range of what came to the minds of its target readership when they thought of monarchic-period prophetic personages, that is, it affected the relative mindshare of various prophetic images that existed in the community. Most importantly, it created a conceptual realm that brought together (1) prophecy, in the "narrow" sense, (2) laws and regulations (associated with the intermediary figures Moses or David, who in Chronicles were also considered to be prophetic characters and, accordingly, their inspired words to be some form of prophecy—and *vice versa*),³⁵ (3) historical writings, and (4) cultic poetry or music.³⁶ In other words, this realm brings together the authoritative repertoire of the community and associated it with prophecy.³⁷

"One Size Does Not Fit All: Notes on the Different Ways in Which Chronicles Dealt with the Authoritative Literature of Its Time," in *What Was Authoritative for Chronicles?* (ed. E. Ben Zvi and D. V. Edelman; Winona Lake, IN: Eisenbrauns, 2011) 13–36. See also 2 Kgs 23:2 and 2 Chr 34:30 and note the exchange between prophets and Levites.

34 See Blenkinsopp, "Ideology and Utopia"; and S. Schweitzer, "Judging a Book by Its Citations: Authority and the Sources in Chronicles," in *What Was Authoritative for Chronicles?* (ed. E. Ben Zvi and D. V. Edelman; Winona Lake, IN: Eisenbrauns, 2011) 37–66.

35 See, for instance, 2 Chr 8:14, noting the concluding expression מצות דויד איש האלהים, and see 2 Chr 30:16. The term איש־האלהים is used in Chronicles for Moses also in 1 Chr 23:14 and for other prophets in 2 Chr 11:2; 25:9. Significantly, the target readership of Chronicles is asked to evoke a memory of David as a person who, like Moses, knew the distant future (see 1 Chr 16:35). I discussed the matter and its implications elsewhere; see "Who Knew What? The Construction of the Monarchic Past in Chronicles and Implications for the Intellectual Setting of Chronicles," in *Judah and the Judeans in the Fourth Century BCE* (ed. O. Lipschits, G. N. Knoppers, and R. Albertz: Winona Lake, IN: Eisenbrauns, 2007) 349–60.

36 See Gerstenberger, "Prophetie in den Chronikbüchern"; and Z. Talshir, "Several Canon-Related Concepts Originating in Chronicles," *ZAW* 111 (2001) 386–403.

37 This is, of course, the beginning of the process that led eventually to the development of an agreed corpus of inspired (i.e., prophetic) writings and eventually to canon(s). See "the law, the prophets, and the rest of the books" in the foreword in Sirach. It is worth stressing that the realm of prophecy in Chronicles included also, as M. Leuchter correctly noted, prophecy as divine דבר, which may "empower history to unfold and direct empires to rise and fall"; M. Leuchter, "Rethinking the 'Jeremiah' Doublet in Ezra–Nehemiah and Chronicles," in *What Was Authoritative for Chronicles?* (ed. E. Ben Zvi and D. V. Edelman; Winona Lake, IN: Eisenbrauns, 2011) 183–200. This concept of prophecy is not necessarily associated with unitemporality, as a divine word may unfold more than one time and in more than one way. See, for instance, understandings of pro-

Moreover, Chronicles brought together and brought to the attention of the community's present memories about both *written texts* and *oral exhortations*, encouraging the community to follow these texts and what they stood for. Oral exhortations served to provide memorable examples of what following YHWH could mean in practical, historically contingent terms (e. g., 2 Chr 28:9 – 15). In any event, readers were reminded that both (inspired/authoritative) written and oral texts were necessary in monarchic Israel and, by extension, in post-monarchic Israel.

In other words, Chronicles did far more than simply legitimize its work by suggesting that pious or "ideologically" appropriate historiographical works such as Chronicles have some kind of prophetic authority and that, by extension, so did the readings and interpretations of existing authoritative literature that Chronicles advanced. Of course, Chronicles did so. But, in addition, it shifted the web of images about the past that existed in the community so as to include memories that evoked a conceptual realm of prophecy consistent with a large and varied authoritative corpus of written works (including those containing interpretations/readings of other written works, for example, Chronicles) and oral speeches. Each of these references to written or oral texts shaped sites of memory that embodied and communicated what was transmitted through divine intermediation.

The implied conceptualization of this realm of prophecy/authoritative corpus and its retrojection to monarchic Israel is consistent with the sense of continuity between the past brought to the present of the community through the reading of Chronicles and its own present, or what should be, according to Chronicles, its present. But, of course, this must be balanced too. There was no room in the present of the target readers of Chronicles, for instance, for a new Moses or David, for new Mosaic commandments or divine laws identifying the place of the temple or establishing its cult. One may note that despite all its differences (e. g., kings, size of population, and so on), the same holds true for the post-David (or David/Solomon) period portrayed in Chronicles. In any event, the Chronistic prophetic landscape of the post-Davidic/Solomonic, monarchic period, and the memories it evoked were consistent with, and a legitimizing force for a present advocated by Chronicles, that is, for its "down-to-earth" utopia.

---

phetic portrayals of the "return" (i. e., the removal of "Exile") as something that has already happened, even if partially in Persian times, but at the same time as something to be fulfilled in the future. On these matters, see pp. 184 – 187 below.

Remembering Also That although the Prophets Were Historical Figures Their Words May Be Transhistorical or Multitemporal and Its Significance

Chronicles is a historiographical work. As expected given its literary genre, all its prophetic characters are explicitly anchored to particular historical circumstances. These anchors are crucial to the memory-shaping function of the book. Remembering these characters would not have contributed to the communal memory of any particular set of circumstances, if it were not for these explicit anchors. Moreover, Chronicles often asked its target readership to imagine these prophetic personages as speakers who addressed concrete, particular historical situations in the present of their addressees.[38] In addition, this Chronistic trend is clearly associated with and even required by the general tendency toward drawing attention to the concept of warning before punishment, which is involved in the shaping of multiple sites of memory in the community about people in the monarchic period who were exhorted to turn back from their sinful path.[39] These tendencies generated a need for the conceptualization of prophecy as anchored in and contingent to the putative historical circumstances of the conveying prophetic voice. After all, prophetic messages and characters had to be imagined as carrying at least the potential to influence the actions of the remembered historical agents in their own (putative) times.

However, Chronicles reminded the community that, whereas the remembered prophets are each to be associated with a particular temporal and spatial place in the array of shared (construed) pasts of the community, prophetic words may and at times did apply to multiple circumstances, including but certainly not limited to those of the prophetic speaker. Thus, prophets in Chronicles may allude to or use words associated with much later prophets in the corpus of prophetic literature,[40] and conversely, prophetic words that refer to the far future in that corpus may be taken as relevant or even partially fulfilled in the mo-

---

[38] Contrast with Amit's assertion that "the prophets of the Deuteronomistic historiography do not react to concrete historical events, ("The Role of Prophecy and Prophets," 88). Amit's statement is a bit too extreme, and she later qualifies it in her essay, but it points at the different balance of attestation of tendencies between Kings and Chronicles.

[39] See Japhet, *Ideology*, 176–91.

[40] E.g. 2 Chr 15:3 (and cf. Hos 3:4), 5 (and cf. Zech 8:10 and Amos 3:9), 6 (and cf. Zech 11:6), 7 (and cf. Jer 31:16 and Zeph 3:16); 2 Chr 16:9 (and cf. Zech 4:10); 20:20 (and cf. Isa 7:9). See P. C. Beentjes, *Tradition and Transformation*, 137–39; Japhet, *Ideology*, 183; Willi, *Auslegung*, 177, 223–29; von Rad, "Levitical Sermon"; Ben Zvi, "Who Knew What."

narchic past, without removing their significance as prophecies for the distant future within the discourse of the community.⁴¹

Thus, Chronicles contributes to a drive toward both close connection and separation between prophet and prophetic words in social memory. For particular purposes and ideological narratives, the two must be remembered together; but at the same time, the prophetic words could be taken as "floating" textual sites of memory by themselves and, as such, be evoked in multiple contexts, to the point that they may significantly contribute to the shaping of memories of multiple events at different times.⁴²

The basic atemporality of the prophetic word, as it becomes a site of memory in and by itself, was necessary for assuming its multitemporality. Again, this is no innovation of Chronicles but a very important feature of the discourse of the period.⁴³ It is reflected, for instance, in the strong tendency toward dehistoricizing the present in the prophetic writings, particularly in the majority of the 12 prophetic books.⁴⁴ Chronicles and these books contributed, even if implicitly, to the development of a community in which evoking prophetic messages did not necessarily evoke temporal constraints and "historical" contingency. This position allowed for the continuous significance of words set in the past, be they reported in the prophetic books, pentateuchal or historical texts or, for that matter, in any book in the authoritative repertoire of the community. This position allowed for the creation of a sea of images and texts that, though set originally in a particular event in the remembered past, were seen as (at least, potentially) relevant and instrumental for multiple or even all times. In other words, it allowed for the social reproduction of a text-centered community.

---

41 For instance, and as A. Warhurst has shown, some of the attributes of the ideal king in Isa 11 contribute to the characterization of Hezekiah in Chronicles. Thus, "the Chronicler retrojects restoration prospects onto descriptions of past history." See Warhurst, "Chronicler's Use of the Prophets," 181. Needless to say, the portrayal of this (partial) fulfillment was not an implied call to reject the future value of the utopian prophecy in Isa 11 or diminish its relative mindshare in the memory of the community. In fact, the opposite is likely to be correct. The allusions to Isa 11 likely served to draw the attention to the text and its (now double) message.
42 This is consistent with the idea of prophecy as a historical force or agent that actually makes things happen in history. See p. 183 n. 37 above; see also Isa 55:10–11.
43 For instance, and as mentioned above, the image of the "return" as both fulfilled in Persian times and yet not fulfilled. See the case of the utopian world of Isa 11, discussed above.
44 I discussed these matters elsewhere; see my "De-historicizing and Historicizing Tendencies in the Twelve Prophetic Books: A Case Study of the Heuristic Value of a Historically Anchored Systemic Approach to the Corpus of Prophetic Literature," in *Israel's Prophets and Israel's Past: Essays on the Relationship of Prophetic Texts and Israelite History in Honor of John H. Hayes* (ed. B. E. Kelle and M. Moore; (OTS 446; London: T&T Clark, 2006) 37–56.

In addition, it allowed the community in the late Persian period to strengthen its sense of continuity between itself and the past communities of Israel that it remembered, as it imagined a shared set of crucial and defining texts. Within a discourse in which Israel was conceived as a transtemporal entity and at the same time as a text-centered community, one can only expect the development of a tendency to associate at least some level of trans-temporality to Israel's texts. Moreover, within this *Sitz im Diskurs*, a tendency of this sort toward trans-temporality is likely to end up evoking some sense of temporal omnipresence concerning the basic sea of texts that define the community or at least to end up creating the conditions in which this sense may have emerged.[45]

To be sure, the concept of atemporal prophetic words uttered by temporally bound prophets carries within itself some degree of tension. This is particularly so because the temporally bound prophets were to be characterized by their prophetic words and remembered as those who uttered them. Tensions like this often carry some degree of generative power within the discourse of the community. In this case, the tension had the potential to generate some instances of partial "leakages" of atemporality from the *prophetic word* to the prophetic figure.[46] These partial leakages allowed for authors, redactors, and interpreters to imagine themselves as taking on, even if partially, the persona of the prophet and shaping prophetic words. This process was central to the development (including redaction) of the prophetic books, but one wonders whether it was not, even if perhaps in a marginal way, at work when the authorship of Chronicles advanced authoritative readings of the divine teachings associated with Moses.[47] One may wonder if the same does not hold true for cases in which prophetic phrases and expressions, or allusions to them, were embedded in the text of Chronicles—even if, and most likely because, these phrases or expressions were known in the community and remembered as associated with acknowledged prophetic voices.

---

[45] Whether this sense of omnipresence is already active in Chronicles, even if in only a partially and strongly balanced way, or whether this book (among others) prepared the way toward its development cannot be answered in any clear way. See my "Who Knew What?"

[46] There is no point in talking about leakage in the other direction. Clearly, there was much room in the discourse of the community for contingent prophetic words, and there was no need of a "leakage" from the image of a contingent prophet to produce this space.

[47] I discussed particular examples and the general issues involved in "One Size Does Not Fit All."

To Conclude

This essay explored ways in which Chronicles influenced social memory about prophets and prophecy in the community within which it emerged. Carrying out this exploration required a *Sitz im Diskurs* approach to Chronicles' relevant data, which included numerous, and at times seemingly contradictory, images of prophets and prophecy. This essay has shown that Chronicles contributed, to the extent of its capabilities, to a process of balancing the relative mindshare of different memories and sets of memories about prophets and prophecy in the late Persian (or early Hellenistic) Yehudite community in which its primary readership is located. The cumulative weight of the five central cases studied strongly suggests that Chronicles' tendencies to rebalance mindshare about prophets and prophecy were deeply interwoven with substantial ideological trends that already existed in the discourse of the community but that were well represented and even particularly salient in Chronicles.

The question of how effective was Chronicles vis à vis other authoritative works (e. g., Kings, prophetic books, pentateuchal books) in shaping mindshare in flesh-and-blood, historical communities in the late Persian or early Hellenistic period remains open. In fact, it cannot be answered with any degree of certainty. Moreover, its degree of influence might have changed from time to time and be dependent on particular settings. One should keep in mind that although Chronicles most likely presented itself as "less authoritative" than the texts in the primary history (Genesis–2 Kings),[48] it could have strongly influenced mindshare, if it successfully convinced the community that it was bringing forward the true meaning of these texts or authoritative, complementary viewpoints and memories. In any event, Chronicles was accepted by the community, or at least the Jerusalem-centred literati of Yehud, and was read and reread by them. Such a read and reread book could not but inform, at least to some extent, social memory among its historical readers.[49]

---

[48] Chronicles was written in Late Biblical Hebrew. I explore elsewhere the communicative message of Late Biblical Hebrew *vis à vis* Standard Biblical Hebrew; see my "Communicative Message of Some Linguistic Choices," in *A Palimpsest: Rhetoric, Ideology, Stylistics and Language Relating to Persian Israel* (ed. E. Ben Zvi, D. V. Edelman, and F. Polak; Piscataway, NJ: Gorgias, 2009) 269–90.

[49] An excellent source for the study of the influence of Chronicles in the shaping of memories of the monarchic period in later periods and communities is I. Kalimi, *The Retelling of Chronicles in Jewish Tradition and Literature: A Historical Journey* (Winona Lake, IN: Eisenbrauns, 2009), and see also bibliography there.

Contributions of the Genealogies in Chronicles to the Shaping of the Memory of the Monarchic Period: The Case of Some Simeonites's Vignettes

In multiple ways, the main historiographical narrative in Chronicles (1 Chr 10–2 Chr 36) construed, shaped, reshaped and explored a monarchic past worth remembering for the Yehudite literati of the Late Persian or Early Hellenistic period. The so-called genealogical section (1 Chr 1–9) contributed much to that endeavor, not only because of its role as an introduction to the main 'historical' narrative, but also as its proleptic summary.[1]

The genealogical section and the main narrative mutually informed each other in multiple ways on matters concerning central meta-narratives in the book (and its target readership), its core mnemonic plots and its main sites of memory (e.g., and prominently, David, his dynasty, and, of course, the temple). There is no doubt that both sections together, in an integrated manner, shaped and communicated a *general*, encompassing communal memory of Israel's past — one that starts from the beginning of human presence in the world to the rebuilding of the Temple in Jerusalem, as commanded by YHWH —and a sense of what the community should learn from it. In addition, at times, the genealogical section and the main narrative together, in an integrated manner, shaped communal memories of *particular*, narrowly defined periods of Israel's past. Of course, these two memory endeavors were mutually reinforcing, because the memories of particular events and periods within the monarchic era that were shaped and evoked among the literati when reading the book (including its two sections) were interwoven into a larger, comprehensive tapestry of memories about Israel's past, and vice versa. The larger comprehensive tapestry contributed much to the 'significance' of the particular threads.

Moreover, since the underlying grammar of preferences and dispreferences for shaping communally shared memories about Israel is not dependent on lit-

---

[1] For the use of this term see Manfred Oeming, *Das wahre Israel: Die 'genealogische Vorhalle' 1 Chronik 1–9* (BWANT, 128; Stuttgart: Kohlhammer, 1990), 217; cf. Pancratius C. Beentjes, "Identity and Community in the Book of Chronicles: The Role and Meaning of the verb *jāḥaś*," *ZAH* 12 (1999), 233–37 (234 n. 8). The said article was published in modified form as "The Importance of Being Registered: The Role and Meaning of the verb יחש in the Book of Chronicles," in Pancratius C. Beentjes, *Tradition and Transformation in the Book of Chronicles* (SSN, 52; Leiden: Brill; 2008), pp. 187–91 (188). "Proleptic summary" is preferred to "genealogical hall" (also used by Oeming) but a discussion of this matter goes beyond the scope of this essay and has no direct bearing on the argument advanced here.

erary genre (such as, 'genealogies' in the first section of Chronicles and 'historiographical narratives' in the second), the same grammars should be working on both sections of the book. Added to this, given that social memory is often a playground on which central issues in the discourse of the community can be safely explored, then one can doubly expect that in both sections, similar issues would be explored.

One of the most noteworthy ways in which reading the genealogy section contributed substantially to shaping and recalling memories of narrowly defined periods within the monarchic past involved the minor 'historical' notes within mainly genealogical material. In what follows, I will focus on a single case and explore its implications for the construction of a monarchic past and through it for our historical reconstruction of the intellectual thought of these literati, especially on political matters.

As the literati read 1 Chr 4:41, they construed the Chronicler[2] as a figure who wanted them to learn and remember, among many other things, (a) written records of the names of Simeonites or Simeonite leaders were drawn during the time of king Hezekiah, and (b) the Simeonites, on their own, conquered some territories and replaced their population with their own during the time of Hezekiah.[3]

---

[2] That is, the authoritative implied author or communicative voice they construed when reading the text, and who they imagined as an authoritative figure who wanted them to learn by reading the book to remember the Israel's past construed by the book.

[3] The text of 1 Chr 4:41 (וַיָּבֹאוּ אֵלֶּה הַכְּתוּבִים בְּשֵׁמוֹת בִּימֵי יְחִזְקִיָּהוּ מֶלֶךְ־יְהוּדָה וַיַּכּוּ אֶת־אָהֳלֵיהֶם וְאֶת־הַמְּעִינִים) is (מְעִינִים Ketiv; מְעוּנִים Qere – אֲשֶׁר נִמְצְאוּ־שָׁמָּה וַיַּחֲרִימֻם עַד־הַיּוֹם הַזֶּה וַיֵּשְׁבוּ תַחְתֵּיהֶם כִּי־מִרְעֶה לְצֹאנָם שָׁם) phrased in such a way that it carries, at the very least by connotation, two *complementary* meanings: (a) They, the ones written by names/whose names have been recorded, came and struck down their [i.e., of the descendants of Ham; see v. 40] tents and the Meunites that were found there in the days of King Hezekiah of Judah, and annihilated them to this day. They settled in their place, because there was pasture there for their flocks" (e.g., LXX; R. W. Klein, *1 Chronicles: A Commentary* [Minneapolis: Fortress Press, 2006], 152; Gary N. Knoppers, *1 Chronicles 1–9* (AB, 12; New York: Doubleday, 2003), 360; Edward L. Curtis and Albert A. Madsen, *The Books of Chronicles* [ICC; New York: Scribner's, 1910], 116–117; and most English translations). (b) "They, the ones written by names/whose names have been recorded in the days of King Hezekiah of Judah, came and struck down their [i.e., of the descendants of Ham; see v. 40] tents and the Meunites that were found there, and annihilated them to this day. They settled in their place, because there was pasture there for their flocks" (cf. Klein, *1 Chronicles: A Commentary*, 360; Curtis and Madsen, *Chronicles*, 116–117). In other words, the, at the very least, connoted polyvalence of the text allowed the community to construe and remember that both (a) the enrolment by names and (b) the action against the descendants of Ham and the Meunites took place in the days of King Hezekiah of Judah. It is worth noting that the relatively awkward position of the temporal clause "in the days of King Hezekiah of Judah" (בִּימֵי יְחִזְקִיָּהוּ מֶלֶךְ־יְהוּדָה) in the Hebrew

The first observation (i.e., 'a') is, as we shall see, very relevant to the present discussion, but certainly unsurprising. It is consistent with: the general tendency in Chronicles to ask its readership to recall and imagine written genealogical records (e.g., 1 Chr 5:7, 17; 7:5, 9, 40 and esp. 9:1) and to associate them with the authority of the royal centre (see esp. 9:1; but in addition to 4:41, see also 5:17 in reference to the days of Jotham of Judah and Jeroboam of Israel), a general, bureaucratic and centralizing ideological viewpoint that socially acceptable identity is, at the end of the day, a matter that depends on written, seemingly objective, 'proof' which is well attested in the repertoire of the literati (e.g, 2 Chr 31:16–19; Ezra 2:62 [cf. Num 3:10]),[4] memories of written genealogical records drawn in Hezekiah's time (see 2 Chr 31:16–19), and (iv) memories of significant scribal activity during Hezekiah's days that existed among the literati and were reflected in their repertoire (see, e.g., Prov 25:1; cf. 2 Kgs 19:2; Isa 22:15; 2 Chr 32:32).

The second observation (i.e., 'b' above) seems, at least on the surface, surprising. The point is not that Simeon maintained some tribal structure within the kingdom of Judah and under a proper Davidic king—a point to which I will return—but that Simeon conducted wars and conquered territories as an independent political agent. After all, is it not the job of the king to conduct wars?

But there is more: verse 41 is not an independent unit. It is part and parcel of 1 Chr 4:38–43 and when this unit was read in a way informed by v 41, the literati learned that they were supposed to consider and remember that matters were not just restricted to a single expedition during Hezekiah's reign. When they read verses 38–40 they were asked to recall that the Simeonites conquered the region of Gedor (or Gerar, see LXX and most scholars[5]) and took control of rich pastures that originally belonged to peaceful Hamites. When they read verses 42–43, they also learned that "some of them, five hundred men of the Simeonites, went to Mount Seir, having as their leaders Pelatiah, Neariah, Rephaiah, and Uzziel, sons of Ishi, and [that] they destroyed שְׁאֵרִית הַפְּלֵטָה לַעֲמָלֵק (i.e., the rem-

---

text (cf. Peter B. Dirksen, 1 Chronicles [HCOT; Leuven: Peeters], 77) may be easily explained by its functional role in shaping a polyvalent text. In other words, the minor awkwardness was a relatively low 'price' to pay for the creation of a preferred, polyvalent text.

4 Cf. Aubrey E. Buster, "Written Record and Membership in Judah and Classical Athens," Niall W. Slater (ed.), *Voice and Voices in Antiquity: Orality and Literacy in the Ancient World, Vol. 11*, (Mnemosyne Supplements, 396; Leiden: Brill, 2016), 297–320.

5 E.g., Knoppers, *1 Chronicles 1–9*, 363, 368. On Gerar see 2 Chr 14:12–14; and cf. the patriarchal stories about Gerar in Gen 20 and 26). The reference to Gerar in the LXX might, however, also relate to its occurrence in 2 Macc 13:24.

nant of the Amalekites [who had escaped destruction] and they live there to this day."

If the first piece of information referred to Gerar, the text here evoked not only references to pastoral spaces and patriarchal stories (cf. Gen 20, 26),[6] but also to a construction of the monarchic period in which the glorious army of King Asa of Judah pursued the Kushite/Egyptian army of Zerah up to Gerar and then defeated all the cities around Gerar (2 Chr 14:13–14). The second of the two observations is particularly relevant, because unlike the case of King Asa, the readers are asked now to remember a case of military conquest by Simeonites, under Simeonite leadership, even if Hezekiah is remembered as the king of Judah at the time, and in the context of the book, as the greatest king of all, in the post-Solomonic period.

It is worth stressing that not only King Hezekiah is explicitly mentioned (and thus his memory recalled) in 1 Chr 4:41, but also that textually inscribed markers linked the account in 1 Chr 4:38–43 with the account of Hezekiah in the main historiographical narrative. Verse 43 serves as a high-note conclusion of 1 Chr 4:38–43 (see below). The verse includes an expression that does not appear elsewhere in the HB, namely שְׁאֵרִית הַפְּלֵטָה ('surviving remnant'). This expression, however, closely resembles and recalls הַפְּלֵיטָה הַנִּשְׁאֶרֶת ('surviving remnant') which appears in Hezekiah's letters to northern Israelites after the fall of their kingdom (2 Chr 30:6).[7] From the perspective of the literati reading Chronicles, who as readers and writers were well aware of the existence of this type of systems of textually-inscribed signpost linking various readings within a book or across books in their repertoire, the presence of these two infrequent expressions was unlikely to be missed. Moreover, from their perspective, it is not just that these signposts connected two narratives associated with King Hezekiah, but also and far more importantly, that these mutually informing signposts shaped and drew attention to another instantiation of the well-known contrast between Amalek and Israel and their fates that existed in the discourse of the community, and which was well attested in its corpus of authoritative texts and in memories about hostile interactions between Israel and Amalek. From their perspective, reference to the final destruction of Amalek at the hands of just some Simeonites (not even all of Simeon) relates, recalls

---

[6] The contrast between the stories of the patriarchs in Gerar and those of the Simeonites, particularly against the background of Yehud and the general discourse of the Yehudite literati requires a separate study that goes beyond the scope of this chapter.

[7] This phrase appears in a completely different context in Exod 10:5, but cf. 2 Kgs 19:39; Isa 37:31; Neh 1:2. In any event, 2 Chr 32:23 is its only occurrence in Chronicles.

and informs the main memory narrative shared by the community, but also the account of Hezekiah in Chronicles, and *vice versa*.

The utter destruction of Amalek was construed by the community of literati as an explicit divine commandment (Exod 17:14–16; Deut 25:19). The literati knew that not observing this commandment could have tragic consequences, as it had for Saul (1 Sam 28:18). Reading Chronicles, however, asked them to remember that even David failed to destroy them (despite 1 Chr 18:11) and so failed all other Davidic kings of Judah, including powerful kings such as Asa who was active in this area (certainly if Gerar is mentioned) and, far more relevant to our case, the great king Hezekiah, who was a man of great piety and whose name was exalted among all the nations (2 Chr 32:23), within their world of memory.

In other words, from the perspective of the literati reading Chronicles, the task of completing the obliteration of Amalek remained to be performed until some Simeonites, acting as their own agents and with no royal intervention, finally carried it out, whereas all Davidic kings, included the best of them, failed. Reading this text, the literati probably assumed that the Simeonites's recompense for their actions was that they avoided exile, because whatever the original meaning of the term עַד הַיּוֹם הַזֶּה in any hypothetical source that might or might not underlie the present text of Chronicles, it is very unlikely that these readers understood it, in the present context of the book, as meaning anything other than 'to this day'.[8]

To be sure, one might argue that within the ideological world shaped and communicated by Chronicles, avoiding exile could have been construed as an implicit, even if partial, hint that the Simeonites did not dwell in 'the land' and that they were not part of the kingdom and subject to the king of Judah.[9] This said, and whatever the case might be about the implied construction/s of Simeon and of its space/s before or at the time of the destruction of the kingdom of Judah,[10] it is impossible to deny that the literati reading 1 Chr 4:38–43 were

---

8 Cf. Knoppers, *1 Chronicles 1–9*, 370–71. See also the other instances of עַד הַיּוֹם הַזֶּה in Chronicles, namely 1 Chr 17:5; 2 Chr 5:9; 8:8; 21:10, all of which are consistent with this pragmatic understanding of the term. Many scholars have noticed that within the world of Chronicles, the Simeonites were not exiled. See, e.g., Yigal Levin, "From Lists to History: Chronological Aspects of the Chronicler's Genealogies," *JBL* 123 (2004), 601–636 (614–615), but compare and contrast with Sara Japhet, *1–2 Chronicles. A Commentary* (OTL; Westminster/John Knox, 1993), 126.
9 See, e.g., 2 Chr 36:20–21 and cf. 1 Chr 5:41.
10 One may remark also that 2 Chr 15:9 and 2 Chr 34:6 seem to suggest a construction of tribal space in which Simeon is not only not outside the boundaries of Judah, but also and more importantly, is inside the territory associated with the northern tribes. This voice in Chronicles is not consistent with that in 1 Chr 4:24–43 or with any construction of remaining in the land and avoiding exile and requires a separate discussion. For the present purposes, it suffices to

explicitly asked to associate the reported events crucial to the present purposes with the reign of Hezekiah. Moreover, the text clearly and overtly communicated to the literati that Hezekiah had authority and ruled over the Simeonites at that time, as demonstrated by his ability to enroll them by name in written records. In addition, the already mentioned mutually reinforcing system of signposts (see שארית הפליטה and הפליטה הנשארת) drew an additional link between the regnal account of Hezekiah and the account of the actions of the Simeonites during Hezekiah's reign. In the world of the literati reading 1 Chr 4:38–43, the Simeonites are not out, but in Hezekiah's kingdom.

1 Chr 4:38–43 is a relatively brief report, but none it communicated to the literati the message that they may safely ignore it. To the contrary, it carried substantial meanings and implications on such a central concept as 'exile', drew much attention to itself by recalling the divine command to destroy Amalek, which within the memory world evoked in the unit remained unfulfilled until the Simeonites' actions, and was directly linked thematically and by textually-inscribed markers to other texts, images and memories of King Hezekiah, the most glorious king since Solomon. To be sure, all in all, it is probably true that it did not carry as much social mindshare among the literati as the construction of the monarchic past in the main historical narrative, but its presence its still significant and suggests the existence of substantial undercurrents or secondary currents of thought concerning the monarchic past, the structure of its state, and the reign of Hezekiah.

This said, the account, and as strongly marked as it is, still represents a kind of 'minority report' within a book in whose main historiographical narrative portrayed time and again the kingdom as a centralized polity in which the Davidic king is the main political and cultic agent.[11] Moreover, this historical narrative describes a political entity that on the one hand is a human kingdom, with often failed rulers, but also, on the other, the kingdom of Yhwh, which was em-

---

state that the case represents one of many positive proofs to the ability of Chronicles and even more importantly of the Chronicler of these literati to embody and communicate multiple voices, which even if they are 'logically' inconsistent with each other, can stand well one beside the other and all together coexist and complement each other, in a stable system characterized by what I called elsewhere, the consistency of inconsistency and the textual and social coherence of seeming incoherence. See, e.g., "Squaring Circles and The Social Benefits of Squaring Them: Joshua as a Case Study for Constrains, Preferences, Balances and Flexibility within the Complex Memory System of the Literati of the late Persian/early Hellenistic Period," in this volume, pp. 232–52.

11 Cultic not in the sense of performing the duties of the priests, but cultic in the sense being responsible for the arrangement and maintenance of the appropriate cult at the only appropriate place. This involved a duty to ensure that the temple and its rites are properly conducted.

bodied in the kingdom of Judah under a proper Davidic king (see 1 Chr 28:5; cf. Ps 2:6[12]). Certainly, Hezekiah was described and imagined as a proper Davidic king and as the central political (and cultic) agent of his time.[13] Yet, remembering the actions of the Simeonites during his reign raised substantial questions and balances images of central control, particularly since there is no reason to believe that the literati construed them as 'renegades'; in fact, the opposite is certainly true.

Before continuing further, it is worth noting that a common approach for studying 1 Chr 4:38–43, and to some extent of removing the strong edge of its implications, has been to set it within a set of references to tribal identity and tribal structures in the main historiographical narrative (1 Chr 10 – 2 Chr 36). It is obviously true that compared to the monarchic pasts evoked by Samuel-Kings and the prophetic books, there is much more room for tribal identity and tribal structures in the monarchic past evoked by Chronicles. This is not the place to discuss at length the complexity of tribal constructions conveyed by Chronicles.[14] For the present purposes, it suffices to notice that, in addition to the usual references to Judah and Benjamin (e.g., 2 Chr 11:1–12; 14:7; 15:2; 25:5; 34:9), the most significant prooftexts concerning tribal structures, identity or leadership in the monarchic Judah construed by Chronicles are 1 Chr 12:24–41; 27:16–22; 2 Chr 11:13–16; 30:1–18; 34:6. But what kind of polity (and implied political thought) do these texts conjure? All of them are about the power, centrality and the unique agency of the Davidic king of Judah.[15] In

---

[12] Cf. Friedhelm Hartenstein, "The King on the Throne of God: The Concept of World Dominion in Chronicles and Psalm 2," in Ben Zvi and Levin (eds.), *Centres and Peripheries in the Early Second Temple Period* (FAT, 108; Tübingen: Mohr-Siebeck, 2016), 315–22.

[13] The political structure of the kingdom of Judah that populated the memory of the literati was different from that of the historical kingdom of Judah, which was most likely not too centralized. On the historical issues, see, e.g., Aren M. Maeir and Itzhaq Shai, "Reassessing the Character of the Judahite Kingdom: Archaeological Evidence for Non-Centralized, Kinship-Based Components," in Saar Ganor, Igor Kreimerman, Katharina Streit, Madeleine Mumcuoglu (eds.), *From Sha'ar Hagolan to Shaaraim Essays in Honor of Prof. Yosef Garfinkel* (Jerusalem: Israel Exploration Society, 2016), 323–40. Of course, what counted for the literati (and for historians studying their world of memory) was what the literai 'knew', not what contemporary archaeology may teach us today.

[14] For instance, the topos of the *twelve* tribes of Israel plays, inter alia, important roles both in memories of the past and of some utopian futures (e.g., Ezek 48:1–29), but one can notice the presence of a strong voice in Chronicles that shows unwillingness to explicitly use, and at times, even willingness to implicitly undermine the importance of the conceptual construction of the *twelve* tribes. But any analysis of these matters and their relation to Chronicles' emphasis on "all Israel" requires a separate discussion.

[15] It is possible that a similar message of central, royal control was implied in 1 Chr 4:31as well.

fact, all of them convey exactly the point that all authority converges or should converge on the Davidic king, whose kingdom is actually a manifestation of Yhwh's kingdom.

Moreover, even references in Chronicles to substantial tribal leadership with actual political authority and power in the northern kingdom—i.e., in cases in which Davidic kingship is not an issue – these references relate to periods in which either there was no king or he was unable to exercise his power over the relevant territory within his kingdom (see, e.g., 1 Chr 5:6; 2 Chr 28:12–15). In other words, not only do none of these usually discussed cases resemble 1 Chr 4:38–43 but, on the contrary, the latter reflected and evoked a memory of a political structure that was diametrically opposed to that of the said texts. Thus, this set of references serves well to draw attention to categorical differences, but does not provide the most suitable research path for understanding the meaning of 1 Chr 4:38–43 per se.

These considerations return us with an additional degree of puzzlement (and of an urge for an explanation) to our original point: The literati reading and rereading 1 Chr 4:38–43 were asked to construe and vicariously experience, through their socially shared reading and imagination, a particular memory of the absolute zenith of the post-Solomonic Judahite kingdom, exactly when it was ruled by a powerful king who was exalted in the sight of all the nations (2 Chr 32:23). At the same time, they were asked to include among their memories of this glorious monarchic period, memories of Simeonites and Simeonite leaders who not only enjoyed total autonomy concerning war, conquest, and settlement, but also fulfilled well-known divinely sanctioned goals that even pious and powerful kings, including Hezekiah, were not able to, or were not bothered to achieve for themselves.

Moreover, they were asked to remember that whereas the celebrated kingdom over which Hezekiah reigned, eventually fell and its inhabitants went into exile, the Simeonites were not exiled. These literati almost certainly construed the fate of the Simeonites in this regard as enjoying a divine reward that was not granted to Judah, despite the grandeur of Hezekiah.

Furthermore, the literati reading these texts and imagining this Hezekianic past construed and remembered that both Hezekiah and Yhwh approved such degree of tribal and even sub-tribal autonomy.

There is no doubt that the literati, by doing so, construed and explored through memory a type of divinely approved political structure that goes so beyond and, in fact, is strongly contrary to the main portrayal (and socially shared memory) of the centralized (and centralizing) monarchy, even if such monarchy

of memory includes 'tribes'.[16] The most promising path to begin exploring the contribution of 1 Chr 4:38–43 to the construction of the Judahite monarchic past and the literati's exploration of political thought through memories of the past requires to turn our attention to a few relevant co-texts of 1 Chr 4:38–43 within the general frame 1 Chr 1–9.

Obviously, the literati who read 1 Chr 4:38–43 also read 1 Chr 5:10 and 1 Chr 5:18–22. Thanks to the first text, they recalled wars of expansion and conquest by the Reubenites acting on their own during the reign of Saul. And thanks to the second text, they recalled similar actions taken by the Reubenites, the Gadites, and the half-tribe of Manasseh, probably at a later time in the monarchic period, and acting on their own again. The account of the Eastern tribes (1 Chr 5:18–22) and that of Simeonites are linked not only by their similar content, but by the textually inscribed and an ideologically significant contrast shaped by their respective endpoints: the Simeonites remained in the land they conquered 'to this day' (עַד הַיּוֹם הַזֶּה), whereas the Eastern tribes, only 'until the exile' עַד־הַגֹּלָה (see 1 Chr 4:43 and 1 Chr 5:22 respectively).[17]

One may correctly argue that the autonomous actions of the Eastern tribes or Reuben alone were not portrayed or remembered as having taken place within the framework of a Davidic polity,[18] or for that matter, during the time of the reign of a pious, powerful king of Judah such as Hezekiah, but still the resemblance between the actions of the Simeonites and the Reubenites and their allies was clear and memorable. The Simeonites were not completely alone, and, actually, the mentioned contrast between the fates of the Simeonites and the others carry an added ideological content that by its very presence interrelates the accounts and their meanings to the remembering community.

Moreover, from a larger perspective of the construction of Israel's past, it is also clear that all of these reports evoking memories concerning independent military actions and conquests taken by a tribe or a set of tribes in Israel are evocative, above all, of memories encoded and recalled in Judges. It is worth noting in this respect that it has been long noticed that the brief report of the conquest of Gerar/Gedor by the Simeonites evoked and played to some extent with

---

[16] As mentioned above, 1 Chr 4:38–43 stands directly against the spirit, rhetorical power, and communicative intention of the set of references about tribes during the Judahite monarchic period in the main historical narrative in Chronicle.

[17] 1 Chr 5:6.

[18] Cf. though the potential meaning evoked by the double reference to "Jotham, king of Judah, and Jeroboam, king of Israel" (1 Chr 5:17) and in that order that the literati read just before 1 Chr 5:18, and which they obviously had still in their minds as they read 1 Chr 5:18–22.

that of the conquest of Laish by the Danites (see esp. Judg 18:7, 27).[19] The report about the Eastern tribes' war in 1 Chr 5:18–22 was also reminiscent of the wars of the period of the Judges. This is particularly the case given the role of 'crying out' to the deity (זעק; 1 Chr 5:20), which although consistent with the worldview of Chronicles, also reminds the readers of some of the stories in Judges (see e.g., Judg 3:15; 6:6; 10:10)[20].

Of course, these reports are part of a larger group of brief historical reports interwoven into the genealogies in Chronicles. It is in this context worth stressing that memories evoked by a significant number of these reports show some generic resemblance to memories associated with Judges. The mini-story about Jabez in 1 Chr 4:9–10, for instance, contains, in a very compacted way, a story like those associated with Judges. The mini-story contains an individual leader, his prayer for help, eventual success and even the seeming paradox of a successful warrior explicitly characterized by his inauspicious name.[21] All of these features/characters find a likely literary/mnemonic counterpart in another successful warrior explicitly characterized by his inability to use his right arm (i.e., Ehud).

In addition, mini-stories in 1 Chr 1–9 asked the literati to remember that another traditional, main royal task was also taken, at times, by individuals mentioned in the genealogies, namely building and, in particular, building cities (and see, e.g., 1 Chr 7:24; 8:12).

In terms of constructions of the past, one may say that these mini-stories evoked among the literati the general atmosphere of the period of Judges. It is not surprising that some of these memories were likely associated with pre-monarchic times, but one has to keep in mind that the genealogical section of Chronicles is at the same time: (a) temporally organized, (b) often very fuzzy about when the remembered 'historical' event occurred (e.g., when did Jabez live?), and also at an ideological level, (c) a-temporal, as it construes Israel as it always is and will be.[22] This being the case, 'incursions' of the atmosphere of the period of the Judges in other periods, especially the monarchic period are not only possible but likely in constructions of Israel's past or future among these literati, and they carry significance.

---

19 See, e.g., R. Klein, *1 Chronicles*, 152.
20 In fact, the expression X זעק ל/אל, in which X stands for the deity, occur elsewhere in Chronicles in 2 Chr 20:9, but note the spatial element created by the reference to the temple (this said, cf. 2 Chr 18:31; 32:20).
21 See the excellent discussion in S. Japhet, *I-II Chronicles*, 108–111.
22 Cf. Jonathan E. Dyck, "The Ideology of Identity in Chronicles," in Mark Brett (ed.) *Ethnicity and the Bible* (Leiden, Leiden: Brill; 1996), 89–116; and Beentjes, "Identity and Community in the Book of Chronicles."

The explicit and emphatic association of the Simeonites actions with the zenith of the post-Solomonic period and the prominence of the case (see references to core ideological topoi such as exile/avoiding exile, and Amalek) strongly suggest that there was something at stake in remembering them precisely at that time in the construed past. From the perspective of political thought, the legitimization of their autonomous deeds by both Yʜᴡʜ and the Davidic Hezekiah at the height of post-Solomonic Judah is particularly relevant.

It is in this context that the location of the literati may also be taken into consideration. They lived in a period in which there was no Davidic king in Jerusalem and in which none was expected in the normal course of the events for a long time.[23] The present conditions of the group, even if in subtle and oblique ways bubbles up in their (remembered) past, through constructions of the past they explore and balance through ideas concerning what we may call political thought, and in this case, the matter of a centralized monarchy.

To be sure, as they were, the literati's reading of 1 Chr 4:38–43 informed but was also informed by their reading of 2 Chr 29–32. These readings, and one may say the genealogies and the main historiographical narrative required, complemented each other. Only when both worked together, each in its own way, did they allow the literati to engage in (implicit) political thought in a manner consistent with their aspirations and historical realities.

From this general perspective, the account of the Simeonites is not so 'odd'. We are dealing with a marginal post-monarchic community that involved itself in constructing memories of their glorious kings of the past, and thus, of a central-

---

23 This is so irrelevant of whichever combination of positions the Chronicler may have communicated regarding the divine promise to David. My own position on the matter, is that Chronicles here, as on many other occasions, displayed a consistency based on inconsistency, a coherence grounded in incoherence. In any event, the authoritative repertoire of the literati reading and rereading Chronicles included texts that explicitly evoked memories of ideal futures in which there are no Davidic kings, but Yʜᴡʜ is king and which at times evoked and projected into the ideal future memories of the period of the Judges (e.g., Obad 21). Chronicles itself explicitly construed a memory of a past in which the disappearance of the monarchic centre in northern Israel leads to the emergence of a type of tribal leadership reminiscent of images associated with the period of the Judges (see esp. 2 Chr 28:12–15 but notice also the importance of the role of prophet in 2 Chr 28:10–11; see also 1 Chr 5:6). On the importance of the prophet/guardian for the political thought of the period, see my "Memory and Political Thought in the Late Persian/Early Hellenistic Yehud/Judah: Some Observations," in Diana V. Edelman and Ehud Ben Zvi (eds.) Leadership, Social Memory and Judean Discourse in the 5th-2nd Centuries BCE (WANEM; London: Equinox, 2016), 9–26.

ized state;[24] but which, here and there balanced them with memories of non-kingly, heroic (as defined within their own discourses), peripheral characters whose very existence assumes the existence of a non-(strongly) centralized polity.[25] It is not so 'odd' for marginal groups engaged in political thought, to explore the possibility of some level of agency outside the main political centre, and in a society in which political thought was carried out through narrating, reading and exploring memories,[26] it was not 'odd' to include some of them in their memory landscape. The account of the Simeonites remains a 'minority report', but one that is prominently marked, placed in proportion by other reports and memories, but still informing them, and at the end, perhaps a bit 'odd', but not so 'odd', and particularly so in a book often displaying a consistency based on inconsistency, a coherence grounded in incoherence.

---

24 As fully anticipated within the discourses of the imperial and monarchic discourses of the ancient Near East, and later periods as well. All these discourses tend to emphasize the power of the king and his court and thus shape images of polities with much central power. Reality, of course, was a different matter in many (most?) cases and the exerting political power often involved negotiations and an awareness of the limits of the power of kings and their statements. These issues require, of course, a separate discussion.
25 Cf. the story of Ruth. The alternative is, of course, to construe characters that maintain agency by managing with the relevant local powers and see the stories of the ancestors in Gen 20; 26 mentioned above.
26 On this see, E. Ben Zvi, "Memory and Political Thought".

A Balancing Act: Settling and Unsettling Issues Concerning Past Divine Promises in Historiographical Texts Shaping Social Memory in the Late Persian Period*

Introduction

Central to the construction of social memory in the late Persian period, at least among the literati of the period, were memories of some core divine promises. Many of these core divine promises were understood and remembered in terms of ברית 'covenant', even in cases in which central texts encoding these memories do not explicitly contain the term ברית. For instance, whether the original writers of 2 Sam 7 (whenever they lived) intended the divine promise to David to be understood as a ברית or not,[1] it is clear that the late Persian- or early Hellenistic-period literati construed the divine promise to David reported and evoked by 2 Sam 7 as a ברית (see 2 Sam 23:5; 1 Kgs 8:23–24 [implicitly]; Jer 33:17–21;[2] Ps 89:29; 2 Chr 13:5; 21:7).[3] Because no text was (or is ever) read

---

* First published in *Covenant in the Persian Period: From Genesis to Chronicles* (eds. R. J. Bautch and G. N. Knoppers; Winona Lake, Ind.: Eisenbrauns, 2015), 109–129.
1 See, for instance, S. L. McKenzie, "The Typology of the Davidic Covenant," in *The Land, That I Will Show You: Essays on the History and Archaeology of the Ancient Near East in Honour of J. Maxwell Miller* (eds. J. A. Dearman and M. P. Graham; JSOTSup 363; Sheffield: Sheffield Academic Press, 2001), 152–78; those who advance this position tend to maintain that for the original (redactionally reconstructed) "Deuteronomist" there was only one Mosaic covenant, the Horeb covenant renewed in Moab (see Deut 28:69; cf. 4:13 and 5:2–19, which is the same that was to be renewed at Mt. Gerizim/Ebal [see Deuteronomy 27]).
2 Jer 33:14–26, and thus Jer 33:17–21, is not present in the LXX Jeremiah, which here may well reflect an earlier version of the text, as it is often proposed–note also the "Chronistic flavor" of the text. See, e.g., B. Gosse, "Les Lévites, Jérémie et les Chroniques," in *ZAW* 123 (2011): 47–56 (52–54); M. Leuchter, *The Polemics of Exile in Jeremiah 26–45* (Cambridge: Cambridge University Press, 2008), 72–81; W. McKane, *Jeremiah 26–52* (ICC; Edinburgh: T&T Clark, 1996), clxii–clxiii, 861–65 and bibliography cited there. In any event, there is no question that questions about "eternal promises" were enduring questions within the discourse of the communities discussed here and, for that matter, within the discourses of many later communities that identified with "Israel."
3 As stated in its title, this essay focuses on "historiographical texts." These texts have, obviously, certain genre characteristics that distinguish them from other texts (such as psalms, proverbs or prophetic texts) that existed within the repertoire of the community, or its literati, and thus it makes sense studying them separately. This said, references will be made, from time to time, in

by itself but within a cultural context and as an integral part of a general discourse, not only did these texts construe the promise to David as a ברית, but they informed the literati's readings of 2 Sam 7 accordingly.

Crucial promises were considered a ברית, and promises raise the issue of obligation, because to make a promise is tantamount to set an obligation on oneself.[4] But the relation between the two is not unproblematic, because a promise

---

this essay to texts that are not historiographical. These references are more than justified. For one, concepts may be encoded and activated by texts, reflected and explored through them, continuously negotiated and renegotiated through (social) readings of texts within a community and the like, but concepts (and ideas and memories for that matter) are held by a community not by a written text. Moreover, no concept exists alone, by itself; instead, they exist and have meaning in relation to other concepts and as an integral component of the social mindscape and intellectual discourse of a community. It is extremely unlikely, and I would say unreasonable, to expect that core communal concepts such as ברית be encoded, explored, activated, shaped and reshaped by the community only within the boundaries of a single literary genre to the exclusion of all others (cf. other core concepts such as *torah*). It is appropriate then to use, when relevant, references to ברית in texts other than "historiographical" to illuminate our historical reconstructions of the ways in which the community, or its literati, at least, constructed the meaning of ברית as they read and read their "historiographical" texts. Moreover, reading is always contextual and historically contingent. Actual readings (and, for that matter, acts of writing/editing, which are to some extent a way of expressing, shaping and communicating particular "readings" and "rereadings") of texts are never carried out in a "vacuum." When the community read and reread the relevant historiographical texts, they did so informed by their world of knowledge, ideological viewpoints and social attitudes, even if, or likely even more so because, the process was dynamic and the reading of texts contributed to the shaping of the latter. Thus, even if our goal were only to understand how a particular text was read in the late Persian period, still we would have to deal with the world of knowledge of the community and be aware of other (non-historiographical) texts within the discourse of the community that informed, in ways known and unbeknownst to the community, its readings of the historiographical texts. Further, most of the non-historiographical texts mentioned here shaped images of the past and evoked and construed (social) memory just as the historiographical texts themselves. The comprehensive social memory of the community about particular events, characters, and the like is influenced by all the relevant texts that it considers "authoritative."

4 Not surprisingly, ברית appears at times in association with other terms within the large semantic/conceptual realm of "obligation." See, for instance, the parallelism between דבר and ברית in 1 Chr 16:15//Ps 105:8; the association between ברית and דבר clearly communicated in 1 Kgs 8:23–24; and similar conceptual developments such as the association between שבועה and [implied] ברית in 1 Chr 16:16//Ps 105:9. It is worth noting that the sense of obligation exists when two parties enter into a ברית, but also in the case of obligations taken by characters on themselves (e.g., 2 Chr 34:31; note that the ברית there is construed as "*before* YHWH," לפני יהוה). It is even more interesting when the term ברית stands for, evokes or even *embodies* a single particular group or entity (see Mal 3:1; Isa 42:6; and Prov 2:17–note especially the parallelisms in the latter two; cf. also Dan 11:22, 28, 30; 1QM 14:4; 1QS 5:11, 18). Even in this case, ברית stands within the general semantic realm of obligation, because the group was essentially construed

seems to create a reason (that is, the obligation) for doing something just by stating the intent to fulfill what was promised.[5] Not only is this conceptually problematic, but rarely would a society consider the value of the act of promising in itself as absolute so as to override completely all socially accepted moral rules. Jephthah is not praised for offering his daughter (see also, for instance, 1 Sam 14:45). Moreover, although YHWH was characterized and remembered both as (a) fulfilling all his promises and not changing his mind, particularly when YHWH is contrasted with human beings (Num 23:19; 1 Sam 15:29; see also Mal 3:6), and as (b) changing his mind and not following through with his promises, particularly *but not exclusively* when he is portrayed as merciful.[6]

Promises, like any performative utterance, are nothing more but nothing less than a socially accepted practice, namely, promising, and as such they receive their meaning from society and generally agreed-on societal norms, which, of course, vary from time to time and are rarely absolute. In any case, this means that promising is to be understood within the social norms and the pragmatic understanding/s of "promise" and "promising" that exist in the relevant society.[7] To illustrate, one may claim that the reason for fulfilling promises may be grounded not in the very act of stating them but in the need not to lose socially granted trust and "honor" in general, and thus the need not to hinder one's own

---

around such an obligation. In the cases relevant to this essay, obligations were understood and remembered as established by divine promises (see, for instance, Deut 7:9; 1 Kgs 8:23–24// 2 Chr 6:14), whether they involve a "contract" or not. To be sure, the idea of a "contract" involving YHWH is somewhat problematic because a "contract" is basically an obligation whose enforcement is implicitly assigned to an external agent and made dependent on some set of "objective" rules to be evaluated by that enforcer. On ברית and obligation, see E. Kutsch "ברית", in *Theological Lexicon of the Old Testament* (eds. E. Jenni and C. Westermann; Peabody, MA: Hendrickson, 1997), 256–66.

5 On general issues regarding promises, see H. Sheinman, *Promises and Agreements: Philosophical Essays* (Oxford: Oxford University Press, 2011).

6 E.g., Hos 11:8–9; contrast the language used here with that of Num 23:19; 1 Sam 15:29. To improve readability, masculine pronouns have been used here in relation to YHWH. Although this deity was construed as beyond the male/female dichotomies that characterized humans and other animals and thus was superior to them (see Gen 1), it was also cast in roles which in human societies were clearly gendered (e.g., warrior, king, husband, father).

7 The crucial promises for the present study are divine promises. But socially shared norms regarding human promises were most likely involved with the construction of divine promises and their meanings. After all, gods were imagined, by necessity, on the basis of attributes, roles and norms that were known to the imagining society because they occurred in society itself (e.g., the god as shepherd, husband, king, mighty warrior, teacher; the god's anger, compassion; the god's council and messengers; and so on–all human roles and characteristics). In fact, the deity was, at least in part, construed as a superhuman and thus based on humans.

future social transactions due to a loss of "status."[8] One may claim that people may be socialized to keep promises in a society, because this facilitates social cooperation and that *mutatis mutandis* this applies to their constructions of the deity; for one who keeps promises is one with whom social cooperation can be easily imagined and remembered. A well-socialized (and one may say well-tamed) "deity" is one with whom a reliable partnership can be struck, and therefore, society may have a stake in constructing and remembering such a deity. These images, though, were balanced by others as we shall see.

In any event, given that promising is above all a social practice, then the pragmatic, not the "semantic" aspects of the remembered promises should be at the forefront of studies of their meanings and significances. "Remembered promises" indicates particular promises within the mnemonic and ideological landscape of the community. One of the best ways to construct a reasonable reconstruction of the pragmatic value of these promises in an ancient society is to examine the memories of these promises this sort of society holds, specifically in our case memories of core divine promises at the center of the social discourse of the literati of the period. This approach also opens the gates for a better understanding of the general discourse of the community. Clearly, the memories of the literati raised both settling and very unsettling issues about core divine promises.

Observations on Some Core Promises within the Community's Mnemonic Landscape

There is no doubt that there were a number of prominent core divine promises within the discourse and mnemonic world of the literati of the time, including the promise not to sweep away the entire world (the promise to Noah, Gen 8:21–22; 9:9–17), the promises of progeny and land for Israel (the promise to the patriarchs[9]), and, among others, promises of the royal and priestly lines. All these promises involved YHWH's obligations. For obvious reasons, the works included in the Deuteronomistic History–or as I prefer to call it, the Deuteronomistic Historical Collection (DHC)–and Chronicles evoked in the remembering

---

8 This line of thinking about "promises" generated and was activated by some memories encoded within the literati's authoritative repertoire of texts in the late Persian/Early Hellenistic periods, e.g., Exod 32:11–13; Jer 14:21.

9 The promise of the land was associated with the patriarchs also in Deuteronomy and the DHC (e.g., Deut 6:10, 23; 8:1; 10:1; 31:7; 34:4; Josh 5:6; 21:41–43). Whether or not אבותם originally referred to the patriarchs or the fathers of the generations who actually entered the land, it is clear that by the late Persian/early Hellenistic period, it was understood to be the patriarchs.

community more memories directly associated with the promises of land and of royal and priestly lines than those of progeny as numerous as the sand of the sea or of not undoing creation.

The land is certainly a central issue in Joshua and plays an important role in Judges as well. The conquest of the entire land was explicitly and saliently presented in the book of Joshua as a fulfillment of a divine promise (e. g., Josh 11:23; 23:14). But the late Persian/early Hellenistic, Jerusalem-centered literati who read the book of Joshua were also asked to construe and vicariously experience a past in which the entire land was conquered and simultaneously not conquered by Joshua (and YHWH; compare Josh 11:23 with Josh 13:1–6; also Josh 23:14 with Josh 23:1–5; and see Judg 1:1–2:5). Significantly, this tension did not lead to less social mindshare (or narrative space, for that matter) for the story. One should stress also that this tension was not hidden but explicit and for all to see. In fact, in the case of the conquest and non-conquest of the entire land, the relevant texts were even set in close literary proximity, so readers could not miss the point.[10]

Tensions such as these served here and elsewhere as attention getters and drew particular attention to the heart of the matter. Thus, they served significant didactic purposes (cf. Jonah).[11] But if so, what was the effect of remembering to-

---

[10] Examples of these and similar "logical" tensions appear in various texts and across genre boundaries. They are particularly common in prophetic literature and within the historiographical books; they appear not only in the DHC but certainly in Chronicles as well. To illustrate, the literati knew about YHWH's promise to Noah not to sweep away the world again (Gen 8:21–22; cf. Gen 9:9–17), but they also remembered a number of divine promises of future sweepings away of the created world, involving the massive killing of humans and animals (e.g., Zeph 1:2–3). Thus, YHWH was remembered as a deity who obligated itself both never to sweep the world away and to sweep it away. Similar cases appear, as it shall be discussed here, in the historiographical works. The existence of a variety of texts encoding and evoking memories that reflected, communicated, and negotiated "divine obligations" in similar ways is *only to be expected* given that (a) the community shared a social mindscape that underlies and makes sense of shared social practices including promises, and (b) systemic preferences and dispreferences in the construction of social memories–including those dealing with promises–are not a function of a particular literary genre or of some rhetorical requirements or preferences in a single or set of related texts.

[11] In its construal of the divine promises, the metaprophetic book of Jonah reminded the readers that the promises were carried out in more than one way, more than once, and at the same time not carried out at all. Accordingly, YHWH was construed in the book as a character who may fulfill its (self-)obligations, may not fulfill them at all, or may fulfill them in what, from the perspective of those receiving the promise, could be described as either a less-than-straightforward manner or even an intentionally deceptive manner–whether for good moral purposes or not. YHWH was construed as a deity doing all the above. See E. Ben Zvi, *Signs of Jonah: Reading*

gether both the presence and the absence of such a total conquest on the community, particularly in the ways it negotiated and thus constructed the meaning of promising as a social and pragmatic practice? Further, what could have been the effect of remembering that the promise of the land was given with full knowledge that its outcome would not last (e. g., Deut 30:20; 31:20–21; Josh 23:15)? Is this a "good faith" promise? And if not, what does it say about promising as a social practice? I will come back to these questions.

The promise of the land was not exclusively, or one may say even mainly, associated with memories of the (construed) period of Joshua within the text/memory-centered community in late Persian/early Hellenistic Judah. It is not by chance that their usual mnemonic cipher was "the land which I swore to Abraham, to Isaac, and to Jacob" or variants of it,[12] not "the land which I swore to Moses" or to "Joshua" or to their generation. To be sure, the remembered patriarchs never held or could have held possession of the "promised" land. The emphasis was thus on remembering the promise and its future fulfillment rather than remembering its fulfillment in a past that exists no more.

There is a second principle at work here as well. The remembering community could see themselves closer to the (for the most part) powerless patriarchs than to a mighty warrior and military leader such as Joshua and his militarily powerful Israel. In fact, the common principle of enhancing "contemporary" identification in shaping social memories was at work even in the characterization of Joshua. The latter was, of course, remembered within this context as the successful leader of a military conquest.[13] But at the same time, this sort of image is balanced in the book of Joshua by a tendency to lessen the weight of his mighty warrior image and attach to him other attributes (for example, a secondary Moses, a prophetic figure, a *torah*/text-centered literati), thus creating a site of memory with which the literati could more readily identify.[14] Do these tenden-

---

and, Rereading in Ancient Yehud (JSOTSup 367; Sheffield: Sheffield Academic Press and Continuum, 2003).
12 E. g., Gen 12:7; 13:15, 17; 15:18; 24:7; 26:3; 28:13; 50:24; Exod 3:8; 6:8; 13:5, 11; 32:13; 33:1; Lev 26:42; Num 14:23; 32:11; Deut 1:8; 6:10; 9:5; 30:20; 34:4; Jer 11:5; cf. Ps 105:9–11; 1 Chr 16:15–18.
13 E. g., Deut 1:38; 3:28; 31:7, 23; Josh 11:7, 10–13, 16, 18, 21, 23, 12:7; and cf. Exod 17:9–13.
14 One may note that mnemonic vignettes that emphasize the warrior-like character of the individual "hero" (e. g., 1 Sam 14:13–15; 18:7; 2 Sam 21:18–22) were not associated with Joshua. Moreover, it is Yhwh who defeats the enemy in all memorable reports. The walls of Jericho fell because of a ritual performance, not Joshua's military heroism. In the case of Ai, the successful ambush is devised by Yhwh, not Joshua (Josh 8:2). Cf. Josh 10:10–14. Significantly, the process of downgrading/lessening the relative weight of military/warrior features of great figures of the past was at work in the construction of Moses and Abraham and even in that of David. See espe-

cies indicate that, within the mnemonic landscape of the community, memories of promises that can be attached to characters with whom the community may more easily identify are more prominent than others?[15] And, in the case of positive promises, because of the principle of hope that is necessary for social reproduction, is it those promises that the society will tend to consider more "fulfillable," even if in the distant future?[16]

Whereas the "promised" land figures prominently in the book of Joshua, and to some extent in Judges as well, the promised king and his line figures prominently in the closely associated books of Samuel and Kings. This being so, it is particularly worth noting that this collection does not begin with David or a failed kingly foil to David such as Saul. Instead, it begins with and shapes a communal memory in which a lengthy apologia for the substitution of priestly with monarchic rule occupied a substantial section of memory-scape.[17] In any event,

---

cially Chronicles and Psalms and note the famous citation from J. Wellhausen (*Prolegomena to the History of Ancient Israel* [trans. A. Menzies and J. S. Black; Cleveland: Meridian, 1957], 182), "See what Chronicles has made out of David! The founder of the kingdom has become the founder of the temple and public worship, the king and hero at the head of his companions in arms has become a singer and master of ceremonies at the head of a swarm of priests and Levites." Of course, ancient Near Eastern warrior kings (for example, neo-Assyrian kings) were also described as pious, praying, and building temples. The issue is the relative weight of certain attributes in the overall construction of the memory of the king, rather than any either/or logic. Chronicles did not innovate as much as it shifted the balance of memory, and because it is also a historiographic work, the matter cannot be explained away as just an issue of genre (cf. Psalms). See G. von Rad, *Old Testament Theology*, vol. 1: *The Theology of Israel's Historical Traditions* (trans. D. M. G. Stalker, with an introduction by W. Brueggemann; Louisville, KY: Westminster John Knox, 2001), 350.

15 Of course, as in all cases of identifications with (construed) characters of the past, there are gaps that cannot be easily bridged. Take, for instance, the identification of the community with the patriarchs. The ancestors of the patriarchs never held–or in the case of Abraham never were in–the land, but the literati in Yehud construed themselves as descendants from those who (at least partially) held it. Their memory of former possessions of the land brought to the forefront a different perspective on the land and its promise. The literati remembered the fall of Jerusalem and its temple, exile, and even an empty land. For them, promises about possession of the land were not only something incongruent with their present situation or a pointer to a distant future but also a reminder of a lost past, whose loss was also promised.

16 Rather than the precise language of a text encoding memories of these promises.

17 It is worth noting that the traditional mnemonic narrative of a new ruler (that is, the "usurper") who brings down an impious regime and brings back order had to be extensively modified in this case. The ideological, generative grammar underlying Samuel–Kings could not allocate to David the traditional role of the "usurper" bringing down Samuel, the last priestly ruler; instead, it had to construe him as a kind of restorer of order supported by Samuel. In other words, it needed a transitional Saul figure to gloss over the fact that David's "restoration" of order is not a return to Samuel's days but a new beginning, by constructing Samuel himself as an active agent supporting David's kingship. Below, I discuss Samuel as a priest and successor of Eli. I

Samuel–Kings reminded the reading community in late Persian/early Hellenistic Judah that monarchy was not a "natural" situation for Israel,[18] and this reminder could not but have an effect on constructions of monarchic promises.[19]

Moreover, although Samuel–Kings contained clear references to the promise to David and evoked it (e. g., 2 Sam 7), the readers were introduced to the general matter of divine promises and their pragmatic meanings as social practices in 1 Sam 2:30. The text is presented as direct divine speech and is associated with a true prophet; in fact, it is the first divine speech in Samuel–Kings and involves the first instance of a prophetic speaker. The text here is blunt and explicit:

> נאם־יהוה אלהי ישראל אמור אמרתי ביתך ובית אביך יתהלכו לפני עד־עולם ועתה
> נאם־יהוה חלילה לי כי־מכבדי אכבד ובזי יקלו

> YHWH the God of Israel declares: "I promised that your [Eli's] family and the family of your ancestor should go in and out before me עד עולם"; but now YHWH declares: "Far be it from me; for those who honor me I will honor, and those who despise me shall be treated with contempt" (NRSV, with slight changes).

The text certainly communicates an interpretative key for negotiating the meaning of divine promises and whether YHWH was construed as necessarily obligated to keep and fulfill them. A few observations sharpen matters further. First, the YHWH of the text does not present the original divine promise as conditional (see vv. 27–28). To be sure, given the reason for annulling it in vv. 29–30, one may claim that the promise was implicitly construed as conditional. But, within this logic, any memory of a past or future "cancellation" of a divine promise that can be explained on account of impious behavior–in other words, almost any memory of a cancellation–would render any promise implicitly conditional. If this is the case here, then it is potentially the case everywhere. The lack of explicit reference to conditionality in vv. 28–29 turns this text into a very substantial interpretive key and a central place for analyzing the ways in which the community negotiated the meaning of divine promises, including core promises.

---

expanded elsewhere on the multiple implications of constructions of Samuel as priest within the discourse of late Persian/early Hellenistic Yehud/Judah. See "The Yehudite Collection of Prophetic Books and Imperial Contexts," in this volume, pp. 143–61.
18 It is worth noting that poignant sites of memory activated memories of explicit, interpretive divine communications (e.g., 1 Sam 8:7) that associated priestly rule over Israel with YHWH's rule over it.
19 The presence of this sort of apologia is not a given or something necessary just because there was no Davidic king in the remembering community, a point demonstrated beyond doubt by the absence of this apologia in Chronicles.

Second and directly related to the first observation, Eli's response to Yhwh's decision to break his promise to him and his house was יהוה הוא הטוב בעינו יעשה ('Yhwh, he will do what is good to him' or 'Yhwh, let him do what seems good to him' or 'He is Yhwh; he will/let him do what is/seems good to him'; 1 Sam 3:18). Although by all means this does not represent a strange position,[20] its implication is that, ultimately, Yhwh can overturn promises as Yhwh pleases.

Third, the explicit use of the expression עד־עולם shows that Yhwh was remembered as a deity for whom yesterday's "perpetual" was not *necessarily* today's or tomorrow's "perpetual." This construction of Yhwh has direct impact on constructions of the social practice of promising and vice-versa, and is at work elsewhere in the discourse of the community.[21] Further, the expression עד־עולם in connection with a divine promise of leadership within the context of the book of Samuel links this verse to divine promises to David (e.g., 2 Sam 7:13, 16; 22:51; cf. 2 Sam 7:25[22] and 1 Kgs 2:45) and comments on what, from the perspective of the remembering community in the late Persian/early Hellenistic period, were considered to be problematic aspects of such a promise; after all, there was no Davidic king over them.

Fourth, the explicit use of the language ובחר אתו מכל־שבטי ישראל 'I [Yhwh] chose him out of all the tribes of Israel' activates not only a reference to David (cf. 1 Kgs 8:16; 2 Chr 6:5; Ps 78:70; see also in relation to Solomon 1 Chr 29:1) but also, and perhaps more importantly, an expression that was mainly used in the historiographical books held by the community in reference to Jerusalem (1 Kgs 8:15–16; 11:32; 14:21; 2 Kgs 21:7; 2 Chr 6:5–6; 33:7; 1 Kgs 8:15–16//2 Chr 6:5–6 share with 1 Sam 2:27–28 also an association between the promise and the Exodus). This web of texts hinted at yet another possible way of negotiating the meaning of the broken promise to Eli, not instead but in addition to the one mentioned above, linking Eli and David. The promise to Eli may be approached as creating a mnemonic path and, one may say, an implied narrative linking the

---

20 Cf. 2 Sam 10:12; 1 Chr 19:13; Isa 45:9; Job 9:12; see also 1 Chr 21:23, which refers not to a divine king but to King David, as perceived from the perspective of Ornan. Note also the idea that no one can tell the king, divine or human, what to do (e.g., Qoh 8:4).

21 Similar considerations apply to the pentateuchal expression ברית עולם (see S. Mason, *"Eternal Covenant" in the Pentateuch: The Contours of an Elusive Phrase* [LHBOTS 494; New York: T&T Clark, 2008], with bibliography). None of this is surprising in view of the previous observation about promises as social practices within a shared social mindscape. It is also not surprising given that עד־עולם does not necessarily mean "eternal" (see, for instance, 1 Sam 1:22; 2 Sam 12:10; 1 Kgs 2:33) and thus its meaning is malleable according to the communicative circumstances in which it is used.

22 Note the different verbal forms used in vv. 24 and 25 and the rhetorical effect to which this difference is used.

broken promise to Eli to the discursively and ideologically far more crucial divine promise regarding Jerusalem. I will return to Jerusalem and the promise to keep it as the city of Yhwh's temple, Yhwh's capital city and as such as the cosmic center of the world, from the perspective of the mentioned community.[23]

Fifth, breaking the promise to Eli was conceptualized in terms of breaking the promise to his biological progeny. But the promise of priesthood was not conceptualized in these terms. After all, the text reported and the community remembered that an "adopted son" who was an Ephraimite, namely, Samuel, succeeded Eli.[24] Even if the community at one level was aware that the House of Eli continued serving as priests before the ark well after the events reported in 1 Sam 2–4 (see esp. 1 Sam 22:20 and 1 Kgs 2:27)–a matter that in itself calls for negotiating the pragmatic meaning of Yhwh's words in 1 Sam 2:2–and even if, contrary to the seeming logic of the narrative in this section of the book of Samuel, the כהן נאמן and בית נאמן of 1 Sam 2:30 were understood as references to Zadok and his house (see 1 Kgs 2:27), still the fact remains that Samuel was remembered as an important priest.[25] After all, he takes the place of the biological sons of Eli.

The implications of remembering Samuel as priest (not only as prophet or judge) were significant in terms of negotiating the meaning of the remembered divine promises of priesthood to a particular line. It certainly raised the issue of whether individuals who were not originally from Levi, or Zadok for that matter, may serve as priest. This issue was, of course, known to the literati and reflected and communicated in other authoritative works within the repertoire of the community (cf. Isa 56:6–7; 66:21, which raise the issue of originally non-Israelites priests). The issue is, of course, taken up also by Chronicles, which attempts to balance the memory of Samuel evoked by the book of Samuel by turning Samuel (and Elkanah, of course) into (genealogical/biological) Levites (1 Chr 6:12–13; most English translations 6:27–28) and thus trying to inform

---

[23] To be sure, Jerusalem was remembered as all these things, but at the same time not necessarily as a city that cannot be conquered or temporarily razed.

[24] Cf. R. Polzin, *Samuel and the Deuteronomist* (Bloomington: Indiana University Press, 1993), 42–43. The logic of the narrative, which contrasts Eli's (biological) sons with Samuel, makes that point unmistakable. To be sure, the community knows that Samuel later on loses his leadership position, but this sort of event was not associated with breaking the promise to Eli (see 1 Sam 2:31–36; 1 Sam 4).

[25] It is true that Samuel is not explicitly called "priest" in the narrative, but 1 Sam 2:11, 18–19; 3:1, and the salient contrast between Samuel and the sons of Eli, who are priests, between the old, corrupt order and the new order about to emerge, serve to characterize Samuel as a priest. The fact that 1 Chr 6:12–13 (most English translations, 6:27–28) turns him into a Levite is proof positive that Samuel was remembered as a priest by the late Persian/early Hellenistic period.

the community's reading of Samuel. The presence of various and conflicting voices attests to the fact that the reading was well inside the boundaries shaped by the social mindscape of the community.

Moreover, this is just one aspect of a more general issue that directly affects the community's understanding of a central, hereditary divine promise within the discourse of the community, namely, the promise/s regarding Israel. Are those who were not genealogically Israel allowed to become Israel? The answer seems not always, but for the most part positive (e. g., Isa 14:1), and given the tendency to "priestize" Israel,[26] this answer was not irrelevant to the pragmatic understanding of the hereditary promise to Levi.[27]

On the surface, at least, to the literati of the late Persian/early Hellenistic period, memories of divine promises to Levi or *some* of his descendants did not seem in need of negotiation in the same way as memories of the promise to David were. After all, there were legitimate priests in Jerusalem at that time, as the literati knew very well,[28] but there was no Davidic king in Jerusalem or hope for one to emerge in the normal course of worldly events.

There is no question that the promise to David figured quite prominently in the memory-scape of the community. Multiple texts, across various literary genres, evoked that site of memory many times, directly and indirectly.[29] The question is, however, how this promise was negotiated by the community in response to their circumstances and their core memory of the fall of Jerusalem and the monarchic polity. The previous survey shows that the memory of the fate of the divine promise to the House of Eli shaped one possible response: namely, the community could construe the divine promise to David as cancelled. This sort of

---

[26] This tendency is encoded in and communicated by texts across genre boundaries, because it played important (and generative roles) within the discourse of the community and thus was bound to emerge in various places. See, for instance, Exod 19:6 and Ps 114:2; cf. Lev 19:2.

[27] Cf. "The Yehudite Collection of Prophetic Books and Imperial Contexts" in this volume, pp. 143–61.

[28] The Jerusalem-centered literati of the late Persian/early Hellenistic period were not only obviously aware of the existence of the temple in Jerusalem, which by itself requires priests to function, but were probably supported by the temple and its priests. On priests and literati at that time see E. Ben Zvi, "Observations on Prophetic Characters, Prophetic Texts, Priests of Old, Persian Period Priests and Literati", in *The Priest in the Prophets. The Portrayal of the Priests, Prophets and Other Religious Specialists in the Latter Prophets* (eds. L. L. Grabbe and A. O. Bellis; JSOTSup 408; London: T&T Clark, 2004), 19–30. (The distribution of roles among the "sons of Levi" and especially that of the "Levites" when this term is used in contradistinction to "priests" was very much a debated issue, but the matter cannot be discussed here.)

[29] See 2 Sam 7:1–17; Ps 89:29; 132:1–18; also 2 Sam 23:5; 1 Kgs 8:23–24; 15:4; 2 Kgs 8:19; Isa 55:3; Jer 33:14–26; 2 Chr 13:5; 21:7.

approach was consistent with other memories of divine promises, with conceptual approaches to promises as social practice, even if projected to the realm of deity, and with some characterizations of and memories of Yhwh.[30]

Moreover, because the promise to David was generally understood as a promise to reign over all Israel, not Judah alone,[31] remembering that Jeroboam could have had an enduring house (בית נאמן)[32] involved already a renegotiation over the meaning of the divine promise to David. In this case, the renegotiation strongly narrowed its scope and, despite explicit rhetoric to the contrary, carried by itself the possibility of further narrowing and renegotiation.[33] To be sure, Chronicles did not shape a mnemonic narrative in which Jeroboam could have had a divinely appointed enduring house.[34] Instead, significantly, Chronicles reshaped causality. Whereas in Kings it is because of sins that the promise is renegotiated, in Chronicles it is quite the opposite; Yhwh decides to divide the kingdom during a pious period. Whereas Kings evoked in the mnemonic community

---

30 Of course, it is also consistent with the generally agreed position, by now, that the covenant of David–and other covenants as well–was conditional. See, for instance, McKenzie, "The Typology of the Davidic Covenant" and M. Avioz, "The Davidic Covenant in 2 Samuel 7: Conditional or Unconditional?" in *The Ancient Near East in the 12th–10th Centuries* BCE: *Culture and, History. Proceedings of the International Conference Held at the University of Haifa, 2–5 May, 2010* (eds. G. Galil, A. Gilboa, A. M. Maeir, and D. Kahn; AOAT 392; Münster: Ugarit-Verlag, 2012), 43–53 and literature cited there. S. L. McKenzie encapsulated the point, stating, "The Davidic promise was always subject to Yahweh, not the other way around" (idem, "The Typology of the Davidic Covenant," 177). I will return to this quotation. For the general conditionality of covenants/promises, see recently S. Mason, "'Eternal Covenant' in the Pentateuch" (and cited literature). Mal 2:4–9 assumes that the covenant is conditional. In fact, readers were asked to imagine and remember Yhwh trying to help the offending party (the priests) to hold the covenant (see esp. Mal 2:4). But one has to keep in mind that within the world that the literati construed covenants–like all types of divine promises–could at least potentially be cancelled by the deity without a humanly understandable reason.
31 The point that David is promised to rule over "(all) Israel" (i.e., not just Judah) is clear from 2 Sam 7 (and its context) and the same position is implied in texts such as Jer 33:14–16; Ezek 37:22–25; Hos 3:5.
32 See 1 Kgs 11:38.
33 In fact, one may claim that the forceful rhetoric to the contrary (see 1 Kgs 11:32, 34, 36) emerged as a response to the implications for the "eternal" value of Yhwh's promise to David and reflected some uneasiness about them. One is reminded of the famous expression "The lady doth protest too much, methinks," *Hamlet*, Act 3, Scene 2, 230.
34 The same holds true for LXX Kings. See A. Schenker, "Jeroboam and the Division of the Kingdom in the Ancient Septuagint: LXX 3 Kingdoms 12.24 a–z, MT 1 Kings 11–12; 14 and the Deuteronomistic History," in *Israel Constructs Its History: Deuteronomistic Historiography in Recent Research* (eds. A. de Pury, T. Römer, and J.-D. Macchi; JSOTSup 306; Sheffield: Sheffield Academic Press, 2000), 214–57.

typical images of punishment for sin (and the conditionality of all divine promises), Chronicles evoked a sense that Yhwh does as Yhwh wishes, and at times Yhwh's decisions cannot be explained by humans, including the implied author of Chronicles.[35] But this being so, and because Yhwh's path was construed as not always explainable or predictable and Yhwh was construed as sovereign, then just as Yhwh can promise, Yhwh can revoke his promises, without any understandable reason. Paraphrasing S. L. McKenzie, one may say that, within the discourse of the community, divine promises were always subject to Yhwh, not the other way around.[36]

But the fact that the community could potentially imagine the promise to David as cancelled does not mean that they always had to imagine it as such. Other ways of negotiating the meaning of the promise to David existed in the community. The promise could be and was at times construed as relevant to the future and yet to be fulfilled. This approach is explicitly manifested in and communicated by some texts in the prophetic books that shaped images and memories of a utopian future in which a highly elevated Davidide plays a central role.[37]

The fact that these images are attested in and evoked by prophetic but not historiographical books is not grounded on discursive or ideological differences within the community but on genre constructions. Prophetic books could and did construe memories of the past and the future; historiographical books were meant to shape memories of the past. The main narrative of the "national" histories was organized around kings and kings' regnal periods. These "national" histories had to conclude, in the main, with the last king of Judah.[38] Prophetic

---

[35] See E. Ben Zvi, *History, Literature and Theology in the Book of Chronicles* (London: Equinox, 2006), 117–43. The underlying ideological stance was common in the general discourse of the period and played an important balancing role in terms of allowing the community to make sense of the world. Its centrality in the social mindscape of the community is attested by the fact that such a stance is reflected in and communicated by, directly and indirectly, various texts held by the community, across boundaries of genre and topic. See, for instance, 1 Sam 3:18; Isa 45:9; Job 9:12; Prov 19:21; 20:24.

[36] See n. 30.

[37] See, for instance, Isa 9:5–6; 11:1–9; Jer 23:5–6; 30:8–11; 33:14–26; Ezek 34:23–30; 37:15–28; Hos 3:5; Amos 9:11–15; Mic 5:1. This Davidide of the utopian future was remembered by the community as a highly elevated human being (see Isa 9:5–7; 11:1–9; Hos 3:5), very different from the community's memories of monarchic David or Solomon as evoked in the "historical" books.

[38] The reason is simple: books such as Kings and Chronicles could not have continued their periodization of history and their organization of time around local kings, as required by their basic character as "national," polity-centered histories. Adopting a strongly ideological, framing structure based on the regnal periods of Achaemenid kings was, for obvious reasons, not a good option and was certainly not taken up. This means that this sort of construction

books certainly did not have such a limitation. The only thing historiographical books could (and did) do was to allow the community to hold the hope for a future, utopian Davidic renewal by leaving open the door for the continuation of the line of David.[39]

But other ways of negotiating the promise existed. For instance, the rebuilder of the temple within social memory at the time, namely Cyrus, had to be both a foreign king and also partially Davidized, because as rebuilder of the temple he is a kind of "second David."[40] This trend is attested by and communicated by books as diverse as Chronicles and Isaiah; it shaped and evoked a basic mnemonic narrative that moved from David to Cyrus, from temple to temple.[41]

It is easy to understand that, within the discourse of the period, the meaning of the promise to David was renegotiated also to mean the promise to Israel. This is due to the related processes of (a) ideological "royalization" of Israel; (b) remembering David, particularly the sinful and heavily punished David, as embodying and symbolically representing Israel, and thus contributing to shaping a shared conceptual realm that includes both David and Israel; (c) numerous memories of a utopian future in which Davidides play no role,[42] but Israel does; and (d) explicit memories of a utopian future that do not mention David

---

and periodization of "national" history can reach only to the end of the monarchy, and indeed both Kings and Chronicles end their main narratives at that point, even if both include an "afterword" notice, and the one in Chronicles is particularly significant. To be sure, books within the repertoire of the community may still contain references to the regnal years of Achaemenid kings (e.g., Ezra, Nehemiah, Haggai, and Zechariah), but obviously these are not comprehensive "national," polity-centered histories as Kings and Chronicles are.

39 See G. N. Knoppers, *I Chronicles 1–9* (AB 12. New York: Doubleday, 2004), 332–36, and literature cited there. As for the end of Kings, see I. D. Wilson, "Joseph, Jehoiachin, and Cyrus: On Book Endings, Exoduses and Exiles, and Yehudite/Judean Social Remembering," in *ZAW* 126 (2014): 521–34 and literature cited there.

40 The same applies to Zerubabbel, the Israelite/Yehudite associated with the building of the temple who ended up being construed as a Davidide in 1 Chr 3:19 and is elevated in Hag 2:21–22. Of course, through the centuries other figures were associated with Davidic lineage (e.g., Jesus, Hillel, R. Judah HaNasi). Processes of Davidization did not completely stop. For a recent example, see the case of David Koresh and his founding of a "davidic kingdom." (One may note that Ben Gurion mused, though very briefly, about a "Third Kingdom of Israel.")

41 The highly elevated character of the construed and remembered Cyrus of the literati contributed to this characterization (and vice versa). On the elevated character of Cyrus, see, for instance, Isa 44:24–28; 45:1–8, 11–13. J. Goldingay describes all of Isa 44:24–45:25 as "the triumph of Cyrus" (idem, *The Message of Isaiah 40–55: A Literary-Theological Commentary* [London: T&T Clark, 2005], 253–300). See also Isa 48:12–15.

42 See, for instance, those evoked by Isa 40–66; Jer 50:4–5, 19–20; Ezek 16:60; Hos 2:18–22; 14:6–9; Obad; Zeph 3.

but in which the ברית is with the people (Jer 50:4–5). The "classical" text expressing this approach is taken to be Isa 55:3–11, but a similar, underlying trend can be detected also in Chronicles. There was a tendency in Chronicles to renegotiate the fulfillment of the promise to David in communal and above all temple-centered terms. Chronicles suggested to its readers that they could construct the fulfillment of the promise to David through the prism of the existence of the (present or future utopian) temple and (present or future utopian) temple-centered Israel.[43] Above all, from a conceptual perspective, Chronicles reminded the community that the typical association between Davidic kings and the temple in Jerusalem and the divine legitimization of monarchic rule associated with temple building/establishing activities were now transferred to the community in Yehud.[44] Some version of this point was made also in Kings,

---

[43] Commonly mentioned texts in this regard are 1 Chr 16:22; 28:20, and the lack of reference to Davidides within the community of 1 Chronicles 9; the common exchange from David's house/kingdom to Yhwh's house/kingdom (e.g., 1 Chr 17:14; 28:5; 29:23; 2 Chr 13:5, 8); and the quasi-royal characterization of Jehoiada the priest in 2 Chr 23–24, which goes as far as possible given the constraints of imagining a priest in the monarchic period but includes even a note about his burial among the kings of Judah (see in particular 2 Chr 23:16, 18–19; 24:3, 12, 14–16). This construction of Jehoiada was likely a projection of a utopian priestly, Jerusalemite ruler like the one the community wanted to have, made to fit within a narrative and mnemonic world of a past, monarchic/Davidic Judah. (For an alternative, but also non-Davidic, non-monarchic Israel and its leadership, see 2 Chr 28:8–15; see E. Ben Zvi, *History, Literature and Theology in the Book of Chronicles*, 223–31.) There is considerable debate as to whether Chronicles shows a royalist, messianic tendency or a non-royalist, non-messianic, communal and temple-centered tendency, and to what extent these agendas are future and possibly utopian and present focused–the latter in particular, but not exclusively, for the non-royalist, communal/temple-centered agenda. For a recent survey of many of the important positions taken in research on the matter and substantial bibliography, see M. Boda, "Gazing through the Cloud of Incense: Davidic and Temple Community in the Chronicler's Perspective," in *Chronicling the Chronicler: The Book of Chronicles and Early Second Temple Historiography* (eds. T. Williams and P. Evans; Winona Lake, IN: Eisenbrauns, 2014). I would argue that all these "voices" are present in Chronicles and that they complement and balance each other, but certainly do not "cancel" each other out. I would further argue that it is the intertwining of these multiple voices that represents both the discourse of the period and the "voice" of the implied author of Chronicles as construed by the literati in the late Persian/early Hellenistic period.

[44] This holds true even if the command to "build" the temple is associated with Cyrus (and through Cyrus with Yhwh) and even as I argued elsewhere, even if the temple was *partially* (and only *partially*) construed as an Achaemenid enterprise. This is not the place for a substantial discussion of these matters; it suffices to notice that to "build/establish" the temple, proper knowledge is necessary–including knowledge of the place where it should be erected, of its basic pattern, and above all of its proper service. It is not by chance that according to Chronicles, the main "builder" of the temple was David, not Solomon, the king who actually built it. In the Persian period, it is the community that is responsible; Cyrus was not imagined as knowing

through the subordination of the temple to *torah* (see the story of Josiah's scroll),⁴⁵ because the *torah* is Israel's and not (only) the Davidic king's.

Tendencies to negotiate the promise to David in communal terms were at work elsewhere in the prophetic books, prominently in the construction of Yhwh's servant, which clearly contains elements of royal and even "imperial" imagery, but also likely in the image of the future king in Zech 9:9.⁴⁶

One may mention also that when a group was engaged in a political project that failed catastrophically (its fall was accompanied with extreme calamity) and that had no chance to succeed under any foreseen circumstances, the group may reconstrue itself and its identity in cultural/religious terms and thus may construe itself as engaged in a cultural/religious project.⁴⁷ This shift from political to cultural/religious project is consistent with the identification/transformation of King David with/to a temple centered community.

This draws attention to a variety of ways in which the community could and did renegotiate the divine promise to David. It could be understood as broken, as yet to be fulfilled, as referring to a highly elevated Davidide or to the people or to Cyrus, and any combination of these. Each of these understandings manifested itself across various literary genres and with subvariations. Each emerged out of

---

Moses' and David's instructions for a proper Jerusalemite temple, as construed by the community. Moreover, the act of "building/establishing" the proper temple/cult was not imagined as complete once for all. In monarchic times, Davidic kings were construed as responsible for ensuring that the temple was established/run properly, that is, according to Moses and David's instructions on their own times–which involved, from time to time and as necessary activities such as cleansing the temple, ensuring proper cult, proper cultic community and (re)building as necessary, or lack thereof when kings failed in their tasks. Within the discourse of the community, all these roles were now construed as Israel's, as was *torah*.

45 E.g., T. Römer, "Du Temple au Livre: L'idéologie de la centralization dans l'historiographie deutéronomiste," in *Rethinking the Foundations: Historiography in the Ancient World and in the Bible* (eds. T. Römer and S. L. McKenzie; BZAW 294; Berlin: De Gruyter, 2000), 207–25.

46 The king may be read as a personification of Israel/the community. See D. L. Petersen, *Zechariah 9–14 and Malachi* (OTL; Louisville, KY: Westminster John Knox, 1995), 58–59; A. M. Leske, "Context and Meaning of Zechariah 9:9," CBQ 62 (2000): 663–78.

47 Cf. the construction of Judaism and Christianity after 70 BCE, and of Judaism in the light of the failure of Bar Kochba's rebellion. From a completely different period and circumstances, compare the recreation of (white) Southern identity after the American civil war. See, for instance, C. R. Wilson, *Baptized in Blood: The Religion of the Lost Cause 1865–1920* (Athens, GA: University of Georgia Press, 2009) and W. Schivelbusch, *The Culture of Defeat: On National Trauma, Mourning and Recovery* (New York: Metropolitan Books, 2001), 37–101; and notice the contrast between the case of the American South with that of other national projects discussed in this volume, which despite national trauma and military defeat, and unlike the case of the American South, continued to be advanced.

a socially shared, implied generative grammar, and each manifestation informed the others. These understandings together provide a representation of the general discourse of the community.

But where do these considerations leave us in terms of better understanding the pragmatic meanings of divine promises? Certainly, remembering the past evoked by the DHC, the Primary History (Genesis–2 Kings), Chronicles, other past-construing texts, as well as remembering the future vicariously experienced by reading prophetic books, raised both "settling" and very "unsettling" issues regarding core divine promises for the community. At the conceptual level, all promises were breakable, but they were also "promises," that is, "obligations."

How could the community approach and negotiate these matters within its discourse? As is well-known, conceptual tensions are often addressed in societies through shared narratives and metaphors that provide them with a "language" to deal with these issues. In our case, the most promising option was to rely on the shared conceptual fields of two constructions that held much mindshare and generated multiple sites of memory in the community: (a) the ברית between Yhwh and Israel and (b) the marriage between Yhwh and Israel, and particularly so because the concepts of ברית and marriage were clearly associated with one another within the social mindscape of the community (Mal 2:14; Prov 2:17). If the concept and social practice of ברית informed those of marriage, then, from the perspective of the community, the latter was likely to, at least partially and implicitly, inform the former.

The community knew well that, in social practice, marriages could be dissolved and promises broken. They "knew" that marriages could be dissolved because of the fault of the bride(/Israel) or just because the husband(/Yhwh) desired so. But they tended to imagine marriage as enduring and hoped that the one between Yhwh and Israel would last or at least would be renewed. Just as they remembered Yhwh as knowing well ahead of time that Israel (/Jerusalem) could not but fail as Yhwh's bride and was thus involved in a social practice that would normally be associated with lack of "good faith" in the performance of promises, they also remembered a Yhwh who will in the future change Israel so it would be able to succeed as Yhwh's bride.

But this metaphorical conceptual frame had its limits too. To illustrate, the community remembered that some divine promises were only partially fulfilled and others were from the outset for a limited time only (such as royal promises for a certain number of generations). None of these work well with the marriage metaphor. Even more importantly, this approach provided no discursive/imaginative tools to address crucial questions such as which divine promises were more or less likely to be broken.

All in all the community construed and remembered promises as breakable, enduring, of short term value, fulfilled, partially fulfilled, not fulfilled, made in good faith and in bad faith. But if so, what can we learn about promises and particularly divine promises and their pragmatic value within the discourse of the community?

Can we discern within this sort of discourse systemic patterns of preference and dispreference that may help us toward a reconstruction of which promises were more easily understood as breakable, which had to be seriously renegotiated and which, although conceptually were considered potentially breakable, were for all practical purposes imagined to be unbreakable or close to unbreakable? Was there a socially shared implied logic governing these matters and thus their pragmatic construction of promises and memories of promises? What does this logic, if it existed, tell us about the community?

Pragmatic Differentiation among Promises in Late Persian/Early Hellenistic Judah

Because potentially all promises could be construed, negotiated, renegotiated and the like in the ways mentioned above, the governing logic is most likely not to be found in variances in the social practice of promising, or in the actual words of the remembered promises. After all, the wording was always influenced by rhetorical needs, and in any case, the same promise could have been reflected in and communicated by various texts, each with its own wording, or for that matter in a semantic attitude toward the meaning of obligation.

The governing logic was more likely grounded in the question of the social cost for the community involved in the various constructions of remembered, core divine promises. For instance, the transtemporal Israel that the literati construed within their discourse and with which they identified could exist and was remembered as existing in the land and outside the land, with a Davidic king on the throne and without him, with a built Jerusalem and functioning temple and without it. The social memory that bonded the group together proved that to be the case. But this Israel could not exist without being imagined as Yhwh's people/wife/son/flock/etc. without divine instruction, without Jerusalem's being construed as Yhwh's wife/selected city/city at the center of the world. The latter required the existence of a divinely approved temple and worship, whether these existed as a shared mental image or as a built space in the "real" world, or both. Thus, promises associated with Yhwh's choice of Israel, Jerusalem and divine instruction, irrelevant of the metaphor or the words involved, strongly tended to be pragmatically remembered as enduring and permanent. The cost of seriously and genuinely doubting whether these promises were or will be in effect in the future carried social and ideological costs too high for processes of shaping self-identity and social reproduction. Doubts of this sort would have raised a strong sense of existential anxiety about the future or identity of the community.[48]

To be sure, a temple required legitimate priests and legitimate teachers (be they priests, prophets, both or none). These were construed as necessary to communicate the divine instruction to the people. Thus, genuinely doubting the continuous existence of priests and teachers carried a very high cost. Surely, negotiating who was or will (or could) be a priest or legitimate teacher is another matter. Accordingly, the pragmatic meaning of the relevant remembered promises could be open for multiple interpretations, within limits: the very existence of priests and teachers could not be at risk.

Unlike promises associated with Yhwh's choice of Israel, Jerusalem and divine instruction, the promise of David was much negotiated.[1] On the one hand, this is consistent with the lower cost for the community of a genuine consideration of the possibility that the promise has been revoked. On the other hand, the fact that it was so saliently negotiated shows that the divine promise to David was a central site of memory and as such attracted to itself multiple interpretations, each encapsulating and communicating main "voices" interacting and complementing each other within the general discourse of the period. In fact, the divine promise to David became a site of memory/tool that facilitated communal thought and imagination about possible futures, the very character of Israel and the ways in which past, present, and future utopian Israel were continuous and discontinuous with each other. Perhaps this is why it was so much negotiated.

---

48 Of course, the promise of progeny belongs to this category as well.
49 To be sure, the community in the late Persian period remembered that monarchic Jerusalem and its temple were destroyed in the past and the people went into exile, a point hammered down time and again, directly and indirectly in the core repertoire of texts of the community. But this was not the point. The point was that the community neither construed nor remembered Yhwh's choice of Jerusalem, Israel, and *torah* as alterable or contingent on human behavior. In other words, the community did not seriously entertain, explore, or consider alternatives such as a resignifying Israel to mean non-Israelites, Jerusalem to mean a city other than Jerusalem, or a divinely ordained "*torah*" different from the one they held to be Yhwh's *torah*. But it could explore whether the promise to David was rescinded or not; whether the promise may have been "democratizèd" or even partially "Persianized."

A Contribution to the Intellectual History of Yehud: The Story of Micaiah and Its Function within the Discourse of Persian-Period Literati*

Stories carry messages. The more salient or memorable a story is in a particular discourse, the more effective it will convey its message; and, conversely, the more a good story reflects and reflects on fundamental concerns and deeply held worldviews within a group, the more likely that the story will become prominent among its members. Stories, and particularly prominent stories, tend to provide a discursive way to relate to "truths" that are explicitly or, more often, implicitly agreed upon within the group, but whose members find difficult to express or to express sharply by other means. As such, these stories are important tools for historians who wish to reconstruct the worldviews of particular groups in the past.[1] The present study focuses on some aspects of the account of Micaiah, for the sake of shedding light into some features of the worldview of ancient Israel.

The story of Micaiah appears both in 1 Kgs 22 and 2 Chr 18, with very minor textual changes–though, unavoidably, not only within a different *Sitz im Buch*, but within a different *Buch* altogether.[2] It is the only prophetic story about the prophets of the kingdom of Israel that is shared between Kings and Chronicles, and one of the very few prophetic stories that are really shared between the Deuteronomistic historical collection/history and Chronicles.[3] This uncharacteristic pattern of occurrences within ancient Israel's histories already suggests that this story is simply not one among many others, but one that played some significant role in the memory and ideological discourse of ancient Israel.

---

* First published in *The Historian and the Bible. Essays in Honour of Lester L. Grabbe* (eds. P. R. Davies and D. V. Edelman; LHBOTS 530; London and New York: T&T Clark, 2010), 89–102.
1 Jonah is an excellent example of a memorable story serving these purposes admirably (see E. Ben Zvi, *Signs of Jonah: Reading and Rereading in Ancient Yehud* [JSOTSup 367; Sheffield: Sheffield Academic, 2003]). It is my contention that the same can be said of the story of Micaiah, the son of Imlah.
2 For a textual comparison of the text of the story in the MT Kings, MT Chronicles, and the LXX versions, see S. J. De Vries, *Prophet Against Prophet: The Role of the Micaiah Narrative (1 Kings 22) in the Development of Early Prophetic Tradition* (Grand Rapids: Eerdmans, 1978), 11–24. On the contextual divergence between Kings and Chronicles, see below.
3 For a discussion of some potential reasons for the inclusion of this story in Chronicles, see below. On this matter, see also A. Rofé, *The Prophetical Stories* (Jerusalem: Magnes, 1988), esp. 205.

The story is certainly at the core of 1 Kgs 22, which in itself is an important section within Kings as it deals with the fall and death of Ahab.[4] The latter is, of course, one of the most prominent northern characters in the book of Kings. Ahab and Jeroboam 1 are in fact the two northern Israelite kings that take the most "real estate" in the social memory of the literati of ancient Israel. Their actions were considered paradigmatic, and their reconstructed reigns and actions served to shape core myths and communicate central ideological positions in Jerusalem-centered historical narratives.

The story may have had a long redactional history and may have originally been associated with a king other than Ahab; moreover, it might have found its way into a forerunner of the present book of Kings at a relatively late stage in the redactional process that led to the present book. Notwithstanding the importance of these debates, the present study focuses on the story as presented to the primary readers of the (present compositional form of the) book of Kings (and of Chronicles, of course). If the primary readers of the book of Kings were somewhat similar to the intended readers of the book–which in itself is a most reasonable assumption–then they would have read the story as associated with Ahab (and Jehoshaphat), as explicitly stated in the text, and as an integral part of the book of Kings in general and its extended account of Ahab. For the intended readers of Chronicles, the story had to do with Jehoshaphat (and Ahab; see below). Whatever previous stories might have existed about Micaiah, by the Persian period these were superseded by the story advanced in both Kings and Chronicles. Moreover, this is the story that became part of the literati's social memory of, and facts agreed upon, the monarchic past. Studies on the intellectual discourse of and social memory in Yehud, such as this one, must focus on that story, not any possible, though by necessity hypothetical, forerunner.

---

4 On these matters, see, among others, De Vries, *Prophet Against Prophet*, 4–6, 25–51; W. Roth, "The Story of the Prophet Micaiah (I Kings 22) in Historical-Critical Interpretation: 1876–1976" in *The Biblical Mosaic: Changing Perspectives* (eds. R.M. Polzin and E. Rothman; Philadelphia: Fortress, 1982), 105–37; G. H. Jones, *1 and 2 Kings*. 2 vols. (NCB; Grand Rapids: Eerdmans, 1984), 2:360–62; B. O. Long, *1 Kings* (FOTL 9; Grand Rapids: Eerdmans, 1984), 233; N. Na'aman, "Prophetic Stories as Sources for the Histories of Jehoshaphat and the Omrides," in *Bib* 78 (1997): 153–73; A.F. Campbell and M. A. O'Brien, *Unfolding the Deuteronomistic History: Origins, Upgrades, Present Text* (Minneapolis: Fortress, 2000), 25, 405–7, and the bibliography cited in these works. For a less common perspective in these matters, see A. G. Auld, "Prophets Shared–But Recycled" in *The Future of the Deuteronomistic History* (ed. T. Römer; BETL 147; Leuven: Leuven University Press/Peeters, 2000), 19–28 (23–24), and for a response to his position, see S. McKenzie, "The Trouble with King Jehoshaphat" in *Reflection and Refraction: Studies in Biblical Historiography in Honour of A. Graeme Auld* (eds. R. Rezetko, T. H. Lim, and W. B. Aucker; VTSup 113; Leiden: Brill, 2004), 299–314 (305–6).

Within 1 Kgs 22 the story of Micaiah takes more narrative space than the actual report about Ahab's death.[5] The story not only leads to, but provides an interpretative frame for, Ahab's death. It shapes the narrative account of his death in Kings and its representation in the social memory of ancient Israel. These features, of course, made the story memorable.

The story (in both Kings and Chronicles) contains, in addition, numerous additional features that enhance its memorable character. These include, among others, a set of impressive personages and settings, both in earth and in heaven, and including one scene in the heavenly court and another–which serves as its counterpoint–in a major open court meeting on earth. These scenes evoke, among others, images of two great kings on earth, of Yhwh, the divine council, hundreds of prophets. The story, in both versions, contains a number of sharp twists and reversals in the plot that accentuate suspense and irony, and keep the attention of the readers by running often against their basic expectations.[6] It carries also numerous visual details meant to engage the imagination of the readers and maintain a hold in their memory, from royal robes to symbolic iron horns. Common popular motifs such as inquiring the deity before battle, reversal of fortunes, the one versus the many, the face-off between the seemingly powerless but pious person and the powerful and sinful man figure prominently in the story. Moreover, the story deals not only with the eventual success of the pious who may observe the heavenly court (see the contrast between Micaiah and Ahab), but also and perhaps far more importantly from the perspective of the readers, with the fate of the struggling pious, who although essentially good, may be temporarily mistaken and misguided (see Jehoshaphat).

The presence of familiar or familiarizing features such as those mentioned above is constantly put in proportion in the story by the presence of de-familiarizing motifs. For instance, rather than bringing forward the image of the lone prophet of Yhwh confronting prophets or worshipers of other deities (see Elijah in 1 Kgs 18, which is also set in the reign of Ahab), it brings forward the image of

---

5 The boundaries of these literary units are porous and can be reconstructed in different ways, but one may say that the story spans from v. 6 (or even v. 3) to 22 and the report of Ahab's death from vv. 29–38.
6 "We expect Jehoshaphat to follow the advice of Micaiah; he does not. We expect Micaiah to tell the truth; he does not, at least not at first. We expect Ahab not to press for the truth; he does. We expect Yahweh to tell the truth; he does not" (D. Robertson, "Micaiah ben Imlah: A Literary View" in *The Biblical Mosaic: Changing Perspectives* (eds. R. M. Polzin and E. Rothman; Philadelphia: Fortress, 1982), 139–46 (146); cf. M. Sternberg, *The Poetics of Biblical Narrative: Ideological Literature and the Drama of Reading* (Bloomington: Indiana University Press, 1987), 406–7). To which we may add, among other things, that in the world of this text the secret divine council carries no secrets, whereas the public meeting of the war council does bear them.

the single godly prophet of YHWH confronting the very same deity's many prophets. Instead of simply narrating a case in which a prophet reveals divine knowledge, it breaks too easy boundaries around what is actually revealed by the deity by projecting a world in which the hidden partially stands for what is actually revealed and what is revealed ends up being partially hidden, at least from the perspective of the characters in the story.

Features like those mentioned above substantially contribute to the continuous revisiting of the story and the associated site of memory by the intended and primary readerships of Kings and Chronicles. But there is more. As if there were not enough markers to substantiate the point that the story was written and set to be memorable and, most likely, well remembered, many aspects of this story were strongly connected to other stories within the world of knowledge of the relevant literati. For instance, it partially echoes aspects of (1) the story about Elijah and his confrontation with the prophets of Baal in 1 Kgs 18,[7] (2) the confrontation between Jeremiah and Hananiah in Jer 28, and (3) other instances of images of meetings at heavenly court (e.g. Isa 6 and Job 1–2, which may be later than Kings, but not necessarily than Chronicles).[8] As the story of Micaiah evoked aspects of other stories and vice versa, attention was drawn to both similarities and dissimilarities, and a web of texts informing each other emerged (see Ben Zvi "Towards an Integrative Study"). This connective character of the story of Micaiah further contributed to its place within the memory of ancient Israel and its repertoire of stories.

Since all the features mentioned above, except the role of the story within Kings, and specifically 1 Kgs 22, apply equally to the story in Chronicles, for the present purposes suffices to note that within Chronicles it is part and parcel

---

[7] Note the motif of the public prophetic confrontation, of the lone genuine prophet vs. the many (even the numbers given to the many echo each other), and of the endangered life of the prophet which raises the issue of potential martyrology, as well as the obvious association of both prophets (Elijah and Micaiah) with the memory of Ahab. To some extent, one may even consider the presence of Micaiah in this story/memory as a replacement for absence/expected presence of Elijah in the central prophetic story about the death of Ahab. The text, however, is "normalized" as the attention of the readers is brought back to Elijah's words in 1 Kgs 22:38, as the story of Ahab comes to a close (cf. 2 Kgs 21:19). At that time, Elijah's presence in the form of his words comes to the forefront, and, as it does, the figure of Micaiah disappears. There are, of course, additional reasons for the reference to Elijah's words (see 1 Kgs 21:23; 2 Kgs 9:36).

[8] Among recent works on the heavenly court (and its secrecy) within an ancient Near Eastern context, see A. Lenzi, *Secrecy and the Gods: Secret Knowledge in Ancient Mesopotamia and Biblical Israel* (SAAS 19; Helsinki: The Neo-Assyrian Text Corpus Project, 2008) and M. S. Kee, "The Heavenly Council and Its Type-scene," in *JSOT* 31 (2007): 259–73.

of the regnal account of Jehoshaphat's reign (not Ahab's).[9] Thus it is not surprising that it contributes to the characterization of this king who is particularly important in Chronicles, though significantly it makes also a very substantial contribution to the shaping of an underlying, connoted characterization of the House of Ahab in Chronicles as one that exerted some irrational attraction for the Davides, even among the best of them, as demonstrated by our very story. Since, according to Chronicles, the Davidic kings were never supposed to become allies or partners of the northern kingdom, the very existence of the House of Ahab and its allure brought incommensurable danger to the House of David. From a more general perspective that takes into account the situation of the intended and primary readers, the House of Ahab becomes as a quasi-mythical symbol of the potentially fatal allure of evildoers for true followers of YHWH.[10] Thus the story of Micaiah plays a prominent role in Chronicles as well.

Since the story of story of Micaiah was repeatedly marked to be so salient, and most likely was so salient within the discourse of Yehud, it is reasonable to assume that it served as a very effective conduit for messages to the community/ies of primary readers of Kings and Chronicles. As other highly connected stories that took much "real estate" in the memory of the past held, at least, among the literati in Yehud, it stands to reason that this story was substantially aligned with fundamental concerns and deeply held worldviews within these literati. But if this is so, which "truths" explicitly or implicitly agreed upon among them were effectively touched on and effectively communicated by this popular story? Or, in other words, what may have these literati dealt with and learned about as they imaginatively visited the imagined, socially shared site of memory created by the story and as they observed Micaiah, Jehoshaphat, Ahab and all the other characters in the story, including, of course, YHWH and the divine council?

---

9 For a study of the story in Chronicles that pays close attention to its language and context, see J. A. Bergman, *Narrative Analogy in the Hebrew Bible: Battle Stories and Their Equivalent Non-Battle Narratives* (VTSup 103; Leiden: Brill, 2004, 181–98. For studies of the account of Jehoshaphat in Chronicles as a whole, see R. Dillard, "The Chronicler's Jehoshaphat," *Trinity Journal* 7 (1986): 17–22; G. N. Knoppers, "Reform and Regression: The Chronicler's Presentation of Jehoshaphat," in *Bib* 72 (1991): 500–24; S. McKenzie, "The Trouble with King Jehoshaphat."
10 See E. Ben Zvi, "The House of Omri/Ahab in Chronicles", in *Ahab Agonistes: The Rise and Fall of the Omri Dynasty* (ed. L. L. Grabbe; LHBOTS 421; ESHM 6. London: T&T Clark, 2007), 41–53. The position of Chronicles on these matters is influenced by the image of the House of Ahab in Kings, on which see idem, "Are there Any Bridges Out There? How Wide Was the Conceptual Gap between the Deuteronomistic History and Chronicles?" in *Community Identity in Judean Historiography: Biblical and Comparative Perspectives* (eds. G. N. Knoppers and K. Ristau; Winona Lake, Ind.: Eisenbrauns, 2009), 59–86.

To be sure, visits to (mental or "real') sites of memory activate and engender social memory, and social memory is about constructing a shared past. Thus the literati could not but learn about the personages that populate their story and their (construed) past, as well as their circumstances. Yet neither Kings nor Chronicles were simply antiquarian; nor were their intended and primary rereaders interested in simply learning and sharing images of the past, for their own sake as it were. Instead, both Kings and Chronicles were didactic histories aimed at teaching ideological/theological lessons, instilling a certain attitude of the mind and socializing the literati and those influenced by them into a particular worldview. Thus the central question returns: What did such a central and significantly remembered story convey to the literati in terms of "truths"?[11]

A good starting point for approaching this matter is the plain observation that Micaiah is characterized by Ahab (and, in fact, presented to the reader for the first time) as a prophet of YHWH who never prophesies anything for Ahab but disaster (1 Kgs 22:8//2 Chr 18:17). This first, salient, and basic presentation of the prophet serves narrative goals: it sets the scene for the central confrontation between two central pairs of characters in the story (Ahab and Micaiah; and Micaiah and the other prophets) and provides the necessary ground for the motif of reversal of fortunes. But this is not all, or even the main issue for the present analysis. Readers were supposed to learn from the experiences of agents populating their historical memory, both their successes and their failures. This didactic aspect is certainly one of the main (systemic or underlying) reasons for asking them to mentally re-visit these sites of memory, and to a large extent for history writing and learning in antiquity. This aspect requires that the reader be aware not only of the eventual decisions of (construed) historical agents, but also the circumstances in which these agents reached their decisions.[12]

This being so, the primary readers of the story cannot but note that Micaiah never prophesied anything for Ahab but disaster, and that at the time of the events Ahab was at the height of his power. Thus, obviously, Micaiah's previous and consistent prophecies of misfortune have not come to pass at that time. If the test for true prophets is that their prophecies come to pass, then from the per-

---

[11] These questions, far from being marginal to the task of reconstructing the historical events during the reigns of Ahab and Jehoshaphat, are central not only to studies of the books of Kings and Chronicles, of ancient Israelite historiography and its social roles in Achaemenid Yehud, but also for the study of the intellectual discourse in Yehud, without which one cannot advance any intellectual history of Yehud.

[12] This is at the core of the widespread approach to past events which uses them as a guide for how to behave (or not to behave) in the present.

spective of Ahab (and Jehoshaphat's as well) Micaiah should have been considered a false prophet at the time when they summoned him, whereas those who prophesied good for Ahab up to this moment should have been considered by them true prophets (cf. Deut 18:22; 1 Sam 3:19; 1 Kgs 8:56; Jer 28:9; Ezek 33:33). Of course, the story clearly shows to the readers, who are all too aware of the eventual fate of Ahab, that fulfillment criteria for truthfulness in prophecy were not only unreliable, but also actually misleading at the time.

But the issue is not left to rest there. Significantly, but not surprisingly in a story full of inversions, the readers were asked to pay attention to the fact that the very same Ahab, and most importantly Micaiah (and likely Jehoshaphat as well), are explicitly described as accepting the very validity of the fulfillment test for prophecy in 1 Kgs 22:27–28//2 Chr 18:26–27, even if they (and Jehoshaphat) seemed to have (correctly) rejected it up to that point. This sudden shift plays a communicative role in the narrative as it serves to characterize the protagonists in the story as believing, correctly again from the perspective of the readers, that this time a final confrontation is about to take place. But whereas the implied author's knowledge of the end of the story may shape the characterization of its literary personages, it is necessarily hidden from historical agents, including the readers as they run their own lives.[13] This being so, the logic of the story suggests that historical agents cannot know when the principle of fulfillment of prophecy is reliable or dangerously misleading. The principle is thus presented to the readers as both valid and invalid, with no clear way of for them in real life to decide which is which, or more precisely, when which is to be held true or untrue.[14]

One may argue that the story of Micaiah suggests that in such circumstances it is wise for agents to hedge their bets and in any case to exercise caution when opposite prophecies are announced. This is what the narrative seems to suggest. Both Ahab and Jehoshaphat are depicted as having kept Micaiah's prophecy well

---

13 Historical agents can never know "the end(s)" of the narrative(s) their lives create.

14 One may argue that the intended and primary readers may have imagined that Ahab (and Jehoshaphat) considered that Micaiah's (earlier) prophecies have not come to pass *yet*, but may come true at some point in the future (cf. Isa 30:8), whereas those of other prophets who prophesied success, although they already came true, might end up "untrue," because of some reversal of fate to take place in the future. But of what use for historical agents are prophecies whose value may shift from one extreme to another in a fully unknown temporal scale? To be sure, such prophecies may fulfill rhetorical purposes in stories about the past and may contribute to the shaping of narratives, but are of no use to historical agents in the "real" world. They are of no use to the primary readers of this story either in Chronicles or Kings in terms of their own formation as (historical) agents and as teachers of (historical) agents in their "real" world.

in their minds, as the story about the disguise during battle indicates. Yet hedging bets is a behavior that implies awareness and knowledge of the impossibility of knowledge on these matters.[15] Moreover, the issue at stake does not actually require multiple or conflicting prophecies. The readers know that no matter what Micaiah would have pronounced, and even without his presence altogether, the prophecies of the 400 would have failed to come true. Whether prophecies are one or many, whether similar or not, the matter raised by the logic of the text concerns the very understanding of prophecy.

But the text does not stop there. The question of prophecy is approached from a second, vivid, attention-getting, complementary and, to a large extent, converging perspective in Micaiah's story. The readers were explicitly asked to construe prophecy as a manifestation of the/a "Empowering Spirit" serving YHWH and therefore as an officer of and in YHWH's heavenly court. The text advances a personification and individualization of that Empowering Spirit (note הרוח in 1 Kgs 22:21//2 Chr 18:20[16]) that makes it comparable to the divinely appointed commissar for examining the loyalty of YHWH's servants referred to as השטן in Job 1–2, while at the same time balancing these features by stressing its ability to morph into (though it would never be fully contained in) a truthful or a misleading spirit in the mouth of prophets, that is, to be manifested among humans as prophecy. Thus the text emphasizes that prophecy truly originating from the divine court may provide both true and false knowledge. Human agents, of course, do not have a clear way to discern, at least in real time, which is which. (Micaiah's reply to Zedakiah [see 1 Kgs 22:24–25// 2 Chr 18:23–24] only emphasizes that such is the case by resorting to the principle of future fulfillment).

The text does not stop there either. The readers were also told in the story that the mentioned un-knowability is not grounded in the abilities of the Empowering Spirit who produces prophecy among human prophets, but in YHWH's character. Not only does the deity fully control this Spirit, as well as

---

15 Cf. J. L. Crenshaw, who concludes that due to the contradictions associated with prophetic conflict, "the public ... found prophecy lacking and turned elsewhere for spiritual direction, namely to apocalyptic and wisdom ..." (*Prophetic Conflict: Its Effect Upon Israelite Religion* [BZAW 124; Berlin: De Gruyter, 1971], 111).

16 To be sure, the use of the article ה does not necessarily mean that the following noun has to refer to a noun/referent specifically defined in the context (see, for instance, B. K. Waltke and M. O'Connor, *An Introduction to Hebrew Syntax* [IBHS] (Winona Lake, Ind.: Eisenbrauns, 1990), § 13.5.1.e). However, if the referent, is an officer in the court, then the metaphor leads to individualization. For another position, see R. B. Chisholm Jr., "Does God Deceive?" in *BibSac* 155 (1998): 11–28 (15).

any of the deity's officers in the divine court, but Yhwh can decide and at times actually comes to an operative decision to provide deceitful knowledge to human beings through prophecy for purposes that Yhwh might find appropriate.

This image of Yhwh was influenced by notions about the power of and the resources lawfully available to the earthly kings, whose courts helped people imagine the heavenly one. Strategic misinformation was an acceptable resort used by kings to achieve their goals. Thus, as one would expect, Yhwh–the ultimate king–was imagined as actually commanding or incurring in the use of misinformation not only in Micaiah's story, but also in other texts, such as Gen 18:12–13; Exod 3:22; 1 Sam 16:2 (see Shemesh 2002, esp. 85–87, and bibliography cited there).

Strategic misinformation could be and was often used to cause harm to opponents. Of course, within a non-dualistic worldview such as the one that existed during the Persian period, this is not a real problem since Yhwh must be conceived of as the creator of good *and* evil (cf. Isa 45:7), and thus able to create knowledge and mis-knowledge among humans, as well as different impediments to their ability to discern between the two as the deity deems appropriate (Exod 9:12; Isa 6:9–10).[17]

At the same time the image of Yhwh creating mis-knowledge is likely to cause some underlying anxieties within the discourse of the literati.[18] Divinely ordained mis-knowledge, or one may say mis-teachings, may take the form of prophetic announcements. Yet there is no reason to stop there. They can certainly take the form of divinely ordained חקים ומשפטים (see Ezek 20:25).

---

17 Cf. Crenshaw, *Prophetic Conflict*, 77–90. Crenshaw's characterization of this aspect of Yhwh as "demonic" and of הרוח in the story as associated (at that time) with notions of an evil spirit or demon, are problematic within the discourse of Persian period Yehud. The same does not hold true, of course, within other discourses. Indeed, although the text clearly refers to this רוח יהוה (see v. 24 and the general context of the divine court), later exegetes working within very different theological discourses and attentive to the latter's logic concluded that הרוח is either Satan (R. L. Mayhue, "False Prophets and the Deceiving Spirit," in *TMSJ* 4, no. 2 (1993): 135–63 and previous works mentioned there) or a demon (e.g. Aquinas, *Summa Theologica*, Question 172, article 6; Aquinas attempts to explain away some of the implications of the text than are mentioned above). It is worth noting, however, that a contrary position, namely that הרוח stands for none other than the Angel Michael was also advanced in antiquity (see Isho'dad of Merv [ca. 850], *Books of Sessions* on 1 Kgs 22:20; ET in M. Conti, *1–2 Kings, 1–2 Chronicles, Ezra, Nehemiah, Esther* [Ancient Christian Commentary on Scriptures; Downers Grove: InterVarsity, 2008], 136). R. Y. Kara maintains that he does not know what this רוח is; Rashi associates it with the spirit of Naboth, following *b. Sanh.* 102b, and see also Rambam, *Mishneh Torah*, Nezakim 4.13. Again, the reasons for this identification are theological.

18 And, of course, in discourses of later times as well. Already Josephus drops the entire court scene in *Ant.* 8 (see esp. § 406).

The most damaging potential discursive and ideological anxieties that such an understanding could have caused were easily fenced off by the association of past mis-teachings to either unworthy messengers or, and most importantly, by assuming that strategic mis-information was aimed only at harming the enemies of the king/YHWH. Thus, even if Moses was also construed as a prophet and divine ordained חקים ומשפטים were central to YHWH's *torah*, there was no real danger within the discourse of the text-centered community in Yehud that the *torah* would be considered "mis-information" or bad teachings meant to hurt Israel.

However, concerns about human inability to discern between divine messages or teachings that carried information and those that carried mis-information were more difficult to be fully dismissed when they, concerned less foundational matters and characters. Moreover, any easy way of solving matters by simply associating mis-information exclusively with sinful individuals is explicitly undermined by the very story of Micaiah, which involved (a) the many prophets who are not characterized as sinful, (b) Jehoshaphat–perhaps a temporally misguided, but not a sinful leader–and in which and not incidentally, (c) Ahab was portrayed much better than his usual image in other texts and in the memory of the literati. The matter is further compounded by the presence and importance in Yehudite ideological discourse of the idea that good characters may be, or even are, likely to be tested by the deity.[19] When does a test become harm, and when is harm a test? How can historical agents go beyond the veil of "unknowability" that may surround divine messages and teachings, whether in the form of oral prophecies or grounded in a "reading" of worldly events as communicative expressions of a divine will and mind?[20] How to deal with these concerns and anxieties?

One way of dealing with these was to explore them from the safe perspective of a very memorable story that comforts its readers by relating, among other things, the fall of the evil king, the triumph of the one over the many, the safe return of a pious, but for once misguided, character (Jehoshaphat), and perhaps even at least a connoted sense of divine willingness to give even a sinner like Ahab one more chance (see Moberly 2003; Hamilton 1994). This story is about

---

[19] I have expanded on this issue in "When YHWH Tests People: General Considerations and Particular Observations regarding the Books of Chronicles and Job," in this volume, pp. 472–81. This image is particularly important in Chronicles, but present in or informing numerous texts as well, including those in the Deuteronomistic History.

[20] That is, the basic approach according to which the world and historical (and personal) events/developments/trajectories are a "book" that can be "read" to learn about the deity and the deity's ways. This approach has a very long history in the ancient Near East, including ancient Israel, and beyond.

Yhwh's power, probably Yhwh's goodness and about "happy endings." It reinforces traditional beliefs about Yhwh's ability to punish evil, destroy villains and overthrow their machinations, just as it unequivocally emphasizes the deity's ability to easily overcome human-made substitutions meant to confuse or derail Yhwh's plans.[21]

Yet, at the same time, as in the case of Gen 18 or Jonah,[22] it is precisely because it provided a safe harbor that it allowed the literati to explore such dangerous waters as what is "true" in divine communication, how an historical agent can know, and, perhaps above all, what "true" may mean in this context. Significantly, the literati, as they reread the story and re-visited this virtual site of memory, encountered again and again a truthful revelation of the events in the heavenly court that can be dismissed on seemingly unassailable logic–given the circumstances–by Yhwh's prophets and Jehoshaphat. Moreover, the divinely planned dismissal of such a true image of the events at the council substantially contributes to the achievement of the goal for which a deceitful divine prophecy was created and sent. Thus, as they read the story and visit this site of memory, they noticed that precisely the word of Yhwh that carries mis-information does *not* return to the deity empty, but accomplishes that which Yhwh has decided, to paraphrase Isa 55:11, and thus fulfills at least one of the tests for truthful prophecy accepted in the discourse of the literati of Yehud.[23] Of course, to stress that test

---

[21] The story about the perceived replacement of Ahab with Jehoshaphat may be (a polemic) play on the theme of a substitute king who takes upon himself the misfortune announced for the king. The story tells the reader that Yhwh can easily frustrate any "crafty" design meant to derail Yhwh's actions.

[22] On Gen 18, see E. Ben Zvi, "The Dialogue between Abraham and Yhwh in Gen 18:23–32," in *JSOT* 53 (1992): 27–46. The memorable story of Jonah also communicates, at one level, a sense of comfort and "happy endings"–no one dies in this prophetic book, everyone can repent, and Jonah is educated by Yhwh. Jonah also provides "safe harbour" that allows it readers to explore "dangerous waters," including those associated with limits to human knowledge and prophecy. Cf. the Micaiah story. (On Jonah, see E. Ben Zvi, *Signs of Jonah: Reading and Rereading in Ancient Yehud* [JSOTSup 367; Sheffield: Sheffield Academic, 2003].)

[23] These considerations along with the characterization of the 400 prophets in the story and the explicit divine origin of their prophecy undermine attempts to frame the story of Micaiah as a confrontation between true and false prophets. Although, as mentioned above, the story evokes other confrontations, it clearly breaks from that model. There are no false prophets/pseudo-prophets in the story. All the prophets here are false to a degree and truthful to a degree–or better, they are true and divinely inspired (and controlled) in their own way. This point contributes much to the very core of the story and its role in ancient Israel. Of course, it is troublesome to decide which of these options is precisely the point (see below). Ii is possible that the LXX already began to neutralize the issue by moving in the direction of disassociating the 400 from Yhwh (see A. Lenzi, *Secrecy and the Gods*, 262 n. 184), a trajectory followed later by

is tantamount to stress the inability of human agents to distinguish in real time between divine mis-information and information, and to underscore the gap between the divine and the human realm and the ability of those in the latter to evaluate the messages that may originate from divine (see Isa 55:8–11).[24]

But how do they know or are even able to explore these matters? By reading authoritative books (such as Kings, Chronicles) and revisiting (virtual) sites of memory both shaped by and reflected in these texts. Of course, books need readers and interpreters, and then comes a book such as Jonah that not only involves itself in meta-prophetic considerations, as in the Micaiah story, but also stresses that the limitations on true knowledge that may affect those who "know scripture," that is, the literati. This may lead us away from, but not necessarily beyond the lessons that the literati could have learned from the story of Micaiah, though we have to keep in mind that the primary readers of Chronicles, at least, most likely read Jonah and were aware of Kings, and that late Persian-period readers of Kings were most likely aware of Chronicles and Jonah.

In a nutshell, the position I advance here is that unsolvable issues/problems within a particular worldview often call for narratives that allow those who uphold such a worldview to explore these matters safely and to express and communicate "truths" that are difficult for them to express. Historians whose aim is to understand the worldview held by a particular group may find these (often memorable and popular) stories to be an excellent source for reconstructing which "truths" were difficult to express in that historical discourse, and which unsolvable matters troubled people at the time, as well as their discourse and particularly its inner logic and cohesion, be these matters at the overt or underlying level. The story of Micaiah, along with Jonah and Gen 18, provides a good example. As in the case of the other stories, the point of the Micaiah story was not to provide a definitive, unequivocal answer, but to allow an exploration of matters that troubled the literati and reflected their awareness of systemic limitations to their knowledge. In these cases, stories served simultaneously both to underlie and undermine the shared discourse of a community. Moreover, and most significantly for studies of intellectual history, these stories and particularly Micaiah's deeply and intricately had interwoven underlying with undermining

---

Josephus. Compare and contrast the positions advanced concerning this matter with, for instance, J. L. Crenshaw, *Prophetic Conflict*; E. G. Dafni, "רוח שקר und falsche Prophetie in I Reg 22," in *ZAW* 112 (2000): 365–86.

24 Isa 55:8–11 is an important meta-prophetic comment. A. Rofé notes in relation to the ideology conveyed by this text that "Rather than the Word being fulfilled, it *fulfills* ... The true purpose of the Word of God can never be known, as His thoughts are beyond human comprehension, just as the heavens are beyond the earth" (*The Prophetical Stories*, 170 [original emphasis]).

and vice versa. When they seem to underlie this shared discourse, they carry messages that seem to undermine it; and, conversely, as they seem to undermine this discourse, they carry messages that buttress it. Just as in Micaiah's story, the hidden may be revealed, the revealed may be hidden, truth may be deception, deception may be truth, multiple tests for true prophecy are both right and wrong at the same time, reliable and misleading, and the readers, the actual historical agents, remain with no sure anchor, except for an awareness about these matters through their continuous reading of communally shared texts and revisiting of communally shared memories.

It is my pleasure to dedicate this essay to Lester, who has contributed so much to the topic of the Historian and the Bible in general, and to the history of Yehud in particular.

When Yhwh Tests People: General Considerations and Particular Observations Regarding the Books of Chronicles and Job*

The King said to the appointed commissar[1] for examining the loyalty of his servants, "Where have you come from?" The commissar answered the King, "From touring and walking about your kingdom in official business." The King said to the commissar, "Did you notice my servant Job? There is no one like him on my kingdom, a blameless and upright man who is fully loyal to me and turns away from treason." Then the commissar answered the King, "Is Job loyal to you for nothing? Have you not put a fence around him and his house and all that he has, on every side? You have blessed the work of his hands, and his possessions have increased in the land. But stretch out your hand now, and touch all that he has, and he will curse you to your face."

This paraphrase of Job 1:7–11 explicitly brings to the forefront the image of a meeting of a royal court in which matters concerning the loyalty of servants to the king are part of the agenda.[2] This image recalls a well attested way by which ancient communities used to imagine or attempted to understand the heavenly kingdom, namely by using representations of earthly kingdoms. Such an approach, however, carried substantial discursive and ideological consequences, because some of the systemic attributes of earthly kingdoms became discursive matrices for the construction of understandings of the heavenly one or its attributes.

The present study does not deal with all possible images, but with the ideological topos of divine testing. The preceding text from the book of Job suggests that at a very basic level the image of divine testing was shaped around, or based on that of the search by earthly kings for (secret) information about the trustworthiness of their servants. If this is the case, one is to expect that: (a) at least some of the considerations that apply to the way in which kings either deal or are imagined to deal with these matters informed to some extent the shaping of images

---

* First published in *Far From Minimal: Celebrating the Work and Influence of Philip R. Davies* (eds. D. Burns and J. W. Rogerson; LHBOTS 484; London and New York: T&T Clark, 2012), 11–20.
1 Gordis used the term "prosecutor attorney." See R. Gordis, *The Book of God and Man* (Chicago: University of Chicago Press, 1965), 70.
2 See L. K. Handy, "The Authorization of Divine Power and the Guilt of God in the Book of Job: Useful Ugaritic Parallels," in *JSOT* 60 (1993): 107–18. Cf. idem, *Among the Host of Heaven* (Winona Lake, Ind.: Eisenbrauns, 1994), 121–22.

of divine testing, and (b) the influence of these considerations on portrayals of YHWH in literary texts be present across different genres or narrowly defined ideological viewpoints within the accepted discourse(s) of the relevant readers, because these consideration are grounded on basic trends within these discourses, and not on singularities of genre or ideological approach.

For obvious systemic reasons, centers of power were concerned with assessing whether its powerful and seemingly loyal servants were indeed trustworthy.[3] Although the allegiance of all inhabitants within the realm to the king was certainly an ideological requirement, that of people in positions of power was considered essential for maintaining and effectively exercising the king's rule. These people included high-level representatives of the king, governors, high military officers, as well as individuals of renown who were influential in society.

YHWH was similarly construed as one for whom the loyalty and love of its subjects[4] is of paramount importance. But just as in the case of earthly kings, not all subjects were equal good candidates for YHWH's testing. To begin with, just as in the earthly realm, there was no conceivable need for a probe into the degree of loyalty of those who evidently rejected the deity and its rules. Their lack of allegiance was known and deserved no further comment, though it may, within these discourses, have merited action. Thus one does not find in the Hebrew Bible, for instance, a report about YHWH's testing of Athaliah's loyalty and devotion to the deity. In fact, it is anticipated that the more a personage seemed to embody the values of loyalty and commitment to YHWH, the more likely candidate she or he will be to stand as the main object of a tradition of a divine test. To be pious or seemingly pious was, however, not the only feature associated with characters who were good candidates for a divine test. The correlation between images of the earthly and heavenly king raised additional criteria. For instance, high-level representatives of the king, regents, governors, high military officers, as well as individuals of renown who were influential in society were far more likely to be tested than ancient counterparts of contemporaries Jane or Joe Doe. As a result, the set of candidates for assessment was likely to consist of characters constructed within the discourse of the community as loyal and effective regents of YHWH on earth, those who either led or seemed to have led society to a greater level of fulfillment of YHWH's laws and the associated blessings, or who by their influential, exemplary role served both as ideo-

---

3 Cf. queries # 150–74, 274–75, 293, 299–305 in I. Starr, *Queries to the Sungod: Divination and Politics in Sargonid Assyria* (SAA IV; Helsinki: Helsinki University Press, 1990), 161–82, 254–55, 276–77, 282–86.

4 All subjects were considered "servants" of the king. No significant distinction between the two terms is made here.

logical role models, and as attestations of the goodness that comes from accepting Yhwh's yoke fully. To be sure, if these characters were to embody, in some way, the mentioned goodness, they were likely to be portrayed as rich, materially or otherwise. But this being so, they became discursive candidates for the suspicion of loving more the good things they received from Yhwh than the deity itself. Just as in the case of earthly individuals who were recipients of the goodness of the monarch, the logic of the discourse suggested that if their love was mainly for the goods provided to them by the king than the king himself, they will be prone to cease to be loyal to the monarch if these goods are taken away, or when some alternative monarch promises them even more goods. In other words, if they fall into this category, they cannot be trusted. Thus, within this type of ideological discourse, as opposed to actual realia,[5] these characters become good candidates for a test that involves the withdrawal of divinely endowed goods.

These general considerations are consistent with the inclusion of characters such as the following within the category of recipients of Yhwh's test: (a) Abraham, after he has been endowed with a particular son; (b) Job who has been blessed continuously with progeny and wealth; (c) kings such as David, Asa, Jehoshaphat, Hezekiah, Josiah in Chronicles, all of whom were tested after receiving substantial blessings of one sort or another; (d) Israel or any Israelite who within certain ancient Israelite worldviews come to assume at least partially the role usually associated with the king in the ancient Near East, after they are given blessings such as divine precepts to live by and the land; and perhaps even (e) Adam and Eve, who are also characterized as regents of the deity on earth.[6]

These didactical stories about divine tests communicated multiple meanings. To be sure, their intended and primary readers (hereafter, for the sake of simplicity only, "the readers") were certainly supposed to learn from them about Yhwh and the manner in which Yhwh governs the world. To some extent,

---

[5] For obvious and systemic reasons, in the socio-political reality kings did not go about systematically depriving their best leaders of their possessions, just to check on them.

[6] See Gen 3; 22; Deut 8:2; 13:2–4; Judg 2:21–22; 3:1–5; the book of Job; 1 Chr 21:1–30; 2 Chr 14:8–14; 16:1–10; 20:1–30; 32:1–23, 31; 35:20–25; cf. Ps 17:3; 26:2. Exod 15:25, at the very least, connoted a sense of divine test of Moses. The story about Joseph and Potiphar's wife in Gen 39 can also be seen as a test story. Significantly, here Joseph passes the test but as a result is thrown into jail rather than being rewarded. To be sure, from the perspective of the target readership, Joseph's time in jail is necessary for the advancement of Yhwh's plan concerning Joseph's future and Israel's future, though the character Joseph is not construed as aware of these divine plans as he is sent to jail for his pious deed.

the readers were supposed to identify with the deity and its concerns about the degree of reliability or loyalty of its representatives on earth, as well as, on questions about whether the actions of these representatives enhanced or diminished the deity's honor in the sight of other human beings. It is worth stressing that these considerations suggest an image of Yhwh as one who is lacking crucial information about some of the deity's most notable servants. For instance, was Yhwh portrayed in Gen 22 as fully cognizant of Abraham's actual willingness to go ahead and sacrifice Isaac, before the actual test? The language of Gen 22:12 clearly suggests that this was not the case.[7] Similarly, it is likely that the readers of Chronicles were not urged to imagine Yhwh as a deity that has sure foreknowledge about how the pious kings being tested in Chronicles were to perform under the stress of the divine test.

These stories also asked their readers to identify with pious heroes of the past such as Abraham, Job, David, Hezekiah, and Josiah. But once matters were seen from this perspective, the discursive and ideological topos of the divine test served to explain a set of troubling issues, namely: Why does pious behavior lead and why has it actually led at times to misfortune for the pious? How should dutiful people conceptually approach and what should they should actually do, if or when they face this type of circumstance? In other words, these reports about divine test served to explain a world that was construed as reflecting a divinely ordained cosmos of law and order, but still one in which pious people and particularly, though not necessarily, leaders not only may not be rewarded for their actions, or even one in which calamity befalls them, but a world in which, from the perspective of the readers, there seems to be a direct relation between dutiful attitude and deeds towards Yhwh and being the target of Yhwh's calamity, contrary to common expectations. In fact, these stories construe Yhwh as free, and to some extent expected to test Yhwh's best servants,[8] and by doing so, to bring misfortune to them.

---

7 Gen 22:12 reads: כִּי עַתָּה יָדַעְתִּי כִּי־יְרֵא אֱלֹהִים אַתָּה וְלֹא חָשַׂכְתָּ אֶת־בִּנְךָ אֶת־יְחִידְךָ מִמֶּנִּי ("for now I know that you fear God, since you have not withheld your son, your only son, from me," NRSV).

8 Of course, if testing is conducted in the opposite direction, namely humans testing Yhwh, then it is construed as a rebellious attitude that significantly would make the testers liable to be disqualified as objects of the only legitimate source of testing. Thus, divine testing is one among a set of ideological and discursive concepts that served to shape and communicate a strongly asymmetrical relationship between Yhwh and human beings, including the most pious. For another example of this set of concepts, when a person in the Hebrew Bible is portrayed as "knowing Yhwh," at the core of that concept is that she or he acknowledges at the very least the rule or power of Yhwh (cf. M. Malul, *Knowledge, Control and Sex: Studies in Biblical Thought, Culture and Worldview* [Tel Aviv–Jaffa: Archaeological Center Publication, 2002],

Significantly, the accounts of these tests seem to imply the presence of a rhetorical shade: that of a "cynical" reader who may wonder about the practical difference between being thrown into a similar severe misfortune as punishment for sins or as a test reserved only for the pious. Many of these didactic texts were deeply involved in persuading their readers that similar or even identical manifestations may be grounded in opposite reasons and behaviors and may be conceptually different. This is, of course, a central point in the book of Job, but it is also clearly present in Chronicles, in which, for instance, a foreign invasion of Judah may reflect either divine punishment of a sinful monarch (e.g. Joash in his later years) or divine testing of a pious one (e.g. Hezekiah).[9] A crucial interpretative question in these cases is, of course: Which is which?

The potential instability of meaning that results from this situation is confronted at the level of the readers but also reflected in the situation of the main characters within the world of the narrative. In the books of Chronicles and Job, this instability is certainly and emphatically erased at the level of the textually inscribed narrators and authorial voices because these voices unequivocally disambiguate the ideological situation. But the same readers were still urged to identify themselves with those being tested, and through their experiences to partake vicariously in the personages' experience of a potentially ambiguous world.[10]

It is well beyond the scope of a single essay to provide a comprehensive study of the many facets of these ideological and rhetorical images of divine testing and their various uses as conduits to address central discursive matters in ancient Israel/Persian Yehud, and above all to make sense of the world as manifested to them, in their constructions of their past, as well as in their conceptualization of their own present and future hopes. This type of study can be carried out only in a monograph fully devoted to these matters, or perhaps in a Ph.D. thesis. But within the scope of the present study it is still possible to show how these general observations hold true across boundaries of literary genres and are relevant to the understanding of books as diverse as Chronicles and

---

passim), but when YHWH knows a person, this certainly does not mean that YHWH acknowledges his or her rule over YHWH's (see, for instance, 2 Sam 7:20; Nah 1:7; 1 Chr 17:18).

9 There is widespread agreement that these and similar invasions represent as a test for the king. See S. Japhet, *The Ideology of the Book of Chronicles and Its Place in Biblical Thought* (BEATAJ 9; 2nd ed.; Frankfurt am Main: Peter Lang, 1997), 191–98.

10 The character Job strongly attempts to disambiguate it as he consistently proclaims his personal innocence from a wrongdoing that is proportional to the calamity. His repeated claims on the matter are to reflect the "objective" ambiguity of his situation.

Job.[11] This observation, in turn, bears significant implications, which will be addressed later.

The following examples from Chronicles suffice to confirm that the main conceptual framework for divine testing described above is at work in Chronicles. The readers of 2 Chr 14:1–4 learned that Asa was a very pious king. Not only did he lead a purge of improper cults and cultic objects (e.g. high places, foreign altars, pillars, *asherim, hammanim*), but also commanded Judah to seek Yhwh and observe the *torah* and the commandments. Further, the readers learn that their evaluation of Asa at this point is shared by Yhwh, for the deity blessed Asa (and his kingdom) with tranquility and peace. Moreover, they noticed that Asa built cities and fortified the kingdom, which are actions that in Chronicles point at divine blessing (2 Chr 14:5–7). But as the narrative seems to reach the climax of the positive description of Asa, the readers are told that Zerah, the Cushite, invaded the land with a million-man army. The same Yhwh who till now given peace and prosperity because of Asa's behavior, is here behind the removal of these blessings, by means of an invasion of the land by the most powerful army within the world of the book, even when Asa's behavior has not changed at all.[12] The poignant paradox is explicitly and strongly underscored by the literary proximity between the climax of the positive characterization of Asa and the account of the invasion, and the explicit reversal motif (i.e. from peace and tranquility to war). As they continue reading,

---

11 For instance, the book of Job includes a large core of poetry; Chronicles is a narrative work. Job is a piece of wisdom literature; Chronicles is a historiographical work. The book of Job, as a whole, centers on a particular test and the actions and words of two main protagonists, Job and Yhwh. (The words of Job's "friends" serve to enhance the characterization of Job and his predicament, and that of readers who identify with him.) Chronicles, on the other hand, is clearly not a book about one divine test, but a history, in which there appear numerous human characters. Unlike Job who is a wealthy leader of much influence in his time, but not a king, the main human, individual characters in Chronicles are kings, and those are the most likely to be tested, if they are pious. Since Job is not a monarch, the main deeds of piety one expects the text to associate with him are personal and relate to him and his family. In the case of the kings who populate the narrative in Chronicles, similar acts of piety would likely involve, among other things, purges of improper cultic behavior, establishment or re-establishment of the proper worship, the leading (back) of Judah/Israel to Yhwh and to the observance of the Yhwh's *torah*, and the like. Whereas the blessings of an individual such as Job are expressed in terms of progeny, material wealth, and honor among his peers, a king's blessing (although it may include all these things) is likely to incorporate peace and tranquility as a major component.

12 From the perspective of the discourse shared by the implied author of Chronicles and the readership, the invasion is not independent of, but rather is a manifestation of Yhwh's will. Normally, Yhwh grants peace and tranquility to those who are loyal, but devastating enemy invasions to those who are disloyal.

the readers learned that Asa did not fail this test and was rewarded with victory. Significantly, the account of Asa in Chronicles then enters into a literary and ideological loop. A new beginning is marked by a call for repentance issued by a prophet and includes a report about a new reform, followed by a new period of peace (2 Chr 15:1–18). Although there is no change in Asa's behavior or that of Judah, the period of peace is again suddenly again by an invasion, which represents a new test for Asa. The readers learned that this time he failed and was punished with wars (16:9), that is the absence of peace, and to series of events that within the discourse of the book directly led to his death (16:10–12).

The readers of Chronicles were informed that Jehoshaphat successfully fulfilled a prophetic role as he was indefatigably traveling back and forth among the people within his entire kingdom to bring them back to YHWH (19:4).[13] Further, they learned that he established judges in all the fortified cities, and reminded them that they judge for YHWH and that the fear of YHWH should be upon them (19:5–7). Thus, these reports served to construe an image of Jehoshaphat not only as fulfilling the role of a prophet, but also the meaning–as understood by the Chronicler–of the laws in Deut 16:18–20. In addition, the text narrates that Jehoshaphat established a central court in Jerusalem (19:8–11). The account of his work as a voice calling for repentance and as judicial reformer is crafted so as to conclude with a quotation of the king's words, ויהי יהוה עם הטוב ("May YHWH be with those who do good"). As the readers completed reading about his great deeds and final words, and reasonably expected YHWH to be with Jehoshaphat, they were immediately told that a great army invaded Judah's territory (20:1–2). The literary proximity along with the explicit ויהי אחריכן ("and it happened after this") urged the readers to relate the two accounts. Jehoshaphat passed the divine test and was given victory (20:3–18), and following it, stable peace (20:29–30) and honor among the nations who now dreaded YHWH (20:29).

Similarly, the account of Hezekiah's reforms (2 Chr 29:3–31:20a), which is highly and explicitly praised in Chronicles (see 31:20b–21), is immediately followed by that of Senacherib's invasion (32:1–23). Literary proximity and the explicit opening of the account of the invasion with, אחרי הדברים והאמת האלה ("after these events and the acts of faithfulness") again relate the two events.[14] Heze-

---

[13] This is a clear prophetic role in Chronicles. See 2 Chr 24:19. The language used here for prophets is exactly that used for Jehoshaphat in 2 Chr 19:4.

[14] The replacement of the note dating the invasion to the fourteenth year of Hezekiah in 2 Kgs 18:13 (//Isa 36:1) with אחרי הדברים והאמת האלה is in itself consistent with this tendency to emphasize the association between the reforms, which began in the first month of the first year, and Sennacherib's campaign.

kiah did not fail this test, and therefore was given victory (32:1–21), then peace[15] and honor among the nations ensued (32:22–23).

The readers were told that Josiah conducted a major and comprehensive purge of improper cults and cultic places and artifacts associated with them, that he reinforced the temple, found the book of the YHWH's instruction by the hand of Moses, and celebrated a passover that served as an example for future generations. As the readers learned that such passover was not celebrated in Israel since the days of the prophet Samuel, and they are reminded that it was in his eighteenth year, that is the year of most of the reforms, they are told, אחרי כל זאת אשר הכין יאשיהו את הבית עלה נכו מלך מצרים ("after all this, when Josiah has set up the temple, Neco, the king of Egypt went up [to wage war]") and thus set up the divine test (2 Chr 35:18–20). Again, literary proximity and the explicit comment in the text create a sense of discursive proximity and relation between the events.[16] Significantly, the fact that the test was constructed as easier than the others mentioned above,[17] only made starker the failure of the pious Josiah in the test. This failure directly led to his death.

These examples from Chronicles and the book of Job not only share the topos of the pious being tested, but of the test as following the most heightened level of pious activity that the readers can imagine. In all these cases, as the piety of the person reaches its climax, severe misfortune is suddenly brought about against the individual. The catastrophe involves the removal of the blessings that the person enjoyed (wealth and children in the case of Job, peace and

---

15 Cf. S. Japhet, *I & II Chronicles: A Commentary* (OTL; Louisville: Westminster John Knox, 1993), 991–92.

16 To be sure, the reference to the eighteenth year of Josiah as the date of the celebration of the passover in 2 Chr 35:19 creates a temporal gap between this event and the campaign of Neco which must be in Josiah's thirty-first year (2 Chr 34:1). Both dates were most likely among the core facts that the Chronicler could not change (on this matter see E. Ben Zvi, "Shifting the Gaze: Historiographic Constraints in Chronicles and Their Implications," in *The Land that I Will Show You: Essays on the History and Archaeology of the Ancient Near East in Honor of J. Maxwell Miller* [eds. M. P. Graham and J. A. Dearman; JSOTSup 343; Sheffield: JSOT Press, 2001], 38–60). The first date refers to the year of the finding of the book, which is the central event that leads to the passover and because of the role of written books in the worldview shaped and reflected by Chronicles. The second date points to the length of a reign (see E. Ben Zvi, "About Time: Observations About the Construction of Time in the Book of Chronicles," in *HBT* 22 [2000]: 17–31). Although the Chronicler cannot change either date, the Chronicler can create a strong sense of literary and discursive proximity between the events–a literary feature that masks the temporal gap. This is achieved by reporting absolutely nothing about events from year eighteenth to the campaign of Neco in year 31.

17 The campaign was not aimed at Judah and Neco explicitly warned Josiah of provoking YHWH to destroy him (2 Chr 35:20–22).

tranquility in the case of the kings) and threatens the very existence of the household/kingdom of the individual being tested. These catastrophes are presented as identical to those that may befall sinners. To be sure, Job claims his innocence and is explicitly supported by the narrator and the character Yhwh in the book, and the readers of Chronicles are told unequivocally that the kings mentioned above were innocent of wrongdoing, at the very least at the beginning of the test, but the point cannot be clearer: actions that can be associated with divine punishment may befall the pious and in fact the most righteousness among the pious. The deity is accordingly construed as one who may choose and is expected to choose freely between blessing and catastrophe to the same person, and to alternate them in a manner that is not dependent on the person's actions. These ideological and discursive positions reflect and communicate a worldview in which the immediate future is unpredictable, and in which no certain conclusions can be reached from the calamity that befall individuals. But at the same time, this is a worldview in which it is certain what a person should do whether she or he enjoys the blessings of Yhwh or whether the same blessings are suddenly withdrawn for no apparent reason: instead of attempting to understand and therefore having at least some degree of discursive control over Yhwh's actions,[18] such a person should think and behave as a loyal servant of Yhwh, and thus fulfill Yhwh's ways. Significantly, this is also a world in which Job's blessings were eventually restored to him when he passed the test, one in which the people are returned to the land in Chronicles even if the text does not claim that they passed the test, and one in which most kings who pass the test may again enjoy peace, though if they remain pious they may still be tested again, for unpredictability still rules.

The fact that Job and Chronicles both share and communicate the main features of a shared discourse, despite all its differences, points at the ubiquity of this type of concerns, of an ideological world populated with images of those who were or may be subjects to a divine test, and by the ideological concepts and images about the divine that were discussed above. To be sure, at the end of the day these texts reinforce "orthodox" positions, as one would expect of authoritative books that were accepted as such in a Jerusalemite center in Persian Yehud; however, significantly, they achieve this reinforcement at the expense of maintaining anxiety, and by means of a clear undermining of any claims that the literati may have entertained about their ability to predict the future. As works

---

[18] In the book of Job such an attempt is not considered sinful per se, but quite the opposite. Still, it is construed as a futile endeavor. The kings of Chronicles do not even attempt to deal with these matters.

written by these literati, they represent a tendency to posit themselves and their explanatory powers in proportion, which in itself is another ubiquitous feature in post-monarchic literature, one that is necessary for keeping the basic ideological tenets alive in a world that was constructed as both cosmically ordered and unpredictable.[19]

---

[19] See E. Ben Zvi, *Signs of Jonah: Reading and Rereading in Ancient Yehud* (JSOTS 367; Sheffield: Sheffield Academic Press/Continuum, 2003), esp. 99–115.

Exploring Jerusalem as a Site of Memory in the Late Persian and Early Hellenistic Periods*

Introduction

The goal of this chapter is to explore, within the context of the relevant period, matters associated with social memories of Jerusalem. The first section discusses interactions between different ways in which Jerusalem served as a site of memory and contributed to the shaping of other sites of memory and core mnemonic narratives in the community. This section deals also with processes by which material signposts in Jerusalem influenced the discourse of the period and the ways in which Jerusalem was remembered and, conversely, the effect that Jerusalems of the mind had on social and political developments. In other words, it traces connections between material Jerusalems and the Jerusalems of the mind and vice versa. The second part of this chapter explores some of the images and concepts that the site of memory Jerusalem embodied and communicated in the late Persian or early Hellenistic period.

Exploring Matters of Social Memory about Jerusalem: Between "Mind" and "Matter," "Matter" and "Mind," and Other Considerations

Urban centers, ancient as well as modern, have populated, socially shared memory-scapes. The multiple associations evoked by cities contributed much to social memory and significantly impacted social mindscapes in the ancient Near East. Ancient cities served as the actual, worldly landscape populated by "material" sites of memory, some of which were personal and others of which were directly and intentionally involved in the shaping of a collective social memory, such as palaces, temples, inscriptions, walls, gates, and the like. Cities were sites of social memory in a very different way. Like Babylon or Nineveh, they served as ciphers that activated and communicated various mnemonic worlds as they integrated multiple images, remembered events, and provided a variety of meanings in diverse ancient communities. Within the community that identified or positively associated itself with them, these cities served as ci-

---

* First published in *Memory and the City in Ancient Israel* (eds. D. V. Edelman and E. Ben Zvi; Winona Lake, Ind.: Eisenbrauns, 2014), 197–217.

https://doi.org/10.1515/9783110547146-024

phers that evoked and communicated a sense of order and construed a past and future that, in turn, played important roles in inner processes of formations of self-identity. These cities embodied and evoked central mythical images and memories that socialized the mnemonic community so that they might share a social mnemonic landscape and a general social mindscape. Social memories affected and to some extent effected not only the way in which people thought and understood the world and themselves but also their actions, including those related to cities. Thus, certain cities emerged to a significant extent the way they did because of social memories; their importance and relevance were at least, in part, the outcome of social memory.

Although cities that serve as sacred cities in "traditional" societies share some important features, whether they are inside or outside the ancient Near East,[1] this essay is primarily about the Jerusalem of the late Persian/Early Hellenistic period.[2] This city was extremely unlike the very large, central, imperial cities of the ancient Near East in terms of its population, political and economic clout, and even its social organization.[3] But it was still a sacred, central city[4] for a par-

---

[1] See, for instance, D. L. Eck, "The City as a Sacred Center," in *The City as a Sacred Center. Essays on Six Asian Contexts* (eds. B. Smith and H. Baker Reynolds; International Studies in Sociology and Social Anthropology 46; Leiden: Brill, 1987), 1–11.

[2] Jerusalem has a long history as a central, sacred city before and after the period discussed here. The chapter, as appropriate to the theme of the volume in which it was first published, is devoted to the late Persian or Early Hellenistic period in Judah/Yehud.

[3] For demographic studies about Jerusalem and its surrounding areas during the Persian period, see, among others, O. Lipschits, "Persian Period Finds from Jerusalem: Facts and Interpretations," in *JHebS* 9/20 (2009): http://www.jhsonline.org/Articles/article_122.pdf; idem, *The Fall and Rise of Jerusalem: Judah under Babylonian Rule* (Winona Lake, IN: Eisenbrauns, 2005), esp. 258–71; idem, "Demographic Changes in Judah between the Seventh and the Fifth Centuries BCE," in *Judah and the Judeans in the Neo-Babylonian Period* (eds. O. Lipschits and J. Blenkinsopp; Winona Lake, IN: Eisenbrauns, 2003), 323–76; I. Finkelstein, "Persian Period Jerusalem and Yehud: A Rejoinder," in *JHebS* 9/24 (2009): http://www.jhsonline.org/Articles/article_126.pdf; idem, "Jerusalem in the Persian (and Early Hellenistic) Period and the Wall of Nehemiah," in *JSOT* 32 (2008): 501–20; idem, "Archaeology and the List of Returnees in the Books of Ezra and Nehemiah," in *PEQ* 140 (2008): 7–16; H. Geva, "Estimating Jerusalem's Population in Antiquity: A Minimalist View," *ErIsr* 28 (Teddy Kollek Volume; 2007, Heb.): 50–65; A. Kloner, "Jerusalem's Environs in the Persian Period," in *New Studies on Jerusalem* (eds. A. Faust and E. Baruch; Ramat Gan: Ingeborg Rennert Center for Jerusalem Studies, 2001), 91–95 [Hebrew]; compare C. E. Carter, *The Emergence of Yehud in the Persian Period: A Social and Demographic Study* (JSOTSup 294; Sheffield, Sheffield Academic Press, 1999); A. Faust, "Judah in the Sixth Century BCE: A Rural Perspective," in *PEQ* 126 (2003): 37–53. See also a summary of the situation in K. Valkama, "What Do Archaeological Remains Reveal of the Settlements in Judah during the Mid-Sixth Century BCE?" in *The Concept of Exile in Ancient Israel and Its Historical Contexts* (eds. E. Ben Zvi and C. Levin; BZAW 404; Berlin: De Gruyter, 2010), 39–59.

ticular community that, unsurprisingly, thought of it as the central city of a future, worldwide empire they believed would certainly come.

Jerusalem served as a central site of memory in late Persian Yehud in two main ways. On the one hand, it was the site that embodied and brought together in some meaningful way multiple material sites of memory the residents of the period encountered in their daily lives. These sites included, for example, a temple whose building and furnishings were much poorer than other central temples and poorer than the Jerusalemite temples that existed in the memory of the community (see Hag 2:3; compare Ezra 3:12). In fact, this material temple was not considered worthy of much writing and, thus, of much remembering in terms of its building or furnishings, as any comparison with descriptions of other temples or sacred cultic buildings of the past or the future (e.g., Ezek 40–44) that existed within the literary repertoire of the community clearly shows (see, for instance, 1 Kgs 5–6; compare Exod 25–28; 35–40).[5] The temple itself was thus conceptualized as a marker of a post-calamity period, a reminder of a glorious past and of a glorious future that is "not yet."

One has to assume that ruins were probably seen in the area in and around Jerusalem throughout the Persian period.[6] These ruins and empty spaces also served to bring home the presence of a past and of its catastrophic fate. These ruins would reinforce a sense that the community is just the "remnant" of a terrible calamity, whose memory probably remained for generations in the com-

---

4 It is important to stress that "cities" and even central "cities" in this context are not necessarily defined by having a large population (see bibliography in the previous note) or by their being walled. Jerusalem was without a wall when the temple was established, and if at a later stage in the Persian period it was surrounded by a wall, the latter was certainly not a massive defensive wall meant to withstand the attack of any significant army. It is worth noting also that, within the social mindscape of the period, cities had "daughters," that is, secondary, small and mainly rural settlements. But conceptually, "daughters" belong to the same category as "mothers." What characterized a central sacred city was neither the size nor the wall but a conceptualization of the city as the place of a "great god," a place connecting "heaven and earth," a central place in the divine economy, and the like. This is discussed in the subsection "Jerusalem, Cities, Houses and Cosmos," below.

5 See D. J. A. Clines, "Haggai's Temple, Constructed, Deconstructed and Reconstructed," in *Interested Parties: The Ideology of Writers and Readers of the Hebrew Bible* (JSOTSup 205; Gender, Culture, Theory 1; Sheffield: Sheffield Academic Press, 1995), 46–75 (esp. 53); originally published in *SJOT* 7 (1993): 19–30.

6 Compare D. Ussishkin, "The Borders and *De Facto* Size of Jerusalem in the Persian Period," in *Judah and the Judeans in the Persian Period* (eds. O. Lipschits and M. Oeming; Winona Lake, IN: Eisenbrauns, 2006), 147–66.

munity.⁷ The buildings of Jerusalem served to shape a collective memory obsessed with a past calamity, which, within the social mindscape of the community, was tantamount to being obsessed with the importance of YHWH's past judgment. It also meant obsession with closely related activities such as (a) construing and remembering the actions of Judah and Jerusalem that made them worthy of such a divine punishment within this discourse and (b) construing hope for a restoration that will return not to the prejudgment situation that led to disaster but to a new hopeful, stable future.⁸ The repertoire of books that carried particular authority within the Jerusalem-centered literati in the late Persian/early Hellenistic period particularly reflected these "obsessions."⁹

Within a province that was called Yehud, not Benjamin, even though its demographic and economic center was Benjamin and its political capital was located at Mizpah in Benjamin for a while, memories that reinforced a sense of continuity with the past enjoyed a systemic preference. Persian-period Jerusalem and its temple evoked and shaped memories of monarchic Jerusalem. Moreover, it evoked memories of monarchic Judah. Without a doubt, one may claim that the

---

7 In a short period, Judah suffered a reduction of 70–75% in its population, and close to 90% in some areas (for example, Jerusalem environs, eastern strip). The city was burned and uninhabited, due to war, famine, associated diseases, deportation, and migration caused by the economic collapse that followed and was engendered by the sociopolitical collapse. Even in Benjamin, which was the least affected of all regions, the population dropped by more than 50%. A catastrophe of this magnitude could not but be remembered and become a site of memory or cipher bearing a weighty significance for generations after the event, particularly among those whose self-identity was grounded in a close identification with those afflicted by the disaster but also within any polity or community that imagined itself and was understood as standing in continuation with the one that had suffered a calamity such as this. See H.-J. Stipp, "The Concept of the Empty Land in Jeremiah 37–43," in *Concept of Exile* (eds. E. Ben Zvi and C. Levin), 103–54. He compares this shrinkage of population with that caused by the Thirty Years' War, which was far less dramatic. To put it in today's numbers, this would be equivalent to the loss of about 25 million Canadians or more than 230 million Americans (144–50). It is worth stressing that there was no demographic or economic recovery to anywhere near the level of late monarchic Judah during the Persian and early Hellenistic periods.
8 A social preference toward the development of discourses of hope (and utopian thinking) in this sort of community is to be expected. See my "Reading and Constructing Utopias: Utopia/s and/in the Collection of Authoritative Texts of Late Yehud. General Considerations and Some Observations," in *Studies in Religion* 42 (2013): 463–76.
9 The underlying assumption is that most of the books included today in the Hebrew Bible in more or less their present forms are representative, to at least a significant degree, of the general authoritative repertoire of these literati in the late Persian/early Hellenistic period. This is a reasonable assumption, at least concerning the pentateuchal collection, the Deuteronomistic Historical collection, the prophetic books collection, Chronicles, and most of the psalms and Proverbs.

ideology according to which Jerusalem stood symbolically for Judah was one that would have been particularly promoted by the incipient temple in Jerusalem, with the likely support of the Persian center. Certainly, it had been at the core of monarchic-period discourse and the perception of Judah outside its borders.[10] Yehud could not have rejected this construction without substantially erasing any claims of continuity between Persian Yehud and monarchic Judah.[11] The very building of the temple evoked and communicated a sense of continuity with the past temple and thus shaped and reshaped a memory of old Jerusalem in which the temple becomes more important than any other building and institution. This process created a core mnemonic metanarrative from temple to temple that, within the discourse of the period, was also one from David to Cyrus and from monarchic Judah to Achaemenid Yehud. At the same time, it also evoked a sense of a third and final movement, from past temple to present temple to future utopian temple, from monarchic Judah to Persian Empire to YHWH's empire on earth; from David to Cyrus to either an elevated David or Israel (or both) at the center of YHWH's kingdom.

Up to this point, I have referenced ways in which encountering material sites of memory in Jerusalem after the city's destruction in 586 BCE shaped a comprehensive site of material memory that affected the production of the intellectual discourse of the literati, their memories, and their general mindscape. Even these material sites of memory had to be socially construed and encoded, but indisputably, there was a material side to them.

At the same time, material sites of memory were not a necessary requisite for a Jerusalem that existed in the mind and the shared imagination of the community. The memories evoked by such a Jerusalem of the mind, with the temple as its center, were most likely the reason that the temple and eventually, Jerusalem were rebuilt in the Persian period. On the surface, the building of a local temple in the midst of a destroyed, unpopulated and unwalled town in an extremely depopulated area rather than in the local political, social, economic, and demographic center does not make much sense. It is an anomaly, further emphasized by the fact that it required not only local but also imperial support. The only reason for rebuilding the temple in Jerusalem rather than (re?)building a temple to YHWH elsewhere in the province was the strong existence of a Jerusalem of the mind whose social memories required that YHWH's house be at the place the

---

10 So, for example, *Texts from Cuneiform Sources [ABC]* (Locust Valley, N.Y.: J. J. Augustin, 1975), 5, rev. l. 12. The text is also available in J.-J. Glassner, *Mesopotamian Chronicles* (SBLWAW 19; Atlanta: Society of Biblical Literature, 2004), 230–31.
11 See "Total Exile, Empty Land and the General Intellectual Discourse in Yehud," in this volume, pp. 599–611.

community remembered YHWH to have selected for that purpose.¹² Building temples in the ancient Near East usually would have occasioned substantial discontinuities with the past,¹³ but they would be construed and accepted as appropriate because they evoked and activated a sense of continuity with a remembered (and thus construed and constantly reshaped) past.¹⁴ The Jerusalem of the mind had a central role in creation of the material Jerusalem of the Persian period.

Of course, various Jerusalems of the mind impacted not only the process of rebuilding an incipient temple but also continued to interact dynamically with the actual city throughout the Persian period. Certainly, repeatedly remembering the preeminence of Jerusalem and its temple likely contributed to the rise of the institution of the temple and, thus, of the city to the position of preeminence it had attained already by the late Persian period.¹⁵ But Jerusalems of the mind and

---

12 R. Klein, "Joshua, Zerubbabel, and Nehemiah Contemporaries? A Response to Diana Edelman's Proposed Late Date for the Second Temple," in *JBL* 127 (2008): 697–701.

13 After all, any activity of building or rebuilding brings something "new" that has to be incorporated and "appropriated" by the past. Moreover, in most cases, (re)building or even "repairing" involves the removal of something considered to be sacred. For this reason, actions of rebuilding, repairing, or even making minor changes in temples or their sacra may be portrayed as acts of impiety or even sacrilege from the perspective of those who negatively construe and remember the (re)builder/repairer agent (e.g., Ahaz, Naram Sin, Nabonaid, "sinful priests," and so on). See, for instance, P.-A. Beaulieu, "Nabonidus the Mad King: A Reconsideration of His Steles from Harran and Babylon," in *Representations of Political Power: Case Histories of Change and Dissolving Order in the Ancient Near East* (eds. M. Heinz and M. H. Feldman; Winona Lake, IN: Eisenbrauns, 2007), 137–66 (143–44). It is worth noting in this regard that despite the negative characterization of Herod, his (re)building activities were not construed as a sacrilege; instead, his role as (re)builder of the temple was deemphasized in literature from the period close to and following the destruction of Jerusalem in 70 CE.

14 One may note the emphasis on the literature of the period on the continuity of ritual, personnel (the same lines of priests), sancta (for example, the vessels), sacred space and sacred (cyclical/ritual) time.

15 Contrast even the case of Samaria, the other main Yahwistic province in which there was also a temple. Note the asymmetry between the Samarian and Yehudite addressees of the letters sent by Jedaniah. For a different position on this matter, see D. V. Edelman, *The Origins of the "Second" Temple: Persian Imperial Policy and the Rebuilding of Jerusalem* (Bible World; London: Equinox, 2005). For a response to Edelman's position, see Klein, "Were Joshua, Zerubbabel and Nehemiah Contemporaries?." The high status of the Jerusalemite temple in Yehud by 407 BCE is unequivocally supported by letters from Elephantine. The letters were sent to "Delaiah and Shelemiah, sons of Sanballat, governor of Samaria" and in first instance, to "Jehohanan the High Priest and his colleagues the priests who are in Jerusalem, and to Ostanes the brother of Anani and the nobles of Judah," and later to Bagavahya, the governor of Yehud. See B. Porten et al., *The Elephantine Papyri in English: Three Millennia of Cross-Cultural Continuity and Change* (Leiden: Brill, 1996), 139–49; B. Porten and A. Yardeni, *Textbook of Aramaic Documents from Ancient Egypt* (4 vols.; Jerusalem: Hebrew University Press, 1986–99), 1:68–75 (B 19 = TAD A4.7 =

social memory did not evolve in a vacuum. They were part of the social memory of a particular historical community and thus historically contingent, both in a narrow and a wider historical sense. The inner Yehudite social processes that led to the religio-cultural-political prominence of Jerusalem over Benjamin shaped and drew much attention to Jerusalem as a site of memory. The sociopolitical and cultural location of Yehud in the Persian Empire also affected the shaping of Jerusalem as a site of memory. Persian kings were brought to memory as supporters of the building and appropriate establishment of the temple, as royal figures lending it prestige, and as instruments in the hands of YHWH for these purposes, as the discourse of Yehud required. At the same time, as the last observation already hints, the very same social and cultural location led to processes of hybridization in which cultural patterns associated with "empire" are turned around to support local identity formation and social reproduction, as well as forms of inner social organization. All this contributed to the shaping of images of Jerusalem. The social, political, and cultural location of Yehud entailed constant interplay with Samaria and their respective elites during the Persian period. These matters also influenced the shaping of social memories about Jerusalem and the mindscape they enjoyed within the Yehudite community. The internal social location of the literati writing and reading the texts in which these memories of Jerusalem were encoded and evoked by reading also played important roles, particularly if these literati were likely supported in one way or another by the Jerusalemite temple.

Because I have discussed some of these issues elsewhere, the next section will focus on various aspects of the Jerusalems of the mind of the late Persian/early Hellenistic period rather than on the historical background from

---

Cowley 30; B 20 = TAD A.4.8 = Cowley 31). Of course, the very presence of the temple required the presence of priests and various services to maintain the cult; the very presence of collected tribute and taxes in the site, at least from some point in the Persian period that of some human and "material" infrastructure to make whatever was collected safe. All these processes could not but affect the "material" city. On the likely roles of the Persian-period temple, see J. Schaper, "The Jerusalem Temple as an Instrument of the Achaemenid Fiscal Administration," in *VT* 45 (1995): 528–39; idem, "The Temple Treasury Committee in the Times of Nehemiah and Ezra," in *VT* 47 (1997): 200–206. The presence of a treasury in Jerusalem may have contributed to the shift of the provincial capital from Mizpah to Jerusalem and the presence of some fortifications. See, for instance, O. Lipschits, "Achaemenid Imperial Policy, Settlement Processes in Palestine, and the Status of Jerusalem in the Middle of the Fifth Century B.C.E.," in *Judah and the Judeans in the Persian Period*, 19–52 (40). Compare C. Tuplin, "The Administration of the Achaemenid Empire," in *Coinage and Administration in the Athenian and Persian Empires* (ed. Ian Carradice; BAR International Series 343; Oxford: B.A.R., 1987), 109–66 (128, 130).

which they emerged and with which they interacted and reshaped themselves, though both aspects should be kept in mind.

Exploring Matters of Social Memory about Jerusalem: Some of the Central Constructions of "Jerusalem"

Introduction and Matters of Mindshare

Jerusalem and related terms (for example, Zion) explicitly appear many more than 800 times in works later included in the HB, which most likely were representative of the repertoire of the time. For obvious reasons, Jerusalem could not appear frequently in the Pentateuch or other historiographical narratives shaping memories of a pre-Davidic, pre-Israelite Jerusalem. S. Talmon noticed many years ago that Jerusalem and related terms are proportionally attested more frequently in this corpus than in late-Second Temple literature, when Jerusalem was a much larger city, or in later rabbinic literature, despite Jerusalem's centrality in rabbinic Judaism, or in the New Testament.[16] The matter is not only numerical; the Deuteronomistic historical collection is largely teleologically oriented toward the catastrophe symbolized by the destruction of Jerusalem and its temple. Jerusalem stands at the center of the collection of prophetic books. Jerusalem and its temple play a central role in Psalms and in Chronicles. All the basic metanarratives of Yehud involved the past and future fate of Jerusalem.

These observations are indicative of the extent of social mindshare among the literati of the period that Jerusalem occupied–the Jerusalems of the mind and memory. Because this mindshare was larger in Yehud in the Persian period than it was both in the Second Temple period and when there was no material (Jewish) Jerusalem or temple as in the rabbinic period, the matter does not appear to be simply or mainly a case of extensive communal remembering about what has been lost and will be regained. The difference between late Persian Yehud and the rabbinic period seems to be that Jerusalem and its temple had to strive to achieve centrality in the Persian period, while it was undoubtedly central in the rabbinic era.

The vast number of references to Jerusalem in the repertoire of the period makes it impossible to undertake here even a basic analysis of Jerusalem as a comprehensive site of memory that embodied and communicated multiple im-

---

16 See S. Talmon, "The Biblical Concept of Jerusalem," in *Journal of Ecumenical Studies* 8 (1971): 300–316.

ages, at times in tension with each other, and integrated them together under a common cipher that embodied and communicated even more meanings and images. The plethora of images, places and contexts in which Jerusalem was evoked and the plethora of manners in which Jerusalem in one way or another was integrated into almost any main metanarrative that existed within the discourse of Yehud makes this sort of endeavor impossible. Thus, I will explore *a few* of the aspects and images that contributed to the construction of this site of memory and to its dominant position in the memory-scape of the community.

Jerusalem, Cities, Houses, Cosmic Order and Divine Wisdom

Creation in the ancient Near East was construed as a "macrocosmic" house. The basic metaphor for social organization was the "house of the father,"[17] and from the macrocosmic perspective, this father/patriarch was the high deity of the group. The "house" included cities, and cities included houses, some of which were houses of deities. All were built/created with wisdom and stood because they were established with wisdom. Houses had to be provisioned and filled with good, appropriate things;[18] if a house is filled with a city or cities, then the latter also should be filled with goods, people, wisdom, and of course, a divine house or houses.

When the divine resident was a high god, then it resided in its house in the city and in the cosmic house at the same time, and a direct connection between the two was construed. The city was included in the house and, at the same time, included it. Moreover, the city was necessary for the maintenance of the house and provided context for it, as the latter was imagined as the central element that filled the city. Conversely, the temple filled the city and the world with the essential goods for its prosperity and maintenance. To illustrate, "Enki's

---

[17] See, for instance, J. D. Schloen, *The House of the Father as Fact and Symbol: Patrimonialism in Ugarit and the Ancient Near East* (Winona Lake, IN: Eisenbrauns, 2001); M. S. Smith, *The Origins of Biblical Monotheism: Israel's Polytheistic Background and the Ugaritic Texts* (New York: Oxford University Press, 2001), 54–66; R. C. van Leeuwen, "Cosmos, Temple, House: Building and Wisdom in Mesopotamia and Israel," in *Wisdom Literature in Mesopotamia and Israel* (ed. R. J. Clifford; SBLSymS 36: Atlanta: Society of Biblical Literature, 2007), 67–90; reprinted and slightly revised, "Cosmos, Temple, House: Building and Wisdom in Ancient Mesopotamia and Israel" in *From the Foundations to the Crenellations: Essays on Temple Building in the Ancient Near East and Hebrew Bible* (eds. M. J. Boda and J. Novotny; AOAT 366; Münster: Ugarit-Verlag, 2010), 399–421.
[18] See van Leeuwen, "Cosmos, Temple, House."

'house' is the entire cosmos, which is made prosperous from out the local temple/Abzu with its gifts of life-giving waters."[19]

Closer to our topic and time, but still standing in relation to these then millennia-old conceptual images, YHWH's future presence in the temple in Jerusalem is associated with fertilizing waters emerging from the place in Ezek 47:1–12 and also with the image of a future fountain in the temple, which appears in texts as different as Joel 4:18; Zech 13:1; 14:8; and Ps 46:5–6 (cf. Isa 33:21). YHWH himself was construed as 'the fountain of living water' (מקור מים חיים; see Jer 2:13; cf. Ps 36:10[most ET, 9] and also Jer 14:8; 17:13[20]), so there is nothing strange in a generative grammar that would give rise to images of his house and city containing a fountain of enlivening waters. One may note also that this sort of image carries Edenic connotations and partially construes future Jerusalem as a second Eden.[21] Within this mnemonic world, the garden thus becomes a city and the city a garden.

To be sure, Jerusalem was construed not only as the source of mythical "water" but also, for example, as the place in which YHWH shines. As a result, it had to be imagined as the site in which מכלל יפי 'the perfection of beauty' was achieved on earth (Ps 50:2). Memories of future Jerusalem as a source of mythical light partially embodying the divine presence, to which nations and rulers (that is, the human world) would come, were reflected in and evoked through the reading of Isa 60:1–3, read in a way informed by Isa 60:19–20.

Multiple, complementary, imaginative acts served to construe memories of utopian Jerusalem. Each of them contributed to and shed light on Jerusalem as a site of memory. Jerusalem was imagined as a fountain of water and of light but also, and in related ways, a fountain of wisdom/divine knowledge for the world. Within the general context of the ancient Near East, the world cannot endure without (divine) wisdom. Within the world of thought of the Jerusalem-centered literati during the late Persian or early Hellenistic period,

---

[19] Citation from ibid., 401.

[20] On the double meaning conveyed by the reference to YHWH as מקוה ישראל in Jer 14:8; 17:13 see, for instance, W. L. Holladay, *Jeremiah* 1 (Hermeneia; Philadelphia: Fortress, 1986), 433.

[21] On Jerusalem as Eden, see T. Stordalen, "Heaven on Earth–Or not? Jerusalem as Eden in Biblical Literature," in *Beyond Eden: The Biblical Story of Paradise (Genesis 2–3) and Its Reception History* (eds. K. Schmid and C. Riedweg; FAT 2; Tübingen: Mohr Siebeck, 2008), 28–57, esp. 36–40; and D. V. Edelman, "City Gardens and Parks in Biblical Social Memory," in *Memory and the City* (eds. D. V. Edelman and E. Ben Zvi; Winona Lake, Ind.: Eisenbrauns, 2014), 115–155. For a recent comparative study of some images and constructions in the (so-called) Akkadian "apocalypses'"and texts such as Ezek 47:1–12; Joel 4:18; and Zech 14:8, see D. Bodi, "Les apocalypses akkadiennes et bibliques: Quelques points communs," in *Revue des Études Juives* 169 (2010): 13–36; and Stordalen, "Heaven on Earth."

this wisdom was identified, in part, as Yhwh's instruction.²² Thus, it is not surprising to note that images of a future, utopian Jerusalem associate the establishment of this sort of place with the spread of 'knowledge' (דעה) of Yhwh (see Isa 11:6–9; 65:17–25).²³ Thus, one finds texts such as כִּי מִצִּיּוֹן תֵּצֵא תוֹרָה וּדְבַר־יְהוָה מִירוּשָׁלָֽם 'For out of Zion shall go forth instruction and the word of Yhwh from Jerusalem' (Isa 2:3; Mic 4:2).

Within this social mindscape, the image of Wisdom as a city dweller calling to people to adopt her ways (Prov 9:1–6) and preaching in and around the city (see Prov 8:1–3) could not but associate her with both (a) "every city, and even the entirety of the inhabited world"²⁴ and (b) Jerusalem, the space associated

---

22 See, for instance, Deut 4:5–6; Ps 19; or texts such as Job 28:28 as read within a community in which "fear of Yhwh" was understood as (at the very least as) following Yhwh's instruction (e.g., Deut 6:2, 24; 13:5; 17:19; 31:12; 1 Sam 12:14). For the potential impact of this correlation on other texts (e.g., Isa 55:1–5), see J. Blenkinsopp, *Isaiah 40–55* (AB 19 A; New York: Doubleday, 2002), 369. For texts likely later than the period discussed here that reflect a similar overlap between wisdom and divine instruction in different ways, compare the language of Ezra 7:14 with that in Ezra 7:25. To be clear, I make the claim not that the concepts of Wisdom and Yhwh's instruction were fully interchangeable during the late Persian/early Hellenistic period but that a most significant ideological overlap existed. As for later periods, for studies on Sirach and (the book of) *Torah*, keeping in mind texts such as Sir 24:23, see, for instance, J. J. Collins, *Jewish Wisdom in the Hellenistic Age* (Louisville, KY: Westminster John Knox, 1997), 54–61. For the proposal that Sir 24:23 reflects Sirach's understanding of Deuteronomy, see G. T. Sheppard, *Wisdom as a Hermeneutical Construct: A Study in the Sapientializing of the Old Testament* (BZAW 151; Berlin: De Gruyter, 1980), 66; and see Sheppard's discussion of Sir 24:3–29 in 19–71. It is possible that Sirach reflected a reading of the text that preceded him. On the various meanings of *torah* in the late Persian period, see also M. Greenberg, "Three Conceptions of the *Torah* in the Hebrew Scriptures," in *Die Hebräische Bibel und ihre zweifache Nachgeschichte: Festschrift für Rolf Rendtorff zum 65. Geburtstag* (eds. E. Blum, C. Macholz, and E. W. Stegemann; Neukirchen-Vluyn: Neukirchener Verlag, 1990), 365–78. For a recent epistemological study of the multiple relations between ciphers such as Wisdom and *Torah*, see R. O'Dowd, *The Wisdom of Torah: Epistemology in Deuteronomy and the Wisdom Literature* (FRLANT 225; Göttingen: Vandenhoeck & Ruprecht, 2009).

23 From the perspective of the late Persian or early Hellenistic period, these two texts informed each other. Significantly, both were associated with the same prophet of old, Isaiah, who was directly associated with Jerusalem. The book of Isaiah reached its compositional form well before Sirach; see Sir 48:18–25, which assumes a memory of the prophet shaped by, and reflecting a reading of the book of Isaiah as a whole and as a book encoding memories about the monarchic-period prophet Isaiah.

24 Michael V. Fox writes in relation to Prov 8:1–3: "The scene and events are atemporal: Wisdom addresses mankind in all cities, inside and outside the city walls, in high places and low grounds, repeatedly and forever. Her city represents every city, and even the entirety of the inhabited world. Ancient Near Eastern mythology often represented the cosmos as a city, and some cities were regarded as microcosms of heaven and earth" (*Proverbs 1–9* [AB 18 A; New York:

with Yhwh's instruction. Divine wisdom is thus cosmic and world-encompassing but also, at least partially, Jerusalem-bound. When construed from the latter perspective, the reference to the heights of the city in Prov 8:2 as the place in which people may encounter Wisdom likely evoked the image of the Jerusalemite temple.[25]

Central cities in the ancient Near East were conceptualized as ordered and ordering sites,[26] embodying and providing divine wisdom/knowledge. This construction carried a flip side that impacted on the way in which cities served as sites of memory. When these cities were construed and remembered as being disordered and thus disordering, they had to be imagined as embodying, providing and propagating "folly" or "misleading knowledge." Given that wisdom/divine knowledge was considered absolutely necessary for the world to endure, the foolish city threatened not only itself but also the world as a whole. The fate of the city was imagined as having larger repercussions.[27]

Within the discourse of Yehud, on the one hand, matters were exacerbated because Yhwh, the only divine being worthy of being called "God," was construed as having only one possible house/city on earth, and the deity could not remain in an unsuitable house/city. The emerging generative grammar of this discourse led to constructions of an effect on the cosmic level for Israel's sinfulness (e.g., Jer 4:22–28; Zeph 1:2–3) and a sense that what happened in or around Jerusalem (Judah) is crucial for the fate of an Israel that includes more than Judah (for example, Chronicles). Above all, it led to a sense that a temple-less or Jerusalem-less condition can only be a temporary situation. Within this discourse, Yhwh will return to Zion/Jerusalem, the city will (and needs to) be rebuilt, and when this happens, the world will finally reach a stable situation. The city will be recognized worldwide as the sacred center of the world and people will come to it, receive its blessings, and honor it by filling it with all kinds of

---

Doubleday, 2000], 267). Compare L. Perdue, *Wisdom & Creation: The Theology of the Wisdom Literature* (Nashville: Abingdon, 1994), 86–87.

25 See L. Perdue, *Proverbs* (Interpretation; Louisville, KY: Westminster John Knox, 2000), 140. The image of Wisdom at the gates was related to the image and administration of justice, which, if done in a way consistent with divine wisdom, provides the harmony and order deemed necessary for the long-term existence of the polity/city. So Perdue, *Wisdom & Creation*, 86.

26 See A. Kuhrt, *The Ancient Near East, c. 3000–330 BC* (2 vols.; London: Routledge, 1995), 2:617.

27 The idea that the fate of a (central) city may affect the cosmos is well attested in the ancient Near East. For an illustration, see, for instance, J. M. Sasson, "An Apocalyptic Vision from Mari? Speculations on ARM X:9," in *Mari: Annales de recherches interdisciplinaires* 1 (1982): 151–67 (164).

(voluntary) gifts, thus contributing to the process of its building (for example, Isa 60:1–18; 61:5; Hag 2:6–9; compare Isa 2:3; Jer 3:17; Mic 4:2).[28]

The images of Jerusalem discussed in this subsection provide excellent examples of how general cultural patterns and even generative grammars that were most often employed in the service of the ideology of dominant political powers of the area were appropriated and reshaped into motifs at the service of local cultural/ideological resistance. They advanced claims that the true center of the universe was not to be found in the imperial cities but in a poor and seemingly marginal city. Contrary to present and past "global" empires that were centered in these cities, they imaginatively experienced and became acquainted with vignettes of a future empire whose center was Jerusalem. They had memories of this certain future Jerusalemite empire, which will come at some undefined future time, but which was already created and consistent with YHWH's will and the true structure of the cosmos. This type of hybridity contributed to the stability and social reproduction of the community in which it evolved and to the long-term stability of the empire.[29]

Hierarchies and Gendered Images: A Few Observations

Within the mindscape of the community in Yehud, the focal point, that is, the house of the higher deity, defines the city, and conversely, the city is imagined

---

28 On the importance of "filling," see R. C. van Leeuwen, "Cosmos, Temple, House." All these images of central cities at the center of the world that existed in the ancient Near East relate to and evoke conceptual images of "world empires." In the case of Babylon or Nineveh, they reflected and related to social constructs of empires as well as to the existence of historical, social, political, and economic empires. In the case of Israel/Yehud, the empire was only one of social imagination, set in the future. But memories of that empire impacted the social mindscape and social memory of the community, which remembered not only the past but also its future, having experienced repeatedly, though vicariously through reading, the shared, communal experience of this future. On the common ancient Near Eastern *topos* of the "city at the center of the world," see, for instance, the classic discussion of M. Liverani, "Memorandum on the Approach to Historiographic Texts," in *Orientalia* 42 (1973): 178–94 (189–91; on bringing gifts, see also 191–93.) The motif of bringing gifts to the imperial center is widely and clearly attested, for instance, in neo-Assyrian and Achaemenid royal texts.

29 This is a point that deserves separate analysis. I have discussed these matters in "On Social Memory and Identity Formation in Late Persian Yehud: A Historian's Viewpoint with a Focus on Prophetic Literature, Chronicles and the Dtr. Historical Collection," in this volume, pp. 28–79; and more extensively in "The Yehudite Prophetic Books and Imperial Context," in this volume, pp. 134–61.

as the house of the deity.³⁰ Both are construed as the center of the cosmic world and of the earthly world in Yehud.³¹ But again, Jerusalem was not imagined and remembered only through the images evoked by the term *house*. As is well-known, in the ancient Near East cities were construed as female figures.³² Although a full discussion of the discursive implications of these gendered associations and the ways in which they may shape social mindscape is beyond the scope of the present work,³³ a few considerations suffice for the present purposes. Given the three most common, structural female roles within the ideational "house," female Jerusalem was to be construed and remembered in the main through the activation of three main generative images: (a) mother, (b) daughter, and (c) wife.³⁴

Jerusalem was explicitly remembered in terms of a mother (e.g., Isa 49:17–18; 54:13). Her children and at times very clearly "sons" are, of course, the residents of the city (whether in the future, past or present) that stands for an Israel. (I will return to this point).

Jerusalem was often remembered in terms of בת ציון 'daughter/female Zion' (*passim*) and at times as 'daughter/female Jerusalem' בת ירושלם (see 2 Kgs 19:21; Isa 37:22; Zeph 3:14; Zech 9:9; Lam 2:15). The term בת evoked the meaning 'daughter', which in turn, evoked "father," which in this case could only be imagined as YHWH.

Jerusalem was also imagined as YHWH's wife (Isa 54:5–8; 62:4), just as Israel is in other texts (for example, Hos 2, and note the "parallel" in Isa 54:5–8). In

---

30 On the blurring of boundaries and terms in relation to Jerusalem, with numerous examples from the Psalms, see S. Gillingham, "The Zion Tradition and the Editing of the Hebrew Psalter," in *Temple Worship in Biblical Israel: Proceedings of the Oxford Old Testament Seminar* (ed. J. Day; LHBOTS 422; London: T&T Clark, 2005), 308–41 (313–16).
31 E.g., Ezek 5:5. Note also previous references to the central fountain that play on the concept of the fountain at the sacred cosmic center. On this matter, see, for instance, C. L. Meyers and E. M. Meyers, *Zechariah 9–14* (AB 25C; New York: Doubleday, 1993), 399.
32 For a discussion of the gender of cities and Jerusalem's unique attribution of a personified biography, see S. Anthonioz, "Cities of Glory and Cities of Pride: Concepts, Gender, and Images of Cities in Mesopotamia and the Bible" in *Memory and the City in Ancient Israel* (eds. D. V. Edelman and E. Ben Zvi), 21–40.
33 The bibliography on these issues is extensive. For a recent study, see, for instance, C. M. Maier, *Daughter Zion, Mother Zion: Gender, Space and the Sacred in Ancient Israel* (Minneapolis: Fortress, 2008). See also J. M. O'Brien, *Challenging Prophetic Metaphor: Theology and Ideology in the Prophets* (Louisville, KY: Westminster John Knox, 2008), 125–51.
34 The motif of the "promiscuous adulteress" (often referred to as "the whore") is in this context a negative variant of the "wife" motif. Sinful Israel/Jerusalem was construed and remembered not only as YHWH's wife but also as "the promiscuous adulteress/whore" who cannot but commit adultery time and again (*passim*). See the ensuing discussion.

either case, within the gendered social mindscape of the period, the imagining of the city as female led the community's generative grammar of imagination to create appropriate males who should "own," protect, and enjoy her.

Even when YHWH was not necessarily or always imagined as Jerusalem's husband, the deity was imagined as rejoicing over her. For instance, readers of Isa 65:18–19 encounter a YHWH who "remembers" his future joy in Jerusalem, when he will create her and complete this creation by filling her with joy, goodness, and goods. But there is also Isa 62:4–5:

לֹא יֵאָמֵר לָךְ עוֹד עֲזוּבָה וּלְאַרְצֵךְ לֹא יֵאָמֵר עוֹד שְׁמָמָה כִּי לָךְ יִקָּרֵא חֶפְצִי־בָהּ וּלְאַרְצֵךְ
בְּעוּלָה כִּי־חָפֵץ יְהוָה בָּךְ וְאַרְצֵךְ תִּבָּעֵל
כִּי־יִבְעַל בָּחוּר בְּתוּלָה יִבְעָלוּךְ בָּנָיִךְ וּמְשׂוֹשׂ חָתָן עַל־כַּלָּה יָשִׂישׂ עָלַיִךְ אֱלֹהָיִךְ

> You shall no more be referred to as a forsaken/divorced woman
> and your land shall no more be referred as desolate/lack in fertility
> but you shall be called "my delight is in her"
> and your land, Married/Intercoursed
> for YHWH delights in you,
> and your land shall be married/intercoursed.
> For as a young man marries/has intercourse with a young woman,
> so shall your sons marry/have intercourse with you,
> and as a groom rejoices over a bride,
> so shall your god rejoice over you.

This text clearly and explicitly advances the image of YHWH as the husband of Jerusalem in a future successful and happy marriage as seen from the perspective of the gendered ideology of the time. But there is more. There is a preferred generative grammar according to which good (male) Israelites are supposed to imitate the deity. Hosea marries Israel and so YHWH. YHWH marries Jerusalem and so the Israelites/Jerusalemites who possess her at the "worldly level" within these utopian (and heavily ideological) acts of imagination. These Jerusalemites/Israelites cannot be other than Jerusalem's sons, that is, her dwellers. The text is not as strange as it may appear at first.[35]

Within this context of strongly gendered images (and social mindscape), it is also worth mentioning that Jerusalem was construed and remembered as YHWH's beautiful, glorious crown; a royal diadem in YHWH's hand (Isa 62:3; cf. Prov 12:4). It was not imagined as a female deity and could not have been imagined as such within the discourse of the community. However, like its counterpart, Israel, when construed in terms evocative of a marriage of eternal faithful-

---

[35] If the reference to "your sons" is exchanged with "your builders," no substantial change occurs, because "your builders" are "your sons." See below.

ness to YHWH,[36] and certainly, given the image of YHWH's permanent presence in its/her midst, which required holiness, some godly attributes had to be assigned to Jerusalem as well, directly and indirectly (see Isa 1:26; 52:1; Jer 3:17; 31:23; Ezek 48:35–the very conclusion of the book of Ezekiel; Zech 8:3).[37]

Just as remembering future Israel, remembering the future Jerusalem within the context of the poor, small city provided hope. Moreover, like other utopian images shared by a community, it facilitated an exploration of alternative "realities," of perceived lacks in the present, and turned a "nowhere" into a "somewhere" that figured prominently in the discourse of the community, which was certain it would become a worldly "somewhere" sometime.

Divine Creation and Building Jerusalem, Secondary Human Partners, and Imago Dei: A Few Observations

Within a discourse in which Jerusalem is construed and remembered as the city of YHWH (e.g., Pss 46:5; 48:2, 9; 87:3; 101:8) that stands at the center of the cosmos and plays cosmic roles such as being its "throne" on earth,[38] it is easy to understand why both its destruction (*passim* in prophetic literature and elsewhere) and its building were imagined to require divine intervention. YHWH was imagined as the builder of the city, and two of YHWH's attributes were 'cre-

---

[36] For a recent study that deals with female, marital, queenly, and crown-related images of Jerusalem in Isaiah, which advances the minority position that Jerusalem never becomes a deity, see C. M. Maier, "Daughter of Zion as Queen and the Iconography of the Female City," in *Images and Prophecy in the Ancient Eastern Mediterranean* (eds. M. Nissinen and C. E. Carter; FRLANT 233; Göttingen: Vandenhoeck & Ruprecht, 2009), 147–62.

[37] Given the discourse of the period, when the "female" city was imagined as disordered and thus disordering, as embodying, providing, and propagating "folly" or "misleading knowledge," as rejecting YHWH and so on, it was imagined as a whore. A comprehensive analysis of central sacred cities (Jerusalem, Babylon, Samaria) cannot omit this aspect. But given that the present study does not and cannot attempt any form of comprehensiveness, and given that the motif is well known and has been discussed in many other contributions, it is fully acknowledged but not addressed here. On these issues, see, for instance, R. P. Carroll, "Whorusalamin: A Tale of Three Cities as Three Sisters," in *On Reading Prophetic Texts: Gender-Specific and Related Studies in Memory of Fokkelien van Dijk-Hemmes* (eds. B. Becking and M. Dijkstra; BibIntS 18; Leiden: Brill, 1996), 67–82 and the works mentioned on 210 n. 33 above.

[38] See Jer 3:17 and compare with 1 Chr 29:23, Ps 132:7, Lam 2:1, and Isa 66:1, which do not negate the need to build and fill the temple and Jerusalem (see the rest of Isa 66) but which set these activities within the context of YHWH's cosmic house that encompasses all. Compare 1 Kgs 8.

ator' (ברא) and 'builder' (בנה; see, for instance, Isa 65:18–19; Pss 102:17; 147:2;[39] cf. Isa 54:5; Ps 51:20). Imagining the cosmic creation of new heavens and a new earth led directly and almost immediately to imagining the creation of a new Jerusalem, both as a place of human dwelling, work, and joy and as a peaceful, Edenic place in which the wolf and the lamb will eat together, and the lion will eat straw (Isa 65:17–25).[40]

But building Jerusalem, just as destroying it (*passim*), also required human hands, as the readership of all of these texts knew (e.g., Isa 62:6–7; 2 Chr 36:23; Haggai). Moreover, the process of building Jerusalem could not have been imagined as complete until the city would be filled with all that belongs to her, including not only the temple but also, among other things, walls, goods, pilgrims, and, of course, joy.[41] Within this inner Yehudite discourse, human beings, both Israelites and non-Israelites, could and at times were imagined as partners with YHWH in building/creating Jerusalem, even if at different levels (e.g., Isa 60; 62:6–7; 65:18–24; Haggai; 2 Chr 36:23). There is an element of *imago dei* or correspondence in actions and feelings; note, for instance, the explicit, textually inscribed tendency to construe an intertwining of YHWH's joy and human joy in, for instance, Isa 65:18–19.

Remembering Monarchic Jerusalem: A Few Observations

As a site of memory, Jerusalem embodied and communicated the memories already mentioned above but also memories of a late monarchic city that was emblematic of chaos and the dissolution of divine knowledge and order. It was remembered as a city in which divine instruction and true prophets were rejected, which was justifiably punished and burned down. As mentioned above, memories of catastrophe associated with the fall of monarchic Judah played a very prominent role in the memory-scape of the community, for obvious reasons. One of the most basic and central Yehudite metanarratives moves from sin to punishment involving destruction, exile, and alienation and on to a future Uto-

---

39 בּוֹנֵה יְרוּשָׁלַ͏ִם יהוה in Ps 147:2 probably should be translated 'the builder of Jerusalem is YHWH' (cf. New Jerusalem Bible).
40 From the perspective of the intended readership, the imagery in this text is supposed to inform and be informed by Gen 2–3. The reference to the snake and its eating dust constitute an obvious, textually inscribed signpost connecting this memory of a future Eden/Jerusalem with that of the past Eden (cf. Gen 3:14). Needless to say, this text is supposed to inform and be informed by Isa 11:6–9.
41 Cf. van Leeuwen, "Cosmos, Temple, House," esp. 399–404.

pia in which YHWH and Israel would be permanently aligned with each other. Remembering Jerusalem was remembering both its past and future, turning Jerusalem into the most memorable site of memory embodying the main narrative of Israel's past and future.

The basic metanarrative appears in multiple forms; it lies at the very core of the prophetic books collection. For instance, the history of Israel is encapsulated in the marital story of Hosea/YHWH and his wife/Israel in Hosea. The woman is Israel. YHWH chose her when she was young (exodus-wilderness) and the couple enjoyed a brief time of faithfulness. She is also a woman who, by nature, cannot but fornicate (that is, sin) and is then punished, but YHWH will bring her back. This time, however, he will provide her with divine attributes that will remove her 'fornicating nature' (אשת זנונים) and allow for a future, stable relationship between them.[42]

Significantly, the metanarrative was constantly reinforced in Yehud by multiple physical sites of memory in ways that the story of YHWH/Hosea with his wife could not. After all, people lived in a city, and in general physical environs that reminded them constantly of a former glory and a past calamity. But there was another important difference between the two. In the basic metanarrative encapsulated in Hosea's story, YHWH found his wife when she/Israel went up from Egypt, in the wilderness (Hos 2:16–17). Jerusalem could not evoke that memory, because within the facts about the past that were agreed on within the community, the city becomes Israelite and a site for memory that stands for Israel (in the main) only after David's conquest.

Thinking of Jerusalem helps to balance a common narrative of the story of Israel. A new foundational event, the building of the temple, and a new central hero, David (and to some extent Solomon), are added to the very foundational events of Exodus and Sinai and their foundational hero, Moses, even if in a secondary position. An entire historiographical work, Chronicles, in part was aimed at achieving this balance. As a site of memory encapsulating the story of Israel, Jerusalem performs a similar work. It draws attention to the foundational roles of the choice of Jerusalem and of David.

A section of the city and, by extension, at times all of Jerusalem was construed and remembered as עיר דוד 'the City of David'.[43] The city was remembered

---

[42] See "Remembering Hosea: The Prophet as a Site of Memory in Persian Period Yehud," in this volume, pp. 274–93.

[43] E.g., 2 Sam 5:7–9; 6:12; 1 Kgs 8:1; Isa 22:9. On the readership's understanding that Jerusalem is the City of David in 2 Sam 5:7–9 and its potential narratological implications, see, for instance, J. P. Fokkelman, *Narrative Art and Poetry in the Books of Samuel: A Full Interpretation Based on Stylistic and Structural Analyses* (4 vols.; Studia Semitica Neerlandica; Assen: Van Gor-

as belonging to both David and Yhwh and as a site of memory, shaped an *ad hoc* conceptual area shared by both.⁴⁴ Another *ad hoc* conceptual area emerges: Yhwh chooses David and Yhwh chooses Jerusalem. The chosen city is directly related to the chosen king, and both choices were construed as intertwined (see explicitly 1 Kgs 8:16 // 2 Chr 6:5) in the past and often across time and into the utopian era (see, for instance, Isa 11 as informed by Isa 65:17–25). Both relate to Israel, who is also chosen by Yhwh.

To remember Jerusalem as David's city was not only to remember a future, utopian city or even a past utopian city (David's Jerusalem) but also to remember the capital of a monarchic polity. It is to remember the fall of that polity and it is to remember that no Davidide is king of Judah in the present. It is both to be reminded of continuity and discontinuity between the kingdom of Judah and the province of Yehud, but of a clear continuity between temple and temple. Significantly, Solomon, the actual builder of the temple, was not construed as a military hero. He fought no wars, just like the leadership of Yehud did not; instead, he was a wise man.⁴⁵

---

cum, 1981–93), 3:162–63. Note also "the Chronicler changed the burial place of King Amaziah of Judah and wrote that he had been buried 'in the city of Judah (בעיר יהודה)' (2 Chr 25:28), while his *Vorlage* relates that Amaziah had been buried 'in the city of David (בעיר דוד)' (2 Kgs 14:20)" (I. Kalimi, "Jerusalem–The Divine City: The Representation of Jerusalem in Chronicles Compared with Earlier and Later Jewish Compositions," in *The Chronicler as Theologian: Essays in Honor of Ralph W. Klein* [eds. M. P. Graham, S. L. McKenzie, and G. N. Knoppers; JSOTSup 371; London: T&T Clark, 2003], 189–205 [191]). For a revised version of this essay as part of a comprehensive elaboration of Kalimi's views about the representation of Jerusalem in Chronicles, see idem, *An Ancient Israelite Historian: Studies in the Chronicler, His Time, Place and Writing* (Assen: Van Gorcum, 2005), 85–157. For a different position regarding עיר דוד in Chronicles, see P. Welten, *Geschichte und Geschichtsdarstellung in den Chronikbüchern* (WMANT 42; Neukirchen-Vluyn: Neukirchener Verlag, 1973), 61–63, 197.

44 Cf. D. V. Edelman, "David in Israelite Social Memory," in *Remembering Biblical Figures in the Late Persian and Early Hellenistic Periods: Social Memory and Imagination* (eds. D. V. Edelman and E. Ben Zvi; Oxford: Oxford University Press, 2013), 141–57, esp. 148–51.

45 This is consistent with a tendency to deemphasize warrior/military features in main heroes within the discourse and the social memory of late Persian/early Hellenistic Judah/Yehud. This tendency impacted on the (main) ways Moses and Abraham were characterized, and in Chronicles, although David remains a military hero, the emphasis is elsewhere. See also the David of Psalms. Even Joshua is imagined as meditating day and night on ספר התורה 'the book of (Yhwh's) instruction' (Josh 1:8). This tendency, with its correlated constructions of "masculinity," is consistent and reflects the mindscape of the literati of a society without any significant military power of its own. Although "traditional" constructions of warrior-like heroes still existed in the period, it is only during the Hasmonean period that this tendency ceases to be dominant. These matters require a separate discussion. I have addressed these issues in relation to remembering Abraham and Moses in the late Persian/early Hellenistic period in "The Memory of

To remember Davidic/Solomonic Jerusalem was to evoke and construe a story about a glorious, Jerusalem-centered, unified Israel under these kings. This story served also to bring together the cultic world of the first foundational past, centered on the Ark, tabernacle, and covenant, with that of the second foundational past when the temple was established and both to the future glorious temple from which light, water, and divine wisdom flow and to whom all flow, while at the same time (ideologically and imaginatively) connecting all of them to the community's, present, Persian-period ('Davidic/Solomonic') temple at the core of their Jerusalem.

But by doing so, the concept and memory of Jerusalem informed and controlled the meaning of the foundational narratives of Exodus and Wilderness that were shared with Samaria in such a way that turned them into unshared and unsharable collections, due to their (exclusivist) Jerusalem-centered perspective (see, for instance, 1 Kgs 8:16 // 2 Chr 6:5). Remembering their Jerusalem together, the literati contributed to their own sense of identity, social cohesion,[46] claims of unique legitimacy, and set ideological and social boundaries around the remembering community. It was a crucial action in their mnemonic struggles with Samaria, where, by the late Persian period, most worshipers of Yhwh in "the land" lived.

The very logic of this process strongly emphasizes Jerusalem's place as the capital of Israel, not of Judah alone. It is a capital that should be inhabited by all pious Israelites (cf. 1 Chr 9:3; 2 Chr 11:13–16). By doing so, it creates a Yehud that stands for and even is Israel while it reinforces a Jerusalem-centered understanding of what Israel (not Yehud) is and should be.

Balancing Images: A Few Observations

Additional aspects of the Jerusalem of mind and memory can be explored,[47] but for present purposes, those advanced above suffice. However, an important feature of this Jerusalem cannot be omitted: the ubiquitous presence of balancing

---

Abraham in Late Persian/Early Hellenistic Yehud/Judah" and "Exploring the Memory of Moses 'The Prophet'" in this volume, pp. 162–98 and pp. 199–231 respectively. For Moses, see T. Römer, "Moses outside the *Torah* and the Construction of a Diaspora Identity," in *JHebS* 8/15 (2008), http://www.jhsonline.org/Articles/article_92.pdf.

46 I discussed the role of "preaching to the choir"-type activities for enhancing social cohesion among the literati in Jerusalem in "On Social Memory and Identity Formation."

47 For example, the Yehudite, construed memory of remembering Jerusalem then and there when Israel was in Exile; see Ps 137:1–6.

images. For example, the unique sacredness of Jerusalem and its role in the divine, cosmic economy shaped a systemic preference to construe the place as designated by Yhwh well before David, so that its selection was also understood as essentially independent of David (see, for instance, the association of Jerusalem and Mt. Moriah in 2 Chr 3:1).[48]

Jerusalem is David's city, but the defining and crucial house in the city, the temple, was built not by him but by the wise Solomon. Chronicles, in turn, balances the memory by emphasizing that David actually provided all that was needed for the temple and set its rules. Many texts bring together the future David and future Jerusalem and associate them with the future, utopian kingdom of Yhwh (for example, Isaiah 11). These texts shape memories of a future kingdom that belongs to both David and Yhwh, with Jerusalem as its capital. Some texts shape memories of a past Davidic kingdom that was Yhwh's kingdom, without clearly stating anything about the future (see 1 Chr 28:5; 2 Chr 13:8), while many other texts remind readers of a utopian, future Jerusalem and a utopian kingdom of Yhwh in which no Davidide appears (for example, Obadiah, Zephaniah, Hos 14).

Jerusalem is Israel and embodies Israel, but it is also remembered as a non-Israelite city, a late conquest. It is a "Canaanite" city where readers of the authoritative repertoire of the period encounter pious people, including a non-Israelite named Melchizedek who was a priest of אל עליון 'the High God' (Gen 14:20), which in turn is then balanced by Ps 110:4, which partially Israelitizes the foreign king.[49] This type of example can be multiplied; another involves Jerusalem in the land of Benjamin but also in Judah; see Josh 15:8, 63; 18:15, and Jerusalem's status as conquered and not conquered in Judg 1:8, 21. Those mentioned above suffice to demonstrate that an element of fuzziness played a part in the construction of Jerusalem as a site of memory, just as in any other site of memory in Yehud.[50]

---

[48] This claimed association is at the core of another "front" in the mnemonic struggles between Yehud and Samaria (or their discourses), since Samarian texts consistently associated Mt. Moriah with Mt. Gerizim. On the struggle over the memory of Mt. Moriah and of Abram, see I. Kalimi, *Early Jewish Exegesis and Theological Controversy: Studies in Scriptures in the Shadow of Internal and External Controversies* (Assen: Van Gorcum, 2002).

[49] See also Judg 19:11–12. In this text the Jebusites are implicitly construed as better than (some) Israelites.

[50] I expanded on this point in my essay "On Social Memory and Identity Formation."

Final Consideration

The preceding observations demonstrate that the city of Jerusalem was a site of memory that did not necessarily foreground images of busy markets, workers, human houses, or an implied urban characterization of labor. Instead, this site of memory communicated a sense of utopian and eternal cosmic sanctity. As such, Jerusalem had to exist eternally but also had a reality outside historical time, just like its foundational streams of waters.[51] This Jerusalem, which populated and generated texts and evoked memories of past and future events, served as a beacon making sense of the past. It provided hope for the future, facilitating a Jerusalem-centered version of traditional ancient Near Eastern motifs consistent with the discourse of the community. At the same time, it turned a potential cognitive dissonance into an argument sustaining the main tenets of the then-present community while simultaneously contributing to the formation of in-group boundaries that separated the community from other communities of Yhwh-worshipers in the vicinity of Yehud as well as the role and centrality of the temple within Yehud.

---

51 Compare M. Nissinen, "City as Lofty as Heaven: Arbela and Other Cities in Neo-Assyrian Prophecy," in *"Every City Shall Be Forsaken: Urbanism and Prophecy in Ancient Israel and the Near East* (eds. L. L. Grabbe and R. D. Haak; JSOTSup 330; Sheffield: Sheffield Academic Press, 2001), 172–209.

Remembering Pre-Israelite Jerusalem in Late Persian Yehud: Mnemonic Preferences, Memories and Social Imagination*

Introduction

The textual repertoire of the literati in late Persian Yehud and the literati themselves seem obsessed with memories of Jerusalem, mainly of a past and glorious Jerusalem, of a late monarchic, sinful and eventually destroyed Jerusalem, and of a future, ideal Jerusalem. Although Jerusalem during the late Persian period was a small town,[1] and perhaps even partially because it was small, it became

---

* First published in *Urban Dreams and Realities in Antiquity: Remains and Representations of the Ancient City* (ed. A. Kemezis; Leiden: Brill, 2014), 413–437.
1 This is not the place to discuss the vast literature on estimates of the population of Persian period Jerusalem. It suffices to state that the city was a relatively small town with less than 2,000 people and probably significantly less than that. For some literature on the matter, see O. Lipschits, "Persian Period Finds from Jerusalem: Facts and Interpretations," *JHebS* 9 (2009), article 20, available online at http://www.jhsonline.org, reprinted under the same title in *Perspectives on Hebrew Scriptures VI: Comprising the Contents of Journal of Hebrew Scriptures, vol. 9* (ed. E. Ben Zvi; Piscataway, NJ: Gorgias Press, 2010), 423–453; I. Finkelstein "Persian Period Jerusalem and Yehud: A Rejoinder." *JHebS* 9 (2009), article 24, available online at http://www.jhsonline.org, reprinted under the same title in *Perspectives on Hebrew Scriptures VI: Comprising the Contents of Journal of Hebrew Scriptures, vol. 9* (ed. E. Ben Zvi. Piscataway, NJ: Gorgias Press, 2010), 529–542; idem, "Jerusalem in the Persian (and Early Hellenistic) Period and the Wall of Nehemiah," *JSOT* 32 (2008): 501–520; idem, "Archaeology and the List of Returnees in the Books of Ezra and Nehemiah," *PEQ* 140 (2008): 1–10; and more recently, I. Finkelstein, I. Koch and O. Lipschits, "The Mound on The Mount: A Possible Solution to the 'Problem With Jerusalem,'" *JHebS* 11 (2011), article 12, available online at http://www.jhsonline.org, reprinted under the same title in *Perspectives in Hebrew Scriptures VIII: Comprising the Contents of Journal of Hebrew Scriptures, vol. 11* (ed. E. Ben Zvi. Piscataway, NJ: Gorgias Press, 2013), 317–339. See also H. Geva "Estimating Jerusalem's Population in Antiquity: A Minimalist View," EI 28 (2007); Teddy Kollek Volume: 50–65 (Hebrew); A. Kloner "Jerusalem's Environs in the Persian Period", in *New Studies on Jerusalem* (eds. A. Faust and E. Baruch; Ramat Gan, Israel: Ingeborg Rennert Center for Jerusalem Studies, 2001), 91–95 (Hebrew); cf. O. Lipschits, "Demographic Changes in Judah between the Seventh and the Fifth Centuries BCE", in *Judah and the Judeans in the Neo-Babylonian Period* (eds. O. Lipschits and J. Blenkinsopp; Winona Lake, Ind.: Eisenbrauns, 2003), 323–376.; C. E. Carter, *The Emergence of Yehud in the Persian Period: A Social and Demographic Study* (JSOTS, 294; Sheffield: Sheffield Academic Press, 1999); A. Faust, "Judah in the Sixth Century BCE: A Rural Perspective," *PEQ* 126 (2003): 37–53. It is worth noting that even those who advance a 'maximalist' view of Persian period Jerusalem–which in itself is a minority viewpoint–agree that the Persian period city was just

a most central site of memory for its literati. Eventually, Jerusalem served as a central site of memory for other, much later communities; as such it both influenced and was shaped by diverse, later Judaic, Christian or Muslim traditions over vast spans of time and space.²

During the approximately two hundred years of Achaemenid rule in the Levant (538–332 BCE)–the same time period within which most of the books that eventually ended up in the Hebrew Bible/Old Testament emerged, at least more or less in their present form–Jerusalem, as a city that populated the social memory of the community, was a central, focal point for shared imagination and for structuring the central mnemonic narratives of the community.

One of the most important of these narratives was the 'from temple to temple' narrative. Its main plot opened with the process leading to establishment of the temple in Jerusalem, then meandered through multiple vignettes of the Judahite monarchic period that took much social mindshare (see Kings, Chronicles) and which, on the whole, portrayed the period as leading to the city's ideologically justifiable destruction. The plot then largely focused on the calamity of destruction and exile and continued with the establishment of a second Jerusalemite temple, which as important as it was, stood a far cry from the glorious temple of the golden past (e. g., Hag 2:3; cf., even if later, Ezra 3:12). It reached its apex and conclusion in the glorious, future, utopian temple that stood at the very heart of an utopian Jerusalem, which at times was imagined as standing at the very heart of an utopian world (e. g., Isa 2:2–4; 56:1–9; 65; Mic 4:1–4; Ezek 40–44; 47:1–2; Hag 2:4–9; Zech 8:3; Ps 46:4–5; 48:2–3, 8–9; *passim*).³ This is not the place to study at length this central mnemonic narrative. It suffices, however, for the present purposes to note its ubiquity in the discourse of Judah/Yehud (or at least, that of its literati) in the late Persian period.

Another narrative, closely intertwined with the preceding one, moved from David, YHWH's chosen king, through many Davidic kings, both good and bad, to a future, utopian Davidic king or even a Davidic community (i. e., a community to whom the promises of David apply and is ruled directly by YHWH). Jerusalem

---

a fraction of the late monarchic Jerusalem. For a 'maximalist' view see G. Barkay, "Additional View of Jerusalem in Nehemiah Days", in *New Studies in the Archaeology of Jerusalem and Its Region II* (eds. D. Amit and G. D. Stiebel; Jerusalem: Israel Antiquities Authority and the Hebrew University, 2008), 48–54 (Hebrew)—Barkay suggests that Persian Jerusalem was about 120 dunam (51)—and for criticism to this position, see works above, esp. those of I. Finkelstein.
2 This said, this essay addresses *only* constructions and memories of Jerusalem that existed within late Persian Yehud.
3 I recently discussed some of these images elsewhere. See "Exploring Jerusalem as a Site of Memory in the Late Persian and Early Hellenistic Period", in this volume, pp. 482–503.

as a complex, condensing and comprehensive site of memory was shaped to evoke the story of the people and their interactions with the deity, both in time and space in the past and future.

The mnemonic Jerusalem at the core of either one of these closely related narratives stood at the center of the literati's construction of Israel in Yehud (i.e., the Persian province of Judah). As such, this Jerusalem of memory played crucial roles in processes of identity formation.[4]

But if this mnemonic system closely interwove the concepts evoked by the terms 'Israel' and 'Jerusalem,' and in doing so, shaped much of their range of meaning, and if Jerusalem embodied and communicated the foundational mnemonic narratives of 'from temple to temple,' and 'from past David to future David' and thus construed a Jerusalem-centered Israel, why did Jerusalem embody and communicate also prominent social memories of a pre-Davidic and pre-Israelite Jerusalem, and what roles did the literati's construed memories of the previous residents of Jerusalem fulfill in their mnemonic system?

Constructing, Imagining and Remembering Differences

As one begins to address these questions, one of the most promising approaches is to place social memories about the previous residents of Jerusalem within a larger context of memories of inhabitants of other cities and regions of 'the land' who were about to be dispossessed by Joshua/Israel/YHWH–according to the basic 'historical' narrative agreed upon by the community at the time. The case is strengthened by additional considerations. For instance, the Jebusites, the previous inhabitants of Jerusalem who were defeated by David, were explicitly referred to time and again in various lists of the dispossessed nations within the authoritative repertoire of the community (see Exod 3:8, 17; 13:5; 23:23; 33:2; 34:11; Deut 7:1; 20:17; Josh 3:10; 9:1; 11:3; 12:8; 24:11).[5] In addition, not only was Jerusalem in 'the land,' but it was also conceived as the very heart of 'the land' and stood symbolically for it numerous times within the discourse of the period.

---

[4] The likely role of the historical temple in Jerusalem in the production and reproduction of their literary repertoire and its struggle to achieve prominence in Judah during the period is consistent and partially, but *only partially* explains these developments in social memory. These issues, however, stand beyond the scope of this essay.

[5] One may add that in Josh 10, the Jerusalemites and their king were explicitly characterized as Amorites' (see vv. 3, 5, 12). On the place of the Amorites in the community's social imagination and memory as a people bound to be dispossessed before Israel due to their sinful behaviour see Gen 15:16; 1 Kgs 21:26; 2 Kgs 21:11.

Thus, for instance, the exile from Jerusalem (and Judah, which in turn was also symbolically represented by its main city, Jerusalem) was conceptually associated with exile from the land.

Although one *might* have anticipated that the conquest of Jerusalem and the portrayal of the Jebusites would be construed and remembered as the culmination of the conquest story and the story of the replacement of the previous residents of the land with the Israelites,[6] and although there was a strong generative grammar that would have led to such a development, the following observations demonstrate that this was not the case; to the contrary, there were very significant points of divergence.

Two central, connective, didactic and very salient differences are particularly relevant for the present purposes.[7] First, the dispossessed were, for the most part, construed as dispossessed because of their wickedness–a preferred systemic choice within the ideological mindscape of ancient Israel. Since their calamity was supposed to match their actions,[8] they became magnets for negative attributes and, as such, excellent candidates for social and ideological processes of 'othering.' They were construed as kind of anti-(ideal) Israel. Accordingly, remembering them served to 'otherize' whatever was characterized as 'anti-Israelite.' Thus, if following Yhwh's instructions/*torah* was considered the epitome of what Israel should do, the dispossessed nations were construed within the discourse of the community as practitioners of and as the embodiment of anti-*torah* behaviour.

In other words, memories of the dispossessed contributed much to the creation of a system of a set of interwoven bipolar, dualistic mental maps, e.g.,

---

6 Cf. Josh 23:4–5.
7 By connective aspects I mean aspects that are clearly connected to other aspects.
8 To be sure, there was not a single mnemonic scenario for the removal of the previous inhabitants of the land within the social memory of the community (or at least, its literati). In fact, there existed several mnemonic scenarios. For instance, there were those involving forced expulsion, either due to Yhwh's manipulation of 'nature' (e.g., Exod 23:28; Josh 24:12) or through other means with Yhwh's support, but there were also scenarios that involved physical extermination (mainly, but not only, in Deuteronomy; e.g. Deut 7:23). All these scenarios involved the removal of the previous inhabitants of the land and thus, from their perspective a terrible catastrophe, which within the discourse of the period was associated with their 'wickedness.' In other words, their dispossession was construed as just punishment. Imagining such a past and such causality at work served obvious didactic/socializing purposes. On the mentioned scenarios see M. Weinfeld, *Deuteronomy 1–11* (AB, 5 A; New York: Doubleday, 1991), 382–384; B. J. Schwartz, "Reexamining the Fate of the 'Canaanites' in the *Torah* Traditions", in *Sefer Moshe. The Moshe Weinfeld Jubilee Volume* (eds. C. Cohen, A. Hurvitz and S. M. Paul; Winona Lake, Ind.: Eisenbrauns, 2004), 151–70 and bibliography.

torah vs. anti-*torah*; Israel vs. the dispossessed nations; ability to stay in the land vs. removal from the land. Memories of repeated warnings given to past Israel to not behave like the dispossessed nations, for if it does it will be dispossessed as well, is a point made time and again (see, among many others, Lev 18:3; Deut 18:9–12; 2 Kgs 16:3; 17:8; 21:2, 6, 8).[9]

Certainly there were texts that evoked social memories that not all the supposedly dispossessed were actually dispossessed (e.g., Josh 13:1–7). But even these memories contributed to the main point, as the remaining previous residents of the land were commonly imagined as being left in the land by YHWH to tempt Israel to do the evil in the sight of its deity (Josh 23:13; Judg 2:21–23; 3:24); in this they played the role of the temptress (female, 'other') to a male Israel (e.g., Num 25; 1 Kgs 11). These texts thus also construe the 'other' as 'anti-Israel' and as certainly worthy of dispossession and complete removal from 'the land.'[10]

As mentioned above, the Jebusites, i.e., the defeated residents of Jerusalem, appear in a general list of dispossessed (and 'worthy of dispossession') nations. But how were they construed and remembered by the community as it read *specific* references about them in its textual repertoire? Which particular portrayals of the Jebusites were encoded in and communicated by these texts?

To begin with, it is particularly significant that despite (a) the explicit inclusion of the Jebusites among the common lists of the nations that were dispossessed before Israel (e.g., Exod 23:23; 33:2; 34:11; *passim*), and (b) the obvious potential to turn them into magnets for negative attributes, this path was not taken. To be sure, there was potential not merely for assigning negative attributes, but for using the Jebusites to construe an anti-Jerusalem so as to project it in portrayals of Jerusalem under particularly sinful kings and thus to shape social memory not only in terms of oppositional dyads such as 'Israel and anti-Israel/dispossessed nations' (see, for instance, 1 Kgs 21:26; 2 Kgs 16:3; 17:8; 21:2, 11; 2 Chr 33:2 and note the comparisons with dispossessed groups, but never with the Jebusites per se), but also dyads of 'Jerusalem and anti- Jerusalem/Jebusite Jerusalem.' But, significantly, this path was not taken.

---

9 To be sure, the point of these maps was not to address the imagined dispossessed nations that populated the social memory of the community nor the non-Israelite Persians, but to remind the Persian period community that the catastrophe of 586 BCE happened because their ancestors, i.e., Israel and thus they themselves, as it were, behaved like the nations that were dispossessed before Israel and thus were also rejected from the land.

10 A minority explanation for their presence was they were left so Israel may learn how to wage warfare (see Judg 3:1–2; but see already Judg 3:4–7).

The community in Yehud developed social memories that failed to include any narratives of the Jebusites developed according to these lines or that served the aforementioned purposes. The obvious rhetorical/didactic benefits that would have resulted had the Jebusites been used in that way, and the systemic preferences for the emergence of the type narrative mentioned above raises the question of what may have countered any tendencies towards creating them. Before addressing these matters, though, the case for the construction (and mnemonic use) of the Jebusites in a manner different from the typical (construed) 'dispossessed nation' within the discourse of the community has to be made, not just stated.

To begin with a negative argument, there are relatively few particular references to (Davidic or pre-Davidic) Jebusites within the authoritative repertoire of the late Persian period community in Judah,[11] and, most significantly, none of the references draw particular attention to their sins. Even among these few references to a pre-(Davidic) conquest Jerusalem there are some that can be easily explained as necessary outcomes of other narratives. To be sure, all these instances carry meanings, but their main thrust was not to evoke substantial social memories about pre-Israelite Jerusalem and its inhabitants.

For instance, according to 1 Sam 17:54, David took the head of Goliath and brought it to Jerusalem, which within the basic world of the narrative was still Jebusite at the time.[12] The reference to this action is not an anachronism, because the term implies "a retrojection of present conditions through ignorance of the past,"[13] but rather a case of departure from temporal consistency for the purpose of shaping a 'better' narrative–in this case, for the purpose of a narrative that successfully brings together the first great victory of David and 'his city,' which is also Israel's and Yhwh's city. A central spatial site of memory (Jerusalem) is thus associated with a communal memory about a core event in the beginning of David's career and thus in the development of the monarchy and the path towards the establishment of the temple.

---

[11] Contrast with the numerous references to the Canaanites, Amorites, and the 'peoples that Yhwh dispossessed' and their 'ways' in the repertoire of the community. Not only the presence of references to these people groups but also a certain density of negative portrayals of them within the discourse of the community is necessary if they are to become successful mnemonic ciphers for Israel when it behaves in 'ungodly' ways within the social mindscape of the community.

[12] David's conquest of Jerusalem was at the time still many years in the future and is many chapters further along in the narration; see 2 Sam 5:6–9

[13] See A. F. Campbell, *1 Samuel* (FOTL 7; Grand Rapids, Mich.: Eerdmans, 2003), 182.

This essay is not the place to analyse this case or other instances in which temporality is less important than symbolic and, above all, mnemonic meanings. It suffices to note, however, that such a reference to Jerusalem does not really evoke memories of a pre-Israelite Jerusalem. This said, it is worth noting that nothing particularly negative about Jebusite Jerusalem transpires from the reference.

A second example: to remember David as *the* king who conquered Jerusalem and turned it into the capital of his/Yhwh's kingdom required, of course, to imagine and remember an enemy to be defeated by David, namely the Jebusites. Yet, the main role of the Jebusites in that story was to be defeated, and their only action was to taunt David–as per the usual, cross-cultural topos of the mistakenly confident group (or person) about to fall. Not only is the matter particularly undeveloped,[14] but also and most significantly, the community when reading Samuel is asked to evoke and remember their taunt, which refers to the 'blind and the lame,' for its implications about later policies of ritual exclusion in (later) Jerusalem (2 Sam 5:6, 8),[15] and when reading Chronicles just to remember that they said to David "You shall not enter here" (1 Chr 11:5).[16] In both cases, mindshare is drawn to the event of the conquest and the city itself, not to the sinful character of the Jebusites.

In addition to the negative evidence, i.e., the lack of a particular negative characterization of the Jebusites or of their construction as 'anti-(ideal) Israel,' there is in fact evidence for a positive characterization of the Jebusites, unlike the case of the other dispossessed nations. For example, there is the characterization of Jebusite Jerusalem in the story of the rape in Gibeah (see Judg 19:10–30). Reading the text evoked in the community the image of a foolish Levite who thought that an Israelite city would be a better place to lodge than Jebusite Jerusalem, just because one was Israelite and the other not. Whatever other messages this story communicated, it certainly created a positive memory of a pre-Israelite, Jebusite Jerusalem. Moreover, if Gibeah was meant to evoke memories of Saul's city within the readership, and Jerusalem meant to evoke memories of David's city, then the Jebusites would have been discursively associated with David.[17]

---

14 Contrast with Josephus, *Ant.* 7.61.
15 See, for instance, S. M. Olyan, "'Anyone Blind or Lame Shall Not Enter The House': On The Interpretation of Second Samuel 5:8b," in *CBQ* 60 (1998): 218–27.
16 Contrast with 1 Sam 17; 2 Kgs 18:19–25; Isa 47:8–13; Ezek 27; Amos 6:1; Obad 3; Zeph 2:15; *passim*.
17 See, for instance Y. Amit, *Hidden Polemics in Biblical Narrative* (Leiden: Brill, 2000), 178–84 and esp. 181.

The latter observation brings up another crucial difference between (construed, social) memories of the conquest of the land during Joshua's time and those of David's conquest of Jerusalem. Unlike the case of the narratives associated with Joshua, the one about his conquest of Jerusalem nowhere states that David expelled, never mind exterminated, the residents of Jerusalem, nor that he would find it desirable to have done so.[18] Moreover, the story of David's conquest of Jerusalem is placed within and particularly informed by its context in both Samuel and Chronicles. Both books portray and ask their readership to remember a post-conquest, prominent Jebusite who was alive and well. This Jebusite possessed a field even after David's conquest (2 Sam 24:16–18; 1 Chr 21:15–28; 21:28). David is not condemned for letting the Jebusites live, and indeed the mentioned Jebusite is portrayed in a positive light and is instrumental to the establishment of the proper site of the temple. David is not remembered as a ruler who dispossessed him, but as one who bought the Jebusite's property for full price.

There are additional divergences between memories of Joshua and his conquest of 'the land' and David's conquest of Jerusalem that impact the way in which the Jebusites were construed and remembered. Joshua was remembered as engaging and defeating many powerful kings.[19] The dispossessed nations were remembered as mighty, many, and often engaging Israel in large coalitions. The characterization of the enemy as mighty was a necessary feature for the construction of the heroic character of the conqueror. Of course, in the case of memories of Joshua and the conquest, the stress was not only or even mainly on the heroic character of Joshua, but on that of YHWH, the one who dispossessed nations.[20] Thus, the community developed and remembered mnemonic narratives

---

[18] Josephus reshapes the biblical text and tells the story as 'it was supposed to be' and thus indirectly confirms that for him the absence of any note about expelling the Jebusites in both Chronicles and Samuel carried a message. For Josephus's version, see *Ant.* 7.65.

[19] See the long list of kings in Josh 12, references to fortifications and to large coalitions in Joshua. It has been widely recognized that some neo Assyrian motifs (including 'the one vs. the many') are present in Josh 1–11/12. See, for instance, J. Van Seters, "Joshua's Campaign of Canaan and Near Eastern Historiography," in *SJOT* 4 (1990): 1–12; T. Römer, *The So-Called Deuteronomistic History. A Sociological, Historical and Literary Introduction* (London: T&T Clark, 2005), 83–90; K. L. Younger Jr., *Ancient Conquest Accounts: A Study in Ancient Near Eastern and Biblical History Writing* (JSOTS 98; Sheffield: JSOT Press, 1990).

[20] The heroic/warrior character of Joshua is balanced by the need to characterize him as a Moses-like leader and his successor and above all, because of the strong systemic preference to emphasize the heroic character of YHWH. It is YHWH who fought for Israel not Joshua (cf. Josh 23:3 and *passim*), just as it was YHWH, not Moses, who separated the waters. The widespread portrayal of the dispossessed people as powerful is most often meant to stress YHWH's

about the deity's taking possession of the land in the far past that explicitly and repeatedly portrayed the events as requiring and involving mighty divine actions.[21] In these narratives Yhwh was both imagined and 'encountered' by the community as a powerful warrior deity whose actions frequently evoked the highest heroic images within the social mindscape of the community, images that were associated with Yhwh's role in the foundational period of Exodus (see, for instance, acts of turning the sea/river into dry land).[22]

Drawing attention to and turning memories of mighty warriors (divine or human) and their deeds into central sites of memory for the group required some detailed narratives. This requirement was obviously fulfilled in the case of the Exodus and the conquest of the land. Even a cursory reading of the books of Exodus and Joshua demonstrates the point beyond any doubt. Moreover, memories of these great heroic deeds were brought to bear and echoed in many different works within the repertoire of the community (e.g., Isa 43:16–17; 63:11–14; Mic 7:15; Ps 66:6; 78:11–14; 106:21–22; 114:3–5; 136:13–16) and one may safely assume that they held a very significant social mindshare.

But what about the conquest of Jerusalem by David or Yhwh? The community believed the city of Jerusalem to be at the center of the 'land' and above all at the center of 'the world.' David, the greatest hero and the leader who took more territory than any other king within the social memory map of the community, conquered Jerusalem. Needless to say, without such an act neither the conquest of the land nor the establishment of the temple, at the core of the world of the community, could have taken place. Taking all this into account, one might have anticipated repeated references to David or at least Yhwh and their heroic deeds in association with the conquest of Jerusalem. One might have expected the existence of detailed narratives commemorating that event time and again and bringing it to the 'present of the community.'[23] Certainly any comparison with memories of the conquest of the land by Yhwh/Joshua would lead us to anticipate all of the above for the conquest of the city that 'embodied' the land, as it were.

---

heroic powers (see, for instance, Num 13:25–33; Deut 7:1; 9:1–2; Josh 23:9; Ps 135:10–12; Neh 9:22–25).

21 The widespread portrayal of the dispossessed people as powerful is most often explicitly meant to stress Yhwh's heroic powers. See, for instance, Num 13:25–33; Deut 7:1; 9:1–2; Josh 23:9; Ps 135:10–12; Neh 9:22–25.

22 See, for instance, and quite explicitly, Josh 2:10; 4:23; 5:1; cf. Ps 114:3, 5; 135:8–12.

23 Cf. portrayals of other conquests of Jerusalem, whether Titus, Crusaders, or Ṣalāḥ ad-Dīn, and their impact on social memory of the relevant communities.

But the story of the conquest of Jerusalem was not allocated much narrative space within the repertoire of the community (see 2 Sam 5:6–9a; 1 Chr 11:4–7a) and not much mindshare would have been allocated to it within a community that construed and remembered its past by reading and rereading the authoritative books in its repertoire. Despite all the considerations mentioned above, the actual conquest narrative of Jerusalem consisted of only three and a half or four verses. From the perspective of the community, there was a lot to read, imagine and remember about Jerusalem, but how it was conquered by David played a very minor role.[24]

Moreover, despite the fact that David was obviously remembered in the community as a warrior hero (e.g., 1 Sam 18:7; 1 Chr 11:2 [// 2 Sam 5:2])[25] and despite the fact that usually great heroes of the past are remembered to have performed at least some acts of heroism when it comes to their most important achievements, the narratives of the conquest of Jerusalem (as reflected and shaped by both Samuel and Chronicles) and the memories that these narratives evoked in the community failed to assign David any particular acts of personal heroism when it comes to this particular event (contrast, for instance, with the extensive narrative and memories associated with his defeat of Goliath).

This is even more noteworthy in Chronicles, a book that reflects and evokes a memory of the conquest of the city as the first royal act of David (1 Chr 11:3–8). Even as the book seems to follow common generative mnemonic grammars and show a distinct preference to associate the main epic-heroic acts of a great king with the beginning of his reign[26] and thus creates anticipation for references to

---

[24] Jerusalem and related terms (e.g., Zion) appear explicitly well over 800 times in works that were later included in the HB and which were most likely among and on the whole representative of the repertoire of the time. Given that, for obvious reasons, Jerusalem could not appear much in the Pentateuch or in historiographical narratives shaping memories of a pre-David and thus pre-Israelite Jerusalem, this is a very large number. Talmon noticed many years ago that Jerusalem and related terms are proportionally more attested in this corpus than in late-Second Temple literature (when Jerusalem was a much larger city) and or later rabbinic literature (despite Jerusalem's centrality in rabbinic Judaism) and needless to say in the New Testament. See S. Talmon, "The Biblical Concept of Jerusalem," in *JES* 8 (1971): 300–16.

[25] To be sure, not only as a warrior hero (see Psalms), but certainly as a warrior hero.

[26] "The author is applying to the figure of David an epic-heroic topos long established in Ancient Near Eastern historiography. Assyrian kings claim to have taken some of their most significant actions at the very outset of their reigns or to have achieved their greatest victories during the first year" (G. N. Knoppers, *I Chronicles 10–29: A New Translation with Introduction and Commentary* [AB, 12; New York: Doubleday, 2004], 545). Of course, since the conquest of Jerusalem is brought to the beginning of his reign, this military campaign is the first of the king (contrast with 2 Sam), and within Chronicles, the first to which the attention of the readership is drawn, but in the past world of Chronicles, David was already a hardened warrior leader when he became king

David's heroism, it fails to do so. The text in 1 Chr 11:3–8 does not evoke any particular memories of his epic-heroic deeds or great military wisdom. Instead of emphasizing David's military heroism,[27] it explicitly brings his building activities after the conquest to the attention of the community (1 Chr 11:8), which makes him the first and most important pious builder king–a very important *topos* in Chronicles. It is not by chance that in Chronicles the first pious, royal building activity in the land takes place in Jerusalem or is conducted by the best king in the book, David.

To be clear, the point I am advancing is *not* that David was not remembered as a powerful military hero within the community, or that the community would not have construed the story of his conquest of Jerusalem as a significant achievement, but that not much textual attention and thus likely not much social mindshare was drawn first to the entire story of the conquest of Jerusalem (in contrast to, for instance, the Exodus, the conquest of the land, or the preparation and building of the temple in Jerusalem) in general and to David's own heroism during the conquest of Jerusalem in particular. When the memory of David the hero was brought to the present of the community, stories like his defeat of Goliath were brought up, but not much about what he did when he conquered Jerusalem.

Most of the book of Samuel is about David and more than a third of the book of Chronicles–which presents itself as a history from Adam to Cyrus–is devoted to David (see 1 Chr 3, most of chs. 6, 11–29). But reports of David's conquest of Jerusalem spanned only three and a half to four verses. This is obviously not a random or accidental distribution of narrative space. The relative lack of stress on the event and the lack of emphasis on David's heroic aspect in relation to this conquest cannot be taken for granted. The absence of emphasis results from and reflects a strong system of preferences and dis-preferences in terms of shaping social memory within the community that clearly overpowered mnemonic tendencies to lionize David's heroic character in association with the conquest of 'his' city or to make the conquest a central site of memory.

(1 Chr 11:2). For a different approach, see J. W. Wright, "The Fight for Peace: Narrative and History in the Battle Accounts in Chronicles", in *The Chronicler as Historian* (eds. M. P. Graham, K. G. Hoglund and S. L. McKenzie; JSOTS 238; Sheffield: JSOT Press, 1997), 150–77 (159–60).

27 No action of personal military heroism or military craftiness is particularly evoked. Instead, if there was a warrior hero in the story in Chronicles, it was Joab not David (1 Chr 11:6). Cf. 2 Sam 5:6–9a and 1 Chr 11:4–7a with Josephus, *Ant.* 7.60–64 and notice how the latter stresses David's heroic character; this is consistent with Josephus' tendency to underscore the courage of David. See L. H. Feldman, *Josephus's Interpretation of the Bible* (Berkeley: University of California Press, 1998), 544–50.

On the surface, one may link these absences with a well-attested tendency in Yehudite social memory to *not* remember some foundational characters (e. g., Abraham, Moses) as the trans-cultural, usual 'manly warrior hero.'[28] This tendency may have been at work in the general construction of David in Chronicles and Psalms, but even if it stands somewhat in the background, it certainly fails to explain why David was not the only main personage that was remembered far more as Jerusalem's builder (esp. by the Chronicler) than as the hero of mighty deeds who conquered Jerusalem.

Unlike narratives about the conquest of the land or the Exodus, there is no reference to mighty deeds of Yhwh in the conquest of Jerusalem. To be sure, texts as Josh 23:4–5 point to the potential within the community for a narrative emphasizing Yhwh's conquest of the last and most important part of 'the land;' there was opportunity for presenting the event as the culmination of the fulfillment of the prophetic words of Joshua, of which late Persian period, Yehudite literati would have been aware, or perhaps associating the successful completion of the conquest with the piousness of the people or its leader, David, who counterbalanced prior acts of rebellion against Yhwh, even if momentarily.[29] Yet, such a narrative is missing from the main set of social memories encoded in, and evoked and virtually experienced through the reading and rereading of their authoritative, past-constructing repertoire of texts. Indeed, in sharp contrast to the numerous references to Yhwh as the deity of wondrous heroic deeds who brought/took Israel up/out from Egypt or gave 'the land' to Israel or removed its previous occupants so as to allow Israel to settle, to the point that these became main attributes of the deity,[30] nothing remotely similar was developed within the community in relation to a Yhwh who conquered or gave Jerusalem to Israel, even if Jerusalem was construed to be the center of 'the land.' Yhwh was imagined as the 'creator' or 'builder' of Jerusalem,[31] but not as its conqueror and the main mighty deeds with which the deity was asso-

---

[28] See, for instance, "The Memory of Abraham," in this volume, T. Römer, "Moses outside the Torah and the Construction of a Diaspora Identity." *JHebS* 8 (2008), article 15; available at www.jhsonline.org, reprinted under the same title in *Perspectives on Hebrew Scriptures v: Comprising the Contents of Journal of Hebrew Scriptures, vol. 8* (ed. E. Ben Zvi; Piscataway, NJ: Gorgias Press, 2009), 293–306.
[29] Cf. Josh 23:4–13; Judg 2:1–3 and the *general* tendency in the social mindscape of the community to associate success with following Yhwh's commandments and failure with rejecting them.
[30] E. g., Exod 6:7; Lev 11:45; Deut 1:25; 2:29; Josh 24:17; Judg 2:12; *passim*.
[31] Being Jerusalem's creator (ברא)/builder (בנה) was one of Yhwh's attributes. See, for instance, Isa 65:18–19; Ps 102:17; 147:2 cf. Isa 54:5; Ps 51:20.

ciated with the city were related to the (re)building of an utopian Jerusalem in the future, not with any conquest of the past.³²

In sum, there is good reason to assume that there was a strong generative grammar that led, against significant odds, to the shaping of a social memory in the community in a way that clearly distinguished between the conquest of the land by Joshua/YHWH and David's conquest of Jerusalem. This generative grammar and its outcome in terms of social memories in late Persian period Yehud could not but play a significant role in the construction of the Jebusites.³³ But before positing explanations for the existence and prevalence of a generative system of preferences and dis-preferences that shaped the community's memories of David's conquest of Jerusalem, two matters must be addressed.

Turning to the first of these matters, one might be tempted to argue that the two conquests ('the land' and Jerusalem) were remembered differently, because they were historically different. Such explanations were relatively common several decades ago, but most scholars today would agree that they hold no water.³⁴

---

32 When it comes to Jerusalem, there is some element of *imitatio dei* in the construction of David. The city is David's city (e.g., 1 Chr 11:7) and also YHWH's city (Isa 60:14; cf. Zech 8:3); moreover, both are its archetypal builders. This issue demands, however, a separate discussion that cannot be carried out within the boundaries of this chapter. (Note also that Israel and the nations other than Israel are also imagined as future builders of the city; e.g., Isa 60.)

33 See below.

34 Several decades ago, the question of whether Jebusite Jerusalem was deeply integrated in and highly influential in the shaping of the Davidic kingdom and its traditions was a 'hot topic.' On this debate see, for instance, J. M. Roberts, "The Davidic Origin of the Zion Tradition," in *JBL* 92 (1973): 329–44; G. H. Jones, *The Nathan Narratives* (JSOTS 90; Sheffield: Sheffield University Press, 1990), 119–142 and the extensive bibliography mentioned in these works. These debates were based on assumptions about the basic 'historicity' of many of the details in the narrative (or some reconstructed, hypothetical precursor of the narrative), which in turn were based on proposed early datings of the relevant texts. Today, most critical historians tend to agree that none of these texts is from the Davidic/Solomonic period. Instead, they maintain that these texts appeared centuries later and represented later viewpoints; moreover, many of these scholars tend to doubt, with very good reason, the existence of a historic Dadivic 'empire' *as described* in the books of Samuel (and Chronicles; e.g., B. Sass, "Four Notes on Taita King of Palistin with an Excursus on King Solomon's Empire," *TA* 37 (2010): 169–74 and bibliography). (For an example of an opposite position with directly bearings on the use of the texts discussed here to reconstruct the history of 'Davidic period,' see M. Cogan, "David's Jerusalem: Notes and Reflections", in *Tehillah le-Moshe. Biblical and Judaic Studies in Honor of Moshe Greenberg* (eds. M. Cogan, B. L. Eichler and J. H. Tigay; Winona Lake, Ind.: Eisenbrauns, 1997), 193–201.) Finally, even if there was some leader of a band of para-social elements named David who took over Jerusalem and established a chiefdom, neither this David nor his Jerusalem were close to the David or Jerusalem of the narratives and above all, the social memory of the community in late Persian period Yehud.

As the narrative of the Israelite conquest of the land demonstrates beyond any doubt, 'historicity,' in our terms, was not a necessary requirement for the development of a preferred narrative or even sets of balancing narratives, as is demonstrated in this case.[35] From a systemic perspective, the main requirements were that the narrative must (a) be consistent with and supportive of the other main narratives of the mnemonic community and (b) be coherent with the general social mindscape of this group (e. g., on matters such as its take on causality, what constitutes pious appropriate behaviour and the like).[36]

Constructions of the character of the society that existed in Jerusalem before it turned into an Israelite (or even Judahite) city, and of the fate of its original inhabitants were part and parcel of the social memory of a community in late Persian Yehud and were not governed by what historically transpired in Jerusalem centuries earlier.[37]

As we turn our attention memories of a pre-Davidic conquest of Jerusalem, the minor report evoking an image of an early Israelite, pre-Davidic conquest of Jerusalem in Judg 1:8 comes to the forefront. There might have been a tradition about an Israelite conquest of Jerusalem well before David (see also Judg 1:7 and cf. Josh 10:1–27; 12:10). But not much attention is drawn to it.[38] It played no substantial role in the construction of memories about Jerusalem in Persian period, Jerusalem-centered Yehud and never developed much social mindshare and ended up with a minimal narrative space in ancient Israelite historiography and its social memory.[39] This is neither because such a tradition would have

---

35 This is not the place to discuss the archaeological data that shows that the narrative in Joshua cannot be taken as a direct representation of historical events. The literature on the matter is extensive and conclusive. For a summary, see, for instance, I. Finkelstein and A. Mazar, *The Quest for the Historical Israel: Debating Archaeology and the History of Early Israel* (Atlanta: Society of Biblical Literature, 2007). To be sure, the quest for historicity in this narrative is misguided to begin with and arises from a misunderstanding of the genre of the book of Joshua.
36 Incidentally, similar criteria tend to influence strongly the chances for integration into social memory of even contemporary groups of particular (construed) memories. This matter, however, stands beyond the scope of this paper and cannot be elaborated here.
37 This holds true whether we today are able to reconstruct the historical society of pre-Judah Jerusalem and the circumstances leading to its fall or perhaps integration into Judah or not.
38 Notice, for instance, the lack of any stress on Jerusalem in Josh 12:10.
39 The statement about the minimal textual space allocated to this memory is correct also if we consider the entire authoritative repertoire of the community at the time. I assume, along with the vast majority of scholars, that the Pentateuchal, the deuteronomistic/historical, and the prophetic collections were part of the authoritative repertoire of the late Persian period literati in Yehud, in a form relatively close to the present one, and that these texts, along with Chronicles, at least some Psalms and Proverbs and books such as Lamentations, constitute for the most part a representative approximation to the contents of that library.

been in direct tension with texts such as Josh 15:8, 63, which associate Jerusalem with Benjamin, not Judah,[40] nor because of the note in Judg 1:21 that the city was not captured by the Israelites (Benjaminites) and that they and the Jebusite live together 'till this day.'[41] Instead, other processes governing systemic selection and dis-selection were at work. To mention some of them: First, scholars working on social memory have noticed a (cross-cultural) tendency towards oneness, that is, characters that already have much mindshare tend to develop further mindshare while at the same time pre-empting the development of memories of potential competitors to their roles, which then tend to be far less remembered and even forgotten.[42] Within the matters discussed here, this means that there was little room within the set of social memories of the late Persian period Yehudite literati for evoking, imagining, and developing much social mindshare for pre-David, earlier Israelite conquerors of Jerusalem. David, only one personage, was *the* conqueror of Jerusalem.

Second, any emphasis on a previous conquest would have led to an image of a Jerusalem that was lost to Israel and then settled by the Jebusites. This image would have stood contrary to the main thrust of the constructions of Jerusalem within the community. Jerusalem, unlike 'the land' (or significant portions of it) was not imagined as a place in which foreigners could potentially settle and displace Israel. This is a community in which post-David Jerusalem was construed

---

40 From the perspective of the literati in late Persian Yehud who were acquainted with Josh 15:63 and Judg 1:21, the city was both Benjaminite (Judg 1:21; see also Josh 18:28) and Judahite (Josh 15:63), and thus, it was Yehudite. Moreover, since from their own perspective Yehud stood for 'Israel,' Jerusalem was also Israelite. This thinking shapes and is reflected in additional constructions of the past. See, for instance, the reference to the residents of Jerusalem in 1 Chr 9:3; and cf. 2 Chr 11:14–16. "For the Chronicler, Jerusalem has always been the centre of 'all Israel', where people from the tribes have lived, both during and after the time of the united kingdom ... [a] list of the inhabitants of Jerusalem should then naturally include Ephraim and Manasseh" (S. Japhet, *1 & 2 Chronicles* [OTL; Louisville, KY: Westminster/John Knox, 1993], 208).
41 Cf. the book of Joshua explicitly states that Joshua conquered the entire land and that he did not. See Josh 11:23, which is followed by a list of defeated kings in Josh 12, and which is immediately followed in the text by Josh 13:1–6. Cf. Josh 23:1–5 and Judg 1:1–2:5. These tensions do not lead to less social mindshare or narrative space. In fact, tensions like these may serve as attention getters and draw particular attention to the matter (and serve well for didactic purposes; see the case mentioned above). But this is not the case here.
42 For an example of tendencies towards mnemonic 'oneness' see B. Schwartz, "Collective Forgetting and the Symbolic Power of Oneness: The Strange Apotheosis of Rosa Parks," in *Social Psychology Quarterly* 72 (2009): 123–42 and see bibliography for the general approach. This tendency is related to the so-called "Matthew Effect." On the "Matthew Effect" see D. Rigney, *The Matthew Effect: How Advantage Begets Further Advantage* (New York, NY: Columbia University Press, 2010).

as either an Israelite city (i.e., Judahite or Yehudite) or not inhabited at all. In other words, if Israel becomes anti-Israel and thus the city is destroyed, it can only be resettled by Israel.

Third, the lateness of the conquest of Jerusalem allows not only for David to conquer Jerusalem for the first time, but also provides an explanation for the (construed) absence of a temple in Israel until the Davidic/Solomonic period.

Fourth, since there existed within the discourse of Persian period Yehud a mental map of Israel that had Jerusalem at its center (see, for instance, Ezekiel and the idea that Jerusalem belongs to 'all Israel;' see also Chronicles[43]) and in which the city symbolized both country and people, the absence of Jerusalem within Israel's map in the pre-Davidic period conveyed a sense that Israel was still in the process of constituting itself, even after the Exodus, Sinai and the conquest of the land by Joshua. Israel's founding figure was Moses, but Israel was still in need of a secondary founding figure, David (and his associate Solomon), because Israel, as understood by the community in Yehud, was not properly constituted until Jerusalem was able to house the temple.[44]

Fifth, the above-mentioned approach is consistent with and generates a tendency to stress the difference between David and previous leaders, and especially the previous Israelite king, Saul, who ruled in the area and was imagined as powerful, but who did not attempt to take Jerusalem. In contrast, and to make the point even more salient, David in Chronicles marches against Jerusalem immediately after he becomes king of Israel.[45]

---

43 See note 38.
44 On the explicit pairing of Moses and David, see Chronicles. On the matter, see S. J. De Vries, "Moses and David as Cult Founders in Chronicles," in *JBL* 107 (1988): 619–39; W. Riley, *King and Cultus in Chronicles. Worship and the Reinterpretation of History* (JSOTS 160; Sheffield: JSOT Press, 1993), 61–63; Cf. J. W. Kleinig, "The Divine Institution of the Lord's Song in Chronicles," in *JSOT* 55 (1992): 75–83; W. M. Schniedewind, "The Chronicler as an Interpreter of Scripture", in *The Chronicler as Author. Studies in Text and Texture* (eds. M. P. Graham and S. L. McKenzie; JSOTS 263; Sheffield: Sheffield Academic Press, 1999), 158–80 (177–78); E. Ben Zvi, "One Size Does Not Fit All: Notes on the Different Ways in Which Chronicles Dealt with the Authoritative Literature of its Time," in *What was Authoritative for Chronicles?* (eds. E. Ben Zvi and D. V. Edelman; Winona Lake, Ind.: Eisenbrauns, 2011), 13–35 (29–32). This construction of the past may not have been a 'radical' innovation of Chronicles, but rather Chronicles may have voiced and developed basic approaches to the past that might have existed before its writing. (For 'Moses' and 'David' in later periods, see E. Mroczek, "Moses, David and Scribal Revelations: Preservation and Renewal in Second Temple Jewish Textual Traditions", in *The Significance of Sinai. Traditions about Sinai and Divine Revelation in Judaism and Christianity* [eds. G. J. Brooke, H. Najman and L. T. Stuckenbruck; Leiden: Brill, 2008], 91–115.)
45 Note also the Saul/Gibeah–David/Jerusalem contrasting pairs and their roles in shaping social memory. See above and Y. Amit, *Hidden Polemics*, 181.

Sixth, the lateness of the setting up of Jerusalem as an Israelite city in the distant past also carried a sense of helical repetition of history, as following the catastrophe of 586 BCE, Jerusalem and its temple was established anew at a time within a map of Yehud that contains well and long-established Benjaminite ('Saulide') centers. Jerusalem, city and temple, is again the 'late comer' who happens to stand at the center of Yehud, Israel and even the world, and displace all earlier Israelite centers.[46]

All these considerations not only pre-empted the development of a strong social memory about a pre-Davidic conquest of Jerusalem, but show the kind of constraints, systems of preferences and dis-preferences, and generative ideological grammars that shaped the ways in which the discourse of Persian Yehud construed David's conquest of Jerusalem and in which this event was remembered, at least by the literati of the period.

This being so, what could have created such a preference for a construction of Jebusite Jerusalem in terms so distinct from those who were construed as dispossessed by Joshua? Why was Jerusalem so different from 'the land' and Joshua from David? Why, although Jerusalem as a site of memory was closely associated with David, did the latter's conquest draw only relatively minor attention in contrast to many other aspects of memories of Jerusalem and David?

Imagining Jerusalem and Jerusalemites, and Construing 'Worlds' through Social Memory

To a large extent one may say that all groups are mnemonic communities, that is, groups shaped around a set of widely shared memories of the past that help to make sense of the group, or in other words, that provide it with an identity and ability to socially reproduce itself. The community in Yehud that construed itself as a 'text/*torah*' centered community was certainly a mnemonic community. What people remembered of their past or future (e.g., the memories of 'experiencing' through acts of imagination the utopian future evoked through the reading and re-reading of prophetic literature) played an important role for the self-understanding of the community and the shaping of their social mindscape. For the purposes advanced, it is particularly important, as mentioned above, that YHWH was remembered as the 'builder' of Jerusalem and not its conqueror.

Within the discourse of late Persian Yehud, Jerusalem was marked as the sacred centre of the world, the place destined to be the site of the only legitimate

---

[46] On 'helical' rather than 'cyclical' see note 60.

temple of Yhwh well before David conquered it, evident in the explicit references to Jerusalem in Abraham stories (see below) and to the 'city that Yhwh will chose' in Deuteronomy, which were read in Yehud as references to Jerusalem.

During the late Persian period Jerusalem was marked as the place for the mythical 'waters' that will emerge from the temple/city (cf. Ezek 47:1–12; Joel 4:18; Zech 13:1 and 14:8; Ps 46:5–6; cf. Isa 33:21), a city on which Yhwh shines, a source of mythical light to which nations and rulers (i.e., the human world) come (see Isa 60:1–3, 19–20) and מכלל יפי 'the perfection of beauty' that can actually be achieved on earth, even if only in the future, and which in the meantime exists in the shared imagination of the community (Ps 50:2). To be sure, the community had only a small, poor temple and city, but none of this could have demoted Jerusalem of its status and place in the divine economy. Moreover, all these utopian attributes were construed as certain to come, because without them, without the cosmic city at the center providing divine 'water,' 'wisdom,' 'light' to the world, the latter could not be imagined as reaching its stable status under the kingship of Yhwh. Similarly, Jerusalem before David was not even Israelite, but already had its place set in the divine economy and was certain to achieve its role and house the temple at some point.

Within this discourse, David's conquest by itself did not change the nature of the place or its relation to Yhwh, nor did the destruction of the city in 586 BCE, for that matter. To be sure, David's conquest like Cyrus' declaration (2 Chr 36:22–23) allowed the materialization of other developments. But they played a secondary, enabling role to the transformation of the city to the place of the temple. Building its proper (i.e., Davidic) temples, which symbolically were one temple, was building Jerusalem and building the ground for the fulfillment of its necessary role in the cosmos.[47] David, Solomon and Yhwh did that in the past,[48] and Yhwh will do that in the future and then 'reside' in the city forever. Social memory is drawn to these central matters and thus shapes what is

---

[47] See "Exploring Jerusalem as a Site of Memory" in this volume, pp. 482–503.
[48] To lesser extent, Cyrus, alongside with Zerubbabel, son of Shealtiel and the high priest Joshua, son of Jehozadak (e.g., 2 Chr 36:22–23; Haggai), did that too within the main mnemonic narratives of the community, but the 'second temple' that they established, as per Yhwh's command, was secondary in importance to the (Davidic/) Solomonic and the future, utopian temple. As usually is the case in main mnemonic narratives, the original and the final points carry more mindshare within the community than what is between them; moreover, the fact that the 'second temple' which the community could see not only with the eyes of their imagination, but also with their physical eyes and with which they interacted in 'material ways' regularly was poor and certainly not 'glorious' may have contributed to the social construction of this temple as a temporary one, to be superseded by the 'glorious' and certain to be utopian temple of future Jerusalem.

important to remember about them. It is far more important to remember David's role in the preparations for the building of the temple and establishing rules for worship within it than to remember his conquest of Jerusalem. In fact, remembering one more than the other served to make a strong point about what is important for the community within its discourse.

In addition, there was a tendency within the social mindscape of the literati to construe the temple as inimical to war (and shedding human blood).[49] The temple tended to be associated with 'rest,' not with military victory (e.g., 1 Chr 22:7–9; 28:3; cf. 1 Kgs 5:17–19)[50]

The association of Jerusalem with sacred space, whether the temple stands on it or not, has implications in terms of preferences and dis-preferences for the construction of its inhabitants. As mentioned above, from David's conquest, through the vicissitudes of multiple generations, including military defeats and even the razing of the city, Jerusalem was remembered as inhabited by Israel or not at all.[51] But what about the time before David's conquest?

The mnemonic community in Yehud had to remember and imagine the existence of a pre-Israelite Jerusalem and Jerusalemites. This went together with the construction of Israel as coming 'from outside the land' and a systemic dis-preference for potential mnemonic narratives about a Jerusalem built on 'virgin soil.'[52] The community encountered not only the Jebusites of the period of David and the Judges but also other non-Israelite inhabitants of Jerusalem. The most salient of them was the non-Israelite Melchizedek who was a priest of אל עליון 'the High God' (Gen 14:20) during the time of Abraham. This foreign king was even partially Israelitized in Ps 110:4. In fact, according to this text, YHWH associates the Davidic king with Melchizedek, and the community of readers is expected to follow.

---

49 See, among others, S. Japhet, *1 & 2 Chronicles*, 397–398, S. Niditch, *War in the Hebrew Bible: A Study in the Ethics of Violence* (New York: Oxford University Press, 1993), 139–40.
50 It is possible that this tendency had a role to play in, at least, readings of Exod 20:25 (cf. Deut 27:5) even if not necessarily on the origins of the instructions set in these verses. Cf. the later readings of these verses reflected in m. Mid. 3:4.
51 Cf. the motif of the 'empty land.'
52 Theoretically, one might imagine a different original myth of Jerusalem, namely as a city built by David on completely new place (cf. the case of Samaria; see 2 Kgs 16:24), but if this were the case, such a Jerusalem will lack continuity with its (imagined) past (e.g., with the city encountered by Abraham, with Mt. Moriah, with the alien city that was much better than Gibeah, which was also the city that became Saul's capital).

David symbolically became Melchizedek, but by the time of Chronicles and most likely earlier, he was also a kind of second Abraham.[53] Most significantly, the story of Abraham's purchase of a burial place from Ephron (Gen 23) and David's purchase of the site of the threshing floor of Araunah/Ornan, that is, the place of the future temple (1 Chr 21:21–22:1; cf. 2 Sam 24:20–25) became mutually evocative, one being the type of the other.[54] The first act of possession of the land in the land (Abraham's purchase of the Cave of Machpelah from Ephron) and the final–and most crucial–act of possession of the land (David's purchase of the place of the future temple) became intertwined. A mnemonic narrative emerges, starting from the purchase of a burial place (the Cave of Machpelah) and leading to the source of (ordered, proper) life, the temple. Significantly, neither of the two changes of possession were imagined (or could have been imagined within the discourse of the community) as involving violent dispossession. By extension, and since Jerusalem is symbolically associated with the temple within the social mindscape of the community, a tendency to draw less attention to the violent/heroic aspect of the conquest of Jerusalem emerged.

Of course, like his predecessor Abraham, David had to encounter a proper, positively construed 'other' after his conquest of Jerusalem with whom he could interact and from whom he could purchase the field. The sacredness of the place shaped a discursive and mnemonic preference for such a narrative.

In addition, the very unique sacredness of Jerusalem and its role in the divine, cosmic economy as the city of the main deity also shaped a systemic preference to construe the place as designated by YHWH well before David's time, and thus its selection was also understood as essentially independent of David (see, for instance, the association of Jerusalem and Mt. Moriah in

---

53 On David and Abraham see also R. E. Clements, *Abraham and David: Genesis xv and its Meaning for Israelite Tradition* (Naperville, Ill: A. R. Allenson, 1967). On the general memory of David in the late Persian and Early Hellenistic periods, see, for instance, D. V. Edelman, "David in Israelite Social Memory", in *Remembering Biblical Figures in the Late Persian and Early Hellenistic Periods: Social Memory and Imagination* (eds. Diana Edelman and E. Ben Zvi; Oxford/New York: Oxford University Press, 2013), 141–157.
54 See, among others, Y. Zakovitch, "Assimilation in Biblical Narratives", in *Empirical Models for Biblical Criticism* (ed. J.H. Tigay; Philadelphia: University of Pennsylvania Press, 1985), 175–96 (181); R. Alter, *The David Story: A Translation with Commentary of 1 and 2 Samuel* (New York: W.W. Norton. 1999), 358–59; S. Japhet, *1 & 2 Chronicles*; S. M. McDonough, "'And David was old, advanced in years': 2 Samuel xxiv 18–25, 1 Kings 1, and Genesis xxiii–xxiv," in *VT* 49 (1999): 128–31; cf. J. E. Harvey, *Retelling the Torah: the Deuteronomistic Historian's Use of Tetrateuchal Narratives* (JSOTS 403; London/New York: T&T Clark, 2004), 60.

2 Chr 3:1).⁵⁵ One may assume that there is a kind of discursive un-ease, and thus there was a systemic dis-preference to imagine a city which stands 'at the center of the world,' and is necessary for its existence, as constantly and only populated by evil characters, who cannot but constantly pollute it. It is more likely to imagine that at least from time to time, it included 'others' with whom Israel/David/Abraham were able to interact positively and even at times partially identify.⁵⁶

Remembering David and his Jerusalem meant construing and remembering a Melchizedek in Jerusalem; remembering David and his Jerusalem meant construing and remembering Araunah/Ornan, and indirectly, Abraham and Ephron; that is, remembering David and his Jerusalem meant remembering a Jerusalem populated by people significantly different from the dispossessed nations of the book of Joshua. These memories construed pre-Davidic Jerusalemites who were not fully 'the Other,' but were in fact partially Israelitized, in Yehudite memory.⁵⁷ Moreover, even if pre-Israelite, partially Israelitized Jerusalem was

---

55 Of course, this claimed association is at the core of another "front" in the mnemonic struggles between Yehud and Samaria (or their discourses), as Samarian text consistently associated Mt. Moriah with Mt. Gerizim. On the struggle over the memory of Mt. Moriah (and of Abram) see I. Kalimi, *Early Jewish Exegesis and Theological Controversy: Studies in Scriptures in the Shadow of Internal and External Controversies* (Assen: Royal Van Gorcum, 2002).
56 A comparison with the mnemonic narratives about the 'conquest of the land' is particularly helpful in this regard. Of course, the land was also conceived as 'selected' for Israel before Joshua. In some texts (esp. those reflecting the thinking of the Holiness Code) the land itself is considered 'holy' (see J. Milgrom, *Leviticus 23–27: A New Translation with Introduction and Commentary* [AB 3B; New Haven; London: Yale University Press, 2008], 2412–13). Abraham and the other patriarchs were remembered as central, foundational figures of Israel who, like David, encountered and interacted with positively portrayed (and remembered) local residents (see "Memory of Abraham", in this volume), but in the case of Abraham and the patriarchs, such encounters reflect the tendency to imagine good residents, at least from time to time, without facing the ideological problem of dispossessing them, for the dispossession is set in the far future, i.e., in the days of Joshua; in the case of David, the narrative has to bring together positive portrayals and dispossession within the same period. The fact, that David's Jebusites are characterized in positive terms unlike Joshua's 'Canaanites' is thus far more remarkable and deserves particular attention. See below.
57 To be sure, the characterization of 'the other' in the land appears in several patriarchal stories not only in relation to Jerusalem. It shapes and reflects accommodation and even appreciation of 'the other' in the land in the present of the world portrayed in the narratives and in the world of the late Persian period community reading these texts, but at the same time in the context of a group that through their shared imagination as they read their authoritative texts experienced vicariously worlds in which any 'other' is displaced from the land. Whereas in the world of the patriarchal narratives, the 'positive other' with whom the patriarchs collaborate is not to be attacked and thus can be easily imagined as behaving properly, 'the other' in Jerusalem at the

not remembered often, some of its characters were memorable and this is especially the case with Melchizedek (see Ps 110).[58]

Remembering Araunah/Ornan was also remembering that the altar was built in a place that was not associated with war or conquest, but with food and life (the threshing floor), the end of pestilence and death, and the image of a sword-holding hand that relaxes and ceases to kill (2 Sam 24:15–25; 1 Chr 21:15–28).

Even if such a Jerusalem took a relatively small mindshare of the community in the Persian period, still Jerusalem could not to be remembered as just another city in the rest of the land *nor* could its inhabitants be remembered like those facing Joshua.

There was strong tendency to balance the discontinuity that was inherent in mnemonic narratives of the Davidic/Israelite conquest of Jerusalem with the continuity in the special status of Jerusalem within the discourse of the community. There was a tendency to prefer narratives that set Jerusalem, as the city of 'the temple,' aside from other cities and lands within 'the land,' and again, this had an indirect influence on the way in which the David's Jebusites and other characters were imagined. There was a tendency to emphasize 'building' over 'conquering' when it comes to Jerusalem and, again, this tendency had an indirect influence on the characterization of the Jebusites of the period. In addition, remembering a future Jerusalem to which all nations will flow (e.g. Isa 2:2–4; 56:1–9) generates tendencies to imagine past Jerusalems in which pious non-Israelites lived and co-existed with Israel.[59] After all, communities in antiquity often tended to construe many of their social memories according to helical, temporal plots, linking past and future;[60] the past was often conceived as some kind of (pregnant) image of the future, and the future of the past.

---

time of David which had to be attacked so as to be conquered according to the main mnemonic narratives of the community is still portrayed unlike the other pre-conquest Canaanites, but has to be partially Israelitized and compared to the dwellers of the land in the patriarchal period (e.g., Araunah/Ornan and Ephron) who lived together in peace with patriarchs. This noteworthy fact sheds light into the memory-scape of the community in late Persian Yehud and the different mnemonic and ideological tendencies that contributed to its shaping.

58 Melchizedek became a significant figure in the late second temple period. See, for instance, 11Q13/11 QMelchizedek. Later still, see references to Melchizedek in Hebrews.

59 See Abraham and Melchizedek; David and Araunah/Ornan; David and the mercenaries who stand loyal to him when Absalom rebels; and cf. with the very significant statement in Judg 1:21b.

60 I prefer 'helical' over the more common 'cyclical' since these plots rarely involve exact returns, but rather return to similar, comparable situations; there is a cycle but also some element of temporal linearity.

Of course, all these were Jerusalems of memory and dreams, imagined and vicariously 'experienced' through reading and rereading by a community in late Persian period Yehud. These Jerusalems were all far removed from any actual, historical Iron Age I city or any of its historical predecessors. Their social memory was not 'history' in any form that we may identify today as 'professional, academic history,' nor could have been. At the same time what this community of shared imagination thought about their past and their (construed) Jerusalem is a subject of interest to historians studying this late Persian community. This essay is a contribution to this type of research.

Re-Negotiating a Putative Utopia and the Stories of the Rejection of Foreign Wives in Ezra–Nehemiah*

1 On the Role of a Social Memory Approach in the Study of the Expulsion of the "Foreign" Wives and Children in Ezra Nehemiah

The stories about the rejection of "foreigners," including "foreign" wives and the children they bore to "Israelites" in Ezra–Nehemiah, have been studied from multiple historical perspectives. Some of this research has focused on the history of the text/s, mainly redactional history, and on the potential implications that the various layers advanced within different models for the development of the text may have for reconstructions of historical shifts in the world of thought of the communities to which the said proposed layers and, above all, their distinct and distinctive proposed authors/redactors may attest.[1]

Others have focused more directly on the possible reasons for the historical expulsion of the "foreign" wives and those of "impure birth (Ezra 9:1–10:44; cf. Neh 9:2; 13:3, 23–29). Such actions relate, for obvious reasons, to matters of "identity formation" and boundaries. These matters are usually, and with very good reason, tackled with social anthropological, political, and economic–essentially transcultural– approaches, and thus it is not surprising that a variety of explanations for the rejection of these mothers and children has been advanced on the basis of these approaches and comparative historical studies. Thus, some scholars approached these issues in light of Pericles's citizenship law and arrived at a number of different explanations,[2] while others thought

---

* First published in *Worlds that Could Not Be. Utopia in Chronicles, Ezra and Nehemiah* (eds. S. J. Schweitzer and F. Uhlenbruch; LHBOTS 620; London: Bloomsbury T&T Clark, 2016), 105–28.
[1] E.g., Y. Dor, "The Composition of the Episode of the Foreign Women in Ezra IX-X," in *VT* 53 (2003): 26–47; and her comprehensive, *Have the "Foreign Women" Really Been Expelled? Separation and Exclusion in the Restoration Period* (Jerusalem: Magnes, 2006) (in Hebrew). The strong presence of these approaches is easy to understand, given (a) that there is more than one story of forced dissolution of "mixed" marriages and expulsions, (b) that it is extremely unlikely that the present Ezra–Nehemiah was written at once, by one author and out of whole cloth and (c) the traditional importance of redactional-critical methods in historical studies of (eventually) "biblical" texts.
[2] E.g., L. S. Fried, "The Concept of 'Impure Birth' in 5th Century Athens and Judea," in *In the Wake of Tikva Frymer-Kensky: Tikva Frymer-Kensky Memorial Volume* (eds. S. Holloway, J. A. Scurlock, and R. Beal; Piscataway, N.J.: Gorgias, 2009), 121–42; Wolfgang Oswald, "Foreign Marriages and Citizenship in Persian Period Judah," in *JHebS* 12, no. 6 (2012), available online:

this comparison at least partially ill-fitting.³ Some researchers addressed the matter in terms of, *inter alia,*" heightened ethnic consciousness as a result of return migration,"⁴ Victor Turner's social drama model,⁵ or "witch-hunting."⁶ Some scholars have accounted for, at least in part, the expulsion of the women in terms of a proposed struggle to avert losses of land holdings,⁷ while others focused on ideologies of purity and their social implementation.⁸ It has also been proposed that the immigrant *golah* community should be understood as "a minority with an ideological [utopian] vision driven by a desire for cultural exclusion and dominance."⁹ Not only the reasons for the dissolutions of the "mixed" marriages, but also the reasons for their existence and seeming popularity in Yehud, in the first place, have been discussed from a variety of social and anthropological perspectives, from hypergamy theory to assumptions about a population gender imbalance in Yehud, with more males than females.¹⁰

---

http://www.jhsonline.org (= Wolfgang Oswald, "Foreign Marriages and Citizenship in Persian Period Judah," in *Perspectives in Hebrew Scriptures IX: Comprising the Contents of Journal of Hebrew Scriptures*, vol. 12 [eds. E. Ben Zvi and C. Nihan; Piscataway, N.J.: Gorgias, 2014], 107–24.
3 E.g., L. L. Grabbe, *A History of the Jews and Judaism in the Second Temple Period. Vol. 1, Yehud: A History of the Persian Province of Judah* (LSTS 47; London: T&T Clark International, 2004), 307.
4 See, e.g., K. E. Southwood, *Ethnicity and the Mixed Marriage Crisis in Ezra 9–10: An Anthropological Approach* (Oxford: Oxford University Press, 2012)–citation from p. 210; and cf. R. Albertz, "Purity Strategies and Political Interests in the Policy of Nehemiah," in *Confronting the Past: Archaeological and Historical Essays on Ancient Israel in Honor of William G. Dever* (eds. S. Gitin, J. E. Wright, and J. P. Dessel; Winona Lake, Ind.: Eisenbrauns, 2006), 199–206.
5 D. P. Moffat, *Ezra's Social Drama: Identity Formation, Marriage and Social Conflict in Ezra 9 and 10* (LHBOTS 579; London: T&T Clark, 2013).
6 D. Janzen, *Witch-hunts, Purity and Social Boundaries: The Expulsion of the Foreign Women in Ezra 9–10* (JSOTSup 350; Sheffield: Sheffield Academic, 2002).
7 E.g., T. C. Eskenazi, "Out from the Shadows: Biblical Women in the Postexilic Era," in *JSOT* 54 (1992): 25–43 (see esp. 35); J. Blenkinsopp, *Ezra–Nehemiah: A Commentary* (Philadelphia: Westminster, 1988), 176–77.
8 E.g., S. M. Olyan, "Purity Ideology in Ezra-Nehemiah as a Tool to Reconstitute the Community," in *JJS* 35 (2004): 1–16 (republished in idem, *Social Inequality in the World of the Text: The Significance of Ritual and Social Distinctions in the Hebrew Bible* [Journal of Ancient Judaism Supplements 4; Göttingen: Vandenhoeck & Ruprecht, 2011], 159–72); H. K. Harrington, "The Use of Leviticus in Ezra- Nehemiah," in *JHebS* 13, no. 3 (2013), available online: http://www.jhsonline.org.
9 E.g., J. W. Cataldo, "Whispered Utopia: Dreams, Agendas, and Theocratic Aspirations in Yehud," in *SJOT* 24 (2010): 53–70 (67).
10 See D. L. Smith-Christopher, "The Mixed Marriage Crisis in Ezra 9–10 and Nehemiah 13: A Study of the Sociology of the Post-Exilic Judaean Community," in *Second Temple Studies 2: Temple Community in the Persian Period* (eds. T. C. Eskenazi and K. H. Richards; JSOTSup 175; Sheffield: JSOT, 1994), 243–65 and bibliography cited there.

The preceding survey of current common approaches to the matter of the expulsion of the "foreign" wives and their children that are particularly informed by social or anthropological models is obviously far from being comprehensive. This said, for the present purposes at least, it suffices to show in broad strokes a reasonably representative image of widespread scholarly tendencies in the field on these matters; an image that is representative enough to raise a number of observations and concerns about the basic assumptions underlying the shared landscape on which the range of common socio-anthropological approaches that are adopted to address matters such as the rejection of the "foreign" wives and their children are grounded.[11]

To begin with, studying the reasons for the *historical* expulsion of the "foreign" wives and the children they had with male members of the community in Yehud during the putative time of Ezra, in contradistinction to studying why a "memory" of such an event emerged and was successfully transmitted, implies an assumption that the expulsion did historically happen.

Second, the often related endeavor of reconstructing the world of thought of a minority *golah* community in the Persian period that stood distinct and against the majority of the population in Yehud implies an assumption that there was such a *golah* community and that its counter-part, a *non-golah* community, existed as well, and that they competed for power, in one way or another for a significant time.

Third, although transcultural studies indicate that a return migration may well lead to a heightened ethnic (or religious) consciousness (as for that matter, diaspora conditions often do among some groups), the point would be moot for historical studies of Persian Yehud, if there was no *substantial* return migration in order to shape a long-term counter-community that stood in contradistinction and opposed to the already existing community for a *significant* time.

Fourth, the explanation of the expulsion in terms of witch-hunting processes assumes (as do several explanations as well) a compelling sense of existential anxiety and the related existence of strong external boundaries within the community.

---

[11] It is worth stressing that the range of proposed approaches is wider than the examples brought up in the text, but to a large extent the basic underlying grounds on which they rest are not necessarily so. See, for instance, the case of comparative studies between the rejection of "foreign women" in Ezra–Nehemiah in Yehud and socio-ideological processes in contemporary Israel: see T. C. Eskenazi and E. P. Judd, "Marriage to a Stranger in Ezra 9–10," in *Second Temple Studies 2* (eds. T. C. Eskenazi and K. H. Richards), 266–85.

At the same time, one may consider that, first, the archaeological evidence does not suggest a massive return.[12] Second, the rise of the temple in Jerusalem to a central position in Yehud would have been unlikely if the small group responsible for running it would have excluded the vast majority of the population in Yehud, which consisted of those who remained in the land. In fact, proposals about a *long term* dual social structure in Yehud are unlikely.[13] Third, the core corpus of authoritative texts that existed in the Persian period does not reflect a community with a strong level of existential anxiety, unlike the one implied in Ezra–Nehemiah.[14] Fourth, the notion of universal matrilinearity (to be distinguished from matrilocal matrilinearity) or alternatively, of universal dual patri-matrilinearity that is crucial to the story of the rejection of the women and their children appears nowhere else until rabbinic literature.[15]

Fifth, neither the notion of זרע הקדש in relation to Israel as a whole and particularly relevant to the rejection of the wives and their children, nor that of the intrinsically (non-contingent and unsolvable) polluting character of the "foreign-

---

12 See, e. g., O. Lipschits, "Demographic Changes in Judah Between the Seventh and the Fifth Centuries BCE," in *Judah and the Judeans in the Neo-Babylonian Period* (eds. O. Lipschits and J. Blenkinsopp; Winona Lake, Ind.: Eisenbrauns, 2003), 323–76 and note in particular the following statement, "the 'return to Zion' did not leave its imprint on the archaeological data, nor is there any demographic testimony of it" (365). Elsewhere Lipschits writes "there is no supporting evidence in the archaeological and historical record for demographic changes to the extent of this list [the 'list of returnees' in Ezra 2 and Neh 9], either at the end of the sixth or the beginning of the fifth centuries, or even during the course of the fifth century." O. Lipschits, "Achaemenid Imperial Policy, Settlement Processes in Palestine, and the Status of Jerusalem in the Middle of the Fifth Century BCE," in *Judah and the Judeans in the Persian Period* (eds. O. Lipschits and M. Oeming; Winona Lake, Ind.: Eisenbrauns, 2006), 19–52 (33 n. 46).
13 See "Total Exile, Empty Land and the General Intellectual Discourse in Yehud," in this volume, pp. 599–611 and bibliography cited there.
14 And unlike the one implied in texts such as *Jubilees*, 1–2 Maccabees or much of the so-called "sectarian" Qumran texts. I have argued on different occasions for the lack of existential anxiety among the literati of the Persian period. See, e. g., "Othering, Selfing, 'Boundarying' and 'Cross-Boundarying' as Interwoven with Socially Shared Memories: Some Observations," in this volume, pp. 580–98; "Exploring the Memory of Moses 'The Prophet' in Late Persian/Early Hellenistic Yehud/Judah," in this volume, pp. 199–231, and "On Social Memory and Identity Formation in Late Persian Yehud: A Historian's Viewpoint with a Focus on Prophetic Literature, Chronicles and the Dtr. Historical Collection," in this volume, pp. 28–79.
15 See Ezra 10:2–3; cf. S. J. D. Cohen, "The Origins of the Matrilineal Principle in Rabbinic Law," *AJSR* 10 (1985): 19–53; idem, *The Beginning of Jewishness: Boundaries, Varieties, Uncertainties* (Berkeley: University of California Press, 1999), esp. 265–69. As mentioned by Cohen, there existed, most likely, a concept of matrilocal matrilinearity. For a different approach, see P. Heger, "Patrilineal or Matrilineal Genealogy in Israel After Ezra," in *JSJ* 43 (2012): 215–48.

er" (Neh 13:4–9) appear elsewhere.¹⁶ In fact, these notions are contradicted by the corpus of authoritative texts of the Persian period and had they been accepted, they would have prevented the inclusion of any "foreigner" in Israel or their descendants.

And, sixth, there is, of course, the matter of the very complex history of composition of Ezra–Nehemiah as a whole and of Ezra 9–10 in particular,¹⁷ and the concerns that such a history of composition and redaction raises in terms of the reliability of these texts for reconstructing the historical Persian Yehud in general and that of the alleged periods of Ezra and Nehemiah in particular.

In sum, the set of common approaches mentioned above, as sophisticated as they are, rely on assuming the basic historicity of the narrative communicated in Ezra–Nehemiah (and particularly Ezra) in its broad strokes. This is their strength, to be sure, but also their weakness, because such an assumption is far from certain. The previous considerations do not "prove" that events somewhat similar to those described in Ezra– Nehemiah did not occur, but certainly raise serious concerns.

---

16 See Olyan, "Purity Ideology," 10–12. It is particularly worth stressing that the conceptually key term זרע הקדש appears in Ezra 9:2 and nowhere else in the entire Hebrew Bible. To be sure, זרע קדש –and notice the absence of the article– appears in Isa 6:13, but it does not carry there the meaning of the זרע הקדש in Ezra 9:2.

17 See, e. g., J. Pakkala, "Intermarriage and Group Identity in the Ezra Tradition (Ezra 7–10 and Nehemiah 8)," in *Mixed Marriages: Intermarriage and Group Identity in the Second Temple Period* (ed. C. Frevel; LHBOTS 547; London: T&T Clark, 2011), 78–88. One cannot but note also that Ezra–Nehemiah has been organized as a work in which two different sections not only exist side by side, but are arranged literarily, more or less, according to a basic parallel structure, which is hardly the product of coincidence. (See L. L. Grabbe, *Ezra–Nehemiah* [New York: Routledge, 1998], 116–19 [esp. 117–18].) If there were influences not only between the texts but also, as likely given the end result, a tendency towards a sense of (partial) convergence and above all interaction between the ways in which Ezra and Nehemiah of memory were shaped, reshaped and remembered, one may engage in questions such as whether, for instance, Ezra 9–10 might not have been dependent on Neh 9–10 (e. g., Grabbe, *History*, 1:314–15), or in general to which extent the existing Ezra and Nehemiah narratives can be considered truly independent sources, even if one were to accept that they began their long textual history in the form of originally independent, though difficult to reconstruct with any precision, forerunners. In any event and as much as there is a sense of partial convergence and memory (and perhaps textual) interaction and as much as both Ezra and Nehemiah share a general exclusionary position concerning membership in the community, it is difficult not to notice the differences between the events narrated in Neh 13:23–29 and Ezra 9–10 as a whole or, for that matter, the lack of any reference to a mass forced divorce and the sending of mothers and children away in both Neh 13:23–29 and in Ezra's prayer (Ezra 9:6–15), even as they advance an anti-"mixed" marriages agenda (cf. Y. Dor, "Composition").

Some would certainly argue that for the purpose of reconstructing the *historical Yehud* of the Persian period, one may well be on far more solid ground if one were to set aside Ezra–Nehemiah as a whole or the "books" of Ezra and Nehemiah, for that matter, and instead, rely solely on reports of Nehemiah's policy and actions against "mixed" marriages in Neh 13:23–29.[18] This is not the place to address in detail the full set of issues associated with such a proposal. It suffices, however, for the present purposes to notice that accepting this proposal carries important implications for matters that underlie the approaches surveyed above.

For example, if one were to rely only on Neh 13:23–29 as an historical source, one would very likely end up with a significantly different reconstruction of the basic historical events. For instance, the nature and scope of the actions of Nehemiah against foreign wives would be up for discussion and would not *necessarily* or even likely include the rejection of children of "mixed marriages."

Moreover, once the focus is on Neh 13:23–29 (and the so-called Nehemiah-Memoir; hereafter and for simplicity abbreviated NM), one cannot but notice the prominent disappearance of the central motif of a separate and exclusivistic community, the בני הגולה, and its necessary counterpart, the counter-community, from the NM.[19] This motif, its centrality–along with, of course, its precondition, namely the long-term historical existence of these two communities–underlie, at least, some of the approaches surveyed above; and therefore, a challenge to the former undermines the argument for the latter.

Furthermore, relying only on Neh 13:23–29 (or the NM) as an historical source cannot but lead historians to prioritize causal explanations for the (differently narrated/reconstructed) events that differ substantially from those advanced in the approaches surveyed above. Whoever follows this path most likely would end up proposing an historical understanding of Nehemiah's actions in terms of, or in association with, his consistent rejection of regional leaders such as Sanballat, Tobiah, and Geshem (see 13:4–9, 28; cf. 2:10, 19; 3:33–35; 4:1; 6:1–19) and his related strong policy in favor of regional "isolation."[20]

---

18 The basic argument would be that Neh 13:23–29 belongs (*in toto?*) to the so-called Nehemiah-Memoir or some (earlier, but relatively close) form of it and to which one may reasonably ascribe more "historicity" than to the other (and likely, later) texts.
19 On this matter, see G. N. Knoppers, "Nehemiah and Sanballat: The Enemy Without or Within?," in *Judah and the Judeans in the Fourth Century BCE* (eds. O. Lipschits, G. N. Knoppers, and R. Albertz; Winona Lake, Ind.: Eisenbrauns, 2007), 305–31, and esp. his discussion on 310–11.
20 See, for instance, Grabbe, *History*, 1:309–10 and *passim*. Of course, this necessarily requires that these regional leaders and particularly Tobiah and Sanballat be considered important historical agents at the time of Nehemiah and not, totally or in the main, literary/mnemonic cy-

In addition, once one focuses on Neh 13:23–29, substantial attention is necessarily drawn to the linguistic reference in Neh 13:24. Here a shared ("authentic") language, "Judah's language," is presented as a major identity marker for the people of Judah (i.e., the יהודים, who play such a crucial role in the NM[21]) and for the construction of the corresponding "Other." This approach is expressed in Herodotus (Hdt. 8.144), who refers to "the kinship of all Greeks in blood and speech," and, of course, in later rabbinic literature (*Lev. Rab.* 32.5), but significantly has no clear parallels in other "biblical" books.

To be sure, one would still have to deal with the usual problems associated with the historicity of the NM, such as that it deploys common ancient Near Eastern patterns of constructing the new ruler,[22] and, as mentioned above, whether Sanballat, Tobiah, and Geshem shape, in the main, literary/mnemonic cyphers aimed at evoking known characters for readers living later than the putative time of Nehemiah. Moreover, there is, of course, the question of the redactional history of the NM and the impact that various reconstructions of this history may (or may not) have on matters of historicity.[23]

---

phers aimed at evoking known characters for readers living later than the putative time of Nehemiah. But, on the latter issues, see S. Grätz, "The Adversaries in Ezra/Nehemiah–Fictitious or Real? A Case Study in Creating Identity in Late Persian and Hellenistic Times," in *Between Cooperation and Hostility: Multiple Identities in Ancient Judaism and the Interaction with Foreign Powers* (eds. R. Albertz and J. Wöhrle; Journal of Ancient Judaism Supplements 11; Göttingen: Vandenhoeck & Ruprecht, 2013), 73–87. See also D. V. Edelman, "Seeing Double: Tobiah the Ammonite as an Encrypted Character," in *RB* 113 (2008): 570–84. See below.

21 See Neh 1:2; 2:16; 3:33, 34; 4:6; 5:1; 6:6; 13:23. This is the core term of the "inner" group in this text, not בני הגולה or the like as in Ezra. See also n. 19.

22 There is no avoiding that Nehemiah's portrayal and memory were shaped according to the traditional Near Eastern pattern of the pious, reforming king who shifts country and people away from the sinful behavior in which they engaged before he came to power. (Nehemiah's building of the walls also reflects a memory associating him with royal activities.) To be sure, the adoption of a common mnemonic narrative frame does not mean that nothing of what is narrated happened in some way or another, but again represents a call for caution, because it explains why a narrative such as the one that exists would have been preferred by those shaping a positive image of Nehemiah.

23 For one example of such reconstructions, see Jacob Wright, *Rebuilding Identity: The Nehemiah Memoir and Its Earliest Readers* (BZAW 348; Berlin: De Gruyter, 2004). For a discussion of his proposals, see G. N. Knoppers, "Revisiting the Composition of Ezra–Nehemiah: In Conversation with Jacob Wright's *Rebuilding Identity: The Nehemiah Memoir and Its Earliest Readers* (BZAW 348; Berlin: De Gruyter, 2004)," in *JHebS* 7, no. 12 (2007), available online: http://www.jhsonline.org, and published also under the same title in *Perspectives in Hebrew Scriptures IV: Comprising the Contents of Journal of Hebrew Scriptures*, vol. 7 (ed. E. Ben Zvi; Piscataway, N.J.: Gorgias, 2008), 323–67.

In sum, the implied claims of historicity underlying the approaches mentioned above is highly debatable; certainly not impossible, but at least highly debatable. But this is not all: even if one were to assume that there was a historical governor named Nehemiah who forcefully coerced the local elite in Jerusalem and its temple by using the power of the empire for a short while and effected the changes that the NM, in whatever textual form, ascribes to him, this historical Nehemiah would have been a minor "flash" or one might say a minor footnote, from the perspective of the history of the Persian period in Yehud. Speaking of this (quite common in research literature) Nehemiah, Lester Grabbe correctly writes, "Nehemiah was a failure, at least in the short term."[24] Hut the Nehemiah of memory was not a minor "flash."

Likewise, if one were to assume for the sake of the argument that Ezra–Nehemiah, or at least the core of it. belongs to the Persian period and that it truthfully represents the ideology and social mindscape of a group at the period, the observations made above about "holy seed" and about the impossibility of non-Israelites (mothers) and the children they have with Israelites ever joining Israel would indicate that it stands almost as an "out-of-the-grid" outlier within the main discourse and main repertoire of core texts of the community in the Persian period (cf., *inter alia*, Pentateuchal traditions, the "historical" books, Ruth and memories they reflect and evoke).[25]

---

[24] The entire quote reads: "Nehemiah was a failure, at least in the short term. Granted he built the city wall and was able to accomplish his goals during the twelve years or so that he was in Jerusalem, but even a temporary absence was sufficient for some of his measures to be abandoned or reversed. Our ignorance of what was happening in Judah in the next two centuries makes it difficult to be precise about the details of how Judaism developed. Yet when we finally find a partial lifting of the veil two centuries later, we find a Judaism which was certainly not in Nehemiah's image ... Nehemiah's attempts to isolate the Jewish community was no more successful ... Most important of all, many of those labelled 'foreigners' in Ezra–Nehemiah seem to have been accepted as Jews by the Jerusalemite community." See Grabbe, *History*, 1:309–10. See also L. L. Grabbe, "Triumph of the Pious or Failure of the Xenophobes? The Ezra–Nehemiah Reforms and the Nachgeschichte," in *Jewish Local Patriotism and Self-Identification in the Graeco-Roman Period* (eds. S. Jones and S. Pearce; JSPSup 31; Sheffield: Sheffield Academic, 1998), 50–65.

[25] One may mention that the demographic increase among Judahites/Jews in the late Hellenistic/Roman period could have hardly taken place without a rejection of the concept of "holy seed" expressed above. Clearly, such a concept stands at odds also with the later rabbinic concept of גיור ("conversion" to Judaism). To be sure this does not mean that proselytes were always welcome (or welcomed by all, for that matter), but that the crucial concepts underlying the narrative of the expulsion of the "foreign" wives and children were not accepted.

(Although it is widely acknowledged, it is still worth stressing in this particular context that in this story neither the wives nor the children were accused of worshiping "foreign" gods or

This being so, I would like to argue that the far more important *historical* Ezra and Nehemiah were those of social memory, that is, those that existed in the minds of later generations. The very (length) and complex) development that eventually led to the book of Ezra–Nehemiah attests beyond any doubt to the high importance of these Ezra/s and Nehemiah/s of memory and that much was at stake in shaping and reshaping them. Whereas their "real" counterparts' actions were, at best, a minor temporary flash, it was for many generations in ancient Israel that memories of Ezra and Nehemiah populated the minds of at least ancient groups that identified with *both* their own Ezras and Nehemiahs as they imagined, construed, and remembered them to be *and* with the viewpoint and deeds they associated with them, including the expulsion of women and children.[26]

But if this is so, and if the historical Ezras and Nehemiahs with the largest impact were those of memory already in the late Second Temple period, would it not make sense that approaches informed by social memory studies be *among* the first to come to mind, among socio-anthropological methods, for the study of these matters?[27]

---

leading the husbands/fathers into such a worship; the crucial reason for which they are expelled is their "foreign" origin.)

26 It is to be stressed that memories of important characters are shaped time and again and are very much historically and communally contingent. For instance, as is widely known, when Ezra becomes remembered as a key founding figure of Judaism, the site of memory "Ezra" turns into a crucial site of memory, subject to multiple mnemonic struggles, involving Jews, Christians and Muslims, over generations. Cf. D. Glatt-Gilat, "Ezra Ben Seraiah the Priest in Ancient and Modern Theological Discourse," in *Or Le-Mayer: Studies in Bible, Semitic Languages, Rabbinic Literature, and Ancient Civilizations* (ed. S. Yona; Beer-Sheva: Ben-Gurion University Press, 2010, Heb.), 87–97. But that later Ezra of memory is not the one addressed here. As anticipated, multiple Ezras of memory appear because he is constantly reshaped and imagined within the particular world of each remembering community. For a less known, in "biblical studies" circles, Ezra of memory, see, for instance, Ibn Khatir's characterization of the prophet Uzair. This said, none of these Ezras of memory were present within the community/ies discussed here; they belong to later times and communities.

27 It is worth noting also that the mentioned approaches may also be at least heuristically helpful in discussing the world of memories of these events. This is so because social-anthropological approaches may well work in worlds of memory and fiction. Even societies or social groups that exist only in literary works may reflect, directly or indirectly, in ways known or unbeknownst, to authors and readers underlying social dynamics and governing grammars underlying actual societies. After all, even imaginary worlds have to be based on known worlds. (This point is widely accepted among those who study, e.g., science fiction and its utopian/ dystopian societies.)

I would like to conclude this section by stressing that I am not claiming in any way or form that the socio-anthropological approaches surveyed above should be disregarded. They are actually helpful and have substantially furthered research in these areas. Instead, I am proposing a complementary approach and a renegotiation of the focus of the research. This renegotiation involves two related aspects: (a) focusing at least for a while as much (or more?) on what was remembered rather than what "actually" happened, which in any case is very difficult to assess and in itself had at best a marginal historical impact on Persian period Yehud (see section 1 of this essay) and (b) focusing on an approach that may help us to explore what was remembered, why and related questions (part 2 of this essay is an example of what such an approach may contribute to the discussion).

2 A Memory Approach to the Story of the Rejection of the "Foreign" Women and Children in Ezra Nehemiah and Utopian Tendencies

The previous section drew attention to the role that studies informed by "Memory Studies" may have for historical studies of stories of the rejections of the "foreign" wives and their children in Ezra–Nehemiah, even if not necessarily for the putative period of Ezra and Nehemiah in Yehud. But, of course, methods are lenses and not important by them-selves but because of what they may allow us to "see," what we may have missed or paid less attention to otherwise. To phrase it differently: the central issue is what kind of new, central questions an approach strongly informed by studies of social memory may either raise or draw particular attention to. In this particular case, several come to mind straight away, such as: Why were Ezra and Nehemiah remembered the way they were? Why were the mentioned expulsions so worthy of being remembered among those who identified with the relevant implied authors? Which systems of grammar of mnemonic preferences were at work in the shaping? What could the community gain by remembering these events in the relatively complex way eventually evoked in Ezra–Nehemiah?

Further, late Second Temple communities involved in constructing and remembering their Ezra and Nehemiah–and by these means in exploring the messages that these sites of memory communicated– could, to be sure, have explored matters of opposition to "mixed marriages" in other ways, but it is particularly significant that the) did so through memories of Ezra and Nehemiah as "encoded" in Ezra– Nehemiah.²⁸

Once one focuses on this book, it is clear that *one* of the most memorable associations evoked by reading Ezra–Nehemiah was the expulsion of "foreign" wives and children and related expulsions of those whom the implied author of Ezra–Nehemiah has construed to be considered "foreigners"²⁹ by the remembering community. One is to take into account, of course, that such an expulsion represents a memorable story,³⁰ partially because of the affective strength of the images it evokes. But at the same time, this was a didactic story about the past of Israel. That is, their past and any emotive appeal and ease of remembrance stood at the service of the message that the story taught them, not the other way around. What the story stood for, in ideological terms, was a complete, unyielding acceptance of the putative logical implications of an approach towards the community as Yhwh's holy seed within a social mindscape in which profanation of what was considered holy was construed as an ultimate threat.

This concept of a "holy seed" is certainly not a minor social matter. Moreover, it is well-grounded in a generative, conceptual grammar at work on a number of occasions. In a nutshell, it is likely that the community in Yehud thought

---

28 One may notice that a strong stance against "mixed marriages" is present, for instance, in Qumran material and *Jubilees*. See, e. g., Hannah Harrington, "Intermarriage in Qumran Texts: The Legacy of Ezra–Nehemiah," in *Mixed Marriages* (ed. C. Frevel), 251–79; C. Frevel, "'Separate Yourself from the Gentiles' (Jubilees 22:16): Intermarriage in the Book of Jubilees," in *Mixed Marriages* (ed. C. Frevel), 220–50. Some of this Qumran material may well be from the third century BCE. See A. Lange, "Your Daughters Do Not Give to Their Sons and Their Daughters Do Not Take for Your Sons (Ezra 9:12): Intermarriage in Ezra 9–10 and in the Pre-Maccabean Dead Sea Scrolls," Part I, in *BN* 137 (2008): 17–39; Part II, in *BN* 139 (2008): 79–98. Often these texts are associated with polemics against what their implied authors (and likely many of their readers) construed as a threatening process of "increased Hellenization" (e. g., Lange, "Your Daughters," 89). All this said, one cannot but notice that Ezra–Nehemiah was not a popular text in the repertoire of the texts found in the Qumran caves and this raises again questions about why the book of Ezra–Nehemiah would not be widely read within groups that strongly rejected any form of exogamy. Of course, when Ezra comes to be remembered as a key founding figure of Judaism, the site of memory "Ezra" turns into a crucial site of memory, subject to multiple mnemonic struggles. See above, n. 26.

29 Cf. "As has long been noted, one of Ezra–Nehemiah's most striking characteristics is its narrative descriptions of expulsions from cult and community of a group of persons of unparalleled size and range who are classed by the text as aliens. These include Yhwh-worshiping male foreigners, women of foreign origin who are married to Judean males, and the children these wives have borne to their Judean husbands" (Olyan, "Purity Ideology," 2).

30 Even transculturally; in fact, one may say that it is still very much "memorable" for many readers and scholars, given the very substantial amount of research devoted to it.

that human reproduction involved either only one seed or only one main (formative) seed, namely the male seed.[31] If so, since women do not produce seeds—or their seeds are of "secondary" importance—and since male seeds do not mix with other male seeds to produce offspring, males within a lineage were imagined as physically carrying and embodying the potential of the male seed of their crucial ancestor. Thus, the seed of David was carried by his descendants and so was the seed of Abraham, or the seed of Aaron. It is obvious that the logic of such an approach to social/biological reproduction leads to the characterization of differences as innate, essentialist, and essentializing. No one could be a Davidide, unless born a Davidide; no one could be an Aaronide except the children of Aaron, and the same would apply to Israel, who were often construed as a "holy people."[32]

---

31 Cf. R. D. Biggs, "Conception, Contraception and Abortion in Ancient Mesopotamia," in *Wisdom, Gods and Literature: Studies in Assyriology in Honour of W. G. Lambert* (eds. A. R. George, and I. L. Finkel; Winona Lake, Ind.: Eisenbrauns, 2000), 1–13; G. Leick, *Sex and Eroticism in Mesopotamian Literature* (New York: Routledge, 2003), 91. Note the antiquity of this view, "Ningirsu rejoiced over Eanatum, semen implanted in the womb by Ningirsu," J. S. Cooper, *Presargonic Inscriptions* (New Haven. Conn.: American Oriental Society, 1986), 34. The only potential evidence for a notion of a female seed in ancient Israel is in MT Lev 12:2–but not the ancient versions, and even the MT does not have to be understood as a reference to the production of a female seed. See, e.g., the discussion in J. Milgrom, *Leviticus 1–16* (AB 3; New York: Doubleday, 1991), 743–44, who nonetheless tends to accept the idea that "the probability rests with the literal translation, 'produces seed'" (743), though at least partially on the basis of rabbinic era ideas about the female production of seed (cf. Aristotle's position on the matter). To be sure, Galen (130–200 CE) advanced the idea of an important female seed and Galenic ideas may have, even if indirectly, influenced rabbinic literature. Real and assumed differences between Galenic and Aristotelian approaches to the matter were at the center of Western European medieval discussions on these issues. For the long history and construction of Aristotelian and Galenic approaches to these matters, see S. M. Connell, "Aristotle and Galen on Sex Difference and Reproduction: A New Approach to an Ancient Rivalry," in *Studies in History and Philosophy of Science* 31 (2000): 405–27.

32 Of course, this explanatory model served well to construe and "account for" continuity through time and multiple generations. But, at the same time, it always had to face the issue of beginnings, which by necessity represent salient cases of discontinuity. For example, how does the seed of Jesse or Boaz or Judah for that matter suddenly transform itself into the seed of David which carries some newly granted properties? Or how did the seed of Aaron become different from the seed of Levi? In these cases, the problem was solved by assuming that the deity granted/provided the new potential for the relevant male seed. Thus, the community constructed and remembered divine acts of genealogical branching. In other words, YHWH shaped something "new" as it were and through this action legitimized the act of branching (and the associated act of marginalizing, as well). It is worth noting that the more mnemonically significant these cases of divinely shaped branching were construed to be within a particular group, the more the same group would tend to consider them foundational events and thus very rare

Within the parameters of this generative conceptual grammar, a "holy" object, such as the male seed of the "priests" (or the "high priest") may be profaned if it is "inserted" and "incubated" in a womb that is not "holy."[33] These considerations, along with conceptual trends towards the construction of "Israel" as "holy" (*passim*) and "priestly" (e. g., Exod 19:6) explain well why the text in Ezra–Nehemiah focused on "foreign wives" and not on "foreign husbands."[34] Within that discourse, the former cannot but profane the "holy seed," but the latter are less of a problem since they do not carry a "holy seed" that can be profaned.

But such an approach, as internally coherent as it might be and thus as "desired" among those who value "internal logical coherence," chanced upon much ambiguity and encountered substantial opposition. There is, for one, the matter of potential adoption by a father (or father figure).[35] There were multiple sites of memory about non-Israelite women who were emphatically not remembered as "profaners" (e. g., Zipporah– daughter of a "foreign" priest, Asenath–also daughter of a "foreign" priest–Ruth, Naamah–mother of Rehoboam and thus of all the kings of Judah). There are also genealogies that stood in direct opposition to the construction of the male seed as the only determinant for identity. Chronicles, for

---

events that belong to the past. In fact, their foundational character required, to a large extent, that the community constructed and remembered them as stable and stabilizing events and this involved by necessity a strong tendency to bracket out the possibility of additional such acts, which could not but undermine such a stability. On genealogical branching and the correlated processes of marginalizing or exclusion from a socio-anthropological and socio-mnemonic perspective, see E. Zerubavel, *Ancestors and Relatives: Genealogy, Identity and Community* (Oxford: Oxford University Press, 2012), *passim*.

33 One may compare and contrast with Lev 21:13–15 and esp. v. 15, which refers to the High Priest and whose scope is expanded to include other priests in Ezek 44:22. It is worth noting that MMT (see MMT B 72–82 = 4Q396 iv: 1–11) follows a logic similar to that underlying Ezra–Nehemiah to its logical conclusion, namely that priests can marry only women from among the priestly families, for, one would assume, only they can provide a "holy container" for the incubation of the "holy seed." One may compare the generative grammar at work here with the one that eventually led to the construction of an elevated Mary in Christianity, who was remembered as providing a "dwelling fit for Christ" (and the like–the cited expression is from Maximus of Turin; she is also compared to the tabernacle) in many Christian traditions.

34 Within this discourse, women were not accorded a direct ability to mark social identity within this socio-biological, ideological construction of seed. They were instead construed as able to uphold or ruin the "seed" through cultural means, i. e., as wives or mothers (see even the case of daughters from the seed of "infamous" Israelites, e. g., Athaliah) or through impurity (the case of the "foreign" wives here).

35 See the case of Samuel in the book of Samuel–though significantly, Chronicles turns him into a Levite–and above all, Isa 56:1–6.

instance, in two cases *explicitly* and *emphatically* assumes the integration of "foreign male seed" in Israel. In 1 Chr 2:17 Amasa, an important character associated with David's time and family, is unequivocally remembered as the son of Jether the Ishmaelite. In 1 Chr 2:34–41, moreover, it is certainly not due to blind chance that the unnamed daughter of a marginal character such as Sheshan and her husband, the Egyptian slave Jarha, are allocated one of the longest genealogies in the Hebrew Bible.[36]

It is within this discursive context or conceptual mindscape[37] that the study of the rejection of the foreign wives and children in Ezra– Nehemiah is to be studied. In what follows and in a nutshell, I argue that later than the putative time of the stories and from the perspective of readers who identified, at least to a large extent, with the characters of Ezra and Nehemiah evoked by these books, the stories of the rejection of the foreign wives in Ezra–Nehemiah contributed to the construction not only of an image of a Utopian "pure" Israel and a memory of a "memorable" attempt to implement it, but also that the stories served as a reminder that implementing "utopia" ran, unsurprisingly, into problems. Thus, these stories served, at least for some ancient readers, as a ground on which they could (safely) explore (perceived to be) Utopian "purifying" constructions and their unfeasibility (both basic and contingent) and thus these constructions contributed to their ability to re-negotiate the boundaries and even the character of their "utopia."

To be sure, any discussion of Utopia or Utopian features has to advance a clear definition of what is meant by them. For the present purposes I will follow an appropriate version of a very pragmatic definition that I have advanced elsewhere, namely,

> a set composed of (a) any (historically-contingent) socially construed memory/image of a future or past "reality" *substantially* better than the present as understood by the community and which, among others, allows for an exploration of a "reality" different than the one it perceives; and … the Utopian "reality" is construed as substantially better than others and

---

[36] See G. N. Knoppers, "'Married into Moab': The Exogamy Practiced by Judah and His Descendants in the Judahite Lineages," in *Mixed Marriages* (ed. C. Frevel), 170–91 (182). Lev 24:10 might be another case of mixed marriage and matrilineal Israelite line, but the case is not as clear as the previous examples and remains open for debate.

[37] The considerations advanced above should suffice for the present purposes. This is not the place to expand on every related aspect or feature of this "universe" of thought and memory, nor on the generative associations to which it may lead (at least potentially), or to the plethora of social ambiguities it generated in the late Second Temple period. See, e.g., the manifold issues that arose out of (forced or voluntary) conversions to Judaism in Hasmonean and later times. A discussion of these matters requires a lengthy and certainly separate discussion.

implies and communicates a critical perspective on the latter, and points to lacks in them. In other words, Utopian representations are one of the ways in which world-critiques can be formulated and "concretized" in the form of socially shared sites of memory (be they texts, images, characters in texts, reported events that are mentally re-enacted through readings or which are integral part of the world of knowledge of a community) and, accordingly, can become memorable and influential in the discourse of the community.[38]

There can be little doubt that Ezra and Nehemiah fit well with the common ancient Near Eastern mnemonic plot characteristic of restoration narratives (e.g., Cyrus's defeat of Nabonidus). The circumstances before their (i.e., Ezra's and Nehemiah's) "heroic" deeds have to be portrayed and remembered as chaotic, abundant in sin and impurity, and their appearance, accordingly, as a crucial turning point, away from chaos, impiety, and rejection of the deity/ies towards order and piety. These restorations often mention cultic and ritual matters and involve constructing a kind of "reboot" of the society of the leader to a previous Utopian or quasi-utopian situation.

Several pillars of the remembered world of Ezra and Nehemiah— principally memories of their deeds of expulsion–contributed in particular to the construction of a Utopian flavor for these memories.[39] To begin with, they remembered a world in which their assumed "proper understanding" of authoritative texts was made effective in the "real" world, through acts of "proper" leadership.[40]

Second, from a transcultural social-anthropological perspective, theirs is the kind of Utopian world for groups that strongly prefer purity, order, and clear-cut boundaries and thus, social segregation. These groups detest potentially intermediate characters and above all ambiguity.[41] It is common for such groups to emphasize purity of lineage and the constructed behavior associated with that lineage, for behaving like a "foreigner" creates an ambiguous taxonomic item, partially internal and partially external; such ambiguous items are detested by these groups, because they shape porous boundaries, which is an anathema for such groups. Within this world, the very existence of the "other," the "foreign-

---

[38] E. Ben Zvi, "Reading and Constructing Utopias: Utopia/s and/in the Collection of Authoritative Texts/Textual Readings of Late Persian Period Yehud," in *SR* 42 (2013): 463–76 (466, original italics).

[39] Of course, "Utopian" only from the perspective of those who identified with the two main characters they shaped through their readings of the relevant texts. In fact, often someone's Utopia may well be someone else's dystopia.

[40] This includes reading the prohibitions of Deut 7:1–6 and 23:4–9 in an expansive way strongly informed by Lev 18:24–30 (see, e.g., M. Fishbane, *Biblical Interpretation in Ancient Israel* [Oxford: Clarendon, 1985], 114–29; Olyan, "Purity Ideology").

[41] See E. Zerubavel, *The Fine Line: Making Distinctions in Every Day Life* (New York: Free Press, 1991), 33–60.

er" within the boundaries of the community, is often perceived as a dangerous impurity to be removed, because it also shapes a sense of ambiguity and porous boundaries.

When lineage is construed as crucial for the construed impermeable taxonomic order, then intermarriage is conceived as a most dangerous threat to order, and mixed children tend to be construed not as ambiguous, but as unambiguous members of the "other"/"foreigner" and thus reaffirming the existence of impermeable boundaries.⁴² Such an approach requires that lineages be construed retroactively and remembered as originally pure and in need of restorative purification, from time to time.

The world of memory evoked by Ezra–Nehemiah includes the forceful expulsion of "foreign" women and "mixed" children. It includes a conceptualization of Israel as a whole, not just the priests, as "the holy seed/lineage" (זרע הקדש) (see Ezra 9:2) which "is illicitly desacralized by … marriages to aliens, which are in fact labeled 'sacrilege' (מעל) in the text at several junctures."⁴³

Within this world the "foreigner" is, as such, not only "profane" and an agent for the profanation of Israel, but also a non-contingent, intrinsic source of ritual pollution that requires purification of holy spaces, such as a temple.⁴⁴ Remembering Ezra, Nehemiah, their exclusionary positions, vicariously experiencing their implementation multiple times in the (construed as) "real" world every time Ezra–Nehemiah was read, and noticing and remembering the ideological underpinnings of these leaders of the past was imagining a Utopian time for those who prefer the type of cross-cultural rigid social mindset, with no room for ambiguity and fuzziness, mentioned above.

But social memory, including (and perhaps particularly) in the case of memories of Utopian periods, serves often also as a playground for exploring ideas and concepts. On the one hand, the main mnemonic narrative in its big contours was about the heroes' "purifying" actions in the past. Remembering them and reading Ezra–Nehemiah was to a significant extent an exercise in construing and remembering a glorious past Utopia of a community in which "proper," clear and rigid boundaries were established and from which ambiguity was driven out. But on the other hand, the very same text evoking all the above carried in itself (and communicated) clear marks of ambiguity on these matters.

---

42 See ibid.
43 See Ezra 9:4; 10:2,6,10; Neh 13:27. Citation from Olyan, "Purity Ideology," 4. See also Milgrom, *Leviticus 1–16*, 359–61, and C. E. Hayes, *Gentile Impurities and Jewish Identities: Intermarriage and Conversion from the Bible to the Talmud* (Oxford: Oxford University Press, 2002).
44 I follow Olyan here, "Purity Ideology," 10–12. For a different position, though still excluding the "foreigner" as profane, see C. E. Hayes, *Gentile Impurities*.

It is not so much that the heroes had to confront opposition from the people or that the offenders were many–this was to be expected, as they had to be imagined as heroes,[45]–but that, for instance, the story of Ezra leads towards its anticipated climactic conclusion in 10:44 yet instead, at least in the MT, concludes in an extremely ambiguous way (10:44b).

Even if, for the sake of argument, one were to argue that such ambiguity was due to an existing ambiguity on these matters in communities substantially later than the original composition of Ezra–Nehemiah, the issue remains that Ezra does not call for an expulsion of mothers and children in his memorable prayer in Ezra 9:5–15 or, for that matter, even in Ezra 10:10 in which the children are not mentioned. The initiative for the expulsion of mothers and children in the story is not an event allocated to Ezra, but to an otherwise unknown character, Shecaniah son of Jehiel, of the descendants of Elam,[46] whose only narrative and mnemonic role is to propose such an action and thus weakening Ezra's responsibility for it (Ezra 10:2–4).[47]

Remembering Ezra and reading the book that encodes his memory also involved reading Ezra 6:21 and its reference to וְכֹל הַנִּבְדָּל מִטֻּמְאַת גּוֹיֵ־הָאָרֶץ אֲלֵהֶם לִדְרֹשׁ לַיהוָה אֱלֹהֵי יִשְׂרָאֵל, which may be translated as "all who keep themselves separate from the impurities (/uncleanness/pollutions) of the nations of the land and join them to seek/worship Yhwh, the God of Israel," obviously stands in tension with the positions, actions, underlying ideology and general social mindset advanced by the main narratives about Ezra and Nehemiah.[48] Fuzziness and balances of various positions are not really eradicated in Ezra–Nehemiah. The book shapes and communicates the mentioned utopia of lack of ambiguity but is in itself a bearer of ambiguity.

---

[45] This also plays into the relatively common ancient Near Eastern characterization of the "heroic" character as one facing the "many"; moreover, the one is pious and the "many" are not.
[46] Of course, the descendants of Elam are Israelites in the world of Ezra (see 2:7; 8:7), but given the rigid social mindscape mentioned above and its fear of ambiguity, one cannot fail to notice the existence of a potential sense of ambiguity evoked by his name or even the connotations hinted at in Ezra 10:26.
[47] Some Karaite commentators claimed that Ezra did not want to expel the children. See Cohen, "Origins of the Matrilineal Principle," 25, 37.
[48] In fact, one may say that Ezra 6:21 is much closer to Isa 56:1–8 than to the rest of Ezra–Nehemiah. Cf. J. Blenkinsopp, *Ezra–Nehemiah*, 133; cf. idem, *Isaiah 56–66* (AB 19B; New York: Doubleday, 2003), 84. According to Blenkinsopp, Ezra 6:21 probably comes from the school to which the author of Chronicles belonged. Whether this is the case or not, the readers of Ezra–Nehemiah read Ezra 6:21 as an integral part of the book of Ezra (and of Ezra–Nehemiah). According to Fried, these might have included "foreign soldiers and Persian officers," see L. S. Fried, *Ezra. A Commentary* (Sheffield: Sheffield Phoenix Press, 2017).

In addition, the book–as any book for that matter–was not read in a vacuum but was in a way informed by other books within the core repertoire of the community. It is impossible to assume that the readers were ignorant of common memories about an Israelite society in which a broad space is allocated to גרים living among and participating in the Israelite "community" or, for that matter, of memories of legal texts dealing with them (e.g., Exod 12:48–49). As mentioned above, their memories included important women (e.g., Zipporah, Asenath, Ruth, Naamah) who were explicitly and emphatically not born of Israelite fathers (see the issue of the seed) or even Israelite mothers, but nonetheless not only were they and their children not rejected, but they and their husbands (who did not expel them) became central to Israel (e.g., Moses–notice also his Cushite wife; Joseph).[1]

To be sure Pentateuchal texts and the memories they evoked were polyphonic on these issues (see, e.g., the case of the killing of Zimri and Cozbi by Phineas, according to Num 25, who was much rewarded for that act). Ambiguity and polyvalence also played important roles in Pentateuchal memories exploring "mixed" marriages. The desire for a "clear cut" Utopia underlying the narratives of the rejection of the "foreign" wives and children in Ezra–Nehemiah, and implicit in the construction of and in acts of remembering a past in which "heroic" figures implement such "un-ambiguous" concepts such as the (male) "holy seed," was again confronted with some remembered situations that, when seen from the relevant perspective, could only be understood as at least seemingly dystopian. Thus, as anticipated, a generative grammar aimed at reshaping, appropriating and "clarifying" these situations emerged This generative grammar underlies much of Ezra Nehemiah and much (but not all) of what it is about.

This said, and although Ezra–Nehemiah clearly evoked (and appropriated as well as reshaped Pentateuchal traditions), the partial text overlap of the ending of Chronicles and the beginning of Ezra–Nehemiah, along with the communicative message of their shared linguistic profile, encouraged a reading of one in the light of the other. But if this is the case, memories of the expulsion of mothers and children and the accompanying ideology and social mindset evoked through readings of Ezra–Nehemiah could not but be balanced by the clear and repeated

---

49 Much has been written on these matters and from various perspectives; see, e.g., K. S. Winslow, "Ethnicity, Exogamy, and Zipporah," in *Women in Judaism* 4, no. 1 (2006), available online: http://wjudaism.library.utoronto.ca/index.php/wjudaism/article/view/225 and idem, "Mixed Marriage in *Torah* Narratives," in *Mixed Marriages* (ed. C. Frevel), 132–49.

rejection of all of the above in Chronicles and thus raise questions about the mentioned Utopia.[50]

In sum, vicariously experiencing the "outlier utopia" evoked by reading Ezra–Nehemiah went hand in hand with remembering that it ran, unsurprisingly, into problems of feasibility, and with remembering that its Utopian character, which relied on conveying un-fuzziness, was actually fuzzy at multiple levels, and in need of much negotiation. To some extent, one may say that remembering that "utopia" served also as an exercise in exploring the boundaries and even the character of "utopia."

---

50 As mentioned above, the cases of Amasa and Jarha explicitly and emphatically call into question the very core of the "biological" approach to "Yhwh's holy seed." To be sure, one may raise the issue of readers of Chronicles strongly informed by Ezra–Nehemiah. On the crucial, for the present purposes, matter of the rejection of "foreigners" and (biological) "lineage purity," the likely influence going in this direction would have been to notice or increase the mindscape of the fact that although the Davidic line and the Judah line are abundant in cases of "mixed-marriages," the same is not true for the lineage of the priests. The story then emerging would have been one stressing the eventual "priestization" of Israel. While this is true when Chronicles was read in a way strongly informed by Ezra– Nehemiah, it is worth noting that Chronicles on its own tends to "royalize" rather than "priestize" Israel. But these matters deserve a separate discussion. In addition, reading Chronicles in a way strongly influenced by Ezra–Nehemiah would lead to an association of the reforms/purges of Hezekiah and Josiah with those of Ezra and Nehemiah and all of these to the motif of restoring temple and community. Cf. J. Clauss, "Understanding the Mixed Marriages of Ezra–Nehemiah in the Light of Temple-Building and the Book's Concept of Jerusalem," in *Mixed Marriages* (ed. C. Frevel), 109–31 (124–30). This said, no matter whether Ezra–Nehemiah is read in the light of Chronicles or vice versa, there is no room to settle in any substantial way the explicit and emphatic construction and memory of Amasa's or Jarha's lineage with the underlying logic governing the concept of (male) holy seed and its putative implementation, as described in Ezra–Nehemiah.

The "Successful, Wise, Worthy Wife" of Proverbs 31:10–31 as a Source for Reconstructing Aspects of Thought and Economy in the Late Persian/Early Hellenistic Period*

Introduction

Studies conducted in the last decades on Prov 31:10–31 have contributed a great deal to a better understanding of the text and the portrayal of the successful, wise, worthy wife at its very center.[1] They have dealt with literary composition and structure (Lichtenstein 1982: 202–11; Hurowitz 2001: 209–18)[2] and addressed, inter alia, gender (Camp 1985: 90–94, 186–208; Fischer 2005: 237–53; cf. Valler 1995: 85–97), imagery (Szlos 2000: 97–103; Novick 2009: 107–13), anthropology (Lang 2004b: 188–207), socioeconomics (Yoder 2001; 2003: 427–47), text criticism (Rofé 2002: 145–55),[3] form criticism (Wolters 1988: 446–57; Nwaoru 2005: 41–66), and various combinations of these matters.[4] In addition, they have been informed by comparative studies with ancient Near Eastern texts (Hurowitz 2005: 221–34), classical texts (esp. Xenophon, *Oeconomicus*; Waegeman 1992: 101–7; Lang 2004b),[5] Ottoman households

---

* First published in *The Economy of Ancient Judah in Its Historical Context* (eds. M. L. Miller, E. Ben Zvi, and G. N. Knoppers; Winona Lake, Ind.: Eisenbrauns, 2015), 27–49.

1 For an excellent study of this pericope, which also includes a survey and critique of most of these studies, see M. V. Fox, *Proverbs 10–31: A New Translation with Introduction and Commentary* (AB 18B; New Haven, CT: Yale University Press, 2009), 882–917.

2 It may be mentioned that readings of Prov 31:10–31 as being closely linked to Prov 31:1–9 have a long history. Yefet ben ʿElī (10th century) maintained that the author of Prov 31:10–31 was the mother of Lemuel–whom he identified with Bathsheba. The proposal for a female authorship of Prov 31:10–31 is noteworthy. On Yefet ben ʿElī's reading of this pericope, see I. Sasson "The Book of Proverbs between Saadia and Yefet," in *Intellectual History of the Islamicate World* 1 (2013): 159–217 (175–76).

3 Compare with Rofé's contribution by the same title published in Hebrew in *Homage to Shmuel: Studies in the World of the Bible* (eds. Z. Talshir, S. Yona and D. Sivan; Jerusalem: Bialik Institute/Beer-sheva: Ben-Gurion University Press, 2001), 382–90.

4 In fact, all the works mentioned thus far could easily have been included in more than one category. This is the case because, in reality, none of these categories excludes the others, and scholars usually deal with multiple issues and approaches.

5 On Xenophon's *Oeconomicus*, see, e.g., S. B. Pomeroy, *Xenophon, Oeconomicus: A Social and Historical Commentary* (Oxford: Clarendon/New York: Oxford University Press, 1994).

https://doi.org/10.1515/9783110547146-027

(Lang 2004a: 140–57), Yoruba *oriki*/recitals (Nwaoru 2005), and Indian parallels (Luke 1991: 131–32).

My contribution to this vast area of studies is from the perspective of a historian of the world of the thought and memory of ancient Israel. Moreover, since the world of thought does not exist in a vacuum, totally unrelated to historical contingencies, and since even imagination must emerge from a "real" world, I conclude with some observations about the ways in which this ideal image may shed light on economy and society in Yehud.

It is obvious that the imagined, remembered, and certainly utopian (from the perspective of the readers) the אשת־חיל portrayed in Prov 31:10–31[6] did not provide a representative portrayal of the activities of historical, average wives in the late Persian/early Hellenistic period in Yehud/Judah–or for that matter, in any period.[7] Instead, it constructed within the community an ideal site of memory.

---

[6] As the title of this contribution shows, I am rendering אשת־חיל a "successful, wise, worthy wife." This is just an attempt to convey a more substantial portion of the semantic realm of אשת־חיל. A. Rofé influences this translation to some extent (cf. idem, "The Valiant Woman, γυνὴ συνετή, and the Redaction of the Book of Proverbs," in *Vergegenwärtigung des Alten Testaments: Beiträge zur biblischen Hermeneutik. Festschrift für Rudolf Smend zum 70. Geburtstag* (eds. C. Bultmann, W. Dietrich, and C. Levin; Göttingen: Vandenhoeck & Ruprecht, 2002), 145–55). Many other renderings have been offered, e.g., "capable wife/woman," "valiant wife/woman," "wife/woman of valor," "wife/woman of substance," "wife/woman of worth," "wife/woman who is a treasure," "wife/woman of strength," "excellent wife/woman," or one may even think of "wonder-wife/woman." Within the pair "wife"–"woman," the preferred term is often "woman," but since the married status of the אשת־חיל plays an important part in her characterization and in the ways in which she was imagined and remembered in the late Persian/early Hellenistic period, I find the term "wife" to be historically more precise. This said, I am aware of concerns related to today's use of biblical text-in settings other than academic attempts to reconstruct a historical past–that have been raised about translations such as the one I am suggesting. See, e.g., D. Yilibuw, "Tampering with Bible Translation in Yap," in *Hidden Truths from Eden: Esoteric Readings of Genesis 1–3* (eds. C. Vander Stichele and S. Scholz; Semeia 76; Atlanta: Scholars Press, 1996), 21–38 (30–32). The goal of this contribution, however, is to advance a (construction of a historically reasonable) reconstruction of the ancient world of thought. Within the world of thought (and memory and imagination) of the literati of Persian or early Hellenistic Yehud/Judah, the אשת־חיל was certainly imagined as a married heterosexual woman and a mother as well. For some lists of translations and brief discussion, see, e.g., V. A. Hurowitz, "The Woman of Valor and a Woman Large of Head: Matchmaking in the Ancient Near East," in *Seeking Out the Wisdom of the Ancients: Essays Offered to Honor Michael V. Fox on the Occasion of His Sixty-Fifth Birthday* (eds. R. L. Troxel, K. G. Friebel, and D. R. Magary; Winona Lake, IN: Eisenbrauns, 2005), 221–34 (esp. 221).

[7] The point is actually partially conceded by the text itself, as it frames the beginning of the pericope with a rhetorical question. On this issue, compare, for instance, M. V. Fox, *Proverbs 10–31*, 890–91; J. Hausmann, "Beobachtungen zu Spr 31,10–31," in *Alttestamentlicher Glaube und Biblische Theologie: Festschrift für Horst Dietrich Preuss* (eds. J. Hausmann and H.-J.

The אשת־חיל became the embodiment of an exemplar.[8] It served processes of socialization within the relevant social group and as a socially approved, guiding lighthouse for single men navigating the sea of marital matchmaking, and likely also for future brides (Crook: 1954: 137–40; Luke 1991; Nwaoru 2005; Fox 2009: 905) within the same group, learning about what they should do to become wives who both were a treasure and created a treasure and to inculcate a direct correspondence between the two—namely, being and creating a treasure.

Before we explore some aspects of the underlying world of thought reflected and communicated by אשת־חיל, two preliminary considerations are in order. First, there is the matter of dating the relevant text. Obviously, if it did not exist during the late Persian/early Hellenistic period in Judah/Yehud, it cannot help us shed much light on this period. But there is a general agreement on dating this text within that range.[9] Of course, there are many attempts to narrow the

---

Zobel. Stuttgart: Kohlhammer, 1992), 261–66 (262); and I. Fischer, *Gotteslehrerinnen: Weise Frauen und Frau Weisheit im Alten Testament* (Stuttgart: Kohlhammer, 2006), 149.

8 The community reading and rereading the text remembers her, her attributes, actions, and her world. As the process continues, the אשת־חיל becomes a site of memory, and I would add, an important site of memory within the community. See below.

9 See C. R. Yoder, *Wisdom as a Woman of Substance: A Socioeconomic Reading of Proverbs 1–9 and 31:10–31* (BZAW 304; Berlin: De Gruyter, 2001), who dates MT Prov 1–9 and Prov 31:10–31 to "a date between the beginning of the sixth century BCE and the end of the third century BCE—most likely sometime in the Persian period" (38). B. Lang suggests that the text may be "roughly contemporaneous with Xenophon's Oeconomicus" and in any case no earlier than the 5th or the 4th centuries BCE (idem, "Women's Work, Household and Property in Two Mediterranean Societies: A Comparative Essay on Proverbs XXXI 10–31," in *VT* 54 (2004): 188–207 [188–89]; idem, "The Hebrew Wife and the Ottoman Wife," in *Anthropology and Biblical Studies: Avenues of Approach* [eds. L. J. Lawrence and M. I. Aguilar; Leiden: Deo, 2004], 140–57 [140]). A. Wolters (*Ṣôpiyyâ* [Prov 31:27] as Hymnic Participle and Play on Sophia", in *JBL* 104 [1985]: 577–87) proposes a date in the 3rd century (but notice also Fox's critique on purported crucial evidence for the dating [Fox, *Proverbs 10–31*, 897]; and the comments in Yoder, *Wisdom as a Woman of Substance*, 33). Finally, one may notice that Waegeman suggests a date no later than the 2nd century BCE (M. Waegeman, "The Perfect Wife of Proverbia 31:10–31," in *Goldene Äpfel in silbernen Schalen: Collected Communications to the XIIIth Congress of the International Organization for the Study of the Old Testament, Leuven 1989* [eds. K.-D. Schunck and M. Augustin; Frankfurt am Main: Peter Lang, 1992], 101–7 [101]). In general, positions concerning these narrower temporal ranges tend to be argued on matters such as the connection between Prov 30:10–31 and Prov 1–9, observations about similar social (and clearly gendered) settings in the Persian period or in Xenophon's *Oeconomicus* (see, e. g., 3.10–15; 6.9; 7.1–41; 8.11–17; 10.10–13), and some linguistic considerations (among other matters). For some additional considerations, see n. 21 below. For the position that Prov 31.10–31 is a premonarchic text, see E. L. Lyons, "A Note on Proverbs 31.10–31," in *The Listening Heart: Essays in Wisdom and the Psalms in Honor of Roland E. Murphy* (ed. K. G. Hoglund, E. F. Huwiler, J. T. Glass, and R. W. Lee; JSOTSup 58; Sheffield: JSOT Press, 1987), 237–45. Lyons contends that the basic "pioneer" conditions of the premonar-

range for the composition of the text, but the arguments in favor of more-precise dates are not necessarily conclusive (Fox 2009: 899–902). In any event, for the present purposes, given the long-term, basic continuity of the relevant socioeconomic setting, a wide range such as "late Persian /early Hellenistic" does not represent a substantial problem.[10]

The second preliminary observation is that, although (a) the wife in Prov 31:10–31 evoked images of Lady Wisdom (e. g., Prov 31:10; cf. 3:15; 8:11), and (b) was likely imagined as partially embodying some of the attributes of Lady Wisdom, and (c) at times an ad hoc potential (though limited) overlap between the two was connoted (e.g., Prov 31:25–26) for the sake of stressing how good she was, the fact remains that the אשת־חיל was still construed and remembered primarily as a wise wife, not an elevated, above-human wife. Unlike the אשת־חיל, Lady Wisdom is not actually and exclusively married to a particular man. Moreover, and most significant, no matter how much the husband of the אשת־חיל was honored among his peers, he certainly did not marry the "daughter of YHWH" who stood before creation (cf. Prov 8:22–36).[11] The אשת־חיל was, after

---

chic period that she associates with this text were also present in the Persian period but decides to support a date in the premonarchic period because of her position that "the extended family did not reappear a self-sufficient economic unit" at any time in Judah, including the Persian period, after the beginning of the monarchy (241). Neither the crucial position nor the related dating has received much support in current research.

10 What about proposals to date the text outside these general parameters? Not only is there is no evidence supporting a Hasmonean date for the text, but both Ben Sira's reliance on Proverbs and commonly suggested dates for LXX Proverbs make such a date less likely. See J. Cook, "The Septuagint as Contextual Bible Translation: Alexandria or Jerusalem as the Context of Proverbs," in *JNSL* 19 (1993): 25–39; idem, "The Law of Moses in Septuagint Proverbs," in *VT* 49 (1999): 448–61; idem, "Semantic Considerations and the Provenance of Translated Units," in *XIII Congress of the International Organization for Septuagint and Cognate Studies: Ljubliana, 2007* (ed. M. K. H. Peters; Atlanta: Society of Biblical Literature, 2008), 67–85. A monarchic date for Prov 31:10–31 is also difficult, given, inter alia, the multiple interrelations between this text and other texts in the book. But, for the present purposes, even if one were to argue that there was some forerunner of Prov 31:10–31, the אשת־חיל evoked through acts of reading Proverbs (again notice, how the relevant text is deeply and carefully interwoven with others) could not have preceded the book itself, which in any case leads us back to the Persian–early Hellenistic period.

11 Of course, when the text is read with very different "lenses," other meanings appear, e. g., when the אשת־חיל is the Church and Christ is her husband (see *Proverbs, Ecclesiastes, Song of Solomon* [ed. J. R. Wright; ACCS; Downers Grove, IL: InterVarsity, 2005], 186–87), or as a type of Mary (a quite common approach, even today in some religious circles), or the "*torah*" (see *Midrash Proverbs*–implicitly, YHWH is her husband), or "Practical Wisdom" or "matter" that serves "Philosophical Wisdom," or "the intellect" (see Ralbag, Proverbs 31; החומר המשרת אל השכל שרות שלם), or Israel (Pesiq. Rab. 31, and Zohar 3.42.b), or the Shekinah and Queen Sabbath

all, an ideal but very human, wife, mother,[12] manager, and entrepreneur whose memory served as an exemplar for other (human) women—not a kind of goddess or just an allegory for Wisdom (McCreesh 1985: 25–46).[13]

Since the אשת־חיל was remembered as an ideal human wife, she could embody and communicate what the community—or better, what the well-off sector of the community—considered ideal economic behavior at the level of a single household. In fact, thinking about and through the אשת־חיל was a way for the community to explore and express its views about ideal economic activity at the level of a single affluent household. This level is particularly important, not only for all the usual reasons for taking into account the activities of agents other than central political leaders or whatever is said about them, but also because it is most likely that the individual household was and was considered by the community to be the basic social and economic unit.[14] In what follows, I will discuss some aspects of these concepts and their potential significance.

(as often understood in traditional Jewish liturgy, influenced by Kabbalistic traditions), or any number of biblical women (e. g., Sarah–passim in rabbinic sources, the wife of Noah, Midrash Eshet Hayil at the beginning), or even, at times, men such as Moses, or the ideal student of *Torah*. According to Saadia Gaon, the text recounts "the attributes of [excellent] men" (though metaphorically), whereas according to Yefet ben ʿElī, it recounts the attributes of excellent people, whether men or women. See I. Sasson, "The Book of Proverbs", 173–76. On rabbinic sources, see S. Valler, "Who Is 'Ēšet Ḥayil' in Rabbinic Literature?," in *A Feminist Companion to Wisdom Literature* (ed. A. Brenner; Sheffield: Sheffield Academic Press, 1995), 85–97; and on general Jewish traditional understandings, see Fox, *Proverbs 10–31*, 905–7; and bibliographical references cited in these two works. For a discussion of the place of the *Eshet Hayil* in contemporary Jewish, liberal and feminist liturgy, see M. Falk, *The Book of Blessings* (Boston: Beacon, 1999), 451–52.

12 Certainly not to be identified with the only woman explicitly characterized as an אשת־חיל in the Hebrew Bible—namely, Ruth—when she was still destitute (Ruth 3:11). Compare and contrast with S. T. S. Goh, "Ruth as a Superior Woman of חיל? A Comparison between Ruth and the 'Capable' Woman in Proverbs 31.10–31," in *JSOT* 38 (2014): 487–500.

13 For a different take on the relation between Lady Wisdom and the אשת־חיל along with a relevant exploration of the concept and role of "personification," see C. V. Camp, *Wisdom and the Feminine in the Book of Proverbs* (Bible and Literature 11; Decatur, GA: Almond, 1985), 96–97, 186–222. For a critique of McCreesh's position and arguments, see M. Gilbert "La Donna Forte di Proverbi 31,10–31," in *"Ritratto o Simbolo,"* in *Libro dei Proverbi: Tradizione, redazione, teologia* (eds. G. Bellia and A. Passaro; Casale Monferrato: Piemme, 1999), 147–67.

14 There is no house of the (local) king to compete for socioeconomic power in the Persian period, and it is unclear whether the Jerusalemite temple played a direct and central role in the *production* of wealth within the province.

Economic Power Brings Honor and the Strongest Endorsement for the Pursuit of Profit and for Profit Itself

The אשת־חיל produced material gain (v. 11) for her husband and household. Not only is the wife's strenuous pursuit of gains–that is, her pursuit of profit (and profit itself)–glorified within the world of thought evoked by the text, but her acquisition of wealth (i.e., economic capital) provides her and him with additional honor, social capital, and power rather than vice versa. This is a rhetorical and mnemonic (at least) partial reversal of the expected situation: namely, that power is the source of wealth, rather than vice versa. In fact, it is often maintained that, whereas wealth is the source of power in capitalistic societies, the opposite was true in more traditional societies (Amin 1991: 349–50). Given the relation between power and social capital, the transformation of her profits into her husband's/household's social capital/honor, the observation made above about wealth's being a source of power holds true in the "story" of the אשת־חיל, even if one were to argue that the community did not construe this wife as one who pursued profit for profit's sake and wealth for wealth's sake.

The same holds true when attention is explicitly drawn to the patronage system headed by the אשת־חיל herself (not her husband) and certainly not restricted to "women and children," but to the poor and needy in general (v. 20; see כַּפָּהּ פָּרְשָׂה לֶעָנִי וְיָדֶיהָ שִׁלְּחָה לָאֶבְיוֹן). Producing and accumulating economic power was conceptualized as leading to increased social capital and power, rather than vice versa, and these matters were explored and embodied in the אשת־חיל.

The reference to her husband and his increased honor (v. 23) may imply an additional redistribution/patronage system, this time managed by the elders of the city.

These references are not insignificant. They serve an ideological need to "normalize" or "balance" her pursuit of profit and wealth (well beyond that required for covering sufficiently the needs of her household) by transforming them into a pursuit that serves purposes other than increasing wealth and by suggesting, implicitly, a potential redistributive system.

To them, one may add the likely later shift in the characterization of the אשת־חיל from a "wise" woman (see LXX Prov 31:30) to a woman who "fears YHWH" (MT), which in another way "normalizes" her memory.[15] But, to be sure, remembering the אשת־חיל meant assigning much more social mindshare

---

[15] An additional potential case of "normalization" that is clearly not a late addition may be discerned in v. 31, if one follows Fox and understands the texts as envisioning "two kinds of recognition: material and verbal" (Fox, *Proverbs 10–31*, 899).

to her work and its constant pursuit of accumulation of wealth within the boundaries of her household and to its partial, glorification, rather than to the social redistribution of the wealth accumulated through an ongoing, constant pursuit of profit, and nowhere is it stated that the main reason for all her labors was to fund the poor and needy.

A final observation: this reversal of expectations—namely, that wealth is construed as leading to power, rather than vice versa—may well be only partial. The אשת־חיל and her husband and those who identified themselves as the addressees of the opening rhetorical question were imagined as members of a high socioeconomic group that already owned considerable resources. One may argue, then, that the society in Yehud as a whole had a power structure that, although it was allowed material wealth to bring about relatively minor shifts of social clout/power among its top echelon, due to restricted social mobility reflected a system in which as a whole, power (i.e., the already existing power of the top echelon of household) led to its increased wealth rather than vice versa. This may well be correct, but one must keep in mind the case of Ta(pe)met and her daughter Yehoshima, which represents a very well attested instance of social mobility in Elephantine.[16] Such cases might have been uncommon, and, in any event, one cannot extrapolate from Elephantine to Yehud. Nevertheless, they raise questions about any claims that social mobility fueled by acquisition of some relative measure of wealth was an impossibility in Yehud.[17] It is worth noting in this con-

---

[16] Compare with, for instance, the situation at the time of the mother's wedding as reflected in B 36 = TAD B3.3 with that of the daughter in B 41 = TAD B3.8. (Social mobility through outstanding service to the crown, esp. but not exclusively in the military, had long been a common path to social mobility in the region and has been well attested in, for instance, Egypt. But we are referring here to a social mobility that is not dependent on the decision of important figures in the court.) See B. Porten et al., *The Elephantine Papyri in English* (Leiden and New York: Brill, 1996) as well as B. Porten and A. Yardeni, *Textbook of Aramaic Documents from Ancient Egypt (TAD)* (4 vols.; Jerusalem: Hebrew University, 1986–1999).

[17] It is worth stressing that there was (some degree of) social mobility in both Egypt and Mesopotamia, and not only at the top (e.g., "commoners" who became royal or high-level military or administrative leaders with "humble" origins). These matters are beyond the scope of this essay, but see, e.g., P. Steinkeller, "The Foresters of Umma: Towards a Definition of Ur III Labor," in *Labor in the Ancient Near East* (ed. M. A. Powell. New Haven, CT: American Oriental Society, 1987), 73–115, e.g., 100; E. C. Stone, "The Constraints on State and Urban Form in Ancient Mesopotamia," in *Urbanism and Economy in the Ancient Near East* (eds. M. Hudson and B. A. Levine; Cambridge: Peabody Museum of Archaeology and Ethnology, 1999), 203–27 (208); E. Frood, "Social Structure and Daily Life: Pharaonic," in *A Companion to Ancient Egypt*, vol. 1 (2 vols.; ed. A. B. Lloyd; Malden, MA: Wiley-Blackwell, 2010), 469–90 (478–79); K. Vandorpe, "The Ptolemaic Period," in *A Companion to Ancient Egypt*, vol. 1 (2 vols.; ed. A. B. Lloyd; Chichester: Wiley-Blackwell, 2010), 159–79. For the present purposes, it suffices to note that assumptions about an

text that Prov 31:10–31 at the very least creates the illusion that any household led by such an אשת־חיל will do well (see below) and that remembering her was still remembering that an increase in profit through the judicious management of a wife was likely to lead to increased social power.

Pursuing Profit Is Wise and It Involves Wisdom about How to Make a Profit: Articulating the Construction of an Economy

How did the imagined, remembered, and, ideally, to be imitated as much as possible אשת־חיל pursue her profit and increase her wealth? The text suggests that this question is important. In fact, within the multiple sites of memory encoded in the authoritative repertoire of the community, thinking about and through the image of the אשת־חיל provided one of the few potential grounds for exploring these matters at the most-relevant level for the community–that is, the single household.

To be sure, the text refers to the proper administration of resources (esp., food and clothing, including the appropriate purchase and production of goods for household use, e.g., food, v. 15; and clothes for herself that communicated her high status, v. 22).[18] But in terms of creating a profit, the stress is first on the sale of value-added products. In particular, she produces clothes and sells (luxury?) linen garments and sashes (or loincloths) to merchants and with her earnings she buys good fields and plants vineyards (v. 16) that, in turn, are supposed to increase her profit. As profit and wealth accumulate, she is able to produce even more profit and wealth. Her position is secure, and she may "laugh" (v. 25) at the time to come (i.e., whatever the future may bring).

The אשת־חיל was imagined as an entrepreneur, as an extremely industrious person who worked day and night (v. 18; compare and contrast with Josh 1:8). She was remembered as "seeking" דרשה wool and flax (v. 13; compare and con-

---

airtight closure of the possibility of social mobility in Persian/early Hellenistic Yehud/Judah are problematic.

18 Imagining her making status clothes for herself makes sense within the world evoked by reading the text among the literati of the time but seems to have raised some uneasiness among some later readers. What about her husband? The LXX "normalizes" the text: "She duplicated cloaks for her husband and for herself clothes of fine linen and purple" (NETS). Another example of the LXX's tendency to "normalize" the text appears in v. 21, which in the LXX reads, "Her husband has no concern for his household, when he spends time somewhere, for all that are hers are being clothed" (NETS). LXX Proverbs emerged in a society that was not identical to that of the original text and in which sensitivity to the partial "absence" of the husband likely led to additional, explicit textual "mitigation," when compared with the MT.

trast with Ezra 7:10), as a master of her trade (vv. 13, 19), a person well aware of quality control (v. 18), and a mistress who wisely and kindly taught her servant-girls to produce very good wares (v. 26; cf. 15). She was recalled as a wise trader, intelligent buyer of farmland,[19] and a planter and owner of vineyards. A set of concepts about ideal economic behavior was thus shaped, formulated, and expressed.

Of course, necessarily, the same holds true for a world of thought and attitudes concerning socioeconomic matters. Within this world, the image of a trade ship evoked strong positive responses, and trade in general not only was viewed in very positive terms but was construed as necessary for the wise management of well-off households. The sense of a Yehudite household's ability to behave wisely in both the economic sphere and in (local and foreign) trade was construed and communicated.

Needless to say, this represents a very different view from the commonly attested ancient (essentially) moralistic, aristocratic disdain for trade and its corrupting influence, as well as for profit produced from trade–all of which were seen as potentially destabilizing forces from the perspective of an established, land-based aristocracy.[20] It is perhaps, not surprising that trade is viewed so highly in a text in which a *wife* is made the exemplar of productive, wealth-creating leadership.[21]

---

19 Note the choice of words in v. 16–namely, זָמְמָה שָׂדֶה וַתִּקָּחֵהוּ, "she plans (/schemes) and executes." Whatever she carefully plans, she executes. These are not impulsive but well-calculated purchases, and within this world of memory and imagery, there is nothing the other side can do to stop her.

20 In terms of ancient Israel, see, for instance, the negative characterization of trade in the oracles against Tyre or other Phoenician cities (e.g., Isa 23; Ezek 27), but see also Nah 3:16 and see the negative reference to Babylon in Ezek 17:4, as a city of merchants. Note that there is no comparable negative, moralizing account of farming in any of the so-called oracles against the nations (OAN). On Ezek 27, see recently I. D. Wilson, "Tyre a Ship," in *ZAW* 125 (2013): 249–62. This tendency existed in many other ancient Mediterranean societies. See the polemic title in P. Horden and N. Purcell, *The Corrupting Sea: A Study of Mediterranean History* (Oxford: Blackwell, 2000); and cf. P. F. Bang, "Imperial Bazaar: Towards a Comparative Understanding of Markets in the Roman Empire," in *Ancient Economies, Modern Methodologies: Archaeology, Comparative History* (eds. P. F. Bang, M. Ikeguchi, and H. G. Ziche; Pragmateiai 12; Bari: Edipuglia, 2006), 51–88 (56–58). It is worth noting that, in Babylonia, "There is no indication that enterprise was considered 'dirty business' or something to be delegated to an underling as in Roman times" (C. Wunsch, "The Šangû-Ninurta Archive" in *Approaching the Babylonian Economy: Proceedings of the START Project Symposium Held in Vienna, 1–3 July 2004* [eds. H. D. Baker and M. Jursa; AOAT 330; Münster: Ugarit-Verlag, 2005], 367–79).

21 There is an element of "transgression" on all these matters. Transgressions or challenges to socially accepted viewpoints are often (construed as) gendered.

Within the world evoked by the אשת־חיל, productive reinvestment was considered a strong virtue, but significantly and not surprisingly, within an agrarian society and economy, land holdings were brought to bear. Within the world of the אשת־חיל, wealthy, well-managed households were supposed to increase their land holdings through well-considered purchases. In this world, fields did not evoke images of ancestral inheritance (cf. 1 Kgs 21:3)[22] but of goods up for purchase by successful, wise household leaders, including wives such as the אשת־חיל.[23]

It should be noticed that, within the "story" of the אשת־חיל and the world it construes, there is nothing the seller can really do to stop her from buying the plot that she planned to purchase. She intelligently planned and industriously carried out her plan. A seller is obviously implied in this story and world, but not worthy of being explicitly mentioned or remembered, since he (or "she"?) had no significant role to play in the story, and his (or her?) perspective was deemed irrelevant.

Wives as Economic Agents and an Economy Imagined as the Arena for Wives' Heroism

Since one is to assume that men were also economic agents, and they also bought fields, the question of preference for the memory of a wife over a husband in the most memorable case of successful management of a household within the community cannot be avoided.

Certainly, the *Sitz im Buch* of Prov 31:10–31 played a role in such a preference (see the multiple links between Prov 1–9, 31:1–9; 31:10–31),[24] and the

---

22 Note also Meyers's observation: "In contrast with the detailed Pentateuchal legal materials dealing with restitution of property, there are no laws that regulate land transfer except for inheritance" (C. Meyers, "The Family in Early Israel," in *Families in Ancient Israel* [eds. L. G. Perdue, J. Blenkinsopp, J. J. Collins, and C. Myers; Louisville: Westminster John Knox, 1997], 1–41 [20]). This absence served to construct an ideal world in which these transfers are not worth thinking about or remembering.
23 Contrast the trader with whom the אשת־חיל continuously collaborates and who is necessary for her creation of wealth. Traders and, for that matter, her "girls" (i.e., maidservants) are construed as being in a situation of ongoing interdependence with the אשת־חיל; sellers of fields are not.
24 For the former (i.e., between Prov 1–9 and Prov 31:10–31) see, e.g., Yoder, *Wisdom as a Woman of Substance*; for the latter (i.e., between Prov 31:1–9 and Prov 31:10–31) see, e.g., V. A. Hurowitz, "The Seventh Pillar: Reconsidering the Literary Structure and Unity of Proverbs 31," in *ZAW* 113 (2001): 209–18.

same holds true for tendencies to recall and incorporate some of the attributes of Lady Wisdom in the אשת־חיל. Prov 31:10–31 was read and the אשת־חיל was imagined and remembered in ways informed by the book of Proverbs as a whole and, vice versa, the way the book was read was informed by the concluding and memorable figure of the אשת־חיל. Just as Lady Wisdom is a caring, reliable provider, so is the אשת־חיל. Within this basic plot, there is not much room for a male provider.

The preference for a wife figure led (within the relevant cultural context) in turn to other preferences, such as an emphasis on clothing (and on the preparation of food and internal administration of the household) or that she be imagined as selling (luxury) clothes (Lang 2004b). Given this emphasis, it is only to be expected that there will be references to her "girls" (rather than her "boys"). Moreover, since within this conceptual world, the household served for production and reproduction, just as the Greek *oikos*, it is not only expected that the successful wife would be imagined as a mother. In addition, since the characterization of the אשת־חיל centers on her success and wisdom in managing the household and increasing its wealth, it is only to be expected that matters of sexual pleasure and desire or the woman's physical looks were construed as irrelevant and thus not worthy of being mentioned.[25]

As usual in all these instances, it is what was not necessarily anticipated that deserves particular attention. In this case, it is the fact that the community was asked to imagine the אשת־חיל as a wife who used *her* profits to purchase fields wisely and plant vineyards. To be sure, unlike Athenian women, elite Persian women owned (and managed) land,[26] but the אשת־חיל was imagined within a community in which the ideal world expressed in its "legal" texts was very unclear about whether wives, under normal circumstances, could buy fields on

---

[25] This is true despite the fact that sexual desire (and to be more precise, the desire of a husband for his wife) was considered very important in other wisdom texts and within the very book of Proverbs (see Prov 5:15–19). Compare and contrast with the social constructions of similar matters in Greece. See, e.g., S. Corner, "Bringing the Outside In: The Andrōn as Brothel and the Symposium's Civic Sexuality," in *Greek Prostitutes in the Ancient Mediterranean, 800 BCE–200 CE* (eds. A. Glazebrook and M. Henry. Madison, WI: University of Wisconsin Press, 2011), 60–85.

[26] As is widely known, Spartan women could own land. See, e.g., S. Hodkinson, "Female Property Ownership and Status in Classical and Hellenistic Sparta," in *Women and Property in Ancient Near Eastern and Mediterranean Societies* (eds. D. Lyons and R. Westbrook; Washington, DC: Center for Hellenic Studies, 2003), published online: *https://chs.harvard.edu/CHS/article/display/1219*.

their own and held them as their property,²⁷ and in which, within this ideal "legal world" (commercial), land transfers were not worthy of much thought (and attention), unless it was in the context of redemption (e. g., Lev 25; Westbrook 1991: 11; see also pp. 90–117).

But the text and the memory of the אשת־חיל that it shaped not only stressed the wife's agency, inside and outside the physical boundaries of her "domestic" space, and into the "male" realm of farming, but also depicted her in terms associated with the masculine/warrior sphere. To some extent, remembering the אשת־חיל involved activating an underlying image of economic activity as war and her agency as heroic behavior. The use of terms such as אשת־חיל (connoting a pair with גבור חיל "mighty warrior" in v. 10), שלל (connoting "booty" in v. 11), the language of v. 17 (namely, חגרה בעוז מתניה ותאמץ זרעותיה "she girds her loins and strengthen her arms")²⁸ all point in this direction. One may even say that there was a connoted, secondary military image when the community remembered that her husband "trusts in her"; for him and his household, she is their fortress and "army," upon whom they can reliably lean (cf., e. g., Wolters 1988; Lawrence 2009: 341–43).

The partial "masculinization" of the necessarily "feminine" image of the אשת־חיל involved multiple processes of "otherization" and "mirroring" and the creation of a conceptual shared "in-between" realm populated by those construed as agents in the production and accretion of wealth, including both wise males and females.²⁹

A study on these matters cannot be carried out within the present essay, but for the present purposes the accompanying characterization of economic activities aimed at increasing wealth as the equivalent of war is of particular significance, and so is the attribution of heroic features to those succeeding in making a profit. It is worth noting that the social background of the text is a local elite who lives in a community without a local king or army and cannot aspire to

---

27 See R. Westbrook, *Property and the Family in Biblical Law* (JSOTSup 113; Sheffield: JSOT Press, 1991), 65 and note, "It is not certain that women could own property at all." See also this: "[T]he limitation of women's property rights is the economic linchpin of patriarchal structure. ... The basic fact that women did not normally own land made them economically dependent on men–first on their fathers, then on their husbands, and ultimately on their sons" (T. Frymer-Kensky, "Parasht Pinchas: Another View," in *The Torah: A Women's Commentary* [eds. T. C. Eskenazi and A. L. Weiss; New York: Women of Reform Judaism, 2008], 983).
28 On this expression, see T. Novick, "'She Binds Her Arms': Rereading Proverbs 31:17," in *JBL* 128 (2009): 107–13.
29 Note also at the basic level of the implied "narrative," the explicitly necessary partnership of the אשת־חיל and male traders, who shared the same goal of acquiring wealth through their respective "trades."

heroism in battle, but only (as the text suggests) to increasing their wealth. Remembering the אשת־חיל works well in the community, because such action embodies in a female body a social mindscape concerning economy and wealth creation shared by the elite, including directly or indirectly (as members of a retainer group) the male literati who read and reread these texts and who may have read them to others, especially non-literati members of the elite.

Obviously, the אשת־חיל is construed as an ancient super-wife and super-mom.[30] This being the case, and despite the many evident differences, contemporary critiques and cross-cultural, social anthropological comparisons between the אשת־חיל and today's image of the (North American) "super-mom" may be heuristically helpful for approaching some aspects of the social and ideological setting in which these "types" emerge and become popular. The ubiquity of the concept/image of the present-day "super-mom" is not dependent at all on whether actual North American mothers can fulfill the too-high expectations or on the systemic reorganization of resources that would be required to allow more than just a few to come close to fulfilling them, and certainly not on whether this image is an oppressive burden on some (elite?) women, because it creates expectations that cannot be matched in reality by most women (even elite women). Instead, its popularity is due to its ability to embody a set of values and ideals about work, pursuit of profit, wealth, and "heroic" agency in the economic world that characterizes a substantial sector of today's society and that, in turn, influences others. It stands to reason that the situation in the case of our ancient "superwife/mom" was not substantially dissimilar. If this is true, the social mindset embodied in the אשת־חיל was not far from that of a significant sector of individuals in the Persian or early Hellenistic period in Judah who remembered her, as they read, reread, and imagined her.

A Different Kind of Potential Cross-Cultural Observation about Wives with Some "Masculine" Features

Yehud was a poor province, and even its elite were relatively poor. The same may be said of early Hellenistic Judah. These circumstances may have facilitated a tendency among the male literati who read these texts and shaped these worlds of imagination and memory to accept and even idealize a slightly "masculinized" feminine image. Cross-culturally societies that live in harsher environments are more predisposed to developing a male preference for women who

---

[30] The point is quite explicitly expressed in, for instance, v. 29; cf. v. 31.

show some "masculine" features, because the latter tend to be construed as communicating a better ability to compete for resources, which is exactly the area in which the אשת־חיל excels (Marcinkowska et al. 2014).

Secure, Predictable Society and Principles of Selection Governing Memories

The אשת־חיל is a site of memory that conjures an entire economic world of activity. The world evoked by the site presupposes a peaceful and stable society. The אשת־חיל could laugh at what the future might bring because, in her world, the future was predictable, controllable, and construed in continuity with the present. She did not need to worry about calamities, about invading armies that might destroy her household or pillage her wealth, or any other chaotic event (e. g., drought). In her world, her wise use of wealth has resulted in secure wealth for years to come.[31] Moreover, since chaos does not play any substantial role in this world, intelligence and industriousness lead necessarily to wealth, blessing, praise, and honor. What characterizes the אשת־חיל is that she is super-intelligent and super-industrious (passim), so she surpasses others (v. 29); but all these wives share in the same secure, nonchaotic world.

One could mention also that the אשת־חיל is a super-reliable wife/entrepreneur/mom. Everything is in order in her household, and chaos has no leg to stand on. Her household and the world in which she lives are *partially* construed as microcosms/macrocosms of each other. If this is true, who is the counterpart of the אשת־חיל in the larger world? One answer would be "Wisdom" (cf. Prov 1–9 and the ways in which it informs and is informed by Prov 31:10–31), but how is Wisdom manifested in the macro-world? Moreover, within the discourse of the period, would it not be possible to imagine Yhwh as the wise leader of a household that contains the entire world and from which chaos is removed? What about the leadership of a temple with cosmic significance (Van Leeuwen 2007; see also "Exploring Jerusalem" in this volume)? Or the Persian king? Or multiple possible combinations of the above? Most significantly, this issue is not explored in Prov 31:10–31 (see below).

To be sure the secure, nonchaotic, reliable world mentioned above could only exist if there were social and political structures to maintain it. It required a sense of social cohesion but also actual political power and ability to control

---

[31] Of course, it is the kind of security and peace that encourages investments in production, training of future workers, and allows for intelligent, long-term planning.

the area to eliminate any substantial chaotic event. In some ways, this orderly, permanently peaceful world was a local reflection of the nonchaotic, peaceful world of Achaemenid royal ideology in which the Persian king provided happiness to humankind (cf. B. Lincoln 2012). But remembering the אשת־חיל meant, not only viewing the world and economic activity in it from the perspective of a single household, but bracketing matters that were not and could not be controlled by such a household (e. g., taxes, Persian imperial rule, temple leadership, and even Yhwh, who from the perspective of the community governed the world).[32] As mentioned above, it is likely that v. 30 did not include the reference to "fearing Yhwh" (see the LXX), but even if it is not the case, Yhwh is not explicitly portrayed as an active agent in the "story" of the אשת־חיל.

The principle of selection governing the memories to be evoked by the אשת־חיל and her activities was that, whatever helped to depict her agency was to be remembered, for the pericope was about her and what she did. But the presence of such a rhetorically and mnemonically helpful focus does not mean that the community remembering such a "great" world in which the אשת־חיל lived and which, to a substantial extent, seemed to "mirror" theirs was not being implicitly socialized into a world of Persian imperial rule, of temple leadership, of Yhwh's rule, or of taxes. "Natural" preconditions are most often not worth mentioning, but still images and "memories" of a world that implicitly assumes them socialize as much as or more than explicit references.[33]

אשת־חיל, Socialization, and Mutually Balancing Voices

The preceding sections explored aspects of intellectual thought, world view, and a general social mindscape reflected and communicated by the "story" of the אשת־חיל and embodied in her. They have shown that remembering this wife involved socialization into a world of ideas concerning the role of elite wives and the economy in general. It involved inculcating certain approaches concerning

---

[32] As mentioned above, it is likely that v. 30 did not include the reference to "fearing Yhwh" (see the LXX), but even if this is not the case, Yhwh is not explicitly portrayed as an active agent in the "story" of the אשת־חיל.

[33] This peaceful, nonchaotic world seems less likely to have been construed as "natural" when the weight of the chaos that followed the fall of the Achaemenid Empire began to affect the social mindscape of the community in Yehud (which usually occurs one generation or two after the events). In my opinion, Prov 31:10–31 seems more at home in the 5th or 4th centuries BCE than the 3rd century. This consideration for dating seems to me far more important than the lack of Greek elements. For proposed dates for this text, see n. 9 above.

profit, trade, industriousness, wealth, land-acquisition and ways to achieve honor in society. It involved also a partial appropriation of the concept of heroism that emphasized, inter alia, how difficult the ongoing pursuit of profit was. It involved a focus on households as the central socioeconomic unit and a general view of society that is devoid of substantial anxiety concerning the power of chaotic powers. Society was construed as stable, predictable, and ordered.

Remembering the אשת־חיל involved recalling and stressing the role of Wisdom. It also involved balancing other texts and messages that existed within the world of thought and knowledge of the remembering community. One may mention, for instance, how the very presence of a view from a "private" household, as opposed to the usual view from the perspective of political figures and centers (kings, governors, etc.) mutually balances, complements, and informs the community's approach to many other texts.

The same can be said for remembering a female hero rather than a male hero, of remembering the less heroic husband (see below) and needless to say, of the mentioned viewpoints concerning economic activity, trade, pursuit of profit, goods, agents, which, from a perspective of the discourse of the community as a whole, mutually complement, inform and balance other views, widely expressed in other texts.

Observations on the Utopian אשת־חיל and Her Orderly World as an Expression of Lacks and Longings

The אשת־חיל and her world represented a utopia. Of course, it was the utopia of a particular group in society and others (e.g., her "girls" or those who sold their fields to her) may not have shared it. Still, it was a utopian world, and such worlds often provided societies ways

to address present lacks and express their longings. Wives are not like the אשת־חיל though, significantly, the ancient male readers would have liked them to be. The latter is not an insignificant observation, given the expanded role that she exerted, the secondary role of the husband in the leadership of the household (note that nowhere is it stated that her husband "allowed" or "commanded" her to do her role; and see the different situation in *Oeconomicus*), and common transcultural attitudes such as those expressed in Sir 25:22 ("There is wrath and impudence and great disgrace when a woman supports her husband").

Similarly, households are not as prosperous as that of the אשת־חיל, and subsistence goods play a larger role in the economy. Even affluent families in an agrarian society located in a stable polity might suffer from lack of rain or pestilence. Farmers rarely "laugh" at what the future may bring, but they would like to.

Of course, the אשת־חיל served some of the transcultural social roles associated with a super-hero, and in this case and most significantly, a masculinized but saliently female super-hero. But who are her "enemies," the "super-villains" that she must confront. They are neither the "others" (whether construed as internal or external to her social group) nor natural forces (e.g., drought, pestilence, etc.), mythological animals, or even "the sword." The "villains" with whom this super-hero has to contend seem to be laziness, lack of understanding, or the proper socialization of those under her. Of course, none of these are substantial hindrances to a person with her wisdom. A super-hero with such enemies is on the one hand the kind of super-hero that emerges from the book of Proverbs as a whole, but on the other hand is a super-hero for a society that even affluent households could only dream of.[34]

From a Utopian אשת־חיל and Her Orderly World to Socioeconomic Realities in Persian or Early Hellenistic Yehud

The interwoven network of images mentioned in the preceding section along with their orderly, predictable, stable and wisdom-full world represent an example within a wide range of sets and arrays of sets of "ideal" images in ancient Israel (Ben Zvi 2006; 2013). All of them were characterized by the absence of some (substantial) "lack," which varied from set to set and array to array, and yet all of them emerged out of a utopianist generative grammar, whose particular manifestations (i.e., the mentioned sets and arrays of sets) informed and balanced each other. Whereas a discussion of these matters goes beyond the scope of this essay, the same does not hold true for some observations on an additional (and complementary) facet of the study of utopian or imaginary worlds in ancient Israel that is particularly relevant to the contribution that the study of images and (utopian) memories evoked by the אשת־חיל makes to the elucidation of some of the matters to which this volume is devoted.

Utopias cannot but be based, to some extent, on existing worlds. There are constraints on social imagination and social communication that affect the production of utopias. The "story" of the אשת־חיל "worked" because the target read-

---

[34] There is nothing to fear in this world and nothing standing against making a profit and the associated accumulation of wealth and honor, except rejection of the wisdom exemplified in the אשת־חיל.

ership was aware of what merchant ships, traders, luxury clothing, maidservants, fields, and vineyards were. All of them existed in the world of the text and in that of the remembering community.

Likewise, the literati in Yehud who were imagining and remembering the אשת־חיל could not have construed her and her world as ideal if they were not willing to accept, at least to some extent, the socioeconomic values that implicitly governed and were reflected and communicated by the אשת־חיל in their own "historical" world–not just in the world evoked by remembering the אשת־חיל.

A society in which relatively affluent groups value industriousness and the ongoing pursuit of profit, and in which wealth is meant to lead to more wealth and to increased honor, in which trade is a positive feature and so is increased land acquisition–this society does not have to be a "pre-capitalist" society. Such societies most likely did not exist in antiquity. Instead, it was a society in which traditional agrarianism was combined with the existence of markets and one in which, despite "moralistic" claims by entrenched land aristocracies, wealth might indeed come from trading value-added products;[35] moreover, wealth from these sources might at times bring in new landowners or further elevate existing ones (see Prov 31:16, 28).

Likewise, although the references to the activities of the אשת־חיל are clearly hyperbolized for obvious literary and mnemonic reasons, it is safe to assume that they reflect in some way actual activities of wives within the relevant socioeconomic circle in Yehud. The fact that women in substantially different but

---

[35] Even a cursory debate on the place of markets in ancient agrarian societies is well beyond the scope of this essay. On these issues, see, e.g., P. F. Bang, "Imperial Bazaar," 51–88; idem, *Roman Bazaar: A Comparative Study of Trade and Markets in a Tributary Empire* (Cambridge: Cambridge University Press, 2011) and the debate it initiated. See also, e.g., R. C. Hunt, "The Role of Bureaucracy in the Provisioning of Cities: A Framework for an Analysis of the Ancient Near East," in *The Organization of Power: Aspects of Bureaucracy in the Ancient Near East* (eds. M. Gibson and R. D. Biggs; SAOC 46; 2nd ed.; Chicago: Oriental Institute, 1991), 153–68 (esp. § 3.1.6.1 "Market Exchange,"158–61). For the present purposes, it suffices to state that markets existed for millennia but that their existence did not turn the relevant economies into "market" or "capitalist" economies. Likewise, concepts that resemble present-day concepts in some form (e.g., loans, interest, shared investments, shared profits) existed in some ancient societies– the obvious case of Old Assyria comes to mind, and see, e.g., K. R. Veenhof, "'Modern' Features in Old Assyrian Trade," in *JESHO* 40 (1997): 336–66, but this is just one example (for a study of another, see C. Wunsch, "Neo-Babylonian Entrepreneurs," in *The Invention of Enterprise: Entrepreneurship from Ancient Mesopotamia to Modern Times* [eds. D. Landes, J. Mokyr, and W. Baumol; Princeton, NJ: Princeton University Press, 2010], 40–61). But none of this means any of the relevant societies were modern capitalist societies. At the same time, the existence of these ancient concepts that somehow resemble contemporary concepts should not be denied solely for fear of seemingly advancing an anachronistic, "modernistic" view.

more-or-less contemporary societies of the period fulfilled similar roles (see esp. Xenophon, *Oeconomicus*, but also the evidence from Elephantine and other areas in the Persian period; e.g., Waegeman 1992; Lang 2004b; Yoder 2001: 59–72) not only reinforces this position but also demonstrates beyond doubt that these socioeconomic patterns were not exclusive of wealthy or "trade-oriented" (groups within) societies (e.g., Athens, Babylonia). The same point emerges from cross-cultural comparisons with societies that were by no means contemporary with the society in Yehud, as the case of households in the blurry boundary between urban and rural in the Ottoman period shows (Lang 2004a).[36]

Studies of socioeconomic realities in mid- to late Yehud (or its continuation in early Hellenistic Judah) have focused, with good reason, on the evidence from the archaeological data. But textual evidence may also contribute a great deal. Unlike other textual evidence often advanced that either focuses on putative, one-time events or scribal legislation,[37] Prov 31:10–31 sheds (indirectly but) very good light on ongoing economic activities and attitudes among affluent households. Moreover, unlike other textual sources, it sheds light not on the center (e.g., the impact on the economy of a governor or of the temple, as a central institution) but on the activities and dreams of multiple, though wealthy agents. In some ways, one can say that Prov 31:10–31 may be one of the very few sources that allows one to come a bit closer toward something even partially resembling what a limited microhistory of the Persian (and early Hellenistic) period in Judah might have looked like, had we sufficient resources to develop one.[38]

---

36 Of course, the אשת־חיל lives and works in that blurry boundary between rural and urban as well.

37 Usually the main texts brought to bear are Ezra–Nehemiah, esp. Neh 5 and, though less often, some pentateuchal literature. The first is substantially shaped by common historiographic tendencies/metanarratives (e.g., those involved in the quasi royalization of Nehemiah); the second deals with literary/ideological examples of legislation that were not necessarily drafted for the purpose of actual implementation. These considerations do not necessarily preclude their use as sources for reconstructing the economic history of Yehud but raise a number of issues that must be addressed–although, for obvious reasons, in a separate study.

38 On microhistory, see, for instance, I. M. Szijártó, "Four Arguments for Microhistory," *Rethinking History: the Journal of Theory and Practice* 6 (2002): 209–15; and the "classical" work in G. Levi, "On Microhistory," in *New Perspectives on Historical Writing* (ed. P. Burke; University Park, PA: Pennsylvania State University Press, 1992), 93–113. For an evaluation of the tendency toward microhistory among a substantial number of contemporary historians, see F. S. Marcos, "Tendencias historiográficas actuales," in *Cultura Histórica* (2009), 80–93, published online and available freely at http://www.culturahistorica.es (University of Barcelona). As I mentioned elsewhere, the attention that characters such as Ta(pe)met or Mibtahiah of Elephantine have received suggests that, had significant, relevant sources been available, a substantial number of historians of ancient Israel would have developed at least some microhistorical practices

when reconstructing the history of Persian period Judah/Yehud. See E. Ben Zvi, "Clio Today and Ancient Israelite History: Some Thoughts and Observations at the Closing Session of the European Seminar for Historical Methodology," in *Even God Cannot Change the Past: Reflections on Seventeen Years of the European Seminar in Historical Methodology* (ed. Lester L. Grabbe; LHBOTS 663; London: T&T Clark, 2018), 20–49.

Monogynistic and Monogamous Tendencies, Memories and Imagination in Late Persian/Early Hellenistic Yehud*

1 General Human and Social Background

Bio-social and genetic studies have shown that human males (and even their hominid biological predecessors) are only mildly polygynous and that their earlier societies, as far as we can reconstruct, must have been predominantly monogamous, or at least that the overall pattern of human mating in them was predominantly, though not exclusively monogamous.[1] Ethnographic studies have shown that in most societies (a) most humans live in monogamous relations, but (b) polygamous and mainly polygynistic marital and/or sexual bonds are socially acceptable.[2] It is customary, though not unproblematic, to refer to such societies in which most individuals are monogamous, as polygamous. In fact, the terminology itself and its sense of either-or as opposed to a continuous spectrum are problematic.

First, one has to distinguish between genetic or biological monogyny and social/cultural monogyny, that is, marital monogamy. Second, as mentioned above, there is an entire spectrum. There are societies, for instance, in which most socially accepted marital bonds involve one male and several females,[3] others in which the majority of marital bonds are monogamous, but there exist some narrow social groups (e. g., royal families and at times, the social stratum immediately below them) that are polygynistic, and there is acceptance of (rather than simply tolerance for) polygynistic marital bonds. Further still, there are other societies in which there is a social (rather than, or in addition to an environmental/

---

* First published in ZAW 125 (2013): 263–77.
1 See, for instance, C. S. Larsen, "Equality for the Sexes in Human Evolution? Early Hominid Sexual Dimorphism and Implications for Mating Systems and Social Behavior," in *Proceedings of the National Academy of Sciences of the United States of America* 100/16 (2003): 9103–04 and bibliography.
2 See, for instance, M. L. Burton et al., "Regions Based on Social Structure," in *Current Anthropology* 37 (1996): 87–111 (89, table 1).
3 Polyandrous societies, in the sense of a society in which the main family unit consists of a woman, her (concurrent) husbands and their children all living together, will not be discussed in this article, because they are very rare and play no role in late Persian Yehud or in ancient Near Eastern societies in general. This said, it is worth noting that women could marry different males, serially.

ecological) imposed universal monogamy but concubines are tolerated, provided that there is no co-habitation (e. g., ancient Greece),[4] but also others in which monogamy is, at least normatively, associated with both social and sexual exclusivity. Moreover, in most (though not all) monogamous societies, monogamy refers to concurrent marital bonds. In these societies both serial, non-concurrent polyandry and polygyny are widely socially accepted, that is, these are societies in which remarriage following divorce or the death of one of the partners is socially and legally allowed.[5]

Given that, at least on the surface, one of the most important factors restricting the ability of men to reproduce is their access to fertile women and the patriarchal character of ancient (and not only ancient) societies, the development of normatively monogamous or even predominantly monogamous societies raise questions about additional factors. This is not the place to survey the very large academic literature on the topic.[6] It suffices for the present purposes, that allocation of resources to the next generation in an agrarian society, social horizontal cohesion (esp. among males) and particularly once the top echelon of the society (i. e., royals) is taken out of consideration, paternal investment of resources, along with restrictions in terms of total family resources (certainly more acute in the case of slaves and of low stratum couples, but not necessarily restricted to them), all seem to have played important roles. In addition, historical contingencies in the form of deeply embedded cultural patterns legitimized by memory and "religion" also play important roles.

2 Particular Background: The Regional Context

Any study of monogynistic or monogamous tendencies in late Persian/early Hellenistic Yehud has to situate this community within its general cultural milieu.

---

[4] See W. Scheidel, "A Peculiar Institution? Greco-Roman Monogamy in Global Context," in *The History of the Family* 14 (2009): 280–291.

[5] Strict (social and biological) monogynistic societies are very rare. Even within the normative world of CD, serial monogamy is acceptable, though not through divorce. See CD-A 4:17–5:1. According to 11QT 57,15–19, a second marriage is not forbidden for the king after the death of the first wife. In other words, while concurrent polygamy and divorce are not acceptable, serial social and biological monogamy is.

[6] See, for instance, L. Fortunato and M. Archetti, "Evolution of Monogamous Marriage by Maximization of Inclusive Fitness," in *Journal of Evolutionary Biology* 23 (2010): 149–156 and bibliography, and Scheidel, "Peculiar Institution". Cf. L. Fortunato, "Reconstructing the History of Marriage Strategies in Indo-European–Speaking Societies: Monogamy and Polygyny," in *Human Biology* 83 (2011): 87–105.

Greece (and later Rome) provides examples of societies in which there was a strict socially imposed universal monogamy, but not necessarily genetical or biological monogyny, as married males had access to women other than their wives (e. g., non-cohabiting concubines, female slaves). The most interesting and relatively unique aspects of their monogamy were that it was socially and culturally enforced and that it did not allow for socially accepted marital polygamy at the highest social level.

Although ancient Egypt and ancient Babylonia are often, but not always, considered polygamous societies, such a labelling reflects mainly the behaviour of the highest stratum in society. As it is well-known, "in ancient Egypt, polygamy was basically restricted to the ruler and his family."[7] Within neo-Assyrian lower and middle classes, most marriages were monogamous[8] and so too seem to have been most marriages in Babylonia.[9] One may also mention that clauses meant to enforce monogamy in marriage contracts are attested over a significant geographical, cultural and temporal range.[10] The most common excep-

---

[7] See, R. Jasnow, "Egypt: Middle Kingdom and Second Intermediate Period," in *A History of Ancient Near Eastern Law* (2 vols.; ed. R. Westbrook; Handbook of Oriental Studies 72, Leiden: Brill, 2003), 255–288 (275); idem, "Egypt: New Kingdom," 289–359 (326); idem, "Egypt: Third Intermediate Period," 777–818 (800); S. Roth, "Harem," in *Encyclopedia of Egyptology* (eds. E. Frood and W. Wendrich, Los Angeles 2012), available online at https://escholarship.org/uc/item/1k3663r3., 1.

[8] See G. Galil, *The Lower Stratum Families in the Neo-Assyrian Period* (Culture and History of the Ancient Near East 27; Leiden: Brill, 2007), esp. 292–301. Cf. K. Radner, "Mesopotamia: Neo-Assyrian Period," in: R. Westbrook (ed.), *History*, 883–910 (895–96).

[9] See, for instance, M. Stol, "Women in Mesopotamia," in *JESHO* 38 (1995): 123–144. Cf. J. Oelsner, B. Wells and C. Wunsch, "Mesopotamia: Neo-Babylonian Period," in *History* (ed. R. Westbrook), 911–974 (933). It is to be stressed that marriage norms and customs varied considerably in Mesopotamia depending on time and place (see Middle Assyrian Laws). On the preponderance of monogamous marriage, along with legal (and social) acceptance of polygamy in the ancient Near East, see also the summary in V. H. Matthews, "Marriage and Family in the Ancient Near East," in *Marriage and Family in the Biblical World* (ed. K. F. Campbell; Downers Grove, IL: InterVarsity Press, 2003), 1–32 (14–16).

[10] See, for instance, the analysis and cases mentioned in Galil, *Lower Stratum Families*, 300–01; see also B 41 (=TAD B3.8) cf. B 28 (=TAD B2.6); and D2 (P. Eleph. 1), which is "the oldest dated Greek document from Egypt" (its date is 310 BCE; citation from B. Porten et al., *The Elephantine Papyri in English: Three Millennia of Cross-Cultural Continuity and Change* (Leiden and New York: Brill, 1996, 408). Explicit contractual penalty clauses meant to pre-empt marital concurrent polygyny appear quite often in Neo-Babylonian contracts. According to Lemos, this development suggests that "polygamy had grown less socially acceptable, and thus in all likelihood less common, in the Neo-Babylonian period." See T. M. Lemos, *Marriage Gifts and Social Change in Ancient Palestine 1200 BCE to 200 CE* (New York: Cambridge University Press, 2010), 150 and bibliography.

tion to this strong tendency was when a couple failed to have children.[11] In addition to divorce or adoption of children – the latter being the most common route taken[12] – there was the option of bringing a secondary wife to the husband (see below).

These considerations apply to the vast majority of the population, but social (and not only genetic/biological) polygyny, was far more common at the highest echelons of the society,[13] and certainly at the level of the king (cf. the traditional situation in Egypt).[14]

Moreover, often social monogyny and polygyny, or what are usually referred to as monogamy and polygamy, may be better understood in marital arrangements in terms of a spectrum rather than as polar opposites.[15] For instance, often in cases of social polygyny, there is a first-ranking wife and a second-ranking wife; from the perspective of the husband, both are wives even if of different rank, but from the perspective of the first-ranking wife, the second is close to, or a kind of servant.[16] Thus, for instance and spanning more than a thousand years, one finds,

> If a man's first ranking wife loses her attractiveness or becomes a paralytic, she will not be evicted from the house; however, her husband may marry a healthy wife, and the second wife shall support the first-ranking wife[17]
>
> If Ṣubetu does not conceive and bear (children), she shall buy a slave-girl in her stead and set her in her place and (so) bring sons into existence. The sons (will be) her sons. If she

---

11 The percentage of infertile, married women was in the range of 15–20%, see Galil, *Lower Stratum Families*, 307; for childless family, see ibid., 302–308. On the general issue, see, for instance, Stol, *Women*, 129–30, and the summary in S. Greengus, "Legal and Social Institutions of Ancient Mesopotamia," in *Civilizations of the Ancient Near East*, vol. 1 (4 vols.; ed. J. M. Sasson; Peabody, Mass.: Hendricks, 2001), 469–484 (478–79). Cf. LH § 145.
12 See Galil, *Lower Stratum Families*, 303.
13 Incidentally, one may assume that the northern Israelite exilee, Hosea, who had two wives (SAA 6, 111) came from an upper social stratum, even if he is now a slave. See Galil, *Lower Stratum Families*, 293; on Hosea's family, see also ibid., 60.
14 Marital polygyny in the case of royal families reflects, inter alia, practical political needs (i.e., political marriages, mapping and communicating power relations among different polities by means of royal wives and concubines) and the role of the harem for "broadcasting" the wealth and power of the royal center to the subjects.
15 I am not referring here to the fact that even in cases of not just socially predominant, but universally imposed social monogyny, husbands could sexually access female servants, or to well-known matters of serial polygyny, involving divorce or death of the first wife. All these create a spectrum, but on another "axis".
16 Or a little (adopted) sister.
17 LL § 28, as translated in M. T. Roth, *Law Collections from Mesopotamia and Asia Minor* (2nd ed., SBLWAW 6; Atlanta: Scholars Press, 1997), 31–32. Cf. LH § 148.

loves the slave-girl she shall keep (her), if she hates her, she shall sell her. If Ṣubetu hates Milki-ramu she shall leave (him), if Milki-ramu hates his wife (?) he shall pay (back the dowry) to her two-fold.[18]

Even in the case of the king's (polygynist) family, similar social tendencies towards a clear hierarchy were at work. For instance, it seems that in the Neo-Assyrian period, there was (at least for the most part) only one queen (MÍ.É.GAL) at the time, and she likely held her queenship for life, even if her king died before her.[19]

3 Late Persian/Early Hellenistic Yehud

There are clear references to social, concurrent marital polygyny within the repertoire of books that were held as authoritative by the community in Yehud. Some polygamous marriages were part and parcel of important memories held by the community (e.g., Jacob and his two wives). Betzig prepared a maximalist list of polygynous patriarchs, judges and kings in the Hebrew Bible that includes slightly above forty entries, beginning with Lemech (Gen 4:19–23).[20] There is no

---

18 The entire case is discussed in S. Svärd, *Power and Women in the Neo-Assyrian Palaces* (PhD diss. University of Helsinki, 2012), 222–23; citation from 222; original translation by Postgate. (Note: After the publication of this essay, the following volume was published, Saana Svärd, *Women and Power in Neo-Assyrian Palaces* [Helsinki: Neo-Assyrian Text Corpus Project, 2015].) It is worth stressing, however, that the bride was of high rank. See also Galil, *Lower Stratum Families*, 301. M. Roth maintains that neo-Babylonian contracts that associate the act taking a second wife with divorce (and financial penalty – in cases that do not involve childlessness) reflect also matters of marital hierarchy. She states "[i]t is not simply the fact of the remarriage that results in divorce, but rather the anticipated superior status of the second wife." In other words, whereas concurrent marital polygyny might have been socially tolerated, shifts in social marital hierarchy were not. See M. T. Roth, *Babylonian Marriage Agreements: 7th–3rd centuries B.C.* (AOAT 222; Kevelaer: Butzon & Bercker, 1989), 12f., and for example, contract 2. On these clauses, see also Lemos, *Marriage Gifts*, 150.
19 See Svärd, *Power, passim*.
20 L. Betzig, "Politics as Sex: The Old Testament Case," in *Evolutionary Psychology* 3 (2005): 326–346; this paper was original delivered at the 2004 Netherlands Organization for Scientific Research (NWO) Workshop "Sexuality and Status Among Males in Human and Animal Societies". The list is in pages 340–342. It may be noted that some entries are based only on the very substantial number of sons attributed to the man (e.g., Abdon in Judg 12:13). Significantly, in these cases, the text stresses and draws direct attention and memory to many sons, *not* to many wives. To be sure, this is a literary/folkloristic topos, but the fact that the topos utilizes the image of multiple sons not wives is worth noting. A few other entries may or may not reflect

doubt that polygynous marriages populated the past remembered by the community, and particularly so in the case of kings (and "judges").[21] At the same time however, it is worth noting already that Betzig's list represents only a small portion of the males mentioned in the Hebrew Bible and even a smaller portion of non-royal males.

Polygynous, concurrent marriages are, of course, implied or directly referred to in legal texts that reflect the ideological horizon of the community in terms of its ideal laws, even if the latter belong to a non-ideal time.[22] The most obvious cases of the latter are Deut 21:15–17 and Exod 21:10–11. The former directly deals with inheritance issues that may occur in case of bigamy and clearly אם יקח לו אחרת in the latter indicates that a male *could* "take" a second wife without violating the ideal norms of the society envisioned in the code. In both cases, socially accepted polygamy is taken for granted. In addition, one may mention that Deut 25:5–10 suggests that even a married man may engage in a levirate marriage, and Deut 21:11–14, that a man may "marry" a captive woman. Similarly, one may argue that the caught-in-the-act rapist portrayed in Deut 22:28–29 may or has to marry his victim, whether he is already married or not.[23] Similar considerations apply to the "seducer" of Exod 22:15–16.[24]

---

serial monogamy rather than concurrent polygamy. All in all, this is a maximalist list and several of the entries are at least arguable. See below.

21 See particularly 1 Kgs 11:3 which asks the community to imagine king Solomon as having 700 wives (all princesses) and 300 concubines. Cf. the implied portrayal of Zedekiah in Jer 38:23; and significantly, on far limited scale and within a context that praises the deed, the case of Joash in 2 Chr 24:3. As for judges, see the case of Gideon (Judg 8:30–31) and with a twist, that of Gilead, the father of Jephthah (Judg 11:1–2).

22 There is a distinction between an intermediate utopia in which the world is still not utopian, but Israel is governed by utopian laws and as such it serves an ordering principle in a chaotic world, and a final utopia in which chaos and the sources for chaos are no more. Intermediate utopias of the type mentioned above or tendencies towards them are reflected in and evoked by the literary and ideological genre of "law codes" in the ancient Near East.

23 It is reasonable to assume that the father of the raped woman had to agree to her marriage to the rapist. On the whole (legal) topos, compare and contrast with MAL A § 55.

24 I am bracketing on purpose Lev 18:18. This text has been understood in two very different ways. According to the first, the verse communicates acceptance for social marital polygyny provided that it does not involve a concurrent marriage of a man to two sisters (as Jacob's case according to ancient Israel's social memory, and as attested in several occasions in ancient Near Eastern documents and literary texts (for examples, see Stol, *Women*, 129) and in many cultures. For sororal polygyny see, G. R. Lee, *Family Structure and Interaction: A Comparative Analysis* (Minneapolis: University of Minnesota Press, 1982), 91–92. If the text is understood in this way, it does not add much to the testimony of the other texts just discussed, all of which were part of the authoritative repertoire of the literati of the late Persian/Early Hellenistic period. According to the second understanding, the text prohibits concurrent (marital?) polygyny. The

Given the survey background in the previous section, neither these laws nor memories about some polygynous men seem to be particularly remarkable. Legal tolerance or acceptance for polygyny was well established in the entire cultural *oikoumene* for a very long time, along with a strong preponderance for monogamous marital relations except in cases of childlessness and among the highest echelons of society and mainly royal figures.

What is more remarkable, is the relatively low number of non-leader males who are characterized as participating in a concurrent polygynic marriage. Even more important for the present purposes is the general trend or, better, "systemic preference" that emerges within the construed memories of main polygynous characters in Israel's past. Abraham had concubines, but social memory ascribed the slot of Abraham's wife to Sarah.[25] Jacob was perhaps the most memorable case of a man with two wives. But the community also remembered that this was not by choice. To be sure, he too had concubines, but these were servants

---

fact that if this were the case, it would stand in tension with other texts within the repertoire of the community (see above) is no argument at all, since texts, including ideal laws within the said repertoire often stand in tension with one another. The crux of the matter is whether to read אֲחֹתָהּ as "her sister" in its narrow sense, meaning "biological/literal sister" (first understanding) or in a wider sense as is obviously the case in Exod 26:3 and cf. with the expression אִישׁ אֶל־אָחִיו in, e.g., Exod 16:15; 25:20; 37:9; Num 14:4; 2 Kgs 7:6. One may argue that from the perspective of the community both meanings may have been "activated" within the discourse of the literati of the period and that, since these "laws" were not to be enforced in practical terms, the community or at least its literati could live well with (and exploit, when necessary) the ambiguity. Already in the late second temple period (and in later periods, see Karaite interpretation), there were attested supporters of the second interpretation, as well, of course, of the first. The debate continues in contemporary scholarship. See, for instance, I. Sassoon, *The Status of Women in Jewish Tradition* (Cambridge: Cambridge University Press, 2011), 4–34; G. P. Hugenberger, *Marriage as a Covenant. Biblical Law and Ethics as Developed from Malachi* (Grand Rapids: Baker, 1998; orig. published in VTSup 52, Leiden/New York: Brill, 1994), 115–118; J. Milgrom, *Leviticus 17–22: A New Translation with Introduction and Commentary* (AB 3 A; New York: Doubleday, 2000), 1548–49 and bibliography. It is true that the second approach mentioned here would support the case advanced in this essay, but given the debated character of the text, I have preferred to base the argument on cases for which there is wide agreement and for very good reason.

25 Significantly, while Genesis seems to suggest that Abraham took Keturah as a wife (Gen 25:1) after Sarah's death (Gen 23; i.e., a case of serial polygyny), Chronicles reflects a reading that considers even this problematic and makes clear that Keturah was no "wife", but a concubine (1 Chr 1:32). As for Hagar, she is Sarah's servant and as such she serves as a surrogate womb to infertile Sarah (Gen 16:2).

(and external wombs) serving his two wives to advance themselves in their inner struggle within the household.[26]

David was of course another memorable marital polygynist. Since he was a king however, this was to be expected. What is far more significant for the present purposes is the social mindscape at work in, implied by and reinforced through Nathan's parable (2 Sam 12:1–10). As expected, the text is clearly patriarchal (see e.g. 12:4,9) and, not surprisingly, Bathsheba is imagined as a little ewe lamb, a woman who is both, a daughter and a wife, a beloved "girl" to a patriarchal father/husband (see 12:3). But less expectedly, the text asks its readers to construe a world in which David, the king, does have many wives, but those below him, including a senior officer in the army are monogamous. The text plays on the opposition between king/extreme wealth/polygyny on the one hand and basically anyone else "non-king"/poor/monogamous on the other. In a society without a local king, such as that of Yehud, imagining such a world is imagining all the community's construed counterparts in that past as monogamous.

It is worth noting in this regard, that even when it comes to very wealthy (non-king) males, the community could still imagine them as having both multiple children and only one wife. The most obvious example is, of course, Job.[27]

The genealogical lists in Chronicles also do not draw attention to cases of concurrent marital polygyny, even when they note many descendants (e.g., 1 Chr 4:27; 25:4–5). Although Chronicles considers numerous offspring to be a sign of divine blessing, it does not reflect or shape, as a whole, a view according to which males should multiply wives so as multiply children, despite seemingly obvious biological reasons to do so. Moreover, contrary to expectations due to the potential use of multiple wives for constructing kinship links among different groups, this path is not taken in this book and the total number of explicit non-royal concurrent marital polygynists in Chronicles is quite minimal.[28]

---

26 Note the precise language ותאמר הנה אמתי בלהה בא אליה ותלד על ברכי ואבנה גם אנכי ממנה in Gen 30:3. The texts here and in Gen 16:2 evoke each other, and it is in this context that the harsher language and far more (reversed) hierarchical language of Gen 30:3 is even more salient (see, for instance, the absence of נא).

27 This example raises questions about the list of polygynists in the HB prepared by Betzig. See above n. 20.

28 Contra Betzig, there is no reference to polygamy in 1 Chr 4:24,27; 8:24; 25:4–5. 1 Chr 2:3–4 is a very special case and even then it does not necessarily involve concurrent polygamous marriage nor raises the matter in any way. 1 Chr 2:19 explicitly involves sequential not concurrent marital polygamy, which of course, is not an issue in most societies. 1 Chr 2:26 may involve concurrent polygyny, but one of the wives is described as a concubine and significantly, she has only one

At times however, the narrative required a second wife for a male who could not be imagined as being a king. The story in 1 Sam 1–2 requires the presence of two wives so as to use the topos of the loved/infertile versus the less-loved/fertile wife. One should take into account, however, that narrative requirements can work both ways. For instance, in Ruth 1 neither one of the sons of Elimelech and Naomi took or could have taken a secondary wife, despite childlessness.

To be sure, one may argue that nothing in either 1 Sam 1–2 or Ruth 1 is too remarkable. Concurrent social bigyny was socially accepted in cases of childlessness but at the same time, childless couples were part of life in the ancient Near East.[29] What is a bit more remarkable, is that once one looks into the details of the "polygynistic" story in 1 Sam 1–2, it becomes abundantly clear that it is not Elkanah's or Peninah's story or a story about a man and two wives. Rather, this is Hannah's story. She is the main and most memorable character (see also 1 Sam 2). The second wife in the story is just a literary prop that serves to characterize and develop the character of Hannah and then disappears quickly from the scene, just as Orpah is a secondary character whose sole role is to contribute to the development of the portrayal of Ruth and thus disappears quickly from the narrative as soon as it fulfils its role. One may notice also that there is a strong, though only at the pragmatic level, monogamous flavour to the presentation of Hannah and Elkanah's marriage, and even one that raises questions about traditional hierarchical roles within that family.[30]

Since narratives and their plots may often carry their own constraints in the way in which they portray their main characters, one may argue that it might be

---

child; that is, adding a concubine is not communicated here as an effective mode of significantly multiplying descendants. Another concubine is mentioned in 1 Chr 7:14.

1 Chr 4:5, 18–19 involve, most likely, a polygamous concurrent marriage, but the main point in the latter report is, however, not that there were two wives, but their different "ethnic" backgrounds. A certain case of concurrent polygyny occurs in 1 Chr 8:8, but the text seems to imply that the entire time the male had two wives he had no offspring, but when he divorced both of them and wedded another (this time only one), he had offspring. One may maintain that the reason that there are so few, *explicit* concurrent polygynists in the genealogies of Chronicles, both in relative and absolute terms, is due to its general tendency to not explicitly include many women to begin with. Yet, even if for the sake of the argument one were to agree that this is all that it is, there still remains the fact that the genealogies of Chronicles do not draw any attention towards concurrent marital polygyny or its ability to increase either the number of the offspring of the male or kinship links or both. On women in the genealogies of Chronicles, see my previous contribution, A. Labahn and E. Ben Zvi, "Observations on Women in the Genealogies of 1 Chronicles 1–9," in *Bib* 84 (2003): 457–478.

29 See Galil, *Lower Stratum Families*, esp. 302–308.

30 A point that the LXX of Samuel notices and finds necessary to correct. See S. D. Walters, "Hannah and Anna: The Greek and Hebrew Texts of 1 Samuel 1," in *JBL* 107 (1988): 385–414.

more productive to focus on the default assumptions underlying non-narrative texts in order to reconstruct the "default" position within the social mindscape of the community concerning (non-kingly) concurrent marital polygyny. Proverbs reflects time and again a social mindscape in which socially accepted, monogamous, marital unions are obviously the default (see Prov 12:4; 18:22; 19:14; 31:10–31; Prov 5:18–23 emphasizes social and biological monogyny[31]). The blessed man who fears Yhwh in Ps 128 is also imagined as monogamous (see v. 3). Qoh 9:9 obviously reflects a social mindscape in which marital monogamy is the social norm.[32]

This monogynistic tendency is strongly present in and communicated by foundational myths of the creation, dealing with the establishment of the human family. It is unequivocally present in Gen 1:27–29, but also in the second account of creation, in Gen 2:22–24.[33] The foundational couple, Adam and Eve, were just two and even the animals are paired two by two in the foundational story of the second beginning, that is, in the story of Noah. Noah himself has only one wife (Gen 6:18–19; 7:7,9,15). Remembering the beginning in that society was remembering and construing a monogamous situation.[34]

Yhwh, the main patriarch and the main father, whose household is the entire earth, was construed as the husband of Israel (e. g., Jer 2:2; Hos 2:16–25; cf.

---

31 On Prov 5:18 in particular see M. V. Fox, *Proverbs 1–9: A New Translation with Introduction and Commentary* (AB 18 A; New York: Doubleday, 2000), 202.

32 Cf. W. Plautz, "Monogamie und Polygynie im Alten Testament," in *ZAW* 75 (1963): 3–27 (4). Most, if not all of the biblical texts brought up in the present essay, are in one way or another discussed in Plautz's essay.

33 Note also the way in which the text of Gen 2:24 is understood and reflected in the LXX, which suggests a strong monogynistic reading of Gen 2:24. Cf. "Therefore a man will leave his father and mother and will be joined to his wife, and the two will become one flesh," (LXX) and see MT, "Therefore a man will leave his father and his mother and clings to his wife, and they become one flesh." Of course, the LXX version is not an innovation, but simply a case in which what is implicit is made explicit. Tendencies to make the implicit explicit are common in translations.

34 The use of texts such as Gen 1:27 and 2:24, as well as Lev 18:18, as key texts for monogynistic/monogamic arguments in the late Second Temple period and its immediate aftermath is well known. See, for instance, CD-A 4:17–5:1; Mark 10:6–9; Matt 19:4–6; cf. 1 Cor 7:2–3. See, inter alia, I. Sassoon, *Status* and D. Instone-Brewer, "Jesus' Old Testament Basis for Monogamy," in *The Old Testament in the New Testament. Essays in Honour of J. L. North* (ed. S. Moyise; JNTSSup 189; Sheffield: Sheffield Academic Press, 2000), 75–105. It goes without saying that the fact that these texts were read in such a way at that time, among particular groups, does not mean that they did not carry a monogynistic message before, in the late Persian/early Hellenistic period. The question of who is "innovating" or not in these matters in the later period has no bearing on the discussion advanced here and requires a separate discussion.

Jer 31:32; Hos 1–2), of Jerusalem (e. g., Isa 54:5–8; 62:4), and of "sisters" Judah/ Jerusalem and northern Israel/Samaria (Jer 3:6–13; Ezek 23). Of course, Jerusalem, northern Israel, Judah, Samaria, all stand for one wife, namely "Israel",[35] who is also construed as Yhwh's (beloved, though often rebellious) son.[36] To be sure, in all these cases, family metaphors served to formulate and express in an intelligible way, and one may also say, think and conceptualize the nature of Yhwh's relation with Israel as understood by the community, which in turn played a central discursive role in processes of identify formation and boundaries.

It is precisely because of the latter that the use of the metaphor can work only within a community whose social mindscape is strongly influenced by monogynistic tendencies. If Yhwh could have had many (conceptually) different wives (e. g., Israel, Egypt, Assyria, etc.), the marital metaphor would not have been easily available. Moreover, and particularly worth stressing, when the "son" metaphor is used, Israel may be imagined as the firstborn of Yhwh (Exod 4:22) or, following the same discursive generative grammar, David, who this time stands for Israel, may also be imagined as a kind of firstborn (Ps 89:28). But whereas other "sons" of Yhwh may be imagined, provided that Israel is the "firstborn", other "wives" are not, even if theoretically, Israel could have been construed Yhwh's main wife. Imagining many sons was *not* like imagining many wives. The fact that Yhwh was imagined having only one "wife" is even more remarkable given that Yhwh was construed as "the king". The general tendency to associate common attributes of earthly kings to Yhwh comes to a halt insofar as it concerns concurrent marital, godly polygyny. Moreover, the general tendency towards *imitatio Dei* in the discourse of the community, would strongly suggest to the community in Yehud in this context that a monogamous marriage was, all things equal, far more appropriate and praiseworthy than a polygynous one.

---

35 This is part and parcel of the ideological construction of "Israel" advanced by the literati in Yehud. This is a Jerusalem-centered Israel in which northern Israel/Samaria are actually coopted by the literati. They are Israel since they are children of Jacob, shared with "all Israel" slavery in Egypt, were in the Exodus, received divine instruction in Sinai, etc. and are bound to follow the same divine instructions in the form of the (readings of the) books held by the literati of Yehud. In fact, the construction of Samaria and Judah and Jerusalem all as the wife of Yhwh serve to embody and communicate this sense of Jerusalem-centered (Jerusalemite-*torah* centered) "all Israel". I have addressed these issues elsewhere, most recently in "Remembering the Prophets through the Reading and Rereading of a Collection of Prophetic Books in Yehud: Methodological Considerations and Explorations," in this volume, pp. 80–108.

36 E. g., Hos 11:1–4; cf. Isa 1:2: Jer 3:14. Note, how the text in Jer 3:14 carries echoes of the image of Yhwh as husband.

4 Additional Considerations about Yehud and Monogynistic Tendencies

The combined weight of the examples mentioned above[37] suffices to demonstrate that although concurrent social, marital polygyny was not deemed illegal (and perhaps in some cases, such as childlessness, a necessary tool to deal with situations in which no one wanted to be to begin with), there were very powerful monogynistic tendencies within the social mindscape of at least the literati whose world was strongly informed by the authoritative texts that they read and reread, and, of course, those influenced by them.

Given (a) the historical depopulation in Yehud at the time, (b) the ideological emphasis on "be fruitful and multiply", (c) the numerous references to divine promises of vast progeny[38] which reflect and ideologically address an at least perceived lack,[39] and (d) the widespread construction of an abundance of children and particularly sons as one of manifestation of divine blessings upon a person (passim), one might have expected a more positive discursive approach towards social (and biological) polygyny within a patriarchal society such as the one in Yehud. After all, for obvious reasons, if patriarchs would marry more than one wife they would increase at the very least the chances of having more children and thus having more sons. Moreover, in traditional societies, increased production tended to go hand in hand with increased reproduction. At least theoretically, a positive feedback linking the two was likely to evolve. All the more wealthy the man would be, the more able he would be to have several concurrent wives (and concubines) and conversely, the more he procreated, the more powerful he (and his clan) would become in relation to others, particularly within a region in which the land could obviously support a much higher population. This positive feedback loop would continue then until another limiting factor (e. g., war, environmental problems, etc.) entered the picture and stopped the cycle.[40]

---

37 There are always more examples that can be brought to bear. See, for instance, Lev 18:18; Ezek 24:15–18; Hos 1–3 (which construes Hosea always as a monogamous husband, just as Yhwh).
38 For the former, see Gen 1:28; 9:1,7; for the latter, e. g., Gen 12:2; 13:16; 15:5; 16:10; 17:2–3; 28:3; 46:3; Exod 32:13; Lev 26:9; Deut 7:13–4; 10:22; 28:11.
39 The same holds true for the promise of the land, which is emphatically repeated through the authoritative repertoire that emerged in Yehud. Cf. also the description of the patriarchs and particularly Abraham, in whom the literati saw as it were themselves.
40 The population of Yehud was just a fraction of that of monarchic Judah, as all recent demographic studies have clearly demonstrated.

But there was no such discursive preference towards concurrent polygyny; neither in general nor, and even more significantly, in relation to the wealthy. Actually, there was a dis-preference. One may notice for instance, the portrayal of the wife in a text such as Prov 31:10–31. Moreover, this systemic dis-preference goes beyond a particular portrayal and is at work as a generative grammar underlying and undermining strong mnemonic associations within the construed past of the community between multiplicity of wives and of children. Solomon's harem served as a site of memory, evoking his power, wealth and his downfall. One may have imagined that Solomon would have had a very large number of descendants, but they are not mentioned anywhere. They are beside the point and not worth remembering. Even Chronicles does not emphasise the connection between multiple wives and multiple descendants for kings. Conversely, the community "knows" that Job had many children, but only one wife. At times, even the couple YHWH-Israel is not necessarily imagined as having sons, but one whose re-union brings fertility to the land (Hos 2:21–25; and note the fertility language).

The studies mentioned in the first section suggest some explanations for these discursive tendencies. For instance, one may mention the tendency to emphasize the horizontal social cohesion within (male) Israel, which appears in other discursive contexts, such as those advancing the "royalization" and "priestization" of all Israel.[41]

One may also take into account that ideologies and memories developed, encoded and communicated by the temple in Jerusalem may have had an impact on the actual behaviour of the community in Yehud, as "religious" ideas often do in terms of social marital organization.

In addition, we may take into account that on the whole, the community was very poor and did not have many resources. Reproduction – which involves not only mating but also parental care and resources – is, of course, an individual activity, but follows clear social patterns that tell us much about the society being reproduced, its socio-cultural preferences and its resources. The presence of potential arable land meant only that this was not the main fact limiting "economic" and thus "demographic" growth, but that there were other limiting factors. It is worth noting, in this regard, that the population of Yehud/Judah did not increase much until the late Hellenistic/Hasmonean and Roman periods.

To be sure, the mentioned social, ideological constructions that strongly favoured the development of monogynistic tendencies within the literature of the

---

[41] See, for instance, Exod 19:6; the royalization of Israel as in the case of the covenant with the people and the identification of the people with David.

period may have had also something to do with the social status, resources and the high valuation of social cohesion within the small group of literati who were the authors, editors and readers of the authoritative repertoire of the period. One has to admit that had we recovered marriage contracts from a broad range of inhabitants of Judah/Yehud during the late Persian/Early Hellenistic period the picture that would have emerged might have been different from the one encoded and communicated in the authoritative repertoire of the community, and especially among the wealthy and powerful within the province.[42]

This said, there is no denying the importance of the world of thought, the social mindscape reflected in the texts discussed here and the social memories evoked by them. Conjugal bonds are a vital component of any society. They create central social units and are directly involved in matters of reproduction (including social reproduction) and in the production necessary for social reproduction. Conjugal relations and families draw directly and indirectly very large amounts of social mindshare and densely populate the world of shared imagination and memories of any group. "Imagined" politics of family, even if most often implied in a society, serve central roles not only for the generative grammars that empower social imagination and memories, but also for the self-understanding and maintenance of a society and thus, to its very ability to socially reproduce.[43]

---

[42] Note the argument advanced by W. Oswald in his "Foreign Marriages and Citizenship in Persian Period Judah," in *JHebS* 12 (2012): article 6, DOI: 10.5508/jhs.2012.v12.a6, available online at http://www.jhsonline.org. The only relevant documents from the period, that are available to us, come from another poor Yhwistic community, the one in Elephantine, and suggest also a tendency towards pragmatic concurrent monogamy, see B 41 (=TAD B3.8) cf. B 28. Of course, the relevant couples whose documents we possess have nothing in common with literati in Jerusalem in terms of social location, intellectual discourse and even horizon of knowledge. It is unwise to draw conclusions from one community to the other.

[43] Monogynistic tendencies continued in the late Second Temple period and found support in many of the texts discussed here, but a study of these tendencies, counter tendencies and social realia at that time is beyond the temporal scope of this essay.

Othering, Selfing, 'Boundarying' and 'Cross-Boundarying' as Interwoven with Socially Shared Memories: Some Observations*

There is a vast corpus of literature on matters of Othering as a discursive strategy of exclusion, as one of dialectical selfing, on whether Othering necessarily involves exaggerations of differences, essentialization of differences and of self, on Othering as a manifestation and/or sharp instrument in power (hierarchical) relations, on Othering as a delegitimizing tool, on the contingent character of Othering, on Othering as a common or even 'natural' cognitive tool, and on various social grammars of Othering. Discussions about self, constructions of sameness, 'strong' or 'weak' concepts of identity, and about processes of social identity formation or categorization and identification are often deeply intertwined with those about Othering.[1]

Being a historian of ancient Israel, my intention is not to contribute to the discussion of disciplinary or cross/inter-disciplinary, explicit or implicit theoretical understandings of Othering evidenced in today's critical literature. Nor is it to discuss the use of constructions of, and social memories about, biblical Israel that served to frame, conceptualize, and justify the Othering of various groups by a wide range of communities, across time and space to the present, that each were strongly influenced by their own Bible and, as they saw it, by 'The Bible'. There can be no doubt that a wide variety of historical instances of oppression, domination, persecution, marginalization, and the like were justified and partially conceptualized in these ways. Such studies, as important as they

---

* First published in *Imagining the Other and Constructing Israelite Identity in the Early Second Temple Period* (eds. D. V. Edelman and E. Ben Zvi; LHBOTS 456; London: Bloomsbury T&T Clark, 2014), 20–40.

1 The literature on these issues, whether discussed directly or indirectly, whether theoretical or based on case-studies, is beyond massive. Moreover, it cuts across multiple disciplines and areas. It plays important roles, for instance, in anthropology, a field that began as an exercise in Othering, social-anthropology, sociology, cognitive studies, history, political science, cultural and postcolonial studies, gender studies, disability studies, contemporary European (and EU) studies, and genocide studies. Against common perception, it should be stressed that, although "processes of negative 'othering' clearly are common aspects of many societies and social groups, ... they are by no means universal and are not built into all theoretical understandings of identity processes" (H. Grad and L. Martín Rojo, "Identities in Discourse: An Integrative View," in *Analysing Identities in Discourse* [eds. R. Dolón and J. Todolí; Philadelphia: J. Benjamins, 2008], 3–28 [13]).

are, are unlikely to contribute to our knowledge of the discourse of ancient Israel in the early Second Temple period, which is my own area of research.

Instead, I will focus on an array of important sites of memories and mnemonic narratives that were shared at least among the community's literati within early Second Temple Israel and which were interwoven in one way or another in processes involving the (partial) Israelitization of Others and (partial) Otherization of Israel. As a whole, these sites and narratives shaped a discursively significant series of 'in-between' realms that communicated and socialized the community in terms of ternary systems rather than simple, clear-cut Us vs. Them systems of categorization.[2]

One may claim that ternary categorizations are ubiquitous in human societies,[3] but the particular features and contours of the 'in-between' realms and the underlying discursive grammar generating them provide significant information about the ideological discourse of the community in question, about what it considered and remembered as being 'Israelite', its rules of classification, and indirectly, its take on matters of 'sameness' and 'identity'.[4] Moreover, since the array of cases discussed here involved cutting across diverse Othering boundaries and binaries like 'ethnic' origin, gender, and 'normal' bodiedness, it seems that the

---

2 For additional examples of ternary systems reflected in texts in the Hebrew Bible, see K. Berge, "Categorical Identities: 'Ethnified Otherness and Sameness'–A Tool for Understanding Boundary Negotiation in the Pentateuch?," in *Imagining the Other* (eds. D. V. Edelman and E. Ben Zvi; LHBOTS 456; London: Bloomsbury T&T Clark, 2014), 70–88.
3 See G. Baumann, "Grammars of Identity/Alterity: A Structural Approach," in *Grammars of Identity/Alterity: A Structural Approach* (eds. G. Baumann and A. Gingrich; EASA Series, 3; New York: Berghahn, 2006), 18–50.
4 The texts to be discussed below do not really construct a 'thirdspace' as the latter is usually understood, because they did not construct a contact zone characterized by concrete intercultural or transcultural encounters involving more than one partner. These texts were written in Hebrew, by and for a very narrow group. They were not primarily aimed at facilitating negotiations with contemporary Others, even if they may have reflected such negotiations in some way. These texts were aimed above all at constructing a sense of self-understanding within the inner group through the partial development of a shared social memory. As was usual in these cases, the endeavour required a discursive, imaginative act of creation of Others. Whether the in-between categories discussed here eventually facilitated the creation of historical thirdspaces or failed to do so in the late Hellenistic or Roman periods is a completely different matter. Had this essay been focused on northern Israel/Samaria, the main historical counterpart and inner-group Other of Yehud, a discussion using "thirdspace" approaches might have been in order. But all the cases discussed here involve Others who were not categorized as "Samarians". On "thirdspace" in general, see, inter alia, *Communicating in the Third Space* (eds. K. Ikas and G. Wagner; Routledge Research in Cultural and Media Studies 18; New York: Routledge, 2009) and the now "classical" work, H. K. Bhabha, *The Location of Culture* (New York: Routledge, 1994).

construction of significant 'in-between' areas and the concomitant construction of boundaries as porous, flexible, and even contingent and contextual were not minor 'accidents' but a reflection of some substantial aspect of the social mindscape of the community, or at least its literati. This shared aspect, in turn, came to be reflected in a tendency to shape and prefer certain types of memories.

The memories discussed here suggest quite complex grammars of constructing 'others' that were far more advanced than a simplistic, binary of Us = good, male, able-bodied, righteous, and pure that included a Them = bad, female, not fully able-bodied, unrighteous, and impure. They suggest multiple grammars were involved in appropriations of the Other; *inter alia*, reciprocal mirroring and discursively contingent rather than categorical Othering. To be sure, the cases discussed here are selective. Certainly, there were other memories that reflected and emerged out of other discursive and ideological needs of the community,[5] which seem to be in clear tension with the patterns observed in and underlying those selected for discussion here. Moreover, the community was well aware that mnemonic narratives were not the only way to explore matters of Otherness. Various 'legal' texts concerning multiple Others and the divine Other existed in the community as well.[6] None of this, however, takes away from the importance of the set of memories discussed and its implications for the study of Othering, Selfing, 'boundarying', and 'cross-boundarying' within the general social mindscape of the remembering community/ies. To the contrary, the explorations advanced provide an important stepping stone for a more integrated ap-

---

5 See, for instance, Num 31; Ezra 10; Neh 13. Interestingly, most of these memories were balanced by other memories that also existed in the community. The case of the Midianites was offset by the memory of Jethro, the priest of Midian. In the case of the foreign wives, remembering that a significant number of central characters in Israel's formative past wedded "foreign" wives (e.g. Moses, Joseph, Judah, Boaz, David, Solomon) and remembering that those "who separated themselves from the pollutions of the nations of the land to worship YHWH, the God of Israel" were fully accepted in the midst of the (early) Second Temple community as encoded and communicated by Ezra 6:21 provide balance to claims about a "holy seed" and its purity implications advanced in other sections of Ezra–Nehemiah.

6 See, for instance, the recent collection of essays in *The Foreigner and the Law: Perspectives from the Hebrew Bible and the Ancient Near East* (eds. R. Achenbach, R. Albertz, and J. Wöhrle; BZAR, 16; Wiesbaden: Harrassowitz, 2011). See also M. A. Christian, "Openness to the Other Inside and Outside of Numbers," in *The Books of Leviticus and Numbers* (ed. T. Römer; BETL 215; Leuven: Peeters, 2008), 579–608; C. van Houten, *The Alien in Israelite Law* (JSOTSup 107; Sheffield: Sheffield Academic Press, 1991); J. Milgrom, "Religious Conversion and the Revolt Model for the Formation of Israel," in *JBL* 101 (1982): 169–76; and *Between Cooperation and Hostility: Multiple Identities in Ancient Judaism and the Interaction with Foreign Powers* (eds. R. Albertz and J. Wöhrle; Journal of Ancient Judaism Supplements 11; Göttingen: Vandenhoeck & Ruprecht, 2013).

proach to the study of the Otherness embodied in the Others who were imagined, remembered, and above all, vicariously encountered by the literati of the early Second Temple period when they read all the texts that served to construe their own past.

Shifting our attention to the cases to be discussed here, one of the most memorable narratives about David that serves as a turning point in the narrative about him involved a central character, Uriah the Hittite. His very name, Uriah, 'Yhwh is my light/fire',[7] asked the community to remember him as an embodiment of a worshiper of Yhwh. What they remembered about him only supported this portrayal. He was remembered as a righteous foil against which an unrighteous David was found extremely lacking. He represents what an Israelite male, never mind an Israelite king, was supposed to be and how he was supposed to behave. Even as he carries his deadly letter,[8] likely aware or at least suspicious of its significance, he faithfully carries out his duty to the king, who fails to carry his own. By doing so, he not only highlights the fault of David but also the illegitimacy of human rebellion against a Davidic king and, by extension, the Davidic dynasty, even when their rulers grievously sin. In addition, he is remembered as faithful to Yhwh, not only by being faithful to the unfaithful David but also by following Yhwh's laws of purity (cf. 1 Sam 21:5–6; see also Exod 19:15; Deut 23:11). His fate, like Bathsheba's, was sealed by a proper observance of purity laws (see 2 Sam 11:4).[9] In all this, Uriah is remembered as an exemplary Is-

---

[7] It has been proposed that the name Uriah was originally derived from Hurrian. Whether this is the case or not is clearly irrelevant to the matters discussed here, because the mnemonic community in the early Second Temple period would not have recognized it as a Hurrian name, even if those advancing such a position in contemporary scholarship were right. The remembering community would have understood Uriah as carrying the meaning, "Yhwh is my light/fire".
[8] The literary/folkloristic topos of the person carrying the "deadly letter" to his putative executioner is well known. In this case, the bearer dies, unlike the case in the Sargon story. On this motif, see B. Alster, "A Note on the Uriah Letter in the Sumerian Sargon Legend," in *Zeitschrift für Assyriologie* 77 (1987): 169–73; idem, "Lugalbanda and the Early Epic Tradition in Mesopotamia", in *Lingering Over Words: Studies in Ancient Near Eastern Literature in Honor of William L. Moran* (eds. T. Abusch, J. Huehnergard, and P. Steinkeller; Atlanta: Scholars Press, 1990), 59–72 (70–71); and W. W. Hallo, "Introduction: Ancient Near Eastern Texts and Their Relevance for Biblical Exegesis", in *The Context of Scripture* (eds. W. W. Hallo and K. L. Younger; Leiden: Brill, 1997), xxvii and bibliography cited there.
[9] This is another site of memory communicating to the remembering community that at times proper behaviour, piety, and faithfulness led to premature death/execution. The individuals were remembered despite or perhaps because their fates were considered positive examples for behaviour. For other examples, see 2 Chr 24:19–22; cf. 2 Chr 16:10. For the general lack of anticipated coherence between behaviour and fate, see Qohelet, passim, but also Psalms, passim. In both cases, the conclusion is similar to that expressed in Qoh 12:13.

raelite man, wrongfully oppressed and persecuted, and yet, or perhaps because of that, one with whom the male remembering community was supposed to identify and aspire to imitate. In fact, in the parable of Nathan, Uriah stands for any proper male in Israel who is good.[10] Thus, within this episode, Uriah stands for male Israel and David for the male Other;[11] Uriah stands for the pious and dispossessed and David for the powerful oppressor and dispossessor, a type of Oriental despot. David/Israel may remain alive only because he undergoes a retributive and punitive process that turns him into a quasi-Uriah (2 Sam 11:12–13).[12]

Given that Uriah stands for any proper male in Israel, and thus, for Israel itself, the existence of a very strong preference to remember him in terms of Uriah the Hittite is particularly noteworthy (2 Sam 11:3, 6, 17, 21, 24; 12:9, 10; 23:29; 1 Kgs 15:5; 1 Chr 11:41). It repeatedly evokes a memory of a notable character who was Us and, at the same time, explicitly and saliently, a Hittite Other.[13]

Uriah is not a unique case. One may note the explicit salience of constructions of Otherness in characters like Doeg the Edomite (1 Sam 21:8; 22:9, 18; Ps 52:2). Doeg was remembered as the head of Saul's entire administration, a loyal servant of the king, and a much stronger defender of his master and his household than Abner. Significantly, Saul, who is chastised elsewhere for not following YHWH, is never censured for having given Doeg such an influential position of leadership over Israel. He was both a faithful and zealous (perhaps overzealous) Saulide Israelite, a zealous (perhaps overzealous) worshiper of Israel's deity, and saliently, an Edomite as well.[14]

---

10 The characterization of Uriah as both a military hero and the "owner" of the ewe-lamb is clearly gendered.

11 Who is significantly, within the gendered discourse of the period, feminized when he prefers to remain in his city and "house" instead of joining his warriors in battle. On shared concepts of masculinity in the ancient Near East, see T. M. Lemos, "'They Have Become Women': Judean Diaspora and Postcolonial Theories of Gender and Migration," in *Social Theory and the Study of Israelite Religion: Essays in Retrospect and Prospect* (ed. S. M. Olyan; Resources for Biblical Study, 71; Atlanta: SBL, 2012), 81–109 (99–101).

12 Cf. from a different perspective, R. M. Schwartz, "Adultery in the House of David: 'Nation' in the Bible and Biblical Scholarship," in *Shadow of Spirit: Postmodernism and Religion* (eds. P. Berry and A. Wernick; New York: Routledge, 1992), 181–97.

13 I am not interested here in the question of the "historical" Uriah. The point is that he is a site of memory that embodies both Israel and the Other. A comparable salient association of ethnic Otherness is present in the case of Ruth, the Moabite, who is constantly remembered as a Moabite and as a mother in Israel, who became one of Us (see Ruth).

14 As an aside, one may mention that, among the constructions of Doeg that were reflected and shaped in rabbinic literature, one finds Doeg, the "ethnic boundary maker", who claims that David was unworthy of even entering the community of Israel, never mind being king over it,

Beyond the memories explicitly evoked by book of Samuel, Ruth is the most obvious figure of the past that is similarly imagined. She is both integral to Israel (see Ruth 1:16b) and serves as a 'mother' for David, for the Davidic, royal/messianic line, and even for Israel itself, because David was identified by the remembering community with Israel and vice versa.[15] At the same time, Ruth is saliently and repeatedly Othered by the repeated attachment of the Othering gentilic, the Moabite (Ruth 1:22; 2:2, 21; 4:5; cf. 1:4).[16]

Significantly, one may note that whereas the Othered is remembered as an Israelite and even a mother in and of David/Israel, within the world evoked by readings of the Ruth's narrative, Elimelech's sons were remembered as Israelites Othering themselves when they married Moabite women, in Moab, which was not part of Israel at that time nor worshiped its deity. So, too, was their father Elimelech, indirectly, due to his role as the head of his household.

'Foreigness' could be evoked by explicit 'foreign' gentilics, as in the case of Ruth, or by the identification of 'foreign' places.[17] But ethnocultural Otherness could be evoked in other ways as well. For instance, a personal name could fulfill that role and, at times, might even add to the texture of the memory/narrative and facilitate its role in communal memorability and socialization. A good example is the story involving Obed-Edom and Amaziah, king of Judah, in 2 Chr 25. This text raises multiple images and a plethora of issues,[18] but for present purposes it suffices to highlight two points. According to 2 Chr 25:24: (a) the treas-

---

because he comes from a Moabite woman. The partners in that imagined "halachic" discussion were Abner and Saul. On Doeg, Uriah, and a few other cases of zealous worshipers of YHWH, see J. Milgrom, *Leviticus 17–22* (AB, 3 A; Garden City: Doubleday, 2000), 1417. Milgrom considers them all *gērim*, because he reads the stories about them in a way informed by (his reading) of Leviticus and related texts and in light of his claim that "religious conversion" was not an option in "biblical times" (1417). But significantly, none of these characters is ever called a *gēr* in the narratives themselves or in references to them elsewhere in the Hebrew Bible. It is likely that they were not imagined as *gērim* by the readers.

15 See, for instance, Isa 55:3 and the increased identification of Israel (the communal I) with David (and vice versa) in the Psalms (e.g. Ps 89:50–51). Note the common exchange between David's house/kingdom and YHWH's house/ kingdom in Chronicles (e.g. 1 Chr 17:14; 28:5; 29:23; 2 Chr 13:5, 8).

16 For an analysis of Ruth using feminist and postcolonial theories see the following contributions in *Imagining the Other* (eds. D. V. Edelman and E. Ben Zvi): C. Walsh, "Women on the Edge," 122–43; for one using ethnic theory, see A.-M. Wetter, "Ruth: A Born-Again Israelite? One Woman's Journey Through Space and Time," 144–62; and for a literary and anthropological analysis, see R. L. Cohn, "Overcoming Otherness in the Book of Ruth," 163–81.

17 See the case of the widow of Zarephath in Sidon. On this example, see below.

18 I have expanded on the matter elsewhere; see E. Ben Zvi, "A House of Treasures: The Account of Amaziah in 2 Chronicles 25–Observations and Implications," in *SJOT* 22 (2008): 63–85.

ures of (the house of) YHWH were under the care of an officer bearing the name Obed-*Edom*, meaning 'servant of Edom', and (b) Amaziah, whose name evokes the sense, 'YHWH is strong', a Davidic king of Judah, worshiped *Edomite* gods and thus caused YHWH's treasures, those kept by Obed-Edom, to be lost. Who is theologically characterized here as 'servant of Edom', but Amaziah? Who is characterized as YHWH's servant, but Obed-Edom?

Moreover, this positive image of YHWH's servant associated with Obed-Edom is reinforced among the readership of the book by the fact that the readers approach the text in a way informed by their image of a second Obed-Edom present in Chronicles. This second Obed-Edom is imagined and remembered by these readers as not only a person whose name communicates the meaning, 'servant of Edom', but also as both a Gittite and a pious Levite (see esp. 1 Chr 13:13–14; 16:5; 26:4–8).[19] Both characters converge and shape together a site of memory, 'Obed-Edom', within readers of Chronicles. This site of memory, or cipher, if one prefers, embodied and communicated a sense of fuzziness, of images and memories of apparent Others who were part of Israel even though they bore and communicated explicit Otherness and, conversely, memories of central Israelites who Otherized themselves.[20] Once again, Otherization has been used here to explore what being Israel and thus a faithful servant of YHWH might entail, but, significantly, through the construction of 'in-between' areas and of Others who are or become Us and of Us who become Others.

It is worth stressing that the Other did not have to be imagined within the remembering community as one of Us to be construed and remembered as a substantially 'Israelitized' individual and thus able to facilitate the kind of 'mirroring' that generates the 'in-between' realms that serve as grounds for exploring, negotiating and constantly reformulating and undermining boundaries. For in-

---

19 Cf. 2 Sam 6:10–12. He is associated here with Edom and with Gath, but, in addition, the readers are asked to imagine him as a proper Israelite. Moreover, readers who would approach 2 Sam 6:10–12 in light of their readings of Chronicles would imagine their Obed–Edom as a Levite. It is possible (and even likely) that the association of Obed–Edom with the Levites in Chronicles does not represent an "innovation", but rather, was a common reading of the story in Samuel that existed among the literati of the late Persian or early Hellenistic period. On readings of Samuel and memories evoked by reading Samuel that were influenced by readings of and memories evoked by reading Chronicles in the late Persian or early Hellenistic period, see "Chronicles and Samuel–Kings: Two Interacting Aspects of One Memory System in the Late Persian/Early Hellenistic Period", in *Rereading the Relecture? The Question of (Post)chronistic Influence in the Latest Redactions of the Books of Samuel* (eds. U. Becker and H. Bezzel; FAT II, 66; Tübingen: Mohr Siebeck, 2014), 41–56. On Obed–Edom in Chronicles see also N. Tan, "The Chronicler's 'Obed-edom': A Foreigner and/or a Levite?," in *JSOT* 32 (2007): 217–30.
20 See also 2 Sam 6:2–12.

stance, the gap between 'proper' Israel and Otherized Israel construed by the story of Elijah carried an interesting mirror gap within the Other. Whereas Jezebel, the Sidonian woman (see 1 Kgs 17:31) who was queen over the Northern Kingdom, persecutes Yhwh's prophets, another Sidonian woman, the widow of Zarephath, supports the prophet. Jezebel and the elite of the kingdom of Israel follow Sidonian gods; the widow acknowledges Yhwh and Yhwh's true prophet. The Israelite elite is Otherized and a non-elite Other woman is 'Israelitized'. Moreover, given that the prophet stands in this story for, and as a representative of, Yhwh, the proper relation between Yhwh and Israel is partially explored through an Israelite prophet and a Sidonian woman who, like Jezebel, is twice Othered as a foreigner and a woman.[21] A system of double mirroring is clearly at work here.

Nebuzaradan, the person who burned the temple and Jerusalem and deported Israel and the temple vessels (2 Kgs 25:8–11; Jer 39:9; 52:12–27), was also remembered as someone who thought and talked like a godly disciple of the prophet Jeremiah,[22] unlike most of Israel at the time. Significantly, Nebuzaradan is not the only case of an enemy military leader who is partially 'Israelitized'. Naaman was remembered as the head of the army of Aram and as a military

---

21 The preference for a story in ancient Israel's social memory in which Jezebel is imagined as the daughter of a Sidonian rather than a Tyrian king, as one might have expected historically, is consistent with, and reinforces the construed anti-pair, Other "Israelitized" Jezebel and still Other Israel, which, by implication, also deals with proper yet Otherized Israel. This preference is at work even in Josephus. He harmonizes his understanding of the biblical story with his reliance on Menander when he refers to Jezebel as the daughter of the king of Tyre and Sidon (see *Ant.* 8:371; for Ethbaal as king of Tyre, see *Ant.* 8:324 and cf. 8:318). Most significantly for our purposes here, he shifts the description of Zarephath from "belonging to Sidon" (1 Kgs 17:9) to 'a city not far from Sidon and Tyre, for it lay between them' (*Ant.* 8:320), closing the circle again. The tendency to conceptualize one's group optimally by constructing and embodying oneself in the remembered figure of someone who is also the Other, along with all the mirroring and crossing of boundaries in multiple directions that is involved, is more common in societies with a low sense of existential anxiety (see below). It is not by chance that in later tradition, the widow of Zarephath becomes a full Israelite and the mother of Jonah (e.g. *y. Sukk.* 5:1; 22b; *Gen. Rab.* 98:11) or even of the Messiah-son-of-Joseph (e.g. *Seder Eliahu Rabba*, ch. 18, *siman* 19); she is eventually included among the twenty-two "women of valour". On Jezebel and the widow as "analogous" characters see D. Pruin, "What Is in a Text?–Searching for Jezebel", in *Ahab Agonistes: The Rise and Fall of the Omri Dynasty* (ed. Lester L. Grabbe; LHBOTS, 421/ ESHM, 6; New York: T&T Clark International, 2007), 208–35 (213–14).

22 "The author wants to persuade us that Nebuzaradan was a pupil of Jeremiah (40:2–3)", K. A. D. Smelik, "The Function of Jeremiah 50 and 51 in the Book of Jeremiah", in *Reading the Book of Jeremiah: A Search for Coherence* (ed. M. Kessler; Winona Lake, IN: Eisenbrauns, 2004), 87–98 (97). Compare also Jer 40:2 with Jer 32:23.

leader who defeated Israel and took captives from it but also as one who came to acknowledge Yhwh and wished to worship Yhwh alone (2 Kgs 5:17).

Naaman was doubly Othered by being made an Aramean and a 'leper'. Particularly relevant to the argument here, whereas Naaman's Otherness is largely overcome in the narrative because he becomes partially 'Israelitized' and also is cured of his leprosy, the latter disease becomes associated subsequently with Gehazi (2 Kgs 5:27), the most central 'insider' aside from the prophet. The community imagined Gehazi as the servant of the servant of Yhwh. Otherness was shifted, as it were, from Naaman to Gehazi. The outsider became an insider, even if a crypto-insider in some ways (2 Kgs 5:18), whereas the insider became the certainly non-cryptic outsider, now and for generations (2 Kgs 5:27).

Moreover, whereas Naaman was remembered as partially 'Israelitized' after he inflicted blows on Israel, Pharaoh Neco was remembered as partially 'Israelitized', fulfilling the role of an Israelite prophet (2 Chr 35:22), *before* he inflicted a severe blow on Israel. He killed Josiah, a pious Israelite who, however, rejected Yhwh's word and thus was construed as a kind of Other. It is not by chance that the memories Chronicles evoked about Josiah's death were partially evocative of those the community had about Ahab's death.[23] To remember Neco as partially 'Israelitized' and as a temporary prophet went hand in hand with remembering Josiah as partially 'Ahabized' and partially Otherized.[24]

Foreign rulers like Hiram of Tyre, the Queen of Sheba, and Cyrus of Persia are all remembered as non-Israelite but also as individuals who, to a substantial extent, understood and were able to participate in the discourse of well-educated Israelites, even able to talk like one of them.[25] Whereas the Queen of Sheba was remembered as going to Jerusalem to hear and learn from Solomon's wisdom, Jethro, the priest of Midian, was remembered as going to Moses to provide him with necessary practical wisdom (Exod 18). In addition, Jethro the Midianite evoked the image of a father figure to Moses, while Cyrus was remembered as

---

[23] See, among others, C. Mitchell, "The Ironic Death of Josiah in 2 Chronicles," in *CBQ* 68 (2006): 421–35; R. W. Klein, *2 Chronicles: A Commentary* (Hermeneia; Minneapolis: Fortress, 2012), 526–27; P. K. Hooker, *First and Second Chronicles* (Westminster Bible Companion; Louisville: Westminster John Knox, 2001), 285.

[24] It is worth noting that, just as in the case of the widow mentioned above, there was an attempt to remove the "foreign prophet" from the mnemonic narrative and replace him with Jeremiah in the story remembered by the community (compare 2 Chr 35:22 with 1 Esd 1:26).

[25] I discussed some of these cases elsewhere; see "When a Foreign Monarch Speaks", in *The Chronicler as Author: Studies in Text and Texture* (eds. M. P. Graham and S. L. McKenzie; JSOTSup 263, Sheffield: Sheffield Academic Press, 1999), 209–28.

Yhwh's anointed king, Hiram as Solomon's brother, and the Queen of Sheba as a female quasi-counterpart to the wise Israelite king.

Most significantly, it was not necessary for the Other to be in direct contact with Israelite territory, its main sites, or even its main heroes to be construed in such a manner, as the case of Job demonstrates. Job was remembered as a man from the land of Uz, a non-Israelite who engaged in direct dialogue with Yhwh and whose discourse and the discourse of all his friends were part and parcel of Israelite discourse.

Of course, there were some limits to these processes of 'Israelitization' of the Other; Cyrus does not know Yhwh (Isa 45:5), and Jethro is not present at the revelation at Sinai. Even so, it is obvious that it is not by chance that all these characters are construed and remembered the way they are. Moreover, memories of this type are encoded in works belonging to multiple literary corpora, across genre and collection. In addition, these memories are not associated with any particular remembered/construed period but cut across temporal lines. They are part and parcel of the entire mnemonic landscape of the community and reflect systemic preferences in terms of both mnemonic narratives and ways of Othering and cross-Othering, which existed in the early Second Temple period.

The above examples demonstrate that, at times, remembering the Other as partially Us was associated with partial Othering of some of Us or even Us.[26] But memories of Israelites who remain Israel but who are partially Othered were certainly not limited to these types of cases. They include the obvious case of Zimri (Num 25), the motif of Israel asking for a king 'like all the other nations' (1 Sam 8; significantly, a request that was remembered as tantamount to rejecting Yhwh and Yhwh's kingship), ubiquitous deuteronomistic memories about Israel following the ways of the other nations and about repeated warnings not to do so, memories of Israel's kings worshiping other gods or their symbols and the like, or even attaching some Othering attributes to some of the more central and pious figures of Israel's constructed past (e.g., Moses, Joseph, David, Solomon). At times, however, the process is far subtler, as when 'Qohelet's king (mnemonically, Solomon) is rendered as one of the Eastern monsters [i.e., monster monarchs] of popular history'.[27] At times, the process involves mirroring characters and groups in substantially different temporal circumstances, evoking

---

26 E.g. Solomon is both implicitly and explicitly compared and contrasted to either the kings or wise people of the other nations (cf. 1 Kgs 5:1–8, 9–14; 10:23; 11:1–3).
27 See J. Barbour, *The Story of Israel in the Book of Qohelet: Ecclesiastes as Cultural Memory* (OTM; Oxford: Oxford University Press, 2012), citation from p. 34.

long-term narratives in which mirroring serves as a main tool to remember and 'experience' manifestations of Us vicariously.[28]

Perhaps one of the most interesting and sophisticated cases of mirror Othering is present in the book of Esther.[29] There are numerous kinds of Othering in the book,[30] but a particularly salient case of Otherness that demands attention involves Israel/Esther/Mordecai vs. Haman/ Amalek. As is well known, the memory of this conflict encoded in the book/s of Esther reflected and evoked an ideological discourse in which Israel and Amalek were construed as mutually genocidal (cf. Exod 17:14–16; Deut 25:17–19, 1 Sam 15; 28:18). Each of the two was remembered as trying to exterminate the other. Thus, when readers were asked to remember that Haman wanted to destroy all the Jews/ Judahites,[31] this would have been a familiar narrative/mnemonic motif. This realization explains the seeming enigma presented by the conceptual rarity in Esther of a political plan to exterminate an entire ethnie from the face of the earth in the ancient

---

28 E.g. Deborah sitting under the tree; Siserah's mother inside a palace; or victorious "judges" as Us and defeated royal courts as They. But as the remembering community knows all too well, "royal courts" became We and We were defeated. Compare Judg 5:28 and 2 Kgs 9:30 and notice the similar language. Multiple forms of mirroring were reflected in and evoked by the memory of the mother of Sisera. A serious examination of them and the ways they complement each other requires a separate discussion that cannot be undertaken here. Beth Hayes is currently working on this and related matters. For another case of mirroring across time, see the Deuteronomistic comparison between social memories about the "nations that YHWH disinherited" and memories of late monarchic Israel.

29 This chapter is not the proper place to address the various proposals for dating of the books of Esther (e.g. MT Esther, proto-AT Esther, LXX Esther and their forerunners or textual successors) critically and their underlying mnemonic stories. The favoured date between 400 and 300 BCE may be in range, but even a date of several decades after 300 BCE will have no substantial bearing on the arguments advanced here. For the 400–300 BCE range, see, among others, A. Berlin, *Esther* (JPS Bible Commentary; Philadelphia: JPS, 2001), xli-xliii, and J. Levenson, *Esther: A Commentary* (OTL; Louisville: Westminster John Knox, 1997), 26–27.

30 For an analysis in this volume of Othering due to power dynamics deriving from minority status in an imperial system, see J.-D. Macchi, "Denial, Deception or Force: How to Deal with Powerful Others," in *Imagining the Other* (eds. D. V. Edelman and E. Ben Zvi), 219–29.

31 I prefer the term "Judahites" over "Judaeans", because it reflects the self- understanding of the readers better and the role of their ideological identification with the kingdom of Judah and its traditions, as they understood them to be, in their inner discourse. Within that discourse there was a substantial level of overlap between "Judahite" and 'Israelite' that involved and effected the appropriation and encompassing of "Israel" under and for Judah/Yehud/the reading community. This process is at work in the case discussed here as well; notice how mnemonic Amalek (i.e. Amalek as a site of memory) was construed around its desire/attempt to exterminate Israel/ (all of the) Judahites/Jews.

Near East.³² What is more telling, however, is the way in which Haman is portrayed as constructing his Other (i.e. Israel) as 'a certain people scattered and separated among the peoples in all the provinces of your kingdom; their laws are different from those of every other people, and they do not keep the king's laws' (Esth 3:8, NRSV). For present purposes, the issue is not that the book, written within the inner group for the use of the inner group, characterized Israel as keeping the king's laws and bringing benefit to him and the like–which it does– but that Haman was remembered as construing his Other, Israel, in terms of its own laws. Moreover, the issue is not that their laws are characterized as different *per se*; every group had somewhat different laws. What stand out is that the Otherness of the laws of the Jews/Judahites was presented as essentially different from that of all Others. Amalek/Haman construed his Other according to Israel's social norms, thus reflecting/refracting self-identities among Yehudites/Judahites/Israel in the Persian and Hellenistic period as a *torah*-centred group. Even more importantly, Mordecai/Israel construed those doomed to destruction in an analogous way. His/Their Other was not necessarily constructed in terms restricted to lineage, even if it included an element of that, because his/their Other consisted of those who wished calamity on Israel, that is, the enemies of the Jews or Judahites, whatever their (original) lineage might be. In other words, Haman's people (the counterpart of Mordecai's people) also were construed as a norm-centered group.³³ Those imagining and remembering this world were involved in mirror Othering at multiple and connected levels.³⁴

All the previous sets of examples have dealt primarily and often exclusively with one common axis of Othering: a construed ethnocultural group with which the in-group identifies itself and then distinguishes outside groups by shaping them as Other in its conceptual world. But this is not the only possible axis for Othering. A very common, transcultural axis is based on gender constructions. In patriarchal societies, it is the inner group that would tend to identify with the hierarchically superior pole, masculinity, and would relegate Others

---

32 This is not to deny that there were some negative constructions of Jews/Judahites in the early Hellenistic period. See P. Schäfer, *Judeophobia: Attitudes Toward the Jews in the Ancient World* (Cambridge: Harvard University Press, 1997).
33 For a different perspective on Israel vs. Amalek in Esther, see A. LaCocque, *Esther Regina: A Bakhtinian Reading* (Evanston: Northwestern University Press, 2008), 65–80.
34 The potential mnemonic significance of the "Jewishization"/"Judahitization" of many Others is likely related to these issues (see Esth 8:17 and note its possible narrative continuation in 9:1). But an analysis of this verse demands a substantial, separate study that cannot be carried out within the scope of this essay. The variegated set of examples brought to bear in this discussion suffices for present purposes.

to the socially construed pole of 'femininity'.³⁵ There are memories of future and past events that clearly reflect this common type of Othering (e. g., 1 Sam 4:9; 8:7; 2 Sam 13:28; Isa 19:16).³⁶ It also is easy to comprehend why constructions of 'exilic'/defeated Israel would at times feminize Israel.³⁷

Nor is it difficult to understand that Israel could identify with both female Esther and male Mordecai in a 'diasporic tale' such as Esther. A fundamental assumption on the narratival level is that the welfare and life of the Israelite/Israel depends, at least on the surface, on the protection and support of a powerful non-Israelite male, the foreign king. Thus, in the narrative world, just as the fate of female Esther is in the hands of her husband, so, too, Israel's future is in the hands of the king of Persia. Both are interwoven; Esther is Israel.

But matters are not so simple. For one, within the ideological discourse of the time, it is not only Israel who is imagined as dependent on the heroic male king for protection, but everyone in the empire. Only the presence of the genocidal Other Amalek makes Israel's dependence more vivid and unique.³⁸ Particularly interesting for the present discussion of Othering within the axis of gender is the fact that the Persian king is not portrayed heroically at all in Esther. While he is de-masculinized in the story, Mordecai becomes more and more masculine as the story progresses, culminating in Esth 10:2–3, and more kingly, even he cannot become the king without breaching the world of the story. Since both Mordecai and Esther stand for Israel, toward the end of the story Esther also begins to be portrayed as fulfilling roles commonly associated with male leaders (Esth 9:29–32).³⁹ Othering through gendered categories proves in this case to be a relatively fluid business; Israel is both Mordecai and Esther, both at the beginning of the narrative and at its conclusion.

Other cases of Othering seem to be even more remarkable. Two come to mind. The first involves discursive negotiations of Otherization by males who construct themselves using obvious female characteristics, thereby shaping their identity and Israel's identity through a construction of qualified, seeming

---

35 E.g. C. R. Chapman, *The Gendered Language of Warfare in the Israelite–Assyrian Encounter* (HSM, 62; Winona Lake, IN: Eisenbrauns, 2004). Cf. Lemos, "They Have Become Women".

36 The motif of the woman in birth can be used in more than one way, though. See Isa 13:8; Jer 30:5–6; Mic 4:9–10; but also and significantly, Isa 42:13–15.

37 See, for instance, Lemos, "They Have Become Women".

38 Thus, in that sense, Israel has a "unique" existence because of Amalek's Othering of Israel, and vice versa (see above).

39 See the shift from an Esther who achieves influence through "feminine wiles" and female beauty to that of a leader who sets up ordinances (Esth 9:32; cf. 9:29 and notice the order of the names).

alterity. The second includes cases in which masculinity itself has to be and actually is reshaped to include a realm that allows the Israelite literati to construct themselves as males who are hierarchically superior to Others.

Turning to the first category, Israel was imagined as Yhwh's bride/wife (Jer 2:2; 31:32; Hos 2:16–25; Isa 54:5–8; 62:3–5). There is nothing strange in the conceptualization of a hierarchical relationship in gendered terms; moreover, the marital imagery is helpful and preferred discursively and mnemonically because it is an easy and fruitful means to characterize Israel negatively. Less obvious features of this metaphorical realm are, however, equally important. For instance, in ancient Israel there was an 'assumption that a virgin woman can be altered like clothing. Once she has sex, however, she becomes unalterable, marked or branded by her husband's "personness"... His [the husband's] person and hers become interwoven through sexual contact.'[40] Israel was certainly imagined as unalterably 'branded' by her husband Yhwh, and to some extent their 'personhood' becomes intertwined. The noted assumption raises at least two important issues.

First, Israel could not be remembered as branded by anyone before Yhwh. She had to be a virgin when meeting Yhwh (cf. Jer 2:2; Hos 2:16). The male literati, then, had to imagine their ancestors in the distant past in terms equivalent not only to women but virgin women, and unborn generations in the distant future as 're-virginized' Israel for whom the ba'als will be erased (Hos 2:19), who will return to the wilderness to be allured by Yhwh once again (cf. Hos 2:16). They also know that bride Israel concerns only a transformative but still fleeting moment in their narrative about their future. The final and permanent state will be Israel as the eternally good wife of Yhwh. Other 'female' characters, each with her own husband, lover/s, or their dead counterparts, are necessary within this discourse to make full sense of the marriage between Yhwh and Israel.[41] Thus, the Othering and hierarchies involved in this process of shaping a sense of self-understanding and boundaries move away from differences shaped around dichotomies of male/female toward a binary consisting of virgin bride/non-virgin bride. The latter then contrasts a wife with the most masculine, powerful husband with wives/lovers or widows of less masculine husbands, which is how nations other than Israel are conceptualized. Within this patriarchal system of hierarchical classification and Othering, the lowest rung is occupied by the whore and cheating wife. Significantly, this was exactly how Israel also remem-

---

[40] S. Niditch, *War in the Hebrew Bible: A Study in the Ethics of Violence* (New York: Oxford University Press, 1993), 85.
[41] Even "I love you" is meaningless if the "unloved" or "not-loved" are not excluded as correctly stressed in Baumann, 'Grammars of Identity/Alterity', 36.

bered itself. Boundaries are not only porous but can be crossed by all at more than one point.

YHWH was the husband of Israel but also 'the king' among all the gods. The self-understanding of Israel construed and remembered YHWH as a male who took no wives in addition to Israel,[42] and yet, since kings were among the relatively few males in society who took multiple wives as a way to broadcast, as it were, their great masculine power, a contradiction arose requiring resolution. To maintain YHWH's conceptualization as the top, most masculine king required the renegotiation of socially constructed norms of masculinity. A conceptual realm was required in which YHWH remained the hierarchically top man who, at the same time, was completely monogynistic.[43]

Re-negotiations of masculinity involved not only YHWH but a self- understanding of Israel and its literati as the top 'man' in the world in the late Persian and early Hellenistic period. Because YHWH was the top 'man', faithfully serving him made the literati and their Israel, who were powerless in worldly terms, the top 'men' of the world and hierarchically superior to the seemingly masculinized, mighty warriors of the other nations, whose fate was and would be eventual defeat. Israel was masculinized and the Other feminized, but mirroring and the reconceptualization of categories had to take place. As a result, the 'great warrior' aspect of main biblical military heroes like David and Joshua has been strongly tempered by remembering them as learners and conveyors of divine knowledge and de-emphasizing their warrior-like personal achievements. A similar tendency shapes the way in which founding figures like Moses and Abraham tended to be remembered in the community. Even a future ideal king was imagined in one case as riding on a donkey rather than in a war chariot or on a horse (Zech 9:9).

This being said, blurring, in-between, overlapping realms were still necessary for the process to work. YHWH still remained a top warrior, not only a teacher; and wisdom, although belonging to YHWH and partially to Israel's literati, was also female. As much as Israel identified with the wife/wives of YHWH in Hosea, it still identified itself with husband YHWH/Hosea; as much as it identi-

---

[42] See "Monogynistic and Monogamous Tendencies, Memories and Imagination in Late Persian/Early Hellenistic Yehud," in this volume, pp. 566–79.
[43] Perhaps some play among various manifestations of transtemporal/ideological "Israel", i.e., as northern and southern, as Jerusalem and the like, may have provided room for a safe acceptance of the monogynistic character of YHWH, but the room for play was minor and ultimately irrelevant. YHWH could never marry Edom, Assyria, Egypt, or the like; none of the "women" of the world except transtemporal/ideological Israel.

fied with Jerusalem as YHWH's wife, it also identified itself as the male children of that union (e. g., Isa 62:4–5).[44]

I will round off this exploration with a brief discussion of another axis that was employed to Other in the biblical texts and continues in use today: bodily ableness and the lack thereof (e. g., Lev 21–22; Deut 15:21 or 17:1). One would assume Israel was supposed to construct itself as bodily able/whole/תם, since this is the normally preferred status, and even more so, given the tendency toward viewing Israel as a nation of priests (e. g. Exod 19:6).[45] Yet, the community remembered Isaac as blind, Moses having a speech impediment, and Jeremiah's rescue by a double Othered individual, Ebed-Melech, a Cushite and a eunuch (Jer 38:7–13). Moreover, it remembered Israel as embodied in a (future) servant of YHWH who was emphatically imagined as far from possessing 'body normalness'.

Although one may claim that, at times, the construction of exilic (though not necessarily exiled) Israel took the form of the Other whose body was not 'normal', even so, YHWH's servant and, indirectly, the Others, point at a *positive Israel in the future* that was characterized at least temporarily as not being whole or able-bodied. Here again is a case of mirrored construction of otherness in which positive images of Israel are associated with the lack of physical wholeness.

These images are also informed and balanced by more usual images. Non-Israelites can be described as not having a complete body (e. g. for the Philistines see Judg 14:3; 1 Sam 14:6, passim), enemy bodies can be maimed (e. g. Judg 1:6 and see also v. 7), and good Israelites who sin may be remembered as symbolically and physically 'othered' (e. g. Uzziah in Chronicles or Miriam).[46] The lack of a complete body is associated with impurity and with social marginalization. These two seemingly contradictory ways of Othering along the body-wholeness axis actually complement one other and together create additional realms of blurring, of in-between and double-edgeness in which the direction of the Othering is basically contextual and contingent rather than categorical.

Examples can be multiplied, additional axes for Othering may be explored (see, for instance, Isa 2:3–4), and each example already given could be analysed

---

44 Cf. "Exploring Jerusalem as a Site of Memory in the Late Persian and Early Hellenistic Period" in this volume, pp. 482–503.
45 Cf. Isa 61:6 and notice the presence of a generative grammar in which "Israelitization" is associated with "priestization". The entire issue of the partial "priestization" and partial "kingization" of the ideological concept of "Israel" in the late Persian/early Hellenistic period (and later) demands a separate discussion.
46 On Gehazi, see above. Gehazi is not construed as a "good Israelite" who sinned.

further. Nevertheless, the cumulative weight of the evidence from these three different axes of Othering indicates that, while Othering was a main tool for shaping constructions of self and corresponding memories of Israel, those Othered or the Othering features used point at the inner group and vice-versa. Boundaries not only were porous but also could be crossed in multiple directions. In-between realms could be expanded and crucial attributes were shifting, contingent, and constantly balanced in terms of the ways in which they served to construct Otherness. Deliberate fuzziness also was a key strategy.

Even when it takes place primarily as internal discourse without involving direct engagement with living 'ethnic' Others,[47] socially shared Othering is enmeshed in processes of identify formation and socialization. Significantly, the literati of the period discussed here were involved, *inter alia*, in imagining and developing memories of a future world empire of Yhwh experienced only through acts of shared readings and imagination.[48] Thus, it is not surprising that a relatively common, cross-cultural, imperial attitude was also at work in their Otherizing. After all, good Israelites or a good 'Israelitized' non-Israelite, like Jethro, Hiram, or the Queen of Sheba, all had to be imagined as complying with what the literati considered to be in line with Yhwh's teachings. In other words, these texts and memories reflect and socialize the Othering community into a variant of a cross-cultural, relatively imperial attitude, where foreigners can be like Us or even Us, provided they think or behave like Us. Yet, this is also a reminder that Us and the Other can and do share an in-between area; the kind of area evoked by memories like those of Moses and Jethro, of Solomon and the Queen of Sheba, or of Solomon and Hiram, of Elijah and the widow, of a Job with whom Israelites can easily identify, of foreigners and eunuchs who are not separate from Yhwh's people (Isa 56:3), and of imagining a glorious future Israel embodied in an impaired body or as both male and female.

The other side of an encompassing grammar of Otherness,[49] where some of Us may (temporarily?) become some of Them if they fail to behave and think like Us, is also a common, cross-cultural topos of Otherization that serves obvious roles in socialization processes. Yet, it also shapes and evokes memories of in-between areas, mirroring, and even double mirroring, which, by necessity, imply a reconceptualization of boundaries as very porous. The Other is often potentially

---

[47] The texts were written in Hebrew and accessible only to a few literati who knew Hebrew.
[48] I expand on this topic in "The Yehudite Collection of Prophetic Books and Imperial Contexts: Some Observations", in this volume, pp. 134–61.
[49] On generative grammars of alterity, see in particular Baumann, "Grammars of Identity/Alterity".

Us and We are often potentially the Other in this type of grammar of Otherization.

The imperial, encompassing grammar of Othering mentioned above cuts across seemingly important boundaries and evokes fuzziness and porous boundaries; at the same time, however, it could not but involve a grammar of rejection. Boundaries still remain and exclude others, like the sinful Israelite and the nations that do not acknowledge or even scorn YHWH. Such preferences in the boundaries used in 'othering' have prioritized following YHWH and YHWH's ways as understood by the community, which one would expect among literati whose Israel was *torah-* (and text-) centred and who explained calamities of the past in terms of forsaking YHWH and YHWH's *torah*. Othering, memories, and systemic mnemonic preferences are all contingent and are an integral component of a larger discourse.

The paragraphs above have stressed encompassing grammars of Othering. But, as is often the case, they were complemented by other grammars at work simultaneously. Segmentation grammars of Othering were clearly at work among the literati who shaped their memories by reading the literature that eventually became the Hebrew Bible. From their perspective, various groups were Us and not Us or Us or not Us, depending on the context in which the We talked about, imagined and construed the Us. Among the most obvious examples of this grammar of Othering are the Northern tribes, Samaria, the generation of the 'wanderings', and even the far more tricky case of Benjamin, which was part not only of Israel but also of a Judah that stood in direct mnemonic continuity with Yehud and yet was, at same time and in the same general discourse, clearly non-Judah, depending on the context.[50] Segmentation grammars, like the others already explored, could not but evoke in-between areas and fuzziness, since the very same sites of memory embodied both Us and the Other at the same time within the general memory-scape of the community.

As shown above, there was much use of reverse mirror Othering, which is another generative grammar for Otherness and for memories that construe and evoke Otherness. Mirroring involves, by its very nature, constructions of Others who were both rejected and emulated. They were rejected when they embodied and helped Us to formulate in our own discourse what was wrong with Us now, in the past, or in the future, and emulated when they embodied and helped Us to formulate in our own discourse what was or could be right with Us, like the sai-

---

50 See "Total Exile, Empty Land and the General Intellectual Discourse in Yehud," in this volume, pp. 599–611, and E. Ben Zvi, "The Concept of Prophetic Books and Its Historical Setting," in *The Production of Prophecy: Constructing Prophecy and Prophets in Yehud* (eds. D. V. Edelman and E. Ben Zvi; BibleWorld; London: Equinox, 2009), 73–95 (83–85).

lors and the repentant Ninevites.⁵¹ Mirror grammars of Othering were ubiquitous in the period. Significantly, the extended use of mirrors and mirrors of mirrors as a means to explore and formulate ways of thinking about Us reflects a sense of comfort with fuzziness. Social preferences for fuzziness and openness, even within limits, are historical, contingent features. They are far more likely to be present in groups that do not face perceived existential threats to their existence and which are relatively secure and 'at ease' in their circumstances.⁵² This observation suggests that in later periods, groups in Israel who were not as 'at ease' may have had different Othering tendencies, but a discussion of these matters is beyond the scope of this essay.⁵³

---

51 For a discussion of the Ninevites "Israelitizing" their behaviour in response to Jonah's delivery of Yhwh's word yet remaining fully Other rather than readjusting or undermining the boundaries of Israel, see Susanne Gillmayr-Bucher, "Jonah and the Other: A Discourse on Interpretative Competence," in *Imagining the Other* (eds. D. V. Edelman and E. Ben Zvi), 201–18.

52 I have discussed these matters elsewhere; see "On Social Memory and Identity Formation in Late Persian Yehud: A Historian's Viewpoint with a Focus on Prophetic Literature, Chronicles and the Dtr. Historical Collection", and "Exploring the Memory of Moses 'The Prophet' in Late Persian/Early Hellenistic Yehud/Judah" pp. 28–79 and 199–231 respectively in this volume.

53 The same holds true for the issue of Yhwh as the Other, which requires an entire monograph. Here, it suffices to note the strong presence in the world of ideas and the imagination of the community of a binary. On the one hand is the principle of *imitatio Dei* (e.g. Lev 19:2), of *imago Dei* and the fact that the ideal/future Israel/Jerusalem is often imagined with godly attributes (e.g. Hos 2:21; Isa 60:3) and, on the other hand, multiple sites of memory that time and again assign human attributes to Yhwh, anthropomorphizing the divine. Multiple levels of negotiating, partially bridging, and leaving open the gap between human and divine or some humans and the divine through explorations of potential "in-between" areas of attributes shared by both are all at work as well. The considerations advanced above all seem, at the very least, heuristically relevant to the study of the divine as the Other within the imagination and historical discourse of the literati of the early Second Temple period, and probably not to them only. This said, a significant difference between this case of Othering and the other cases discussed above should be noted: trends that enhance a measure of "fuzziness" in this case are less common in societies that are "at ease" and more common in those that are not, but his matter demands a separate study. For some strategies used to make the divine one of Us and also for the Divine to assert its Otherness, see the D. V. Edelman, "Yhwh's Othering of Israel," in *Imagining the Other* (eds. D. V. Edelman and E. Ben Zvi), 41–69.

Total Exile, Empty Land and the General Intellectual Discourse in Yehud*

The ubiquitous concepts of "Empty Land" and "Total Exile" along with their associated metanarratives in the pre-late-Persian period required, and resulted in, the creation of social memory and forgetfulness that demands exploration, and an explanation for its success. This chapter addresses these matters and as it does so, it draws attention to ways in which claims for a total exile and an empty land were deeply involved in the ideological discourse of Yehud at the time.

Cultural memories are created by and within societies that are anchored in particular historical circumstances. It is usually agreed, even among scholars who tend to disagree on many areas, that the area of Benjamin was substantially less affected by the destruction associated with the Babylonian campaign of 586 BCE, and that its population constituted by far the largest group in neo-Babylonian Judah and early Yehud and their economic center.[1] If this is the case,

---

* First published in *The Concept of Exile in Ancient Israel and its Historical Contexts* (eds. E. Ben Zvi and C. Levin; BZAW 404; Berlin/New York: De Gruyter, 2010), 155–68.

1 See, for instance, O. Lipschits, *The Fall and Rise of Jerusalem* (Winona Lake, Ind.: Eisenbrauns, 2005); idem, "The History of the Benjamin Region Under Babylonian Rule," in *TA* 26 (1999): 155–90; idem, "Demographic Changes in Judah between the 7th and the 5th Centuries BCE," in *Judah and the Judeans in the Neo-Babylonian Period* (eds. O. Lipschits and J. Blenkinsopp; Winona Lake, Ind.: Eisenbrauns, 2003), 323–376; CE Carter, *The Emergence of Yehud in the Persian Period: A Social and Demographic Study* (JSOTSup 294; Sheffield: Sheffield Academic Press, 1999); idem, "Ideology and Archaeology in the neo-Babylonian Period: Excavating Text and Tell," in *Judah and the Judeans in the Neo-Babylonian Period*, 301–22; E. Stern, *Archaeology of the Land of the Bible, II: The Assyrian, Babylonian and Persian Periods (732–332 BCE)* (ABRL; New York: Doubleday, 2001), 321–26. Despite all their differences, compare on this matter, E. Stern, "The Babylonian Gap: The Archaeological Reality," in *JSOT* 28 (2004): 273–277 (esp. 276); and J. Blenkinsopp, "The Bible, Archaeology and Politics; or The Empty Land Revisited," in *JSOT* 27, no. 2 (2002): 169–187 (esp. 183–84); or B. Oded, "Where is the 'Myth of the Empty Land' to be Found? History versus Myth," in *Judah and the Judeans in the Neo-Babylonian Period*, 55–74; and H. M. Barstad, "After the 'Myth of the Empty Land': Major Challenges in the Study of Neo-Babylonian Judah," in *Judah and the Judeans in the Neo-Babylonian Period*, 3–20. On the general issue of the Benjaminite area during the neo-Babylonian period see also, among others, J. Zorn, "Tell en-Naṣbeh and the Problem of the Material Culture of the 6th Century," in *Judah and the Judeans in the Neo-Babylonian Period*, 413–447; idem, "Estimating the Population Size of Ancient Settlements: Methods, Problems, Solutions and a Case Study," in *BASOR* 295 (1994): 31–48; J. Zorn, J. Yellin and J. Hayes, "The M(W)SH Stamp Impressions and the Neo-Babylonian Period," in *IEJ* 44 (1994): 161–183; and the survey and bibliography in L. L. Grabbe, *A*

then those living in Benjamin and some other areas in Judah that were not completely depopulated after 586 BCE certainly knew that the land was not empty after the destruction of the monarchic polity; after all, they themselves remained in the land.[2] One would expect that actual continuity would have led to the development of social memories that stress such a continuity, but instead, the dominant metanarrative about the past and its related social memory that developed in Yehud was one that stressed total exile, an empty land, and a (partial) return.[3]

History of the Jews and Judaism in the Second Temple Period, Volume 1: Yehud: A History of the Persian Province of Judah (LSTS 47; London: T&T Clark, 2004), 22–30.

2 In addition to Benjamin, the Bethlehem-Tekoa area, and perhaps the Beth Zur area, is often mentioned among the regions in which a settlement remained. See O. Lipschits, "The Rural Settlement in Judah in The Sixth Century BCE: A Rejoinder," in *PEQ* 136 (2004): 99–107 and bibliography cited. It should be mentioned that there is considerable debate about the archaeology of the Persian period – Lipschits' article itself was a rejoinder to A. Faust, "Judah in the Sixth Century BCE: A Rural Perspective," in *PEQ* 135 (2003): 37–53. There is a substantial debate concerning particular sites such as Beth Zur, Gibeon, and in general about the extent of settlement in the Persian period and its total population. Among recent works on these matters, see I. Finkelstein, "Archaeology and the List of Returnees in the Books of Ezra and Nehemiah," in *PEQ* 140 (2008): 1–10; and idem, "Jerusalem in the Persian (and Early Hellenistic) Period and the Wall of Nehemiah," in *JSOT* 32 (2008): 501–520. It is worth noting that the main gist of my argument would not be affected if the position argued by Finkelstein is accepted; there would still be the matter of memory and forgetfulness and its deep involvement in discourses of empty land and full exile (see below) since (a) no one denies that there is evidence for some settlement during the Persian period and (b) a very large section of the (if Finkelstein's position is correct, much smaller) population would still likely consist of the descendants of those who remained in the land. In fact, one of Finkelstein's points is that the main text supporting a massive return (namely, the list in Ezra 2:1–67; Neh 7:6–68) cannot be used to reconstruct demographic shifts in Persian Yehud. Finally, most of the texts reflecting and shaping the discourse mentioned in this article belong to the Persian period, and in fact, to the pre-Chronicles period, which I date to the late Persian and perhaps very early Hellenistic period; in other words, they belong to the pre-late Persian period.

3 Numerous recent works have approached the mythical role of the concept of total exile and empty land. See, for instance, R. P. Carroll, "The Myth of the Empty Land," in *Semeia* 59 (1992): 79–93; H. M. Barstad, *The Myth of the Empty Land: A Study in the History and Archaeology of Judah during the 'Exilic' Period* (Oslo: Scandinavian University Press, 1996). I would like to stress that the present study focuses on early Yehud, before the putative time of Ezra or Nehemiah and well before the time of the writing of Ezra 1–6 and Ezra–Nehemiah. I also do not base any argument in this essay on the assumption that the world depicted in Ezra–Nehemiah reflects the historical circumstances of the shared discourse of literati in the pre-late Persian period. To reconstruct the latter, I prefer to use pentateuchal, the (so-called) dtr. history and prophetic literature. See my "Towards an Integrative Study of the Production of Authoritative Books in Ancient Israel," in *The Production of Prophecy: Constructing Prophecy and Prophets in Yehud* (eds. D. V. Edelman and E. Ben Zvi; London: Equinox, 2009), 15–28.

A number of explanations for this seemingly unlikely development are possible. One may argue, for instance, that the dominant metanarrative represented the viewpoint and worldview of hegemonic social/political group(s) that actually came back from the Babylonian exile.[4] If one follows this approach, the following scenario evolves.

To sustain this group's hegemonic position from an ideological perspective, it developed a discourse in which the presence of "others" (that is, those who remained in the land) was ideologically and narratively erased resulting in the "empty land," which was to be filled by them. Since "no one" remained, the entire period before the arrival of the returnees becomes of no relevance to the "national" history, which in fact, continues through those who have been exiled, and mainly to Babylonia.[5] Within this discourse of exclusion, the history of renewal and return set about by YHWH is understood as involving only "exilic Israel."[6] Israel thus becomes "exilic Israel" and any other group becomes a kind of evolutionary dead end, in any case certainly not "Israel."

Moreover, this scenario emphasizes that the discourse included a moral dimension, as the erasure of those remaining in the land through discursive extermination or total eradication from the land involved also the denigration and marginalization of groups that might have remained.[7] Not only do they go no-

---

4 Among recent works, see D. Rom-Shiloni, "Exiles and Those Who Remained: Strategies of Exclusivity in the Early Sixth Century BCE," in *Shai le-Sara Japhet: Studies in the Bible, its Exegesis and its Language* (eds. M. Bar-Asher, D. Rom-Shiloni, E. Tov and N. Wazana; Jerusalem: Bialik Institute, 2007), 119–38 (Hebrew). Rom-Shiloni reconstructs a multi-generational social and ideological conflict between two communities, the exilees/returnees on the one hand and those who remained in the land on the other. According to her, both groups developed a separatist, exclusivist ideologies that carried a sense of self-supremacy, and eventually due to social, political, economic and other related reasons, the community of exilees/returnees overcame the other.

5 See 2 Kgs 25:11–12, 25–26 and note how the national narrative moves outside the land, to the Babylonian exile (2 Kgs 25:27–29). Although in many ways different, according to Chronicles the national narrative resumes with the note about Cyrus encouraging exilees to return to Judah to contribute to the building of the temple that YHWH has charged him to build.

6 This concept does not necessarily support the scenario that I will depict and criticize below. On this matter, see my "Inclusion in and Exclusion from Israel as Conveyed by the Use of the Term 'Israel' in Postmonarchic Biblical Texts," in *The Pitcher is Broken: Memorial Essays for Gösta W. Ahlström* (eds. S. W. Holloway and L. K. Handy; JSOTSup 190; Sheffield: JSOT Press, 1995), 95–149, in which I dealt with some of the issues I raise here from a different, but overall complementary perspective.

7 Negative characterization may serve as a prelude to discursive extermination; see, for instance, Jer 24. For a different approach, but which ends in a narrative, total eradication of the presence of "those who may have remained," see Jer 40:1–41:18.

where and are eventually removed from the land, they also fully deserve it. Furthermore, the obvious typological links in Yehudite discourse between Babylonian return and the Exodus on the one hand, and the first conquest of the land and the second settlement of the land on the other, would associate non-returnees with non-Israelites whose sins made them unworthy of living in the land.[8]

This scenario is obviously about a discourse made to discriminate among groups in society. One may argue that narratives of erasure of the other were related to socio-political realities such as exclusive membership in the (Persian sponsored) *golah*/temple/charter-community in whose hands rested the regional power.[9] One may connect these narratives of erasure to the economy and maintain that they reflected a struggle over land between the returnees and those who remained, with the Persian center supporting the former.[10]

There is no doubt that a large number of texts in the HB (e.g., Jer 24; Ezek 33:21–29) *might* be understood within this explanatory frame and that aspects of this scenario are reflected in the main metanarrative present in the HB and most likely the social memory at least among Yehudite literati.[11]

This scenario, however, still has to explain why the Benjaminites and other non-returnee groups that constituted the vast majority of the population accepted these narratives.[12] Again, on the surface, this does not seem to be so difficult. Three possible approaches to the question emerge within this scenario; groups

---

[8] Cf., among many others, R. P. Carroll, "The Myth of the Empty Land," esp. 85; K. W. Whitelam, "Israel's Traditions of Origin: Reclaiming the Land," in *JSOT* 14 (1989): 19–42. See also M. Liverani, *Israel's History and the History of Israel* (London: Equinox, 2005), esp. 250–91. Among the many biblical references that associate the sins of Israel that caused the latter's total exile with those of the nations that were before Israel in the land, see Lev 18:24–28; Deut 18:9–13; 1 Kgs 14:24; 2 Kgs 21:2.

[9] Cf. R. P. Carroll, "The Myth of the Empty Land," 85; and D. Rom-Shiloni, "Exiles and Those Who Remained." Cf. the earlier work in J. Weinberg, *The Citizen-Temple Community* (JSOTSup 151; Sheffield: Sheffield Academic Press, 1992); cf. CE Carter, *Emergence of Yehud*, 296. For the suggestion of a chartered community see J. Kessler, "Persia's Loyal Yahwists: Power Identity and Ethnicity in Achaemenid Yehud," in *Judah and the Judeans in the Persian Period* (eds. O. Lipschits and M. Oeming; Winona Lake, Ind.: Eisenbrauns, 2006), 91–121. (Kessler does not think that the charter proposal accounts for the quasi-ubiquity of the empty land motif.)

[10] This narrative is relatively common and has influenced even recently, among others, G. A. Yee, *Poor Banished Children of Eve: Woman as Evil in the Hebrew Bible* (Minneapolis: Fortress Press, 2003), 140–43.

[11] See, for instance, R. P. Carroll, "The Myth of the Empty Land." For a comparative study of the most significant discussion of these texts, see J. Kessler, "Images of Exile: Representations of the 'Exile' and 'Empty Land' in the Sixth to Fourth Century BCE Yehudite Literature," in (eds. E. Ben Zvi and C. Levin; BZAW 404; Berlin/New York: De Gruyter, 2010), 309–52.

[12] See, for instance, the population estimates in O. Lipschits, *Fall and Rise of Jerusalem*, 270.

that were discriminated against by the returnees eventually co-opted the memories of those whom they would have seen as their oppressors and rejected their own might have done so because of, a) a kind of social "Stockholm syndrome," b) a more lengthy process by means of which disenfranchised groups attempt to improve their lot by identifying with those in power and eventually end up fully assimilating to them, or c) forceful assimilation of the disenfranchised group by the center. One may support options b) and c) in particular by bringing up other cases in history in which marginal groups ended up joining the dominant socio-cultural group and through the process either co-opted or were co-opted into memories that not only were originally foreign to them, but also contradicted their previous self-understanding and memories.[13] In other words, new identities could lead and very often do lead to new memories. Images of the past are reshaped by the present of those who create and revisit them.

Did I convince you? I hope not, since, despite all its appeal, this scenario as a whole is very unlikely. To begin with, it is based on the assumption of a central conflict between a few returnees supported by the Persian center and much larger local communities – hat is, between Jerusalem and its temple, and, for the most part, the rest of Yehud. It is also based on the assumption that such conflict occurred in the early Persian period and was likely resolved through the exercise of power with the following features: a) it was resolved in a matter of a few generations – unless one would maintain that the Pentateuch, dtr-H, and prophetic literature were a kind of sectarian literature that was accepted only by Temple centered and *torah* centered returnees in Jerusalem, but not elsewhere in

---

13 It may be noticed, however, that for the most part, these processes took time. There is not so much time from the beginning of the incipient temple in Jerusalem in the early Persian period to the moment in which the temple and its leadership became central to Yehud (see TAD A 4.8), and the cultural memory processes I am referring to and which were related to the success of Jerusalem and its temple are to be associated with the period in between; the same holds true for the wide acceptance in Yehud and Yehud's literature of the concept of Jerusalem's absolute centrality. On the latter, cf. M. D. Knowles, *Centrality Practiced: Jerusalem and the Religious Practice of Yehud & the Diaspora in the Persian Period* (Atlanta: Society of Biblical Literature, 2006). (D. Edelman dates the resettlement of Jerusalem and the building of the temple later. See D. Edelman, *The Origins of the 'Second Temple': Persian Imperial Policy and the Rebuilding of Jerusalem* [London: Equinox, 2005]. I remain convinced that a small incipient temple/cultic institution was established early in the Persian period and that around that temple, Jerusalem began to develop in a manner commensurate with its temple. Because of the people associated with this incipient temple, the city was resettled at the time, even if by relatively few people.)

Yehud;[14] b) it was resolves with those remaining in the land (i.e., the vast majority) fully capitulating and not only accepting the social, political, and economic primacy of the returnees over them, but also adopting their "enemies'" memories, identity, and ideology as their own.

Several considerations work against this construction. To begin with, at the very core of this scenario stands a Jerusalemite temple community, a local center supported by the Persians that excludes most of the residents of the province. The historical likelihood of such a community during the early Persian period is very slim. An incipient temple with no agricultural lands would likely try to bring in the residents of the province, rather than keeping them out. The demographic situation in Jerusalem and its rural surrounding areas[15] makes exclusion a very unlikely policy for officials at the temple. From the perspective of the imperial center, the well-known tendency to support and befriend local elites was meant to stabilize provinces and ethnic groups, but forceful, long term support for a small minority of returnees over and against the vast majority of the population of the province is not consistent with such a goal; moreover, if a central temple was supposed to serve as a fiscal center in the province, what would be the point of excluding most of its inhabitants?[16] One may note that the likely role

---

14 Cf. K. L. Noll, "Was There Doctrinal Dissemination in Early Yahweh Religion?," in *BibInt* 16 (2008): 395–427, who maintains that these texts do not necessarily reflect the beliefs of the scribal community that produced and read them and that such a community never intended to disseminate the contents of its literary repertoire.

15 H. Geva recently estimated that the population of Persian period Jerusalem reached no more than 1,000 people, as does O. Lipschits, whereas I. Finkelstein estimates about 400–500 people, "that is, not much more than 100 adult men." C. E. Carter's earlier estimates mentioned 1,500–3,000 people. Similarly, the total population of Yehud has been estimated between a low of 15,000 to 20,000 to a high of 30,000 people. See H. Geva, "Estimating Jerusalem's Population in Antiquity: A Minimalist View," in *EI* 28 [Teddy Kollek Volume] (2007): 50–65 (Hebrew); I. Finkelstein, "Jerusalem in the Persian (and Early Hellenistic) Period;" idem, "Archaeology and the List of Returnees;" O. Lipschits, "Jerusalem between Two Periods of Greatness: The Size and Status of the City in the Babylonian, Persian and Early Hellenistic Periods," in *Judah between East and West: The Transition from Persian to Greek Rule (ca. 400–200 BCE)* (eds. O. Lipschits and L. L. Grabbe; LSTS; London/New York: T&T Clark, 2012), 163–75; idem, *Fall and Rise of Jerusalem*; and CE Carter, *Emergence of Yehud*. Given that the degree of development of the environs of an ancient city serves as indirect evidence for the size and population of the city, see also A. Kloner, "Environs in the Persian Period," in *New Studies on Jerusalem* (eds. A. Faust and E. Baruch; Ramat Gan, Israel: Ingeborg Rennert Center for Jerusalem Studies, 2001), 91–95 (Hebrew), which provides a picture coherent with the one advanced in the studies mentioned above.

16 On the matter of temples as fiscal centers see, for instance, J. Schaper, "The Jerusalem Temple as an Instrument of the Achaemenid Fiscal Administration," in *VT* 45 (1995): 528–39; idem "The Temple Treasury Committee in the Times of Nehemiah and Ezra," in *VT* 47 (1997): 200–06.

of Mizpah in Benjamin as the capital of the province during the early and decisive period also speaks strongly against this scenario. Finally, there is no account of such practices in the HB, and no significant text in Haggai, Zechariah, or Malachi refers to them.[17] Furthermore, if one were to argue from Ezra 1–6, a text clearly later than the period covered here,[18] one should note that it incorporates *the entire population* of Yehud into the community as returnees.[19]

Of course, there were negative characterizations of Benjamin in the Jerusalem-centered discourse of the period, as one would expect from literature shaped in an incipient temple that had to stand competition,[20] but these attacks were not only set well in the past, but also fully integrated within a general discourse that emphasized social and regional cohesion in the form of central con-

---

The presence of a treasury in Jerusalem may have contributed to the shift of the provincial capital from Mizpah to Jerusalem. Cf. C. Tuplin, "The Administration of the Achaemenid Empire," in *Coinage and Administration in the Athenian and Persian Empires* (ed. Ian Carradice; BAR International Series 343; Oxford: B. A. R., 1987), 109–66 (128, 130).

17 On Zech 1–8 see J. Kessler, "Diaspora and Homeland in the Early Achaemenid Period: Community, Geography and Demography in Zechariah 1–8," in *Approaching Yehud: New Approaches to the Study of the Persian Period* (ed. J. L. Berquist; SemeiaSt 50; Atlanta: Society of Biblical Literature, 2007), 137–66 (158–66).

18 On Ezra 1–6, see, among others, H. G. M. Williamson, "The Composition of Ezra i–vi," in *JTS* NS 34 (1983): 1–30; reprinted in idem, *Studies in Persian Period History and Historiography* (FAT, 38; Tübingen: Mohr Siebeck, 2004), 244–70.

19 Ezra 10:29 constructs a later period, but it is worth noting that it suggests that membership into the community was open to those who identify with its ideology and socio-cultural (including cultic) norms.

20 For the general tendencies discussed here see C. Edenburg, *The Story of the Outrage at Gibeah (Judg 19–21): Composition, Sources and Historical Context* (Phd Thesis, Tel Aviv University, 2003), passim. Edenburg relates some of the ideological tendencies of the story to tensions between a Jerusalem centered group and Benjamin during the early Persian period. Particularly relevant to the case here are the multiple negative references to Bethel and Beth-El in prophetic books and elsewhere (particularly in Kings, and probably in a "hidden way" in the episode of Bochim; see Judg 2:1–5). (Note: After the publication of this essay, an updated, translated and edited version of Edenburg's dissertation was published as Cynthia Edenburg, *Dismembering the Whole. Composition and Purpose of Judges 19–21* [SBLAIL, 24; Atlanta: SBL Press, 2016].) On these issues see also J. Blenkinsopp, "Benjamin Traditions Read in the Early Persian Period," in *Judah and the Judeans in the Persian Period*, 629–45; Y. Amit, "The Saul Polemic in the Persian Period," in *Judah and the Judeans in the Persian Period*, 647–61. For an argument in favor of a Saulide-Davidic rivalry in the early Persian period, see D. Edelman, "Did Saulide-Davidic Rivalry Resurface in Early Persian Yehud?" in *The Land that I Will Show You: Essays on the History and Archaeology of the Ancient Near East in Honour of J. Maxwell Miller* (eds. J. A. Dearman and M. P. Graham; JSOTSup 343; Sheffield: Sheffield Academic Press, 2001), 69–91.

nective concepts such as transtemporal Israel and memory of a kingdom of Judah that involved both Judah and Benjamin.[21]

In summary, the "Empty Land" motif and its related concepts of exile and return, present us with a good case in which discursive erasure most likely did not arise as a mystified representation from the worldly ambitions for power of a colonizing or elite group. Significantly, the same can be said of the (partial) erasure of the Canaanites in Joshua.

But if so, how to explain the social and ideological process that led to a systemic preference for "Empty Land" over its alternatives (e.g. continuity) within the discourse of Yehud, particularly since the images of "Empty Land" and "Return" stood so strong against the historical experience of the majority of the population, including its political and economic centers? Why would people develop and turn into a core feature of their self-understanding a counterfactual social memory, of whose counterfactualness they were well aware? Why would a group adopt a social memory that erases its experience in the recent past, if not under duress (be it political, economic, associated with a sense of dishonor,[22] or any combination of the above)?

I would like to advance that the explanation may have much to do with discursive and ideological needs. Of course, the latter do not exist in a vacuum, but are experienced, developed, and imagined within particular historical settings – I will return to this point. To begin with, the concept of "Empty Land" was deeply

---

[21] The ubiquitous, collective memory of a Judahite monarchy that included both Judah and Benjamin contributed to the social cohesion of Yehud (see 1 Kgs 12:21, 23; Jer 17:26). P.R. Davies associates the development of the concept of biblical Israel in Judah/Yehud with processes of social cohesion in neo-Babylonian and Persian period Judah/Yehud. See, for instance, his "The Origin of Biblical Israel," in *JHebS* 5 (2005): available at http://www.jhsonline.org. By the time of Chronicles, the pair Judah – Benjamin is attested numerous times (e.g., 2 Chr 11:1, 3, 10, 12, 23; 2 Chr 15:2, 8, 9; 25:5; 31:1) and serves above all to communicate a sense of boundary and separation between Yehud (i.e., Judah and Benjamin, which are conceived as inseparable) and Samaria. This historical tendency towards integration, which clearly reflects the actual historical necessities of the period, may also be responsible for the fact that, eventually, the priestly line of the second temple was construed as being Aaronide, a line that seems to have been originally associated with Bethel. It is possible that non-Jerusalemite centered Aaronides were eventually co-opted by the Jerusalem center, or that they took it over and contributed to its shaping. In either case, the end result is social and ideological integration. See J. Blenkinsopp, "Bethel in the Neo-Babylonian Period," in *Judah and the Judeans in the Neo-Babylonian Period*, 93–107; idem, "The Judaean Priesthood during the Neo-Babylonian and Achaemenid Periods: A Hypothetical Reconstruction," in *CBQ* 60 (1998): 25–43.

[22] It is difficult to imagine that those who remained in the land associated dis-honor with remaining in the land, unless they already accepted the metanarrative about Israel's total exile. But in that case, they would be "exilees/returnees," along with the rest of Israel/Yehud.

interwoven with a significant number of other central metaphors, and metanarratives associated with the concept of "Exile." A result of this high connectedness was that people could not easily reject the "Empty Land" motif without rejecting so many central motifs and ways of thinking about the past binding the community together; after all, Yehudite Israel was a text and memory centered community.

As is well-known, Yhwh's anger on account of the sin of Israel/Judah and their leaders was seen as the fundamental reason for the collapse of the monarchic polity, the destruction of Jerusalem, and the severe blow to the rural population in Judah. This type of explanation is common in the ancient Near East and consistent with the motif of the foundational role of the divine in human affairs. Although it was used by imperial powers and conquerors, it also served in the interest of those defeated, who despite the adversity they faced could through this narrative not only maintain the centrality and power of their own deity/deities but even further extol it. In addition, an emphasis on previous sin provided a sense of agency to the defeated community and a poignant story meant to socialize it in terms consistent with the local elites' understanding of sin and piety, which is now presented as unequivocally supported by a tragic divine action in history. Significantly, this basic metanarrative tends to conclude with some form of restoration of proper order. The "grammar" of this metanarrative requires an element of closure. In this regard and not surprisingly it fits well the postmonarchic discourse in Judah/Yehud.[23]

The image of Yhwh's wrath and abandonment of the place used to explain the disaster of 586 BCE was related to and partially evocative of, from another perspective, a claim concerning the presence of impurity. After all, impurity is that which repels divine presence. Once the matter is approached from this perspective, then the pollution created by sinful human activity during the monarchic period must be driven out of the land, for if this is not the case, the community will certainly fall. The logic of this line of thinking requires that the land passes through a purification period. This leads to the image of the land as resting, replenishing, and purging itself. The ready metaphor for this process is that of the fallow land.[24] A lack of people is more consistent with that image

---

[23] Metanarratives that could interweave the goals of the local and imperial/hegemonic elites were often preferred, given the tendency for the latter to rely on the former and vice versa. For examples of the basic narrative mentioned above see the Curse of Agade, the epic of Tukulti-Ninurta (and his explanation of his victory over Kashtiliash II), Nebuchadnezzar I's epic, Esarhaddon's explanation for the destruction of Babylon, Adad-guppi's autobiography, and the Mesha Inscription.

[24] Cf. Lev 26:34–35, 43; 2 Chr 36:31.

than their presence or diminished presence.[25] In any case, any community living on the still polluted land cannot but fail and disappear. Within the logic of this approach, remaining in the land was either not an option or path to a dead end. A viable community, as Persian period Yehud would have imagined itself, would be more likely to be construed within this line of thought as (mythically) refound on a purified land.

Another consideration: one of the results of the postmonarchic attribution of kingly features to Israel (the so-called "democratization")[26] is that Israel is the child of the deity. But "child" is only one common type of family subordinate; the other is "wife." Given common hierarchical gender constructions and the "maleness" of king/shepherd YHWH, it is only expected that Israel be construed in this discourse as YHWH's wife. In this context, Israel's sin was imagined in terms of adultery, exile associated with divorce or at least expulsion of Israel from YHWH's space, and the hope for the future in terms of marital reconciliation.[27] Now, within the social and ideological logic of this image, Israel/the wife could not have been imagined as half expelled from the matrimonial house, that is, the land. Israel as whole must be expelled from the land. This basic and common metaphor leads necessarily to a construction of the exile as full and complete, and to that of an empty land.

Of course, female Israel can also be construed in terms of Jerusalem (see Ezek 23), in which case it has to be imagined as both fully destroyed and as rebuilt or about to be rebuilt; after all, the metanarrative cannot conclude with the story of a final, irrevocable estrangement and permanent divorce between wife Israel and husband YHWH. The image of female Jerusalem is, of course, an example of the widespread ancient Near Eastern topos of the city as a woman. This topos, in the context of lamented past destruction and present rebuilding, is central to "City Laments." Expectations associated with City Laments include references to the destruction of the city due to the wrath of a male deity/deities, divine abandonment, and *total destruction*, irrelevant of the actual historical

---

[25] Cf. Lev 18:24–28; 20:22.

[26] The idea of a covenant between the people and YHWH instead of the king and YHWH is at the core of Deuteronomy and Exodus–Numbers and serves as the most salient example of this tendency. Another example involves the "democratization" of royal myths of origin; see, for instance, J. Van Seters, "The Creation of Man and the Creation of the King," in *ZAW* 101 (1989): 333–42. Within Chronicles there is a clear trend to reshape the narratives of Samuel-Kings in a way consonant with these "democratization" tendencies; see S. Japhet, *The Ideology of Chronicles and Its Place in Biblical Thought* (BEATAJ 9; 2nd rev. ed.; Frankfurt a. M.: Lang, 1997), 416–28.

[27] An obvious example for the use(s) of this metaphor is Hos 1–3.

situation.²⁸ But if both Jerusalem and the land stand symbolically for Israel, and the capital city stands for its territory and polity (as usual in the ancient Near East), then both Jerusalem and the land have to be imagined as fully destroyed, and Israel as exiled in its entirety.

Without doubt one may claim that the ideology according to which Jerusalem can and does stand symbolically for Judah is one that would have been particularly promoted by the incipient temple in Jerusalem, with the likely support of the Persian center. But certainly, it was at the core of monarchic period discourse and the perception of Judah outside its borders (cf. ABC 5, rev. l. 12). Yehud could not have rejected this construction without substantially erasing any claims of continuity between Persian Yehud and monarchic Judah. But already the name "Yehud" (not Benjamin) points to an internal and external ideology of continuity and to a self-identity based on that continuity, and external recognition and support for it.²⁹

This sense of self-identity is directly and deeply involved in a metanarrative of restoration that moves from "David" to "Cyrus," and from monarchic Judah to provincial Yehud, and from monarchic temple to Persian temple – including a return of the presence of Yhwh and symbols of continuity in the form of vessels claimed to be from the first temple in the second one. Metanarratives of continuity between two different periods, tend to de-emphasize the element and period of discontinuity. This explains why there is little narrative space allocated to the neo-Babylonian period or any aspect of the early Persian period that was not related with the re-establishment of the temple and Jerusalem in ancient Israelite historiography.³⁰ Little narrative space in authoritative historiography creates

---

28 See D. Edelman, "The 'Empty Land' as a Motif in City Laments," in *Ancient and Modern Scriptural Historiography/L'Historiographie Biblique, Ancienne et Moderne* (eds. G. J. Brooke and T. Römer, BETL 207; Leuven: Leuven University Press, 2007), 127–49 and bibliography.

29 Cf. the area surrounding Babylon after the destruction of the city by Sennacherib. The surrounding population and the "external world" kept a sense of self-identity associated with Babylon at the center. Cf. the closer case of Rabbat Ammon, which was likely destroyed by the Babylonians and ceased to be the capital of the province for a while (O. Lipschits, "Ammon in Transition from Vassal Kingdom to Babylonian Province," in *BASOR* 335 [2004]: 37–52), but eventually became again the center of the area afterwards. There are numerous comparable cases both from ancient times to the present (e.g., few think that Bonn had a real chance of remaining the capital of Germany for long after unification; cases of moving the capital by a local/national elite/ruler are different; e.g., Dur Sarrukhin, Brazilia).

30 Cf., among others, S. Japhet, *From the Rivers of Babylon to the Highlands of Judah: Collected Studies on the Restoration Period* (Winona Lake, Ind.: Eisenbrauns, 2006), 353–66, 416–31; E. Ben Zvi, "What is New in Yehud? Some Considerations," in *Yahwism after the Exile* (eds. R. Albertz and B. Becking; STAR 5; Assen: Van Gorcum, 2003), 32–48. Of course, as usual, there are a few exceptions to the rule; see the story of Gedaliah, a matter I deal with elsewhere: "The Voice

less sites of memory within the world of the community shaped around the reading of the relevant historical narratives. The memory of the community centered in Mizpah, of neo-Babylonian Judah/Benjamin, is thus less and less evoked and becomes more and more absent from the main shared discourse. In the metanarrative of Jerusalem to Jerusalem, Judah to Judah/Yehud, temple to temple there is very little room for Mizpah. The "original" memories of the Benjaminites become more and more marginal, as those who may evoke them see or imagine themselves as Israel/Yehud.[31]

This of course does not mean that the Benjaminites themselves become marginal, but that their self-identity becomes subsumed under a more general one. The temple in Jerusalem would have encouraged such a process. The literature produced by literati associated with the Temple most likely co-opted traditions from the area (see the Pentateuch). Even some of the Bethel leadership (sons of Aaron?) may have been co-opted and might eventually taken leadership positions in Jerusalem.[32] But neither the incipient and poor temple of Jerusalem nor a small number of returnees (even if supported by the Persian center for a while) could have forced the long term acceptance of an extraneous self-identity and ideology upon the vast majority of the population during the early Persian period against their will and through oppression. The Benjaminites and others were most likely not passive objects, rather, they are historical agents too.

Historical communities do not develop a full discursive logical consistency. But at least in the case of Yehud, it seems that the logic of a particular discourse and the sort of narrative plots and typological connections that evolved out of a widely accepted metanarrative had an important impact in terms of systemic preference and dis-preference for social memories. This is not surprising, since the latter are closely associated with matters of social cohesion and self-identity. Those living in Benjamin and others whose ancestors remained in the land knew that the land was not empty after the destruction of the monarchic polity, and so

---

and Role of a Counterfactual Memory in the Construction of Exile and Return: Considering Jeremiah 40: 7–12," in this volume, pp. 612–30.

[31] In other words, a discursive and ideological "need" to stress continuity between two different periods contributes to, and shapes elements of social memory forgetfulness. For a comparative study of this type of social (and historiographical) processes, see K. M. Stott, "A Comparative Study of the Exilic Gap in Ancient Israelite, Messenian and Zionist Collective Memory," in *Community Identity in Judean Historiography* (eds. G. N. Knoppers and K. A. Ristau; Winona Lake, Ind.: Eisenbrauns, 2009), 41–58.

[32] See J. Blenkinsopp, "Bethel in the Neo-Babylonian Period," in *Judah and the Judeans in the Neo-Babylonian Period*, 93–107; and note above. One may note that it is reasonable to assume that some of the Mizpah elite were likely co-opted by Jerusalem, when the latter became the capital of the province.

did the few returnees and the literati in Jerusalem. But preference for a social memory that they knew to be counterfactual–despite the tensions and at times faulting lines that the situation creates – can be explained in terms of discursive needs, and particularly since the preferred memory became necessary to sustain and support numerous concepts, plots, and metaphors enabling the community to understand itself and maintain a sense of hope for the future expressed in terms of purified land, marriage with Yhwh, permanent cultic divine presence, or the like.

In sum, the social success of the concepts of "Total Exile" and "Empty Land" cannot be explained in terms of their supposed function in an exclusivist, discriminatory, and oppressive social system imposed by a community of exiles/returnees over and against a community of remainees that included the vast majority of Yehud. The successful (for the most part) erasure of social memories of continuity among Benjaminites and other groups of remainees and their replacement with memories that they knew to be in one sense counterfactual had less to do with long term oppression or exclusion of the vast majority of the population – and even less with an ideological, mystified representation of an historical oppression – than with the inner logic of the shared central discourse that evolved through time and through social negotiation among local groups living a few hours walk from each other in early Persian Yehud. To be sure, this social negotiation included tensions and processes of co-opting and being co-opted, but also contributed, through the integrative discourse it created, to social cohesion and to a construction of self-identity in Persian Yehud. Because it involved a shared discourse about the fall of the monarchic polity, causality in history, and strong claims of continuity with monarchic Judah, the discourse had to bear a strong message of settlement discontinuity, exile, and empty land.

A final word: Benjamin is no Samaria. No process comparable to the inner Yehudite, which involved above all Benjamin and Jerusalem but perhaps other groups as well, developed between Samaria and Yehud, despite their sharing of the Pentateuch. Several factors may have contributed to this historical, separate process. Among them one may mention a) matters of provincial boundaries, b) Persian policies, c) an internal and external sense of socio-political continuity – Samaria and Judah were always two different polities, and were perceived as such but other groups, and d) the question of Jerusalem's uniqueness within Judah, but not beyond its borders. But the matter is for another talk.

The Voice and Role of a Counterfactual Memory in the Construction of Exile and Return: Considering Jeremiah 40:7–12*

Some Considerations of Counterfactual History/Thinking

Counterfactual histories are common in popular culture today.[1] To a large extent, the popularity of the genre is a function of the role of these stories in shaping and reshaping evaluations of the present.[2] Counterfactual narratives about the past[3] frequently provide a way to imagine a better, alternative past leading to a better present, though at times a dystopian past/present is advanced. In any event, these narratives tend to carry a strong component of presentism, even if on the surface they deal only with alternate pasts.[4]

From a methodological perspective, alternate histories written by professional scholars, although often attacked by members of our guild, serve important roles. For instance, they help to raise issues of historical causality, of long-term processes, and of chaos in history. Alternate histories serve to undermine deterministic narratives and metanarratives. They raise awareness of the problematic nature of reductive historical approaches, though at times indulging in it. Counterfactual historical simulations come as close as possible to arranging an "ex-

---

* First published in *The Concept of Exile in Ancient Israel and its Historical Contexts* (eds. E. Ben Zvi and C. Levin; BZAW 404; Berlin/New York: De Gruyter, 2010), 155–68.
1 The bibliographic database of a main website for alternate history, Uchronia, claims to contain "over 2800 novels, stories, essays and other printed material involving the 'what ifs' of history." See http://www.uchronia.net/. A search under "Canada" retrieves more than twenty volumes, while a similar search for "Germany" retrieves, as expected, several times more.
2 See G. Rosenfeld, "Why Do We Ask 'What if'? Reflections on the Function of Alternate History," in *History and Theory* 41 (2002): 90–103.
3 The bibliography on virtual/alternate/counterfactual history, at times called allohistory, is immense and varied. See, among others, *Virtual History: Alternatives and Counterfactuals* (ed. N. Ferguson; Papermac: London, 1998), esp. N. Ferguson, "Introduction," 1–90; A. Demandt, *History That Never Happened: A Treatise on the Question, What Would Have Happened If...?* (3rd rev. ed.; Jefferson, NC: McFarland & Company, 1993); J. Bulhof, "What If? Modality and History," in *History and Theory* 38 (1999): 145–68; M. Bunzl, "Counterfactual History: A User's Guide," in *American Historical Review* 109 (2004): 845–58; and the forum on "Counterfactual Realities" in *Representations* 98 (2007): 51–134, that includes contributions of Catherine Gallagher, Sarah Jain, Mark Maslan, Paul K. Saint-Amour and Andrew Miller. For a volume devoted to counterfactual history of ancient Israel, see *Virtual History and the Bible* (ed. J. Cheryl Exum; Leiden: E. J. Brill, 2000).
4 See G. Rosenfeld, "Why Do We Ask 'What if?'"

periment" which looks at (or better, imagines) the behaviour of a system or outcomes as particular variable changes.[5] They carry the potential of contributing to the reconstruction of the world of historical agents, for the future these agents imagined and sought to bring about through their actions is by necessity a kind of an alternate history, which rarely if ever turned into "actual" history.[6]

Significantly, studies in experimental social psychology have concluded that counterfactuals are important for certain mental processes: "People often evaluate story or situation outcomes by mentally altering preceding events and simulating what impact this would have had on the outcome... [t]his mental simulation process plays an important role in cognition and emotion."[7] Similarly, counterfactuals play important roles in assessing (perceived) causality.[8] Counterfactuals are important cognitive tools, because they allow mental simulations in which some variable can be manipulated.[9] Such simulations played important roles for historical agents (i.e. human beings) in ancient times as well, contributing to their decision-making and affective response to events and to their constructions of their virtually re-lived past as they read narratives about it.

It is therefore not surprising that antiquity attests to both explicit and implicit counterfactual historical thinking.[10] Perhaps the most obvious and well-discussed case of explicit counterfactual musings is Livy's discussion of what would have happened if Rome and Alexander would have faced each other in war (*Ab Urbe Condita* 9.17–19).[11] At a deeper level, however, Kagan is correct when he states:

> To my mind, no one who aims to write a history rather than a chronicle can avoid discussing what might have happened; the only question is how explicitly one reveals what one is doing...Historians interpret what they recount, that is, they make judgments about it. There is no way that the historian can judge that one action or policy was wise or foolish without

---

[5] On this type of simulations in daily life see below.
[6] See D. Carr, "Place and Time: On the Interplay of Historical Points of View," in *History and Theory* 40 (2001): 153–67, esp. 158–67.
[7] I. Gavanski and G. L. Wells, "Counterfactual Processing of Normal and Exceptional Events," in *Journal of Experimental Social Psychology* 25 (1989): 314–25 and bibliography (citation from 314).
[8] G. L. Wells and I. Gavanski, "Mental Simulation of Causality," in *Journal of Personality and Social Psychology* 56 (1989): 161–169.
[9] D. Kahneman and A. Tversky, "The Simulation Heuristic," in *Judgment Under Uncertainty: Heuristics and Biases* (eds. D. Kahneman, P. Slovic, and A. Tversky; New York: Cambridge University Press, 1982), 201–08.
[10] This holds true even if the particular genre of extensive counter-historical narrative seems to be a relatively new phenomenon.
[11] On this text see R. Morello, "Livy's Alexander Digression (9.17–19): Counterfactuals and Apologetics," in *Journal of Roman Studies* 92 (2002): 62–85.

saying, or implying, that it was better or worse than some other that might have been employed, which is, after all, "counterfactual history." No doubt my method has been influenced by the great historian whom I have been studying for three decades, who engages in this practice very frequently and more openly than most. Let two examples suffice. In his explanation of the great length of the Greek's siege of Troy, Thucydides says: "But if they had taken with them an abundant supply of food, and ... had carried the war *continuously, they would easily have prevailed in battle and taken the city*" [1.11.2]. Again, in the conclusion to this summation and judgment of Pericles' career, he says: "Such abundant grounds had Pericles at that time for his own forecast that Athens might quite easily have triumphed in this war over the Peloponnesians alone" [2.65.13]. I believe that there are important advantages to such explicitness: it puts the reader on notice that that statement in question is a judgment, an interpretation, rather than a fact, and it helps avoid the excessive power of the fait accompli, making clear that what really occurred was not the inevitable outcome of superhuman forces but the result of decisions by human beings and suggesting that both the decisions and their outcomes could well have been different.[12]

To be sure, in ancient Israelite historiography and in ancient Israelite constructions of the past reflected and shaped in other literary genres such as prophetic literature, divine causality had an important role, but so did individual or collective choice and human agency. In fact, the entire didactic value of these texts was predicated on the assumption of individual and collective choice and agency, a matter duly stressed also in books such as Deuteronomy. It would be beyond the scope of this chapter to investigate the interaction between these two types of causalities in the discourse of at least the literati of ancient Israel/Yehud, or even in a particular book or episode, no matter how central.[13] It suffices to notice that the presence of an undisputable sense of human agency in this discourse, even if balanced or informed by other ideological considerations, implies that these ancient literati almost certainly involved themselves in counterfactual thinking.

Some Considerations of Ancient Yehudite Memory and the Concept of Exile

The methodological considerations mentioned above carry important potential for reconstructing the intellectual discourse of ancient Israel/Yehud and should

---

12 D. Kagan, *The Fall of the Athenian Empire* (Ithaca, NY: Cornell University Press, 1987), x–xi.
13 Cf. my "Observations on Josiah's Account in Chronicles and Implications for Reconstructing the Worldview of the Chronicler," in *Essays on Ancient Israel in Its Near Eastern Context: A Tribute to Nadav Na'aman* (eds. Y. Amit, E. Ben Zvi, I. Finkelstein and O. Lipschits; Winona Lake, Ind.: Eisenbrauns, 2006), 89–106.

be consistently pursued in the future.¹⁴ As studies advance in this area, it would be advisable, however, to bring the term "memory" into the discussion. Although somewhat oversimplifying matters, one may say that history, at least as usually understood in contemporary discourse, tends to separate the past from the present and focus on the unique, unrepeatable character of the past or the past event,¹⁵ whereas memory tends to construe a past that is presently alive in the community, to fuse past and present, and to shape the past in terms of a basic metanarrative/myth that is constantly reused to interpret and provide significance to a recounted past, which accordingly becomes, to some extent, both cyclical and recyclable.¹⁶ It is memory that plays an important role in the formation and maintenance of group identity by shaping common myths, teleology, and basic structuring, which are interpretative tools to assign meaning to events, past, present and future. It is memory rather than history that counts most in the world of at least the literati of ancient Yehud. Thus, if one focuses on reconstructing their views, it is more appropriate to address the question of counterfactual memory at least as much as that of counterfactual history.

Given the theme of this volume, I will focus on a certain concept that served to generate much cyclical structure in the basic memory of the past held by the Yehudite literati, and provide significance to memories of past, present and future circumstances. The memory shaped through the main discourse of the Yehudite literati associated the return from Babylon with the Exodus from Egypt, and thus Babylonian exile with the stay in Egypt, while the latter also served as the main archetype for constructing exile in general. Within a discourse in which the opposite of exile is secure life in the land and full access to the fulfilled potential of its agrarian gifts, a point usually made in prophetic literature, the Exodus/Conquest motif embodies a main story of overcoming exile and establishing the ground for non-exilic conditions. This being so, the main patriarchal stories are largely transformed into memories of "exile" (i.e., of "exilic conditions"), even when their characters were portrayed as being in the land.¹⁷ Within this

---

14 To the best of my knowledge, they have not yet impacted historical studies on the intellectual world of Yehud. The only book on counterfactual history in HB studies follows, in the main, a different approach.
15 This holds true even if by necessity every past historically reconstructed is a present past, that is, a past that exists only in the present and within a present discourse. See my "Reconstructing the Intellectual Discourse of Ancient Yehud," in *SR* 39 (2010): 7–23 and bibliography there.
16 Cf. G. M. Spiegel, "Memory and History: Liturgical Time and Historical Time," in *History and Theory* 41 (2002): 149–62.
17 Thus one may say that Abraham (except in Gen 14) is a kind of archetype of the exilic Israelite in the land. The concept of "exile" in the land existed also in the later Hellenistic period, see

logic, monarchic Israel becomes, as it were, pregnant with exile, carries it in its midst, and eventually gives birth to it. If this is true, then postmonarchic Israel, and particularly Yehud, can be imagined as pregnant with overcoming exile, carrying it in its midst and eventually giving birth to it at some point in the far future. But this is not the entire story. The concept of secure life in the land and full access to the fulfilled potential of its agrarian gifts is ideologically associated with that of proper relationship between Yhwh and Israel. Thus, exile stands for partial estrangement between the two.[18]

Of course, secure life in the land and full access to the fulfilled potential of its agrarian gifts are ideal, unrealizable conditions and therefore the image of completely overcoming exile becomes intertwined with utopian thinking, while at the same time raising and leaving open the issue of what level of control over the land may be seen as at least a partial undoing of exile and estrangement from Yhwh.

Since exile was used to structure periodizations of the past, and the corresponding stories of conclusions and new beginnings, these considerations point to the suitability of this discourse to construe temporal and social boundaries and at the same time to undermine them.

It is against this background that I plan to approach the counterfactual memory regarding exile that is implied, reflected in and evoked by Jer 40:7–12, and reveal the light it sheds on the discourse of Yehudite literati.

Some Considerations of Jeremiah 40:7–12 and its Interrelated Immediate Cotext

Although Jer 40:7–12 is illuminated and informed by its immediate cotexts in the book of Jeremiah (Jer 40:1–6 and Jer 40:13–41:18),[19] it is common to study it as a

---

the classic M. A. Knibb, "The Exile in the Literature of the Intertestamental Period," in *HeyJ* 17 (1976): 253–72. Cf. J. R. Linville, "Rethinking the 'Exilic' Book of Kings," in *JSOT* 75 (1997): 21–42.
18 The discourse of the period did not allow for a final separation/divorce between Yhwh and Israel.
19 I wish to stress that this essay discusses the counterfactual memory of the intended and primary readers of these texts in their present compositional form, not of any, by necessity, hypothetical forerunners of these units that have been proposed in research. Although I am convinced that these texts underwent a redactional history, the intended and primary readers of the version I deal with were not asked to approach these texts and construct their memory (factual or counterfactual) on any redactional history, but rather on the basis of the world construed by the texts in their present form. For a proposed redactional history of these and related texts and significant bibliography see O. Lipschits, *The Fall and Rise of Jerusalem* (Winona Lake, Ind.:

textual, literary/ideological unit or subunit.[20] This understanding of Jer 40:7–12 is already attested to in the MT system of unit delimitation that explicitly separates Jer 40:7–12 from the previous and following subunits in the book by two *setumah* divisions. This traditional delimitation of the subunit reflects an awareness of, and a reading that highlights some thematic and ideological concerns that strongly characterize and set it apart, due to their divergence from commonly attested concepts and images of the exile,[21] as well as from the usual constructions of the situation in Judah following the fall of Jerusalem in biblical literature.[22]

Eisenbrauns, 2005), 304–47, esp. 325–34, 39–44. See also W. McKane, *Jeremiah. Volume II: Commentary on Jeremiah XXVI–LII* (ICC; Edinburgh: T&T Clark, 1996), 1005–1011. As is well known, the present compositional form of these units is attested in two main versions the MT and LXX. In this study I investigate the voice and role of a counterfactual memory evoked among intended and primary readers by and through rereading MT Jer 40:7–12 in a way informed by its cotexts in that book (i.e., MT Jeremiah), but when relevant, notes concerning the LXX are included. To be sure, a similar study could have focused on the counterfactual memories evoked by and through the rereading of the LXX version. Although some differences between these two studies are bound to come up concerning particular details and in one case on matters of potentially connoted versus explicitly stated (and magnified) portrayals, I doubt that a study similar to this one but focused on the LXX text would reach conclusions substantially different from the present one. I take for granted in this essay that the basic social group who read and reread the texts discussed here consisted of literati in Persian period Yehud who shared a Jerusalem-centered ideology, but if the precise form of the texts discussed here belongs to the early Hellenistic period, it would not affect the argument in any major way. To date these passages to the monarchic, neo-Babylonian, Hasmonean (/late Hellenistic) or Roman periods is either difficult or impossible. It may be mentioned at this point that texts of Jeremiah close to the MT (i.e. texts that are 'proto-masoretic') are clearly attested in Qumran (see E. Tov, "Jeremiah," in *Qumran Cave 4, vol X: The Prophets* [eds. E. Ulrich et. al.; DJD XV; Oxford: Clarendon Press, 1997], 145–70, 171–76, 177–201, 202–5). 4Q Jer^a, which is usually dated to the late third or the early second century, attests to a text close to the MT not only in general, but also in orthography (see E. Tov, "Jeremiah," 150). 4Q Jer^c is also close to the MT and even its paragraphing is comparable to the latter (even if not identical, see E. Tov, "Jeremiah," 181). 4Q Jer^d is not only similar in orthography but seems to reflect the MT version of Jer 43:5 (E. Tov, "Jeremiah," 203–4).

20 E.g., R. P. Carroll, *Jeremiah: A Commentary* (OTL; Philadelphia: Westminster, 1986), 703–5; L. Stulman, *Jeremiah* (AOTC; Nashville: Abingdon, 2005), 323–24; W. Brueggemann, *Jeremiah 26–52: To Build, To Plant* (ITC; Grand Rapids, MI: Eerdmans, 1991), 163–67.
21 Cf. R. Albertz, *Israel in Exile: The History and Literature of the Sixth Century BCE* (Atlanta: SBL, 2003), 6.
22 A point stressed, among others, in R. P. Carroll, *Jeremiah*, 705. I would like to stress that I am not advancing a claim that the only possible structure of this section of the book of Jeremiah is one in which Jer 40:7–12 is understood as a separate unit. Prophetic books are texts to be read and reread and as such, they tend to show multiple, complementary reading structures that encouraged and allowed the intended and primary rereaders to develop an understanding of the

But what makes Jer 40:7–12 so different? To begin with, it portrays a brief, hope-charged age and a polity: Gedaliah's governorship.[23] Moreover, the intended and primary rereaders of vv. 11–12 could have hardly missed that the language of these verses is evocative of an image of a return of the exiles from all lands. At first the text refers to Judahites who found refuge among Judah's eastern neighbors, but it immediately adds a reference to Judahites אֲשֶׁר בְּכָל־הָאֲרָצוֹת, "in all the (other) lands" (v. 11a), which allows and perhaps encourages the intended and primary rereaders to imagine a larger scenario. The point is clearly developed as the prophetic reading moves into a climactic bipartite conclusion in v. 12 וַיָּשֻׁבוּ כָל־הַיְּהוּדִים מִכָּל־הַמְּקֹמוֹת אֲשֶׁר נִדְּחוּ־שָׁם וַיָּבֹאוּ אֶרֶץ־יְהוּדָה "*all the Judahites returned from all the places to which they had been scattered*

---

text in which meanings abstracted from one perceived structure of a text inform those of another structure. Within this system, it is most reasonable to assume that there existed readings of this section of the book of Jeremiah in which Jer 40:7–12 was understood as a prophetic reading within a set of prophetic readings. It can be read as a prophetic reading in its own, but at the same time it is clearly marked as interrelated with its immediate cotexts in the book, as is often the case with many prophetic readings. For the general positions concerning prophetic books that underlie this paragraph, see, for instance, my *Hosea* (FOTL 21 A, part 1; Grand Rapids: Eerdmans, 2005) and "The Prophetic Book: A Key Form of Prophetic Literature," in *The Changing Face of Form Criticism for the Twenty-First Century* (eds. Marvin A. Sweeney and Ehud Ben Zvi; Grand Rapids: Eerdmans, 2003), 276–97.

23 Whether Gedaliah was appointed as governor or to a higher or lower office has been a matter of some debate in recent research. For the proposal that Gedaliah "was not a governor … but only an officially installed representative of the Jewish 'remnant' before the Babylonian authorities in Judah" see J. Weinberg, "Gedaliah, the Son of Ahikam in Mizpah: His Status and Role, Supporters and Opponents," in *ZAW* 119 (2007): 356–68 (360). For the proposal that Gedaliah was crowned as king of Judah see J. M. Miller and J. H. Hayes, *A History of Ancient Israel and Judah* (Philadelphia: Westminster, 1987), 423, 445. The 2nd rev. ed. of the work (Louisville: Westminster John Knox, 2006) is less assertive on the issue (see 483, and cf. 445 in the original ed. with 510 in the 2nd rev. ed.), but has not abandoned the proposal. In any event, J. H. Hayes is not alone. See H. Niehr, "Religio-Historical Aspects of the 'Early Post-Exilic' Period," in *The Crisis of Israelite Religion: Transformation of Religious Tradition in Exilic and Post-Exilic Times* (eds. B. Becking, M. Korpel, C. A. Marjo; Oudtestamentische Studiën 42; Leiden: Brill, 1999), 228–44 (230). I tend to think that it is more likely that Judah did not remain as a vassal kingdom, albeit with a king who was not a member of the previous ruling dynasty, and that it became a province after 586 with Gedaliah as its governor. See O. Lipschits, *The Fall and Rise of Jerusalem*, 88–92 and bibliography. One should mention, however, that although the Babylonian policy towards Judah was very similar to that against Ammon after its rebellion was quashed, it is unclear whether the Babylonians ended the monarchy in Ammon at that time. See O. Lipschits, "Ammon in Transition from Vassal Kingdom to Babylonian Province," in *BASOR* 335 (2004): 37–52, and notice the comment on 44. In any event, it is not the historical Gedaliah/Gedaliah's community that stands at the center of the investigation here, but their ideological representation in Jer 40:7–12.

and came to the *land of Judah* (v. 12).²⁴ This wording most likely was meant to evoke, and actually did evoke among the primary and intended rereaders of this unit, an image of overcoming exile, of return. Such a reading is supported by the back reference to the returnees in Jer 43:5: אֲשֶׁר־שָׁבוּ מִכָּל־הַגּוֹיִם אֲשֶׁר נִדְּחוּ־שָׁם לָגוּר בְּאֶרֶץ יְהוּדָה "who have returned from all the nations to which they have scattered to live in the land of Judah." One may also note that the wording of Jer 40:12 not only communicated the matter by itself, but was reminiscent of divine promises such as those in Jer 16:15; 23:3, 8; 29:14, and a reversal of the situation portrayed in Jer 24:9.²⁵

---

24 J. G. Janzen has proposed that the Hebrew *Vorlage* attested by the LXX had ארץ in the singular, and that the text read בכל הארץ. See J. G. Janzen, *Studies in the Text of Jeremiah* (Cambridge: Harvard University Press, 1973), 208. W. L. Holladay, *Jeremiah 2* (Hermeneia; Minneapolis: Fortress, 1989), 271, follows J. G. Janzen, but see W. McKane, *Jeremiah*, vol. 2, 1003. Pietersma and Saunders translate the relevant section of the verse in the LXX as follows: "and all the Judeans, those in Moab, who were in Moab, and those among the sons of Ammon and those in Idumea and those in any other land, heard that the king of Babylon ...and they came to Godolias." See A. Pietersma and M. Saunders, *Ieremias* (NETS; Oxford University Press, 2007), available at http://ccat.sas.upenn.edu/nets/edition/34–ieremias-nets.pdf.

25 Jer 43:5 plays on the reminiscent power of this language for rhetorical purposes, namely to emphasize the failure of such elevated hopes. On this issue, see below. A word about the LXX is in order at this point. As is well known, the text in Jer LXX 47 (40):12 lacks a counterpart for וַיֵּשְׁבוּ כָל־הַיְּהוּדִים מִכָּל־הַמְּקֹמוֹת אֲשֶׁר נִדְּחוּ־שָׁם וַיָּבֹאוּ אֶרֶץ־יְהוּדָה אֶל־גְּדַלְיָהוּ and for the related expression in MT Jer 43:5 (LXX Jer 50:5). The phrase מִכָּל־הַגּוֹיִם אֲשֶׁר נִדְּחוּ־שָׁם "from all the nations to which they have scattered" in Jer 43:5 is not attested in LXX Jer 50 (MT 43):5. The LXX text here may be translated as "...all those remaining from Iouda who had returned to settle in the land." See A. Pietersma and M. Saunders, *Ieremias*. The relevant phrase seems to be reflected in 4QJerᵈ; see E. Tov, "Jeremiah," (DJD XV), 203–4. For another potential difference see previous note. Whether the LXX here reflects a Hebrew *Vorlage* earlier than the one represented by MT (as probably is the case) or not, the latter is still worth studying. Moreover, the MT may well reflect an ancient reading of an earlier text in which the return referred to in vv. 11–12 was understood, at least at a connotative level, as more extensive and partially in mythical terms. Janzen correctly noted that "the sentence [missing in the LXX] refers to the dispersion proper" elsewhere in the book of Jeremiah (with the exception of 43:5, see below). But then he stated, "the occurrences in 40:12 and 43:5 are out of place, for here the reference is only to those who temporarily took refuge in the hills when danger struck, and who filtered back when the fighting was over" (see Janzen, *Studies*, 53; cf. W. McKane, *Jeremiah*, vol. 2, 1003). There is no doubt that the sentence would be out of place for readers who understood it in the "historical" way Janzen, McKane or Holladay, (*Jeremiah 2*, 271, 295–96) do. But the fact that the sentence appears in the MT, whether "originally" or "redactionally added" indicates that at least some ancient literati did not share his reading of the text. Surely, Janzen's reading is far more likely to reflect the historical reality of Gedaliah's community than any expansive, mythic-laced reading, but this text was in the main not about historical reality – however one understands "historical reality" today – but about stirring images in the readers, about causing them to virtually relive and partake in the past community they

An elevated image of the return (at least by connotation) and of the returning community of Gedaliah is also conveyed, though in a different way, by the second part of the conclusion of the prophetic reading in v. 12.[26] As Stulman, among others, maintains, the text here portrayed a state of prosperity that carried an idyllic quality,[27] and was reminiscent of the promise in Jer 31:11–12 (cf. Jer 32:5).[28] The implied and the primary readers most likely understood such a state as connoting divine blessing.[29]

The text surely acknowledges exile (see the conclusion of v. 7[30] and Jer 40:1–6, which informs the present text; see below), but balances this acknowledgment with an elevated description of Gedaliah's community. The community is a שְׁאֵרִית, that is, a remnant, but one that carries much hope, and one which, from the perspective of a rereading community of the prophetic literature that is well aware of signposts for readings informing each other, not only called to mind the שְׁאֵרִית in Jer 31:7, but also and particularly the one in Jer 23:3, given the use of the phrases מִכָּל־הַמְּקֹמוֹת אֲשֶׁר נִדְּחוּ־שָׁם "from all the places where they had been scattered there" in 40:12 and הָאֲרָצוֹת אֲשֶׁר־הִדַּחְתִּי אֹתָם שָׁם מִכָּל "from of all

---

construe through their readings, and as they do so, to involve themselves in a didactic and ideologically-oriented thinking. Of course, even if one were to maintain that the MT drastically innovated here and departed from any previous denoted or connoted possible understanding of the verse in ancient Israel, it would still be worthy of study for the present purposes; after all, it had its own intended and primary rereaders. Significantly, it is always the book *as reread*, i.e., as understood by a community that was part and parcel of the community's authoritative written tradition, immaterial of whether such a reading was considered "proper" or "mistaken" by any other community. On these matters cf. B. Shuter, "Tradition as Rereading," in *Second Thoughts: A Focus on Rereading* (ed. D. Galef; Detroit: Wayne State University Press, 1998), 74–112. With Shutter, I have reservations on the usual dichotomy of *traditum* (i.e. the content of the tradition) and *traditio* (i.e. the process of transmission), because transmission not only makes whatever is transmitted "tradition" but also contributes much to the shaping of its meaning (through processes involving contingent "reading competence," see below) for a particular group. Cf. and partially contrast with the now classic, M. Fishbane, *Biblical Interpretation in Ancient Israel* (Oxford: Clarendon, 1985), passim.

26 The text here is essentially shared by the LXX and the MT. Both project an elevated image.
27 See L. Stulman, *Jeremiah*, 323.
28 Cf. Isa 43:5–6; see K. Baltzer, "Das Ende des Staates Juda und die Messias-Frage," in *Studien zur Theologie der alttestamentlichen Überlieferungen* (eds. R. Rendtorff and K. Koch; Neukirchen: Neukirchener Verlag, 1961), 33–43 (33–37); idem, *Deutero-Isaiah* (Hermeneia; Minneapolis: Augsburg Fortress, 2001), 160. For a very different position of the characterization of the period see W. McKane, *Jeremiah*, vol. 2, 1002–3.
29 See R. Albertz, *A History of Israelite Religion in the Old Testament Period*, vol. 1 (OTL; Louisville: Westminster John Knox, 1994), 242; idem, *Israel in Exile*, 6.
30 ... וּמִדַּלַּת הָאָרֶץ מֵאֲשֶׁר לֹא־הָגְלוּ בָּבֶלָה "those of the poorest of the land who had not been taken into exile to Babylon."

the lands where I have driven them there in 23:3, and the fact that the exchange between מִכָּל־הַמְּקֹמוֹת "from all the places" and מִכָּל הָאֲרָצוֹת "from all the lands" existed already in Jer 40:11–12. In other words, Gedaliah's community is skillfully portrayed as co-existing and to a large extent a result of exile, but at the same time as bearing the potential to overcome exile, at least a form of it, for the "remnant" of Judah, in Judah.[31]

An additional, positive feature of the construction of Gedaliah's community and his governorship is worth mentioning at this point. It appears as an aside in the following subunit, but it could hardly have been ignored when the rereaders of Jeremiah imagined and virtually revisited Gedaliah's community through their rereadings of the books. According to Jer 41:5, eighty people from Samaria, Shechem and Shiloh came to the House of the Lord bringing grain offerings and incense to present at the temple of YHWH. To be sure, they came with their beards shaved and their clothes torn, and their bodies gashed, but come they did. This image carried both an acknowledgment of the calamity that preceded the establishment of Gedaliah's polity, but also construed Gedaliah's governorship as one in which people from the main centers of northern Israel/Samaria came to YHWH's house[32] in Judah, such as in the days of Josiah, or, according to Chronicles, Hezekiah and Asa.[33] This construction of Gedaliah's polity skillfully balanced a sense of mourning with an idyllic scenario of an at least embryonic cultic reunification during his governorship.

It is worth noting that when a similar acknowledgment of the supremacy of Jerusalem appears in Zech 7:1–7–the delegation is from Bethel in this text–there is not only an allusion to the community of Gedaliah, but also a reference to a continuous remembering of this community and its fall (v. 5).[34] This being the

---

31 One may wonder also whether the exile of the elite that supported the rebellion against Babylon was not construed as particularly conducive to the creation of a remnant/polity with the potential to be pious, and blessed by YHWH. Cf. the sentiment in Zeph 3:11–13. See below.
32 The reference to בית יהוה in this context was most likely understood by the Jerusalem-centered literati responsible for the book(s) of Jeremiah as pointing to the place of the Jerusalemite temple. In any event, it is difficult to imagine that such a reading of the text would not have arisen within the process of continuous rereading of the book. For a different position see J. Weinberg, "Gedaliah."
33 Also cf. 2 Chr 11:13–17. For the position of Chronicles concerning Northern Israel see H. G. M. Williamson, *Israel in the Books of Chronicles* (Cambridge: Cambridge University Press, 1977); S. Japhet, *The Ideology of the Book of Chronicles and its Place in Biblical Thought* (2nd rev. ed.; BEATAJ 9; Frankfurt a. M.: Lang, 1997); E. Ben Zvi, *History, Literature and Theology in the Book of Chronicles* (London: Equinox, 2006).
34 I assume here that the reference to fasting and lamentation in the seventh month was understood as pointing to and constituted acts of remembering the assassination of Gedaliah (see

case, one may conclude that the literati responsible for Zech 7:5, who likely also lived in the Persian period, and their intended readers, had a highly elevated image of Gedaliah and his community, to the point that their loss was construed as worth of leading to a remembrance similar to that of the loss of the Temple and Jerusalem.[35]

It is also worth mentioning that Jer 40:10–12 communicates an understanding of "(the land of) Judah" that obviously includes Benjamin (see the references to Mizpah as its new center), and thus of "Benjaminites" who are construed as Judahites. Given the tensions between Benjamin and Judah/Jerusalem in at least the early Persian period, such an integrative world represents a fulfillment, retrojected into the past, of the desires of Persian period, Jerusalem-centered literati.[36] Again, there is something idyllic about such a construction of the community of Gedaliah.

As indicated above, the meaning of Jer 40:7–12 is strongly informed by its links to the preceding unit, namely Jer 40:1–6. The repetition of the motif of the appointment of Gedaliah by the Babylonian king (vv. 5, 7, 11) using consistently similar language, and not incidentally always followed in the narrative by a report about a positive Judahite response, bound the two subunits together. The reference to Mizpah (vv. 6, 10, 12) contributed to this sense of textual coherence. Moreover, the presence of a continuous series of *wyqtol* sentences across the boundary between the two units provided an unmistakable textually inscribed marker linking the two. All these features indicated to the intended and primary rereaders that they should see read, or at least include among their rereading, the text of vv. 7–12 as the continuation of vv. 1–6.

What issues emerged as consequence of this reading? First, the *wyqtol* sequence served now to alert the readers to continuity at the levels of plot and ideology. Thus, the text moves seamlessly from the report about Jeremiah's

---

Jer 41:1–3; 2 Kgs 25:25). This is a widely held position, and for good reason. For a recent treatment, see M. A. Sweeney, *The Twelve Prophets*, vol. 2 (Berit Olam; Collegeville, MN: Liturgical, 2000), 639–41. On these acts of remembrance (and the association with Gedaliah's murder) see also Y. Hoffman, "The Fasts in the Book of Zechariah and the Fashioning of National Remembrance," in *Judah and the Judeans in the Neo-Babylonian Period* (eds. O. Lipschits and J. Blenkinsopp; Winona Lake, Ind.: Eisenbrauns, 2003), 169–218. Cf. R. Albertz, *History of Israelite Religion*, vol. 1, 242.

35 See the reference to the fast and mourning in the fifth month (Zech 7:3, 5) and cf. 2 Kgs 25:8–9//Jer 52:12–13.

36 The point is strengthened by the association of the leader of the polity with Mizpah, that is, even the center in Mizpah/Benjamin acknowledges and internalizes this world.

choice to join the community and settling in it (v. 6),³⁷ to a report about a similar action taken by military leaders (vv. 7–8) and then by the general population. Thus, the text moves from prophetic to military leadership to general population, just in an order consistent with a hierarchy of legitimization.

To be sure, Jeremiah is not explicitly mentioned in vv. 7–12, or in Jer 40:13–41:18, for that matter. Although the lack of explicit reference to the prophet links the latter two units (see below), the rhetorical purposes of the lacking references are different. The text in vv. 7–12 is about Gedaliah's, not Jeremiah's, community. The prophet's choice legitimizes the polity and its leader (v. 6), just as Yhwh indirectly does so by means of prosperity and ingathering (vv. 11–12). Direct, human, political agency, which is at the center of the narrative here, however, belongs to Gedaliah and so he takes all the initiatives. At the same time, although neither Jeremiah nor Yhwh are directly mentioned in vv. 7–12, their positive presence is implied and construed as consistent with the actions taken by Gedaliah. In fact, one may describe Gedaliah in vv. 7–12 as a Jeremianic character insofar as his positions reflect closely those advocated by Jeremiah's attitude. Moreover, these positions are construed as a representation of Yhwh's word and thus, Gedaliah–like Jeremiah – is characterized as a godly personage associated and aligned with the deity.³⁸ In sum, the absence of explicit references to Yhwh and Jeremiah in vv. 7–12 concerns a rhetorical foregrounding of the central political figure and its positive characterization and a corresponding backgrounding of the legitimizing characters in these promising, dreamy times.

Since the prophet, the military/social leadership, and the people all rally around Gedaliah, and so seems to do Yhwh, and since Gedaliah is not only portrayed as the mediator between the king of Babylon and the people (v. 10), but also explicitly and emphatically characterized as the person whom the king of Babylon appointed and whose authority as governor derives from that of the

---

37 Of course, the book of Jeremiah contains another report about the release of Jeremiah by Nebuzaradan; see Jer 39:11–14. It is worth noting that, despite the differences between the account, and the fact that they asked their readers to visit different virtual sites of memory, both of them are consistent with the position that it was Jeremiah's choice to remain with Gedaliah (see Jer 39:11–12). The presence of different accounts/constructions of the same event is not peculiar to the book of Jeremiah, but a relatively common feature that appears also in ancient Israelite historiographical works (e.g. Judges and Samuel). Jeremiah's choice is consistent to a large extent with the portrayal of his "political" ideas in the book. "Gedaliah's modest, moderate regime seems to give concrete political embodiment to Jeremiah's expectations" (W. Brueggemann, *Jeremiah 26–52*, 166).

38 Cf. D. R. Jones, *Jeremiah* (NCB; Grand Rapids: Eerdmans, 1992), 469–70. Jones maintains that Gedaliah appears as an *alter ego* of Jeremiah.

Babylonian king, an ideological/rhetorical need to present these two central aspects of Gedaliah's characterization as not merely compatible, but supporting each other, arises. The matter demanded particular explanation since the empowering powers (the king of Babylon and his main representative, Nebuzaradan) were also directly associated in the minds of the rereaders with the destruction of Jerusalem and the burning of the temple.³⁹

The text in Jer 40 addresses the issue in two ways. First, there is the emphatic and consistent repetition of the sequence of a reference to Gedaliah's appointment followed by a report about a positive Judahite response. In fact, this sequence is one of the features that bind Jer 40:1–6 and Jer 40:7–12. Second, and more importantly, the text found a way to portray the foreign king who provided the legitimacy and authorization for the governorship of Gedaliah in a positive way. As in the case of the destruction of Jerusalem/Temple or the implementation of the exile, the king is represented by Nebuzaradan.⁴⁰ Like the virtuous foreign kings of Chronicles,⁴¹ Nebuzaradan is explicitly characterized as a pious foreigner leader, who not only acknowledge Yhwh's power and justice, but also thinks and talks like a pious Israelite/Judahite/Yehudite. In fact, according to Jer 40:2–3, Nebuzaradan thought and talked as a godly disciple of the prophet Jeremiah would have thought and talked.⁴²

Thus, within the discourse represented in the text, Jeremiah provides legitimacy to Gedaliah directly by choosing to settle in his community; but also indirectly, because Nebuzaradan–and therefore the king of Babylon as well–is imagined as a Jeremianic figure. Not accidentally, their Jeremianic character is communicated to the literati in Yehud through an instance of Yhwh's word to

---

39 2 Kgs 25:8–9//Jer 52:12–13.
40 2 Kgs 25:8–9 and Jer 52:12–13; 2 Kgs 25:11–12; Jer 39:9–10.
41 See E. Ben Zvi, *History, Literature and Theology in the Book of Chronicles*, 270–88; previously published as "When a Foreign Monarch Speaks," in *The Chronicler as Author: Studies in Text and Texture* (eds. M. P. Graham and S. L. McKenzie; JSOTSup 263; Sheffield: Sheffield Academic Press, 1999), 209–28.
42 "The author wants to persuade us that Nebuzaradan was a pupil of Jeremiah (40:2–3)." See K. A. D. Smelik, "The Function of Jeremiah 50 and 51 in the Book of Jeremiah," in *Reading the Book of Jeremiah: A Search for Coherence* (ed. M. Kessler; Winona Lake, Ind.: Eisenbrauns, 2004), 87–98 (citation from 97). Compare also Jer 40:2 with Jer 32:23. The question of how likely (or unlikely) it is that the historical Nebuzaradan would have uttered such a speech has bearing only on the historical reconstruction of the fall of Jerusalem, but not to any study of the world that the intended and primary rereaders of the book of Jeremiah, many years later after the events, were asked to and likely imagined through their reading and rereading of the book. From their perspective, it would have been unthinkable to imagine an unreliable narrator or a deceitful implied author in a text presented as Yhwh's word, accepted as such by them, and included in the book of Jeremiah.

Jeremiah (see 40:1), which in turn is available to them in a prophetic book associated with Jeremiah (i. e. the book of Jeremiah). Thus, the text textures a chain of links binding together in multiple ways the characters of YHWH, Jeremiah, Nebuzaradan, and Nebuchadnezzar...and all of them, in an empowering, authorizing way to Gedaliah.[43] All of this is consistent with an ideology in which the ultimate source of authority and legitimacy cannot be Jeremiah, Gedaliah, Nebuzaradan, or Nebuchadnezzar, but a deity whose "word" is available to the literati through the book of Jeremiah and similar books.[44]

Before moving forward, it is necessary to deal with the fact that even according to Jer 40:1, Nebuzaradan is associated with the exile of בְּבָלָה הַמֻּגְלִים וִיהוּדָה יְרוּשָׁלַם כָּל־גָּלוּת "all the exiles of Jerusalem and Judah who were being exiled to Babylon." One may wonder, however, whether the text was not read from a perspective informed by the ideological theme of a poor, humble (and pious) remnant, which assumes the necessity of the exile/removal of sinful elites from Judah/Jerusalem and sees it as an essential requirement for life under YHWH's blessing in the land (cf. Zeph 3:11–13). Converging evidence supporting the fact that the implied and primary rereaders were asked to approach the text here from this particular ideological perspective includes: (a) the characterization of Gedaliah's community as including דַּלַּת הָאָרֶץ "the poorest of the land" (v. 7)[45]; (b) the reference to the taking over of cities, which assumes that members of Gedaliah's community did not have power over them before; (c) the basic fact that these readers knew that had the king remained in the land, Gedaliah could not have been appointed governor; and (d) that the community failed because people such as Ishmael son of Nethaniah, a Davide,[46] were not exiled to Baby-

---

[43] It is worth stressing that the characterization of Nebuzaradan (and indirectly, Nebuchadnezzar) in Jer 40:2–3, 12 is different from the elevated figure of Nebuchadnezzar in other sections of the book of Jeremiah (e. g. Jer 25:1–14; Jer 27), even if Nebuchadnezzar is explicitly referred to as YHWH's servant (Jer 25:9; 27:6). In none of these texts is Nebuchadnezzar portrayed as a Jeremianic figure. On these elevated (but not Jeremianic) characterizations of Nebuchadnezzar in the book of Jeremiah, see J. Hill, "'Your Exile Will Be Long': The Book of Jeremiah and the Unended Exile," in *Reading the Book of Jeremiah: A Search for Coherence* (ed. M. Kessler; Winona Lake, Ind.: Eisenbrauns, 2004), 149–61 (152–56); and esp. J. Hill, *Friend or Foe? The Figure of Babylon in the Book of Jeremiah MT* (BibInt Series; Leiden: Brill, 1999), 103–10, 130–39, 198–99, 203–5.

[44] Given other constructions of the image of the Babylonian king among the literati of Yehud, it is not surprising that the book of Jeremiah includes also Jer 50–52, and in fact concludes with them in the MT version.

[45] Cf. Jer 39:10.

[46] מִזֶּרַע הַמְּלוּכָה "from the royal family" (Jer 41:1). The characterization of Ishmael as a Davide is important in the text; "the exploits of Ishmael-ben-Nethaniah-ben-Elishama (Jer. xl 13–xli 18)

lon. In addition, the language of "remnant" (v. 11) carries in itself, by logical necessity, the notion of exile or removal of the majority. To place hope in the character of a remnant that follows Yhwh, is to view exile as a necessary step. To overcome exile in the land goes, in this discourse, hand in hand with maintaining exile outside the land. This tension was imagined to be as resolvable only when a second utopia (the first concerns the pious remnant) would become reality, in the far future.

Of course, the literati who read and reread Jer 40:7–12 were well aware that Gedaliah's community collapsed. Thus, it is not surprising that Jer 40:7–12 is deeply interwoven not only with the immediately preceding unit (Jer 40:1–6), but also the following one (Jer 40:13–41:18). Explicit text markers of cohesion such as the transition in v. 12, the shared repertoire of main characters, the lack of any explicit reference to Jeremiah, and a sense of continuing plot all contributed to explicitly mark Jer 40:7–12 as deeply associated with 40:13–41:18 and communicated to the intended and primary rereaderships of Jer 40:7–12 that they should read the text in a way informed by the ensuing narrative in the book of Jeremiah.

As the ancient rereaders of Jer 40:7–12 imagined and revisited in their minds Gedaliah's polity, as they paid close attention to and rejoiced in the high hopes for stability and prosperity, they could not avoid the thought that all these great expectations were *all* dashed by the tragic collapse of Gedaliah's community. The elevated portrayal of the community in the text and the readers' imagination serves to increase the emotive impact of its fall. It is not by chance that neither Jeremiah nor Yhwh are explicitly referred to in Jer 40:13–41:18. The world portrayed in 40:13–41:18 is one of shattering of dreams, of lost potential, of blood and violence. Their absence contributes a sense of divine occultation or hiddenness, of unmitigated chaos, and enhances further the emotive impact of the narrative.[47]

---

complete the picture of the House of David's inimical opposition to Yahweh's purposes" (J. Applegate, "The Fall of Zedekiah: Redactional Debate in the Book of Jeremiah, Part 1," in *VT* 48 (1998): 137–60 (142). For the suggestion that the story of Ishamael and Gedaliah overturns as it were the story of David and Saul, see G. E. Yates, "Ishmael's Assassination of Gedaliah: Echoes of the Saul-David Story in Jeremiah 40:7–41:1–18," in *WTJ* 67 (2005): 103–13.

47 Cf. L. Stulman, *Jeremiah*, 326–29.

Back to Counterfactual Memory

Memories of past elevated hopes that not only were never fulfilled, but that led to a dystopian situation following a tragic event are the most common material for counterfactual questions. What if the tragic event might have been averted? What if the elevated hopes had been fulfilled, even if only partially? Albertz clearly engages in counterfactual thinking when he writes:

Certainly, we do not know what would have become of this experiment [Gedaliah's polity] had it had time to develop longer. Possibly the social and religious history of Israel would have taken a different course ... Only as a result of it [the murder of Gedaliah] did the history of Israel as a state break off completely after more than 400 years. The darkness of the exilic period fell over people and land.[48]

Albertz, however, is not alone. In fact, he is simply responding to the implied questions raised by the text. There is much reason to assume that the literati who read, continuously reread, and pondered about the lessons to be learned from Jer 40:7–12 would have also responded to the implied invitation of the text to engage in such counterfactual thinking. In fact, it hardly seems possible that these literati virtually visited their constructed community of Gedaliah and identified with him–as the implied author asked them to do–and never engaged with "what if" questions.

Given the issues involved and the authority of the prophetic books among the ancient literati, and the considerations advanced above about counterfactual thinking, any reading of Jer 40:1–12 by these literati that was strongly informed by counterfactual motifs must have interacted and involved central aspects of their intellectual, ideological discourse. This is so, because as pointed out in section one, there exists a relationship between counterfactual historical thinking and the construction of the present by those involved in imagining alternative scenarios in the past. Moreover, one has to take into account that simulated past trajectories play a necessary, cognitive role and have important instructional bearings, and that this type of thinking cannot but raise and discuss issues of historical causality.

In fact, readings strongly informed by a counterfactual approach most likely carried important ideological implications within the discourse of the literati of Yehud. For instance, they could not have missed that had Gedaliah's community survived, it would have looked very similar to the literati's Persian period society. "Serve the king of Babylon/Persia and it will go well with you" is certainly a text

---

48 R. Albertz, *History of Israelite Religion*, vol. 1, 242.

that talked about their own situation. The same holds for the idea that a governor may be appointed by a foreign, imperial king, or that a foreign, imperial king may actually be associated with Yhwh (see the construction of Cyrus; if a foreign king may order the rebuilding of Temple, he may certainly appoint governors).

In other words, neo-Babylonian Yehud would have been similar to a Persian Yehud. Of course, as historians we know today that such was the historical case, but from the perspective of literati who internalized a concept of Exile and Return and the related image of the empty land (see Jer 43:5–7), the only way to entertain such thoughts was through a playful, though ideologically significant, counterfactual memory.

Of course, as the literati did so, given that Gedaliah's community was imagined in idyllic terms, they could not but retroject into that past community that looked like theirs some of the expectations of their own Jerusalem-centered, Yehudite discourse–among them, a Judah that includes Benjamin, and whose cultic center is in Yhwh's house in Jerusalem, a world in which people from the province of Samaria would accept the centrality of Jerusalem.

Other aspects of their ideological discourse come to light through the examination of this counterfactual, alternate memory. Had Gedaliah's community remained in the land and fulfilled its hope, to some extent they would have overcome exile, that is, they would have lived safely in the land, enjoyed Yhwh's blessing and the related bounty of their land. Yet, other Judahites would have remained in Babylon. Again, the counterfactual world was construed as somewhat similar to the circumstances of the literati's times. People have returned to the land, the temple has been rebuilt, and anxiety over a potential, future, communal exile from it has vanished. Although they did not necessarily see themselves as living under Yhwh's blessing or fully overcoming exile, some postexilic traits existed in Yehud and co-existed with exile in Babylon.

But what if, in at least some of their rereading, these literati took a more radical path and followed the cue of textually inscribed references such as אֲשֶׁר בְּכָל־הָאֲרָצוֹת, "in all the (other) lands" (v. 11) or the following verse, וַיָּשֻׁבוּ כָל־הַיְּהוּדִים מִכָּל־הַמְּקֹמוֹת אֲשֶׁר נִדְּחוּ־שָׁם וַיָּבֹאוּ אֶרֶץ־יְהוּדָה "*all* the *Judahites* returned from *all* the places to which they had been scattered and came to the *land of Judah*" (v. 12)? What if Gedaliah's success would have involved the creation of a community much larger than the literati's and a real "return," even if some people remained in exile? After all, some were exiled with Jehoiachin, but Israel did not go into exile at the time. In addition, of course, unlike Zedekiah's polity, Gedaliah's would have been pious, blessed by Yhwh, and fundamentally stable, because it aligned itself with Yhwh's will, both internally and in terms of foreign, vassal relations. Within this scenario, Israel/Judah would have never gone into "exile," and would have prospered under Yhwh and the king to whom Yhwh had given power. But if Israel/Judah never went into exile, then it could have never returned, and as a consequence, the central ideological metanarrative of exile and return would have no place in Israel's discourse. The authoritative repertoire of books and readings[49] held by the community would have had then a substantially different profile. Since the books and readings are Yhwh's word, then Yhwh's word had to be considered at least potentially contingent. Had it been a different history, then a different set of Yhwh's words would have existed.[50]

But could a different history have occurred? As mentioned above, counterfactual historical thought brings up by necessity questions of causality. Could have it worked for Gedaliah's group? The literati, as almost any imaginable reader of the text, could not have failed to note the presence of a strong, explicit trend in Jer 40:13–41:18 that emphasized human agency. Gedaliah is consistently portrayed as someone who made a tragic mistake and paid with his life and the life of his polity for it. Exile and catastrophe came to Israel/Judah, according to this line of thought, because of a leader's inability to believe ill of a sinner (Ishmael), recognize the true speech of a pious person (Johanan), and act accordingly (Jer 40:15–16).[51]

But was this the entire story? Did the ancient literati in Yehud understand history as only a matter of human agency? It is extremely unlikely that the literati understood historical causality only in human terms. Not only would this have been a unique instance in ancient historiography, but it would have been at odds with the literati's very understanding of the world and of their deity. Both the so-called DtrH and Chronicles balanced human agency with divine determination,[52] as in all prophetic books. Gedaliah had freedom to act and fail, but Yhwh knew already that Israel will go into exile.[53]

---

[49] As mentioned above, it is the book *as reread* by a community that is part and parcel of the core of its sacred textual tradition.
[50] Is Albertz thinking, at least in part, of this scenario, when he engages in his own counterhistorical thinking?
[51] The basic issue involved in the mistake is of the type often discussed in wisdom literature.
[52] See my "Are There Any Bridges Out There? How Wide Was the Conceptual Gap Between the Deuteronomistic History and Chronicles?" in *Community Identity in Judean Historiography: Biblical and Comparative Perspectives* (eds. G. N. Knoppers and K. Ristau; Winona Lake, Ind.: Eisenbrauns, 2009), 59–86; and "Observations on Josiah's Account in Chronicles and Implications for Reconstructing the Worldview of the Chronicler," in *Essays on Ancient Israel in Its Near Eastern Context: A Tribute to Nadav Na'aman* (eds. Y. Amit, E. Ben Zvi, I. Finkelstein and O. Lipschits; Winona Lake, Ind.: Eisenbrauns, 2006), 89–106.
[53] This may be why Chronicles erased references to memories of Gedaliah in its own account. After all, the land had to "make up for its Sabbaths" (2 Chr 36:20–21) and could not have done

As mentioned above, counterfactual thinking allows people to attempt to reconstruct the view of historical agents. Did the literati imagine Gedaliah as thinking that he alone decided on the course of action he has taken, or that he thought that no matter which decision he would take, it would fit somehow into some divinely established path, unbeknownst to him or any of his contemporaries? The second option is far more likely, and by itself carries also implications about their own understanding of themselves and its manifestation through their identification with Gedaliah, as they imagined him to be.

In sum, the literati's exploration of an important counterfactual memory following the cue of Jer 40:1–12 led them to discuss, among many others, matters of human agency and historical/divine determinism in relation to exile, to explore the concept of exile in terms of contingency and the implications of such considerations, to reflect on the very boundaries of the concept of exile, remnant, inside and outside the land and their interrelations, and to examine aspects of their own society through the mirror of one that failed to exist in their memories, though existed to a large extent in history. The analysis of counterfactual memories in ancient Israel provides a powerful tool that can help us to reconstruct aspects of the intellectual discourse in Yehud, including its concept of exile.[54]

---

so had Gedaliah's community been successful. It is worth noting the erasure, although it refers to Jeremiah in the relevant text, advocates a double, human/divine agency, and maintains that the exile that eventually resulted did not change a thing in what matters most, since the rules governing Yhwh's relationship with Israel, and Yhwh's instructions remained unchanged. Of course, these issues go beyond the limits of this essay and require a separate discussion.

[54] This is only one illustration of the potential that studies on counterfactual memory in ancient Israel have for the reconstruction of the intellectual history in particular and for that of the history of ancient Israel in general. I hope more studies of this type will be developed in the coming years.

Potential Intersections Between Research Frames Informed by Social-Memory and 'Bourdieusian' Approaches/Concepts: The Study of Socio-Historical Features of the Literati of the early Second Temple Period

Introduction

The goal of this chapter is to explore potential intersections and dialogues between these two research frames/approaches (i.e., social memory and Bourdieusian), both in terms of what they may might contribute to the study of socio-historical characteristics of the literati of the late Persian/Early Hellenistic Period and in terms of the potential significance of some, even partial, convergences.[1]

Thus, in what follows I will address issues such as 'cultural capital,' 'memory capital,' habitus, social mindscape, taste, grammars of preference, literatidicy (as a form of sociodicy), power, Temple controls and the possibility of effecting social change, and the related matter of social reproduction, insofar as they facilitate our understanding of the mentioned literati. Towards the end of this contribution I will address some methodological implications of convergences and intersections between Social Memory and Bourdieusian approaches for furthering studies on socio-historical characteristics of the literati in Yehud/Judah at the time and as a group.

---

[1] For a clear example of Bourdieusian approaches to these matters, see, e.g., Amy Erickson, "Jonah and the Scribal *Habitus*," David J. Chalcraft, Frauke Uhlenbruch and Rebecca S. Watson (eds.) *Methods, Theories, Imaginations: Social Scientific Approaches in Biblical Studies* (Bible in the Modern World, 60; Sheffield: Sheffield Phoenix, 2014), 59–78. This chapter emerged out of two talks on these matters, one at a Symposium on Bourdieu and Biblical Studies held in Oslo (September 2014) and the other at the PNW-SBL meeting held in Calgary (2017). I thank the participants at these meetings for their questions and feedback and Terje Stordalen, in particular, for inviting me to the first of these two meetings and asking me to deal with these questions. Basic understanding of Bourdieu's conceptual framework is assumed throughout the chapter. Those interested in further readings on Bourdieu's thought, may consult, *inter alia*, Pierre Bourdieu, *Distinction: A Social Critique of the Judgement of Taste* (transl. Richard Nice; London: Routledge & Kegan Paul, 1986); idem, *Homo Academicus* (transl. Peter Collier; Stanford, CA: Stanford University Press, 1988); idem, *The Logic of Practice* (transl. Richard Nice; Stanford, CA: Stanford University Press, 1980); idem, *The Field of Cultural Production* (ed. and introduced Randal Johnson; New York, NY: Columbia University Press, 1993), and, of course, his original works in French. Needless to say, the corpus of studies on Bourdieu's thought is extremely vast.

Before addressing these matters, a few general remarks on matters of contingency and applicability are in order. A common challenge that often confronts current social-anthropological models as they are applied to the study of ancient Israel is particularly relevant to research strongly informed by both concepts such as social memory or social mindscape and Bourdieusian approached. The basic matter relates to concerns raises about the use of conceptual and methodological frameworks that (a) emerged out of, were aimed at, and overwhelmingly used for understanding contemporary societies for a better understanding of ancient societies, and relatedly (b) arose to deal with and make sense of data drastically different from that exists about ancient societies.[2]

Bourdieu's conceptual framework emerged out of studies of society in mid-late 20th century France and there is no doubt that it was deeply interwoven into a very particular, historically contingent discourse. Although Memory Studies, as an academic field of studies, goes back to the first half of the 20th century, it flourished mainly in the last decades, and both its emergence and later flourishing are closely inter-related with sets of historically contingent discourses.

The kind and extent of historical sources accessible to researchers in a particular area/topic cannot but have a significant impact on the pragmatic range of approaches that these scholars may use. There is a most substantial, qualitative gap between the world of potential 'data' for the study of the intellectual world of the literati in Yehud—the main sources are sets of books—and for that of the groups studied by Bourdieu, or for that matter, by other contemporary sociologists, social-anthropologists, as well as most memory studies scholars or historians whose research focuses on relatively recent periods, such as the 20th century or even the long 19th century, for that matter.[3]

These observations may seem too self-evident, but their underlying implications are not. The reason is that if theoretical models that emerged from studies recent and contemporary societies and approaches that have emerged to construe, organize and 'make sense' of 'data' 'gathered' from a wealth of sources

---

[2] Similar considerations apply, for instance, to any research on ancient Israel that is grounded on such widely used concepts as 'hybridity' or 'third space.'

[3] The type of sources available to the historians of the world of ideas of the (ideologically) Jerusalemite centered literati of the late Persian/early Hellenistic period is to a large extent restricted to a relatively narrow number of written sources. In fact, historians who desire to construct a reconstruction of the world of knowledge of the mentioned literati, including their memoryscape, have no alternative but to infer them, mostly, from those of the constructed target literary (re)readerships of a textual repertoire that is likely to be representative in broad strokes of the core repertoire of the historical literati. In terms of general approach, cf. David Kraemer, "The Intended Reader as a Key to Interpreting the Bavli," *Prooftexts* 13 (1993), 125–140.

and from types of sources drastically different from those of ancient societies are indeed heuristically helpful for reconstructing the social history of the latter, even if in some 'fine-tuned' manner, this would say something about the role and place of *trans-cultural* tendencies in social-anthropology and historical analysis? In the case of historians—which is the closest to my own heart, this cannot but say something, even if indirectly on matters of both historical contingency and its limits, particularly in terms of the potential roles of some trans-contingent, even if always historically contingently manifested tendencies. These matters bear on issues of history, historiography, and I would add, on the formation, development and social reproduction of historical worlds of social memory.

But, alternatively, if the sole matter linking such extremely diverse groups and societies has nothing to do with them themselves, but only with desires of contemporary researchers, even unbeknownst to them, to 'universalize' the approaches they happen to like, and thus express their desire 'conquer' via their scholarly constructions of human societies in the past, then proceeding in this way would only serve to undermine 'otherness' through partial assimilation of these older societies to the researchers' anticipated 'norms.'

Clearly these are not marginal matters, but at the core of any methodologically self-reflective approach to scholarly reconstructions of ancient societies. Studies like the one advanced here contribute to an informed dialogue on these issues.

Brief Survey of Some Aspects of the World of the Mentioned Literati

In the next section, which represents the core of this essay, consists of observations meant to open a substantial conversation about potential intersections between research frameworks informed by Social-Memory and 'Bourdieusian' approaches and concepts. These observations, however, require some knowledge of the historical world of the mentioned literati.

Although there is room for a debate on possible late monarchic period forerunners of some of the books that were eventually included in the Hebrew Bible, there is general agreement among historians of ancient Israel that by the late Persian period/early Hellenistic period in Yehud/Judah there existed a particular repertoire of books that included, *inter alia*, the pentateuchal books, the deuteronomistic historical collection, the prophetic book collection, Chronicles, Ruth, Lamentations, possibly Proverbs and many Psalms. It is reasonable to assume that on the whole (a) the present *forms* of these books[4] and collections of books are on the whole representative of the texts read by the literati in Yehud at that time and (b) this repertoire as a whole is reasonably representative of the core repertoire of these literati, that is, what they considered to be their authoritative repertoire of textual repertoire. [5]

This authoritative repertoire consisted of an open, flexible literary 'canon' that served didactic, socializing roles. The dynamic aspect of this 'canon' is particularly worth stressing. The texts were often multivocal and existed at least at times in more than one version. They were collections of works, but they often had areas of overlap and some books were likely included in more than collection of books (e.g., the Pentateuch, the Hexateuch, the Deuteronomic Historical Collection, hereafter, DHC; the Prophetic Book Collection [Isaiah-Malachi], hereafter PBC], the Primary Historical Collection or Enneateuch [Gen-2Kings]). Since whether a book was read as part of a collection or another or by itself impacted the way in which was read, this allowed the relevant books to read in multiple, complementary ways.[6]

---

[4] Note the plural.

[5] The term 'authoritative' is not meant to evoke the later concept of canon, or of canonicity. The point I want to make is that in the late Persian/early Hellenistic period there existed a particular group of individuals who served, within the constructed world in which they imagined themselves to be, as *authorities* selecting, composing, redacting, shaping, reading, rereading and even developing the literary genres of what they construed as the 'core repertoire' of texts for Israel. This repertoire was in their sight 'authoritative' because in one way or another they associated the relevant texts included in it (even if in various instantiations) with godly instruction and thus linked in one way or another to a character Yhwh, who in their ideological world transcended their own social location, but with whom they wished to partially identify and whose voice they voiced through acts of writing and reading (*imago dei*). These texts were, for them, both godly and didactic and they stood at the center of their image of a textually centred 'Israel', with whom they identified. The texts were authoritative because they 'embodied' and communicated within the world of these literati, even if indirectly, the authority of Yhwh and Yhwh's didactic works and their messages for the community, and of those writing, editing, copying, shaping and reshaping, interpreting and voicing them.

[6] For instance, reading Ruth as part of the DHC meant balancing the main metanarrative in the last chapters of Judges that serve, inter alia, to construe a memory of a horrific and horrifying period as the background for the necessary establishment of a true king (i.e., David), with that an image and memory of a peaceful period of Judges characterized by substantial personal safety (note the cross-cultural image of women travelling distances alone and unmolested), but which still leads to David, though on different grounds. Here like in the case of reading Joshua as an integral part of the Hexateuch or not makes a difference to both the way in which the book and collection, as a whole, are read and understood. The outcome in all these cases is similar, namely complementary polyvalence emerges. (Cf. the case of reading Deuteronomy *also* as a prophetic book.)

In addition, redactional processes were at work and at times reshaped texts or versions of texts. New works could be added to the repertoire and, in some cases, these new texts shaped memories that interacted, informed and were informed by memories shaped by other texts already existing in the repertoire. Moreover, and to be stressed, what was authoritative were the 'read' texts, that is the texts as read by the community, which were in turn flexible, multiple, multivalent and always informed and informing each other within the repertoire. There is no doubt that the creation of such a dynamic and flexible corpus of read texts involved very high cognitive costs.

Of course, the same can be said of the complex array of social memories evoked through the reading of these text. This is a group with two co-existing 'national' histories, each going back to the creation of the world, with multiple prophetic characters that served each as sites of memory, even if they are associated with similar periods, with, at least, two founders of the temple and more than one main myth of origin. All this is contrary to transcultural tendencies towards 'oneness' in social memory and most significantly, all this takes place within a very small group and relatively homogeneous, at least from a social perspective, group of literati. Why would there be a strong systemic preference for very high cognitive costs in such a group?

I will return to this system of preferences. But first I would like to emphasize some basic social pre-requisites for the existence of such a group. For one, these relatively few literati had to be trained. Obviously, to fulfill their 'job,' they had to learn how to write, edit and proficiently read the appropriate works.[7] To learn how to write and read proficiently, the literati in training had to become aware of the different literary genres in their repertoire, and their main literary and linguistic features. To do so, students had to actually read, and study works written in these genres. Of course, this process of learning by reading, studying—probably including some memorizing—taught the students more than reading (and writing) competence. The continuous involvement with, at least partial internalization of these works along with their 'proper', though often interwoven in multiple ways, interpretations served to inculcate in the literati social and ideological norms.

---

7 Of course, "proficiency" is a socially-contingent category. To read a text proficiently within a particular community means reading the text in a way consistent with the expectations and interpretative rules that govern such activity within the community. Thus, for instance, a proficient reading of the book of Habakkuk among the followers of the Teacher of Righteousness is certainly very different from what would count as proficient reading of the book in any community today.

In fact, from a social viewpoint that the main goal of this education was to shape the minds of these literati in training in a way consonant with the ideology of their social-cultural center, both in direct, explicit ways and more importantly, indirectly by imprinting in them, among others, a set of terms, images and metaphors, a fully developed 'language' with which to understand 'naturally' the world and their role in them.

Moreover, as through the process of education in this cultural system became more and more 'natural' and 'moral' to them, it is most likely that they developed self-policing tendencies so as to keep (substantial) deviancy or the potential of (substantial) deviancy at bay.[8]

Whether the actual instruction was from a father or father figure, to sons, or son-figures, in a private home/school or at some (central) room in the temple; whether instruction was directly under control of, and administrated by the temple, or indirectly controlled by the temple through the internalization of the temple ideology/worldviews among individual Jerusalemite teachers/masters, many of whom were priests or at least involved in the temple; there is no doubt that the end result of this educational process would have been the 'production' of a necessarily small, but from a sociological perspective, relatively homogeneous group evolving out of a relatively homogeneous learning process.

There is much of this learning process that one cannot reconstruct. But one knows, for instance, that these few literati learned how to read texts, even if one cannot identify with any certainty which ones were learned first and which later. One may safely assume that memorization played some role in text acculturation, though not necessarily the same one in the different phases of the educational process those literati would have to pass through. For instance, it is likely that memorization played a more important role in earlier than later stages of the process. Given the ideological emphasis on written texts and the aura surrounding 'sacred' written texts in the discourses of Achaemenid period Yehud, and given that the literati were taught how to write, edit and proficiently *read written texts*, one cannot but conclude that at some point, and likely at the more advanced level, the written texts took center stage in the educational curriculum.[9]

---

[8] This is the most reasonable, given general transcultural roles of education, and that the social role of these writers, readers, rereaders and readers to others of the central texts of the community was to ideologically sustain the community and socialize its members into what were deemed to be acceptable worldviews by the center.

[9] An ongoing conversation on matters of memorization and its roles in ancient Israel emerged in the field of Hebrew Bible following the publication of David Carr, *Writing on the Tablet of the Heart: Origins of Scripture and Literature* (Oxford: Oxford University Press, 2005). This is not the place to engage the entire gamut of issues associated with this conversation. This said, as men-

Moreover, it is possible to reconstruct a likely image of their central educational canon. To learn how to properly write or 'edit' and to proficiently read works in various literary genres, the (future) literati had to get acquainted and to achieve this goal, they had to carefully read works written in, and often playing with the relevant genres and their conventions. Thus, it is very likely that the (high level) literati's scholarly, educational curriculum as a whole had to include all the major literary genres that were central to the cultural and religious discourse of their community and which participated in the aforementioned core repertoire. In other words, the (future) literati had to learn different types of psalms, proverbs, prophetic texts, historical texts and the like. Moreover, since the point of the educational process was meant to imprint their minds with the worldview of Jerusalem-centered Yehud, and to turn them into upholders and developers of the constructed, communal memory of their ideological center, one must assume that most if not all of the authoritative texts of that center were learned and studied. If in ancient Mesopotamia, textbooks of the scribal curriculum became part of cultural canons,[10] in Yehudite Jerusalem the authoritative, written texts were the formative 'textbooks' at least at the core of the advanced level studies of the literati and vice versa, 'textbooks' were likely to become authoritative.[11]

Of course, the mentioned education of the literati involved social resources. Even if the literati were few, resources had to be invested in their education, and later, on the maintenance of such group and its learned activities. These resources involved not only substantial time for the higher level of studies and later for ongoing reading, re-reading, composing, editing and re-editing and copying, but also the existence of some 'library' that included on the one hand a physical space and the relevant physical scrolls, but also a set of conceptual rules governing and organizing its contents. The latter involved matters such as ways for recalling scrolls, such as titles/incipits, which often served also as introductions, and at times also colophons. It is worth stressing that at times a scroll may in-

---

tioned above, the written text played at least in the world imagined by these literati (/scribes) also a very substantial role (see, e.g., Exod 31:18; Deut 9:10; 17:18–19; 2 Kgs 14:6; 22–23; 2 Chr 17:9; Neh 8).

10 Cf. Karel van der Toorn, *Scribal Culture and the Making of the Hebrew Bible* (Cambridge, Mass.: Harvard University Press, 2007), 244–47. For a survey of the production and dissemination of scholarly knowledge in Mesopotamia—including training—and bibliography see Eleanor Robson, "The Production and Dissemination of Scholarly Knowledge," in K. Radner and E. Robson (eds.), *The Oxford Handbook of Cuneiform Culture* (Oxford: Oxford University Press, 2011), 557–576. Of course, the circumstances in Mesopotamia were very different from those in Persian period Yehud.

11 Of course, the process could still have worked both ways. Cf. van der Toorn, *Scribal Culture*.

clude more than one 'book' and one single work may include a title and a number of subtitles. Moreover, as mentioned above, collections served as 'shelves of the mind' and had overlaps. In any event, even in these matters, the systemic preference for high complexity was full at work.

Clearly, the existence of a temple in Jerusalem and the process that led to its growing importance in the province of Yehud, of which it eventually becomes its acknowledged center towards the end of the Persian period and later in the early Hellenistic period, and the existence of a Persian system that facilitated this very process—beginning already with its allowing the building of the temple—were important and, given the low resources of the province, necessary conditions for the existence of the mentioned literati. Bourdieu would maintain that academics—and the entire educational system of which they are an integral part—need the state. I would maintain the existence, generation after generation, of this cadre of literati needed the temple and indirectly the empire.[12] At the same time, it is obvious that neither temple nor empire were sufficient conditions for the development of the mentioned literati or their authoritative repertoire. Other factors have to be examined to explain these matters historically and sociologically.

Likewise, as important as the complex interactions between Jerusalemite Yehud and Samaria, working at multiple levels,[13] were for the shape of the core of ideological, mnemonic and narrative components of the messages communicated by the authoritative repertoire of the Yehudite literati, focusing on them alone would only fail to shed light on many significant socio-historical aspects of the literati's world.

I would argue that at the very least, heuristically, it is better to approach them from a perspective informed by social and socio-anthropological trans-cultural studies: a matter that leads me directly a series of observations and explorations directly related to the core matter of this essay.

---

12 Elsewhere I elaborated on this point and the related one of the influence that this relation with the temple, and indirectly with empire, had on some aspects of the literati's repertoire; from the more obvious such as its strong Jerusalem-centredness, the general lack of negative references to the Achaemenid empire, to the less obvious such as the ways in which this repertoire is involved in processes of local cultural resistance, hybridity and utopianizing images of YHWH's imperial kingdom. See, e.g., "The Yehudite Collection of Prophetic Books and Imperial Contexts: Some Observations," in this volume, pp. 134–61.

13 From, e.g., shared priest families to ideological boundaries, from shared texts to un-sharable interpretations of these texts (e.g., the Pentateuch).

A Network of Selected Observations On Cultural and Memory Capital

There can be no doubt that the literati possessed 'cultural capital.' They had unequal, and to a large extent monopolistic access to a corpus of core literature, i.e. 'cultural goods'. If others wanted to have access to it, they had to receive it in a partial and interpreted form by the literati, who were not only gatekeepers of these goods but also both its producers and 'users'.

One may also talk of institutionalized goods at work in this field, for although the literati did not receive 'degrees' in any modern sense, they were likely recognizable products of a learning system, and for the most advanced a lifelong learning (informal, but still 'real' system). There was an unequal distribution of cultural resources or goods, as in any other ancient society.

There is room also for discussing the financing of the education of the literati and their production of goods in terms of transformation of economic capital into cultural capital and discuss the impact of scarcity (i.e., the low number of literati) in their social status and impact.

In addition, there is the matter of the transformation of cultural capital into social capital that is directly impacted by value assigned to cultural capital or better particular types of cultural capital in society, since transformation of capital require some form of implied exchange rate.[14]

A focus on memory studies would bring particular attention to the issue of 'memory capital.' Although memory capital might be included within the general category of 'cultural capital', it has its own distinct elements as an individual and above all, in our case, as group asset in the general memory market of a society. Wearing Bourdieusian lenses allow historians of ancient Israel informed by Memory Studies to perceive and then focus on the question of how memory markets worked in this period. In other words, these lenses facilitate the development of a set of research questions. For instance, the memory market never lacks memories. To make the memories held by the literati valuable for the community as a whole or its leadership at least, required 'marketing' within the general memory market of the population. This meant, for instance, fostering what we may call a niche market about memories of the community as a whole—as

---

14 This process is transcultural. For instance, the current downturn in the number of students in the humanities in contemporary Western societies is directly associated with a presently 'widely agreed' reduced exchange rate for the cultural capital obtained by studying humanities. Cf. John Guillory, *Cultural Capital: The Problem of Literary Canon Formation* (Chicago/London: University of Chicago Press, 1993). See "the professional-managerial class ...no longer requires the (primarily literary) cultural capital of the old the bourgeoisie" (op. cit, p. xii).

opposed to personal or sub-group memories— and increasing its mindshare.[15] One may approach cultic events, rituals and public readings from this perspective. Significantly, the same holds true for the world in which the literati lived and for the past worlds they imagined and which in various ways intersected and interacted with their own.

In addition, such an approach would lead to research questions about 'memory embodying goods' seemingly open to all (e. g., ruins of monarchic Jerusalem, the temple as a building), but whose significance is construed on the grounds of mnemonic narratives, or those that are not open to all, though discursively are presented as belong to the entire community such as books embodying and encoding memory.

In any event, it is worth noting that for memory capital to be worthwhile, it has to be partially, carefully and in a controlled way spent in the market. Enough of it must be spent so the 'others' should be able to understand its value and not too much to challenge the unequal distribution of assets in that market. After all, the literati as a group are bound to keep their own memory capital.

Reflecting on the Use of the term Capital for the Study of Ancient Societies and the Literati of the Early Second Temple Period

Concepts such as cultural, social, symbolic, mnemonic, body (including, but not limited to sexual), and so on, 'capital' are helpful to scholars in multiple areas and for the study of various historical societies, including ancient societies and groups within them, precisely because the term 'capital' evokes images of exchanges and markets, of unequal social distribution of 'goods', and of deploying capital by those who have it for various purposes that they deem appropriate to achieve their goals that. Using the set of 'capital' terms (and evoking the concept of 'capital') is indeed heuristically more helpful than, for instance, using cultural terms such as cultural wealth, social recognition, or the like.

In addition, occasionally, other benefits might come about from evoking the 'capital' concept. For Bourdieu the use of the term 'cultural capital' and the like served rhetorically as a call to his fellow intellectuals to distance themselves from and be critical of rarified, idealized and lionized concepts of (high) 'culture'

---

15 On these issues, from a complementary perspective, see the observations on the matter of literatidicy below.

that served them so well.¹⁶ To be sure, the terms he used were particularly suited to the intended addressees of his academic work, within his historical situation, social location, general politico-cultural mission and the matters that they evoke (e.g., 'capitalism'. But, one may argue that in the field of ancient Israelite history (and in the related field of Biblical Studies) there is still, among some scholars, a rarefication and idealization of the cultural goods of the literate, that is, 'biblical books', due to theological, historical and sociological reasons that may be similarly addressed.

All this said, the unavoidable question about the 'costs' involved in using a model rooted in the experience of contemporary 'capitalism' and Western capitalistic societies, such as France, be used to study a very different and clearly not a 'capitalistic' society or some groups within it remains. Can they be used without bringing about, at least, some potential 'complications'?

I full discussion on these matters is well beyond the scope of the chapter, but one example suffices to draw attention to some matters, insofar as they related to the world of the mentioned literati. Let me begin with a quote from Bourdieu, ... it should not be forgotten that it [cultural capital] exists as symbolically and materially active, effective capital only insofar as it is appropriated by agents and implemented and invested as a weapon and a stake in the struggles which go on in the fields of cultural production (the artistic field, the scientific field, etc.) and, beyond them, in the field of the social classes – struggles in which the agents wield strengths and obtain profits proportionate to their mastery of this objectified capital, and therefore to the extent of their embodied capital.¹⁷

A historian of ancient Israel cannot but wonder what does one know about the struggles that went on in the fields of cultural production in Yehud among the very few literati and the weaponization of their personal cultural goods. To what extent did individual literati constantly and systemically compete with each other within their own small group in the pursuit of their personal increased cultural capital, i.e., their cultural profit.

To be sure, humans being humans, there can be no doubt that most likely there was some degree of individual competition among the literati, but the real question does not concern this obvious and all too human point, but whether the system in which these literati worked was grounded on the pursuit of individual, ever increasing profit so as to maximize one's own capital as is the

---

16 Cf. David L. Swartz, "Metaprinciples for Sociological Research in Bourdieusian Perspective," in Philip S. Gorski (ed.), *Bourdieu and Historical Analysis* (Durham, N.C.: Duke University Press, 2013), 19–35.
17 P. Bourdieu, "Forms of Capital," in John G. Richardson (ed.) *Handbook of Theory of Research for the Sociology of Education* (New York: Greenwood Press, 1986), 46–58 (50).

case, to a significant extent, in the contemporary capitalist societies about which Bourdieu wrote.

Several considerations work strongly against such an assumption. For one, the shared discourse, or if one prefers and from another perspective, social mindscape allowed no room for the lionization of the individual author or redactor or literati. Anonymity was undisputed and there was a very strong generative grammar of ideas and memories at work that involved the erasure of actual and implied authors and of individual creativity claims. This preference conveyed a sense that individual literati as opposed to their works were not worth of being remembered, unlike kings, prophets and number of other figures of old that the community turned into important site of memory. A social mindscape in which individual literati are not worth being remembered is one unlikely to construct individual literati as agents constantly and mainly vying for increased cultural capital as a weapon in inner struggles.

This preference for the literati's self-erasure, which lasted at least until Ben Sira's time, was deeply intertwined with a social/cultural/ideological preference for communal 'ownership' of such core cultural goods as the books at the center of the authoritative repertoire of the community. Here unequal access to (cultural) goods was balanced with (ideological) tendencies towards horizontal social cohesion that construed these very same goods as belonging to the larger community.[18]

Practical considerations such as the very low number of literati in Yehud, scarcity of resources in Yehud and the need of institutional support, along with the ability of the center to control small groups and their output all likely played a role in diminishing any tendencies towards an emphasis on individual and struggle-centered behaviors within the group. But this is not the whole picture.

The generative grammar of preferences and dis-preferences underlying and governing the production and reproduction of the very goods considered to be valuable among these literati, that is, their texts strongly preferred multivocality and integrative fuzziness. As a result, the literati reading these texts ended up construing and remembering the major mnemonic characters populating their memory-scape, including the deity Yhwh, Moses and other prophetic characters, as embodying in one person multiple and seemingly contradictory positions, and even multiple dictions. If the heroes in their shared social memory and the anonymous implied authors of their works were construed as embodiments

---

[18] I will return and expand on this point below, when I discuss 'literatidicy,' a concept emerging from a Bourdieusian analysis.

of integrative tendencies, it stands to reason the literati themselves were socialized from an early age to favor these tendencies.[19] A strong preference for such integrative constructions suggests a vision for the group that is not consistent with systemically ingrained in-group struggle over 'cultural capital.'

Furthermore, it is worth noting that the very same literati had no problem imagining, constructing and remembering individual agents who focused on the pursuit of profit or accumulated increased capital in most *other* fields. For instance, אשת חיל provides an excellent example within the realm of economic capital, and interestingly enough, remembering her was remembering how economic capital may be transferred from economic to symbolic and social capital, to advance her and her husband's standing and power.[20] Likewise memories of individual kings and prophets provided excellent mnemonic examples of instances in which symbolic capital was used to effect change among those who have less symbolic capital, for better or worse. Against this background, the lack of any references to individual literati pursuing profit and increased cultural capital or using it to advance their own standing and power are even more glaring.[21]

Finally, there is no doubt that the choice of the term 'capital' evokes some common contemporary discourses about 'capitalism' and class struggle, about 'oppression' and 'resistance to oppressors', about understanding them as a, or the dominant, historical theme through time about inequality as a moral wrong and a moral imperative to revolutionize society. It is in this context that one must keep in mind that within the world of ideas of ancient Israel or in general in the ancient Near East, persistent inequality of resources, be they cultural, economic, or political, was widely considered an obvious given, a 'natural' social feature, not a problematic issue that requires explanation, never mind solution, provided that it existed within the boundaries of a society in which the powerful fulfilled their (construed) 'responsibilities', including caring for the needy and powerless and upholding 'justice'.

---

19 Elsewhere I suggested that such preference reflects a society with a low level of existential anxiety. See, e. g., "On Social Memory and Identity Formation in Late Persian Yehud: A Historian's Viewpoint with a Focus on Prophetic Literature, Chronicles and the Dtr. Historical Collection," in this volume, pp. 28–79. I will return to this point in the section about social reproduction vs historical change.
20 See "The 'Successful, Wise, Worthy Wife' of Prov 31:10–31 as a Source for Reconstructing Aspects of Thought and Economy in the Late Persian/Early Hellenistic Period," in this volume, pp. 546–65.
21 This conclusion should be at least partially balanced, as particularly in Chronicles, the literati may have identified with prophetic voices, but this requires a separate discussion.

At the core of their discourse about who the world should be, there was a conceptual construction of a divinely-ordained and maintained balance between vertical hierarchy and social horizontal cohesion. Moreover, within the discourse of the Yehudite literati, the dominant tensions in the Yehudite community were not along inner economic/social lines or divides, but more along those of a local, communal ideological resistance to general imperial discourses, by way of hybridity and the like, and to some extent along the line of resistance to the social and cultic discursive power of Samaria, the far more powerful sibling Yhwistic province.

Of course, it is possible, and some would undoubtedly argue, that the discourse of these literati, and those for whom they serve as a retainer class, reflects an intentional obfuscation of existing inner social tensions and that processes of 'misrecognition' held the day. But even if this were to be the case, such arguments are not heuristically helpful for reconstructing the historical social mindscape of the literati or the ways in which they interacted with other groups in society.

In contradistinction, transcultural studies of minorities and relatively disempowered ethnocultural groups interacting with large and relatively more powerful groups tend to show that in these cases, the main divide between 'us' and the 'other' is often the one construed around 'ethnocultural' not inner socioeconomic lines, and significantly, much of the discourse and social mindshare within the community revolves around 'us' and the closest possible 'other' (in this case, Samaria). Transcultural social, anthropological and historical studies discussing these matters may provide more heuristically helpful insights on these issues (and see studies on hybridity, on conceptualizations and problematizations of images of the Other, on fluid, continuous and multiple processes of identify formation, on the social roles of social memory and the like that have flourished in the last decades and which are beginning to have an impact in studies of ancient Israel in recent decades).

In sum, for the present case, the concept of 'cultural capital' (and similar 'capitals') is helpful in raising a number of questions and issues and likely in a (possibly) Bourdieusian sense of general resources that might be used to exert power, a concept that in itself may be used for a large spectrum of potential influences on 'others'. As one might have anticipated, just as wearing these methodological lenses facilitates 'seeing' many important aspects of the historical literati, but as it is often the case, might at times blur the vision concerning some other aspects. Bringing matters of social memory, generative grammars, and social mindscape to bear helps in these cases. In addition, since the cultural and symbolic capital of the literati was not only inseparable from their mnemonic capital, but also interwoven with the latter at all levels, the two research frameworks discussed here not only inform each other, but partially converge.

On the Matter of Taste

As their core literary corpus evidently shows, the literati had a clear set of manifested preferences or 'taste' to use Bourdieu's terms. They liked and valued texts written in a highly sophisticated language that made them directly inaccessible to the vast majority of the population, and set themselves as controllers and brokers of these texts. They liked balancing figures that embodied and integrated multiple positions and texts continuously informing and balancing each other.

Obviously, they rejected univocal books and univocal main characters and one may wonder whether they found the latter only 'not-their cup of tea' or also 'un-cultured' and thus perhaps somewhat *'repulsive'* to members of their social group. In this context, it is worth stressing that for purposes of setting social boundaries, or even personal boundaries, constructions of distaste, *repulsion* and the like are far more important factors than positive constructions of taste (e. g., the rejection of pork was more important that widespread preference of meat dishes over vegetables in Yehudite society).

The uniform *rejection* of univocal books and univocal main characters across the entire literary repertoire, despite all its inner variety of genres, idiolects, and the putative circumstances of the worlds they construe and evoke, is strongly suggestive, at least, of a very strong 'distaste,' bordering in repulsion on these matters, if not, and perhaps as or more likely, repulsion.

Clearly, as the literati embodied and performed their taste in Bourdieusian terms—which includes preferences along a whole spectrum from 'taboo' and 'disgusting' to simple distaste to positive taste, to extreme positive preference—they publicly claimed an 'education' or to use Bourdieu's concepts, a 'socio-cultural conditioning' that only very few could have in their society. Their aesthetic taste (and the world-view it conveyed) shaped a sense of social difference. Each time they manifested it, the literati positioned themselves as members of a particular social group, which from their perspective constituted a 'cultural aristocracy.' Each time they manifested their taste, they performed a claim to the power associated with their being members of that group—even if they were not self-aware of doing so.

As all social, performative claims for power, this one raises also the socio-historical question of power over whom, and in the eyes of whom. If power is, in a nutshell, the ability to impose, dominate or asymmetrically influence others, there might be various estimates among different groups of such claims for power, depending on their social location.

Working from a perspective informed by Social Memory studies I often refer (and have done so above) to a contingent generative grammar that set systems of contingent generative grammars that govern or control systems of preferences and dis-preferences among the literati (and those influenced by them) and which governed the production and consumption of social memories and texts—every time a text is read, it is reshaped and thus 're-produced' as well as 'reproduced'.

To be sure, social generative grammars consisting of system of preferences and dis-preferences were not restricted to solely shaping social memories. Social generative grammars of preferences and dis-preferences governed the production, reproduction and 'consumption' of any aspect of socially 'appropriate' behavior within the group.

Thus, from a pragmatic perspective, the concept of grammars of preference and dis-preferences seem to converge, at least to some extent with that of Bourdieu's 'taste'. In addition, to what is stated above, one may notice also that both stress social and historical contingency rather than supposed 'universality'. 'Taste' like any socially-construed system of preferences is by necessity historically and group contingent, and claims of 'universality', if made, are only rhetorical and ideological claims for increased legitimacy or socio-cultural domination of a particular 'taste' and against potential or real others.

Likewise, from a functionalistic or systemic perspective, groups tend to end up, at least in the long term, adopting a taste/generative system of preferences and dis-preferences that contribute to their social legitimization and power. This is so, because the latter contribute to their ability to socially reproduce itself over time.

At the same time, although the authoritative textual repertoire of the literati stands as an obvious cultural embodiment of their distinctive 'taste' or their grammar or grammars of preferences and dis-preferences, these relate only to very narrow aspect of their professional lives. In fact, it relates only to a particular field within their professional lives, since it is reasonable to assume that most of them had additional socio-professional roles to fulfil in the community, e.g., priests, scribes, landholders, or any combination of the above. Certainly, if one of these literati wrote, for instance, contracts, the latter would have embodied a different set of preferences and writing them would be an act of positioning, but different than reading the books in their authoritative repertoire.

In other words, the manifested preference or 'taste' was always contingent on the social role being performed by the individual and the same person could have performed various social roles. Given their integrative tendencies and taste for fuzziness in their worlds of imagination and memory, it seems reasonable to assume that they could have easily interwoven multiple preferences or tastes into their general, collective sense of taste, which in itself raises interesting questions about porousness of distinctions, and about overlapping and in-between realms.

The 'taste' or mentioned generative grammars that historians of the intellectual world and the social memories about Israel that they construed and communicated focus on them are therefore both a narrow slice of the 'taste'/generative grammar at work among the literati as a social group and, at the same time, one that is likely to shed some light on other realms subject also to socially shared, group 'taste'/grammars.

On the Matter of Habitus

The mentioned shared generative social grammars imply an underlying concept of a shared 'social mindscape,' as used in some socio-anthropologic approaches to social memory, including my own. The study of social mindscapes involves, inter alia, that of accepted and shared ways of thinking, of generating ideas, questions and ways of addressing them, of providing meaning to 'data' and actually construing 'data' by focusing on particular matters and not others, of assigning significance to memories, stories, and actually shaping the production of memories according to particular patterns. Moreover, it involves the study of how all these are deeply interconnected.[22]

As in the previous case, despite all the obvious differences and extremely wide gap between the literati of the LPEH period and the groups that Bourdieu studied, there still seems to be some partial convergence between the concept of 'social mindscape' and a Bourdieusian concept of 'habitus,' when the latter is understood as the way "things are" or "are done" in a particular social setting; that is, a certain 'feel for the game' held and acted upon by members of a particular group, whether consciously or unconsciously.

---

[22] On "social mindscapes" see E. Zerubavel, *Social Mindscapes: An Invitation to Cognitive Sociology* (Cambridge, Mass.: Harvard University Press, 1997); E. Zerubavel, *Time Maps: Collective Memory and the Social Shape of the Past* (Chicago: University of Chicago Press, 2003). The concept of "mindscape" precedes, of course, Zerubavel and goes back to M. Maruyama who used "the term 'mindscape' to mean a structure of reasoning, cognition, perception, conceptualization, design, planning, and decision making that may vary from one individual, profession, culture, or social group to another," M. Maruyama, "Mindscapes and Science Theories," *Current Anthropology* 21 (1980), 589–99 (591).

For the present purposes, one important converging feature seems to be that both allow for human agency, and that both channel it in terms of a very contingent, systemic variant of rational choice, in which choices are regulated by (a) boundaries around what is considered 'natural' behaviour in a particular social setting/'field of practice' and thus most often 'naturally' engaged, (b) a sense of the degree to which a participant may improvise and adapt that is closely associated with their 'knowing the game', and thus being well socialized into a shared social mindscape and (c) a (conscious or unconscious) awareness of the heavy cost for acting, speaking, expressing feelings or tastes, or thinking, for that matter, in ways that are eminently inconsistent with what the community 'naturally' considers to be proper according to its shared 'feel of the game'/social mindscape.

This systemic variant of rational choice may be manifested in instances of both conscious and unconscious choices by individuals and certainly does not have to be understood in terms of individual interests/choices as opposed to group interests/choices, because from the perspective of those making the choice most often what was considered proper for the group (in our case, the literati) would often be considered for the individual (in our case the learned person).[23]

On the Matter of Literatidicy (as a form of sociodicy)

The term sociodicy does not originate with Bourdieu, but with Raymond Aron. It is nevertheless likely to play some significant role in any Bourdieusian approach. Societies in which resources are limited are societies in which justification is very much required for the allocation of resources. Certainly, the investment of the necessary resources for the development and maintenance of the cadre of literati in such a poor province as Yehud required justification. Thus, one may speak of a literatidicy in Yehud.

---

[23] On Bourdieu and rational choice, along with explorations on what a Bourdieusian approach to this matter might be see Ivan Ermakoff, "Rational Choice May Take Over," in Philip S. Gorski (ed.), *Bourdieu and Historical Analysis* (Durham, N.C.: Duke University Press, 2013), 89–107. It is worth mentioning that a similar version of 'rational choice' explains why individuals may construct and uphold socially shared memories of events that can be easily 'proven' to be factually wrong, if to admit to the mistake and correct it (i.e., to adopt a new, more factually correct social memory), carries the high social cost of losing membership in their group. Moreover, since being aware of the trade raises significant personal costs, it is likely that mechanism of 'rational choice' will, in ways unbeknownst to the individual, be triggered to inhibit this awareness of the tension by finding ways to uphold the group social memory and contest the historical evidence against it. Memory Studies have often dealt with these matters.

The very concept of Israel as a text-centered community, which stands at the very centre of the ideological discourse of the community provides a literatidicy, as it constructs the literati as absolutely essential to the very existence of the community. The related concept of the 'guardian' as essential to the well-being of the community or polity, and which I discussed elsewhere,[24] serves a similar purpose and often the two were interwoven.

But this literatidicy had to be conveyed to and accepted by the larger community. It is in this context that the preference for communal 'ownership' of such core cultural goods as the books at the center of the authoritative repertoire of the community may play a role. On the one hand, they draw attention away from unequal access to these goods and the 'persistence of inequality,' but on the other, though complementary hand, they shaped a 'sociodicy of competence'.

Of course, a sociodicy of competence works only if the relevant competence is in a field that the community is to consider relevant to them. One has to assume that to some extent the text-centered vision had to be successfully communicated to and shared by groups other than the literati. The story of Jehoshaphat's mobile teaching committee in 2 Chr 17:7–9, and references to public readings of divine teachings (e.g., Deut 31:9–13; cf. Neh 8) show that communication to the larger group was associated with important memories of the past. They indicate also some of the ways in which such a communication may have actually been carried out.

It is worth stressing that teaching the (textually inscribed) divine instruction to the larger population was portrayed and remembered as involving a negotiation between the inherent vertical hierarchy of competence between those reading and instructing and those being read to and instructed, on the one hand, and claims for horizontal cohesion so strong that overcome, even if partially, barriers of gender, age and, in the case of Deut 31:12, also of origin (see the reference to the *ger* there).

Memories and ideological claims that divine instruction was given to Israel as a whole are clearly part and parcel of this stressed construction of horizontal social cohesion. The same holds true, obviously, for tendencies towards the priestization and royalization of 'all Israel.'[25]

---

24 I expanded elsewhere on the closely interrelated concept of the 'guardian' essential to the well-being of the community or polity. See my "Memory and Political Thought in the Late Persian/Early Hellenistic Yehud/Judah: Some Observations," Diana V. Edelman and Ehud Ben Zvi (eds.) *Leadership, Social Memory and Judean Discourse in the 5th-2nd Centuries BCE* (WANEM; London: Equinox, 2016), 9–26.
25 Considerations of horizontal social cohesion seemed to have had impacted multiple fields of social interaction in Yehud, including family construction. See "Monogynistic and Monogamous

In addition, among the tenets that were communicated to the general population, there was an understanding of past catastrophes as resulting from the communal and the community's leaders forsaking of divine instruction, that was closely interwoven with comforting memories of a glorious, utopian future for 'Israel' (see esp. the Prophetic Book Collection; Isaiah-Malachi). It is worth stressing that in some versions of this utopian future that the literati shaped, shared and communicated, they imagined themselves as becoming unnecessary and were thus again erased, or self-erased, in their own utopian imagination.[26]

These images, in all their versions, along with the worlds of shared imagination and the socially shared memories of the utopian future/s, served well, from a systemic perspective, to increase the persuasive appeal of this literatidicy. In sum, claims advancing literatidicy were rooted on core elements of the literati's discourse, and on the social memory and mindscape of those in Yehud who were socialized to accept them. Moreover, these claims were communicated in ways that from a systemic perspective maximized their affective appeal and thus their social effect.

To be sure, this literatidicy, as all successful sociodicies, was not the outcome of manipulative, cynic agents finding ways of supporting themselves, but of a convergence of (a) agency by the literati who were educated/socialized in particular ways and who partook in a social mindscape in which these positions were 'natural,' and (b) social systemic reasons that would confer an advantage in social reproduction for groups conditioned to think and act in such ways.

Symbolic Power, Temple Controls and Possibility of Effecting Social Change

It was noted in the background survey that the literati needed the temple, and there were references to their internalization of the temple ideology/worldviews including an overwhelming Jerusalem-centredness. These comments seem reminiscent of Kant's comments, which in turn informed Bourdieu,[27] on the 'higher

---

Tendencies, Memories and Imagination in Late Persian/Early Hellenistic Yehud in this volume, pp. 566–79.
26 See, e.g., Jer 31:31–34 and cf. with the lack of prophets in the utopian future, see "Prophetic Memories in the Deuteronomistic Historical and the Prophetic Collections of Books," in this volume, pp. 109–33.
27 E.g., and explicitly in P. Bourdieu, *Homo Academicus* (Cambridge: Polity Press, 1988), 62–69.

faculties/ disciplines' that have a strong influence on people and thus are more directly controlled by the government.

For Kant, as one may easily anticipate given his historical context, these were theology, law and medicine. It seems reasonable to assume that in the world of Yehud, the faculty producing and controlling the core, authoritative books would be considered a 'higher faculty.' The lack of texts within the controlled core repertoire of the community that deal with other 'faculties' that likely existed at the time, e.g., medicine (even only in the form of charms to warn against diseases) seems to support such a contention. In addition, transcultural studies have shown that those in a position of power have at least attempted to control the interpretation of texts deemed to be authoritative within a community. Studies of the reception of the Old Testament and the Tanakh (or 'the written *torah*') in Christian and Jewish communities respectively across time and space have proven that point again and again.

This said, questions still emerge. For instance, did the literati have the actual power that they imply they had in their own literature and if so when? The much later sages at the beginning of rabbinic Judaism also construed a world in which they carried a lot of power, but most historians of the period agree that their positioning within their own discourse often did not reflect historical realities, except when they were associated with the figure of the 'nasi' in Roman Palestine and the exilarch of Parthian and Sassanid Babylon.[28] But with less potential social authority comes a lessened need for social control by the centre.

In other words, the issue of central control over the literati is associated with that of their actual social authority. If as it is possible, many (most?) of the literati were priests or levites, and in any event, if the literati and their education was supported by the Jerusalemite temple, it stands to reason that as this temple became more and more important in Yehud and particularly when it became the main local center of power, eventually with the High Priest even taking most of the roles previously assigned to governors appointed by the 'empire', the authority of the literati increased and with the controls over them.

Another consideration about central control of 'authoritative texts', whereas the polyphonic texts of the authoritative repertoire held by the literati were at least to be theoretically open to the public, the interpretation of them was not (and see again the case of the Jehoshaphat's committee and the presence of a combination of royally appointed officials, levites and priests, or the controlled

---

[28] See, for instance, S. Schwartz, *The Ancient Jews from Alexander to Muhammad* (Cambridge: Cambridge University Press, 2014), idem, *Imperialism and Jewish Society, 200 BCE to 640 CE* (Princeton: Princeton University Press, 2001) and bibliography.

teaching of *torah* in Neh 8). Moreover, if some or many of the literati were priests, it is significant that there is no concrete manual for professional priestly activites (or for Levites singing for that matter) in this seemingly open 'repertoire' of texts. There are plenty of legitimizing references, but much of the necessary practical knowledge remained 'secret' and thus well controlled.[29]

Moreover, some balance between secrecy and openness was often implicated in constructions of professional identity, after all, if one's professional goods were imagined as theoretically open to all, one's cultural capital cannot be imagined as at least potentially transitory. This may not be a problem from the perspective of the literati who imagined themselves as eventually socially unnecessary, though only in the far away, distant utopian future, but it would present a problem for priests. After all, the temple was imagined at the time as necessary and actually as a central, world space in the utopian future.

On the Matter of Historical Change/Transformation vs. Social Reproduction

I would like to conclude this list of observations with brief considerations on matters of historical change or transformation.[30] Taste, the production of canons as central cultural goods that provide their owners with much cultural capital, social mindscapes, social memories, sociodicies and even controls over cultural goods tend to draw much attention to matters of social reproduction.

But social groups exist in a larger 'ecology', as one of many in the system. Significant changes to one important element in the system are bound to create changes in other elements. The process of elevation of the temple, as mentioned above, was likely to have an influence on the literati, their cultural capital, their powers and controls over them and, needless to say, over the very cultural good they held. Yet, the most drastic changes to the system occurred after conquest by Alexander. There was the catastrophe that befell Samaria, the powerful 'frenemy' of Yehud, and also the impact of the eventual interaction with a network of Hellenistic cultural, political and economic centres. Moreover, following the perse-

---

[29] Cf., though for comparative purposes only, see K. Stevens, "Secrets in the Library: Protected Knowledge and Professional Identity in Late Babylonian Uruk," *Iraq* 75 (2013), 211–53.

[30] One may note that in the Anglophone academic world, Bourdieu is often considered a theorist of social reproduction rather than of transformation. On the problematic character of such a position, see Philip S. Gorski, "Introduction," in Philip S. Gorski (eds.), *Bourdieu and Historical Analysis* (Durham, N.C.: Duke University Press; 2013).

cutions of Antiochos IV, a major cultural/mnemonic trauma developed.[31] The low level of existential anxiety that shaped in multiple ways the discourse of the Yehudite literati of the Persian period eventually gave way to a high level of existential anxiety which was reflected in and to a large extent shaped much of the discourses of the late Second Temple period.

To this transformation, one may add the eventual transformation of Jerusalem from a minor town to the capital of a regional power during the Hasmonean period, along with a very substantial increase in the number of literati, the correlated decrease in abilities of the centre to control them,[32] and for the first time the potential, duly realized, for the creation of socially-separate 'sects,' each of which saw itself as either 'Israel' or its 'proper' centre. Struggles within, outside or against the Hasmonean centre contributed their own and had no parallel in previous periods. Changes of such magnitude[33] could not but lead to very substantial changes over taste and judgment, over social mindscape or habitus, 'required' related forms of social distinction and not surprisingly, new or 'renewed' (e. g., through interpretation) 'cultural goods'. An analysis of these matters is beyond the scope of this essay, but this does not hold true for the observation that the conceptual frames discussed here serve well to study not only continuity and processes of social reproduction but also of drastic social transformation.

On the Matter of Partial Conceptual Convergences

The preceding observations involving, e. g., 'mnemonic capital', 'taste', 'habitus' and 'literatidicy' as a form of 'sociodicy' have all explored intersections at which concepts commonly used within a set of social memory approaches and concepts that belong to Bourdeusian research frames interacted (or were made to interact) with each other in a manner that shed light on the historical literati of the Late Persian or Early Hellenistic period. At times, concepts illuminated each other in a particular light, at times they become partially interwoven and at times they even seemed to converge, even if only partially. In all these

---

31 This is not the place to discuss the reasons, extent or any 'historical' or 'historiographical' aspect of them. Much has been written on these issues. For the present purposes suffices to notice that a traumatic memory evolved among the Judahites (Jews?) who resided in Judah at the time.
32 Cf. Albert Baumgarten, *The Flourishing of Jewish Sects in the Maccabean Era: An Interpretation* (Leiden, E. J. Brill, 1997), esp., pp. 114–151.
33 And many more may be added, e. g., demographic changes; the development of Judeo-Hellenistic diasporas, etc.

cases, two research frames interacted with each other and led to a better understanding of a particular, historically contingent group.

These observations raise an important 'theoretical' issue. According to some contemporary, pragmatic approaches towards the possibility of knowledge of the past, "consensus in a uniquely heterogeneous, large, and uncoerced group of historians is a *likely* indicator of knowledge;"[34] or, as I prefer, a "likely indicator of a 'reasonable' reconstruction of a likely (though necessarily partial) past,"[35] and in either case may serve historians as pragmatic gate to the concept of historical 'external referentiality'.

Would then intersections and interactions involving uncoerced, heterogeneous groups of scholars, or their research frames, each with its own terminology and history be able to serve as a kind of indicator for potential reasonability when historical social processes and traits become observable or more easily observable by wearing these double lenses?

Since none of the above applies only to ancient Yehudite society or its literati, but seem transcultural and not necessarily dependent of historical contingencies, may them point to the reasonability of proposing them from a general socio-anthropological methodological approach[36]?

At the same time, critically aware scholars cannot avoid the nagging question of whether the relevant groups of scholars—that is, those following Bourdieusian approaches and terminology and those following Memory Studies—may not be so 'heterogeneous' after all? Claims and balances remain part of our methodological culture.

---

[34] Citation from Aviezer Tucker, *Our Knowledge of the Past. A Philosophy of Historiography* (Cambridge: Cambridge Univ. Press, 2004), 39; emphasis added.

[35] E. Ben Zvi, "Clio Today and Ancient Israelite History: Some Thoughts and Observations at the Closing Session of The European Seminar for Historical Methodology," in Lester L. Grabbe (ed.), *"Even God Cannot Change the Past": Reflections on Seventeen Years of the European Seminar in Historical Methodology* (LHBOTS, 663, London: T&T Clark, 2018) 20–49.

[36] I include 'historical sociology' within the realm of 'history'. To be sure, some would include it in 'sociology', but being 'included' within the constructed 'box' of 'sociology' does not preempt it from being not only included but also quite central to 'history'.

Social Sciences Models and Mnemonic/Imagined Worlds: Exploring Their Interrelations in Ancient Israel*

Introduction

Undoubtedly and unsurprisingly from a methodological viewpoint, models and concepts from the social sciences have shed much light on contemporary societies and also on historical worlds of the ancient past/s. The reason that they work effectively for contemporary societies as well as reconstructions of ancient historical ones, including ancient Israel, is that matters as diverse as ancient communities, kings and other political leaders, prophets, priests, literati, prophecies, laws, marriage, divorce, temples, cultic practices, historical narratives, and group memories share one thing in common: they are all social entities of one sort or another and, therefore, are all amenable to approaches from the social sciences.[1]

Even more, these very approaches often work well for imagined social worlds that existed only in the shared, social memory of a group or set of groups in antiquity.[2] This is especially important for analyses of those texts that depict constructed memories of what an (ideal) political community should look like. At times, the mentioned methods not only work in these worlds of constructed and shared memory, but seem to work far better within them than in the 'counterpart' historical worlds, which for ancient contexts are typically reconstructed by historians.

---

* First published in Jeremiah W. Cataldo (ed.), *Imagined Worlds and Constructed Differences in the Hebrew Bible* (LHBOTS, 677; London: Bloomsbury, 2019), 9–26, with permission.

[1] My use of the term 'social entity' reflects an understanding of it in line with the following: "A social entity is not a fixed thing with stable properties .... It is rather a continuing swirl of linked social activities and practices, themselves linked to other 'separate' social traditions" and that all "social facts are carried by socially construed individuals in action." Citation from David Little, "The Heterogeneous Social: New Thinking about the Foundations of the Social Sciences" in C. Mantzavinos (ed.) *Philosophy of the Social Sciences: Philosophical Theory and Scientific Practice* (Cambridge University Press, 2009), 154–178 (159), and cf. also Andrew Abbott, *Department & Discipline: Chicago Sociology at One Hundred* (Chicago, IL: University of Chicago Press, 1999), esp. 222–23.

[2] They work also in memory worlds held by groups in other societies, including contemporary ones, but the focus here is in ancient Israel.

To illustrate my point, I will first draw attention to several substantially different, illustrative examples that all together serve as an indication that the issue raised above is not marginal, but a major one for future research. Then I will begin to explore the implications of these observations and suggest some research paths to which they lead. On the whole, the goal of this contribution is to draw attention to these matters and encourage further conversations and explorations on them.

A Set of Diverse Examples

The case of well-known social constructions and structures.

There is no denying the presence and underlying importance of more broadly understood social constructions such as honor-shame, patron-client and 'the house of the father' (and in some cases, its subdivisions into 'houses of mothers') in numerous narratives or worlds of memory.[3] Social-scientific and comparative studies on all the above are relevant and provide good heuristic tools for studies of both narrative worlds and most likely 'historical' societies in ancient Israel in which all the above played important roles.

The reason for congruence in these cases is relatively simple: communities imagined worlds in terms of what they implicitly construed as 'natural' and therefore, such social constructions were part and parcel of the world of communities, across time and both in their 'real' world and their worlds memory and imagination. Although relatively easy to understand, these cases are certainly not meaningless. They do provide us crucial information about that which was

---

[3] Concerning honor and shame, see, e.g., Saul M. Olyan, "Honor, Shame, and Covenantal Relations in Ancient Israel and its Environment," *JBL* 115 (1996), 201–218; and in relation to, e.g., Esther see, e.g., Timothy S. Laniak, *Shame and Honor in the Book of Esther* (SBLDS, 65; Atlanta, GA: Scholars Press, 1988); and Lillian R. Klein, "Honor and Shame in Esther," in Athalya Brenner (ed.) *Feminist Companion to Esther, Judith and Susanna* (Sheffield: Sheffield Academic Press, 1995), 149–75; for multiple cases of narratives and prophecies involving accounts of past or future mutilations of enemies see, T. M. Lemos, "Shame and Mutilation of Enemies in the Hebrew Bible," *JBL* 125 (2006), 225–24. Examples may be easily multiplied. On imagined/construed patron client relationships, see e.g., J. Schäder, "Patronage and Clientage between God, Israel and the Nations: A Social-Scientific Investigation of Psalm 47," *Journal for Semitics* 19 (2010), 235–262. On literary constructions of the house of the mother, see Cynthia R. Chapman, *The House of the Mother: The Social Roles of Maternal Kin in Biblical Hebrew Narrative and Poetry* (New Haven: CT: Yale University Press, 2016). The motif of the house of the father is ubiquitous in the Hebrew Bible narratives, wisdom texts, poetry and prophetic literature.

so 'natural' as to be transparent to particular communities, and even so 'natural' that it permeated and constrained their social imagination.[4]

The case of state (and chiefdom) formation

The next example is, appropriately, of a different type. Rather than socially construed non-dynamic constant conditions and transparent continuity, this example unequivocally relates to change and discontinuity. Without entering much into the details and shortcomings of various theories of state formation[5] and

---

[4] Cf. "What is familiar is what we are used to, and what we are used to is what is most difficult to know. The greater discovery lies in becoming aware of our most basic assumptions, so that we can question them and make them strange," David Nirenberg, 527th Convocation Address University of Chicago, "A Time of Mind," available at http://eventbeat.org/the-527th-convocation-address-the-university-of-chicago/. The larger issue of constraints on imagination cannot be discussed here. It suffices to mention that such constraints are based on cognitive matters (e.g., humans cannot really imagine what seven dimensions may look like) and on the basic fact that imaginaries (just like memories, for that matter) are not construed by individuals or social groups in a vacuum. Imaginaries are strongly grounded on the world of knowledge held among those construing them, i.e. the imagination agents, and on their group's social mindscape, and its social, political and cultural circumstances. Moreover, imaginaries have to relate in some way directly or indirectly to the world of those that imagine them, if the act of imagining is to have some epistemic function and thus help those involved in to learn something. The range of research on these and the related and much larger matters concerning imagination, usually with an eye into the present, may be exemplified by the following works and the works cited in them, Amy Kind and Peter Kung (eds.), *Knowledge through Imagination* (Oxford: Oxford University Press, 2016) and see esp. in this collection, Amy Kind, "Imagining under Constraints," 145–59, and Neil Van Leeuwen, "The Imaginative Agent," 85–110; the journal issue introduced by Joanna Latimer and Beverley Skeggs, "The Politics of Imagination: Keeping Open and Critical," *The Sociological Review* 59 (2011), 393–410; Rita Carter, "The Limits of Imagination," in Robin Headlam Wells and Johnjoe McFadden (eds) *Human Nature: Fact and Fiction: Literature, Science and Human Nature*, (London: Continuum, 2006), 128–43; Greg Currie, "Imagination and Learning," in Amy Kind (ed.), *The Routledge Handbook of Philosophy of Imagination* (New York: Routledge, 2016); 407–19; Natalie M. Fletcher, "Imagination and The Capabilities Approach), in A. Kind (ed.), *op. cit*, 392–404.

[5] Those advanced by Elman R. Service (see, e.g., *Origins of the State and Civilization: The Process of Cultural Evolution* [New York: Norton, 1975]), along with the emphasis on chiefdom as the stage between tribal and state political organization) and thus also, those of e.g., Colin Renfrew (see, e.g., "Beyond a Subsistence Economy: The Evolution of Social Organization in Prehistoric Europe," in Charlotte B. Moore (ed.) *Reconstructing Complex Societies An Archaeological Colloquium* [BASORSup, 20; Cambridge, MA: ASOR, 1974], 69–88) had a significant impact on studies of ancient Israelite history. See e.g., James W. Flanagan, "Chiefs in Israel," in David J. Chalcraft

without any need to accept unilineal, evolutionary paths,⁶ it is safe to say that there is a wide agreement that transitions from chiefdom to state usually involved, *inter alia*, a shift towards socio-political complexity, which often includes the development of state bureaucracy, law and the ability to enforce it, 'urban' centres; strong and permanent armies; more complex redistribution systems than those of chiefs (including tax systems and an ability to administer them); building and tendencies towards enhancing the role of central temples and administrative centralization.

Are these not all part and parcel of a world of memory in which a polity that we may call today a 'state' emerged out of clashes between two original chiefs, Saul and David, during the late reign of David and especially Solomon, from the perspective of ancient readers of Samuel and Kings?

Surely, when the literati who read the books of Samuel and Kings recalled and imagined Saul, David and Solomon, the polity that their readings evoked shifted from one in which features consistent with models of chiefdom are dominant to one in which features consistent with a polity we may call 'state' are obviously prevalent—obviously using our own terminology.⁷

In addition, we may consider the influential model of Carneiro, which argues that warfare (or the threat thereof) played an important role in the establishment of chiefdoms.⁸ David's kingdom is often, and with good reasons, characterized as a 'chiefdom'. Certainly, Saul's kingdom as portrayed in the book of Samuel qualifies as a 'chiefdom'. This being the case, it is worth noting that the narrative communicated by the Book of Samuel and the set of socially shared memories encoded and evoked by this book about the establishment of Saul's kingdom, and even David's, conform with Carneiro's model. In fact, one might approach the emer-

---

(ed.), *Social Scientific Old Testament Criticism. A Sheffield Reader* (BibSem, 47; Sheffield: Sheffield Academic Press, 1997), 136–61.

6 The models mentioned above have been critiqued on these grounds.

7 For the present purposes, it is not necessary to enter the debate about archaeological data dealing with the emergence of states in the Southern Levant during the Iron Age or reconstructions of 'historical' Iron Age Sauls, Davids, or Solomons, or whether the wars of David were constructed and remembered in terms associated with those of Hazael in the 9th century (see, e.g., N. Na'aman, "In Search of Reality Behind the Account of David's Wars with Israel's Neighbours," *IEJ* 52 [2002], 200–224) or whether the portrayal of the Solomon of Kings was based on Omride sources portraying Omride kings (see E. Axel Knauf, "King Solomon's Copper Supply," in E. Lipiński [ed.], *Phoenicia and the Bible. Proceedings of the Conference held at the University of Leuven on the 15th and 16th of March 1990* [Studia Phoenicia, XI, Leuven: Peeters, 1991], 167–86).

8 Robert L. Carneiro, "Chiefdom: Precursor of the State," in Grant D. Jones and Robert R. Kautz (eds.), *The Transition to Statehood in the New World* (Cambridge: Cambridge University Press, 1981), 37–75 (63–65).

gence of the short-lived 'chiefdoms' of Gideon and Jephtah, as portrayed in Judges, in the same manner.

To be sure, scholars of previous generations have been very much aware that the narratives in Samuel, Kings, and Chronicles as well, portray a world and socio-political processes that conform, to a significant extent, with some widely-known general social-scientific models.[9] These scholars, however, have been challenged, over time and *inter alia*, because they relied on the 'historicity' of literary texts much later than the putative time they were portraying. Moreover, these texts often had a long redactional history. Today, even if one were to argue that these texts might contain a kernel of historicity, few historians would take them as reliable sources for historical reconstructions of the process of state formation for the historical, Iron Age kingdoms of (northern) Israel, first, and Judah later. Moreover, the process of state formation portrayed in these sources is not that of either one of these historical kingdoms, but of the Israel that serves as the main site of memory and character in the Primary History (Gen-2 Kings), the Deuteronomistic History Collection (hereafter, DHC), or Chronicles, and which is a social and ideological construction that evolved much later than the establishment of these kingdoms.

I would like to stress that I consider neither the narratives nor the world they evoke as reliable sources for reconstructions of the events that led to the forma-

---

9 Jim Flanagan wrote about 35 years ago, as follows: To summarize militia, kinship ties, redistribution, and appeals to religious legitimacy all figured as strands in the warp and woof of the social, political, economic, and religious fabric of the day. Studies of the cultural evolutionary and succession patterns of other societies have described similar transitional circumstances and have concluded that such times were periods when the society was led by chiefs. The descriptions drawn from those non-Yahwistic and primary societies fit the evidence found in the literature of Yahwistic, secondary Israel. In fact, most of the elements on Renfrew's list of twenty characteristics of chiefdoms cited above can be documented in Israel. These indicate both the presence of chiefs and the absence of a strong centralized monopoly of force equipped with laws during the time of Saul and the early years of David. Since the parallels between Renfrew's list and the biblical evidence are not random, and because the evolutionary process outlined by Service is clearly evident in Israel, the cross-cultural comparisons are valid and productive. They have helped us understand the processes al work in ancient Israel and have aided in dismissing conjectures about the immediate transition from tribal league to full-blown monarchy." (See James W. Flanagan, "Chiefs in Israel," in David J. Chalcraft [ed.], *Social Scientific Old Testament Criticism*, pp. 136–61; citation, 157–58; the original article was published as James W. Flanagan, "Chiefs in Israel," *JSOT* 20 [1981], 47–63; and was republished in additional volumes, e.g. in Charles E. Carter and Carol L. Meyers [eds.], *Community, Identity, and Ideology: Social Science Approaches to the Hebrew Bible* [Winona Lake, Ind.: Eisenbrauns, 1996], 311–34 and in J. Cheryl Exum [ed.], *The Historical Books* [Biblical Seminar, 40; Sheffield: Sheffield Academic Press, 1997], 142–66.)

tion of the state polities referred to as the kingdoms of Judah and Israel. They are products of imagined identities, not intentional historical reflections. But the basic observations made above still hold true; the narratives in the DHC and Chronicles, and the worlds of imagination and memory that they shaped and evoked when these books were read—both separately and in a way in which each one informs the other—do indeed show some degree of coherence with what one would anticipate from models of processes by which chiefdoms end up becoming state polities.

Whereas these narratives and worlds of memory may not be a good mimetic reflection of historical processes in the Iron Age, the fact that they conform in broad strokes with what models in 20th and 21st century social sciences project is still a very meaningful piece of information. Moreover, the fact that the relatively simple, uni-directional and teleological manner in which the narrative in these textual sources moved first towards chiefdom and then to a state polity is far more consonant with both the simplified lines of 'theoretical models' and with construed narratives of social memory that existed among the much later literati who produced, reproduced, redacted and read and reread these texts than the far more complex, chaotic historical realities.

It is worth noting in this context that relative lack of complexity in comparison with historical 'realities' tends also to characterize social memory.[10] Since both social memory and socio-anthropological models involve simplification, even if for different reasons, their confluence in the case mentioned above is not necessarily perplexing. Before discussing these matters further, a few additional examples/case studies are needed.

The case of prophetic (and a few other) figures of old

The next case focuses on prophetic figures of memory that were evoked through readings and rereadings of the Prophetic Book Collection (hereafter, PBC) or the DHC in the late Persian/early Hellenistic period and some common socio-anthropological characterizations of prophets. For instance, prophets are considered a type of 'intermediary' between the deity and humans. This holds well for prophets in general and for the prophets of memory evoked by the literati's reading of the PBC, DHC or Chronicles. The same holds true for the distinction between cen-

---

10 See, for instance, Norman Yoffee, *Myths of the Archaic State: Evolution of the Earliest Cities, States, and Civilizations* (Cambridge: Cambridge University Press, 2004), 91–100, and his comments about the construed and remembered dynastic cycle and the unification of China.

tral and peripheral prophets, which is also at work within their world of memory of these literati.[11] In addition, the Elijah and Elisha of memory that were encoded in the book of Kings and whose memory was evoked through rereadings of the book clearly show some well-known shamanistic behaviours.[12] Likewise, there can be little doubt that the prophetic characters of memory were imagined, for the most past, as 'spontaneous' diviners, that is, a class of diviners who do not need to use a particular form of learned technical knowledge, except in some cases trance-inducing techniques (see 2 Kgs 3:15; cf. 1 Sam 10:5; 1 Chr 25:1) and unlike 'technical diviners' such as astronomers or priests using the ephod.[13]

When Lester Grabbe discussed and summarized a well-known case in which comparative anthropological studies substantially impacted research on prophecy in ancient Israel,[14] he stated:

The prophetic persona of Handsome Lake has many parallels with those of the OT prophets... [h]e had a divine call to preach to his people at a time of crisis in the community...[h]is message was not necessarily a popular one but called for repentance and a change of life on the part of hearers ... [s]everal of his messages were received in visions, at least one seems to fit the characteristics of an apocalypse... [h]is message was a moral one...[15]

---

[11] For instance, the Nathan of memory and the Isaiah of memory conform—in the main, in the case of Isaiah— to general matters present in central prophets, and the Elisha of memory to those of peripheral prophets. On central and peripheral prophets in this context, the foundational contribution has been Robert R. Wilson, *Prophecy and Society in Ancient Israel* (Philadelphia: Fortress, 1980). See, e.g., how this distinction is used in relation to Micah in Paul L. Reddit, *Introduction to the Prophets* (Grand Rapids, Mich.: Eerdmans; 2008), 274–75.

[12] See, e.g., Thomas W. Overholt, *Cultural Anthropology and the Old Testament* (Minneapolis: Fortress, 1996), 24–68. Grabbe elsewhere draws on social sciences models of prophecy when he compares the prophets populating the texts of the Hebrew Bible ('the Israelite prophet') and Joseph Smith, the Latter-Day Saints' prophet. See Lester L. Grabbe, "Joseph Smith and the *Gestalt* of the Israelite Prophet" in Philip F. Esler (ed.), *Ancient Israel. The Old Testament in its Social Context* (Minneapolis: Fortress, 2006), 111–27.

[13] Cf. Jonathan Stökl, *Prophecy in the Ancient Near East: A Philological and Sociological Comparison* (Culture and History of the Ancient Near East, 56; Leiden/Boston: Brill, 2012), 9–10.

[14] See, e.g., Thomas W. Overholt, "Prophecy: The Problem of Cross-Cultural Comparison," Semeia 21 (1982), 55–78 and idem, *Channels of Prophecy. The Social Dynamics of Prophetic Activity* (Minneapolis: Fortress, 1989).

[15] Lester L. Grabbe, *Priests, Prophets, Diviners, Sages. A Socio-Historical Study of Religious Specialists in Ancient Israel* (Valley Forge, Pa.: Trinity Press International, 1995), 97.

Everything cited above fits well the prophets of memory evoked through readings and rereadings of the PBC by the mentioned literati.[16] In fact, what he states in the text above seems to fit these prophets of memory much better than the average historical prophet of the monarchic period. For one, there is no reason to assume that the prophets of the monarchic period lived or spoke only or mainly at times of crisis, nor that they called the people to repentance, or that they were unpopular because of that. Moreover, one has to keep in mind that the topos of the rejected prophet is also a variant of the 'one against the many' topos (and cf. Micaiah, Elijah, to a significant extent, Jeremiah). This ideological and literary topos often serves legitimization purposes.

Legitimation may also occur through vision narratives. There is no denying that some flesh and blood prophets may indeed have experienced visions/ dreams in the ancient Near East (including, of course, ancient Israel), but the prophets whose visions are always reliable and uncontestable are those (archetypal) characters populating the memory landscape of the literati who read the relevant texts within the context of their authoritative repertoire.[17] The visions here serve to legitimize the (literary and memory-world) messenger, but above all the message that such a messenger conveys. Memories of visions play important roles as sites of memory by themselves whose contribution to the memory landscape and to the social mindscape of the group was to socialize it to some 'godly' messages.

In addition, Grabbe and others tend to focus on the images of prophets construed in the PBC. As mentioned earlier, there are plenty of prophets (נביא) portrayed in texts of the Hebrew Bible written memories about which were shaped and communicated through the literati's reading and rereading who do not fit well with Grabbe's description (e.g., Gen 20:7; Exod 15:20; Num 11:24–29; Deut 13:2–6; 1 Sam 9:9; 10:10–13; 22:5; 1 Kgs 14:1–18; Isa 3:2; Mic 3:5; Lam 2:14; 1 Chr 25:1 and notice also the way in which these literati remembered, e.g. Ahab's prophets [except Micaiah], Elisha, Hulda, Hananiah, the son of Azzur and so on; cf. the later Noadiah).

In addition, the emphasis on prophets who are not listened to by their contemporaries is indisputably present in the PBC, but is just one 'voice' among oth-

---

16 It is worth noting that Grabbe himself refers to them as the 'OT prophets' rather than as 'ancient Israel prophets' in the text cited above. This said, there are also plenty of prophets (נביא) portrayed in texts of the Hebrew Bible and whose memory was shaped and communicated through the literati's reading and rereading of the respective books and texts that do not fit well with Grabbe's description. See below.

17 This is so, because the literati construed and remembered the implied authors and narrators of texts within their core repertoire as reliable characters.

ers in Chronicles. In fact, the memory of the monarchic past encoded and communicated by Chronicles includes many prophetic voices that were listened to.[18]

To be sure, one may argue that this memory is not necessarily reliable for reconstructing the historical circumstances in the kingdom of Judah. But the books in the PBC are much later than the putative time of the prophet and represent the outcome of a very lengthy compositional and redactional process, which is impossible to track with any certitude. Further, the characterizations of the monarchic-period prophets in the PBC sets them apart from much of what we know of other prophets in the ancient Near East,[19] a fact that cannot but raise questions about the 'historicity' of their portrayal. These kinds of concerns are not restricted to the PBC. For instance, the Elijah and Elisha narratives, at least in their present form, should be dated to the Persian period. And few scholars would consider literary personages Nathan or Samuel as characterized in Kings and Samuel respectively, to be reliable guides for the reconstruction of historical prophets at the time of the formation of the Iron Age kingdoms of Israel and Judah.

It is not surprising therefore, that as in the case of state (and chiefdom) formation, one of the main critiques raised against colleagues who use 'social sciences' models for historical studies of monarchic period prophets is that they root their analysis on an assumed 'historicity' of, in most cases, the characterization of prophets in the PBC, and less frequently on selected characterizations of particular prophets in the DHC (e.g., Samuel, Nathan, Elijah, Elisha).

One might argue that such a critique may be addressed, even if one were to accept at least some of the concerns about the reliability of these characterizations for the purpose of reconstructing historical prophets in their putative periods, by maintaining that these characterizations were rooted in well-known aspects of realia from ancient times, even if these characterizations were indeed the outcome of long editorial processes and were informed by the eventual circumstances of the readership of the relevant books, as they emerged in their final compositional versions.

The same type of response may be advanced against critiques of using socio-anthropological analysis for characters that clearly existed in literary and memory worlds such as Qohelet.[20] In other words, one might claim that even if Qo-

---

18 See "Chronicles and its Reshaping of Memories of Monarchic Period Prophets: Some Observations," in this volume, pp. 407–27.
19 Cf. Martti Nissinen, *Ancient Prophecy: Near Eastern, Greek, and Biblical Perspectives* (Oxford: Oxford University Press, 2017), esp. 189–216.
20 Cf. Mark R. Sneed, *The Politics of Pessimism in Ecclesiastes. A Social-Science* Perspective (SBLAIL, 12; Atlanta: SBL, 2012).

helet is a character in the book, his characterization and the related memory evoked by reading the book are deeply rooted in the actual realia of a sage or sages.

For the present purposes, it is crucial to note that within this framework, it is only to be expected that the worlds portrayed in these books would include social roles, agents and processes that fit corresponding, in type, socio-anthropological models and concepts. This is so, because within this argument (a) models and concepts 'work' in the 'actual' world, (b) since the world of memory encoded in the relevant texts is mimetically rooted in the former, therefore (c) these models and concepts must 'work' on the world of memory evoked by reading the relevant texts.

The problem with this approach is that social memory rarely mimetically reflects the 'actual' world. Communities do not remember events and characters in particular ways only or even mainly because they just 'happened' that way. This is so because the shaping of social memories involves, *inter alia*, ongoing processes of selection, remembering and forgetting, attaching significance by plotting characters and events in larger (implicit or explicit) core narratives or metanarratives, and creatively developing sites of memory and their own network of connections.

Moreover, socially constructing and remembering what 'happened' always brings the present of the community to bear and by necessity the use of social-ideological lenses that draw attention to some matters and away from others and thus, not surprisingly, the past is always the presently remembered past. In addition, as is well known, transculturally communities may, did and continue to construe, remember and celebrate past events, personages and circumstances that 'historically' never happened. There is plenty of historical evidence for these social processes. A simple cross-cultural case one may mention in this context is the Passover story told and retold every year.

In addition, and using again the example of prophets, the comprehensive world of memory shared by the literati who read and reread their entire corpus of authoritative books included a general construction of what a prophet is that emerged strongly informed by the PBC, but which stood in sharp contrast with general conceptualizations of prophets in the ANE and in other memories held by the literati (compare and contrast the PBC prophets as a whole with those in Chronicles or in the DHC [e.g., a prophet like Joel with Hulda, or the singer prophets in Chronicles]), or for that matter Neo-Assyrian and Mari prophets, and notice, *inter alia*, that the prophecies of the PBC former tend to focus on a utopian, far away future of 'the people', their characters are encoded in a particular and unique literary genre 'the ancient Israelite prophetic book' and their words are expressed in such a matter that contain signposts to words appearing in other sections of the book associated with them, and other texts within the core corpus of texts of the literati.[21]

It is worth noting also that the vast range of prophetic characters populating the comprehensive memory-scape of the community is far more diverse and chaotic than the often narrow sets of collections of texts at the center of many social-scientific studies. However, the mentioned models work well within the particular worlds of memory evoked by each of these sets.

To be sure, one may argue that this is just because people imagine worlds on the basis of what they know and that 'naturally' they would construe prophets as diviners and so on. Although there is an element of truth in this argument (see 2.1), this is certainly not the entire story.

For one, in the world of the relevant literati prophets could be imagined as singers (see 1 Chr 25:1–8) or individuals who recorded (and interpreted) monarchic history (see 1 Chr 29:30; 2 Chr 9:29; 12:15; 13:22; 23:32; 33:19) and conversely books consisting of historical (royal) record included prophetic texts (2 Chr 20:34; 32:32; 33:18).[22] None of the above are necessarily the most common roles of prophets from a socio-anthropological perspective or transculturally.

In addition, at times the prophets of memory were imagined in even more significant ways unlike those of actual monarchic polities, such as when remembering them as focusing much of their message on an ideal future set at a fully indeterminate period well beyond the period of the relevant king, or in ways that strongly communicate a 'historically-blurred,' vague and potential 'trans-historical' context.[23] Most significantly, in all these aspects, many of the prophets included in Chronicles but absent from the DHC (e.g., Shemaiah, Azariah the son of Oded, Jahaziel the son of Zechariah, Oded) and whose prophecies and thus their portrayals in the book are considered to be unreliable sources for historical reconstructions of the monarchic period, with good reason, fit much better with the usual models or roles of a prophet than many of the prophets in the PBC. In other words, worlds of memory may or may not conform with social-anthropological expectations about prophets in ancient Near Eastern societies and the dis-

---

[21] Cf. Martti Nissinen, *Ancient Prophecy*.

[22] See "Chronicles and its Reshaping of Memories of Monarchic Period Prophets" in this volume.

[23] See E. Ben Zvi, "Balancing Shades of 'Historical', Historically-blurred', and 'Trans-historical' Contexts and Temporal Contingency in Late Persian/Early Hellenistic Yehudite Memories of YHWH's Words and Prophets of Old in the Prophetic Book Collection and its Subcollections," forthcoming in *Major and Minor Prophets Compared* (eds. Guido Benzi, Elena Di Pede, and Donatella Scaiola; Rome: Ateneo Salesiano).

tinction between one case and the other is not grounded on matters of historicity or lack thereof.

In addition, it is worth keeping in mind that prophetic characters were never imagined as standing alone, but rather as part of a closely interrelated system that included many other figures of memory (e. g., kings, 'the people'). As in all systems, grammars of preference shaping the memories associated with some members could not but impact the way in which others were remembered. These systemic considerations constrain the ways in which prophets may or may not be remembered in particular cases, narratives and general meta-narratives.[24] In none of these cases, the constraints are based on adherence to 'historicity' in our contemporary terms.

The case of memory agents and transfer of social roles across time

This case relates to the social role of 'memory agents'. Such agents are at work in any social group.[25] The literati who composed, edited, read and reread texts belonging to their authoritative repertoire clearly served the social roles of actual, historical 'memory agents' in their societies. But, for reasons that deserve a separate discussion, they construed themselves as not worthy of being remembered and erased themselves, as it were, from their own texts.[26] These texts, however, evoked and construed social memories of characters of old that were worth remembering as those explicitly and saliently fulfilling the social role of 'memory agents' for both their putative world and that of the literati.

One finds them, most obviously as the speakers proclaiming purported historical, social memory résumés (e. g., Josh 24; 1 Sam 12; Ezek 20; Ps 105; Ps 106; Neh 9).[27] In this context, it is worth mentioning also the numerous related calls to remember the past in particular ways that existed within the world of memory of the literati and were encoded in texts such as Deut 6:20–25; 26:5–9. In all

---

[24] See E. Ben Zvi, "Memories of Kings of Israel and Judah within the Mnemonic Landscape of the Literati of the Late Persian/early Hellenistic Period: Exploratory Considerations," in *SJOT* 33 (2019), 1–14.

[25] Cf. 'reputation entrepreneurs' in the works of the influential sociologist Gary Alan Fine. See, e. g., Gary Alan Fine, *Sticky Reputations: The Politics of Collective Memory in Midcentury America* (New York: Routledge, 2012).

[26] The situation changes dramatically by the time of Ben Sira.

[27] On these see, e. g., Carol Newsom, "Rhyme and Reason: The Historical Résumé in Israelite and Early Jewish Thought," in B. E. Kelle and M. B. Moore, *Israel's Prophets and Israel's Past: Essays on the Relationship of Prophetic Texts and Israelite History in Honor of John H. Hayes* (LHBOTS 446; London; New York: T&T Clark: 2006), 293–310.

these instances, remembered, but not-historical (in the professional sense) characters served, at least on the surface, the necessary role of socially authoritative 'memory agents,' and were accepted by the community as such.

The case of expelled wives and children

Whereas the previous example refers to social roles in two worlds, this one deals with processes of social causation at work in non-historical, mnemonic worlds. Elsewhere I joined several other scholars in the field and raised major concerns about the 'historicity' of the narrative of the expulsion of foreign wives and children reported in Ezra 9–10. I argued that in some circles such a mnemonic narrative served to remember and explore seemingly utopian circumstances, as per the understanding of the group, as well as the limitations of that utopia. [28] This said, since what is at stake in the story concerns matters of social identity and boundary makers, and particularly in times envisioned as 'crisis time', it is not a surprise that the underlying socio-political process in the world of the text, taken more or less literally, have been explained productively in terms of a number of socio-anthropological models, many of which may actually complement each other. [29]

Moreover, these explanations are usually supported not by the text of Ezra 9–10, per se, but by the world evoked by their co-texts, that is, when Ezra 9–10 is read in the context of Ezra-Nehemiah. Since both Ezra 9–10 and Ezra-Nehemiah represent a closing stage of a long and complicated compositional and redactional textual process, one may correctly argue that the process led, in a way unbeknownst to those involved, to a final text and memory world that fits well with certain trans-cultural social processes that can be modeled and explained through the mentioned socio-anthropological models. In other words, the outcome of the generative grammar governing the redactional processes was a text and a socially shared memory that is explainable by socio-anthropological approaches, despite its lack of 'historicity'.

---

[28] On all these issues see "Re-negotiating a Putative Utopia and the Stories of the Rejection of the Foreign Wives in Ezra-Nehemiah," in this volume, pp. 527–45.
[29] For a summary of many of these approaches, see "Re-negotiating."

The case of a supposed split in the inner group

As I discussed elsewhere, the Pentateuch encodes and communicates the foundational, 'national' collective memory of two historical groups that saw themselves as 'Israel', and which participated in shaping the collection, namely Yehudites and Samarians. Usually, in cases of two groups that construe themselves as sharing a common past, the existence of the two groups is explained and remembered as the outcome of a split in an original group. Often in such instances, the post-split groups tend to claim that they (but not the other) represent the proper continuation of the pre-split group and frequently—though not always— express a hope for a future re-unification, in which the 'wrong' side will recant and be re-incorporated into the 'proper' group.[30]

The story of the Pentateuch, and one may say with some reason the entire Hebrew Bible, and later related literature informed by books and texts included in these collections fit extremely well into this model. Israel was one and split up. Each side blames the other, and often delegitimizes its claims and post-split memories. Expressions of hope for a future re-unification appear and are usually construed as narratives of appropriation, in which one side adopts finally the 'proper' path, i.e., the path that characterizes one of the two groups, but not the other. There are good historical and socio-anthropological (including social memory) reasons for the wide distribution of these models.

However, the 'biblical' main narrative of an 'all Israel' that consisted of the twelve tribes, was together in Egypt, experienced the Exodus, revelation during its wanders in the desert, and the entrance to the land under Joshua, and which eventually split into two following the end of Solomon's reign over 'all Israel' does not reflect history.

---

[30] I discussed this in E. Ben Zvi, "The Pentateuch as/and Social Memory of 'Israel' in the Late Persian Period," in J. Baden and C. Nihan (eds.), *The Oxford Handbook of the Pentateuch* (forthcoming). Examples of the mentioned strong tendencies include the case of Christianity and Judaism sharing the Old Testament/Miqra as a collection embodying the memory of 'Israel, and despite all their differences, Western and Eastern Germany, North and South Vietnam; North and South Korea. See also the dispute over who is 'true' to the (American) Constitution in the process leading to, and even during the American Civil War (cf., e.g., Michael G. Kammen, *A Machine That Would Go of Itself: The Constitution in American Culture* [New Brunswick, NJ: Transaction Publishers, 2006], esp. 95–124). Comparable examples of splits within political parties are a myriad and well-attested in Europe. The identity, character, and even historical context of the players may be widely different, but the grammars of preference for construing and remembering the foundational events that led to a situation of two groups sharing a past and the usual hopes of unification, identity fears and the associated processes of 'otherization' tend to appear in the vast majority of these cases.

In this case, the social memory of 'Israel' as agreed upon by the group fits well into transcultural, socio-anthropological models and expectations, but the historical reality as reconstructed by professional historians does not at all. The 'all Israel' of the Pentateuch (and other 'biblical' texts) is not the result of one unified group that eventually split, but to the contrary, of two groups that under circumstances that cannot be discussed here, eventually grew to understand themselves as one, with a shared memory about themselves and their foundational events.

The point I wish to advance here is that the eventual main narrative of 'Israel' about itself and its origins in the Pentateuch fits very well with what one would anticipate from socio-anthropological models and concepts, yet it is non-historical. These models and concepts work here only in a world of imagination and memory.

A later but illustrative case about the role of language in social identity strategies

The last example comes for a later period. As is well-known, selective use of language plays an important role in identity strategies. Examples abound and come from various periods and areas of the world. Given the context here, it is worth noting that Diana Edelman has recently explored this matter, from a strong historical perspective, in relation to the early second Temple period.[31]

That said, I would like to draw attention to a rabbinic tradition embodied in Lev Rab. 32.5 (and in Song Rab. 4.25), according to which Israel was redeemed from Egypt because they maintained four things. Two of these directly address this issue, namely 'language' and 'names,'[32] the latter being directly related to the former. I doubt there are many professional historians of ancient Israel who would accept the 'historicity' of this mnemonic narrative, but it certainly works well within the parameters of accepted socio-linguistic approaches and their bearings on matters of social identity and of strategies of producing and socially reproducing identity by minority groups across time and space.[33]

---

[31] Diana Edelman, "Identities within a Central and Peripheral Perspective: The Use of Aramaic in the Hebrew Bible," E. Ben Zvi and C. Levin (eds.) *Centres and Peripheries in the Early Second Temple* Period (FAT, 108; Tübingen: Mohr-Siebeck, 2016), 109–31.
[32] The other two are gossip and 'licentious' sexual behavior. A discussion of why these two were also included is beyond the scope of this contribution, as much as is of interest in itself.
[33] Language distinctiveness is often a key marker of social identity (see the importance of speaking Greek in the Hellenistic world), both for insiders and outsiders. In general, it is usually

Implications and Further Research

The preceding examples may be easily multiplied.[34] Paraphrasing Qohelet, there is no end to examples, and the multiplications of examples is a weariness of the flesh. I am certainly not interested in wearing out the reader. I hope that the examples above suffice to make the point that socio-anthropological or social-scientific models and concepts may work not only for 'historical' worlds, but also for worlds of imagination and memory. Moreover, given that socio-anthropological models require, by necessity, process simplification, at times they may work better in worlds of memory than in 'historical' worlds. Historical worlds are always chaotic, whereas the models tend not to be. Remembered worlds are often less chaotic than 'real' worlds, due to cognitive reasons, and therefore may provide a better playground for the aforementioned models to work. The same holds true in terms of a reduction in the number of agents and their interactions.

This being so, and given our focus on ancient Israel, what are the implications and potential paths for future research that emerge from these considerations in terms of the use of 'social-scientific' approaches in our field? The following remarks are meant to open a wide discussion on these matters.[35]

The historicity in the sense of 'mimetic external referentiality' of narratives about the past cannot be proven by arguing that the processes and events that it portrays fit with general explanatory models and expectations derived from cross-cultural, socio-anthropologic studies.

Conversely, claiming that the historical prophets of the monarchic period were not as portrayed in the PBC, or that the process of state formation in Israel and Judah did not proceed as described in Samuel (and Kings), or that Israel was not historically a unified group that split into two does not require that we abandon social-anthropological models and concepts. In fact, we may find much of

---

agreed that the ability to maintain heritage languages in minority contexts contributes to the development of a strong sense of group identity and boundaries, and that the latter, in turn, contribute much to the ability to maintain the heritage language, and thus shaping a positive feedback loop. Edelman writes, reflecting a long tradition in scholarship, "[l]anguage is often a marker of group identity ... language is one means by which group identity is often defined and expressed ... [i]t cements solidarity among members by eliciting feelings of belonging, appreciation and attraction." See Edelman, "Identities within a Central and Peripheral Perspective." 110–11.

34 For instance, one may discuss the choice of Jerusalem as the city located in a peripheral space or cognitive dissonance in the prophets of memory and their putative worlds.

35 The oral presentation out of which this contribution emerged was given in a forum about the future of Social-Scientific approaches in our field.

interest in the work of scholars who used social-scientific models a generation ago.

These models and expectations have indeed much to contribute to the study of mnemonic narratives and the imaginary worlds of memory that they construe, even when they are devoid of 'historicity.'

As mentioned above, and given that theoretical modelling is by inner necessity a simplifying process, the mnemonic narratives, which by themselves, tend to simplify complex events and processes so as to make them memorable and reduce the associated cognitive costs, might resemble these models more than historical events/processes as professional historians are able to reconstruct them (e. g., less chaos, fewer characters, and so on).[36] Further, whereas memories evoked within particular contexts and through the reading and rereading of certain books or sections thereof may activate worlds of memory in which certain models work well, memories evoked in other contexts and through the reading and rereading of other books or passages may activate other worlds of memory, in which this does not hold true.

The previous consideration raises the issue of how the comprehensive social memory of a group, which includes all these worlds of memory, balances these worlds and how social-anthropological models and concepts may heuristically help us to imagine and construct these balancing processes.

Imagination has its limits. The world of knowledge of those shaping imaginary worlds is to a significant extent constrained by their own world of knowledge, social mindscape and of course, social memory. This means both that (i) 'realities' in the present past of the remembering group influence their construed worlds of memory, though in a highly mediated way, namely via its reflections in memory, including and in some cases mainly via shaping and evoking memory texts, either oral or written and (ii) all other socio-cultural 'realities', and matters of social location and ideology in the present also influence their construed worlds of memory. Both (i) and (ii) may serve as mechanisms through which

---

[36] From a different perspective, one may approach these matters from the perspective of the difference between 'history' and 'historical narrative'. To address this perspective in this context requires a full discussion on historical methodology and on the relation between social memory and professionally written historical narratives, which cannot be carried out here. For my own position on some of these issues, see E. Ben Zvi, "Clio Today and Ancient Israelite History: Some Thoughts and Observations at the Closing Session of The European Seminar for Historical Methodology," Lester L. Grabbe (ed.), *"Even God Cannot Change the Past": Reflections on Seventeen Years of the European Seminar in Historical Methodology* (LHBOTS 663, London: Bloomsbury T&T Clark, 2018), 20–49.

models from the social-sciences that might have worked in these 'realities' are transferred, at least partially, to the community's world of memory.[37]

Within the social mindscape of the group, there exist underlying generative grammars of preference or dis-preference for social production and reproduction of narratives about the past, including both matters related to basic features of plots and, *inter alia*, underlying, implicit rules concerning basic expectations and conceptualizations of causality and the potential ways in which the latter may be instantiated. When the community shaping its world of memory implicitly, likely in ways unbeknownst to them, internalized expectations that we today relate directly or indirectly with those to which social anthropological approaches lead us, the latter are likely to, in one way or another, be understood as 'at work' in the world of memory of the group, even if they never formulated them. The literati followed some transcultural models we have now about how certain social and political processes and roles tend to develop. It seems that in these cases our social-anthropological models represented, at the very least, an approximation of the 'natural' order, that is, 'the way things are/work out' from the perspective of the literati, and thus, by shaping their memories accordingly, they increased the memories' verisimilitude within their ideological discourse, world of knowledge and social mindscape.

The 'natural' rules of the world may well be transparent to the literati. There is a need for social-anthropological studies that emphasize that which was transparent in their social mindscape and how it influenced the worlds of memory.

The community imagining and remembering a past and past characters and processes must be able to feel connected with, and emotionally care about the past world they are creating in their own present; it must be able to 'engage' as it were and this requires that which is 'natural' and thus 'invisible' in their world to be so in the other. The outcome is the creation of a partially shared realm either conveying a sense of underlying continuity or, at the very least, shaping a conceptually in-between area in which the same basic rules apply. In other words, it requires the construction of sites of memory that serve as transtemporal bridges. Through this process the imagined, remembered past may be influenced by the interpretive framework of social models and roles at work in the present of the literati, as it imagines itself, and *vice versa*.

Social memories are most often shaped as explicit or implicit narratives. The mnemonic narratives of a group (including their characters and plots) do not

---

[37] Cf. the case of the Book of Mormon, and notice the role of the present past of the community in which the book emerged (i.e., their 'biblical past') contributed to the shaping of other memories of their (later) past, and eventual future, and how both were associated with the identity, location and ideology of the group.

exist in silos, but informed each other, and all together create a system or world of memory, which by necessity is also an imaginary, literary (in the widest sense of the term) world. This being so, cross-cultural and cognitive studies on (a) (imaginary) world shaping, (b) the ways in which they serve necessary social roles, as social memories in ancient Israel, providing playgrounds on which members of the group may safely explore various ideas and (c) the ways in which texts may induce readers to care about characters that are a product of social imagination. All the above types of studies may make an important heuristic contribution to the study of the intellectual world of ancient Israel, even if these studies are focused on contemporary societies and their socio-cultural production.[38]

Instead of a conclusion

In sum, there is much work before us. Socio-anthropological approaches are as needed now as they were one or two generations ago for studies of ancient Israel. This said, a wider focus is also needed. Conversations as the one I hope to initiate with this contribution represent a step in that direction.

---

38 E.g., Mark J. P. Wolf, *Building Imaginary Worlds: The Theory and History of* Subcreation (Routledge: New York, 2012); Isabel Jaén and Julies Jacques Simon (eds.), *Cognitive Literary Studies Current Themes and New Directions* (Austin, TX: University of Texas Press, 2012); Blakey Vermeule, *Why De We Care about Literary Characters?* (Baltimore: John Hopkins University Press, 2010).

Bibliography

Abadie, Philippe. "From the Impious Manasseh (2 Kings 21) to the Convert Manasseh (2 Chronicles 33)," in *The Chronicler as Theologian: Essays in Honor of Ralph W. Klein* (eds. M. Patrick Graham, Steven L. McKenzie and Gary N. Knoppers; JSOTSup 371; London: T&T Clark, 2003), 89–104.

Abate, Emma. *La fine del regno di Sedecia* (Textos y estudios "Cardenal Cisneros" 76; Madrid: CSIC, 2008).

Abbott, Andrew. *Department & Discipline: Chicago Sociology at One Hundred* (Chicago, IL: University of Chicago Press, 1999).

Achenbach, Reinhard, Rainer Albertz, and Jacob Wöhrle, eds. *The Foreigner and the Law: Perspectives from the Hebrew Bible and the Ancient Near East* (BZAR, 16; Wiesbaden: Harrassowitz, 2011).

Ackroyd, Peter R. "The Biblical Interpretation of the Reigns of Ahaz and Hezekiah," in *In the Shelter of Elyon: Essays on Ancient Palestinian Life and Literature in Honor of G. W. Ahlström* (eds. W. Boyd Barrick and John R. Spencer; JSOTSup 31; Sheffield: JSOT Press, 1984), 247–59.

Aharoni, Yohanan. *The Land of the Bible* (rev. ed.; Philadelphia: Westminster, 1979).

Albertz, Rainer. *A History of Israelite Religion in the Old Testament Period*, vol. 1 (OTL; Louisville: Westminster John Knox, 1994).

Albertz, Rainer. "An End to the Confusion? Why the Old Testament Cannot Be a Hellenistic Book", in *Did Moses Speak Attic?* (ed. Lester L. Grabbe; JSOTSup 317; Sheffield: Sheffield Academic Press, 2001), 30–46.

Albertz, Rainer. *Israel in Exile: The History and Literature of the Sixth Century BCE* (Atlanta: SBL, 2003).

Albertz, Rainer. "Darius in Place of Cyrus: The First Edition of Deutero-Isaiah (Isaiah 40.1–52.12)," in *JSOT* 27 (2003): 371–83.

Albertz, Rainer. "Purity Strategies and Political Interests in the Policy of Nehemiah," in *Confronting the Past: Archaeological and Historical Essays on Ancient Israel in Honor of William G. Dever* (eds. Seymour Gitin, J. Edward Wright and J. P. Dessel; Winona Lake, IN: Eisenbrauns, 2006), 199–206.

Albertz, Rainer and Jakob Wöhrle, eds. *Between Cooperation and Hostility: Multiple Identities in Ancient Judaism and the Interaction with Foreign Powers* (Journal of Ancient Judaism Supplements; Göttingen: Vandenhoeck & Ruprecht, 2013).

Alster, Bendt. "A Note on the Uriah Letter in the Sumerian Sargon Legend", in *Zeitschrift für Assyriologie* 77 (1987): 169–73.

Alster, Bendt. "Lugalbanda and the Early Epic Tradition in Mesopotamia", in *Lingering Over Words: Studies in Ancient Near Eastern Literature in Honor of William L. Moran* (eds. Tzvi Abusch, John Huehnergard and Piotr Steinkeller; Atlanta: Scholars Press, 1990), 59–72.

Alter, Robert. *The David Story: A Translation with Commentary of 1 and 2 Samuel* (New York: W.W. Norton, 1999).

Amar, Itzhak. "Chaotic Writing as a Literary Element in the Story of Ahaz in 2 Chronicles 28," in *VT* 66 (2016): 349–364.

Amin, Samir. "The Ancient World-Systems versus the Modern Capitalist World-System," in *Review Fernand Braudel Center* 14 (1991): 349–85.

Amit, Yairah. "'The Glory of Israel Does Not Deceive or Change His Mind': On the Reliability of Narrator and Speakers in Biblical Narrative," in *Proof* 12 (1992): 201–12.
Amit, Yairah. *Hidden Polemics in Biblical Narrative* (Leiden: Brill, 2000).
Amit, Yairah. "The Saul Polemic in the Persian Period," in *Judah and the Judeans in the Neo-Babylonian Period* (eds. Oded Lipschits and Joseph Blenkinsopp; Winona Lake, IN: Eisenbrauns, 2003), 647–61.
Amit, Yairah. "The Role of Prophecy and Prophets in the Chroniclers World," in *Prophets, Prophecy, and Prophetic Texts in Second Temple Judaism* (eds. Michael H. Floyd and Robert D. Haak; LHBOTS 427; London: T&T Clark, 2006), 80–101.
Andersen, Francis I. and David Noel Freedman. *Hosea: A New Translation with Introduction and Commentary* (AB 24; New York, NY: Doubleday, 1980).
Anderson, Benedict. *Imagined Communities: Reflections on the Origin and Spread of Nationalism* (Rev. ed.; London and New York: Verso, 2006).
Anthonioz, Stéphanie. "Cities of Glory and Cities of Pride: Concepts, Gender, and Images of Cities in Mesopotamia and the Bible" in *Memory and the City in Ancient Israel* (eds. Diana V. Edelman and Ehud Ben Zvi; Winona Lake, IN: Eisenbrauns, 2014), 21–40.
Aperghis, Gerassimos G. "Jewish Subjects and Seleukid Kings: A Case Study of Economic Interaction," in *The Economies of Hellenistic Societies, Third to First Centuries BC* (eds. Zosia H. Archibald, John K. Davies and Vincent Gabrielsen; Oxford/New York: Oxford University Press, 2011), 19–41.
Applegate, John. "The Fall of Zedekiah: Redactional Debate in the Book of Jeremiah, Part I," in *VT* 48 (1998): 137–60.
Applegate, John. "The Fate of Zedekiah: Redactional Debate in the Book of Jeremiah, Part II," in *VT* 58 (1998): 301–8.
Assmann, Aleida. *Cultural Memory and Western Civilization: Functions, Media, Archives* (Cambridge/New York: Cambridge University Press, 2011).
Assmann, Jan. *Religion and Cultural Memory* (Stanford: Stanford University Press, 2006).
Auld, A. Graeme. "Prophets Shared–But Recycled" in *The Future of the Deuteronomistic History* (ed. Thomas C. Römer; BETL 147; Leuven: Leuven University Press/Peeters, 2000), 19–28.
Austin, Michael M. "Hellenistic Kings, War and the Economy," in *Classical Quarterly* 36 (1986): 450–66.
Avioz, Michael. "A Rhetorical Analysis of Jeremiah 7:1–15," in *TynB* 57 (2006): 173–189.
Avioz, Michael. "The Davidic Covenant in 2 Samuel 7: Conditional or Unconditional?" in *The Ancient Near East in the 12th–10th Centuries B.C.E.: Culture and, History. Proceedings of the International Conference Held at the University of Haifa, 2–5 May, 2010* (eds. Gershon Galil, Ayelet Gilboa, Aren M. Maeir and Dan'el Kahn; AOAT 392; Münster: Ugarit-Verlag, 2012), 43–53.
Bae, Hee-Sook. *Vereinte Suche nach JHWH. Die Hiskianische und Josianische Reform in der Chronik* (BZAW 355; Berlin: De Gruyter, 2005).
Balogh, Csaba. "'He Filled Zion with Justice and Righteousness.' The Composition of Isaiah 33", in *Bib* 89 (2008): 477–504
Baltzer, Klaus. "Das Ende des Staates Juda und die Messias-Frage," in *Studien zur Theologie der alttestamentlichen Überlieferungen* (eds. Rolf Rendtorff and Klaus Koch; Neukirchen: Neukirchener Verlag, 1961), 33–43.
Baltzer, Klaus. *Deutero-Isaiah* (Hermeneia; Minneapolis: Augsburg Fortress, 2001).

Bang, Peter Fibiger. "Imperial Bazaar: Towards a Comparative Understanding of Markets in the Roman Empire," in *Ancient Economies, Modern Methodologies: Archaeology, Comparative History* (eds. Peter Fibiger Bang, Mamoru Ikeguchi and Hartmut G. Ziche; Pragmateiai 12; Bari: Edipuglia, 2006), 51–88.

Bang, Peter Fibiger. *Roman Bazaar: A Comparative Study of Trade and Markets in a Tributary Empire* (Cambridge: Cambridge University Press, 2011).

Barbour (Grillo), Jennifer. *The Story of Israel in the Book of Qohelet: Ecclesiastes as Cultural Memory* (OTM; Oxford: Oxford University Press, 2012).

Barkay, Gabriel. "Additional View of Jerusalem in Nehemiah Days", in *New Studies in the Archaeology of Jerusalem and Its Region II* (eds. David Amit and Guy D. Stiebel; Jerusalem: Israel Antiquities Authority and the Hebrew University, 2008), 48–54.

Barkin, Steve M. "The Journalist as Story-teller. An Interdisciplinary Perspective," in *American Journalism* 1 (1984): 27–33.

Bar-Kochva, Bezalel. *Pseudo-Hecataeus, On the Jews* (Berkeley: University of California Press, 1996).

Barstad, Hans M. *The Myth of the Empty Land: A Study in the History and Archaeology of Judah during the 'Exilic' Period* (Oslo: Scandinavian University Press, 1996).

Barstad, Hans M. "After the 'Myth of the Empty Land': Major Challenges in the Study of Neo-Babylonian Judah," in *Judah and the Judeans in the Neo-Babylonian Period* (eds. Oded Lipschits and Joseph Blenkinsopp; Winona Lake, IN: Eisenbrauns, 2003), 3–20.

Bar-Tal, Daniel, Lily Chernyak-Hai, Noa Schori and Ayelet Gundar, "A Sense of Self-Perceived Collective Victimhood in Intractable Conflicts," in *International Review of the Red Cross* 91/874 (2009): 229–258.

Bar-Tal, Daniel, *Intractable Conflicts: Socio-Psychological Foundations and* Dynamics (Cambridge: Cambridge University Press, 2013).

Barton, John. *Joel and Obadiah: A Commentary* (OTL; Louisville: Westminster John Knox, 2001).

Basirov, Oric. "The Achemenian Practice of Primary Burial: An Argument against Their Zoroastrianism? Or a Testimony of Their Religious Tolerance?" in *The World of Achaemenid Persia. History, Art and Society in Iran and the Ancient Near East* (eds. John Curtis and St John Simpson; London: Tauris, 2010), 75–83.

Baumann, Gerd. "Grammars of Identity/Alterity: A Structural Approach," in *Grammars of Identity/Alterity: A Structural Approach* (eds. Gerd Baumann and André Gingrich; EASA Series, 3; New York: Berghahn, 2006), 18–50.

Baumgarten, Albert I. "'But Touch the Law and the Sect Will Split': Legal Dispute as the Cause of Sectarian Schism," in *Review of Rabbinic Judaism* 5 (2002): 301–315.

Baumgarten, Albert. *The Flourishing of Jewish Sects in the Maccabean Era: An Interpretation* (Leiden: Brill, 1997).

Bautch, Richard J. *Developments in Genre between Post-exilic Penitential Prayers and the Psalms of Communal Lament* (Academia Biblica 7; Atlanta, GA: SBL, 2003).

Beaulieu, Paul-Alain. "Nabonidus the Mad King: A Reconsideration of His Steles from Harran and Babylon," in *Representations of Political Power: Case Histories of Change and Dissolving Order in the Ancient Near East* (eds. Marlies Heinz and Marian H. Feldman; Winona Lake, IN: Eisenbrauns, 2007), 137–66.

Becking, Bob. "More than a Pawn in Their Game: Zedekiah and the Fall of Jerusalem in 2 Chronicles 36:11–21," in *Rewriting Biblical History: Essays on Chronicles and Ben Sira in Honor of Pancratius C. Beentjes* (eds. Jeremy Corley and Harm van Grol; Deuterocanonical and Cognate Literature Studies 7; Berlin: De Gruyter, 2011), 257–71.

Becking, Bob. "Zedekiah, Josephus and the Dating of the Books of Chronicles," in *SJOT* 25 (2011): 217–33.

Bedford, Peter R. "The Economic Role of the Jerusalem Temple in Achaemenid Judah: Comparative Perspectives," in *Shai le-Sara Japhet: Studies in the Bible, its Exegesis and its Language* (eds. Moshe Bar-Asher et al.; Jerusalem: Bialik Institute, 2007).

Beentjes, Pancratius C., "Identity and Community in the Book of Chronicles: The Role and Meaning of the verb *jāḥaś*," in *ZAH* 12 (1999): 233–37.

Beentjes, Pancratius C., "Prophets in the Book of Chronicles" in *The Elusive Prophet: The Prophet as a Historical Person, Literary Character, and Anonymous Artist* (ed. J. C. de Moor; OTS 45; Leiden: Brill, 2001), 45–53.

Beentjes, Pancratius C. "Ben Sira 44:19–23–the Patriarchs: Text, Tradition, Theology," in *Studies in the Book of Ben Sira* (eds. Géza G. Xeravits and József Zsengellér; JSJSup 127; Leiden: Brill, 2008), 209–28.

Beentjes, Pancratius C. *Tradition and Transformation in the Book of Chronicles* (SSN 52; Leiden: Brill, 2008).

Beentjes, Pancratius C. "The Importance of Being Registered: The Role and Meaning of the verb יחש in the Book of Chronicles," in *Tradition and Transformation in the Book of Chronicles* (ed. Pancratius C. Beentjes; SSN 52; Leiden: Brill; 2008), pp. 187–91.

Begg, C. T."The Classical Prophets in the Chronistic History," in *BZ* 32 (1988): 100–107.

Begg, C. T. "The Chronicler's Non-mention of Elisha," in *BN* 45 (1988): 100–107.

Ben Zvi, Ehud. *A Historical-Critical Study of The Book of Zephaniah* (BZAW 198; Berlin: De Gruyter, 1991).

Ben Zvi, Ehud. "The Dialogue between Abraham and YHWH in Gen 18:23–32," in *JSOT* 53 (1992): 27–46.

Ben Zvi, Ehud. "Prophets and Prophecy in the Compositional and Redactional Notes in I–II Kings," in *ZAW* 105 (1993): 331–51.

Ben Zvi, Ehud. "Inclusion in and Exclusion from Israel as Conveyed by the Use of the Term 'Israel' in Postmonarchic Biblical Texts," in *The Pitcher is Broken: Memorial Essays for Gösta W. Ahlström* (eds. Steven W. Holloway and Lowell K. Handy; JSOTSup 190; Sheffield: JSOT Press, 1995), 95–149.

Ben Zvi, Ehud. "Prelude to a Reconstruction of the Historical Manassic Judah," in *BN* 81 (1996): 31–44.

Ben Zvi, Ehud. *A Historical-Critical Study of The Book of Obadiah* (BZAW 242; Berlin: De Gruyter, 1996).

Ben Zvi, Ehud. "The Chronicler as a Historian: Building Texts," in *The Chronicler as Historian* (eds. M. Patrick Graham, Kenneth G. Hoglund and Steven L. McKenzie; JSOTSup 238; Sheffield: JSOT Press, 1997), 132–49.

Ben Zvi, Ehud. "When a Foreign Monarch Speaks," in *The Chronicler as Author: Studies in Text and Texture* (eds. M. Patrick Graham and Steven L. McKenzie; JSOTSup 263; Sheffield: Sheffield Academic Press, 1999), 209–28.

Ben Zvi, Ehud. "About Time: Observations About the Construction of Time in the Book of Chronicles," in *HBT* 22 (2000): 17–31.

Ben Zvi, Ehud. "Shifting the Gaze: Historiographic Constraints in Chronicles and Their Implications," in *The Land That I Will Show You: Essays on the History and Archaeology* of the Ancient Near East in Honor of J. Maxwell Miller (eds. M. Patrick Graham and J. Andrew Dearman; JSOTSup 343; Sheffield: JSOT Press, 2001), 38–60.

Ben Zvi, Ehud. *Signs of Jonah: Reading and Rereading in Ancient Yehud* (JSOTSup 367; London: Sheffield Academic Press, 2003).

Ben Zvi, Ehud. "The Prophetic Book: A Key Form of Prophetic Literature', in *The Changing Face of Form Criticism for the Twenty-First Century* (eds. Marvin A. Sweeney and Ehud Ben Zvi; Grand Rapids, MI: Eerdmans, 2003), 276–97.

Ben Zvi, Ehud. "The Secession of the Northern Kingdom in Chronicles: Accepted 'Facts' and New Meanings," in *The Chronicler as a Theologian: Essays in Honor of Ralph W. Klein* (eds. M. Patrick Graham, Steven L. McKenzie and Gary N. Knoppers; JSOTSup 371; London: T& T Clark, 2003), 61–88.

Ben Zvi, Ehud. "What is New in Yehud? Some Considerations," in *Yahwism after the Exile* (eds. Rainer Albertz and Bob Becking; STAR 5; Assen: Van Gorcum, 2003), 32–48.

Ben Zvi, Ehud. "Malleability and its Limits. Sennacherib's Campaign against Judah as a Case Study," in *Like a Bird in a Cage. The Invasion of Sennacherib in 701 BCE* (ed. Lester L. Grabbe; JSOTSup 363; Sheffield: Sheffield Academic Press, 2003), 73–105.

Ben Zvi, Ehud. "Analogical Thinking and Ancient Israel Intellectual History: The Case for an 'Entropy Model' in the Study of Israelite Thought" in *Relating to the Text. Interdisciplinary and Form-Critical Insights on the Bible* (eds. Timothy J. Sandoval and Carleen Mandolfo; JSOTSup 384; London: T&T Clark, 2003), 321–332.

Ben Zvi, Ehud and Antje Labahn. "Observations on Women in the Genealogies of 1 Chronicles 1–9," in *Bib* 84 (2003): 457–478.

Ben Zvi, Ehud. "'The Prophets'–Generic Prophets and their Role in the Construction of the Image of the 'Prophets of Old' within the Postmonarchic Readership of the Book of King," in *ZAW* 116 (2004): 555–67.

Ben Zvi, Ehud. "Observations on Prophetic Characters, Prophetic Texts, Priests of Old, Persian Period Priests and Literati," in *The Priest in the Prophets. The Portrayal of the Priests, Prophets and Other Religious Specialists in the Latter Prophets* (eds. Lester L. Grabbe and Alice O. Bellis. Journal for the Study of the Old Testament Supplement 408. London: T&T Clark, 2004), 19–30.

Ben Zvi, Ehud. *Hosea* (FOTL 21 A/1; Grand Rapids, MI: Eerdmans, 2005).

Ben Zvi, Ehud. "Josiah and the Prophetic Books: Some Observations", in *Good Kings and Bad Kings* (ed. Lester L. Grabbe; LHBOTS 393; European Seminar in Historical Methodology 5; London: T&T Clark, 2005), 47–64.

Ben Zvi, Ehud. "Revisiting 'Boiling in Fire' in 2 Chr 35:13 and Related Passover Questions Text, Exegetical Needs, Concerns, and General Implications," in *Biblical Interpretation in Judaism and Christianity* (eds. Isaac Kalimi and Peter J. Haas; LHBOTS, 439; London and New York: T&T Clark, 2006) 238–50.

Ben Zvi, Ehud. "Observations on Josiah's Account in Chronicles and Implications for Reconstructing the Worldview of the Chronicler," in *Essays on Ancient Israel in Its Near Eastern Context: A Tribute to Nadav Na'aman* (eds. Yairah Amit, Ehud Ben Zvi, Israel Finkelstein and Oded Lipschits; Winona Lake, IN: Eisenbrauns, 2006), 89–106.

Ben Zvi, Ehud. "De-historicizing and Historicizing Tendencies in the Twelve Prophetic Books: A Case Study of the Heuristic Value of a Historically Anchored Systemic Approach to the Corpus of Prophetic Literature" in *Israel's Prophets And Israel's Past: Essays on the*

Relationship of Prophetic Texts And Israelite History in Honor of John H. Hayes (eds. Brad E. Kelle and Megan Bishop Moore; LHBOTS 446; London: T&T Clark, 2006), 37–56.
Ben Zvi, Ehud. "Utopias, Multiple Utopias, and Why Utopias at All? The Social Roles of Utopian Visions in Prophetic Books within Their Historical Context," in *Utopia and Dystopia in Prophetic Literature* (ed. Ehud Ben Zvi; PFES 92; Helsinki: Finnish Exegetical Society / Göttingen: Vandenhoeck & Ruprecht, 2006), 55–85.
Ben Zvi, Ehud. *History, Literature and Theology in the Book of Chronicles* (London: Equinox, 2006).
Ben Zvi, Ehud. "Who Knew What? The Construction of the Monarchic Past in Chronicles and Implications for the Intellectual Setting of Chronicles," in *Judah and the Judeans in the Fourth Century B.C.E.* (eds. Oded Lipschits, Gary N. Knoppers and Rainer Albertz; Winona Lake, IN: Eisenbrauns, 2007), 349–360.
Ben Zvi, Ehud. "The House of Omri/Ahab in Chronicles," in *Ahab Agonistes: The Rise and Fall of the Omri Dynasty* (ed. Lester L. Grabbe; LHBOTS 421; European Seminar in Historical Methodology 6; London/New York: T&T Clark, 2007), 41–53.
Ben Zvi, Ehud. "Reading Hosea and Imagining YHWH," in *HBT* 30 (2008): 43–57.
Ben Zvi, Ehud. "Imagining Josiah's Book and the Implications of Imagining it in Early Persian Yehud," in *Berührungspunkte: Studien zur Sozial- und Religionsgeschichte Israels und seiner Umwelt: Festschrift für Rainer Albertz zu seinem 65. Geburtstag* (eds. Rüdiger Schmitt, Ingo Kottsieper and Jakob Wöhrle; AOAT 250; Münster: Ugarit Verlag, 2008), 193–212.
Ben Zvi, Ehud. "A House of Treasures: The Account of Amaziah in 2 Chronicles 25– Observations and Implications," in *SJOT* 22 (2008): 63–85.
Ben Zvi, Ehud and James D. Nogalski (with an introduction by Thomas C. Römer). *Two Sides of a Coin: Juxtaposing Views on Interpreting the Book of the Twelve/the Twelve Prophetic Books* (Analecta Gorgiana 201; Piscataway, N.J: Gorgias Press, 2009).
Ben Zvi, Ehud. "Are There Any Bridges Out There? How Wide Was the Conceptual Gap between the Deuteronomistic History and Chronicles?" in *Community Identity in Judean Historiography: Biblical and Comparative Perspectives* (eds. Gary N. Knoppers and Kenneth A. Ristau; Winona Lake, IN: Eisenbrauns, 2009), 59–86.
Ben Zvi, Ehud. "Towards an Integrative Study of the Production of Authoritative Books in Ancient Israel," in *The Production of Prophecy: Constructing Prophecy and Prophets in Yehud* (eds. Diana V. Edelman and Ehud Ben Zvi; London: Equinox, 2009), 15–28.
Ben Zvi, Ehud. "The Communicative Message of Some Linguistic Choices," in *A Palimpsest: Rhetoric, Ideology, Stylistics and Language Relating to Persian Israel* (eds. Ehud Ben Zvi, Diana V. Edelman and Frank Polak; Piscataway, NJ: Gorgias, 2009), 269–90.
Ben Zvi, Ehud. "The Concept of Prophetic Books and Its Historical Setting", in *The Production of Prophecy: Constructing Prophecy and Prophets in Yehud* (eds. Diana V. Edelman and Ehud Ben Zvi; BibleWorld; London: Equinox, 2009), 73–95.
Ben Zvi, Ehud. "Is the Twelve Hypothesis Likely from an Ancient Readers' Perspective?" in *Two Sides of a Coin* (eds. Ehud Ben Zvi and James D. Nogalski; Analecta Gorgiana 201; Piscataway, NJ: Gorgias, 2009), 47–96.
Ben Zvi, Ehud. "A Contribution to Intellectual History of Yehud: The Story of Micaiah and Its Function within the Discourse of Persian Period Literati," in *The Historian and the Bible* (eds. Philip R. Davies and Diana V. Edelman; LHBOTS 530; London and New York: T&T Clark, 2010), 89–102.

Ben Zvi, Ehud. "On the Term 'Deuteronomistic' in Relation to Joshua–Kings in the Persian Period", in *Raising Up a Faithful Exegete* (eds. Kurt L. Noll and Brooks Schramm; Winona Lake, IN: Eisenbrauns, 2010), 61–71.

Ben Zvi, Ehud. "Reconstructing the Intellectual Discourse of Ancient Yehud," in *SR* 39 (2010): 7–23.

Ben Zvi, Ehud. "Total Exile, Empty Land and the General Intellectual Discourse in Yehud," in *The Concept of Exile in Ancient Israel and Its Historical Contexts* (eds. Ehud Ben Zvi and Christoph Levin; BZAW 404; Berlin: De Gruyter, 2010), 155–68.

Ben Zvi, Ehud. "One Size Does Not Fit All: Notes on the Different Ways in Which Chronicles Dealt with the Authoritative Literature of its Time," in *What was Authoritative for Chronicles?* (eds. Ehud Ben Zvi and Diana V. Edelman; Winona Lake, IN: Eisenbrauns, 2011), 13–35.

Ben Zvi, Ehud. "On Social Memory and Identity Formation in Late Persian Yehud: A Historian's Viewpoint with a Focus on Prophetic Literature, Chronicles, and the Dtr. Historical Collection," in *Texts, Contexts and Readings in Postexilic Literature: Explorations into Historiography and Identity Negotiation in Hebrew Bible and Related Texts* (ed. Louis C. Jonker; FAT II/53; Tübingen: Mohr Siebeck, 2011), 95–148.

Ben Zvi, Ehud. "Constructing the Past: The Recent History of Jewish Biblical Theology," in *Jewish Bible Theology. Perspectives and Case Studies* (ed. I. Kalimi; Winona Lake, Ind.: Eisenbrauns, 2012), 31–50.

Ben Zvi, Ehud. "Remembering the Prophets through the Reading and Rereading of a Collection of Written Prophetic Books in Yehud: Methodological Considerations and Explorations," in *Remembering and Forgetting in Judah's Early Second Temple Period* (eds. Ehud Ben Zvi and Christoph Levin; FAT 85; Tübingen: Mohr Siebeck, 2012), 17–44.

Ben Zvi, Ehud. "When YHWH Tests People: General Considerations and Particular Observations regarding the Books of Chronicles and Job," in *Far from Minimal: Celebrating the Work and Influence of Philip R. Davies* (eds. Duncan Burns and John W. Rogerson; LHBOTS; London: T&T Clark, 2012), 11–20.

Ben Zvi, Ehud. "The Study of Forgetting and the Forgotten in Ancient Israelite Discourse/s: Observations and Test Cases," in *Cultural Memory in Biblical Exegesis* (eds. Pernille Carstens, Trine Hasselbach and Niels Peter Lemche; Perspectives on Hebrew Scriptures and Its Contexts 17; Piscataway, NJ: Gorgias, 2012), 139–57.

Ben Zvi, Ehud. "How 'Historical' is Ancient Israel?" in *The Wiley-Blackwell Companion to the History of Jews and Judaism* (ed. Alan T. Levenson; Malden, MA: Wiley-Blackwell, 2012), 25–34.

Ben Zvi, Ehud. "Observations on Lines of Thought Concerning the Concepts of Prophecy and Prophets in Yehud, with an Emphasis on Deuteronomy–2 Kings and Chronicles," in *Words, Ideas, Worlds: Biblical Essays in Honour of Yairah Amit* (eds. Athalya Brenner and Frank H. Polak; Sheffield: Sheffield Phoenix, 2012), 1–19.

Ben Zvi, Ehud. "Toward a Sense of Balance: Remembering the Catastrophe of Monarchic Judah/(Ideological) Israel and Exile through Reading Chronicles in late Yehud," in *Chronicling the Chronicler: The Book of Chronicles and Early Second Temple Historiography* (eds. Paul S. Evans and Tyler Williams; Winona Lake, IN: Eisenbrauns, 2013), 247–65.

Ben Zvi, Ehud. "The Memory of Abraham in the Late Persian/Early Hellenistic Yehud/Judah", in *Remembering Biblical Figures in the Late Persian and Early Hellenistic Periods: Social*

Memory and Imagination (eds. Diana Edelman and Ehud Ben Zvi; Oxford/New York: Oxford University Press, 2013), 3–37; republication with minor changes of "The Memory of Abraham in the Late Persian/Early Hellenistic Yehud/Judah", in *The Reception and Remembrance of Abraham* (eds. Pernille Carstens and Niels-Peter Lemche; Piscataway, NJ: Gorgias Press, 2011), 13–60.

Ben Zvi, Ehud. "Purity Matters in the Book of Chronicles: A Kind of Prolegomenon," in *Purity, Holiness, and Identity in Judaism and Christianity* (eds. Carl S. Ehrlich, Anders Runesson and Eileen Schuller; WUNT, 305; Tübingen: Mohr Siebeck, 2013), 37–52.

Ben Zvi, Ehud. "Reading and Constructing Utopias: Utopia/s and/in the Collection of Authoritative Texts/Textual Readings of Late Persian Period Yehud," in *SR* 42 (2013): 463–76.

Ben Zvi, Ehud. "Reading Chronicles and Reshaping the Memory of Manasseh," in *Chronicling the Chronicler. The Book of Chronicles and Early Second Temple Historiography* (eds. Paul S. Evans and Tyler F. Williams; Winona Lake, IN: Eisenbrauns, 2013), 121–140.

Ben Zvi, Ehud. "Chronicles and Its Reshaping of Memories of Monarchic Period Prophets: Some Observations," in *Prophets, Prophecy, and Ancient Israelite Historiography* (eds. Mark J. Boda and Lissa M. Wray Beal; Winona Lake, IN: Eisenbrauns, 2013), 167–88.

Ben Zvi, Ehud. "Exploring the Memory of Moses 'The Prophet' in Late Persian/Early Hellenistic Yehud/Judah," in *Remembering Biblical Figures in the Late Persian & Early Hellenistic Periods: Social Memory and Imagination* (eds. Diana V. Edelman and Ehud Ben Zvi; Oxford: Oxford University Press, 2013), 335–64.

Ben Zvi, Ehud. "Isaiah, a Memorable Prophet: Why Was Isaiah So Memorable in the Late Persian/Early Hellenistic Periods? Some Observations," in *Remembering Biblical Figures in the Late Persian & Early Hellenistic Periods: Social Memory and Imagination* (eds. Diana V. Edelman and Ehud Ben Zvi; Oxford: Oxford University Press, 2013), 365–383.

Ben Zvi, Ehud. "Monogynistic and Monogamous Tendencies, Memories and Imagination in Late Persian/Early Hellenistic Yehud," in *ZAW* 125:2 (2013): 263–77.

Ben Zvi, Ehud. "Prophetic Memories in the Deuteronomistic Historical and the Prophetic Collections of Books," in *Israelite Prophecy and the Deuteronomistic History; Portrait, Reality and the Formation of a History* (eds. Mignon R. Jacobs and Raymond F. Person Jr.; AIL 314; Atlanta: SBL, 2013), 75–102.

Ben Zvi, Ehud. "Othering, Selfing, 'Boundarying' and 'Cross-Boundarying' as Interwoven with Socially Shared Memories: Some Observations," in *Imagining the Other and Constructing Israelite Identity in the Early Second Temple Period* (eds. Diana V. Edelman and Ehud Ben Zvi; LHBOTS 456; London: Bloomsbury T&T Clark, 2014), 20–40.

Ben Zvi, Ehud. "Exploring Jerusalem as a Site of Memory in the Late Persian and Early Hellenistic Period", in *Memory and the City in Ancient Israel* (eds. Diana V. Edelman and Ehud Ben Zvi; Winona Lake, IN: Eisenbrauns, 2014), 197–217.

Ben Zvi, Ehud. "Chronicles and Samuel–Kings: Two Interacting Aspects of One Memory System in the Late Persian/Early Hellenistic Period," in *Rereading the Relecture? The Question of (Post)chronistic Influence in the Latest Redactions of the Books of Samuel* (eds. Uwe Becker and Hannes Bezzel; FAT II, 66; Tubingen: Mohr Siebeck, 2014), 41–56.

Ben Zvi, Ehud. "Remembering Pre-Israelite Jerusalem in Late Persian Yehud: Mnemonic Preferences, Memories and Social Imagination," in *Urban Dreams and Realities in Antiquity: Remains and Representations of the Ancient City* (ed. Adam Kemezis; Leiden: E.J. Brill, 2014), 413–437.

Ben Zvi, Ehud. "The Yehudite Prophetic Books and Imperial Context," in *Divination, Politics and Ancient Near Eastern Empires* (eds. Jonathan Stökl and Alan Lenzi; ANEM/MACO 7; Atlanta: Society of Biblical Literature, 2014), 145–69.

Ben Zvi, Ehud. "Reshaping the Memory of Zedekiah and his Period in Chronicles," in *Congress Volume Munich 2013* (ed. Christl M. Maier; VTSup 163; Leiden: Brill, 2014), 370–95.

Ben Zvi, Ehud. "Remembering Hosea: The Prophet as a Site of Memory in Persian Period Yehud," in *Poets, Prophets, and Texts in Play. Studies in Biblical Poetry and Prophecy in Honour of Francis Landy* (eds. Ehud Ben Zvi, Claudia V. Camp, David M. Gunn and Aaron W. Hughes, LHBOTS 597; London: Bloomsbury T&T Clark, 2015), 37–57.

Ben Zvi, Ehud. "A Balancing Act: Settling and Unsettling Issues Concerning Past Divine Promises in Historiographical Texts Shaping Social Memory in the Late Persian Period," in *Covenant in the Persian Period: From Genesis to Chronicles* (eds. Richard J. Bautch and Gary N. Knoppers; Winona Lake, IN: Eisenbrauns, 2015), 109–29.

Ben Zvi, Ehud. "Late Historical Books and Rewritten History" in *The Cambridge Companion to the Hebrew Bible/Old Testament* (eds. Stephen B. Chapman and Marvin A. Sweeney; Cambridge: Cambridge University Press, 2016), 292–313.

Ben Zvi, Ehud. "Introductory Centre/Core-Periphery Considerations and the Case of Interplaying of Rigid and Flexible Constructions of Centre and Periphery among the Literati of the Late Persian/Early Hellenistic Period," in *Centres and Peripheries in the Early Second Temple Period* (eds. Ehud Ben Zvi and Christoph Levin; FAT, 108; Tübingen: Mohr-Siebeck, 2016), 21–41.

Ben Zvi, Ehud. "Remembering Twelve Prophetic Characters from the Past," in *The Book of the Twelve – One Book or Many?* (eds. Elena Di Pede and Donatella Scaiola; FAT II; Tübingen: Mohr-Siebeck, 2016), 6–36.

Ben Zvi, Ehud. "Memory and Political Thought in the Late Persian/Early Hellenistic Yehud/Judah: Some Observations," in *Leadership, Social Memory and Judean Discourse in the 5th-2nd Centuries BCE* (eds. Diana V. Edelman and Ehud Ben Zvi; WANEM; London: Equinox, 2016), 9–26

Ben Zvi, Ehud. "Chronicles and Social Memory," in *ST* 71 (2017): 69–90.

Ben Zvi, Ehud. "Clio Today and Ancient Israelite History: Some Thoughts and Observations at the Closing Session of the European Seminar for Historical Methodology," in *Even God Cannot Change the Past: Reflections on Seventeen Years of the European Seminar in Historical Methodology* (ed. Lester L. Grabbe; LHBOTS 663; London: T&T Clark, 2018), 20–49.

Ben Zvi, Ehud and Christoph Levin, eds. *The Concept of Exile in Ancient Israel and its Historical Contexts* (BZAW, 404; Berlin/New York: de Gruyter, 2010).

Ben Zvi, Ehud and Christoph Levin, eds. *Remembering and Forgetting in Early Second Temple Judah* (FAT, 85; Tübingen: Mohr-Siebeck, 2012).

Ben Zvi, Ehud and Christoph Levin, eds., *Thinking of Water in the Early Second Temple Period* (BZAW, 461; Berlin/New York: de Gruyter, 2014).

Ben Zvi, Ehud and Christoph Levin, eds. *Centres and Peripheries in the Early Second Temple Period* (FAT, 108; Tübingen: Mohr-Siebeck, 2016).

Berge, Kåre. "Categorical Identities: 'Ethnified Otherness and Sameness' – A Tool for Understanding Boundary Negotiation in the Pentateuch?" in *Imagining the Other and*

Constructing Israelite Identity in the Early Second Temple Period (eds. Diana V. Edelman and Ehud Ben Zvi; LHBOTS 456; London: Bloomsbury T&T Clark, 2014), 70–88.
Bergman, Joshua A. *Narrative Analogy in the Hebrew Bible: Battle Stories and Their Equivalent Non-battle Narratives* (VTSup 103; Leiden: Brill, 2004).
Berlejung, Angelika. "The Assyrians in the West: Assyrianization, Colonialism, Indifference, or Development Policy?" in *Congress Volume Helsinki 2010* (ed. Martti Nissinen; VTSup 148, Leiden: Brill, 2012), 21–60.
Bernheimer, R. "The Martyrdom of Isaiah," in *The Art Bulletin* 34 (1952): 19–34.
Berlin, Adele. *Esther* (JPS Bible Commentary; Philadelphia: JPS, 2001).
Berquist, Jon L. "Constructions of Identity in Postcolonial Yehud" in *Judah and the Judeans in the Persian Period* (eds. Oded Lipschits and Manfred Oeming; Winona Lake, IN: Eisenbrauns, 2006), 53–56.
Berquist, Jon L. "Identities and Empire. Historiographic Questions for the Deuteronomistic History in the Persian Period" in *Historiography and Identity: (Re)formulation in Second Temple Historiographical Literature* (ed. Louis C. Jonker; LHBOTS 534; London: T&T Clark, 2010), 3–13
Betzig, Laura. "Politics as Sex: The Old Testament Case," in *Evolutionary Psychology* 3 (2005): 326–346.
Bhabha, Homi K. *The Location of Culture* (New York: Routledge, 1994).
Biale, David. "Counter-History and Jewish Polemics Against Christianity: The *Sefer Toldot Yeshu* and the *Sefer Zerubavel*," *Jewish Social Studies* 6 (1999): 130–45.
Bichler, Reinhold. "Some Observations on the Image of the Assyrian and Babylonian Kingdoms within the Greek Tradition", in *Commerce and Monetary Systems in the Ancient World* (eds. Robert Rollinger and Christoph Ulf; Melammu 5; Stuttgart: Steiner, 2004), 499–518.
Biggs, Robert D. "Conception, Contraception and Abortion in Ancient Mesopotamia," in *Wisdom, Gods and Literature: Studies in Assyriology in Honour of W. G. Lambert* (eds. Andrew R. George and Irving L. Finkel; Winona Lake, IN: Eisenbrauns, 2000), 1–13.
Bird, S. Elizabeth and Robert W. Dardenne, "Myth, Chronicle and Story: Exploring the Narrative Quality of News," in *Media, Myths, and Narratives: Television and the Press* (ed. James W. Carey; London: Sage, 1988), 67–85.
Blenkinsopp, Joseph. *Prophecy and Canon* (Notre Dame, IN/London: University of Notre Dame Press, 1977).
Blenkinsopp, Joseph. *Ezra–Nehemiah: A Commentary* (Philadelphia: Westminster, 1988).
Blenkinsopp, Joseph. "The Judaean Priesthood during the Neo-Babylonian and Achaemenid Periods: A Hypothetical Reconstruction," in *CBQ* 60 (1998): 25–43.
Blenkinsopp, Joseph. *Isaiah 40–55: A New Translation with Introduction and Commentary* (AB 19 A; New York: Doubleday, 2002).
Blenkinsopp, Joseph. "The Bible, Archaeology and Politics; or The Empty Land Revisited," in *JSOT* 27:2 (2002): 169–187.
Blenkinsopp, Joseph. "Benjamin Traditions Read in the Early Persian Period," in *Judah and the Judeans in the Neo-Babylonian Period* (eds. Oded Lipschits and Joseph Blenkinsopp; Winona Lake, IN: Eisenbrauns, 2003), 629–45.
Blenkinsopp, Joseph. "Bethel in the Neo-Babylonian Period," in *Judah and the Judeans in the Neo-Babylonian Period* (eds. Oded Lipschits and Joseph Blenkinsopp; Winona Lake, IN: Eisenbrauns, 2003), 93–107.

Blenkinsopp, Joseph. *Isaiah 56–66. A New Translation with Introduction and Commentary* (AB 19B; New York: Doubleday, 2003).

Blenkinsopp, Joseph. "Abraham as Paradigm in the Priestly History in Genesis," in *JBL* 128 (2009): 225–41.

Blenkinsopp, Joseph. "Ideology and Utopia in 1–2 Chronicles," in *What Was Authoritative for Chronicles?* (ed. E. Ben Zvi and D. V. Edelman; Winona Lake, IN: Eisenbrauns, 2011) 89–104.

Blum, Erhard. "Historiography or Poetry? The Peculiarities of the Hebrew Prose Tradition," in *Memory in the Bible and Antiquity: The Fifth Durham-Tübingen Research Symposium (Durham, September 2004)* (eds. Loren T. Stuckenbruck, Stephen C. Barton and Benjamin G. Wold; WUNT 212; Tübingen: Mohr Siebeck, 2007.

Blum, Erhard. "Would Ancient Readers of the Books of Hosea or Micah be 'Competent' to Read the Book of Jeremiah?" in *Jeremiah (Dis)Placed. New Directions in Writing/Reading Jeremiah* (eds. A. R. Peter Diamond and Louis Stulman; LHBOTS 529; London: T&T Clark, 2010), 80–98.

Boase, Elizabeth and Christopher G. Frechette (eds.), *Bible Through the Lenses of Trauma* (Atlanta: SBL Press, 2016).

Boda, Mark J. "Gazing Through the Cloud of Incense: Davidic and Temple Community in the Chronicler's Perspective," in *Chronicling the Chronicler: The Book of Chronicles and Early Second Temple Historiography* (eds. Paul S. Evans and Tyler Williams; Winona Lake, IN: Eisenbrauns, 2013), 215–46.

Bodi, Daniel. "Les apocalypses akkadiennes et bibliques: Quelques points communs," in *Revue des Études Juives* 169 (2010): 13–36.

Bos, James M. *Reconsidering the Date and Provenance of the Book of Hosea: The Case for Persian Period Yehud* (LHBOTS 580; London: Bloomsbury T&T Clark, 2013.

Bourdieu, Pierre. *Distinction: A Social Critique of the Judgement of Taste* (transl. Richard Nice; London: Routledge & Kegan Paul, 1986).

Bourdieu, Pierre. "Forms of Capital," in *Handbook of Theory of Research for the Sociology of Education* (ed. John G. Richardson; New York: Greenwood Press, 1986), 46–58.

Bourdieu, Pierre. *Homo Academicus* (transl. Peter Collier; Stanford, CA: Stanford University Press, 1988.

Bourdieu, Pierre. *The Logic of Practice* (transl. Richard Nice; Stanford, CA: Stanford University Press, 1980).

Bourdieu, Pierre. *The Field of Cultural Production* (ed. and introduced Randal Johnson; New York, NY: Columbia University Press, 1993).

Braun, Roddy L. "Solomon, The Chosen Temple Builder. The Significance of 1 Chronicles 22, 28 and 29 for the Theology of Chronicles," in *JBL* 95 (1976): 581–90.

Brett, Mark G. "National Identity as Commentary and as Metacommentary" in *Historiography and Identity: (Re)formulation in Second Temple Historiographical Literature* (ed. Louis C. Jonker; LHBOTS 534; London: T&T Clark, 2010), 29–40.

Breytenbach, Andries. "Who Is Behind the Samuel Narrative?" in *Past, Present, Future: The Deuteronomistic History and the Prophets* (eds. Johannes C. de Moor and Harry F. van Rooy; OTS 44; Leiden: Brill, 2000), 50–61.

Briant, Pierre. "Des Achéménides aux rois hellénistiques: continuités et ruptures," in *Annali della Scuola Normale Superiori di Pisa* 9 (1979): 1375–414.

Briant, Pierre. *Rois, Tributs et Paysans*: études sur les formations tributaires du Moyen-Orient ancient (Annales littéraires de l'Université de Besançon 269 / Centre de recherches d'histoire ancienne 43; Paris: Les Belles lettres, 1982).
Briant, Pierre. "Des Achémenides aux rois hellénistiques: Continuités et ruptures," in *Rois, tributs et paysans* (ed. P. Briant; Paris: Les Belles lettres, 1982), 291–330).
Briant, Pierre. "Histoire impériale et histoire régionale: À propos de l'histoire de Juda dans l'Empire achéménide," in *Congress Volume: Oslo 1998* (eds. André Lemaire and Magne Sæbø; VTSup 80; Leiden: Brill, 2000), 235–45.
Briant, Pierre. *From Cyrus to Alexander: A History of the Persian Empire* (Winona Lake, IN: Eisenbrauns, 2002).
Brosius, Maria. "Greeks at the Persian Court," in *Ktesias' Welt = Ctesias' World* (eds. Josef Wiesehöfer, Robert Rollinger and Giovanni B. Lanfranchi; Classica et orientalia 1; Wiesbaden: Harrassowitz, 2011), 69–80.
Brueggemann, Walter. *Jeremiah 26–52: To Build, To Plant* (ITC; Grand Rapids, MI: Eerdmans, 1991).
Bulhof, Johannes. "What If? Modality and History," in *History and Theory* 38 (1999): 145–68.
Bunzl, Martin. "Counterfactual History: A User's Guide," in *American Historical Review* 109 (2004): 845–58.
Burns, J. B. "Is Neco Also among the Prophets?" in *Proceedings, Eastern Great Lakes and Midwest Biblical Society* 14 (1994) 113–22.
Burton, Michael L. et al. "Regions Based on Social Structure," in *Current Anthropology* 37 (1996): 87–111.
Buster, Aubrey E. "Written Record and Membership in Judah and Classical Athens," in *Voice and Voices in Antiquity: Orality and Literacy in the Ancient World, Vol. 11*, (ed. Niall W. Slater; Mnemosyne Supplements, 396; Leiden: Brill, 2016), 297-320.
Camp, Claudia V. *Wisdom and the Feminine in the Book of Proverbs* (Bible and Literature 11; Decatur, GA: Almond, 1985).
Campbell, Antony F. and Mark A. O'Brien. *Unfolding the Deuteronomistic History: Origins, Upgrades, Present Text* (Minneapolis, MN: Fortress, 2000).
Campbell, Antony F. *1 Samuel* (FOTL 7; Grand Rapids, MI: Eerdmans, 2003).
Carneiro, Robert L. "Chiefdom: Precursor of the State," in *The Transition to Statehood in the New World* (ed. Grant D. Jones and Robert R. Kautz; Cambridge: Cambridge University Press, 1981), 37–75.
Carr, David. "Place and Time: On the Interplay of Historical Points of View," in *History and Theory* 40 (2001): 153–67.
Carr, David. *Writing on the Tablet of the Heart: Origins of Scripture and Literature* (Oxford: Oxford University Press, 2005).
Carroll, Robert P. *Jeremiah: A Commentary* (OTL; Philadelphia: Westminster, 1986).
Carroll, Robert P. "The Myth of the Empty Land", in *Semeia* 59 (1992): 79–93.
Carroll, Robert P. "Whorusalamin: A Tale of Three Cities as Three Sisters," in *On Reading Prophetic Texts: Gender-Specific and Related Studies in Memory of Fokkelien van Dijk-Hemmes* (eds. Bob Becking and Meindert Dijkstra; BibIntS 18; Leiden: Brill, 1996), 67–82.
Carter, Charles E. *The Emergence of Yehud in the Persian Period: A Social and Demographic Study* (JSOTSup 294; Sheffield, Sheffield Academic Press, 1999).

Carter, Charles E. "Ideology and Archaeology in the Neo-Babylonian Period: Excavating Text and Tell," in *Judah and the Judeans in the Neo-Babylonian Period* (eds. Oded Lipschits and Joseph Blenkinsopp; Winona Lake, IN: Eisenbrauns, 2003), 301–22.

Carter, Rita. "The Limits of Imagination," in *Human Nature: Fact and Fiction: Literature, Science and Human Nature* (eds. Robin Headlam Wells and Johnjoe McFadden; London: Continuum, 2006), 128–43

Cataldo, Jeremiah W. "Whispered Utopia: Dreams, Agendas, and Theocratic Aspirations in Yehud," in *SJOT* 24 (2010): 53–70.

Cattell, Maria G. and Jacob J. Climo. "Meaning in Social Memory and History: Anthropological Perspectives," in *Social Memory and History. Anthropological Perspectives* (eds. Jacob J. Climo and Maria G. Cattell; Walnut Creek: Altamira, 2002), 1–36.

Chalcraft, David J. "Sociology and the Book of Chronicles: Risk, Ontological Security, Moral Panics and Types of Narrative" in *What Was Authoritative for Chronicles?* (eds. Ehud Ben Zvi and Dianne V. Edelman; Winona Lake, IN: Eisenbrauns, 2011), 201–227.

Chang, Shelley Hsueh-lun. *History and Legend: Ideas and Images in the Ming Historical Novels* (Ann Arbor: University of Michigan Press, 1990).

Chapman, Cynthia R. *The Gendered Language of Warfare in the Israelite–Assyrian Encounter* (HSM, 62; Winona Lake, IN: Eisenbrauns, 2004).

Chapman, Cynthia R. *The House of the Mother: The Social Roles of Maternal Kin in Biblical Hebrew Narrative and Poetry* (New Haven: Yale University Press, 2016).

Chapman, Stephen B. *The Law and the Prophets* (FAT 27; Tübingen: Mohr Siebeck, 2000).

Charlesworth, James H., ed. *Old Testament Pseudepigrapha* (New York: Doubleday, 1985).

Chavalas, Mark. "The Age of Empires: 3100–900 BCE," in *A Companion to the Ancient Near East* (ed. Daniel C. Snell; Malden/Oxford: Blackwell, 2005), 34–47

Chisholm, Robert B., Jr. "Does God Deceive?" in *BibSac* 155 (1998): 11–28.

Christian, Mark A. "Openness to the Other Inside and Outside of Numbers," in *The Books of Leviticus and Numbers* (ed. Thomas C. Römer; BETL 215; Leuven: Peeters, 2008), 579–608.

Claassens, L. Juliana. "God and Violence in the Prophets," in *The Oxford Handbook of the Prophets* (ed. Carolyn Sharp; New York: Oxford University Press, 2016), 334–49.

Clauss, Jan. "Understanding the Mixed Marriages of Ezra-Nehemiah in the Light of Temple-Building and the Book's Concept of Jerusalem," in *Mixed Marriages: Intermarriage and Group Identity in the Second Temple Period* (ed. Christian Frevel; LHBOTS 547; London: T&T Clark, 2011), 109–31.

Clements, Ronald E. *Abraham and David: Genesis xv and its Meaning for Israelite Tradition* (Naperville, Ill: A.R. Allenson, 1967).

Clines, David J. A. *Interested Parties: The Ideology of Writers and Readers of the Hebrew Bible* (JSOTSup 205; Gender, Culture, Theory 1; Sheffield: Sheffield Academic Press, 1995), 46–75; originally published in *SJOT* 7 (1993): 19–30.

Cogan, Mordechai. "David's Jerusalem: Notes and Reflections", in *Tehillah le-Moshe. Biblical and Judaic Studies in Honor of Moshe Greenberg* (eds. Mordechai Cogan, Barry L. Eichler and Jeffrey H. Tigay; Winona Lake, IN: Eisenbrauns, 1997), 193–201.

Cohen, Shaye J. D. "Alexander the Great and Jaddua the High Priest According to Josephus," in *AJSR* 7–8 (1982–83): 41–68.

Cohen, Shaye J. D. "The Origins of the Matrilineal Principle in Rabbinic Law," in *AJSR* 10 (1985): 19–53.

Cohen, Shaye J. D. *The Beginning of Jewishness: Boundaries, Varieties, Uncertainties* (Berkeley: University of California Press, 1999).
Cohn, Robert L. "Negotiating (with) the Natives: Ancestors and Identity in Genesis," in *Harvard Theological Review* 96 (2003): 147–66
Collins, John J. *Jewish Wisdom in the Hellenistic Age* (Louisville, KY: Westminster John Knox, 1997).
Coman, Mihai. "New Stories and Myth – The Impossible Reunion?" in *Media Anthropology* (eds. Eric W. Rothenbuhler and Mihai Coman; Thousand Oaks, CA: Sage, 2005), 111–120.
Connell, Sophia M. "Aristotle and Galen on Sex Difference and Reproduction: A New Approach to an Ancient Rivalry," in *Studies in History and Philosophy of Science* 31 (2000): 405–27.
Conti, Marco. *1–2 Kings, 1–2 Chronicles, Ezra, Nehemiah, Esther* (Ancient Christian Commentary on Scriptures; Downers Grove: InterVarsity, 2008).
Cook, Johann. "The Septuagint as Contextual Bible Translation: Alexandria or Jerusalem as the Context of Proverbs," in *JNSL* 19 (1993): 25–39.
Cook, Johann. "The Law of Moses in Septuagint Proverbs," in *VT* 49 (1999): 448–61.
Cook, Johann. "Semantic Considerations and the Provenance of Translated Units," in *XIII Congress of the International Organization for Septuagint and Cognate Studies: Ljubliana, 2007* (ed. Melvin K. H. Peters; Atlanta: Society of Biblical Literature, 2008), 67–85.
Cooper, Jerrold S. *Presargonic Inscriptions* (New Haven, CT: American Oriental Society, 1986).
Corner, Sean. "Bringing the Outside In: The Andrōn as Brothel and the Symposium's Civic Sexuality," in *Greek Prostitutes in the Ancient Mediterranean, 800 BCE–200 CE* (eds. Allison Glazebrook and Madeleine M. Henry; Madison, WI: University of Wisconsin Press, 2011), 60–85.
Creangă, Ovidiu. "Variations on the Theme of Masculinity: Joshua's Gender In/stability in the Conquest Narrative," in *Men and Masculinities in the Hebrew Bible and Beyond* (ed. O. Creangă; The Bible in the Modern World, 33; Sheffield: Sheffield Phoenix, 2010), 83–109.
Crenshaw, James L. *Prophetic Conflict: Its Effect Upon Israelite Religion* (BZAW 124; Berlin: De Gruyter, 1971).
Crook, Margaret B. "The Marriageable Maiden of Proverbs 31:10–31," in *JNES* 13 (1954): 137–40.
Currie, Greg. "Imagination and Learning," in *The Routledge Handbook of Philosophy of Imagination* (ed. Amy Kind; New York: Routledge, 2016), 407–19.
Curtis Edward L. and Albert A. Madsen. *The Books of Chronicles* (ICC; New York: Scribner's, 1910).
Cypess, Sandra Messinger. *Uncivil Wars: Elena Garro, Octavio Paz, and the Battle for Cultural Memory* (Austin: University of Texas Press, 2012).
Dafni, Evangelia G. "רוח שקר und falsche Prophetie in I Reg 22," in *ZAW* 112 (2000): 365–86.
Dandamaev. M. A. *A Political History of the Achaemenid Empire* (trans. W. J. Vogelsang; Leiden: Brill, 1989).
Davies, John K. "The Interpenetration of Hellenistic Sovereignties," in *The Hellenistic World: New Perspectives* (ed. Daniel Ogden; London: Duckworth and The Classical Press of Wales, 2002), 1–21

Davies, Philip R. "The Origin of Biblical Israel," in *JHebS* 5/17 (2005): available online at http://www.jhsonline.org; republished with some changes in *Essays on Ancient Israel in Its Near Eastern Context: A Tribute to Nadav Na'aman* (eds. Yairah Amit, Ehud Ben Zvi, Israel Finkelstein and Oded Lipschits; Winona Lake, IN: Eisenbrauns, 2006), 141–148.

Davies, Philip R. *Memories of Ancient Israel: An Introduction to Biblical History – Ancient and Modern* (Louisville, KY: Westminster John Knox; 2008), 113.

Davila, James R. "Is the Prayer of Manasseh a Jewish Work?" in *Heavenly Tablets: Interpretation, Identity and Tradition in Ancient Judaism* (eds. Lynn R. LiDonnici and Andrea Lieber; JSJSup 119; Leiden: Brill, 2007), 75–85.

De Breucker, Geert. "Heroes and Sinners: Babylonian Kings in Cuneiform Historiography of the Persian and Hellenistic Periods," in *Political Memory in and after the Persian Empire* (eds. Jason M. Silverman and Caroline Waerzeggers; ANEM/MACO, 13; Atlanta: SBL Press, 2015), 75–94.

De Pury, Albert. "Abraham: The Priestly Writer's 'Ecumenical' Ancestor," in *Rethinking the Foundations: Historiography in the Ancient World and in the Bible* (eds. Steven L. McKenzie and Thomas C. Römer; BZAW 294; Berlin/New York: De Gruyter, 2000), 163–81.

De Vries, Simon J. *Prophet Against Prophet: The Role of the Micaiah Narrative (1 Kings 22) in the Development of Early Prophetic Tradition* (Grand Rapids, MI: Eerdmans, 1986).

De Vries, Simon J. "The Forms of Prophetic Address in Chronicles," in *HAR* 10 (1986): 15–36.

De Vries, Simon J. "Moses and David as Cult Founders in Chronicles," in *JBL* 107 (1988): 619–639.

De Vries, Simon J. *1 and 2 Chronicles* (FOTL 11; Grand Rapids, MI: Eerdmans, 1989).

Demandt, Alexander. *History That Never Happened: A Treatise on the Question, What Would Have Happened If...?* (3rd rev. ed.; Jefferson, NC: McFarland & Company, 1993).

Deurloo, Karel A. "The One God and All Israel" in *Studies in Deuteronomy in Honour of C. J. Labuschagne* (eds. Florentino García Martínez et al.; VTSup 53; Leiden: Brill, 1994), 31–46.

Dicou, Bert. *Edom, Israel's Brother and Antagonist: The Role of Edom in Biblical Prophecy and Story* (JSOTSup 169; Sheffield: JSOT Press, 1994).

Dillard, Ray. "The Chronicler's Jehoshaphat," in *Trinity Journal* 7 (1978): 17–22.

Di Pede, Elena. "Jérémie et les rois de Juda, Sédécias et Joaqim," in *VT* 56 (2006): 452–69.

Dirksen, Peter B. *1 Chronicles* (HCOT; Leuven: Peeters, 2005).

Dor, Yonina. "The Composition of the Episode of the Foreign Women in Ezra IX–X," in *VT* 53 (2003): 26–47.

Dor, Yonina. *Have the "Foreign Women" Really Been Expelled? Separation and Exclusion in the Restoration Period* (Jerusalem: Magnes, 2006).

Dozeman, Thomas B. *Joshua 1-12* (AB 6B; New Haven, Yale Univ. Press, 2015).

Dusinberre, Elspeth R. M. *Aspects of Empire in Achaemenid Sardis* (Cambridge: Cambridge University Press, 2003.

Dyck, Jonathan E. "The Ideology of Identity in Chronicles," in *Ethnicity and the Bible* (ed. Mark Brett ' Leiden, Leiden: Brill; 1996), 89–116.

Dyck, Jonathan E. *Theocratic Ideology* (Biblical Interpretation Series 33; Leiden: Brill, 1998).

Eck, Diana L. "The City as a Sacred Center," in *The City as a Sacred Center. Essays on Six Asian Contexts* (eds. Bardwell Smith and Holly Baker Reynolds; International Studies in Sociology and Social Anthropology 46; Leiden: Brill, 1987), 1–11.

Edelman, Diana V. "Did Saulide-Davidic Rivalry Resurface in Early Persian Yehud?" in *The Land that I Will Show You: Essays on the History and Archaeology of the Ancient Near East in Honour of J. Maxwell Miller* (eds. J. Andrew Dearman and M. Patrick Graham; JSOTSup 343; Sheffield: Sheffield Academic Press, 2001), 69–91.

Edelman, Diana V. *The Origins of the "Second" Temple: Persian Imperial Policy and the Rebuilding of Jerusalem* (Bible World; London: Equinox, 2005).

Edelman, Diana V. "The 'Empty Land' as a Motif in City Laments," in *Ancient and Modern Scriptural Historiography / L'Historiographie Biblique, Ancienne et Moderne* (eds. George J. Brooke and Thomas C. Römer, BETL 207; Leuven: Leuven University Press, 2007), 127–49.

Edelman, Diana V. "Seeing Double: Tobiah the Ammonite as an Encrypted Character," in *RB* 113 (2008): 570–84.

Edelman, Diana V. and Ehud Ben Zvi, eds. *Remembering Biblical Figures in the Late Persian and Early Hellenistic Periods: Social Memory and Imagination* (Oxford: Oxford University Press, 2013).

Edelman, Diana V. "Introduction" in *Remembering Biblical Figures in the Late Persian and Early Hellenistic Periods: Social Memory and Imagination* (eds. Diana V. Edelman and Ehud Ben Zvi; Oxford: Oxford University Press, 2013), xi–xxiv.

Edelman, Diana V. "David in Israelite Social Memory," in *Remembering Biblical Figures in the Late Persian and Early Hellenistic Periods: Social Memory and Imagination* (eds. Diana V. Edelman and Ehud Ben Zvi; Oxford: Oxford University Press, 2013), 141–57.

Edelman, Diana V. "City Gardens and Parks in Biblical Social Memory," in *Memory and the City in Ancient Israel* (eds. Diana V. Edelman and Ehud Ben Zvi; Winona Lake, IN: Eisenbrauns, 2014), 115–155.

Edelman, Diana V. and E. Ben Zvi, eds. *Memory and the City in Ancient Israel* (Winona Lake, Ind.: Eisenbrauns, 2014).

Edelman, Diana V. and E. Ben Zvi, eds. *Imagining the Other and Constructing Israelite Identity in the Early Second Temple Period.* (LHBOTS 456; London: Bloomsbury T&T Clark, 2014).

Edelman, Diana V. and E. Ben Zvi, eds. *Leadership, Social Memory and Judean Discourse in the 5th-2nd Centuries BCE* (WANEM; London: Equinox, 2016).

Edenburg, Cynthia. *The Story of the Outrage at Gibeah (Judg 19–21): Composition, Sources and Historical Context* (Phd Thesis, Tel Aviv University, 2003).

Edenburg Cynthia. *Dismembering the Whole. Composition and Purpose of Judges 19–21* (SBLAIL 24; Atlanta: SBL Press, 2016).

Emerton, John A. "The Site of Salem, the City of Melchizedek (Genesis XIV 18)," in *Studies in the Pentateuch* (ed. John A. Emerton; VTSup 41; Leiden: Brill, 1990).

Emmerson, Grace I. *Hosea: An Israelite Prophet in Judean Perspective* (JSOTSup 28; Sheffield: JSOT, 1984).

Endres, John C. "The Spiritual Vision of Chronicles: Wholehearted, Joy-Filled Worship of God," in *CBQ* 69 (2007), 1–21.

Erickson, Amy. "Jonah and the Scribal *Habitus*," in *Methods, Theories, Imaginations: Social Scientific Approaches in Biblical Studies* (eds. David J. Chalcraft, Frauke Uhlenbruch and Rebecca S. Watson; Bible in the Modern World, 60; Sheffield: Sheffield Phoenix, 2014), 59–78.

Ermakoff, Ivan. "Rational Choice May Take Over," in *Bourdieu and Historical Analysis* (ed. Philip S. Gorski; Durham, N.C.: Duke University Press, 2013), 89–107.
Eskenazi, Tamara C. "Out from the Shadows: Biblical Women in the Postexilic Era," in *JSOT* 54 (1992): 25–43.
Eskenazi, Tamara C. and Eleanore P. Judd, "Marriage to a Stranger in Ezra 9–10," in *Second Temple Studies 2: Temple Community in the Persian Period* (eds. Tamara C. Eskenazi and Kent H. Richards; JSOTSup 175; Sheffield: JSOT, 1994), 266–85.
Evans, Craig A. "From Gospel to Gospel: The Function of Isaiah in the New Testament" in *Writing and Reading the Scroll of Isaiah* (eds. Craig C. Broyles and Craig A. Evans; VTSup 70.2; Leiden/ New York: Brill, 1997), 651–91.
Exum, J. Cheryl, ed. *The Historical Books* (Biblical Seminar 40; Sheffield: Sheffield Academic Press, 1997).
Exum, J. Cheryl, ed. *Virtual History and the Bible* (Leiden: Brill, 2000).
Eyerman, Ron. "Social Movements and Memory," in *Routledge International Handbook of Memory Studies* (eds. Trever Hagen and Anna Lisa Tota; London: Routledge; 2015), 100–105.
Falk, Marcia. *The Book of Blessings* (Boston: Beacon, 1999).
Farber, Zev. *Images of Joshua in the Bible and Their* Reception (BZAW, 457; Berlin: de Gruyter, 2016).
Faust, Avraham. "Judah in the Sixth Century B.C.E.: A Rural Perspective," in *PEQ* 126 (2003): 37–53.
Feldman, Louis H. "Josephus's Portrait of Joshua," in *HTR* 82 (1989): 351–76.
Feldman, Louis H. *Josephus's Interpretation of the Bible* (Berkeley: University of California Press, 1998).
Feldman, Louis H. "Prophets and Prophecy in Josephus," in *Prophets, Prophecy, and Prophetic Texts in Second Temple Judaism* (eds. Michael H. Floyd and Robert D. Haak; London/New York: T&T Clark, 2006), 210–39.
Feldman, Louis H. *Philo's Portrayal of Moses in the Context of Ancient Judaism* (Notre Dame, Ind.: Univ. of Notre Dame Press, 2007).
Feldman, Louis H. and Steve Mason, eds. *Judean Antiquities 1–4* (Flavius Josephus Translation and Commentary 3; Leiden: Brill, 2000).
Ferguson, Niall, ed. *Virtual History: Alternatives and Counterfactuals* (Papermac: London, 1998).
Fine, Gary Alan. *Difficult Reputations. Collective Memories of the Evil, Inept and Controversial* (Chicago: Chicago University Press, 2001).
Fine, Gary Alan. *Sticky Reputations: The Politics of Collective Memory in Midcentury America* (New York: Routledge, 2012).
Finkelstein, Israel. "The Archaeology of the Days of Manasseh," in *Scriptures and Other Artifacts: Essays on Bible and Archaeology in Honor of Philip J. King* (eds. Michael D. Coogan et al.; Louisville: Westminster John Knox, 1994), 169–87.
Finkelstein, Israel and Amihai Mazar. *The Quest for the Historical Israel: Debating Archaeology and the History of Early Israel* (Atlanta: Society of Biblical Literature, 2007).
Finkelstein, Israel. "Archaeology and the List of Returnees in the Books of Ezra and Nehemiah," in *PEQ* 140 (2008): 1–10
Finkelstein, Israel. "Jerusalem in the Persian (and Early Hellenistic) Period and the Wall of Nehemiah," in *JSOT* 32 (2008): 501–520.

Finkelstein, Israel. "Persian Period Jerusalem and Yehud: A Rejoinder," in *JHebS* 9/24 (2009); available online at http://www.jhsonline.org; republished in *Perspectives on Hebrew Scriptures VI: Comprising the Contents of Journal of Hebrew Scriptures, vol. 9* (ed. Ehud Ben Zvi. Piscataway, NJ: Gorgias Press, 2010), 529–542.

Finkelstein, Israel, Ido Koch and Oded Lipschits. "The Mound on the Mount: A Possible Solution to the 'Problem with Jerusalem'," in *JHebS* 11/12 (2011); republished in *Perspectives on Hebrew Scriptures VIII* (ed. Ehud Ben Zvi; Piscataway: Gorgias Press, 2012), 317–39.

Finkelstein, Jacob J. "Mesopotamia," in *JNES* 21 (1962), 73–92.

Fischer, Irmtraud. "Gotteslehrerin: Ein Streifzug durch Spr 31,10–31 auf den Pfaden unterschiedlicher Methodik," in *BZ* 49 (2005): 237–53.

Fischer, Irmtraud. *Gotteslehrerinnen: Weise Frauen und Frau Weisheit im Alten Testament* (Stuttgart: Kohlhammer, 2006).

Fishbane, Michael. *Biblical Interpretation in Ancient Israel* (Oxford: Clarendon, 1985).

Fishbane, Michael. *Haftarot* (JPS Bible Commentary; Philadelphia: The Jewish Publication Society), 2002.

Flanagan, James W. "Chiefs in Israel," in *Social Scientific Old Testament Criticism. A Sheffield Reader* (ed. David J. Chalcraft; BibSem, 47; Sheffield: Sheffield Academic Press, 1997), 136-61.

Fletcher, Natalie M. "Imagination and The Capabilities Approach," in *The Routledge Handbook of Philosophy of Imagination* (ed. Amy Kind; New York: Routledge, 2016), 392–404.

Fokkelman, Jan P. *Narrative Art and Poetry in the Books of Samuel: A Full Interpretation Based on Stylistic and Structural Analyses,* 4 vols. (Studia Semitica Neerlandica; Assen: Van Gorcum, 1981–93).

Fortunato, Laura. "Reconstructing the History of Marriage Strategies in Indo-European-Speaking Societies: Monogamy and Polygyny," in *Human Biology* 83 (2011): 87–105.

Fortunato, Laura and Marco Archetti. "Evolution of Monogamous Marriage by Maximization of Inclusive Fitness," in *Journal of Evolutionary Biology* 23 (2010): 149–156.

Fox, Michael V. *Proverbs 1–9: A New Translation with Introduction and Commentary* (AB 18 A; New York: Doubleday, 2000).

Fox, Michael V. *Proverbs 10–31: A New Translation with Introduction and Commentary* (AB 18B; New Haven, CT: Yale University Press, 2009).

Fox, Robin Lane. "Alexander the Great: 'Last of the Achaemenids'?" in *Persian Responses* (ed. Christopher Tuplin; Swansea: Classical Press of Wales, 2007), 267–311.

Freedman, David Noel, A. Dean Forbes, and Francis I. Andersen. *Studies in Hebrew and Aramaic Orthography* (BibJS 2; Winona Lake, IN: Eisenbrauns, 1992).

Frevel, Christian. "'Separate Yourself from the Gentiles' (Jubilees 22:16): Intermarriage in the Book of Jubilees," in *Mixed Marriages: Intermarriage and Group Identity in the Second Temple Period* (ed. Christian Frevel; LHBOTS 547; London: T&T Clark, 2011), 220–50.

Friebel, Kelvin. *Jeremiah's and Ezekiel's Sign-Acts* (JSOTSup 283; Sheffield: Sheffield Academic Press, 1999).

Fried, Lisbeth S. "The Concept of 'Impure Birth' in 5th Century Athens and Judea," in *In the Wake of Tikva Frymer-Kensky: Tikva Frymer-Kensky Memorial Volume* (eds. Stephen W. Holloway, Jo Ann Scurlock and Richard Beal; Piscataway, NJ: Gorgias, 2009), 121–42.

Fried, Lisbeth S. *Ezra. A Commentary* (Sheffield: Sheffield Academic Press, 2017).

Frolov, Serge. "The Prophecy of Jeremiah in Esr 1,1," in *ZAW* 116 (2004): 595–601.
Frood, Elizabeth. "Social Structure and Daily Life: Pharaonic," in *A Companion to Ancient Egypt*, vol. 1 (2 vols.; ed. Alan B. Lloyd; Malden, MA: Wiley-Blackwell, 2010), 469–90.
Frymer-Kensky, Tikva. "Parasht Pinchas: Another View," in *The Torah: A Women's Commentary* (eds. Tamara C. Eskenazi and Andrea L. Weiss; New York: Women of Reform Judaism, 2008), 983.
Galil, Gershon. *The Lower Stratum Families in the Neo-Assyrian Period* (Culture and History of the Ancient Near East 27; Leiden: Brill, 2007).
Gallagher, Catherine et al. "Counterfactual Realities" in *Representations* 98 (2007): 51–134.
García Martínez, Florentino. *The Dead Sea Scrolls Study Edition* (Grand Rapids, MI: Eerdmans, 1997–1998).
Garland, Robert. *Wandering Greeks: The Ancient Greek Diaspora from the Age of Homer to the Death of Alexander the Great* (Princeton, NJ: Princeton University Press, 2014).
Gerstenberger, Erhard S. "Prophetie in den Chronikbüchern: Jahwes Wort in zweierlei Gestalt?" in *Schriftprophetie Festschrift für Jörg Jeremias zum 65. Geburtstag* (ed. Freidhelm Hartenstein et al.; Neukirchen-Vluyn: Neukirchener Verlag, 2004), 351–67.
Gerstenberger, Erhard S. "Persian Empire, Spirituality and the Genesis of the Prophetic Books" in *Production of Prophecy* (eds. Diana V. Edelman and Ehud Ben Zvi; London: Equinox, 2009), 110–130.
Geva, Hillel. "Estimating Jerusalem's Population in Antiquity: A Minimalist View," in *ErIsr* 28 (Teddy Kollek Volume; 2007): 50–65 (Heb.).
Geyer, John B. "Ezekiel 27 and the Cosmic Ship," in *Among the Prophets: Language, Image and Structure in the Prophetic Writings* (eds. Philip R. Davies and David J. A. Clines; JSOTSup 144; Sheffield: JSOT Press, 1993), 105–26.
Giddens, Anthony. *The Consequences of Modernity* (Cambridge: Polity, 1990).
Gilbert, Maurice. "La Donna Forte di Proverbi 31,10–31," in *'Ritratto o Simbolo,' Libro dei Proverbi: Tradizione, redazione, teologia* (eds. Giuseppe Bellia and Angelo Passaro; Casale Monferrato: Piemme, 1999), 147–67.
Gillingham, Susan. "The Zion Tradition and the Editing of the Hebrew Psalter," in *Temple Worship in Biblical Israel: Proceedings of the Oxford Old Testament Seminar* (ed. John Day; LHBOTS 422; London: T&T Clark, 2005), 308–41.
Gillmayr-Bucher, Susanne. "Jonah and the Other: A Discourse on Interpretative Competence," in *Imagining the Other and Constructing Israelite Identity* (eds. Diana V. Edelman and Ehud Ben Zvi; LHBOTS 456; London: Bloomsbury T&T Clark, 2014), 201–18.
Glassner, Jean-Jacques. *Mesopotamian Chronicles* (SBLWAW 19; Atlanta: Society of Biblical Literature, 2004).
Glatt-Gilat, David. "Ezra Ben Seraiah the Priest in Ancient and Modern Theological Discourse," in *Or Le-Mayer: Studies in Bible, Semitic Languages, Rabbinic Literature, and Ancient Civilizations* (ed. Shamir Yona; Beer-Sheva: Ben-Gurion University Press, 2010), 87–97 (Heb.)
Goh, Samuel T. S. "Ruth as a Superior Woman of חיל? A Comparison between Ruth and the 'Capable' Woman in Proverbs 31.10–31," in *JSOT* 38 (2014): 487–500.
Goldingay, John. *The Message of Isaiah 40–55. A Literary-Theological Commentary* (2 vols.; London: T&T Clark, 2005–06).
Gordis, Robert. *The Book of God and Man* (Chicago: University of Chicago Press, 1965).

Gorski, Philip S. "Introduction," in *Bourdieu and Historical Analysis* (ed. Philip S. Gorski; Durham, N.C.: Duke University Press; 2013).
Gosse, Bernard. "Les Lévites, Jérémie et les Chroniques," in *ZAW* 123 (2011): 47–56.
Grabbe, Lester L. *Priests, Prophets, Diviners, Sages. A Socio-Historical Study of Religious Specialists in Ancient Israel* (Valley Forge, Pa.: Trinity Press International, 1995).
Grabbe, Lester L. "Triumph of the Pious or Failure of the Xenophobes? The Ezra–Nehemiah Reforms and the Nachgeschichte," in *Jewish Local Patriotism and Self-Identification in the Graeco-Roman Period* (eds. Siân Jones and Sarah Pearce; JSPSup 31; Sheffield: Sheffield Academic, 1998), 50–65.
Grabbe, Lester L. *Ezra–Nehemiah* (New York: Routledge, 1998).
Grabbe, Lester L. *A History of the Jews and Judaism in the Second Temple Period, Volume 1. Yehud: A History of the Persian Province of Judah* (LSTS 47; London / New York: T&T Clark, 2004).
Grabbe, Lester L. "Joseph Smith and the *Gestalt* of the Israelite Prophet" in *Ancient Israel. The Old Testament in its Social Context* (ed. Philip F. Esler; Minneapolis: Fortress, 2006), 111–27.
Grabbe, Lester L. "Hecataeus of Abdera and the Jewish Law: The Question of Authenticity," in *Berührungspunkte. Studien zur Sozial- und Religionsgeschichte Israels und seiner Umwelt. Festschrift für Rainer Frolov zu seinem 65. Geburtstag* (eds. Ingo Kottsieper, Rüdiger Schmitt and Jacob Wöhrle; AOAT, 350; Münster, Ugarit-Verlag, 2008), 613-626.
Grad, Hector and Luisa Martín Rojo. "Identities in Discourse: An Integrative View," in *Analysing Identities in Discourse* (eds. Rosana Dolón and Júlia Todolí; Philadelphia: J. Benjamins, 2008), 3–28.
Grätz, Sebastian. "The Adversaries in Ezra/Nehemiah–Fictitious or Real? A Case Study in Creating Identity in Late Persian and Hellenistic Times," in *Between Cooperation and Hostility: Multiple Identities in Ancient Judaism and the Interaction with Foreign Powers* (eds. Rainer Albertz and Jakob Wöhrle; Journal of Ancient Judaism Supplements 11; Göttingen: Vandenhoeck & Ruprecht, 2013), 73–87.
Green, Douglas J. *'I Undertook Great Works.' The Ideology of Domestic Achievements in West Semitic Royal Inscriptions* (FAT II 41, Tübingen 2010).
Greenberg, Moshe. "Three Conceptions of the Torah in the Hebrew Scriptures," in *Die Hebräische Bibel und ihre zweifache Nachgeschichte: Festschrift für Rolf Rendtorff zum 65. Geburtstag* (eds. Erhard Blum, Christian Macholz and Ekkehard W. Stegemann; Neukirchen-Vluyn: Neukirchener Verlag, 1990), 365–78.
Greengus, Samuel. "Legal and Social Institutions of Ancient Mesopotamia," in *Civilizations of the Ancient Near East*, vol. 1 (4 vols.; ed. Jack M. Sasson; Peabody, MA: Hendricks, 2001), 469–484.
Gregory, Bradley C. "Abraham as the Jewish Ideal: Exegetical Traditions in Sirach 44:19–21," in *CBQ* 70 (2008): 66–81.
Greifenhagen, Franz V. *Egypt on the Pentateuch's Ideological Map* (JSOTSup 361; Sheffield: Sheffield Academic Press, 2002).
Gruen, Erich S. "Persia Through the Jewish Looking-Glass," in *Cultural Borrowings and Ethnic Appropriations in Antiquity* (ed. Erich S. Gruen; Oriens et Occidens 8; Stuttgart: Franz Steiner, 2005), 90–104; reprinted in *Jewish Perspectives on Hellenistic Rulers* (ed. Tessa Rajak et al.; Hellenistic Culture and Society 50; Berkeley: University of California Press, 2007), 53–75.

Guillory, John. *Cultural Capital: The Problem of Literary Canon Formation* (Chicago/London: University of Chicago Press, 1993).
Gunneweg, Antonius H. J. "Das Gesetz und die Propheten: eine Auslegung von Ex 33,7–11; Num 11,4–12,8; Dtn 31,14 f.; 34,10," in *ZAW* 102 (1990): 169–80.
Guo, Xuezhi. *The Ideal Chinese Political Leader: A Historical and Cultural Perspective* (Westport, CT: Praeger, 2002).
Hadas-Lebel, Mireille. "Hezekiah as King Messiah: Traces of an Early Jewish-Christian Polemic in the Tannaitic Tradition," in *Jewish Studies at the Turn of the Twentieth Century, vol. 1: Biblical, Rabbinical, and Medieval Studies* (eds. Judit Targarona Borrás and Ángel Sáenz-Badillos; Leiden: Brill, 1999), 275–81.
Hagedorn, Anselm C. "Local Law in an Imperial Context: The Role of Torah in the (Imagined) Persian Period," in *The Pentateuch as Torah: New Models for Understanding its Promulgation and Acceptance* (eds. Gary N. Knoppers and Bernard M. Levinson; Winona Lake, IN: Eisenbrauns, 2007), 57–76.
Hallo, William W. and K. Lawson Younger, eds. *The Context of Scripture: Canonical Compositions, Monumental Inscriptions and Archival Documents from the Biblical World* (3 vols., Boston and Leiden: Brill, 2003).
Halpern, Baruch. "Why Manasseh Is Blamed for the Babylonian Exile: The Evolution of a Biblical Tradition," in *VT* 48 (1998): 473–514.
Halvorson-Taylor, Martien A. *Enduring Exile: The Metaphorization of Exile in the Hebrew Bible* (VTSup 141; Leiden: Brill, 2011).
Hamilton, Jeffries M. "Caught in the Nets of Prophecy? The Death of King Ahab and the Character of God," in *CBQ* 56 (1994): 649–63.
Hammond Meghan Marie and Sue J. Kim (eds.) *Rethinking Empathy through Literature* (Routledge Interdisciplinary Perspectives on Literature, 31; London/New York: Routledge, 2014).
Handy, Lowell K. "The Authorization of Divine Power and the Guilt of God in the Book of Job: Useful Ugaritic Parallels," in *JSOT* 60 (1993): 107–18.
Handy, Lowell K. *Among the Host of Heaven* (Winona Lake, IN: Eisenbrauns, 1994).
Handy, Lowell K. "One Problem Involved in Translating to Meaning: An Example of Acknowledging Time and Tradition," in *SJOT* 10 (1996): 16–27.
Handy, Lowell K. "Biblical Bronze Age Memories: The Abraham Cycle as Usable Past," in *Biblical Research* 42 (1997): 43–56.
Handy, Lowell K. "Rehabilitating Manasseh: Remembering King Manasseh in the Persian and Hellenistic Periods," in *Remembering Biblical Figures in the Late Persian & Early Hellenistic Periods: Social Memory and Imagination* (eds. Diana V. Edelman and Ehud Ben Zvi; Oxford: Oxford University Press, 2013), 221–235.
Hanspach, Alexander. *Inspirierte Interpreten: Das Prophetenverständnis der Chronikbücher und sein Ort in der Religion und Literatur zur Zeit des Zweiten Tempels* (ATAT 64; St. Otillien: EOS, 2000).
Harrington, Hannah K. "Intermarriage in Qumran Texts: The Legacy of Ezra–Nehemiah," in *Mixed Marriages: Intermarriage and Group Identity in the Second Temple Period* (ed. Christian Frevel; LHBOTS 547; London: T&T Clark, 2011), 251–79.
Harrington, Hannah K. "The Use of Leviticus in Ezra–Nehemiah," in *JHebS* 13/3 (2013), available online at: http://www.jhsonline.org.

Hartenstein, Friedhelm. "The King on the Throne of God: The Concept of World Dominion in Chronicles and Psalm 2," in *Centres and Peripheries in the Early Second Temple Period* (eds. E. Ben Zvi and C. Levin; FAT, 108; Tübingen: Mohr-Siebeck, 2016), 315–22.
Harvey, John E. *Retelling the Torah: the Deuteronomistic Historian's Use of Tetrateuchal Narratives* (JSOTSup 403; London: T&T Clark, 2004).
Hausmann, Jutta. "Beobachtungen zu Spr 31,10–31," in *Alttestamentlicher Glaube und Biblische Theologie: Festschrift für Horst Dietrich Preuss* (eds. Jutta Hausmann and Hans-Jürgen Zobel; Stuttgart: Kohlhammer, 1992), 261–66.
Hayes, Christine E. *Gentile Impurities and Jewish Identities: Intermarriage and Conversion from the Bible to the Talmud* (Oxford: Oxford University Press, 2002).
Heger, Paul. "Patrilineal or Matrilineal Genealogy in Israel After Ezra," in *JSJ* 43 (2012): 215–48.
Hendel, Ronald. *Remembering Abraham* (Oxford: Oxford University Press, 2005).
Hess, Richard S. "The Dead Sea Scrolls and Higher Criticism of the Hebrew Bible: The Case of 4QJudga," in *The Scrolls and the Scriptures: Qumran Fifty Years After* (eds. Stanley E. Porter and Craig A. Evans; Sheffield: Sheffield Academic Press, 1997), 122–28.
Hill, John. "'Your Exile Will Be Long': The Book of Jeremiah and the Unended Exile," in *Reading the Book of Jeremiah: A Search for Coherence* (ed. Martin Kessler; Winona Lake, IN: Eisenbrauns, 2004), 149–161.
Hill, John. *Friend or Foe? The Figure of Babylon in the Book of Jeremiah MT* (BibIntSup 40; Leiden: Brill, 1999).
Hodkinson, Stephen. "Female Property Ownership and Status in Classical and Hellenistic Sparta," in *Women and Property in Ancient Near Eastern and Mediterranean Societies* (eds. Deborah Lyons and Raymond Westbrook; Washington, DC: Center for Hellenic Studies, 2003), available online at: https://chs.harvard.edu/CHS/article/display/1219.
Höffken, Peter. "Der Prophet Jesaja beim Chronisten," in *BN* 81 (1996) 82–90.
Hoffman, Yair. "The Fasts in the Book of Zechariah and the Fashioning of National Remembrance," in *Judah and the Judeans in the Neo-Babylonian Period* (eds. Oded Lipschits and Joseph Blenkinsopp; Winona Lake, IN: Eisenbrauns, 2003), 169–218.
Holladay, William L. *Jeremiah 1* (Hermeneia; Philadelphia: Fortress, 1986).
Holladay, William L. *Jeremiah 2* (Hermeneia; Minneapolis, MN: Fortress, 1989).
Holt, Else K. "Jeremiah's Temple Sermon and the Deuteronomists: An Investigation of the Redactional Relationship between Jeremiah 7 and 26," in *JSOT* 36 (1986): 78–81.
Holt, Else K. *Prophesying the Past* (JSOTSup 194; Sheffield: Sheffield Academic Press, 1995).
Hooker, Paul. *First and Second Chronicles* (Westminster Bible Companion; Louisville: Westminster John Knox, 2001).
Horden, Peregrine, and Nicholas Purcell. *The Corrupting Sea: A Study of Mediterranean History* (Oxford: Blackwell, 2000).
Hugenberger, Gordon P. *Marriage as a Covenant. Biblical Law and Ethics as Developed from Malachi* (Grand Rapids, MI: Baker, 1998; orig. published in VTSup 52, Leiden/New York: Brill, 1994).
Hunt, Robert C. "The Role of Bureaucracy in the Provisioning of Cities: A Framework for an Analysis of the Ancient Near East," in *The Organization of Power: Aspects of Bureaucracy in the Ancient Near East* (eds. McGuire Gibson and Robert D. Biggs; SAOC 46; 2nd ed.; Chicago: Oriental Institute, 1991), 153–68.

Hurowitz, Victor A. "*kæsæp 'ober lassoḥer* (Genesis 23,16)," in *ZAW* 108 (1996): 12–19.
Hurowitz, Victor A. "The Seventh Pillar: Reconsidering the Literary Structure and Unity of Proverbs 31," in *ZAW* 113 (2001): 209–18.
Hurowitz, Victor A. "The Woman of Valor and a Woman Large of Head: Matchmaking in the Ancient Near East," in *Seeking Out the Wisdom of the Ancients: Essays Offered to Honor Michael V. Fox on the Occasion of His Sixty-Fifth Birthday* (eds. Ronald L. Troxel, Kelvin Friebel and Dennis R. Magary; Winona Lake, IN: Eisenbrauns, 2005), 221–34.
Ikas, Karin and Gerhard Wagner, eds. *Communicating in the Third Space* (Routledge Research in Cultural and Media Studies 18; New York: Routledge, 2009).
Instone-Brewer, David. "Jesus' Old Testament Basis for Monogamy," in *The Old Testament in the New Testament: Essays in Honour of J. L. North* (ed. Steve Moyise; JNTSSup 189; Sheffield: Sheffield Academic Press, 2000), 75–105.
Jaén Isabel and Julies Jacques Simon (eds.), *Cognitive Literary Studies Current Themes and New Directions* (Austin, TX: University of Texas Press, 2012).
Janzen, David. *Witch-hunts, Purity and Social Boundaries: The Expulsion of the Foreign Women in Ezra 9–10* (JSOTSup 350; Sheffield: Sheffield Academic, 2002).
Janzen, David. *The Social Meanings of Sacrifice in the Hebrew Bible* (BZAW 344; Berlin: De Gruyter, 2004).
Janzen, J. Gerald. *Studies in the Text of Jeremiah* (Cambridge: Harvard University Press, 1973).
Janzen, J. Gerald. "The 'Wandering Aramean' Reconsidered," in *VT* 44 (1994): 359–75.
Japhet, Sara. *I & II Chronicles: A Commentary* (OTL; Louisville: Westminster John Knox, 1993).
Japhet, Sara. *The Ideology of the Book of Chronicles and Its Place in Biblical Thought* (BEATAJ 9; 2nd ed.; Frankfurt am Main: Peter Lang, 1997).
Japhet, Sara. *From the Rivers of Babylon to the Highlands of Judah: Collected Studies on the Restoration Period* (Winona Lake, IN: Eisenbrauns, 2006).
Jarick, John. *2 Chronicles* (Readings; Sheffield: Sheffield Phoenix, 2007).
Jedlowski, Paolo. "Memories of the Future," in *Routledge International Handbook of Memory Studies* (eds. Trever Hagen and Anna Lisa Tota; London: Routledge, 2015), 145–54.
Jenni, Ernst and Claus Westermann, eds. *Theologisches Handwörterbuch zum Alten Testament (THAT)*, 2 vols. (Munich: Chr. Kaiser, 1971–76).
Johnson, Lyman L. "Digging Up Cuauhtémoc," in *Death, Dismemberment, and Memory: Body Politics in Latin America* (ed. Lyman L. Johnson; Albuquerque: University of New Mexico Press, 2004), 207–44.
Johnston, Laurie. "Religion and the Balkans–Blessing or Curse?" in *Understanding the War in Kosovo* (eds. Florian Bieber and Židas Daskalovski; London/Portland, OR: Frank Cass, 2003), 184–95.
Johnstone, William. *1 and 2 Chronicles, vol. 2: 2 Chronicles 10–36: Guilt and Atonement* (JSOTSup 254; Sheffield: Sheffield Academic Press, 1997).
Jones, Douglas R. *Jeremiah* (NCB; Grand Rapids, MI: Eerdmans, 1992).
Jones, Gwilym H. *1 and 2 Kings* (2 vols.; NCB; Grand Rapids, MI: Eerdmans, 1984).
Jones, Gwilym H. *The Nathan Narratives* (JSOTSup 90; Sheffield: Sheffield University Press, 1990).
Jonker, Louis C. *Reflections of King Josiah in Chronicles: Late Stages of the Josiah Reception in 2 Chr 34f* (Textpragmatische Studien zur Hebräischen Bibel 2; Gütersloh: Gütersloher Verlagshaus, 2003).

Jonker, Louis C. "The Exile as Sabbath Rest: The Chronicler's Interpretation of the Exile," *OTE* 20 (2007): 703–19.
Jonker, Louis C. "Refocusing the Battle Accounts of the Kings: Identity Formation in the Books of Chronicles," in *Behutsames Lesen: Alttestamentliche Exegese im Gespräch mit Literaturwissenschaft und Kulturwissenschaften: Festschrift für Christof Hardmeier zum 65. Geburtstag* (ed. S. Lubs et al.; Arbeiten zur Bibel und Ihrer Geschichte 28; Leipzig: Evangelische Verlagsanstalt, 2007), 245–74.
Jonker, Louis C. "What Constitutes Society? Yehud's Self-Understanding in the Late Persian Era as Reflected in the Books of Chronicles," in *JBL* 127 (2008): 703–24.
Jonker, Louis C. "The Chronicler's Reinterpretation of Hezekiah's Reformation Efforts," in *From Ebla to Stellenbosch* (eds. Izak Cornelius and Louis C. Jonker; Wiesbaden: Harrassowitz, 2008), 116–40.
Jonker, Louis C. "The Chronicler and the Prophets: Who Were his Authoritative Sources?" in *What Was Authoritative for Chronicles?* (eds. Ehud Ben Zvi and Diana V. Edelman; Winona Lake, IN: Eisenbrauns, 2011), 145–64.
Jonker, Louis C. "Manasseh in Paradise, or Not? The Influence of ANE Palace Garden Imagery in LXX 2 Chronicles 33:20," in *Thinking of Water in the Early Second Temple Period* (eds. Ehud Ben Zvi and Christoph Levin; BZAW, 461; Berlin/New York: De Gruyter, 2014), 339–58.
Joüon, Paul. *A Grammar of Biblical Hebrew* (trans. and rev. by Takamitsu Muraoka; SubBib, 27; 2nd ed.; Rome: Pontifical Biblical Institute, 2006).
Jursa, Michael (with contributions by Céline Debourse). "A Babylonian Priestly Martyr, a King-like Priest, and the Nature of Late Babylonian Priestly Literature," in *Wiener Zeitschrift für die Kunde des Morgenlandes* 107 (2017), 77–98.
Kagan, Donald. *The Fall of the Athenian Empire* (Ithaca, NY: Cornell University Press, 1987).
Kahneman, Daniel and Amos Tversky. "The Simulation Heuristic," in *Judgment Under Uncertainty: Heuristics and Biases* (eds. Daniel Kahneman, Paul Slovic and Amos Tversky; New York: Cambridge University Press, 1982), 201–08.
Kalimi, Isaac. *Early Jewish Exegesis and Theological Controversy: Studies in Scriptures in the Shadow of Internal and External Controversies* (Assen: Van Gorcum, 2002).
Kalimi, Isaac. "Jerusalem–The Divine City: The Representation of Jerusalem in Chronicles Compared with Earlier and Later Jewish Compositions," in *The Chronicler as Theologian: Essays in Honor of Ralph W. Klein* (eds. M. Patrick Graham, Steven L. McKenzie and Gary N. Knoppers; JSOTSup 371; London: T&T Clark, 2003), 189–205.
Kalimi, Isaac. *The Reshaping of Ancient Israelite History in Chronicles* (Winona Lake, IN: Eisenbrauns, 2004).
Kalimi, Isaac. *An Ancient Israelite Historian: Studies in The Chronicler, His Time, Place and Writing* (SSN 46; Assen: Van Gorcum, 2005).
Kalimi, Isaac. *The Retelling of Chronicles in Jewish Tradition and Literature: A Historical Journey* (Winona Lake, IN: Eisenbrauns, 2009).
Kallai, Zecharia. "The Boundaries of Canaan and the Land of Israel in the Bible," in *Eretz Israel* 12 (1975): 27–34.
Kallai, Zecharia. "The Patriarchal Boundaries, Canaan and the Land of Israel: Patterns and Application in Biblical Historiography," in *Israel Exploration Journal* 47 (1997): 69–82.
Kammen, Michael G. *A Machine That Would Go of Itself: The Constitution in American Culture* (New Brunswick, NJ: Transaction Publishers, 2006).

Kaplonski, Christopher. *Truth, History and Politics in Mongolia: The Memory of Heroes* (London: Routledge, 2004).

Kegler, Jürgen. "Prophetengestalten im Deuteronomistischen Geschichtswerk und in den Chronikbüchern: Ein Beitrag zur Kompositions- und Redaktionsgeschichte der Chronikbücher," in *ZAW* 105 (1993): 481–97.

Kee, Min Suc. "The Heavenly Council and Its Type-Scene," in *JSOT* 31 (2007): 259–73.

Kelly, Brian E. "Manasseh in the Books of Kings and Chronicles (2 Kings 21:1–18; 2 Chr 33:1–20)," in *Windows into Old Testament History: Evidence, Argument, and the Crisis of "Biblical Israel"* (eds. V. Philips Long, David W. Baker and Gordon J. Wenham; Grand Rapids, MI: Eerdmans, 2002), 131–46.

Kessler, John. "Persia's Loyal Yahwists: Power Identity and Ethnicity in Achaemenid Yehud" in *Judah and the Judeans in the Persian Period* (eds. Oded Lipschits and Manfred Oeming; Winona Lake, IN: Eisenbrauns, 2006), 91–121.

Kessler, John. "Diaspora and Homeland in the Early Achaemenid Period: Community, Geography and Demography in Zechariah 1–8," in *Approaching Yehud: New Approaches to the Study of the Persian Period* (ed. Jon L. Berquist; SemeiaSt 50; Atlanta: Society of Biblical Literature, 2007), 137–66.

Kessler, John. "Images of Exile: Representations of 'Exile' and 'Empty Land' in Sixth to Fourth Century BCE Yehudite Literature," in *The Concept of Exile in Ancient Israel and Its Historical Contexts* (eds. Ehud Ben Zvi and Christoph Levin; BZAW 404; Berlin/New York: De Gruyter, 2010), 308–51.

Kim, Tae Hun. "The Dream of Alexander in Josephus *Ant.* 11.325–39," in *JSS* 34 (2003): 425–442.

Kind, Amy. "Imagining Under Constraints," in *Knowledge through Imagination* (eds. Amy Kind and Peter Kung; Oxford: Oxford University Press, 2016), 145–59.

Kind, Amy and Peter Kung (eds.), *Knowledge through Imagination* (Oxford: Oxford University Press, 2016).

Klein Lillian R. "Honor and Shame in Esther," in *Feminist Companion to Esther, Judith and Susanna* (ed. Athalya Brenner; Sheffield: Sheffield Academic Press, 1995).

Klein, Ralph W. "Prophets and Prophecy in the Books of Chronicles," in *TBT* 36 (1998) 227–32.

Klein, Ralph W. *1 Chronicles* (Hermeneia; Minneapolis, MN: Fortress, 2006).

Klein, Ralph W. "Were Joshua, Zerubbabel, and Nehemiah Contemporaries? A Response to Diana V. Edelman's Proposed Late Date for the Second Temple," in *JBL* 127 (2008): 697–701.

Klein, Ralph W. *2 Chronicles: A Commentary* (Hermeneia; Minneapolis, MN: Fortress, 2012).

Kleinig, John W. "The Divine Institution of the Lord's Song in Chronicles," in *JSOT* 55 (1992): 75–83.

Kloner, Amos. "Jerusalem's Environs in the Persian Period," in *New Studies on Jerusalem* (eds. Avraham Faust and Eyal Baruch; Ramat Gan: Ingeborg Rennert Center for Jerusalem Studies, 2001), 91–95.

Knauf, E. Axel. "King Solomon's Copper Supply," in *Phoenicia and the Bible. Proceedings of the Conference held at the University of Leuven on the 15th and 16th of March 1990* (ed. E. Lipiński; Studia Phoenicia, XI, Leuven: Peeters, 1991), 167–86.

Knauf, E. Axel. "The Glorious Days of Manasseh," in *Good Kings and Bad Kings* (ed. Lester L. Grabbe; LHBOTS 393; London: T&T Clark, 2005), 164–88.

Knauf, E. Axel. *Josua* (ZB 6; Zürich: Theologischer Verlag Zürich, 2008).
Knauf, E. Axel. "Remembering Joshua" in *Remembering Biblical Figures in the Late Persian and Early Hellenistic Periods: Social Memory and Imagination* (eds. Diana V. Edelman and Ehud Ben Zvi; Oxford: Oxford University Press, 2013), 106–27.
Knauf, E. Axel. "Why 'Joshua'"?, in *Deuteronomy-Kings as Emerging Authoritative Books. A Conversation* (ed. Diana V. Edelman; ANEM 6; Atlanta, Ga.: SBL; 2014), 73–84.
Knibb, Michael A. "The Exile in the Literature of the Intertestamental Period," in *HeyJ* 17 (1976): 253–72.
Knibb, Michael A. "Isaianic Traditions in the Aprocrypha and Pseudepigrapha," in *Writing and Reading the Scroll of Isaiah* (eds. Craig C. Broyles and Craig A. Evans; VTSup 70.2; Leiden/ New York: Brill, 1997), 633–50, republished in Michael A. Knibb, *Essays on the Book of Enoch and Other Early Jewish Texts and Traditions* (Studia in Veteris Testamenti Pseudepigrapha 22; Leiden/New York: Brill, 2009), 289–306.
Knoppers, Gary N. "Review of W. M. Schniedewind, *The Word of God in Transition: From Prophet to Exegete in the Second Temple Period*," in *JJS* 49 (1998): 133–35.
Knoppers, Gary N. "Rehoboam in Chronicles," in *JBL* 109 (1990): 423–40.
Knoppers, Gary N. "Reform and Regression: The Chronicler's Presentation of Jehoshaphat," in *Bib* 72 (1991): 500–24.
Knoppers, Gary N. "Images of David in Early Judaism: David as Repentant Sinner in Chronicles," in *Bib* 76 (1995): 449–70.
Knoppers, Gary N. "'Great Among His Brothers,' But Who is He? Social Complexity and Ethnic Diversity in the Genealogy of Judah," in *JHebS* 3/6 (2000), available online at http://www.jhsonline.org.
Knoppers, Gary N. "Intermarriage, Social Complexity and Ethnic Diversity in the Genealogy of Judah," in *JBL* 120 (2001): 15–30.
Knoppers, Gary N. *I Chronicles 1–9: A New Translation with Introduction and Commentary* (AB 12; New York: Doubleday, 2003).
Knoppers, Gary N. *I Chronicles 10–29: A New Translation with Introduction and Commentary* (AB 12; New York: Doubleday, 2004).
Knoppers, Gary N. "Revisiting the Samarian Question in the Persian Period" in *Judah and the Judeans in the Persian Period* (eds. Oded Lipschits and Manfred Oeming; Winona Lake, IN: Eisenbrauns, 2006), 265–289.
Knoppers, Gary N. "Nehemiah and Sanballat: The Enemy Without or Within?" in *Judah and the Judeans in the Fourth Century B.C.E.* (eds. Oded Lipschits, Gary N. Knoppers and Rainer Albertz; Winona Lake, IN: Eisenbrauns, 2007), 305–31.
Knoppers, Gary N. "Revisiting the Composition of Ezra–Nehemiah: In Conversation with Jacob Wright's *Rebuilding Identity: The Nehemiah Memoir and Its Earliest Readers* (BZAW 348; Berlin: De Gruyter, 2004)," in *Perspectives in Hebrew Scriptures IV: Comprising the Contents of Journal of Hebrew Scriptures*, vol. 7 (ed. Ehud Ben Zvi; Piscataway, NJ: Gorgias, 2008), 323–67.
Knoppers, Gary N. "Aspects of Samaria's Religious Culture During the Early Hellenistic Period" in *The Historian and the Bible. Essays in Honour of Lester L. Grabbe* (eds. Philip R. Davies and Diana V. Edelman; LHBOTS 530; London: T&T Clark, 2010), 159–174.
Knoppers, Gary N. "'Married into Moab': The Exogamy Practiced by Judah and His Descendants in the Judahite Lineages," in *Mixed Marriages: Intermarriage and Group*

Identity in the Second Temple Period (ed. Christian Frevel; LHBOTS 547; London: T&T Clark, 2011), 170–91.
Knoppers, Gary N. "Saint or Sinner? Manasseh in Chronicles," in *Rewriting Biblical History: Essays on Chronicles and Ben Sira in Honor of Pancratius C. Beentjes* (eds. Jeremy Corley and Harm van Grol; Deuterocanonical and Cognate Literature Studies 7; Berlin: De Gruyter, 2011), 211–29.
Knoppers, Gary N. "The Relationship of the Deuteronomistic History to Chronicles. Was the Chronicler a Deuteronomist?" in *Congress Volume Helsinki 2010* (ed. Martti Nissinen; VTSup 148, Leiden: Brill, 2012), 307–341.
Knoppers, Gary N. *Jews and Samaritans: The Origins and History of Their Early Relations* (Oxford: Oxford University Press, 2013).
Knowles, Melody D. *Centrality Practiced: Jerusalem in the Religious Practice of Yehud & the Diaspora in the Persian Period* (Atlanta: Society of Biblical Literature, 2006).
Kraemer, David. "The Intended Reader as a Key to Interpreting the Bavli," in *Prooftexts* 13 (1993): 125–140.
Kugel, James L. *Traditions of the Bible* (Cambridge, MA: Harvard University, 1998)
Kuhrt, Amélie. "The Cyrus Cylinder and Achaemenid Policy," in *JSOT* 25 (1983): 83–97.
Kuhrt, Amélie. *The Ancient Near East, c. 3000–330 BC* (2 vols.; London: Routledge, 1995).
Kuhrt, Amélie. "Israelite and Near Eastern Historiography" in *Congress Volume: Oslo 1998* (eds. André Lemaire and Magne Sæbø; VTSup 80; Leiden: Brill, 2000), 257–79.
Kuhrt, Amélie. *The Persian Empire: A Corpus of Sources from the Achaemenid Period* (2 vols.; London: Routledge, 2007).
Kuhrt, Amélie and Susan M. Sherwin-White, *From Samarkhand to Sardis: A New Approach to the Seleucid Empire* (London: Duckworth, 1993).
Kutsch, Ernst. "ברית", in *Theological Lexicon of the Old Testament* (eds. Ernst Jenni and Claus Westermann. Peabody, MA: Hendrickson, 1997), 256–66.
LaCocque, André. *Esther Regina: A Bakhtinian Reading* (Evanston: Northwestern University Press, 2008.
Landy, Francis. *Hosea* (2nd ed. Sheffield: Sheffield Phoenix, 2011; 1st ed. Sheffield: Sheffield Academic, 1995).
Landy, Francis. "Notes Towards a Poetics of Memory in Ancient Israel," in *Remembering and Forgetting in Early Second Temple Judah* (eds. Ehud Ben Zvi and Christoph Levin; FAT 85; Tubingen: Mohr Siebeck, 2012), 331–45.
Laniak, Timothy S. *Shame and Honor in the Book of Esther* (SBLDS 65; Atlanta, Ga.: Scholars Press, 1988).
Lang, Bernhard. "The Hebrew Wife and the Ottoman Wife," in *Anthropology and Biblical Studies: Avenues of Approach* (eds. Louise. J. Lawrence and Mario I. Aguilar; Leiden: Deo, 2004), 140–57.
Lang, Bernhard. "Women's Work, Household and Property in Two Mediterranean Societies: A Comparative Essay on Proverbs XXXI 10–31," in *VT* 54 (2004): 188–207.
Lange, Armin. "Your Daughters Do Not Give to Their Sons and Their Daughters Do Not Take for Your Sons (Ezra 9,12): Intermarriage in Ezra 9–10 and in the Pre-Maccabean Dead Sea Scrolls," Part I, in *BN* 137 (2008): 17–39; Part II, in *BN* 139 (2008): 79–98.
Larsen, Clark S. "Equality for the Sexes in Human Evolution? Early Hominid Sexual Dimorphism and Implications for Mating Systems and Social Behavior," in *Proceedings*

of the National Academy of Sciences of the United States of America 100/16 (2003): 9103 f.

Larson, Erik, Lawrence H. Schiffman, and John Strugnell. "4QText Mentioning Hezekiah," in *Qumran Cave 4, XIV: Parabiblical Texts, Part 2* (eds. Magen Broshi et al.; DJD 19; Oxford: Clarendon Press, 1995), 235–44.

Larson, Erik. "4Q470 and the Angelic Rehabilitation of King Zedekiah," in *DSD* 1 (1994): 210–18.

Latimer, Joanna and Beverley Skeggs, "The Politics of Imagination: Keeping Open and Critical," in *The Sociological Review* 59 (2011): 393–410.

Lawrence, Beatrice. "Gender Analysis: Gender and Method in Biblical Studies," in *Method Matters: Essays on the Interpretation of the Hebrew Bible in Honor of David L. Petersen* (eds. Joel M. LeMon and Kent H. Richards; Atlanta: Society of Biblical Literature, 2009), 333–48.

Lee, Gary R. *Family Structure and Interaction: A Comparative Analysis* (Minneapolis: University of Minnesota Press, 1982).

Leick, Gwendolyn. *Sex and Eroticism in Mesopotamian Literature* (New York: Routledge, 2003).

Lemche, Niels Peter. *The Canaanites and Their Land* (JSOTSup 110; Sheffield: JSOT, 1991).

Lemos, Tracy M. "Shame and Mutilation of Enemies in the Hebrew Bible," in *JBL* 125 (2006): 225–24.

Lemos, Tracy M. *Marriage Gifts and Social Change in Ancient Palestine 1200 BCE to 200 CE* (New York: Cambridge University Press, 2010).

Lemos, Tracy M. "'They Have Become Women': Judean Diaspora and Postcolonial Theories of Gender and Migration", in *Social Theory and the Study of Israelite Religion: Essays in Retrospect and Prospect* (ed. Saul M. Olyan; Resources for Biblical Study, 71; Atlanta: SBL, 2012), 81–109 (99–101).

Lenzi, Alan. *Secrecy and the Gods: Secret Knowledge in Ancient Mesopotamia and Biblical Israel* (SAAS 19; Helsinki: The Neo-Assyrian Text Corpus Project, 2008).

Leske, Adrian M. "Context and Meaning of Zechariah 9:9," in *CBQ* 62 (2000): 663–78.

Leuchter, Mark. "Jeremiah's 70-Year Prophecy and the לב קמי / ששך *Atbash* Codes," in *Bib* 85 (2004): 503–22.

Leuchter, Mark. "The Temple Sermon and the Term מקום in the Jeremianic Corpus," in *JSOT* 30 (2005): 93–109.

Leuchter, Mark. *The Polemics of Exile in Jeremiah 26–45* (Cambridge: Cambridge University Press, 2008).

Leuchter, Mark. "Rethinking the 'Jeremiah' Doublet in Ezra–Nehemiah and Chronicles," in *What Was Authoritative for Chronicles?* (ed. E. Ben Zvi and D. V. Edelman; Winona Lake, IN: Eisenbrauns, 2011) 183–200.

Leuchter, Mark. *Samuel and the Shaping of Tradition* (Biblical Refigurations, Oxford 2013).

Levene, Mark. "Introduction," in *The Massacre in History* (eds. Mark Levene and Penny Roberts; New York: Berghahn Books, 1999), 1–38.

Levenson, Jon D. *Esther: A Commentary* (OTL; Louisville: Westminster John Knox, 1997).

Levenson, Jon D. "The Universal Horizon of Biblical Particularism," in *Ethnicity and the Bible* (ed. Mark G. Brett; Leiden: Brill, 2002), 143–69.

Levenson, Jon D. "The Conversion of Abraham to Judaism, Christianity and Islam," in *The Idea of Biblical Interpretation* (eds. Hindy Najman and Judith H. Newman; JSJSup 83; Leiden: Brill, 2004), 3–40.
Levenson, Jon D. *The Love of God: Divine Gift, Human Gratitude, and Mutual Faithfulness in Judaism* (Princeton: Princeton University Press, 2016).
Levi, Giovanni. "On Microhistory," in *New Perspectives on Historical Writing* (ed. Peter Burke; University Park, PA: Pennsylvania State University Press, 1992), 93–113.
Levin, Christoph. "The 'Word of Yahweh': A Theological Concept in the Book of Jeremiah" in *Re-Reading the Scriptures* (ed. Christoph Levin; FAT 87; Tübingen: Mohr Siebeck, 2013), 221–243.
Levin, Christoph. *Re-Reading the Scriptures* (FAT 87; Tübingen: Mohr Siebeck, 2013).
Levin, Yigal. "From Lists to History: Chronological Aspects of the Chronicler's Genealogies," in *JBL* 123 (2004): 601–636.
Levine, Baruch A. *Numbers 1–20: A New Translation with Introduction and Commentary* (AB 4 A; New York: Doubleday, 1993).
Levitt Kohn, Risa. *A New Heart and a New Soul* (JSOTSup 358; London/New York/Sheffield: Sheffield Academic Press, 2002.
Lichtenstein, Murray H. "Chiasm and Symmetry in Proverbs 31," in *CBQ* 44 (1982): 202–11.
Lierman, John. *The New Testament Moses: Christian Perceptions of Moses and Israel in the Setting of Jewish Religion* (Tübingen: Mohr Siebeck, 2004).
Lincoln, Bruce. *'Happiness for Mankind': Achaemenian Religion and the Imperial Project* (Acta Iranica 53; Leuven: Peeters, 2012).
Linville, James R. "Rethinking the 'Exilic' Book of Kings," in *JSOT* 75 (1997): 21–42.
Lipschits, Oded. "The History of the Benjamin Region Under Babylonian Rule," in *TA* 26 (1999): 155–90.
Lipschits, Oded. "Demographic Changes in Judah between the Seventh and the Fifth Centuries B.C.E." in *Judah and the Judeans in the Neo-Babylonian Period* (eds. Oded Lipschits and Joseph Blenkinsopp; Winona Lake, IN: Eisenbrauns, 2003), 323–76.
Lipschits, Oded. "Ammon in Transition from Vassal Kingdom to Babylonian Province," in *BASOR* 335 (2004): 37–52.
Lipschits, Oded. "The Rural Settlement in Judah in The Sixth Century B.C.E.: A Rejoinder," in *PEQ* 136 (2004): 99–107.
Lipschits, Oded. *The Fall and Rise of Jerusalem* (Winona Lake, IN: Eisenbrauns, 2005).
Lipschits, Oded. "Achaemenid Imperial Policy, Settlement Processes in Palestine, and the Status of Jerusalem in the Middle of the Fifth Century B.C.E.," in *Judah and the Judeans in the Persian Period* (eds. Oded Lipschits and Manfred Oeming; Winona Lake, IN: Eisenbrauns, 2006), 19–52.
Lipschits, Oded. "Persian Period Finds from Jerusalem: Facts and Interpretations," *JHebS* 9/20 (2009), available online at http://www.jhsonline.org, republished in *Perspectives on Hebrew Scriptures VI: Comprising the Contents of Journal of Hebrew Scriptures, vol. 9* (ed. Ehud Ben Zvi; Piscataway, NJ: Gorgias Press, 2010), 423–453.
Lipschits, Oded and David S. Vanderhoft, *The Yehud Stamp Impressions: A Corpus of Inscribed Impressions from the Persian and Hellenistic Periods in Judah* (Winona Lake, IN: Eisenbrauns, 2011).
Lipschits, Oded, Omer Sergi, and Ido Koch. "Judahite Stamped and Incised Jar Handles: A Tool for Studying the History of Late Monarchic Judah," in *TA* 38 (2011): 5–41.

Lipschits, Oded. "Jerusalem between Two Periods of Greatness: The Size and Status of the City in the Babylonian, Persian and Early Hellenistic Periods," in *Judah between East and West: The Transition from Persian to Greek Rule (ca. 400–200 BCE)* (eds. Oded Lipschits and Lester L. Grabbe; LSTS; London/New York: T&T Clark, 2012), 163–75.

Liss, Hanna. "'Describe the Temple to the House of Israel': Preliminary Remarks on the Temple Vision in the Book of Ezekiel and the Question of Fictionality in Priestly Literatures," in *Utopia and Dystopia in Prophetic Literature* (ed. Ehud Ben Zvi; Publications of the Finnish Exegetical Society 92; Helsinki: Finnish Exegetical Society and Göttingen: Vandenhoeck & Ruprecht, 2006), 122–43.

Little, David. "The Heterogeneous Social: New Thinking About the Foundations of the Social Sciences" in *Philosophy of the Social Sciences: Philosophical Theory and Scientific Practice* (ed. C. Mantzavinos; Cambridge University Press, 2009).

Liverani, Mario. "Memorandum on the Approach to Historiographic Texts," in *Orientalia* 42 (1973): 178–94.

Liverani, Mario. "Kitru, Kataru," in *Mesopotamia* 17 (1982): 43–66.

Liverani, Mario. *Israel's History and the History of Israel* (London: Equinox, 2005).

Livneh, Atar. "With my Sword and Bow: Jacob as Warrior in Jubilees," in *Rewriting and Interpretation: The Biblical Patriarchs in Light of the Dead Sea Scrolls* (eds. Deborah Dimant and Reinhard Kratz; BZAW 439; Berlin: de Gruyter, 2013), 189–213.

Long, Burke O. *1 Kings* (FOTL 9; Grand Rapids, MI: Eerdmans, 1984).

Lowery, Richard H. *The Reforming Kings: Cults and Society in First Temple Judah* (JSOTSup 120; Sheffield: JSOT Press, 1991).

Luke, K. "The Ideal Wife (Prov 31:10–31)," in *Jeevadhara* 21 (1991): 118–32.

Lust, Johan. "Messianism and the Greek Version of Jeremiah: Jer 23,5–6 and 33,14–26," in *Messianism and the Septuagint: Collected Essays* (eds. Johan Lust and Katrin Hauspie; BETL 178; Leuven: Leuven University Press, 2004), 41–67.

Lyons, Ellen L. "A Note on Proverbs 31.10–31," in *The Listening Heart: Essays in Wisdom and the Psalms in Honor of Roland E. Murphy* (ed. Kenneth G. Hoglund et al.; JSOTSup 58; Sheffield: JSOT Press, 1987), 237–45.

Ma, John. "Kings," in *A Companion to the Hellenistic World* (ed. Andrew Erskine; Oxford: Blackwell, 2003), 177–195.

Ma, John. *Antiochos III and the Cities of Western Asia Minor* (Oxford: Oxford University Press, 2000).

Macchi, Jean-Daniel. "Denial, Deception or Force: How to Deal with Powerful Others", in *Imagining the Other and Constructing Israelite Identity in the Early Second Temple Period* (eds. Diana V. Edelman and Ehud Ben Zvi; LHBOTS 456; London: Bloomsbury T&T Clark, 2014), 219–29.

Macintosh, Andrew A. *Hosea* (ICC; Edinburgh: T&T Clark, 1997).

Maddox, Donald. *Semiotics of Deceit* (Lewisburg, PA: Bucknell University, 1984).

Mahr Johannes B. and Gergely Csibra. "Why Do We Remember? The Communicative Function of Episodic Memory," in *Behavioral and Brain Sciences* 41 (2018) E1. doi:10.1017/S0140525X17000012.

Maeir Aren M. and Itzhaq Shai, "Reassessing the Character of the Judahite Kingdom: Archaeological Evidence for Non-Centralized, Kinship-Based Components," in *From Sha'ar Hagolan to Shaaraim Essays in Honor of Prof. Yosef Garfinkel* (eds. Saar Ganor,

Igor Kreimerman, Katharina Streit, Madeleine Mumcuoglu; Jerusalem: Israel Exploration Society, 2016), 323–40.

Maier, Christl M. *Daughter Zion, Mother Zion: Gender, Space and the Sacred in Ancient Israel* (Minneapolis, MN: Fortress, 2008).

Maier, Christl M. "Daughter of Zion as Queen and the Iconography of the Female City," in *Images and Prophecy in the Ancient Eastern Mediterranean* (eds. Martti Nissinen and Charles E. Carter; FRLANT 233; Göttingen: Vandenhoeck & Ruprecht, 2009), 147–62.

Malul, Meir. *Knowledge, Control and Sex: Studies in Biblical Thought, Culture and Worldview* (Tel Aviv–Jaffa: Archaeological Center Publication, 2002).

Manning, Joseph G. *The Last Pharaohs: Egypt under the Ptolemies, 305–30 BC* (Princeton: Princeton University Press, 2010).

Marcinkowska, Urszula. M., et al. "Cross-Cultural Variation in Men's Preference for Sexual Dimorphism in Women's Faces," in *Biology Letters* (2014), available online at http://dx.doi.org/10.1098/rsbl.2013.0850.

Marcos, Fernando S. "Tendencias historiográficas actuales," in *Cultura Histórica* (2009), available online at http://www.culturahistorica.es.

Maruyama, Magoroh. "Mindscapes and Science Theories," in *Current Anthropology* 21 (1980): 589–99.

Mason, Rex. *Preaching the Tradition: Homily and Hermeneutics after the Exile* (Cambridge: Cambridge University Press, 1990).

Mason, Steve. *'Eternal Covenant' in the Pentateuch: The Contours of an Elusive Phrase* (LHBOTS 494; New York: T&T Clark, 2008).

Matthews, Victor H. "Marriage and Family in the Ancient Near East," in *Marriage and Family in the Biblical World* (ed. Ken M. Campbell; Downers Grove, IL: InterVarsity Press, 2003), 1–32.

Mayhue, Richard L. "False Prophets and the Deceiving Spirit," in *TMSJ* 4, no. 2 (1993): 135–63.

McCreesh, Thomas P. "Wisdom as Wife: Proverbs 31:10–31," in *RB* 92 (1985): 25–46.

McDonough, Sean M. "'And David was Old, Advanced in Years': 2 Samuel xxiv 18–25, 1 Kings 1, and Genesis xxiii–xxiv," in *VT* 49 (1999): 128–131.

McKane, William. *Jeremiah 26–52* (ICC. Edinburgh: T&T Clark, 1996).

McKeating, Henry. "Ezekiel the 'Prophet Like Moses'?" JSOT 101 (1994): 7–109.

McKenzie, John L. *Second Isaiah: A New Translation with Introduction and Commentary* (AB 20; Garden City, NY: Doubleday, 1968).

McKenzie, Steven L. "The Typology of the Davidic Covenant," in *The Land, That I Will Show You: Essays on the History and Archaeology of the Ancient Near East in Honour of J. Maxwell Miller* (eds. J. Andrew Dearman and M. Patrick Graham; Journal for the Study of the Old Testament Supplement 363; Sheffield: Sheffield Academic Press, 2001), 152–78.

McKenzie, Steven L. "The Trouble with King Jehoshaphat" in *Reflection and Refraction: Studies in Biblical Historiography in Honour of A. Graeme Auld* (eds. Robert Rezetko, Timothy H. Lim and W. Brian Aucker; VTSup 113; Leiden: Brill, 2004), 299–314.

McKenzie, Steven L. *1–2 Chronicles* (AOTC; Nashville: Abingdon, 2004).

Meeks, Wayne A. *The Prophet-King: Moses Traditions and the Johannine Christology* (NovTSup 14; Leiden: Brill, 1967).

Mendels, Doron. "Hecataeus of Abdera and a Jewish 'Patrios Politeia' of the Persian Period (Diodorus Siculus XL, 3)," in *ZAW* 95 (1983): 96–110.

Mettinger, Tryggve. N. D. "In Search of the Hidden Structure: YHWH as King in Isaiah 40–55," in *Writing and Reading the Scroll of Isaiah* (eds. Craig C. Broyles and Craig A. Evans; VTSup 70; Leiden/New York: Brill, 1997), 143–54.
Meyers, Carol L. "The Family in Early Israel," in *Families in Ancient Israel* (eds. L. G. Perdue, Joseph Blenkinsopp, John J. Collins and Carol L. Myers; Louisville: Westminster John Knox, 1997), 1–41.
Meyers, Carol L. and Eric M. Meyers, *Zechariah 9–14: A New Translation with Introduction and Commentary* (AB 25C; New York: Doubleday, 1993).
Micheel, Rosemarie. *Die Seher- und Prophetenüberlieferungen in der Chronik* (BBET 18; Frankfurt am Main: Peter Lang, 1983).
Michaelian Kourken and John Sutton. "Collective Mental Time Travel: Remembering the Past and Imagining the Future Together," in *Synthese. An International Journal for Epistemology, Methodology and Philosophy of Science*. Special issue: Thinking (about) groups); 2017; https://doi.org/10.1007/s11229-017-1449-1.
Milgrom, Jacob. "Religious Conversion and the Revolt Model for the Formation of Israel," in *JBL* 101 (1982): 169–76.
Milgrom, Jacob. *Leviticus 1–16: A New Translation with Introduction and Commentary* (AB 3; New York: Doubleday, 1991).
Milgrom, Jacob. *Leviticus 17–22: A New Translation with Introduction and Commentary* (AB 3 A; New York: Doubleday, 2000).
Milgrom, Jacob. *Leviticus 23–27: A New Translation with Introduction and Commentary* (AB 3B; New Haven / London: Yale University Press, 2008).
Miller, James C. "Ethnicity and the Hebrew Bible: Problems and Prospects," in *CurBS* 6 (2008): 170–213.
Miller, James M. and John H. Hayes, *A History of Ancient Israel and Judah* (Philadelphia: Westminster, 1987; 2nd rev. ed. Louisville: Westminster John Knox, 2006).
Misztal, Barbara A. *Theories of Social Remembering* (Maidenhead: Open University Press, 2003).
Mitchell, Christine. "The Ironic Death of Josiah in 2 Chronicles", in *CBQ* 68 (2006): 421–35.
Mitchell, Christine. "Otherness and Historiography in Chronicles" in *Historiography and Identity: (Re)formulation in Second Temple Historiographical Literature* (ed. Louis C. Jonker; LHBOTS 534; London: T&T Clark, 2010), 93–109.
Mitchell, Lynette "Remembering Cyrus the Persian: Exploring Monarchy and Freedom in Classical Greece," in *Remembering Biblical Figures in the Late Persian and Early Hellenistic Periods: Social Memory and Imagination* (ed. Diana V. Edelman and Ehud Ben Zvi; Oxford: Oxford University Press, 2013), 283–92.
Moberly, R. Walter L. "Does God Lie to His Prophets? The Story of Micaiah ben Imlah as a Test Case," in *HTR* 96 (2003): 1–23
Moffat, Donald P. *Ezra's Social Drama: Identity Formation, Marriage and Social Conflict in Ezra 9 and 10* (LHBOTS 579; London: T&T Clark, 2013).
Momigliano, A. *Essays in Ancient and Modern Historiography* (Middletown: Wesleyan University Press, 1977).
Morello, Ruth. "Livy's Alexander Digression (9.17–19): Counterfactuals and Apologetics," in *Journal of Roman Studies* 92 (2002): 62–85.
Mosis, Rudolf. *Untersuchungen zur Theologie des chronistischen Geschichtswerkes* (Freiburger theologische Studien 92; Freiburg: Herder, 1973).

Mroczek, Eva. "Moses, David and Scribal Revelations: Preservation and Renewal in Second Temple Jewish Textual Traditions", in *The Significance of Sinai. Traditions about Sinai and Divine Revelation in Judaism and Christianity* (eds. George J. Brooke, Hindy Najman and Loren T. Stuckenbruck; Leiden: Brill, 2008), 91–115.

Müller, Reinhard. "The Altar on Mount Gerizim (Deuteronomy 27:1–8). Center or Periphery?," in *Centres and Peripheries in the Early Second Temple Period* (eds. Ehud Ben Zvi and Christoph Levin, FAT 108; Tübingen: Mohr-Siebeck, 2016), 197–214.

Mullally Sinéad L. and Eleanor A. Maguire, "Memory, Imagination, and Predicting the Future: A Common Brain Mechanism?" in *The Neuroscientist* 20 (2014): 220–234.

Na'aman, Nadav. "Prophetic Stories as Sources for the Histories of Jehoshaphat and the Omrides," in *Bib* 78 (1997): 153–73.

Na'aman, Nadav. *Borders and Districts in Biblical Historiography* (Jerusalem Biblical Studies 4; Tel Aviv: Simor, 1986).

Na'aman, Nadav. "In Search of Reality Behind the Account of David's Wars with Israel's Neighbours," in *IEJ* 52 (2002) 200–24.

Na'aman, Nadav. *Ancient Israel and Its Neighbors: Interaction and Counteraction* (Winona Lake, IN: Eisenbrauns, 2005).

Na'aman, Nadav. *Canaan in the Second Millennium B.C.E. Collected Essays, Volume Two* (Winona Lake, IN: Eisenbrauns, 2005).

Na'aman, Nadav. "Saul, Benjamin and the Emergence of 'Biblical Israel'," in *ZAW* 121 (2009): 211–224.

Na'aman, Nadav. "The Israelite-Judahite Struggle for the Patrimony of Ancient Israel," in *Bib* 91 (2010): 1–23.

Na'aman, Nadav. "Memories of Monarchical Israel in the Narratives of David's Wars with Israel's Neighbours," in *HebAI* 6 (2017): 308–28.

Nelson, Richard D. "Josiah in the Book of Joshua," in *JBL* 100 (1981): 531–540.

Neusner, Jacob. *In the Aftermath of Catastrophe: Founding Judaism 70–640* (M-QSHR 2/51; Montreal: McGill-Queen's University Press, 2009).

Newsom, Carol. "Rhyme and Reason: The Historical Résumé in Israelite and Early Jewish Thought," in *Israel's Prophets and Israel's Past: Essays on the Relationship of Prophetic Texts and Israelite History in Honor of John H. Hayes* (eds. B. E. Kelle and M. B. Moore; LHBOTS 446; London; New York: T&T Clark: 2006), 293–310.

Newsome, J. D. "Toward a New Understanding of the Chronicler and His Purposes," in *JBL* 94 (1975): 201–17.

Niditch, Susan. *War in the Hebrew Bible: A Study in the Ethics of Violence* (New York: Oxford University Press, 1993).

Niehr, Herbert. "Religio-Historical Aspects of the 'Early Post-Exilic' Period," in *The Crisis of Israelite Religion: Transformation of Religious Tradition in Exilic and Post-Exilic Times* (eds. Bob Becking, Marjo C. A. Korpel; Oudtestamentische Studiën 42; Leiden: Brill, 1999), 228–44.

Nihan, Christophe. "The Torah between Samaria and Judah: Shechem and Gerizim in Deuteronomy and Joshua," in *The Pentateuch as Torah: New Models for Understanding Its Promulgation and Acceptance* (eds. Gary N. Knoppers and Bernard M. Levinson; Winona Lake, IN: Eisenbrauns, 2007), 187–223.

Nihan, Christophe. "The Memory of Ezekiel in Postmonarchic Yehud," in *Remembering Biblical Figures in the Late Persian & Early Hellenistic Periods: Social Memory and*

Imagination (eds. Diana V. Edelman and Ehud Ben Zvi; Oxford: Oxford University Press, 2013), 415–48.
Nissinen, Martti. "City as Lofty as Heaven: Arbela and Other Cities in Neo-Assyrian Prophecy," in *'Every City Shall Be Forsaken': Urbanism and Prophecy in Ancient Israel and the Near East* (eds. Lester L. Grabbe and Robert D. Haak; JSOTSup 330; Sheffield: Sheffield Academic Press, 2001), 172–209.
Nissinen, Martti. *Ancient Prophecy: Near Eastern, Greek, and Biblical Perspectives* (Oxford: Oxford University Press, 2017).
Noegel, Scott B. "God of Heaven and Sheol: The 'Unearthing of Creation," in *HS* 58 (2017): 119–44.
Noll, Kurt L. "Was There Doctrinal Dissemination in Early Yahweh Religion?" in *BibInt* 16 (2008): 395–427.
Nora, Pierre. "Between Memory and History: Les Lieux de Mémoire," in *Representations* 26 (1989): 7–24.
Nora, Pierre. "General Introduction: Between Memory and History," in *Realms of Memory Volume 1: Conflicts and Divisions* (ed. Pierre Nora; New York: Columbia University Press, 1996), 1–20 (xvii).
Novick, Tzvi. "'She Binds Her Arms': Rereading Proverbs 31:17," in *JBL* 128 (2009): 107–13.
Nwaoru, Emmanuel O. "Image of the Woman of Substance in Proverbs 31:10–31 and African Context," in *BN* 127 (2005): 41–66.
O'Brien, Julia M. "Nahum-Habakkuk-Zephaniah: Reading the 'Former Prophets' in the Persian Period," in *Interpretation* 61 (2007): 168–83.
O'Brien, Julia M. *Challenging Prophetic Metaphor: Theology and Ideology in the Prophets* (Louisville, KY: Westminster John Knox, 2008).
O'Connor, Kathleen M. *Jeremiah: Pain and Promise* (Minneapolis: Fortress, 2011).
O'Connor, Kathleen M. "Reclaiming Jeremiah's Violence," in *The Aesthetics of Violence in the Prophets* (eds. Julia M. O'Brien and Chris Franke; LHBOTS, 517; New York: T&T Clark, 2010), 37–49.
O'Dowd, Ryan. *The Wisdom of Torah: Epistemology in Deuteronomy and the Wisdom Literature* (FRLANT 225; Göttingen: Vandenhoeck & Ruprecht, 2009).
Oberschall, Anthony. *Conflict and Peace Building in Divided Societies: Responses to Ethnic Violence* (New York: Routledge, 2007).
Oded, Bustenay. *War, Peace and Empire. Justifications for War in Assyrian Royal Inscriptions* (Wiesbaden: Reichert Verlag, 1992).
Oded, Bustenay. "Where is the 'Myth of the Empty Land' to be Found? History versus Myth," in *Judah and the Judeans in the Neo-Babylonian Period* (eds. Oded Lipschits and Joseph Blenkinsopp; Winona Lake, IN: Eisenbrauns, 2003), 55–74.
Oeming, Manfred. *Das wahre Israel: Die 'genealogische Vorhalle' 1 Chronik 1-9* (BWANT, 128; Stuttgart: Kohlhammer, 1990).
Olyan, Saul M. "Honor, Shame, and Covenantal Relations in Ancient Israel and its Environment," in *JBL* 115 (1996): 201–18.
Olyan, Saul M. "'Anyone Blind or Lame Shall Not Enter The House': On The Interpretation of Second Samuel 5:8b," in *CBQ* 60 (1998): 218–227.
Olyan, Saul M. "Purity Ideology in Ezra–Nehemiah as a Tool to Reconstitute the Community," in *JJS* 35 (2004): 1–16.

Olyan, Saul M. *Social Inequality in the World of the Text: The Significance of Ritual and Social Distinctions in the Hebrew Bible* (Journal of Ancient Judaism Supplements 4; Göttingen: Vandenhoeck & Ruprecht, 2011).
Olyan, Saul M. "Is Isaiah 40–55 Really Monotheistic?," in *JANER* 12 (2012), 190–201.
Oswald, Wolfgang. "Foreign Marriages and Citizenship in Persian Period Judah," in *JHebS* 12/6 (2012), DOI: 10.5508/jhs.2012.v12.a6, available online at http://www.jhsonline.org; republished in *Perspectives in Hebrew Scriptures IX: Comprising the Contents of Journal of Hebrew Scriptures*, vol. 12 (eds. Ehud Ben Zvi and Christophe Nihan; Piscataway, NJ: Gorgias, 2014), 107–24.
Overholt, Thomas W. "Prophecy: The Problem of Cross-Cultural Comparison," in *Semeia* 21 (1982), 55–78.
Overholt, Thomas W. *Channels of Prophecy. The Social Dynamics of Prophetic Activity* (Minneapolis: Fortress, 1989).
Overholt, Thomas W. *Cultural Anthropology and the Old Testament* (Minneapolis: Fortress, 1996).
Pakkala, Juha. "Intermarriage and Group Identity in the Ezra Tradition (Ezra 7–10 and Nehemiah 8)," in *Mixed Marriages: Intermarriage and Group Identity in the Second Temple Period* (ed. Christian Frevel; LHBOTS 547; London: T&T Clark, 2011), 78–88.
Pakkala, Juha. "Zedekiah's Fate and the Dynastic Succession," in *JBL* 125 (2006): 443–52.
Palmquist, Stephen R. and Philip McPherson Rudisill, "Three Perspectives on Abraham's Defense against Kant's Charge of Immoral Conduct," in *Journal of Religion* 89 (2009): 467–97.
Panaino, Antonio. "The Mesopotamian Heritage of Achaemenian Kingship," in *The Heirs of Assyria* (eds. Sanna Aro and Robert M. Whiting; Melammu 1; Helsinki: The Neo-Assyrian Text Corpus Project 2000), 35–49.
Patton, Corrine L. "Pan-Deuteronomism and the Book of Ezekiel," in L. S. Schearing and S. L. McKenzie (eds.), *Those Elusive Deuteronomists* (JSOTSup, 268; Sheffield Academic Press: Sheffield, 1999) 200–215.
Paz, Octavio. *The Labyrinth of Solitude: Life and Thought in Mexico* (New York: Grove Press, 1961).
Peltonen, Kai. "A Jigsaw without a Model? The Date of Chronicles," in *Did Moses Speak Attic?* (ed. Lester L. Grabbe; JSOTSup, 317; Sheffield: Sheffield Academic Press, 2001), 225–71.
Perdue, Leo. *Wisdom & Creation: The Theology of the Wisdom Literature* (Nashville: Abingdon, 1994).
Perdue, Leo. *Proverbs* (Interpretation; Louisville, KY: Westminster John Knox, 2000).
Perrin, Denis and Kourken Michaelian. "Memory as Mental Time Travel," in *Routledge Handbook of Philosophy of Memory* (eds. Sven Bernecker & Kourken Michaelian; London: Routledge; 2017), 228–239.
Person, Raymond F. "II Kings 24,18–25,30 and Jeremiah 52: A Text-Critical Case Study in the Redaction History of the Deuteronomistic History," in *ZAW* 105 (1993): 174–205.
Petersen, David L. *Late Israelite Prophecy: Studies in Deutero-prophetic Literature and in Chronicles* (SBLMS 23; Missoula, MT: Scholars Press, 1977).
Petersen, David L. *Zechariah 9–14 and Malachi* (OTL; Louisville, KY: Westminster John Knox, 1995).
Pietersma, Albert and Marc Saunders. *Ieremias* (NETS; Oxford University Press, 2007), available online at http://ccat.sas.upenn.edu/nets/edition/34-ieremias-nets.pdf.

Pioske, Daniel. "Retracing a Remembered Past Methodological Remarks on Memory, History, and the Hebrew Bible," in *BibInt* 23 (2015): 291–315.
Plautz, Werner. "Monogamie und Polygynie im Alten Testament," in *ZAW* 75 (1963): 3–27.
Polak, Frank H. "David's Kingship–A Precarious Equilibrium," in *Politics and Theopolitics in the Bible and Postbiblical Literature* (eds. Henning Graf Reventlow, Yair Hoffman and Benjamin Uffenheimer; JSOTSup 171; Sheffield: Sheffield Academic Press, 1994), 119–47.
Polzin, Robert and Eugene Rothman, eds. *The Biblical Mosaic: Changing Perspectives* (Philadelphia: Fortress, 1982).
Polzin, Robert. *Samuel and the Deuteronomist* (Bloomington: Indiana University Press, 1993).
Pomeroy, Sarah B. *Xenophon, Oeconomicus: A Social and Historical Commentary* (Oxford: Clarendon / New York: Oxford University Press, 1994).
Porten, Bezalel and Ada Yardeni, eds. *Textbook of Aramaic Documents from Ancient Egypt* (4 vols.; Jerusalem: Hebrew University Press, 1986–99).
Porten, Bezalel et al., eds. *The Elephantine Papyri in English: Three Millennia of Cross-Cultural Continuity and Change* (Leiden: Brill, 1996).
Poser, Ruth. *Das Ezechielbuch als Trauma-Literatur* (VTSup, 154; Leiden: Brill, 2012).
Pruin, Dagmar. "What Is in a Text? – Searching for Jezebel", in *Ahab Agonistes: The Rise and Fall of the Omri Dynasty* (ed. Lester L. Grabbe; LHBOTS, 421/ESHM, 6; New York: T&T Clark, 2007), 208–35.
Raabe, Paul R. *Obadiah: A New Translation with Introduction and Commentary* (AB 24D; New York: Doubleday, 1996).
Ramet, Sabrina P. "Dead Kings and National Myths: Why Myths of Founding and Martyrdom are Important," in *Civic and Uncivic Values: Serbia in the Post-Milošević Era* (eds. Ola Listhaug et al.; Budapest/New York: Central European University Press, 2011), 267–98.
Reddit, Paul L. *Introduction to the Prophets* (Grand Rapids, Mich.: Eerdmans; 2008).
Reddit, Paul. *Zechariah 9-14* (IECOT; Stuttgart: Kohlhammer, 2012).
Renfrew, Colin. "Beyond a Subsistence Economy: The Evolution of Social Organization in Prehistoric Europe," in *Reconstructing Complex Societies An Archaeological Colloquium* (ed. Charlotte B. Moore; BASORSup, 20; Cambridge, MA: ASOR, 1974), 69–88.
Renkema, Johan. *Obadiah* (HCOT; Leuven: Peeters, 2003).
Rezetko, Robert. "The (Dis)Connection between Textual and Linguistic Developments in the Book of Jeremiah: Hebrew Bible Textual Criticism Challenges Biblical Hebrew Historical Linguistics," in *Empirical Models Challenging Biblical Criticism* (eds. R. F. Person Jr. and R. Rezetko; SBLAIL, 25; Atlanta: SBL Press, 2016), 239–69.
Rigney, Daniel. *The Matthew Effect: How Advantage Begets Further Advantage* (New York, NY: Columbia University Press, 2010).
Riley, William. *King and Cultus in Chronicles. Worship and the Reinterpretation of History* (JSOTSup 160; Sheffield: JSOT Press, 1993).
Ristau, Ken A. "Reading and Rereading Josiah: The Chronicler's Representation of Josiah for the Postexilic Community," in *Community Identity in Judean Historiography: Biblical and Comparative Perspectives* (eds. Gary N. Knoppers and Ken A. Ristau; Winona Lake, IN: Eisenbrauns, 2009), 219–47.
Roberts, J. J. M. "The Davidic Origin of the Zion Tradition," in *JBL* 92 (1973): 329–344.
Robertson, D. "Micaiah ben Imlah: A Literary View" in *The Biblical Mosaic: Changing Perspectives* (eds. Robert Polzin and Eugene Rothman; Philadelphia: Fortress, 1982), 139–46.

Robson, Eleanor. "The Production and Dissemination of Scholarly Knowledge," in *The Oxford Handbook of Cuneiform Culture* (eds. K. Radner and E. Robson; Oxford: Oxford University Press, 2011), 557–576.
Rofé, Alexander. *The Prophetical Stories* (Jerusalem: Magnes, 1988).
Rofé, Alexander. "The Monotheistic Argumentation in Deuteronomy 4,32–40: Contents, Composition and Text," in *VT* 35 (1985): 434–45.
Rofé, Alexander. *Deuteronomy: Issues and Interpretation* (London/New York: T&T Clark, 2002).
Rofé, Alexander. "The Valiant Woman, γυνὴ συνετή, and the Redaction of the Book of Proverbs," in *Vergegenwärtigung des Alten Testaments: Beiträge zur biblischen Hermeneutik. Festschrift für Rudolf Smend zum 70. Geburtstag* (eds. Christoph Bultmann, Walter Dietrich and Christoph Levin; Göttingen: Vandenhoeck & Ruprecht, 2002), 145–55.
Römer, Thomas C. "Transformations in Deuteronomistic and Biblical Historiography: On 'Book-Finding' and other Literary Strategies," in *ZAW* 109 (1997): 1–11.
Römer, Thomas C. "How Did Jeremiah Become a Convert to Deuteronomistic Ideology?," in *Those Elusive Deuteronomists* (eds. L. S. Schearing and S. L. McKenzie; JSOTSup, 268; Sheffield Academic Press: Sheffield, 1999), 189–199.
Römer, Thomas C. "Du temple au livre: L'idéologie de la centralization dans l'historiographie deutéronomiste," in *Rethinking the Foundations: Historiography in the Ancient World and in the Bible* (eds. Thomas C. Römer and Steven L. McKenzie; Beihefte zur ZAW 294; Berlin: De Gruyter, 2000), 207–25.
Römer, Thomas C. *The So-Called Deuteronomistic History. A Sociological, Historical and Literary Introduction* (London: T&T Clark, 2005).
Römer, Thomas C. "Moses outside the Torah and the Construction of a Diaspora Identity," in *JHebS* 8/15 (2008), available online at www.jhsonline.org; republished under the same title in *Perspectives on Hebrew Scriptures v: Comprising the Contents of Journal of Hebrew Scriptures, vol. 8* (ed. Ehud Ben Zvi; Piscataway, NJ: Gorgias Press, 2009), 293–306.
Römer, Thomas C. "Moses, the Royal Lawgiver," in *Remembering Biblical Figures in the Late Persian and Early Hellenistic Periods: Social Memory and Imagination* (eds. Diana Edelman and Ehud Ben Zvi; Oxford/New York: Oxford University Press, 2013), 81–94.
Römer, Thomas C. "Joshua's Encounter with the Commander of Yhwh's Army (Josh 5:13–15): Literary Construction or Reflection of a Royal Ritual?," in *Warfare, Ritual, and Symbol in Biblical and Modern Contexts* (eds. Brad E. Kelle, Frank Ritchel Ames, and Jacob L. Wright; AIL 18; Atlanta: SBL, 2014), 49–64.
Rom-Shiloni, Dalit. "Exiles and Those Who Remained: Strategies of Exclusivity in the Early Sixth Century BCE," in *Shai le-Sara Japhet: Studies in the Bible, its Exegesis and its Language* (eds. Moshe Bar-Asher et al.; Jerusalem: Bialik Institute, 2007), 119–38.
Rom-Shiloni, Dalit. "Group Identities in Jeremiah: Is it the Persian Period Conflict," in *A Palimpsest: Rhetoric, Ideology, Stylistics and Language Relating to Persian Israel* (eds. Ehud Ben Zvi, Diana V. Edelman and Frank Polak. Piscataway: Gorgias Press, 2009), 11–46
Roncace, Marc. *Jeremiah, Zedekiah, and the Fall of Jerusalem: A Study of Prophetic Narrative* (LHBOTS 423; London: T&T Clark, 2005).

Rosenfeld, Gavriel. "Why do we ask 'What if'? Reflections on the Function of Alternate History," in *History and Theory* 41 (2002): 90–103.
Roth, Martha T. *Babylonian Marriage Agreements: 7th–3rd Centuries B.C.* (AOAT 222; Kevelaer: Butzon & Bercker, 1989).
Roth, Martha T. *Law Collections from Mesopotamia and Asia Minor* (2nd ed., SBLWAW 6; Atlanta: Scholars Press, 1997).
Roth, Silke. "Harem," in *UCLA Encyclopedia of Egyptology* (eds. Elizabeth Frood, Willeke Wendrich, Los Angeles 2012), available online at https://escholarship.org/uc/item/1k3663r3.
Roth, Wolfgang. "The Story of the Prophet Micaiah (I Kings 22) in Historical-Critical Interpretation: 1876–1976" in *The Biblical Mosaic: Changing Perspectives* (eds. Robert Polzin and Eugene Rothman; Philadelphia: Fortress, 1982), 105–37.
Rusch, Gebhard. "Comprehension vs. Understanding of Literature," in *The Systemic and Empirical Approach to Literature and Culture as Theory and Application* (eds. Steven Tötösy de Zepetnek and Irene Sywenky: Siegen 1997), 107–119.
Sandmel, Samuel. *Philo's Place in Judaism* (New York: KTAV, 1971).
Sandoval, Timothy J. and Carleen Mandolfo, eds. *Relating to the Text. Interdisciplinary and Form-Critical Insights on the Bible* (JSOTSup 384; London: T&T Clark, 2003).
Sarna, Nahum M. *Exodus* (The JPS Torah Commentary; Philadelphia: Jewish Publication Society, 1991).
Sass, Benjamin. "Four Notes on Taita King of Palistin with an Excursus on King Solomon's Empire," in *Tel Aviv* 37 (2010): 169–174.
Sasson, Ilana. "The Book of Proverbs between Saadia and Yefet," in *Intellectual History of the Islamicate World* 1 (2013): 159–217.
Sasson, Jack M. "An Apocalyptic Vision from Mari? Speculations on ARM X:9,"in *Mari: Annales de recherches interdisciplinaires* 1 (1982): 151–67.
Sassoon, Isaac. *The Status of Women in Jewish Tradition* (Cambridge: Cambridge University Press, 2011).
Schäder, Jo-Mari. "Patronage and Clientage Between God, Israel and the Nations: A Social-Scientific Investigation of Psalm 47," in *Journal for Semitics* 19 (2010), 235-262.
Schäfer, Peter. *Judeophobia: Attitudes Toward the Jews in the Ancient World* (Cambridge: Harvard University Press, 1997).
Schäfer, Peter, Michael Meerson, and Yaacov Deutsch, eds. *Toledot Yeshu ('The Life Story of Jesus') Revisited: A Princeton Conference* (TSAJ 143; Tübingen: Mohr Siebeck, 2011).
Schäfer-Lichtenberger, Christa. *Josua und Salomo. Eine Studie zu Autorität und Legitimität des Nachfolgers im Alten Testament* (VTSup, 58; Leiden: Brill, 1995).
Schaper, Joachim. "The Jerusalem Temple as an Instrument of the Achaemenid Fiscal Administration," in *VT* 45 (1995): 528–39.
Schaper, Joachim. "The Temple Treasury Committee in the Times of Nehemiah and Ezra," in *VT* 47 (1997): 200–06.
Scheidel, Walter. "A Peculiar Institution? Greco-Roman Monogamy in Global Context," in *The History of the Family* 14 (2009): 280–291.
Schenker, Adrian. "Jeroboam and the Division of the Kingdom in the Ancient Septuagint: LXX 3 Kingdoms 12.24 a–z, MT 1 Kings 11–12; 14 and the Deuteronomistic History," in *Israel Constructs Its History: Deuteronomistic Historiography in Recent Research* (eds. Albert de

Pury, Thomas C. Römer, and Jean-Daniel Macchi; JSOTSup 306; Sheffield: Sheffield Academic Press, 2000), 214–57.
Schivelbusch, Wolfgang. *The Culture of Defeat: On National Trauma, Mourning and Recovery* (New York: Metropolitan Books, 2001).
Schloen, J. David. *The House of the Father as Fact and Symbol: Patrimonialism in Ugarit and the Ancient Near East* (Winona Lake, IN: Eisenbrauns, 2001).
Schmid, Konrad. "Persian Imperial Authorization as a Historical Problem and as a Biblical Construct: A Plea for Distinctions in the Current Debate," in *The Pentateuch as Torah: New Models for Understanding its Promulgation and Acceptance* (eds. Gary N. Knoppers and Bernard M. Levinson; Winona Lake, IN: Eisenbrauns, 2007), 23–38.
Schmid, Konrad. "Abraham's Sacrifice: Gerhard von Rad's Interpretation of Genesis 22," in *Interpretation* 62 (2008): 268–76.
Schmid, Konrad. *The Old Testament. A Literary History* (Minneapolis: Fortress, 2012).
Schniedewind, William M. "The Source Citations of Manasseh: King Manasseh in History and Homily," in *VT* 41 (1991): 450–61.
Schniedewind, William M. *The Word of God in Transition: From Prophet to Exegete in the Second Temple Period* (JSOTSup 197; Sheffield: Sheffield Academic Press, 1995).
Schniedewind, William M. "Prophets and Prophecy in the Books of Chronicles," in *The Chronicler as Historian* (eds. M. Patrick Graham, Kenneth G. Hoglund, and Steven L. McKenzie; JSOTSup 238; Sheffield: Sheffield Academic Press, 1997), 204–224.
Schniedewind, William M. "The Chronicler as an Interpreter of Scripture", in *The Chronicler as Author. Studies in Text and Texture* (eds. M. Patrick Graham and Steven L. McKenzie; JSOTSup 263; Sheffield: Sheffield Academic Press, 1999), 158–180.
Schniedewind, William. M. *Society and the Promise to David: The Reception History of 2 Samuel 7:1–17* (Oxford: Oxford University Press, 1999).
Schultz, Richard L. *The Search for Quotation* (JSOTSup 180; Sheffield: Sheffield Academic Press, 1999).
Schwartz, Barry. "Collective Forgetting and the Symbolic Power of Oneness: The Strange Apotheosis of Rosa Parks," in *Social Psychology Quarterly* 72 (2009): 123–142.
Schwartz, Barry. *Abraham Lincoln and the Forge of National Memory* (Chicago: University of Chicago Press, 2000).
Schwartz, Baruch J. "Reexamining the Fate of the 'Canaanites' in the Torah Traditions," in *Sefer Moshe. The Moshe Weinfeld Jubilee Volume* (eds. Chaim Cohen, Avi Hurvitz and Shalom M. Paul; Winona Lake, IN: Eisenbrauns, 2004), 151–170.
Schwartz, Daniel R. "Diodorus Siculus 40.3 – Hecataeus or Pseudo-Hecataeus?," in *Jews and Gentiles in the Holy Land in the Days of the Second Temple, the Mishnah and the Talmud* (eds. Menachem Mor et al.; Jerusalem: Yad Ben-Zvi, 2003), 181–97.
Schwartz, Regina M. "Adultery in the House of David: 'Nation' in the Bible and Biblical Scholarship", in *Shadow of Spirit: Postmodernism and Religion* (eds. Philippa Berry and Andrew Wernick; New York: Routledge, 1992), 181–97.
Schwartz Seth. *Imperialism and Jewish Society, 200 B.C.E. to 640 C.E.* (Princeton: Princeton University Press, 2001).
Schwartz Seth. *The Ancient Jews from Alexander to Muhammad* (Cambridge: Cambridge University Press, 2014).
Schweitzer, Steven J. *Reading Utopia in Chronicles* (OTS 442; New York: T&T Clark, 2007).

Schweitzer, Steven J. "Judging a Book by Its Citations: Authority and the Sources in Chronicles," in *What Was Authoritative for Chronicles?* (ed. E. Ben Zvi and D. V. Edelman; Winona Lake, IN: Eisenbrauns, 2011) 37–66.

Seeligmann, I. L., "Die Auffassung von der Prophetie in der Deuteronomistischen und Chronistischen Geschichtsschreibung," in *VT* 29 (1978): 254–84.

Seitz, Christopher R. "The Prophet Moses and the Canonical Shape of Jeremiah," in *ZAW* 101 (1989): 3–27.

Seniavskii, Aleksandr S. and Elena S. Seniavskaia. "The Historical Memory of Twentieth-Century Wars as an Arena of Ideological, Political, and Psychological Confrontation," in *Russian Studies in History* 49 (2010), 53–91.

Service, Elman R. *Origins of the State and Civilization: The Process of Cultural Evolution* (New York: Norton, 1975).

Sheinman, Hanoch. *Promises and Agreements: Philosophical Essays* (Oxford: Oxford University Press, 2011).

Shemesh, Yael. "Lies by Prophets and Other Lies in the Hebrew Bible," in *JANES* 29 (2002): 81–95.

Sheppard, Gerald T. *Wisdom as a Hermeneutical Construct: A Study in the Sapientializing of the Old Testament* (BZAW 151; Berlin: De Gruyter, 1980).

Shuter, Bill. "Tradition as Rereading," in *Second Thoughts: A Focus on Rereading* (ed. David Galef; Detroit: Wayne State University Press, 1998), 74–112.

Sinopoli, Carla M. "The Archaeology of Empires," in *Annual Review of Anthropology* 23 (1994): 159–80.

Ska, Jean-Louis. "Essai sur la nature et la signification du cycle d'Abraham (Gn. 11,27–25,11)," in *Studies in the Book of Genesis* (ed. André Wénin; Leuven: Peeters, 2001), 153–77.

Skehan, Patrick W. and Alexander A. Di Lella. *The Wisdom of Ben Sira: A New Translation with Introduction and Commentary* (AB 39; Garden City, NY: Doubleday, 1987).

Smelik, Klaas A. D. "The Portrayal of King Manasseh," in *Converting the Past: Studies in Ancient Israelite and Moabite Historiography* (ed. Klaas A. D. Smelik; OtSt 28; Leiden: Brill, 1992), 129–89.

Smelik, Klaas A. D. "The Representation of King Ahaz in 2 Kings 16 and 2 Chronicles 28," in *Intertextuality in Ugarit and Israel* (ed. Johannes C. de Moor; OtSt, 40; Leiden: Brill, 1998), 143–185.

Smelik, Klaas A. D. "The Function of Jeremiah 50 and 51 in the Book of Jeremiah," in *Reading the Book of Jeremiah: A Search for Coherence* (ed. Martin Kessler; Winona Lake, IN: Eisenbrauns, 2004), 87–98.

Smith, Anthony D. *The Nation in History: Historiographical Debates about Ethnicity and Nationalism* Hanover: University Press of New England, 2000).

Smith, Mark S. *The Origins of Biblical Monotheism: Israel's Polytheistic Background and the Ugaritic Texts* (New York: Oxford University Press, 2001).

Smith, Mark S. *God in Translation: Deities in Cross-Cultural Discourse in the Biblical World* (Tübingen: Mohr Siebeck, 2008; Grand Rapids, MI: Eerdmans, 2010).

Smith-Christopher, Daniel L. "The Mixed Marriage Crisis in Ezra 9–10 and Nehemiah 13: A Study of the Sociology of the Post-Exilic Judaean Community," in *Second Temple Studies 2: Temple Community in the Persian Period* (eds. Tamara C. Eskenazi and Kent H. Richards; JSOTSup 175; Sheffield: JSOT, 1994), 243–65.

Sneed, Mark R. *The Politics of Pessimism in Ecclesiastes. A Social-Science* Perspective (SBLAIL, 12; Atlanta: SBL, 2012).
Snell, Daniel C. "Intellectual Freedom in the Ancient Near East?" in *Intellectual Life of the Ancient Near East* (ed. Jiří Prosecky; Prague: Academy of Sciences of the Czech Republic-Oriental Institute, 1998), 359–63.
Sommer, Benjamin D. *A Prophet Reads Scripture* (Stanford, CA: Stanford University Press, 1998).
Southwood, Katherine E. *Ethnicity and the Mixed Marriage Crisis in Ezra 9–10: An Anthropological Approach* (Oxford: Oxford University Press, 2012).
Spiegel, Gabrielle M. "Memory and History: Liturgical Time and Historical Time," in *History and Theory* 41 (2002): 149–62.
Starr, Ivan. *Queries to the Sungod: Divination and Politics in Sargonid Assyria* (SAA IV; Helsinki: Helsinki University Press, 1990).
Stavrakopoulou, Francesca. *King Manasseh and Child Sacrifice: Biblical Distortions of Historical Realities* (BZAW 338; Berlin: De Gruyter, 2004).
Stavrakopoulou, Francesca. "The Blackballing of Manasseh," in *Good Kings and Bad Kings* (ed. Lester L. Grabbe; LHBOTS 393; London: T&T Clark, 2005), 248–63.
Stavrakopoulou, Francesca. "Ancestor Ideologies and the Territoriality of the Dead in Genesis," in *A Palimpsest: Rhetoric, Ideology, Stylistics and Language Relating to Persian Israel* (eds. Ehud Ben Zvi, Diana V. Edelman and Frank Polak; Piscataway, NJ: Gorgias, 2009), 61–80.
Steinkeller, Piotr. "The Foresters of Umma: Towards a Definition of Ur III Labor," in *Labor in the Ancient Near East* (ed. Marvin A. Powell; New Haven, CT: American Oriental Society, 1987), 73–115.
Stern, Ephraim. *Archaeology of the Land of the Bible, II: The Assyrian, Babylonian and Persian Periods (732–332 BCE)* (ABRL; New York: Doubleday, 2001).
Stern, Ephraim. "The Babylonian Gap: The Archaeological Reality," in *JSOT* 28 (2004): 273–277.
Stern, Menahem. *Greek and Latin Authors on Jews and Judaism, Volume One* (Jerusalem: Israel Academy of Sciences and Humanities, 1974), 26–35.
Sternberg, Meir. *The Poetics of Biblical Narrative: Ideological Literature and the Drama of Reading* (Bloomington: Indiana University Press, 1987).
Sternberg, Meir. "Double Cave, Double Talk: The Indirections of Biblical Dialogue," in *'Not in Heaven': Coherence and Complexity in Biblical Narrative* (eds. Jason P. Rosenblatt and Joseph C. Sitterson, Jr; Bloomington, IN: Indiana University Press, 1991), 28–57.
Stevens, Kathryn. "Secrets in the Library: Protected Knowledge and Professional Identity in Late Babylonian Uruk," in *Iraq* 75 (2013): 211–53.
Stipp, Hermann-Josef. "Zedekiah in the Book of Jeremiah: On the Formation of a Biblical Character," in *CBQ* 58 (1996): 627–48.
Stipp, Hermann-Josef. "The Concept of the Empty Land in Jeremiah 37–43," in *The Concept of Exile in Ancient Israel and Its Historical Contexts* (eds. Ehud Ben Zvi and Christoph Levin; BZAW 404; Berlin: De Gruyter, 2010), 103–54.
Stipp, Hermann-Josef. "Remembering Josiah's Reforms in Kings," in *Remembering and Forgetting in Early Second Temple Judah* (eds. Ehud Ben Zvi and Christoph Levin; FAT 85; Tübingen: Mohr Siebeck, 2012), 225–38.

Stökl, Jonathan. *Prophecy in the Ancient Near East: A Philological and Sociological Comparison* (Culture and History of the Ancient Near East, 56; Leiden/Boston: Brill, 2012).
Stol, Marten. "Women in Mesopotamia," in *JESHO* 38 (1995), 123–144.
Stone Charles B. and William Hirst. "(Induced) Forgetting to Form a Collective Memory," in *Memory Studies* 7 (2014): 314–27.
Stone, Elizabeth C. "The Constraints on State and Urban Form in Ancient Mesopotamia," in *Urbanism and Economy in the Ancient Near East* (eds. Michael Hudson and Baruch A. Levine; Cambridge: Peabody Museum of Archaeology and Ethnology, 1999), 203–27.
Stordalen, Terje. "Heaven on Earth—Or not? Jerusalem as Eden in Biblical Literature," in *Beyond Eden: The Biblical Story of Paradise (Genesis 2–3) and Its Reception History* (eds. Konrad Schmid and Christoph Riedweg; FAT 2/34; Tübingen: Mohr Siebeck, 2008), 28–57.
Stott, Katherine. "A Comparative Study of the Exilic Gap in Ancient Israelite, Messenian, and Zionist Collective Memory," in *Community Identity in Judean Historiography: Biblical and Comparative Perspectives* (eds. Gary N. Knoppers and Kenneth A. Ristau; Winona Lake, IN: Eisenbrauns, 2009), 41–58.
Strootman, Rolf. "Kings and Cities in the Hellenistic Age," in *Political Culture in the Greek City After the Classical Age* (eds. Richard Alston, Onno van Nijf and Christina Williamson; Groningen-Royal Holloway Studies on the Greek City After the Classical Age 2; Leuven: Peeters, 2011), 141–53.
Stulman, Louis. *Jeremiah* (AOTC; Nashville: Abingdon, 2005).
Svärd, Saana. *Power and Women in the Neo-Assyrian Palaces* (PhD diss. University of Helsinki, 2012).
Svärd, Saana. *Women and Power in Neo-Assyrian Palaces* (Helsinki : Neo-Assyrian Text Corpus Project, 2015).
Swartz, David L. "Metaprinciples for Sociological Research in Bourdieusian Perspective," in *Bourdieu and Historical Analysis* (ed. Philip S. Gorski; Durham, N.C.: Duke University Press, 2013), 19–35.
Sweeney, Marvin A. *The Twelve Prophets*, vol. 2 (Berit Olam; Collegeville, MN: Liturgical, 2000).
Sweeney, Marvin A. *King Josiah of Judah. The Lost Messiah of Israel* (Oxford: Oxford Univ. Press, 2001).
Sweeney, Marvin A. "King Manasseh of Judah and the Problem of Theodicy in the Deuteronomistic History," in *Good Kings and Bad Kings* (ed. Lester L. Grabbe; LHBOTS 393; London: T&T Clark, 2005), 264–78.
Szijártó, István M. "Four Arguments for Microhistory," in *Rethinking History: the Journal of Theory and Practice* 6 (2002): 209–15.
Szlos, M. Beth. "A Portrait of Power: A Literary-Critical Study of the Depiction of the Woman in Proverbs 31:10–31," in *USQR* 54 (2000): 97–103.
Szpunar Piotr M. and Karl K. Szpunar, "Collective Future Thought: Concept, Function, and Implications for Collective Memory Studies," in *Memory Studies* 9 (2016): 376–389.
Taggar-Cohen, Ada. "Between Ḥerem, Ownership, and Ritual: Biblical and Hitttite Perspectives," in *Current Issues in Priestly and Related Literature: The Legacy of Jacob Milgrom and Beyond* (eds. Roy Gane and Ada Taggar-Cohen; RBS 82; Atlanta: SBL Press, 2015), 419–34.

Taggar-Cohen, Ada. "The Holiness School—Creativity and Editorial Activity in the Book of Joshua: The Case of Joshua 24," in *Marbeh Hokma: Studies in the Bible and the Ancient Near East in Memory of Victor Avigdor* Hurowitz (eds. Shamir Yona et al.; Winona Lake, IN: Eisenbrauns, 2015), vol. I, 541–557.

Talmon, Shemaryahu. "The Biblical Concept of Jerusalem," in *Journal of Ecumenical Studies* 8 (1971): 300–316.

Talshir, Zipora. "Several Canon-Related Concepts Originating in Chronicles," *ZAW* 111 (2001): 386–403.

Talshir, Zipora, Shamir Yona and Daniel Sivan, eds. *Homage to Shmuel: Studies in the World of the Bible* (Jerusalem: Bialik Institute / Beer-Sheva: Ben-Gurion University Press, 2001).

Tan, Nancy. "The Chronicler's 'Obededom': A Foreigner and/or a Levite?', in *JSOT* 32 (2007), 217–30.

Taylor, Charles. *A Secular Age* (Cambridge, MA: Belknap Press of Harvard University Press, 2007).

Thareani-Sussely, Yifat. "The Archaeology of the Days of Manasseh Reconsidered in the Light of Evidence from the Beersheba Valley," in *PEQ* 139 (2007): 69–77.

Thelle, Rannfrid I. "Babylon in the Book of Jeremiah (MT): Negotiating a Power Shift," in *Prophecy in the Book of Jeremiah* (eds. Hans Barstad and Reinhard G. Kratz; BZAW 388; Berlin/New York: De Gruyter, 2009), 187–232.

Thompson, Thomas L. *The Messiah Myth: The Near Eastern Roots of Jesus and David* (New York: Basic Books, 2005).

Throntveit, Mark A. "The Relationship of Hezekiah to David and Solomon in the Books of Chronicles," in *The Chronicler as Theologian: Essays in Honor of Ralph W. Klein* (eds. M. Patrick Graham, Steven L. McKenzie, and Gary N. Knoppers; JSOTSup 371; London: T&T Clark, 2003), 105–21.

Tiemeyer, Lena-Sofia. "Abraham–A Judahite Prerogative," in *ZAW* 120 (2008), 49–66.

Tiemeyer, Lena-Sofia. *For the Comfort of Zion* (VTSup 139; Leiden/Boston, 2011).

Tigay, Jeffrey H. *Deuteronomy* (JPS Torah Commentary; Philadelphia: Jewish Publication Society, 1996).

Tov, Emanuel. *The Text-Critical Use of the Septuagint in Biblical Research* (Jerusalem: Simor, 1981).

Trebolle Barrera, Julio C. "Textual Variants in 4QJudg^a and the Textual and Editorial History of the Book of Judges," in *RevQ* 14 (1990): 229–45

Trotter, James M. *Reading Hosea in Achaemenid Yehud* (JSOTSup 328; Sheffield: Sheffield Academic Press, 2001).

Troxel, Ronald L. *LXX-Isaiah as Translation and Interpretation* (JSJSup 124; Leiden/Boston: Brill, 2008).

Tucker, Aviezer. Our *Knowledge of the Past. A Philosophy of Historiography* (Cambridge: Cambridge Univ. Press, 2004).

Tuell, Steven S. *First and Second Chronicles* (Interpretation; Louisville: John Knox, 2001).

Tuplin, Christopher. "The Administration of the Achaemenid Empire," in *Coinage and Administration in the Athenian and Persian Empires* (ed. Ian Carradice; BAR International Series 343; Oxford: B.A.R., 1987), 109–66.

Ulrich, Eugene et. al., eds. *Qumran Cave 4, vol. X: The Prophets* (DJD XV; Oxford: Clarendon Press, 1997).

Ussishkin, David. "The Borders and *De Facto* Size of Jerusalem in the Persian Period," in *Judah and the Judeans in the Persian Period* (eds. Oded Lipschits and Manfred Oeming; Winona Lake, IN: Eisenbrauns, 2006), 147–66.
Valkama, Kirsi. "What Do Archaeological Remains Reveal of the Settlements in Judah during the Mid-Sixth Century BCE?" in *The Concept of Exile in Ancient Israel and Its Historical Contexts* (eds. Ehud Ben Zvi and Christoph Levin; BZAW 404; Berlin: De Gruyter, 2010), 39–59.
Valler, Shulamit. "Who Is '*Ēšet Ḥayil*' in Rabbinic Literature?" in *A Feminist Companion to Wisdom Literature* (ed. Athalya Brenner; Sheffield: Sheffield Academic Press, 1995), 85–97.
Van der Toorn, Karel. "The Exodus as Charter Myth," in *Religious Identity and the Invention of Tradition* (eds. Jan Willem van Henten and Anton W. J. Houtepen; STAR 3; Assen: Royal Van Gorcum, 2001), 113–27.
Van der Toorn, Karel. *Scribal Culture and the Making of the Hebrew Bible* (Cambridge, MA: Harvard University Press, 2007).
van Dijk, Teun A. *Macrostructures* (Hillsdale, NJ: Erlbaum, 1980).
van Dijk, Teun A. and Walter Kintsch, *Strategies of Discourse Comprehension* (New York: Academic Press, 1983).
Van Houten, Christiana. *The Alien in Israelite Law* (JSOTSup 107; Sheffield: Sheffield Academic Press, 1991).
Van Leeuwen, Neil, "The Imaginative Agent," in *Knowledge through Imagination* (eds. Amy Kind and Peter Kung; Oxford: Oxford University Press, 2016), 85–110.
Van Leeuwen, Raymond C. "Cosmos, Temple, House: Building and Wisdom in Mesopotamia and Israel," in *Wisdom Literature in Mesopotamia and Israel* (ed. Richard J. Clifford; SBLSymS 36: Atlanta: Society of Biblical Literature, 2007), 67–90; reprinted and slightly revised, "Cosmos, Temple, House: Building and Wisdom in Ancient Mesopotamia and Israel" in *From the Foundations to the Crenellations: Essays on Temple Building in the Ancient Near East and Hebrew Bible* (eds. Mark J. Boda and Jamie Novotny; AOAT 366; Münster: Ugarit-Verlag, 2010), 399–421.
van Rooy, H. F. "Prophet and Society in the Persian Period according to Chronicles," in *Second Temple Studies*, vol. 2: *Temple Community in the Persian Period* (ed. T. C. Eskenazi and K. H. Richards; JSOTSup 175; Sheffield: Sheffield Academic Press, 1994), 163–79.
Van Seters, John. *Abraham in History and Tradition* (New Haven, CT: Yale University Press, 1975).
Van Seters, John. "The Creation of Man and the Creation of the King," in *ZAW* 101 (1989): 333–42.
Van Seters, John. "Joshua's Campaign of Canaan and Near Eastern Historiography," in *SJOT* 4 (1990): 1–12.
Van Seters, John. "Creative Imitation in the Hebrew Bible," in *SR* 29 (2000): 395–409
Van Seters, John. *The Pentateuch. A Social-Science Commentary* (Sheffield: Sheffield Academic Press, 1999).
Van Staalduine-Sulman, Eveline. *The Targum of Samuel* (Leiden: Brill, 2002).
Vandorpe, Katelijn. "The Ptolemaic Period," in *A Companion to Ancient Egypt*, vol. 1 (2 vols.; ed. Alan B. Lloyd; Chichester: Wiley-Blackwell, 2010), 159–79.
Veenhof, Klaas R. "'Modern' Features in Old Assyrian Trade," in *JESHO* 40 (1997): 336–66.

Vermeule, Blakey. *Why De We Care about Literary Characters?* (Baltimore: John Hopkins University Press, 2010).

Veyne, Paul. *Did the Greeks Believe in Their Myths?* (Chicago: University of Chicago Press, 1988).

Visotzky, Burton L. *The Genesis of Ethics* (New York: Crown, 1996).

Volkan, Vamik D. "Transgenerational Transmissions and Chosen Traumas: An Aspect of Large-Group Identity," in *Group Analysis* 34 (2001): 79–97.

Von Rad, Gerhard. "Die levitische Predigt in den Büchern der Chronik," in *Festschrift für Otto Procksch* (ed. A. Alt; Leipzig: Deichertsche Verlag und Hinrichssche Buchhandlung, 1934), 113–24.

Von Rad, Gerhard. *Studies in Deuteronomy* (London: SCM Press, 1953).

Von Rad, Gerhard. *The Problem of the Hexateuch and Other Essays*, translated by E. W. Trueman Dicken (Edinburgh: Oliver & Boyd, 1966).

Von Rad, Gerhard. "The Levitical Sermon in I and II Chronicles," in *The Problem of the Hexateuch and Other Essays* (ed. G. von Rad; Edinburgh: Oliver & Boyd, 1966), 267–80.

Von Rad, Gerhard. *Old Testament Theology*, translated by D. M. G. Stalker. 2 vols. (Louisville, KY: Westminster John Knox, 2001).

Waegeman, Maryse. "The Perfect Wife of Proverbia 31:10–31," in *Goldene Äpfel in silbernen Schalen: Collected Communications to the XIIIth Congress of the International Organization for the Study of the Old Testament, Leuven 1989* (eds. Klaus-Dietrich Schunck and Matthias Augustin; Frankfurt am Main: Peter Lang, 1992), 101–7.

Waerzeggers, Caroline. "Facts, Propaganda or History? Shaping Political Memory in the Nabonidus Chronicle," in *Political Memory in and after the Persian Empire* (eds. Jason M. Silverman and Caroline Waerzeggers; ANEM/MACO, 13; Atlanta: SBL Press, 2015), 95–124.

Wagenaar, Jan. "Crossing the Sea of Reeds (Exod 13–14) and the Jordan (Josh 3–4): A Priestly Framework for the Wilderness Wandering Studies in the Book of Exodus," in *Studies in the Book of Exodus: Redaction, Reception, Interpretation* (ed. Marc Vervenne; BETL 126; Leuven: Peelers, 1996, 461–470.

Walsh, Carey. "Women on the Edge," in *Imagining the Other and Constructing Israelite Identity in the Early Second Temple Period* (eds. E. Ben Zvi and D. V. Edelman; LHBOTS 456; London: Bloomsbury T&T Clark, 2014), 122–43.

Walsh, Jerome T. *1 Kings* (Berit Olam; Collegeville, MN: Liturgical Press, 1996).

Walters, Stanley D. "Hannah and Anna: The Greek and Hebrew Texts of 1 Samuel 1," JBL 107 (1988): 385–414.

Waltke, Bruce K. and Michael Patrick O'Connor, *An Introduction to Biblical Hebrew Syntax (IBHS)* (Winona Lake, IN: Eisenbrauns, 1990).

Warhurst, Amber K. "The Chronicler's Use of the Prophets," in *What Was Authoritative for Chronicles?* (eds. Ehud Ben Zvi and Diana V. Edelman; Winona Lake, IN.: Eisenbrauns, 2012), 165–82.

Watts, James W. *Psalm and Story: Inset Hymns in Hebrew Narrative* (JSOTSup 139; Sheffield: JSOT, 1992), 30–32.

Watts, James W., ed. *Persia and Torah: The Theory of Imperial Authorization of the Pentateuch* (SBLSymS 17; Atlanta: Society of Biblical Literature, 2001).

Weinberg, Joel. "Die 'ausser kanonischen Prophezeiungen' in den Chronikbüchern," in *Acta Antiqua* 26 (1978): 387–404.

Weinberg, Joel. "Gedaliah, the Son of Ahikam in Mizpah: His Status and Role, Supporters and Opponents," in *ZAW* 119 (2007): 356–68.
Weinberg, Joel. *The Citizen-Temple Community* (JSOTSup 151; Sheffield: Sheffield Academic Press, 1992).
Weinfeld, Moshe. "The Extent of the Promised Land: The Status of Transjordan," in *Das Land Israel in biblischer Zeit* (ed. Georg Strecker; Göttingen: Vandenhoeck & Ruprecht, 1983), 59–75.
Weinfeld, Moshe. *Deuteronomy 1–11: A New Translation with Introduction and Commentary* (AB 5 A; New York: Doubleday, 1991).
Wellhausen, Julius. *Prolegomena to the History of Israel* (Edinburgh: Adam & Charles Black, 1885).
Wellhausen, Julius. *Skizzen und Vorarbeiten Fünftes Heft. Die Kleinen Propheten* (Berlin: Georg Reimer, 1893).
Wells, Gary L. "Counterfactual Processing of Normal and Exceptional Events," in *Journal of Experimental Social Psychology* 25 (1989): 314–25.
Wells, Gary L. and Igor Gavanski, "Mental Simulation of Causality," in *Journal of Personality and Social Psychology* 56 (1989): 161–169.
Welten, Peter. *Geschichte und Geschichtsdarstellung in den Chronikbüchern* (WMANT 42; Neukirchen-Vluyn: Neukirchener Verlag, 1973).
Wertsch, James V. "Collective Memory and Narrative Templates," in *Social Research* 75 (2008): 133–56.
Wertsch, James V. *Voices of Collective Remembering* (Cambridge/New York: Cambridge University Press, 2002).
Westbrook, Raymond. *Property and the Family in Biblical Law* (JSOTSup 113; Sheffield: JSOT Press, 1991).
Westbrook, Raymond, ed. *A History of Ancient Near Eastern Law* (2 vols.; Handbook of Oriental Studies 72, Leiden: Brill, 2003).
Whitelam, Keith W. "Israel's Traditions of Origin: Reclaiming the Land," in *JSOT* 14 (1989): 19–42.
Widmer, Michael. *Moses, God, and the Dynamics of Intercessory Prayer* (FAT 2.8; Tübingen: Mohr Siebeck, 2004).
Wiesehöfer, Josef. *Ancient Persia: From 550 BC to 650 AD* (London: Tauris, 1996).
Willey, Patricia T. *Remember the Former Things* (SBL Dissertation Series 161; Atlanta, GA: Scholars Press, 1997).
Willi, Thomas. *Die Chronik als Auslegung; Untersuchungen zur literarischen Gestaltung der historischen Überlieferung Israels* (FRLANT 106; Göttingen: Vandenhoeck & Ruprecht, 1972).
Williamson, Hugh G. M. "The Accession of Solomon in the Books of Chronicles," in *VT* 26 (1976): 351-71.
Williamson, Hugh G. M. *Israel in the Books of Chronicles* (Cambridge: Cambridge University Press, 1977).
Williamson, Hugh G. M. *1–2 Chronicles* (NCB; Grand Rapids, MI: Eerdmans, 1982).
Williamson, Hugh G. M. "The Messianic Texts in Isa 1–39", in *King and Messiah in Israel and the Ancient Near East: Proceedings of the Oxford Old Testament Seminar* (ed. John Day; JSOTSup 270; Sheffield: Sheffield Academic Press, 1998), 238–70.

Williamson, Hugh. G. M. "The Composition of Ezra i–vi," in *JTS* NS 34 (1983): 1–30; reprinted in Hugh G. M. Williamson, *Studies in Persian Period History and Historiography* (FAT, 38; Tübingen: Mohr Siebeck, 2004), 244–70.
Wilson, Charles R. *Baptized in Blood: The Religion of the Lost Cause 1865–1920* (Athens, GA: University of Georgia Press, 2009).
Wilson, Ian D. "Tyre, a Ship: The Metaphorical World of Ezekiel 27 in Ancient Judah," in *ZAW* 125 (2013): 249–62.
Wilson, Ian D. "Joseph, Jehoiachin, and Cyrus: On Book Endings, Exoduses and Exiles, and Yehudite/Judean Social Remembering," in *ZAW* 126 (2014): 521–34.
Wilson, Ian D. *Kingship and Memory in Ancient Judah* (New York: Oxford University Press, 2017).
Wilson, Robert R. *Prophecy and Society in Ancient Israel* (Philadelphia: Fortress, 1980).
Winslow, Karen Strand. "Ethnicity, Exogamy, and Zipporah," in *Women in Judaism* 4, no. 1 (2006), available online at http://wjudaism.library.utoronto.ca/index.php/wjudaism/article/view/225.
Winslow, Karen Strand. "Mixed Marriage in Torah Narratives," in *Mixed Marriages: Intermarriage and Group Identity in the Second Temple Period* (ed. Christian Frevel; LHBOTS 547; London: T&T Clark, 2011), 132–49.
Wolf, Mark J. P. *Building Imaginary Worlds: The Theory and History of Subcreation* (Routledge: New York, 2012).
Wolters, Albert. "Ṣôpiyyâ (Prov 31:27) as Hymnic Participle and Play on Sophia", in *JBL* 104 (1985): 577–87.
Wolters, Albert. "Proverbs XXXI 10–31 as Heroic Hymn: A Form Critical Analysis," in *VT* 38 (1988): 446–57.
Wright, J. Robert. *Proverbs, Ecclesiastes, Song of Solomon* (ACCS; Downers Grove, IL: InterVarsity, 2005).
Wright, Jacob L. *Rebuilding Identity: The Nehemiah Memoir and Its Earliest Readers* (BZAW 348; Berlin: De Gruyter, 2004).
Wright, Jacob L. "Continuing These Conversations" in *Historiography and Identity: (Re)formulation in Second Temple Historiographical Literature* (ed. Louis C. Jonker; LHBOTS 534; London: T&T Clark, 2010), 149–167.
Wright, John W. "The Innocence of David in I Chronicles 21," in *JSOT* 60 (1993): 87–105.
Wright, John W. "The Fight for Peace: Narrative and History in the Battle Accounts in Chronicles," in *The Chronicler as Historian* (eds. M. Patrick Graham, Kenneth G. Hoglund and Steven L. McKenzie; JSOTSup 238; Sheffield: JSOT Press, 1997), 150–177.
Wunsch, Cornelia. "The Šangû-Ninurta Archive" in *Approaching the Babylonian Economy: Proceedings of the START Project Symposium Held in Vienna, 1–3 July 2004* (eds. Heather D. Baker and Michael Jursa; AOAT 330; Münster: Ugarit-Verlag, 2005), 367–79.
Wunsch, Cornelia. "Neo-Babylonian Entrepreneurs," in *The Invention of Enterprise: Entrepreneurship from Ancient Mesopotamia to Modern Times* (eds. David S. Landes, Joel Mokyr, and William J. Baumol; Princeton, NJ: Princeton University Press, 2010), 40–61.
Yates, Gary E. "Ishmael's Assassination of Gedaliah: Echoes of the Saul-David Story in Jeremiah 40:7–41:1–18," in *WTJ* 67 (2005): 103–13.
Yee, Gale A. *Poor Banished Children of Eve: Woman as Evil in the Hebrew Bible* (Minneapolis, MN: Fortress Press, 2003).

Yilibuw, Dolores. "Tampering with Bible Translation in Yap," in *Hidden Truths from Eden: Esoteric Readings of Genesis 1–3* (eds. Caroline Vander Stichele and Suzanne Scholz; Semeia 76; Atlanta: Scholars Press, 1996), 21–38.

Yoder, Christine R. *Wisdom as a Woman of Substance: A Socioeconomic Reading of Proverbs 1–9 and 31:10–31* (BZAW 304; Berlin: De Gruyter, 2001).

Yoffee, Norman. *Myths of the Archaic State: Evolution of the Earliest Cities, States, and Civilizations* (Cambridge: Cambridge University Press, 2004).

Younger, K. Lawson, Jr. *Ancient Conquest Accounts: A Study in Ancient Near Eastern and Biblical History Writing* (JSOTSup 98; Sheffield: JSOT Press, 1990).

Zakovitch, Yair. "Assimilation in Biblical Narratives", in *Empirical Models for Biblical Criticism* (ed. Jeffrey H. Tigay; Philadelphia: University of Pennsylvania Press, 1985), 175–196.

Zamagni, Claudio. "La tradition sur Moïse d'Hécatée d'Abdère d'après Diodore et Photius," in *Interprétations de Möise: Égypte, Judée, Grèce et Rome* (ed. Thomas Römer et al.; Leiden / Boston: Brill, 2010), pp. 133-69.

Zerubavel, Eviatar. *The Fine Line: Making Distinctions in Every Day Life* (New York: Free Press, 1991).

Zerubavel, Eviatar. *Social Mindscapes. An Invitation to Cognitive Sociology* (Cambridge, MA: Harvard University Press, 1997).

Zerubavel, Eviatar. *Time Maps: Collective Memory and the Social Shape of the Past* (Chicago: University of Chicago Press, 2003).

Zerubavel, Eviatar. *Ancestors and Relatives: Genealogy, Identity, and Community* (Oxford: Oxford University Press, 2012).

Zlotnick-Sivan, Helena. "Moses the Persian? Exodus 2, the Other and Biblical Mnemohistory," in *ZAW* 116 (2004): 189–205.

Zorn, Jeffrey R. "Estimating the Population Size of Ancient Settlements: Methods, Problems, Solutions and a Case Study," in *BASOR* 295 (1994): 31–48.

Zorn, Jeffrey R. "Tell en-Naṣbeh and the Problem of the Material Culture of the 6th Century," in *Judah and the Judeans in the Neo-Babylonian Period* (eds. Oded Lipschits and Joseph Blenkinsopp; Winona Lake, IN: Eisenbrauns, 2003), 413–447.

Zorn, Jeffrey R., Joseph Yellin and John W. Hayes. "The M(W)SH Stamp Impressions and the Neo-Babylonian Period," in *IEJ* 44 (1994): 161–183.

Index of Authors

Abadie, Philippe 367, 372
Abate, Emma 351, 354
Abbott, Andrew 655
Ackroyd, Peter R. 385
Albertz, Rainer 146, 168, 236, 266, 267, 388, 392, 528, 617, 620, 622, 627, 629
Alster, Bendt 583
Alter, Robert 176, 329, 523
Amar, Itzhak 333
Amin, Samir 551
Amit, Yairah 120, 121, 375, 407, 424, 510, 519, 605
Andersen, Francis I. 208, 296
Anderson, Benedict 64
Anthonioz, Stéphanie 495
Aperghis, Gerassimos G. 142
Applegate, John 354, 626
Archetti, Marco 567
Assmann, Aleida 13, 317, 343
Assmann, Jan 13, 317, 343
Auld, A. Graeme 460
Austin, Michael M. 137
Avioz, Michael 310, 451

Bae, Hee-Sook 352
Balogh, Csaba 272
Baltzer, Klaus 267, 620
Bang, Peter Fibiger 554, 563
Bar-Kochva, Bezalel 168
Bar-Tal, Daniel 303
Barbour (Grillo), Jennifer 589
Barkay, Gabriel 505
Barkin, Steve M. 261
Barstad, Hans M. 599, 600
Barton, John 72, 84, 95, 131
Basirov, Oric 78
Baumann, Gerd 350, 581, 593, 596
Baumgarten, Albert 78, 653
Bautch, Richard J. 166
Beaulieu, Paul-Alain 487
Becking, Bob 358
Bedford, Peter R. 142

Beentjes, Pancratius C. 185, 337, 407, 424, 428, 437
Begg, C. T. 407
Ben Zvi, Ehud 6, 22, 24, 27, 29–30, 34–35, 38, 44–46, 55, 57, 62, 65, 70, 72–73, 79, 92, 96, 110, 113–14, 119, 122, 124, 126, 129, 131, 153, 155, 159–161, 165, 179–181, 184, 200, 202, 214, 217, 222, 227, 253, 257, 274–75, 278, 281, 283, 285, 292, 294, 299, 304, 306, 319–321, 323–325, 336, 346, 352, 372, 386, 389–390, 411, 424, 439, 444, 450, 452, 454, 459, 462–63, 469, 479, 519, 541, 562, 565, 574, 585, 597, 609, 621, 624, 654, 665–66, 668, 671
Bergman, Joshua A. 463
Berlejung, Angelika 153
Berlin, Adele 590
Bernheimer, R. 414
Berquist, Jon L. 28, 71
Betzig, Laura 570, 573
Bhabha, Homi K. 581
Biale, David 144
Bichler, Reinhold 264
Biggs, Robert D. 538
Bird, S. Elizabeth 102, 261, 413
Blenkinsopp, Joseph 145–147, 170, 176, 211, 267, 272, 352, 418, 422, 492, 528, 543, 599, 605–6, 610
Blum, Erhard 84, 313
Boase, Elizabeth 302
Boda, Mark J. 365, 406, 454,
Bodi, Daniel 491
Bos, James M. 275, 285
Bourdieu, Pierre 631–32, 638, 640–42, 645–648, 650, 652
Braun, Roddy L. 237
Brett, Mark G. 48, 65
Breytenbach, Andries 122
Briant, Pierre 134, 137, 162, 409
Brosius, Maria 155
Brueggemann, Walter 446, 617, 623
Bulhof, Johannes 612

https://doi.org/10.1515/9783110547146-035

Bunzl, Martin 612
Burns, J. B. 408, 472
Burton, Michael L. 566
Buster, Aubrey E. 430

Camp, Claudia V. 274, 546, 550
Campbell, Antony F. 460, 509, 568
Carneiro, Robert L. 658
Carr, David 613, 636
Carroll, Robert P. 227, 310, 497, 600, 602, 617
Carter, Charles E. 394, 483, 504, 599, 602, 604
Carter, Rita 657
Carvalho, Corrine L. 311
Cataldo, Jeremiah W. 528, 655
Cattell, Maria G. 68
Chalcraft, David J. 40, 631, 657
Chang, Shelley Hsueh-lun 347
Chapman, Cynthia R. 592, 656
Chapman, Stephen B. 211
Charlesworth, James H. 368
Chavalas, Mark 136
Chernyak-Hai, Lily 303
Chisholm, Robert B. 466
Christian, Mark A. 582
Claassens, L. Juliana 302
Clauss, Jan 545
Clements, Ronald E. 177, 329, 523
Climo, Jacob J. 68
Clines, David J. A. 157, 484
Cogan, Mordechai 516
Cohen, Shaye J. D. 70, 530, 543
Cohn, Robert L. 176, 585
Collins, John J. 492, 555
Coman, Mihai 102, 261
Connell, Sophia M. 538
Conti, Marco 467
Cook, Johann 549
Cooper, Jerrold S. 538
Corner, Sean 556
Creangă, Ovidiu 239
Crenshaw, James L. 271, 466–67, 470
Crook, Margaret B. 548
Csibra, Gergely 8
Currie, Greg 657

Curtis, Edward L. 429
Cypess, Sandra Messinger 348

Dafni, Evangelia G. 470
Dandamaev, M. A. 409
Dardenne, Robert W. 102, 261
Davies, John K. 154
Davies, Philip R. 52, 103, 107, 606
Davila, James R. 368
De Breucker, Geert 23
De Pury, Albert 170
De Vries, Simon J. 30, 254, 323, 372, 408, 421, 459–60, 519
Debourse, Céline 23
Deurloo, Karel A. 64
Deutsch, Yaacov 144
Di Lella, Alexander A. 253
Di Pede, Elena 3, 354
Dicou, Bert 95
Dillard, Ray 463
Dirksen, Peter B. 430
Dor, Yonina 527, 531
Dozeman, Thomas B. 243, 245
Dusinberre, Elspeth R. M. 136
Dyck, Jonathan E. 254, 437

Eck, Diana L. 483
Eco, Umberto 25
Edelman, Diana V. 13, 31, 258, 270, 487, 491, 500, 523, 533, 598, 603, 605, 609, 669–70
Edenburg, Cynthia 605
Emerton, John A. 177, 329
Emmerson, Grace I. 282
Endres, John C. 379
Erickson, Amy 631
Ermakoff, Ivan 648
Eskenazi, Tamara C. 407, 528–29
Evans, Craig A. 253
Eyerman, Ron 7

Falk, Marcia 550
Farber, Zev 233, 244
Faust, Avraham 369, 394, 483, 504, 600, 604
Feldman, Louis H. 163, 195, 201, 238, 514
Ferguson, Niall 612

Fine, Gary Alan   12, 19, 332, 337, 666
Finkelstein, Israel   142, 369, 394, 483, 504, 505, 517, 600, 604
Finkelstein, Jacob J.   191
Fischer, Irmtraud   546, 548
Fishbane, Michael   27, 389, 541, 620
Flanagan, James W.   657, 659
Fletcher, Natalie M.   657
Fokkelman, Jan P.   499
Forbes, A. Dean   390
Fortunato, Laura   567
Fox, Michael V.   492, 546–51, 575
Fox, Robin Lane   162
Freedman, David Noel   208, 296, 390
Frevel, Christian   537
Friebel, Kelvin   205
Fried, Lisbeth S.   527, 543
Frolov, Serge   388
Frood, Elizabeth   552
Frymer-Kensky, Tikva   557

Galil, Gershon   568–70, 574
Gallagher, Catherine   612
García Martínez, Florentino   356
Garland, Robert   247
Gavanski, Igor   613
Gerstenberger, Erhard S.   77, 229, 407, 422
Geva, Hillel   394, 483, 504, 604
Geyer, John B.   157
Giddens, Anthony   39
Gillingham, Susan   495
Gillmayr-Bucher, Susanne   598
Glassner, Jean-Jacques   486
Glatt-Gilat, David   535
Goh, Samuel T. S.   550
Goldingay, John   60, 145, 147, 189, 267, 269, 453
Gordis, Robert   472
Gorski, Philip S.   641, 648, 652
Gosse, Bernard   440
Grabbe, Lester L.   134, 528, 531–32, 534, 599, 661, 662
Grad, Hector   580
Grätz, Sebastian   533
Green, Douglas J.   330
Greenberg, Moshe   492
Greengus, Samuel   569

Gregory, Bradley C.   185
Greifenhagen, Franz V.   268
Gruen, Erich S.   147
Guillory, John   639
Gundar, Ayelet   303
Gunneweg, Antonius H. J.   211
Guo, Xuezhi   347

Hadas-Lebel, Mireille   385
Hagedorn, Anselm C.   136
Hallo, William W.   167, 583
Halpern, Baruch   367
Halvorson-Taylor, Martien A.   106, 265, 390
Hamilton, Jeffries M.   468
Hammond, Meghan Marie   11
Handy, Lowell K.   21, 179, 337, 472
Hanspach, Alexander   408
Harrington, Hannah K.   528, 537
Hartenstein, Friedhelm   434
Harvey, John E.   30, 176, 329, 523
Hausmann, Jutta   547
Hayes, Beth   590
Hayes, Christine E.   542
Hayes, John H.   618
Hayes, John W.   599
Heger, Paul   530
Hendel, Ronald   163, 203
Hess, Richard S.   121
Hill, John   43, 159, 261, 625
Hirst, William   9
Hodkinson, Stephen   556
Höffken, Peter   408
Hoffman, Yair   622
Holladay, William L.   491, 619
Holt, Else K.   202, 310
Honigman, Sylvie   3, 137
Hooker, Paul   588
Horden, Peregrine   554
Hugenberger, Gordon P.   572
Hunt, Robert C.   563
Hurowitz, Victor A.   176, 546, 547, 555

Ikas, Karin   581
Instone-Brewer, David   575

Jaén, Isabel   673
Jain, Sarah   612

Janzen, David 177, 528
Janzen, J. Gerald 192, 619
Japhet, Sara 30, 176, 254, 329, 359, 364, 369, 372, 379, 381, 388–91, 395–96, 407, 413, 424, 432, 437, 476, 479, 518, 522, 523, 608–9, 621
Jarick, John 388
Jedlowski, Paolo 8
Jenni, Ernst 323
Johnson, Lyman L. 348
Johnston, Laurie 348
Johnstone, William 368
Jones, Douglas R. 623
Jones, Gwilym H. 460, 516
Jonker, Louis C. 28, 37, 352, 367, 384, 388–89, 407, 411, 420
Joüon, Paul 202
Jursa, Michael 23

Kagan, Donald 613, 614
Kahneman, Daniel 613
Kalimi, Isaac 30, 62, 178, 254, 328, 389–90, 427, 500, 502, 524
Kallai, Zecharia 171
Kammen, Michael G. 668
Kaplonski, Christopher 145, 199
Kee, Min Suc 462
Kegler, Jürgen 407
Kelly, Brian E. 369
Kessler, John 46, 47, 268, 602, 605
Kim, Sue J. 11
Kim, Tae Hun 70
Kind, Amy 657
Kintsch, Walter 27
Klein, Lillian R. 656
Klein, Ralph W. 254, 391, 408, 429, 437, 487, 588
Kleinig, John W. 323, 519
Kloner, Amos 394, 483, 504, 604
Knauf, E. Axel 224, 234–35, 242, 369, 658
Knibb, Michael A. 253, 616
Knoppers, Gary N. 70, 103, 177, 219, 254, 284, 321, 337, 362, 365, 367, 371, 372, 400, 408, 429, 430, 432, 453, 463, 513, 532–33, 540
Knowles, Melody D. 603
Koch, Ido 142, 369, 504

Kraemer, David 632
Kugel, James L. 184, 185
Kuhrt, Amélie 65, 137, 151, 154, 264, 493
Kung, Peter 657
Kutsch, Ernst 442

Labahn, Antje 574
LaCocque, André 591
Landy, Francis 274, 275
Lang, Bernhard 546–48, 556, 564
Lange, Armin 537
Laniak, Timothy S. 656
Larsen, Clark S. 566
Larson, Erik 356
Latimer, Joanna 657
Lawrence, Beatrice 557
Lee, Gary R. 350, 548, 571
Leick, Gwendolyn 538
Lemche, Niels Peter 171
Lemos, Tracy M. 568, 570, 584, 592, 656
Lenzi, Alan 462, 469
Leske, Adrian M. 455
Leuchter, Mark 263, 310, 322, 326, 388, 422, 440
Levene, Mark 42
Levenson, Jon D. 181, 185, 246, 248, 590
Levi, Giovanni 564
Levin, Christoph 120, 315
Levin, Yigal 432
Levine, Baruch A. 205, 225
Levitt Kohn, Risa 257
Lichtenstein, Murray H. 546
Lierman, John 115, 122, 201, 225, 327
Lincoln, Bruce 560
Linville, James R. 616
Lipschits, Oded 142, 155, 369, 394, 483, 488, 504, 530, 599, 600, 602, 604, 609, 616, 618
Liss, Hanna 89, 219
Little, David 655
Liverani, Mario 43, 58, 74, 151, 157, 170, 261, 494, 602
Livneh, Atar 249
Long, Burke O. 460
Lowery, Richard H. 375
Luke, K. 547–48

Lust, Johan 308, 356
Lyons, Ellen L. 548–49

Ma, John 137, 154, 472, 608
Macchi, Jean-Daniel 590
Macintosh, Andrew A. 282
Maddox, Donald 172
Madsen, Albert A. 429
Maeir, Aren M. 434
Maguire, Eleanor A. 8
Mahr Johannes B. 8
Maier, Christl M. 495, 497
Malul, Meir 475
Manning, Joseph G. 137, 154
Marcinkowska, Urszula M. 559
Marcos, Fernando S. 564
Martín Rojo, Luisa 580
Maruyama, Magoroh 6, 32, 135, 647
Maslan, Mark 612
Mason, Rex 407
Mason, Steven D. 448, 451
Matthews, Victor H. 568
Mayhue, Richard L. 467
Mazar, Amihai 517
McCreesh, Thomas P. 550
McDonough, Sean M. 30, 176, 329, 523
McKane, William 440, 617, 619, 620
McKeating, Henry 128, 218, 258, 311
McKenzie, John L. 267
McKenzie, Steven L. 370, 389, 440, 451–52, 460, 463
Meeks, Wayne A. 122, 225
Meerson, Michael 144
Mendels, Doron 61, 168, 236
Mettinger, Tryggve 272
Meyers, Carol L. 495, 555
Meyers, Eric M. 495
Michaelian, Kourken 8
Micheel, Rosemarie 407
Milgrom, Jacob 69, 360, 397, 524, 538, 542, 572, 582, 585
Miller, Andrew 612
Miller, James C. 33
Miller, James Maxwell 618
Misztal, Barbara A. 33
Mitchell, Christine 67, 70, 588
Mitchell, Lynette 145

Moberly, R. Walter L. 468
Moffat, Donald P. 528
Momigliano, A. 65
Morello, Ruth 613
Mosis, Rudolf 372
Mroczek, Eva 519
Mullally, Sinéad L. 8
Müller, Reinhard 247

Na'aman, Nadav 25, 52, 171, 460, 58
Nelson, Richard D. 249
Neusner, Jacob 367, 401
Newsom, Carol 666
Newsome, J. D. 407
Niditch, Susan 522, 593
Niehr, Herbert 618
Nihan, Christophe 103, 357
Nirenberg, David 657
Nissinen, Martti 503, 663, 665
Noegel, Scott B. 296
Nogalski, James D. 92
Noll, Kurt L. 604
Nora, Pierre 89
Novick, Tzvi 546, 557
Nwaoru, Emmanuel O. 546–48

Oberschall, Anthony 42
O'Brien, Julia M. 263, 302, 412, 495
O'Brien, Mark A. 460
O'Connor, Kathleen M. 302
O'Connor, Michael Patrick 202, 466
Oded, Bustenay 67, 599
O'Dowd, Ryan 492
Oeming, Manfred 428
Olyan, Saul M. 270, 510, 528, 531, 537, 541–42, 656
Oswald, Wolfgang 527–28, 579
Overholt, Thomas W. 661

Pakkala, Juha 308, 351, 354, 531
Palmquist, Stephen R. 182
Panaino, Antonio 264
Passaro, Angelo 550
Patton, Corrine L.(see Carvalho, Corrine L.)
Paz, Octavio 348
Peltonen, Kai 254
Perdue Leo G. 493

Perrin, Denis 8
Person, Raymond F. Jr. 351
Petersen, David L. 407, 455
Pietersma, Albert 619
Pioske, Daniel 13
Plautz, Werner 575
Polak, Frank 43, 123
Polzin, Robert 449

Porten, Bezalel 29, 191, 487, 552, 568
Poser, Ruth 302
Pruin, Dagmar 587
Purcell, Nicholas 554

Raabe, Paul R. 72, 95, 131
Ramet, Sabrina P. 348
Reddit, Paul L. 295, 661
Renkema, Johan 72, 95, 131
Rezetko, Robert 306
Rigney, Daniel 92, 518
Riley, William 323, 519
Ristau, Kenneth A. 352
Roberts, J. J. M. 516
Robertson, D. 461
Robson, Eleanor 637
Rofé, Alexander 203, 414, 459, 470, 546–47
Rom-Shiloni, Dalit 47, 601–2
Römer, Thomas C. 45, 153, 168, 194–95, 200, 237–38, 245, 310, 319, 324, 455, 501, 511, 515
Roncace, Marc 128, 218, 258
Rosenfeld, Gavriel 612
Roth, Martha T 569–70
Roth, Silke 568
Roth, Wolfgang 460
Rudisill, Philip McPherson 182
Rusch, Gebhard 306, 318

Saint-Amour, Paul K. 612
Sandmel, Samuel 163
Sarna, Nahum M. 206
Sass, Benjamin 516
Sasson, Ilana 546, 550
Sasson, Jack M. 493
Sassoon, Isaac 572, 575
Saunders, Marc 619

Schäder, Jo-Mari 656
Schäfer, Peter 144, 591
Schäfer-Lichtenberger, Christa 237
Schaper, Joachim 142, 488, 604
Scheidel, Walter 567
Schenker, Adrian 451
Schiffman, Lawrence H. 356
Schivelbusch, Wolfgang 455
Schloen, J. David 490
Schmid, Konrad 142, 183, 306
Schniedewind, William M. 120, 323, 368–69, 372, 408, 421, 519
Schori, Noa 303
Schultz, Richard L. 255
Schwartz, Barry 12, 14, 19, 93, 102, 259, 317, 343, 518
Schwartz, Baruch J. 180, 236, 242, 247, 507
Schwartz, Daniel R. 61, 168, 236
Schwartz, Regina M. 584
Schwartz Seth 651
Schweitzer, Steven J. 418, 422
Seeligmann, I. L. 407
Seitz, Christopher R. 128, 218, 258
Seniavskaia, Elena S. 261
Seniavskii, Aleksandr S. 261
Sergi, Omer 369
Service, Elman R. 657, 659
Shai, Itzhaq 434
Sheinman, Hanoch 442
Shemesh, Yael 467
Sheppard, Gerald T. 492
Sherwin-White, Susan M. 154
Shuter, Bill 620
Silverman, Jason M. 23
Simon, Julies Jacques 673
Sinopoli, Carla M. 136
Ska, Jean-Louis 170
Skeggs, Beverly 657
Skehan, Patrick W. 253
Smelik, Klaas A. D. 43, 160, 262, 333, 367, 380, 587, 624
Smith, Anthony D. 32–33, 35
Smith, Mark S. 270, 490
Smith-Christopher, Daniel L. 302, 528
Sneed, Mark R. 663
Snell, Daniel C. 188
Sommer, Benjamin D. 255

Southwood, Katherine E. 528
Spiegel, Gabrielle M. 615
Starr, Ivan 473
Stavrakopoulou, Francesca 170, 176, 368–69, 372
Steinkeller, Piotr 552
Stern, Ephraim 599
Stern, Menahem 168, 236
Sternberg, Meir 176, 461
Stevens, Kathryn 652
Stipp, Hermann-Josef 308, 354–56, 367, 394, 485
Stökl, Jonathan 661
Stol, Marten 568–69, 571
Stone Charles B. 9
Stone, Elizabeth C. 552
Stordalen, Terje 151, 491, 631
Stott, Katherine 96, 266, 395, 610
Strootman, Rolf 154
Strugnell, John 356
Stulman, Louis 302, 617, 620, 626
Sutton, John 8
Svärd, Saana 570
Swartz, David L. 641
Sweeney, Marvin A. 249, 375, 622
Szijártó, István M. 564
Szlos, M. Beth 546
Szpunar, Karl K. 8
Szpunar, Piotr M. 8

Taggar-Cohen, Ada 239
Talmon, Shemaryahu 489, 513
Talshir, Zipora 422
Tan, Nancy 586
Taylor, Charles 48
Thareani-Sussely, Yifat 369
Thelle, Rannfrid I. 354
Thompson, Thomas L. 385
Throntveit, Mark A. 384
Tiemeyer, Lena-Sofia 163, 268–69
Tigay, Jeffrey H. 74, 176, 192,
Tov, Emanuel 355, 617, 619
Trebolle Barrera, Julio C. 121
Trotter, James M. 275
Troxel, Ronald L. 255
Tucker, Aviezer 654
Tuell, Steven S. 379

Tuplin, Christopher 488, 605
Tversky, Amos 613

Ussishkin, David 56, 395, 484

Valkama, Kirsi 394, 483
Valler, Shulamit 546, 550
Van der Toorn, Karel 36, 208
van Dijk, Teun A. 27
Van Houten, Christiana 582
Van Leeuwen, Neil 657
Van Leeuwen, Raymond C. 490, 494, 498, 559
van Rooy, H. F. 407
Van Seters, John 60, 163, 171, 189, 191, 238, 386, 511, 608
Van Staalduine-Sulman, Eveline 121
Vanderhoft, David S. 155
Vandorpe, Katelijn 552
Veenhof, Klaas R. 563
Vermeule, Blakey 673
Veyne, Paul 261
Visotzky, Burton L. 190
Volkan, Vamik D. 302
Von Rad, Gerhard 82, 120, 222, 408, 421, 423, 446

Waegeman, Maryse 546, 548, 564
Waerzeggers, Caroline 23
Wagenaar, Jan 116
Wagner, Gerhard 581
Walsh, Carey 585
Walsh, Jerome T. 124
Walters, Stanley D. 121, 574
Waltke, Bruce 202, 466
Warhurst, Amber K. 96, 255, 384, 407, 425
Watts, James W. 121, 142
Weinberg, Joel 46, 407, 602, 618, 621
Weinfeld, Moshe 180, 391, 507
Wellhausen, Julius 44, 296, 370, 446
Wells, Bruce 568
Wells, Gary L. 613
Welten, Peter 375, 500
Wertsch, James V. 12–13, 19, 317, 325, 343
Westbrook, Raymond 557
Westermann, Claus 323
Whitelam, Keith W. 602

Widmer, Michael   201, 227
Wiesehöfer, Josef   155
Willey, Patricia T.   269
Willi, Thomas   407, 424
Williamson, Hugh G. M.   73, 131, 237, 254, 360, 372, 388–89, 397, 605, 621
Wilson, Charles R.   455
Wilson, Ian D.   13, 157, 453, 554
Wilson, Robert R.   661
Winslow, Karen Strand   544
Wolf, Mark J. P.   673
Wolters, Albert   546, 548, 557
Wright, J. Robert   549
Wright, Jacob L.   65, 533
Wright, John W.   372, 406, 514
Wunsch, Cornelia   554, 563, 568

Yardeni, Ada   29, 191, 487, 552
Yates, Gary E.   626
Yee, Gale A.   302, 602
Yellin, Joseph   599
Yilibuw, Dolores   547
Yoder, Christine R.   546, 548, 555, 564
Yoffee, Norman   660
Younger, K. Lawson, Jr.   238, 241, 511

Zakovitch, Yair   30, 176, 329, 523
Zamagni, Claudio   236
Zerubavel, Eviatar   6, 12, 19, 32–33, 36, 48–49, 56, 61, 79, 81, 112, 135, 146, 212, 260, 266, 279, 317–18, 322, 343, 539, 541, 647
Zlotnick-Sivan, Helena   77

Index of References to Ancient Sources

Hebrew Bible

Genesis
Gen 1 442
Gen 1:27 575
Gen 1:27–29 575
Gen 1:28 577
Gen 2–3 498
Gen 2:22–24 575
Gen 2:24 575
Gen 3 474
Gen 3:14 498
Gen 4:17 168
Gen 4:19–23 570
Gen 5:22 195
Gen 5:24 195
Gen 6:18–19 575
Gen 7:7 575
Gen 7:9 575
Gen 7:15 575
Gen 8:21–22 443, 444
Gen 9:1 577
Gen 9:7 577
Gen 9:9–17 443, 444
Gen 10:15–19 170
Gen 11:27 163
Gen 11:27–32 196
Gen 11:27–25:10 163
Gen 11:31 191
Gen 11:31–12:3 181
Gen 11:32–12:1 191
Gen 12 182, 197
Gen 12:1 190, 191
Gen 12:1–3 182, 196, 197
Gen 12:2 577
Gen 12:3 181
Gen 12:4 182
Gen 12:5–6 176, 196
Gen 12:7 167, 445
Gen 12:16 190
Gen 12:17 190
Gen 12:20 190
Gen 13:1–2 190
Gen 13:15 167, 445
Gen 13:16 577
Gen 13:17 167, 445
Gen 14 45, 178, 193–195, 615
Gen 14:14–15 193
Gen 14:18–20 177
Gen 14:18–22 179
Gen 14:20 502, 522
Gen 14:22 179
Gen 15:1 211
Gen 15:5 577
Gen 15:14 185
Gen 15:16 180, 506
Gen 15:18 167, 170, 180, 445
Gen 15:19 180
Gen 16:2 572–73
Gen 16:10 577
Gen 17 186
Gen 17:2–3 577
Gen 17:5 166
Gen 17:8 168, 170
Gen 17:10–11 185
Gen 17:12 186
Gen 18 469–70
Gen 18:12–13 467
Gen 18:18 181
Gen 18:23–32 187–88, 469
Gen 19 187
Gen 20 70, 430–31, 439
Gen 20:3–7 179
Gen 20:7 179, 191, 226, 662
Gen 20:11 179
Gen 20:14 190
Gen 20:17 226
Gen 20:17–18 191
Gen 21:22–34 178
Gen 21:4 186
Gen 22 176–77, 182, 474, 475
Gen 22:2 177
Gen 22:12 183, 475
Gen 22:16–18 184
Gen 22:16–19 166
Gen 22:17 174

Gen 22:18   184
Gen 23   176, 179, 329, 523, 572
Gen 23:6   179, 194
Gen 23:14–20   176
Gen 23:19   177
Gen 24:4   191
Gen 24:7   167, 445
Gen 24:10   191
Gen 25:1   572
Gen 25:20   191
Gen 26   430–31, 439
Gen 26:3   167, 445
Gen 26:3–5   182
Gen 26:4   174
Gen 26:5   60, 184, 323
Gen 26:24   183
Gen 28:3   577
Gen 28:13   167, 445
Gen 28:14   181
Gen 30:3   573
Gen 31:52   85
Gen 33:18   177, 196
Gen 33:18–19   176
Gen 34:14   186
Gen 34:30   173
Gen 35:20   85
Gen 39   474
Gen 46:3   577
Gen 49:29–33   169
Gen 50:5   169
Gen 50:13   169
Gen 50:24   167, 445

Exodus
Exod 1:5   174
Exod 2:24   185
Exod 3:5   69, 117
Exod 3:6   167, 185
Exod 3:7   196
Exod 3:8   66, 167–69, 445, 506
Exod 3:15   167, 185
Exod 3:16   185
Exod 3:17   169, 506
Exod 3:22   467
Exod 4:5   167
Exod 4:10   207
Exod 4:20   224

Exod 4:22   576
Exod 4:22–3   167
Exod 4:28–31   210
Exod 5:22–23   226
Exod 6:7   203, 515
Exod 6:8   167, 185, 445
Exod 6:12   207
Exod 6:30   207
Exod 7:1   206
Exod 7:2–5   206
Exod 7:3   203, 204
Exod 7:10   204
Exod 8:15   340
Exod 8:32   340
Exod 9:7   340
Exod 9:12   467
Exod 9:34   340
Exod 10:1   340
Exod 10:1–2   204
Exod 10:5   203
Exod 12:9   321
Exod 12:11   60, 189, 204, 267
Exod 12:14   85
Exod 12:25–36   190
Exod 12:31–34   60, 204
Exod 12:37–38   174
Exod 12:40–41   185
Exod 12:42   82
Exod 12:48   186
Exod 12:48–49   544
Exod 13:3   85
Exod 13:5   66, 167, 169, 445, 506
Exod 13:8–9   203
Exod 13:8–10   85
Exod 13:11   167, 445
Exod 13:21–22   60, 189, 204, 267
Exod 14:11–12   207, 226
Exod 14:13   201
Exod 14:19   60, 189, 204, 267
Exod 14:31   185
Exod 15   206, 226
Exod 15:2   255
Exod 15:11   75
Exod 15:13   66
Exod 15:20   120, 662
Exod 15:20–21   226
Exod 15:25   474

Exod 15:26   184
Exod 16:15   572
Exod 16:28   184
Exod 17:4   207, 226
Exod 17:8–14   195, 237, 244
Exod 17:9   224
Exod 17:9–10   243
Exod 17:9–13   445
Exod 17:11   243
Exod 17:13   244
Exod 17:14   244
Exod 17:14–16   432, 590
Exod 18   70, 224, 588
Exod 19:5–6   288
Exod 19:6   365, 450, 539, 578, 595
Exod 19:15   583
Exod 20:2   203
Exod 20:6   184
Exod 20:8   85
Exod 20:12   370, 376
Exod 20:18–21   206
Exod 20:25   522
Exod 21:10–11   571
Exod 22:15–16   571
Exod 23:20   207
Exod 23:20–23   245
Exod 23:21–22   207
Exod 23:23   207, 506, 508
Exod 23:27–31   247
Exod 23:28   507
Exod 23:30   207
Exod 23:31–33   336
Exod 24:12   21, 184, 228
Exod 25:20   572
Exod 25–28   484
Exod 26:3   572
Exod 31:18   228, 637
Exod 31–34   189, 267
Exod 32:1   203
Exod 32:1–44   226
Exod 32:9   364
Exod 32:11–13   443
Exod 32:11–14   226
Exod 32:13   85, 166, 167, 174, 183, 185, 445, 577
Exod 32:15–16   228
Exod 32:21–33   206
Exod 32:23   203
Exod 32:32   228
Exod 33:1   167, 203, 445
Exod 33:1–6   245
Exod 33:2   169, 207, 506, 508
Exod 33:3   364
Exod 33:5   364
Exod 33:7–11   205-5
Exod 33:11   206, 211, 216
Exod 33:12   203
Exod 34:1   228
Exod 34:11   169, 245, 247, 506, 508
Exod 34:27–28   228
Exod 34:29–35   205
Exod 34:34–35   206
Exod 35–40   484
Exod 37:9   572
Exod 40:34–35   323

Leviticus
Lev 8:3   168
Lev 9:4   323
Lev 9:6   323
Lev 9:23–24   323
Lev 9:24   321
Lev 10:8   377
Lev 11:44–45   206
Lev 11:45   59, 200, 203, 205, 515
Lev 12:2   538
Lev 12:3   186
Lev 13:1   377
Lev 15:1   377
Lev 16:2   206, 326
Lev 17:8–9   155
Lev 18:3   508
Lev 18:18   571, 575, 577
Lev 18:24–28   390, 602, 608
Lev 18:24–30   541
Lev 18:25–28   242, 247
Lev 19:2   64, 186, 450, 598
Lev 20:22   242, 247, 390, 608
Lev 21:13–15   539
Lev 21:15   539
Lev 21–22   595
Lev 22:8   219
Lev 22:31–33   206
Lev 22:33   59, 203, 205

Lev 24:10   540
Lev 25   557
Lev 25:23   66
Lev 26:9   577
Lev 26:15   184
Lev 26:33–35   388, 390
Lev 26:34–35   66, 388, 390, 607
Lev 26:41   186
Lev 26:42   166, 168, 445
Lev 26:43   388, 607

Numbers
Num 1:46–47   174
Num 2:32   174
Num 3:10   430
Num 11:2   226
Num 11:12   212
Num 11:21   174
Num 11:24–29   662
Num 11:25–9   211
Num 12:6   211
Num 12:6–8   205
Num 12:7   185, 225
Num 12:8   216
Num 12:13   206
Num 13:25–33   512
Num 14:4   572
Num 14:23   167, 445
Num 15:14   155
Num 15:41   59
Num 16:20   377
Num 18:8   377
Num 19:1   377
Num 21:7   226
Num 21:17   26
Num 21:21–35   45, 168, 194, 237
Num 21:25   168
Num 21:31   168
Num 23:19   442
Num 25   508, 544, 589
Num 26:51   174
Num 27:16–17   241
Num 27:17   241
Num 28:20–21   219
Num 29:3–4   219
Num 29:14–15   219
Num 31   582

Num 32:11   167, 445
Num 33:2   221, 228
Num 33:54   242
Num 33:55   72
Num 34:1–12   170
Num 34:1–15   391
Num 34:17   242

Deuteronomy
Deut 1:1   215
Deut 1:5   227
Deut 1:8   166, 167, 445
Deut 1:10   173
Deut 1:25   515
Deut 1:38   242, 445
Deut 2:26–3:13   45, 168, 194, 237
Deut 2:29   515
Deut 3:14   168
Deut 3:28   445
Deut 4   62, 381
Deut 4:1   227
Deut 4:1–15   228
Deut 4:4   227
Deut 4:5–6   69, 70, 200, 492
Deut 4:6   59
Deut 4:10   227
Deut 4:12   216
Deut 4:13   228, 440
Deut 4:14   206, 207, 216, 227
Deut 4:14–19   207
Deut 4:15   207
Deut 4:16   368
Deut 4:25–28   62
Deut 4:25–31   62
Deut 4:27   174
Deut 4:31   166
Deut 4:32–34   200, 203
Deut 4:32–40   206
Deut 4:34   203, 204
Deut 4:35   381
Deut 4:37   182, 203
Deut 4:41–49   62
Deut 4:47   169
Deut 5:1   227
Deut 5:2–19   440
Deut 5:6   203
Deut 5:10   184

Deut 5:16   370, 376
Deut 5:22   228
Deut 5:22–33   206
Deut 5:29   184
Deut 5:31   184, 227
Deut 5:31–33   228
Deut 5:33   376
Deut 6:1   227
Deut 6:1–2   184
Deut 6:2   184, 370, 492
Deut 6:5   182
Deut 6:10   167, 443, 445
Deut 6:20–25   203, 205, 666
Deut 6:22   203, 204
Deut 6:22–25   206
Deut 6:23   443
Deut 6:24   492
Deut 7:1   169, 506, 512
Deut 7:1–6   541
Deut 7:2   241
Deut 7:6   59
Deut 7:7–8   182
Deut 7:9   442
Deut 7:13   182, 577
Deut 7:13–14
Deut 7:16   241, 336
Deut 7:18   85
Deut 7:18–21   200
Deut 7:19   203, 204
Deut 7:23   241, 507
Deut 8:1   443
Deut 8:2   210, 474
Deut 8:6   184
Deut 8:7–9   66
Deut 9   227
Deut 9:1–2   512
Deut 9:3   241, 245
Deut 9:5   167, 445
Deut 9:6   364
Deut 9:7   85
Deut 9:10   228, 637
Deut 9:13   364
Deut 9:16   364
Deut 9:18–19   226
Deut 9:25–29   226
Deut 9:27   85, 166, 183
Deut 10:1   443

Deut 10:2   228
Deut 10:4   228
Deut 10:10–11   226
Deut 10:15   182
Deut 10:15–16   186
Deut 10:22   174, 577
Deut 11:1   60, 182, 184, 323
Deut 11:3   204
Deut 11:13   182
Deut 11:22   182
Deut 11:24   241
Deut 12:10–12   250
Deut 12:13–14   320
Deut 12:30–31   336
Deut 13:1–12   205, 211
Deut 13:2   204
Deut 13:2–4   221, 474
Deut 13:2–6   210, 662
Deut 13:5   184, 492
Deut 13:6   203
Deut 13:14–17   336
Deut 14:1   167
Deut 15:21   595
Deut 16:3   60, 189, 204, 267
Deut 16:7   321
Deut 16:18–20   478
Deut 17:1   209, 595
Deut 17:14   194
Deut 17:14–20   122, 194, 224, 321, 324
Deut 17:16   268
Deut 17:18   249
Deut 17:18–19   637
Deut 17:18–20   194
Deut 17:19   184, 492
Deut 17:20   376
Deut 18:9   335
Deut 18:9–12   508
Deut 18:9–13   602
Deut 18:10   335
Deut 18:10–11   368
Deut 18:10–14   320
Deut 18:14   210
Deut 18:14–22   119
Deut 18:15   116, 207, 210, 211
Deut 18:15–19   209
Deut 18:16   206
Deut 18:18   116, 207

Deut 18:18–19   210, 211
Deut 18:22   221, 465
Deut 20:16–17   241
Deut 20:16–18   336
Deut 20:17   506
Deut 20:18   335
Deut 21:11–14   571
Deut 21:15–17   571
Deut 22:7   376
Deut 22:28–29   571
Deut 23:4–9   541
Deut 23:6   182
Deut 23:11   583
Deut 24:9   85
Deut 24:16   320
Deut 25:5–10   571
Deut 25:16   376
Deut 25:17   85
Deut 25:17–19   590
Deut 25:19   432
Deut 26:5   173, 191, 192
Deut 26:5–9   666
Deut 26:7   167
Deut 26:8   203, 204
Deut 27:1–8   247
Deut 27:2–4   247
Deut 27:3   21, 228
Deut 27:4   247
Deut 27:5   320, 522
Deut 27:8   21, 228
Deut 28   200
Deut 28:11   577
Deut 28:15–68   216, 222, 249, 313, 354
Deut 28:58   228
Deut 28:62   174
Deut 28:69   440
Deut 29:2   203
Deut 29:13–27   216, 222, 249, 313, 354
Deut 29:19–20   228
Deut 29:21–23   390
Deut 29:26   228
Deut 29:27   390
Deut 29:28   62
Deut 30:1   133, 206, 394
Deut 30:1–5   62, 216, 222, 249, 313, 354
Deut 30:1–10   62, 200
Deut 30:2–10   133, 222, 313, 394

Deut 30:6   63, 186, 403
Deut 30:6–9   186
Deut 30:10   228
Deut 30:16   418
Deut 30:17–19   216, 222, 249, 313, 354
Deut 30:20   167, 185, 445
Deut 31   118
Deut 31:7   118, 443, 445
Deut 31:7–8   242
Deut 31:9   21, 228
Deut 31:9–13   26, 649
Deut 31:10   118
Deut 31:12   184, 227, 492, 649
Deut 31:14   118
Deut 31:14–21   118
Deut 31:16   62, 118
Deut 31:16–21   200
Deut 31:16–22   206
Deut 31:19   118, 227, 228
Deut 31:19–22   216, 222, 249, 313, 354
Deut 31:20–21   445
Deut 31:22   120, 118, 227, 228
Deut 31:23   118
Deut 31:24   21, 228
Deut 31:25   118
Deut 31:26–29   133, 394
Deut 31:27   364
Deut 31:30   120
Deut 32   120, 167
Deut 32:8   74, 75
Deut 32:19–25   206, 222, 249, 313, 354
Deut 32:19–43   200
Deut 32:26–43   222, 313
Deut 32:43   75
Deut 33:1   116, 201
Deut 33:4–5   224
Deut 33:5   224
Deut 34:4   167, 443, 445
Deut 34:5–10   117
Deut 34:7   117
Deut 34:10   116, 204, 205, 207, 210, 211, 214
Deut 34:10–12   202, 204, 205, 210, 211
Deut 34:11   203
Deut 34:11–12   204, 211
Deut 34:12   203, 204

Joshua
Josh 1:1   117, 118
Josh 1:1–2   116
Josh 1:1–5   241
Josh 1:1–6   240, 242
Josh 1:2   185
Josh 1:3–4   241
Josh 1:6   118
Josh 1:7   185, 241
Josh 1:7–8   210, 240, 245
Josh 1:8   45, 110, 116, 193, 194, 224, 228, 239, 249, 500, 553
Josh 1–11   238, 511
Josh 1–12   245, 250, 511
Josh 1:13   85, 117, 185
Josh 1:15   117, 185
Josh 2   70
Josh 2:1   242
Josh 2:10   512
Josh 2:23   242
Josh 3:7   242
Josh 3:10   169, 242, 506
Josh 3:15   242
Josh 4:1–24   250
Josh 4:20–24   85
Josh 4:23   512
Josh 5:1   512
Josh 5:3   85
Josh 5:6   443
Josh 5:13–15   238, 245
Josh 5:15   69, 117
Josh 7   239
Josh 8:1–2   243
Josh 8:2   445
Josh 8:18   243
Josh 8:19   243
Josh 8:23–24   249
Josh 8:26   243
Josh 8:30–35   247, 249, 250
Josh 8:31   117, 247, 320
Josh 8:31–32   116
Josh 8:31–34   21
Josh 8:32   228, 239
Josh 8:33   117
Josh 8:34   228, 249
Josh 9   250
Josh 9:1   506

Josh 9:9–10   250
Josh 9–12   238
Josh 10   243, 506
Josh 10:1–27   517
Josh 10:3   506
Josh 10:5   506
Josh 10:10–11   243
Josh 10:10–14   445
Josh 10:12   506
Josh 10:12–14   243
Josh 10:41–42   241
Josh 11:3   506
Josh 11:7   445
Josh 11:10–13   445
Josh 11:12   117
Josh 11:16   445
Josh 11:18   445
Josh 11:21   445
Josh 11:23   72, 241, 444, 445, 518
Josh 12   511, 518
Josh 12:6   117, 237
Josh 12:7   445
Josh 12:8   506
Josh 12:10   517
Josh 13:1   250
Josh 13:1–6   241, 444, 518
Josh 13:1–7   72, 508
Josh 13:1–13   170
Josh 13:2–6   173
Josh 13:8   117
Josh 13–24   250
Josh 14:7   117
Josh 15:8   502, 518
Josh 15:13–19   241
Josh 15:63   72, 241, 502, 518
Josh 16:10   72, 241
Josh 17:11–13   241
Josh 17:12–13   72
Josh 18:1   241, 250
Josh 18:7   117
Josh 18:15   502
Josh 18:28   285, 518
Josh 19:47   241
Josh 20:1   219, 377
Josh 21:41–43   443
Josh 21:43   72
Josh 21:45   118

Josh 22:2   117
Josh 22:4   117
Josh 22:5   116, 117, 210
Josh 22:10–34   250
Josh 22:19   66, 69, 300
Josh 22:26–28   85
Josh 22:43   241
Josh 23   245
Josh 23–24   249
Josh 23:1   250
Josh 23:1–5   444, 518
Josh 23:3   511
Josh 23:3–4   119
Josh 23:4   242
Josh 23:4–5   507, 515
Josh 23:4–13   515
Josh 23:6   116, 210
Josh 23:9   512
Josh 23:12–26   62
Josh 23:13   72, 508
Josh 23:14   118, 444
Josh 23:14–16   249
Josh 23:15   445
Josh 24   239, 249, 666
Josh 24:1–28   250
Josh 24:2–3   196
Josh 24:2–4   191
Josh 24:2–13   119, 246
Josh 24:6   21
Josh 24:11   506
Josh 24:11–12   245
Josh 24:12   507
Josh 24:15   196
Josh 24:15–20   62
Josh 24:17   203, 515
Josh 24:19–20   118
Josh 24:19–21   249
Josh 24:25–26   119
Josh 24:29   117
Josh 24:29–30   117

Judges
Judg 1   72, 173, 186, 241, 525, 595, 605
Judg 1:1–2:5   444, 518
Judg 1:6   595
Judg 1:7   517, 595
Judg 1:8   72, 502, 517

Judg 1:21   72, 502, 518, 525
Judg 2:1–3   72, 121, 515
Judg 2:1–5   605
Judg 2:6   62
Judg 2:8–9   117
Judg 2:12   203, 515
Judg 2:13   62
Judg 2:18–19   62
Judg 2:20–23   72
Judg 2:21–22   474
Judg 2:21–23   508
Judg 3:1–2   245, 508
Judg 3:1–5   173
Judg 3:4–7   508
Judg 3:12   62
Judg 3:15   437, 474
Judg 3:24   508
Judg 4:1   62
Judg 4:4   120, 276
Judg 4:4–5   120
Judg 5:1   121
Judg 5:28   590
Judg 6:1   62
Judg 6:2–6   121
Judg 6:6   437
Judg 6:8–10   119, 121
Judg 6:11–13   121
Judg 8:30–31   571
Judg 9   122
Judg 9:8–15   122
Judg 10:10   437
Judg 10:11–14   119
Judg 11:1–2   571
Judg 11:12–24   49
Judg 11:12–26   49
Judg 12:13   570
Judg 14:3   595
Judg 15:18   186
Judg 18:7   437
Judg 18:27   437
Judg 19:10–30   510
Judg 19:11–12   502

1 Samuel
1 Sam 1:1   322
1 Sam 1–2   574
1 Sam 1–8   325

1 Sam 1:22   448
1 Sam 2   121, 574
1 Sam 2:1   121
1 Sam 2:1–10   120
1 Sam 2:2   449
1 Sam 2–4   449
1 Sam 2:11   449
1 Sam 2:18   326, 327
1 Sam 2:18–19   449
1 Sam 2:22–34   62
1 Sam 2:27–28   447, 448
1 Sam 2:27–36   122, 123
1 Sam 2:28–29   447
1 Sam 2:29–30   447
1 Sam 2:30   123, 447, 449
1 Sam 2:31–36   449
1 Sam 2:34   204
1 Sam 3:1   209
1 Sam 3:18   448, 452
1 Sam 3:19   465
1 Sam 3:20   174
1 Sam 4   449
1 Sam 4:9   592
1 Sam 4:10–18   62
1 Sam 6:6   340
1 Sam 6:14   327
1 Sam 8:1–3   62
1 Sam 8:7   325, 447, 592
1 Sam 8:11–18   156
1 Sam 8:25–27   238
1 Sam 9:9   662
1 Sam 10:5   661
1 Sam 10:10–13   662
1 Sam 12   119, 121, 325, 666
1 Sam 12:8–15   119
1 Sam 12:14   183, 492
1 Sam 14:6   186, 595
1 Sam 14:13–15   445
1 Sam 14:45   442
1 Sam 15   590
1 Sam 15:20   211
1 Sam 15:22   310
1 Sam 15:29   442
1 Sam 16:2   467
1 Sam 17   510
1 Sam 17:26   186
1 Sam 17:36   186, 238

1 Sam 17:54   509
1 Sam 18:7   238, 445, 513
1 Sam 21:5–6   583
1 Sam 21:8   584
1 Sam 21:11   238
1 Sam 22:5   662
1 Sam 22:9   584
1 Sam 22:14   225
1 Sam 22:18   326, 327, 584
1 Sam 22:20   449
1 Sam 28:18   432, 590
1 Sam 29:5   238
1 Sam 31:4   186

2 Samuel
2 Sam 2:11   329
2 Sam 3:10   174
2 Sam 5:2   146, 241, 513
2 Sam 5:6   510
2 Sam 5:6–9   509, 513, 514
2 Sam 5:7–9   499
2 Sam 5:8   510
2 Sam 5:9   168
2 Sam 6:2–12   586
2 Sam 6:10–12   586
2 Sam 6:12   499
2 Sam 6:13–18   327
2 Sam 6:14   326
2 Sam 7   321, 440, 441, 447, 451
2 Sam 7:1–17   450
2 Sam 7:4   211
2 Sam 7:7   146
2 Sam 7:9   238
2 Sam 7:13   448
2 Sam 7:16   123, 448
2 Sam 7:20   476
2 Sam 7:24   448
2 Sam 7:25   448
2 Sam 8:13   238
2 Sam 8:18   327, 327, 328
2 Sam 10:12   448
2 Sam 11:3   584
2 Sam 11:4   583
2 Sam 11:6   584
2 Sam 11:12–13   584
2 Sam 11:17   584
2 Sam 11:21   584

2 Sam 11:24   584
2 Sam 12:1–10   573
2 Sam 12:3   573
2 Sam 12:4   573
2 Sam 12:9   573, 584
2 Sam 12:10   448, 584
2 Sam 13:28   592
2 Sam 17:11   174
2 Sam 18:18   85
2 Sam 19:22   146
2 Sam 21:18–22   445
2 Sam 22:51   448
2 Sam 23:1   146
2 Sam 23:5   321, 440, 450
2 Sam 23:29   584
2 Sam 24:2   174
2 Sam 24:11   219
2 Sam 24:12–13   190
2 Sam 24:15–25   525
2 Sam 24:16   168
2 Sam 24:16–18   511
2 Sam 24:17   327
2 Sam 24:20–25   30, 176, 523
2 Sam 24:20–26   329

1 Kings
1 Kgs 1   123, 150, 152
1 Kgs 2:3   210, 320
1 Kgs 2:11   329
1 Kgs 2:27   449
1 Kgs 2:33   448
1 Kgs 2:45   448
1 Kgs 3:6–9   227
1 Kings 5–6   484
1 Kgs 5:1   75
1 Kgs 5:1–8   589
1 Kgs 5:4   250
1 Kgs 5:5   174
1 Kgs 5:9–14   150, 152, 589
1 Kgs 5:17–19   522
1 Kgs 5:27–32   72
1 Kgs 6–7   90
1 Kgs 8   118, 497
1 Kgs 8:1   499
1 Kgs 8:10–11   323
1 Kgs 8:14   327
1 Kgs 8:15–16   448

1 Kgs 8:16   448, 500, 501
1 Kgs 8:23–24   321, 440–442, 450
1 Kgs 8:25   209, 401
1 Kgs 8:46   373
1 Kgs 8:46–53   118
1 Kgs 8:55–56   327
1 Kgs 8:56   118, 250, 465
1 Kgs 8:66   117
1 Kgs 9:6   401
1 Kgs 9:20–22   72
1 Kgs 10   150, 152
1 Kgs 10:1–13   250
1 Kgs 10:23   589
1 Kgs 10:24–25   250
1 Kgs 11   508
1 Kgs 11:1–3   589
1 Kgs 11:3   571
1 Kgs 11:28   72
1 Kgs 11:31–35   119
1 Kgs 11:32   448, 451
1 Kgs 11:34   451
1 Kgs 11:36   451
1 Kgs 11:38   184, 451
1 Kgs 12:15   119, 221
1 Kgs 12:21   606
1 Kgs 12:23   606
1 Kgs 13:16   205
1 Kgs 14:1–18   662
1 Kgs 14:7–11   119
1 Kgs 14:18   117, 118, 119. 222
1 Kgs 14:21   448
1 Kgs 14:24   169, 602
1 Kgs 15:4   450
1 Kgs 15:5   584
1 Kgs 15:26   335
1 Kgs 15:29   117, 118, 119, 222
1 Kgs 15:34   335
1 Kgs 16:8–10   352
1 Kgs 16:12   119, 222
1 Kgs 16:24   168, 169
1 Kgs 16:26   335
1 Kgs 16:34   118
1 Kgs 17:9   587
1 Kgs 17:16   118, 119, 222
1 Kgs 17:20   226
1 Kgs 17:31   587
1 Kgs 18   129, 461, 462

1 Kgs 18:4   43, 226
1 Kgs 18:13   43
1 Kgs 18:36   167
1 Kgs 19:15–16   123
1 Kgs 19:22–28   157
1 Kgs 21:3   555
1 Kgs 21:23   462
1 Kgs 21:26   506, 508
1 Kgs 22   121, 459–462
1 Kgs 22:3–22   461
1 Kgs 22:6–22   461
1 Kgs 22:8   464
1 Kgs 22:20   467
1 Kgs 22:21   466
1 Kgs 22:24   467
1 Kgs 22:24–25   466
1 Kgs 22:27–28   465
1 Kgs 22:29–38   461
1 Kgs 22:38   462
1 Kgs 22:44   380
1 Kgs 22:53   335

2 Kings
2 Kgs 3:3   335
2 Kgs 3:11   124
2 Kgs 3:15   661
2 Kgs 4:33   227
2 Kgs 5:17   588
2 Kgs 5:18   588
2 Kgs 5:27   588
2 Kgs 7:6   572
2 Kgs 8:19   450
2 Kgs 9:7   43, 117, 118, 226
2 Kgs 9:21   168
2 Kgs 9:30   590
2 Kgs 9:36   117, 119, 222, 462
2 Kgs 10:10   117, 118, 119, 222
2 Kgs 10:16–19   336
2 Kgs 10:29   335
2 Kgs 10:30   119
2 Kgs 10:31   335
2 Kgs 12:4   380
2 Kgs 13:2   335
2 Kgs 13:11   335
2 Kgs 13:23   166
2 Kgs 14:4   380
2 Kgs 14:6   110, 210, 228, 320, 637

2 Kgs 14:20   500
2 Kgs 14:24   335
2 Kgs 14:25   117, 118, 119, 222, 391
2 Kgs 14:25–27   129
2 Kgs 14:29   352
2 Kgs 15:4   380
2 Kgs 15:8–11   352
2 Kgs 15:9   335
2 Kgs 15:12   119
2 Kgs 15:18   335
2 Kgs 15:24   335
2 Kgs 15:28   335
2 Kgs 16:3   169, 335, 508
2 Kgs 16:24   522
2 Kgs 17   336, 352
2 Kgs 17:2   329, 352, 353
2 Kgs 17:6   391
2 Kgs 17:7   203
2 Kgs 17:7–18   283
2 Kgs 17:7–23   393
2 Kgs 17:8   169, 335, 508
2 Kgs 17:11   169
2 Kgs 17:13   116–118, 124, 125, 184, 208–210, 263, 322, 354, 413
2 Kgs 17:13–15   226
2 Kgs 17:14   364
2 Kgs 17:17   335
2 Kgs 17:23   117, 119, 222
2 Kgs 17:34   320
2 Kgs 17:37   21
2 Kgs 18:11   391
2 Kgs 18:12   117
2 Kgs 18:13   478
2 Kgs 18:19–25   510
2 Kgs 19:2   430
2 Kgs 19:15   227
2 Kgs 19:21   495
2 Kgs 19:39   431
2 Kgs 20:1–7   370
2 Kgs 20:2   227
2 Kgs 20:3   85
2 Kgs 20:9   204
2 Kgs 20:12–19   271
2 Kgs 21   271
2 Kgs 21:1–10   368
2 Kgs 21:1–18   369
2 Kgs 21:1–20   105, 334, 367

2 Kgs 21:2   169, 335, 508, 602
2 Kgs 21:3   335, 352
2 Kgs 21:3–7   334
2 Kgs 21:4   368
2 Kgs 21:6   320, 335, 368, 508
2 Kgs 21:7   146, 324–326, 368, 448
2 Kgs 21:8   210, 508
2 Kgs 21:8–9   354
2 Kgs 21:9   336
2 Kgs 21:10   117, 118, 368
2 Kgs 21:11   335, 506, 508
2 Kgs 21:11–14   397
2 Kgs 21:12–14   42
2 Kgs 21:13   335, 352
2 Kgs 21:14   41
2 Kgs 21:15   336
2 Kgs 21:16   335
2 Kgs 21:18   330, 368
2 Kgs 21:19   462
2 Kgs 22:1   111
2 Kgs 22:6–20   228
2 Kgs 22:8–10   310
2 Kgs 22:10–11   110
2 Kgs 22:14   276
2 Kgs 22–23   637
2 Kgs 23:2   249, 422
2 Kgs 23:4–14   334
2 Kgs 23:12   105, 334, 335
2 Kgs 23:15   335
2 Kgs 23:23   210
2 Kgs 23:26   105, 266, 334, 385
2 Kgs 23:26–27   397
2 Kgs 24:1–25:21   217
2 Kgs 24:2   117, 118, 119, 222
2 Kgs 24:3   334, 361, 385, 397, 419
2 Kgs 24:9   351
2 Kgs 24:13–14   241
2 Kgs 24:18–25:21   313, 355
2 Kgs 24:20   354, 360
2 Kgs 25   314
2 Kgs 25:1–18   217
2 Kgs 25:1–21   42
2 Kgs 25:3–7   364
2 Kgs 25:4–5   351
2 Kgs 25:5–7   399
2 Kgs 25:7   364
2 Kgs 25:8–9   622, 624
2 Kgs 25:8–11   160, 587
2 Kgs 25:11–12   601, 624
2 Kgs 25:21–26   390
2 Kgs 25:22–25   313, 314, 316
2 Kgs 25:25   622
2 Kgs 25:25–26   601
2 Kgs 25:27–29   601
2 Kgs 25:27–30   125, 313, 351, 357, 365
2 Kgs 25:28   62

Isaiah
Isa 1:1   22
Isa 1:2   167, 576
Isa 1:26   497
Isa 2:1–4   255, 270
Isa 2:2–4   63, 73, 149, 151, 152, 181, 265, 288, 418, 505, 525
Isa 2:3   105, 132, 149, 492, 494
Isa 2:3–4   595
Isa 2:4   96
Isa 3:2   662
Isa 6   462
Isa 6:1   260
Isa 6:9–10   263, 271, 467
Isa 6:11–12   390
Isa 6:13   531
Isa 7   260
Isa 7:8–9   296
Isa 7:9   96, 424
Isa 7:11   205
Isa 7:14   204
Isa 9:5–6   72, 131, 148, 452
Isa 9:5–7   72, 131, 148, 452
Isa 10:5   159
Isa 10:10–11   157
Isa 11   63, 130, 265, 272, 418, 425, 500
Isa 11:1–9   72, 131, 148, 452
Isa 11:6–9   492, 498
Isa 11:11   300
Isa 12:2   255
Isa 13   158
Isa 13:8   592
Isa 14   158, 255
Isa 14–27   134, 136
Isa 14:1   155, 450
Isa 14:3–23   157
Isa 14:3–24   158

Isa 14:21–24   158
Isa 14:24–27   152
Isa 14:28   260
Isa 15   307
Isa 19:16   592
Isa 19:20   131, 156, 204
Isa 20:3   117, 118
Isa 22:9   499
Isa 22:15   430
Isa 23   255, 554
Isa 25   255
Isa 26   255
Isa 30:8   465
Isa 30:27–33   158
Isa 33   272
Isa 33:17–24   272
Isa 33:21   491, 521
Isa 36:1   478
Isa 36–39   147
Isa 37:22   495
Isa 37:23–29   157
Isa 37:31   431
Isa 37:35   117
Isa 39   266, 271, 385
Isa 39:1–8   127
Isa 39:6–8   336
Isa 40   127, 266, 271
Isa 40–48   147
Isa 40–55   76, 152, 268, 385
Isa 40–66   73, 131, 148, 453
Isa 40:1   336
Isa 40:1–52:12   146, 266
Isa 40:18–20   270
Isa 41:8   163, 166, 182, 260
Isa 41:8–9   117, 269
Isa 41:8–10   269
Isa 41:9   147
Isa 42:1   73, 117, 149
Isa 42:1–7   269
Isa 42:5–7   265
Isa 42:6   73, 74, 147, 149, 151, 441
Isa 42:13–15   592
Isa 42:39   117
Isa 43:1–2   265
Isa 43:5–6   620
Isa 43:10–11   270
Isa 43:16–17   512

Isa 44–55   272
Isa 44:1–5   269
Isa 44:6   270
Isa 44:9   270
Isa 44:9–15   270
Isa 44:9–20   67
Isa 44:21   85, 269
Isa 44:21–22   269
Isa 44:24–28   147, 453
Isa 44:24–45:7   267
Isa 44:24–45:25   147, 453
Isa 44:26   121, 208
Isa 44:28   75, 145, 146, 147, 179
Isa 45:1   146, 179
Isa 45:1–4   58, 75
Isa 45:1–5   270
Isa 45:1–7   75, 145
Isa 45:1–8   147, 453
Isa 45:4   147, 269
Isa 45:5   75, 76, 149, 589
Isa 45:5–7   149, 270
Isa 45:7   77, 467
Isa 45:9   448, 452
Isa 45:11–13   453
Isa 45:12–13   145, 147
Isa 45:13   145, 179
Isa 45:14   73, 149, 151, 270
Isa 45:18   270
Isa 45:21   270
Isa 46:8   85
Isa 46:9   85, 270
Isa 47:8–13   510
Isa 48:12–15   147, 453
Isa 48:15   147
Isa 48:20   269
Isa 49:1   147
Isa 49:1–6   269
Isa 49:3–4   269
Isa 49: 6–7   181
Isa 49:7   73, 149
Isa 49:14–18   146
Isa 49:17–18   495
Isa 49:23   73, 149
Isa 51:1–3   174
Isa 51:2   147, 163, 174, 175, 178, 260
Isa 51:3   146
Isa 51:4   181

Isa 51:4–5   73, 149, 265
Isa 52:1   55, 60, 186, 189, 204, 267, 497
Isa 52:11   267
Isa 52:11–12   60, 189, 267, 383
Isa 52:12   60, 190, 204, 267
Isa 52:13   117
Isa 52:13–15   269
Isa 53:11   117
Isa 54:5   498, 515
Isa 54:5–8   495, 576, 593
Isa 54:13   495
Isa 55:1–5   492
Isa 55:3   450, 585
Isa 55:3–5   145, 151, 288
Isa 55:3–11   454
Isa 55:8–11   470
Isa 55:10–11   425
Isa 55:11   469
Isa 56–66   134, 136, 255, 271
Isa 56:1–6   539
Isa 56:1–7   265
Isa 56:1–8   74, 153, 155, 181, 288, 543
Isa 56:1–9   505, 525
Isa 56:3   596
Isa 56:3–7   70
Isa 56:3–8   322
Isa 56:6   117
Isa 56:6–7   73, 74, 149, 449
Isa 56:9–12   271
Isa 57:3–13   271
Isa 58:1–14   271
Isa 58:3–4   271
Isa 58:6–10   271
Isa 59:1–15   271
Isa 59:9–15   271
Isa 60   265, 498, 516
Isa 60:1–3   149, 491, 521
Isa 60:1–18   494
Isa 60:3   598
Isa 60:8–9   300
Isa 60:9   73, 149
Isa 60:10–16   151
Isa 60:11–12   418
Isa 60:14   516
Isa 60:19–20   149, 491, 521
Isa 60:19–22   265
Isa 61:1   121

Isa 61:5   494
Isa 61:6   595
Isa 62:3   496
Isa 62:3–5   593
Isa 62:4   495, 576
Isa 62:4–5   496, 595
Isa 62:6–7   498
Isa 63:7–64:11   271
Isa 63:11–12   128, 260
Isa 63:11–14   512
Isa 63:16   163, 166, 167, 260
Isa 64:7   167
Isa 65   505
Isa 65:1–12   271
Isa 65:17   63, 130, 418
Isa 65:17–25   492, 498, 500
Isa 65:18–19   496, 498, 515
Isa 65:18–24   498
Isa 66   497
Isa 66:1   497
Isa 66:17   271
Isa 66:21   155, 449

Jeremiah
Jer 1:1   213, 215
Jer 1:2   211
Jer 1:4   211
Jer 2:2   575, 593
Jer 2:13   491
Jer 2:15   307
Jer 3:6–13   576
Jer 3:14   576
Jer 3:17   151, 494, 497
Jer 4:1–2   308
Jer 4:4   186
Jer 4:7   307
Jer 4:22–28   493
Jer 5:1   308
Jer 6:12   300
Jer 7   310
Jer 7:1–15   310
Jer 7:3   310
Jer 7:7   310
Jer 7:12   310
Jer 7:14   310
Jer 7:25   117, 118, 127, 226, 263, 307, 310, 412, 413

Jer 7:26   364
Jer 9:11   307
Jer 9:25   186
Jer 10:13   307
Jer 10:25   307
Jer 11   119
Jer 11:1–8   308
Jer 11:5   166, 167, 445
Jer 11:7–8   308
Jer 11:14   307
Jer 11:18–21   43
Jer 12:7   180
Jer 14:8   491
Jer 14:21   443
Jer 15:1   122
Jer 15:1–4   307
Jer 15:4   266, 330, 361, 367, 397
Jer 15:14   105, 334, 385
Jer 16:10–13   119
Jer 16:15   619
Jer 17:13   491
Jer 17:23   364
Jer 17:26   606
Jer 18:1–11   308
Jer 18:1–12   308
Jer 20:1–2   43
Jer 22:1–5   308
Jer 22:28–30   308, 354, 357
Jer 23:3   619, 620, 621
Jer 23:5–6   72, 131, 148, 308, 356, 452
Jer 23:8   619
Jer 24   106, 268, 357, 601, 602
Jer 24:7   63, 403, 418
Jer 24:9   619
Jer 25:1–14   159, 625
Jer 25:4   117, 127, 226, 263, 412, 413
Jer 25:4–5   307
Jer 25:9   43, 75, 159, 261, 392, 625
Jer 25:9–11   42
Jer 25:11–12   159
Jer 25:12   388
Jer 26:2–3   307
Jer 26:5   117, 118
Jer 26:7–9   43
Jer 26:9   127, 226, 263, 307, 412, 413
Jer 26:11   43
Jer 26:18   110, 260, 263

Jer 26:18–19   413
Jer 27   625
Jer 27:6   43, 75, 117, 159, 261, 625
Jer 27:11–12   159
Jer 27:12–15   308
Jer 27:18   227
Jer 27:22   189
Jer 28   462
Jer 28:9   465
Jer 29   159
Jer 29:10   388
Jer 29:14   619
Jer 29:19   117
Jer 30:5–6   592
Jer 30:8–11   72, 131, 148, 452
Jer 30:10   117
Jer 31:2   182
Jer 31:7   620
Jer 31:9   167
Jer 31:11–12   620
Jer 31:16   96, 424
Jer 31:20   167
Jer 31:23   497
Jer 31:29   307
Jer 31:31–34   63, 100, 101 130, 131, 298, 308, 312, 403, 418, 650
Jer 31:31–40   308
Jer 31:32   576, 593
Jer 31:33–34   290
Jer 32:5   356, 362, 620
Jer 32:20–21   203
Jer 32:23   43, 160, 262, 587, 624
Jer 32:38–41   63, 130, 298, 403, 418
Jer 32:43   390
Jer 33:6   390
Jer 33:14–16   451
Jer 33:14–26   72, 131, 148, 308, 356, 440, 450, 452
Jer 33:15–17   308
Jer 33:17–21   321, 440
Jer 33:26   166
Jer 34:2–5   356
Jer 34:5   307, 362
Jer 34:8–11   355
Jer 34:8–22   308
Jer 34:11   356
Jer 34:21–22   356

Jer 35:15   117, 118, 127, 209, 220, 226, 263, 412, 413
Jer 36:2–7   307
Jer 36:10–26   356
Jer 36:19   356
Jer 36:25   356
Jer 37:3   226
Jer 37:12–21   43
Jer 37:17–21   355
Jer 37:18–21   355
Jer 38:4–28   355
Jer 38:7–13   595
Jer 38:9   355
Jer 38:17–18   355, 359
Jer 38:17–23   308
Jer 38:23   571
Jer 39:1–10   217, 355
Jer 39:2–7   364
Jer 39:7   364
Jer 39:9   160, 587
Jer 39:9–10   624
Jer 39:10   625
Jer 39:11–12   623
Jer 39:11–14   623
Jer 40   624
Jer 40–41   217
Jer 40–42   217
Jer 40:1   625
Jer 40:1–6   43, 616, 620, 622, 624, 626
Jer 40:1–12   627, 630
Jer 40:1–41:18   601
Jer 40:1–43:7   313, 314, 316
Jer 40:2   43, 160, 262, 587, 624
Jer 40:2–3   43, 160, 262, 624, 625
Jer 40:5   622
Jer 40:6   622, 623
Jer 40:6–12   314
Jer 40:7   620, 622, 625
Jer 40:7–8   623
Jer 40:7–12   612–30
Jer 40:7–41:18   159, 268
Jer 40:10   622, 623
Jer 40:10–12   622
Jer 40:11   618, 622, 626, 628
Jer 40:11–12   618, 619, 621, 623
Jer 40:12   618, 619, 620, 622, 625, 626, 628
Jer 40:13–41:18   616, 623, 625, 626, 629

Jer 40:15–16   629
Jer 40–41   217
Jer 40–42   217
Jer 41:1   625
Jer 41:1–3   622
Jer 41:5   621
Jer 42:1–22   159, 268
Jer 42:7–12   314
Jer 43:1–13   159, 268
Jer 43:5   617, 619
Jer 43:5–7   628
Jer 43:6   315
Jer 44:1–30   159, 268
Jer 44:2   390
Jer 44:4   117, 118, 127, 226, 263, 412, 413
Jer 44:18–21   355
Jer 45:9   355
Jer 48   307
Jer 49:7–22   307
Jer 50   158
Jer 50:4–5   73, 131, 148, 308, 453
Jer 50:5   619
Jer 50:19–20   73, 131, 148, 453, 454
Jer 50–52   625
Jer 51   314
Jer 51:19   69
Jer 51:24–28   158
Jer 52:1–27   217, 313, 355
Jer 52:6–11   364
Jer 52:7   351
Jer 52:12–13   622, 624
Jer 52:12–27   160, 587
Jer 52:31–34   313, 357, 365

Ezekiel
Ezek 1:2   357
Ezek 1:3   211
Ezek 3:16–27   413
Ezek 3:18   307
Ezek 4:13   300
Ezek 5:5   495
Ezek 7:26   209
Ezek 8:3   368
Ezek 8:5   368
Ezek 11:14–21   106
Ezek 11:15   163
Ezek 11:19–20   63, 130, 298, 403, 418

Ezek 12   42
Ezek 12:12–14   357
Ezek 12:13   364
Ezek 16:3   188
Ezek 16:60   453
Ezek 17:4   554
Ezek 17:11–21   357
Ezek 17:15   398
Ezek 17:16   364
Ezek 17:19   360
Ezek 17:22–24   357
Ezek 18   218, 258
Ezek 18:2   307
Ezek 20   119, 311, 666
Ezek 20:5   311
Ezek 20:25   467
Ezek 20:31   335
Ezek 20:33–38   204
Ezek 21:30   357
Ezek 23   280, 576, 608
Ezek 23:34   307
Ezek 24:15–18   577
Ezek 26:5   307
Ezek 26:16–18   159
Ezek 27   157, 510, 554
Ezek 27–28   159
Ezek 28   157
Ezek 28:10   307
Ezek 31   157
Ezek 32   186
Ezek 32:9   311
Ezek 33:8   307
Ezek 33:21–29   106, 159, 602
Ezek 33:23   163
Ezek 33:24   174
Ezek 33:33   465
Ezek 34:23   117
Ezek 34:23–30   72, 131, 148, 452
Ezek 36:17   360, 364
Ezek 36:20   66
Ezek 36:25–28   63, 298, 403, 418
Ezek 36:26   100
Ezek 36:26–27   308
Ezek 37:1–28   131
Ezek 37:15–28   72, 130, 148, 452
Ezek 37:22–25   451
Ezek 37:25   179

Ezek 38:10–12   67
Ezek 38:17   117, 118
Ezek 39   152
Ezek 39:1–20   152
Ezek 39:5   307
Ezek 40–43   89
Ezek 40–44   484, 505
Ezek 40–48   89, 90, 218, 258
Ezek 43:9   90
Ezek 44:3   179
Ezek 44:7   155, 186
Ezek 44:9   186
Ezek 44:22   539
Ezek 44:31   219
Ezek 45:24   219
Ezek 47:1–2   505
Ezek 47:1–12   491, 521
Ezek 47:13–20   170
Ezek 47:13–23   391
Ezek 48:1   170
Ezek 48:1–29   434
Ezek 48:28   170
Ezek 48:35   497

Hosea
Hos 1:1   213, 286, 291
Hos 1–2   101, 287, 576
Hos 1–3   41, 577, 608
Hos 1:2–2:2   295
Hos 1:2–2:25   292
Hos 1:4   295
Hos 1:4–5   295, 296
Hos 1:7   280, 283
Hos 2   130, 265, 495
Hos 2:1   289, 291, 295, 593
Hos 2:1–2   292
Hos 2:1–3   291, 296
Hos 2:2   106, 167, 292, 295, 296
Hos 2:4–15   291
Hos 2:4–25   297–299
Hos 2:5–15   42
Hos 2:10–15   291
Hos 2:13   299
Hos 2:15   128, 295
Hos 2:16   289, 593
Hos 2:16–17   182, 284, 288, 499
Hos 2:16–25   216, 283, 291, 292, 575, 593

Hos 2:17   60, 85
Hos 2:18–22   73, 131, 148, 453
Hos 2:19   593
Hos 2:20   298
Hos 2:20–22   292
Hos 2:21   63, 152, 403, 418, 598
Hos 2:21–22   100, 130, 269, 288, 289, 290, 298
Hos 2:21–23   287
Hos 2:21–25   289, 296, 578
Hos 2:23–25   289, 295
Hos 2:24   295
Hos 2:24–25   297
Hos 2:25   295, 298
Hos 3:1–5   299
Hos 3:3–5   291
Hos 3:4   96, 424
Hos 3:4–5   282, 292
Hos 3:5   72, 131, 148, 292, 451, 452
Hos 4:1   280
Hos 4:6   298
Hos 6:6   310
Hos 7:11   286
Hos 7:16   291
Hos 8   283
Hos 8:1   180, 283, 298, 299
Hos 8:4   283
Hos 8:4–6   283
Hos 8:13   299
Hos 9:1–13   299
Hos 9:3   106, 280, 286, 291, 299, 300
Hos 9:3–4   265
Hos 9:3–5   289, 291
Hos 9:3–6   299
Hos 9:4   283
Hos 9:4–5   291
Hos 9:6   291
Hos 9:9–10   128
Hos 9:9–11   297
Hos 9:10   85, 289, 291
Hos 9:15   180, 289, 297
Hos 10:1   291
Hos 10:1–2   291
Hos 10:5–6   280
Hos 10:7   283
Hos 10:9   128, 283
Hos 10:11   280

Hos 10:11–13   291
Hos 10:14   85
Hos 11   300, 301
Hos 11:1   85, 151, 182, 284, 292
Hos 11:1–2   297
Hos 11:1–4   287, 288, 291, 576
Hos 11:1–11   300
Hos 11:4   300
Hos 11:5   280, 286, 300
Hos 11:5–6   291
Hos 11:7–11   292
Hos 11:8   287
Hos 11:8–9   41, 175, 442
Hos 11:10   300
Hos 11:10–11   300
Hos 11:11   286, 291, 300
Hos 12:1   283
Hos 12:2   286
Hos 12:3   60, 280
Hos 12:3–5   280
Hos 12:4–5   284
Hos 12:9   291
Hos 12:9–10   291
Hos 12:10   284
Hos 12:13   107, 286
Hos 12:13–14   284
Hos 12:14   128, 202, 207–209, 216, 248, 291
Hos 13:4–6   291
Hos 13:5–6   288
Hos 13:11   283
Hos 14   502
Hos 14:2–9   292
Hos 14:5   182
Hos 14:5–8   299
Hos 14:5–9   290
Hos 14:6–8   291
Hos 14:6–9   73, 131, 148
Hos 14:8   73, 131

Joel
Joel 4:9–21   152
Joel 4:10   96, 255
Joel 4:18   491, 521

Amos
Amos 1:1   213, 215

Amos 1:3–5   286
Amos 2:10   169, 208
Amos 3:2   182
Amos 3:7   117, 118, 127, 222
Amos 3:9   96, 424
Amos 6:1   510
Amos 7:2–3   226
Amos 7:5–6   226
Amos 7:17   66, 69, 300
Amos 8:11–12   209
Amos 9:7   189
Amos 9:11–15   72, 131, 148, 452

Obadiah
Obad   43, 73, 148, 453
Obad 1–7   307
Obad 3   67, 510
Obad 19–21   72, 131
Obad 20   156, 300
Obad 21   438

Jonah
Jonah 3:2–3   160

Micah
Mic 1:1   213, 260
Mic 3:5   662
Mic 4:1–3   73, 149, 255
Mic 4:1–4   151, 152, 418, 505
Mic 4:1–5   63, 72, 181, 418
Mic 4:2   105, 132, 149, 492, 494
Mic 4:3   96
Mic 4:5   74
Mic 4:9–10   592
Mic 5:1   72, 131, 148, 452
Mic 5:6   41, 72
Mic 5:6–8   41
Mic 5:7–8   72
Mic 6:4   128
Mic 6:5   85
Mic 6:16   352
Mic 7:8   41
Mic 7:15   512
Mic 7:17   72

Nahum
Nah 1:7   476

Nah 2   158
Nah 3:4   67
Nah 3:16   554

Zephaniah
Zeph 1:2–3   390, 444, 493
Zeph 1:2–6   42
Zeph 2:4–15   158
Zeph 2:11   73, 75, 149
Zeph 2:13–15   158
Zeph 2:15   510
Zeph 3   73, 131, 148, 453
Zeph 3:6   307
Zeph 3:8–20   152
Zeph 3:11–13   41, 621, 625
Zeph 3:14   495
Zeph 3:16   96, 424
Zeph 3:20   72

Haggai
Hag 1:1   392
Hag 1:12   392
Hag 1:13   121
Hag 1:14   392
Hag 1:33   208
Hag 2:2   392
Hag 2:2–3   90
Hag 2:3   484, 505
Hag 2:4   392
Hag 2:4–9   505
Hag 2:6–7   152
Hag 2:6–9   90, 181, 494
Hag 2:7–8   73, 149, 151
Hag 2:21–22   146, 453

Zechariah
Zech 1–8   47, 134, 605
Zech 1:4   110, 209, 220, 226, 400, 412, 413
Zech 1:4–5   85
Zech 1:4–6   127, 263
Zech 1:6   117, 118
Zech 1:8–17   76, 149
Zech 4:10   96, 424
Zech 6:11   392
Zech 6:14   85
Zech 7:1–7   621
Zech 7:3   622

Zech 7:5   621, 622
Zech 7:7   110, 400, 412
Zech 7:12   400, 412
Zech 7:12–14   127, 263
Zech 8:3   497, 505, 516
Zech 8:10   96, 424
Zech 8:20–23   181
Zech 8:20–22   73, 149
Zech 9:8   180
Zech 9:9   455, 495, 594
Zech 9:9–10   72, 76, 131, 152
Zech 9:10   149
Zech 9:11   66
Zech 10:9   295
Zech 10:20–22   151
Zech 11:6   96, 424
Zech 13:1   491, 521
Zech 14   152
Zech 14:1   152
Zech 14:8   491, 521

Malachi
Mal 1:1   121
Mal 1:2   182
Mal 2:4   451
Mal 2:4–9   451
Mal 2:7   299
Mal 2:14   456
Mal 3:1   441
Mal 3:6   442
Mal 3:22   85, 128, 129, 131, 223
Mal 3:22–24   210, 211
Mal 3:23   124

Psalms
Ps 1   68, 122, 225
Ps 1:6   291
Ps 2:6   434
Ps 17:3   474
Ps 18:1   117
Ps 19   492
Ps 22:30   73, 150
Ps 24:1   74
Ps 26:2   474
Ps 29:1   75
Ps 36:1   117
Ps 36:10   491

Ps 44:1–3   245
Ps 46:4–5   505
Ps 46:5   497
Ps 46:5–6   491, 521
Ps 47:5   166, 182
Ps 47:10   166, 167
Ps 48:2   497
Ps 48:2–3   505
Ps 48:8–9   505
Ps 48:9   497
Ps 50   310
Ps 50:2   491, 521
Ps 51:1   81
Ps 51:16   310
Ps 51:20   498, 515
Ps 52:2   584
Ps 66:6   512
Ps 68:30   73, 150
Ps 72:8–10   73, 150
Ps 74:2   85
Ps 74:9   209
Ps 76:3   177, 329
Ps 78   81, 85, 119, 246
Ps 78:10   298
Ps 78:11–14   512
Ps 78:70   448
Ps 78:71–72   146
Ps 79:6–7   307
Ps 82   75
Ps 87:3   497
Ps 89   321, 440, 450
Ps 89:12   74
Ps 89:28   576
Ps 89:29   440
Ps 89:50–51   585
Ps 90:1   201
Ps 91:14–16   370
Ps 96:5   75
Ps 96:7–10   73, 150
Ps 97:6–7   73, 150
Ps 97:7   75
Ps 99:6   122
Ps 100:3   74
Ps 101:8   497
Ps 102:17   498, 515
Ps 105   81, 119, 666
Ps 105:6   183

Ps 105:8 441
Ps 105:8–15 174
Ps 105:9 441
Ps 105:9–11 167, 445
Ps 105:11 168
Ps 105:12 173
Ps 105:14–15 175, 179
Ps 105:42 166, 183
Ps 105:44 169
Ps 106 81, 119
Ps 106 403, 666
Ps 106:21–22 512
Ps 106:34 241, 246
Ps 107 119
Ps 110 326, 525
Ps 110:2–4 177
Ps 110:4 327, 328, 502, 522
Ps 114:2 450
Ps 114:3 512
Ps 114:3–5 512
Ps 114:5 512
Ps 115 67
Ps 118:14 255
Ps 119 209, 401
Ps 128 575
Ps 128:3 575
Ps 132:1–18 450
Ps 132:7 497
Ps 132:10 117
Ps 135:7 307
Ps 135:8–12 512
Ps 135:10–12 512
Ps 136 119
Ps 136:13–16 512
Ps 137:1 268
Ps 137:1–6 501
Ps 137:4 265
Ps 137:7 85
Ps 147:2 498, 515

Job
Job 1–2 462, 466
Job 1:7–11 472
Job 1:8 117
Job 9:12 448, 452
Job 28:28 492
Job 38 184
Job 40 184

Proverbs
Prov 1:1 81
Prov 1–9 548, 555, 559
Prov 2:17 441, 456
Prov 2:20–22 291
Prov 3:1–2 370
Prov 3:15 549
Prov 3:33 291
Prov 4:18–19 291
Prov 5:15–19 556
Prov 5:18 575
Prov 5:18–23 575
Prov 8:1–3 492
Prov 8:2 493
Prov 8:11 549
Prov 8:22–36 549
Prov 9:1–6 492
Prov 10:2 370, 376
Prov 10:28 291
Prov 11:4 376
Prov 11:21 291
Prov 11:23 291
Prov 12:4 496, 575
Prov 12:28 370
Prov 18:22 575
Prov 19:14 575
Prov 19:21 452
Prov 20:24 452
Prov 24:16 291
Prov 25:1 81, 430
Prov 29:18 209
Prov 30:10–31 548
Prov 31:1–9 546, 555
Prov 31:10 549, 553, 557, 559
Prov 31:10–31 2, 546–65, 575, 578, 643
Prov 31:11 551, 557
Prov 31:13 553, 554
Prov 31:15 553, 554
Prov 31:16 553, 554, 563
Prov 31:17 557
Prov 31:18 553, 554
Prov 31:19 554
Prov 31:20 551
Prov 31:21 553

Prov 31:22   553
Prov 31:23   551
Prov 31:25   553
Prov 31:25–26   549
Prov 31:26   554
Prov 31:27   548
Prov 31:28   563
Prov 31:29   558, 559
Prov 31:30   551, 560
Prov 31:31   558

Ruth
Ruth 1   574, 585
Ruth 1:4   585
Ruth 1:16   585
Ruth 1:22   585
Ruth 2:2   585
Ruth 2:21   585
Ruth 3:11   550
Ruth 4:5   585

Song of Songs
Song 1:1   81

Qohelet
Qoh 1:1   81
Qoh 7:20   373
Qoh 8:4   448
Qoh 9:9   575
Qoh 12:1   85
Qoh 12:13   405, 583

Lamentations
Lam 1:5   42
Lam 1:8–9   42
Lam 1:14   42
Lam 1:18   42
Lam 2:1   497
Lam 2:9   209
Lam 2:14   662
Lam 2:15   495
Lam 3:42   42
Lam 4:13   42
Lam 4:15   189
Lam 4:22   42
Lam 5:1   85

Lam 5:7   42
Lam 5:21   42

Esther
Esth 2:5   349
Esth 2:5–6   51
Esth 3:8   591
Esth 8:17   591
Esth 9:1   591
Esth 9:29   592
Esth 9:29–32   592
Esth 9:32   592
Esth 10:2–3   592

Daniel
Dan 4   373
Dan 4:34   373
Dan 9:6   117
Dan 9:10   117
Dan 9:11   117
Dan 11:22   441
Dan 11:28   441
Dan 11:30   441

Ezra-Nehemiah

Ezra
Ezra 1   145
Ezra 1:4   190
Ezra 1–6   600, 605
Ezra 2   530
Ezra 2:1–67   600
Ezra 2:7   543
Ezra 2:62   430
Ezra 3:12   484, 505
Ezra 4:3   145
Ezra 6:21   543, 582
Ezra 6:22   264
Ezra 7:10   554
Ezra 7:14   492
Ezra 7:25   492
Ezra 8:7   543
Ezra 9–10   527–45, 667
Ezra 9:2   531, 542
Ezra 9:4   542
Ezra 9:5–15   543
Ezra 9:6–15   531

Ezra 9:11   117
Ezra 10   582
Ezra 10:2   530, 542, 605
Ezra 10:2–3   530
Ezra 10:2–4   543
Ezra 10:6   542
Ezra 10:10   542, 543
Ezra 10:26   543
Ezra 10:29   605
Ezra 10:44   527

Nehemiah
Neh 1:2   431, 533
Neh 2:10   532
Neh 2:16   533
Neh 2:19   532
Neh 3:33   533
Neh 3:33–35   532
Neh 3:34   533
Neh 4:1   532
Neh 4:6   533
Neh 4:14   85
Neh 5   564
Neh 5:1   533
Neh 5:19   85
Neh 6:1–19   532
Neh 6:6   533
Neh 6:14   276
Neh 7:6–68   600
Neh 8   26, 27 637, 649, 652
Neh 8:17   392
Neh 9   163, 530, 531, 666
Neh 9–10   531
Neh 9:2   527
Neh 9:6–37   119
Neh 9:8   169, 181
Neh 9:22–25   512
Neh 9:24–25   246
Neh 9:26   414
Neh 9:27   72, 131
Neh 9:30   127, 263
Neh 10:30   117
Neh 13   582
Neh 13:3   527
Neh 13:4–9   531, 532
Neh 13:23   533
Neh 13:23–29   527, 531–533

Neh 13:24   533
Neh 13:27   542
Neh 13:28   532

1 Chronicles
1 Chr 1–9   392, 428, 436, 437
1 Chr 10–2 Chr 36   428
1 Chr 1:1–2:2   177
1 Chr 1:32   572
1 Chr 2:3   413
1 Chr 2:3–4   573
1 Chr 2:17   540
1 Chr 2:19   573
1 Chr 2:26   573
1 Chr 2:34–41   540
1 Chr 3   514
1 Chr 3:4   329
1 Chr 3:19   146, 453
1 Chr 4:3   434
1 Chr 4:5   574
1 Chr 4:9–10   437
1 Chr 4:18–19   574
1 Chr 4:24   432, 573
1 Chr 4:24–43   432
1 Chr 4:27   573
1 Chr 4:31   434
1 Chr 4:38–40   430
1 Chr 4:38–43   428–439
1 Chr 4:40
1 Chr 4:41   429, 430, 431
1 Chr 4:42–43   430
1 Chr 4:43   431, 436
1 Chr 5:6   390, 400, 435, 436, 438
1 Chr 5:7   430
1 Chr 5:10   436
1 Chr 5:17   430, 436
1 Chr 5:18   436
1 Chr 5:18–22   436, 437
1 Chr 5:20   437
1 Chr 5:22   436
1 Chr 5:25   391
1 Chr 5:25–26   390
1 Chr 5:26   390, 391, 400
1 Chr 5:41   391, 392, 432
1 Chr 6   514
1 Chr 6:12–13   449
1 Chr 6:13   322

1 Chr 6:18   322
1 Chr 6:34   117
1 Chr 7:5   430
1 Chr 7:9   430
1 Chr 7:14   574
1 Chr 7:24   437
1 Chr 7:27   251
1 Chr 7:40   430
1 Chr 8:6–7   392, 400
1 Chr 8:8   574
1 Chr 8:12   437
1 Chr 8:24   573
1 Chr 9   391, 454
1 Chr 9:1   361, 391, 396, 397, 400, 430
1 Chr 9:2–34   391, 400
1 Chr 9:2–44   396
1 Chr 9:3   361, 397, 501, 518
1 Chr 9:22   326
1 Chr 10–2 Chr 36   428, 434
1 Chr 10:13   349, 391
1 Chr 10:13–11:1   349
1 Chr 11   329, 513, 514
1 Chr 11–29   514
1 Chr 11:2   146, 241, 513, 514
1 Chr 11:3–8   513, 514
1 Chr 11:4–7   513, 514
1 Chr 11:5   510
1 Chr 11:6   514
1 Chr 11:7   516
1 Chr 11:8   514
1 Chr 11:41   584
1 Chr 12:18   167
1 Chr 12:24–41   434
1 Chr 13:13–14   586
1 Chr 15:27   326, 327
1 Chr 16:5   586
1 Chr 16:12   85
1 Chr 16:15   85, 441
1 Chr 16:15–18   167, 445
1 Chr 16:15–22   174
1 Chr 16:16   441
1 Chr 16:19   173
1 Chr 16:21–22   175, 179
1 Chr 16:22   454
1 Chr 16:35   118, 119, 217, 324, 346, 390, 392, 400, 422
1 Chr 17:5   432

1 Chr 17:6   146
1 Chr 17:14   454, 585
1 Chr 17:18   476
1 Chr 18:11   432
1 Chr 18:17   327
1 Chr 19:13   448
1 Chr 21   169, 220
1 Chr 21:1–30   474
1 Chr 21:9   219, 377
1 Chr 21:15–28   511, 525
1 Chr 21:16   220
1 Chr 21:21–22:1   30, 176, 523
1 Chr 21:21–26   329
1 Chr 21:22   169
1 Chr 21:23   448
1 Chr 21:26   321
1 Chr 21:28   511
1 Chr 22:7–9   522
1 Chr 23:14   422
1 Chr 25:1   120, 206, 226, 661, 662
1 Chr 25:1–8   422, 665
1 Chr 25:4–5   573
1 Chr 26:4–8   586
1 Chr 27:16–22   434
1 Chr 27:23   174
1 Chr 28:3   522
1 Chr 28:5   30, 434, 454, 502, 585
1 Chr 28:19   258, 421
1 Chr 28:20   454
1 Chr 29:1   448
1 Chr 29:18   167
1 Chr 29:23   30, 454, 497, 585
1 Chr 29:27   329
1 Chr 29:29   313
1 Chr 29:30   207, 422, 665

2 Chronicles
2 Chr 1:3   117
2 Chr 2:10–15   70
2 Chr 3:1   30, 169, 177, 328, 502, 524
2 Chr 3–4   90
2 Chr 5:9   432
2 Chr 6:5   448, 500, 501
2 Chr 6:5–6   448
2 Chr 6:14   442
2 Chr 6:15–17   117
2 Chr 6:16   209, 401

2 Chr 6:36–39   118
2 Chr 6:42   85, 117, 146
2 Chr 7:1   321
2 Chr 7:14   381
2 Chr 7:19   184
2 Chr 8:7–8   169
2 Chr 8:8   432
2 Chr 8:14   422
2 Chr 9:5–8   70
2 Chr 9:29   207, 422, 665
2 Chr 11:1   606
2 Chr 11:1–4   415
2 Chr 11:1–12   434
2 Chr 11:2   422
2 Chr 11:3   606
2 Chr 11:10   606
2 Chr 11:12   606
2 Chr 11:13–16   434, 501
2 Chr 11:13–17   30, 283, 621
2 Chr 11:14–16   518
2 Chr 11:23   606
2 Chr 12:2   391
2 Chr 12:5–6   415
2 Chr 12:15   207, 313, 422, 665
2 Chr 12:22   382
2 Chr 13:2   371
2 Chr 13:4–12   283
2 Chr 13:5   321, 440, 450, 454, 585
2 Chr 13:8   454, 502, 585
2 Chr 13:9–12   327
2 Chr 13:22   85, 207, 313, 420, 422, 665
2 Chr 14:1–4   477
2 Chr 14:2   72
2 Chr 14:4   72
2 Chr 14:5–7   477
2 Chr 14:7   434
2 Chr 14:8–14   474
2 Chr 14:10   227
2 Chr 14:12–14   430
2 Chr 14:13–14   431
2 Chr 15:1–7   415
2 Chr 15:1–18   478
2 Chr 15:2   434, 606
2 Chr 15:3   96, 424
2 Chr 15:5   424
2 Chr 15:6   424
2 Chr 15:7   424
2 Chr 15:8   606
2 Chr 15:9   432, 606
2 Chr 15:17   72
2 Chr 16:1–10   474
2 Chr 16:7   420
2 Chr 16:7–10   414
2 Chr 16:9   96, 424, 478
2 Chr 16:10   43, 583
2 Chr 16:10–12   478
2 Chr 17:6   72
2 Chr 17:7–8   228
2 Chr 17:7–9   26, 27, 649
2 Chr 17:9   110, 637
2 Chr 18   121, 459
2 Chr 18:17   464
2 Chr 18:20   466
2 Chr 18:23–24   466
2 Chr 18:26–27   465
2 Chr 18:31   437
2 Chr 19:2   420
2 Chr 19:4   478
2 Chr 19:5–7   478
2 Chr 19:8–11   478
2 Chr 20:1–2   478
2 Chr 20:1–30   474
2 Chr 20:3–18   478
2 Chr 20:6–12   227
2 Chr 20:7   166, 182
2 Chr 20:9   437
2 Chr 20:14   420
2 Chr 20:14–17   421
2 Chr 20:20   424
2 Chr 20:29   478
2 Chr 20:29–30   478
2 Chr 20:33   72
2 Chr 20:34   207, 422, 665
2 Chr 20:37   420
2 Chr 21:2   30
2 Chr 21:7   321, 440, 450
2 Chr 21:10   432
2 Chr 21:11–15   420
2 Chr 21:12–15   124, 284
2 Chr 23–24   454
2 Chr 23:16   454
2 Chr 23:18   30, 210, 258, 323
2 Chr 23:18–19   454
2 Chr 23:32   207, 422, 665

2 Chr 24:3   454, 571
2 Chr 24:6   117
2 Chr 24:12   454
2 Chr 24:14 – 16   454
2 Chr 24:15   325, 370
2 Chr 24:19   110, 413, 415, 420, 478
2 Chr 24:19 – 22   583
2 Chr 24:19 – 25   414
2 Chr 24:20   207, 420
2 Chr 24:20 – 22   43, 371, 414, 421
2 Chr 25   70, 416, 585
2 Chr 25:4   210, 321
2 Chr 25:5   434, 606
2 Chr 25:7 – 9   415
2 Chr 25:7 – 10   420
2 Chr 25:9   422
2 Chr 25:24   585
2 Chr 25:28   500
2 Chr 26:5   415
2 Chr 26:10   330
2 Chr 26:16   391
2 Chr 26:16 – 21   327
2 Chr 26:22 – 23   179
2 Chr 28   315, 333, 341, 364
2 Chr 28:1   370, 371
2 Chr 28:1 – 27   358
2 Chr 28:5 – 7   371
2 Chr 28:6 – 7   339
2 Chr 28:8 – 15   402, 415, 454
2 Chr 28:9   420
2 Chr 28:9 – 15   315, 365, 423
2 Chr 28:10 – 11   438
2 Chr 28:12 – 15   435, 438
2 Chr 28:18   280
2 Chr 28:19   30, 391
2 Chr 28:22   391
2 Chr 28:24   339, 373, 392
2 Chr 28:27   30, 416
2 Chr 29 – 31   416
2 Chr 29 – 32   438
2 Chr 29:3   339, 416, 478
2 Chr 29:3 – 5   392
2 Chr 29:3 – 31:20   478
2 Chr 29:6   391
2 Chr 29:6 – 9   392, 398
2 Chr 29:7   391
2 Chr 29:25   323, 324, 421

2 Chr 30:1 – 18   434
2 Chr 30:1 – 31:1   391
2 Chr 30:6   167, 210, 431
2 Chr 30:7   391
2 Chr 30:8   364
2 Chr 30:16   422
2 Chr 30:18 – 20   79
2 Chr 30:22   380
2 Chr 31:1   606
2 Chr 31:16 – 19   430
2 Chr 31:20 – 21   478
2 Chr 32:1   380
2 Chr 32:1 – 21   479
2 Chr 32:1 – 23   474, 478
2 Chr 32:5   380
2 Chr 32:20   227, 437
2 Chr 32:22 – 23   479
2 Chr 32:23   431, 432, 435
2 Chr 32:24   227
2 Chr 32:25 – 26   271
2 Chr 32:26   380, 382
2 Chr 32:31   474
2 Chr 32:32   207, 313, 422, 430, 665
2 Chr 33:1 – 9   416
2 Chr 33:1 – 10   368
2 Chr 33:1 – 20   358, 369
2 Chr 33:2   508
2 Chr 33:4   368
2 Chr 33:5   368
2 Chr 33:7   368, 448
2 Chr 33:8   210
2 Chr 33:10   219, 220, 362, 368, 377, 378, 381, 399
2 Chr 33:11   362, 378, 399
2 Chr 33:11 – 17   368
2 Chr 33:12   220, 362, 378, 380, 399
2 Chr 33:12 – 13   382
2 Chr 33:13   227, 381
2 Chr 33:14   210, 380
2 Chr 33:15 – 16   382
2 Chr 33:15 – 17   382
2 Chr 33:16   380, 381
2 Chr 33:17   380
2 Chr 33:18   207, 362, 365, 377 – 379, 422, 665
2 Chr 33:19   207, 227, 379, 382, 442, 665
2 Chr 33:20   367

2 Chr 34:1   370, 479
2 Chr 34:6   432, 434
2 Chr 34:6–9   391
2 Chr 34:9   434
2 Chr 34:14   110
2 Chr 34:22   276
2 Chr 34:23–28   392, 397
2 Chr 34:30   422
2 Chr 34:31   441
2 Chr 34:33   380, 382
2 Chr 35:4   323
2 Chr 35:12   210
2 Chr 35:13   22
2 Chr 35:15   323
2 Chr 35:18––20   479
2 Chr 35:19   479
2 Chr 35:20–22   479
2 Chr 35:20–24   421
2 Chr 35:20–25   474
2 Chr 35:21   70
2 Chr 35:22   421, 588
2 Chr 35:25   422
2 Chr 36   220, 359, 362, 364, 378, 398, 399, 434
2 Chr 36:1–3   359
2 Chr 36:1–19   358
2 Chr 36:4–8   359
2 Chr 36:6   362, 378, 399
2 Chr 36:9   363
2 Chr 36:9–10   359
2 Chr 36:11   360, 397
2 Chr 36:11–13   359, 362
2 Chr 36:11–21   342–366
2 Chr 36:12   220, 263, 314, 359, 362, 378, 399, 420
2 Chr 36:13   359, 364, 398
2 Chr 36:14   360, 391
2 Chr 36:14–16   360, 363
2 Chr 36:14–21   359
2 Chr 36:15   208, 220, 378, 399, 406
2 Chr 36:15–16   43, 121, 209, 220, 263, 400, 413, 414
2 Chr 36:20–21   388–390, 392, 432, 629
2 Chr 36:20–23   396
2 Chr 36:21   66, 339, 360
2 Chr 36:22   145, 339, 421
2 Chr 36:22–23   75, 521
2 Chr 36:23   70, 380, 383, 390, 498
2 Chr 36:31   607

New Testament

Mark
Mark 10:6–9   575

Matthew
Matt 2:11   194
Matt 19:4–6   575
Matt 25:29   92

Acts
Acts 7   312
Acts 8:1–3   337
Acts 9:1–18   337
Acts 26:9–18   337

1 Corinthians
1 Cor 7:2–3   575

Deuterocanonical Works and Pseudepigrapha

1 Esdras
1 Esd 1:26   588
1 Esd 1:28   421

Judith
Jdt 5:3–23   119
Jdt 5:6   196

1 Maccabees
1 Macc 1   42
1 Macc 2:50–68   119
1 Macc 9:22   140
1 Macc 14:4–14   140
1 Macc 14:4–15   96
1 Macc 16:23   140

Index of References to Ancient Sources

2 Maccabees
2 Macc 6   42
2 Macc 9:12   373
2 Macc 9:17   373
2 Mac 9:13–17   337
2 Mac 13:24   430

Wisdom of Solomon
Wis 11:1   201

Sirach
Sir 17:17   74
Sir 24:3–29   492
Sir 24:23   492
Sir 25:22   561
Sir 44–49   113
Sir 45:3–5   205
Sir 46:1   201, 238
Sir 48:18–25   253, 255, 492
Sir 48:23–25   91

Sir 48:24–25   108, 413
Sir 49:4–7   363
Sir 49:6–7   363
Sir 49:10   108

2 Baruch
2 Bar 1:3   351, 356

Jubilees
Jub 11:16–17   196
Jub 12:2–8   196
Jub 12:12–14   196
Jub 34:1–9   249
Jub 37:1–38:14   249
Jub 38   194

Assumption of Moses
As. Mos. 5:1–6   42
As. Mos. 8:1–5   42
As. Mos. 9:1–10:10   42

Philo

Decal. 175   201
Gig. 56   201
Mos. 1:334   225

Mut. 103   201
Mut. 125   201
Leg. 2.1.1   201

Josephus

Antiquities
Ant. 1.154–157   196
Ant. 1.159–160   195
Ant. 1.177–179   195
Ant. 2.213–214   195
Ant. 2.327   201
Ant. 3.59   238
Ant. 4.165   201, 238
Ant. 4.320   201
Ant. 4.324   238
Ant. 4.329   201
Ant. 6.84   238
Ant. 7.60–64   514
Ant. 7.61   510
Ant. 7.65   511
Ant. 7.68   238
Ant. 7.294   238

Ant. 8   467
Ant. 8.318   587
Ant. 8.320   587
Ant. 8.324   587
Ant. 8.371   587
Ant. 8.406   467
Ant. 9.207   238
Ant. 9.280   238
Ant. 10.100   351
Ant. 10.103–105   356
Ant. 10.120   356
Ant. 11.112   238
Ant. 11.325–339   70, 147

Jewish War
War 4.459   238

Elephantine

B 19 = TAD A4.7   487
B 20 = TAD A.4.8   488, 603
B 23 = TAD B 2.1   191
B 24 = TAD B 2.2   191
B 28 = TAD B 2.6   568, 579

B 29 = TAD B.2.7.3   191
B 36 = TAD B 3.3   191, 552
B 39 = TAD B 3.6   191
B 41 = TAD B3.8   552, 568, 579
D2 (P. Eleph. 1)   568

Qumran

1Q GenAp col. 22 l. 13   177
1QIsa^a 272
1QM 14:4   441
1QS 5:11   441
1QS 5:18   441
4Q Jer^a 617
4Q Jer^d 617
4Q381 frg. 33, 8–11   368

4Q470   356
4QDeut^j 74, 75
4QDeut^q 75
4QJudg^a 121
11Q 13/11 QMelchizedek   525
11QT 57.15–19   567
CD–A 4:17–5:1   567, 575
MMT B 72–82 = 4Q396 iv: 1–11   539

Mishnah and Talmuds (alphabetic order)

m. Mid. 3:4   522

b. 'Abod. Zar. 20a   337
b. 'Arak. 17a   356
b. B. Bat. 15a.   333
b. Ḥag. 13a.   219
b. Pes. 49b   337
b. Šabb. 13b   219
b. Sanh. 94a   333, 385
b. Sanh. 98b   385

b. Sanh. 99a   333, 385
b. Sanh. 99b   336
b. Sanh. 102b   467
b. Sanh. 102b–103a   367, 373
b. Sanh. 103a   356
b. Sanh. 103b   336
b. Zebah. 102a   122, 225

y. Sukk. 5:1; 22b   587

Midrash Rabbah

Gen Rab. 38.13   196
Gen Rab. 98:11   587

Exod Rab. 40:2   225
Exod Rab. 48:4   225

Lev Rab. 32.5   553, 669

Num Rab. 15:13   225

Deut Rab. 5.11   360

Song Rab. 4.25   669

Other Midrashim and Later Literature

Midr. *Tehillim*/Psalms Ps 1   225
Pesiq. Rab. 31   549

Seder Eliahu Rabba, ch. 18, *siman* 19   587
Zohar 3.42.b   549

Achaemenid Royal Inscriptions

DB 32–33   158
DE   74, 137, 151
DNa   74, 151
DSb   74
DZc   151
XE   137, 151

Some additional ancient Near Eastern Sources

ABC 5, rev. l. 12   609
Borsippa Cylinder of Antiochos I   154
LH § 148   569
LL § 28   569
MAL A § 55   571
Queries to the Sun God # 150–74   473
Queries to the Sun God # 274–75   473
Queries to the Sun God # 293   473
Queries to the Sun God # 299–305   473

Greco-Roman Historians

Herodotus
Hdt. 4.11   170, 235, 247
Hdt. 4.173   170
Hdt. 8.144   533

Xenophon
Oec. 4.13   151
Oec. 3.10–15   548
Oec. 6.9   548
Oec. 7.1–41   548
Oec. 8.11–17   548
Oec. 10.10–13   548

Diodorus Siculus
Bibliotheca historica 40.3   61, 168, 236

www.ingramcontent.com/pod-product-compliance
Lightning Source LLC
Chambersburg PA
CBHW021217300426
44111CB00007B/338